Annual Abstract of Statistics

No 153
2017 Edition
Volume 1 of 2
Compiled by: Dandy Booksellers

Contacts

For information about the content of this publication, contact Dandy Booksellers: Tel 020 7624 2993
Email: dandybooksellers@btconnect.com

Publications orders
To obtain the print version of this publication, please contact
Dandy Booksellers
Tel: 0207 624 2993
Email: dandybooksellers@btconnect.com
Fax: 0207 624 5049
Post: Unit 3&4, 31-33 Priory Park Road, London, NW6 7UP
Web: www.dandybooksellers.com

Contents

Page:

12: Banking and Finance

Page:

13: Service industry

Units of measurement

Length

1 millimetre (mm)	= 0.03937 inch	
1 centimetre (cm)	= 10 millimetres	= 0.3937 inch
1 metre (m)	= 1,000 millimetres	= 1.094 yards
1 kilometre (km)	= 1,000 metres	= 0.6214 mile
1 inch (in.)		= 25.40 millimetres or 2.540 centimetres
1 foot (ft.)	= 12 inches	= 0.3048 metre
1 yard (yd.)	= 3 feet	= 0.9144 metre
1 mile	= 1,760 yards	= 1.609 kilometres

Area

1 square millimetre (mm2)		= 0.001550 square inch
1 square metre (m2)	= one million square millimetres	= 1.196 square yards
1 hectare (ha)	= 10,000 square metres	= 2.471 acres
1 square kilometre (km2)	= one million square metres	= 247.1 acres
1 square inch (sq. in.)		= 645.2 square millimetres or 6.452 square centimetres
1 square foot (sq. ft.)	= 144 square inches	= 0.09290 square metre or 929.0 square centimetres
1 square yard (sq. yd.)	= 9 square feet	= 0.8361 square metre
1 acre	= 4,840 square yards	= 4,046 square metres or 0.4047 hectare
1 square mile (sq. mile)	= 640 acres	= 2.590 square kilometres or 259.0 hectares

Volume

1 cubic centimetre (cm3)		= 0.06102 cubic inch
1 cubic decimetre (dm3)	= 1,000 cubic centimetres	= 0.03531 cubic foot
1 cubic metre (m3)	= one million cubic centimetres	= 1.308 cubic yards
1 cubic inch (cu.in.)		=16.39 cubic centimetres
1 cubic foot (cu. ft.)	= 1,728 cubic inches	= 0.02832 cubic metre or 28.32 cubic decimetres
1 cubic yard (cu. yd.)	= 27 cubic feet	= 0.7646 cubic metre

Capacity

1 litre (l)	= 1 cubic decimetre	= 0.2200 gallon
1 hectolitre (hl)	= 100 litres	= 22.00 gallons
1 pint		= 0.5682 litre
1 quart	= 2 pints	= 1.137 litres
1 gallon	= 8 pints	= 4.546 litres
1 bulk barrel	= 36 gallons (gal.)	= 1.637 hectolitres

Weight

1 gram (g)		= 0.03527 ounce avoirdupois
1 hectogram (hg)	= 100 grams	= 3.527 ounces or 0.2205 pound
1 kilogram (kg)	= 1,000 grams or 10 hectograms	= 2.205 pounds
1 tonne (t)	= 1,000 kilograms	= 1.102 short tons or 0.9842 long ton
1 ounce avoirdupois (oz.)	= 437.5 grains	= 28.35 grams
1 pound avoirdupois (lb.)	= 16 ounces	= 0.4536 kilogram
1 hundredweight (cwt.)	= 112 pounds	= 50.80 kilograms
1 short ton	= 2,000 pounds	= 907.2 kilograms or 0.9072 tonne
1 long ton (referred to as ton)	= 2,240 pounds	= 1,016 kilograms or 1.016 tonnes
1 ounce troy	= 480 grains	= 31.10 grams

Energy

British thermal unit (Btu)	= 0.2520 kilocalorie (kcal) = 1.055 kilojoule (kj)
Therm	= 105 British thermal units = 25,200 kcal = 105,506 kj
Megawatt hour (MWh)	= 106 watt hours (Wh)
Gigawatt hour (GWh)	= 106 kilowatt hours = 34,121 therms

Food and drink

Butter	23,310 litres milk	= 1 tonne butter (average)
Cheese	10,070 litres milk	= 1 tonne cheese
Condensed milk	2,550 litres milk	= 1 tonne full cream condensed milk
	2,953 litres skimmed milk	= 1 tonne skimmed condensed milk
Milk	1 million litres	= 1,030 tonnes
Milk powder	8,054 litres milk	= 1 tonne full cream milk powder
	10,740 litres skimmed milk	= 1 tonne skimmed milk powder
Eggs	17,126 eggs	= 1 tonne (approximate)
Sugar	100 tonnes sugar beet	= 92 tonnes refined sugar
	100 tonnes cane sugar	= 96 tonnes refined sugar

Shipping

Gross tonnage	= The total volume of all the enclosed spaces of a vessel, the unit of measurement being a 'ton' of 100 cubic feet.
Deadweight tonnage	= Deadweight tonnage is the total weight in tons of 2,240 lb. that a ship can legally carry, that is the total weight of cargo, bunkers, stores and crew.

Introduction

Welcome to the 2017 edition of the Annual Abstract of Statistics. This compendium draws together statistics from a wide range of official and other authoritative sources.

Dandy Booksellers have sourced and formatted these tables under instruction from various government departments/ organisations

Current data for many of the series appearing in this Annual Abstract are contained in other ONS publications, such as Economic & Labour Market Review, Population Trends, Health Statistics Quarterly and Financial Statistics. These titles can be purchased through Dandy Booksellers.

The name (and telephone number, where this is available) of the organisation providing the statistics are shown under each table. In addition, a list of Sources is given at the back of the book, which sets out the official publications or other sources to which further reference can be made.

Identification codes

The four-letter identification code at the top of each data column, or at the side of each row is the ONS reference for this series of data on their database. Please quote the relevant code if you contact them requiring any further information about the data. On some tables it is not possible to include these codes, so please quote the table number in these cases.

Definitions and classification

Time series
So far as possible annual totals are given throughout, but quarterly or monthly figures are given where these are more suitable to the type of series.

Standard Industrial Classification

A Standard Industrial Classification (SIC) was first introduced into the UK in 1948 for use in classifying business establishments and other statistical units by the type of economic activity in which they are engaged. The classification provides a framework for the collection, tabulation, presentation and analysis of data about economic activities. Its use promotes uniformity of data collected by various government departments and agencies.

Since 1948 the classification has been revised in 1958, 1968, 1980, 1992, 2003 and 2007. One of the principal objectives of the 1980 revision was to eliminate differences from the activity classification issued by the Statistical Office of the European Communities (Eurostat) and entitled 'Nomenclature générale des activités économiques dans les Communautés Européennes', usually abbreviated to NACE.

In 1990 the European Communities introduced a new statistical classification of economic activities (NACE Rev 1) by regulation. The regulation made it obligatory for the UK to introduce a new Standard Industrial Classification SIC(92), based on NACE Rev 1. UK SIC(92) was based exactly on NACE Rev 1 but, where it was thought necessary or helpful, a fifth digit was added to form subclasses of the NACE 1 four digit system. Classification systems need to be revised periodically because, over time, new products, processes and industries emerge. In January 2003 a minor revision of NACE Rev 1, known as NACE Rev 1.1, was published in the Official Journal of the European Communities.

Consequently, the UK was obliged to introduce a new Standard Industrial Classification, SIC(2003) consistent with NACE Rev 1.1. The UK took the opportunity of the 2003 revision also to update the national Subclasses. Full details are available in UK Standard Industrial Classification of Economic Activities 2003 and the Indexes to the UK Standard Industrial Classification of Economic Activities 2003. These are the most recent that are currently used. The most up to date version is the UK Standard Industrial Classification of Economic activities 2007 (SIC2007). It will be implemented in five stages and came into effect on 1 January 2008.

- For reference year 2008, the Annual Business Inquiry (parts 1 & 2) will be based on SIC 2007
- PRODCOM will also be based on SIC 2007 from reference year 2008
- Other annual outputs will be based on SIC 2007 from reference year 2009, unless otherwise determined by regulation
- Quarterly and monthly surveys will be based on SIC 2007 from the first reference period in 2010, unless otherwise determined by regulation
- National Accounts will move to SIC 2007 in September 2011

Symbols and conventions used

Change of basis
Where consecutive figures have been compiled on different bases and are not strictly comparable, a footnote is added indicating the nature of the difference.

Geographic coverage
Statistics relate mainly to the UK. Where figures relate to other areas, this is indicated on the table.

Units of measurement
The various units of measurement used are listed after the Contents.

Rounding of figures
In tables where figures have been rounded to the nearest final digit, the constituent items may not add up exactly to the total.

Symbols
The following symbols have been used throughout:

.. = not available or not applicable (also information supressed to avoid disclosure)

- = nil or less than half the final digit shown

Office for National Statistics online: www.ons.gov.uk

Web-based access to time series, cross-sectional data and metadata from across the Government Statistical Service (GSS), is available using the site search function from the homepage. Download many datasets, in whole or in part, or consult directory information for all GSS statistical resources, including censuses, surveys, periodicals and enquiry services. Information is posted as PDF electronic documents or in XLS and CSV formats, compatible with most spreadsheet packages.

Contact point

Dandy Booksellers welcomes any feedback on the content of the Annual Abstract, including comments on the format of the data and the selection of topics. Comments and requests for general information should be addressed to:

Dandy Booksellers
Unit 3&4
31-33 Priory Park Road
London
NW6 7UP
or
enquiries@dandybooksellers.com

this page is intentionally blank

Chapter 1

Area

Area

The United Kingdom (UK) comprises Great Britain and Northern Ireland. Great Britain comprises England, Wales and Scotland.

Physical Features

The United Kingdom (UK) constitutes the greater part of the British Isles. The largest of the islands is Great Britain. The next largest comprises Northern Ireland and the Irish Republic. Western Scotland is fringed by the large island chain known as the Hebrides, and to the north east of the Scottish mainland are the Orkney and Shetland Islands. All these, along with the Isle of Wight, Anglesey and the Isles of Scilly, form part of the UK, but the Isle of Man, in the Irish Sea and the Channel Islands, between Great Britain and France are largely self-governing and are not part of the UK. The UK is currently one of the 28 member states of the European Union. With an area of about 243 000 sq km (about 94 000 sq miles), the UK is just under 1 000 km (about 600 miles) from the south coast to the extreme north of Scotland and just under 500 km (around 300 miles) across at the widest point.

- Highest mountain: Ben Nevis, in the highlands of Scotland, at 1 343 m (4 406 ft)
- Longest river: the Severn, 354 km (220 miles) long, which rises in central Wales and flows through Shrewsbury, Worcester and Gloucester in England to the Bristol Channel
- Largest lake: Lough Neagh, Northern Ireland, at 396 sq km (153 sq miles)
- Deepest lake: Loch Morar in the Highlands of Scotland, 310 m (1 017 ft) deep
- Highest waterfall: Eas a'Chual Aluinn, from Glas Bheinn, in the highlands of Scotland, with a drop of 200 m (660 ft)
- Deepest cave: Ogof Ffynnon Ddu, Wales, at 308 m (1 010 ft) deep
- Most northerly point on the British mainland: Dunnet Head, north-east Scotland
- Most southerly point on the British mainland: Lizard Point, Cornwall
- Closest point to mainland continental Europe: Dover, Kent. The Channel Tunnel, which links England and France, is a little over 50 km (31 miles) long, of which nearly 38 km (24 miles) are actually under the Channel

Area Measurements

I'd like to get area figures for all the local authorities in the UK. Where do I look?

UK Standard Area Measurements (SAM) are now available to download free of charge from the Open Geography portal in both MS Excel and CSV formats for a variety of administrative areas (countries, counties, local authority districts, electoral wards/divisions, regions, output areas, super output areas and workplace zones). The two questions below show some statistics taken from SAM 2016 (Extent of the Realm figures).

Which is the largest local authority in the UK?

- The largest anywhere in the UK is Highland (Scotland), at 2,647,291.08 hectares (ha).
- The largest in England is Northumberland, at 507,818.03 ha.
- The largest in Wales is Powys, at 519,545.61 ha.
- The largest in Northern Ireland is Fermanagh, at 303,596.58 ha.

Which is the smallest local authority in the UK?

- The smallest anywhere in the UK is the City of London, at 314.96 ha
- The smallest in Scotland is Dundee City, at 6,222.38 ha.
- The smallest in Wales is Blaenau Gwent, at 10,872.79 ha
- The smallest in Northern Ireland is Belfast at 13,247.62 ha.

UK Standard Area Measurements (SAM)

About UK Standard Area Measurements (SAM)

The SAM product provides a definitive list of measurements for administrative, health, Census, electoral and other geographic areas in the UK. SAM will change annually for some geographies, but for others it will be 'frozen' for several years.

The land measurement figures provided are defined by topographic boundaries (coastline and inland water), where available.

Measurements are reviewed annually and include information up to the end of December.

The measurements have been produced in conjunction with the following UK government statistical organisations and independent mapping agencies: National Records of Scotland (NRS), Northern Ireland Statistics and Research Agency (NISRA), Ordnance Survey®(OS) and Land & Property Services (LPS).

The SAM User Guide explains differences in methodology and base mapping between these agencies.

Product details

If you have any queries about this dataset, please contact:

ONS Geography Customer Services
Office for National Statistics
Segensworth Road
Titchfield
Fareham
Hampshire
PO15 5RR

Tel: 01329 444 971
Email: ons.geography@ons.gov.uk

1.1 Standard Area Measurement for Local Authority Districts as at 31/12/2016

Local Authority Name	Code	Extent of the realm (km^2)	Area to mean high water (km^2)	Inland water (km^2)	Land only (km^2)
United Kingdom	**K02000001**	**248531**	**244188**	**1643**	**242545**
Great Britain	**K03000001**	**234397**	**230055**	**1098**	**228957**
England	**E92000001**	**132946**	**130462**	**152**	**130310**
Hartlepool	E06000001	98	94	0	94
Middlesbrough	E06000002	55	54	0	54
Redcar and Cleveland	E06000003	254	245	0	245
Stockton-on-Tees	E06000004	210	205	0	205
Darlington	E06000005	197	197	0	197
Halton	E06000006	90	79	0	79
Warrington	E06000007	182	181	0	181
Blackburn with Darwen	E06000008	137	137	0	137
Blackpool	E06000009	43	35	0	35
Kingston upon Hull, City of	E06000010	81	71	0	71
East Riding of Yorkshire	E06000011	2495	2406	1	2405
North East Lincolnshire	E06000012	204	192	0	192
North Lincolnshire	E06000013	876	846	0	846
York	E06000014	272	272	0	272
Derby	E06000015	78	78	0	78
Leicester	E06000016	73	73	0	73
Rutland	E06000017	394	394	12	382
Nottingham	E06000018	75	75	0	75
Herefordshire, County of	E06000019	2180	2180	0	2180
Telford and Wrekin	E06000020	290	290	0	290
Stoke-on-Trent	E06000021	93	93	0	93
Bath and North East Somerset	E06000022	351	351	5	346
Bristol, City of	E06000023	235	110	0	110
North Somerset	E06000024	391	375	1	374
South Gloucestershire	E06000025	537	497	0	497
Plymouth	E06000026	84	80	0	80
Torbay	E06000027	119	63	0	63
Bournemouth	E06000028	47	46	0	46
Poole	E06000029	75	65	0	65
Swindon	E06000030	230	230	0	230
Peterborough	E06000031	343	343	0	343
Luton	E06000032	43	43	0	43
Southend-on-Sea	E06000033	68	42	0	42
Thurrock	E06000034	184	163	0	163
Medway	E06000035	269	194	0	194
Bracknell Forest	E06000036	109	109	0	109
West Berkshire	E06000037	704	704	0	704
Reading	E06000038	40	40	0	40
Slough	E06000039	33	33	0	33
Windsor and Maidenhead	E06000040	198	198	2	197
Wokingham	E06000041	179	179	0	179
Milton Keynes	E06000042	309	309	0	309
Brighton and Hove	E06000043	85	83	0	83
Portsmouth	E06000044	60	40	0	40
Southampton	E06000045	56	50	0	50
Isle of Wight	E06000046	395	380	0	380
County Durham	E06000047	2233	2232	6	2226
Cheshire East	E06000049	1166	1166	0	1166
Cheshire West and Chester	E06000050	941	917	0	917
Shropshire	E06000051	3197	3197	0	3197
Cornwall	E06000052	3613	3550	4	3546
Isles of Scilly	E06000053	23	16	0	16

1.1 Standard Area Measurement for Local Authority Districts as at 31/12/2016

Local Authority Name	Code	Extent of the realm (km^2)	Area to mean high water (km^2)	Inland water (km^2)	Land only (km^2)
Wiltshire	E06000054	3255	3255	0	3255
Bedford	E06000055	476	476	0	476
Central Bedfordshire	E06000056	716	716	0	716
Northumberland	E06000057	5078	5026	12	5014
Aylesbury Vale	E07000004	903	903	0	903
Chiltern	E07000005	196	196	0	196
South Bucks	E07000006	141	141	0	141
Wycombe	E07000007	325	325	0	325
Cambridge	E07000008	41	41	0	41
East Cambridgeshire	E07000009	652	651	0	651
Fenland	E07000010	547	546	0	546
Huntingdonshire	E07000011	913	912	6	906
South Cambridgeshire	E07000012	902	902	0	902
Allerdale	E07000026	1321	1258	16	1242
Barrow-in-Furness	E07000027	132	78	0	78
Carlisle	E07000028	1054	1039	0	1039
Copeland	E07000029	776	738	6	732
Eden	E07000030	2156	2156	14	2142
South Lakeland	E07000031	1743	1553	19	1534
Amber Valley	E07000032	265	265	0	265
Bolsover	E07000033	160	160	0	160
Chesterfield	E07000034	66	66	0	66
Derbyshire Dales	E07000035	795	795	3	792
Erewash	E07000036	110	110	0	110
High Peak	E07000037	540	540	1	539
North East Derbyshire	E07000038	276	276	0	276
South Derbyshire	E07000039	338	338	0	338
East Devon	E07000040	824	814	0	814
Exeter	E07000041	48	47	0	47
Mid Devon	E07000042	913	913	0	913
North Devon	E07000043	1105	1086	0	1086
South Hams	E07000044	905	886	0	886
Teignbridge	E07000045	681	674	0	674
Torridge	E07000046	996	985	1	984
West Devon	E07000047	1165	1161	1	1160
Christchurch	E07000048	52	50	0	50
East Dorset	E07000049	354	354	0	354
North Dorset	E07000050	609	609	0	609
Purbeck	E07000051	428	404	0	404
West Dorset	E07000052	1087	1082	0	1082
Weymouth and Portland	E07000053	43	42	0	42
Eastbourne	E07000061	46	44	0	44
Hastings	E07000062	31	30	0	30
Lewes	E07000063	294	292	0	292
Rother	E07000064	518	512	2	509
Wealden	E07000065	836	835	2	833
Basildon	E07000066	110	110	0	110
Braintree	E07000067	612	612	0	612
Brentwood	E07000068	153	153	0	153
Castle Point	E07000069	64	45	0	45
Chelmsford	E07000070	343	342	3	339
Colchester	E07000071	347	333	4	329
Epping Forest	E07000072	339	339	0	339
Harlow	E07000073	31	31	0	31
Maldon	E07000074	427	359	0	359
Rochford	E07000075	263	169	0	169
Tendring	E07000076	366	338	0	338
Uttlesford	E07000077	641	641	0	641
Cheltenham	E07000078	47	47	0	47

1.1 Standard Area Measurement for Local Authority Districts as at 31/12/2016

Local Authority Name	Code	Extent of the realm (km^2)	Area to mean high water (km^2)	Inland water (km^2)	Land only (km^2)
Cotswold	E07000079	1165	1165	0	1165
Forest of Dean	E07000080	561	526	0	526
Gloucester	E07000081	41	41	0	41
Stroud	E07000082	476	461	0	461
Tewkesbury	E07000083	415	414	0	414
Basingstoke and Deane	E07000084	634	634	0	634
East Hampshire	E07000085	514	514	0	514
Eastleigh	E07000086	85	80	0	80
Fareham	E07000087	78	74	0	74
Gosport	E07000088	28	25	0	25
Hart	E07000089	215	215	0	215
Havant	E07000090	79	55	0	55
New Forest	E07000091	777	753	0	753
Rushmoor	E07000092	39	39	0	39
Test Valley	E07000093	628	628	0	628
Winchester	E07000094	661	661	0	661
Broxbourne	E07000095	51	51	0	51
Dacorum	E07000096	212	212	0	212
Hertsmere	E07000098	101	101	0	101
North Hertfordshire	E07000099	375	375	0	375
Three Rivers	E07000102	89	89	0	89
Watford	E07000103	21	21	0	21
Ashford	E07000105	581	581	0	581
Canterbury	E07000106	321	309	0	309
Dartford	E07000107	76	73	0	73
Dover	E07000108	321	315	0	315
Gravesham	E07000109	105	99	0	99
Maidstone	E07000110	393	393	0	393
Sevenoaks	E07000111	370	370	1	369
Shepway	E07000112	366	357	0	357
Swale	E07000113	422	374	0	374
Thanet	E07000114	112	103	0	103
Tonbridge and Malling	E07000115	241	240	0	240
Tunbridge Wells	E07000116	331	331	0	331
Burnley	E07000117	111	111	0	111
Chorley	E07000118	203	203	0	203
Fylde	E07000119	183	166	0	166
Hyndburn	E07000120	73	73	0	73
Lancaster	E07000121	654	576	0	576
Pendle	E07000122	169	169	0	169
Preston	E07000123	143	142	0	142
Ribble Valley	E07000124	584	584	1	583
Rossendale	E07000125	138	138	0	138
South Ribble	E07000126	115	113	0	113
West Lancashire	E07000127	381	347	0	347
Wyre	E07000128	329	282	0	282
Blaby	E07000129	130	130	0	130
Charnwood	E07000130	279	279	0	279
Harborough	E07000131	593	593	1	592
Hinckley and Bosworth	E07000132	297	297	0	297
Melton	E07000133	481	481	0	481
North West Leicestershire	E07000134	279	279	0	279
Oadby and Wigston	E07000135	24	24	0	24
Boston	E07000136	398	365	0	365
East Lindsey	E07000137	1831	1765	0	1765
Lincoln	E07000138	36	36	0	36
North Kesteven	E07000139	922	922	0	922
South Holland	E07000140	816	751	0	751
South Kesteven	E07000141	943	943	0	943

1.1 Standard Area Measurement for Local Authority Districts as at 31/12/2016

Local Authority Name	Code	Extent of the realm (km^2)	Area to mean high water (km^2)	Inland water (km^2)	Land only (km^2)
West Lindsey	E07000142	1158	1156	0	1156
Breckland	E07000143	1305	1305	0	1305
Broadland	E07000144	553	552	0	552
Great Yarmouth	E07000145	182	174	0	174
King's Lynn and West Norfolk	E07000146	1528	1439	0	1439
North Norfolk	E07000147	990	964	2	962
Norwich	E07000148	41	39	0	39
South Norfolk	E07000149	909	908	0	908
Corby	E07000150	80	80	0	80
Daventry	E07000151	666	666	3	663
East Northamptonshire	E07000152	510	510	0	510
Kettering	E07000153	233	233	0	233
Northampton	E07000154	81	81	0	81
South Northamptonshire	E07000155	634	634	0	634
Wellingborough	E07000156	163	163	0	163
Craven	E07000163	1179	1179	1	1177
Hambleton	E07000164	1311	1311	0	1311
Harrogate	E07000165	1309	1309	1	1308
Richmondshire	E07000166	1319	1319	0	1319
Ryedale	E07000167	1507	1507	0	1507
Scarborough	E07000168	826	816	0	816
Selby	E07000169	602	599	0	599
Ashfield	E07000170	110	110	0	110
Bassetlaw	E07000171	639	638	0	638
Broxtowe	E07000172	80	80	0	80
Gedling	E07000173	120	120	0	120
Mansfield	E07000174	77	77	0	77
Newark and Sherwood	E07000175	652	651	0	651
Rushcliffe	E07000176	409	409	0	409
Cherwell	E07000177	589	589	0	589
Oxford	E07000178	46	46	0	46
South Oxfordshire	E07000179	679	679	0	679
Vale of White Horse	E07000180	579	579	1	578
West Oxfordshire	E07000181	714	714	0	714
Mendip	E07000187	739	739	0	739
Sedgemoor	E07000188	606	564	0	564
South Somerset	E07000189	959	959	0	959
Taunton Deane	E07000190	463	462	0	462
West Somerset	E07000191	747	727	1	725
Cannock Chase	E07000192	79	79	0	79
East Staffordshire	E07000193	390	390	3	387
Lichfield	E07000194	331	331	0	331
Newcastle-under-Lyme	E07000195	211	211	0	211
South Staffordshire	E07000196	407	407	0	407
Stafford	E07000197	598	598	0	598
Staffordshire Moorlands	E07000198	576	576	0	576
Tamworth	E07000199	31	31	0	31
Babergh	E07000200	612	595	1	594
Forest Heath	E07000201	378	378	0	378
Ipswich	E07000202	40	40	0	40
Mid Suffolk	E07000203	871	871	0	871
St Edmundsbury	E07000204	657	657	0	657
Suffolk Coastal	E07000205	921	892	0	892
Waveney	E07000206	375	370	0	370
Elmbridge	E07000207	96	96	1	95
Epsom and Ewell	E07000208	34	34	0	34
Guildford	E07000209	271	271	0	271
Mole Valley	E07000210	258	258	0	258
Reigate and Banstead	E07000211	129	129	0	129

1.1 Standard Area Measurement for Local Authority Districts as at 31/12/2016

Local Authority Name	Code	Extent of the realm (km^2)	Area to mean high water (km^2)	Inland water (km^2)	Land only (km^2)
Runnymede	E07000212	78	78	0	78
Spelthorne	E07000213	51	51	6	45
Surrey Heath	E07000214	95	95	0	95
Tandridge	E07000215	248	248	0	248
Waverley	E07000216	345	345	0	345
Woking	E07000217	64	64	0	64
North Warwickshire	E07000218	284	284	0	284
Nuneaton and Bedworth	E07000219	79	79	0	79
Rugby	E07000220	354	354	2	351
Stratford-on-Avon	E07000221	978	978	0	978
Warwick	E07000222	283	283	0	283
Adur	E07000223	44	42	0	42
Arun	E07000224	224	221	0	221
Chichester	E07000225	812	786	0	786
Crawley	E07000226	45	45	0	45
Horsham	E07000227	531	530	0	530
Mid Sussex	E07000228	334	334	0	334
Worthing	E07000229	34	33	0	33
Bromsgrove	E07000234	217	217	0	217
Malvern Hills	E07000235	577	577	0	577
Redditch	E07000236	54	54	0	54
Worcester	E07000237	33	33	0	33
Wychavon	E07000238	664	664	0	664
Wyre Forest	E07000239	195	195	0	195
St Albans	E07000240	161	161	0	161
Welwyn Hatfield	E07000241	130	130	0	130
East Hertfordshire	E07000242	476	476	0	476
Stevenage	E07000243	26	26	0	26
Bolton	E08000001	140	140	0	140
Bury	E08000002	99	99	0	99
Manchester	E08000003	116	116	0	116
Oldham	E08000004	142	142	0	142
Rochdale	E08000005	158	158	0	158
Salford	E08000006	97	97	0	97
Stockport	E08000007	126	126	0	126
Tameside	E08000008	103	103	0	103
Trafford	E08000009	106	106	0	106
Wigan	E08000010	188	188	0	188
Knowsley	E08000011	87	87	0	87
Liverpool	E08000012	134	112	0	112
St. Helens	E08000013	136	136	0	136
Sefton	E08000014	205	155	0	155
Wirral	E08000015	256	157	0	157
Barnsley	E08000016	329	329	0	329
Doncaster	E08000017	569	568	0	568
Rotherham	E08000018	287	287	0	287
Sheffield	E08000019	368	368	0	368
Newcastle upon Tyne	E08000021	115	113	0	113
North Tyneside	E08000022	85	82	0	82
South Tyneside	E08000023	67	64	0	64
Sunderland	E08000024	140	137	0	137
Birmingham	E08000025	268	268	0	268
Coventry	E08000026	99	99	0	99
Dudley	E08000027	98	98	0	98
Sandwell	E08000028	86	86	0	86
Solihull	E08000029	178	178	0	178
Walsall	E08000030	104	104	0	104
Wolverhampton	E08000031	69	69	0	69
Bradford	E08000032	366	366	0	366

1.1 Standard Area Measurement for Local Authority Districts as at 31/12/2016

Local Authority Name	Code	Extent of the realm (km^2)	Area to mean high water (km^2)	Inland water (km^2)	Land only (km^2)
Calderdale	E08000033	364	364	0	364
Kirklees	E08000034	409	409	0	409
Leeds	E08000035	552	552	0	552
Wakefield	E08000036	339	339	0	339
Gateshead	E08000037	144	142	0	142
City of London	E09000001	3	3	0	3
Barking and Dagenham	E09000002	38	36	0	36
Barnet	E09000003	87	87	0	87
Bexley	E09000004	64	61	0	61
Brent	E09000005	43	43	0	43
Bromley	E09000006	150	150	0	150
Camden	E09000007	22	22	0	22
Croydon	E09000008	86	86	0	86
Ealing	E09000009	56	56	0	56
Enfield	E09000010	82	82	1	81
Greenwich	E09000011	50	47	0	47
Hackney	E09000012	19	19	0	19
Hammersmith and Fulham	E09000013	17	16	0	16
Haringey	E09000014	30	30	0	30
Harrow	E09000015	50	50	0	50
Havering	E09000016	114	112	0	112
Hillingdon	E09000017	116	116	0	116
Hounslow	E09000018	57	56	0	56
Islington	E09000019	15	15	0	15
Kensington and Chelsea	E09000020	12	12	0	12
Kingston upon Thames	E09000021	37	37	0	37
Lambeth	E09000022	27	27	0	27
Lewisham	E09000023	35	35	0	35
Merton	E09000024	38	38	0	38
Newham	E09000025	39	36	0	36
Redbridge	E09000026	56	56	0	56
Richmond upon Thames	E09000027	59	57	0	57
Southwark	E09000028	30	29	0	29
Sutton	E09000029	44	44	0	44
Tower Hamlets	E09000030	22	20	0	20
Waltham Forest	E09000031	39	39	0	39
Wandsworth	E09000032	35	34	0	34
Westminster	E09000033	22	21	0	21
Northern Ireland	**N92000002**	14133	14133	545	13588
Antrim and Newtownabbey	N09000001	728	728	156	572
Armagh City, Banbridge and Craigavon	N09000002	1436	1436	99	1337
Belfast	N09000003	132	132	0	132
Causeway Coast and Glens	N09000004	1980	1980	0	1980
Derry City and Strabane	N09000005	1239	1239	0	1238
Fermanagh and Omagh	N09000006	3006	3006	149	2857
Lisburn and Castlereagh	N09000007	510	510	5	505
Mid and East Antrim	N09000008	1049	1049	2	1046
Mid Ulster	N09000009	1955	1955	128	1827
Newry, Mourne and Down	N09000010	1637	1637	5	1633
Ards and North Down	N09000011	461	461	0	461

1.1 Standard Area Measurement for Local Authority Districts as at 31/12/2016

Local Authority Name	Code	Extent of the realm (km^2)	Area to mean high water (km^2)	Inland water (km^2)	Land only (km^2)
Scotland	**S92000003**	80226	78811	900	77911
Clackmannanshire	S12000005	164	159	0	159
Dumfries and Galloway	S12000006	6676	6438	11	6427
East Ayrshire	S12000008	1270	1270	8	1262
East Lothian	S12000010	701	679	0	679
East Renfrewshire	S12000011	174	174	0	174
Na h-Eileanan Siar	S12000013	3268	3100	41	3059
Falkirk	S12000014	315	297	0	297
Fife	S12000015	1374	1325	0	1325
Highland	S12000017	26473	26163	506	25657
Inverclyde	S12000018	174	162	2	160
Midlothian	S12000019	355	355	2	354
Moray	S12000020	2257	2238	0	2238
North Ayrshire	S12000021	904	885	0	885
Orkney Islands	S12000023	1086	1013	25	989
Perth and Kinross	S12000024	5419	5384	98	5286
Scottish Borders	S12000026	4743	4739	7	4732
Shetland Islands	S12000027	1657	1469	1	1468
South Ayrshire	S12000028	1235	1224	2	1222
South Lanarkshire	S12000029	1774	1774	2	1772
Stirling	S12000030	2255	2253	66	2187
Aberdeen City	S12000033	206	186	0	186
Aberdeenshire	S12000034	6338	6318	5	6313
Argyll and Bute	S12000035	7164	7008	99	6909
City of Edinburgh	S12000036	273	263	0	263
Renfrewshire	S12000038	269	261	0	261
West Dunbartonshire	S12000039	183	177	19	159
West Lothian	S12000040	432	429	1	428
Angus	S12000041	2203	2185	4	2182
Dundee City	S12000042	62	60	0	60
North Lanarkshire	S12000044	472	472	2	470
East Dunbartonshire	S12000045	174	174	0	174
Glasgow City	S12000046	176	175	0	175
Wales	**W92000004**	21225	20782	46	20736
Isle of Anglesey	W06000001	749	714	3	711
Gwynedd	W06000002	2622	2548	13	2535
Conwy	W06000003	1153	1130	4	1126
Denbighshire	W06000004	846	839	2	837
Flintshire	W06000005	489	437	0	437
Wrexham	W06000006	504	504	0	504
Ceredigion	W06000008	1806	1789	3	1786
Pembrokeshire	W06000009	1650	1619	0	1619
Carmarthenshire	W06000010	2439	2371	1	2370
Swansea	W06000011	421	380	0	380
Neath Port Talbot	W06000012	452	442	1	441
Bridgend	W06000013	255	251	0	251
Vale of Glamorgan	W06000014	340	331	0	331
Cardiff	W06000015	150	142	1	141
Rhondda Cynon Taf	W06000016	424	424	0	424
Caerphilly	W06000018	277	277	0	277
Blaenau Gwent	W06000019	109	109	0	109
Torfaen	W06000020	126	126	1	126
Monmouthshire	W06000021	886	850	1	849
Newport	W06000022	218	191	0	191
Powys	W06000023	5195	5195	15	5181
Merthyr Tydfil	W06000024	112	112	1	111

Source: ONS Geography Codes
Standard Area Measurement for UK Local Authority District

Parliamentary elections

Chapter 2

Parliamentary elections

This chapter covers parliamentary elections, by-elections and devolved assembly elections in the UK, Wales, Scotland and Northern Ireland.

Parliamentary elections (Table 2.1)

Information is supplied on the total electorate, average electorate and valid votes as a percentage of electorate. The number of seats by party is also listed.

Parliamentary by-elections (Table 2.2)

Information can be found on the votes recorded for each party and General Elections and subsequent by-elections between General Elections.

Devolved assembly elections (Tables 2.3 and 2.4)

Table 2.3 provides information on the devolved assembly elections in Wales and Scotland, listing information on the number of votes, percentage share and number of seats per party.

Table 2.4 provides information on the devolved assembly elections in Northern Ireland, listing information the number of seats by party and percentage share of the vote.

2.1 Parliamentary elections[1]

United Kingdom Thousands and percentages

		15-Oct 1964	31-Mar 1966	18-Jun 1970[1]	28-Feb 1974		10-Oct 1974	03-May 1979	09-Jun 1983	11-Jun 1987	09-Apr 1992	01-May 1997	07-Jun 2001	05-May 2005	06-May 2010	07-May 2015	08-Jun 2017
United Kingdom																	
Electorate	**DZ5P**	35894	35957	39615	40256	**DZ6V**	40256	41573	42704	43666	43719	43846	44403	44246	45597	46354	46844
Average-electors per seat	**DZ5T**	57	57.1	62.9	63.4	**DZ6R**	63.4	65.5	66.7	67.2	67.2	66.5	67.4	68.5	70.1	71.3	72.1
Valid votes counted	**DZ5X**	27657	27265	28345	31340	**DZ6N**	29189	31221	30671	32530	33614	31286	26367	27149	29688	30698	32204
As percentage of electorate	**DZ63**	77.1	75.8	71.5	77.9	**DZ6J**	72.5	75.1	71.8	74.5	76.7	71.4	59.4	61.4	65.1	66.2	68.7
England and Wales																	
Electorate	**DZ5Q**	31610	31695	34931	35509	**DZ6W**	35509	36695	37708	38568	38648	38719	39228	39266	40565	40968	41613
Average-electors per seat	**DZ5U**	57.8	57.9	63.9	64.3	**DZ6S**	64.3	66.5	67.2	68.8	68.8	68	68.9	69	70.8	71.6	72.7
Valid votes counted	**DZ5Y**	24384	24116	24877	27735	**DZ6O**	25729	27609	27082	28832	29897	27679	23243	24097	26548	27034	28732
As percentage of electorate	**DZ64**	77.1	76.1	71.2	78.1	**DZ6K**	72.5	75.2	71.8	74.8	77.5	71.5	59.3	61.4	65.4	66.0	69.0
Scotland																	
Electorate	**DZ5R**	3393	3360	3659	3705	**DZ6X**	3705	3837	3934	3995	3929	3949	3984	3840	3863	4100	3988
Average-electors per seat	**DZ5V**	47.8	47.3	51.5	52.2	**DZ6T**	52.2	54	54.6	55.5	54.6	54.8	55.3	65.1	65.5	69.5	67.6
Valid votes counted	**DZ5Z**	2635	2553	2688	2887	**DZ6P**	2758	2917	2825	2968	2931	2817	2313	2334	2466	2910	2650
As percentage of electorate	**DZ65**	77.6	76	73.5	77.9	**DZ6L**	74.5	76	71.8	74.3	74.2	71.3	58.1	60.8	63.8	71.0	66.4
Northern Ireland																	
Electorate	**DZ5S**	891	902	1025	1027	**DZ6Y**	1037	1028	1050	1090	1141	1178	1191	1140	1169	1237	1243
Average-electors per seat	**DZ5W**	74.2	75.2	85.4	85.6	**DZ6U**	86.4	85.6	61.8	64.1	67.1	65.4	66.2	63.3	65.0	68.7	69
Valid votes counted	**DZ62**	638	596	779	718	**DZ6Q**	702	696	765	730	785	791	810	718	674	718	857
As percentage of electorate	**DZ66**	71.7	66.1	76	69.9	**DZ6M**	67.7	67.7	72.9	67	68.8	67.1	68	62.9	57.6	58.1	65.4
Members of Parliament elected: (numbers)	**DZV7**	630	630	630	635	**DZV8**	635	635	650	650	651	659	659	646	650	650	650
Conservative	**DZ67**	303	253	330	296	**DZ6D**	276	339	396	375	336	165	166	198	306	331	317
Labour	**DZ68**	317	363	287	301	**DZ6E**	319	268	209	229	271	418	412	355	258	232	262
Liberal Democrat[2]	**DZ69**	9	12	6	14	**DZ6F**	13	11	23	22	20	46	52	62	57	8	12
Scottish National Party	**DZ6A**	–	–	1	7	**DZ6G**	11	2	2	3	3	6	5	6	6	56	35
Plaid Cymru	**DZ6B**	–	–	–	2	**DZ6H**	3	2	2	3	4	4	4	3	3	3	4
Other[3]	**DZ6C**	1	2	6	15	**DZ6I**	13	13	18	18	17	20	20	22	20	20	20

1 The Representation of the People Act 1969 lowered the minimum voting age from 21 to 18 years with effect from 16 February 1970.

2 Liberal before 1992. The figures for 1983 and 1987 include six and five MPs respectively who were elected for the Social Democratic Party.

3 Including the Speaker.

Source: British Electoral Facts 1832-2012

Plymouth University for the Electoral Commission: 01752 233207

2.2a Summary of Parliamentary by-elections in Great Britain (excluding Northern Ireland), 1945-2018

		Net Seat Gains and Losses						Average change in share of vote since previous election					
	Number of by-elections	CON	LAB	LD	PC/ SNP	Other	No change	CON	LAB	LD	PC/ SNP	Other	Average turnout
1945-50	50	+4	-1	...	...	-3	45	3.7%	-2.3%	-1.1%	1.4%	-1.0%	67.3%
1950-51	14	...	...	...	...	...	14	+6.8%	-2.0%	-4.6%		-0.2%	68.8%
1951-55	44	+1	-1	...	...	...	43	-0.6%	+0.3%	-0.6%	+0.6%	+0.3%	58.6%
1955-59	49	-2	+4	...	...	-2	34	-8.7%	+1.3%	+6.2%	+0.3%	+0.9%	63.5%
1959-64	61	-5	+4	+1	...	...	54	-14.1%	-2.1%	+13.7%	+1.2%	+1.5%	62.9%
1964-66	13	...	-1	+1	...	...	11	+1.3%	-1.8%	+0.5%	+0.3%	+0.4%	58.2%
1966-70	37	+11	-15	+1	+2	+1	22	+6.8%	-17.3%	+3.3%	+5.5%	+1.7%	62.1%
1970-74	30	-5	...	+5	+1	-1	20	-10.7%	-4.2%	+9.0%	+4.0%	+1.9%	56.5%
1974	1	...	...	...	...	...	1	-1.1%	-3.4%	-2.3%	...	+6.8%	25.9%
1974-79	30	+6	-6	+1	...	-1	23	+9.9%	-9.3%	-4.9%	-0.3%	+4.6%	57.5%
1979-83	17	-3	+1	+4	...	-2	11	-11.4%	-10.2%	+18.6%	+1.6%	+1.4%	56.7%
1983-87	16	-4	...	+4	...	...	11	-14.0%	+0.4%	+12.3%	+0.1%	+1.2%	63.5%
1987-92	23	-7	+3	+3	+1	...	15	-11.0%	-0.8%	-0.6%	+5.7%	+6.6%	57.4%
1992-97	17	-8	+3	+4	+1	...	9	-19.9%	+7.4%	+5.2%	+2.4%	+4.9%	52.7%
1997-2001	15	-2	+1	+2	...	-1	14	-0.6%	-11.1%	+5.0%	+3.1%	+3.6%	42.4%
2001-05	6	...	-2	+2	...	...	4	-4.2%	-19.8%	+15.8%	+1.1%	+7.0%	39.3%
2005-10	14	...	-1	+1	...	...	9	+2.6%	-10.4%	+2.0%	+4.3%	+5.3%	48.8%
2010-15	19	-3	...	...	...	+3	13	-6.4%	+5.4%	-7.6%	+1.1%	+17.9%	39.6%
2015-17	10	...	...	+1	...	...	8	-4.7%	+3.9%	+7.7%	+5.7%	-6.6%	44.1%
2017 - Dec. 2018	1	...	...	...	...	...	1	-8.6%	-17.0%	+20.2%	...	+6.2%	32.2%

Sources:

1. F.W.S. Craig, Chronology of British Parliamentary By-elections 1833-1987
2. Colin Rallings and Michael Thrasher, British Electoral Facts 1832-2006
3. House of Commons Library, RP10/50 By-election results 2005-10; SN05833 By-elections since 2010 General Election; CBP 7417 By-elections since the 2015 General Election; CBP-8280 By-elections since the 2017 General Election

2.2b Parliamentary by-elections in Northern Ireland, 1974 - 2018[5]

			Change in vote share since previous election:					
Date	Constituency	Result	DUP	UUP	SF	SDLP	Other	Turnout
GENERAL ELECTION 1974 (FEB)								
None								
GENERAL ELECTION 1974 (OCT)								
None								
GENERAL ELECTION 1979								
09/04/1981	Fermanagh and South Tyrone	Anti-H Block gain from Ind Rep	...	+41.0%	...	...	+51.2%	82.4%
20/08/1981	Fermanagh and South Tyrone	Anti-H Block hold	...	-3.2%	...	...	+3.2%	87.5%
04/03/1982	Belfast South	UUP hold	+22.6%	-22.4%	...	+0.9%	+29.3%	65.7%
GENERAL ELECTION 1983[6]								
23/01/1986	East Antrim	UUP hold	...	+47.5%	...	...	-4.8%	58.9%
23/01/1986	North Antrim	DUP hold	+43.2%	...	...	...	...	53.5%
23/01/1986	South Antrim	UUP hold	...	+48.5%	...	...	...	52.2%
23/01/1986	Belfast East	DUP hold	+35.6%	...	...	...	-6.1%	63.6%
23/01/1986	Belfast North	UUP hold	...	+35.3%	...	...	+13.7%	54.7%
23/01/1986	Belfast South	UUP hold	...	+21.4%	...	...	+2.4%	56.6%
23/01/1986	North Down	UPU hold	...	...	...	...	+21.9%	60.5%
23/01/1986	South Down	UUP hold	...	+8.1%	-2.2%	+5.6%	-0.6%	73.8%
23/01/1986	Fermanagh and South Tyrone	UUP hold	...	+2.1%	-7.6%	+5.0%	+0.5%	80.4%
23/01/1986	Lagan Valley	UUP hold	...	+31.5%	...	...	+7.3%	81.4%
23/01/1986	East Londonderry	UUP hold	...	+56.0%	...	...	...	47.0%
23/01/1986	Mid Ulster	DUP hold	+16.1%	...	-2.6%	+3.0%	-0.1%	77.0%
23/01/1986	Newry and Armagh	SDLP gain from UUP	...	+0.2%	-7.7%	+8.7%	-1.2%	76.6%
23/01/1986	Strangford	UUP hold	...	+45.4%	...	...	...	55.1%
23/01/1986	Upper Bann	UUP hold	...	+23.9%	...	...	+13.8%	57.2%
GENERAL ELECTION 1987								
17/05/1990	Upper Bann	UUP hold	...	-3.5%	-1.7%	-1.6%	-4.8%	53.4%
GENERAL ELECTION 1992								
15/06/1995	North Down	UKU gain from UPU	...	...	...	...	-19.3%	38.6%
GENERAL ELECTION 1997								
21/09/2000	South Antrim	DUP gain from UUP	...	-22.2%	+3.0%	-4.7%	-5.0%	43.0%
GENERAL ELECTION 2001								
None								
GENERAL ELECTION 2005								
None								
GENERAL ELECTION 2010 (up to July 2011)								
09/06/2011	Belfast West	SF hold	-1.5%	-1.4%	-0.4%	-2.9%	+6.3%	37.4%
07/03/2013	Mid Ulster	SF hold	...	...	-5.1%	+3.1%	+1.9%	55.4%
GENERAL ELECTION 2015								
None								
GENERAL ELECTION 2017 (as at December 2018)								
03/05/2018	West Tyrone	SF hold	-3.0%	+3.1%	-4.1%	+4.9%	+1.9%	54.6%

2.2b Parliamentary by-elections in Northern Ireland, 1974 - 2018[5]

Notes for table 2.2b:

1. The formation of new parties in the early 1970s altered the pattern of party competition at Westminster elections. The SDLP (formed 1970) and the DUP (formed 1971) are included in Table 14b (1974-2012). Ulster Unionists are listed as Conservatives up to 1972 when they stopped taking the Conservative whip.
2. Irish Nationalist/Anti-Partitionist
3. Sinn Féin (SF) candidate T.J. Mitchell was elected as MP for Mid-Ulster at the 1955 General Election, but was in prison at the time of election and hence was disqualified from being an MP. No petition was lodged but a by-election writ was subsequently issued; in the 31 August 1955 by-election Mitchell again stood for Sinn Féín and topped the poll (therefore the by-election is here recorded as a Sinn Féin hold). However on this occasion a petition was lodged and since Mitchell was disqualified, the Conservative candidate was elected instead.
4. Prior to the by-election the seat was held by a Conservative (see footnote 1). Changes in vote share are as compared to the 1955 General Election.
* Constituency returned two MPs at previous general election. Change in vote share between general election and by-election is calculating using the total vote received by a party's candidate in the previous general election. However some electors will only voted for one candidate in the general election and of those who cast two votes, some will have voted for candidates from different parties. Additionally some parties will only have stood one candidate in a multimember seat.
5. The formation of new parties in the early 1970s altered the pattern of party competition at Westminster elections. The SDLP (formed 1970) and the DUP (formed 1971) are included in this table but not in Table 14a. The Ulster Unionist Party (UUP) took the Conservative whip at Westminster until 1972 and so in Table 14a are listed under Conservatives.
6. Multiple by-elections were held in January 1986 after fifteen unionist Members resigned their seats in protest at the Anglo-Irish Agreement.

Party descriptions:

DUP - Democratic Unionist Party
UUP - Ulster Unionist Party
SF - Sinn Fein
SDLP - Social Democratic and Labour Party
UPU - Ulster Popular Unionist Party
UKU - United Kingdom Unionist

Sources:

1. F.W.S. Craig, British Parliamentary Election Results 1918-1949
2. F.W.S. Craig, British Parliamentary Election Results 1950-1973
3. F.W.S. Craig, British Parliamentary Election Results 1974-1983
4. Colin Rallings and Michael Thrasher, British Parliamentary Election Results 1983-1997
5. House of Commons Library RP01/36, By-election results 1997-2000; RP05/34, By-election results 2001-05;
6. RP10/50, By-election results 2005-10; SN05833, By-elections since 2010 General Election, By-elections since 2015 General Election; CBP-8280 By-elections since the 2017 General Election

2.3a National Assembly for Wales elections, 1999-2016

	Number of Votes					% share				
	1999	2003	2007	2011	2016	1999	2003	2007	2011	2016
Constituency votes										
LAB	384,671	340,515	314,925	401,677	353,865	37.6%	40.0%	32.2%	42.3%	34.7%
PC	290,565	180,185	219,121	182,907	209,374	28.4%	21.2%	22.4%	19.3%	20.5%
CON	162,133	169,832	218,730	237,389	215,597	15.8%	20.0%	22.4%	25.0%	21.1%
UKIP		19,795	18,047		127,038		2.3%	1.8%		12.5%
LD	137,657	120,250	144,410	100,259	78,165	13.5%	14.1%	14.8%	10.6%	7.7%
Others	47,992	20,266	62,859	27,021	35,341	4.7%	2.4%	6.4%	2.8%	3.5%
Total	1,023,018	850,843	978,092	949,253	1,019,380	100%	100%	100%	100%	100%
Constituency seats										
LAB	27	30	24	28	27	67.5%	75.0%	60.0%	70.0%	67.5%
PC	9	5	7	5	6	22.5%	12.5%	17.5%	12.5%	15.0%
CON	1	1	5	6	6	2.5%	2.5%	12.5%	15.0%	15.0%
UKIP	0	0	0	0	0	0.0%	0.0%	0.0%	0.0%	0.0%
LD	3	3	3	1	1	7.5%	7.5%	7.5%	2.5%	2.5%
Others	0	1	1	0	0	0.0%	2.5%	2.5%	0.0%	0.0%
Total:	**40**	**40**	**40**	**40**	**40**	**100%**	**100%**	**100%**	**100%**	**100%**
Regional votes										
LAB	361,657	310,658	288,955	349,935	319,196	35.4%	36.6%	29.6%	36.9%	31.5%
PC	312,048	167,653	204,757	169,799	211,548	30.5%	19.7%	21.0%	17.9%	20.8%
CON	168,206	162,725	209,154	213,773	190,846	16.5%	19.2%	21.5%	22.5%	18.8%
UKIP		29,427	38,349	43,256	132,138		3.5%	3.9%	4.6%	13.0%
LD	128,008	108,013	114,500	76,349	65,504	12.5%	12.7%	11.7%	8.0%	6.5%
Others	51,938	71,076	119,071	95,776	95,511	5.1%	8.4%	12.2%	10.1%	9.4%
Total	**1,021,857**	**849,552**	**974,786**	**948,888**	**1,014,743**	**100%**	**100%**	**100%**	**100%**	**100%**
Regional seats										
LAB	1	0	2	2	2	5.0%	0.0%	10.0%	10.0%	10.0%
PC	8	7	8	6	6	40.0%	35.0%	40.0%	30.0%	30.0%
CON	8	10	7	8	5	40.0%	50.0%	35.0%	40.0%	25.0%
UKIP	0	0	0	0	7	0.0%	0.0%	0.0%	0.0%	35.0%
LD	3	3	3	4	0	15.0%	15.0%	15.0%	20.0%	0.0%
Others	0	0	0	0	0	0.0%	0.0%	0.0%	0.0%	0.0%
Total:	**20**	**20**	**20**	**20**	**20**	**100%**	**100%**	**100%**	**100%**	**100%**
Total seats										
LAB	28	30	26	30	29	46.7%	50.0%	43.3%	50.0%	48.3%
PC	17	12	15	11	12	28.3%	20.0%	25.0%	18.3%	20.0%
CON	9	11	12	14	11	15.0%	18.3%	20.0%	23.3%	18.3%
UKIP	0	0	0	0	7	0.0%	0.0%	0.0%	0.0%	11.7%
LD	6	6	6	5	1	10.0%	10.0%	10.0%	8.3%	1.7%
Others	0	1	1	0	0	0.0%	1.7%	1.7%	0.0%	0.0%
Total:	**60**	**60**	**60**	**60**	**60**	**100%**	**100%**	**100%**	**100%**	**100%**
Constituency turnout										
	46.4%	38.2%	43.5%	41.5%	45.5%					
Regional turnout										
	46.3%	38.1%	43.4%	41.4%	45.3%					

Sources

Colin Rallings and Michael Thrasher, *British Electoral Facts 1832-2006*

Electoral Commission, *Report on the National Assembly for Wales general election 5 May 2016*

House of Commons Library Briefing Paper CBP 7594 , *National Assembly for Wales Elections: 2016*

The next National Assembly for Wales election is expected in 2021

2.3b Scottish Parliament elections, 1999-2016

	Number of votes and seats					% Share				
	1999	2003	2007	2011	2016	1999	2003	2007	2011	2016
Constituency votes										
SNP	672,768	455,742	664,227	902,915	1,059,898	28.7%	23.8%	32.9%	45.4%	46.5%
CON	364,425	318,279	334,742	276,652	501,844	15.6%	16.6%	16.6%	13.9%	22.0%
LAB	908,346	663,585	648,374	630,461	514,261	38.8%	34.6%	32.1%	31.7%	22.6%
LD	333,179	294,347	326,232	157,714	178,238	14.2%	15.4%	16.2%	7.9%	7.8%
GRN			2,971		13,172			0.1%		0.6%
Others	63,770	184,641	43,402	21,534	11,741	2.7%	9.6%	2.2%	1.1%	0.5%
Total	**2,342,488**	**1,916,594**	**2,016,977**	**1,989,276**	**2,279,154**	**100%**	**100%**	**100%**	**100%**	**100.0%**
Constituency seats										
SNP	7	9	21	53	59	9.6%	12.3%	28.8%	72.6%	80.8%
CON	0	3	4	3	7	0.0%	4.1%	5.5%	4.1%	9.6%
LAB	53	46	37	15	3	72.6%	63.0%	50.7%	20.5%	4.1%
LD	12	13	11	2	4	16.4%	17.8%	15.1%	2.7%	5.5%
GRN										
Others	1	2	0	0	0	1.4%	2.7%	0.0%	0.0%	0.0%
Total	**73**	**73**	**73**	**73**	**73**	**100%**	**100%**	**100%**	**100%**	**100%**
Regional votes										
SNP	638,644	399,659	633,401	876,421	953,587	27.3%	20.9%	31.0%	44.0%	41.7%
CON	359,109	296,929	284,005	245,967	524,220	15.4%	15.5%	13.9%	12.4%	22.9%
LAB	786,818	561,375	595,415	523,469	435,919	33.6%	29.3%	29.2%	26.3%	19.1%
LD	290,760	225,774	230,671	103,472	119,284	12.4%	11.8%	11.3%	5.2%	5.2%
GRN	84,023	132,138	82,584	86,939	150,426	3.6%	6.9%	4.0%	4.4%	6.6%
Others	179,560	299,976	215,973	154,568	102,315	7.7%	15.7%	10.6%	7.8%	4.5%
Total	**2,338,914**	**1,915,851**	**2,042,049**	**1,990,836**	**2,285,751**	**100%**	**100%**	**100%**	**100%**	**100%**
Regional Seats										
SNP	28	18	26	16	4	50.0%	32.1%	46.4%	28.6%	7.1%
CON	18	15	13	12	24	32.1%	26.8%	23.2%	21.4%	42.9%
LAB	3	4	9	22	21	5.4%	7.1%	16.1%	39.3%	37.5%
LD	5	4	5	3	1	8.9%	7.1%	8.9%	5.4%	1.8%
GRN	1	7	2	2	6	1.8%	12.5%	3.6%	3.6%	10.7%
Others	1	8	1	1	0	1.8%	14.3%	1.8%	1.8%	0.0%
Total	**56**	**56**	**56**	**56**	**56**	**100%**	**100%**	**100%**	**100%**	**100%**
Total seats										
SNP	35	27	47	69	63	62.5%	48.2%	83.9%	123.2%	112.5%
CON	18	18	17	15	31	32.1%	32.1%	30.4%	26.8%	55.4%
LAB	56	50	46	37	24	100.0%	89.3%	82.1%	66.1%	42.9%
LD	17	17	16	5	5	30.4%	30.4%	28.6%	8.9%	8.9%
GRN	1	7	2	2	6	1.8%	12.5%	3.6%	3.6%	10.7%
Others	2	10	1	1		3.6%	17.9%	1.8%	1.8%	0.0%
Total	**129**	**129**	**129**	**129**	**129**	**100%**	**100%**	**100%**	**100%**	**100%**
Constituency Turnout										
	58.8%	49.4%	51.7%	50.4%	55.6%					
Regional Turnout										
	58.7%	49.4%	52.4%	50.4%	55.7%					

Sources

Colin Rallings and Michael Thrasher, *British Electoral Facts 1832-2006*

Electoral Commission, *Report on the Scottish Parliament election on 5 May 2011*

House of Commons Library Research Paper RP07/46, *Scottish Parliament Elections: 3 May 2007*

House of Commons Library Research Paper RP11/41, *Scottish Parliament Elections: 2011*

House of Commons Library Briefing Paper CBP-7529, Scottish Parliament Elections: 2016

The next Scottish Parliament election is expected in 2021

2.4 Northern Ireland Assembly elections: 1998-2017

	1st Pref Votes and seats won						% of votes and seats won					
	1998	2003	2007	2011	2016	2017	1998	2003	2007	2011	2016	2017
Votes												
DUP	146,917	177,944	207,721	198,436	202,567	225,413	18.1%	25.3%	30.1%	30.0%	29.2%	28.1%
Sinn Féin	142,858	162,758	180,573	178,222	166,785	224,245	17.6%	23.2%	26.2%	26.9%	24.0%	27.9%
UUP	172,225	156,931	103,145	87,531	87,302	103,314	21.3%	22.3%	14.9%	13.2%	12.6%	12.9%
SDLP	177,963	117,547	105,164	94,286	83,364	95,958	22.0%	16.7%	15.2%	14.2%	12.0%	11.9%
Alliance	52,636	25,372	36,139	50,875	48,447	72,717	6.5%	3.6%	5.2%	7.7%	7.0%	9.1%
UK Unionists	36,541	5,700	10,452	...	...	...	4.5%	0.8%	1.5%	...	...	...
PUP	20,634	8,032	3,822	1,493	5,955	5,590	2.5%	1.1%	0.6%	0.2%	0.9%	0.7%
People before Profit Alliance	...	...	774	5,438	13,761	14,100	...	...	0.1%	0.8%	2.0%	1.8%
TUV	...	...	...	16,480	23,776	20,523	...	...	...	2.5%	3.4%	2.6%
UKIP	...	...	...	4,152	10,109	1,579	...	...	...	0.6%	1.5%	0.2%
Green Party	510	2,688	11,985	6,031	18,718	18,527	0.1%	0.4%	1.7%	0.9%	2.7%	2.3%
Others	59,961	45,277	30,538	18,790	33,526	21,349	7.4%	6.4%	4.4%	2.8%	4.8%	2.7%
Total	**810,245**	**702,249**	**690,313**	**661,734**	**694,310**	**803,315**	**100.0%**	**100.0%**	**100.0%**	**100.0%**	**100.0%**	**100.0%**
Seats von												
DUP	20	30	36	38	38	28	18.5%	27.8%	33.3%	35.2%	35.2%	31.1%
Sinn Féin	18	24	28	29	28	27	16.7%	22.2%	25.9%	26.9%	25.9%	30.0%
UUP	28	27	18	16	16	10	25.9%	25.0%	16.7%	14.8%	14.8%	11.1%
SDLP	24	18	16	14	12	12	22.2%	16.7%	14.8%	13.0%	11.1%	13.3%
Alliance	6	6	7	8	8	8	5.6%	5.6%	6.5%	7.4%	7.4%	8.9%
UK Unionists	5	1	0	...	...	...	4.6%	0.9%	0.0%	...	...	...
PUP	2	1	1	0	0	0	1.9%	0.9%	0.9%	0.0%	0.0%	0.0%
People before Profit Alliance	...	...	0	0	2	1	...	...	0.0%	0.0%	1.9%	1.1%
TUV	...	...	...	1	1	1	...	...	...	0.9%	0.9%	1.1%
UKIP	...	...	...	0	0	0	...	...	...	0.0%	0.0%	0.0%
Green Party	0	0	1	1	2	2	0.0%	0.0%	0.9%	0.9%	1.9%	2.2%
Others	5	1	1	1	1	1	4.6%	0.9%	0.9%	0.9%	0.9%	1.1%
Total	**108**	**108**	**108**	**108**	**108**	**90**	**100.0%**	**100.0%**	**100.0%**	**100.0%**	**100.0%**	**100.0%**
Electorate	1,178,556	1,097,526	1,107,904	1,210,009	1,281,595	1,254,709						
Turnout	68.7%	64.0%	62.3%	54.7%	54.2%	64.0%						

Sources:
Colin Rallings and Michael Thrasher, *British Electoral Facts 1832-2006*
Electoral Office for Northern Ireland, www.eoni.org.uk

The next Scottish Parliament election is expected in 2022

this page is intentionally blank

Chapter 3

International development

International development

Overseas development assistance

The Department for International Development (DFID) is the UK Government Department with lead responsibility for overseas development. DFID's aim is to eliminate poverty in poorer countries through achievement of the Millennium Development Goals (MDG's). Statistics relating to international development are published on a financial year basis and on a calendar year basis. Statistics on a calendar year basis allow comparisons of aid expenditure with other donor countries. Aid flows can be measured before (gross) or after (net) deductions of repayments of principal on past loans. These tables show only the gross figures.

Aid is provided in two main ways: Bilateral funding is provided directly to partner countries while multilateral funding is provided through international organisations.

Funds can only be classified as multilateral if they are channelled through an organisation on a list in the OECD –

Development Assistance Committee (DAC) Statistical Reporting Directives – which identifies all multilateral organisations. This list also highlights some bodies that might appear to be multilateral but are actually bilateral (in particular this latter category includes some international non-governmental organisations such as the International Committee of the Red Cross and some Public-Private Partnerships). The DAC list of multilaterals is updated annually based on members nominations; organisations must be engaged in development work to be classified as multilateral aid channels although money may be classified as bilateral while a case is being made for a new multilateral organisation to be recognised.

While core funding to multilateral organisations is always classified as multilateral expenditure, additional funding channelled through multilaterals is often classified as bilateral expenditure. This would be the case in circumstances where a DFID country office transfers some money to a multilateral organisation (for example UN agency) for a particular programme in that country (or region). That is where DFID has control over what the money is being spent on and/or where it is being spent. Likewise, if DFID responds to an emergency appeal from an agency for a particular country or area, the funds will be allocated as bilateral spend to that country or region. As a result, some organisations, such as UN agencies have some of their DFID funding classified as bilateral and some as multilateral.

Bilateral assistance takes various forms:

Financial Aid – Poverty Reduction Budget Support (PRBS) – Funds provided to developing countries for them to spend in support of their expenditure programmes whose long-term objective is to reduce poverty; funds are spent using the overseas governments' own financial management, procurement and accountability systems to increase ownership and long term sustainability. PRBS can take the form of a general contribution to the overall budget – general budget support – or support with a more restricted focus which is earmarked for a specific sector – sector budget support.

Other Financial Aid – Funding of projects and programmes such as Sector Wide Programmes not classified as PRBS. Financial aid in its broader sense covers all bilateral aid expenditure other than technical cooperation and administrative costs but in SID we separately categorise this further.

Technical Co-operation – Activities designed to enhance the knowledge, intellectual skills, technical expertise or the productive capability of people in recipient countries. It also covers funding of services which contribute to the design or implementation of development projects and programmes.

This assistance is mainly delivered through research and development, the use of consultants, training (generally overseas partners visiting the UK or elsewhere for a training programme) and employment of 'other Personnel' (non-DFID experts on fixed term contracts). This latter category is growing less significant over time as existing contracted staff reach the end of their assignments.

Bilateral Aid Delivered Through a Multilateral Organisation – This category covers funding that is channelled through a multilateral organisation and DFID has control over the country, sector or theme that the funds will be spent on. For example, where a DFID country office transfers money to a multilateral organisation for a particular piece of work in that country. This also includes aid delivered through multi donor funds such as the United Nations Central Emergency Response Fund (CERF).

Bilateral Aid Delivered Through a Non-Governmental Organisation (NGO) – This category covers support to the international development work of UK and international not for profit organisations such as NGOs or Civil Society Organisations. This covers Partnership Programme Arrangements (PPAs), the Civil Society Challenge Fund and other grants.

Other Bilateral Aid – This category includes any aid not elsewhere classified such as funding to other donors for shared development purposes. More information on all of the above aid types is provided in the Glossary.

Humanitarian Assistance – Provides food, aid and other humanitarian assistance including shelter, medical care and advice in emergency situations and their aftermath. Work of the conflict pools is also included.

DFID Debt Relief – This includes sums for debt relief on DFID aid loans and cancellation of debt under the Commonwealth Debt Initiative (CDI). The non-CDI DFID debt relief is reported on the basis of the 'benefit to the recipient country'. This means that figures shown represent the money available to the country in the year in question that would otherwise have been spent on debt servicing. The CDI debt cancellation is reported on a 'lump sum' basis where all outstanding amounts on a loan are shown at the time the agreement to cancel is made.

CDC Gross Investments – CDC Group PLC is wholly government owned. Its investments must have a clear development objective. The net amount (that is equity purchase less equity sales) of

CDC investments in official development assistance (ODA)-eligible countries is reported as ODA and the gross amount (that is equity purchase only) is reported in GPEX.

Non-DFID Debt Relief – Comprises CDC Debt and ECGD Debt. CDC has a portfolio of loans to governments which can become eligible for debt relief under the Heavily Indebted Poor Countries (HIPC) or other debt relief deals. UK Export Finance (UKEF) is the UK's official export credit agency providing insurance for exporters against the main risks in selling overseas and guarantees to banks providing export finance. It also negotiates debt relief arrangements on commercial debt.

The Foreign and Commonwealth Office (FCO) contributes to UK GPEX in a number of ways:

The FCO Strategic Programme Fund supports a range of the UK government's international goals. Where the programme funds projects which meet the required OECD definition these projects are included in UK GPEX statistics.

The FCO supports the British Council through grant-in-aid funding. This funding goes to support a range of initiatives including building the capacity and quality of English language teaching; supporting education systems; and using cultural exchange to improve economic welfare. UK GPEX statistics include the proportion of this work which is clearly focussed on delivering economic welfare and development in ODA eligible countries.

The British Council also manages, on behalf of the FCO, the Chevening Scholarships programme, which provides funding for postgraduate students or researchers from developing countries to study in UK universities. Funding from this scheme to students from ODA eligible countries are included in UK ODA and GPEX statistics.

The FCO makes annual contributions to UN and Commonwealth organisations. A proportion of these contributions are allowed to score as ODA in line with Annex 2 of the DAC Statistical Reporting Directives.

The FCO is responsible for the UK contribution to the UN Department for Peacekeeping Operations (UNDPKO). In line with DAC rules 6 per cent of donor funding to UNDPKO is allowed to score as ODA. FCO also funds other bilateral peacekeeping missions including the Organisation for Security and Cooperation in Europe (OSCE) and the European Security and Defence Policy (ESDP) civilian missions; a proportion of which is reported as bilateral GPEX.

Conflict Stability and Security Fund (CSSF) formerly The Conflict Pool (CP) –The CSSF replaced the Conflict Pool (CP) - the Conflict Pool was a cross-departmental fund that supported a range of activities designed to reduce the number of people around the world whose lives are or might be affected by violent conflict. Unlike the CSSF, however, access to Conflict Pool funding was limited to just three Departments, namely the Foreign and Commonwealth Office (FCO), the Department for International Development (DFID) and the Ministry of Defence (MOD). As with the Conflict Pool, the CSSF combines Official Development Assistance (ODA) with non-ODA funding, enabling a wider range of responses to conflict and instability overseas . https://publications.parliament.uk/pa/jt201617/jtselect/jtnatsec/208/20805.htm#_idTextAnchor007

Other –includes contributions from other government departments including: Department of Energy and Climate Change; Department of Health; Department for Environment, Food & Rural

Affairs; Department for Culture, Media and Sport; Scottish Government; and the Welsh Assembly Government. It also includes estimates of the UK Border Agency's costs of supporting refugees in the UK; as well as estimates of gift aid to NGOs and other official funding to NGOs.

Further details on the UK's development assistance can be found in the Department for International Developments publication Statistics on International Development which can be found on the website www.dfid.gov.uk

Comparisons are available in the OECD Development Assistance Committee's annual report.

3.1 DFID Gross Public Expenditure 2010/11 - 2015/16

£ thousands

	2010/11	2011/12[R]	2012/13[R]	2013/14[R]	2014/15[R]	2015/16
DFID Bilateral Programme[1]						
Poverty Reduction Budget Support	643,671	536,662	410,133	567,073	434,844	119,723
of which						
General Budget Support	*360,467*	*242,290*	*167,343*	*106,600*	*49,698*	49,706
Sector Budget Support	*283,204*	*294,372*	*242,790*	*460,474*	*385,146*	70,017
Other Financial Aid	550,728	544,778	686,257	601,626	468,856	734,877
Technical Co-operation	467,939	527,907	638,258	901,383	1,003,205	1,173,155
Bilateral Aid Delivered through a Multilateral Organisation[2]	1,465,789	1,433,498	1,095,717	1,500,719	1,267,365	1,201,232
Bilateral Aid Delivered through a NGO	626,752	739,558	747,302	999,809	1,029,908	1,047,968
of which:						
Partnership Programme Agreements	*119,097*	*119,625*	*110,347*	*124,309*	*24,000*	50,131
Other CSO's	*507,655*	*619,933*	*636,955*	*875,500*	*1,005,908*	997,836
Other Bilateral Aid[3]	76,009	81,372	119,120	172,378	143,202	628,203
Humanitarian Assistance	350,669	354,293	476,878	866,485	1,071,957	1,187,007
DFID Debt Relief	66,460	14,954	17,169	9,172	11,384	-
Total DFID Bilateral Programme	**4,248,018**	**4,233,021**	**4,190,834**	**5,618,647**	**5,430,720**	**6,092,164**
DFID Multilateral Programme						
European Commission	1,268,563	1,220,076	1,085,769	1,095,770	711,663	825,691
World Bank	926,713	1,038,568	1,025,431	1,206,227	1,407,938	1,262,581
UN Agencies	355,337	376,708	360,304	441,269	392,631	367,994
Other Multilateral	671,061	622,373	809,804	1,563,745	1,416,051	1,031,312
Total DFID Multilateral Programme	**3,221,673**	**3,257,724**	**3,281,308**	**4,277,012**	**3,928,283**	**3,487,578**
Total DFID Programme (excl. Total Operating Costs)	**7,469,691**	**7,490,745**	**7,472,142**	**9,895,659**	**9,359,003**	**9,579,742**
DFID Total Operating Costs[4]	219,457	220,352	220,220	226,743	231,973	210,093
Total DFID Programme	**7,689,149**	**7,682,191**	**7,670,916**	**10,057,810**	**9,598,783**	**9,789,834**

Source: Department for International Development (DFID)

1. Descriptions of aid types given in Technical Note 1.
2 This covers earmarked funding provided through multilateral organisations where the recipient country, region, sector, theme or specific project are known. This figure does not include all bilateral aid spent through a multilateral organisation – other types of aid such as humanitarian assistance or debt relief also include aid spent through a multilateral organisation. In total in 2015/16 £1,979 million of bilateral aid was spent through multilateral organisations. Table 6 has a more detailed breakdown of this spend.
3. Other Bilateral Aid, for example UK Aid using other governments delivery partners (for instance Sweden)
4. Includes Front Line Delivery costs and Administration spend.
R Revised

3.2 DFID Bilateral Gross Public Expenditure by Region and Country Groupings 2011/12 - 2015/16[1]

£ thousands

		Financial Aid			Bilateral aid						
		General Poverty Reduction Budget Support	Sector Poverty Reduction Budget Support	Other Financial Aid[4]	Bilateral aid delivered through a Multilateral	Bilateral aid Delivered through an NGO	Other Bilateral Aid[2]	Technical Co-operation	Humanitarian Assistance	DFID Debt Relief	Total DFID Bilateral Programme[5]
TOTAL ALL COUNTRIES	**2011/12**	**242,290**	**294,372**	**544,778**	**1,433,498**	**739,558**	**81,372**	**527,907**	**354,293**	**14,954**	**4,233,021**
	2012/13	**167,343**	**242,790**	**686,257**	**1,095,717**	**747,302**	**119,120**	**638,258**	**476,878**	**17,169**	**4,190,834**
	2013/14	**106,600**	**460,474**	**601,626**	**1,500,719**	**999,809**	**172,378**	**901,383**	**866,485**	**9,172**	**5,618,647**
	2014/15	**49,698**	**385,146**	**468,856**	**1,267,365**	**1,029,908**	**143,202**	**1,003,205**	**1,071,957**	**11,384**	**5,430,720**
	2015/16	**49,706**	**70,017**	**734,877**	**1,201,232**	**1,047,968**	**628,203**	**1,173,155**	**1,187,007**	**0**	**6,092,164**
Africa	2011/12	222,290	242,372	222,158	386,727	213,000	45,046	298,059	260,329	1,713	1,891,694
	2012/13	167,343	213,090	297,050	316,222	207,660	76,600	368,762	317,865	1,124	1,965,716
	2013/14	106,600	301,524	255,996	419,387	308,233	78,176	491,619	379,607	0	2,341,141
	2014/15	49,698	266,896	159,625	397,398	291,669	45,574	530,160	642,456	0	2,383,476
	2015/16	19,706	40,217	368,601	449,333	341,155	69,256	585,255	536,377	0	2,409,899
of which:	*2011/12*	*222,290*	*242,372*	*222,158*	*356,386*	*190,709*	*38,047*	*285,327*	*248,159*	*1,713*	1,807,161
Africa: South of Sahara	*2012/13*	*167,343*	*213,090*	*297,050*	*265,232*	*180,258*	*70,965*	*340,240*	*266,401*	*1,124*	1,801,704
	2013/14	*106,600*	*301,524*	*255,996*	*369,362*	*274,171*	*458,274*	*377,742*	*0*	*0*	2,143,668
	2014/15	*49,698*	*266,896*	*159,623*	*316,186*	*258,450*	*34,758*	*480,926*	*574,999*	*0*	2,141,536
	2015/16	*19,706*	*40,217*	*368,601*	*360,496*	*295,237*	*46,946*	*533,687*	*513,116*	*0*	2,178,006
Americas	2011/12	0	0	26,576	14,004	2,215	526	3,932	2,537	0	49,789
	2012/13	0	0	30,440	11,979	1,947	364	2,552	6,383	0	53,665
	2013/14	0	0	26,857	8,503	1,522	154	1,028	7,273	3,535	48,872
	2014/15	0	0	23,231	5,059	1,509	841	2,905	3,945	0	37,490
	2015/16	0	0	28,905	6,147	756	415	1,386	2,978	0	40,586
Asia	2011/12	20,000	52,000	293,140	413,386	130,578	15,342	142,103	88,841	9,218	1,164,608
	2012/13	0	29,700	349,146	230,559	154,291	17,503	158,565	147,882	9,781	1,097,427
	2013/14	0	158,950	308,699	357,438	180,964	54,985	207,705	439,868	0	1,708,610
	2014/15	0	118,250	275,918	221,946	178,572	63,215	208,528	391,541	0	1,457,970
	2015/16	30,000	29,800	326,857	265,347	183,107	65,657	252,103	533,911	0	1,686,782
Europe	2011/12	0	0	0	244	344	-14	3,230	425	378	4,607
	2012/13	0	0	6,746	782	193	12	2,305	7	0	10,046
	2013/14	0	0	6,340	66	0	12	25	129	0	6,573
	2014/15	0	0	5,915	1,389	0	500	261	6,410	0	14,475
	2015/16	0	0	5,450	3,992	0	511	4,853	17,052	0	31,858
Pacific	2011/12	0	0	2,738	0	0	0	36	0	212	2,986
	2012/13	0	0	2,883	0	0	0	11	150	166	3,210
	2013/14	0	0	2,839	0	0	0	0	0	44	2,883
	2014/15	0	0	3,070	570	218	0	106	1,300	0	5,264
	2015/16	0	0	2,907	0	0	0	0	1,348	0	4,256

3.2 DFID Bilateral Gross Public Expenditure by Region and Country Groupings 2011/12 - 2015/16[1]

£ thousands

		Financial Aid			Bilateral aid						
		General Poverty Reduction Budget Support	Sector Poverty Reduction Budget Support	Other Financial Aid[4]	Bilateral aid delivered through a Multilateral	Bilateral aid Delivered through an NGO	Other Bilateral Aid[2]	Technical Co-operation	Humanitarian Assistance	DFID Debt Relief	Total DFID Bilateral Programme[5]
Non Region Specific	2011/12	0	0	167	619,137	393,421	20,473	80,546	2,161	3,433	1,119,337
	2012/13[R]	0	0	-10	536,175	383,211	24,640	106,063	4,591	6,097	1,060,769
	2013/14[R]	0	0	894	715,325	509,090	39,051	201,007	39,608	5,593	1,510,569
	2014/15[R]	0	0	1,097	641,002	557,940	33,072	261,245	26,305	11,384	1,532,045
	2015/16	0	0	2,156	476,413	522,950	492,365	329,559	95,340	0	1,918,783
Other groups											
Total Developing Countries[3]	2011/12	242,290	294,372	538,531	743,312	312,187	53,281	424,512	342,464	11,521	2,962,470
	2012/13	167,343	242,790	676,208	507,266	331,487	82,253	492,518	403,905	11,072	2,914,843
	2013/14	106,600	460,474	587,736	696,783	450,321	92,426	657,599	612,184	3,578	3,667,700
	2014/15	49,698	385,146	456,806	505,451	432,096	98,890	672,587	851,193	0	3,451,867
	2015/16	49,706	70,017	718,559	583,608	469,384	113,170	765,562	1,059,637	0	3,829,643
Least Developed Countries	2011/12	210,000	210,372	196,839	459,436	236,335	37,951	177,206	244,447	4,782	1,777,367
	2012/13	153,235	203,090	329,843	273,248	232,812	66,016	220,994	282,805	4,857	1,766,900
	2013/14	93,668	299,024	302,854	426,444	298,523	59,634	295,780	344,688	44	2,120,659
	2014/15	49,698	287,403	237,567	330,156	286,036	49,313	316,108	613,048	0	2,169,329
	2015/16	9,706	37,727	502,714	335,976	280,756	56,287	356,469	637,567	0	2,217,203
Commonwealth	2011/12	222,290	147,539	444,034	305,730	192,060	30,273	279,811	94,825	1,305	1,717,867
	2012/13	167,343	114,290	487,666	204,792	208,203	52,367	329,497	80,472	1,291	1,645,921
	2013/14	106,600	260,824	414,936	303,174	309,900	61,085	443,382	97,907	3,578	2,001,386
	2014/15	49,698	162,496	320,137	180,079	305,409	68,811	465,901	308,257	0	1,860,788
	2015/16	49,706	66,244	374,883	235,353	324,830	80,014	508,362	228,830	0	1,868,222
of which	*2011/12[R]*	*0*	*0*	*91,166*	*0*	*298*	*0*	*5,962*	*0*	*0*	*97,426*
Overseas Territories[7]	*2012/13[R]*	*0*	*0*	*130,123*	*0*	*201*	*0*	*3,581*	*0*	*0*	*133,905*
	2013/14[R]	*0*	*0*	*117,901*	*0*	*252*	*0*	*1,546*	*0*	*0*	*119,699*
	2014/15[R]	*0*	*0*	*94,294*	*0*	*216*	*0*	*2,572*	*0*	*0*	*97,083*
	2015/16	*0*	*0*	*82,451*	*0*	*199*	*0*	*3,326*	*0*	*0*	*85,976*
HIPC Countries[6]	2011/12	222,290	242,372	156,929	344,625	137,161	30,654	131,226	229,373	0	1,494,629
	2012/13	167,343	213,090	303,951	190,153	122,886	59,125	171,428	245,884	0	1,473,861
	2013/14	106,600	301,524	254,558	266,066	187,735	39,630	234,391	302,209	0	1,692,713
	2014/15	49,698	266,896	187,047	250,065	191,153	30,810	277,856	570,905	0	1,824,430
	2015/16	19,706	40,217	478,419	246,680	211,900	40,878	317,701	498,793	0	1,854,294

Source: Department for International Development (DFID)

1. Descriptions of aid types given in Technical Note 1.
2. Other Bilateral Aid, for example UK Aid using other governments delivery partners (for instance Sweden)
3. Developing Countries are those countries and regions in the DAC List of Recipients of Official Development Assistance.
4. Pension payments have been reclassified from "Other Financial Aid" to "Aid from other UK Official Sources". This is consistent with the classification of spending under Department Expenditure Limits (DEL) agreed with Treasury.
5. Includes Non Region Specific
6. Highly Indebted Poor Countries
7. Overseas territories in GPEX 15/16 were Anguilla, Cyprus, Gibraltar, Montserrat, Pitcairn Island, St Helena (including Tristan da Cunha) and Turks and Caicos Islands

R. Revised

3.3 DFID Gross Public Expenditure by Input Sector Code and Delivery Channel, 2015/16

£ thousands

Input Sector Code	DFID Bilateral through a Multilateral GPEX	DFID Other Bilateral GPEX	Total DFID Bilateral GPEX
Education:			
11010 Education Poverty Reduction Budget Support	0	23,463	23,463
11020 Education Unallocable/Unspecified	7,994	18,135	26,130
11110 Education Policy and Administrative Management	1,867	44,813	46,680
11120 Facilities and Training Education	654	13,540	14,194
11130 Teacher Training	19,303	32,531	51,834
11220 Primary Education	36,693	195,217	231,910
11230 Basic Life Skills for Youth and Adults Education	676	44,038	44,713
11240 Pre-School	100	289	389
11320 Secondary Education	18,370	65,336	83,706
11330 Vocational Training	6,460	18,888	25,348
11420 Higher Education	0	39,631	39,631
11430 Advanced Technical and Managerial Training	0	7,964	7,964
Education Total	**92,117**	**503,846**	**595,963**
Health:			
12010 Health Poverty Reduction Budget Support	0	5,468	5,468
12020 Health Unallocable/Unspecified	622	16,697	17,320
12110 Health Policy and Administrative Management	10,705	44,197	54,903
12220 Basic Health Care	21,749	97,396	119,145
12240 Basic Nutrition	32,447	32,575	65,023
12250 Infectious Disease Control	69,657	35,910	105,568
12261 Health Education	10,258	22,208	32,466
12262 Malaria Control	17,681	50,749	68,430
12263 Tuberculosis Control	2,670	9,925	12,595
12281 Health Personnel Development	1,973	13,387	15,361
13010 Population Policy and Administrative Management	2,229	885	3,113
13021 Reproductive Health Care	17,543	28,746	46,290
13022 Maternal and Neonatal Health	48,415	76,331	124,746
13030 Family Planning	56,841	64,112	120,953
13041 HIV/AIDS including STD Prevention	3,105	18,387	21,492
13042 HIV/AIDS including STD Treatment and Care	3,920	1,747	5,667
13081 Personnel Development for Population and Reproductive Health	881	17,723	18,604
Health Total	**300,697**	**536,444**	**837,141**
Social Infrastructure and Services:			
16011 Social Protection	28,939	168,604	197,543
16012 Social Other	8,733	26,519	35,252
16020 Employment Policy & Admin Management	715	748	1,463
16030 Housing Policy and Admin Management	0	825	825
16040 Low-cost Housing	0	5,772	5,772
16070 Poverty Reduction Budget Support-Social infrastructure and services	0	5,278	5,278
52010 Food Aid and Food Security Programmes	13,069	12,803	25,872
Social Infrastructure and Services Total	**51,456**	**220,550**	**272,006**
Water Supply and Sanitation:			
14010 Water Resources Policy and Administrative Management	10,015	14,783	24,798
14015 Water Resources Protection	1,911	4,675	6,586
14020 Water Supply and Sanitation Large Systems	166	6,791	6,957
14021 Water Supply – Large Systems	0	3,628	3,628
14022 Sanitation - large systems, (MDG Water and Sanitation)	0	109	109
14030 Basic Drinking Water	15,925	13,588	29,513
14031 Basic drinking water supply	13,016	36,270	49,286
14032 Basic sanitation	9,523	38,365	47,888
14040 River Development	3,100	1,236	4,336
14050 Waste Management and Disposal	780	1,840	2,620
14060 Water Poverty Reduction Budget Support	0	2,082	2,082
14070 Water Unallocable/Unspecified	-951	4,687	3,736
14081 Education and Training	4,001	1,717	5,719
Water Supply and Sanitation Total	**57,486**	**129,770**	**187,256**

3.3 DFID Gross Public Expenditure by Input Sector Code and Delivery Channel, 2015/16

£ thousands

Input Sector Code	DFID Bilateral through a Multilateral GPEX	DFID Other Bilateral GPEX	Total DFID Bilateral GPEX
Government and Civil Society:			
15010 Government Poverty Reduction Budget Support	0	9,029	9,029
15020 Government Unallocated/ Unspecified	20,695	22,881	43,576
15110 Economic and Development Policy/Planning	17,775	82,774	100,549
15114 Tax policy and tax administration support	7,162	23,939	31,101
15121 Public Sector Financial Management	33,221	52,309	85,529
15122 Corruption - Public Sector Financial Management	2,979	22,053	25,032
15130 Legal and Judicial Development	6,506	20,972	27,477
15141 National Government Administration	65,908	21,939	87,847
15142 Local Government Administration	11,843	29,112	40,955
15150 Strengthening Civil Society	5,064	75,899	80,963
15152 Legislatures and political parties (Governance and Security)	500	6,553	7,053
15161 Elections	4,229	16,404	20,634
15162 Human Rights	6,377	20,567	26,943
15163 Free Flow of Information	982	10,226	11,208
15164 Women's Equality Organisations and Institutions	5,698	28,013	33,711
15172 Statistical Capacity Building	20,023	4,127	24,150
15173 Narcotics Control	0	587	587
15180 Ending violence against women and girls	0	443	443
15210 Security System Management and Reform	8,339	20,237	28,576
15220 Civilian Peace-Building, Conflict Prevention and Resolution	24,936	33,458	58,394
15230 Post-Conflict Peace-Building (UN)	294	1,108	1,402
15240 Reintegration and SALW Control	0	902	902
15250 Land Mine Clearance	0	6,048	6,048
Government and Civil Society Total	**242,530**	**509,581**	**752,111**
Economic:			
Economic Infrastructure			
21010 Transport Policy and Administrative Management	1,179	17,354	18,534
21021 Road Transport: Excluding Rural Feeder Roads	28,350	7,509	35,859
21022 Road Transport: Rural Feeder Roads	13,900	17,336	31,236
21031 Other Transport	1,685	16,051	17,736
22010 Communications Policy and Administrative Management	0	1,203	1,203
22020 Telecommunications	0	332	332
22030 Radio/Television/Print Media: Communications	0	173	173
22040 Information and Communication Technology (ICT)	780	436	1,216
23010 Energy Policy and Administrative Management	9,424	12,499	21,922
23020 Power Generation/Non-Renewable Sources: Energy	10,180	2,628	12,808
23030 Power Generation/Renewable Sources: Energy	3,028	38,321	41,349
23040 Energy Access for Households, Enterprises and Communities: Energy (Wealth Creation)	3,163	6,367	9,529
24010 Financial Policy and Administrative Management	8,007	336,501	344,507
24020 Monetary Institutions	3,034	1,282	4,316
24030 Formal Sector Financial Intermediaries	8,898	24,963	33,861
24040 Informal/Semi-Formal Financial Intermediaries	12,877	24,148	37,026
24081 Education/Training in Banking and Financial Services	554	3,960	4,515
25010 Business Support Services and Institutions	14,301	51,025	65,326
25020 Privatisation	1,097	1,115	2,212
Production Sectors			
31110 Agriculture Policy and Administrative Management	9,086	15,142	24,227
31120 Agricultural Development	99,455	50,369	149,824
31130 Agricultural Land Resources	7,250	35,665	42,915
31163 Livestock: Agriculture	3,771	5,441	9,212
31191 Agricultural Services	9,956	14,939	24,895
31210 Forestry Policy and Administrative Management	3,300	17,672	20,973
31220 Forestry Development	0	2,935	2,935
31310 Fishing Policy and Administrative Management	0	0	0
31320 Fishery Development	0	672	672
32110 Industrial Policy and Administrative Management	824	1,700	2,524
32120 Industrial Development	1,519	4,971	6,489
32130 Small and Medium-Sized Enterprises (SME): Development	5,492	191,800	197,292
32210 Mineral/Mining Policy and Administrative Management	1,642	6,781	8,422

3.3 DFID Gross Public Expenditure by Input Sector Code and Delivery Channel, 2015/16

£ thousands

Input Sector Code	DFID Bilateral through a Multilateral GPEX	DFID Other Bilateral GPEX	Total DFID Bilateral GPEX
32310 Construction Policy and Administrative Management	25	1,997	2,022
32350 Production Poverty Reduction Budget Support	0	7,768	7,768
33110 Trade Policy and Administrative Management	3,318	16,935	20,253
33120 Trade Facilitation	10,997	17,697	28,694
33130 Regional Trade Agreements (RTAs)	1,020	8,037	9,057
33140 Multilateral Trade Negotiations	0	4,902	4,902
33181 Trade Education/Training	2,321	914	3,235
33210 Tourism Policy and Administrative Management	0	1,926	1,926
43050 Non-Agricultural Alternative Development	0	1,694	1,694
Development Planning			
43020 Poverty Reduction Budget Support for Econ. Infrastructure & Dev. Planning	1,730	19,302	21,032
43030 Urban Development and Management	15,871	41,632	57,503
43040 Rural Development	3,537	42,368	45,905
Economic Total	**301,570**	**1,076,462**	**1,378,031**
Environment Protection:			
41010 Environmental Policy and Administrative Management	546	5,580	6,126
41031 Bio-Diversity	0	438	438
41032 Climate Change	34,751	87,286	122,037
41033 Desertification, Environment	0	497	497
41050 Flood Prevention/Control	21	3,081	3,102
41060 Environment: Poverty Reduction Budget Support	0	400	400
41070 Environment Unallocable/Unspecified	50	1,695	1,745
41081 Environmental Education/ Training	0	804	804
41090 Climate Change - Low Carbon Emissions	2,453	17,781	20,234
41092 Climate Change - Cross Cutting	52	0	52
41093 Climate Change - Adaptation	10,714	36,788	47,502
Environment Protection Total	**48,586**	**154,350**	**202,936**
Research:			
80010 Economic Research	10,139	26,426	36,566
80011 Education Research	1,370	16,957	18,328
80012 Health Research	12,323	67,827	80,150
80013 Water Supply and Sanitation Research	0	3,483	3,483
80014 Governance Research	1,522	13,516	15,038
80015 Social Research	2,497	11,053	13,551
80016 Humanitarian Research	1,687	8,283	9,969
80017 Renewable Natural Resources Research	1,771	1,648	3,419
80018 Environment Research	2,797	11,851	14,647
80019 Energy Research	3,291	3,133	6,424
80020 Agricultural Research	9,188	34,166	43,354
80021 Forestry Research	0	484	484
80022 Fishery Research	0	0	0
80023 Technological Research and Development	1,013	4,326	5,339
80024 Unspecified/Unallocated Research	4,491	25,067	29,558
Research Total	**52,090**	**228,219**	**280,309**
Humanitarian Assistance:			
72010 Material Relief Assistance and Services	348,424	254,039	602,463
72040 Emergency Food Aid	248,721	48,211	296,932
72050 Relief Coordination, Protection and Support Services	63,757	126,976	190,733
73010 Reconstruction Relief and Rehabilitation	20,737	34,726	55,463
74010 Disaster Prevention and Preparedness	27,651	39,220	66,870
Humanitarian Assistance Total	**709,290**	**503,172**	**1,212,462**

3.3 DFID Gross Public Expenditure by Input Sector Code and Delivery Channel, 2015/16

£ thousands

Input Sector Code	DFID Bilateral through a Multilateral GPEX	DFID Other Bilateral GPEX	Total DFID Bilateral GPEX
Non Sector Allocable:			
88888 Core Contributions to Multilateral Institutions - Global Partnerships	368	0	368
88802 Core Contributions to Multilateral Institutions - Governance & Security	5,400	0	5,400
88805 Core Contributions to Multilateral Institutions - MDG Humanitarian	55,473	7,742	63,215
88807 Core Contributions to Multilateral Institutions - MDG Other Health	364	2,523	2,887
88811 Core Contributions to Multilateral Institutions - MDG Water & Sanitation	6,494	0	6,494
88814 Core Contributions to Multilateral Institutions - Wealth Creation	0	3,874	3,874
88816 Core Contributions to Multilateral Institutions - Climate Change ICF	1,000	0	1,000
88803 Core Contributions to Multilateral Institutions- Education	18,000	0	18,000
88804 Core Contributions to Multilateral Institutions- HIV/Aids	0	65	65
88806 Core Contributions to Multilateral Institutions- Malaria	0	42	42
88813 Core Contributions to Multilateral Institutions - Multiple Pillars	131	0	131
88815 Core Contributions to Multilateral Institutions - Climate and Environment	1,627	0	1,627
88889 Multilateral Capacity Building and Administration	1,404	218	1,622
88890 Multilateral Institutions: Secondees to & Staffing of	45	5,019	5,064
60010 Action Relating to Debt	0	0	0
90010 Programme Partnership Agreements	0	113,668	113,668
91020 Front Line Delivery Costs	0	91	91
92000 Support to Non-Governmental Organisations (NGOs)	521	106,545	107,067
93020 Aid to Refugees in Recipient Countries	1,760	2,516	4,276
88888 Multilateral Core Contribution	30,461	420	30,881
99820 Promotion of Development Awareness	576	7,600	8,177
Others			
Non Sector Allocable Total	**123,624**	**250,325**	**373,949**

Source: Department for International Development (DFID)

Notes

1. Figues may not sum to totals due to rounding.

Chapter 4

Labour market

Labour Market

Labour Force Survey

Background

The Labour Force Survey (LFS) is the largest regular household survey in the UK. LFS interviews are conducted continuously throughout the year. In any three-month period, nationally representative samples of approximately 110,000 people aged 16 and over in around 50,000 households are interviewed. Each household is interviewed five times, at three-monthly intervals. The initial interview is done face-to-face by an interviewer visiting the address, except for residents north of the Caledonian Canal in Scotland. The other interviews are done by telephone wherever possible. The survey asks a series of questions about respondents' personal circumstances and their labour market activity. Most questions refer to activity in the week before the interview.

The LFS collects information on a sample of the population. To convert this information to give estimates for the population, the data must be grossed. This is achieved by calculating weighting factors (often referred to simply as weights) which can be applied to each sampled individual in such a way that the weighted-up results match estimates or projections of the total population in terms of age distribution, sex, and region of residence. There is a considerable amount of ongoing research to improve methodologies. Whenever methodologies are implemented the estimates may be revised.

The concepts and definitions used in the LFS are agreed by the International Labour Organisation (ILO) – an agency of the United Nations. The definitions are used by European Union member countries and members of the Organisation for Economic Co-operation and Development (OECD). The LFS was carried out every two years from 1973 to 1983. The ILO definition was first used in 1984. This was also the first year in which the survey was conducted on an annual basis with results available for every spring quarter (representing an average of the period from March to May). The survey moved to a continuous basis in spring 1992 in Great Britain and in winter 1994/95 in Northern Ireland, with average quarterly results published four times a year for seasonal quarters: spring (March to May), summer (June to August), autumn (September to November) and winter (December to February). From April 1998, results are published 12 times a year for the average of three consecutive months.

Strengths and limitations of the LFS

The LFS produces coherent labour market information on the basis of internationally standard concepts and definitions. It is a rich source of data on a wide variety of labour market and personal characteristics. It is the most suitable source for making comparisons between countries. The LFS is designed so that households interviewed in each three month period constitute a representative sample of UK households. The survey covers those living in private households and nurses in

National Health Service accommodation. Students living in halls of residence have been included since 1992, as information about them is collected at their parents' address.

However the LFS has its limitations. It is a sample survey and is therefore subject to sampling variability. The survey does not include people living in institutions such as hostels, hotels, boarding houses, mobile home sites or residential homes. 'Proxy' reporting (when members of the household are not present at the interview, another member of the household answers the questions on their behalf) can affect the quality of information on topics such as earnings, hours worked, benefit receipt and qualifications. Around a third of interviews are conducted 'by proxy', usually by a spouse or partner but sometimes by a parent or other near relation. LFS estimates are also potentially affected by non-response.

Sampling Variability

Survey estimates are prone to sampling variability. The easiest way to explain this concept is by example. In the September to November 1997 period, ILO unemployment in Great Britain (seasonally adjusted) stood at 1,847,000. If we drew another sample for the same period we could get a different result, perhaps 1,900,000 or 1,820,000.

In theory, we could draw many samples, and each would give a different result. This is because each sample would be made up of different people who would give different answers to the questions. The spread of these results is the sampling variability. Sampling variability is determined by a number of factors including the sample size, the variability of the population from which the sample is drawn and the sample design. Once we know the sampling variability we can calculate a range of values about the sample estimate that represents the expected variation with a given level of assurance. This is called a confidence interval. For a 95 per cent confidence interval we expect that in 95 per cent of the samples (19 times out of 20) the confidence interval will contain the true value that would be obtained by surveying the entire population. For the example given above, we can be 95 per cent confident that the true value was in the range 1,791,000 to 1,903,000.

Unreliable estimates

Estimates of small numbers have relatively wide confidence intervals making them unreliable. For this reason, the Office for National Statistics (ONS) does not currently publish LFS estimates below 10,000.

Non-response

All surveys are subject to non-response – that is respondents in the sample who either refuse to take part in the survey or who cannot be contacted. Non-response can introduce bias to a survey, particularly if the people not responding have characteristics that are different from those who do respond.

The LFS has a response rate of around 65 per cent to the first interview, and over 90 per cent of those who are interviewed once go on to complete all five interviews. These are relatively high levels for a household survey.

Any bias from non-response is minimised by weighting the results. Weighting (or grossing) converts sample data to represent the full population. In the LFS, the data are weighted separately by age, sex and area of residence to population estimates based on the census. Weighting also adjusts for people not in the survey and thus minimises non-response bias.

LFS concepts and definitions

Discouraged worker - A sub-group of the economically inactive population who said although they would like a job their main reason for not seeking work was because they believed there were no jobs available.

Economically active – People aged 16 and over who are either in employment or unemployed.

Economic activity rate – The number of people who are in employment or unemployed expressed as a percentage of the relevant population.

Economically inactive – People who are neither in employment nor unemployed. These include those who want a job but have not been seeking work in the last four weeks, those who want a job and are seeking work but not available to start, and those who do not want a job.

Employment – People aged 16 and over who did at least one hour of paid work in the reference week (as an employee or self-employed), those who had a job that they were temporarily away from, those on government-supported training and employment programmes, and those doing unpaid family work.

Employees – The division between employees and self employed is based on survey respondents' own assessment of their employment status.

Full Time – The classification of employees, self-employed and unpaid family workers in their main job as full-time or part-time is on the basis of self-assessment. However, people on government supported employment and training programmes that are at college in the reference week are classified, by convention, as part-time.

Government -supported training and employment programmes – Comprise all people aged 16 and over participating in one of the government's employment and training programmes (Youth Training, Training for Work and Community Action), together with those on similar programmes administered by Training and Enterprise Councils in England and Wales, or Local Enterprise Companies in Scotland.

Hours worked – Respondents to the LFS are asked a series of questions enabling the identification of both their usual hours and their actual hours. Total hours include overtime (paid and unpaid) and exclude lunch breaks.

Actual Hours Worked – Actual hours worked statistics measure how many hours were actually worked. These statistics are directly affected by changes in the number of people in employment and in the number of hours that individual works.

Usual Hours Worked – Usual hours worked statistics measure how many hours people usually work per week. Compared with actual hours worked, they are not affected by absences and so can provide a better measure of normal working patterns.

Unemployment – The number of unemployed people in the UK is measured through the LFS following the internationally agreed definition recommended by the International Labour Organisation (ILO), an agency of the United Nations.

Unemployed people are:

Without a job, have actively sought work in the last four weeks and are available to start work in the next two weeks, or

Out of work, have found a job and are waiting to start in the next two weeks

Unemployment (rate) – The number of unemployed people expressed as a percentage of the relevant economically active population.

Unemployment (duration) – The duration of respondents unemployment is defined as the shorter of the following two periods:

Duration of active search for work

Length of time since employment

Part-time – see full-time.

Second jobs – Jobs which LFS respondents hold in addition to a main full-time or part-time job.

Self-employment – See Employees.

Temporary employees – In the LFS these are defined as those employees who say that their main job is non permanent in one of the following ways: fixed period contract, agency temping, casual work, seasonal work or other temporary work.

Unpaid family workers – Persons doing unpaid work for a business they own or for a business that a relative owns.

International Employment Comparisons

All employment rates for European Union (EU) countries published by Eurostat (including the rate for the UK) are based on the population aged 15–64. The rates for Canada and Japan are also based on the population aged 15–64, but the rate for the US is for those aged 16–64. The employment rate for the UK published by ONS is based on the working age population aged 16–64 and therefore takes into account both the current school leaving age and state pension ages.

The unemployment rate published by Eurostat for most EU countries (but not for the UK), are calculated by extrapolating from the most recent LFS data using monthly registered unemployment data. A standard population basis (15–74) is used by Eurostat except for Spain and the UK (16–74). The unemployment rate for the US is based on those aged 16 and over, but the rates for Canada and Japan are for those aged 15 and over. All unemployment rates are seasonally adjusted.

The unemployment rate for the UK published by Eurostat is based on the population aged 16–74 while the unemployment rate for the UK published by ONS is based on those aged 16 and over. There are other minor definitional differences.

Jobseekers allowance claimant count

This is a count of all those people who are claiming Jobseeker's Allowance (JSA) at Jobcentre Plus local offices. People claiming JSA must declare that they are:

- out of work
- capable of work
- available for work
- actively seeking work

during the week in which the claim is made.
All people claiming JSA on the day of the monthly count are included in the claimant count, irrespective of whether they are actually receiving benefits. Also see table 5.6 in Social protection chapter.

Annual Survey of Hours and Earnings

The Annual Survey of Hours and Earnings (ASHE) is based on a one per cent sample of employee jobs taken from HM Revenue & Customs (HMRC) PAYE records. Information on earnings and paid hours worked is obtained from employers and treated confidentially. ASHE does not cover the self-employed nor does it cover employees not paid during the reference period.

The headline statistics for ASHE are based on the median rather than the mean. The median is the value below which 50 per cent of employees fall. It is ONS's preferred measure of average earnings as it is less affected by a relatively small number of very high earners and the skewed distribution of earnings. It therefore gives a better indication of typical pay than the mean.

The earnings information presented relates to gross pay before tax, National Insurance or other deductions, and excludes payments in kind. With the exception of annual earnings, the results are restricted to earnings relating to the survey pay period and so exclude payments of arrears from another period made during the survey period; any payments due as a result of a pay settlement but not yet paid at the time of the survey will also be excluded.

Average Weekly Earnings

The Average Weekly Earnings (AWE) indicator measures changes in the level of earnings in Great Britain. Average earnings are calculated as the total wages and salaries paid by firms, divided by the number of employees paid. It is given as a level, in pounds per employee per week. Annual growth rates are derived from the level of average weekly earnings.

The AWE data are now published on a SIC 2007 basis, and the historic time series have been re-estimated as a result.

AWE is based on the Monthly wages and Salaries Survey (MWSS). As such, it is a timely indicator of changes in the level of earnings. The survey does not cover businesses with fewer than 20 employees; an adjustment is made to AWE to reflect these businesses. Note that the survey does not include Northern Ireland.

Unlike the previous measure of average earnings (the Average Earnings Index), changes in the composition of the workforce have an impact on AWE. If a high-paying sector of the economy employs more people, other things staying the same, average earnings will increase.

Average Weekly Earnings, like AEI before it, is a measure based on earnings per employee. If the number of paid hours worked per employee change, average earnings will also change.

Trade unions

The statistics relate to all organisations of workers known to the Certification Officer with head offices in Great Britain that fall within the appropriate definition of a trade union in the Trade Union and Labour Relations (Consolidation) Act 1992. Included in the data are home and overseas membership figures of contributory and non-contributory members. Employment status of members is not provided and the figures may therefore include some people who are self-employed, unemployed or retired.

4.1 Labour Force Survey Summary: economic activity for those aged 16 and over and those aged from 16 to 64

United Kingdom (thousands) seasonally adjusted

	All aged 16 & over								
	All aged 16 & over level	Total economically active level	Total in employ-ment level	Unemployed level	Economically inactive level	Economic activity rate (%)	Employment rate (%)	Unemploy-ment rate (%)	Economic inactivity rate (%)
People	**MGSL**	**MGSF**	**MGRZ**	**MGSC**	**MGSI**	**MGWG**	**MGSR**	**MGSX**	**YBTC**
Aug-Oct 2013	51,378	32,627	30,223	2,404	18,751	63.5	58.8	7.4	36.5
Aug-Oct 2014	51,769	32,802	30,848	1,953	18,967	63.4	59.6	6.0	36.6
Aug-Oct 2015	52,170	33,152	31,436	1,715	19,019	63.5	60.3	5.2	36.5
Nov-Jan 2016	52,269	33,225	31,541	1,684	19,044	63.6	60.3	5.1	36.4
Feb-Apr 2016	52,369	33,269	31,603	1,666	19,099	63.5	60.3	5.0	36.5
May-Jul 2016	52,468	33,414	31,779	1,635	19,054	63.7	60.6	4.9	36.3
Aug-Oct 2016	**52,535**	**33,407**	**31,794**	**1,613**	**19,128**	**63.6**	**60.5**	**4.8**	**36.4**
Men	**MGSM**	**MGSG**	**MGSA**	**MGSD**	**MGSJ**	**MGWH**	**MGSS**	**MGSY**	**YBTD**
Aug-Oct 2013	25,029	17,445	16,098	1,348	7,583	69.7	64.3	7.7	30.3
Aug-Oct 2014	25,241	17,490	16,404	1,086	7,751	69.3	65.0	6.2	30.7
Aug-Oct 2015	25,465	17,705	16,769	937	7,760	69.5	65.8	5.3	30.5
Nov-Jan 2016	25,522	17,751	16,829	922	7,771	69.6	65.9	5.2	30.4
Feb-Apr 2016	25,580	17,756	16,860	896	7,824	69.4	65.9	5.0	30.6
May-Jul 2016	25,637	17,826	16,921	905	7,811	69.5	66.0	5.1	30.5
Aug-Oct 2016	**25,672**	**17,774**	**16,889**	**885**	**7,898**	**69.2**	**65.8**	**5.0**	**30.8**
Women	**MGSN**	**MGSH**	**MGSB**	**MGSE**	**MGSK**	**MGWI**	**MGST**	**MGSZ**	**YBTE**
Aug-Oct 2013	26,349	15,182	14,125	1,057	11,167	57.6	53.6	7.0	42.4
Aug-Oct 2014	26,528	15,311	14,444	867	11,217	57.7	54.4	5.7	42.3
Aug-Oct 2015	26,705	15,446	14,668	779	11,259	57.8	54.9	5.0	42.2
Nov-Jan 2016	26,747	15,474	14,712	762	11,273	57.9	55.0	4.9	42.1
Feb-Apr 2016	26,789	15,514	14,743	770	11,275	57.9	55.0	5.0	42.1
May-Jul 2016	26,831	15,588	14,857	731	11,243	58.1	55.4	4.7	41.9
Aug-Oct 2016	**26,863**	**15,634**	**14,905**	**728**	**11,229**	**58.2**	**55.5**	**4.7**	**41.8**

United Kingdom (thousands) seasonally adjusted

	All aged 16 to 64								
	All aged 16 to 64 level	Total economically active level	Total in employ-ment level	Unemployed level	Economically inactive level	Economic activity rate (%)	Employment rate (%)	Unemploy-ment rate (%)	Economic inactivity rate (%)
People	**LF2O**	**LF2K**	**LF2G**	**LF2I**	**LF2M**	**LF22**	**LF24**	**LF2Q**	**LF2S**
Aug-Oct 2013	40,560	31,532	29,152	2,379	9,028	77.7	71.9	7.5	22.3
Aug-Oct 2014	40,702	31,649	29,715	1,934	9,053	77.8	73.0	6.1	22.2
Aug-Oct 2015	40,904	31,956	30,261	1,695	8,949	78.1	74.0	5.3	21.9
Nov-Jan 2016	40,954	32,008	30,343	1,665	8,947	78.2	74.1	5.2	21.8
Feb-Apr 2016	41,005	32,065	30,422	1,643	8,940	78.2	74.2	5.1	21.8
May-Jul 2016	41,055	32,206	30,588	1,618	8,850	78.4	74.5	5.0	21.6
Aug-Oct 2016	**41,080**	**32,174**	**30,577**	**1,596**	**8,907**	**78.3**	**74.4**	**5.0**	**21.7**
Men	**YBTG**	**YBSL**	**YBSF**	**YBSI**	**YBSO**	**MGSP**	**MGSV**	**YBTJ**	**YBTM**
Aug-Oct 2013	20,111	16,782	15,452	1,330	3,329	83.4	76.8	7.9	16.6
Aug-Oct 2014	20,191	16,801	15,729	1,072	3,390	83.2	77.9	6.4	16.8
Aug-Oct 2015	20,307	16,978	16,054	924	3,329	83.6	79.1	5.4	16.4
Nov-Jan 2016	20,338	17,001	16,089	912	3,337	83.6	79.1	5.4	16.4
Feb-Apr 2016	20,369	17,022	16,137	885	3,347	83.6	79.2	5.2	16.4
May-Jul 2016	20,400	17,075	16,178	896	3,326	83.7	79.3	5.2	16.3
Aug-Oct 2016	**20,413**	**17,025**	**16,148**	**877**	**3,388**	**83.4**	**79.1**	**5.2**	**16.6**
Women	**LF2P**	**LF2L**	**LF2H**	**LF2J**	**LF2N**	**LF23**	**LF25**	**LF2R**	**LF2T**
Aug-Oct 2013	20,449	14,749	13,700	1,049	5,700	72.1	67.0	7.1	27.9
Aug-Oct 2014	20,511	14,848	13,986	862	5,663	72.4	68.2	5.8	27.6
Aug-Oct 2015	20,598	14,978	14,207	771	5,620	72.7	69.0	5.1	27.3
Nov-Jan 2016	20,617	15,007	14,254	753	5,610	72.8	69.1	5.0	27.2
Feb-Apr 2016	20,636	15,043	14,285	758	5,593	72.9	69.2	5.0	27.1
May-Jul 2016	20,655	15,131	14,410	722	5,524	73.3	69.8	4.8	26.7
Aug-Oct 2016	**20,668**	**15,149**	**14,429**	**719**	**5,519**	**73.3**	**69.8**	**4.7**	**26.7**

Source: Labour Force Survey

Labour market statistics enquiries: labour.market@ons.gsi.gov.uk

4.1 Labour Force Survey Summary: economic activity for those aged 16 and over and those aged from 16 to 64

United Kingdom (thousands) seasonally adjusted

Note: When comparing quarterly changes ONS recommends comparing with the previous non-overlapping 3-month average time period (eg, compare Apr-Jun with Jan-Mar, not with Mar-May).

The headline employment rate is the number of people aged 16 to 64 in employment divided by the population aged 16 to 64.
The headline unemployment rate is the number of unemployed people (aged 16+) divided by the economically active population (aged 16+).
The economically active population is defined as those in employment plus those who are unemployed.
The headline inactivity rate is the number of economically inactive people aged 16 to 64 divided by the population aged 16 to 64.

Note on headline employment, unemployment and inactivity rates

The headline employment and inactivity rates are based on the population aged 16 to 64 but the headline unemployment rate is based on the economically active population aged 16 and over. The employment and inactivity rates for those aged 16 and over are affected by the inclusion of the retired population in the denominators and are therefore less meaningful than the rates for those aged from 16 to 64. However, for the unemployment rate for those aged 16 and over, no such effect occurs as the denominator for the unemployment rate is the economically active population which only includes people in work or actively seeking and able to work.

Note on headline employment, unemployment and inactivity levels

The headline employment and unemployment levels are for those aged 16 and over; they measure all people in work or actively seeking and able to work. However, the headline inactivity level is for those aged 16 to 64. The inactivity level for those aged 16 and over is less meaningful as it includes elderly people who have retired from the labour force.

4.2 Full-time, part-time and temporary workers

United Kingdom (thousands) seasonally adjusted

	All in employment					Full-time and part-time workers[1]							Temporary employees (reasons for temporary working)							Part-time workers (reasons for working part-time)[3]					
	Total	Employ- ees	Self employed	Unpaid family workers	Government supported training & employment pro- grammes[2]	Total people working full-time	Total people working part- time	Employ- ees working full-time	Employ- ees working part-time	Self- employed people working full-time	Self- employed people working part-time	Total workers with second jobs	Total	Total as % of all employ- ees	Could not find perman- ent job	% that could not find perman- ent job	Did not want perman- ent job	Had a contract with period of training	Some other reason	Total[4]	Could not find full- time job	% that could not find full-time job	Did not want full-time job	Ill or dis- abled	Student or at school
People (16+)	MGSA	MGRO	MGRR	MGRU	MGRX	YCBF	YCBI	YCBL	YCBO	YCBR	YCBU	YCBX	YCCA	YCCD	YCCG	YCCJ	YCCM	YCCP	YCCS	YCCV	YCCY	YCDB	YCDE	YCDH	YCDK
Nov-Jan 2006	28,934	25,046	3,692	92	104	21,660	7,274	18,746	6,300	2,842	851	1,038	1,432	5.7	364	25.4	388	105	575	7,151	612	8.6	5,226	169	1,107
Dec-Feb 2006	28,988	25,092	3,714	88	94	21,678	7,309	18,761	6,331	2,851	863	1,047	1,451	5.8	364	25.1	401	102	584	7,194	620	8.6	5,233	177	1,125
Jan-Mar 2006	29,048	25,143	3,724	89	93	21,704	7,344	18,774	6,369	2,865	859	1,029	1,486	5.9	374	25.2	410	114	588	7,227	620	8.6	5,256	175	1,133
Feb-Apr 2006	29,085	25,170	3,738	85	92	21,757	7,328	18,818	6,352	2,874	865	1,035	1,484	5.9	369	24.9	416	115	584	7,216	619	8.6	5,245	172	1,142
Mar-May 2006	29,063	25,179	3,703	86	95	21,745	7,319	18,833	6,347	2,852	850	1,025	1,478	5.9	369	25.0	412	115	582	7,197	610	8.5	5,228	171	1,147
Apr-Jun 2006	29,106	25,210	3,711	91	94	21,745	7,360	18,831	6,379	2,853	858	1,048	1,462	5.8	370	25.3	417	110	565	7,237	623	8.6	5,243	170	1,163
May-Jul 2006	29,140	25,226	3,726	99	90	21,769	7,371	18,847	6,379	2,858	869	1,053	1,439	5.7	359	24.9	414	99	566	7,247	632	8.7	5,233	176	1,170
Jun-Aug 2006	29,224	25,283	3,749	105	87	21,821	7,402	18,875	6,408	2,880	869	1,060	1,469	5.8	363	24.7	432	96	577	7,277	644	8.9	5,236	186	1,183
Jul-Sep 2006	29,183	25,211	3,771	104	98	21,763	7,421	18,817	6,394	2,877	895	1,068	1,466	5.8	367	25.0	433	94	573	7,288	646	8.9	5,227	186	1,197
Aug-Oct 2006	29,189	25,195	3,795	98	101	21,709	7,480	18,755	6,440	2,888	908	1,067	1,479	5.9	385	26.1	428	88	577	7,348	660	9.0	5,259	188	1,203
Sep-Nov 2006	29,204	25,200	3,788	101	115	21,745	7,459	18,779	6,421	2,895	893	1,059	1,495	5.9	391	26.2	437	94	573	7,313	662	9.1	5,240	190	1,177
Oct-Dec 2006	29,214	25,217	3,789	102	106	21,749	7,466	18,787	6,431	2,896	893	1,081	1,512	6.0	392	25.9	450	92	579	7,324	664	9.1	5,244	194	1,180
Nov-Jan 2007	29,202	25,186	3,809	100	107	21,753	7,449	18,762	6,424	2,924	885	1,072	1,529	6.1	399	26.1	442	105	583	7,309	668	9.1	5,235	198	1,166
Dec-Feb 2007	29,175	25,155	3,816	99	105	21,748	7,427	18,760	6,394	2,922	894	1,076	1,522	6.0	397	26.1	440	105	579	7,288	646	8.9	5,255	192	1,158
Jan-Mar 2007	29,194	25,169	3,821	103	100	21,756	7,438	18,782	6,387	2,908	914	1,074	1,534	6.1	405	26.4	435	112	583	7,300	660	9.0	5,257	189	1,162
Feb-Apr 2007	29,232	25,211	3,821	101	100	21,797	7,435	18,829	6,382	2,905	915	1,095	1,514	6.0	403	26.6	426	104	581	7,297	671	9.2	5,264	178	1,152
Mar-May 2007	29,314	25,310	3,801	99	104	21,896	7,419	18,926	6,384	2,907	894	1,100	1,513	6.0	407	26.9	422	101	584	7,278	685	9.4	5,246	176	1,140
Apr-Jun 2007	29,322	25,310	3,803	98	111	21,902	7,420	18,935	6,375	2,907	896	1,107	1,507	6.0	417	27.7	409	97	583	7,271	682	9.4	5,251	174	1,131
May-Jul 2007	29,352	25,319	3,811	104	118	21,921	7,431	18,965	6,355	2,897	914	1,118	1,501	5.9	411	27.4	412	92	586	7,269	697	9.6	5,228	181	1,130
Jun-Aug 2007	29,376	25,330	3,830	102	113	21,947	7,428	18,983	6,347	2,904	926	1,117	1,491	5.9	406	27.2	417	87	582	7,274	697	9.6	5,247	165	1,128
Jul-Sep 2007	29,420	25,380	3,832	97	111	21,989	7,431	19,026	6,354	2,902	930	1,103	1,485	5.9	393	26.4	421	84	587	7,284	694	9.5	5,258	169	1,127
Aug-Oct 2007	29,470	25,422	3,841	97	111	22,038	7,433	19,067	6,355	2,911	930	1,115	1,462	5.8	385	26.3	422	84	571	7,285	701	9.6	5,256	168	1,123
Sep-Nov 2007	29,527	25,471	3,843	103	110	22,054	7,472	19,086	6,385	2,901	942	1,116	1,478	5.8	380	25.7	432	83	583	7,326	698	9.5	5,287	173	1,136
Oct-Dec 2007	29,576	25,521	3,834	106	114	22,075	7,501	19,104	6,417	2,899	936	1,126	1,495	5.9	380	25.4	449	81	585	7,353	729	9.9	5,261	170	1,152
Nov-Jan 2008	29,614	25,546	3,847	109	112	22,083	7,531	19,108	6,438	2,901	947	1,112	1,473	5.8	367	24.9	440	78	588	7,385	739	10.0	5,273	174	1,160
Dec-Feb 2008	29,676	25,557	3,892	110	117	22,130	7,546	19,100	6,457	2,955	937	1,125	1,445	5.7	363	25.1	428	83	572	7,394	728	9.8	5,276	177	1,170
Jan-Mar 2008	29,684	25,582	3,878	109	115	22,134	7,549	19,123	6,459	2,946	932	1,103	1,430	5.6	363	25.4	426	83	558	7,391	705	9.5	5,290	184	1,168
Feb-Apr 2008	29,706	25,623	3,851	115	117	22,160	7,546	19,150	6,473	2,939	911	1,121	1,439	5.6	358	24.9	431	86	564	7,385	696	9.4	5,275	187	1,183
Mar-May 2008	29,749	25,657	3,856	116	119	22,227	7,522	19,216	6,441	2,941	915	1,116	1,420	5.5	357	25.1	404	85	574	7,356	671	9.1	5,281	193	1,165
Apr-Jun 2008	29,722	25,641	3,859	111	110	22,189	7,533	19,176	6,465	2,947	912	1,130	1,396	5.4	348	24.9	404	85	560	7,377	679	9.2	5,283	203	1,168
May-Jul 2008	29,696	25,629	3,854	101	112	22,170	7,526	19,166	6,463	2,942	912	1,131	1,385	5.4	351	25.3	391	88	555	7,375	689	9.3	5,267	215	1,162
Jun-Aug 2008	29,612	25,591	3,826	90	105	22,081	7,531	19,117	6,473	2,913	913	1,120	1,383	5.4	353	25.5	404	83	543	7,387	702	9.5	5,292	216	1,138
Jul-Sep 2008	29,580	25,566	3,818	90	107	22,061	7,519	19,097	6,469	2,915	903	1,126	1,390	5.4	360	25.9	402	88	540	7,372	715	9.7	5,280	207	1,130
Aug-Oct 2008	29,535	25,545	3,794	91	105	22,010	7,525	19,075	6,469	2,886	908	1,127	1,370	5.4	351	25.6	407	83	530	7,377	732	9.9	5,279	197	1,127
Sep-Nov 2008	29,556	25,532	3,830	91	103	21,959	7,597	19,016	6,516	2,900	930	1,145	1,403	5.5	364	26.0	399	84	555	7,447	753	10.1	5,312	199	1,138
Oct-Dec 2008	29,528	25,507	3,828	94	100	21,951	7,578	19,007	6,499	2,898	930	1,142	1,411	5.5	380	26.9	392	86	554	7,429	770	10.4	5,282	198	1,133
Nov-Jan 2009	29,539	25,508	3,845	88	99	21,952	7,587	18,994	6,514	2,918	927	1,152	1,425	5.6	397	27.8	390	91	546	7,441	815	11.0	5,256	191	1,134

4.2 Full-time, part-time and temporary workers

United Kingdom (thousands) seasonally adjusted

	All in employment					Full-time and part-time workers[1]							Temporary employees (reasons for temporary working)							Part-time workers (reasons for working part-time)[3]					
	Total	Employees	Self employed	Unpaid family workers	Government supported training & employment programmes[2]	Total people working full-time	Total people working part-time	Employees working full-time	Employees working part-time	Self-employed people working full-time	Self-employed people working part-time	Total workers with second jobs	Total	Total as % of all employees	Could not find permanent job	% that could not find permanent job	Did not want permanent job	Had a contract with period of training	Some other reason	Total[4]	Could not find full-time job	% that could not find full-time job	Did not want full-time job	Ill or disabled	Student or at school
People (16+)	MGSA	MGRO	MGRR	MGRU	MGRX	YCBF	YCBI	YCBL	YCBO	YCBR	YCBU	YCBX	YCCA	YCCD	YCCG	YCCJ	YCCM	YCCP	YCCS	YCCV	YCCY	YCDB	YCDE	YCDH	YCDK
Dec-Feb 2009	29,429	25,416	3,826	85	102	21,843	7,586	18,867	6,549	2,919	907	1,155	1,427	5.6	420	29.5	386	84	537	7,457	850	11.4	5,258	183	1,123
Jan-Mar 2009	29,366	25,335	3,844	87	101	21,768	7,598	18,794	6,540	2,918	926	1,161	1,428	5.6	426	29.8	386	81	536	7,466	875	11.7	5,257	184	1,111
Feb-Apr 2009	29,272	25,220	3,860	88	103	21,715	7,557	18,747	6,474	2,911	949	1,156	1,417	5.6	419	29.6	381	87	530	7,423	902	12.1	5,199	190	1,090
Mar-May 2009	29,155	25,096	3,856	101	102	21,585	7,570	18,641	6,455	2,892	964	1,143	1,404	5.6	417	29.7	384	92	512	7,419	936	12.6	5,163	191	1,087
Apr-Jun 2009	29,087	25,043	3,843	98	104	21,479	7,609	18,553	6,490	2,869	974	1,126	1,430	5.7	431	30.2	386	89	524	7,464	963	12.9	5,166	189	1,094
May-Jul 2009	29,018	24,962	3,858	91	107	21,412	7,606	18,462	6,500	2,895	963	1,121	1,429	5.7	443	31.0	371	84	531	7,463	972	13.0	5,175	181	1,086
Jun-Aug 2009	29,076	24,987	3,894	84	110	21,446	7,630	18,466	6,521	2,923	971	1,139	1,435	5.7	446	31.1	376	89	524	7,492	981	13.1	5,176	184	1,099
Jul-Sep 2009	29,069	25,002	3,881	78	109	21,388	7,681	18,434	6,568	2,903	978	1,143	1,450	5.8	464	32.0	377	85	525	7,546	1,001	13.3	5,195	189	1,115
Aug-Oct 2009	29,084	25,019	3,881	83	102	21,349	7,734	18,392	6,627	2,909	971	1,146	1,438	5.7	468	32.5	369	86	516	7,598	1,017	13.4	5,200	190	1,148
Sep-Nov 2009	29,092	25,013	3,896	76	107	21,344	7,748	18,401	6,611	2,898	998	1,129	1,437	5.7	490	34.1	365	76	506	7,609	1,038	13.6	5,199	183	1,144
Oct-Dec 2009	29,102	24,988	3,912	87	115	21,349	7,753	18,382	6,606	2,917	995	1,129	1,445	5.8	497	34.4	362	78	508	7,601	1,038	13.7	5,196	187	1,138
Nov-Jan 2010	29,057	24,947	3,906	86	119	21,291	7,766	18,335	6,612	2,906	999	1,094	1,451	5.8	499	34.4	370	77	505	7,612	1,045	13.7	5,197	185	1,141
Dec-Feb 2010	29,024	24,902	3,909	92	122	21,281	7,743	18,320	6,583	2,913	996	1,081	1,481	5.9	513	34.6	366	83	519	7,578	1,051	13.9	5,160	179	1,148
Jan-Mar 2010	29,013	24,844	3,954	90	124	21,234	7,778	18,247	6,598	2,940	1,014	1,067	1,482	6.0	513	34.6	366	79	524	7,612	1,071	14.1	5,187	168	1,140
Feb-Apr 2010	29,048	24,857	3,973	91	126	21,221	7,827	18,221	6,635	2,949	1,024	1,097	1,501	6.0	539	35.9	361	82	519	7,659	1,090	14.2	5,220	172	1,134
Mar-May 2010	29,144	24,960	3,959	93	131	21,265	7,878	18,278	6,683	2,932	1,027	1,134	1,541	6.2	554	36.0	375	80	532	7,710	1,073	13.9	5,280	167	1,148
Apr-Jun 2010	29,192	25,019	3,949	90	133	21,301	7,891	18,315	6,704	2,928	1,021	1,136	1,578	6.3	573	36.3	380	82	543	7,725	1,076	13.9	5,303	172	1,134
May-Jul 2010	29,325	25,094	3,989	103	139	21,335	7,991	18,323	6,771	2,949	1,040	1,134	1,577	6.3	571	36.2	383	80	543	7,811	1,115	14.3	5,311	171	1,174
Jun-Aug 2010	29,339	25,105	3,993	109	132	21,314	8,025	18,291	6,814	2,962	1,031	1,121	1,578	6.3	591	37.5	369	86	532	7,845	1,138	14.5	5,302	170	1,188
Jul-Sep 2010	29,385	25,106	4,046	105	129	21,341	8,044	18,294	6,812	2,990	1,055	1,121	1,588	6.3	600	37.8	370	87	531	7,867	1,153	14.7	5,310	165	1,190
Aug-Oct 2010	29,308	25,101	3,980	99	127	21,289	8,019	18,306	6,795	2,932	1,048	1,114	1,598	6.4	592	37.0	374	92	540	7,843	1,174	15.0	5,311	164	1,142
Sep-Nov 2010	29,284	25,056	4,003	94	131	21,282	8,001	18,285	6,771	2,944	1,059	1,114	1,575	6.3	589	37.4	354	94	538	7,830	1,178	15.0	5,342	172	1,086
Oct-Dec 2010	29,324	25,098	4,009	93	125	21,326	7,999	18,337	6,761	2,938	1,071	1,121	1,546	6.2	577	37.3	340	95	534	7,832	1,192	15.2	5,321	164	1,102
Nov-Jan 2011	29,391	25,138	4,025	100	129	21,387	8,004	18,406	6,732	2,929	1,096	1,151	1,567	6.2	579	37.0	341	93	553	7,828	1,180	15.1	5,349	164	1,080
Dec-Feb 2011	29,442	25,192	4,026	98	126	21,433	8,009	18,472	6,720	2,916	1,109	1,174	1,577	6.3	573	36.3	352	95	557	7,830	1,180	15.1	5,354	172	1,065
Jan-Mar 2011	29,441	25,235	3,983	98	125	21,437	8,005	18,507	6,728	2,883	1,100	1,166	1,595	6.3	579	36.3	357	100	558	7,828	1,188	15.2	5,338	182	1,063
Feb-Apr 2011	29,436	25,217	4,009	93	117	21,414	8,021	18,474	6,743	2,893	1,116	1,153	1,601	6.3	583	36.4	356	94	568	7,859	1,230	15.6	5,321	185	1,069
Mar-May 2011	29,466	25,249	4,022	91	104	21,451	8,016	18,519	6,731	2,891	1,131	1,151	1,605	6.4	582	36.3	363	92	568	7,862	1,259	16.0	5,312	180	1,056
Apr-Jun 2011	29,447	25,247	4,008	96	96	21,476	7,971	18,527	6,720	2,906	1,102	1,136	1,616	6.4	609	37.7	361	88	558	7,822	1,270	16.2	5,268	180	1,047
May-Jul 2011	29,345	25,162	4,001	94	88	21,452	7,893	18,502	6,660	2,915	1,086	1,142	1,568	6.2	578	36.9	354	85	551	7,746	1,287	16.6	5,186	182	1,032
Jun-Aug 2011	29,299	25,069	4,049	100	81	21,441	7,858	18,453	6,616	2,951	1,099	1,123	1,532	6.1	583	38.1	317	82	550	7,715	1,278	16.6	5,179	181	1,026
Jul-Sep 2011	29,281	24,972	4,121	105	83	21,408	7,873	18,387	6,586	2,978	1,142	1,143	1,524	6.1	581	38.1	326	86	532	7,728	1,275	16.5	5,177	190	1,034
Aug-Oct 2011	29,300	24,948	4,154	110	88	21,401	7,900	18,326	6,622	3,021	1,133	1,142	1,539	6.2	607	39.4	326	86	521	7,754	1,286	16.6	5,194	184	1,041
Sep-Nov 2011	29,325	24,965	4,150	114	97	21,381	7,945	18,309	6,656	3,009	1,141	1,146	1,554	6.2	593	38.2	350	90	521	7,797	1,333	17.1	5,187	184	1,048
Oct-Dec 2011	29,342	25,016	4,118	112	97	21,365	7,977	18,317	6,699	2,992	1,125	1,126	1,546	6.2	602	39.0	345	92	507	7,824	1,363	17.4	5,188	188	1,042
Nov-Jan 2012	29,346	25,003	4,127	111	106	21,364	7,982	18,316	6,686	2,995	1,132	1,116	1,560	6.2	611	39.1	343	97	509	7,819	1,395	17.8	5,168	188	1,025
Dec-Feb 2012	29,381	25,007	4,156	99	120	21,345	8,036	18,298	6,708	2,990	1,166	1,147	1,589	6.4	630	39.6	351	97	512	7,874	1,406	17.9	5,191	181	1,048

4.2 Full-time, part-time and temporary workers

United Kingdom (thousands) seasonally adjusted

	All in employment					Full-time and part-time workers[1]							Temporary employees (reasons for temporary working)							Part-time workers (reasons for working part-time)[3]					
	Total	Employ-ees	Self employed	Unpaid family workers	Government supported training & employment pro-grammes[2]	Total people working full-time	Total people working part-time	Employ-ees working full-time	Employ-ees working part-time	Self-employed people working full-time	Self-employed people working part-time	Total workers with second jobs	Total	Total as % of all employ-ees	Could not find perman-ent job	% that could not find perman-ent job	Did not want perman-ent job	Had a contract with period of training	Some other reason	Total[4]	Could not find full-time job	% that could not find full-time job	Did not want full-time job	Ill or dis-abled	Student or at school
People (16+)	MGSA	MGRO	MGRR	MGRU	MGRX	YCBF	YCBI	YCBL	YCBO	YCBR	YCBU	YCBX	YCCA	YCCD	YCCG	YCCJ	YCCM	YCCP	YCCS	YCCV	YCCY	YCDB	YCDE	YCDH	YCDK
Jan-Mar 2012	29,454	25,042	4,186	96	129	21,372	8,082	18,319	6,724	2,992	1,194	1,152	1,569	6.3	618	39.4	341	90	521	7,918	1,414	17.9	5,215	191	1,048
Feb-Apr 2012	29,492	25,064	4,195	98	134	21,410	8,081	18,340	6,725	3,010	1,185	1,149	1,557	6.2	610	39.2	333	95	518	7,910	1,413	17.9	5,214	192	1,041
Mar-May 2012	29,564	25,120	4,185	111	148	21,475	8,089	18,381	6,739	3,019	1,166	1,141	1,575	6.3	638	40.5	322	94	521	7,905	1,398	17.7	5,222	191	1,045
Apr-Jun 2012	29,667	25,187	4,222	112	146	21,513	8,154	18,402	6,785	3,032	1,190	1,124	1,615	6.4	644	39.9	331	101	539	7,975	1,427	17.9	5,244	184	1,071
May-Jul 2012	29,744	25,222	4,252	117	153	21,542	8,202	18,414	6,808	3,036	1,216	1,125	1,651	6.5	659	39.9	346	101	545	8,023	1,429	17.8	5,298	181	1,067
Jun-Aug 2012	29,779	25,280	4,232	112	155	21,566	8,213	18,464	6,816	3,013	1,220	1,117	1,637	6.5	648	39.6	343	100	547	8,036	1,418	17.6	5,315	182	1,072
Jul-Sep 2012	29,759	25,255	4,232	110	161	21,568	8,191	18,456	6,800	3,016	1,216	1,109	1,625	6.4	656	40.3	328	93	548	8,015	1,412	17.6	5,316	182	1,054
Aug-Oct 2012	29,744	25,244	4,224	109	167	21,560	8,185	18,440	6,804	3,024	1,200	1,124	1,633	6.5	657	40.2	325	93	559	8,004	1,405	17.6	5,318	185	1,039
Sep-Nov 2012	29,849	25,336	4,236	113	164	21,665	8,184	18,536	6,800	3,035	1,201	1,122	1,651	6.5	655	39.6	339	90	568	8,001	1,406	17.6	5,329	182	1,022
Oct-Dec 2012	29,908	25,369	4,258	115	166	21,736	8,172	18,590	6,779	3,049	1,209	1,146	1,656	6.5	660	39.8	339	97	560	7,988	1,392	17.4	5,337	184	1,010
Nov-Jan 2013	29,891	25,414	4,206	107	164	21,753	8,138	18,643	6,771	3,008	1,198	1,138	1,640	6.5	656	40.0	335	95	554	7,969	1,405	17.6	5,331	185	989
Dec-Feb 2013	29,815	25,339	4,222	102	153	21,699	8,116	18,590	6,749	3,012	1,210	1,121	1,602	6.3	643	40.1	334	101	523	7,959	1,422	17.9	5,302	183	995
Jan-Mar 2013	29,839	25,398	4,185	102	154	21,734	8,105	18,623	6,774	3,018	1,167	1,111	1,612	6.3	649	40.3	337	104	522	7,942	1,418	17.9	5,278	178	1,014
Feb-Apr 2013	29,884	25,400	4,219	105	160	21,723	8,160	18,612	6,788	3,028	1,191	1,100	1,592	6.3	631	39.7	343	100	517	7,978	1,443	18.1	5,269	182	1,029
Mar-May 2013	29,861	25,411	4,185	103	162	21,725	8,136	18,638	6,773	3,012	1,173	1,122	1,584	6.2	626	39.5	331	101	525	7,946	1,466	18.4	5,223	181	1,016
Apr-Jun 2013	29,938	25,462	4,196	115	165	21,769	8,169	18,672	6,790	3,013	1,184	1,124	1,569	6.2	605	38.5	329	104	531	7,974	1,455	18.2	5,259	189	1,010
May-Jul 2013	29,994	25,519	4,204	108	163	21,867	8,127	18,746	6,773	3,033	1,171	1,132	1,564	6.1	604	38.6	312	112	536	7,944	1,464	18.4	5,223	186	1,009
Jun-Aug 2013	30,024	25,501	4,243	117	164	21,893	8,131	18,731	6,769	3,066	1,176	1,157	1,573	6.2	604	38.4	300	123	547	7,945	1,460	18.4	5,263	193	968
Jul-Sep 2013	30,106	25,579	4,244	113	171	21,944	8,162	18,786	6,794	3,066	1,178	1,160	1,602	6.3	603	37.6	306	126	566	7,972	1,462	18.3	5,258	194	993
Aug-Oct 2013	30,223	25,638	4,297	119	169	21,997	8,226	18,813	6,824	3,095	1,203	1,170	1,598	6.2	596	37.3	318	124	560	8,027	1,462	18.2	5,305	195	1,003
Sep-Nov 2013	30,302	25,631	4,409	115	147	22,111	8,191	18,854	6,777	3,177	1,232	1,184	1,606	6.3	583	36.3	322	129	571	8,009	1,445	18.0	5,296	191	1,022
Oct-Dec 2013	30,290	25,615	4,424	111	141	22,140	8,151	18,862	6,753	3,192	1,232	1,176	1,623	6.3	602	37.1	334	118	568	7,984	1,430	17.9	5,289	190	1,025
Nov-Jan 2014	30,329	25,586	4,501	110	132	22,165	8,164	18,836	6,749	3,247	1,254	1,174	1,620	6.3	594	36.7	349	115	562	8,004	1,436	17.9	5,298	192	1,027
Dec-Feb 2014	30,492	25,709	4,538	115	130	22,243	8,249	18,887	6,822	3,270	1,268	1,157	1,629	6.3	586	36.0	361	116	567	8,090	1,421	17.6	5,397	193	1,032
Jan-Mar 2014	30,532	25,706	4,579	123	123	22,277	8,255	18,919	6,787	3,272	1,307	1,180	1,653	6.4	591	35.7	365	117	580	8,094	1,419	17.5	5,421	192	1,020
Feb-Apr 2014	30,640	25,821	4,574	124	121	22,376	8,264	19,022	6,799	3,270	1,305	1,184	1,681	6.5	600	35.7	379	119	582	8,104	1,405	17.3	5,440	188	1,032
Mar-May 2014	30,743	25,906	4,599	118	120	22,451	8,291	19,102	6,804	3,268	1,331	1,192	1,680	6.5	606	36.1	377	119	579	8,134	1,367	16.8	5,506	194	1,032
Apr-Jun 2014	30,705	25,858	4,606	114	127	22,400	8,305	19,058	6,799	3,262	1,344	1,211	1,653	6.4	603	36.5	378	113	559	8,143	1,347	16.5	5,544	195	1,016
May-Jul 2014	30,702	25,886	4,568	118	131	22,395	8,308	19,066	6,820	3,251	1,317	1,201	1,666	6.4	609	36.5	371	120	567	8,138	1,342	16.5	5,559	181	1,013
Jun-Aug 2014	30,786	26,004	4,527	128	128	22,507	8,279	19,171	6,833	3,258	1,269	1,222	1,685	6.5	610	36.2	386	120	570	8,102	1,349	16.7	5,518	174	1,017
Jul-Sep 2014	30,833	26,058	4,530	122	123	22,566	8,267	19,238	6,820	3,258	1,272	1,203	1,702	6.5	599	35.2	410	123	570	8,092	1,336	16.5	5,524	172	1,016
Aug-Oct 2014	30,848	26,066	4,543	118	121	22,588	8,261	19,258	6,808	3,260	1,283	1,209	1,694	6.5	572	33.8	421	122	578	8,091	1,309	16.2	5,564	175	994
Sep-Nov 2014	30,850	26,094	4,539	103	114	22,565	8,285	19,263	6,832	3,238	1,302	1,200	1,683	6.5	569	33.8	414	121	579	8,133	1,314	16.2	5,577	187	1,008
Oct-Dec 2014	30,944	26,216	4,516	103	110	22,632	8,312	19,359	6,857	3,209	1,307	1,200	1,716	6.5	581	33.8	412	115	609	8,164	1,310	16.1	5,587	189	1,029
Nov-Jan 2015	31,003	26,244	4,542	113	104	22,691	8,312	19,400	6,844	3,223	1,318	1,194	1,681	6.4	573	34.1	394	121	593	8,162	1,324	16.2	5,594	195	1,006
Dec-Feb 2015	31,122	26,355	4,550	113	105	22,745	8,378	19,466	6,888	3,212	1,337	1,219	1,685	6.4	591	35.1	379	120	595	8,226	1,354	16.5	5,616	196	1,013
Jan-Mar 2015	31,156	26,409	4,525	119	102	22,769	8,387	19,491	6,918	3,207	1,318	1,222	1,681	6.4	585	34.8	374	123	599	8,236	1,325	16.1	5,641	213	1,011

4.2 Full-time, part-time and temporary workers

United Kingdom (thousands) seasonally adjusted

	All in employment					Full-time and part-time workers[1]							Temporary employees (reasons for temporary working)							Part-time workers (reasons for working part-time)[3]					
	Total	Employ-ees	Self employed	Unpaid family workers	Government supported training & employment pro-grammes[2]	Total people working full-time	Total people working part-time	Employ-ees working full-time	Employ-ees working part-time	Self-employed people working full-time	Self-employed people working part-time	Total workers with second jobs	Total	Total as % of all employ-ees	Could not find perman-ent job	% that could not find perman-ent job	Did not want perman-ent job	Had a contract with period of training	Some other reason	Total[4]	Could not find full-time job	% that could not find full-time job	Did not want full-time job	Ill or dis-abled	Student or at school
People (16+)	MGSA	MGRO	MGRR	MGRU	MGRX	YCBF	YCBI	YCBL	YCBO	YCBR	YCBU	YCBX	YCCA	YCCD	YCCG	YCCJ	YCCM	YCCP	YCCS	YCCV	YCCY	YCDB	YCDE	YCDH	YCDK
Feb-Apr 2015	31,129	26,420	4,495	110	104	22,783	8,346	19,509	6,912	3,194	1,301	1,221	1,681	6.4	583	34.7	374	125	599	8,212	1,308	15.9	5,626	213	1,015
Mar-May 2015	31,057	26,384	4,473	103	97	22,756	8,302	19,514	6,870	3,157	1,316	1,199	1,671	6.3	559	33.5	398	120	594	8,185	1,280	15.6	5,620	217	1,015
Apr-Jun 2015	31,110	26,385	4,518	101	106	22,793	8,317	19,514	6,872	3,195	1,324	1,195	1,642	6.2	566	34.5	382	129	566	8,195	1,291	15.7	5,615	224	1,018
May-Jul 2015	31,188	26,447	4,530	100	111	22,801	8,387	19,545	6,901	3,183	1,347	1,187	1,666	6.3	561	33.7	400	126	578	8,248	1,277	15.5	5,653	229	1,039
Jun-Aug 2015	31,220	26,503	4,513	93	111	22,855	8,366	19,614	6,889	3,170	1,343	1,164	1,644	6.2	579	35.2	399	128	538	8,232	1,268	15.4	5,643	221	1,051
Jul-Sep 2015	31,333	26,554	4,576	94	108	22,894	8,439	19,593	6,961	3,227	1,349	1,162	1,668	6.3	571	34.2	411	127	559	8,310	1,255	15.1	5,715	215	1,077
Aug-Oct 2015	31,436	26,616	4,631	88	101	22,990	8,446	19,661	6,956	3,268	1,363	1,163	1,656	6.2	579	35.0	405	119	552	8,319	1,277	15.3	5,676	218	1,100
Sep-Nov 2015	31,513	26,673	4,653	95	92	23,053	8,460	19,722	6,951	3,273	1,381	1,165	1,647	6.2	570	34.6	392	137	549	8,332	1,240	14.9	5,726	225	1,092
Oct-Dec 2015	31,540	26,666	4,680	95	98	23,081	8,459	19,719	6,947	3,302	1,378	1,142	1,634	6.1	554	33.9	400	137	544	8,325	1,236	14.8	5,706	233	1,089
Nov-Jan 2016	31,541	26,689	4,662	96	93	23,035	8,506	19,676	7,013	3,299	1,363	1,125	1,655	6.2	554	33.5	409	138	554	8,377	1,213	14.5	5,765	237	1,103
Dec-Feb 2016	31,555	26,668	4,688	103	97	23,076	8,479	19,685	6,983	3,323	1,364	1,124	1,648	6.2	542	32.9	413	123	571	8,347	1,190	14.3	5,761	248	1,088
Jan-Mar 2016	31,572	26,665	4,714	100	93	23,094	8,478	19,685	6,980	3,345	1,369	1,120	1,648	6.2	561	34.0	410	116	560	8,349	1,198	14.3	5,745	251	1,096
Feb-Apr 2016	31,603	26,693	4,706	110	94	23,091	8,513	19,669	7,024	3,360	1,346	1,127	1,633	6.1	536	32.8	429	128	540	8,370	1,194	14.3	5,779	243	1,094
Mar-May 2016	31,712	26,726	4,778	118	91	23,173	8,539	19,714	7,012	3,400	1,377	1,138	1,615	6.0	511	31.7	428	132	544	8,389	1,187	14.2	5,823	238	1,081
Apr-Jun 2016	31,747	26,757	4,785	120	85	23,183	8,564	19,729	7,028	3,396	1,389	1,131	1,666	6.2	529	31.8	433	135	569	8,417	1,154	13.7	5,870	239	1,100
May-Jul 2016	31,779	26,834	4,754	110	82	23,255	8,524	19,801	7,033	3,396	1,358	1,135	1,651	6.2	524	31.7	430	133	564	8,391	1,149	13.7	5,874	246	1,075
Jun-Aug 2016	31,811	26,829	4,786	124	72	23,234	8,576	19,753	7,077	3,427	1,359	1,167	1,643	6.1	506	30.8	431	129	576	8,436	1,139	13.5	5,915	249	1,094
Jul-Sep 2016	31,810	26,826	4,787	128	68	23,254	8,557	19,793	7,033	3,402	1,386	1,154	1,621	6.0	483	29.8	429	132	578	8,419	1,144	13.6	5,899	252	1,085
Aug-Oct 2016	31,794	26,833	4,762	128	70	23,235	8,559	19,816	7,017	3,353	1,409	1,131	1,614	6.0	489	30.3	426	123	576	8,427	1,151	13.7	5,916	249	1,067
Sep-Nov 2016	31,808	26,822	4,782	128	75	23,262	8,546	19,799	7,023	3,391	1,392	1,120	1,622	6.0	493	30.4	421	111	597	8,415	1,143	13.6	5,887	256	1,078
Oct-Dec 2016	31,845	26,836	4,803	123	83	23,300	8,545	19,807	7,029	3,421	1,382	1,121	1,621	6.0	473	29.1	411	112	626	8,411	1,116	13.3	5,885	257	1,097

Source: Labour Force Survey

Note: When comparing quarterly changes ONS recommends comparing with the previous non-overlapping 3-month average time period (eg, compare Apr-Jun with Jan-Mar, not with Mar-May).

1. The split between full-time and part-time employment is based on respondents' self-classification.
2. This series does not include all people on these programmes; it only includes those engaging in any form of work, work experience or work-related training.
3. These series cover Employees and Self-employed only. These series include some temporary employees.
4. The total includes those who did not give a reason for working part-time and it therefore does not equal the sum of the other columns in this section of the table.

4.2 Full-time, part-time and temporary workers

United Kingdom (thousands) seasonally adjusted

	All in employment					Full-time and part-time workers[1]							Temporary employees (reasons for temporary working)							Part-time workers (reasons for working part-time)[3]					
	Total	Employees	Self employed	Unpaid family workers	Government supported training & employment programmes[2]	Total people working full-time	Total people working part-time	Employees working full-time	Employees working part-time	Self-employed people working full-time	Self-employed people working part-time	Total workers with second jobs	Total	Total as % of all employees	Could not find permanent job	% that could not find permanent job	Did not want permanent job	Had a contract with period of training	Some other reason	Total[4]	Could not find full-time job	% that could not find full-time job	Did not want full-time job	Ill or disabled	Student or at school
Men (16+)	MGSA	MGRO	MGRR	MGRU	MGRX	YCBF	YCBI	YCBL	YCBO	YCBR	YCBU	YCBX	YCCA	YCCD	YCCG	YCCJ	YCCM	YCCP	YCCS	YCCV	YCCY	YCDB	YCDE	YCDH	YCDK
Nov-Jan 2006	15,604	12,797	2,717	31	58	13,961	1,642	11,564	1,233	2,354	363	455	652	5.1	195	30.0	163	50	244	1,596	245	15.3	786	76	476
Dec-Feb 2006	15,614	12,809	2,717	29	59	13,960	1,654	11,566	1,244	2,351	365	457	660	5.2	191	28.9	168	55	247	1,609	250	15.5	786	76	484
Jan-Mar 2006	15,609	12,820	2,700	31	58	13,966	1,642	11,579	1,241	2,345	355	440	666	5.2	192	28.8	168	60	247	1,596	247	15.4	778	76	482
Feb-Apr 2006	15,656	12,859	2,710	30	57	14,015	1,641	11,612	1,247	2,362	348	442	669	5.2	194	29.0	175	55	245	1,595	247	15.5	775	72	489
Mar-May 2006	15,639	12,853	2,696	33	56	13,991	1,648	11,597	1,256	2,356	340	434	666	5.2	187	28.1	173	55	251	1,596	248	15.5	775	73	490
Apr-Jun 2006	15,652	12,864	2,697	36	54	13,993	1,659	11,601	1,263	2,355	343	449	654	5.1	187	28.7	173	53	241	1,606	252	15.7	770	70	504
May-Jul 2006	15,683	12,894	2,698	38	53	14,013	1,670	11,626	1,268	2,346	352	452	643	5.0	179	27.9	168	48	248	1,620	256	15.8	772	75	509
Jun-Aug 2006	15,722	12,922	2,711	42	48	14,057	1,665	11,657	1,265	2,360	351	449	663	5.1	186	28.1	172	47	258	1,616	263	16.3	760	77	507
Jul-Sep 2006	15,740	12,909	2,731	42	58	14,040	1,700	11,629	1,280	2,366	365	455	667	5.2	193	28.9	173	47	254	1,645	270	16.4	769	74	519
Aug-Oct 2006	15,738	12,894	2,743	42	59	14,007	1,731	11,591	1,303	2,372	371	456	687	5.3	206	30.0	176	46	259	1,674	279	16.7	789	75	518
Sep-Nov 2006	15,744	12,880	2,756	40	68	14,035	1,709	11,602	1,279	2,389	367	450	700	5.4	211	30.1	182	49	258	1,646	280	17.0	780	76	498
Oct-Dec 2006	15,751	12,902	2,747	41	60	14,048	1,703	11,621	1,281	2,386	362	462	707	5.5	214	30.2	185	48	259	1,643	278	16.9	785	78	492
Nov-Jan 2007	15,760	12,886	2,773	39	63	14,064	1,696	11,606	1,280	2,416	356	447	712	5.5	209	29.3	187	56	260	1,636	281	17.2	770	83	491
Dec-Feb 2007	15,752	12,885	2,768	40	58	14,052	1,700	11,609	1,276	2,403	366	461	703	5.5	212	30.2	185	51	255	1,642	267	16.2	787	82	495
Jan-Mar 2007	15,758	12,885	2,775	43	56	14,034	1,724	11,597	1,288	2,399	376	463	713	5.5	215	30.1	183	53	261	1,664	274	16.5	798	81	500
Feb-Apr 2007	15,782	12,913	2,772	40	57	14,064	1,718	11,635	1,278	2,392	380	461	696	5.4	211	30.3	177	48	260	1,658	273	16.5	799	80	496
Mar-May 2007	15,846	12,979	2,771	38	59	14,134	1,712	11,703	1,275	2,393	377	457	696	5.4	219	31.4	174	43	261	1,653	277	16.8	804	76	487
Apr-Jun 2007	15,839	12,965	2,775	36	62	14,126	1,713	11,696	1,269	2,393	382	456	693	5.3	223	32.2	172	40	258	1,652	275	16.7	821	75	469
May-Jul 2007	15,846	12,969	2,771	37	68	14,120	1,726	11,705	1,264	2,378	393	460	689	5.3	219	31.8	177	39	255	1,658	281	17.0	832	79	453
Jun-Aug 2007	15,861	12,991	2,771	38	61	14,137	1,724	11,714	1,278	2,388	383	456	694	5.3	218	31.4	185	38	252	1,660	290	17.5	828	70	460
Jul-Sep 2007	15,884	13,027	2,760	37	60	14,141	1,742	11,733	1,294	2,374	386	450	682	5.2	206	30.2	189	37	249	1,680	293	17.4	831	72	471
Aug-Oct 2007	15,903	13,036	2,774	37	56	14,176	1,726	11,754	1,282	2,390	384	458	668	5.1	202	30.3	187	38	241	1,666	292	17.5	817	71	474
Sep-Nov 2007	15,942	13,061	2,783	37	61	14,181	1,762	11,755	1,306	2,385	398	454	684	5.2	203	29.6	192	42	247	1,704	288	16.9	834	72	498
Oct-Dec 2007	15,947	13,057	2,787	39	63	14,182	1,766	11,741	1,317	2,395	392	450	696	5.3	200	28.8	193	45	258	1,709	291	17.0	836	71	498
Nov-Jan 2008	15,968	13,074	2,789	39	66	14,180	1,788	11,733	1,341	2,398	391	453	685	5.2	188	27.4	189	43	265	1,732	292	16.9	858	69	501
Dec-Feb 2008	15,993	13,054	2,825	40	74	14,197	1,796	11,714	1,340	2,435	390	461	663	5.1	181	27.4	181	43	258	1,730	292	16.9	857	69	498
Jan-Mar 2008	16,005	13,070	2,822	40	73	14,209	1,796	11,739	1,331	2,427	395	451	657	5.0	185	28.1	182	39	251	1,726	289	16.7	860	69	494
Feb-Apr 2008	16,024	13,106	2,805	42	70	14,229	1,795	11,769	1,337	2,415	391	458	656	5.0	179	27.3	183	42	252	1,727	287	16.6	860	73	492
Mar-May 2008	16,019	13,101	2,809	40	68	14,254	1,764	11,792	1,309	2,419	390	458	648	4.9	178	27.5	165	45	259	1,699	268	15.8	859	76	479
Apr-Jun 2008	16,011	13,097	2,810	40	64	14,221	1,790	11,758	1,340	2,423	387	461	628	4.8	176	28.1	159	46	247	1,727	271	15.7	864	78	499
May-Jul 2008	15,987	13,089	2,798	36	64	14,178	1,809	11,726	1,363	2,415	383	451	611	4.7	182	29.7	143	47	239	1,746	290	16.6	858	82	503
Jun-Aug 2008	15,927	13,059	2,775	30	64	14,105	1,822	11,685	1,374	2,389	386	451	615	4.7	180	29.2	154	44	238	1,760	303	17.2	858	83	504
Jul-Sep 2008	15,910	13,049	2,769	28	64	14,081	1,829	11,664	1,385	2,387	382	456	633	4.8	184	29.1	158	46	244	1,766	315	17.8	860	81	497
Aug-Oct 2008	15,864	13,029	2,736	33	67	14,024	1,840	11,639	1,390	2,355	381	452	627	4.8	177	28.2	170	42	239	1,772	322	18.2	857	80	498
Sep-Nov 2008	15,885	13,017	2,766	37	65	14,045	1,840	11,634	1,383	2,381	385	471	635	4.9	186	29.4	155	42	251	1,768	333	18.8	847	79	492
Oct-Dec 2008	15,870	12,991	2,774	41	64	14,012	1,858	11,598	1,393	2,386	388	473	639	4.9	195	30.5	152	42	250	1,780	353	19.9	840	80	490
Nov-Jan 2009	15,859	12,977	2,784	38	61	13,995	1,865	11,572	1,405	2,399	385	479	659	5.1	215	32.6	153	47	243	1,790	379	21.2	832	77	485

4.2 Full-time, part-time and temporary workers

United Kingdom (thousands) seasonally adjusted

	All in employment					Full-time and part-time workers[1]							Temporary employees (reasons for temporary working)							Part-time workers (reasons for working part-time)[3]					
	Total	Employ-ees	Self employed	Unpaid family workers	Government supported training & employment pro-grammes[2]	Total people working full-time	Total people working part-time	Employ-ees working full-time	Employ-ees working part-time	Self-employed people working full-time	Self-employed people working part-time	Total workers with second jobs	Total	Total as % of all employ-ees	Could not find perman-ent job	% that could not find perman-ent job	Did not want perman-ent job	Had a contract with period of training	Some other reason	Total[4]	Could not find full-time job	% that could not find full-time job	Did not want full-time job	Ill or dis-abled	Student or at school
Men (16+)	MGSA	MGRO	MGRR	MGRU	MGRX	YCBF	YCBI	YCBL	YCBO	YCBR	YCBU	YCBX	YCCA	YCCD	YCCG	YCCJ	YCCM	YCCP	YCCS	YCCV	YCCY	YCDB	YCDE	YCDH	YCDK
Dec-Feb 2009	15,786	12,921	2,771	33	61	13,935	1,851	11,504	1,417	2,399	372	483	662	5.1	225	34.1	158	38	240	1,789	385	21.5	830	78	481
Jan-Mar 2009	15,739	12,876	2,773	32	58	13,900	1,839	11,475	1,402	2,394	379	492	664	5.2	232	35.0	155	37	239	1,781	394	22.1	821	77	474
Feb-Apr 2009	15,678	12,807	2,779	33	59	13,841	1,836	11,417	1,391	2,391	388	500	662	5.2	228	34.4	155	40	238	1,779	405	22.8	812	79	464
Mar-May 2009	15,577	12,711	2,774	36	56	13,718	1,859	11,318	1,393	2,369	405	489	649	5.1	219	33.7	153	48	229	1,798	425	23.6	806	80	467
Apr-Jun 2009	15,513	12,658	2,756	40	59	13,646	1,866	11,268	1,390	2,341	415	480	676	5.3	231	34.1	156	47	243	1,805	438	24.3	793	79	472
May-Jul 2009	15,465	12,607	2,761	36	61	13,618	1,847	11,229	1,379	2,356	405	480	680	5.4	231	34.0	151	45	253	1,783	438	24.6	789	72	466
Jun-Aug 2009	15,471	12,608	2,770	33	61	13,616	1,856	11,206	1,402	2,375	395	491	679	5.4	235	34.7	151	47	246	1,797	432	24.0	802	70	472
Jul-Sep 2009	15,447	12,608	2,749	29	61	13,606	1,841	11,215	1,392	2,359	390	489	671	5.3	240	35.8	146	44	241	1,782	433	24.3	785	79	468
Aug-Oct 2009	15,448	12,588	2,769	33	58	13,591	1,857	11,189	1,400	2,373	396	494	672	5.3	245	36.5	140	49	237	1,796	435	24.2	778	79	486
Sep-Nov 2009	15,438	12,593	2,757	32	56	13,568	1,870	11,188	1,405	2,354	403	483	685	5.4	262	38.2	145	43	235	1,808	449	24.8	788	76	479
Oct-Dec 2009	15,436	12,570	2,770	37	60	13,558	1,879	11,168	1,402	2,363	407	485	690	5.5	268	38.8	146	42	235	1,809	447	24.7	799	77	471
Nov-Jan 2010	15,407	12,538	2,773	36	60	13,514	1,893	11,127	1,411	2,360	413	467	683	5.4	259	37.9	147	41	236	1,823	449	24.6	812	75	471
Dec-Feb 2010	15,404	12,539	2,763	41	63	13,511	1,893	11,129	1,409	2,354	408	457	709	5.7	273	38.5	149	46	241	1,817	457	25.2	800	72	474
Jan-Mar 2010	15,397	12,516	2,775	41	66	13,486	1,911	11,096	1,420	2,363	411	434	707	5.6	268	37.9	151	43	245	1,832	463	25.3	808	69	479
Feb-Apr 2010	15,417	12,527	2,780	42	69	13,501	1,917	11,103	1,425	2,368	412	452	715	5.7	283	39.6	151	42	239	1,836	463	25.2	807	68	487
Mar-May 2010	15,499	12,593	2,787	42	77	13,551	1,948	11,152	1,441	2,365	422	476	733	5.8	291	39.7	158	41	244	1,863	459	24.6	834	63	497
Apr-Jun 2010	15,539	12,633	2,788	41	77	13,567	1,972	11,165	1,468	2,368	420	472	760	6.0	304	40.0	163	40	253	1,888	468	24.8	847	70	492
May-Jul 2010	15,634	12,684	2,820	43	87	13,622	2,012	11,206	1,478	2,379	441	467	753	5.9	300	39.8	160	40	253	1,919	480	25.0	847	70	508
Jun-Aug 2010	15,654	12,690	2,839	42	83	13,617	2,036	11,182	1,508	2,396	442	458	760	6.0	314	41.3	157	43	246	1,950	492	25.2	851	77	515
Jul-Sep 2010	15,696	12,706	2,864	43	83	13,635	2,061	11,183	1,523	2,414	450	465	756	5.9	319	42.2	150	44	243	1,973	501	25.4	859	72	525
Aug-Oct 2010	15,658	12,726	2,808	43	81	13,590	2,068	11,202	1,524	2,357	451	459	761	6.0	314	41.3	156	48	242	1,975	522	26.4	867	72	500
Sep-Nov 2010	15,644	12,704	2,825	33	82	13,587	2,057	11,189	1,514	2,367	458	462	744	5.9	303	40.7	151	52	238	1,973	520	26.4	878	78	483
Oct-Dec 2010	15,679	12,736	2,834	34	75	13,623	2,057	11,217	1,519	2,375	459	469	718	5.6	289	40.3	147	53	228	1,977	519	26.3	882	73	488
Nov-Jan 2011	15,711	12,774	2,823	35	80	13,672	2,039	11,281	1,493	2,363	460	488	738	5.8	299	40.5	145	51	244	1,953	511	26.2	880	73	471
Dec-Feb 2011	15,717	12,786	2,820	33	77	13,695	2,022	11,322	1,464	2,350	470	509	741	5.8	296	40.0	145	51	249	1,935	513	26.5	871	76	454
Jan-Mar 2011	15,692	12,791	2,795	31	76	13,670	2,022	11,326	1,465	2,323	472	496	752	5.9	300	40.0	146	56	250	1,937	523	27.0	869	81	441
Feb-Apr 2011	15,742	12,817	2,827	28	70	13,689	2,053	11,323	1,494	2,345	481	488	769	6.0	314	40.8	145	51	259	1,975	540	27.3	880	83	452
Mar-May 2011	15,739	12,816	2,832	31	60	13,690	2,049	11,335	1,480	2,336	495	490	771	6.0	311	40.4	149	49	262	1,976	554	28.0	889	74	438
Apr-Jun 2011	15,728	12,795	2,838	38	56	13,687	2,041	11,316	1,479	2,350	488	488	792	6.2	329	41.6	151	46	265	1,967	564	28.7	877	71	437
May-Jul 2011	15,655	12,731	2,836	38	49	13,628	2,027	11,257	1,474	2,353	483	498	760	6.0	304	40.0	154	45	257	1,957	578	29.5	865	71	423
Jun-Aug 2011	15,621	12,688	2,847	40	46	13,647	1,974	11,256	1,432	2,372	475	476	746	5.9	308	41.3	135	42	260	1,907	568	29.8	841	67	415
Jul-Sep 2011	15,591	12,611	2,896	42	42	13,618	1,972	11,199	1,413	2,399	497	487	735	5.8	303	41.3	139	43	250	1,909	555	29.1	851	67	420
Aug-Oct 2011	15,610	12,607	2,918	41	44	13,620	1,990	11,159	1,448	2,433	485	494	737	5.8	313	42.5	134	41	249	1,933	563	29.1	850	68	433
Sep-Nov 2011	15,624	12,610	2,919	44	51	13,599	2,025	11,141	1,470	2,426	493	493	734	5.8	302	41.1	149	41	242	1,963	579	29.5	856	68	440
Oct-Dec 2011	15,632	12,648	2,889	42	53	13,599	2,033	11,161	1,487	2,406	483	480	728	5.8	308	42.4	142	42	236	1,970	595	30.2	852	69	437
Nov-Jan 2012	15,634	12,641	2,892	42	59	13,601	2,034	11,162	1,479	2,408	484	463	732	5.8	313	42.7	140	46	234	1,963	602	30.7	848	73	428
Dec-Feb 2012	15,686	12,677	2,905	37	66	13,589	2,096	11,147	1,530	2,407	498	488	737	5.8	326	44.3	135	46	231	2,029	626	30.9	860	73	456

4.2 Full-time, part-time and temporary workers

United Kingdom (thousands) seasonally adjusted

	All in employment					Full-time and part-time workers[1]							Temporary employees (reasons for temporary working)							Part-time workers (reasons for working part-time)[3]					
	Total	Employ-ees	Self employed	Unpaid family workers	Government supported training & employment pro-grammes[2]	Total people working full-time	Total people working part-time	Employ-ees working full-time	Employ-ees working part-time	Self-employed people working full-time	Self-employed people working part-time	Total workers with second jobs	Total	Total as % of all employ-ees	Could not find perman-ent job	% that could not find perman-ent job	Did not want perman-ent job	Had a contract with period of training	Some other reason	Total[4]	Could not find full-time job	% that could not find full-time job	Did not want full-time job	Ill or dis-abled	Student or at school
Men (16+)	MGSA	MGRO	MGRR	MGRU	MGRX	YCBF	YCBI	YCBL	YCBO	YCBR	YCBU	YCBX	YCCA	YCCD	YCCG	YCCJ	YCCM	YCCP	YCCS	YCCV	YCCY	YCDB	YCDE	YCDH	YCDK
Jan-Mar 2012	15,720	12,688	2,916	43	74	13,598	2,123	11,154	1,534	2,404	512	487	740	5.8	319	43.1	140	44	237	2,045	635	31.0	867	73	457
Feb-Apr 2012	15,754	12,701	2,930	44	79	13,621	2,132	11,159	1,542	2,423	507	488	739	5.8	311	42.0	138	47	243	2,049	641	31.3	867	75	450
Mar-May 2012	15,801	12,713	2,945	47	97	13,662	2,139	11,164	1,549	2,447	497	485	737	5.8	323	43.8	136	46	233	2,046	633	30.9	869	76	452
Apr-Jun 2012	15,866	12,761	2,970	43	92	13,702	2,165	11,186	1,575	2,465	506	485	753	5.9	325	43.1	137	50	241	2,081	651	31.3	875	73	462
May-Jul 2012	15,874	12,754	2,978	43	99	13,722	2,152	11,185	1,568	2,472	506	476	761	6.0	333	43.7	137	50	242	2,074	643	31.0	881	72	459
Jun-Aug 2012	15,903	12,785	2,970	46	102	13,743	2,159	11,228	1,557	2,453	518	470	755	5.9	325	43.1	135	49	245	2,075	631	30.4	888	75	458
Jul-Sep 2012	15,897	12,767	2,972	50	108	13,754	2,143	11,229	1,537	2,453	519	463	760	6.0	337	44.3	125	45	253	2,056	630	30.7	885	70	447
Aug-Oct 2012	15,906	12,772	2,971	47	116	13,779	2,127	11,249	1,522	2,456	515	464	767	6.0	342	44.5	122	45	258	2,037	631	31.0	889	69	426
Sep-Nov 2012	15,937	12,833	2,947	46	110	13,818	2,119	11,303	1,530	2,447	501	454	780	6.1	346	44.4	131	40	263	2,030	636	31.3	893	62	411
Oct-Dec 2012	15,945	12,836	2,954	45	110	13,833	2,113	11,314	1,522	2,451	503	454	786	6.1	358	45.5	135	43	251	2,025	641	31.7	887	65	402
Nov-Jan 2013	15,925	12,847	2,922	44	113	13,811	2,114	11,325	1,521	2,418	504	440	775	6.0	349	45.1	138	42	246	2,025	637	31.5	902	62	396
Dec-Feb 2013	15,868	12,786	2,938	37	107	13,773	2,095	11,292	1,494	2,415	523	437	765	6.0	342	44.7	140	46	237	2,017	642	31.8	892	62	399
Jan-Mar 2013	15,871	12,806	2,920	36	109	13,788	2,082	11,308	1,498	2,415	505	434	751	5.9	337	45.0	141	41	231	2,003	637	31.8	878	61	404
Feb-Apr 2013	15,891	12,811	2,936	35	109	13,750	2,141	11,283	1,528	2,414	522	447	746	5.8	329	44.1	147	36	234	2,050	665	32.4	879	64	416
Mar-May 2013	15,885	12,831	2,916	33	105	13,761	2,124	11,314	1,518	2,405	511	452	751	5.9	324	43.1	142	42	243	2,029	665	32.7	868	65	406
Apr-Jun 2013	15,933	12,862	2,921	44	107	13,785	2,148	11,341	1,521	2,398	523	457	738	5.7	313	42.4	143	40	242	2,044	659	32.3	883	68	410
May-Jul 2013	15,964	12,895	2,929	40	101	13,831	2,134	11,376	1,519	2,414	515	468	742	5.8	312	42.1	134	49	247	2,033	659	32.4	880	65	408
Jun-Aug 2013	15,995	12,900	2,948	45	101	13,852	2,142	11,377	1,523	2,433	515	490	736	5.7	306	41.6	132	60	237	2,038	661	32.5	891	68	397
Jul-Sep 2013	16,053	12,964	2,946	40	102	13,887	2,166	11,414	1,551	2,431	515	492	754	5.8	309	41.0	129	67	249	2,065	665	32.2	901	72	403
Aug-Oct 2013	16,098	12,969	2,978	44	107	13,922	2,176	11,422	1,547	2,453	525	496	743	5.7	302	40.6	132	61	247	2,072	659	31.8	904	74	412
Sep-Nov 2013	16,157	12,975	3,043	44	94	13,982	2,174	11,434	1,541	2,501	542	502	760	5.9	298	39.2	131	62	269	2,083	657	31.6	905	75	426
Oct-Dec 2013	16,133	12,950	3,049	46	88	13,965	2,168	11,406	1,544	2,508	541	509	773	6.0	301	38.9	142	63	268	2,085	641	30.7	915	76	435
Nov-Jan 2014	16,168	12,934	3,109	46	78	14,001	2,167	11,389	1,545	2,561	548	511	768	5.9	299	39.0	147	60	262	2,093	648	31.0	915	76	433
Dec-Feb 2014	16,239	12,982	3,133	44	81	14,064	2,175	11,421	1,561	2,587	546	515	764	5.9	295	38.7	153	57	258	2,107	640	30.4	932	78	436
Jan-Mar 2014	16,264	12,989	3,144	56	76	14,077	2,187	11,421	1,567	2,598	546	517	777	6.0	301	38.8	147	58	270	2,113	642	30.4	950	80	421
Feb-Apr 2014	16,314	13,046	3,134	61	73	14,155	2,159	11,498	1,548	2,597	537	508	778	6.0	304	39.1	149	61	264	2,085	612	29.3	954	82	421
Mar-May 2014	16,358	13,095	3,136	61	67	14,197	2,161	11,547	1,547	2,593	542	504	776	5.9	310	39.9	147	61	259	2,090	600	28.7	965	90	417
Apr-Jun 2014	16,336	13,068	3,137	57	74	14,194	2,143	11,553	1,515	2,582	555	509	769	5.9	313	40.8	144	57	254	2,070	590	28.5	964	85	413
May-Jul 2014	16,325	13,064	3,124	56	82	14,168	2,156	11,536	1,528	2,573	551	492	777	5.9	319	41.0	141	63	254	2,079	589	28.3	977	86	408
Jun-Aug 2014	16,378	13,133	3,115	55	75	14,224	2,154	11,586	1,547	2,582	533	520	797	6.1	323	40.6	155	58	261	2,080	591	28.4	972	80	416
Jul-Sep 2014	16,409	13,167	3,119	54	70	14,264	2,146	11,624	1,542	2,593	526	510	800	6.1	310	38.7	171	63	256	2,068	583	28.2	974	79	415
Aug-Oct 2014	16,404	13,181	3,102	53	68	14,270	2,134	11,648	1,532	2,580	522	520	807	6.1	291	36.0	185	66	265	2,054	566	27.5	983	75	411
Sep-Nov 2014	16,400	13,201	3,084	48	67	14,241	2,158	11,647	1,554	2,555	530	495	798	6.0	297	37.2	177	65	260	2,084	573	27.5	990	84	420
Oct-Dec 2014	16,441	13,269	3,060	47	64	14,294	2,146	11,725	1,544	2,534	526	489	826	6.2	311	37.7	172	61	281	2,070	565	27.3	994	84	411
Nov-Jan 2015	16,474	13,286	3,079	49	61	14,326	2,149	11,736	1,550	2,553	525	483	807	6.1	310	38.5	161	63	272	2,076	573	27.6	997	85	405
Dec-Feb 2015	16,557	13,341	3,105	51	60	14,374	2,183	11,776	1,565	2,565	540	518	812	6.1	319	39.3	155	66	272	2,105	589	28.0	1,019	84	402
Jan-Mar 2015	16,585	13,390	3,082	53	60	14,389	2,196	11,806	1,584	2,545	537	524	810	6.0	312	38.6	159	67	272	2,121	579	27.3	1,030	88	412

4.2 Full-time, part-time and temporary workers

United Kingdom (thousands) seasonally adjusted

	All in employment					Full-time and part-time workers[1]							Temporary employees (reasons for temporary working)							Part-time workers (reasons for working part-time)[3]					
	Total	Employ-ees	Self employed	Unpaid family workers	Government supported training & employment pro-grammes[2]	Total people working full-time	Total people working part-time	Employ-ees working full-time	Employ-ees working part-time	Self-employed people working full-time	Self-employed people working part-time	Total workers with second jobs	Total	Total as % of all employ-ees	Could not find perman-ent job	% that could not find perman-ent job	Did not want perman-ent job	Had a contract with period of training	Some other reason	Total[4]	Could not find full-time job	% that could not find full-time job	Did not want full-time job	Ill or dis-abled	Student or at school
Men (16+)	MGSA	MGRO	MGRR	MGRU	MGRX	YCBF	YCBI	YCBL	YCBO	YCBR	YCBU	YCBX	YCCA	YCCD	YCCG	YCCJ	YCCM	YCCP	YCCS	YCCV	YCCY	YCDB	YCDE	YCDH	YCDK
Feb-Apr 2015	16,544	13,364	3,068	51	61	14,367	2,177	11,790	1,574	2,532	537	536	804	6.0	313	38.9	159	64	268	2,110	563	26.7	1,029	88	416
Mar-May 2015	16,491	13,345	3,039	45	62	14,359	2,132	11,797	1,548	2,508	531	530	791	5.9	294	37.2	174	55	267	2,080	548	26.4	1,009	90	418
Apr-Jun 2015	16,534	13,342	3,086	45	62	14,374	2,160	11,795	1,547	2,525	560	542	768	5.8	298	38.8	164	60	246	2,107	558	26.5	1,024	94	418
May-Jul 2015	16,588	13,390	3,091	42	65	14,393	2,195	11,836	1,554	2,515	576	525	775	5.8	285	36.8	171	57	262	2,130	555	26.0	1,036	96	428
Jun-Aug 2015	16,636	13,461	3,071	38	66	14,426	2,210	11,891	1,570	2,492	580	498	758	5.6	295	38.9	170	59	234	2,149	557	25.9	1,052	88	433
Jul-Sep 2015	16,676	13,452	3,120	41	63	14,438	2,238	11,851	1,601	2,543	577	491	792	5.9	298	37.7	182	58	253	2,178	556	25.5	1,073	81	451
Aug-Oct 2015	16,769	13,525	3,145	41	58	14,527	2,241	11,913	1,612	2,571	574	491	787	5.8	308	39.2	182	47	250	2,185	560	25.6	1,055	86	469
Sep-Nov 2015	16,803	13,553	3,156	48	46	14,562	2,241	11,950	1,602	2,577	580	501	774	5.7	297	38.3	175	60	242	2,182	543	24.9	1,073	90	461
Oct-Dec 2015	16,834	13,564	3,169	48	53	14,583	2,251	11,944	1,620	2,602	567	494	769	5.7	287	37.3	182	61	238	2,187	547	25.0	1,062	95	462
Nov-Jan 2016	16,829	13,563	3,170	45	51	14,555	2,274	11,917	1,646	2,601	568	495	773	5.7	289	37.4	185	63	235	2,214	539	24.3	1,086	99	472
Dec-Feb 2016	16,848	13,543	3,200	51	54	14,594	2,255	11,922	1,621	2,633	567	483	772	5.7	285	36.8	184	55	249	2,188	530	24.2	1,064	103	471
Jan-Mar 2016	16,848	13,538	3,210	50	50	14,609	2,240	11,923	1,615	2,649	561	479	772	5.7	297	38.5	173	51	251	2,176	528	24.3	1,047	110	472
Feb-Apr 2016	16,860	13,533	3,222	54	52	14,623	2,237	11,917	1,616	2,671	551	483	768	5.7	273	35.6	184	66	245	2,167	531	24.5	1,037	100	473
Mar-May 2016	16,879	13,524	3,247	57	52	14,624	2,256	11,901	1,623	2,687	560	487	748	5.5	256	34.2	180	70	243	2,182	533	24.4	1,079	92	456
Apr-Jun 2016	16,913	13,551	3,253	58	51	14,616	2,297	11,903	1,648	2,677	576	471	781	5.8	272	34.9	178	76	254	2,224	534	24.0	1,110	95	463
May-Jul 2016	16,921	13,609	3,214	49	49	14,675	2,246	11,976	1,633	2,664	549	480	776	5.7	271	35.0	177	76	252	2,182	514	23.6	1,113	97	440
Jun-Aug 2016	16,961	13,614	3,243	59	45	14,680	2,281	11,963	1,651	2,682	561	491	768	5.6	265	34.5	174	70	259	2,212	516	23.3	1,127	101	454
Jul-Sep 2016	16,926	13,611	3,216	60	39	14,659	2,267	11,969	1,642	2,651	565	498	753	5.5	250	33.1	175	68	261	2,206	516	23.4	1,123	103	450
Aug-Oct 2016	16,889	13,607	3,181	59	42	14,597	2,292	11,958	1,649	2,599	581	494	741	5.4	249	33.7	171	59	261	2,231	515	23.1	1,161	101	441
Sep-Nov 2016	16,886	13,576	3,209	56	46	14,605	2,282	11,930	1,646	2,631	577	489	743	5.5	255	34.4	174	50	264	2,223	511	23.0	1,140	104	453
Oct-Dec 2016	16,901	13,569	3,227	54	51	14,620	2,280	11,921	1,648	2,654	572	485	728	5.4	235	32.3	165	49	279	2,220	498	22.4	1,142	103	461

Source: Labour Force Survey

Note: When comparing quarterly changes ONS recommends comparing with the previous non-overlapping 3-month average time period (eg, compare Apr-Jun with Jan-Mar, not with Mar-May).

1. The split between full-time and part-time employment is based on respondents' self-classification.
2. This series does not include all people on these programmes; it only includes those engaging in any form of work, work experience or work-related training.
3. These series cover Employees and Self-employed only. These series include some temporary employees.
4. The total includes those who did not give a reason for working part-time and it therefore does not equal the sum of the other columns in this section of the table.

4.2 Full-time, part-time and temporary workers

United Kingdom (thousands) seasonally adjusted

	All in employment					Full-time and part-time workers[1]							Temporary employees (reasons for temporary working)							Part-time workers (reasons for working part-time)[3]					
	Total	Employ-ees	Self employed	Unpaid family workers	Government supported training & employment pro-grammes[2]	Total people working full-time	Total people working part-time	Employ-ees working full-time	Employ-ees working part-time	Self-employed people working full-time	Self-employed people working part-time	Total workers with second jobs	Total	Total as % of all employ-ees	Could not find perman-ent job	% that could not find perman-ent job	Did not want perman-ent job	Had a contract with period of training	Some other reason	Total[4]	Could not find full-time job	% that could not find full-time job	Did not want full-time job	Ill or dis-abled	Student or at school
Women (16+)	MGSA	MGRO	MGRR	MGRU	MGRX	YCBF	YCBI	YCBL	YCBO	YCBR	YCBU	YCBX	YCCA	YCCD	YCCG	YCCJ	YCCM	YCCP	YCCS	YCCV	YCCY	YCDB	YCDE	YCDH	YCDK
Nov-Jan 2006	13,330	12,249	975	60	46	7,699	5,632	7,182	5,067	488	488	583	780	6.4	169	21.7	225	55	331	5,555	368	6.6	4,440	93	631
Dec-Feb 2006	13,374	12,282	998	58	35	7,718	5,656	7,195	5,087	500	498	589	791	6.4	173	21.9	233	48	337	5,585	370	6.6	4,447	101	642
Jan-Mar 2006	13,439	12,322	1,024	58	35	7,738	5,701	7,195	5,128	520	504	589	820	6.7	182	22.2	242	54	341	5,631	373	6.6	4,478	98	651
Feb-Apr 2006	13,429	12,311	1,029	55	35	7,742	5,686	7,206	5,105	512	517	592	816	6.6	175	21.5	242	60	339	5,621	371	6.6	4,470	100	653
Mar-May 2006	13,424	12,326	1,006	53	39	7,754	5,671	7,236	5,090	496	510	591	812	6.6	181	22.4	239	60	331	5,601	363	6.5	4,454	97	657
Apr-Jun 2006	13,454	12,346	1,013	55	39	7,753	5,701	7,230	5,116	499	515	599	808	6.5	182	22.6	245	57	324	5,631	370	6.6	4,473	101	659
May-Jul 2006	13,457	12,331	1,029	60	37	7,757	5,701	7,221	5,110	512	517	601	795	6.5	179	22.5	247	51	318	5,627	376	6.7	4,461	102	661
Jun-Aug 2006	13,502	12,361	1,038	64	39	7,764	5,738	7,219	5,143	520	518	611	806	6.5	177	22.0	260	49	319	5,660	381	6.7	4,476	109	676
Jul-Sep 2006	13,443	12,301	1,040	62	39	7,722	5,721	7,188	5,114	511	529	613	799	6.5	174	21.7	260	47	318	5,643	376	6.7	4,458	112	677
Aug-Oct 2006	13,451	12,302	1,052	56	42	7,702	5,749	7,164	5,137	516	536	612	792	6.4	180	22.7	252	42	317	5,674	381	6.7	4,470	113	685
Sep-Nov 2006	13,459	12,319	1,032	60	47	7,710	5,749	7,177	5,142	507	525	609	795	6.5	181	22.7	255	45	315	5,667	382	6.7	4,459	114	679
Oct-Dec 2006	13,463	12,315	1,042	60	46	7,701	5,763	7,166	5,149	511	531	619	805	6.5	178	22.1	265	43	319	5,680	386	6.8	4,459	116	688
Nov-Jan 2007	13,441	12,299	1,036	62	44	7,689	5,752	7,155	5,144	507	529	625	817	6.6	190	23.2	256	49	322	5,673	388	6.8	4,465	115	675
Dec-Feb 2007	13,423	12,269	1,048	59	47	7,696	5,727	7,151	5,118	520	528	616	818	6.7	185	22.6	254	55	324	5,646	380	6.7	4,468	110	663
Jan-Mar 2007	13,436	12,284	1,047	61	44	7,721	5,715	7,186	5,099	509	538	611	821	6.7	190	23.1	251	58	321	5,636	386	6.9	4,459	107	662
Feb-Apr 2007	13,450	12,298	1,048	61	43	7,734	5,717	7,194	5,104	513	535	634	817	6.6	192	23.5	249	56	320	5,639	399	7.1	4,465	98	655
Mar-May 2007	13,468	12,331	1,030	61	45	7,762	5,706	7,223	5,109	513	517	643	817	6.6	189	23.1	248	58	323	5,626	408	7.3	4,443	101	653
Apr-Jun 2007	13,483	12,344	1,027	62	49	7,776	5,706	7,239	5,106	514	514	651	814	6.6	194	23.9	237	57	326	5,619	406	7.2	4,430	99	662
May-Jul 2007	13,506	12,350	1,040	66	50	7,801	5,705	7,260	5,090	519	521	658	812	6.6	192	23.6	235	54	331	5,611	415	7.4	4,396	102	678
Jun-Aug 2007	13,514	12,339	1,060	64	52	7,810	5,704	7,269	5,070	516	544	661	798	6.5	188	23.5	232	49	329	5,613	407	7.3	4,420	95	668
Jul-Sep 2007	13,536	12,353	1,072	59	52	7,847	5,689	7,293	5,061	529	543	653	803	6.5	186	23.2	232	47	337	5,604	401	7.2	4,427	97	656
Aug-Oct 2007	13,568	12,386	1,066	60	56	7,861	5,706	7,313	5,073	520	546	657	794	6.4	182	23.0	235	46	330	5,619	409	7.3	4,439	97	650
Sep-Nov 2007	13,584	12,410	1,060	66	49	7,874	5,711	7,331	5,079	516	543	661	794	6.4	177	22.3	240	41	336	5,622	409	7.3	4,453	102	638
Oct-Dec 2007	13,628	12,464	1,047	67	51	7,893	5,735	7,364	5,100	503	544	676	799	6.4	179	22.4	256	36	327	5,644	438	7.8	4,426	99	654
Nov-Jan 2008	13,646	12,472	1,058	70	45	7,903	5,743	7,375	5,097	503	556	659	788	6.3	179	22.7	250	35	324	5,653	447	7.9	4,416	105	660
Dec-Feb 2008	13,683	12,503	1,067	70	43	7,932	5,751	7,386	5,117	520	547	665	782	6.3	181	23.2	247	40	314	5,664	437	7.7	4,419	108	671
Jan-Mar 2008	13,678	12,511	1,056	69	42	7,925	5,753	7,384	5,128	519	537	652	773	6.2	178	23.1	244	44	307	5,665	416	7.3	4,431	115	674
Feb-Apr 2008	13,682	12,517	1,045	73	47	7,931	5,751	7,381	5,136	524	521	663	783	6.3	179	22.8	248	44	312	5,657	409	7.2	4,415	114	690
Mar-May 2008	13,730	12,556	1,047	76	51	7,972	5,758	7,424	5,132	523	524	658	772	6.1	179	23.1	239	39	316	5,657	402	7.1	4,422	117	686
Apr-Jun 2008	13,710	12,544	1,048	72	47	7,968	5,742	7,418	5,125	524	524	669	767	6.1	171	22.3	245	38	313	5,650	408	7.2	4,419	126	670
May-Jul 2008	13,709	12,540	1,056	65	48	7,993	5,716	7,441	5,100	527	529	680	774	6.2	169	21.9	248	40	316	5,629	399	7.1	4,410	134	659
Jun-Aug 2008	13,684	12,532	1,052	60	41	7,976	5,709	7,433	5,099	525	527	670	768	6.1	173	22.6	251	39	305	5,626	399	7.1	4,435	133	634
Jul-Sep 2008	13,670	12,518	1,049	61	43	7,980	5,690	7,434	5,084	528	521	670	757	6.0	176	23.2	244	42	295	5,606	399	7.1	4,419	126	633
Aug-Oct 2008	13,671	12,515	1,058	58	38	7,986	5,685	7,437	5,079	532	527	675	743	5.9	174	23.4	237	41	291	5,606	409	7.3	4,423	117	629
Sep-Nov 2008	13,672	12,516	1,064	54	37	7,914	5,758	7,382	5,134	519	545	673	768	6.1	178	23.1	244	42	304	5,679	420	7.4	4,465	120	646
Oct-Dec 2008	13,659	12,515	1,054	53	36	7,939	5,720	7,409	5,106	511	542	670	772	6.2	185	24.0	240	44	303	5,649	417	7.4	4,442	118	643
Nov-Jan 2009	13,680	12,530	1,061	50	39	7,957	5,722	7,421	5,109	519	542	673	766	6.1	182	23.7	237	44	303	5,651	437	7.7	4,424	114	648

4.2 Full-time, part-time and temporary workers

United Kingdom (thousands) seasonally adjusted

	All in employment					Full-time and part-time workers[1]							Temporary employees (reasons for temporary working)							Part-time workers (reasons for working part-time)[3]					
	Total	Employees	Self employed	Unpaid family workers	Government supported training & employment programmes[2]	Total people working full-time	Total people working part-time	Employees working full-time	Employees working part-time	Self-employed people working full-time	Self-employed people working part-time	Total workers with second jobs	Total	Total as % of all employees	Could not find permanent job	% that could not find permanent job	Did not want permanent job	Had a contract with period of training	Some other reason	Total[4]	Could not find full-time job	% that could not find full-time job	Did not want full-time job	Ill or disabled	Student or at school
Women (16+)	MGSA	MGRO	MGRR	MGRU	MGRX	YCBF	YCBI	YCBL	YCBO	YCBR	YCBU	YCBX	YCCA	YCCD	YCCG	YCCJ	YCCM	YCCP	YCCS	YCCV	YCCY	YCDB	YCDE	YCDH	YCDK
Dec-Feb 2009	13,643	12,495	1,055	52	41	7,908	5,735	7,363	5,133	520	535	671	765	6.1	195	25.5	227	46	297	5,667	465	8.2	4,428	105	643
Jan-Mar 2009	13,627	12,458	1,071	55	43	7,868	5,759	7,320	5,139	524	547	669	764	6.1	193	25.3	230	44	297	5,686	481	8.5	4,436	107	638
Feb-Apr 2009	13,594	12,413	1,081	56	45	7,874	5,721	7,330	5,083	520	561	656	755	6.1	191	25.3	226	47	292	5,644	497	8.8	4,387	112	626
Mar-May 2009	13,578	12,386	1,082	64	46	7,867	5,711	7,324	5,062	523	559	655	755	6.1	198	26.2	231	44	282	5,621	511	9.1	4,357	111	620
Apr-Jun 2009	13,575	12,385	1,087	58	46	7,832	5,742	7,285	5,100	527	559	646	754	6.1	200	26.6	230	42	282	5,660	525	9.3	4,373	110	622
May-Jul 2009	13,553	12,355	1,097	55	46	7,793	5,759	7,234	5,121	539	559	641	750	6.1	212	28.3	220	39	279	5,680	534	9.4	4,386	108	620
Jun-Aug 2009	13,604	12,379	1,124	51	50	7,830	5,774	7,260	5,119	548	576	648	756	6.1	211	27.9	225	42	279	5,695	549	9.6	4,374	114	627
Jul-Sep 2009	13,622	12,394	1,132	48	48	7,782	5,840	7,218	5,176	544	588	654	779	6.3	223	28.7	230	41	284	5,764	569	9.9	4,411	110	648
Aug-Oct 2009	13,636	12,430	1,111	50	44	7,759	5,877	7,203	5,227	536	575	652	767	6.2	223	29.0	228	36	279	5,802	583	10.0	4,422	112	662
Sep-Nov 2009	13,654	12,420	1,139	43	52	7,777	5,877	7,213	5,207	544	595	647	752	6.1	228	30.3	220	34	271	5,801	589	10.2	4,412	107	666
Oct-Dec 2009	13,665	12,418	1,142	50	55	7,791	5,874	7,214	5,204	555	588	644	755	6.1	229	30.4	216	36	273	5,792	591	10.2	4,398	110	667
Nov-Jan 2010	13,650	12,409	1,133	50	59	7,777	5,873	7,207	5,201	546	587	627	768	6.2	240	31.2	223	36	269	5,788	596	10.3	4,385	109	671
Dec-Feb 2010	13,620	12,364	1,146	51	59	7,770	5,850	7,190	5,174	559	587	624	772	6.2	240	31.1	217	37	278	5,761	594	10.3	4,360	107	674
Jan-Mar 2010	13,616	12,329	1,180	50	58	7,749	5,867	7,151	5,177	577	603	633	775	6.3	245	31.6	215	37	278	5,780	608	10.5	4,379	99	661
Feb-Apr 2010	13,630	12,329	1,194	50	58	7,720	5,910	7,119	5,211	581	613	645	786	6.4	256	32.6	210	40	280	5,823	627	10.8	4,413	104	647
Mar-May 2010	13,645	12,367	1,172	51	54	7,715	5,930	7,125	5,242	567	605	658	808	6.5	263	32.6	217	39	289	5,847	613	10.5	4,446	104	651
Apr-Jun 2010	13,653	12,387	1,161	49	56	7,734	5,919	7,151	5,236	560	601	664	818	6.6	269	32.9	217	42	290	5,837	608	10.4	4,456	102	642
May-Jul 2010	13,691	12,410	1,169	60	52	7,712	5,979	7,117	5,293	570	599	667	824	6.6	272	33.0	222	40	289	5,892	635	10.8	4,464	101	666
Jun-Aug 2010	13,686	12,415	1,154	67	49	7,697	5,989	7,109	5,306	566	589	662	818	6.6	277	33.9	211	43	286	5,895	646	11.0	4,451	93	673
Jul-Sep 2010	13,689	12,400	1,181	62	46	7,706	5,983	7,111	5,289	576	606	656	832	6.7	281	33.8	220	42	288	5,894	652	11.1	4,451	93	665
Aug-Oct 2010	13,650	12,375	1,172	57	46	7,699	5,950	7,104	5,271	575	597	655	836	6.8	277	33.2	217	44	297	5,868	652	11.1	4,444	92	642
Sep-Nov 2010	13,640	12,352	1,177	61	49	7,695	5,945	7,095	5,257	577	600	652	831	6.7	286	34.4	203	42	300	5,857	658	11.2	4,464	94	603
Oct-Dec 2010	13,645	12,362	1,174	59	50	7,703	5,942	7,120	5,242	562	612	653	828	6.7	287	34.7	193	42	306	5,854	673	11.5	4,439	91	614
Nov-Jan 2011	13,680	12,364	1,202	65	49	7,715	5,965	7,126	5,238	565	636	663	829	6.7	281	33.9	196	43	309	5,875	669	11.4	4,469	91	609
Dec-Feb 2011	13,725	12,406	1,205	65	49	7,739	5,987	7,150	5,256	566	639	666	836	6.7	277	33.1	208	44	308	5,895	668	11.3	4,483	96	611
Jan-Mar 2011	13,749	12,444	1,189	66	50	7,767	5,982	7,181	5,263	561	628	670	843	6.8	279	33.1	211	45	308	5,891	665	11.3	4,469	100	622
Feb-Apr 2011	13,694	12,400	1,182	65	46	7,726	5,968	7,151	5,249	548	634	665	831	6.7	269	32.4	210	43	309	5,884	689	11.7	4,441	102	617
Mar-May 2011	13,728	12,434	1,191	60	43	7,761	5,967	7,183	5,251	555	636	661	834	6.7	271	32.5	214	43	306	5,886	705	12.0	4,423	106	617
Apr-Jun 2011	13,719	12,452	1,171	58	39	7,789	5,930	7,211	5,241	556	615	648	824	6.6	280	34.0	210	41	293	5,855	707	12.1	4,391	109	611
May-Jul 2011	13,690	12,431	1,164	56	39	7,824	5,866	7,245	5,186	562	603	644	807	6.5	274	34.0	200	40	293	5,789	709	12.2	4,321	111	610
Jun-Aug 2011	13,678	12,381	1,202	60	35	7,794	5,884	7,197	5,184	579	623	647	785	6.3	274	34.9	182	40	289	5,808	711	12.2	4,338	114	611
Jul-Sep 2011	13,690	12,361	1,225	63	42	7,789	5,900	7,188	5,173	579	646	655	789	6.4	278	35.2	187	43	282	5,819	720	12.4	4,326	123	614
Aug-Oct 2011	13,690	12,341	1,236	69	44	7,781	5,909	7,167	5,174	588	648	649	802	6.5	293	36.6	192	44	272	5,822	723	12.4	4,344	116	608
Sep-Nov 2011	13,702	12,354	1,232	69	46	7,781	5,920	7,168	5,186	583	649	653	820	6.6	292	35.6	201	49	279	5,835	754	12.9	4,331	116	608
Oct-Dec 2011	13,710	12,368	1,229	70	44	7,766	5,944	7,156	5,212	586	642	646	818	6.6	294	35.9	204	50	271	5,854	768	13.1	4,336	119	605
Nov-Jan 2012	13,712	12,361	1,235	69	47	7,763	5,948	7,154	5,207	586	648	653	828	6.7	298	36.0	203	52	275	5,855	794	13.6	4,319	116	598
Dec-Feb 2012	13,695	12,329	1,250	62	54	7,756	5,939	7,151	5,178	583	668	659	852	6.9	303	35.6	216	51	281	5,845	780	13.3	4,331	108	592

4.2 Full-time, part-time and temporary workers

United Kingdom (thousands) seasonally adjusted

	All in employment					Full-time and part-time workers[1]							Temporary employees (reasons for temporary working)							Part-time workers (reasons for working part-time)[3]					
	Total	Employ-ees	Self employed	Unpaid family workers	Government supported training & employment pro-grammes[2]	Total people working full-time	Total people working part-time	Employ-ees working full-time	Employ-ees working part-time	Self-employed people working full-time	Self-employed people working part-time	Total workers with second jobs	Total	Total as % of all employ-ees	Could not find perman-ent job	% that could not find perman-ent job	Did not want perman-ent job	Had a contract with period of training	Some other reason	Total[4]	Could not find full-time job	% that could not find full-time job	Did not want full-time job	Ill or dis-abled	Student or at school
Women (16+)	MGSA	MGRO	MGRR	MGRU	MGRX	YCBF	YCBI	YCBL	YCBO	YCBR	YCBU	YCBX	YCCA	YCCD	YCCG	YCCJ	YCCM	YCCP	YCCS	YCCV	YCCY	YCDB	YCDE	YCDH	YCDK
Jan-Mar 2012	13,733	12,355	1,271	53	55	7,774	5,959	7,165	5,190	588	682	665	829	6.7	299	36.1	201	46	284	5,872	779	13.3	4,348	117	591
Feb-Apr 2012	13,738	12,364	1,265	55	55	7,789	5,949	7,181	5,183	587	678	661	818	6.6	299	36.6	195	48	275	5,861	772	13.2	4,346	116	591
Mar-May 2012	13,763	12,407	1,241	64	52	7,813	5,950	7,217	5,190	572	669	656	838	6.8	316	37.7	186	49	288	5,859	765	13.1	4,353	116	592
Apr-Jun 2012	13,801	12,426	1,252	69	54	7,812	5,989	7,216	5,210	567	685	639	862	6.9	320	37.1	194	51	297	5,895	776	13.2	4,369	110	610
May-Jul 2012	13,870	12,468	1,274	74	54	7,821	6,049	7,229	5,239	564	710	650	890	7.1	326	36.6	210	51	303	5,949	786	13.2	4,417	110	608
Jun-Aug 2012	13,876	12,495	1,262	66	53	7,822	6,054	7,236	5,259	560	702	646	882	7.1	323	36.6	208	50	301	5,961	786	13.2	4,427	107	614
Jul-Sep 2012	13,862	12,489	1,260	61	53	7,814	6,048	7,226	5,262	563	697	646	866	6.9	319	36.8	204	48	295	5,959	782	13.1	4,431	112	607
Aug-Oct 2012	13,838	12,472	1,253	62	51	7,781	6,057	7,191	5,281	568	685	660	866	6.9	315	36.4	202	47	301	5,966	774	13.0	4,429	117	612
Sep-Nov 2012	13,912	12,503	1,289	67	54	7,847	6,065	7,233	5,270	588	701	668	871	7.0	308	35.4	208	50	305	5,971	771	12.9	4,436	120	610
Oct-Dec 2012	13,962	12,533	1,304	70	56	7,903	6,059	7,276	5,257	598	706	691	869	6.9	302	34.7	204	54	310	5,963	751	12.6	4,451	119	608
Nov-Jan 2013	13,966	12,567	1,285	63	51	7,942	6,024	7,318	5,249	590	695	698	865	6.9	307	35.5	197	53	308	5,944	768	12.9	4,428	122	594
Dec-Feb 2013	13,947	12,553	1,285	64	46	7,926	6,021	7,299	5,254	597	687	684	837	6.7	301	35.9	194	56	286	5,942	781	13.1	4,411	121	595
Jan-Mar 2013	13,969	12,592	1,265	66	45	7,946	6,023	7,316	5,276	603	662	677	862	6.8	312	36.2	196	62	291	5,938	780	13.1	4,400	117	610
Feb-Apr 2013	13,993	12,589	1,283	69	52	7,973	6,020	7,329	5,260	614	669	653	846	6.7	303	35.8	196	65	283	5,929	778	13.1	4,390	119	612
Mar-May 2013	13,975	12,580	1,268	70	57	7,964	6,011	7,324	5,255	607	661	670	833	6.6	302	36.3	189	59	283	5,917	801	13.5	4,356	116	610
Apr-Jun 2013	14,005	12,600	1,276	71	58	7,985	6,020	7,332	5,268	615	661	667	831	6.6	291	35.1	186	65	289	5,929	796	13.4	4,376	121	600
May-Jul 2013	14,030	12,625	1,275	68	62	8,037	5,994	7,370	5,254	619	656	663	822	6.5	291	35.4	178	63	289	5,911	804	13.6	4,343	121	601
Jun-Aug 2013	14,030	12,600	1,294	72	63	8,041	5,989	7,354	5,246	633	661	667	837	6.6	297	35.5	167	63	310	5,907	799	13.5	4,371	125	571
Jul-Sep 2013	14,053	12,615	1,298	72	68	8,057	5,996	7,372	5,243	634	664	667	848	6.7	294	34.7	177	60	317	5,907	797	13.5	4,357	121	590
Aug-Oct 2013	14,125	12,668	1,320	76	62	8,076	6,049	7,391	5,277	642	678	674	855	6.7	294	34.4	186	63	313	5,955	803	13.5	4,401	121	591
Sep-Nov 2013	14,145	12,656	1,366	70	53	8,129	6,016	7,420	5,237	675	690	682	846	6.7	286	33.8	191	66	303	5,927	788	13.3	4,391	116	596
Oct-Dec 2013	14,157	12,664	1,375	66	53	8,174	5,983	7,456	5,208	685	690	667	850	6.7	302	35.5	192	55	300	5,899	789	13.4	4,374	114	590
Nov-Jan 2014	14,161	12,651	1,391	64	54	8,164	5,997	7,447	5,205	685	706	663	852	6.7	295	34.6	203	55	300	5,911	788	13.3	4,383	116	593
Dec-Feb 2014	14,253	12,727	1,405	71	50	8,179	6,074	7,466	5,261	684	722	642	865	6.8	290	33.6	208	58	308	5,983	781	13.1	4,465	115	596
Jan-Mar 2014	14,268	12,718	1,436	67	47	8,200	6,068	7,498	5,220	674	761	663	876	6.9	289	33.0	218	59	310	5,981	777	13.0	4,472	112	599
Feb-Apr 2014	14,326	12,775	1,440	64	48	8,221	6,105	7,524	5,251	673	767	676	903	7.1	296	32.8	230	59	318	6,018	793	13.2	4,487	106	611
Mar-May 2014	14,385	12,811	1,463	57	53	8,254	6,130	7,555	5,257	675	788	687	904	7.1	296	32.8	230	58	320	6,045	767	12.7	4,541	104	615
Apr-Jun 2014	14,369	12,789	1,469	58	53	8,206	6,162	7,505	5,285	680	789	703	885	6.9	289	32.7	234	56	305	6,074	757	12.5	4,580	110	603
May-Jul 2014	14,378	12,822	1,444	62	49	8,226	6,151	7,530	5,292	678	766	709	889	6.9	290	32.6	229	58	312	6,058	753	12.4	4,582	94	605
Jun-Aug 2014	14,408	12,871	1,412	72	53	8,283	6,125	7,584	5,286	676	736	702	888	6.9	286	32.3	231	62	309	6,022	758	12.6	4,546	94	601
Jul-Sep 2014	14,424	12,892	1,411	69	52	8,302	6,121	7,614	5,278	665	746	693	902	7.0	289	32.1	238	60	314	6,024	753	12.5	4,551	94	601
Aug-Oct 2014	14,444	12,886	1,441	65	52	8,318	6,127	7,610	5,276	680	761	689	887	6.9	282	31.7	236	56	313	6,037	744	12.3	4,582	99	584
Sep-Nov 2014	14,451	12,894	1,455	56	47	8,324	6,126	7,616	5,278	683	772	705	885	6.9	273	30.8	236	57	320	6,050	741	12.3	4,587	103	588
Oct-Dec 2014	14,503	12,947	1,456	55	45	8,337	6,166	7,634	5,313	675	781	712	891	6.9	270	30.3	239	54	328	6,093	745	12.2	4,593	105	618
Nov-Jan 2015	14,529	12,958	1,463	64	44	8,366	6,164	7,665	5,294	670	793	710	874	6.7	263	30.1	233	57	321	6,087	751	12.3	4,597	110	600
Dec-Feb 2015	14,565	13,014	1,445	62	45	8,370	6,195	7,690	5,323	647	797	700	873	6.7	272	31.1	224	54	323	6,121	765	12.5	4,597	112	611
Jan-Mar 2015	14,571	13,020	1,443	65	42	8,379	6,191	7,686	5,334	663	781	698	871	6.7	273	31.3	215	57	327	6,115	746	12.2	4,611	125	599

4.2 Full-time, part-time and temporary workers

United Kingdom (thousands) seasonally adjusted

	All in employment					Full-time and part-time workers[1]							Temporary employees (reasons for temporary working)							Part-time workers (reasons for working part-time)[3]					
	Total	Employ-ees	Self employed	Unpaid family workers	Government supported training & employment pro-grammes[2]	Total people working full-time	Total people working part-time	Employ-ees working full-time	Employ-ees working part-time	Self-employed people working full-time	Self-employed people working part-time	Total workers with second jobs	Total	Total as % of all employ-ees	Could not find perman-ent job	% that could not find perman-ent job	Did not want perman-ent job	Had a contract with period of training	Some other reason	Total[4]	Could not find full-time job	% that could not find full-time job	Did not want full-time job	Ill or dis-abled	Student or at school
Women (16+)	MGSA	MGRO	MGRR	MGRU	MGRX	YCBF	YCBI	YCBL	YCBO	YCBR	YCBU	YCBX	YCCA	YCCD	YCCG	YCCJ	YCCM	YCCP	YCCS	YCCV	YCCY	YCDB	YCDE	YCDH	YCDK
Feb-Apr 2015	14,585	13,056	1,426	59	43	8,416	6,169	7,718	5,338	662	764	685	877	6.7	271	30.8	215	61	331	6,102	744	12.2	4,598	125	599
Mar-May 2015	14,566	13,039	1,434	58	35	8,397	6,169	7,718	5,321	650	785	669	881	6.8	265	30.1	224	65	327	6,106	732	12.0	4,611	128	597
Apr-Jun 2015	14,576	13,044	1,433	56	44	8,419	6,157	7,719	5,325	669	764	653	874	6.7	268	30.7	218	69	319	6,089	732	12.0	4,591	129	600
May-Jul 2015	14,600	13,056	1,439	59	46	8,408	6,192	7,709	5,347	668	771	663	891	6.8	276	31.0	229	70	317	6,118	722	11.8	4,617	133	611
Jun-Aug 2015	14,584	13,042	1,441	55	46	8,429	6,155	7,723	5,319	678	763	667	886	6.8	284	32.1	228	69	304	6,082	711	11.7	4,590	133	618
Jul-Sep 2015	14,657	13,102	1,456	54	46	8,456	6,202	7,742	5,360	684	772	672	877	6.7	273	31.1	229	69	306	6,132	699	11.4	4,642	134	626
Aug-Oct 2015	14,668	13,092	1,486	47	43	8,463	6,205	7,748	5,344	696	790	672	869	6.6	271	31.1	223	72	303	6,134	717	11.7	4,622	132	631
Sep-Nov 2015	14,710	13,120	1,497	48	46	8,492	6,219	7,771	5,349	696	801	664	873	6.7	273	31.3	216	76	307	6,150	697	11.3	4,653	135	631
Oct-Dec 2015	14,706	13,102	1,511	48	45	8,498	6,208	7,775	5,327	700	811	648	866	6.6	267	30.8	217	75	306	6,139	689	11.2	4,644	137	626
Nov-Jan 2016	14,712	13,126	1,492	51	42	8,480	6,232	7,759	5,367	697	795	630	882	6.7	266	30.1	223	75	319	6,162	674	10.9	4,679	139	631
Dec-Feb 2016	14,707	13,125	1,487	52	43	8,482	6,225	7,763	5,362	690	798	641	876	6.7	257	29.4	229	68	322	6,159	660	10.7	4,697	145	618
Jan-Mar 2016	14,724	13,126	1,504	50	43	8,485	6,238	7,762	5,365	696	808	641	877	6.7	264	30.1	238	66	309	6,173	670	10.9	4,698	141	623
Feb-Apr 2016	14,743	13,161	1,485	56	42	8,468	6,276	7,752	5,409	689	795	644	865	6.6	262	30.3	245	62	295	6,204	662	10.7	4,742	143	620
Mar-May 2016	14,833	13,202	1,531	61	39	8,549	6,283	7,812	5,389	713	818	651	867	6.6	255	29.4	249	62	301	6,207	655	10.5	4,744	146	626
Apr-Jun 2016	14,834	13,206	1,532	63	33	8,568	6,267	7,826	5,380	719	814	660	885	6.7	257	29.0	255	59	314	6,193	620	10.0	4,759	145	637
May-Jul 2016	14,857	13,225	1,540	61	32	8,579	6,278	7,825	5,400	731	809	656	875	6.6	253	28.9	254	57	312	6,208	635	10.2	4,762	149	634
Jun-Aug 2016	14,850	13,216	1,543	64	27	8,554	6,295	7,789	5,426	745	798	676	875	6.6	242	27.6	257	59	317	6,224	623	10.0	4,789	147	640
Jul-Sep 2016	14,885	13,215	1,572	69	30	8,594	6,290	7,823	5,392	751	821	656	868	6.6	234	26.9	254	64	317	6,213	628	10.1	4,776	150	635
Aug-Oct 2016	14,905	13,226	1,582	70	29	8,638	6,267	7,858	5,368	754	828	638	873	6.6	240	27.4	255	64	315	6,196	636	10.3	4,755	147	625
Sep-Nov 2016	14,921	13,246	1,573	72	30	8,657	6,264	7,868	5,377	759	814	631	879	6.6	238	27.1	247	61	333	6,191	632	10.2	4,747	152	625
Oct-Dec 2016	14,944	13,267	1,577	69	32	8,680	6,264	7,886	5,381	767	810	636	893	6.7	237	26.6	247	62	347	6,191	618	10.0	4,743	154	637

Source: Labour Force Survey

Note: When comparing quarterly changes ONS recommends comparing with the previous non-overlapping 3-month average time period (eg, compare Apr-Jun with Jan-Mar, not with Mar-May).

1. The split between full-time and part-time employment is based on respondents' self-classification.
2. This series does not include all people on these programmes; it only includes those engaging in any form of work, work experience or work-related training.
3. These series cover Employees and Self-employed only. These series include some temporary employees.
4. The total includes those who did not give a reason for working part-time and it therefore does not equal the sum of the other columns in this section of the table.

4.3 Employment by sex and age group: United Kingdom

United Kingdom (thousands) seasonally adjusted

	Aged 16 and over								Aged 16-64							
	Employment		Unemployment		Activity		Inactivity		Employment		Unemployment		Activity		Inactivity	
	level	rate (%)	level	rate (%)	level	rate (%)	level	rate (%)	level	rate (%)	level	rate (%)	level	rate (%)	level	rate (%)
People	**MGRZ**	**MGSR**	**MGSC**	**MGSX**	**MGSF**	**MGWG**	**MGSI**	**YBTC**	**LF2G**	**LF24**	**LF2I**	**LF2Q**	**LF2K**	**LF22**	**LF2M**	**LF2S**
Oct-Dec 2012	29,908	58.5	2,535	7.8	32,443	63.5	18,652	36.5	28,925	71.4	2,512	8.0	31,438	77.6	9,072	22.4
Oct-Dec 2013	30,290	58.9	2,357	7.2	32,648	63.5	18,795	36.5	29,215	72.0	2,326	7.4	31,542	77.7	9,038	22.3
Oct-Dec 2014	30,944	59.7	1,870	5.7	32,814	63.3	19,023	36.7	29,820	73.2	1,851	5.8	31,671	77.7	9,064	22.3
Jan-Mar 2016	31,572	60.3	1,687	5.1	33,259	63.5	19,077	36.5	30,387	74.1	1,665	5.2	32,052	78.2	8,937	21.8
Apr-Jun 2016	31,747	60.5	1,643	4.9	33,390	63.7	19,045	36.3	30,540	74.4	1,625	5.1	32,165	78.4	8,874	21.6
Jul-Sep 2016	31,810	60.6	1,618	4.8	33,428	63.7	19,085	36.3	30,577	74.4	1,601	5.0	32,178	78.3	8,895	21.7
Oct-Dec 2016	31,845	60.6	1,585	4.7	33,430	63.6	19,151	36.4	30,645	74.6	1,568	4.9	32,213	78.4	8,885	21.6
Men	**MGSA**	**MGSS**	**MGSD**	**MGSY**	**MGSG**	**MGWH**	**MGSJ**	**YBTD**	**YBSF**	**MGSV**	**YBSI**	**YBTJ**	**YBSL**	**MGSP**	**YBSO**	**YBTM**
Oct-Dec 2012	15,945	64.1	1,420	8.2	17,365	69.8	7,509	30.2	15,343	76.4	1,401	8.4	16,744	83.4	3,337	16.6
Oct-Dec 2013	16,133	64.4	1,322	7.6	17,455	69.6	7,609	30.4	15,484	77.0	1,304	7.8	16,788	83.4	3,334	16.6
Oct-Dec 2014	16,441	65.0	1,041	6.0	17,482	69.2	7,796	30.8	15,758	78.0	1,027	6.1	16,785	83.1	3,425	16.9
Oct-Dec 2015	16,834	66.0	921	5.2	17,755	69.6	7,748	30.4	16,096	79.2	911	5.4	17,007	83.7	3,320	16.3
Jan-Mar 2016	16,848	65.9	915	5.1	17,763	69.5	7,798	30.5	16,118	79.2	905	5.3	17,024	83.6	3,335	16.4
Apr-Jun 2016	16,913	66.0	891	5.0	17,804	69.5	7,815	30.5	16,168	79.3	883	5.2	17,051	83.6	3,339	16.4
Jul-Sep 2016	16,926	66.0	884	5.0	17,810	69.4	7,851	30.6	16,167	79.2	876	5.1	17,042	83.5	3,366	16.5
Oct-Dec 2016	16,901	65.8	873	4.9	17,773	69.2	7,923	30.8	16,181	79.2	864	5.1	17,045	83.5	3,376	16.5
Women	**MGSB**	**MGST**	**MGSE**	**MGSZ**	**MGSH**	**MGWI**	**MGSK**	**YBTE**	**LF2H**	**LF25**	**LF2J**	**LF2R**	**LF2L**	**LF23**	**LF2N**	**LF2T**
Oct-Dec 2012	13,962	53.3	1,115	7.4	15,078	57.5	11,142	42.5	13,583	66.5	1,111	7.6	14,694	71.9	5,734	28.1
Oct-Dec 2013	14,157	53.7	1,036	6.8	15,193	57.6	11,185	42.4	13,731	67.1	1,022	6.9	14,753	72.1	5,704	27.9
Oct-Dec 2014	14,503	54.6	829	5.4	15,332	57.7	11,226	42.3	14,062	68.5	825	5.5	14,886	72.5	5,640	27.5
Oct-Dec 2015	14,706	55.0	766	5.0	15,472	57.9	11,261	42.1	14,244	69.1	758	5.1	15,001	72.8	5,609	27.2
Jan-Mar 2016	14,724	55.0	772	5.0	15,496	57.9	11,279	42.1	14,268	69.2	760	5.1	15,028	72.8	5,602	27.2
Apr-Jun 2016	14,834	55.3	752	4.8	15,586	58.1	11,230	41.9	14,371	69.6	742	4.9	15,113	73.2	5,535	26.8
Jul-Sep 2016	14,885	55.4	734	4.7	15,618	58.2	11,234	41.8	14,410	69.7	725	4.8	15,135	73.2	5,528	26.8
Oct-Dec 2016	14,944	55.6	713	4.6	15,657	58.2	11,228	41.8	14,464	70.0	704	4.6	15,168	73.4	5,509	26.6

	Aged 16-17								Aged 18-24							
	Employment		Unemployment		Activity		Inactivity		Employment		Unemployment		Activity		Inactivity	
	level	rate (%)	level	rate (%)	level	rate (%)	level	rate (%)	level	rate (%)	level	rate (%)	level	rate (%)	level	rate (%)
People	**YBTO**	**YBUA**	**YBVH**	**YBVK**	**YBZL**	**YCAG**	**YCAS**	**LWEX**	**YBTR**	**YBUD**	**YBVN**	**YBVQ**	**YBZO**	**YCAJ**	**YCAV**	**LWFA**
Oct-Dec 2012	332	22.0	203	37.9	535	35.4	976	64.6	3,392	58.2	788	18.9	4,180	71.7	1,646	28.3
Oct-Dec 2013	325	21.5	190	36.9	515	34.1	994	65.9	3,382	58.4	741	18.0	4,123	71.2	1,670	28.8
Oct-Dec 2014	346	23.2	160	31.6	506	33.9	988	66.1	3,479	60.2	591	14.5	4,070	70.4	1,711	29.6
Jan-Mar 2016	369	25.2	127	25.6	496	33.8	971	66.2	3,582	62.3	500	12.2	4,082	71.0	1,663	29.0
Apr-Jun 2016	353	24.2	143	28.8	496	34.0	965	66.0	3,580	62.4	475	11.7	4,055	70.7	1,678	29.3
Jul-Sep 2016	340	23.3	124	26.7	463	31.9	991	68.1	3,567	62.4	473	11.7	4,040	70.7	1,678	29.3
Oct-Dec 2016	372	25.8	122	24.6	494	34.2	952	65.8	3,556	62.4	440	11.0	3,996	70.1	1,704	29.9
Men	**YBTP**	**YBUB**	**YBVI**	**YBVL**	**YBZM**	**YCAH**	**YCAT**	**LWEY**	**YBTS**	**YBUE**	**YBVO**	**YBVR**	**YBZP**	**YCAK**	**YCAW**	**LWFB**
Oct-Dec 2012	143	18.4	111	43.7	254	32.8	522	67.2	1,735	59.0	465	21.1	2,200	74.9	739	25.1
Oct-Dec 2013	145	18.8	99	40.6	245	31.6	529	68.4	1,731	59.1	445	20.5	2,176	74.2	755	25.8
Oct-Dec 2014	148	19.3	86	36.7	233	30.5	531	69.5	1,802	61.5	343	16.0	2,145	73.2	787	26.8
Oct-Dec 2015	174	23.1	72	29.3	246	32.7	508	67.3	1,866	63.8	281	13.1	2,147	73.4	779	26.6
Jan-Mar 2016	173	23.1	70	28.7	243	32.3	509	67.7	1,848	63.3	282	13.2	2,130	72.9	791	27.1
Apr-Jun 2016	160	21.4	77	32.4	237	31.6	512	68.4	1,829	62.7	282	13.4	2,112	72.4	805	27.6
Jul-Sep 2016	151	20.2	67	30.7	217	29.2	528	70.8	1,809	62.2	288	13.7	2,097	72.1	813	27.9
Oct-Dec 2016	176	23.7	66	27.3	242	32.6	500	67.4	1,808	62.3	277	13.3	2,085	71.8	818	28.2
Women	**YBTQ**	**YBUC**	**YBVJ**	**YBVM**	**YBZN**	**YCAI**	**YCAU**	**LWEZ**	**YBTT**	**YBUF**	**YBVP**	**YBVS**	**YBZQ**	**YCAL**	**YCAX**	**LWFC**
Oct-Dec 2012	189	25.7	92	32.7	281	38.2	454	61.8	1,657	57.4	324	16.3	1,980	68.6	907	31.4
Oct-Dec 2013	180	24.5	91	33.6	271	36.8	465	63.2	1,651	57.7	296	15.2	1,947	68.0	915	32.0
Oct-Dec 2014	199	27.3	74	27.2	273	37.4	456	62.6	1,677	58.9	248	12.9	1,925	67.6	924	32.4
Oct-Dec 2015	190	26.5	61	24.4	251	35.0	467	65.0	1,733	61.2	210	10.8	1,943	68.6	889	31.4
Jan-Mar 2016	196	27.4	57	22.5	253	35.3	462	64.7	1,735	61.4	218	11.2	1,952	69.1	872	30.9
Apr-Jun 2016	193	27.1	66	25.6	259	36.4	453	63.6	1,751	62.2	193	9.9	1,944	69.0	873	31.0
Jul-Sep 2016	189	26.7	57	23.2	246	34.7	463	65.3	1,758	62.6	185	9.5	1,943	69.2	864	30.8
Oct-Dec 2016	197	27.9	56	22.1	253	35.8	452	64.2	1,748	62.5	163	8.5	1,911	68.3	886	31.7

4.3 Employment by sex and age group: United Kingdom

United Kingdom (thousands) seasonally adjusted

	Aged 25-34								Aged 35-49							
	Employment		Unemployment		Activity		Inactivity		Employment		Unemployment		Activity		Inactivity	
	level	rate (%)	level	rate (%)	level	rate (%)	level	rate (%)	level	rate (%)	level	rate (%)	level	rate (%)	level	rate (%)
People	YBTU	YBUG	YCGM	YCGP	YBZR	YCAM	YCAY	LWFD	YBTX	YBUJ	YCGS	YCGV	YBZU	YCAP	YCBB	LWFG
Oct-Dec 2012	6,721	78.9	529	7.3	7,251	85.1	1,274	14.9	10,774	82.0	614	5.4	11,387	86.7	1,753	13.3
Oct-Dec 2013	6,875	79.7	487	6.6	7,362	85.4	1,260	14.6	10,680	82.0	539	4.8	11,219	86.2	1,802	13.8
Oct-Dec 2014	6,998	80.5	381	5.2	7,379	84.9	1,315	15.1	10,836	83.7	421	3.7	11,256	86.9	1,691	13.1
Jan-Mar 2016	7,188	81.7	351	4.7	7,539	85.7	1,261	14.3	10,792	83.7	361	3.2	11,153	86.5	1,743	13.5
Apr-Jun 2016	7,251	82.2	340	4.5	7,591	86.0	1,232	14.0	10,785	83.7	368	3.3	11,153	86.5	1,734	13.5
Jul-Sep 2016	7,247	82.0	344	4.5	7,591	85.9	1,248	14.1	10,790	83.8	364	3.3	11,154	86.6	1,720	13.4
Oct-Dec 2016	7,264	82.1	346	4.5	7,610	86.0	1,240	14.0	10,780	83.8	361	3.2	11,142	86.6	1,719	13.4
Men	YBTV	YBUH	YCGN	YCGQ	YBZS	YCAN	YCAZ	LWFE	YBTY	YBUK	YCGT	YCGW	YBZV	YCAQ	YCBC	LWFH
Oct-Dec 2012	3,652	86.5	280	7.1	3,932	93.1	290	6.9	5,698	87.9	300	5.0	5,998	92.5	483	7.5
Oct-Dec 2013	3,714	86.9	278	7.0	3,992	93.5	280	6.5	5,644	87.9	269	4.5	5,913	92.1	511	7.9
Oct-Dec 2014	3,768	87.3	203	5.1	3,972	92.1	343	7.9	5,708	89.3	217	3.7	5,925	92.7	464	7.3
Oct-Dec 2015	3,882	88.9	198	4.8	4,080	93.4	289	6.6	5,700	89.5	177	3.0	5,877	92.3	493	7.7
Jan-Mar 2016	3,928	89.6	173	4.2	4,100	93.5	284	6.5	5,694	89.4	183	3.1	5,877	92.3	489	7.7
Apr-Jun 2016	3,947	89.7	165	4.0	4,113	93.5	288	6.5	5,713	89.8	179	3.0	5,892	92.6	471	7.4
Jul-Sep 2016	3,935	89.2	169	4.1	4,104	93.1	306	6.9	5,704	89.7	178	3.0	5,881	92.5	475	7.5
Oct-Dec 2016	3,926	88.9	177	4.3	4,103	92.9	313	7.1	5,699	89.8	172	2.9	5,871	92.5	478	7.5
Women	YBTW	YBUI	YCGO	YCGR	YBZT	YCAO	YCBA	LWFF	YBTZ	YBUL	YCGU	YCGX	YBZW	YCAR	YCBD	LWFI
Oct-Dec 2012	3,070	71.3	249	7.5	3,319	77.1	984	22.9	5,076	76.2	313	5.8	5,390	80.9	1,269	19.1
Oct-Dec 2013	3,161	72.7	209	6.2	3,370	77.5	981	22.5	5,036	76.3	270	5.1	5,306	80.4	1,291	19.6
Oct-Dec 2014	3,230	73.7	178	5.2	3,408	77.8	972	22.2	5,128	78.2	204	3.8	5,331	81.3	1,227	18.7
Oct-Dec 2015	3,287	74.6	184	5.3	3,471	78.8	936	21.2	5,073	77.6	187	3.6	5,260	80.5	1,274	19.5
Jan-Mar 2016	3,260	73.8	179	5.2	3,439	77.9	976	22.1	5,098	78.1	178	3.4	5,276	80.8	1,253	19.2
Apr-Jun 2016	3,303	74.7	175	5.0	3,478	78.6	944	21.4	5,071	77.7	189	3.6	5,260	80.6	1,263	19.4
Jul-Sep 2016	3,313	74.8	175	5.0	3,487	78.7	941	21.3	5,087	78.0	186	3.5	5,273	80.9	1,245	19.1
Oct-Dec 2016	3,338	75.3	170	4.8	3,507	79.1	927	20.9	5,081	78.0	190	3.6	5,271	80.9	1,241	19.1

	Aged 50-64								Age 65+							
	Employment		Unemployment		Activity		Inactivity		Employment		Unemployment		Activity		Inactivity	
	level	rate (%)	level	rate (%)	level	rate (%)	level	rate (%)	level	rate (%)	level	rate (%)	level	rate (%)	level	rate (%)
People	LF26	LF2U	LF28	LF2E	LF3A	LF2C	LF2A	LF2W	LFK4	LFK6	K5HU	K5HW	LFK8	LFL2	LFL4	LFL6
Oct-Dec 2012	7,706	67.0	379	4.7	8,084	70.2	3,424	29.8	983	9.3	23	2.2	1,005	9.5	9,580	90.5
Oct-Dec 2013	7,954	68.4	369	4.4	8,322	71.5	3,312	28.5	1,075	9.9	31	2.8	1,106	10.2	9,756	89.8
Oct-Dec 2014	8,161	69.1	299	3.5	8,460	71.6	3,359	28.4	1,124	10.1	19	1.6	1,143	10.3	9,958	89.7
Jan-Mar 2016	8,455	70.0	326	3.7	8,781	72.7	3,299	27.3	1,186	10.4	22	1.8	1,207	10.6	10,140	89.4
Apr-Jun 2016	8,571	70.6	298	3.4	8,869	73.1	3,264	26.9	1,207	10.6	18	1.5	1,225	10.8	10,171	89.2
Jul-Sep 2016	8,632	70.8	296	3.3	8,929	73.3	3,259	26.7	1,233	10.8	17	1.3	1,250	10.9	10,190	89.1
Oct-Dec 2016	8,673	70.8	298	3.3	8,971	73.3	3,271	26.7	1,200	10.5	17	1.4	1,217	10.6	10,266	89.4
Men	MGUX	YBUN	MGVM	MGXF	YBZY	MGWQ	MGWB	LWFK	MGVA	YBUQ	MGVP	MGXI	YCAE	MGWT	MGWE	LWFN
Oct-Dec 2012	4,115	72.7	245	5.6	4,360	77.0	1,304	23.0	603	12.6	19	3.0	621	13.0	4,172	87.0
Oct-Dec 2013	4,250	74.3	213	4.8	4,463	78.0	1,260	22.0	649	13.1	17	2.6	666	13.5	4,275	86.5
Oct-Dec 2014	4,332	74.6	178	4.0	4,510	77.6	1,299	22.4	683	13.5	14	2.1	697	13.8	4,372	86.2
Oct-Dec 2015	4,475	75.7	182	3.9	4,657	78.8	1,252	21.2	738	14.3	11	1.4	748	14.5	4,428	85.5
Jan-Mar 2016	4,475	75.4	198	4.2	4,673	78.7	1,261	21.3	730	14.0	9	1.2	739	14.2	4,463	85.8
Apr-Jun 2016	4,518	75.8	179	3.8	4,697	78.8	1,262	21.2	744	14.2	8	1.1	752	14.4	4,476	85.6
Jul-Sep 2016	4,568	76.3	174	3.7	4,743	79.2	1,243	20.8	759	14.5	8	1.0	767	14.6	4,485	85.4
Oct-Dec 2016	4,572	76.0	172	3.6	4,744	78.9	1,268	21.1	720	13.6	9	1.2	728	13.8	4,546	86.2
Women	LF27	LF2V	LF29	LF2F	LF3B	LF2D	LF2B	LF2X	LFK5	LFK7	K5HV	K5HX	LFK9	LFL3	LFL5	LFL7
Oct-Dec 2012	3,591	61.4	134	3.6	3,724	63.7	2,120	36.3	380	6.6	*	*	384	6.6	5,408	93.4
Oct-Dec 2013	3,704	62.6	156	4.0	3,860	65.3	2,052	34.7	426	7.2	13	3.1	440	7.4	5,481	92.6
Oct-Dec 2014	3,829	63.7	121	3.1	3,949	65.7	2,060	34.3	441	7.3	*	*	446	7.4	5,586	92.6
Oct-Dec 2015	3,961	64.7	115	2.8	4,076	66.6	2,042	33.4	462	7.5	8	1.8	470	7.7	5,652	92.3
Jan-Mar 2016	3,979	64.8	129	3.1	4,108	66.8	2,037	33.2	456	7.4	12	2.6	468	7.6	5,677	92.4
Apr-Jun 2016	4,053	65.6	119	2.9	4,172	67.6	2,002	32.4	463	7.5	10	2.2	473	7.7	5,695	92.3
Jul-Sep 2016	4,064	65.5	122	2.9	4,186	67.5	2,015	32.5	474	7.7	9	1.8	483	7.8	5,706	92.2
Oct-Dec 2016	4,101	65.8	126	3.0	4,226	67.8	2,003	32.2	480	7.7	9	1.8	489	7.9	5,719	92.1

Source: Labour Force Survey

Labour market statistics enquiries: labour.market@ons.gsi.gov.uk

Note: When comparing quarterly changes ONS recommends comparing with the previous non-overlapping 3-month average time period (eg, compare Apr-Jun with Jan-Mar, not with Mar-May).

4.4 All in employment by industry

United Kingdom (thousands) not seasonally adjusted

				Standard Industrial Classification (SIC) 2007															
	All in employment1	Public sector	Private sector	Agri-culture, forestry & fishing A	Mining, energy and water supply B, D, E	Manu-facturing C	Con-struction F	Wholesale, retail & repair of motor vehicles G	Transport & storage H	Accom-modation & food services I	Infor-mation & commun-ication J	Financial & insurance activities K	Real estate activities L	Prof-essional, scientific & technical activities M	Admin-istrative & support services N	Public admin & defence; social security O	Edu-cation P	Human health & social work activities Q	Other services R, S, T
People																			
Jan-Mar 2007	29,108	6,954	22,040	288	450	3,216	2,527	4,120	1,566	1,324	1,056	1,263	257	1,874	1,304	1,980	2,798	3,500	1,473
Apr-Jun 2007	29,242	6,987	22,131	294	464	3,281	2,544	4,034	1,559	1,371	1,051	1,272	245	1,883	1,347	1,985	2,823	3,461	1,513
Jul-Sep 2007	29,525	6,919	22,466	297	469	3,269	2,558	4,090	1,556	1,406	1,062	1,304	266	1,912	1,432	1,990	2,782	3,505	1,512
Oct-Dec 2007	29,640	7,018	22,479	307	461	3,216	2,537	4,187	1,576	1,395	1,019	1,312	279	1,952	1,399	1,996	2,840	3,531	1,517
Jan-Mar 2008	29,596	7,047	22,404	334	452	3,148	2,535	4,184	1,605	1,382	1,024	1,288	263	1,939	1,398	2,011	2,847	3,566	1,509
Apr-Jun 2008	29,637	7,101	22,383	321	446	3,087	2,512	4,195	1,590	1,355	1,033	1,287	253	1,969	1,417	2,035	2,861	3,642	1,519
Jul-Sep 2008	29,685	7,039	22,508	313	463	3,068	2,583	4,248	1,606	1,355	1,063	1,272	259	1,919	1,404	2,033	2,805	3,648	1,533
Oct-Dec 2008	29,593	7,167	22,289	306	507	2,981	2,564	4,221	1,626	1,335	1,036	1,244	252	1,849	1,347	2,037	2,848	3,748	1,584
Jan-Mar 2009	29,277	7,224	21,913	322	489	2,857	2,482	4,107	1,571	1,324	1,035	1,227	273	1,842	1,309	2,009	2,919	3,772	1,579
Apr-Jun 2009	29,003	7,238	21,624	311	483	2,777	2,385	3,989	1,510	1,360	1,015	1,235	268	1,882	1,301	1,967	2,929	3,739	1,583
Jul-Sep 2009	29,170	7,278	21,745	329	491	2,813	2,311	4,031	1,463	1,428	1,020	1,246	265	1,890	1,301	1,977	2,960	3,778	1,599
Oct-Dec 2009	29,167	7,324	21,691	323	482	2,799	2,311	4,017	1,455	1,406	1,014	1,223	254	1,886	1,328	1,944	3,045	3,846	1,579
Jan-Mar 2010	28,924	7,255	21,488	336	472	2,815	2,208	3,943	1,462	1,388	1,011	1,210	263	1,882	1,319	1,930	3,062	3,824	1,549
Apr-Jun 2010	29,110	7,325	21,586	341	463	2,875	2,207	4,004	1,443	1,461	979	1,175	262	1,893	1,326	1,925	3,129	3,848	1,532
Jul-Sep 2010	29,484	7,298	21,973	369	474	2,888	2,234	4,112	1,483	1,503	1,045	1,165	301	1,852	1,341	1,925	3,120	3,821	1,594
Oct-Dec 2010	29,390	7,278	21,929	366	489	2,902	2,238	4,082	1,436	1,427	1,030	1,171	300	1,882	1,379	1,867	3,120	3,884	1,555
Jan-Mar 2011	29,350	7,315	21,842	357	497	2,860	2,212	4,034	1,451	1,417	1,059	1,179	299	1,857	1,299	1,875	3,121	3,967	1,544
Apr-Jun 2011	29,367	7,183	22,021	342	521	2,868	2,198	4,051	1,445	1,458	1,073	1,173	308	1,851	1,321	1,844	3,129	3,931	1,587
Jul-Sep 2011	29,376	7,009	22,216	370	519	2,841	2,237	4,019	1,428	1,498	1,061	1,192	300	1,888	1,339	1,852	2,986	3,981	1,639
Oct-Dec 2011	29,405	6,970	22,276	357	527	2,884	2,172	4,078	1,432	1,499	1,083	1,215	293	1,898	1,353	1,864	3,021	3,927	1,583
Jan-Mar 2012	29,365	6,952	22,209	374	534	2,851	2,148	4,017	1,430	1,438	1,124	1,199	333	1,903	1,369	1,847	3,088	3,865	1,554
Apr-Jun 2012	29,587	6,846	22,517	353	532	2,921	2,171	4,103	1,416	1,496	1,098	1,229	328	1,945	1,357	1,803	3,078	3,871	1,574
Jul-Sep 2012	29,851	6,883	22,722	356	547	2,934	2,175	4,129	1,457	1,527	1,113	1,216	329	1,983	1,372	1,827	3,021	3,948	1,607
Oct-Dec 2012	29,974	6,984	22,752	316	518	2,911	2,150	4,105	1,482	1,523	1,146	1,169	346	1,968	1,376	1,824	3,140	3,992	1,592
Jan-Mar 2013	29,750	6,989	22,504	304	537	2,921	2,102	4,031	1,487	1,504	1,161	1,150	344	2,000	1,354	1,852	3,114	3,985	1,587
Apr-Jun 2013	29,861	6,965	22,638	308	526	2,868	2,155	4,021	1,456	1,504	1,162	1,144	344	2,024	1,423	1,864	3,103	4,029	1,591
Jul-Sep 2013	30,194	7,012	22,933	324	510	2,954	2,188	3,999	1,520	1,566	1,177	1,178	326	2,073	1,450	1,880	3,081	4,036	1,642
Oct-Dec 2013	30,362	6,904	23,226	322	511	2,957	2,200	4,097	1,543	1,555	1,198	1,172	341	2,096	1,437	1,817	3,094	4,068	1,639
Jan-Mar 2014	30,446	6,934	23,311	379	508	2,945	2,229	4,063	1,490	1,579	1,150	1,171	369	2,169	1,388	1,851	3,107	4,076	1,663
Apr-Jun 2014	30,628	6,936	23,497	395	511	2,997	2,217	3,994	1,467	1,633	1,174	1,158	359	2,141	1,441	1,806	3,218	4,105	1,693
Jul-Sep 2014	30,918	6,914	23,808	386	543	3,019	2,242	3,976	1,470	1,665	1,237	1,207	340	2,139	1,487	1,853	3,197	4,062	1,781
Oct-Dec 2014	31,018	6,901	23,914	375	537	3,077	2,268	4,124	1,479	1,594	1,250	1,182	339	2,136	1,452	1,798	3,233	4,142	1,753
Jan-Mar 2015	31,074	6,980	23,915	348	567	3,007	2,266	4,066	1,512	1,618	1,276	1,185	334	2,189	1,414	1,845	3,285	4,170	1,765
Apr-Jun 2015	31,035	6,929	23,913	340	552	3,016	2,196	3,998	1,537	1,663	1,243	1,222	339	2,146	1,499	1,831	3,265	4,155	1,756
Jul-Sep 2015	31,416	6,851	24,377	349	553	2,968	2,223	4,095	1,576	1,698	1,275	1,254	348	2,173	1,539	1,841	3,266	4,162	1,812
Oct-Dec 2015	31,615	6,900	24,528	383	546	2,992	2,264	4,207	1,610	1,638	1,261	1,279	347	2,204	1,563	1,878	3,329	4,130	1,756
Jan-Mar 2016	31,499	6,924	24,414	351	528	3,008	2,271	4,131	1,608	1,663	1,225	1,262	358	2,243	1,525	1,856	3,357	4,143	1,744
Apr-Jun 2016	31,673	6,939	24,564	337	519	3,034	2,315	4,167	1,609	1,707	1,207	1,269	356	2,294	1,496	1,898	3,300	4,158	1,773
Jul-Sep 2016	31,890	6,908	24,830	357	516	3,013	2,290	4,253	1,638	1,766	1,302	1,260	354	2,250	1,511	1,936	3,336	4,100	1,809
Oct-Dec 2016	31,920	6,853	24,898	375	528	2,948	2,316	4,226	1,603	1,768	1,321	1,196	352	2,350	1,530	1,964	3,284	4,148	1,789

4.4 All in employment by industry

United Kingdom (thousands) not seasonally adjusted

				Standard Industrial Classification (SIC) 2007															
	All in employment1	Public sector	Private sector	Agri-culture, forestry & fishing A	Mining, energy and water supply B, D, E	Manu-facturing C	Con-struction F	Wholesale, retail & repair of motor vehicles G	Transport & storage H	Accom-modation & food services I	Infor-mation & commun-ication J	Financial & insurance activities K	Real estate activities L	Prof-essional, scientific & technical activities M	Admin-istrative & support services N	Public admin & defence; social security O	Edu-cation P	Human health & social work activities Q	Other services R, S, T
Men																			
Jan-Mar 2007	15,691	2,436	13,197	204	346	2,452	2,210	2,135	1,242	587	758	662	125	1,024	735	1,001	770	717	661
Apr-Jun 2007	15,789	2,459	13,259	208	359	2,506	2,216	2,084	1,244	618	749	658	116	1,024	771	991	788	709	684
Jul-Sep 2007	15,964	2,423	13,465	214	363	2,464	2,244	2,103	1,245	647	754	681	126	1,052	827	1,005	784	703	686
Oct-Dec 2007	15,987	2,444	13,467	210	358	2,429	2,225	2,131	1,268	648	713	703	133	1,064	823	1,021	799	720	678
Jan-Mar 2008	15,938	2,483	13,374	223	352	2,379	2,204	2,132	1,293	631	722	692	130	1,060	804	1,039	786	756	664
Apr-Jun 2008	15,961	2,509	13,371	222	349	2,354	2,181	2,144	1,274	633	730	675	131	1,082	823	1,053	780	800	659
Jul-Sep 2008	15,990	2,488	13,422	218	370	2,316	2,249	2,177	1,275	620	752	648	143	1,066	802	1,037	741	805	704
Oct-Dec 2008	15,909	2,538	13,293	219	409	2,252	2,233	2,161	1,292	616	744	629	137	1,022	774	1,028	777	830	717
Jan-Mar 2009	15,670	2,572	13,020	247	390	2,144	2,213	2,103	1,255	604	722	624	132	1,069	715	1,003	803	828	722
Apr-Jun 2009	15,464	2,558	12,828	240	383	2,102	2,127	2,056	1,208	620	717	635	124	1,105	710	985	791	812	710
Jul-Sep 2009	15,526	2,572	12,867	252	389	2,128	2,065	2,089	1,171	645	725	642	122	1,094	695	996	831	805	726
Oct-Dec 2009	15,477	2,581	12,814	246	384	2,122	2,070	2,069	1,173	633	722	637	115	1,064	706	995	868	820	719
Jan-Mar 2010	15,326	2,533	12,694	252	380	2,154	1,971	2,037	1,181	643	710	628	118	1,089	707	984	857	792	693
Apr-Jun 2010	15,493	2,576	12,807	264	373	2,207	1,961	2,094	1,160	681	692	622	113	1,092	725	1,003	864	810	697
Jul-Sep 2010	15,773	2,601	13,047	284	381	2,213	1,992	2,159	1,173	684	748	624	132	1,070	760	994	872	804	735
Oct-Dec 2010	15,720	2,582	13,035	283	394	2,214	1,991	2,147	1,133	668	748	640	130	1,097	788	949	843	852	702
Jan-Mar 2011	15,620	2,582	12,930	270	413	2,179	1,955	2,115	1,167	643	756	647	133	1,091	724	963	848	855	697
Apr-Jun 2011	15,685	2,547	13,050	262	428	2,170	1,940	2,112	1,172	651	766	644	144	1,100	752	913	887	863	725
Jul-Sep 2011	15,666	2,453	13,136	271	422	2,167	2,005	2,082	1,149	678	752	650	154	1,105	741	904	842	851	758
Oct-Dec 2011	15,672	2,436	13,158	262	424	2,196	1,939	2,124	1,154	710	788	654	151	1,104	732	922	838	843	714
Jan-Mar 2012	15,649	2,426	13,113	270	434	2,153	1,910	2,093	1,158	678	812	635	177	1,116	741	912	867	823	696
Apr-Jun 2012	15,822	2,358	13,329	257	436	2,203	1,928	2,155	1,140	674	802	660	162	1,146	745	889	866	836	735
Jul-Sep 2012	15,969	2,385	13,424	256	440	2,220	1,942	2,159	1,173	681	803	671	156	1,151	754	922	849	841	746
Oct-Dec 2012	15,985	2,403	13,431	236	404	2,199	1,916	2,160	1,190	677	814	642	164	1,138	765	952	897	853	724
Jan-Mar 2013	15,800	2,378	13,262	220	418	2,226	1,858	2,082	1,202	696	827	638	169	1,178	743	955	865	828	706
Apr-Jun 2013	15,888	2,359	13,373	234	419	2,198	1,894	2,092	1,175	701	848	635	163	1,183	782	953	836	849	715
Jul-Sep 2013	16,121	2,402	13,573	236	400	2,241	1,912	2,109	1,227	750	849	650	149	1,211	804	956	857	860	740
Oct-Dec 2013	16,174	2,321	13,724	233	409	2,225	1,936	2,125	1,251	733	842	653	144	1,242	805	918	847	859	763
Jan-Mar 2014	16,198	2,344	13,743	271	414	2,199	1,948	2,130	1,207	756	819	666	161	1,270	769	927	842	872	767
Apr-Jun 2014	16,290	2,356	13,823	286	414	2,240	1,947	2,064	1,171	764	850	657	152	1,263	816	922	884	889	780
Jul-Sep 2014	16,473	2,373	13,981	291	437	2,255	1,968	2,067	1,152	788	891	677	162	1,256	818	947	901	873	823
Oct-Dec 2014	16,481	2,383	13,979	279	422	2,308	2,003	2,139	1,141	728	892	657	168	1,254	791	924	928	889	794
Jan-Mar 2015	16,525	2,408	14,019	267	444	2,264	1,998	2,139	1,159	755	901	638	173	1,261	776	944	948	918	813
Apr-Jun 2015	16,486	2,359	14,017	259	439	2,274	1,931	2,104	1,195	778	894	670	169	1,232	813	933	940	905	801
Jul-Sep 2015	16,737	2,351	14,287	252	442	2,223	1,968	2,163	1,231	810	930	686	173	1,227	819	915	971	931	846
Oct-Dec 2015	16,874	2,365	14,406	267	432	2,269	2,004	2,224	1,277	789	925	707	174	1,241	834	925	976	912	789
Jan-Mar 2016	16,795	2,334	14,384	252	426	2,291	2,002	2,164	1,281	787	907	710	180	1,278	814	912	938	933	794
Apr-Jun 2016	16,864	2,356	14,421	250	418	2,304	2,034	2,176	1,291	820	873	706	173	1,321	812	927	925	915	780
Jul-Sep 2016	16,982	2,391	14,528	260	413	2,255	2,005	2,239	1,305	814	941	718	174	1,298	810	943	958	915	819
Oct-Dec 2016	16,942	2,363	14,494	287	426	2,203	2,016	2,212	1,276	799	950	683	172	1,351	820	949	900	950	815

4.4 All in employment by industry

United Kingdom (thousands) not seasonally adjusted

Standard Industrial Classification (SIC) 2007

	All in employment1	Public sector	Private sector	Agri-culture, forestry & fishing A	Mining, energy and water supply B, D, E	Manu-facturing C	Con-struction F	Wholesale, retail & repair of motor vehicles G	Transport & storage H	Accom-modation & food services I	Infor-mation & commun-ication J	Financial & insurance activities K	Real estate activities L	Prof-essional, scientific & technical activities M	Admin-istrative & support services N	Public admin & defence; social security O	Edu-cation P	Human health & social work activities Q	Other services R, S, T
Women																			
Jan-Mar 2007	13,417	4,519	8,842	85	104	764	317	1,985	324	737	298	601	131	851	569	979	2,029	2,783	812
Apr-Jun 2007	13,453	4,528	8,872	87	105	775	328	1,950	315	753	301	614	129	858	576	993	2,035	2,752	830
Jul-Sep 2007	13,561	4,496	9,001	83	105	805	314	1,986	311	759	308	623	139	860	604	986	1,998	2,802	826
Oct-Dec 2007	13,653	4,574	9,012	98	103	787	312	2,056	308	747	306	609	145	888	576	975	2,041	2,811	839
Jan-Mar 2008	13,658	4,563	9,030	112	100	769	331	2,052	311	751	302	595	133	879	594	972	2,061	2,810	845
Apr-Jun 2008	13,677	4,593	9,011	99	97	733	331	2,051	316	722	302	612	122	887	594	982	2,081	2,842	860
Jul-Sep 2008	13,695	4,551	9,086	95	93	753	334	2,071	332	734	310	624	117	853	602	996	2,065	2,843	828
Oct-Dec 2008	13,683	4,629	8,996	88	98	728	331	2,060	334	719	292	614	115	827	574	1,009	2,071	2,917	866
Jan-Mar 2009	13,606	4,652	8,894	75	99	713	270	2,004	316	719	313	603	142	773	594	1,006	2,116	2,944	857
Apr-Jun 2009	13,539	4,680	8,796	71	100	674	258	1,933	302	740	298	600	145	778	591	982	2,138	2,927	872
Jul-Sep 2009	13,644	4,705	8,878	77	102	686	246	1,942	291	783	295	605	143	796	606	981	2,130	2,973	873
Oct-Dec 2009	13,690	4,743	8,877	77	98	677	241	1,948	282	773	292	586	139	822	622	950	2,177	3,026	860
Jan-Mar 2010	13,597	4,721	8,794	84	92	661	237	1,906	281	745	301	583	144	793	613	946	2,206	3,032	856
Apr-Jun 2010	13,616	4,748	8,780	78	89	668	246	1,910	283	780	287	553	149	801	601	923	2,266	3,039	835
Jul-Sep 2010	13,710	4,697	8,926	86	93	676	241	1,953	309	819	297	542	169	782	581	931	2,247	3,017	859
Oct-Dec 2010	13,670	4,696	8,894	84	95	688	247	1,935	303	759	281	531	171	785	592	918	2,277	3,032	853
Jan-Mar 2011	13,730	4,732	8,912	87	85	681	257	1,919	285	774	303	532	167	766	575	913	2,273	3,112	847
Apr-Jun 2011	13,682	4,636	8,972	80	93	698	258	1,939	273	807	307	529	164	751	569	932	2,242	3,068	862
Jul-Sep 2011	13,710	4,556	9,080	98	96	675	232	1,937	279	820	308	542	147	783	598	948	2,144	3,130	881
Oct-Dec 2011	13,733	4,534	9,118	95	103	688	234	1,954	278	789	295	561	143	794	621	942	2,183	3,084	869
Jan-Mar 2012	13,716	4,526	9,095	104	100	698	237	1,924	272	760	312	564	156	787	628	935	2,221	3,042	858
Apr-Jun 2012	13,765	4,488	9,188	96	97	718	243	1,948	275	823	297	569	166	799	611	914	2,211	3,035	839
Jul-Sep 2012	13,882	4,499	9,298	100	107	715	233	1,970	284	846	310	545	173	832	619	905	2,172	3,107	861
Oct-Dec 2012	13,989	4,581	9,321	80	114	712	233	1,945	292	846	332	527	182	830	611	872	2,244	3,139	867
Jan-Mar 2013	13,949	4,611	9,242	84	119	695	244	1,949	285	808	333	512	175	823	611	897	2,250	3,158	880
Apr-Jun 2013	13,972	4,606	9,266	74	107	670	262	1,929	281	803	314	510	180	840	641	911	2,268	3,181	877
Jul-Sep 2013	14,073	4,610	9,359	88	110	713	276	1,891	292	816	328	527	177	862	646	924	2,224	3,176	903
Oct-Dec 2013	14,189	4,583	9,501	88	102	732	264	1,972	292	821	356	518	197	854	632	899	2,248	3,209	876
Jan-Mar 2014	14,248	4,591	9,567	108	94	746	281	1,933	283	823	332	506	208	898	620	924	2,265	3,204	896
Apr-Jun 2014	14,338	4,581	9,674	109	97	757	270	1,930	296	869	324	500	207	878	626	884	2,333	3,216	913
Jul-Sep 2014	14,445	4,541	9,827	95	106	764	274	1,909	318	877	346	530	178	884	669	906	2,296	3,190	958
Oct-Dec 2014	14,537	4,519	9,934	96	115	770	265	1,985	339	866	358	525	171	882	660	875	2,305	3,253	959
Jan-Mar 2015	14,550	4,571	9,897	81	123	743	267	1,927	353	863	375	547	161	928	639	900	2,336	3,252	952
Apr-Jun 2015	14,549	4,571	9,896	81	113	742	265	1,894	342	885	349	552	170	914	687	898	2,325	3,249	955
Jul-Sep 2015	14,679	4,500	10,090	98	111	745	256	1,932	345	888	346	568	175	945	720	926	2,295	3,231	966
Oct-Dec 2015	14,740	4,535	10,122	116	114	722	260	1,983	333	849	336	572	173	964	730	953	2,352	3,218	966
Jan-Mar 2016	14,704	4,590	10,031	99	103	717	270	1,966	327	876	319	552	178	965	711	943	2,419	3,210	950
Apr-Jun 2016	14,808	4,582	10,143	87	101	730	281	1,991	318	886	333	564	183	973	683	971	2,375	3,243	993
Jul-Sep 2016	14,908	4,517	10,302	97	103	758	285	2,014	334	953	361	543	180	952	700	994	2,378	3,185	990
Oct-Dec 2016	14,978	4,491	10,404	88	101	745	300	2,014	327	970	371	513	180	999	710	1,015	2,384	3,198	974

4.4 All in employment by industry

Source: Labour Force Survey

1 The breakdown by industry sector for Q1 2009 onwards is not entirely consistent with those of previous quarters. This is because:
(a) LFS data on industrial activity were coded directly to SIC 1992 for all quarters up to and including Q4 2008 and then mapped to the new industrial classification, SIC 2007, according to the assumed relationship between the two classifications;
(b) data for Q1 2009 onwards have been coded directly to SIC 2007; and
(c) a new, automatic coding tool was introduced in January 2009.

The effect of these changes on the time series was significant for some of the industry sectors shown. Consequently some adjustments have been made to the pre-2009 estimates to account for the estimated combined effects of the new classification and the new coding tool. This also means that the pre-2009 estimates in this table are not the same as those obtained from LFS microdata.
More information and analysis of these effects are available in the Labour Force Survey User Guide (Volume 1) and from Labour Force Assessment Branch (tel 01633 455839 or email labour.market.assessment@ons.gov.uk).
Includes people with workplace outside UK and those who did not state their industry.
In the LFS the distinction between public and private sector is based on respondents' views about the organisation for which they work. The public sector estimates provided here do not correspond to the official Public Sector Employment estimates which are based on National Accounts definitions.

4.5a International Comparisons of Employment and Unemployment

		Latest period	Employment rate (%)[1 2]	Change on year %
Employment rates as published by EUROSTAT: (not seasonally adjusted)				
European Union (EU)				
Austria	YXSN	Jul-Sep 16	72.6	0.5
Belgium	YXSO	Jul-Sep 16	62.2	0.1
Bulgaria	A495	Jul-Sep 16	64.2	-0.3
Croatia	GUMI	Jul-Sep 16	58.4	0.9
Cyprus	A4AC	Jul-Sep 16	64.0	1.5
Czech Republic	A4AD	Jul-Sep 16	72.2	1.7
Denmark	YXSP	Jul-Sep 16	75.2	1.5
Estonia	A4AE	Jul-Sep 16	73.2	-0.8
Finland	YXSQ	Jul-Sep 16	70.5	0.6
France	YXSR	Jul-Sep 16	64.6	0.3
Germany	YXSS	Jul-Sep 16	75.0	0.8
Greece	YXST	Jul-Sep 16	53.0	1.3
Hungary	A4AF	Jul-Sep 16	67.1	2.3
Ireland	YXSU	Jul-Sep 16	65.4	1.6
Italy	YXSV	Jul-Sep 16	57.6	0.9
Latvia	A4AG	Jul-Sep 16	68.9	0.3
Lithuania	A4AH	Jul-Sep 16	70.0	2.0
Luxembourg	YXSW	Jul-Sep 16	65.1	-0.4
Malta	A4AI	Jul-Sep 16	66.5	1.3
Netherlands	YXSX	Jul-Sep 16	75.3	0.8
Poland	A4AJ	Jul-Sep 16	64.9	1.4
Portugal	YXSY	Jul-Sep 16	66.0	1.6
Romania	A494	Jul-Sep 16	63.1	-0.1
Slovak Republic	A4AK	Jul-Sep 16	65.1	2.1
Slovenia	A4AL	Jul-Sep 16	66.4	-0.3
Spain	YXSZ	Jul-Sep 16	60.2	1.8
Sweden	YXTA	Jul-Sep 16	77.3	0.4
United Kingdom (	ANZ6	Jul-Sep 16	73.7	0.8
Total EU 4	**A496**	**Jul-Sep 16**	**67.1**	**1.0**
Eurozone 4	YXTC	Jul-Sep 16	65.9	1.0
Employment rates published by the OECD (seasonally adjusted)				
Canada	A48O	Oct-Dec 16	72.9	0.5
Japan	A48P	Oct-Dec 16	74.7	1.1
United States	A48Q	Oct-Dec 16	69.5	0.6

		Latest Period	Un-employment rate (%)[3]	Change on month %	Change on year %
Unemployment rates as published by EUROSTAT on 31 January 2017 (seasonally adjusted)					
European Union (EU)					
Austria	ZXDS	Dec 16	5.7	0.0	-0.3
Belgium	ZXDI	Dec 16	7.6	0.0	-1.0
Bulgaria	A492	Dec 16	7.1	0.0	-0.8
Croatia	GUMJ	Dec 16	11.4	0.0	-3.6
Cyprus	A4AN	Dec 16	14.3	0.1	1.2
Czech Republic	A4AO	Dec 16	3.5	-0.1	-1.0
Denmark	ZXDJ	Dec 16	6.2	-0.1	0.1
Estonia	A4AP	Nov 16	6.7	-0.5	0.1
Finland	ZXDU	Dec 16	8.7	0.0	-0.6
France	ZXDN	Dec 16	9.6	0.1	-0.6
Germany	ZXDK	Dec 16	3.9	0.0	-0.5
Greece	ZXDL	Oct 16	23.0	-0.1	-1.5
Hungary	A4AQ	Nov 16	4.5	-0.1	-1.8
Ireland	ZXDO	Dec 16	7.2	-0.1	-1.7
Italy	ZXDP	Dec 16	12.0	0.0	0.4
Latvia	A4AR	Dec 16	9.8	0.2	-0.2
Lithuania	A4AS	Dec 16	8.1	0.2	-0.8
Luxembourg	ZXDQ	Dec 16	6.3	0.1	-0.2
Malta	A4AT	Dec 16	4.5	-0.1	-0.6
Netherlands	ZXDR	Dec 16	5.4	-0.2	-1.2
Poland	A4AU	Dec 16	5.9	-0.1	-1.0
Portugal	ZXDT	Dec 16	10.2	-0.3	-2.0
Romania	A48Z	Dec 16	5.5	-0.2	-1.2
Slovak Republic	A4AV	Dec 16	8.8	-0.2	-1.9
Slovenia	A4AW	Dec 16	7.5	-0.1	-0.9
Spain	ZXDM	Dec 16	18.4	-0.3	-2.3
Sweden5	ZXDV	Dec 16	6.9	0.0	-0.3
United Kingdom (	ZXDW	Oct 16	4.8	0.0	-0.2
Total EU 4	**A493**	**Dec 16**	**8.2**	**0.0**	**-0.8**
Eurozone 4	ZXDH	Dec 16	9.6	-0.1	-0.9
Unemployment rates as published by national statistical offices (seasonally adjusted)					
Canada	ZXDZ	Jan 17	6.8	-0.1	-0.4
Japan	ZXDY	Dec 16	3.1	0.0	-0.2
United States	ZXDX	Jan 17	4.8	0.1	-0.1

Sources: EUROSTAT, OECD, national statistical offices.
Labour market statistics enquiries: labour.market@ons.gsi.gov.uk

(*) Note: The UK rates shown in this table are as published by EUROSTAT (the EUs statistical office). See Table 1 for the latest rates

1. All employment rates shown in this table are for those aged from 15 to 64 except for the rate for the United States published by OECD which are for those aged from 16 to 64.

2. The employment rates for the EU are published by EUROSTAT and are not seasonally adjusted. EUROSTAT do not publish seasonally adjusted (SA) employment rates but SA rates for some EU countries are published by OECD. These OECD employment rates are available at data table A10.

3. Unemployment rates published by EUROSTAT for most EU countries (but not for the UK), are calculated by extrapolating from the most recent LFS data using monthly registered unemployment data. A standard population basis (15-74) is used by EUROSTAT except for Spain, Italy and the UK (16-74). The unemployment rate for the US is based on those aged 16 and over, but the rates for Canada and Japan are for those aged 15 and over. All unemployment rates shown in this table are seasonally adjusted.

4. The "Total EU" series consist of all 28 EU countries. The Eurozone figures consist of the following EU countries: Austria, Belgium, Cyprus, Estonia, Finland, France, Germany, Greece, Ireland, Italy, Latvia, Lithuania, Luxembourg, Malta, Netherlands, Portugal, Slovak Republic, Slovenia and Spain.

5. The EU unemployment rates are as published on the EUROSTAT database. For Sweden the rates on the database differ from those shown in the EUROSTAT News Release published on 31 January 2017. This is because the figures for Sweden on the database are seasonally adjusted estimates but the figures for Sweden shown in the News Release are the trend component.

4.5b Labour Disputes

United Kingdom, not seasonally adjusted

	Working days lost (thousands)	Working days lost cumulative 12 month totals (thousands)	Number of stoppages	Workers involved (thousands)	Working days lost in the Public Sector (thousands)	Working days lost in the Private Sector (thousands)	Number of stoppages in the Public Sector	Number of stoppages in the Private Sector
	1	2	3	4	5	6	7	8
	BBFW		BLUU	BLUT	F8XZ	F8Y2	F8Y3	F8Y4
2014 Dec	13	788	15	11	11	3	8	7
2015 Dec	9	170	10	11	1	8	4	6
2016 Jan	20	167	9	20	18	2	4	5
2016 Feb	18	161	11	19	16	2	8	3
2016 Mar	35	174	14	23	33	3	8	6
2016 Apr	73	240	15	23	71	2	7	8
2016 May	22	250	18	11	4	17	8	10
2016 Jun	16	258	18	8	2	14	4	14
2016 Jul	76	316	16	87	64	12	3	13
2016 Aug	5	299	9	1	0	5	1	8
2016 Sep	8	299	12	5	4	4	4	8
2016 Oct	8	304	11	4	2	6	3	8
2016 Nov	22	312	14	17	17	5	5	9
2016 Dec	19	322	11	4	9	10	5	6

Source: ONS Labour Disputes Survey
Labour Disputes Statistics Helpline 01633 456724

1. Due to rounding the working days lost for the public and private sector may not add up to the working days lost.
Please note: data for workers is only available from Jan-86

4.6 Civil Service employment; regional distribution by government department[12]

All employees — Headcount

	North East	North West	Yorkshire and The Humber	East Midlands	West Midlands	East	London	South East	South West	Wales	Scotland	Northern Ireland	Overseas	Not reported
31 March 2016														
Attorney General's Departments														
Attorney General's Office	0	0	0	0	0	0	30	0	0	0	0	0	0	0
Crown Prosecution Service	310	870	790	350	530	400	1,470	590	260	320	0	0	20	0
Crown Prosecution Service Inspectorate	0	0	10	0	0	0	20	0	0	0	0	0	0	0
Government Legal Department[5]	..	20	20	0	0	..	1,700	0	50	0	0	0	0	0
Serious Fraud Office	0	0	0	0	0	0	410	0	0	0	0	0	0	0
Business, Innovation and Skills														
Business, Innovation and Skills (excl. agencies)[12]	30	60	290	30	60	30	2,540	10	20	60	20	0	0	0
Advisory Conciliation and Arbitration Service	70	120	60	60	60	40	220	50	50	60	80	0	0	0
Companies House	0	0	0	0	0	0	10	0	0	850	20	20	0	0
Competition and Markets Authority	0	0	0	0	0	0	630	0	0	..	..	..	0	0
Insolvency Service	40	210	80	40	400	90	360	100	90	50	40	0	0	0
Land Registry	430	580	230	690	420	230	310	0	1,130	470	0	0	0	0
Met Office	0	30	20	50	10	50	40	90	1,710	20	110	10	30	0
National Measurement and Regulation Office[14]	0	0	0	0	0	0	90	0	..	0	..	0	0	0
Skills Funding Agency	50	70	70	20	420	20	120	70	30	0	0	0	0	0
UK Intellectual Property Office	0	0	0	0	0	0	40	0	0	1,110	0	0	0	0
UK Space Agency	0	0	0	0	0	0	10	0	70	0	0	0	0	0
Cabinet Office														
Cabinet Office (excl. agencies)	..	10	20	10	0	30	2,000	30	..	0	0	0	0	0
Other Cabinet Office agencies														
Crown Commercial Service	0	250	30	..	..	160	150	..	20	110	..	0	0	0
Government in Parliament	0	0	0	0	0	0	100	0	0	0	0	0	0	0
Chancellor's other departments														
Government Actuary's Department	0	0	0	0	0	0	160	0	0	0	..	0	0	0
National Savings and Investments	..	10	0	0	0	0	150	0	0	0	10	0	0	0
Charity Commission														
Charity Commission	0	150	0	0	0	0	80	0	80	10	0	0	0	0
Communities and Local Government														
Department for Communities and Local Government	40	70	50	40	80	80	1,260	20	70	0	0	0	0	0
Planning Inspectorate	0	0	0	0	0	0	0	0	720	40	0	0	0	0
Queen Elizabeth II Centre	0	0	0	0	0	0	50	0	0	0	0	0	0	0
Culture, Media and Sport														
Department for Culture Media and Sport	0	0	10	0	0	0	520	0	0	..	0	0	0	0
National Archives[13]	0	0	0	0	0	0	620	0	0	0	0	0	0	0
Royal Parks	0	0	0	0	0	0	120	0	0	0	0	0	0	0
Defence														
Ministry of Defence[10]	270	1,450	2,590	1,410	2,230	3,600	3,210	7,730	6,970	1,170	3,410	1,240	1,230	230
Defence Science and Technology Laboratory	0	0	0	10	0	10	0	1,910	1,790	0	0	0	0	0

4.6 Civil Service employment; regional distribution by government department[12]

All employees — *Headcount*

	North East	North West	Yorkshire and The Humber	East Midlands	West Midlands	East	London	South East	South West	Wales	Scotland	Northern Ireland	Overseas	Not reported
Defence Equipment and Support[11]	..	280	20	140	210	190	270	580	7,670	10	510	..	60	..
Royal Fleet Auxiliary	0	0	0	0	0	0	0	0	0	0	0	0	0	1,950
UK Hydrographic Office	0	0	0	0	0	..	0	0	940	0	..	0	..	0
Education														
Department for Education	310	170	350	40	90	10	1,270	0	20	0	0	0	0	0
Education Funding Agency	100	80	110	30	160	..	380	0	20	0	0	0	0	0
Standards and Testing Agency	..	..	..	..	70	0	50	0	0	0	0	0	0	0
The National College for Teaching and Leadership	10	90	10	110	50	0	30	0	0	0	0	0	0	0
Energy and Climate Change														
Department of Energy and Climate Change	0	0	0	0	0	0	1,390	0	0	0	90	0	0	0
Oil and Gas Authority[9]	0	0	0	0	0	0	70	0	0	0	60	0	0	0
Environment, Food and Rural Affairs														
Department for Environment Food and Rural Affairs	10	20	220	10	80	30	1,210	30	90	0	..	0	0	0
Animal and Plant Health Agency	40	190	160	90	340	150	80	650	280	230	120	0	0	0
Centre for Environment Fisheries and Aquaculture Science	0	..	..	0	0	400	..	0	140	0	0	0	0	0
Office of Water Services	0	0	0	0	130	0	40	0	0	0	0	0	0	0
Rural Payments Agency	290	700	210	40	50	40	10	400	310	0	0	..	0	0
Veterinary Medicines Directorate	0	0	0	0	0	0	0	150	0	0	0	0	0	0
ESTYN														
ESTYN	0	0	0	0	0	0	0	0	0	120	0	0	0	0
Food Standards Agency														
Food Standards Agency	20	90	200	70	90	130	210	80	80	90	10	50	..	0
Foreign and Commonwealth Office														
Foreign and Commonwealth Office (excl. agencies)	0	0	0	0	0	0	2,450	270	0	0	0	0	1,610	0
FCO Services	0	0	0	0	0	0	150	650	0	0	0	0	120	0
Wilton Park Executive Agency	0	0	0	0	0	0	0	70	0	0	0	0	0	0
Health														
Department of Health (excl. agencies)	0	40	670	0	0	0	1,300	20	0	0	0	0	0	0
Medicines and Healthcare Products Regulatory Agency	0	0	10	0	0	370	870	0	0	0	0	0	0	..
Public Health England	140	430	280	100	380	410	2,090	550	960	..	20	0	..	..
HM Revenue and Customs														
HM Revenue and Customs	10,900	12,210	4,430	3,330	3,880	2,850	8,850	3,820	2,090	3,510	9,140	1,570	0	60
Valuation Office Agency	270	440	480	240	280	240	720	460	400	280	60	0	0	0
HM Treasury														
HM Treasury	0	0	0	0	0	40	1,290	0	0	0	..	0	0	0
Debt Management Office	0	0	0	0	0	0	110	0	0	0	0	0	0	0
Government Internal Audit Agency[8]	10	10	10	10	10	..	90	..	10	20	..	0	0	0
Office for Budget Responsibility	0	0	0	0	0	0	20	0	0	0	0	0	0	0

4.6 Civil Service employment; regional distribution by government department[12]

All employees — *Headcount*

	North East	North West	Yorkshire and The Humber	East Midlands	West Midlands	East	London	South East	South West	Wales	Scotland	Northern Ireland	Overseas	Not reported
Home Office														
Home Office[3]	1,260	4,490	2,660	200	840	1,950	11,700	2,990	310	500	760	460	500	10
International Development														
Department for International Development	0	0	0	0	0	0	870	0	0	0	630	0	500	0
Justice														
Ministry of Justice (excl. agencies)	20	100	80	40	120	20	2,370	20	30	90	10	..	0	0
Criminal Injuries Compensation Authority	0	0	0	0	0	0	0	0	0	0	270	0	0	0
Her Majesty's Courts and Tribunals Service	800	2,320	1,460	1,460	1,690	1,190	4,060	1,590	1,000	940	200	0	0	0
Legal Aid Agency	290	300	60	210	130	20	400	30	100	60	0	0	0	0
National Offender Management Service	2,830	6,160	5,650	4,610	4,360	4,490	5,790	7,070	3,440	1,530	0	0	0	0
Office of the Public Guardian	0	0	0	270	790	0	30	0	0	0	0	0	0	0
National Crime Agency														
National Crime Agency	70	790	170	130	350	150	1,450	500	240	50	40	80	150	70
Northern Ireland Office														
Northern Ireland Office	0	0	0	0	0	0	50	0	0	0	0	60	0	0
Office for Standards in Education														
Office for Standards in Education, Children's Services and Skills	0	450	100	130	120	70	360	0	220	0	0	0	0	0
Office of Gas and Electricity Markets														
Office of Gas and Electricity Markets	0	0	0	0	0	0	720	0	0	..	110	0	0	0
Office of Qualifications and Examinations Regulation														
Ofqual	0	0	0	0	180	0	0	0	0	0	0	..	0	0
Scotland Office														
Scotland Office (incl. Office of the Advocate General for Scotland)	0	0	0	0	0	0	30	0	0	0	80	0	0	0
Scottish Government														
Scottish Government (excl. agencies)	0	0	0	0	0	0	0	0	0	0	5,380	0	10	0
Accountant in Bankruptcy	0	0	0	0	0	0	0	0	0	0	140	0	0	0
Crown Office and Procurator Fiscal Service	0	0	0	0	0	0	0	0	0	0	1,740	0	0	0
Disclosure Scotland	0	0	0	0	0	0	0	0	0	0	330	0	0	0
Education Scotland	0	0	0	0	0	0	0	0	0	0	280	0	0	0
Food Standards Scotland[4]	0	0	0	0	0	0	0	0	0	0	160	0	0	0
National Records of Scotland	0	0	0	0	0	0	0	0	0	0	380	0	0	0
Office of the Scottish Charity Regulator	0	0	0	0	0	0	0	0	0	0	50	0	0	0
Registers of Scotland	0	0	0	0	0	0	0	0	0	0	1,060	0	0	0
Revenue Scotland[4]	0	0	0	0	0	0	0	0	0	0	50	0	0	0
Scottish Courts and Tribunals Service[6]	0	0	0	0	0	0	0	0	0	0	1,670	0	0	0
Scottish Housing Regulator	0	0	0	0	0	0	0	0	0	0	50	0	0	0
Scottish Prison Service	0	0	0	0	0	0	0	0	0	0	4,640	0	0	0
Scottish Public Pensions Agency	0	0	0	0	0	0	0	0	0	0	300	0	0	0

4.6 Civil Service employment; regional distribution by government department[12]

All employees — *Headcount*

	North East	North West	Yorkshire and The Humber	East Midlands	West Midlands	East	London	South East	South West	Wales	Scotland	Northern Ireland	Overseas	Not reported
Student Awards Agency for Scotland	0	0	0	0	0	0	0	0	0	0	260	0	0	0
Transport Scotland	0	0	0	0	0	0	0	0	0	0	400	0	0	0
Transport														
Department for Transport (excl. agencies)	10	0	10	20	..	0	1,810	200	10	10	0	0	..	0
Driver and Vehicle Licensing Agency	..	..	..	..	10	..	10	0	10	6,110	10	0	0	0
Driver and Vehicle Standards Agency	340	420	420	460	370	400	410	450	520	420	310	0	0	0
Maritime and Coastguard Agency	20	20	50	..	0	10	20	540	70	110	150	40	0	0
Office of Rail and Road[7]	..	20	20	..	10	..	230	10	10	..	20	0	0	0
Vehicle Certification Agency	0	0	0	40	0	..	0	..	100	0	0	0	10	0
United Kingdom Statistics Authority														
United Kingdom Statistics Authority	0	0	0	0	0	0	50	1,810	..	1,910	0	0	0	0
UK Export Finance														
UK Export Finance	..	..	..	..	..	..	230	..	..	..	..	..	0	0
UK Supreme Court														
UK Supreme Court	0	0	0	0	0	0	50	0	0	0	0	0	0	0
Wales Office														
Wales Office	0	0	0	0	0	0	30	0	0	20	0	0	0	0
Welsh Government														
Welsh Government	0	0	0	0	0	0	10	0	0	5,430	0	0	10	0
Work and Pensions														
Department for Work and Pensions	9,300	17,050	8,910	4,450	7,570	4,090	8,120	5,410	4,940	5,380	9,670	..	0	30
The Health and Safety Executive	70	950	350	480	80	130	150	110	90	100	260	0	0	0
All employees	28,370	51,690	31,360	19,420	26,630	22,110	78,230	39,060	37,110	31,170	43,050	3,530	4,260	2,350

Source: Annual Civil Service Employment Survey

1 Numbers are rounded to the nearest ten, and cells containing between one and five employees are represented by "..".
2 Workplace postcode data are used to derive geographical information.
3 Home Office estimates for 31 March 2016 include staff paid via the Foreign and Commonwealth Office employee records system (PRISM).
4 As of 1 April 2015, there are two new departments under Scottish Government - Revenue Scotland and Food Standards Scotland.
5 As of 1 April 2015 Treasury Solicitors has become the Government Legal Department.
6 As of 1 April 2015 Scottish Court Service has become Scottish Courts and Tribunals Service.
7 As of 1 April 2015 Office of Rail Regulation has become Office of Rail and Road.
8 As of 1 April 2015 Government Internal Audit Agency was launched as an executive agency of HM Treasury.
9 As of 1 April 2015 Oil and Gas Authority became a new executive agency of Department of Energy and Climate Change.
10 As of 1 April 2015 Defence Electronics and Components Agency (DECA) are now reported within core MOD figures.
11 As of 1 April 2015 Defence, Equipment and Support previously reported within core MOD figures are now reported as a separate entity under the MOD umbrella.
12 Although Business, Innovation and Skills figures exclude agencies, figures are included for UK Trade and Investment.
13 National Archives previously reported under Ministry of Justice umbrella, now reported under the Department for Culture, Media and Sport umbrella.
14 As of 1 April 2015 National Measurement Office has become National Measurement and Regulation Office.

4.7 Unemployment by age and duration

United Kingdom (thousands) seasonally adjusted

	All aged 16 & over							All aged 16 - 64						
	All level	rate (%)[1]	Up to 6 months level	Over 6 and up to 12 months level	All over 12 months level	% over 12 months level	All over 24 months level	All level	rate (%)[1]	Up to 6 months level	Over 6 and up to 12 months level	All over 12 months level	% over 12 months level	All over 24 months level
People	**MGSC**	**MGSX**	**YBWF**	**YBWG**	**YBWH**	**YBWI**	**YBWL**	**LF2I**	**LF2Q**	**LF2Y**	**LF32**	**LF34**	**LF36**	**LF38**
Jul-Sep 2013	2,483	7.6	1,164	425	893	36.0	460	2,461	7.8	1,155	423	883	35.9	457
Aug-Oct 2013	2,404	7.4	1,132	399	873	36.3	446	2,379	7.5	1,121	396	861	36.2	444
Sep-Nov 2013	2,340	7.2	1,103	397	841	35.9	450	2,316	7.3	1,085	392	839	36.2	447
Oct-Dec 2013	2,357	7.2	1,111	399	847	35.9	453	2,326	7.4	1,089	394	843	36.2	449
Nov-Jan 2014	2,340	7.2	1,117	393	829	35.4	452	2,309	7.3	1,098	389	822	35.6	448
Dec-Feb 2014	2,256	6.9	1,073	373	810	35.9	433	2,225	7.0	1,059	368	798	35.9	429
Jan-Mar 2014	2,212	6.8	1,042	353	817	36.9	447	2,185	6.9	1,031	349	805	36.8	442
Feb-Apr 2014	2,161	6.6	1,027	341	793	36.7	433	2,132	6.7	1,013	337	783	36.7	428
Mar-May 2014	2,112	6.4	1,012	347	753	35.7	419	2,084	6.6	999	345	739	35.5	412
Apr-Jun 2014	2,061	6.3	990	331	740	35.9	408	2,035	6.4	977	328	731	35.9	403
May-Jul 2014	2,010	6.1	968	318	723	36.0	400	1,990	6.3	961	316	713	35.8	394
Jun-Aug 2014	1,972	6.0	946	313	713	36.1	389	1,953	6.2	942	313	698	35.7	383
Jul-Sep 2014	1,961	6.0	954	317	690	35.2	377	1,940	6.1	948	317	675	34.8	371
Aug-Oct 2014	1,953	6.0	937	332	685	35.1	377	1,934	6.1	931	330	672	34.8	371
Sep-Nov 2014	1,924	5.9	950	317	657	34.1	355	1,904	6.0	938	312	653	34.3	350
Oct-Dec 2014	1,870	5.7	930	302	638	34.1	340	1,851	5.8	920	298	633	34.2	333
Nov-Jan 2015	1,858	5.7	945	285	628	33.8	339	1,837	5.8	933	281	623	33.9	333
Dec-Feb 2015	1,840	5.6	934	283	623	33.9	352	1,820	5.7	928	280	612	33.6	343
Jan-Mar 2015	1,826	5.5	954	283	589	32.2	342	1,803	5.7	947	278	578	32.0	333
Feb-Apr 2015	1,813	5.5	949	290	574	31.6	327	1,793	5.6	944	286	563	31.4	318
Mar-May 2015	1,848	5.6	974	304	570	30.9	318	1,830	5.8	970	301	559	30.6	311
Apr-Jun 2015	1,849	5.6	967	304	577	31.2	325	1,826	5.7	958	301	567	31.1	318
May-Jul 2015	1,822	5.5	981	295	546	30.0	309	1,799	5.7	974	291	534	29.7	303
Jun-Aug 2015	1,779	5.4	961	290	529	29.7	302	1,755	5.5	953	286	516	29.4	298
Jul-Sep 2015	1,760	5.3	965	279	516	29.3	290	1,740	5.5	959	275	505	29.0	287
Aug-Oct 2015	1,715	5.2	938	265	512	29.8	288	1,695	5.3	931	262	502	29.6	283
Sep-Nov 2015	1,687	5.1	938	258	491	29.1	269	1,668	5.2	925	254	489	29.3	263
Oct-Dec 2015	1,688	5.1	946	252	490	29.0	261	1,669	5.2	934	248	487	29.2	256
Nov-Jan 2016	1,684	5.1	946	257	481	28.6	258	1,665	5.2	934	254	477	28.6	253
Dec-Feb 2016	1,700	5.1	966	264	471	27.7	264	1,679	5.2	956	259	464	27.6	258
Jan-Mar 2016	1,687	5.1	949	270	468	27.7	264	1,665	5.2	937	268	461	27.7	259
Feb-Apr 2016	1,666	5.0	951	254	461	27.7	262	1,643	5.1	939	252	452	27.5	257
Mar-May 2016	1,648	4.9	950	235	462	28.0	258	1,626	5.1	940	234	452	27.8	253
Apr-Jun 2016	1,643	4.9	959	237	447	27.2	253	1,625	5.1	949	235	441	27.2	249
May-Jul 2016	1,635	4.9	957	230	448	27.4	257	1,618	5.0	952	229	437	27.0	252
Jun-Aug 2016	1,668	5.0	968	256	445	26.6	247	1,653	5.1	965	256	433	26.2	243
Jul-Sep 2016	1,618	4.8	945	239	434	26.8	241	1,601	5.0	941	239	421	26.3	237
Aug-Oct 2016	1,613	4.8	951	245	418	25.9	227	1,596	5.0	944	244	408	25.6	223
Sep-Nov 2016	1,602	4.8	958	237	407	25.4	215	1,585	4.9	944	235	406	25.6	213
Oct-Dec 2016	1,585	4.7	937	244	404	25.5	210	1,568	4.9	923	242	403	25.7	208
Men	**MGSD**	**MGSY**	**MGYK**	**MGYM**	**MGYO**	**YBWJ**	**YBWM**	**YBSI**	**YBTJ**	**YBWP**	**YBWS**	**YBWV**	**YBWY**	**YBXB**
Jul-Sep 2013	1,387	8.0	600	234	553	39.9	306	1,372	8.2	592	232	548	39.9	304
Aug-Oct 2013	1,348	7.7	598	217	533	39.6	292	1,330	7.9	586	214	530	39.8	290
Sep-Nov 2013	1,311	7.5	577	218	517	39.4	299	1,296	7.7	563	215	517	39.9	298
Oct-Dec 2013	1,322	7.6	576	226	520	39.3	306	1,304	7.8	561	224	520	39.9	304
Nov-Jan 2014	1,290	7.4	551	227	512	39.7	303	1,271	7.6	537	226	508	40.0	300
Dec-Feb 2014	1,262	7.2	538	214	509	40.3	289	1,242	7.4	528	212	502	40.4	286
Jan-Mar 2014	1,230	7.0	518	198	515	41.8	299	1,212	7.2	511	196	504	41.6	294
Feb-Apr 2014	1,205	6.9	516	184	505	41.9	290	1,185	7.0	507	182	495	41.8	286
Mar-May 2014	1,159	6.6	495	182	482	41.6	283	1,137	6.8	487	180	470	41.3	278
Apr-Jun 2014	1,139	6.5	492	180	467	41.0	267	1,121	6.7	484	178	459	41.0	263
May-Jul 2014	1,117	6.4	490	168	459	41.1	267	1,103	6.6	486	167	449	40.8	262
Jun-Aug 2014	1,096	6.3	484	165	447	40.8	251	1,083	6.4	481	164	438	40.4	247
Jul-Sep 2014	1,088	6.2	491	171	426	39.2	233	1,072	6.4	486	170	417	38.9	228
Aug-Oct 2014	1,086	6.2	486	178	422	38.9	233	1,072	6.4	480	175	417	38.9	228
Sep-Nov 2014	1,069	6.1	489	173	408	38.1	225	1,054	6.3	479	168	406	38.5	221
Oct-Dec 2014	1,041	6.0	477	163	401	38.5	221	1,027	6.1	471	160	396	38.6	216
Nov-Jan 2015	1,025	5.9	481	151	393	38.3	223	1,009	6.0	475	148	386	38.3	218
Dec-Feb 2015	1,014	5.8	474	152	388	38.3	234	1,000	5.9	471	150	380	38.0	227
Jan-Mar 2015	1,004	5.7	479	154	371	36.9	232	988	5.9	476	151	361	36.6	226
Feb-Apr 2015	1,007	5.7	486	159	362	36.0	217	992	5.9	483	157	352	35.5	211
Mar-May 2015	1,007	5.8	493	161	354	35.1	208	992	5.9	490	158	345	34.7	203
Apr-Jun 2015	1,014	5.8	498	160	356	35.1	211	1,001	5.9	492	158	350	35.0	207
May-Jul 2015	988	5.6	504	151	332	33.7	194	974	5.8	501	150	323	33.1	190
Jun-Aug 2015	976	5.5	500	152	323	33.2	190	960	5.7	496	150	315	32.8	188

4.7 Unemployment by age and duration

United Kingdom (thousands) seasonally adjusted

	All aged 16 & over							All aged 16 - 64						
	All level	rate (%)[1]	Up to 6 months level	Over 6 and up to 12 months level	All over 12 months level	% over 12 months	All over 24 months level	All level	rate (%)[1]	Up to 6 months level	Over 6 and up to 12 months level	All over 12 months level	% over 12 months level	All over 24 months level
Men *(contd.)*	**MGSD**	**MGSY**	**MGYK**	**MGYM**	**MGYO**	**YBWJ**	**YBWM**	**YBSI**	**YBTJ**	**YBWP**	**YBWS**	**YBWV**	**YBWY**	**YBXB**
Jul-Sep 2015	962	5.5	503	144	314	32.7	184	948	5.6	499	142	308	32.4	181
Aug-Oct 2015	937	5.3	485	144	307	32.8	186	924	5.4	479	141	303	32.8	182
Sep-Nov 2015	924	5.2	493	141	290	31.4	173	914	5.4	484	138	292	31.9	169
Oct-Dec 2015	921	5.2	490	141	291	31.5	172	911	5.4	482	138	290	31.9	169
Nov-Jan 2016	922	5.2	488	145	290	31.4	170	912	5.4	481	142	288	31.6	168
Dec-Feb 2016	933	5.2	495	149	289	31.0	180	922	5.4	490	146	286	31.0	178
Jan-Mar 2016	915	5.1	473	156	286	31.3	175	905	5.3	468	155	282	31.1	173
Feb-Apr 2016	896	5.0	469	142	284	31.7	174	885	5.2	464	142	280	31.6	172
Mar-May 2016	898	5.1	485	133	280	31.2	173	888	5.2	480	133	276	31.0	170
Apr-Jun 2016	891	5.0	489	132	269	30.2	171	883	5.2	484	131	268	30.3	169
May-Jul 2016	905	5.1	503	130	272	30.0	178	896	5.2	501	131	264	29.5	175
Jun-Aug 2016	901	5.0	490	133	277	30.8	170	894	5.2	488	134	272	30.4	168
Jul-Sep 2016	884	5.0	487	126	270	30.6	168	876	5.1	485	127	264	30.2	165
Aug-Oct 2016	885	5.0	495	129	261	29.5	156	877	5.2	488	129	259	29.5	154
Sep-Nov 2016	883	5.0	500	131	252	28.5	143	873	5.1	489	129	255	29.1	142
Oct-Dec 2016	873	4.9	495	132	246	28.2	138	864	5.1	486	131	247	28.6	138
Women	**MGSE**	**MGSZ**	**MGYL**	**MGYN**	**MGYP**	**YBWK**	**YBWN**	**LF2J**	**LF2R**	**LF2Z**	**LF33**	**LF35**	**LF37**	**LF39**
Jul-Sep 2013	1,095	7.2	564	191	340	31.0	153	1,089	7.4	563	191	335	30.8	153
Aug-Oct 2013	1,057	7.0	534	182	340	32.2	154	1,049	7.1	535	182	331	31.6	154
Sep-Nov 2013	1,029	6.8	526	179	325	31.5	150	1,020	6.9	522	177	322	31.6	149
Oct-Dec 2013	1,036	6.8	535	173	327	31.6	147	1,022	6.9	528	171	324	31.6	145
Nov-Jan 2014	1,050	6.9	566	166	317	30.2	149	1,038	7.0	561	163	314	30.3	148
Dec-Feb 2014	995	6.5	535	158	302	30.3	144	983	6.6	531	155	296	30.1	143
Jan-Mar 2014	981	6.4	524	155	302	30.8	148	973	6.6	520	152	300	30.9	148
Feb-Apr 2014	956	6.3	512	156	288	30.1	143	947	6.4	505	154	288	30.4	142
Mar-May 2014	953	6.2	517	164	271	28.5	135	946	6.4	512	165	269	28.4	134
Apr-Jun 2014	922	6.0	498	151	273	29.6	142	914	6.2	492	150	271	29.7	140
May-Jul 2014	892	5.8	479	150	264	29.6	133	887	6.0	475	149	263	29.7	132
Jun-Aug 2014	875	5.7	461	148	265	30.3	138	869	5.9	461	149	260	29.9	137
Jul-Sep 2014	874	5.7	463	146	264	30.2	144	868	5.8	463	147	258	29.7	143
Aug-Oct 2014	867	5.7	451	153	263	30.3	144	862	5.8	451	155	256	29.7	143
Sep-Nov 2014	855	5.6	461	144	249	29.2	130	850	5.7	459	144	247	29.1	129
Oct-Dec 2014	829	5.4	453	139	237	28.6	119	825	5.5	450	138	237	28.7	118
Nov-Jan 2015	833	5.4	464	134	236	28.3	116	828	5.6	459	133	237	28.6	115
Dec-Feb 2015	826	5.4	460	131	235	28.4	118	820	5.5	457	130	232	28.3	115
Jan-Mar 2015	822	5.3	475	129	218	26.5	110	815	5.5	471	128	217	26.6	107
Feb-Apr 2015	806	5.2	464	130	212	26.3	110	801	5.4	461	129	211	26.3	107
Mar-May 2015	841	5.5	481	143	217	25.8	110	838	5.6	480	143	214	25.6	108
Apr-Jun 2015	835	5.4	470	145	221	26.4	114	826	5.5	466	142	217	26.3	111
May-Jul 2015	834	5.4	477	144	213	25.6	115	825	5.5	473	141	211	25.6	112
Jun-Aug 2015	804	5.2	460	138	206	25.6	112	795	5.3	457	136	201	25.3	110
Jul-Sep 2015	798	5.2	462	135	201	25.2	106	791	5.3	460	133	197	25.0	106
Aug-Oct 2015	779	5.0	453	121	205	26.3	102	771	5.1	452	120	199	25.8	101
Sep-Nov 2015	763	4.9	445	118	201	26.3	96	754	5.0	441	116	197	26.2	94
Oct-Dec 2015	766	5.0	456	111	199	26.0	90	758	5.1	452	110	197	25.9	88
Nov-Jan 2016	762	4.9	458	112	192	25.1	88	753	5.0	453	112	189	25.1	85
Dec-Feb 2016	767	5.0	471	115	181	23.6	83	757	5.0	466	114	178	23.5	80
Jan-Mar 2016	772	5.0	476	114	182	23.6	89	760	5.1	468	113	179	23.6	86
Feb-Apr 2016	770	5.0	482	111	177	23.0	88	758	5.0	475	110	173	22.8	85
Mar-May 2016	749	4.8	465	103	181	24.2	85	738	4.9	460	102	176	23.9	83
Apr-Jun 2016	752	4.8	469	105	178	23.7	82	742	4.9	465	103	173	23.4	80
May-Jul 2016	731	4.7	454	100	177	24.2	79	722	4.8	450	98	173	24.0	77
Jun-Aug 2016	768	4.9	478	122	167	21.8	77	759	5.0	477	122	160	21.1	75
Jul-Sep 2016	734	4.7	457	112	164	22.3	73	725	4.8	456	112	157	21.6	71
Aug-Oct 2016	728	4.7	456	115	157	21.5	71	719	4.7	455	115	149	20.7	69
Sep-Nov 2016	719	4.6	457	106	156	21.7	72	711	4.7	454	105	152	21.3	71
Oct-Dec 2016	713	4.6	442	112	158	22.2	72	704	4.6	437	111	155	22.1	71

4.7 Unemployment by age and duration

United Kingdom (thousands) seasonally adjusted

	16-17							18-24						
	All level	rate (%)[1]	Up to 6 months level	Over 6 and up to 12 months level	All over 12 months level	% over 12 months level	All over 24 months level	All level	rate (%)[1]	Up to 6 months level	Over 6 and up to 12 months level	All over 12 months level	% over 12 months level	All over 24 months level
People	**YBVH**	**YBVK**	**YBXD**	**YBXG**	**YBXJ**	**YBXM**	**YBXP**	**YBVN**	**YBVQ**	**YBXS**	**YBXV**	**YBXY**	**YBYB**	**YBYE**
Jul-Sep 2013	193	36.7	136	29	28	14.3	*	794	19.2	397	139	258	32.5	113
Aug-Oct 2013	193	36.3	131	32	30	15.4	*	764	18.6	387	137	240	31.4	105
Sep-Nov 2013	197	36.5	138	35	24	12.4	*	742	18.0	375	134	233	31.4	106
Oct-Dec 2013	190	36.9	129	36	25	13.1	*	741	18.0	376	132	234	31.6	113
Nov-Jan 2014	190	36.9	139	31	20	10.7	*	731	17.7	377	130	225	30.7	104
Dec-Feb 2014	181	36.4	127	32	22	12.3	*	705	17.1	361	122	222	31.5	103
Jan-Mar 2014	181	36.0	128	30	24	13.1	*	686	16.8	347	115	224	32.6	104
Feb-Apr 2014	174	34.7	118	31	26	14.7	*	670	16.2	348	108	214	32.0	103
Mar-May 2014	168	34.1	118	26	25	14.6	*	646	15.7	348	105	192	29.7	91
Apr-Jun 2014	162	33.5	113	23	25	15.7	*	600	14.7	319	101	180	30.0	86
May-Jul 2014	161	33.7	112	25	24	15.0	*	588	14.5	311	98	180	30.5	84
Jun-Aug 2014	163	33.6	111	31	21	13.1	*	571	14.0	291	91	190	33.2	88
Jul-Sep 2014	162	33.1	115	30	16	10.0	*	587	14.4	305	89	192	32.8	87
Aug-Oct 2014	160	32.8	111	32	17	10.6	*	598	14.7	308	87	202	33.8	96
Sep-Nov 2014	158	32.3	110	29	18	11.7	*	614	15.2	332	95	187	30.4	84
Oct-Dec 2014	160	31.6	113	28	18	11.6	*	591	14.5	325	83	183	31.0	84
Nov-Jan 2015	154	30.8	110	24	20	12.7	*	591	14.5	332	78	180	30.5	83
Dec-Feb 2015	155	30.9	114	22	19	12.1	*	586	14.3	327	80	179	30.6	92
Jan-Mar 2015	146	29.5	108	21	17	11.6	*	584	14.2	343	86	155	26.6	81
Feb-Apr 2015	149	29.9	109	22	18	12.2	*	582	14.2	349	87	145	25.0	71
Mar-May 2015	145	28.6	109	20	15	10.7	*	574	14.1	343	92	140	24.3	66
Apr-Jun 2015	143	28.6	109	18	16	10.9	*	581	14.1	343	93	145	24.9	65
May-Jul 2015	145	28.1	113	20	12	8.4	*	569	13.9	344	89	136	24.0	62
Jun-Aug 2015	144	28.1	111	21	12	8.5	*	536	13.1	327	83	126	23.5	54
Jul-Sep 2015	141	27.0	106	21	14	9.6	*	516	12.6	321	76	120	23.2	51
Aug-Oct 2015	127	24.9	98	18	11	8.5	*	498	12.2	312	71	116	23.2	52
Sep-Nov 2015	129	25.7	97	17	15	11.6	*	503	12.3	316	74	114	22.6	47
Oct-Dec 2015	134	26.8	102	17	14	10.7	*	492	12.0	307	74	111	22.7	44
Nov-Jan 2016	133	26.9	98	21	14	10.6	*	499	12.2	311	78	110	22.1	43
Dec-Feb 2016	129	26.0	101	16	12	9.5	*	502	12.3	323	80	99	19.7	46
Jan-Mar 2016	127	25.6	105	14	8	6.5	*	500	12.2	318	87	95	19.0	46
Feb-Apr 2016	133	27.2	109	14	9	6.9	*	482	11.9	312	79	92	19.0	44
Mar-May 2016	139	28.3	112	17	9	6.7	*	472	11.6	308	72	92	19.5	42
Apr-Jun 2016	143	28.8	116	17	10	7.1	*	475	11.7	313	72	90	19.0	40
May-Jul 2016	143	29.1	113	16	14	9.8	*	480	11.9	321	67	92	19.1	42
Jun-Aug 2016	140	28.7	112	15	13	9.2	*	488	12.0	313	81	94	19.2	41
Jul-Sep 2016	124	26.7	96	15	13	10.2	*	473	11.7	305	78	90	19.0	43
Aug-Oct 2016	126	27.4	100	14	13	10.0	*	458	11.4	289	86	83	18.2	40
Sep-Nov 2016	124	25.7	94	17	13	10.2	*	446	11.1	289	74	83	18.6	33
Oct-Dec 2016	122	24.6	92	17	12	9.9	*	440	11.0	281	78	81	18.5	32
Men	**YBVI**	**YBVL**	**YBXE**	**YBXH**	**YBXK**	**YBXN**	**YBXQ**	**YBVO**	**YBVR**	**YBXT**	**YBXW**	**YBXZ**	**YBYC**	**YBYF**
Jul-Sep 2013	102	40.1	72	18	12	11.9	*	468	21.4	217	84	167	35.7	80
Aug-Oct 2013	103	40.4	70	19	14	13.6	*	459	21.2	221	84	154	33.6	73
Sep-Nov 2013	109	41.9	76	20	12	11.4	*	440	20.2	206	82	151	34.5	77
Oct-Dec 2013	99	40.6	67	20	12	12.3	*	445	20.5	204	83	158	35.4	84
Nov-Jan 2014	96	39.1	69	17	10	10.2	*	432	19.9	198	84	150	34.8	75
Dec-Feb 2014	90	39.3	60	18	13	14.3	*	427	19.6	199	80	148	34.7	74
Jan-Mar 2014	90	38.8	58	18	15	16.4	*	414	19.1	190	74	150	36.3	77
Feb-Apr 2014	92	40.0	58	18	17	18.0	*	409	18.7	193	66	149	36.4	77
Mar-May 2014	85	37.4	55	14	17	19.8	*	391	18.0	190	62	139	35.6	69
Apr-Jun 2014	78	35.6	48	12	17	22.2	*	367	17.0	180	64	123	33.5	63
May-Jul 2014	76	36.0	50	11	15	19.4	*	361	17.0	179	63	120	33.1	59
Jun-Aug 2014	78	35.5	52	12	13	17.1	*	352	16.4	169	58	126	35.8	62
Jul-Sep 2014	79	36.1	56	11	11	13.7	*	357	16.6	168	60	130	36.3	59
Aug-Oct 2014	78	35.5	53	14	11	13.5	*	356	16.6	165	57	134	37.6	63
Sep-Nov 2014	81	36.2	55	16	9	11.7	*	353	16.5	172	57	124	35.0	55
Oct-Dec 2014	86	36.7	62	15	9	10.5	*	343	16.0	174	44	125	36.4	57
Nov-Jan 2015	85	37.0	62	12	10	12.3	*	345	16.0	176	42	127	36.8	64
Dec-Feb 2015	92	39.0	69	12	12	12.6	*	339	15.6	170	42	127	37.4	69
Jan-Mar 2015	86	37.3	66	11	9	11.0	*	340	15.7	182	48	111	32.5	61
Feb-Apr 2015	87	37.3	66	11	10	11.1	*	343	15.9	187	53	103	30.1	53
Mar-May 2015	81	34.8	63	10	8	9.3	*	338	15.8	187	52	98	29.1	49
Apr-Jun 2015	80	34.3	61	11	8	10.1	*	338	15.7	188	51	100	29.5	47
May-Jul 2015	81	33.4	62	11	8	9.6	*	333	15.5	193	46	94	28.3	42
Jun-Aug 2015	77	32.6	57	13	8	10.3	*	317	14.6	188	44	85	27.0	36

4.7 Unemployment by age and duration

United Kingdom (thousands) seasonally adjusted

	16-17							18-24						
	All level	rate (%)[1]	Up to 6 months level	Over 6 and up to 12 months level	All over 12 months level	% over 12 months level	All over 24 months level	All level	rate (%)[1]	Up to 6 months level	Over 6 and up to 12 months level	All over 12 months level	% over 12 months level	All over 24 months level
Men *(contd.)*	**YBVI**	**YBVL**	**YBXE**	**YBXH**	**YBXK**	**YBXN**	**YBXQ**	**YBVO**	**YBVR**	**YBXT**	**YBXW**	**YBXZ**	**YBYC**	**YBYF**
Jul-Sep 2015	79	32.4	56	14	9	11.9	*	293	13.6	180	36	77	26.4	34
Aug-Oct 2015	74	29.9	53	14	7	10.1	*	278	12.9	170	33	74	26.7	35
Sep-Nov 2015	75	30.3	51	12	12	16.4	*	289	13.4	180	39	70	24.3	32
Oct-Dec 2015	72	29.3	51	11	11	14.6	*	281	13.1	172	40	68	24.3	27
Nov-Jan 2016	73	30.5	47	15	10	14.2	*	288	13.4	176	42	70	24.4	27
Dec-Feb 2016	71	29.2	50	12	9	12.7	*	285	13.3	174	45	66	23.2	30
Jan-Mar 2016	70	28.7	51	11	8	10.8	*	282	13.2	171	47	64	22.8	30
Feb-Apr 2016	69	29.4	53	10	7	9.7	*	275	13.0	170	45	60	21.8	28
Mar-May 2016	73	31.3	58	10	*	*	*	273	12.9	168	42	63	23.1	28
Apr-Jun 2016	77	32.4	63	11	*	*	*	282	13.4	176	44	62	21.9	30
May-Jul 2016	81	34.5	65	11	6	6.8	*	297	14.1	190	44	63	21.2	33
Jun-Aug 2016	79	33.4	62	11	6	7.1	*	291	13.8	180	46	65	22.2	32
Jul-Sep 2016	67	30.7	51	11	5	7.4	*	288	13.7	178	45	65	22.6	33
Aug-Oct 2016	64	30.0	52	9	*	*	*	285	13.6	169	55	62	21.6	31
Sep-Nov 2016	65	27.5	52	10	*	*	*	280	13.4	168	52	60	21.4	23
Oct-Dec 2016	66	27.3	52	11	*	*	*	277	13.3	168	54	55	20.0	21
Women	**YBVJ**	**YBVM**	**YBXF**	**YBXI**	**YBXL**	**YBXO**	**YBXR**	**YBVP**	**YBVS**	**YBXU**	**YBXX**	**YBYA**	**YBYD**	**YBYG**
Jul-Sep 2013	91	33.5	64	11	15	16.9	*	327	16.7	180	55	91	27.9	32
Aug-Oct 2013	90	32.4	61	14	16	17.4	*	305	15.7	166	53	85	28.1	32
Sep-Nov 2013	88	31.5	62	14	12	13.7	*	302	15.6	168	53	82	27.0	29
Oct-Dec 2013	91	33.6	62	16	13	14.0	*	296	15.2	171	49	77	25.8	29
Nov-Jan 2014	95	34.8	70	14	11	11.2	*	299	15.3	178	46	74	24.9	29
Dec-Feb 2014	91	34.0	67	14	9	10.3	*	279	14.3	163	42	74	26.7	29
Jan-Mar 2014	91	33.6	70	12	9	9.8	*	272	14.1	157	41	73	27.0	28
Feb-Apr 2014	82	30.2	60	13	9	10.9	*	262	13.5	154	42	65	25.0	26
Mar-May 2014	83	31.2	63	12	8	9.2	*	254	13.1	159	43	53	20.7	22
Apr-Jun 2014	84	31.8	66	10	8	9.7	*	233	12.1	139	37	57	24.4	23
May-Jul 2014	85	31.9	62	13	9	11.0	*	227	11.8	132	35	60	26.4	25
Jun-Aug 2014	85	31.9	59	18	8	9.5	*	219	11.3	122	34	64	29.0	27
Jul-Sep 2014	83	30.7	59	19	6	6.6	*	230	11.9	137	29	63	27.3	28
Aug-Oct 2014	82	30.7	58	18	6	7.9	*	242	12.6	143	31	68	28.2	32
Sep-Nov 2014	77	29.0	55	13	9	11.7	*	262	13.7	160	38	63	24.3	29
Oct-Dec 2014	74	27.2	52	13	10	12.9	*	248	12.9	150	39	59	23.7	26
Nov-Jan 2015	69	25.5	48	12	9	13.1	*	246	12.7	156	37	53	21.7	19
Dec-Feb 2015	63	23.7	45	11	7	11.3	*	248	12.8	157	38	53	21.3	23
Jan-Mar 2015	60	22.6	42	10	7	12.5	*	244	12.6	161	38	45	18.4	20
Feb-Apr 2015	62	23.3	42	11	9	13.9	*	239	12.3	162	34	42	17.6	18
Mar-May 2015	63	23.2	46	10	8	12.4	*	236	12.2	156	39	42	17.6	16
Apr-Jun 2015	63	23.6	48	8	8	11.9	*	242	12.4	155	42	45	18.6	18
May-Jul 2015	64	23.4	51	8	*	*	*	236	12.1	152	42	42	17.8	20
Jun-Aug 2015	66	24.2	54	8	*	*	*	219	11.3	139	39	41	18.5	18
Jul-Sep 2015	61	22.2	50	7	*	*	*	223	11.5	141	39	42	19.0	17
Aug-Oct 2015	53	20.1	45	5	*	*	*	220	11.4	142	37	42	18.8	17
Sep-Nov 2015	54	21.2	46	5	*	*	*	215	11.0	136	35	44	20.3	16
Oct-Dec 2015	61	24.4	51	6	*	*	*	210	10.8	134	33	43	20.5	17
Nov-Jan 2016	60	23.6	51	6	*	*	*	211	10.8	135	37	40	18.9	16
Dec-Feb 2016	58	22.9	51	*	*	*	*	217	11.1	149	35	33	15.2	16
Jan-Mar 2016	57	22.5	53	*	*	*	*	218	11.2	147	40	31	14.2	17
Feb-Apr 2016	63	25.2	56	5	*	*	*	207	10.7	142	33	32	15.3	16
Mar-May 2016	66	25.6	54	7	5	7.6	*	199	10.2	140	30	29	14.7	14
Apr-Jun 2016	66	25.6	53	7	7	10.3	*	193	9.9	137	27	29	14.8	10
May-Jul 2016	61	24.0	48	*	8	13.7	*	183	9.4	131	24	29	15.7	9
Jun-Aug 2016	61	24.3	50	*	7	11.9	*	197	10.1	133	35	29	14.7	9
Jul-Sep 2016	57	23.2	46	*	8	13.5	*	185	9.5	127	33	25	13.4	10
Aug-Oct 2016	62	25.0	48	5	9	14.6	*	173	8.9	120	31	22	12.5	9
Sep-Nov 2016	59	23.9	42	6	11	17.9	*	166	8.6	121	22	23	14.0	11
Oct-Dec 2016	56	22.1	40	6	9	16.7	*	163	8.5	114	24	26	15.9	12

4.7 Unemployment by age and duration

United Kingdom (thousands) seasonally adjusted

	25-49							50 and over						
	All level	rate (%)[1]	Up to 6 months level	Over 6 and up to 12 months level	All over 12 months level	% over 12 months level	All over 24 months level	All level	rate (%)[1]	Up to 6 months level	Over 6 and up to 12 months level	All over 12 months level	% over 12 months level	All over 24 months level
People	**MGVI**	**MGXB**	**YBYH**	**YBYK**	**YBYN**	**YBYQ**	**YBYT**	**YBVT**	**YBVW**	**YBYW**	**YBYZ**	**YBZC**	**YBZF**	**YBZI**
Jul-Sep 2013	1,086	5.8	469	199	418	38.5	234	410	4.4	162	58	190	46.4	109
Aug-Oct 2013	1,036	5.6	454	171	412	39.7	230	411	4.4	160	59	192	46.7	107
Sep-Nov 2013	1,011	5.4	437	169	405	40.0	234	391	4.2	153	59	179	45.8	107
Oct-Dec 2013	1,026	5.5	447	170	409	39.9	232	400	4.2	159	62	179	44.7	106
Nov-Jan 2014	1,017	5.5	440	171	406	40.0	241	401	4.3	162	61	178	44.3	104
Dec-Feb 2014	971	5.2	422	159	389	40.1	226	399	4.2	163	60	177	44.2	101
Jan-Mar 2014	957	5.1	415	152	391	40.8	233	388	4.1	153	57	178	46.0	108
Feb-Apr 2014	935	5.0	412	152	371	39.7	222	381	4.0	150	49	182	47.7	108
Mar-May 2014	917	4.9	401	163	353	38.5	212	381	4.0	145	52	184	48.3	115
Apr-Jun 2014	922	4.9	404	161	356	38.6	207	377	4.0	153	45	179	47.5	113
May-Jul 2014	904	4.8	402	156	347	38.4	198	356	3.7	144	39	173	48.5	113
Jun-Aug 2014	890	4.8	400	151	339	38.1	190	347	3.6	144	40	162	46.8	107
Jul-Sep 2014	872	4.7	385	156	331	38.0	183	340	3.6	148	42	150	44.2	103
Aug-Oct 2014	860	4.6	376	166	317	36.9	174	336	3.5	141	46	149	44.3	104
Sep-Nov 2014	828	4.4	375	147	305	36.9	167	324	3.4	133	46	146	45.0	100
Oct-Dec 2014	802	4.3	370	144	287	35.8	155	317	3.3	121	47	149	46.9	101
Nov-Jan 2015	808	4.3	378	136	294	36.4	160	306	3.2	125	47	134	43.8	94
Dec-Feb 2015	793	4.2	364	133	295	37.2	164	307	3.2	129	48	130	42.4	94
Jan-Mar 2015	785	4.2	376	129	280	35.6	164	310	3.2	127	47	137	44.1	95
Feb-Apr 2015	781	4.2	365	134	282	36.2	167	302	3.1	127	47	128	42.4	89
Mar-May 2015	813	4.4	387	137	289	35.5	169	317	3.3	135	55	127	40.0	84
Apr-Jun 2015	803	4.3	375	135	293	36.5	176	322	3.3	140	59	123	38.3	83
May-Jul 2015	780	4.2	379	124	277	35.5	162	327	3.3	144	63	120	36.7	83
Jun-Aug 2015	768	4.1	383	125	260	33.9	156	331	3.4	141	60	131	39.4	90
Jul-Sep 2015	775	4.2	399	124	252	32.5	146	328	3.3	140	58	130	39.7	92
Aug-Oct 2015	757	4.1	392	120	245	32.4	141	333	3.4	137	56	140	42.1	93
Sep-Nov 2015	726	3.9	383	117	226	31.1	132	329	3.3	142	50	136	41.5	88
Oct-Dec 2015	746	4.0	399	116	231	31.0	135	316	3.2	139	45	133	41.9	81
Nov-Jan 2016	737	3.9	399	118	219	29.8	125	316	3.2	138	40	138	43.6	87
Dec-Feb 2016	733	3.9	397	118	218	29.8	124	336	3.4	145	50	141	42.0	91
Jan-Mar 2016	712	3.8	379	116	216	30.4	122	348	3.5	147	53	148	42.6	93
Feb-Apr 2016	705	3.8	382	111	212	30.1	123	345	3.4	148	50	148	42.7	94
Mar-May 2016	707	3.8	391	101	215	30.4	124	329	3.3	139	46	145	44.0	93
Apr-Jun 2016	708	3.8	394	108	206	29.0	125	317	3.1	136	40	141	44.5	88
May-Jul 2016	693	3.7	382	107	204	29.4	120	320	3.2	140	41	139	43.4	92
Jun-Aug 2016	720	3.8	400	119	200	27.8	114	321	3.2	142	41	138	43.0	89
Jul-Sep 2016	708	3.8	400	108	199	28.1	109	313	3.1	143	37	132	42.3	87
Aug-Oct 2016	710	3.8	411	108	191	26.9	107	319	3.1	151	37	131	40.9	78
Sep-Nov 2016	723	3.9	421	106	196	27.1	106	309	3.0	153	40	116	37.5	73
Oct-Dec 2016	708	3.8	407	107	193	27.3	101	316	3.1	157	42	117	37.2	75
Men	**MGVJ**	**MGXC**	**YBYI**	**YBYL**	**YBYO**	**YBYR**	**YBYU**	**YBVU**	**YBVX**	**YBYX**	**YBZA**	**YBZD**	**YBZG**	**YBZJ**
Jul-Sep 2013	575	5.8	227	97	251	43.7	149	243	4.8	84	36	123	50.6	74
Aug-Oct 2013	543	5.5	218	80	246	45.2	147	242	4.7	89	34	119	49.3	70
Sep-Nov 2013	536	5.4	211	83	243	45.2	151	227	4.4	83	33	110	48.6	69
Oct-Dec 2013	547	5.5	214	90	243	44.4	151	230	4.5	90	33	107	46.6	69
Nov-Jan 2014	528	5.3	197	90	240	45.6	160	234	4.6	86	37	111	47.5	66
Dec-Feb 2014	508	5.1	193	84	232	45.6	147	236	4.6	87	33	116	49.2	67
Jan-Mar 2014	496	5.0	189	75	232	46.7	148	231	4.5	81	32	118	51.1	73
Feb-Apr 2014	481	4.8	186	73	222	46.1	141	224	4.3	78	27	118	52.8	71
Mar-May 2014	458	4.6	175	76	207	45.2	134	225	4.4	75	31	119	52.9	78
Apr-Jun 2014	468	4.7	185	74	209	44.6	125	226	4.4	78	30	118	52.2	77
May-Jul 2014	459	4.6	181	70	209	45.5	126	220	4.3	80	24	116	52.7	80
Jun-Aug 2014	455	4.6	182	72	202	44.3	117	211	4.1	81	24	106	50.2	71
Jul-Sep 2014	444	4.5	177	77	190	42.8	107	208	4.0	89	23	96	46.0	65
Aug-Oct 2014	444	4.5	182	83	179	40.4	98	209	4.0	86	25	98	47.1	69
Sep-Nov 2014	430	4.3	180	74	176	40.9	98	206	4.0	82	25	98	47.9	69
Oct-Dec 2014	420	4.2	173	77	170	40.5	96	193	3.7	68	28	97	50.4	66
Nov-Jan 2015	414	4.2	173	71	170	41.0	98	181	3.5	70	26	85	47.1	60
Dec-Feb 2015	406	4.1	166	71	168	41.5	103	178	3.4	69	27	82	46.0	61
Jan-Mar 2015	396	4.0	163	68	165	41.6	106	183	3.5	69	28	86	47.2	63
Feb-Apr 2015	400	4.0	163	68	169	42.3	107	177	3.4	70	28	80	45.2	55
Mar-May 2015	404	4.1	166	68	171	42.2	106	184	3.5	77	30	77	42.0	51
Apr-Jun 2015	411	4.1	171	66	174	42.3	112	185	3.5	78	33	75	40.5	51
May-Jul 2015	391	3.9	170	60	162	41.3	102	183	3.5	80	34	69	37.6	50
Jun-Aug 2015	389	3.9	178	60	151	38.8	98	192	3.6	77	36	79	41.1	56

4.7 Unemployment by age and duration

United Kingdom (thousands) seasonally adjusted

	25-49							50 and over						
	All level	rate (%)[1]	Up to 6 months level	Over 6 and up to 12 months level	All over 12 months level	% over 12 months level	All over 24 months level	All level	rate (%)[1]	Up to 6 months level	Over 6 and up to 12 months level	All over 12 months level	% over 12 months level	All over 24 months level
***Men** (contd.)*	MGVJ	MGXC	YBYI	YBYL	YBYO	YBYR	YBYU	YBVU	YBVX	YBYX	YBZA	YBZD	YBZG	YBZJ
Jul-Sep 2015	392	4.0	185	60	147	37.6	93	197	3.7	82	34	80	40.7	57
Aug-Oct 2015	383	3.9	183	60	139	36.3	89	202	3.8	78	37	86	42.8	60
Sep-Nov 2015	364	3.7	180	58	126	34.6	84	196	3.6	83	32	81	41.4	56
Oct-Dec 2015	375	3.8	188	59	129	34.3	86	193	3.6	79	31	83	43.0	56
Nov-Jan 2016	367	3.7	184	60	123	33.5	83	194	3.6	80	29	86	44.1	58
Dec-Feb 2016	370	3.7	188	59	124	33.4	86	206	3.8	83	33	91	43.9	62
Jan-Mar 2016	356	3.6	174	60	122	34.2	80	207	3.8	77	38	92	44.6	62
Feb-Apr 2016	348	3.5	172	54	122	35.1	81	203	3.7	74	34	95	46.8	63
Mar-May 2016	354	3.5	185	51	119	33.6	79	198	3.6	74	30	94	47.5	65
Apr-Jun 2016	344	3.4	178	53	113	32.9	77	187	3.4	73	24	91	48.3	63
May-Jul 2016	335	3.3	175	51	109	32.4	73	191	3.5	73	24	94	49.5	70
Jun-Aug 2016	345	3.4	177	53	115	33.3	74	185	3.4	71	22	92	49.6	63
Jul-Sep 2016	347	3.5	187	47	113	32.6	73	182	3.3	72	23	87	47.9	61
Aug-Oct 2016	347	3.5	195	44	108	31.2	71	188	3.4	79	21	87	46.4	54
Sep-Nov 2016	359	3.6	202	45	111	31.0	69	179	3.3	77	23	79	43.9	50
Oct-Dec 2016	348	3.5	195	44	109	31.3	68	181	3.3	80	22	79	43.7	49
Women	MGVK	MGXD	YBYJ	YBYM	YBYP	YBYS	YBYV	YBVV	YBVY	YBYY	YBZB	YBZE	YBZH	YBZK
Jul-Sep 2013	511	5.9	242	102	166	32.5	85	167	4.0	77	23	67	40.3	35
Aug-Oct 2013	493	5.7	236	91	166	33.7	84	169	4.0	71	25	73	42.9	37
Sep-Nov 2013	474	5.5	226	86	162	34.2	83	164	3.8	70	26	69	42.0	38
Oct-Dec 2013	479	5.5	233	80	167	34.8	81	170	3.9	69	29	72	42.2	37
Nov-Jan 2014	489	5.6	242	81	166	33.9	81	167	3.9	76	25	67	39.8	38
Dec-Feb 2014	462	5.3	229	76	157	34.1	79	163	3.8	76	27	60	37.0	34
Jan-Mar 2014	462	5.3	226	77	159	34.5	85	157	3.6	72	25	60	38.4	35
Feb-Apr 2014	455	5.2	226	80	149	32.9	81	158	3.6	72	22	64	40.5	37
Mar-May 2014	459	5.2	226	88	146	31.7	78	156	3.6	70	21	65	41.8	37
Apr-Jun 2014	453	5.2	219	87	147	32.4	82	152	3.5	75	15	61	40.4	36
May-Jul 2014	445	5.1	221	86	138	31.1	72	135	3.1	64	15	56	41.7	34
Jun-Aug 2014	435	5.0	218	80	137	31.6	72	136	3.1	63	16	56	41.6	36
Jul-Sep 2014	428	4.9	208	79	141	32.9	76	132	3.0	59	19	55	41.3	38
Aug-Oct 2014	416	4.7	194	83	138	33.2	76	128	2.9	55	22	51	39.6	35
Sep-Nov 2014	398	4.5	196	73	129	32.5	70	119	2.7	51	20	47	39.9	31
Oct-Dec 2014	382	4.4	197	67	117	30.6	59	125	2.8	54	19	52	41.5	34
Nov-Jan 2015	393	4.5	205	64	124	31.6	62	125	2.8	56	21	49	39.0	34
Dec-Feb 2015	387	4.4	198	62	127	32.7	62	129	2.9	60	21	48	37.6	34
Jan-Mar 2015	390	4.5	213	61	115	29.5	59	128	2.9	58	19	51	39.7	32
Feb-Apr 2015	381	4.4	202	66	113	29.7	60	125	2.8	58	19	48	38.4	33
Mar-May 2015	409	4.7	222	69	118	28.9	63	133	3.0	58	25	49	37.3	32
Apr-Jun 2015	393	4.5	204	69	120	30.5	64	137	3.1	62	26	48	35.3	31
May-Jul 2015	389	4.5	210	64	116	29.7	60	144	3.2	64	29	51	35.5	34
Jun-Aug 2015	379	4.4	204	65	109	28.9	58	140	3.1	63	25	52	37.0	33
Jul-Sep 2015	383	4.4	214	64	105	27.4	53	131	2.9	57	24	50	38.1	34
Aug-Oct 2015	374	4.3	209	60	106	28.3	52	132	2.9	58	19	54	41.0	33
Sep-Nov 2015	362	4.1	203	59	100	27.5	48	132	2.9	59	18	55	41.6	32
Oct-Dec 2015	371	4.2	211	58	103	27.6	48	123	2.7	60	14	50	40.3	25
Nov-Jan 2016	369	4.2	215	59	96	26.0	42	121	2.7	58	11	52	42.8	29
Dec-Feb 2016	363	4.2	210	59	95	26.1	38	129	2.8	62	17	50	38.9	29
Jan-Mar 2016	356	4.1	206	56	95	26.5	42	141	3.1	70	15	56	39.7	31
Feb-Apr 2016	358	4.1	210	57	90	25.2	43	142	3.1	74	16	52	36.9	30
Mar-May 2016	353	4.0	207	50	96	27.3	45	132	2.8	65	16	51	38.7	27
Apr-Jun 2016	364	4.2	216	55	93	25.4	48	129	2.8	63	16	50	38.9	25
May-Jul 2016	358	4.1	207	55	95	26.7	47	129	2.8	68	17	44	34.3	22
Jun-Aug 2016	374	4.3	223	66	85	22.8	40	135	2.9	71	18	46	33.9	25
Jul-Sep 2016	361	4.1	213	62	86	23.8	36	131	2.8	71	14	45	34.6	26
Aug-Oct 2016	363	4.1	216	64	83	22.9	37	131	2.8	72	16	43	33.1	25
Sep-Nov 2016	364	4.1	219	61	84	23.2	37	130	2.8	76	17	37	28.7	23
Oct-Dec 2016	359	4.1	212	63	84	23.5	33	134	2.9	77	19	38	28.4	26

Source: Labour Force Survey

Note: When comparing quarterly changes ONS recommends comparing with the previous non-overlapping 3-month average time period (eg, compare Apr-Jun with Jan-Mar, not with Mar-May).

[1] Denominator = economically active for that age group.

*** Sample size too small for reliable estimate.**

4.8 Regional Labour Force Survey Summary (employment, unemployment, economic activity, inactivity)

Headline estimates for November 2016 to January 2017

Thousands, seasonally adjusted

		Economically active [1]		Employment		Unemployment		Economically inactive	
		Aged 16+	Aged 16-64	Aged 16+	Aged 16-64	Aged 16+	Aged 16+	Aged 16-64	Aged 16-64
Area Codes	Area Names	Level	Rate (%)[2]	Level	Rate (%)[2]	Level	Rate (%)[3]	Level	Rate (%)[2]
K02000001	United Kingdom	33,438	78.4	31,854	74.6	1,584	4.7	8,874	21.6
K03000001	Great Britain	32,548	78.5	31,015	74.7	1,533	4.7	8,567	21.5
E92000001	England	28,294	78.7	26,956	74.9	1,339	4.7	7,353	21.3
E12000001	North East	1,296	75.9	1,209	70.7	88	6.8	399	24.1
E12000002	North West	3,573	76.9	3,399	73.1	173	4.9	1,039	23.1
E12000003	Yorkshire and The Humber	2,700	77.1	2,556	72.9	144	5.3	775	22.9
E12000004	East Midlands	2,391	79.1	2,288	75.7	103	4.3	611	20.9
E12000005	West Midlands	2,855	76.8	2,696	72.4	160	5.6	827	23.2
E12000006	East	3,161	80.2	3,023	76.6	138	4.4	742	19.8
E12000007	London	4,774	78.0	4,506	73.5	268	5.6	1,306	22.0
E12000008	South East	4,701	81.4	4,538	78.5	163	3.5	1,030	18.6
E12000009	South West	2,843	81.2	2,742	78.2	101	3.6	625	18.8
W92000004	Wales	1,518	76.7	1,451	73.3	66	4.4	443	23.3
S92000003	Scotland	2,736	77.4	2,608	73.7	129	4.7	770	22.6
N92000002	Northern Ireland	889	73.8	838	69.4	51	5.7	307	26.2

Change on quarter (change since August to October 2016)

Note: Changes on quarter at regional level are particularly subject to sampling variability and should be interpreted in the context of changes over several quarters rather than in isolation.

Thousands, seasonally adjusted

		Economically active [1]		Employment		Unemployment		Economically inactive	
		Aged 16+	Aged 16-64	Aged 16+	Aged 16-64	Aged 16+	Aged 16+	Aged 16-64	Aged 16-64
Area Codes	Area Names	Level	Rate (%)[2]	Level	Rate (%)[2]	Level	Rate (%)[3]	Level	Rate (%)[2]
K02000001	United Kingdom	61	0.1	92	0.2	-31	-0.1	-34	-0.1
K03000001	Great Britain	59	0.1	91	0.2	-32	-0.1	-34	-0.1
E92000001	England	56	0.1	73	0.1	-17	-0.1	-27	-0.1
E12000001	North East	5	0.0	1	-0.2	4	0.3	1	0.0
E12000002	North West	12	0.2	29	0.6	-17	-0.5	-10	-0.2
E12000003	Yorkshire and The Humber	-13	-0.5	-14	-0.4	0	0.0	16	0.5
E12000004	East Midlands	-7	0.0	2	0.4	-9	-0.4	-1	0.0
E12000005	West Midlands	-10	-0.2	-18	-0.4	9	0.3	7	0.2
E12000006	East	2	-0.2	11	0.0	-9	-0.3	8	0.2
E12000007	London	24	0.0	15	-0.2	9	0.2	3	0.0
E12000008	South East	15	0.5	15	0.4	0	0.0	-25	-0.5
E12000009	South West	28	0.8	32	0.9	-3	-0.2	-26	-0.8
W92000004	Wales	3	0.4	2	0.4	1	0.1	-8	-0.4
S92000003	Scotland	0	0.0	16	0.4	-16	-0.6	1	0.0
N92000002	Northern Ireland	2	0.0	1	-0.1	1	0.1	0	0.0

Change on year (change since November 2015 to January 2016)

Thousands, seasonally adjusted

		Economically active [1]		Employment		Unemployment		Economically inactive	
		Aged 16+	Aged 16-64	Aged 16+	Aged 16-64	Aged 16+	Aged 16+	Aged 16-64	Aged 16-64
Area Codes	Area Names	Level	Rate (%)[2]	Level	Rate (%)[2]	Level	Rate (%)[3]	Level	Rate (%)[2]
K02000001	United Kingdom	209	0.2	315	0.5	-106	-0.3	-59	-0.2
K03000001	Great Britain	206	0.2	310	0.5	-104	-0.4	-56	-0.2
E92000001	England	270	0.4	320	0.5	-50	-0.2	-101	-0.4
E12000001	North East	-9	-0.6	5	0.2	-14	-1.0	10	0.6
E12000002	North West	20	-0.1	23	-0.1	-3	-0.1	10	0.1
E12000003	Yorkshire and The Humber	23	0.4	43	1.0	-20	-0.8	-11	-0.4
E12000004	East Midlands	25	1.1	28	1.3	-3	-0.2	-31	-1.1
E12000005	West Midlands	77	1.5	69	1.3	8	0.1	-50	-1.5
E12000006	East	-7	-0.7	-31	-1.3	24	0.8	29	0.7
E12000007	London	67	0.3	87	0.7	-20	-0.5	-11	-0.3
E12000008	South East	35	0.4	50	0.6	-15	-0.3	-17	-0.4
E12000009	South West	39	1.0	45	1.2	-7	-0.3	-31	-1.0
W92000004	Wales	-1	1.0	11	1.6	-12	-0.8	-20	-1.0
S92000003	Scotland	-63	-1.9	-21	-0.7	-42	-1.4	65	1.9
N92000002	Northern Ireland	3	0.3	5	0.6	-2	-0.3	-3	-0.3

The Labour Force Survey is tabulated by region of residence.

Source: Labour Force Survey

1. Economically active = Employment plus Unemployment.
2. Denominator = all persons aged 16 to 64.
3. Denominator = total economically active

4.9 Claimant count rates: by region

ONS Crown Copyright Reserved [from Nomis on 18 April 2019]

Sex: Total
Rate: Workplace-based estimates
Seasonally adjusted

Area		Jan - Dec 2005 (inclusive)		Jan - Dec 2006 (inclusive)		Jan - Dec 2007 (inclusive)		Jan - Dec 2008 (inclusive)	
		number	rate	number	rate	number	rate	number	rate
England	E92000001	706,092	2.6	785,550	2.8	723,100	2.6	754,108	2.7
United Kingdom	K02000001	861,775	2.7	944,967	2.9	864,467	2.6	906,083	2.7
North East	E12000001	45,942	3.8	50,233	4.0	49,275	3.9	53,717	4.3
North West	E12000002	101,242	2.9	115,550	3.3	110,092	3.1	119,708	3.4
Yorkshire and The Humber	E12000003	76,017	2.9	87,358	3.3	81,158	3.0	88,033	3.3
East Midlands	E12000004	54,083	2.5	61,975	2.8	58,483	2.6	61,408	2.7
West Midlands	E12000005	93,958	3.4	108,325	3.8	102,525	3.6	106,167	3.7
East	E12000006	58,100	2.1	65,583	2.2	61,225	2.1	63,625	2.2
London	E12000007	162,950	3.4	166,833	3.4	145,450	2.9	137,658	2.7
South East	E12000008	71,625	1.6	81,675	1.8	71,950	1.6	76,942	1.7
South West	E12000009	42,175	1.6	48,017	1.8	42,942	1.6	46,850	1.7
Wales	W92000004	41,200	2.9	44,217	3.0	40,692	2.8	45,517	3.1
Scotland	S92000003	85,892	3.1	87,258	3.1	76,300	2.7	78,633	2.7
Northern Ireland	N92000002	28,592	3.3	27,875	3.2	24,375	2.8	27,825	3.1

Area		Jan - Dec 2009 (inclusive)		Jan - Dec 2010 (inclusive)		Jan - Dec 2011 (inclusive)		Jan - Dec 2012 (inclusive)	
		number	rate	number	rate	number	rate	number	rate
England	E92000001	1,275,583	4.5	1,230,708	4.4	1,258,225	4.5	1,301,583	4.6
United Kingdom	K02000001	1,527,683	4.6	1,496,358	4.5	1,534,408	4.6	1,585,575	4.7
North East	E12000001	83,775	6.6	81,417	6.5	85,367	6.9	93,425	7.6
North West	E12000002	191,708	5.3	184,017	5.1	190,200	5.3	200,275	5.6
Yorkshire and The Humber	E12000003	149,817	5.6	148,008	5.5	153,267	5.7	164,075	6.1
East Midlands	E12000004	108,300	4.8	101,492	4.5	103,142	4.5	108,842	4.7
West Midlands	E12000005	173,775	6.2	163,667	5.9	164,025	5.9	164,983	5.8
East	E12000006	115,992	3.9	111,067	3.8	111,800	3.8	115,075	3.8
London	E12000007	211,150	4.1	217,283	4.3	228,000	4.5	226,708	4.2
South East	E12000008	149,225	3.3	139,858	3.1	137,242	3.0	139,333	3.0
South West	E12000009	91,842	3.3	83,900	3.0	85,183	3.1	88,867	3.2
Wales	W92000004	77,133	5.2	73,192	5.1	74,850	5.2	79,600	5.5
Scotland	S92000003	125,958	4.5	135,733	5.0	141,508	5.1	141,433	5.1
Northern Ireland	N92000002	49,008	5.5	56,725	6.2	59,825	6.6	62,958	7.1

Area		Jan - Dec 2013 (inclusive)		Jan - Dec 2014 (inclusive)		Jan - Dec 2015 (inclusive)		Jan - Dec 2016 (inclusive)	
		number	rate	number	rate	number	rate	number	rate
England	E92000001	1,157,878	4.1	828,677	2.8	631,171	2.1	615,959	2.0
United Kingdom	K02000001	1,421,326	4.2	1,036,114	3.0	797,916	2.3	772,818	2.2
North East	E12000001	84,494	6.8	61,856	5.0	47,595	3.8	50,055	4.1
North West	E12000002	179,102	5.0	128,476	3.5	106,321	2.9	104,886	2.8
Yorkshire and The Humber	E12000003	149,861	5.6	110,499	4.1	82,997	3.0	75,162	2.7
East Midlands	E12000004	95,520	4.2	67,760	2.9	49,353	2.1	45,197	1.9
West Midlands	E12000005	149,178	5.3	109,445	3.8	81,154	2.8	82,132	2.8
East	E12000006	101,690	3.4	68,618	2.2	49,607	1.6	47,056	1.5
London	E12000007	202,011	3.7	148,091	2.6	114,913	2.0	111,375	1.9
South East	E12000008	119,459	2.6	81,401	1.7	60,382	1.2	59,959	1.2
South West	E12000009	76,563	2.7	52,532	1.8	38,848	1.3	40,137	1.4
Wales	W92000004	72,896	5.0	56,857	3.8	45,380	3.0	43,025	2.8
Scotland	S92000003	127,998	4.6	96,569	3.4	78,407	2.8	77,755	2.7
Northern Ireland	N92000002	62,555	7.0	54,012	6.0	42,959	4.8	36,079	3.9

Source: Office for National Statistics

From May 2013 onwards these figures are not designated as National Statistics.

From May 2013 onwards these figures are considered Experimental Statistics.

Under Universal Credit a broader span of claimants are required to look for work than under Jobseeker's Allowance. As Universal Credit Full Service is rolled out in particular areas, the number of people recorded as being on the Claimant Count is therefore likely to rise.

Rate figures for dates from 2015 onwards are calculated using mid-2015 workforce estimates.

4.10 Claimant count by Sex and Unitary and Local Authority

ONS Crown Copyright Reserved [from Nomis on 18 April 2019]

Age 16+

	Claimant Count December 2016						Change on year					
	Levels			Claimants as a proportion of residents aged 16-64			Levels			Claimants as a proportion of residents aged 16-64		
Area	Total	Male	Female	Total	Male	Female	Total	Male	Female	Total	Male	Female
United Kingdom	**747,420**	**473,220**	**274,205**	**1.8**	**2.3**	**1.3**	**13,620**	**565**	**13,060**	**0.0**	**0.0**	**0.0**
Great Britain	**715,425**	**450,995**	**264,430**	**1.8**	**2.2**	**1.3**	**19,870**	**5,225**	**14,645**	**0.1**	**0.0**	**0.1**
England and Wales	**640,515**	**400,115**	**240,395**	**1.7**	**2.2**	**1.3**	**16,130**	**3,680**	**12,445**	**0.0**	**0.0**	**0.1**
England	**600,915**	**374,865**	**226,050**	**1.7**	**2.2**	**1.3**	**18,535**	**5,330**	**13,205**	**0.0**	**0.1**	**0.1**
North East	**50,615**	**33,470**	**17,145**	**3.0**	**4.1**	**2.0**	**3,885**	**1,465**	**2,420**	**0.2**	**0.2**	**0.2**
Darlington	**2,175**	**1,445**	**725**	**3.3**	**4.5**	**2.2**	**315**	**180**	**130**	**0.5**	**0.5**	**0.4**
County Durham	**7,835**	**5,000**	**2,835**	**2.4**	**3.1**	**1.7**	**890**	**470**	**420**	**0.3**	**0.3**	**0.2**
Hartlepool	**2,690**	**1,805**	**885**	**4.7**	**6.4**	**3.0**	**95**	**-20**	**115**	**0.2**	**0.0**	**0.4**
Middlesbrough	**4,230**	**2,965**	**1,265**	**4.7**	**6.7**	**2.8**	**170**	**35**	**135**	**0.1**	**0.1**	**0.3**
Northumberland	**4,640**	**2,950**	**1,685**	**2.4**	**3.1**	**1.7**	**370**	**145**	**220**	**0.2**	**0.1**	**0.2**
Redcar and Cleveland	**3,235**	**2,250**	**985**	**4.0**	**5.7**	**2.3**	**-210**	**-380**	**170**	**-0.2**	**-0.9**	**0.4**
Stockton-on-Tees	**3,920**	**2,670**	**1,250**	**3.2**	**4.4**	**2.0**	**165**	**-10**	**175**	**0.1**	**0.0**	**0.3**
Tyne and Wear (Met County)	**21,900**	**14,380**	**7,520**	**3.0**	**4.0**	**2.1**	**2,100**	**1,045**	**1,060**	**0.3**	**0.3**	**0.3**
Gateshead	3,490	2,305	1,185	2.7	3.6	1.8	**465**	**270**	**200**	**0.3**	**0.4**	**0.3**
Newcastle upon Tyne	5,495	3,585	1,910	2.7	3.5	2.0	**580**	**250**	**330**	**0.2**	**0.2**	**0.4**
North Tyneside	3,215	2,205	1,010	2.5	3.5	1.5	**325**	**190**	**140**	**0.2**	**0.3**	**0.2**
South Tyneside	4,115	2,705	1,410	4.4	5.9	3.0	**170**	**20**	**150**	**0.2**	**0.0**	**0.4**
Sunderland	5,585	3,580	2,005	3.2	4.1	2.2	**560**	**315**	**240**	**0.4**	**0.4**	**0.2**
North West	100,490	63,895	36,595	2.2	2.8	1.6	**-610**	**-1,930**	**1,320**	**0.0**	**-0.1**	**0.0**
Blackburn with Darwen	**2,380**	**1,535**	**845**	**2.6**	**3.3**	**1.8**	**-60**	**-60**	**0**	**0.0**	**-0.1**	**0.0**
Blackpool	**3,500**	**2,385**	**1,115**	**4.1**	**5.5**	**2.6**	**105**	**45**	**60**	**0.2**	**0.1**	**0.1**
Cheshire East	**2,390**	**1,520**	**870**	**1.1**	**1.4**	**0.8**	**-60**	**-100**	**40**	**0.0**	**0.0**	**0.1**
Cheshire West and Chester	**2,785**	**1,720**	**1,065**	**1.4**	**1.7**	**1.0**	**90**	**-15**	**105**	**0.1**	**0.0**	**0.1**
Halton	**2,175**	**1,305**	**870**	**2.7**	**3.3**	**2.1**	**55**	**5**	**50**	**0.0**	**0.0**	**0.1**
Warrington	**1,950**	**1,230**	**720**	**1.5**	**1.9**	**1.1**	**-250**	**-195**	**-55**	**-0.2**	**-0.3**	**-0.1**
Cumbria	**4,390**	**2,885**	**1,500**	**1.5**	**1.9**	**1.0**	**-150**	**-180**	**25**	**0.0**	**-0.1**	**0.0**
Allerdale	1,045	675	365	1.8	2.3	1.3	**-15**	**-35**	**15**	**0.0**	**-0.2**	**0.1**
Barrow-in-Furness	1,120	760	360	2.7	3.7	1.7	**-50**	**-65**	**10**	**-0.1**	**-0.2**	**0.0**
Carlisle	790	510	280	1.2	1.6	0.8	**-70**	**-40**	**-35**	**-0.1**	**-0.1**	**-0.1**
Copeland	910	610	300	2.1	2.8	1.4	**25**	**10**	**10**	**0.0**	**0.1**	**0.0**
Eden	205	130	75	0.7	0.9	0.5	**5**	**-5**	**10**	**0.1**	**0.0**	**0.1**
South Lakeland	320	200	120	0.5	0.7	0.4	**-45**	**-50**	**5**	**-0.1**	**-0.1**	**0.0**
Greater Manchester (Met County)	**43,360**	**27,255**	**16,105**	**2.4**	**3.1**	**1.8**	**150**	**-740**	**890**	**0.0**	**-0.1**	**0.1**
Bolton	5,125	3,210	1,910	2.9	3.7	2.2	**215**	**40**	**170**	**0.1**	**0.1**	**0.2**
Bury	2,650	1,625	1,030	2.3	2.8	1.7	**-30**	**-95**	**70**	**0.0**	**-0.2**	**0.1**
Manchester	9,665	6,090	3,580	2.5	3.1	1.9	**-350**	**-400**	**55**	**-0.2**	**-0.3**	**0.0**
Oldham	3,835	2,330	1,505	2.7	3.3	2.1	**-35**	**-50**	**15**	**0.0**	**-0.1**	**0.0**
Rochdale	3,710	2,270	1,440	2.7	3.4	2.1	**290**	**155**	**135**	**0.2**	**0.2**	**0.2**
Salford	4,245	2,725	1,520	2.6	3.3	1.9	**75**	**-40**	**115**	**0.0**	**-0.1**	**0.1**
Stockport	3,230	2,160	1,070	1.8	2.5	1.2	**-160**	**-130**	**-30**	**-0.1**	**-0.1**	**0.0**
Tameside	3,590	2,210	1,380	2.6	3.2	2.0	**-20**	**-120**	**100**	**0.0**	**-0.2**	**0.2**
Trafford	2,220	1,380	840	1.5	1.9	1.1	**-30**	**-120**	**90**	**-0.1**	**-0.2**	**0.1**
Wigan	5,090	3,260	1,835	2.5	3.2	1.8	**195**	**30**	**175**	**0.1**	**0.0**	**0.2**
Lancashire	**13,315**	**8,435**	**4,880**	**1.8**	**2.3**	**1.3**	**820**	**270**	**545**	**0.1**	**0.1**	**0.1**
Burnley	1,605	985	620	3.0	3.7	2.3	**210**	**85**	**125**	**0.4**	**0.3**	**0.5**
Chorley	1,060	690	370	1.5	1.9	1.1	**140**	**110**	**30**	**0.2**	**0.3**	**0.1**
Fylde	605	390	215	1.3	1.7	1.0	**40**	**45**	**-5**	**0.0**	**0.2**	**0.0**
Hyndburn	1,145	710	430	2.3	2.9	1.7	**80**	**10**	**70**	**0.1**	**0.0**	**0.2**
Lancaster	1,845	1,170	675	2.1	2.6	1.5	**225**	**75**	**150**	**0.3**	**0.1**	**0.3**
Pendle	1,060	650	410	1.9	2.4	1.5	**-35**	**-60**	**25**	**-0.1**	**-0.2**	**0.1**
Preston	1,835	1,190	645	2.0	2.5	1.4	**35**	**-5**	**40**	**0.1**	**0.0**	**0.1**
Ribble Valley	220	130	90	0.6	0.7	0.5	**-30**	**-35**	**5**	**-0.1**	**-0.2**	**0.0**
Rossendale	830	505	325	1.9	2.3	1.5	**-20**	**-35**	**15**	**-0.1**	**-0.2**	**0.1**
South Ribble	815	515	305	1.2	1.5	0.9	**55**	**50**	**10**	**0.1**	**0.1**	**0.0**
West Lancashire	1,275	825	450	1.8	2.4	1.3	**-10**	**-40**	**30**	**-0.1**	**-0.2**	**0.1**
Wyre	1,025	680	345	1.6	2.2	1.1	**125**	**80**	**45**	**0.2**	**0.3**	**0.2**

4.10 Claimant count by Sex and Unitary and Local Authority

ONS Crown Copyright Reserved [from Nomis on 18 April 2019]
Age 16+

	Claimant Count December 2016						Change on year					
	Levels			Claimants as a proportion of residents aged 16-64			Levels			Claimants as a proportion of residents aged 16-64		
Area	**Total**	**Male**	**Female**	**Total**	**Male**	**Female**	**Total**	**Male**	**Female**	**Total**	**Male**	**Female**
Merseyside (Met County)	**24,245**	**15,625**	**8,620**	**2.7**	**3.5**	**1.9**	**-1,310**	**-970**	**-340**	**-0.2**	**-0.3**	**-0.1**
Knowsley	2,875	1,750	1,120	3.1	3.9	2.3	-180	-125	-60	-0.2	-0.3	-0.1
Liverpool	10,590	6,870	3,720	3.2	4.1	2.2	-235	-195	-40	-0.1	-0.2	-0.1
Sefton	4,005	2,615	1,390	2.4	3.2	1.7	-320	-210	-110	-0.2	-0.3	-0.1
St. Helens	2,960	1,880	1,080	2.7	3.4	1.9	-235	-190	-45	-0.2	-0.4	-0.1
Wirral	3,815	2,510	1,305	2.0	2.7	1.3	-335	-245	-90	-0.1	-0.2	-0.1
Yorkshire and The Humber	**71,630**	**45,920**	**25,710**	**2.1**	**2.7**	**1.5**	**-1,360**	**-1,935**	**570**	**0.0**	**-0.1**	**0.0**
East Riding of Yorkshire	**2,880**	**1,880**	**1,000**	**1.5**	**1.9**	**1.0**	**-150**	**-120**	**-30**	**0.0**	**-0.1**	**0.0**
Kingston upon Hull, City of	**5,990**	**3,890**	**2,100**	**3.5**	**4.5**	**2.5**	**-855**	**-745**	**-105**	**-0.5**	**-0.8**	**-0.1**
North East Lincolnshire	**3,315**	**2,120**	**1,195**	**3.4**	**4.4**	**2.4**	**-150**	**-185**	**35**	**-0.1**	**-0.3**	**0.1**
North Lincolnshire	**2,275**	**1,485**	**790**	**2.2**	**2.8**	**1.5**	**-135**	**-120**	**-15**	**-0.1**	**-0.3**	**0.0**
York	**910**	**610**	**305**	**0.7**	**0.9**	**0.4**	**5**	**-10**	**20**	**0.0**	**0.0**	**0.0**
North Yorkshire	**4,125**	**2,570**	**1,555**	**1.1**	**1.4**	**0.9**	**590**	**295**	**295**	**0.1**	**0.1**	**0.2**
Craven	285	180	105	0.9	1.1	0.6	50	30	20	0.2	0.2	0.1
Hambleton	475	305	170	0.9	1.1	0.6	70	20	50	0.1	0.0	0.1
Harrogate	880	530	350	0.9	1.1	0.7	355	190	170	0.4	0.4	0.3
Richmondshire	290	155	135	0.8	0.8	0.9	90	30	60	0.2	0.1	0.4
Ryedale	360	200	160	1.1	1.3	1.0	90	40	55	0.2	0.3	0.3
Scarborough	1,205	790	415	1.9	2.6	1.3	-40	0	-40	-0.1	0.1	-0.1
Selby	630	415	215	1.2	1.6	0.8	-35	-10	-25	0.0	0.0	-0.1
South Yorkshire (Met County)	**20,855**	**13,615**	**7,240**	**2.4**	**3.1**	**1.6**	**-650**	**-535**	**-120**	**-0.1**	**-0.1**	**-0.1**
Barnsley	3,215	1,980	1,235	2.1	2.6	1.6	-140	-145	5	-0.1	-0.2	0.0
Doncaster	4,730	2,985	1,745	2.5	3.1	1.8	-260	-155	-110	-0.1	-0.2	-0.2
Rotherham	4,115	2,670	1,450	2.6	3.3	1.8	-5	-85	85	0.0	-0.1	0.1
Sheffield	8,795	5,980	2,815	2.3	3.1	1.5	-245	-150	-100	-0.1	-0.2	-0.1
West Yorkshire (Met County)	**31,275**	**19,745**	**11,525**	**2.1**	**2.7**	**1.6**	**-25**	**-520**	**490**	**-0.1**	**-0.1**	**0.1**
Bradford	8,785	5,465	3,320	2.7	3.3	2.0	10	-70	80	0.0	-0.1	0.0
Calderdale	2,550	1,630	920	2.0	2.5	1.4	65	-40	100	0.1	-0.1	0.2
Kirklees	5,385	3,385	2,000	2.0	2.5	1.5	-70	-145	75	0.0	-0.1	0.1
Leeds	10,845	6,995	3,850	2.1	2.8	1.5	-120	-280	160	-0.1	-0.1	0.1
Wakefield	3,710	2,270	1,435	1.8	2.2	1.4	95	10	75	0.1	0.0	0.1
East Midlands	**41,410**	**26,095**	**15,310**	**1.4**	**1.8**	**1.0**	**-1,575**	**-1,435**	**-140**	**-0.1**	**-0.1**	**0.0**
Derby	**2,190**	**1,330**	**860**	**1.4**	**1.6**	**1.1**	**-5**	**0**	**-5**	**0.0**	**-0.1**	**0.0**
Leicester	**3,605**	**2,210**	**1,395**	**1.5**	**1.9**	**1.2**	**-825**	**-505**	**-320**	**-0.4**	**-0.5**	**-0.3**
Nottingham	**6,535**	**4,340**	**2,195**	**2.9**	**3.7**	**2.0**	**-310**	**-290**	**-20**	**-0.2**	**-0.4**	**0.0**
Rutland	**100**	**60**	**40**	**0.4**	**0.5**	**0.4**	**-25**	**-20**	**0**	**-0.1**	**-0.2**	**0.0**
Derbyshire	**5,680**	**3,615**	**2,065**	**1.2**	**1.5**	**0.8**	**240**	**105**	**135**	**0.1**	**0.0**	**0.0**
Amber Valley	890	570	320	1.2	1.5	0.8	35	50	-20	0.1	0.1	-0.1
Bolsover	680	410	270	1.4	1.7	1.1	85	35	50	0.2	0.2	0.2
Chesterfield	1,125	765	360	1.7	2.3	1.1	55	15	45	0.1	0.0	0.1
Derbyshire Dales	250	160	95	0.6	0.8	0.5	35	25	15	0.1	0.2	0.1
Erewash	1,115	720	395	1.6	2.0	1.1	10	-5	15	0.1	-0.1	0.1
High Peak	575	350	225	1.0	1.2	0.8	-60	-65	5	-0.1	-0.2	0.0
North East Derbyshire	720	445	270	1.2	1.5	0.9	50	15	30	0.1	0.1	0.1
South Derbyshire	325	200	125	0.5	0.6	0.4	25	40	-10	0.0	0.1	0.0
Leicestershire	**3,065**	**1,825**	**1,240**	**0.7**	**0.9**	**0.6**	**-280**	**-265**	**-15**	**-0.1**	**-0.1**	**0.0**
Blaby	365	215	150	0.6	0.7	0.5	-55	-45	-10	-0.1	-0.2	0.0
Charnwood	850	540	315	0.7	0.9	0.6	0	10	-5	0.0	0.0	0.0
Harborough	255	150	105	0.5	0.5	0.4	-5	-15	5	0.0	-0.1	0.0
Hinckley and Bosworth	625	355	270	0.9	1.1	0.8	-55	-75	20	-0.1	-0.2	0.1
Melton	280	155	130	0.9	1.0	0.8	-15	-45	35	-0.1	-0.3	0.2
North West Leicestershire	415	260	155	0.7	0.8	0.5	-105	-70	-30	-0.2	-0.3	-0.1
Oadby and Wigston	275	150	120	0.8	0.9	0.7	-45	-25	-25	-0.1	-0.1	-0.1
Lincolnshire	**7,045**	**4,495**	**2,550**	**1.6**	**2.0**	**1.1**	**-185**	**-240**	**55**	**0.0**	**-0.2**	**0.0**
Boston	595	380	215	1.4	1.8	1.0	-15	-15	0	-0.1	-0.2	-0.1
East Lindsey	1,725	1,065	665	2.2	2.8	1.7	0	-65	65	0.0	-0.2	0.2
Lincoln	1,460	1,015	440	2.2	3.1	1.3	-70	-55	-20	-0.1	-0.2	-0.1
North Kesteven	635	415	220	0.9	1.2	0.6	50	30	20	0.0	0.0	0.0
South Holland	580	320	260	1.1	1.2	0.9	5	-10	15	0.0	0.0	0.0
South Kesteven	1,010	645	365	1.2	1.6	0.8	5	10	-5	0.0	0.0	-0.1
West Lindsey	1,040	655	385	1.9	2.4	1.3	-155	-135	-15	-0.3	-0.5	-0.1

4.10 Claimant count by Sex and Unitary and Local Authority

ONS Crown Copyright Reserved [from Nomis on 18 April 2019]

Age 16+

	Claimant Count December 2016						Change on year					
	Levels			Claimants as a proportion of residents aged 16-64			Levels			Claimants as a proportion of residents aged 16-64		
Area	**Total**	**Male**	**Female**	**Total**	**Male**	**Female**	**Total**	**Male**	**Female**	**Total**	**Male**	**Female**
Northamptonshire	**6,035**	**3,730**	**2,305**	**1.3**	**1.6**	**1.0**	-160	-125	-35	-0.1	-0.1	0.0
Corby	625	380	245	1.4	1.8	1.1	-135	-140	5	-0.4	-0.6	0.0
Daventry	545	340	205	1.1	1.4	0.8	105	65	40	0.2	0.3	0.1
East Northamptonshire	480	305	180	0.9	1.1	0.6	-50	-15	-25	-0.1	-0.1	-0.1
Kettering	915	570	345	1.5	1.9	1.1	-90	-55	-40	-0.2	-0.2	-0.2
Northampton	2,460	1,530	925	1.7	2.1	1.3	70	70	-5	0.0	0.1	0.0
South Northamptonshire	270	165	105	0.5	0.6	0.4	10	5	5	0.0	0.0	0.0
Wellingborough	735	440	295	1.6	1.9	1.2	-80	-60	-20	-0.1	-0.3	-0.1
Nottinghamshire	**7,155**	**4,495**	**2,660**	**1.4**	**1.8**	**1.1**	-25	-85	60	0.0	0.0	0.1
Ashfield	1,410	890	520	1.8	2.3	1.3	-25	0	-20	-0.1	0.0	-0.1
Bassetlaw	1,125	670	460	1.6	1.9	1.3	0	-40	40	0.0	-0.1	0.1
Broxtowe	935	575	360	1.3	1.6	1.0	60	30	35	0.1	0.0	0.1
Gedling	1,020	645	370	1.4	1.8	1.0	45	10	35	0.0	0.0	0.1
Mansfield	1,225	800	425	1.8	2.4	1.3	-120	-80	-40	-0.2	-0.2	-0.1
Newark and Sherwood	870	530	340	1.2	1.5	0.9	0	10	-5	0.0	0.1	-0.1
Rushcliffe	570	385	185	0.8	1.1	0.5	10	-10	20	0.0	0.0	0.0
West Midlands	**80,055**	**50,315**	**29,735**	**2.2**	**2.8**	**1.7**	5,900	2,970	2,920	0.1	0.2	0.2
Herefordshire, County of	**1,175**	**730**	**450**	**1.0**	**1.3**	**0.8**	280	160	125	0.2	0.3	0.2
Shropshire	**1,880**	**1,220**	**660**	**1.0**	**1.3**	**0.7**	45	15	30	0.0	0.0	0.0
Stoke-on-Trent	**3,065**	**1,950**	**1,115**	**1.9**	**2.4**	**1.4**	160	125	35	0.1	0.1	0.0
Telford and Wrekin	**1,675**	**1,055**	**620**	**1.5**	**1.9**	**1.1**	210	150	60	0.2	0.2	0.1
Staffordshire	**4,735**	**2,985**	**1,750**	**0.9**	**1.1**	**0.7**	270	230	45	0.1	0.1	0.1
Cannock Chase	700	425	275	1.1	1.4	0.9	5	20	-15	0.0	0.1	0.0
East Staffordshire	575	355	220	0.8	1.0	0.6	55	40	15	0.1	0.2	0.0
Lichfield	385	245	135	0.6	0.8	0.5	20	20	-5	0.0	0.1	0.0
Newcastle-under-Lyme	890	570	320	1.1	1.4	0.8	30	25	5	0.0	0.1	0.0
South Staffordshire	680	425	255	1.0	1.2	0.8	-5	-15	10	0.0	-0.1	0.1
Stafford	615	410	205	0.7	1.0	0.5	70	75	-5	0.0	0.2	0.0
Staffordshire Moorlands	440	285	155	0.8	1.0	0.5	15	15	0	0.1	0.1	0.0
Tamworth	450	265	180	0.9	1.1	0.7	80	40	35	0.1	0.2	0.1
Warwickshire	**3,445**	**2,040**	**1,410**	**1.0**	**1.2**	**0.8**	385	150	240	0.1	0.1	0.1
North Warwickshire	390	220	170	1.0	1.1	0.9	50	5	45	0.1	0.0	0.3
Nuneaton and Bedworth	1,345	775	570	1.7	2.0	1.4	20	-5	25	0.0	0.0	0.0
Rugby	865	485	380	1.3	1.5	1.2	270	125	145	0.4	0.4	0.5
Stratford-on-Avon	270	165	105	0.4	0.5	0.3	5	-5	10	0.0	0.0	0.0
Warwick	575	395	185	0.6	0.9	0.4	40	35	15	0.0	0.1	0.0
West Midlands (Met County)	**59,880**	**37,630**	**22,250**	**3.3**	**4.2**	**2.5**	4,250	1,995	2,255	0.2	0.2	0.3
Birmingham	29,815	19,085	10,730	4.1	5.3	2.9	1,710	845	865	0.2	0.1	0.2
Coventry	4,035	2,490	1,545	1.7	2.1	1.4	120	5	115	0.0	0.0	0.1
Dudley	5,575	3,530	2,045	2.9	3.7	2.1	370	135	240	0.2	0.2	0.2
Sandwell	7,040	4,360	2,680	3.5	4.3	2.7	735	360	375	0.3	0.3	0.4
Solihull	2,200	1,330	870	1.7	2.1	1.3	280	115	165	0.2	0.1	0.2
Walsall	4,805	2,890	1,910	2.8	3.4	2.2	520	280	235	0.3	0.3	0.2
Wolverhampton	6,415	3,945	2,470	4.0	4.8	3.1	525	255	270	0.3	0.2	0.3
Worcestershire	**4,190**	**2,710**	**1,480**	**1.2**	**1.5**	**0.8**	290	150	140	0.1	0.0	0.0
Bromsgrove	565	360	205	1.0	1.2	0.7	40	25	15	0.1	0.0	0.0
Malvern Hills	430	275	155	1.0	1.3	0.7	55	5	50	0.1	0.0	0.2
Redditch	825	495	325	1.5	1.9	1.2	35	-10	40	0.0	0.0	0.1
Worcester	1,000	670	325	1.5	2.0	1.0	135	90	40	0.2	0.2	0.1
Wychavon	645	415	230	0.9	1.2	0.6	35	10	20	0.1	0.1	0.0
Wyre Forest	735	495	240	1.3	1.7	0.8	5	30	-30	0.1	0.1	-0.1
East	**45,925**	**28,360**	**17,565**	**1.2**	**1.5**	**0.9**	1,165	400	765	0.0	0.0	0.0
Bedford	**1,895**	**1,165**	**735**	**1.8**	**2.2**	**1.4**	-150	-95	-50	-0.2	-0.2	-0.1
Central Bedfordshire	**1,270**	**780**	**490**	**0.7**	**0.9**	**0.6**	-90	-70	-20	-0.1	-0.1	0.0
Luton	**2,330**	**1,390**	**940**	**1.7**	**2.0**	**1.4**	-115	-60	-55	-0.1	-0.1	-0.1
Peterborough	**1,475**	**865**	**610**	**1.2**	**1.4**	**1.0**	-55	-40	-10	0.0	-0.1	0.0
Southend-on-Sea	**2,215**	**1,415**	**805**	**2.0**	**2.5**	**1.4**	90	20	75	0.1	0.0	0.1
Thurrock	**1,975**	**1,100**	**875**	**1.8**	**2.1**	**1.6**	70	-30	100	0.0	0.0	0.2
Cambridgeshire	**2,655**	**1,675**	**980**	**0.7**	**0.8**	**0.5**	-60	0	-60	0.0	0.0	0.0

4.10 Claimant count by Sex and Unitary and Local Authority

ONS Crown Copyright Reserved [from Nomis on 18 April 2019]

Age 16+

	Claimant Count December 2016						Change on year					
	Levels			Claimants as a proportion of residents aged 16-64			Levels			Claimants as a proportion of residents aged 16-64		
Area	Total	Male	Female	Total	Male	Female	Total	Male	Female	Total	Male	Female
Cambridge	720	485	235	0.8	1.0	0.6	**25**	**25**	**0**	**0.0**	**0.0**	**0.0**
East Cambridgeshire	290	175	115	0.5	0.7	0.4	**-50**	**-35**	**-15**	**-0.1**	**-0.1**	**-0.1**
Fenland	550	335	215	0.9	1.1	0.7	**-60**	**-10**	**-50**	**-0.1**	**-0.1**	**-0.2**
Huntingdonshire	660	400	265	0.6	0.7	0.5	**50**	**15**	**40**	**0.0**	**0.0**	**0.1**
South Cambridgeshire	430	280	150	0.5	0.6	0.3	**-30**	**10**	**-35**	**0.0**	**0.0**	**-0.1**
Essex	**11,520**	**6,995**	**4,525**	**1.3**	**1.6**	**1.0**	**-55**	**-130**	**75**	**0.0**	**0.0**	**0.0**
Basildon	1,930	1,140	795	1.7	2.0	1.4	**-50**	**-40**	**-5**	**0.0**	**-0.1**	**0.0**
Braintree	995	600	395	1.1	1.3	0.8	**-35**	**-20**	**-20**	**0.0**	**0.0**	**-0.1**
Brentwood	380	230	150	0.8	1.0	0.6	**65**	**50**	**20**	**0.1**	**0.2**	**0.0**
Castle Point	655	385	270	1.2	1.5	1.0	**-15**	**-15**	**0**	**-0.1**	**0.0**	**0.0**
Chelmsford	1,140	725	415	1.1	1.3	0.8	**40**	**55**	**-15**	**0.1**	**0.1**	**0.0**
Colchester	1,355	845	510	1.1	1.4	0.9	**-65**	**-55**	**-10**	**-0.1**	**-0.1**	**0.0**
Epping Forest	950	515	435	1.2	1.3	1.1	**30**	**15**	**15**	**0.0**	**0.0**	**0.1**
Harlow	950	570	385	1.8	2.1	1.4	**-5**	**-15**	**15**	**0.0**	**-0.1**	**0.0**
Maldon	310	185	125	0.8	1.0	0.7	**-30**	**-30**	**0**	**-0.1**	**-0.1**	**0.0**
Rochford	415	255	160	0.8	1.0	0.6	**-30**	**-40**	**10**	**-0.1**	**-0.2**	**0.0**
Tendring	2,185	1,390	795	2.8	3.7	2.0	**15**	**-45**	**60**	**0.0**	**-0.1**	**0.1**
Uttlesford	250	160	90	0.5	0.6	0.3	**15**	**10**	**5**	**0.1**	**0.0**	**0.0**
Hertfordshire	**7,665**	**4,695**	**2,970**	**1.0**	**1.3**	**0.8**	**185**	**220**	**-35**	**0.0**	**0.1**	**0.0**
Broxbourne	715	400	310	1.2	1.4	1.0	**20**	**30**	**-20**	**0.0**	**0.1**	**-0.1**
Dacorum	1,020	640	380	1.1	1.3	0.8	**20**	**50**	**-30**	**0.1**	**0.1**	**-0.1**
East Hertfordshire	625	400	220	0.7	0.9	0.5	**20**	**35**	**-15**	**0.0**	**0.1**	**0.0**
Hertsmere	760	455	305	1.2	1.5	0.9	**20**	**-5**	**25**	**0.0**	**0.0**	**0.0**
North Hertfordshire	895	530	365	1.1	1.3	0.9	**-10**	**-15**	**5**	**0.0**	**0.0**	**0.0**
St Albans	710	445	265	0.8	1.0	0.6	**135**	**95**	**40**	**0.2**	**0.2**	**0.1**
Stevenage	835	540	295	1.5	1.9	1.0	**5**	**40**	**-35**	**0.0**	**0.1**	**-0.2**
Three Rivers	495	315	180	0.9	1.1	0.6	**40**	**40**	**0**	**0.1**	**0.1**	**0.0**
Watford	785	470	315	1.2	1.5	1.0	**-5**	**-25**	**20**	**-0.1**	**-0.1**	**0.1**
Welwyn Hatfield	820	495	325	1.0	1.2	0.8	**-65**	**-35**	**-30**	**-0.1**	**-0.2**	**-0.1**
Norfolk	**7,130**	**4,570**	**2,560**	**1.3**	**1.7**	**1.0**	**675**	**220**	**455**	**0.1**	**0.0**	**0.2**
Breckland	835	530	305	1.0	1.3	0.8	**45**	**10**	**40**	**0.0**	**0.0**	**0.1**
Broadland	490	320	170	0.7	0.9	0.5	**45**	**30**	**15**	**0.1**	**0.1**	**0.1**
Great Yarmouth	2,350	1,485	865	4.0	5.1	3.0	**555**	**240**	**315**	**0.9**	**0.8**	**1.1**
King`s Lynn and West Norfolk	825	510	315	0.9	1.2	0.7	**-5**	**-20**	**20**	**0.0**	**0.0**	**0.0**
North Norfolk	515	345	165	0.9	1.3	0.6	**0**	**10**	**-15**	**0.0**	**0.1**	**0.0**
Norwich	1,560	1,035	525	1.6	2.2	1.1	**15**	**-50**	**65**	**0.0**	**-0.1**	**0.1**
South Norfolk	555	345	210	0.7	0.9	0.5	**20**	**5**	**15**	**0.0**	**0.0**	**0.0**
Suffolk	**5,790**	**3,710**	**2,080**	**1.3**	**1.7**	**0.9**	**665**	**365**	**300**	**0.2**	**0.2**	**0.1**
Babergh	400	240	160	0.8	0.9	0.6	**10**	**10**	**0**	**0.0**	**0.0**	**0.0**
Forest Heath	275	160	115	0.7	0.8	0.6	**-5**	**-15**	**5**	**0.0**	**-0.1**	**0.0**
Ipswich	1,700	1,150	550	1.9	2.6	1.3	**80**	**65**	**15**	**0.1**	**0.2**	**0.1**
Mid Suffolk	435	265	175	0.7	0.9	0.6	**15**	**25**	**-5**	**0.0**	**0.1**	**0.0**
St Edmundsbury	640	400	235	0.9	1.1	0.7	**5**	**-25**	**25**	**0.0**	**-0.1**	**0.1**
Suffolk Coastal	465	305	160	0.6	0.9	0.4	**45**	**30**	**15**	**0.0**	**0.1**	**0.0**
Waveney	1,875	1,195	685	2.8	3.7	2.0	**520**	**280**	**245**	**0.7**	**0.9**	**0.7**
London	**111,435**	**64,125**	**47,310**	**1.9**	**2.1**	**1.6**	**5,120**	**2,540**	**2,580**	**0.1**	**0.0**	**0.1**
Inner London	**50,965**	**29,775**	**21,190**	**2.0**	**2.3**	**1.7**	**755**	**335**	**420**	**0.0**	**0.0**	**0.0**
Camden	2,645	1,525	1,120	1.5	1.7	1.3	**50**	**-10**	**60**	**0.0**	**0.0**	**0.1**
City of London	55	35	20	1.1	1.2	1.0	**5**	**0**	**5**	**0.0**	**-0.3**	**0.3**
Hackney	4,645	2,735	1,910	2.4	2.8	1.9	**40**	**15**	**25**	**0.0**	**0.0**	**0.0**
Hammersmith and Fulham	3,085	1,760	1,320	2.4	2.7	2.0	**125**	**-45**	**165**	**0.2**	**0.0**	**0.3**
Haringey	4,535	2,705	1,830	2.4	2.8	1.9	**60**	**-25**	**90**	**0.0**	**-0.1**	**0.0**
Islington	3,615	2,125	1,490	2.1	2.4	1.7	**320**	**165**	**155**	**0.2**	**0.1**	**0.1**
Kensington and Chelsea	1,615	935	680	1.5	1.7	1.3	**20**	**20**	**0**	**0.1**	**0.0**	**0.1**
Lambeth	5,550	3,350	2,200	2.3	2.7	1.8	**-215**	**-60**	**-155**	**-0.1**	**-0.1**	**-0.2**
Lewisham	4,900	2,925	1,975	2.3	2.8	1.9	**-75**	**10**	**-85**	**-0.1**	**-0.1**	**-0.1**
Newham	4,530	2,555	1,975	1.9	1.9	1.8	**220**	**55**	**165**	**0.1**	**-0.1**	**0.1**
Southwark	5,490	3,135	2,355	2.4	2.7	2.1	**520**	**265**	**255**	**0.2**	**0.2**	**0.2**
Tower Hamlets	4,730	2,775	1,960	2.1	2.4	1.9	**-220**	**-50**	**-165**	**-0.2**	**-0.1**	**-0.2**
Wandsworth	3,125	1,835	1,285	1.3	1.6	1.1	**-85**	**-20**	**-65**	**-0.1**	**0.0**	**0.0**
Westminster	2,450	1,380	1,070	1.4	1.5	1.3	**-20**	**10**	**-30**	**0.0**	**0.0**	**-0.1**

4.10 Claimant count by Sex and Unitary and Local Authority

ONS Crown Copyright Reserved [from Nomis on 18 April 2019]

Age 16+

	Claimant Count December 2016						Change on year					
	Levels			Claimants as a proportion of residents aged 16-64			Levels			Claimants as a proportion of residents aged 16-64		
Area	Total	Male	Female	Total	Male	Female	Total	Male	Female	Total	Male	Female
Outer London	60,470	34,350	26,120	1.8	2.0	1.5	4,365	2,205	2,160	0.1	0.1	0.1
Barking and Dagenham	3,175	1,750	1,420	2.4	2.7	2.1	75	65	5	0.0	0.0	-0.1
Barnet	3,515	2,050	1,465	1.4	1.7	1.2	-90	-15	-75	-0.1	0.0	0.0
Bexley	2,025	1,100	925	1.3	1.5	1.2	215	105	110	0.1	0.2	0.2
Brent	5,065	3,130	1,935	2.3	2.8	1.8	-480	-190	-290	-0.2	-0.1	-0.3
Bromley	2,270	1,275	995	1.1	1.3	0.9	150	30	120	0.1	0.0	0.1
Croydon	6,560	3,675	2,885	2.6	3.1	2.3	1,830	880	950	0.7	0.8	0.8
Ealing	4,750	2,815	1,935	2.1	2.4	1.7	-140	-150	15	0.0	-0.1	0.0
Enfield	4,505	2,430	2,070	2.1	2.3	1.9	145	60	80	0.0	0.0	0.1
Greenwich	3,870	2,175	1,695	2.0	2.3	1.8	35	-15	55	-0.1	0.0	0.0
Harrow	1,840	1,035	805	1.2	1.3	1.0	15	20	-10	0.1	0.0	0.0
Havering	2,570	1,435	1,135	1.6	1.9	1.4	245	130	115	0.1	0.2	0.1
Hillingdon	2,580	1,455	1,125	1.3	1.5	1.2	70	40	30	0.0	0.1	0.1
Hounslow	3,880	2,120	1,760	2.2	2.3	2.0	1,060	440	620	0.6	0.5	0.7
Kingston upon Thames	1,190	710	485	1.0	1.2	0.8	105	95	15	0.1	0.1	0.0
Merton	2,175	1,230	945	1.6	1.8	1.4	200	105	100	0.2	0.2	0.2
Redbridge	2,740	1,535	1,205	1.4	1.6	1.2	50	55	-5	0.0	0.1	-0.1
Richmond upon Thames	1,400	820	580	1.1	1.3	0.9	200	115	85	0.1	0.1	0.1
Sutton	2,225	1,215	1,010	1.7	1.9	1.5	635	375	260	0.5	0.6	0.4
Waltham Forest	4,135	2,400	1,735	2.2	2.5	1.9	45	55	-15	0.0	0.0	0.0
South East	59,135	37,100	22,035	1.1	1.3	0.8	2,995	1,810	1,185	0.1	0.0	0.1
Bracknell Forest	570	335	235	0.7	0.9	0.6	-5	-10	10	0.0	0.0	0.0
Brighton and Hove	2,950	1,845	1,100	1.5	1.8	1.1	60	15	40	0.1	0.0	0.0
Isle of Wight	1,610	1,065	545	2.0	2.7	1.3	-90	-35	-60	-0.1	-0.1	-0.2
Medway	3,345	2,075	1,265	1.9	2.3	1.4	-120	-95	-30	-0.1	-0.2	-0.1
Milton Keynes	2,190	1,360	830	1.3	1.6	1.0	140	120	20	0.1	0.1	0.1
Portsmouth	1,990	1,290	695	1.4	1.7	1.0	0	-20	15	0.0	-0.1	0.0
Reading	1,585	980	610	1.4	1.7	1.1	175	90	90	0.1	0.1	0.1
Slough	1,295	755	540	1.4	1.6	1.1	35	15	20	0.1	0.1	0.0
Southampton	2,220	1,485	735	1.3	1.7	0.9	-105	-75	-30	-0.1	-0.1	0.0
West Berkshire	590	345	245	0.6	0.7	0.5	110	50	55	0.1	0.1	0.1
Windsor and Maidenhead	730	455	280	0.8	1.0	0.6	80	45	40	0.1	0.1	0.1
Wokingham	605	380	225	0.6	0.8	0.4	100	85	20	0.1	0.2	0.0
Buckinghamshire	2,620	1,640	985	0.8	1.0	0.6	295	225	75	0.1	0.1	0.0
Aylesbury Vale	880	530	350	0.7	0.9	0.6	190	125	65	0.1	0.2	0.1
Chiltern	360	220	140	0.7	0.8	0.5	95	55	35	0.2	0.2	0.1
South Bucks	300	185	115	0.7	0.9	0.5	45	40	5	0.1	0.2	0.0
Wycombe	1,080	705	375	1.0	1.3	0.7	-35	5	-40	0.0	0.0	-0.1
East Sussex	4,265	2,680	1,585	1.3	1.7	1.0	-150	-155	5	-0.1	-0.1	0.0
Eastbourne	1,045	645	395	1.7	2.2	1.3	-50	-55	-5	-0.1	-0.2	0.0
Hastings	1,415	915	500	2.5	3.2	1.7	-60	-55	0	-0.1	-0.2	0.0
Lewes	650	420	230	1.1	1.5	0.8	5	-15	20	0.0	0.0	0.1
Rother	600	375	225	1.2	1.5	0.9	-5	-5	0	0.0	-0.1	0.0
Wealden	555	320	235	0.6	0.7	0.5	-40	-30	-10	-0.1	-0.1	0.0
Hampshire	5,890	3,715	2,175	0.7	0.9	0.5	-145	-45	-100	0.0	0.0	0.0
Basingstoke and Deane	810	510	300	0.7	0.9	0.5	60	55	5	0.0	0.1	0.0
East Hampshire	400	250	150	0.6	0.7	0.4	-30	-5	-25	0.0	0.0	-0.1
Eastleigh	505	325	185	0.6	0.8	0.5	-10	-15	5	0.0	-0.1	0.1
Fareham	395	245	145	0.6	0.7	0.4	-35	-45	5	0.0	-0.1	0.0
Gosport	535	345	190	1.0	1.3	0.7	-45	-20	-25	-0.1	-0.1	-0.1
Hart	240	160	80	0.4	0.6	0.3	5	10	-5	0.0	0.1	0.0
Havant	1,035	640	395	1.4	1.8	1.0	-85	-70	-15	-0.1	-0.2	-0.1
New Forest	630	405	225	0.6	0.8	0.4	-25	10	-40	-0.1	0.0	-0.1
Rushmoor	535	345	190	0.8	1.1	0.6	-25	20	-40	-0.1	0.1	-0.1
Test Valley	425	260	165	0.6	0.7	0.4	15	5	15	0.0	0.0	0.0
Winchester	375	225	150	0.5	0.6	0.4	20	5	15	0.0	0.0	0.0
Kent	14,785	9,275	5,510	1.6	2.0	1.2	1,435	820	615	0.2	0.2	0.2
Ashford	1,125	720	405	1.5	1.9	1.0	125	90	35	0.2	0.2	0.0
Canterbury	1,330	825	500	1.3	1.6	1.0	260	130	130	0.3	0.2	0.3
Dartford	740	415	325	1.1	1.2	1.0	70	55	15	0.1	0.1	0.1
Dover	1,400	925	475	2.0	2.7	1.4	155	95	60	0.2	0.2	0.2

4.10 Claimant count by Sex and Unitary and Local Authority

ONS Crown Copyright Reserved [from Nomis on 18 April 2019]
Age 16+

	Claimant Count December 2016						Change on year					
	Levels			Claimants as a proportion of residents aged 16-64			Levels			Claimants as a proportion of residents aged 16-64		
Area	**Total**	**Male**	**Female**	**Total**	**Male**	**Female**	**Total**	**Male**	**Female**	**Total**	**Male**	**Female**
Gravesham	1,240	780	460	1.9	2.4	1.4	5	0	5	0.0	0.0	0.0
Maidstone	1,185	705	485	1.2	1.4	0.9	115	55	65	0.1	0.1	0.1
Sevenoaks	510	315	195	0.7	0.9	0.5	-5	0	0	0.0	0.0	0.0
Shepway	1,355	875	475	2.1	2.7	1.5	70	30	35	0.1	0.1	0.1
Swale	1,915	1,145	770	2.2	2.6	1.7	145	55	90	0.2	0.1	0.2
Thanet	2,735	1,780	960	3.3	4.5	2.3	385	230	160	0.4	0.6	0.4
Tonbridge and Malling	730	465	265	0.9	1.2	0.7	50	45	5	0.0	0.1	0.0
Tunbridge Wells	520	325	195	0.7	0.9	0.5	55	35	20	0.1	0.1	0.0
Oxfordshire	**2,645**	**1,670**	**980**	**0.6**	**0.8**	**0.5**	145	105	45	0.0	0.1	0.1
Cherwell	500	315	180	0.5	0.7	0.4	60	60	-5	0.0	0.1	0.0
Oxford	980	650	330	0.9	1.1	0.6	60	30	30	0.1	0.0	0.0
South Oxfordshire	400	235	165	0.5	0.6	0.4	35	25	10	0.1	0.1	0.0
Vale of White Horse	415	260	160	0.5	0.7	0.4	10	10	5	0.0	0.1	0.0
West Oxfordshire	350	205	145	0.5	0.6	0.4	-20	-20	0	-0.1	-0.1	0.0
Surrey	**4,495**	**2,775**	**1,720**	**0.6**	**0.8**	**0.5**	575	380	195	0.1	0.1	0.1
Elmbridge	415	260	160	0.5	0.6	0.4	70	35	40	0.1	0.0	0.1
Epsom and Ewell	320	190	130	0.7	0.8	0.5	65	25	40	0.2	0.1	0.1
Guildford	535	330	200	0.6	0.7	0.4	40	10	25	0.1	0.0	0.0
Mole Valley	260	175	80	0.5	0.7	0.3	10	20	-15	0.0	0.1	-0.1
Reigate and Banstead	655	405	250	0.7	0.9	0.6	30	30	0	0.0	0.1	0.0
Runnymede	330	210	120	0.6	0.8	0.4	30	35	-5	0.1	0.2	0.0
Spelthorne	560	320	240	0.9	1.0	0.8	110	80	30	0.2	0.2	0.1
Surrey Heath	310	195	115	0.6	0.7	0.4	105	65	40	0.2	0.2	0.1
Tandridge	365	200	165	0.7	0.8	0.6	35	10	25	0.1	0.1	0.1
Waverley	345	230	115	0.5	0.6	0.3	10	20	-10	0.0	0.0	0.0
Woking	395	255	140	0.6	0.8	0.5	55	40	10	0.1	0.1	0.1
West Sussex	**4,755**	**2,985**	**1,770**	**0.9**	**1.2**	**0.7**	460	305	155	0.0	0.1	0.1
Adur	440	270	170	1.2	1.5	0.9	10	10	5	0.1	0.1	0.0
Arun	985	610	375	1.1	1.4	0.8	90	40	45	0.1	0.1	0.1
Chichester	645	410	235	0.9	1.2	0.7	80	65	15	0.1	0.2	0.1
Crawley	930	550	375	1.3	1.5	1.0	50	15	25	0.1	0.0	0.0
Horsham	535	355	180	0.6	0.9	0.4	80	55	25	0.0	0.1	0.0
Mid Sussex	430	270	155	0.5	0.6	0.3	50	45	-5	0.1	0.1	-0.1
Worthing	800	520	280	1.2	1.6	0.8	115	75	40	0.2	0.2	0.1
South West	**40,220**	**25,580**	**14,640**	**1.2**	**1.5**	**0.9**	3,020	1,440	1,580	0.1	0.1	0.1
Bath and North East Somerset	**1,410**	**875**	**535**	**1.2**	**1.5**	**0.9**	400	210	190	0.3	0.4	0.3
Bournemouth, Christchurch and Poole	**3,220**	**2,080**	**1,140**	**1.3**	**1.7**	**1.0**	370	235	135	0.1	0.2	0.2
Bristol, City of	**5,105**	**3,275**	**1,830**	**1.6**	**2.1**	**1.2**	320	120	200	0.0	0.1	0.1
Cornwall	**4,785**	**3,050**	**1,730**	**1.5**	**1.9**	**1.0**	365	170	195	0.1	0.1	0.1
Isles of Scilly	**5**	**5**	**0**	**0.5**	**0.8**	**#**	0	0	0	0.0	0.1	#
North Somerset	**1,225**	**775**	**450**	**1.0**	**1.3**	**0.7**	30	-10	40	0.0	0.0	0.0
Plymouth	**3,475**	**2,285**	**1,190**	**2.1**	**2.7**	**1.4**	320	150	170	0.2	0.2	0.2
South Gloucestershire	**1,485**	**900**	**580**	**0.9**	**1.0**	**0.7**	35	0	30	0.1	0.0	0.1
Swindon	**1,640**	**980**	**660**	**1.2**	**1.4**	**0.9**	-130	-90	-40	-0.1	-0.1	-0.1
Torbay	**1,500**	**1,045**	**460**	**1.9**	**2.7**	**1.2**	-15	20	-30	-0.1	0.0	0.0
Wiltshire	**2,525**	**1,575**	**950**	**0.8**	**1.1**	**0.6**	205	120	85	0.0	0.1	0.0
Devon	**4,190**	**2,640**	**1,550**	**0.9**	**1.2**	**0.7**	330	190	140	0.1	0.1	0.1
East Devon	635	395	245	0.8	1.1	0.6	35	35	5	0.0	0.1	0.0
Exeter	865	550	315	1.0	1.2	0.7	155	85	70	0.2	0.1	0.1
Mid Devon	425	255	170	0.9	1.1	0.7	80	45	35	0.2	0.2	0.1
North Devon	520	335	185	1.0	1.2	0.7	-20	-15	-5	0.0	-0.1	0.0
South Hams	315	200	115	0.7	0.8	0.5	-5	-5	0	0.0	-0.1	0.0
Teignbridge	670	405	265	0.9	1.1	0.7	50	20	30	0.1	0.1	0.1
Torridge	495	340	160	1.3	1.8	0.8	-30	-15	-10	-0.1	-0.1	-0.1
West Devon	260	165	95	0.8	1.1	0.6	55	45	10	0.2	0.3	0.1
Dorset	**1,735**	**1,110**	**630**	**0.8**	**1.1**	**0.6**	65	20	50	0.0	0.1	0.0
Christchurch	250	150	100	0.9	1.1	0.7	30	10	20	0.1	0.0	0.1
East Dorset	300	200	105	0.6	0.9	0.4	25	25	5	0.0	0.1	0.0
North Dorset	245	135	110	0.6	0.6	0.5	20	-15	40	0.1	-0.1	0.1
Purbeck	185	115	75	0.7	0.9	0.6	10	-5	20	0.0	0.0	0.2
West Dorset	390	255	135	0.7	0.9	0.5	40	45	-5	0.1	0.1	0.0
Weymouth and Portland	610	405	205	1.6	2.1	1.1	-35	-25	-10	-0.1	-0.1	0.0

4.10 Claimant count by Sex and Unitary and Local Authority

ONS Crown Copyright Reserved [from Nomis on 18 April 2019]

Age 16+

	Claimant Count December 2016						Change on year					
	Levels			Claimants as a proportion of residents aged 16-64			Levels			Claimants as a proportion of residents aged 16-64		
Area	**Total**	**Male**	**Female**	**Total**	**Male**	**Female**	**Total**	**Male**	**Female**	**Total**	**Male**	**Female**
Gloucestershire	**3,950**	**2,530**	**1,415**	**1.0**	**1.3**	**0.7**	**80**	**-50**	**125**	**0.0**	**-0.1**	**0.0**
Cheltenham	750	490	260	1.0	1.3	0.7	35	0	30	0.0	0.0	0.1
Cotswold	315	190	125	0.6	0.8	0.5	10	-10	20	0.0	0.0	0.1
Forest of Dean	585	380	205	1.1	1.5	0.8	-55	-45	-15	-0.2	-0.2	0.0
Gloucester	1,315	845	465	1.6	2.1	1.1	100	30	65	0.1	0.1	0.1
Stroud	490	325	165	0.7	0.9	0.5	-20	-15	-5	0.0	-0.1	0.0
Tewkesbury	495	300	195	0.9	1.1	0.7	15	-15	30	0.0	-0.1	0.1
Somerset	**3,965**	**2,455**	**1,510**	**1.2**	**1.5**	**0.9**	**635**	**350**	**285**	**0.2**	**0.2**	**0.1**
Mendip	805	490	315	1.2	1.5	0.9	230	130	105	0.3	0.4	0.3
Sedgemoor	1,380	830	550	1.9	2.3	1.5	315	185	130	0.4	0.5	0.3
South Somerset	835	525	305	0.9	1.1	0.6	60	35	20	0.1	0.1	0.0
Taunton Deane	785	505	280	1.1	1.5	0.8	40	10	30	0.0	0.0	0.1
West Somerset	160	105	55	0.9	1.2	0.6	-10	-5	-5	0.0	0.0	0.0
Wales	**39,600**	**25,250**	**14,350**	**2.1**	**2.6**	**1.5**	**-2,410**	**-1,655**	**-755**	**-0.1**	**-0.2**	**-0.1**
Anglesey, Isle of	1,115	740	375	2.8	3.7	1.9	-135	-105	-30	-0.3	-0.4	-0.1
Gwynedd	1,440	970	470	1.9	2.6	1.3	-55	-30	-20	-0.1	-0.1	0.0
Conwy	1,435	945	485	2.2	2.9	1.4	-80	-65	-20	-0.1	-0.2	-0.1
Denbighshire	1,185	775	410	2.1	2.8	1.5	-125	-85	-35	-0.3	-0.3	-0.1
Flintshire	1,480	915	565	1.6	2.0	1.2	-30	-20	-5	0.0	0.0	0.0
Wrexham	1,465	930	535	1.8	2.2	1.3	-215	-140	-75	-0.2	-0.4	-0.2
Powys	795	525	270	1.0	1.4	0.7	-20	-15	-5	-0.1	0.0	0.0
Ceredigion	520	335	190	1.2	1.4	0.9	-25	-15	-5	0.0	-0.1	0.0
Pembrokeshire	1,665	1,100	565	2.3	3.1	1.6	-65	-80	15	-0.1	-0.2	0.1
Carmarthenshire	1,995	1,255	740	1.8	2.3	1.3	90	60	30	0.1	0.1	0.0
Swansea	3,105	2,065	1,045	2.0	2.6	1.4	-70	-5	-60	-0.1	0.0	-0.1
Neath Port Talbot	1,985	1,240	745	2.3	2.8	1.7	5	15	-10	0.0	0.0	0.0
Bridgend	1,840	1,130	710	2.1	2.5	1.6	45	5	40	0.1	0.0	0.1
Vale of Glamorgan	1,345	885	460	1.7	2.3	1.2	-85	-45	-40	-0.1	-0.1	-0.1
Cardiff	4,975	3,290	1,680	2.0	2.7	1.4	-435	-260	-180	-0.2	-0.2	-0.1
Rhondda Cynon Taff	3,250	1,985	1,265	2.2	2.7	1.7	-255	-210	-45	-0.2	-0.3	0.0
Merthyr Tydfil	965	575	385	2.6	3.1	2.0	-35	-55	15	-0.1	-0.3	0.1
Caerphilly	3,050	1,835	1,215	2.7	3.3	2.1	-500	-325	-170	-0.5	-0.6	-0.3
Blaenau Gwent	1,510	935	575	3.4	4.3	2.6	-120	-60	-60	-0.3	-0.3	-0.3
Torfaen	1,200	750	450	2.1	2.7	1.6	-250	-180	-65	-0.4	-0.6	-0.2
Monmouthshire	610	390	220	1.1	1.4	0.8	-15	10	-25	0.0	0.0	-0.1
Newport	2,665	1,680	985	2.9	3.6	2.1	-45	-40	-5	0.0	-0.2	0.0
Scotland	**74,915**	**50,880**	**24,035**	**2.1**	**3.0**	**1.4**	**3,750**	**1,545**	**2,200**	**0.1**	**0.1**	**0.2**
Aberdeen City	3,420	2,425	995	2.1	3.0	1.3	895	565	330	0.5	0.7	0.5
Aberdeenshire	2,365	1,615	750	1.4	1.9	0.9	605	360	245	0.3	0.4	0.3
Angus	1,405	970	435	2.0	2.8	1.2	175	115	55	0.3	0.4	0.2
Argyll and Bute	855	590	265	1.6	2.2	1.0	-20	-25	5	-0.1	-0.1	0.0
Clackmannanshire	840	560	285	2.6	3.5	1.7	60	15	50	0.2	0.1	0.3
Dumfries and Galloway	1,455	920	535	1.6	2.1	1.2	-80	-115	40	-0.1	-0.3	0.1
Dundee City	3,215	2,320	895	3.3	4.8	1.8	325	210	115	0.4	0.4	0.3
East Ayrshire	2,510	1,715	795	3.3	4.6	2.0	-30	-70	40	0.0	-0.1	0.1
East Dunbartonshire	725	485	240	1.1	1.5	0.7	55	10	40	0.1	0.0	0.1
East Lothian	1,270	775	495	2.0	2.5	1.5	270	140	130	0.4	0.4	0.4
East Renfrewshire	685	460	225	1.2	1.7	0.8	125	80	45	0.2	0.3	0.2
Edinburgh, City of	4,930	3,280	1,650	1.4	1.9	0.9	-135	-170	35	-0.1	-0.1	0.0
Na h-Eileanan Siar	305	235	70	1.9	2.9	0.9	-25	-15	-10	-0.2	-0.2	-0.1
Falkirk	2,190	1,465	730	2.2	2.9	1.4	125	45	80	0.2	0.1	0.1
Fife	5,445	3,715	1,725	2.3	3.3	1.5	515	290	220	0.2	0.3	0.2
Glasgow City	13,145	9,015	4,130	3.0	4.2	1.9	475	185	290	0.0	0.0	0.1
Highland	2,465	1,660	805	1.7	2.3	1.1	235	80	155	0.2	0.1	0.2
Inverclyde	1,215	840	375	2.4	3.5	1.5	-75	-65	-10	-0.1	-0.2	0.0
Midlothian	860	580	280	1.6	2.2	1.0	-35	-40	5	0.0	-0.1	0.0
Moray	960	675	285	1.6	2.2	1.0	210	140	70	0.3	0.4	0.3
North Ayrshire	3,295	2,135	1,160	3.9	5.4	2.7	-85	-125	45	-0.1	-0.2	0.2
North Lanarkshire	5,610	3,740	1,875	2.6	3.5	1.7	-160	-160	5	0.0	-0.1	0.0
Orkney Islands	130	90	40	1.0	1.3	0.6	45	25	15	0.4	0.4	0.3
Perth and Kinross	995	690	305	1.1	1.5	0.7	40	30	10	0.1	0.1	0.1
Renfrewshire	2,700	1,885	815	2.4	3.4	1.4	-5	-25	20	0.0	-0.1	0.0

4.10 Claimant count by Sex and Unitary and Local Authority

ONS Crown Copyright Reserved [from Nomis on 18 April 2019]

Age 16+

	Claimant Count December 2016						Change on year					
	Levels			Claimants as a proportion of residents aged 16-64			Levels			Claimants as a proportion of residents aged 16-64		
Area	**Total**	**Male**	**Female**	**Total**	**Male**	**Female**	**Total**	**Male**	**Female**	**Total**	**Male**	**Female**
Scottish Borders	1,080	725	355	1.6	2.2	1.0	**10**	**10**	**0**	**0.0**	**0.1**	**0.0**
Shetland Islands	120	95	25	0.8	1.3	0.4	**-5**	**5**	**-10**	**-0.1**	**0.1**	**-0.1**
South Ayrshire	1,685	1,145	540	2.5	3.5	1.5	**5**	**-15**	**20**	**0.0**	**-0.1**	**0.0**
South Lanarkshire	4,255	2,890	1,370	2.1	2.9	1.3	**180**	**110**	**75**	**0.1**	**0.1**	**0.1**
Stirling	945	605	340	1.6	2.1	1.1	**100**	**55**	**45**	**0.2**	**0.2**	**0.2**
West Dunbartonshire	1,960	1,340	615	3.4	4.8	2.0	**-165**	**-180**	**10**	**-0.3**	**-0.7**	**0.0**
West Lothian	1,875	1,250	630	1.6	2.2	1.1	**125**	**95**	**30**	**0.1**	**0.2**	**0.1**
Northern Ireland	**31,995**	**22,220**	**9,775**	**2.7**	**3.8**	**1.6**	**-6,250**	**-4,665**	**-1,590**	**-0.6**	**-0.8**	**-0.3**
Antrim and Newtownabbey	1,910	1,335	570	2.2	3.1	1.3	**-205**	**-195**	**-15**	**-0.2**	**-0.4**	**0.0**
Armagh City, Banbridge and Craigavon	2,560	1,700	860	1.9	2.6	1.3	**-770**	**-565**	**-205**	**-0.6**	**-0.9**	**-0.3**
Belfast	8,105	5,925	2,180	3.6	5.4	1.9	**-1,315**	**-1,020**	**-295**	**-0.6**	**-1.0**	**-0.3**
Causeway Coast and Glens	2,705	1,830	880	3.0	4.1	2.0	**-560**	**-425**	**-130**	**-0.6**	**-0.9**	**-0.2**
Derry City and Strabane	5,070	3,460	1,605	5.3	7.4	3.3	**-965**	**-720**	**-250**	**-1.0**	**-1.5**	**-0.5**
Fermanagh and Omagh	1,695	1,115	575	2.3	3.1	1.6	**-495**	**-365**	**-135**	**-0.7**	**-1.0**	**-0.4**
Lisburn and Castlereagh	1,490	1,035	455	1.7	2.4	1.0	**-290**	**-170**	**-125**	**-0.3**	**-0.4**	**-0.3**
Mid and East Antrim	2,165	1,505	660	2.5	3.5	1.5	**-75**	**-75**	**0**	**-0.1**	**-0.2**	**0.0**
Mid Ulster	1,465	920	545	1.6	2.0	1.2	**-420**	**-290**	**-130**	**-0.5**	**-0.6**	**-0.3**
Newry, Mourne and Down	2,520	1,745	775	2.3	3.2	1.4	**-800**	**-575**	**-220**	**-0.7**	**-1.0**	**-0.4**
Ards and North Down	2,315	1,650	665	2.4	3.5	1.3	**-355**	**-265**	**-85**	**-0.3**	**-0.5**	**-0.2**

Source: ONS Labour Market Statistics; Nomisweb

These figures are suppressed as value is 1 or 2.

Under Universal Credit a broader span of claimants are required to look for work than under Jobseeker's Allowance. As Universal Credit Full Service is rolled out in particular areas, the number of people recorded as being on the Claimant Count is therefore likely to rise.

This dataset only includes claimant records with information to sufficiently classify them within the dataset. Totals from this dataset may not tally with the total number of claim records shown elsewhere as a small number of records do not have this information.

All data are rounded to the nearest 5 and may not precisely add to the sum of the number of people claiming JSA, published on Nomis, and the number of people claiming Universal Credit required to seek work, published by DWP, due to independent rounding.

4.11a Weekly pay - Gross (£) - For all employee jobs[a]: United Kingdom, 2016

Description	Code	Number of jobs[b] (000's)	Median	Annual % change	Mean	Annual % change	Percentiles 10	20	25	30	40	60	70	75	80	90
ALL EMPLOYEES		25,758	438.4	3.1	525.0	3.5	141.2	231.2	275.9	307.9	371.1	516.1	611.1	670.8	736.7	953.5
All Industries and Services		25,752	438.4	3.1	525.1	3.5	141.3	231.2	276.0	307.9	371.2	516.2	611.2	670.8	736.7	953.5
All Index of Production Industries		2,800	545.2	2.4	632.2	4.0	294.7	360.0	387.8	418.4	479.0	621.7	713.2	765.0	828.5	1,046.0
All Manufacturing		2,439	532.6	2.5	617.1	4.5	290.3	353.3	381.0	408.2	467.6	607.6	695.0	747.3	808.0	1,012.1
All Service Industries		21,915	420.0	4.1	508.5	3.4	128.5	212.7	254.3	289.8	351.5	495.0	589.7	650.6	721.1	932.9
AGRICULTURE, FORESTRY AND FISHING	A	133	371.5	3.8	404.2	3.4	146.1	224.7	265.5	296.9	337.4	413.3	473.4	499.9	539.5	659.6
Crop and animal production, hunting and related service activities	1	119	364.8	4.4	384.4	1.9	143.9	218.2	254.2	291.9	330.7	402.4	460.0	484.8	522.7	635.6
Forestry and logging	2	9	474.3	7.8	548.2	8.2	x	325.0	352.7	373.6	430.8	521.6	x	x	x	x
Fishing and aquaculture	3	x	x		634.9		x	x	x	x	x	x	x	x	x	x
MINING AND QUARRYING	B	44	704.8	-2.1	845.0	-3.7	418.6	520.3	545.8	578.6	649.1	759.7	876.5	971.5	x	x
Mining of coal and lignite	5	x	x		841.1		x	x	x	x	x	732.8	x	x	x	x
Extraction of crude petroleum and natural gas	6	6	x		1,368.5	-4.5	x	722.3	x	843.0	961.8	x	x	x	x	x
Mining of metal ores	7	..														
Other mining and quarrying	8	22	636.8	2.4	684.3	2.0	388.6	497.6	521.8	543.7	591.4	688.4	737.2	769.2	799.4	x
Mining support service activities	9	13	732.5	-7.2	875.2	-4.6	429.8	519.6	544.7	580.6	643.2	784.9	1,005.2	x	x	x
MANUFACTURING	C	2,439	532.6	2.5	617.1	4.5	290.3	353.3	381.0	408.2	467.6	607.6	695.0	747.3	808.0	1,012.1
Manufacture of food products	10	375	419.4	4.1	504.0	3.1	250.1	299.8	316.8	336.0	371.4	478.2	557.8	603.7	655.6	841.5
Manufacture of beverages	11	44	615.1	0.4	723.4	2.6	287.1	412.1	445.6	490.0	547.2	713.5	805.7	879.6	945.9	x
Manufacture of tobacco products	12	:														
Manufacture of textiles	13	45	394.7	4.5	479.4	3.7	227.5	280.8	289.8	318.6	352.6	445.5	502.4	545.1	603.7	x
Manufacture of wearing apparel	14	16	280.7	3.6	358.1	-0.7	148.9	172.6	195.2	216.0	258.8	307.0	375.8	x	x	x
Manufacture of leather and related products	15	9	350.4	-1.8	393.4	6.8	x	277.1	285.0	301.1	325.4	391.2	441.8	x	x	x
Manufacture of wood and of products of wood and cork, except furniture; manufacture of articles of straw and plaiting materials	16	59	458.7	6.8	497.1	6.5	270.6	332.0	348.0	371.0	408.2	495.4	571.7	613.3	646.8	x
Manufacture of paper and paper products	17	58	537.7	3.3	616.7	8.8	315.8	372.3	402.4	429.5	481.7	596.9	674.9	709.8	765.2	x
Printing and reproduction of recorded media	18	102	472.2	1.5	562.4	4.1	258.3	332.5	359.4	384.4	432.6	519.7	589.4	651.6	707.5	x
Manufacture of coke and refined petroleum products	19	10	962.9	3.8	1,000.8	1.2	479.2	656.4	764.8	804.5	884.6	1,029.5	1,160.5	x	x	x
Manufacture of chemicals and chemical products	20	85	605.4	2.2	680.3	3.2	315.6	382.9	416.9	456.1	518.2	667.5	766.7	816.5	896.4	1,148.7
Manufacture of basic pharmaceutical products and pharmaceutical preparations	21	50	690.7	9.9	986.8	31.5	371.4	459.6	492.7	537.1	605.4	791.3	887.3	1,033.1	1,133.0	x
Manufacture of rubber and plastic products	22	152	460.0	2.6	547.3	1.8	288.0	331.5	352.0	372.4	418.9	520.6	583.8	628.3	674.8	842.4
Manufacture of other non-metallic mineral products	23	76	516.7	-0.1	563.0	0.0	291.2	355.6	390.4	421.0	466.3	580.1	636.6	673.0	722.1	x
Manufacture of basic metals	24	81	659.7	1.2	687.0	2.8	354.5	455.3	493.1	526.1	603.7	726.4	784.8	834.9	896.4	979.5
Manufacture of fabricated metal products, except machinery and equipment	25	278	502.3	0.6	568.7	4.3	280.8	351.0	378.9	403.6	450.9	574.2	637.5	681.7	734.9	916.7
Manufacture of computer, electronic and optical products	26	132	613.3	3.5	687.6	2.7	324.7	389.1	415.9	454.3	527.9	698.6	781.9	834.4	906.8	1,124.5
Manufacture of electrical equipment	27	97	517.8	1.8	617.5	6.9	297.4	345.6	378.7	412.1	465.4	590.0	677.2	734.5	815.5	x
Manufacture of machinery and equipment n.e.c.	28	193	584.6	3.4	644.5	2.0	339.4	402.4	432.6	457.3	516.7	651.5	721.1	766.1	807.0	996.4
Manufacture of motor vehicles, trailers and semi-trailers	29	193	665.9	6.0	741.5	6.3	369.6	440.6	479.9	521.6	587.0	738.1	831.6	901.7	978.1	1,191.1
Manufacture of other transport equipment	30	166	733.6	4.0	781.6	3.7	440.7	530.8	572.4	601.5	673.0	802.6	877.7	915.2	962.5	1,158.5
Manufacture of furniture	31	66	410.9	3.3	495.3	11.2	263.7	312.1	329.4	344.7	382.3	470.0	536.7	582.6	624.9	x
Other manufacturing	32	68	442.5	-2.2	521.2	3.1	228.1	304.9	328.3	355.5	401.2	498.3	591.2	632.4	692.1	x
Repair and installation of machinery and equipment	33	86	590.8	-4.4	693.1	1.0	307.8	397.9	436.3	466.1	515.0	666.5	770.9	828.2	916.8	x
ELECTRICITY, GAS, STEAM AND AIR CONDITIONING SUPPLY	D	168	713.1	3.1	801.0	3.3	364.6	448.6	495.7	542.9	620.2	815.3	936.5	1,000.0	1,085.9	1,344.0
Electricity, gas, steam and air conditioning supply	35	168	713.1	3.1	801.0	3.3	364.6	448.6	495.7	542.9	620.2	815.3	936.5	1,000.0	1,085.9	1,344.0
WATER SUPPLY; SEWERAGE, WASTE MANAGEMENT AND REMEDIATION ACTIVITIES	E	148	555.6	4.3	625.5	2.0	307.7	387.4	412.1	440.3	495.6	618.4	686.2	737.5	778.9	956.4
Water collection, treatment and supply	36	43	603.3	-0.8	675.2	0.1	388.6	446.6	471.6	486.4	558.7	658.7	742.2	779.6	812.5	x
Sewerage	37	13	605.8	7.7	631.2	0.8	329.3	413.6	442.9	496.6	527.0	652.1	716.5	737.6	x	x

4.11a Weekly pay - Gross (£) - For all employee jobs[a]: United Kingdom, 2016

Description	Code	Number of jobs[b] (000's)	Median	Annual % change	Mean	Annual % change	Percentiles 10	20	25	30	40	60	70	75	80	90
Waste collection, treatment and disposal activities; materials recovery	38	89	523.0	5.1	605.1	3.9	293.6	355.9	384.2	409.3	453.9	590.9	657.9	702.1	758.0	x
Remediation activities and other waste management services	39	x	x		514.8	-7.5	x	x	x	x	x	x	x	x	x	x
CONSTRUCTION	F	905	542.8	2.6	612.5	3.4	225.7	351.1	394.1	424.7	485.2	611.4	694.2	755.7	824.1	1,041.3
Construction of buildings	41	272	566.7	5.9	671.2	6.4	253.3	380.1	417.2	441.9	500.0	651.5	766.2	842.8	927.4	1,188.6
Civil engineering	42	170	587.8	0.4	663.8	1.6	288.0	392.2	421.6	460.0	525.8	661.3	767.8	820.0	877.7	1,079.8
Specialised construction activities	43	463	517.3	2.0	559.2	2.4	204.7	330.5	364.1	400.0	460.0	576.9	650.0	690.1	748.8	919.9
WHOLESALE AND RETAIL TRADE; REPAIR OF MOTOR VEHICLES AND MOTORCYCLES	G	3,715	340.0	6.1	416.4	5.3	113.7	166.1	197.3	230.0	292.0	395.3	471.7	517.4	574.9	771.0
Wholesale and retail trade and repair of motor vehicles and motorcycles	45	461	433.8	4.7	480.5	3.2	198.7	292.1	316.0	337.6	383.3	482.2	538.2	571.7	609.0	753.8
Wholesale trade, except of motor vehicles and motorcycles	46	1,033	470.1	2.2	580.9	4.6	248.5	321.1	345.0	365.8	415.0	536.9	625.9	685.3	766.5	1,002.1
Retail trade, except of motor vehicles and motorcycles	47	2,221	267.4	9.1	326.7	5.5	88.9	128.4	147.4	167.9	215.0	309.4	359.8	397.5	448.5	616.8
TRANSPORTATION AND STORAGE	H	1,104	529.7	1.8	596.9	0.1	288.4	368.1	400.0	420.9	473.9	590.7	664.4	711.8	775.3	960.6
Land transport and transport via pipelines	49	489	538.4	1.5	573.5	0.8	264.3	367.3	400.0	427.2	479.7	592.5	659.7	705.8	765.2	927.2
Water transport	50	13	526.0	-0.3	601.1	1.7	230.3	304.0	369.6	406.6	463.7	579.7	652.6	x	x	x
Air transport	51	75	607.9	-2.8	754.6	-8.8	316.1	375.7	405.1	445.1	528.1	729.1	826.8	895.6	992.2	x
Warehousing and support activities for transportation	52	331	567.1	4.6	649.5	2.0	309.5	381.0	408.3	436.4	496.5	632.4	711.8	771.5	841.6	1,099.2
Postal and courier activities	53	197	466.9	-0.7	506.7	-1.1	273.7	353.0	383.3	402.5	425.7	506.0	558.1	591.9	632.9	747.8
ACCOMMODATION AND FOOD SERVICE ACTIVITIES	I	1,437	232.7	8.9	267.6	6.1	60.0	104.8	120.0	143.5	181.3	283.6	330.5	357.5	389.2	486.6
Accommodation	55	298	296.1	10.3	319.6	5.7	86.1	147.8	174.6	202.3	264.3	331.5	371.4	402.5	432.2	546.3
Food and beverage service activities	56	1,139	214.1	9.7	254.0	6.7	56.1	97.4	114.8	130.0	170.1	264.0	314.4	345.0	376.3	476.0
INFORMATION AND COMMUNICATION	J	1,019	670.8	3.4	772.1	3.7	304.0	412.0	456.1	493.5	574.9	768.7	885.6	962.9	1,057.9	1,341.6
Publishing activities	58	132	560.7	3.4	661.1	3.5	256.6	373.7	402.5	439.6	483.0	658.4	762.5	816.7	873.3	x
Motion picture, video and television programme production, sound recording and music publishing activities	59	49	497.1	3.4	626.8	9.4	133.6	227.3	298.0	351.4	423.5	580.0	742.7	815.7	925.6	x
Programming and broadcasting activities	60	47	783.0	6.7	888.0	5.8	423.4	538.6	575.8	619.7	710.0	873.0	982.5	1,046.6	1,147.7	x
Telecommunications	61	228	670.8	1.6	760.3	1.9	342.1	449.9	491.0	533.2	586.2	750.3	842.6	901.3	1,008.1	1,245.7
Computer programming, consultancy and related activities	62	494	696.7	3.5	804.4	3.2	294.9	414.0	460.0	503.1	592.8	804.9	938.4	1,028.0	1,127.5	1,422.5
Information service activities	63	69	724.8	3.6	817.9	2.1	341.1	434.1	470.9	501.3	634.3	855.8	975.4	1,044.1	1,159.0	x
FINANCIAL AND INSURANCE ACTIVITIES	K	937	632.7	0.6	871.6	0.2	298.3	372.2	407.8	448.5	534.1	772.3	958.2	1,072.6	1,226.0	1,724.9
Financial service activities, except insurance and pension funding	64	501	656.7	-2.4	911.5	-1.3	301.5	376.6	413.3	452.0	545.1	814.3	1,008.9	1,132.5	1,301.0	1,782.3
Insurance, reinsurance and pension funding, except compulsory social security	65	104	629.6	3.9	764.4	-0.3	334.9	382.7	418.6	458.9	536.6	730.4	840.3	915.4	1,024.4	1,370.9
Activities auxiliary to financial services and insurance activities	66	332	606.1	2.2	844.6	1.7	286.0	357.5	394.9	440.8	511.7	733.9	911.9	1,044.7	1,169.1	1,724.9
REAL ESTATE ACTIVITIES	L	348	461.1	2.3	529.9	2.3	167.6	287.5	321.2	347.8	406.7	515.0	579.8	634.7	691.6	919.1
Real estate activities	68	348	461.1	2.3	529.9	2.3	167.6	287.5	321.2	347.8	406.7	515.0	579.8	634.7	691.6	919.1
PROFESSIONAL, SCIENTIFIC AND TECHNICAL ACTIVITIES	M	1,751	574.9	3.9	690.1	3.4	210.8	330.4	368.6	408.6	487.7	670.4	781.4	862.4	958.2	1,274.5
Legal and accounting activities	69	492	517.5	1.9	652.1	2.0	210.8	306.6	335.4	366.4	437.0	613.3	747.4	822.7	916.6	1,274.5
Activities of head offices; management consultancy activities	70	429	551.9	6.7	729.8	5.5	191.6	310.5	345.5	383.3	460.0	655.5	799.2	878.1	1,017.3	1,405.8
Architectural and engineering activities; technical testing and analysis	71	408	632.4	3.1	712.8	1.7	287.5	402.5	456.6	490.1	560.7	724.4	819.5	891.7	969.9	1,193.8
Scientific research and development	72	126	723.2	-0.5	824.5	-0.8	383.3	501.1	539.3	570.2	642.2	789.1	910.7	998.3	1,111.4	1,363.4
Advertising and market research	73	132	584.8	6.8	697.5	9.2	210.8	356.7	402.5	440.8	522.8	670.8	768.6	845.8	951.6	1,246.2
Other professional, scientific and technical activities	74	116	483.0	0.4	574.7	5.1	153.3	248.5	297.5	344.0	421.6	574.9	664.9	728.3	814.5	x
Veterinary activities	75	50	372.6	3.8	446.8	3.4	143.0	209.8	230.7	258.1	324.5	454.6	550.5	596.7	671.5	x
ADMINISTRATIVE AND SUPPORT SERVICE ACTIVITIES	N	1,641	347.2	2.5	417.4	3.7	101.9	171.7	214.5	251.3	299.0	403.4	479.1	524.0	579.4	760.7
Rental and leasing activities	77	147	488.9	4.5	563.3	8.0	238.5	335.0	358.0	383.3	430.4	540.3	628.6	670.8	729.7	949.9
Employment activities	78	626	321.3	3.1	378.9	2.4	118.9	199.5	230.0	252.4	287.3	364.1	426.1	470.7	517.4	670.8

4.11a Weekly pay - Gross (£) - For all employee jobs[a]: United Kingdom, 2016

Description	Code	Number of jobs[b] (000's)	Median	Annual % change	Mean	Annual % change	Percentiles 10	20	25	30	40	60	70	75	80	90
Travel agency, tour operator and other reservation service and related activities	79	76	431.2	4.7	529.2	0.2	187.3	269.5	288.0	313.0	373.2	479.1	552.9	620.2	670.8	x
Security and investigation activities	80	113	389.9	-3.0	404.0	0.7	121.7	240.0	280.4	306.3	347.8	432.4	478.1	506.1	545.2	639.3
Services to buildings and landscape activities	81	403	261.6	9.9	331.7	8.5	71.5	98.5	112.5	128.5	180.0	328.6	403.8	448.1	508.7	682.1
Office administrative, office support and other business support activities	82	277	420.3	1.3	526.9	2.6	149.0	244.6	276.0	300.0	350.3	481.7	586.5	644.4	715.1	1,025.5
PUBLIC ADMINISTRATION AND DEFENCE; COMPULSORY SOCIAL SECURITY	O	1,359	560.0	0.4	588.3	0.8	258.9	357.1	386.5	425.5	485.8	623.3	706.8	745.0	795.0	936.1
Public administration and defence; compulsory social security	84	1,359	560.0	0.4	588.3	0.8	258.9	357.1	386.5	425.5	485.8	623.3	706.8	745.0	795.0	936.1
EDUCATION	P	3,683	435.1	1.7	486.3	2.4	117.5	209.5	247.3	285.4	361.9	522.3	627.5	682.8	729.1	889.5
Education	85	3,683	435.1	1.7	486.3	2.4	117.5	209.5	247.3	285.4	361.9	522.3	627.5	682.8	729.1	889.5
HUMAN HEALTH AND SOCIAL WORK ACTIVITIES	Q	3,897	396.2	4.2	478.2	3.0	155.2	226.4	257.7	287.4	341.2	461.3	545.5	598.2	655.4	829.5
Human health activities	86	2,539	463.3	2.7	552.5	2.0	193.2	281.9	315.7	344.5	403.3	540.1	621.1	674.6	731.0	920.6
Residential care activities	87	687	298.3	5.0	342.5	3.4	130.1	181.3	203.5	223.5	260.4	336.3	384.0	419.4	460.7	597.9
Social work activities without accommodation	88	671	294.7	4.2	336.3	3.3	99.9	154.8	179.4	207.0	254.5	340.1	401.1	435.8	479.1	617.1
ARTS, ENTERTAINMENT AND RECREATION	R	508	306.6	4.6	428.3	15.3	41.6	100.8	135.5	165.3	244.6	359.2	428.9	477.2	536.3	728.3
Creative, arts and entertainment activities	90	48	423.1	-6.7	553.5	2.4	x	176.6	230.0	292.6	353.3	518.2	617.9	690.8	766.6	x
Libraries, archives, museums and other cultural activities	91	63	388.4	-6.8	419.6	-3.6	85.3	168.4	220.1	260.2	319.5	460.0	520.9	567.0	600.3	x
Gambling and betting activities	92	95	323.3	5.8	369.3	7.8	130.1	188.6	217.5	245.6	294.4	362.8	411.0	445.7	483.7	x
Sports activities and amusement and recreation activities	93	302	263.5	11.6	429.0	26.0	27.3	57.6	81.1	114.7	179.4	321.4	384.9	428.9	482.0	680.2
OTHER SERVICE ACTIVITIES	S	444	353.6	5.4	418.1	3.1	103.6	156.0	184.7	215.0	287.6	421.6	483.4	534.7	595.8	792.9
Activities of membership organisations	94	209	410.5	0.0	453.3	-0.4	77.0	161.5	198.1	245.1	337.8	463.9	538.7	595.7	666.5	856.8
Repair of computers and personal and household goods	95	37	476.7	-0.5	581.3	2.8	239.1	335.4	357.9	383.3	425.6	530.0	641.9	729.1	804.6	x
Other personal service activities	96	198	281.9	5.1	350.5	5.9	114.7	146.9	161.0	184.0	224.7	335.4	400.2	440.8	480.8	652.4
ACTIVITIES OF HOUSEHOLDS AS EMPLOYERS; UNDIFFERENTIATED GOODS-AND SERVICES-PRODUCING ACTIVITIES OF HOUSEHOLDS FOR OWN USE	T	71	138.3	7.5	203.6	5.6	30.2	48.0	63.1	78.0	103.6	199.3	255.4	299.1	349.9	x
Activities of households as employers of domestic personnel	97	71	138.3	7.5	203.6	5.6	30.2	48.0	63.1	78.0	103.6	199.3	255.4	299.1	349.9	x
Undifferentiated goods- and services-producing activities of private households for own use	98	:														
ACTIVITIES OF EXTRATERRITORIAL ORGANISATIONS AND BODIES	U	x	x		558.6	13.3	x	x	x	x	x	x	x	x	x	x
Activities of extraterritorial organisations and bodies	99	x	x		558.6	13.3	x	x	x	x	x	x	x	x	x	x
NOT CLASSIFIED		6	x		x		x	x	x	x	x	x	x	x	x	x

a Employees on adult rates whose pay for the survey pay-period was not affected by absence.

Source: Annual Survey of Hours and Earnings, Office for National Statistics.

b Figures for Number of Jobs are for indicative purposes only and should not be considered an accurate estimate of employee job counts.

KEY - The colour coding indicates the quality of each estimate; jobs, median, mean and percentiles but not the annual percentage change.

The quality of an estimate is measured by its coefficient of variation (CV), which is the ratio of the standard error of an estimate to the estimate.

Key	Statistical robustness
CV <= 5%	Estimates are considered precise
CV > 5% and <= 10%	Estimates are considered reasonably precise
CV > 10% and <= 20%	Estimates are considered acceptable
x = CV > 20%	Estimates are considered unreliable for practical purposes
.. = disclosive	
: = not applicable	
- = nil or negligible	

4.11b Hourly pay - Gross (£) - For all employee jobs[a]: United Kingdom, 2016

Description	Code	Number of jobs[b] (000's)	Median	Annual % change	Mean	Annual % change	Percentiles 10	20	25	30	40	60	70	75	80	90
ALL EMPLOYEES		25,758	12.16	3.3	15.73	3.1	7.30	8.18	8.69	9.22	10.50	14.20	16.77	18.37	20.33	26.43
All Industries and Services		25,752	12.16	3.3	15.73	3.1	7.30	8.18	8.69	9.22	10.51	14.20	16.77	18.37	20.33	26.43
All Index of Production Industries		2,800	13.50	2.8	16.14	4.1	7.98	9.21	9.86	10.50	11.92	15.43	17.88	19.39	21.20	27.09
All Manufacturing		2,439	13.22	3.0	15.77	4.7	7.87	9.03	9.64	10.26	11.65	15.04	17.40	18.91	20.61	26.31
All Service Industries		21,915	11.93	3.7	15.71	2.9	7.25	8.03	8.51	9.05	10.27	14.02	16.68	18.28	20.28	26.42
AGRICULTURE, FORESTRY AND FISHING	A	133	9.37	4.8	10.88	3.0	7.20	7.50	7.71	8.00	8.61	10.06	11.16	12.00	12.78	16.45
Crop and animal production, hunting and related service activities	1	119	9.12	4.8	10.32	2.1	7.20	7.43	7.60	7.96	8.43	9.93	10.64	11.45	12.13	15.14
Forestry and logging	2	9	12.53	2.1	14.87	1.3	7.99	9.29	x	10.67	11.82	13.10	x	x	x	x
Fishing and aquaculture	3	x	x		18.49	29.5	x	x	9.64	9.76	10.01	x	x	x	x	x
MINING AND QUARRYING	B	44	16.32	-7.2	20.21	-5.0	10.40	11.40	12.15	13.02	14.47	19.11	21.67	24.59	26.49	x
Mining of coal and lignite	5	x	x		x		x	x	x	x	x	x	x	x	x	x
Extraction of crude petroleum and natural gas	6	6	28.79		36.93	-5.5	x	21.00	23.31	24.12	25.14	x	x	x	x	x
Mining of metal ores	7	..														
Other mining and quarrying	8	22	13.51	2.0	15.55	1.1	9.35	10.63	10.90	11.25	12.33	15.32	17.51	18.90	19.49	x
Mining support service activities	9	13	18.96	-6.8	22.27	-4.4	10.88	13.19	13.94	14.85	16.01	20.55	25.27	x	x	x
MANUFACTURING	C	2,439	13.22	3.0	15.77	4.7	7.87	9.03	9.64	10.26	11.65	15.04	17.40	18.91	20.61	26.31
Manufacture of food products	10	375	10.07	5.3	12.67	2.8	7.27	7.75	8.01	8.38	9.06	11.26	13.19	14.40	16.00	20.94
Manufacture of beverages	11	44	15.89	-0.3	19.69	5.4	8.75	11.38	11.97	12.74	14.38	17.84	21.41	22.97	24.62	x
Manufacture of tobacco products	12	:														
Manufacture of textiles	13	45	9.80	3.6	12.58	4.8	7.20	7.64	8.00	8.29	9.00	10.88	12.32	13.85	14.86	x
Manufacture of wearing apparel	14	16	8.20	3.7	11.30	2.0	x	x	7.20	7.21	7.79	9.42	x	x	x	x
Manufacture of leather and related products	15	9	9.06	-1.4	11.03	6.1	7.20	7.66	x	8.10	8.44	10.81	x	x	x	x
Manufacture of wood and of products of wood and cork, except furniture; manufacture of articles of straw and plaiting materials	16	59	11.00	9.0	12.25	6.4	7.68	8.56	9.00	9.37	10.04	11.91	12.75	13.86	15.31	x
Manufacture of paper and paper products	17	58	13.31	3.4	15.82	8.5	8.11	9.41	10.29	10.80	12.20	14.77	17.23	18.29	19.83	x
Printing and reproduction of recorded media	18	102	11.97	1.2	14.99	5.5	8.00	9.03	9.56	10.06	10.91	13.21	15.45	16.73	18.06	x
Manufacture of coke and refined petroleum products	19	10	25.72	5.0	25.68	1.6	13.18	16.41	19.67	22.00	23.46	27.11	29.54	32.07	x	x
Manufacture of chemicals and chemical products	20	85	15.28	0.3	17.55	1.4	8.32	10.04	10.70	11.44	13.27	17.04	19.36	21.31	24.11	x
Manufacture of basic pharmaceutical products and pharmaceutical preparations	21	50	18.28	10.9	26.09	30.9	9.81	12.00	12.87	13.67	15.85	21.01	23.52	26.97	31.00	x
Manufacture of rubber and plastic products	22	152	11.16	2.1	13.72	1.2	7.67	8.44	8.89	9.31	10.16	12.72	14.42	15.55	16.71	21.76
Manufacture of other non-metallic mineral products	23	76	12.04	0.1	13.86	-1.2	7.97	9.25	9.70	10.06	10.92	13.40	15.35	16.34	17.94	x
Manufacture of basic metals	24	81	16.30	1.8	17.25	4.1	9.11	11.27	12.27	13.06	14.65	17.87	19.80	21.36	22.70	25.34
Manufacture of fabricated metal products, except machinery and equipment	25	278	12.47	3.6	14.32	5.5	7.92	9.12	9.59	10.06	11.09	13.80	15.28	16.29	17.75	22.50
Manufacture of computer, electronic and optical products	26	132	16.13	4.8	18.17	3.2	8.50	10.18	11.06	12.00	13.88	18.19	20.79	22.26	23.98	29.58
Manufacture of electrical equipment	27	97	13.31	5.2	15.81	6.7	7.91	9.20	9.99	10.53	11.95	14.76	17.13	18.42	20.36	x
Manufacture of machinery and equipment n.e.c.	28	193	14.47	2.6	16.52	2.3	8.89	10.36	11.13	11.85	13.24	16.09	18.16	19.43	20.78	26.52
Manufacture of motor vehicles, trailers and semi-trailers	29	193	16.67	6.2	18.48	6.1	9.37	10.96	11.93	12.94	14.89	19.09	21.33	22.43	23.83	29.41
Manufacture of other transport equipment	30	166	18.87	3.9	20.22	4.3	11.36	13.60	14.41	15.43	17.15	20.63	22.73	23.87	25.28	31.54
Manufacture of furniture	31	66	10.00	1.3	12.43	10.8	7.42	8.03	8.40	8.67	9.36	11.00	12.50	13.46	14.84	x
Other manufacturing	32	68	12.03	0.7	14.51	5.2	7.71	8.61	9.13	9.79	11.00	13.40	15.40	17.19	18.74	x
Repair and installation of machinery and equipment	33	86	14.22	-4.8	17.51	2.3	8.65	10.40	11.00	11.80	12.99	16.20	18.92	20.21	22.42	x
ELECTRICITY, GAS, STEAM AND AIR CONDITIONING SUPPLY	D	168	18.57	0.3	21.36	2.7	10.28	12.28	13.37	14.66	16.43	20.81	24.27	26.51	28.95	35.33
Electricity, gas, steam and air conditioning supply	35	168	18.57	0.3	21.36	2.7	10.28	12.28	13.37	14.66	16.43	20.81	24.27	26.51	28.95	35.33
WATER SUPPLY; SEWERAGE, WASTE MANAGEMENT AND REMEDIATION ACTIVITIES	E	148	13.01	3.3	15.33	1.4	8.16	9.53	10.00	10.49	11.58	14.51	16.76	17.87	19.84	24.79
Water collection, treatment and supply	36	43	15.46	0.5	17.54	-0.6	10.16	11.85	12.32	12.97	14.34	17.07	18.00	20.08	20.90	x
Sewerage	37	13	14.35	1.3	16.33	1.3	9.27	10.00	10.56	11.31	13.81	17.40	19.32	20.21	x	x

4.11b Hourly pay - Gross (£) - For all employee jobs[a]: United Kingdom, 2016

Description	Code	Number of jobs[b] (000's)	Median	Annual % change	Mean	Annual % change	Percentiles 10	20	25	30	40	60	70	75	80	90
Waste collection, treatment and disposal activities; materials recovery	38	89	11.41	2.6	14.27	2.9	7.75	8.85	9.27	9.68	10.50	12.75	14.52	16.06	17.59	x
Remediation activities and other waste management services	39	x	10.90	-5.0	14.13	1.0	x	x	x	9.86	10.36	x	x	x	x	x
CONSTRUCTION	F	905	13.30	2.7	15.59	3.2	8.18	9.71	10.25	10.96	12.00	14.73	16.56	17.72	19.30	25.31
Construction of buildings	41	272	14.00	5.2	17.46	5.0	8.68	10.09	10.86	11.39	12.58	16.00	18.79	20.64	22.88	30.23
Civil engineering	42	170	13.62	2.1	16.03	2.6	8.26	10.00	10.57	11.20	12.43	15.00	17.05	18.79	20.33	26.37
Specialised construction activities	43	463	12.93	2.6	14.34	2.2	8.00	9.41	10.00	10.50	11.70	14.14	15.54	16.50	17.50	21.19
WHOLESALE AND RETAIL TRADE; REPAIR OF MOTOR VEHICLES AND MOTORCYCLES	G	3,715	9.24	4.7	12.74	4.0	7.20	7.40	7.58	7.83	8.41	10.40	12.08	13.18	14.65	20.34
Wholesale and retail trade and repair of motor vehicles and motorcycles	45	461	10.51	4.3	12.31	2.7	7.20	7.67	8.05	8.47	9.51	11.56	12.92	13.68	14.65	18.52
Wholesale trade, except of motor vehicles and motorcycles	46	1,033	12.02	4.2	15.44	4.3	7.64	8.50	8.99	9.49	10.57	13.69	16.00	17.76	19.78	26.92
Retail trade, except of motor vehicles and motorcycles	47	2,221	8.30	5.6	11.23	4.0	7.05	7.20	7.37	7.48	7.84	9.01	10.04	10.84	12.00	16.54
TRANSPORTATION AND STORAGE	H	1,104	12.35	1.3	14.84	-0.5	8.33	9.50	10.00	10.44	11.24	13.74	15.68	16.99	18.89	25.35
Land transport and transport via pipelines	49	489	11.77	2.4	13.69	0.7	8.06	9.07	9.56	10.00	10.83	12.91	14.56	15.76	17.27	23.44
Water transport	50	13	14.04	1.9	16.40	4.9	8.42	9.77	10.23	10.88	12.20	15.32	16.87	x	x	x
Air transport	51	75	17.91	-1.2	21.94	-10.9	9.35	11.63	12.92	13.63	15.47	20.87	25.59	27.23	29.23	x
Warehousing and support activities for transportation	52	331	13.50	4.4	16.25	1.7	8.38	9.58	10.03	10.68	12.00	15.37	17.57	19.23	21.31	28.76
Postal and courier activities	53	197	11.48	-3.2	13.03	-2.8	8.62	10.21	10.39	10.49	10.88	12.44	13.42	13.88	14.79	17.69
ACCOMMODATION AND FOOD SERVICE ACTIVITIES	I	1,437	7.50	7.1	9.21	5.1	6.00	6.91	7.19	7.20	7.21	7.93	8.57	9.00	9.66	12.02
Accommodation	55	298	7.98	8.5	9.91	3.9	6.70	7.20	x	7.20	7.50	8.61	9.51	10.05	10.89	13.93
Food and beverage service activities	56	1,139	7.45	7.0	9.00	5.7	5.80	6.71	7.14	x	7.20	7.77	8.35	8.76	9.33	11.57
INFORMATION AND COMMUNICATION	J	1,019	18.09	3.7	21.41	3.2	9.55	11.75	12.78	13.80	15.74	20.64	23.69	25.72	28.12	35.78
Publishing activities	58	132	16.23	4.8	19.84	3.9	9.25	11.22	11.89	12.60	14.02	18.40	21.43	22.99	24.92	31.43
Motion picture, video and television programme production, sound recording and music publishing activities	59	49	13.68	4.4	18.65	7.7	7.20	8.52	9.54	10.04	11.72	16.31	19.55	21.43	25.16	x
Programming and broadcasting activities	60	47	21.63	5.8	24.68	7.3	12.24	15.10	15.84	17.51	20.12	23.96	26.88	29.19	30.66	x
Telecommunications	61	228	17.14	2.8	20.04	1.5	9.70	12.00	13.03	14.04	15.42	19.62	21.60	23.14	25.55	31.84
Computer programming, consultancy and related activities	62	494	19.00	3.3	22.29	2.9	9.66	12.04	13.22	14.31	16.56	21.72	25.01	27.19	29.95	38.12
Information service activities	63	69	19.48	3.9	22.18	1.0	9.73	11.97	12.79	13.93	16.86	22.32	25.70	27.37	30.01	x
FINANCIAL AND INSURANCE ACTIVITIES	K	937	18.17	1.4	25.50	0.7	9.59	11.22	12.16	13.13	15.33	22.05	27.19	30.58	34.97	48.55
Financial service activities, except insurance and pension funding	64	501	18.97	-1.0	26.98	-0.6	9.92	11.46	12.31	13.34	15.81	23.16	28.80	32.57	37.21	51.12
Insurance, reinsurance and pension funding, except compulsory social security	65	104	17.97	4.1	21.88	-0.5	9.59	11.17	12.39	13.19	15.31	20.62	24.07	26.83	29.27	38.44
Activities auxiliary to financial services and insurance activities	66	332	17.32	2.5	24.45	2.1	9.11	10.81	11.79	12.77	14.80	20.88	25.76	29.00	32.80	47.44
REAL ESTATE ACTIVITIES	L	348	12.81	0.9	15.80	1.9	8.04	9.30	9.90	10.43	11.66	14.22	16.35	17.52	19.70	26.33
Real estate activities	68	348	12.81	0.9	15.80	1.9	8.04	9.30	9.90	10.43	11.66	14.22	16.35	17.52	19.70	26.33
PROFESSIONAL, SCIENTIFIC AND TECHNICAL ACTIVITIES	M	1,751	16.02	3.0	20.03	2.6	8.47	10.16	11.01	12.00	13.88	18.47	21.67	23.94	26.39	35.06
Legal and accounting activities	69	492	15.33	1.5	19.86	2.0	8.35	9.86	10.57	11.49	13.14	18.12	21.58	24.12	26.54	36.00
Activities of head offices; management consultancy activities	70	429	15.69	6.0	21.13	1.9	8.11	9.56	10.22	11.16	13.24	18.04	21.90	24.92	28.10	38.55
Architectural and engineering activities; technical testing and analysis	71	408	16.79	3.0	19.52	1.9	9.40	11.49	12.33	13.10	14.97	19.15	22.05	23.97	25.94	32.10
Scientific research and development	72	126	19.55	-0.6	22.90	-0.9	11.13	13.83	14.58	15.54	17.63	21.58	24.77	27.81	30.35	37.56
Advertising and market research	73	132	16.10	7.2	20.31	8.7	8.97	10.71	11.67	12.46	14.37	18.56	21.06	23.00	25.84	34.60
Other professional, scientific and technical activities	74	116	13.77	1.5	17.33	3.5	7.95	9.37	10.00	10.60	12.07	15.76	18.17	19.90	22.27	29.34
Veterinary activities	75	50	11.03	3.7	13.97	1.6	7.31	8.07	8.48	8.89	9.78	13.31	15.80	17.03	20.17	x
ADMINISTRATIVE AND SUPPORT SERVICE ACTIVITIES	N	1,641	9.50	2.7	12.58	3.5	7.20	7.30	7.53	7.90	8.62	10.73	12.52	13.75	15.29	20.42
Rental and leasing activities	77	147	11.52	4.3	13.97	7.1	7.50	8.55	9.00	9.42	10.38	12.94	14.44	15.65	16.87	22.66
Employment activities	78	626	9.25	2.7	11.50	3.3	7.20	7.22	7.48	7.80	8.46	10.28	11.98	13.05	14.63	19.22

4.11b Hourly pay - Gross (£) - For all employee jobs[a]: United Kingdom, 2016

Description	Code	Number of jobs[b] (000's)	Median	Annual % change	Mean	Annual % change	Percentiles 10	20	25	30	40	60	70	75	80	90
Travel agency, tour operator and other reservation service and related activities	79	76	11.69	4.0	15.22	0.6	7.45	8.15	8.69	9.15	10.28	13.09	14.65	16.68	17.65	x
Security and investigation activities	80	113	8.88	1.8	10.17	3.9	7.20	7.50	7.70	7.90	8.25	9.45	10.00	10.74	11.43	14.06
Services to buildings and landscape activities	81	403	8.20	5.2	11.70	7.9	7.19	x	7.20	7.25	7.65	9.25	10.54	11.51	12.98	17.32
Office administrative, office support and other business support activities	82	277	11.50	-2.2	15.58	2.9	7.22	8.00	8.53	8.99	10.00	13.29	15.84	17.43	19.50	28.11
PUBLIC ADMINISTRATION AND DEFENCE; COMPULSORY SOCIAL SECURITY	O	1,359	15.03	0.8	16.53	1.1	9.44	10.61	11.50	12.21	13.61	16.62	18.47	19.41	20.53	24.33
Public administration and defence; compulsory social security	84	1,359	15.03	0.8	16.53	1.1	9.44	10.61	11.50	12.21	13.61	16.62	18.47	19.41	20.53	24.33
EDUCATION	P	3,683	14.33	2.0	17.02	2.4	7.99	8.94	9.42	10.20	12.00	17.15	19.97	21.62	23.34	28.22
Education	85	3,683	14.33	2.0	17.02	2.4	7.99	8.94	9.42	10.20	12.00	17.15	19.97	21.62	23.34	28.22
HUMAN HEALTH AND SOCIAL WORK ACTIVITIES	Q	3,897	12.22	3.9	15.06	2.9	7.50	8.40	8.91	9.40	10.67	14.36	16.43	17.82	18.97	23.43
Human health activities	86	2,539	14.56	1.2	17.21	2.1	8.83	10.00	10.53	11.37	12.94	16.43	18.21	19.46	21.12	25.53
Residential care activities	87	687	8.45	4.1	10.44	3.6	7.20	7.27	7.40	7.54	7.95	9.15	10.45	11.45	12.73	15.95
Social work activities without accommodation	88	671	9.29	3.1	11.45	2.2	7.20	7.50	7.75	8.00	8.57	10.42	11.98	12.98	14.09	17.96
ARTS, ENTERTAINMENT AND RECREATION	R	508	9.40	3.3	15.23	15.3	6.92	7.24	7.51	7.89	8.51	10.55	12.40	13.65	15.32	20.50
Creative, arts and entertainment activities	90	48	12.77	-3.9	17.74	-0.7	7.61	8.69	9.37	10.00	11.08	15.39	18.22	19.67	21.02	x
Libraries, archives, museums and other cultural activities	91	63	11.26	-2.1	13.66	-0.1	7.20	7.96	8.36	8.68	10.01	12.79	13.99	15.62	16.58	x
Gambling and betting activities	92	95	8.51	2.3	10.94	6.9	7.17	7.24	7.50	7.79	8.07	9.36	10.52	11.02	12.06	x
Sports activities and amusement and recreation activities	93	302	9.09	4.6	16.95	25.1	6.70	7.20	7.30	7.52	8.30	10.09	11.77	13.00	14.58	20.11
OTHER SERVICE ACTIVITIES	S	444	10.54	2.9	13.80	2.9	7.20	7.50	7.98	8.30	9.34	11.98	13.85	15.31	17.05	22.81
Activities of membership organisations	94	209	12.25	-1.2	15.75	-0.9	7.50	8.55	9.15	9.82	10.95	13.90	16.23	17.90	19.91	24.70
Repair of computers and personal and household goods	95	37	12.39	-2.4	15.51	1.5	7.50	8.84	9.50	10.20	11.26	14.25	16.72	18.16	20.17	x
Other personal service activities	96	198	8.63	4.1	11.46	5.8	6.90	x	7.20	7.40	8.00	9.63	10.93	11.95	12.98	17.30
ACTIVITIES OF HOUSEHOLDS AS EMPLOYERS; UNDIFFERENTIATED GOODS-AND SERVICES-PRODUCING ACTIVITIES OF HOUSEHOLDS FOR OWN USE	T	71	9.07	0.8	10.19	-1.0	7.45	7.96	8.00	8.30	8.70	9.71	10.09	10.80	11.59	x
Activities of households as employers of domestic personnel	97	71	9.07	0.8	10.19	-1.0	7.45	7.96	8.00	8.30	8.70	9.71	10.09	10.80	11.59	x
Undifferentiated goods- and services-producing activities of private households for own use	98	:														
ACTIVITIES OF EXTRATERRITORIAL ORGANISATIONS AND BODIES	U	x	x		15.52	7.0	x	x	x	x	x	x	x	x	x	x
Activities of extraterritorial organisations and bodies	99	x	x		15.52	7.0	x	x	x	x	x	x	x	x	x	x
NOT CLASSIFIED		6	8.41	0.8	x		x	7.25	7.51	7.52	8.22	9.90	x	x	x	x

Source: Annual Survey of Hours and Earnings, Office for National Statistics.

a Employees on adult rates whose pay for the survey pay-period was not affected by absence.

b Figures for Number of Jobs are for indicative purposes only and should not be considered an accurate estimate of employee job counts.

KEY - The colour coding indicates the quality of each estimate; jobs, median, mean and percentiles but not the annual percentage change.

The quality of an estimate is measured by its coefficient of variation (CV), which is the ratio of the standard error of an estimate to the estimate.

Key	Statistical robustness
CV <= 5%	Estimates are considered precise
CV > 5% and <= 10%	Estimates are considered reasonably precise
CV > 10% and <= 20%	Estimates are considered acceptable
x = CV > 20%	Estimates are considered unreliable for practical purposes
.. = disclosive	
: = not applicable	
- = nil or negligible	

4.12a - Weekly pay - Gross (£) - For all employee jobs[a]: United Kingdom, 2016

Description	Number of jobs[b] (thousand)	Median	Annual % change	Mean	Annual % change	Percentiles 10	20	25	30	40	60	70	75	80	90
ALL EMPLOYEES	25,758	438.4	3.1	525.0	3.5	141.2	231.2	275.9	307.9	371.1	516.1	611.1	670.8	736.7	953.5
Male	12,997	530.4	2.5	632.7	3.3	219.6	325.8	359.1	392.0	460.0	610.3	711.6	770.4	849.2	1,109.7
Female	12,760	349.1	3.5	415.4	3.7	110.4	172.8	204.9	234.6	294.2	415.4	494.9	545.5	610.0	784.2
Full-Time	18,571	538.6	2.2	644.9	2.9	308.9	363.0	389.2	418.7	475.3	613.3	704.5	762.5	826.6	1,058.8
Part-Time	7,186	177.1	6.4	215.2	5.6	54.7	94.0	111.3	123.8	152.6	205.1	236.1	259.8	290.9	405.0
Male Full-Time	11,201	577.5	1.8	699.3	2.8	328.9	389.0	420.4	448.8	509.6	658.9	757.0	815.6	894.4	1,162.7
Male Part-Time	1,797	166.8	7.3	217.1	8.6	47.4	84.5	100.4	115.2	145.8	192.5	221.7	244.8	278.2	402.5
Female Full-Time	7,371	480.5	2.2	562.3	2.9	290.0	334.1	354.6	378.3	426.4	547.4	630.0	678.1	733.9	901.1
Female Part-Time	5,390	181.2	5.9	214.6	4.6	57.4	97.9	114.8	127.0	154.3	209.1	240.7	264.0	296.3	405.0

a Employees on adult rates whose pay for the survey pay-period was not affected by absence. Source: Annual Survey of Hours and Earnings, Office for National Statistics.

b Figures for Number of Jobs are for indicative purposes only and should not be considered an accurate estimate of employee job counts.

The quality of an estimate is measured by its coefficient of variation (CV), which is the ratio of the standard error of an estimate to the estimate.

4.12b Hourly pay - Excluding overtime (£) - For all employee jobs[a]: United Kingdom, 2016

Description	Code	Number of jobs[b] (000's)	Median	Annual % change	Mean	Annual % change	Percentiles 10	20	25	30	40	60	70	75	80	90
ALL EMPLOYEES		25,758	12.09	3.1	15.77	3.1	7.29	8.14	8.64	9.19	10.46	14.16	16.75	18.33	20.28	26.43
All Industries and Services		25,752	12.09	3.1	15.77	3.1	7.29	8.14	8.64	9.19	10.47	14.16	16.75	18.33	20.28	26.43
All Index of Production Industries		2,800	13.31	2.9	16.11	4.2	7.84	9.08	9.70	10.35	11.74	15.26	17.73	19.25	21.04	27.07
All Manufacturing		2,439	13.00	2.9	15.74	4.8	7.75	8.91	9.50	10.12	11.48	14.88	17.24	18.75	20.49	26.28
All Service Industries		21,915	11.90	3.5	15.77	3.0	7.24	8.00	8.50	9.01	10.23	14.00	16.67	18.25	20.26	26.42
AGRICULTURE, FORESTRY AND FISHING	A	133	9.18	5.0	10.83	3.4	7.20	7.41	7.60	8.00	8.50	9.97	11.05	11.89	12.73	16.45
Crop and animal production, hunting and related service activities	1	119	9.00	5.0	10.24	2.5	7.20	7.32	7.50	7.74	8.30	9.63	10.45	11.19	12.02	15.08
Forestry and logging	2	9	12.53	2.1	14.84	1.3	7.99	9.29	10.15	10.64	11.63	13.02	x	x	x	x
Fishing and aquaculture	3	x	x		18.45	32.9	x	x	9.38	9.70	10.01	x	x	x	x	x
MINING AND QUARRYING	B	44	16.22	-6.6	20.38	-4.7	9.88	10.98	11.92	12.78	14.41	19.16	21.67	24.27	26.38	x
Mining of coal and lignite	5	x	x		x		x	x	x	x	x	x	x	x	x	x
Extraction of crude petroleum and natural gas	6	6	28.79		36.72	-6.2	x	21.00	23.31	24.12	25.14	x	x	x	x	x
Mining of metal ores	7	..														
Other mining and quarrying	8	22	13.37	1.3	15.53	1.8	9.20	10.36	10.54	10.79	11.97	15.30	17.09	19.02	19.58	x
Mining support service activities	9	13	18.96	-7.5	22.26	-4.2	10.88	13.14	13.76	14.85	15.86	20.55	25.27	x	x	x
MANUFACTURING	C	2,439	13.00	2.9	15.74	4.8	7.75	8.91	9.50	10.12	11.48	14.88	17.24	18.75	20.49	26.28
Manufacture of food products	10	375	9.94	5.9	12.65	2.7	7.20	7.62	7.91	8.20	8.91	11.12	13.09	14.36	15.77	20.91
Manufacture of beverages	11	44	15.94	0.0	19.71	5.4	8.75	11.25	11.87	12.74	14.25	17.71	21.29	22.94	24.62	x
Manufacture of tobacco products	12	:														
Manufacture of textiles	13	45	9.70	2.7	12.54	4.7	7.20	7.57	7.86	8.10	8.98	10.82	12.23	13.29	14.38	x
Manufacture of wearing apparel	14	16	8.20	3.7	11.21	1.9	x	x	7.20	7.21	7.79	9.38	10.83	x	x	x
Manufacture of leather and related products	15	9	9.06	0.4	11.00	6.4	7.20	7.62	x	8.10	8.36	10.29	x	x	x	x
Manufacture of wood and of products of wood and cork, except furniture; manufacture of articles of straw and plaiting materials	16	59	10.94	9.7	12.16	6.7	7.50	8.37	8.67	9.21	10.00	11.72	12.50	13.66	15.10	x
Manufacture of paper and paper products	17	58	13.29	5.3	15.85	9.1	8.00	9.22	10.23	10.72	12.12	14.79	17.25	18.23	19.83	x
Printing and reproduction of recorded media	18	102	11.96	1.8	15.02	5.9	7.89	8.88	9.47	9.92	10.78	13.13	15.34	16.67	17.91	x
Manufacture of coke and refined petroleum products	19	10	25.41	7.4	25.32	2.0	13.04	16.20	19.67	22.00	23.46	26.86	28.24	30.85	x	x
Manufacture of chemicals and chemical products	20	85	14.99	0.3	17.53	1.5	8.17	9.89	10.56	11.29	13.14	16.88	19.32	21.16	23.46	x
Manufacture of basic pharmaceutical products and pharmaceutical preparations	21	50	17.91	9.2	26.17	31.4	9.67	11.69	12.85	13.50	15.77	21.01	23.34	26.38	31.00	x
Manufacture of rubber and plastic products	22	152	11.10	3.6	13.73	1.2	7.52	8.32	8.75	9.15	10.00	12.54	14.34	15.27	16.56	21.19
Manufacture of other non-metallic mineral products	23	76	11.94	-0.5	13.80	-1.5	7.79	9.04	9.50	9.99	10.79	13.28	15.10	16.29	17.94	x
Manufacture of basic metals	24	81	16.25	3.1	17.30	4.4	9.03	11.08	12.05	12.83	14.50	17.67	19.80	21.27	22.70	25.34
Manufacture of fabricated metal products, except machinery and equipment	25	278	12.06	2.6	14.23	6.1	7.80	8.98	9.40	9.98	10.97	13.42	15.00	16.09	17.67	22.45
Manufacture of computer, electronic and optical products	26	132	16.02	5.4	18.14	3.0	8.35	10.13	11.04	11.97	13.80	18.14	20.67	22.07	23.95	29.70
Manufacture of electrical equipment	27	97	13.08	5.6	15.77	6.9	7.92	9.05	9.84	10.44	11.79	14.72	16.77	18.42	20.29	x
Manufacture of machinery and equipment n.e.c.	28	193	14.20	2.7	16.48	2.6	8.76	10.17	11.00	11.61	12.87	15.82	18.01	19.39	20.75	26.52
Manufacture of motor vehicles, trailers and semi-trailers	29	193	16.48	6.6	18.29	6.0	9.20	10.72	11.76	12.74	14.53	18.72	21.00	22.25	23.80	29.50
Manufacture of other transport equipment	30	166	18.75	5.2	20.23	4.6	11.14	13.35	14.24	15.40	16.80	20.51	22.60	23.81	25.29	31.54
Manufacture of furniture	31	66	9.93	1.7	12.32	11.2	7.39	7.88	8.15	8.50	9.20	10.80	12.22	13.08	14.33	x
Other manufacturing	32	68	12.01	0.7	14.49	5.5	7.60	8.57	9.03	9.65	10.82	13.33	15.36	16.97	18.61	x
Repair and installation of machinery and equipment	33	86	14.04	-4.7	17.37	2.4	8.47	10.17	10.99	11.59	12.84	16.05	18.39	20.03	21.89	x
ELECTRICITY, GAS, STEAM AND AIR CONDITIONING SUPPLY	D	168	18.27	0.1	21.14	2.5	10.28	12.23	13.26	14.39	16.27	20.52	24.12	26.39	28.52	34.80
Electricity, gas, steam and air conditioning supply	35	168	18.27	0.1	21.14	2.5	10.28	12.23	13.26	14.39	16.27	20.52	24.12	26.39	28.52	34.80
WATER SUPPLY; SEWERAGE, WASTE MANAGEMENT AND REMEDIATION ACTIVITIES	E	148	12.85	3.6	15.32	1.6	8.07	9.35	9.84	10.34	11.21	14.38	16.40	17.81	19.72	24.74
Water collection, treatment and supply	36	43	15.19	1.4	17.49	-0.7	10.11	11.66	12.27	12.94	14.03	16.47	17.98	20.06	20.87	x
Sewerage	37	13	14.56	4.6	16.50	2.4	9.15	10.00	10.42	11.00	13.14	17.40	19.35	20.21	x	x

4.12b Hourly pay - Excluding overtime (£) - For all employee jobs[a]: United Kingdom, 2016

Description	Code	Number of jobs[b] (000's)	Median	Annual % change	Mean	Annual % change	Percentiles 10	20	25	30	40	60	70	75	80	90
Waste collection, treatment and disposal activities; materials recovery	38	89	11.15	2.2	14.22	3.0	7.64	8.63	9.07	9.50	10.38	12.60	14.52	15.83	17.47	x
Remediation activities and other waste management services	39	x	10.85	-5.4	14.26	1.7	x	x	x	9.62	10.05	x	x	x	x	x
CONSTRUCTION	F	905	13.11	2.3	15.54	3.3	8.12	9.61	10.16	10.86	11.99	14.50	16.35	17.61	19.23	25.23
Construction of buildings	41	272	13.96	6.0	17.53	5.2	8.61	10.00	10.79	11.28	12.49	15.95	18.81	20.54	22.92	30.23
Civil engineering	42	170	13.50	2.6	16.02	2.7	8.16	9.84	10.50	11.07	12.18	14.83	16.95	18.56	20.22	26.30
Specialised construction activities	43	463	12.72	1.8	14.19	2.2	7.95	9.20	10.00	10.48	11.54	13.94	15.33	16.25	17.32	21.19
WHOLESALE AND RETAIL TRADE; REPAIR OF MOTOR VEHICLES AND MOTORCYCLES	G	3,715	9.16	5.1	12.80	4.0	7.20	7.39	7.54	7.79	8.34	10.27	12.01	13.08	14.57	20.31
Wholesale and retail trade and repair of motor vehicles and motorcycles	45	461	10.43	4.2	12.26	2.4	7.20	7.62	8.00	8.44	9.44	11.50	12.78	13.56	14.55	18.45
Wholesale trade, except of motor vehicles and motorcycles	46	1,033	11.98	4.2	15.47	4.3	7.54	8.45	8.91	9.43	10.53	13.56	15.94	17.66	19.75	26.97
Retail trade, except of motor vehicles and motorcycles	47	2,221	8.21	5.5	11.30	4.1	7.07	7.20	7.36	7.46	7.80	8.92	9.91	10.73	11.96	16.45
TRANSPORTATION AND STORAGE	H	1,104	12.28	1.1	14.92	-0.7	8.23	9.35	9.93	10.36	11.18	13.71	15.66	17.01	18.91	25.34
Land transport and transport via pipelines	49	489	11.67	1.9	13.69	0.6	8.00	8.96	9.43	9.88	10.78	12.79	14.52	15.67	17.31	23.42
Water transport	50	13	14.04	2.1	16.47	5.3	8.42	9.73	10.14	10.80	12.03	15.32	16.87	x	x	x
Air transport	51	75	17.59	-3.6	21.94	-11.7	9.04	11.48	12.91	13.60	15.38	20.79	25.65	27.35	29.23	x
Warehousing and support activities for transportation	52	331	13.48	5.1	16.35	1.8	8.33	9.45	9.97	10.60	11.91	15.38	17.58	19.25	21.37	28.66
Postal and courier activities	53	197	11.49	-3.5	13.09	-3.3	8.62	10.17	10.36	10.47	10.86	12.43	13.44	13.98	14.87	17.75
ACCOMMODATION AND FOOD SERVICE ACTIVITIES	I	1,437	7.50	7.1	9.21	5.2	6.00	6.91	7.19	7.20	7.21	7.92	8.56	9.00	9.66	12.02
Accommodation	55	298	7.97	8.4	9.92	4.0	6.70	x	x	7.20	7.50	8.59	9.50	10.06	10.89	13.93
Food and beverage service activities	56	1,139	7.44	7.0	9.00	5.8	5.79	6.71	7.15	x	7.20	7.77	8.35	8.76	9.32	11.59
INFORMATION AND COMMUNICATION	J	1,019	18.03	3.7	21.43	3.3	9.53	11.72	12.78	13.75	15.55	20.55	23.61	25.64	28.11	35.78
Publishing activities	58	132	16.20	4.6	19.85	3.9	9.25	11.20	11.89	12.60	14.02	18.40	21.43	22.99	24.92	31.67
Motion picture, video and television programme production, sound recording and music publishing activities	59	49	13.68	4.0	18.77	8.2	7.20	8.36	9.53	10.04	11.64	15.97	19.55	21.43	25.16	x
Programming and broadcasting activities	60	47	21.56	5.9	24.63	7.3	12.11	14.90	15.79	17.48	20.04	23.80	26.68	29.19	30.66	x
Telecommunications	61	228	16.78	3.1	19.99	1.7	9.68	11.75	12.94	13.85	15.23	19.49	21.47	23.11	25.55	31.94
Computer programming, consultancy and related activities	62	494	19.02	3.5	22.35	3.1	9.58	12.01	13.22	14.31	16.56	21.71	25.01	27.17	29.81	38.32
Information service activities	63	69	19.48	3.9	22.16	0.7	9.72	11.97	12.78	13.93	16.79	22.32	25.70	27.36	29.79	x
FINANCIAL AND INSURANCE ACTIVITIES	K	937	18.09	1.1	25.56	0.7	9.58	11.17	12.06	13.08	15.32	21.99	27.20	30.53	34.83	48.55
Financial service activities, except insurance and pension funding	64	501	18.94	-1.1	27.06	-0.7	9.91	11.40	12.22	13.29	15.77	23.05	28.77	32.53	37.18	51.12
Insurance, reinsurance and pension funding, except compulsory social security	65	104	17.81	4.5	21.89	-0.4	9.52	11.06	12.18	13.13	15.21	20.53	24.07	26.83	29.27	38.44
Activities auxiliary to financial services and insurance activities	66	332	17.27	2.6	24.52	2.1	9.06	10.80	11.76	12.77	14.84	20.85	25.76	29.00	32.81	47.44
REAL ESTATE ACTIVITIES	L	348	12.81	0.9	15.82	1.8	8.02	9.23	9.87	10.42	11.66	14.19	16.35	17.51	19.70	26.47
Real estate activities	68	348	12.81	0.9	15.82	1.8	8.02	9.23	9.87	10.42	11.66	14.19	16.35	17.51	19.70	26.47
PROFESSIONAL, SCIENTIFIC AND TECHNICAL ACTIVITIES	M	1,751	15.95	2.9	20.08	2.7	8.45	10.13	11.00	11.98	13.82	18.44	21.66	23.93	26.39	35.10
Legal and accounting activities	69	492	15.33	1.6	19.89	2.1	8.33	9.85	10.55	11.47	13.14	18.07	21.59	24.13	26.54	36.09
Activities of head offices; management consultancy activities	70	429	15.59	5.4	21.21	2.1	8.12	9.51	10.21	11.16	13.20	18.03	21.89	24.91	28.10	38.55
Architectural and engineering activities; technical testing and analysis	71	408	16.77	3.3	19.56	2.1	9.38	11.37	12.26	13.03	14.85	19.15	22.03	23.97	25.94	32.10
Scientific research and development	72	126	19.54	-0.4	22.97	-0.8	11.02	13.77	14.55	15.54	17.60	21.58	24.77	27.58	30.35	37.56
Advertising and market research	73	132	16.10	7.0	20.33	8.7	8.97	10.73	11.68	12.45	14.37	18.56	21.06	23.00	25.84	34.73
Other professional, scientific and technical activities	74	116	13.73	1.0	17.35	3.6	7.95	9.37	10.00	10.60	12.07	15.78	18.30	19.90	22.27	29.34
Veterinary activities	75	50	11.06	4.5	13.99	1.6	7.31	8.04	8.43	8.82	9.71	13.26	15.77	17.03	20.17	x
ADMINISTRATIVE AND SUPPORT SERVICE ACTIVITIES	N	1,641	9.49	3.0	12.59	3.5	7.20	7.28	7.50	7.85	8.57	10.66	12.49	13.67	15.17	20.44
Rental and leasing activities	77	147	11.45	5.1	13.93	6.9	7.50	8.47	8.93	9.39	10.30	12.69	14.36	15.45	16.81	22.41
Employment activities	78	626	9.19	2.1	11.49	3.1	x	7.20	7.40	7.73	8.40	10.22	11.95	13.00	14.51	19.23

4.12b Hourly pay - Excluding overtime (£) - For all employee jobs[a]: United Kingdom, 2016

Description	Code	Number of jobs[b] (000's)	Median	Annual % change	Mean	Annual % change	Percentiles 10	20	25	30	40	60	70	75	80	90
Travel agency, tour operator and other reservation service and related activities	79	76	11.65	4.0	15.22	0.4	7.44	8.15	8.69	9.11	10.27	13.11	14.65	16.68	17.65	x
Security and investigation activities	80	113	8.89	1.9	10.14	3.9	7.20	7.50	7.69	7.90	8.25	9.46	10.03	10.82	11.39	14.10
Services to buildings and landscape activities	81	403	8.20	5.8	11.70	8.1	7.20	x	7.20	7.24	7.62	9.23	10.50	11.48	12.96	17.33
Office administrative, office support and other business support activities	82	277	11.50	-1.9	15.63	3.0	7.21	8.00	8.50	8.94	10.00	13.22	15.75	17.32	19.48	28.13
PUBLIC ADMINISTRATION AND DEFENCE; COMPULSORY SOCIAL SECURITY	O	1,359	15.10	1.4	16.58	1.6	9.44	10.59	11.50	12.22	13.64	16.70	18.42	19.34	20.44	24.32
Public administration and defence; compulsory social security	84	1,359	15.10	1.4	16.58	1.6	9.44	10.59	11.50	12.22	13.64	16.70	18.42	19.34	20.44	24.32
EDUCATION	P	3,683	14.30	1.9	17.06	2.3	7.99	8.94	9.40	10.18	12.00	17.12	19.96	21.64	23.34	28.24
Education	85	3,683	14.30	1.9	17.06	2.3	7.99	8.94	9.40	10.18	12.00	17.12	19.96	21.64	23.34	28.24
HUMAN HEALTH AND SOCIAL WORK ACTIVITIES	Q	3,897	12.23	3.8	15.07	2.9	7.50	8.40	8.92	9.40	10.71	14.37	16.43	17.81	18.93	23.40
Human health activities	86	2,539	14.56	1.2	17.17	2.1	8.82	10.00	10.54	11.37	12.94	16.43	18.19	19.41	21.10	25.49
Residential care activities	87	687	8.44	4.1	10.49	3.6	7.20	7.27	7.40	7.54	7.94	9.17	10.50	11.50	12.84	15.96
Social work activities without accommodation	88	671	9.30	3.1	11.51	2.3	7.20	7.50	7.75	8.00	8.58	10.49	11.98	13.02	14.11	18.01
ARTS, ENTERTAINMENT AND RECREATION	R	508	9.39	3.1	15.36	15.1	6.93	7.23	7.50	7.88	8.51	10.54	12.31	13.68	15.25	20.49
Creative, arts and entertainment activities	90	48	12.78	-3.7	17.82	-0.7	7.61	8.83	9.37	9.98	11.05	15.33	18.22	19.44	20.78	x
Libraries, archives, museums and other cultural activities	91	63	11.15	-3.1	13.68	-0.3	7.20	7.97	8.36	8.64	9.98	12.69	14.00	15.62	16.53	x
Gambling and betting activities	92	95	8.51	2.4	11.05	6.4	x	7.20	7.47	7.79	8.05	9.36	10.43	11.06	12.16	x
Sports activities and amusement and recreation activities	93	302	9.06	4.1	17.04	25.2	6.70	7.20	7.30	7.51	8.30	10.09	11.73	13.00	14.58	20.24
OTHER SERVICE ACTIVITIES	S	444	10.53	3.0	13.81	3.0	7.20	7.50	7.96	8.28	9.32	11.97	13.85	15.29	17.06	22.78
Activities of membership organisations	94	209	12.25	-1.3	15.78	-0.8	7.50	8.55	9.13	9.80	10.95	13.91	16.23	17.86	19.91	24.76
Repair of computers and personal and household goods	95	37	12.45	-1.8	15.52	1.6	7.50	8.82	9.50	10.11	11.31	14.22	16.42	17.94	20.48	x
Other personal service activities	96	198	8.62	4.3	11.46	6.1	6.90	x	7.20	7.39	8.00	9.58	10.90	11.86	12.98	17.30
ACTIVITIES OF HOUSEHOLDS AS EMPLOYERS; UNDIFFERENTIATED GOODS-AND SERVICES-PRODUCING ACTIVITIES OF HOUSEHOLDS FOR OWN USE	T	71	9.08	0.9	10.20	-0.8	7.44	7.98	8.00	8.31	8.72	9.71	10.02	10.80	11.59	x
Activities of households as employers of domestic personnel	97	71	9.08	0.9	10.20	-0.8	7.44	7.98	8.00	8.31	8.72	9.71	10.02	10.80	11.59	x
Undifferentiated goods- and services-producing activities of private households for own use	98	:														
ACTIVITIES OF EXTRATERRITORIAL ORGANISATIONS AND BODIES	U	x	x		15.50	6.7	x	x	x	x	x	x	x	x	x	x
Activities of extraterritorial organisations and bodies	99	x	x		15.50	6.7	x	x	x	x	x	x	x	x	x	x
NOT CLASSIFIED		6	8.41	0.8	x		x	7.25	7.51	7.52	8.22	9.90	x	x	x	x

a Employees on adult rates whose pay for the survey pay-period was not affected by absence.

Source: Annual Survey of Hours and Earnings, Office for National Statistics.

b Figures for Number of Jobs are for indicative purposes only and should not be considered an accurate estimate of employee job counts.

KEY - The colour coding indicates the quality of each estimate; jobs, median, mean and percentiles but not the annual percentage change.

The quality of an estimate is measured by its coefficient of variation (CV), which is the ratio of the standard error of an estimate to the estimate.

Key	Statistical robustness
CV <= 5%	Estimates are considered precise
CV > 5% and <= 10%	Estimates are considered reasonably precise
CV > 10% and <= 20%	Estimates are considered acceptable
x = CV > 20%	Estimates are considered unreliable for practical purposes
.. = disclosive	
: = not applicable	
- = nil or negligible	

4.13 Average weekly earnings: main industrial sectors Great Britain

Great Britain

Standard Industrial Classification 2007

	Whole economy		Manufacturing		Construction		Services		Distribution Hotels and Restuarants	
	Actual	Seasonally adjusted	Actual	Seasonally adjusted	Actual	Seasonally adjusted	Actual	Seasonally adjusted	Actual	Seasonally adjusted
	KA46	**KAB9**	**K55I**	**K5CA**	**K55L**	**K5CD**	**K55O**	**K5BZ**	**K55R**	**K5CG**
2000	313	313	363	364	370	370	298	297	212	212
2001	329	330	377	377	399	398	315	314	221	220
2002	340	340	390	391	409	409	326	324	229	229
2003	350	351	405	405	427	427	336	335	234	234
2004	366	366	425	424	439	439	352	351	242	242
2005	382	383	440	440	452	452	369	369	251	252
2006	400	401	457	457	480	480	387	386	260	260
2007	420	420	476	475	512	512	406	405	276	276
2008	436	435	490	490	520	521	422	421	283	283
2009	435	435	495	496	525	525	420	420	286	286
2010	445	444	516	515	525	525	430	430	293	293
2011	455	455	524	522	534	534	442	441	296	296
2012	461	461	533	532	538	538	447	447	304	304
2013	466	466	545	544	536	535	452	452	312	311
2014	472	471	555	554	542	541	457	456	316	315
2015	482	482	564	563	555	554	468	468	328	328
2016	494	493	576	576	583	582	479	478	336	336

	Finance and Business Industries		Private Sector		Public Sector		Private Sector Excl Financial Services	
	Actual	Seasonally adjusted	Actual	Seasonally adjusted	Actual	Seasonally adjusted	Actual	Seasonally adjusted
	K55U	**K5C4**	**KA4O**	**KAC4**	**KA4R**	**KAC7**	**KA4U**	**KAD8**
2000	380	382	312	312	314	314	314	314
2001	408	408	328	328	331	330	331	330
2002	414	414	338	338	344	343	344	342
2003	424	424	347	348	360	360	360	359
2004	447	448	363	363	376	375	375	374
2005	474	475	378	379	396	395	395	394
2006	507	507	397	398	410	409	410	408
2007	534	532	419	419	424	422	424	421
2008	560	557	434	434	439	437	438	436
2009	540	541	429	429	452	452	450	448
2010	566	566	438	437	467	467	459	459
2011	597	596	448	448	479	479	468	467
2012	597	596	454	454	487	487	476	475
2013	598	598	460	460	490	489	480	479
2014	599	599	467	466	493	492	487	486
2015	616	616	479	479	497	497	492	492
2016	631	630	492	491	505	505	501	500

Source: Office for National Statistics: 01633 456780

4.14a Average Weekly Earnings by Industry (Not Seasonally Adjusted)

All figures are in pounds (£)

	Agriculture, Forestry and Fishing (A)			Mining and Quarrying (B)			Manufacturing - Food Products, Beverages and Tobacco (C1)			Manufacturing - Textiles, Leather and Clothing (C2)		
	Average Weekly Earnings	of which		Average Weekly Earnings	Of which		Average Weekly Earnings	Of which		Average Weekly Earnings	Of which	
		Bonuses	Arrears		Bonuses	Arrears		Bonuses	Arrears		Bonuses	Arrears
CDID	K57A	K57B	K57C	K57D	K57E	K57F	K57G	K57H	K57I	K57J	K57K	K57L
2012 Jan	322	3	0	1247	260	6	456	8	0	367	9	0
2012 Feb	325	6	0	1138	160	0	459	10	0	381	19	0
2012 Mar	337	17	0	1534	548	2	506	46	0	380	21	0
2012 Apr	312	2	0	1133	137	0	469	15	1	371	10	0
2012 May	312	5	0	1069	60	0	466	12	1	379	10	0
2012 Jun	321	3	0	1032	54	0	473	12	0	381	16	0
2012 Jul	342	14	0	1036	57	0	462	8	0	393	15	0
2012 Aug	336	8	0	1021	36	0	461	4	0	387	9	0
2012 Sep	334	6	0	1025	36	1	486	23	0	394	11	0
2012 Oct	327	4	1	1039	42	3	468	11	0	392	10	0
2012 Nov	333	5	0	1069	59	5	461	4	0	400	18	0
2012 Dec	358	28	2	1073	83	4	497	27	0	407	29	0
2013 Jan	339	6	0	1207	226	0	467	7	8	387	10	0
2013 Feb	344	6	0	1197	198	3	482	16	0	392	13	0
2013 Mar	342	3	0	1534	538	3	533	46	2	408	27	0
2013 Apr	351	4	0	1266	271	1	491	14	0	397	15	0
2013 May	347	3	0	1183	165	0	483	5	1	393	10	0
2013 Jun	335	3	0	1088	57	2	489	9	1	397	10	0
2013 Jul	336	2	0	1083	39	0	479	7	1	395	8	0
2013 Aug	335	3	0	1098	45	6	475	5	0	395	13	0
2013 Sep	342	3	0	1127	51	1	493	18	0	407	16	0
2013 Oct	346	2	0	1133	52	3	484	10	0	398	10	1
2013 Nov	335	3	0	1112	48	1	485	4	0	404	10	0
2013 Dec	390	53	0	1144	84	0	527	44	0	411	35	0
2014 Jan	340	3	0	1181	114	2	490	6	0	389	8	0
2014 Feb	350	5	0	1200	142	8	503	20	1	388	10	0
2014 Mar	352	2	1	1614	574	3	517	53	0	393	16	0
2014 Apr	345	3	0	1297	233	0	483	9	0	385	11	0
2014 May	334	3	0	1265	176	1	478	5	1	378	6	0
2014 Jun	335	5	0	1137	77	0	486	16	0	384	7	0
2014 Jul	346	13	0	1117	59	1	477	8	0	382	8	0
2014 Aug	330	2	0	1105	44	3	474	4	0	378	6	0
2014 Sep	335	5	0	1118	54	0	491	19	0	385	9	0
2014 Oct	342	3	0	1125	62	0	473	6	0	388	11	0
2014 Nov	339	3	0	1094	45	0	491	22	0	395	8	0
2014 Dec	390	42	1	1134	92	1	514	42	0	411	23	0
2015 Jan	348	13	0	1119	103	0	478	10	0	398	13	0
2015 Feb	347	4	0	1155	126	0	487	18	0	397	11	0
2015 Mar	364	7	0	1507	481	0	514	51	0	414	27	0
2015 Apr	367	4	0	1211	170	1	480	13	0	402	21	1
2015 May	355	5	0	1130	92	0	473	9	0	390	12	0
2015 Jun	350	8	0	1124	72	0	469	9	0	393	7	0
2015 Jul	361	17	0	1077	36	1	467	6	0	399	12	0
2015 Aug	360	9	0	1089	38	0	463	2	1	393	6	0
2015 Sep	358	7	0	1107	59	0	485	18	0	399	10	0
2015 Oct	354	6	0	1097	49	0	478	9	0	400	10	0
2015 Nov	370	3	0	1094	61	0	481	10	1	400	11	0
2015 Dec	377	16	0	1108	71	0	518	38	3	421	33	0
2016 Jan	377	20	0	1170	132	0	481	9	1	399	9	0
2016 Feb	373	4	0	1331	303	2	492	18	1	388	8	0
2016 Mar	387	6	0	1621	592	2	558	79	1	396	23	0
2016 Apr	388	11	0	1220	178	2	498	16	0	401	15	0
2016 May	371	5	0	1086	51	2	496	11	0	392	10	0
2016 Jun	362	3	0	1103	71	1	485	8	0	388	7	0
2016 Jul	374	14	0	1090	53	0	484	7	0	389	7	0
2016 Aug	362	3	0	1073	43	1	482	3	1	384	5	0
2016 Sep	382	2	0	1058	51	3	508	26	0	390	7	0
2016 Oct	389	5	0	1066	40	1	491	6	0	392	9	0
2016 Nov	375	2	0	1086	62	1	490	5	0	401	11	0
2016 Dec	410	37	0	1105	73	1	517	27	0	417	29	0
2017 Jan	376	4	0	1153	125	0	486	7	0	403	7	0
2017 Feb	386	5	0	1426	402	1	499	18	0	396	10	0
2017 Mar	387	1	1	1395	368	1	562	82	0	421	31	0
2017 Apr	396	6	0	1280	240	1	514	21	0	405	13	0
2017 May	389	5	0	1090	49	0	499	10	0	403	8	0
2017 Jun	391	4	0	1090	48	0	499	10	1	407	10	0
2017 Jul	394	15	0	1084	51	0	494	8	1	431	30	0
2017 Aug	402	7	0	1062	25	0	493	3	1	405	6	0
2017 Sep	404	4	0	1093	57	0	516	26	1	409	10	0
2017 Oct	399	4	0	1094	53	0	500	7	2	410	8	1
2017 Nov	393	5	0	1095	52	2	498	6	2	410	7	0
2017 Dec	419	37	0	1109	65	0	518	25	2	440	39	0
2018 Jan	388	3	0	1191	150	0	496	7	1	403	8	1
2018 Feb	384	3	0	1401	359	1	495	7	1	409	14	0
2018 Mar	380	3	0	1441	393	0	542	48	1	431	34	0

p = Provisional r = Revised

Source: Monthly Wages and Salaries Survey

Inquiries: Email: earnings@ons.gov.uk Tel: 01633 456120

4.14a Average Weekly Earnings by Industry (Not Seasonally Adjusted)

All figures are in pounds (£)

	Manufacturing - Chemicals and Man-made Fibres (C3)			Manufacturing - Basic Metals and Metal Products (C4)			Manufacturing - Engineering and Allied Industries (C5)			Other Manufacturing (C6)		
	Average Weekly Earnings	Of which Bonuses	Of which Arrears	Average Weekly Earnings	Of which Bonuses	Of which Arrears	Average Weekly Earnings	Of which Bonuses	Of which Arrears	Average Weekly Earnings	Of which Bonuses	Of which Arrears
CDID	K57M	K57N	K57O	K57P	K57Q	K57R	K57S	K57T	K57U	K57V	K57W	K57X
2012 Jan	672	25	10	525	19	0	582	19	1	463	14	0
2012 Feb	662	25	2	520	16	0	601	41	1	468	17	0
2012 Mar	901	265	0	548	39	0	631	65	1	504	45	1
2012 Apr	729	84	1	549	36	1	596	26	2	478	20	0
2012 May	669	19	0	537	24	1	589	17	1	472	13	0
2012 Jun	678	24	1	526	21	0	601	28	1	472	13	1
2012 Jul	677	21	4	532	21	0	590	16	0	469	11	0
2012 Aug	672	19	1	510	8	0	584	13	1	470	10	0
2012 Sep	662	13	1	511	9	0	580	7	4	471	10	0
2012 Oct	667	17	0	515	11	0	585	8	1	473	13	0
2012 Nov	682	17	2	522	13	2	588	14	1	478	15	0
2012 Dec	715	36	1	529	23	4	598	26	0	485	22	0
2013 Jan	696	21	6	523	12	6	593	19	0	472	12	0
2013 Feb	700	31	0	518	17	3	604	28	0	479	16	0
2013 Mar	946	270	0	547	41	1	655	76	1	511	44	0
2013 Apr	811	149	1	534	25	0	621	35	1	492	26	1
2013 May	690	22	2	526	20	0	603	16	1	479	13	0
2013 Jun	693	15	0	524	21	0	632	42	1	477	11	0
2013 Jul	689	12	0	518	16	0	614	22	2	478	12	0
2013 Aug	696	17	0	502	6	0	600	15	0	476	9	1
2013 Sep	685	20	1	517	11	0	589	6	0	478	11	1
2013 Oct	684	16	1	526	12	0	598	11	1	481	10	1
2013 Nov	686	16	0	533	16	0	608	14	1	486	15	2
2013 Dec	704	28	1	551	33	9	614	23	1	499	25	0
2014 Jan	670	20	0	527	14	0	629	30	3	485	13	1
2014 Feb	682	23	0	533	19	0	629	25	2	488	17	1
2014 Mar	1019	351	1	549	33	0	679	75	1	525	52	1
2014 Apr	779	114	1	532	18	0	640	31	1	504	28	1
2014 May	692	14	1	535	17	1	623	20	1	494	15	1
2014 Jun	689	15	1	541	22	0	655	45	3	494	13	0
2014 Jul	704	34	1	539	18	0	626	22	0	487	13	1
2014 Aug	700	28	0	518	6	1	608	8	1	488	12	0
2014 Sep	696	24	1	536	12	4	609	9	0	491	12	1
2014 Oct	687	15	1	542	14	0	614	9	0	489	11	0
2014 Nov	669	13	0	544	15	0	618	10	1	491	13	0
2014 Dec	686	31	0	562	38	1	649	40	2	505	30	0
2015 Jan	678	25	0	539	17	0	629	15	2	489	19	0
2015 Feb	712	38	1	532	12	6	631	18	1	490	16	0
2015 Mar	1030	348	1	569	44	6	700	81	2	540	69	0
2015 Apr	793	117	1	551	21	0	656	30	2	508	31	0
2015 May	705	13	0	538	11	1	638	17	1	492	13	0
2015 Jun	707	17	0	552	18	0	679	56	1	500	19	0
2015 Jul	730	44	2	558	16	3	640	17	1	508	22	1
2015 Aug	706	15	1	540	6	1	625	9	1	504	17	0
2015 Sep	719	19	4	553	11	0	624	7	0	495	10	0
2015 Oct	718	24	1	555	13	1	627	8	0	497	12	1
2015 Nov	702	15	0	558	16	0	631	9	0	505	14	0
2015 Dec	734	42	1	574	37	0	650	25	0	523	34	0
2016 Jan	702	14	2	549	10	0	647	18	1	504	18	0
2016 Feb	710	22	0	557	19	1	644	18	1	504	19	0
2016 Mar	1125	430	1	577	40	0	699	71	1	539	49	1
2016 Apr	796	89	0	567	25	0	673	34	1	521	27	0
2016 May	737	23	0	573	29	1	657	17	0	509	16	0
2016 Jun	739	16	1	572	24	0	692	50	0	512	20	0
2016 Jul	752	26	0	556	10	0	669	22	1	511	17	1
2016 Aug	709	16	0	550	9	0	656	12	1	504	13	0
2016 Sep	715	19	0	561	10	1	647	8	1	507	13	1
2016 Oct	713	28	0	555	8	1	652	11	0	505	11	0
2016 Nov	711	27	0	558	17	0	653	10	1	514	19	0
2016 Dec	739	47	0	573	40	0	677	31	4	526	32	1
2017 Jan	707	30	0	559	14	2	665	16	1	509	17	0
2017 Feb	727	32	6	565	22	0	670	25	1	511	21	1
2017 Mar	969	274	1	588	44	0	744	92	1	537	43	0
2017 Apr	825	114	4	575	26	0	687	33	1	523	29	1
2017 May	742	32	1	572	23	1	666	16	1	512	15	0
2017 Jun	729	24	1	565	21	0	702	45	1	517	19	1
2017 Jul	732	31	1	576	27	0	688	30	2	514	21	1
2017 Aug	733	14	0	556	5	1	669	15	2	508	12	1
2017 Sep	737	13	1	554	7	2	669	11	0	513	13	0
2017 Oct	734	18	1	561	9	0	683	23	1	512	13	0
2017 Nov	760	34	1	576	16	0	678	14	2	522	20	1
2017 Dec	773	45	0	599	38	5	707	39	1	531	30	1
2018 Jan	740	11	0	563	13	0	697	23	1	516	17	0
2018 Feb	758	31	0	568	16	0	697	27	1	517	18	0
2018 Mar	981	249	0	598	46	1	799	127	2	551	47	2

p = Provisional r = Revised

Source: Monthly Wages and Salaries Survey

Inquiries: Email: earnings@ons.gov.uk Tel: 01633 456120

4.14a Average Weekly Earnings by Industry (Not Seasonally Adjusted)

All figures are in pounds (£)

	Electricity, Gas and Water Supply (D , E)			Construction (F)			Wholesale Trade (G46)			Retail Trade and Repairs (G45 & G47)		
	Average Weekly Earnings	Of which		Average Weekly Earnings	Of which		Average Weekly Earnings	Of which		Average Weekly Earnings	Of which	
		Bonuses	Arrears		Bonuses	Arrears		Bonuses	Arrears		Bonuses	Arrears
CDID	K57Y	K57Z	K582	K583	K584	K585	K586	K587	K588	K589	K58A	K58B
2012 Jan	600	24	0	533	13	0	527	55	0	268	12	0
2012 Feb	600	32	1	534	14	0	522	53	0	272	18	0
2012 Mar	657	87	1	582	49	3	573	101	1	291	34	0
2012 Apr	617	36	0	538	16	0	516	41	0	277	18	1
2012 May	593	17	2	542	13	0	516	39	1	277	16	0
2012 Jun	659	80	1	547	22	0	532	53	0	279	16	0
2012 Jul	637	58	2	538	15	0	523	42	1	275	15	0
2012 Aug	591	15	1	519	8	0	522	42	0	273	15	0
2012 Sep	596	17	2	531	17	0	514	33	0	270	10	0
2012 Oct	611	19	6	529	14	0	525	37	1	274	15	0
2012 Nov	617	24	2	534	17	0	518	31	0	270	14	0
2012 Dec	613	22	1	532	24	0	532	48	1	268	14	0
2013 Jan	601	20	0	519	12	1	547	57	0	272	13	0
2013 Feb	613	26	4	530	13	1	549	62	0	273	19	0
2013 Mar	656	74	0	550	28	1	575	80	2	294	35	0
2013 Apr	641	48	1	557	28	1	583	81	0	282	21	1
2013 May	612	24	0	537	13	1	541	41	1	285	23	0
2013 Jun	668	71	1	541	20	1	555	52	0	282	16	0
2013 Jul	642	54	0	533	15	1	562	59	1	285	18	0
2013 Aug	616	24	1	528	11	1	550	50	0	287	21	0
2013 Sep	602	11	2	542	23	1	538	38	0	278	11	0
2013 Oct	613	18	2	526	12	1	545	37	0	283	18	0
2013 Nov	617	14	7	534	16	1	536	42	0	277	13	0
2013 Dec	619	20	3	540	24	1	565	64	0	276	13	0
2014 Jan	624	19	1	546	15	1	583	59	1	283	14	0
2014 Feb	625	18	1	533	14	0	543	48	0	280	14	0
2014 Mar	697	83	5	554	39	0	604	108	1	306	38	0
2014 Apr	667	49	12	531	18	0	556	61	1	296	24	0
2014 May	628	23	2	526	12	0	526	31	0	298	24	0
2014 Jun	676	72	1	541	21	0	547	53	0	288	14	0
2014 Jul	663	57	3	551	27	0	539	48	1	288	15	0
2014 Aug	637	27	2	531	14	1	526	41	1	288	14	0
2014 Sep	621	18	2	551	28	1	533	37	0	288	11	0
2014 Oct	623	14	2	537	14	0	533	39	0	294	17	0
2014 Nov	637	18	8	547	22	0	529	38	0	290	16	0
2014 Dec	624	13	1	556	33	1	557	65	1	287	13	0
2015 Jan	627	21	1	534	15	0	556	59	0	303	17	0
2015 Feb	646	37	6	538	12	0	555	65	0	298	15	0
2015 Mar	697	89	2	583	44	0	668	169	1	326	39	0
2015 Apr	670	56	4	546	20	0	551	57	0	317	25	0
2015 May	642	24	2	555	28	0	542	39	0	316	26	0
2015 Jun	694	71	2	551	19	0	552	51	0	307	18	0
2015 Jul	665	51	1	568	29	0	560	57	0	309	20	0
2015 Aug	646	29	1	546	13	0	545	39	0	304	16	0
2015 Sep	626	15	3	559	26	0	529	35	0	303	15	0
2015 Oct	625	11	1	553	16	1	530	36	0	306	19	0
2015 Nov	631	17	2	561	20	1	536	40	1	302	16	0
2015 Dec	633	13	4	565	33	0	575	71	1	302	16	0
2016 Jan	627	16	1	566	21	1	556	51	0	307	18	0
2016 Feb	660	33	4	565	19	0	586	71	0	306	17	0
2016 Mar	713	90	1	598	48	1	642	120	1	326	35	0
2016 Apr	708	77	1	577	27	0	577	49	0	328	30	1
2016 May	661	18	5	584	37	0	560	31	1	326	29	1
2016 Jun	721	66	12	571	22	0	570	44	1	316	15	1
2016 Jul	706	63	2	590	34	1	568	43	0	322	24	1
2016 Aug	670	26	2	567	14	0	559	36	0	316	16	1
2016 Sep	658	14	2	589	32	0	559	35	1	315	14	1
2016 Oct	659	13	2	603	43	0	570	45	0	320	21	1
2016 Nov	672	20	2	592	27	1	568	44	0	319	18	0
2016 Dec	667	19	5	595	39	1	582	60	0	316	18	0
2017 Jan	663	20	1	574	15	1	588	45	1	319	20	0
2017 Feb	675	28	2	579	22	0	610	79	1	312	16	0
2017 Mar	734	82	1	605	50	1	675	137	1	333	34	1
2017 Apr	744	90	1	576	22	0	581	49	0	339	31	0
2017 May	676	21	5	577	21	0	561	32	1	339	31	0
2017 Jun	736	81	2	581	21	1	566	38	0	326	18	0
2017 Jul	705	50	2	593	26	1	571	40	1	321	21	0
2017 Aug	668	16	1	581	15	0	569	38	0	319	16	0
2017 Sep	667	17	2	611	38	0	559	32	0	326	17	0
2017 Oct	661	10	2	605	31	0	569	41	0	329	21	1
2017 Nov	665	12	1	602	26	0	589	50	1	326	21	0
2017 Dec	672	12	6	611	30	1	614	72	0	319	16	0
2018 Jan	671	15	2	600	19	0	597	53	0	324	16	0
2018 Feb	683	30	1	596	18	0	603	68	0	327	21	0
2018 Mar	736	82	2	641	57	0	690	155	1	342	30	0

p = Provisional r = Revised

Source: Monthly Wages and Salaries Survey
Inquiries: Email: earnings@ons.gov.uk Tel: 01633 456120

4.14a Average Weekly Earnings by Industry (Not Seasonally Adjusted)

All figures are in pounds (£)

	Transport and Storage (H)			Accommodation and Food Service Activities (I)			Information and Communication (J)			Financial & Insurance Activities (K)		
	Average Weekly Earnings	Of which Bonuses	Of which Arrears	Average Weekly Earnings	Of which Bonuses	Of which Arrears	Average Weekly Earnings	Of which Bonuses	Of which Arrears	Average Weekly Earnings	Of which Bonuses	Of which Arrears
CDID	K58F	K58G	K58H	K58C	K58D	K58E	K5E9	K5EA	K5EB	K58I	K58J	K58K
2012 Jan	507	7	0	220	6	0	728	78	1	1080	323	0
2012 Feb	518	17	0	224	10	0	748	93	1	1467	703	2
2012 Mar	528	25	0	217	6	0	821	161	2	1483	716	3
2012 Apr	528	17	1	217	4	1	724	67	1	884	115	0
2012 May	523	9	1	221	8	0	736	77	2	863	94	1
2012 Jun	542	26	2	219	3	0	783	131	2	988	223	3
2012 Jul	524	6	1	221	5	0	736	76	1	849	87	0
2012 Aug	536	17	1	222	4	0	746	77	1	830	66	1
2012 Sep	527	11	0	219	3	0	735	67	3	844	84	1
2012 Oct	528	13	1	217	4	0	715	48	1	808	46	1
2012 Nov	522	7	2	220	6	0	733	62	1	808	41	1
2012 Dec	544	23	2	223	7	1	724	53	1	886	113	0
2013 Jan	519	7	0	212	5	1	744	74	2	1120	351	1
2013 Feb	523	14	0	216	8	0	773	99	1	1511	736	1
2013 Mar	539	26	1	217	6	0	799	131	1	1528	750	0
2013 Apr	543	21	5	219	8	0	775	95	2	1045	259	1
2013 May	534	9	1	224	9	0	742	59	2	956	168	0
2013 Jun	558	34	1	219	4	0	795	108	5	1037	257	0
2013 Jul	531	10	1	221	5	0	744	61	1	853	73	0
2013 Aug	531	12	1	221	3	0	755	68	1	840	64	0
2013 Sep	526	4	1	220	4	0	745	63	1	863	86	0
2013 Oct	531	6	2	220	3	0	736	51	2	828	50	1
2013 Nov	535	7	5	222	6	0	729	47	1	829	52	1
2013 Dec	566	34	1	227	8	1	740	51	1	927	140	0
2014 Jan	527	7	0	222	6	1	757	72	2	1125	350	0
2014 Feb	627	38	68	224	7	0	780	93	2	1632	841	3
2014 Mar	550	29	1	223	7	0	815	135	2	1619	813	3
2014 Apr	550	20	1	223	6	0	788	102	2	928	129	1
2014 May	545	13	1	229	10	0	750	67	1	948	154	1
2014 Jun	562	33	2	223	8	0	804	111	2	979	186	1
2014 Jul	552	23	0	223	6	0	741	46	3	853	59	2
2014 Aug	534	5	0	222	4	0	767	72	2	890	65	2
2014 Sep	534	5	1	219	4	1	730	37	1	920	90	1
2014 Oct	543	13	1	222	4	0	753	55	1	884	52	3
2014 Nov	543	7	1	224	8	1	753	56	2	885	53	0
2014 Dec	573	31	0	232	11	1	780	61	2	1041	198	2
2015 Jan	541	9	3	227	5	1	790	80	4	1174	337	1
2015 Feb	547	18	0	231	10	1	819	102	3	1568	721	5
2015 Mar	548	19	1	233	9	1	883	163	1	1785	940	1
2015 Apr	556	20	4	229	8	1	795	76	1	1045	185	2
2015 May	550	12	0	237	11	1	794	77	2	1011	154	1
2015 Jun	571	37	1	230	5	1	821	103	1	990	125	7
2015 Jul	543	10	1	233	5	1	797	78	0	954	93	3
2015 Aug	550	10	2	231	4	0	807	95	1	949	90	1
2015 Sep	546	8	1	228	5	0	758	49	2	949	89	1
2015 Oct	544	6	0	233	5	0	784	75	1	923	62	1
2015 Nov	547	10	1	234	8	0	767	57	2	915	48	1
2015 Dec	572	32	0	239	12	0	785	72	3	1083	205	2
2016 Jan	549	8	2	231	5	0	805	93	1	1252	379	0
2016 Feb	555	20	1	234	8	0	792	89	1	1441	559	5
2016 Mar	570	34	0	237	11	0	848	143	1	1927	1050	5
2016 Apr	560	22	0	233	7	0	789	75	2	1058	168	4
2016 May	546	10	1	238	10	0	791	78	1	1070	181	1
2016 Jun	574	29	6	233	6	0	804	87	2	1072	184	1
2016 Jul	551	11	2	236	5	0	798	80	1	1018	124	2
2016 Aug	558	16	1	237	4	0	798	82	1	954	71	2
2016 Sep	552	9	1	237	5	0	770	50	1	960	76	2
2016 Oct	547	7	1	236	4	0	783	63	1	956	71	1
2016 Nov	558	12	2	237	8	0	784	61	1	945	57	0
2016 Dec	581	35	1	243	10	0	796	68	1	1105	217	1
2017 Jan	549	10	1	234	4	1	824	94	1	1255	375	0
2017 Feb	563	21	4	238	10	0	817	94	1	1520	629	2
2017 Mar	570	29	1	243	11	0	878	149	2	2140	1247	5
2017 Apr	568	19	0	238	6	0	810	83	1	1092	190	1
2017 May	570	19	1	242	12	0	795	64	2	1096	188	7
2017 Jun	578	28	0	239	6	0	850	117	1	1172	263	2
2017 Jul	565	12	1	241	6	0	806	70	1	1011	100	1
2017 Aug	572	18	1	241	5	0	822	83	2	1007	87	4
2017 Sep	567	13	2	241	6	0	781	47	1	1053	134	2
2017 Oct	560	6	1	241	5	1	810	69	4	997	79	1
2017 Nov	567	10	1	244	8	0	809	64	1	975	53	1
2017 Dec	590	31	1	251	10	0	832	82	1	1194	263	3
2018 Jan	566	9	0	239	4	0	845	86	1	1334	400	1
2018 Feb	573	18	3	246	10	0	842	98	2	1608	664	3
2018 Mar	584	31	1	251	12	0	907	160	1	2170	1223	3

p = Provisional r = Revised

Source: Monthly Wages and Salaries Survey

Inquiries: Email: earnings@ons.gov.uk Tel: 01633 456120

4.14a Average Weekly Earnings by Industry (Not Seasonally Adjusted)

All figures are in pounds (£)

	Real Estate Activities (L)			Professional, Scientific & Technical Activities (M)			Administrative and Support Service Activities (N)			Public Administration (O)		
	Average Weekly Earnings	Of which		Average Weekly Earnings	Of which		Average Weekly Earnings	Of which		Average Weekly Earnings	Of which	
		Bonuses	Arrears		Bonuses	Arrears		Bonuses	Arrears		Bonuses	Arrears
CDID	K58L	K58M	K58N	K5EC	K5ED	K5EE	K5EF	K5EG	K5EH	K58O	K58P	K58Q
2012 Jan	464	29	0	664	37	1	345	12	0	535	1	0
2012 Feb	474	36	0	678	48	1	347	13	0	538	1	0
2012 Mar	576	133	0	766	132	1	375	39	0	541	2	0
2012 Apr	476	32	0	675	40	0	345	12	0	545	0	0
2012 May	466	30	0	663	30	0	344	10	0	543	1	0
2012 Jun	488	49	0	667	28	0	341	9	0	550	5	0
2012 Jul	491	53	0	691	59	1	345	12	0	551	5	0
2012 Aug	460	28	0	658	26	1	346	9	0	547	3	0
2012 Sep	473	36	1	650	23	1	340	9	0	554	7	1
2012 Oct	475	39	0	645	23	1	343	10	0	547	2	1
2012 Nov	472	36	0	651	28	1	340	8	0	544	2	0
2012 Dec	485	51	0	691	70	1	352	20	0	543	2	2
2013 Jan	477	47	2	640	22	0	342	11	0	546	1	1
2013 Feb	457	32	1	663	35	1	344	12	0	535	0	0
2013 Mar	512	81	1	719	87	2	366	37	0	536	3	0
2013 Apr	511	79	0	686	54	2	351	20	0	537	1	0
2013 May	481	45	0	653	32	1	351	15	0	537	0	0
2013 Jun	484	46	0	657	38	1	339	8	0	540	3	0
2013 Jul	501	65	0	671	46	2	349	15	0	543	6	0
2013 Aug	481	44	1	642	23	0	345	9	0	540	1	4
2013 Sep	473	44	0	650	29	1	337	9	0	547	7	0
2013 Oct	480	48	0	650	24	1	338	10	0	537	1	0
2013 Nov	466	41	0	647	22	1	337	8	0	537	1	0
2013 Dec	491	50	0	692	65	0	357	25	0	540	2	1
2014 Jan	467	39	0	647	21	1	352	18	1	545	1	1
2014 Feb	459	32	0	655	33	0	342	16	0	541	1	1
2014 Mar	537	101	1	727	100	1	363	34	0	548	2	4
2014 Apr	502	65	2	673	44	1	345	17	0	553	7	3
2014 May	487	51	0	664	41	1	348	12	0	547	1	1
2014 Jun	494	50	2	678	55	1	348	13	0	549	3	0
2014 Jul	515	76	1	669	46	1	354	13	0	549	4	3
2014 Aug	475	38	0	650	26	1	358	10	0	547	3	1
2014 Sep	475	30	1	651	26	1	360	10	0	555	7	0
2014 Oct	487	40	1	660	26	1	367	12	0	552	1	1
2014 Nov	478	34	0	655	24	1	357	10	0	549	1	1
2014 Dec	518	67	1	716	83	1	370	26	0	554	1	1
2015 Jan	484	35	0	653	21	1	362	14	0	551	0	1
2015 Feb	482	38	1	690	53	0	373	23	1	551	2	1
2015 Mar	600	155	1	763	122	1	390	34	0	548	2	0
2015 Apr	484	39	1	679	45	1	379	18	0	552	1	1
2015 May	502	61	0	666	36	1	383	13	1	552	1	0
2015 Jun	509	61	3	677	45	1	381	13	1	551	2	0
2015 Jul	536	91	1	683	49	1	378	13	0	554	4	0
2015 Aug	476	33	1	665	33	1	378	10	0	552	2	1
2015 Sep	477	30	0	653	20	0	373	11	0	561	8	1
2015 Oct	480	35	1	660	29	1	379	12	0	556	2	1
2015 Nov	470	27	0	658	22	1	377	11	0	553	1	1
2015 Dec	489	42	0	722	78	1	389	22	0	550	1	0
2016 Jan	479	31	0	670	25	1	389	17	1	556	0	1
2016 Feb	486	36	0	696	57	1	399	22	0	555	1	0
2016 Mar	652	198	1	773	128	3	413	37	0	553	2	1
2016 Apr	518	63	0	717	67	1	404	18	0	566	6	0
2016 May	514	64	0	667	32	0	400	21	0	557	1	0
2016 Jun	510	54	1	678	43	1	401	18	0	561	1	1
2016 Jul	538	88	0	690	62	1	400	17	0	556	1	0
2016 Aug	477	27	2	663	33	2	394	10	0	570	8	1
2016 Sep	478	34	0	653	22	1	396	11	0	562	2	0
2016 Oct	478	32	0	652	29	1	400	15	0	566	2	1
2016 Nov	472	25	0	656	27	1	398	10	0	564	1	1
2016 Dec	490	40	1	679	50	0	415	24	1	562	0	0
2017 Jan	486	34	0	670	28	1	402	15	0	563	0	0
2017 Feb	485	35	1	677	41	1	416	27	0	562	0	0
2017 Mar	620	169	1	740	101	0	451	60	0	561	1	0
2017 Apr	496	39	0	686	41	1	415	20	0	567	7	0
2017 May	518	62	2	681	33	1	412	14	0	561	1	0
2017 Jun	509	54	1	695	49	1	420	24	0	563	1	0
2017 Jul	538	85	1	708	60	2	410	12	1	564	1	2
2017 Aug	478	28	1	675	30	1	413	16	0	569	6	1
2017 Sep	481	31	0	676	32	0	413	14	0	564	3	1
2017 Oct	485	30	0	674	30	0	412	15	0	572	3	1
2017 Nov	476	27	1	673	30	1	411	11	0	568	2	2
2017 Dec	497	36	0	707	65	1	427	28	0	564	1	1
2018 Jan	505	36	0	678	36	1	412	15	0	572	1	1
2018 Feb	507	36	0	692	37	1	422	26	0	568	0	0
2018 Mar	654	183	1	766	109	1	446	51	0	569	1	1

p = Provisional r = Revised

Source: Monthly Wages and Salaries Survey

Inquiries: Email: earnings@ons.gov.uk Tel: 01633 456120

4.14a Average Weekly Earnings by Industry (Not Seasonally Adjusted)

All figures are in pounds (£)

	Education (P)			Health and Social Work (Q)			Arts, Entertainment and Recreation (R)			Other Service Activities (S)		
	Average Weekly Earnings	Of which		Average Weekly Earnings	Of which		Average Weekly Earnings	Of which		Average Weekly Earnings	Of which	
		Bonuses	Arrears		Bonuses	Arrears		Bonuses	Arrears		Bonuses	Arrears
CDID	K58R	K58S	K58T	K58U	K58V	K58W	K5EI	K5EJ	K5EK	K58X	K58Y	K58Z
2012 Jan	390	0	0	398	0	0	345	16	0	345	14	1
2012 Feb	391	1	0	400	1	0	334	7	0	342	19	0
2012 Mar	393	1	0	399	2	0	343	27	0	341	21	0
2012 Apr	396	1	0	401	0	0	333	10	1	335	12	0
2012 May	394	1	0	404	0	0	336	11	0	333	11	0
2012 Jun	397	1	0	401	0	0	365	25	0	337	15	0
2012 Jul	397	1	0	402	1	0	348	11	1	333	13	0
2012 Aug	404	1	0	401	1	0	361	10	0	336	12	0
2012 Sep	406	1	0	400	1	0	364	13	0	323	7	0
2012 Oct	402	0	0	400	1	0	352	6	0	320	8	0
2012 Nov	401	0	0	403	0	0	358	13	0	328	13	0
2012 Dec	402	1	1	404	1	0	374	14	0	331	13	0
2013 Jan	397	1	1	406	0	0	366	16	0	332	11	0
2013 Feb	394	0	0	398	1	0	356	5	0	328	11	0
2013 Mar	395	2	0	400	1	0	358	19	0	333	20	0
2013 Apr	398	0	0	407	1	0	364	18	0	336	13	0
2013 May	399	1	0	404	1	0	367	19	0	335	9	0
2013 Jun	399	1	0	403	1	0	375	18	0	337	6	0
2013 Jul	401	1	0	402	1	0	363	10	0	335	9	0
2013 Aug	405	1	1	398	0	0	366	13	0	336	8	0
2013 Sep	408	0	0	400	1	0	365	19	0	329	6	0
2013 Oct	408	1	1	400	1	0	349	4	0	340	5	5
2013 Nov	406	1	1	400	1	0	350	13	0	342	9	1
2013 Dec	410	1	1	402	1	0	346	14	0	346	9	0
2014 Jan	402	0	0	404	1	0	363	12	1	347	12	1
2014 Feb	404	0	0	401	1	0	334	6	0	420	76	0
2014 Mar	405	3	0	399	1	0	329	13	0	373	28	2
2014 Apr	406	1	1	404	1	0	351	14	0	353	14	0
2014 May	407	1	2	404	1	0	344	13	0	352	11	1
2014 Jun	406	1	0	404	1	0	354	15	0	348	7	0
2014 Jul	408	1	0	401	0	0	350	7	0	353	12	0
2014 Aug	415	1	0	399	1	0	338	6	1	357	11	0
2014 Sep	418	1	0	404	1	0	344	16	0	357	7	0
2014 Oct	415	1	0	403	0	0	333	8	1	356	8	0
2014 Nov	413	1	0	404	1	0	336	8	1	341	9	0
2014 Dec	420	2	2	405	1	0	341	18	1	348	14	0
2015 Jan	413	1	0	406	1	0	351	14	1	344	15	0
2015 Feb	411	0	0	404	0	0	330	11	0	346	17	0
2015 Mar	413	3	0	404	1	0	341	22	0	365	33	0
2015 Apr	413	1	0	408	1	0	347	25	0	353	18	0
2015 May	412	0	0	410	1	0	336	11	0	350	13	0
2015 Jun	415	2	0	410	0	0	366	18	0	353	11	0
2015 Jul	416	1	0	408	0	0	372	17	0	358	15	0
2015 Aug	421	1	0	404	0	0	365	20	0	355	15	0
2015 Sep	424	1	0	408	1	0	381	29	0	347	10	0
2015 Oct	420	1	0	404	0	0	347	11	0	348	9	0
2015 Nov	421	1	2	407	1	0	346	7	0	349	10	0
2015 Dec	422	1	1	408	1	0	358	15	3	356	17	0
2016 Jan	418	2	1	408	1	0	365	10	0	375	23	1
2016 Feb	418	1	0	409	0	1	356	10	0	372	20	0
2016 Mar	418	1	0	408	1	1	361	14	0	386	31	0
2016 Apr	419	1	0	413	0	0	382	37	0	396	27	1
2016 May	417	1	0	413	1	0	363	17	0	384	14	0
2016 Jun	421	1	1	415	0	1	376	20	0	389	19	0
2016 Jul	419	1	1	412	0	0	399	15	0	388	14	0
2016 Aug	426	1	0	412	0	0	398	35	0	389	17	0
2016 Sep	430	1	0	413	1	0	394	25	0	385	13	0
2016 Oct	427	1	1	413	0	0	377	13	0	390	12	0
2016 Nov	425	1	1	416	2	1	383	10	1	394	18	1
2016 Dec	427	1	1	415	1	0	380	17	0	403	20	0
2017 Jan	423	1	0	415	1	0	386	20	0	382	17	0
2017 Feb	423	0	0	415	1	0	449	91	0	385	17	0
2017 Mar	424	1	0	414	1	0	376	23	0	400	27	0
2017 Apr	427	1	0	420	1	0	376	20	0	405	28	0
2017 May	427	1	0	424	1	1	378	16	0	390	14	0
2017 Jun	428	1	0	422	1	0	407	28	1	387	10	1
2017 Jul	430	2	0	421	1	0	420	28	0	399	20	2
2017 Aug	439	1	1	420	0	0	403	21	0	390	16	0
2017 Sep	441	1	1	423	1	0	407	21	1	375	8	0
2017 Oct	440	1	1	425	1	0	391	12	0	370	15	0
2017 Nov	438	2	1	427	2	0	396	12	0	375	13	0
2017 Dec	440	2	1	426	1	0	396	17	0	384	16	0
2018 Jan	436	1	1	426	1	0	374	13	1	383	15	0
2018 Feb	437	1	0	425	0	0	380	11	0	381	19	0
2018 Mar	438	2	0	426	1	0	392	28	0	399	25	0

p = Provisional r = Revised

Source: Monthly Wages and Salaries Survey

Inquiries: Email: earnings@ons.gov.uk Tel: 01633 456120

4.14b Average Weekly Earnings (nominal) - Regular Pay
(Great Britain, seasonally adjusted)

Standard Industrial Classification (2007)

	Whole Economy			Private sector [3 4 5]			Public sector [3 4 5]			Services, SIC 2007 sections G-S		
	Weekly Earnings (£)	% changes year on year: Single month	% changes year on year: 3 month average [2]	Weekly Earnings (£)	% changes year on year: Single month	% changes year on year: 3 month average [2]	Weekly Earnings (£)	% changes year on year: Single month	% changes year on year: 3 month average [2]	Weekly Earnings (£)	% changes year on year: Single month	% changes year on year: 3 month average [2]
	KAI7	KAI8	KAI9	KAJ2	KAJ3	KAJ4	KAJ5	KAJ6	KAJ7	K5DL	K5DM	K5DN
Jan 04	340	3.4	3.8	333	3.1	3.5	364	4.3	4.6	325	3.5	4.0
Feb 04	340	3.3	3.7	333	2.8	3.3	366	4.7	4.6	325	3.3	3.8
Mar 04	341	3.4	3.4	334	3.1	3.0	367	4.4	4.5	326	3.3	3.4
Apr 04	343	3.5	3.4	336	3.2	3.0	369	4.6	4.6	328	3.6	3.4
May 04	344	3.6	3.5	337	3.2	3.2	370	5.0	4.7	329	3.7	3.5
Jun 04	345	3.6	3.6	337	3.3	3.3	372	4.5	4.7	330	3.8	3.7
Jul 04	346	3.8	3.7	339	3.7	3.4	373	3.8	4.4	331	3.9	3.8
Aug 04	348	3.9	3.8	340	4.0	3.7	375	3.6	4.0	333	3.9	3.8
Sep 04	348	3.7	3.8	340	3.5	3.8	376	4.1	3.8	334	3.8	3.9
Oct 04	350	3.9	3.8	342	3.7	3.8	378	4.6	4.1	336	4.2	4.0
Nov 04	351	3.7	3.8	343	3.5	3.6	379	4.5	4.4	336	3.9	4.0
Dec 04	353	4.1	3.9	346	4.1	3.8	379	4.1	4.4	339	4.5	4.2
Jan 05	354	4.2	4.0	346	3.9	3.8	382	5.0	4.5	339	4.4	4.2
Feb 05	354	4.2	4.1	347	4.2	4.1	382	4.3	4.5	341	4.7	4.5
Mar 05	357	4.6	4.3	349	4.4	4.2	386	5.3	4.9	343	5.1	4.7
Apr 05	357	4.1	4.3	349	3.8	4.1	389	5.4	5.0	344	4.8	4.8
May 05	358	4.2	4.3	349	3.7	4.0	391	5.7	5.4	345	4.7	4.8
Jun 05	359	4.2	4.2	351	3.9	3.8	391	5.2	5.4	346	4.7	4.7
Jul 05	361	4.4	4.3	353	4.2	3.9	392	5.2	5.4	348	5.0	4.8
Aug 05	363	4.4	4.3	354	4.1	4.1	394	5.0	5.1	349	4.8	4.8
Sep 05	364	4.6	4.5	355	4.4	4.2	396	5.2	5.1	350	5.0	4.9
Oct 05	365	4.2	4.4	356	4.0	4.2	397	5.1	5.1	351	4.4	4.7
Nov 05	366	4.2	4.3	357	4.0	4.1	399	5.2	5.2	351	4.5	4.6
Dec 05	366	3.7	4.0	358	3.3	3.8	400	5.5	5.3	352	3.8	4.2
Jan 06	368	4.1	4.0	360	4.0	3.8	400	4.7	5.1	354	4.4	4.2
Feb 06	369	4.3	4.0	361	4.0	3.8	402	5.3	5.2	355	4.1	4.1
Mar 06	370	3.6	4.0	362	3.7	3.9	400	3.6	4.5	356	3.8	4.1
Apr 06	371	3.9	3.9	363	4.2	4.0	400	3.1	4.0	356	3.6	3.9
May 06	373	4.0	3.8	365	4.5	4.1	401	2.6	3.1	357	3.7	3.7
Jun 06	375	4.2	4.0	366	4.5	4.4	404	3.4	3.0	360	4.1	3.8
Jul 06	374	3.6	3.9	366	3.7	4.2	405	3.5	3.2	360	3.4	3.7
Aug 06	375	3.4	3.7	367	3.6	3.9	405	2.9	3.3	360	3.3	3.6
Sep 06	377	3.5	3.5	369	3.9	3.7	406	2.7	3.0	362	3.4	3.3
Oct 06	379	4.0	3.7	371	4.4	4.0	408	2.8	2.8	364	4.0	3.5
Nov 06	380	4.0	3.8	372	4.4	4.2	410	2.8	2.8	365	4.0	3.8
Dec 06	381	4.1	4.1	374	4.5	4.4	411	3.0	2.8	367	4.2	4.1
Jan 07	382	3.7	4.0	373	3.8	4.2	414	3.7	3.1	366	3.5	3.9
Feb 07	384	3.9	3.9	376	4.2	4.1	413	2.7	3.1	369	4.1	3.9
Mar 07	385	4.1	3.9	377	4.3	4.1	415	3.7	3.3	370	4.1	3.9
Apr 07	386	4.0	4.0	378	4.2	4.2	414	3.3	3.2	371	4.2	4.1
May 07	388	4.2	4.1	381	4.4	4.3	416	3.7	3.6	374	4.6	4.3
Jun 07	390	4.2	4.1	383	4.5	4.3	417	3.2	3.4	375	4.3	4.4
Jul 07	392	4.6	4.3	385	5.1	4.7	417	2.8	3.2	376	4.5	4.5
Aug 07	393	4.9	4.6	386	5.2	4.9	419	3.5	3.1	378	4.8	4.6
Sep 07	394	4.5	4.7	387	4.8	5.1	420	3.3	3.2	378	4.6	4.6
Oct 07	394	3.9	4.4	387	4.1	4.7	421	3.1	3.3	379	3.9	4.4
Nov 07	396	4.2	4.2	389	4.5	4.5	422	3.1	3.2	381	4.3	4.3

4.14b Average Weekly Earnings (nominal) - Regular Pay
(Great Britain, seasonally adjusted)

Standard Industrial Classification (2007)

	Whole Economy			Private sector [3 4 5]			Public sector [3 4 5]			Services, SIC 2007 sections G-S		
	Weekly Earnings (£)	% changes year on year: Single month	% changes year on year: 3 month average [2]	Weekly Earnings (£)	% changes year on year: Single month	% changes year on year: 3 month average [2]	Weekly Earnings (£)	% changes year on year: Single month	% changes year on year: 3 month average [2]	Weekly Earnings (£)	% changes year on year: Single month	% changes year on year: 3 month average [2]
	KAI7	KAI8	KAI9	KAJ2	KAJ3	KAJ4	KAJ5	KAJ6	KAJ7	K5DL	K5DM	K5DN
Dec 07	397	4.0	4.0	389	4.1	4.3	425	3.4	3.2	381	4.0	4.1
Jan 08	398	4.1	4.1	390	4.5	4.4	426	2.9	3.1	382	4.3	4.2
Feb 08	400	4.2	4.1	392	4.4	4.3	429	3.7	3.3	384	4.1	4.1
Mar 08	402	4.3	4.2	394	4.4	4.4	431	3.8	3.5	386	4.3	4.2
Apr 08	404	4.6	4.4	396	4.6	4.4	432	4.4	4.0	389	4.9	4.4
May 08	403	3.8	4.2	395	3.7	4.2	431	3.7	4.0	388	3.7	4.3
Jun 08	404	3.5	4.0	397	3.7	4.0	429	2.9	3.7	388	3.5	4.0
Jul 08	405	3.4	3.6	397	3.2	3.5	434	4.0	3.6	390	3.7	3.6
Aug 08	406	3.3	3.4	398	3.1	3.3	434	3.6	3.5	392	3.6	3.6
Sep 08	407	3.3	3.3	399	3.1	3.2	436	3.8	3.8	392	3.6	3.7
Oct 08	408	3.6	3.4	401	3.6	3.3	436	3.5	3.6	393	3.9	3.7
Nov 08	409	3.2	3.4	401	3.0	3.3	437	3.6	3.6	394	3.3	3.6
Dec 08	409	3.2	3.3	401	3.1	3.2	438	3.0	3.4	394	3.3	3.5
Jan 09	409	2.8	3.1	401	2.8	3.0	439	3.0	3.2	394	3.0	3.2
Feb 09	410	2.6	2.9	402	2.4	2.8	442	3.1	3.0	396	3.1	3.1
Mar 09	410	2.0	2.5	402	2.0	2.4	439	2.0	2.7	395	2.3	2.8
Apr 09	411	1.9	2.2	402	1.7	2.0	444	2.8	2.6	397	2.0	2.5
May 09	412	2.3	2.0	403	1.9	1.9	446	3.4	2.7	397	2.6	2.3
Jun 09	412	2.0	2.1	402	1.4	1.7	448	4.3	3.5	398	2.4	2.3
Jul 09	411	1.4	1.9	400	0.6	1.3	450	3.8	3.8	397	1.8	2.3
Aug 09	411	1.3	1.6	400	0.4	0.8	452	4.0	4.0	397	1.4	1.9
Sep 09	413	1.4	1.4	401	0.5	0.5	452	3.7	3.8	398	1.5	1.6
Oct 09	413	1.0	1.2	401	0.1	0.3	453	3.7	3.8	398	1.1	1.3
Nov 09	413	1.0	1.1	401	0.0	0.2	455	3.9	3.8	398	1.1	1.2
Dec 09	415	1.3	1.1	403	0.4	0.2	455	3.9	3.8	399	1.2	1.1
Jan 10	417	1.8	1.4	405	1.0	0.5	457	4.0	3.9	401	1.8	1.4
Feb 10	416	1.5	1.6	404	0.6	0.7	459	3.8	3.9	401	1.2	1.4
Mar 10	418	2.1	1.8	407	1.3	1.0	457	4.1	4.0	403	1.8	1.6
Apr 10	417	1.4	1.7	405	0.6	0.9	459	3.4	3.8	402	1.2	1.4
May 10	417	1.2	1.6	404	0.4	0.8	461	3.5	3.6	402	1.1	1.4
Jun 10	418	1.4	1.3	405	0.8	0.6	459	2.6	3.1	403	1.2	1.2
Jul 10	420	2.2	1.6	407	1.9	1.0	462	2.7	2.9	405	2.1	1.5
Aug 10	421	2.3	2.0	409	2.2	1.6	462	2.3	2.5	406	2.3	1.9
Sep 10	422	2.2	2.2	409	1.9	2.0	465	2.9	2.6	407	2.3	2.2
Oct 10	422	2.2	2.2	409	2.0	2.0	466	2.9	2.7	407	2.3	2.3
Nov 10	423	2.4	2.3	410	2.2	2.0	467	2.8	2.8	408	2.6	2.4
Dec 10	423	1.9	2.2	409	1.6	1.9	468	2.9	2.8	408	2.4	2.5
Jan 11	426	2.2	2.2	413	2.0	1.9	470	2.9	2.9	412	2.6	2.5
Feb 11	425	2.1	2.1	412	1.9	1.8	470	2.6	2.8	411	2.5	2.5
Mar 11	425	1.7	2.0	411	1.2	1.7	472	3.2	2.9	411	2.1	2.4
Apr 11	426	2.1	2.0	412	1.9	1.6	471	2.6	2.8	412	2.5	2.4
May 11	427	2.3	2.0	413	2.3	1.8	472	2.2	2.7	413	2.7	2.4
Jun 11	426	2.0	2.1	413	1.9	2.0	472	2.7	2.5	412	2.3	2.5
Jul 11	427	1.6	2.0	414	1.7	2.0	471	1.9	2.3	412	1.8	2.3
Aug 11	427	1.5	1.7	414	1.4	1.7	473	2.3	2.3	413	1.6	1.9
Sep 11	429	1.7	1.6	416	1.8	1.6	474	1.9	2.0	414	1.7	1.7
Oct 11	430	1.9	1.7	417	1.9	1.7	475	2.1	2.1	415	2.1	1.8

4.14b Average Weekly Earnings (nominal) - Regular Pay
(Great Britain, seasonally adjusted)

Standard Industrial Classification (2007)

	Whole Economy			Private sector [3 4 5]			Public sector [3 4 5]			Services, SIC 2007 sections G-S		
	Weekly Earnings (£)	% changes year on year		Weekly Earnings (£)	% changes year on year		Weekly Earnings (£)	% changes year on year		Weekly Earnings (£)	% changes year on year	
		Single month	3 month average [2]		Single month	3 month average [2]		Single month	3 month average [2]		Single month	3 month average [2]
	KAI7	KAI8	KAI9	KAJ2	KAJ3	KAJ4	KAJ5	KAJ6	KAJ7	K5DL	K5DM	K5DN
Nov 11	430	1.8	1.8	418	2.0	1.9	476	1.8	1.9	416	1.9	1.9
Dec 11	431	1.9	1.9	418	2.3	2.1	475	1.4	1.7	416	2.0	2.0
Jan 12	430	1.0	1.6	418	1.2	1.8	473	0.7	1.3	416	1.0	1.6
Feb 12	432	1.7	1.5	420	1.9	1.8	477	1.3	1.1	418	1.7	1.5
Mar 12	433	1.9	1.5	421	2.2	1.8	478	1.3	1.1	418	1.8	1.5
Apr 12	433	1.7	1.7	420	2.0	2.0	478	1.4	1.3	418	1.5	1.7
May 12	434	1.7	1.7	421	1.9	2.0	479	1.6	1.4	419	1.5	1.6
Jun 12	435	1.9	1.8	422	2.2	2.0	482	2.2	1.7	420	1.9	1.6
Jul 12	435	1.8	1.8	422	1.9	2.0	483	2.7	2.2	420	1.8	1.7
Aug 12	436	2.1	2.0	423	2.1	2.0	487	3.1	2.7	422	2.2	2.0
Sep 12	435	1.5	1.8	422	1.6	1.8	484	2.2	2.6	421	1.6	1.9
Oct 12	435	1.2	1.6	422	1.3	1.7	484	1.8	2.4	421	1.2	1.7
Nov 12	436	1.3	1.4	424	1.5	1.5	484	1.8	2.0	422	1.4	1.4
Dec 12	436	1.2	1.3	423	1.2	1.3	484	1.9	1.8	422	1.2	1.3
Jan 13	434	1.0	1.2	422	1.0	1.2	483	2.0	1.9	420	1.1	1.3
Feb 13	435	0.7	1.0	423	0.8	1.0	481	1.0	1.6	420	0.5	1.0
Mar 13	436	0.7	0.8	424	0.7	0.8	483	1.1	1.4	420	0.4	0.7
Apr 13	438	1.1	0.9	425	1.2	0.9	485	1.4	1.2	423	1.1	0.7
May 13	438	1.0	0.9	426	1.1	1.0	486	1.5	1.3	423	0.9	0.8
Jun 13	438	0.8	1.0	426	1.0	1.1	484	0.5	1.1	423	0.8	0.9
Jul 13	439	0.9	0.9	427	1.2	1.1	485	0.4	0.8	424	0.9	0.9
Aug 13	438	0.5	0.7	427	0.9	1.0	484	-0.7	0.0	423	0.3	0.7
Sep 13	438	0.7	0.7	426	0.9	1.0	485	0.1	-0.1	423	0.6	0.6
Oct 13	439	0.9	0.7	428	1.2	1.0	487	0.6	0.0	424	0.9	0.6
Nov 13	439	0.5	0.7	428	0.8	1.0	486	0.3	0.3	423	0.4	0.6
Dec 13	441	1.1	0.9	429	1.5	1.2	487	0.8	0.6	426	1.0	0.7
Jan 14	441	1.6	1.1	431	2.0	1.4	487	0.9	0.7	425	1.2	0.8
Feb 14	440	1.1	1.3	428	1.3	1.6	487	1.1	1.0	424	0.8	1.0
Mar 14	439	0.7	1.1	427	0.7	1.3	490	1.4	1.2	424	0.8	1.0
Apr 14	440	0.4	0.7	429	0.7	0.9	487	0.4	1.0	424	0.3	0.7
May 14	440	0.5	0.5	430	0.9	0.8	488	0.3	0.7	425	0.5	0.5
Jun 14	441	0.7	0.5	430	0.9	0.9	488	0.7	0.5	426	0.6	0.5
Jul 14	442	0.6	0.6	431	0.9	0.9	489	0.7	0.6	426	0.5	0.5
Aug 14	443	1.0	0.8	432	1.3	1.0	489	1.0	0.8	427	1.0	0.7
Sep 14	446	1.7	1.1	435	2.2	1.5	490	1.0	0.9	430	1.7	1.1
Oct 14	447	1.8	1.5	437	2.3	1.9	490	0.6	0.9	432	1.8	1.5
Nov 14	445	1.6	1.7	436	2.0	2.1	489	0.7	0.8	430	1.7	1.8
Dec 14	447	1.5	1.6	437	1.8	2.0	492	0.9	0.7	433	1.6	1.7
Jan 15	448	1.5	1.5	439	1.9	1.9	491	0.8	0.8	434	2.0	1.8
Feb 15	450	2.3	1.8	440	2.7	2.1	493	1.1	0.9	435	2.7	2.1
Mar 15	451	2.8	2.2	442	3.5	2.7	492	0.5	0.8	436	2.9	2.5
Apr 15	452	2.7	2.6	442	3.1	3.1	493	1.4	1.0	436	2.9	2.8
May 15	452	2.7	2.7	443	3.2	3.3	493	1.2	1.0	437	2.9	2.9
Jun 15	453	2.7	2.7	444	3.2	3.2	494	1.3	1.3	438	3.0	2.9
Jul 15	454	2.9	2.8	445	3.4	3.3	495	1.2	1.2	439	3.0	3.0
Aug 15	454	2.5	2.7	445	2.9	3.2	494	1.2	1.2	438	2.6	2.9
Sep 15	454	1.8	2.4	444	2.0	2.8	497	1.5	1.3	438	1.8	2.5

4.14b Average Weekly Earnings (nominal) - Regular Pay
(Great Britain, seasonally adjusted)

Standard Industrial Classification (2007)

	Whole Economy			Private sector [3 4 5]			Public sector [3 4 5]			Services, SIC 2007 sections G-S		
	Weekly Earnings (£)	% changes year on year		Weekly Earnings (£)	% changes year on year		Weekly Earnings (£)	% changes year on year		Weekly Earnings (£)	% changes year on year	
		Single month	3 month average [2]		Single month	3 month average [2]		Single month	3 month average [2]		Single month	3 month average [2]
	KAI7	KAI8	KAI9	KAJ2	KAJ3	KAJ4	KAJ5	KAJ6	KAJ7	K5DL	K5DM	K5DN
Oct 15	454	1.6	2.0	445	1.8	2.2	496	1.3	1.3	439	1.6	2.0
Nov 15	455	2.2	1.9	446	2.4	2.0	497	1.6	1.5	440	2.1	1.8
Dec 15	457	2.0	1.9	448	2.4	2.2	497	1.1	1.4	441	2.0	1.9
Jan 16	459	2.4	2.2	450	2.5	2.4	499	1.5	1.4	443	2.2	2.1
Feb 16	460	2.3	2.2	452	2.6	2.5	500	1.4	1.4	445	2.3	2.1
Mar 16	461	2.1	2.3	452	2.3	2.5	500	1.7	1.6	445	2.0	2.2
Apr 16	463	2.5	2.3	454	2.6	2.5	503	1.9	1.7	448	2.6	2.3
May 16	462	2.1	2.2	453	2.3	2.4	500	1.4	1.6	446	1.9	2.2
Jun 16	464	2.3	2.3	455	2.5	2.5	503	1.8	1.7	448	2.2	2.2
Jul 16	464	2.1	2.2	456	2.3	2.4	502	1.4	1.5	448	2.0	2.0
Aug 16	465	2.3	2.3	456	2.5	2.4	503	1.8	1.7	448	2.3	2.2
Sep 16	466	2.7	2.4	458	3.0	2.6	503	1.3	1.5	450	2.6	2.3
Oct 16	466	2.6	2.5	458	2.9	2.8	503	1.4	1.5	450	2.5	2.5
Nov 16	467	2.7	2.7	460	3.0	3.0	505	1.5	1.4	452	2.8	2.6
Dec 16	467	2.3	2.5	459	2.5	2.8	504	1.5	1.5	451	2.3	2.5
Jan 17	468	1.9	2.3	460	2.2	2.6	505	1.3	1.4	452	1.9	2.3

Source: Monthly Wages & Salaries Survey

Inquiries: Email: labour.market@ons.gov.uk

Earnings enquiries: 01633 456773

1. Estimates of regular pay exclude bonuses and arrears of pay.

2. The three month average figures are the changes in the average seasonally adjusted values for the three months ending with the relevant month compared with the same period a year earlier.

3. From July 2009 Royal Bank of Scotland Group plc is classified to the public sector; for earlier time periods it is classified to the private sector. Between July 2009 and March 2014 Lloyds Banking Group plc is classified to the public sector; it is classified to the private sector for earlier and later time periods.

4. Between June 2010 and May 2012 English Further Education Corporations and Sixth Form College Corporations are classified to the public sector. Before June 2010 and after May 2012 they are classified to the private sector.

5. From October 2013 Royal Mail plc is classified to the private sector; previously it is in the public sector.

4.14b Average Weekly Earnings (nominal) - Regular Pay
(Great Britain, seasonally adjusted)

Standard Industrial Classification (2007)

	Finance and business services, SIC 2007 sections K-N			Public sector excluding financial services[4 5]			Manufacturing, SIC 2007 section C			Construction, SIC 2007 section F			Wholesaling, retailing, hotels & restaurants, SIC 2007 sections G & I		
	Weekly Earnings (£)	% changes year on year: Single month	% changes year on year: 3 month average [2]	Weekly Earnings (£)	% changes year on year: Single month	% changes year on year: 3 month average [2]	Weekly Earnings (£)	% changes year on year: Single month	% changes year on year: 3 month average [2]	Weekly Earnings (£)	% changes year on year: Single month	% changes year on year: 3 month average [2]	Weekly Earnings (£)	% changes year on year: Single month	% changes year on year: 3 month average [2]
	K5DO	K5DP	K5DQ	KAK6	KAK7	KAK8	K5DU	K5DV	K5DW	K5DX	K5DY	K5DZ	K5E2	K5E3	K5E4
Jan 04	390	2.5	3.3	363	4.3	4.6	399	4.4	4.2	417	4.6	4.8	224	1.7	2.3
Feb 04	389	1.7	2.8	366	4.7	4.6	401	4.5	4.3	418	3.9	4.8	224	2.6	2.5
Mar 04	391	2.1	2.1	367	4.5	4.5	403	5.2	4.7	423	4.8	4.4	225	2.8	2.4
Apr 04	393	2.1	2.0	369	4.6	4.6	402	4.4	4.7	423	4.3	4.3	227	3.3	2.9
May 04	396	2.6	2.3	370	5.0	4.7	406	4.6	4.8	422	4.6	4.6	227	3.1	3.1
Jun 04	395	2.6	2.5	371	4.5	4.7	407	4.6	4.5	417	1.9	3.6	228	3.7	3.4
Jul 04	396	3.0	2.8	372	3.9	4.4	409	4.9	4.7	419	3.2	3.2	229	4.2	3.7
Aug 04	398	3.6	3.1	375	3.6	4.0	410	4.7	4.7	424	4.4	3.2	229	4.1	4.0
Sep 04	399	3.4	3.3	376	4.1	3.9	412	4.4	4.7	418	1.5	3.0	230	3.8	4.0
Oct 04	401	3.1	3.4	378	4.6	4.1	414	5.0	4.7	415	0.6	2.2	231	4.7	4.2
Nov 04	402	3.2	3.2	379	4.5	4.4	415	4.8	4.7	417	1.2	1.1	231	4.2	4.2
Dec 04	406	4.1	3.5	379	4.0	4.4	415	4.0	4.6	420	0.4	0.7	234	4.5	4.5
Jan 05	407	4.2	3.8	382	5.0	4.5	415	4.0	4.2	430	3.0	1.5	234	4.5	4.4
Feb 05	411	5.5	4.6	382	4.3	4.5	416	3.9	3.9	416	-0.4	1.0	235	4.5	4.5
Mar 05	412	5.4	5.0	386	5.3	4.9	419	3.9	3.9	421	-0.6	0.7	235	4.6	4.5
Apr 05	413	5.2	5.4	388	5.4	5.0	420	4.5	4.1	420	-0.6	-0.5	236	4.1	4.4
May 05	414	4.5	5.0	391	5.7	5.4	420	3.7	4.0	423	0.3	-0.3	234	3.0	3.9
Jun 05	413	4.7	4.8	390	5.2	5.4	422	3.6	3.9	424	1.6	0.4	236	3.3	3.5
Jul 05	419	5.9	5.0	392	5.2	5.4	423	3.4	3.5	426	1.7	1.2	237	3.6	3.3
Aug 05	419	5.3	5.3	394	5.1	5.1	426	3.7	3.6	434	2.3	1.9	240	4.6	3.8
Sep 05	420	5.3	5.5	396	5.2	5.1	427	3.7	3.6	434	4.0	2.7	239	4.0	4.1
Oct 05	421	4.9	5.1	397	5.1	5.1	427	3.2	3.5	438	5.4	3.9	241	4.3	4.3
Nov 05	421	4.7	5.0	398	5.2	5.2	428	3.1	3.3	440	5.5	5.0	242	4.6	4.3
Dec 05	420	3.5	4.4	399	5.5	5.3	430	3.7	3.3	437	4.1	5.0	242	3.4	4.1
Jan 06	425	4.5	4.3	400	4.7	5.1	429	3.3	3.4	443	3.0	4.2	243	3.7	3.9
Feb 06	423	3.1	3.7	402	5.4	5.2	435	4.5	3.8	447	7.3	4.8	243	3.5	3.5
Mar 06	429	4.0	3.8	400	3.6	4.5	434	3.5	3.8	445	5.9	5.3	243	3.1	3.4
Apr 06	429	3.9	3.7	400	3.1	4.0	436	3.7	3.9	451	7.2	6.8	242	2.6	3.1
May 06	430	4.0	4.0	401	2.6	3.1	439	4.3	3.8	457	7.9	7.0	245	4.6	3.4
Jun 06	433	4.9	4.3	404	3.4	3.0	437	3.6	3.9	458	8.0	7.7	245	3.8	3.7
Jul 06	433	3.3	4.0	405	3.5	3.2	435	2.7	3.5	463	8.6	8.2	245	3.5	4.0
Aug 06	435	3.8	4.0	405	2.9	3.3	439	3.2	3.2	458	5.6	7.4	245	2.3	3.2
Sep 06	436	3.6	3.6	406	2.7	3.0	441	3.4	3.1	462	6.5	6.9	248	3.7	3.1
Oct 06	437	4.0	3.8	408	2.8	2.8	443	3.7	3.4	465	6.2	6.1	250	3.6	3.2
Nov 06	437	3.9	3.8	409	2.8	2.8	444	3.7	3.6	464	5.4	6.0	252	4.3	3.9
Dec 06	441	5.0	4.3	411	3.0	2.9	443	3.0	3.5	466	6.8	6.1	253	4.8	4.2
Jan 07	434	2.2	3.7	414	3.7	3.1	449	4.6	3.8	466	5.3	5.8	251	3.5	4.2
Feb 07	440	4.0	3.7	413	2.7	3.1	450	3.4	3.7	462	3.4	5.1	254	4.8	4.3
Mar 07	442	3.1	3.1	414	3.7	3.4	453	4.5	4.2	470	5.6	4.7	255	5.1	4.5
Apr 07	445	3.7	3.6	413	3.3	3.2	450	3.3	3.7	469	4.1	4.4	257	5.9	5.3
May 07	448	4.2	3.6	415	3.6	3.5	451	2.9	3.6	471	3.1	4.3	256	4.8	5.3
Jun 07	450	4.0	3.9	416	3.1	3.3	453	3.7	3.3	475	3.8	3.7	258	5.3	5.4
Jul 07	452	4.5	4.2	417	2.8	3.1	455	4.7	3.8	495	7.1	4.7	259	5.6	5.2
Aug 07	453	4.1	4.2	419	3.5	3.1	455	3.6	4.0	497	8.5	6.5	260	6.2	5.7
Sep 07	456	4.8	4.5	420	3.3	3.2	455	3.2	3.8	499	7.8	7.8	260	5.0	5.6
Oct 07	457	4.6	4.5	421	3.1	3.3	457	3.2	3.3	491	5.7	7.3	261	4.4	5.2
Nov 07	461	5.3	4.9	422	3.1	3.2	457	3.0	3.1	494	6.5	6.6	261	3.7	4.3

4.14b Average Weekly Earnings (nominal) - Regular Pay
(Great Britain, seasonally adjusted)

Standard Industrial Classification (2007)

	Finance and business services, SIC 2007 sections K-N			Public sector excluding financial services[4 5]			Manufacturing, SIC 2007 section C			Construction, SIC 2007 section F			Wholesaling, retailing, hotels & restaurants, SIC 2007 sections G & I		
	Weekly Earnings (£)	% changes year on year: Single month	% changes year on year: 3 month average[2]	Weekly Earnings (£)	% changes year on year: Single month	% changes year on year: 3 month average[2]	Weekly Earnings (£)	% changes year on year: Single month	% changes year on year: 3 month average[2]	Weekly Earnings (£)	% changes year on year: Single month	% changes year on year: 3 month average[2]	Weekly Earnings (£)	% changes year on year: Single month	% changes year on year: 3 month average[2]
	K5DO	K5DP	K5DQ	KAK6	KAK7	KAK8	K5DU	K5DV	K5DW	K5DX	K5DY	K5DZ	K5E2	K5E3	K5E4
Dec 07	462	4.7	4.8	425	3.4	3.2	458	3.3	3.2	494	5.8	6.0	260	2.8	3.6
Jan 08	459	5.8	5.2	426	2.8	3.1	462	2.8	3.0	483	3.7	5.3	262	4.4	3.6
Feb 08	465	5.5	5.3	428	3.6	3.3	464	3.3	3.1	492	6.5	5.3	262	3.0	3.4
Mar 08	465	5.2	5.5	430	3.8	3.4	465	2.5	2.8	489	4.1	4.8	265	3.7	3.7
Apr 08	468	5.2	5.3	431	4.4	3.9	466	3.6	3.1	494	5.3	5.3	268	4.2	3.6
May 08	466	4.0	4.8	431	3.7	4.0	466	3.3	3.2	496	5.4	4.9	266	3.6	3.8
Jun 08	472	4.7	4.6	428	2.9	3.7	468	3.1	3.3	499	4.9	5.2	265	2.9	3.6
Jul 08	475	5.1	4.6	433	4.0	3.6	469	3.0	3.2	499	0.8	3.7	264	2.0	2.8
Aug 08	478	5.4	5.1	434	3.6	3.5	468	2.9	3.0	493	-0.9	1.6	266	2.1	2.3
Sep 08	478	4.7	5.1	435	3.8	3.8	468	2.9	2.9	500	0.3	0.1	267	2.9	2.3
Oct 08	479	4.7	4.9	436	3.5	3.6	470	2.8	2.9	504	2.6	0.7	266	2.2	2.4
Nov 08	479	4.0	4.5	437	3.6	3.6	473	3.5	3.1	503	1.8	1.6	265	1.5	2.2
Dec 08	477	3.3	4.0	438	3.0	3.4	472	3.2	3.2	503	1.9	2.1	268	2.9	2.2
Jan 09	479	4.4	3.9	439	3.0	3.2	471	2.1	2.9	505	4.6	2.8	268	2.2	2.2
Feb 09	480	3.4	3.7	441	3.1	3.1	470	1.2	2.2	503	2.3	2.9	271	3.5	2.8
Mar 09	482	3.6	3.8	439	2.0	2.7	470	1.3	1.5	504	3.0	3.3	269	1.7	2.4
Apr 09	482	3.1	3.4	443	2.8	2.7	472	1.3	1.2	506	2.3	2.6	268	0.1	1.7
May 09	483	3.6	3.4	445	3.3	2.7	474	1.6	1.4	504	1.6	2.3	269	1.1	1.0
Jun 09	483	2.5	3.1	447	4.3	3.5	477	2.0	1.6	496	-0.7	1.1	269	1.3	0.8
Jul 09	483	1.6	2.5	446	2.8	3.5	473	0.8	1.4	503	0.7	0.6	269	2.0	1.4
Aug 09	483	1.2	1.7	448	3.1	3.4	476	1.7	1.5	507	2.9	1.0	269	1.3	1.5
Sep 09	483	1.2	1.3	447	2.8	2.9	478	2.1	1.5	506	1.1	1.6	271	1.2	1.5
Oct 09	484	1.0	1.1	448	2.9	2.9	480	2.2	2.0	510	1.2	1.7	271	1.9	1.4
Nov 09	487	1.6	1.3	450	2.8	2.8	481	1.7	2.0	510	1.3	1.2	271	2.2	1.8
Dec 09	487	2.0	1.5	451	2.8	2.8	491	4.0	2.6	513	2.0	1.5	273	1.9	2.0
Jan 10	490	2.3	1.9	452	2.9	2.9	491	4.2	3.3	512	1.3	1.5	272	1.7	1.9
Feb 10	486	1.3	1.8	453	2.7	2.8	493	4.8	4.3	512	1.8	1.7	274	1.1	1.6
Mar 10	495	2.7	2.1	452	3.1	2.9	496	5.4	4.8	510	1.1	1.4	276	2.4	1.8
Apr 10	492	1.9	2.0	455	2.5	2.8	494	4.5	4.9	512	1.2	1.3	273	2.1	1.9
May 10	493	2.0	2.2	456	2.4	2.6	493	4.1	4.7	506	0.4	0.9	272	1.4	2.0
Jun 10	492	1.9	1.9	453	1.5	2.1	494	3.7	4.1	504	1.6	1.1	274	2.2	1.9
Jul 10	500	3.5	2.4	457	2.5	2.1	493	4.4	4.1	502	-0.2	0.6	275	2.0	1.9
Aug 10	502	3.8	3.1	457	2.0	2.0	496	4.2	4.1	502	-1.1	0.1	276	2.6	2.3
Sep 10	504	4.3	3.9	459	2.7	2.4	496	3.7	4.1	504	-0.3	-0.5	276	2.0	2.2
Oct 10	506	4.7	4.2	460	2.6	2.4	496	3.2	3.7	508	-0.5	-0.6	274	1.2	1.9
Nov 10	508	4.3	4.4	462	2.7	2.7	496	3.2	3.4	506	-0.7	-0.5	275	1.4	1.5
Dec 10	511	5.0	4.7	463	2.8	2.7	497	1.2	2.5	502	-2.2	-1.1	274	0.3	1.0
Jan 11	518	5.6	5.0	464	2.8	2.8	498	1.5	1.9	514	0.4	-0.8	276	1.3	1.0
Feb 11	513	5.5	5.4	465	2.5	2.7	497	0.9	1.2	516	0.8	-0.3	275	0.2	0.6
Mar 11	513	3.7	4.9	466	3.1	2.8	499	0.6	1.0	514	0.9	0.7	275	-0.2	0.4
Apr 11	515	4.7	4.7	465	2.3	2.6	498	0.9	0.8	509	-0.5	0.4	277	1.4	0.5
May 11	519	5.4	4.6	465	2.0	2.5	499	1.1	0.8	512	1.3	0.6	278	2.1	1.1
Jun 11	519	5.3	5.1	465	2.5	2.3	500	1.1	1.0	515	2.3	1.0	277	0.8	1.4
Jul 11	519	3.8	4.8	464	1.6	2.1	501	1.6	1.3	516	2.8	2.1	277	0.7	1.2
Aug 11	517	3.0	4.0	466	2.1	2.1	502	1.2	1.3	518	3.3	2.8	277	0.5	0.7
Sep 11	520	3.3	3.3	467	1.6	1.8	504	1.7	1.5	518	2.7	2.9	277	0.5	0.6
Oct 11	525	3.7	3.3	467	1.5	1.8	503	1.5	1.5	516	1.6	2.5	279	1.6	0.9

4.14b Average Weekly Earnings (nominal) - Regular Pay

(Great Britain, seasonally adjusted)

Standard Industrial Classification (2007)

	Finance and business services, SIC 2007 sections K-N			Public sector excluding financial services[4 5]			Manufacturing, SIC 2007 section C			Construction, SIC 2007 section F			Wholesaling, retailing, hotels & restaurants, SIC 2007 sections G & I		
	Weekly Earnings (£)	% changes year on year: Single month	% changes year on year: 3 month average[2]	Weekly Earnings (£)	% changes year on year: Single month	% changes year on year: 3 month average[2]	Weekly Earnings (£)	% changes year on year: Single month	% changes year on year: 3 month average[2]	Weekly Earnings (£)	% changes year on year: Single month	% changes year on year: 3 month average[2]	Weekly Earnings (£)	% changes year on year: Single month	% changes year on year: 3 month average[2]
	K5DO	K5DP	K5DQ	KAK6	KAK7	KAK8	K5DU	K5DV	K5DW	K5DX	K5DY	K5DZ	K5E2	K5E3	K5E4
Nov 11	524	3.3	3.4	467	1.1	1.4	506	1.9	1.7	518	2.2	2.2	281	2.2	1.4
Dec 11	528	3.3	3.4	467	0.8	1.1	505	1.6	1.6	516	2.8	2.2	280	2.5	2.1
Jan 12	525	1.3	2.7	466	0.4	0.8	504	1.2	1.5	518	0.7	1.9	282	2.2	2.3
Feb 12	527	2.7	2.5	469	0.9	0.7	505	1.7	1.5	519	0.5	1.4	283	2.9	2.5
Mar 12	530	3.3	2.4	470	0.8	0.7	508	1.9	1.6	524	1.8	1.0	283	2.8	2.6
Apr 12	528	2.5	2.8	470	1.0	0.9	509	2.2	1.9	523	2.7	1.7	283	1.9	2.5
May 12	528	1.7	2.5	470	1.2	1.0	511	2.4	2.1	529	3.3	2.6	284	2.0	2.2
Jun 12	530	2.1	2.1	474	2.1	1.4	511	2.2	2.3	523	1.6	2.6	286	3.3	2.4
Jul 12	528	1.7	1.8	476	2.6	2.0	512	2.1	2.2	522	1.2	2.0	285	3.1	2.8
Aug 12	529	2.4	2.1	479	2.7	2.5	513	2.2	2.2	516	-0.5	0.8	285	2.7	3.0
Sep 12	528	1.4	1.9	477	2.1	2.5	513	1.7	2.0	515	-0.6	0.1	285	2.8	2.8
Oct 12	526	0.2	1.3	477	2.1	2.3	514	2.1	2.0	515	-0.2	-0.4	285	2.3	2.6
Nov 12	527	0.5	0.7	477	2.0	2.1	513	1.4	1.7	516	-0.3	-0.4	287	2.4	2.5
Dec 12	526	-0.5	0.1	476	1.9	2.0	516	2.1	1.9	512	-0.8	-0.4	286	2.0	2.2
Jan 13	525	0.0	0.0	476	2.0	2.0	514	2.0	1.8	504	-2.6	-1.2	284	0.7	1.7
Feb 13	526	-0.2	-0.2	473	1.0	1.7	518	2.5	2.2	516	-0.6	-1.4	284	0.3	1.0
Mar 13	526	-0.8	-0.3	475	1.1	1.4	521	2.6	2.3	518	-1.1	-1.4	286	1.3	0.8
Apr 13	527	-0.1	-0.4	477	1.5	1.2	521	2.4	2.5	527	0.6	-0.4	288	1.8	1.1
May 13	526	-0.3	-0.4	478	1.6	1.4	521	2.1	2.3	524	-1.0	-0.5	288	1.5	1.5
Jun 13	523	-1.2	-0.5	477	0.6	1.2	523	2.3	2.2	518	-1.0	-0.5	291	1.8	1.7
Jul 13	525	-0.4	-0.6	478	0.4	0.9	522	2.0	2.1	515	-1.3	-1.1	293	2.7	2.0
Aug 13	523	-1.1	-0.9	477	-0.3	0.2	522	1.6	2.0	520	0.9	-0.5	293	2.8	2.4
Sep 13	522	-1.2	-0.9	478	0.4	0.2	522	1.7	1.8	520	1.0	0.2	293	2.8	2.7
Oct 13	522	-0.7	-1.0	481	0.9	0.3	524	2.1	1.8	514	-0.2	0.5	294	3.0	2.9
Nov 13	522	-1.1	-1.0	480	0.7	0.7	527	2.8	2.2	515	-0.2	0.2	293	1.9	2.6
Dec 13	526	0.1	-0.6	482	1.2	1.0	528	2.3	2.4	519	1.5	0.4	294	2.8	2.6
Jan 14	522	-0.5	-0.5	482	1.4	1.1	530	3.0	2.7	528	4.8	2.0	297	4.7	3.1
Feb 14	519	-1.4	-0.6	482	1.8	1.5	533	2.9	2.8	518	0.4	2.2	293	3.3	3.6
Mar 14	524	-0.3	-0.7	482	1.4	1.5	529	1.6	2.5	508	-1.9	1.1	293	2.2	3.4
Apr 14	521	-1.2	-0.9	482	1.2	1.4	530	1.7	2.1	515	-2.3	-1.3	292	1.6	2.4
May 14	522	-0.9	-0.8	483	1.2	1.2	530	1.8	1.7	514	-1.8	-2.0	294	2.2	2.0
Jun 14	523	-0.1	-0.7	484	1.4	1.3	532	1.8	1.8	518	0.0	-1.4	293	0.7	1.5
Jul 14	525	-0.1	-0.3	484	1.2	1.3	529	1.3	1.6	522	1.2	-0.2	292	-0.1	0.9
Aug 14	530	1.3	0.4	484	1.4	1.3	530	1.6	1.6	520	-0.1	0.4	294	0.3	0.3
Sep 14	534	2.5	1.2	486	1.5	1.4	532	2.0	1.6	523	0.6	0.6	297	1.2	0.5
Oct 14	539	3.3	2.3	486	1.0	1.3	533	1.7	1.7	524	1.9	0.8	297	0.9	0.8
Nov 14	535	2.5	2.8	485	1.1	1.2	532	0.9	1.5	523	1.5	1.3	297	1.3	1.2
Dec 14	535	1.6	2.5	488	1.4	1.2	532	0.9	1.1	526	1.4	1.6	298	1.4	1.2
Jan 15	536	2.7	2.3	487	1.1	1.2	532	0.5	0.8	517	-2.2	0.2	302	1.7	1.5
Feb 15	538	3.7	2.7	488	1.4	1.3	536	0.4	0.6	525	1.4	0.2	303	3.3	2.1
Mar 15	542	3.3	3.2	489	1.4	1.3	535	1.0	0.7	533	4.9	1.3	304	4.0	3.0
Apr 15	543	4.2	3.8	489	1.4	1.4	537	1.4	1.0	528	2.7	3.0	303	3.7	3.7
May 15	544	4.3	4.0	489	1.2	1.4	537	1.2	1.2	528	2.7	3.4	305	3.6	3.8
Jun 15	545	4.3	4.3	491	1.4	1.4	538	1.2	1.3	531	2.5	2.6	304	3.8	3.7
Jul 15	546	4.0	4.2	491	1.3	1.3	541	2.2	1.5	536	2.8	2.7	306	4.5	4.0
Aug 15	546	3.1	3.8	491	1.5	1.4	542	2.2	1.9	535	3.0	2.8	306	4.1	4.1
Sep 15	546	2.2	3.1	493	1.6	1.4	542	2.0	2.1	533	1.9	2.6	303	2.3	3.6

4.14b Average Weekly Earnings (nominal) - Regular Pay
(Great Britain, seasonally adjusted)

Standard Industrial Classification (2007)

	Finance and business services, SIC 2007 sections K-N			Public sector excluding financial services [4 5]			Manufacturing, SIC 2007 section C			Construction, SIC 2007 section F			Wholesaling, retailing, hotels & restaurants, SIC 2007 sections G & I		
	Weekly Earnings (£)	% changes year on year: Single month	3 month average [2]	Weekly Earnings (£)	% changes year on year: Single month	3 month average [2]	Weekly Earnings (£)	% changes year on year: Single month	3 month average [2]	Weekly Earnings (£)	% changes year on year: Single month	3 month average [2]	Weekly Earnings (£)	% changes year on year: Single month	3 month average [2]
	K5DO	K5DP	K5DQ	KAK6	KAK7	KAK8	K5DU	K5DV	K5DW	K5DX	K5DY	K5DZ	K5E2	K5E3	K5E4
Oct 15	549	1.8	2.3	493	1.4	1.5	543	1.8	2.0	537	2.5	2.5	305	2.7	3.0
Nov 15	551	3.1	2.3	494	1.7	1.6	545	2.3	2.0	538	2.8	2.4	306	3.1	2.7
Dec 15	555	3.8	2.9	494	1.1	1.4	547	2.7	2.3	536	1.8	2.4	308	3.3	3.0
Jan 16	557	3.8	3.5	495	1.6	1.5	547	2.7	2.6	542	4.9	3.2	308	1.8	2.7
Feb 16	557	3.4	3.7	496	1.6	1.4	547	2.0	2.5	546	4.0	3.6	311	2.6	2.5
Mar 16	557	2.7	3.3	497	1.7	1.6	547	2.4	2.4	547	2.7	3.9	310	2.0	2.1
Apr 16	561	3.3	3.2	499	2.0	1.8	551	2.6	2.3	549	3.8	3.5	313	3.0	2.5
May 16	555	2.0	2.7	496	1.5	1.7	554	3.1	2.7	549	3.9	3.5	313	2.7	2.6
Jun 16	559	2.5	2.6	499	1.8	1.7	553	2.8	2.8	550	3.4	3.7	314	3.4	3.0
Jul 16	557	2.0	2.2	497	1.4	1.5	555	2.7	2.9	552	2.9	3.4	314	2.8	3.0
Aug 16	557	1.9	2.1	500	1.8	1.6	554	2.3	2.6	556	3.8	3.4	316	3.4	3.2
Sep 16	558	2.2	2.0	500	1.3	1.5	554	2.2	2.4	557	4.5	3.7	317	4.4	3.5
Oct 16	557	1.5	1.9	500	1.5	1.5	554	2.0	2.2	559	4.2	4.2	317	4.0	3.9
Nov 16	560	1.7	1.8	501	1.5	1.4	553	1.6	1.9	561	4.3	4.3	319	4.2	4.2
Dec 16	560	0.9	1.4	501	1.4	1.5	554	1.3	1.6	559	4.3	4.3	317	3.2	3.8
Jan 17	563	1.1	1.2	502	1.3	1.4	556	1.7	1.5	557	2.7	3.8	318	3.3	3.6

Source: Monthly Wages & Salaries Survey

Inquiries: Email: labour.market@ons.gov.uk

Earnings enquiries: 01633 456773

1. Estimates of regular pay exclude bonuses and arrears of pay.

2. The three month average figures are the changes in the average seasonally adjusted values for the three months ending with the relevant month compared with the same period a year earlier.

3. From July 2009 Royal Bank of Scotland Group plc is classified to the public sector; for earlier time periods it is classified to the private sector. Between July 2009 and March 2014 Lloyds Banking Group plc is classified to the public sector; it is classified to the private sector for earlier and later time periods.

4. Between June 2010 and May 2012 English Further Education Corporations and Sixth Form College Corporations are classified to the public sector. Before June 2010 and after May 2012 they are classified to the private sector.

5. From October 2013 Royal Mail plc is classified to the private sector; previously it is in the public sector.

4.14c Average Weekly Earnings (nominal) - Bonus Pay
(Great Britain, seasonally adjusted)

Standard Industrial Classification (2007)

	Whole Economy			Private sector [2 3 4]			Public sector [2 3 4]			Services, SIC 2007 sections G-S		
	Weekly Earnings (£)	% changes year on year: Single month	% changes year on year: 3 month average [1]	Weekly Earnings (£)	% changes year on year: Single month	% changes year on year: 3 month average [1]	Weekly Earnings (£)	% changes year on year: Single month	% changes year on year: 3 month average [1]	Weekly Earnings (£)	% changes year on year: Single month	% changes year on year: 3 month average [1]
	KAF4	KAF5	KAF6	KAF7	KAF8	KAF9	KAG2	KAG3	KAG4	K5CS	K5CT	K5CU
Jan 04	20	18.2	6.3	27	84.7	26.2	3	17.5	-4.1	19	29.5	6.6
Feb 04	18	6.1	8.0	21	7.4	27.2	3	-2.7	6.5	15	-9.1	4.7
Mar 04	21	8.1	10.6	24	5.5	26.3	3	12.2	8.9	19	10.8	9.6
Apr 04	21	23.4	12.3	24	21.5	11.1	3	6.3	5.3	22	37.5	12.6
May 04	20	19.8	16.7	25	31.9	18.7	3	7.4	8.7	19	16.5	21.3
Jun 04	20	18.6	20.6	23	20.7	24.7	3	-20.7	-4.9	19	14.3	22.6
Jul 04	20	15.7	18.0	23	5.6	18.9	3	-5.1	-8.1	19	10.4	13.7
Aug 04	21	19.4	17.9	23	15.0	13.5	3	11.6	-6.4	19	19.6	14.7
Sep 04	22	22.5	19.2	25	17.6	12.7	3	-4.9	0.5	21	24.6	18.1
Oct 04	25	21.0	21.0	27	11.0	14.4	3	1.7	2.8	23	21.9	22.1
Nov 04	22	20.7	21.4	25	15.2	14.5	3	35.5	8.5	21	26.3	24.2
Dec 04	22	19.1	20.3	24	11.8	12.6	3	12.2	14.7	21	28.1	25.3
Jan 05	23	13.6	17.7	28	5.7	10.6	3	-3.4	12.4	21	10.4	21.1
Feb 05	22	18.7	17.0	25	19.8	11.8	3	3.4	3.9	19	25.1	20.6
Mar 05	22	2.4	11.1	25	2.6	8.7	3	-11.0	-4.1	20	3.0	11.9
Apr 05	22	6.4	8.7	26	8.0	9.6	3	19.4	3.3	22	-0.9	7.5
May 05	23	11.2	6.6	25	0.8	3.7	3	17.8	7.8	21	12.8	4.7
Jun 05	22	7.4	8.3	25	8.2	5.6	4	16.3	17.8	21	8.6	6.5
Jul 05	23	11.7	10.1	26	13.8	7.4	4	35.0	22.8	21	12.5	11.3
Aug 05	26	26.3	15.2	29	26.6	16.2	4	33.0	27.9	25	28.4	16.6
Sep 05	24	8.5	15.3	27	8.8	16.2	4	55.7	40.9	23	9.8	16.7
Oct 05	25	-2.2	9.9	27	1.8	11.8	4	42.9	43.3	23	-2.3	11.0
Nov 05	26	14.3	6.5	29	15.8	8.7	4	23.6	40.4	24	14.2	6.9
Dec 05	25	14.7	8.4	28	17.0	11.2	5	36.0	34.2	24	15.2	8.7
Jan 06	24	4.2	11.0	28	-1.7	9.8	5	69.9	43.1	21	0.9	10.1
Feb 06	25	18.3	12.2	29	17.8	10.4	4	58.8	54.3	23	22.3	12.5
Mar 06	27	24.7	15.5	31	24.5	12.9	4	45.8	58.3	26	29.3	17.1
Apr 06	26	17.1	20.0	30	18.0	20.1	5	35.6	46.0	25	15.1	22.0
May 06	27	18.3	20.0	30	16.7	19.7	5	42.4	41.0	25	19.3	21.0
Jun 06	29	32.7	22.6	33	32.2	22.2	5	28.2	35.2	28	35.4	23.1
Jul 06	29	27.0	25.9	33	29.1	26.0	5	22.3	30.5	28	32.5	29.0
Aug 06	28	8.3	21.9	32	9.7	23.0	5	5.8	18.0	27	8.5	24.5
Sep 06	25	5.3	13.1	29	5.1	14.2	3	-22.5	0.7	24	4.8	14.7
Oct 06	27	9.5	7.7	31	14.6	9.8	5	17.7	0.1	26	12.3	8.5
Nov 06	28	9.4	8.1	33	11.8	10.5	3	-19.4	-7.7	27	11.4	9.5
Dec 06	31	26.3	15.0	37	30.9	19.1	5	7.0	2.8	34	40.6	21.7
Jan 07	33	41.0	25.2	37	35.4	25.8	4	-27.8	-13.8	29	38.5	29.8
Feb 07	32	26.8	31.2	37	28.5	31.5	3	-29.3	-17.2	30	27.1	35.4
Mar 07	30	9.8	25.2	33	7.9	23.4	5	13.7	-15.6	28	8.4	23.8
Apr 07	28	8.0	14.7	34	11.9	15.9	5	4.0	-4.0	28	11.9	15.5
May 07	30	11.6	9.8	34	14.0	11.2	5	8.9	8.8	28	10.6	10.3
Jun 07	30	4.0	7.8	35	4.6	9.9	6	23.2	12.0	29	2.7	8.2
Jul 07	31	6.3	7.2	36	7.9	8.6	5	4.2	12.1	30	5.0	5.9

4.14c Average Weekly Earnings (nominal) - Bonus Pay
(Great Britain, seasonally adjusted)

Standard Industrial Classification (2007)

	Whole Economy			Private sector [2 3 4]			Public sector [2 3 4]			Services, SIC 2007 sections G-S		
	Weekly Earnings (£)	% changes year on year		Weekly Earnings (£)	% changes year on year		Weekly Earnings (£)	% changes year on year		Weekly Earnings (£)	% changes year on year	
		Single month	3 month average [1]		Single month	3 month average [1]		Single month	3 month average [1]		Single month	3 month average [1]
	KAF4	KAF5	KAF6	KAF7	KAF8	KAF9	KAG2	KAG3	KAG4	K5CS	K5CT	K5CU
Aug 07	31	10.1	6.8	36	12.8	8.4	4	-1.5	8.7	30	11.8	6.4
Sep 07	34	33.1	15.8	39	35.4	18.0	4	26.8	8.2	34	40.3	18.0
Oct 07	30	11.4	17.8	36	16.0	21.0	2	-50.1	-12.8	31	21.1	23.9
Nov 07	32	16.0	19.8	39	18.0	22.7	5	57.9	1.1	31	15.9	25.3
Dec 07	28	-9.5	5.3	35	-6.6	8.3	4	-7.5	-9.0	29	-14.5	5.4
Jan 08	36	7.4	4.3	39	3.8	4.5	4	-3.0	10.8	30	1.2	-0.4
Feb 08	33	3.0	0.5	39	4.6	0.6	5	49.1	9.2	31	2.7	-4.1
Mar 08	33	9.9	6.7	35	6.0	4.7	3	-28.4	0.5	30	9.5	4.3
Apr 08	29	3.7	5.5	37	10.3	6.9	4	-22.2	-7.0	30	9.3	7.0
May 08	34	13.8	9.2	40	17.3	11.2	5	-5.5	-18.5	32	13.6	10.8
Jun 08	30	-0.4	5.7	36	3.4	10.3	5	-12.0	-13.0	30	3.7	8.8
Jul 08	31	-0.8	4.1	36	0.4	6.9	6	24.0	1.1	30	0.7	5.9
Aug 08	30	-4.6	-2.0	35	-1.8	0.6	5	17.9	8.5	30	-0.8	1.2
Sep 08	29	-15.6	-7.3	34	-13.3	-5.2	5	16.6	19.6	29	-13.3	-4.8
Oct 08	30	-2.1	-7.7	36	-0.6	-5.4	5	86.5	32.5	32	4.8	-3.4
Nov 08	26	-20.3	-12.9	32	-18.2	-10.9	6	25.4	35.3	27	-15.5	-8.2
Dec 08	26	-7.3	-10.2	33	-4.4	-8.0	5	19.9	36.4	29	-0.7	-3.9
Jan 09	23	-36.1	-22.3	24	-37.2	-20.5	5	37.7	27.0	29	-3.2	-6.6
Feb 09	17	-50.0	-32.4	21	-47.4	-30.6	5	3.4	18.9	19	-37.2	-13.9
Mar 09	26	-21.5	-36.0	26	-27.3	-37.6	6	81.0	36.8	18	-39.2	-26.7
Apr 09	27	-6.8	-26.9	37	-1.9	-25.9	6	48.8	40.3	24	-20.5	-32.3
May 09	26	-24.8	-18.2	29	-26.3	-18.5	4	-11.7	33.8	24	-24.9	-28.1
Jun 09	26	-15.2	-16.1	32	-11.6	-13.5	4	-23.8	0.5	22	-26.8	-24.0
Jul 09	24	-21.4	-20.7	30	-17.6	-18.7	4	-38.0	-25.4	24	-20.3	-24.0
Aug 09	24	-19.7	-18.8	30	-14.2	-14.4	3	-41.1	-34.6	24	-18.4	-21.8
Sep 09	25	-13.9	-18.4	30	-11.0	-14.3	6	14.8	-22.7	25	-14.9	-17.9
Oct 09	24	-17.8	-17.2	30	-15.7	-13.7	5	0.2	-9.5	25	-22.3	-18.7
Nov 09	25	-2.4	-11.7	32	2.5	-8.4	5	-20.7	-3.0	27	1.5	-12.7
Dec 09	25	-6.6	-9.3	33	-0.3	-4.9	4	-33.3	-18.8	29	-1.3	-8.2
Jan 10	21	-6.5	-5.1	23	-7.7	-1.3	6	16.6	-13.3	24	-17.5	-6.0
Feb 10	24	45.9	6.7	32	56.9	12.4	5	10.0	-3.0	29	49.2	5.2
Mar 10	25	-2.9	8.3	35	34.8	26.6	4	-30.6	-3.7	26	41.2	18.0
Apr 10	24	-12.2	5.1	29	-20.2	16.0	5	-6.7	-10.8	20	-18.3	20.4
May 10	26	-0.1	-5.2	33	13.7	6.1	6	29.9	-6.3	25	2.5	5.6
Jun 10	24	-5.0	-5.9	28	-13.2	-7.8	5	36.5	16.8	25	15.3	-0.8
Jul 10	23	-4.5	-3.2	28	-7.0	-2.5	5	27.0	31.1	23	-5.2	3.8
Aug 10	23	-1.8	-3.8	28	-8.2	-9.5	4	41.7	34.7	23	-5.8	1.0
Sep 10	25	1.8	-1.5	31	3.5	-3.9	4	-35.6	1.9	25	2.3	-2.8
Oct 10	25	2.9	1.0	31	1.2	-1.2	6	26.6	3.6	25	0.6	-0.9
Nov 10	26	1.7	2.1	31	-4.7	-0.1	6	31.7	4.4	26	-3.0	-0.1
Dec 10	26	6.7	3.7	31	-6.3	-3.4	5	37.0	31.3	26	-11.1	-4.7
Jan 11	27	24.8	10.4	34	50.9	8.9	5	-20.4	11.4	33	38.3	6.5
Feb 11	28	14.4	14.9	33	1.2	11.1	6	7.1	3.4	28	-3.3	6.2

4.14c Average Weekly Earnings (nominal) - Bonus Pay
(Great Britain, seasonally adjusted)

Standard Industrial Classification (2007)

	Whole Economy			Private sector [2 3 4]			Public sector [2 3 4]			Services, SIC 2007 sections G-S		
	Weekly Earnings (£)	% changes year on year: Single month	% changes year on year: 3 month average [1]	Weekly Earnings (£)	% changes year on year: Single month	% changes year on year: 3 month average [1]	Weekly Earnings (£)	% changes year on year: Single month	% changes year on year: 3 month average [1]	Weekly Earnings (£)	% changes year on year: Single month	% changes year on year: 3 month average [1]
	KAF4	KAF5	KAF6	KAF7	KAF8	KAF9	KAG2	KAG3	KAG4	K5CS	K5CT	K5CU
Mar 11	27	8.0	15.3	35	1.2	13.7	6	47.7	8.2	28	8.8	13.3
Apr 11	25	4.0	8.8	31	6.5	2.8	5	-3.7	15.2	22	10.7	4.7
May 11	26	-0.3	3.9	33	-0.7	2.2	5	-8.1	9.5	25	2.7	7.2
Jun 11	30	22.9	8.8	35	26.4	10.0	6	21.8	3.1	31	22.8	12.2
Jul 11	31	37.1	19.2	35	26.1	16.1	17	272.7	86.8	32	42.6	22.1
Aug 11	27	15.5	25.1	33	18.0	23.5	5	5.9	98.6	28	20.9	28.5
Sep 11	26	1.7	17.6	31	0.2	14.2	5	26.5	109.0	26	2.2	21.1
Oct 11	27	6.3	7.7	33	6.2	7.8	4	-32.9	-4.9	28	9.1	10.4
Nov 11	27	4.4	4.2	32	4.9	3.8	5	-11.3	-10.5	27	4.1	5.1
Dec 11	26	-0.6	3.3	31	1.0	4.0	5	-1.6	-16.0	26	3.0	5.4
Jan 12	25	-6.7	-1.0	31	-10.1	-1.7	7	46.5	8.9	27	-17.0	-4.4
Feb 12	26	-7.4	-4.9	31	-5.4	-5.0	4	-31.3	1.9	26	-6.9	-7.8
Mar 12	26	-4.0	-6.1	33	-6.4	-7.3	5	-21.2	-5.9	28	-2.7	-9.3
Apr 12	27	7.3	-1.6	33	6.3	-2.1	4	-13.8	-22.4	26	17.5	1.4
May 12	26	0.4	1.1	32	-3.4	-1.4	6	9.2	-9.6	25	-0.5	3.9
Jun 12	27	-8.2	-0.7	33	-6.4	-1.4	6	-9.3	-5.0	28	-10.4	0.6
Jul 12	29	-8.0	-5.6	34	-0.9	-3.6	4	-74.2	-45.1	30	-7.5	-6.5
Aug 12	28	4.8	-4.2	33	-0.1	-2.5	8	72.7	-35.4	29	5.9	-4.4
Sep 12	27	6.3	0.5	32	3.9	0.9	6	17.9	-32.3	28	9.8	2.0
Oct 12	27	-0.4	3.5	31	-3.7	0.0	9	120.7	67.6	27	-2.1	4.4
Nov 12	27	0.4	2.0	32	-1.0	-0.3	6	10.4	43.8	27	1.0	2.8
Dec 12	26	-1.2	-0.4	30	-2.9	-2.5	8	57.1	56.9	26	0.3	-0.3
Jan 13	27	6.3	1.8	32	4.3	0.1	5	-21.0	11.0	28	1.3	0.9
Feb 13	26	3.2	2.7	32	3.6	1.6	3	-29.3	1.0	27	4.0	1.9
Mar 13	24	-7.2	0.7	30	-9.0	-0.6	5	-2.5	-17.1	26	-6.3	-0.4
Apr 13	41	51.5	16.4	50	50.3	15.3	5	3.9	-8.3	41	61.5	19.1
May 13	30	18.9	21.5	37	17.3	19.6	5	-16.4	-5.8	30	20.8	24.6
Jun 13	29	4.2	24.8	34	5.2	24.4	6	-1.7	-5.4	29	4.3	28.4
Jul 13	28	-4.9	5.6	33	-3.7	6.0	3	-30.7	-15.1	29	-4.0	6.3
Aug 13	28	-0.9	-0.6	34	3.4	1.5	3	-57.6	-33.4	29	-2.3	-0.8
Sep 13	28	4.6	-0.5	34	5.5	1.6	5	-13.0	-37.3	30	4.0	-0.9
Oct 13	27	0.8	1.5	32	2.0	3.6	3	-65.4	-49.6	27	1.5	1.0
Nov 13	27	-0.4	1.7	32	-0.2	2.5	3	-44.8	-45.0	28	1.0	2.2
Dec 13	27	6.1	2.1	33	6.9	2.8	2	-69.7	-61.3	28	4.6	2.3
Jan 14	28	4.4	3.3	33	3.4	3.3	5	-14.7	-46.2	28	2.0	2.5
Feb 14	30	11.7	7.4	35	10.0	6.7	4	58.7	-28.1	30	12.7	6.4
Mar 14	26	7.8	8.0	32	6.1	6.5	5	10.3	10.3	28	6.8	7.1
Apr 14	29	-27.9	-7.0	35	-30.1	-8.9	6	32.2	29.4	30	-27.8	-6.8
May 14	29	-5.1	-11.6	35	-7.1	-13.5	2	-47.6	-1.8	29	-3.8	-11.2
Jun 14	29	-0.2	-13.0	38	9.6	-11.8	2	-56.0	-26.6	28	-3.1	-13.5
Jul 14	26	-4.9	-3.4	31	-7.3	-1.7	5	46.8	-29.3	26	-9.2	-5.3
Aug 14	26	-7.9	-4.3	31	-8.1	-1.9	1	-61.8	-31.4	26	-8.9	-7.1
Sep 14	27	-5.1	-6.0	32	-5.8	-7.1	3	-30.5	-18.8	27	-8.9	-9.0

4.14c Average Weekly Earnings (nominal) - Bonus Pay
(Great Britain, seasonally adjusted)

Standard Industrial Classification (2007)

	Whole Economy			Private sector [2 3 4]			Public sector [2 3 4]			Services, SIC 2007 sections G-S		
	Weekly Earnings (£)	% changes year on year Single month	3 month average [1]	Weekly Earnings (£)	% changes year on year Single month	3 month average [1]	Weekly Earnings (£)	% changes year on year Single month	3 month average [1]	Weekly Earnings (£)	% changes year on year Single month	3 month average [1]
	KAF4	KAF5	KAF6	KAF7	KAF8	KAF9	KAG2	KAG3	KAG4	K5CS	K5CT	K5CU
Oct 14	28	3.2	-3.4	33	2.7	-3.9	3	-7.8	-34.0	29	4.3	-4.7
Nov 14	29	7.1	1.6	34	6.8	1.0	3	-24.4	-22.6	29	5.5	0.1
Dec 14	32	15.6	8.7	37	14.3	7.9	3	49.2	0.9	32	14.8	8.2
Jan 15	28	-0.4	7.4	33	-0.3	6.9	2	-61.6	-24.7	28	-0.1	6.7
Feb 15	28	-4.9	3.2	33	-4.7	2.9	3	-37.0	-29.6	29	-4.3	3.2
Mar 15	29	12.7	2.1	36	12.6	2.3	2	-56.3	-52.1	31	11.8	2.2
Apr 15	29	-0.6	1.9	35	1.0	2.7	2	-60.7	-52.6	30	0.0	2.2
May 15	29	1.5	4.2	35	1.4	4.8	2	-3.4	-48.9	30	1.8	4.4
Jun 15	27	-5.9	-1.7	35	-7.7	-1.9	2	-16.3	-37.7	25	-9.5	-2.4
Jul 15	31	17.6	4.0	37	20.4	3.7	3	-41.3	-25.0	32	22.6	4.5
Aug 15	31	20.9	10.3	37	20.4	9.8	1	8.3	-26.1	32	23.3	11.6
Sep 15	30	9.4	15.9	35	7.8	16.1	6	72.7	7.2	31	13.7	19.8
Oct 15	29	6.7	12.2	35	6.6	11.5	2	-18.1	27.5	31	7.8	14.7
Nov 15	28	-1.7	4.7	34	-1.7	4.1	2	-2.7	21.6	29	-0.1	7.0
Dec 15	31	-3.2	0.4	36	-2.3	0.7	1	-60.0	-30.1	31	-0.6	2.2
Jan 16	31	10.7	1.7	37	11.3	2.2	5	164.7	10.4	31	11.1	3.3
Feb 16	27	-5.8	0.4	32	-5.5	1.0	3	-0.2	10.8	27	-7.1	1.0
Mar 16	30	2.2	2.4	36	1.0	2.2	2	-15.9	36.4	31	0.0	1.2
Apr 16	32	8.2	1.7	38	8.4	1.4	2	4.4	-3.8	33	8.8	0.6
May 16	32	8.2	6.2	38	7.7	5.7	3	26.3	4.9	32	7.6	5.4
Jun 16	28	5.0	7.2	36	2.5	6.2	3	20.0	16.8	27	6.5	7.7
Jul 16	34	8.8	7.4	41	9.9	6.8	2	-24.1	5.5	35	9.9	8.1
Aug 16	30	-3.9	3.2	36	-5.1	2.4	3	82.7	15.3	31	-4.6	3.7
Sep 16	29	-1.1	1.3	35	0.3	1.7	3	-54.5	-26.6	30	-3.7	0.6
Oct 16	31	5.6	0.1	37	5.9	0.3	2	-15.2	-24.6	31	1.0	-2.5
Nov 16	31	11.0	5.1	37	11.2	5.8	3	3.5	-32.5	32	9.6	2.2
Dec 16	29	-4.9	3.7	35	-4.7	4.0	3	95.4	17.1	29	-6.8	1.1
Jan 17	30	-1.7	1.2	36	-1.7	1.4	2	-54.6	-13.7	31	-0.9	0.4

Source: Monthly Wages & Salaries Survey

Inquiries: Email: labour.market@ons.gov.uk

Earnings enquiries: 01633 456773

1. The three month average figures are the changes in the average seasonally adjusted values for the three months ending with the relevant month compared with the same period a year earlier.

2. From July 2009 Royal Bank of Scotland Group plc is classified to the public sector; for earlier time periods it is classified to the private sector. Between July 2009 and March 2014 Lloyds Banking Group plc is classified to the public sector; it is classified to the private sector for earlier and later time periods.

3. Between June 2010 and May 2012 English Further Education Corporations and Sixth Form College Corporations are classified to the public sector. Before June 2010 and after May 2012 they are classified to the private sector.

4. From October 2013 Royal Mail plc is classified to the private sector; previously it is in the public sector.

4.14c Average Weekly Earnings (nominal) - Bonus Pay
(Great Britain, seasonally adjusted)

Standard Industrial Classification (2007)

	Finance and business services, SIC 2007 sections K-N			Public sector excluding financial services [4 5]			Manufacturing, SIC 2007 section C			Construction, SIC 2007 section F			Wholesaling, retailing, hotels & restaurants, SIC 2007 sections G & I		
	Weekly Earnings (£)	% changes year on year: Single month	3 month average [1]	Weekly Earnings (£)	% changes year on year: Single month	3 month average [1]	Weekly Earnings (£)	% changes year on year: Single month	3 month average [1]	Weekly Earnings (£)	% changes year on year: Single month	3 month average [1]	Weekly Earnings (£)	% changes year on year: Single month	3 month average [1]
	K5CV	K5CW	K5CX	KAH3	KAH4	KAH5	K5D3	K5D4	K5D5	K5D6	K5D7	K5D8	K5D9	K5DA	K5DB
Jan 04	48	57.0	10.5	2	11.2	-8.5	17	8.4	11.7	20	-3.7	10.1	14	-12.5	-3.4
Feb 04	37	-7.0	6.9	2	-3.2	2.5	14	-18.1	-5.0	20	1.7	2.0	15	-0.1	2.4
Mar 04	49	21.0	20.8	2	8.4	5.3	16	-0.3	-3.9	22	-2.6	-1.6	13	-3.5	-5.5
Apr 04	53	44.1	18.7	2	3.8	2.9	16	23.8	-0.3	20	5.1	1.2	16	24.0	6.2
May 04	53	39.9	34.6	2	6.8	6.4	19	19.8	13.7	24	52.4	15.1	14	8.9	9.4
Jun 04	46	27.8	37.4	2	-23.4	-7.2	16	24.7	22.6	19	7.3	20.1	14	6.1	12.9
Jul 04	49	26.0	31.3	2	-7.7	-10.4	17	3.1	15.1	21	12.9	23.1	14	0.9	5.1
Aug 04	37	0.5	18.2	2	5.4	-10.3	18	6.9	10.5	17	-10.6	2.9	15	14.4	6.9
Sep 04	45	21.9	16.4	2	-7.3	-3.3	20	27.8	12.2	14	-33.3	-11.5	16	17.4	10.7
Oct 04	63	39.2	21.9	2	-2.5	-1.5	18	16.4	16.7	18	-23.7	-23.0	14	-1.7	9.7
Nov 04	50	22.9	28.6	2	32.3	5.4	17	-12.1	9.0	25	21.1	-12.7	14	11.0	8.7
Dec 04	52	70.5	41.7	2	7.3	10.7	21	45.2	13.9	20	-1.9	-2.3	15	-14.1	-2.9
Jan 05	53	11.0	30.3	2	-5.5	9.4	18	7.8	11.1	23	14.3	11.3	15	13.2	1.6
Feb 05	50	32.9	33.7	2	2.4	1.3	17	19.9	23.6	22	14.0	8.8	15	4.1	-0.2
Mar 05	51	4.4	14.7	2	-6.5	-3.4	17	5.7	10.7	25	10.7	12.9	14	3.4	6.8
Apr 05	53	0.1	10.4	2	10.1	1.8	18	16.1	13.7	23	14.5	13.0	14	-8.6	-0.7
May 05	50	-6.6	-0.9	2	12.5	5.0	16	-11.7	2.5	26	4.6	9.6	15	7.8	0.4
Jun 05	58	27.5	6.0	2	3.1	8.4	16	-0.5	0.5	22	16.8	11.4	14	-2.4	-1.5
Jul 05	53	7.8	8.7	2	30.6	14.8	18	6.8	-2.2	23	10.0	10.0	14	-4.4	0.2
Aug 05	65	77.4	34.1	3	25.8	19.3	18	1.5	2.6	19	11.4	12.7	14	-5.5	-4.1
Sep 05	62	37.0	37.4	3	48.5	34.6	16	-16.8	-3.4	20	41.9	19.1	15	-9.6	-6.6
Oct 05	58	-8.2	27.6	3	51.0	41.3	17	-4.6	-6.9	23	33.6	28.2	15	2.1	-4.6
Nov 05	66	31.9	17.4	2	18.6	39.0	19	13.7	-3.3	25	-1.2	20.3	14	-0.1	-2.8
Dec 05	60	16.8	11.8	3	29.7	32.7	19	-11.3	-1.6	24	20.3	15.4	16	4.7	2.3
Jan 06	56	4.6	17.5	3	71.5	39.3	19	6.9	2.0	25	7.9	8.1	14	-6.1	-0.5
Feb 06	64	28.0	16.2	3	73.6	57.3	21	22.7	4.7	26	17.3	14.9	13	-15.7	-5.7
Mar 06	69	35.8	22.5	3	51.3	65.5	19	13.0	14.1	23	-8.2	5.2	15	7.0	-5.3
Apr 06	68	28.8	30.9	3	35.6	53.0	20	10.8	15.4	23	0.8	2.9	15	1.8	-2.6
May 06	69	39.0	34.4	3	34.9	40.3	19	14.5	12.7	24	-5.0	-4.3	14	-7.3	0.4
Jun 06	94	60.5	43.5	3	25.5	31.9	19	20.1	15.0	26	16.4	3.6	15	5.1	-0.3
Jul 06	80	51.7	51.0	3	17.0	25.5	18	2.8	12.1	27	16.6	8.7	16	18.8	5.2
Aug 06	75	15.5	41.3	3	6.4	15.8	18	-1.9	6.4	27	37.7	22.8	14	3.8	9.2
Sep 06	59	-4.8	19.1	2	-21.6	-0.2	20	25.0	8.0	20	-1.2	17.3	14	-1.4	6.9
Oct 06	72	23.3	11.2	3	17.7	1.1	24	36.7	19.5	24	2.0	11.9	15	0.4	0.9
Nov 06	79	20.6	12.9	2	-22.0	-7.5	19	1.0	20.2	22	-12.0	-4.0	15	1.5	0.2
Dec 06	105	73.7	38.8	3	4.8	1.6	19	2.7	12.8	24	1.4	-3.0	15	-4.3	-0.9
Jan 07	80	43.5	45.2	3	-22.1	-13.3	21	9.7	4.5	24	-2.0	-4.3	16	9.2	1.9
Feb 07	81	27.9	48.1	2	-24.7	-15.1	22	4.5	5.6	44	68.0	23.7	16	27.0	9.5
Mar 07	73	4.8	24.0	3	-0.1	-16.3	20	7.9	7.3	25	9.8	26.7	19	28.7	21.5
Apr 07	76	10.9	14.2	3	-3.7	-10.3	20	1.4	4.6	28	20.0	34.3	18	23.5	26.4
May 07	72	3.9	6.5	3	6.3	0.9	22	17.6	8.8	30	25.7	18.7	19	37.0	29.6
Jun 07	73	-22.5	-4.7	3	20.4	7.6	23	21.3	13.2	35	34.3	27.0	20	37.5	32.6
Jul 07	76	-4.9	-9.2	3	1.5	9.3	23	24.7	21.2	28	5.3	21.5	20	20.6	31.2

4.14c Average Weekly Earnings (nominal) - Bonus Pay
(Great Britain, seasonally adjusted)

Standard Industrial Classification (2007)

	Finance and business services, SIC 2007 sections K-N			Public sector excluding financial services[4 5]			Manufacturing, SIC 2007 section C			Construction, SIC 2007 section F			Wholesaling, retailing, hotels & restaurants, SIC 2007 sections G & I		
	Weekly Earnings (£)	% changes year on year: Single month	% changes year on year: 3 month average[1]	Weekly Earnings (£)	% changes year on year: Single month	% changes year on year: 3 month average[1]	Weekly Earnings (£)	% changes year on year: Single month	% changes year on year: 3 month average[1]	Weekly Earnings (£)	% changes year on year: Single month	% changes year on year: 3 month average[1]	Weekly Earnings (£)	% changes year on year: Single month	% changes year on year: 3 month average[1]
	K5CV	K5CW	K5CX	KAH3	KAH4	KAH5	K5D3	K5D4	K5D5	K5D6	K5D7	K5D8	K5D9	K5DA	K5DB
Aug 07	79	4.4	-8.7	3	2.2	8.0	22	23.4	23.1	27	0.8	13.3	17	20.6	26.0
Sep 07	89	49.9	13.5	3	25.3	8.4	23	10.9	19.3	31	56.5	17.6	20	41.0	27.1
Oct 07	73	1.5	16.4	2	-50.5	-13.4	22	-5.6	8.2	27	13.0	20.8	21	42.4	34.7
Nov 07	79	-0.9	14.2	3	54.2	-2.3	24	24.2	8.8	31	44.4	36.6	19	30.5	38.0
Dec 07	74	-29.4	-11.9	3	-9.1	-12.1	24	23.3	12.6	33	38.0	31.4	19	23.1	31.9
Jan 08	79	-1.0	-12.3	2	-3.8	8.7	21	2.9	16.4	31	28.6	36.8	17	7.4	20.1
Feb 08	85	4.4	-10.6	2	-13.4	-8.7	22	3.8	9.6	30	-31.8	2.1	18	9.2	13.1
Mar 08	81	11.6	4.8	2	-40.7	-20.2	19	-6.1	0.3	27	8.6	-5.4	22	13.8	10.4
Apr 08	77	2.2	5.9	3	-0.3	-18.8	23	14.0	3.9	25	-10.8	-15.4	18	0.4	7.9
May 08	87	21.1	11.5	3	-8.1	-16.6	34	54.2	21.6	27	-11.1	-5.1	20	4.1	6.2
Jun 08	89	22.1	14.9	3	-13.5	-7.8	24	1.9	23.2	23	-34.7	-19.8	18	-10.2	-2.1
Jul 08	78	2.1	14.9	3	21.3	-0.9	27	16.3	23.6	23	-18.1	-22.0	18	-8.5	-5.1
Aug 08	72	-8.4	4.9	3	19.9	8.1	21	-3.6	5.0	25	-6.3	-21.0	17	-2.6	-7.3
Sep 08	80	-9.3	-5.4	3	16.4	19.2	21	-5.2	2.7	27	-14.5	-13.1	16	-21.3	-11.2
Oct 08	87	19.1	-0.4	3	80.5	32.7	24	5.3	-1.1	21	-24.1	-15.0	15	-26.4	-17.5
Nov 08	63	-19.4	-4.0	4	26.9	35.5	19	-20.4	-7.1	21	-34.2	-24.3	18	-6.5	-18.4
Dec 08	80	7.8	2.0	3	15.7	35.4	21	-11.9	-9.3	20	-40.0	-33.3	16	-12.3	-15.4
Jan 09	76	-3.5	-5.3	2	-1.9	14.2	21	-3.8	-12.3	18	-43.1	-39.1	18	5.5	-4.8
Feb 09	43	-49.5	-16.4	3	60.5	23.1	18	-18.5	-11.5	20	-34.3	-39.2	17	-2.5	-3.4
Mar 09	46	-43.1	-32.5	3	91.9	44.7	21	10.4	-4.7	23	-13.9	-31.1	16	-25.0	-8.8
Apr 09	85	9.1	-28.7	4	49.9	64.3	24	5.1	-1.5	24	-4.5	-18.5	17	-6.7	-12.3
May 09	49	-43.2	-26.7	2	-11.7	36.0	20	-41.2	-14.1	18	-33.8	-17.8	17	-14.2	-15.9
Jun 09	52	-41.0	-26.4	2	-24.4	3.9	18	-22.2	-22.3	19	-14.8	-18.3	16	-9.4	-10.2
Jul 09	61	-20.7	-35.5	2	-45.7	-28.6	18	-33.9	-33.5	19	-18.3	-23.0	16	-11.9	-11.9
Aug 09	67	-7.7	-24.3	1	-54.9	-42.7	18	-13.7	-24.1	19	-24.2	-19.3	18	4.1	-5.9
Sep 09	59	-26.8	-18.7	3	-11.1	-37.9	19	-9.7	-20.3	17	-36.1	-26.6	17	5.1	-1.2
Oct 09	63	-27.6	-21.3	2	-39.9	-35.8	18	-25.8	-16.7	18	-11.2	-24.9	17	9.8	6.3
Nov 09	68	6.8	-17.8	2	-53.5	-35.7	20	7.1	-10.7	21	-0.8	-17.8	17	-5.3	2.8
Dec 09	83	4.3	-7.0	2	-43.5	-46.1	20	-3.7	-8.7	20	-1.4	-4.5	17	0.7	1.4
Jan 10	61	-19.8	-3.3	2	-10.6	-38.7	20	-3.0	-0.1	21	18.7	4.9	18	-1.1	-2.0
Feb 10	73	70.4	9.3	2	-54.1	-38.7	22	18.2	3.2	20	-0.3	5.2	19	7.1	2.2
Mar 10	64	38.8	20.0	4	15.7	-17.7	22	4.2	6.0	24	5.7	7.5	23	41.8	15.3
Apr 10	62	-27.0	14.6	1	-70.9	-39.1	19	-22.9	-2.2	15	-34.9	-10.5	19	9.4	19.1
May 10	72	46.7	10.1	2	-25.9	-30.5	20	-1.0	-7.5	17	-6.4	-12.5	16	-4.1	15.5
Jun 10	66	25.1	7.2	2	-13.2	-43.8	15	-19.4	-14.9	15	-24.1	-23.1	16	-1.3	1.4
Jul 10	56	-8.4	19.0	1	-22.3	-20.6	22	23.0	0.5	16	-14.9	-15.4	16	2.8	-0.9
Aug 10	65	-2.3	3.6	2	1.7	-12.2	22	18.9	7.2	16	-13.2	-17.5	15	-12.3	-3.9
Sep 10	72	22.3	3.4	1	-49.3	-28.5	22	12.7	18.0	16	-5.4	-11.4	16	-3.1	-4.5
Oct 10	71	12.8	10.4	2	-2.7	-22.7	25	43.3	24.4	12	-33.3	-17.5	16	-3.3	-6.3
Nov 10	72	5.6	13.2	2	-4.4	-23.8	20	-2.3	16.7	16	-22.2	-20.7	18	6.6	0.1
Dec 10	68	-18.5	-1.7	1	-10.7	-5.9	22	10.2	15.8	17	-10.6	-21.8	19	13.0	5.4
Jan 11	98	59.4	11.7	1	-39.8	-20.2	23	17.1	8.2	19	-10.5	-14.4	17	-4.7	4.8
Feb 11	74	1.0	10.0	2	20.4	-13.1	21	-2.8	7.9	25	26.4	1.6	18	-3.8	1.2

4.14c Average Weekly Earnings (nominal) - Bonus Pay
(Great Britain, seasonally adjusted)

Standard Industrial Classification (2007)

	Finance and business services, SIC 2007 sections K-N			Public sector excluding financial services [4 5]			Manufacturing, SIC 2007 section C			Construction, SIC 2007 section F			Wholesaling, retailing, hotels & restaurants, SIC 2007 sections G & I		
	Weekly Earnings (£)	% changes year on year Single month	% changes year on year 3 month average [1]	Weekly Earnings (£)	% changes year on year Single month	% changes year on year 3 month average [1]	Weekly Earnings (£)	% changes year on year Single month	% changes year on year 3 month average [1]	Weekly Earnings (£)	% changes year on year Single month	% changes year on year 3 month average [1]	Weekly Earnings (£)	% changes year on year Single month	% changes year on year 3 month average [1]
	K5CV	K5CW	K5CX	KAH3	KAH4	KAH5	K5D3	K5D4	K5D5	K5D6	K5D7	K5D8	K5D9	K5DA	K5DB
Mar 11	76	18.5	24.7	2	-57.5	-36.0	22	0.7	4.7	21	-14.2	-0.7	19	-19.7	-10.3
Apr 11	68	9.5	9.3	2	51.2	-19.1	22	15.1	3.8	17	11.7	5.9	17	-9.8	-11.8
May 11	68	-6.0	6.8	1	-20.4	-28.8	20	2.3	5.7	16	-4.9	-4.4	17	6.8	-9.2
Jun 11	86	30.4	10.8	1	-42.0	-11.3	19	31.0	14.8	20	35.8	13.3	23	40.6	11.4
Jul 11	85	50.8	22.8	3	129.1	14.1	22	0.4	9.1	14	-13.1	5.0	20	22.4	23.3
Aug 11	69	6.7	28.3	2	9.9	25.7	19	-12.7	3.3	16	-2.1	6.0	18	13.4	25.6
Sep 11	70	-2.9	15.9	2	12.9	50.1	24	11.4	-0.3	17	4.7	-3.5	18	10.3	15.4
Oct 11	71	0.8	1.3	1	-28.5	-3.6	20	-18.8	-7.3	18	43.9	12.9	18	11.6	11.7
Nov 11	75	4.4	0.7	2	4.2	-5.4	21	6.3	-1.5	22	38.8	27.8	17	-4.3	5.5
Dec 11	69	2.2	2.5	1	-6.4	-10.9	21	-5.7	-7.1	19	6.3	27.7	18	-1.5	1.6
Jan 12	71	-27.5	-9.4	2	41.7	11.6	21	-8.7	-3.1	17	-6.9	11.5	19	13.9	2.4
Feb 12	65	-11.9	-14.2	2	-19.1	1.6	24	14.5	-0.4	18	-27.6	-11.6	19	5.5	5.7
Mar 12	73	-4.6	-15.8	1	-13.0	-0.7	19	-14.9	-3.5	20	-5.1	-14.3	18	-4.0	4.8
Apr 12	75	11.6	-2.1	1	-30.2	-20.9	22	2.6	0.4	20	13.0	-9.0	17	2.7	1.3
May 12	56	-17.8	-3.7	2	9.0	-12.7	25	21.4	2.5	19	16.0	6.9	19	7.8	2.0
Jun 12	66	-22.8	-10.8	2	47.7	2.5	21	8.2	10.6	24	21.8	17.2	20	-10.6	-1.0
Jul 12	75	-11.1	-17.2	2	-48.1	-16.3	21	-4.9	7.9	17	22.9	20.3	18	-11.0	-5.4
Aug 12	74	7.3	-10.0	2	27.2	-10.2	24	28.0	9.7	16	-2.2	14.4	23	28.4	0.7
Sep 12	67	-3.9	-3.2	2	52.1	-4.7	21	-14.5	1.1	15	-9.7	2.5	20	10.8	8.5
Oct 12	66	-7.3	-1.4	3	180.8	78.5	22	6.9	5.1	20	11.7	0.1	20	10.5	16.5
Nov 12	66	-11.4	-7.6	2	19.0	75.9	23	7.8	-0.7	18	-20.4	-7.3	19	11.4	10.9
Dec 12	69	-0.8	-6.6	2	72.7	83.6	20	-5.7	3.0	17	-7.1	-6.5	19	1.0	7.6
Jan 13	72	2.1	-3.5	1	-21.5	19.4	19	-10.5	-2.8	16	-8.0	-12.4	20	2.7	4.9
Feb 13	68	4.3	1.8	1	-25.6	5.0	22	-10.0	-8.8	17	-6.5	-7.2	20	5.8	3.2
Mar 13	66	-8.5	-0.9	2	14.9	-12.2	20	7.4	-5.0	12	-41.2	-19.5	18	0.2	2.9
Apr 13	127	68.5	22.7	2	35.1	5.8	27	22.4	6.1	34	73.4	8.6	25	43.2	15.9
May 13	79	42.2	33.9	2	16.2	21.3	22	-11.2	5.5	19	2.5	11.3	23	21.8	21.5
Jun 13	74	12.5	42.3	2	16.4	21.6	23	7.2	5.5	23	-6.0	21.3	21	1.6	21.1
Jul 13	67	-11.4	11.7	2	4.0	12.0	21	0.7	-1.7	17	-3.2	-2.6	23	29.7	17.0
Aug 13	70	-5.9	-2.2	1	-35.0	-7.8	24	0.3	2.6	20	29.4	4.6	28	24.7	18.4
Sep 13	73	9.1	-3.2	2	-11.1	-15.2	21	1.7	0.9	20	29.9	18.0	22	8.4	20.8
Oct 13	69	4.8	2.4	1	-74.2	-45.0	22	2.6	1.5	16	-20.3	10.3	21	6.4	13.6
Nov 13	69	4.9	6.3	1	-56.0	-50.5	23	-1.4	0.9	17	-3.2	0.1	21	9.6	8.1
Dec 13	70	2.3	4.0	1	-69.6	-68.3	22	11.8	4.0	18	1.7	-7.8	21	11.1	9.0
Jan 14	71	-1.2	1.9	1	-14.3	-51.4	25	32.3	13.3	20	26.5	7.8	21	7.2	9.3
Feb 14	76	11.3	4.0	1	2.3	-37.4	22	3.7	15.4	19	11.3	12.8	16	-20.9	-1.2
Mar 14	68	1.7	3.8	1	-16.9	-10.7	22	10.5	14.9	17	45.4	25.7	20	10.7	-1.5
Apr 14	69	-45.7	-18.9	1	-10.7	-9.6	23	-16.1	-2.1	22	-36.3	-8.1	24	-4.6	-5.4
May 14	72	-8.8	-23.4	1	-32.9	-20.6	22	2.8	-2.4	17	-9.9	-13.7	21	-7.8	-1.5
Jun 14	69	-7.2	-25.1	2	-15.8	-20.1	24	7.5	-2.9	25	8.7	-16.0	22	5.7	-2.5
Jul 14	61	-8.5	-8.2	2	31.7	-6.0	23	10.1	6.8	28	71.4	20.4	20	-14.2	-5.8
Aug 14	68	-2.5	-6.1	1	-36.7	-4.8	21	-12.4	1.1	26	25.8	31.9	21	-25.9	-13.0
Sep 14	70	-4.4	-5.1	1	-32.2	-12.0	24	16.0	3.7	24	20.4	37.2	21	-3.0	-15.4

4.14c Average Weekly Earnings (nominal) - Bonus Pay
(Great Britain, seasonally adjusted)

Standard Industrial Classification (2007)

	Finance and business services, SIC 2007 sections K-N			Public sector excluding financial services [4 5]			Manufacturing, SIC 2007 section C			Construction, SIC 2007 section F			Wholesaling, retailing, hotels & restaurants, SIC 2007 sections G & I		
	Weekly Earnings (£)	% changes year on year: Single month	% changes year on year: 3 month average [1]	Weekly Earnings (£)	% changes year on year: Single month	% changes year on year: 3 month average [1]	Weekly Earnings (£)	% changes year on year: Single month	% changes year on year: 3 month average [1]	Weekly Earnings (£)	% changes year on year: Single month	% changes year on year: 3 month average [1]	Weekly Earnings (£)	% changes year on year: Single month	% changes year on year: 3 month average [1]
	K5CV	K5CW	K5CX	KAH3	KAH4	KAH5	K5D3	K5D4	K5D5	K5D6	K5D7	K5D8	K5D9	K5DA	K5DB
Oct 14	69	-0.7	-2.6	2	73.4	-12.0	21	-6.3	-1.6	17	6.4	18.5	21	-0.8	-11.4
Nov 14	72	3.5	-0.6	1	63.8	13.6	24	6.3	5.1	23	33.1	20.4	22	4.0	0.0
Dec 14	85	20.1	7.7	2	153.8	93.9	27	23.1	7.6	24	37.4	26.3	21	3.9	2.4
Jan 15	65	-8.4	5.0	1	-42.3	41.4	24	-6.6	6.9	20	-0.5	22.1	23	8.7	5.5
Feb 15	70	-7.2	1.2	4	212.5	99.1	20	-9.5	1.9	16	-12.9	7.1	19	22.4	10.7
Mar 15	71	4.9	-3.8	1	-2.7	51.9	25	10.7	-2.0	20	16.7	0.6	25	28.7	19.5
Apr 15	74	7.2	1.3	0	-76.2	33.4	24	5.7	2.4	23	9.0	4.1	23	-2.5	14.6
May 15	69	-5.3	2.1	1	4.1	-27.7	20	-9.6	2.3	39	125.7	47.2	23	8.2	10.6
Jun 15	54	-21.9	-6.6	1	-27.2	-35.3	27	10.2	2.3	23	-9.0	33.4	23	7.0	4.0
Jul 15	74	20.2	-3.2	1	-41.0	-26.1	23	1.1	0.8	30	6.0	29.8	24	20.1	11.6
Aug 15	84	22.7	6.4	1	4.5	-28.1	23	7.0	6.1	23	-9.4	-3.7	23	8.8	11.8
Sep 15	69	-1.9	13.3	3	79.1	4.7	21	-12.9	-2.0	22	-8.9	-3.6	23	10.7	13.1
Oct 15	72	4.9	8.4	1	-11.5	25.7	24	12.6	1.5	18	10.4	-4.2	21	0.9	6.8
Nov 15	68	-5.6	-1.0	1	-1.3	21.3	21	-11.0	-4.6	21	-7.7	-3.4	22	1.7	4.4
Dec 15	77	-8.7	-3.6	1	-56.7	-26.1	24	-10.9	-4.1	24	0.6	0.2	24	11.1	4.6
Jan 16	75	14.4	-0.9	2	193.9	7.2	22	-5.1	-9.1	28	37.3	8.8	22	-2.7	3.2
Feb 16	62	-10.8	-2.5	2	-55.3	-27.5	22	7.9	-3.6	25	53.7	27.1	21	10.1	5.8
Mar 16	74	5.0	2.6	2	41.4	-2.1	25	0.1	0.6	23	15.0	34.2	22	-14.9	-3.6
Apr 16	80	7.6	0.7	1	315.9	-7.2	23	-4.5	0.8	32	34.2	33.1	22	-6.2	-4.8
May 16	78	13.4	8.6	2	44.7	76.1	26	28.8	6.9	50	29.4	27.3	22	-2.4	-8.1
Jun 16	68	27.0	14.9	2	69.3	89.6	26	-4.2	5.1	26	16.6	27.3	21	-9.3	-6.0
Jul 16	88	20.1	19.7	1	-13.2	30.9	20	-14.8	1.8	35	17.3	22.2	24	0.1	-3.9
Aug 16	72	-14.2	8.3	2	103.6	45.3	25	10.5	-2.9	24	4.1	13.0	21	-5.6	-4.9
Sep 16	67	-2.9	0.4	1	-41.9	-6.3	26	20.0	4.8	26	18.3	13.5	22	-2.7	-2.7
Oct 16	74	2.4	-5.4	1	-8.6	-5.0	21	-9.6	6.5	46	152.6	51.8	24	10.2	0.4
Nov 16	74	9.5	3.0	2	20.5	-17.1	24	14.7	7.7	29	36.3	64.8	24	5.9	4.3
Dec 16	68	-12.4	-0.7	2	106.8	28.9	24	-0.4	1.1	29	20.0	63.6	22	-6.5	2.9
Jan 17	72	-3.4	-2.6	1	-46.4	4.4	23	2.9	5.4	20	-28.7	6.2	22	-0.3	-0.4

Source: Monthly Wages & Salaries Survey

Inquiries: Email: labour.market@ons.gov.uk

Earnings enquiries: 01633 456773

1. The three month average figures are the changes in the average seasonally adjusted values for the three months ending with the relevant month compared with the same period a year earlier.

2. From July 2009 Royal Bank of Scotland Group plc is classified to the public sector; for earlier time periods it is classified to the private sector. Between July 2009 and March 2014 Lloyds Banking Group plc is classified to the public sector; it is classified to the private sector for earlier and later time periods.

3. Between June 2010 and May 2012 English Further Education Corporations and Sixth Form College Corporations are classified to the public sector. Before June 2010 and after May 2012 they are classified to the private sector.

4. From October 2013 Royal Mail plc is classified to the private sector; previously it is in the public sector.

4.14d Average Weekly Earnings in the public sector for selected activities

All figures are in pounds (£) — *Not Seasonally Adjusted*

	Public Administration (Public Sector) (O)			Education (Public Sector) (P)			Health and Social Work (Public Sector) (Q)			Arts, Entertainment and Recreation (Public Sector) (R)		
	Average Weekly Earnings	Of which Bonuses	Of which Arrears	Average Weekly Earnings	Of which Bonuses	Of which Arrears	Average Weekly Earnings	Of which Bonuses	Of which Arrears	Average Weekly Earnings	Of which Bonuses	Of which Arrears
CDID	K5BE	K5BF	K5BG	K5BH	K5BI	K5BJ	K5BK	K5BL	K5BM	K5BN	K5BO	K5BP
2012 Jan	535	1	0	375	0	0	534	0	0	435	1	0
2012 Feb	538	1	0	377	0	0	537	0	0	463	0	0
2012 Mar	541	2	0	377	0	0	536	0	0	462	0	0
2012 Apr	545	0	0	381	0	0	540	0	0	463	1	1
2012 May	543	1	0	379	0	0	543	0	0	501	44	0
2012 Jun	550	5	0	381	0	0	541	0	0	463	5	0
2012 Jul	551	5	0	382	1	0	542	0	0	461	0	2
2012 Aug	547	3	0	387	0	0	536	0	0	455	0	0
2012 Sep	554	7	1	388	0	0	537	0	0	437	3	1
2012 Oct	547	2	1	385	0	0	536	0	0	462	41	0
2012 Nov	544	2	0	385	0	0	538	0	0	442	1	2
2012 Dec	543	2	2	385	0	0	537	0	0	444	5	0
2013 Jan	546	1	1	381	0	0	540	0	0	442	0	2
2013 Feb	535	0	0	380	0	0	538	0	0	441	0	0
2013 Mar	536	3	0	379	0	0	538	0	0	451	0	0
2013 Apr	537	1	0	384	0	0	547	0	0	450	3	0
2013 May	537	0	0	383	0	0	546	0	0	447	5	0
2013 Jun	540	3	0	382	0	0	545	0	0	449	4	1
2013 Jul	543	6	0	384	1	0	546	0	0	449	4	3
2013 Aug	540	1	4	386	0	1	536	0	0	442	1	1
2013 Sep	547	7	0	390	0	1	541	0	0	439	1	0
2013 Oct	537	1	0	390	0	1	543	0	0	441	1	1
2013 Nov	537	1	0	387	0	1	543	0	0	450	1	0
2013 Dec	540	2	1	391	0	1	543	0	0	444	0	0
2014 Jan	545	1	1	386	0	0	545	0	0	447	0	3
2014 Feb	541	1	1	388	0	0	544	0	1	450	0	0
2014 Mar	548	2	4	387	0	0	539	0	0	448	0	0
2014 Apr	553	7	3	392	0	2	547	0	0	454	1	0
2014 May	547	1	1	392	0	3	550	0	1	454	2	0
2014 Jun	549	3	0	390	0	0	549	0	0	453	5	0
2014 Jul	549	4	3	391	0	0	547	0	0	451	5	1
2014 Aug	547	3	1	393	1	0	538	0	0	448	6	0
2014 Sep	555	7	0	397	0	0	545	0	0	451	0	0
2014 Oct	552	1	1	395	0	0	540	0	0	448	1	3
2014 Nov	549	1	1	394	0	1	542	0	0	448	2	0
2014 Dec	554	1	1	405	2	3	543	0	0	456	3	1
2015 Jan	551	0	1	394	0	0	545	0	0	452	0	0
2015 Feb	551	2	1	395	0	0	545	0	0	447	0	0
2015 Mar	548	2	0	395	0	0	543	0	0	459	2	5
2015 Apr	552	1	1	398	0	1	550	0	0	455	2	0
2015 May	552	1	0	395	0	0	551	0	0	454	0	0
2015 Jun	552	2	0	394	0	0	555	0	0	451	4	0
2015 Jul	554	4	1	396	0	0	547	0	0	456	7	1
2015 Aug	553	2	1	398	0	0	540	0	0	443	4	0
2015 Sep	561	8	1	403	0	0	548	0	0	447	1	1
2015 Oct	556	2	1	400	0	1	544	0	0	443	1	1
2015 Nov	553	1	1	401	0	2	549	0	0	447	1	0
2015 Dec	550	1	0	403	0	1	550	0	1	455	5	5
2016 Jan	556	0	1	398	0	1	549	0	0	451	0	0
2016 Feb	555	1	0	399	0	0	551	0	1	455	0	3
2016 Mar	553	2	1	401	0	0	546	0	0	455	2	0
2016 Apr	566	6	0	401	0	0	554	0	0	458	2	0
2016 May	557	1	0	398	0	0	552	0	0	461	16	0
2016 Jun	561	1	1	401	0	1	556	0	0	454	4	0
2016 Jul	556	1	0	400	0	1	550	0	0	466	18	2
2016 Aug	570	8	1	404	0	0	547	0	0	455	4	1
2016 Sep	562	2	0	406	0	0	549	0	0	458	0	1
2016 Oct	566	2	1	404	0	1	547	0	0	452	0	0
2016 Nov	564	1	1	406	0	1	551	0	0	460	1	0
2016 Dec	562	0	0	408	0	1	549	0	0	464	0	0

p = Provisional
r = Revised

Source: Monthly Wages and Salaries Survey

Inquiries: Email: earnings@ons.gov.uk Tel: 01633 456120

4.15a Weekly pay - Gross (£) - For all employee jobs[a]: United Kingdom, 2016

Description	Code	Number of jobs[b] (000s)	Median	Annual % change	Mean	Annual % change	Percentiles 10	20	25	30	40	60	70	75	80	90
All employees		25,758	438.4	3.1	525.0	3.5	141.2	231.2	275.9	307.9	371.1	516.1	611.1	670.8	736.7	953.5
18-21		1,273	206.8	3.8	219.6	4.8	44.3	79.5	97.2	114.9	155.5	256.7	293.6	311.2	333.9	393.7
22-29		4,471	400.0	4.4	433.4	5.7	160.8	259.5	288.0	311.0	352.9	450.3	504.8	537.6	577.4	697.7
30-39		5,916	498.3	1.9	567.3	2.5	180.6	288.2	327.0	360.7	429.4	577.4	669.3	719.7	779.3	977.4
40-49		6,300	503.7	2.4	606.5	3.0	172.6	272.0	310.7	347.0	422.3	596.8	709.1	769.2	844.7	1,107.7
50-59		5,581	473.4	3.4	581.6	4.2	163.1	255.1	296.6	331.9	399.8	563.1	672.7	733.4	806.7	1,057.8
60+		1,974	348.8	2.9	436.7	2.6	97.7	154.1	183.7	216.6	287.0	419.7	502.3	560.0	624.1	848.0
18-21 ALL OCCUPATIONS		1,273	206.8	3.8	219.6	4.8	44.3	79.5	97.2	114.9	155.5	256.7	293.6	311.2	333.9	393.7
18-21 Managers, directors and senior officials	1	19	338.5	3.4	354.0	0.8	x	271.2	296.6	304.8	326.2	347.5	367.1	384.2	388.5	x
18-21 Corporate managers and directors	11	16	337.1	3.9	361.4	10.7	x	270.7	292.2	299.4	324.8	346.8	383.5	386.1	x	x
18-21 Other managers and proprietors	12	x	334.9	-4.9	316.1	-23.6	x	x	x	x	x	x	x	x	x	x
18-21 Professional occupations	2	42	345.0	2.1	371.4	3.9	x	273.9	287.5	302.3	331.4	385.6	426.3	457.0	479.1	545.1
18-21 Science, research, engineering and technology professionals	21	16	345.0	3.2	372.0	-3.6	x	289.1	300.4	314.6	338.2	353.1	387.8	x	x	x
18-21 Health professionals	22	8	x		313.3	-1.0	x	x	x	x	x	x	x	x	x	x
18-21 Teaching and educational professionals	23	x	x		410.0	77.8	x	x	x	x	398.2	x	x	x	x	x
18-21 Business, media and public service professionals	24	13	359.8	-0.3	391.6	-6.0	x	288.3	295.1	307.4	331.4	378.7	420.9	x	x	x
18-21 Associate professional and technical occupations	3	110	310.6	0.7	302.6	2.2	x	x	167.5	221.5	287.5	335.2	366.4	387.8	412.0	487.5
18-21 Science, engineering and technology associate	31	31	334.8	6.4	352.9	9.3	x	268.9	287.5	297.6	319.6	352.6	383.3	398.0	424.4	x
18-21 Health and social care associate professionals	32	11	x		198.3		x	x	x	x	x	x	x	x	x	x
18-21 Protective service occupations	33	x	446.4	-11.0	461.1	-6.5	x	x	x	x	x	461.7	x	x	x	x
18-21 Culture, media and sports occupations	34	15	x		248.0	10.2	x	x	x	x	x	x	x	x	x	x
18-21 Business and public service associate professionals	35	49	309.6	-6.2	298.1	-2.0	x	x	x	213.0	285.3	332.4	364.1	376.9	406.3	x
18-21 Administrative and secretarial occupations	4	123	275.4	3.6	255.5	2.7	61.2	129.7	151.4	186.7	239.2	298.2	322.8	333.2	348.4	388.9
18-21 Administrative occupations	41	100	287.5	6.3	265.6	4.1	71.7	140.0	176.2	198.1	251.9	305.7	326.1	340.0	353.6	392.9
18-21 Secretarial and related occupations	42	23	224.1	-0.5	211.7	-1.1	41.6	93.7	107.9	131.0	172.2	261.3	283.3	299.7	320.5	x
18-21 Skilled trades	5	83	305.3	0.1	324.4	1.3	170.8	216.1	237.2	255.2	281.4	339.4	377.0	402.6	419.3	473.2
18-21 Skilled agricultural and related trades	51	x	300.0	3.2	280.1	-2.3	x	x	x	x	287.0	308.4	x	x	x	x
18-21 Skilled metal, electrical and electronic trades	52	45	337.5	-1.7	364.5	-0.4	212.0	253.4	267.8	279.9	300.3	375.7	410.1	424.6	447.8	546.2
18-21 Skilled construction and building trades	53	12	305.9	5.7	329.9	-0.5	187.2	218.9	228.0	250.0	281.5	337.8	387.4	417.0	x	x
18-21 Textiles, printing and other skilled trades	54	23	256.6	-3.0	249.9	-2.5	x	147.8	170.8	185.4	222.0	284.4	307.5	325.1	356.7	x
18-21 Caring, leisure and other service occupations	6	166	211.1	-2.8	206.6	2.1	39.9	87.0	110.4	131.9	173.3	240.1	270.1	282.7	300.0	349.3
18-21 Caring personal service occupations	61	127	226.1	-0.8	217.0	2.0	43.7	100.8	124.5	146.7	192.6	253.0	276.5	291.6	303.7	358.0
18-21 Leisure, travel and related personal service	62	39	156.0	5.7	172.4	2.1	x	63.4	81.1	96.6	125.6	195.4	226.0	248.3	272.0	x
18-21 Sales and customer service occupations	7	299	136.6	8.8	167.5	8.1	48.3	69.0	81.2	90.1	112.5	167.8	214.3	240.4	268.2	325.1
18-21 Sales occupations	71	254	126.9	6.4	156.3	7.8	45.1	64.7	75.2	85.6	104.5	155.0	195.8	217.6	243.2	304.9
18-21 Customer service occupations	72	45	240.4	9.2	230.5	3.9	74.8	109.7	127.7	141.6	182.5	276.2	299.1	315.0	333.3	374.7
18-21 Process, plant and machine operatives	8	33	306.0	3.5	318.4	4.2	114.1	206.9	240.5	261.1	288.0	329.4	365.6	380.9	411.1	538.0
18-21 Process, plant and machine operatives	81	26	311.0	3.9	329.3	7.0	173.0	239.6	259.5	274.8	292.1	336.7	366.0	380.8	401.5	536.4
18-21 Transport and mobile machine drivers and operatives	82	7	x		278.8	-6.3	x	x	x	x	x	307.3	x	x	x	x
18-21 Elementary occupations	9	398	148.1	4.8	177.6	6.9	34.5	56.5	69.0	84.5	112.7	191.8	242.0	268.1	289.3	345.1
18-21 Elementary trades and related occupations	91	32	306.5	11.0	310.3	10.5	x	227.2	241.0	264.2	284.7	335.5	363.9	387.0	412.4	x
18-21 Elementary administration and service occupations	92	366	134.0	2.8	166.2	6.4	33.0	53.6	64.8	79.3	106.4	171.5	222.1	249.1	273.6	331.0

4.15a Weekly pay - Gross (£) - For all employee jobs[a]: United Kingdom, 2016

Description	Code	Number of jobs[b] (000s)	Median	Annual % change	Mean	Annual % change	Percentiles 10	20	25	30	40	60	70	75	80	90
22-29 ALL OCCUPATIONS		4,471	400.0	4.4	433.4	5.7	160.8	259.5	288.0	311.0	352.9	450.3	504.8	537.6	577.4	697.7
22-29 Managers, directors and senior officials	1	229	487.3	1.7	563.0	0.5	302.7	351.9	373.7	388.8	440.8	538.4	613.1	662.8	718.7	910.3
22-29 Corporate managers and directors	11	174	510.5	1.8	593.0	-0.9	306.6	364.0	385.6	406.9	460.0	574.9	651.6	710.0	769.4	982.6
22-29 Other managers and proprietors	12	54	421.6	-0.4	467.1	4.9	281.8	320.2	345.0	360.3	387.0	460.4	508.3	536.6	568.7	x
22-29 Professional occupations	2	935	553.6	3.1	582.8	2.3	354.6	426.3	456.1	475.2	513.6	592.5	643.9	675.3	721.5	848.4
22-29 Science, research, engineering and technology professionals	21	212	574.9	3.4	613.5	3.5	383.3	456.2	469.5	491.1	535.9	613.3	670.8	712.0	752.9	877.8
22-29 Health professionals	22	249	547.5	2.2	564.3	0.5	336.5	437.1	465.8	487.6	516.5	583.3	624.1	650.4	682.6	808.3
22-29 Teaching and educational professionals	23	218	510.7	1.1	515.9	3.2	312.3	x	426.3	431.7	465.8	544.5	578.8	616.9	634.7	719.6
22-29 Business, media and public service professionals	24	256	583.2	1.4	632.6	1.3	354.6	431.2	460.0	479.1	536.6	641.9	707.2	754.7	804.9	958.2
22-29 Associate professional and technical occupations	3	692	481.5	0.5	546.2	7.5	308.7	365.0	388.1	410.3	445.7	527.0	574.9	606.8	643.1	766.6
22-29 Science, engineering and technology associate	31	134	471.9	2.5	480.9	0.4	306.6	349.0	367.2	385.8	429.6	498.3	541.1	567.8	605.1	695.1
22-29 Health and social care associate professionals	32	46	399.6	-0.5	396.4	-0.8	163.5	281.9	325.4	342.6	372.4	422.2	459.7	477.6	494.4	x
22-29 Protective service occupations	33	42	572.9	0.8	569.7	1.9	400.8	459.7	475.7	494.9	524.6	600.5	630.1	647.9	670.5	x
22-29 Culture, media and sports occupations	34	59	413.7	4.2	x		x	267.4	316.4	345.0	383.3	440.6	479.1	508.6	536.6	x
22-29 Business and public service associate professionals	35	412	504.1	1.2	547.9	2.3	333.4	384.2	408.6	429.2	465.7	547.9	598.8	638.9	680.7	821.1
22-29 Administrative and secretarial occupations	4	512	360.0	3.3	373.9	4.4	169.3	265.8	287.5	306.6	335.4	390.8	429.0	450.2	478.8	555.8
22-29 Administrative occupations	41	421	369.9	3.2	387.8	5.0	194.9	287.0	305.3	319.0	345.0	402.5	439.6	459.0	480.5	563.9
22-29 Secretarial and related occupations	42	91	302.1	2.4	309.6	3.1	110.2	170.6	200.5	233.7	277.9	335.4	372.9	391.1	425.4	513.6
22-29 Skilled trades	5	380	440.8	3.1	468.8	3.8	275.6	328.5	347.4	364.1	400.0	479.9	523.2	563.5	594.9	703.0
22-29 Skilled agricultural and related trades	51	20	346.9	0.3	361.1	4.7	280.4	303.6	306.8	314.9	331.3	363.6	379.9	387.5	407.8	x
22-29 Skilled metal, electrical and electronic trades	52	190	504.4	0.9	534.9	1.9	328.0	383.0	400.1	421.6	466.5	547.1	600.9	629.4	671.9	787.7
22-29 Skilled construction and building trades	53	61	477.1	6.0	491.0	2.5	298.5	363.0	389.0	403.0	441.0	504.5	550.1	574.9	597.0	x
22-29 Textiles, printing and other skilled trades	54	109	360.0	5.3	361.3	9.4	210.1	274.0	294.0	310.5	336.5	384.0	412.2	431.8	453.6	496.5
22-29 Caring, leisure and other service occupations	6	474	280.2	3.9	277.3	4.1	112.1	161.7	187.3	212.0	251.5	305.1	335.2	351.5	371.6	433.9
22-29 Caring personal service occupations	61	389	278.6	3.5	273.8	4.0	110.4	162.9	187.6	212.1	249.0	301.5	331.1	347.4	368.2	427.1
22-29 Leisure, travel and related personal service	62	86	292.2	8.2	293.0	4.8	115.2	155.8	184.3	211.4	264.1	320.0	353.9	365.1	394.4	462.0
22-29 Sales and customer service occupations	7	509	287.9	6.2	286.5	6.3	111.9	152.9	175.2	202.5	250.8	317.6	346.1	366.1	387.5	452.9
22-29 Sales occupations	71	361	260.9	5.9	261.8	5.6	98.9	134.2	151.2	172.2	216.6	291.5	325.1	344.0	361.9	422.5
22-29 Customer service occupations	72	148	338.7	2.4	346.7	3.6	174.3	244.6	269.1	290.4	316.2	362.7	392.5	414.7	432.9	502.2
22-29 Process, plant and machine operatives	8	207	402.6	5.0	434.7	5.6	250.7	301.4	317.7	332.2	365.0	441.2	495.2	531.3	576.0	657.8
22-29 Process, plant and machine operatives	81	137	397.2	4.5	430.8	4.8	267.4	300.0	314.6	330.2	360.3	435.8	490.3	526.9	563.8	640.0
22-29 Transport and mobile machine drivers and operatives	82	70	415.6	7.2	442.3	7.1	197.4	304.4	324.0	339.8	371.8	453.4	501.3	546.8	584.2	698.7
22-29 Elementary occupations	9	533	280.8	8.0	279.9	7.6	85.0	137.6	164.2	193.6	244.1	310.1	342.8	361.3	385.0	459.5
22-29 Elementary trades and related occupations	91	68	354.4	7.5	367.6	9.9	213.1	275.6	287.5	301.8	327.6	383.6	421.1	440.0	457.8	526.6
22-29 Elementary administration and service occupations	92	465	268.0	8.7	267.0	7.8	78.8	125.6	150.0	174.7	226.6	297.9	331.2	347.4	369.0	440.7
30-39 ALL OCCUPATIONS		5,916	498.3	1.9	567.3	2.5	180.6	288.2	327.0	360.7	429.4	577.4	669.3	719.7	779.3	977.4
30-39 Managers, directors and senior officials	1	610	721.8	0.7	869.1	0.2	345.9	453.0	493.3	536.6	625.5	844.7	1,005.7	1,107.4	1,240.9	1,557.2
30-39 Corporate managers and directors	11	509	788.6	1.8	929.0	0.3	359.9	479.1	527.1	579.5	683.0	919.9	1,096.7	1,205.9	1,319.6	1,665.0
30-39 Other managers and proprietors	12	102	532.2	1.8	568.9	1.2	309.0	385.7	408.8	437.2	482.0	576.9	638.4	670.0	713.6	846.7
30-39 Professional occupations	2	1,562	689.9	1.9	732.7	2.3	371.1	483.9	527.0	566.5	629.2	754.7	829.3	878.4	934.0	1,110.7

4.15a Weekly pay - Gross (£) - For all employee jobs[a]: United Kingdom, 2016

Description	Code	Number of jobs[b] (000s)	Median	Annual % change	Mean	Annual % change	Percentiles 10	20	25	30	40	60	70	75	80	90
30-39 Science, research, engineering and technology professionals	21	385	767.1	2.3	816.0	3.3	479.1	582.3	613.5	644.7	716.5	838.2	926.4	969.9	1,025.3	1,180.9
30-39 Health professionals	22	370	597.1	0.3	660.6	1.8	294.7	407.5	443.5	478.7	540.1	654.0	728.3	786.9	851.3	1,081.8
30-39 Teaching and educational professionals	23	391	683.5	2.3	658.3	3.0	308.1	439.5	497.0	539.4	623.0	725.8	787.3	814.3	852.5	948.3
30-39 Business, media and public service professionals	24	416	712.4	0.5	789.4	1.0	418.7	520.7	557.2	590.2	653.5	776.6	862.7	919.9	978.8	1,226.8
30-39 Associate professional and technical occupations	3	1,007	585.7	0.2	652.2	0.3	331.3	421.4	446.7	479.1	530.8	646.1	718.7	764.1	816.5	996.8
30-39 Science, engineering and technology associate	31	168	536.1	-0.4	570.3	0.3	344.5	406.3	439.1	460.0	498.3	574.9	623.4	665.6	706.6	837.7
30-39 Health and social care associate professionals	32	90	426.7	-2.3	423.1	-3.0	193.9	261.6	301.8	341.1	389.3	466.6	506.3	529.1	550.9	631.2
30-39 Protective service occupations	33	125	708.8	4.0	716.0	4.5	488.8	576.1	602.9	627.9	664.9	741.4	793.9	817.6	853.3	949.5
30-39 Culture, media and sports occupations	34	60	494.2	-0.1	630.7	3.1	x	324.4	381.4	411.7	460.0	539.6	611.5	632.4	653.6	x
30-39 Business and public service associate professionals	35	564	613.3	-0.5	701.2	-0.6	350.2	432.1	462.0	493.9	556.3	677.6	766.6	824.1	900.8	1,132.2
30-39 Administrative and secretarial occupations	4	605	373.2	0.7	397.2	1.5	154.5	210.9	245.9	280.7	329.7	415.7	469.0	498.3	536.6	651.6
30-39 Administrative occupations	41	501	383.3	0.2	409.3	1.2	159.8	226.6	263.0	297.1	345.0	426.1	479.1	508.6	544.4	667.9
30-39 Secretarial and related occupations	42	105	310.0	4.5	339.7	3.6	134.0	178.2	195.6	214.0	268.3	352.0	410.9	440.8	479.1	593.5
30-39 Skilled trades	5	440	482.7	0.9	509.1	1.4	276.5	347.0	369.5	396.4	440.8	531.7	584.6	611.9	648.6	770.8
30-39 Skilled agricultural and related trades	51	19	380.9	3.2	388.1	-2.1	290.8	320.0	326.5	342.3	353.8	397.9	413.3	442.4	453.5	x
30-39 Skilled metal, electrical and electronic trades	52	220	565.0	2.7	597.1	2.5	363.2	434.0	455.9	480.3	523.0	608.5	668.3	709.1	749.7	859.5
30-39 Skilled construction and building trades	53	71	500.0	0.3	515.5	0.3	341.1	399.0	415.1	434.5	472.3	541.3	576.8	595.4	622.5	x
30-39 Textiles, printing and other skilled trades	54	131	364.8	1.2	374.4	1.1	172.2	254.2	278.4	298.8	335.1	402.4	440.8	460.0	480.2	562.9
30-39 Caring, leisure and other service occupations	6	469	272.1	5.8	288.6	6.3	115.2	162.0	181.3	199.7	234.4	311.0	350.9	373.2	396.3	473.7
30-39 Caring personal service occupations	61	392	265.5	4.5	280.2	6.1	111.2	159.0	179.1	196.6	229.7	304.3	344.7	365.6	384.8	455.6
30-39 Leisure, travel and related personal service	62	77	308.8	5.9	331.4	7.0	124.6	175.8	194.2	215.9	272.0	348.8	394.1	428.1	461.6	571.8
30-39 Sales and customer service occupations	7	389	294.6	5.4	313.5	4.5	117.3	154.8	173.5	198.2	250.6	335.9	373.2	402.5	436.0	538.5
30-39 Sales occupations	71	254	259.7	6.1	281.7	6.5	113.4	139.1	154.1	171.5	214.8	300.0	342.6	361.3	391.0	481.1
30-39 Customer service occupations	72	134	350.0	-1.2	373.8	-0.4	153.6	212.3	243.2	275.5	321.1	392.2	447.2	477.1	511.8	597.7
30-39 Process, plant and machine operatives	8	310	448.0	5.1	478.0	4.7	273.9	326.6	348.3	368.3	406.8	498.3	550.0	583.9	622.4	724.3
30-39 Process, plant and machine operatives	81	164	423.1	4.9	454.4	4.5	277.2	316.7	335.3	353.9	387.0	469.3	523.1	554.2	589.6	672.4
30-39 Transport and mobile machine drivers and operatives	82	147	476.1	4.4	504.5	4.6	263.9	342.1	367.8	395.4	432.3	523.1	575.6	621.7	662.2	771.0
30-39 Elementary occupations	9	525	292.2	5.8	295.6	4.5	82.0	127.0	152.1	179.3	246.6	329.6	372.0	397.9	422.8	511.5
30-39 Elementary trades and related occupations	91	67	360.9	3.5	380.2	6.1	229.8	286.5	294.8	310.1	337.4	395.1	420.6	447.7	469.7	544.9
30-39 Elementary administration and service occupations	92	458	278.9	7.5	283.3	4.3	72.5	117.4	138.0	161.5	216.2	316.8	358.8	386.6	414.4	501.5
40-49 ALL OCCUPATIONS		6,300	503.7	2.4	606.5	3.0	172.6	272.0	310.7	347.0	422.3	596.8	709.1	769.2	844.7	1,107.7
40-49 Managers, directors and senior officials	1	802	860.0	4.0	1,046.0	4.5	345.0	500.1	563.2	615.2	733.2	1,009.4	1,202.2	1,308.8	1,446.6	1,916.5
40-49 Corporate managers and directors	11	704	910.8	4.4	1,096.2	4.4	365.2	536.6	593.1	653.5	773.5	1,073.2	1,258.6	1,368.4	1,533.1	1,960.6
40-49 Other managers and proprietors	12	98	593.1	2.3	686.0	1.0	268.0	382.1	423.2	455.2	533.2	666.0	772.1	822.9	881.4	x
40-49 Professional occupations	2	1,477	731.5	2.3	790.3	2.4	337.5	477.5	534.3	577.4	665.9	806.2	895.3	952.4	1,027.2	1,270.6
40-49 Science, research, engineering and technology professionals	21	340	837.0	1.4	885.9	1.5	509.9	614.4	662.0	706.1	774.4	915.7	1,005.9	1,054.1	1,117.2	1,300.9
40-49 Health professionals	22	419	628.4	1.4	730.8	2.2	270.0	391.1	440.5	482.2	551.8	696.8	785.1	822.6	908.7	1,375.3
40-49 Teaching and educational professionals	23	380	725.0	2.2	707.8	2.9	270.0	420.0	478.8	539.9	659.7	777.2	849.6	891.2	943.5	1,115.3
40-49 Business, media and public service professionals	24	338	767.3	2.0	860.6	2.5	406.0	531.0	575.2	622.5	695.3	854.9	955.1	1,026.8	1,102.8	1,364.3
40-49 Associate professional and technical occupations	3	929	615.5	-0.8	683.4	-0.9	325.2	421.6	454.2	484.8	555.8	689.9	766.6	813.8	871.0	1,071.8

4.15a Weekly pay - Gross (£) - For all employee jobs[a]: United Kingdom, 2016

Description	Code	Number of jobs[b] (000s)	Median	Annual % change	Mean	Annual % change	Percentiles 10	20	25	30	40	60	70	75	80	90
40-49 Science, engineering and technology associate	31	143	575.5	0.0	600.2	-0.4	338.6	413.7	448.1	472.5	527.9	628.0	683.7	722.8	760.3	869.5
40-49 Health and social care associate professionals	32	90	445.8	3.5	445.0	0.8	181.6	244.9	293.8	334.8	398.9	488.6	522.0	547.9	582.6	714.1
40-49 Protective service occupations	33	137	751.1	0.9	766.0	0.8	538.5	597.7	634.4	670.4	721.3	801.0	844.5	871.4	912.5	1,013.2
40-49 Culture, media and sports occupations	34	38	517.3	9.2	524.1	7.9	x	239.6	305.8	381.1	446.8	579.7	632.9	683.4	745.9	x
40-49 Business and public service associate professionals	35	521	632.4	-1.6	737.1	-2.8	345.0	429.6	461.2	490.9	566.9	703.9	804.9	870.7	958.3	1,259.8
40-49 Administrative and secretarial occupations	4	718	364.1	1.2	396.2	2.2	154.5	213.1	243.7	272.9	322.0	409.4	461.6	495.8	536.6	665.7
40-49 Administrative occupations	41	564	377.8	1.3	409.6	2.0	161.3	230.1	259.8	289.3	337.7	421.6	476.3	506.8	548.5	676.8
40-49 Secretarial and related occupations	42	154	313.5	5.0	347.2	3.5	144.2	181.5	201.3	218.8	268.7	354.6	405.1	430.4	480.0	621.8
40-49 Skilled trades	5	470	502.6	0.9	536.6	1.5	259.2	348.4	378.2	406.9	452.5	551.8	614.7	651.6	697.2	827.5
40-49 Skilled agricultural and related trades	51	25	388.1	1.7	408.4	3.0	270.1	304.8	317.0	332.9	361.0	417.0	440.9	465.4	489.0	x
40-49 Skilled metal, electrical and electronic trades	52	242	586.7	2.0	636.8	2.8	391.0	447.0	475.4	498.8	539.7	638.3	700.6	738.3	778.0	935.8
40-49 Skilled construction and building trades	53	76	520.7	0.7	553.7	-1.1	341.1	415.6	430.3	448.4	480.3	558.7	601.1	631.9	661.2	x
40-49 Textiles, printing and other skilled trades	54	127	338.8	4.3	359.7	4.3	154.9	202.1	228.8	256.2	301.0	380.0	421.9	451.8	479.3	571.4
40-49 Caring, leisure and other service occupations	6	597	275.6	4.8	292.7	3.7	114.1	170.0	190.5	210.9	242.5	309.6	348.5	371.3	401.1	475.9
40-49 Caring personal service occupations	61	516	270.8	4.2	284.7	4.4	114.8	170.4	190.9	210.6	239.5	302.8	343.1	361.8	390.0	458.5
40-49 Leisure, travel and related personal service	62	81	317.6	5.4	343.9	-0.8	107.6	165.0	188.7	212.3	265.9	354.7	406.9	444.4	490.9	656.5
40-49 Sales and customer service occupations	7	337	279.1	7.4	309.6	4.8	115.2	152.6	172.2	191.6	235.1	316.5	361.3	390.5	426.2	540.4
40-49 Sales occupations	71	238	244.3	9.7	271.1	5.9	110.2	140.0	153.1	171.1	204.8	284.4	320.7	341.4	370.7	466.1
40-49 Customer service occupations	72	99	364.7	-0.9	401.7	0.0	162.8	225.3	256.8	281.1	321.2	399.7	454.3	492.4	543.0	695.9
40-49 Process, plant and machine operatives	8	395	476.8	2.1	508.5	2.6	285.7	333.7	357.8	378.3	425.4	525.5	586.0	624.2	661.1	788.7
40-49 Process, plant and machine operatives	81	178	441.1	2.7	481.5	1.9	278.7	314.3	331.7	348.3	391.3	489.3	544.9	576.8	628.6	750.0
40-49 Transport and mobile machine drivers and operatives	82	217	505.2	1.4	530.7	3.1	299.6	359.9	381.7	402.3	447.4	552.5	614.7	646.3	683.3	816.7
40-49 Elementary occupations	9	574	273.5	7.6	283.8	4.3	66.1	109.1	127.8	154.1	208.8	316.0	365.0	397.6	424.0	519.9
40-49 Elementary trades and related occupations	91	66	359.4	1.6	385.4	4.1	219.3	284.7	294.4	307.6	334.9	391.7	428.9	456.0	491.7	588.3
40-49 Elementary administration and service occupations	92	509	247.3	7.5	270.6	5.0	60.8	100.9	115.9	138.7	185.6	299.4	352.1	383.9	414.2	509.3
50-59 ALL OCCUPATIONS		5,581	473.4	3.4	581.6	4.2	163.1	255.1	296.6	331.9	399.8	563.1	672.7	733.4	806.7	1,057.8
50-59 Managers, directors and senior officials	1	706	806.9	2.3	1,004.0	2.9	318.9	470.3	527.0	578.1	689.9	948.9	1,149.0	1,265.3	1,405.9	1,843.3
50-59 Corporate managers and directors	11	601	862.4	1.1	1,064.2	2.9	330.9	495.1	561.5	613.2	735.6	1,014.2	1,229.3	1,341.6	1,504.3	1,932.0
50-59 Other managers and proprietors	12	106	584.2	0.6	662.1	0.4	295.2	382.5	419.5	462.6	526.5	671.4	755.0	806.0	880.9	1,091.0
50-59 Professional occupations	2	1,235	711.6	1.1	775.3	1.2	305.2	440.7	498.3	551.4	642.6	791.3	876.4	924.4	998.7	1,235.2
50-59 Science, research, engineering and technology professionals	21	244	825.0	1.9	884.0	1.8	487.9	605.7	651.1	683.4	751.8	901.3	998.8	1,066.4	1,119.7	1,346.2
50-59 Health professionals	22	388	622.8	3.6	724.2	0.9	267.2	371.8	413.5	452.5	545.5	686.4	784.4	810.2	864.3	1,139.3
50-59 Teaching and educational professionals	23	331	725.8	1.0	718.4	-0.6	237.6	408.8	462.7	535.2	652.5	788.2	862.8	908.9	948.6	1,124.5
50-59 Business, media and public service professionals	24	271	724.7	2.2	820.0	3.0	360.9	483.2	536.6	582.0	660.3	809.5	921.2	987.0	1,057.9	1,321.6
50-59 Associate professional and technical occupations	3	702	590.3	0.3	667.8	1.4	301.2	400.5	436.4	467.4	529.8	667.0	750.9	803.4	869.3	1,089.9
50-59 Science, engineering and technology associate	31	132	589.1	2.7	619.7	3.8	344.3	412.2	441.4	465.6	534.3	639.3	708.1	742.9	782.6	937.1
50-59 Health and social care associate professionals	32	93	440.6	-1.6	441.4	-0.8	191.5	273.3	312.8	356.4	389.7	475.2	518.7	537.4	561.2	662.9
50-59 Protective service occupations	33	60	734.2	1.6	734.2	1.2	426.3	535.1	560.0	583.8	660.3	791.6	851.1	878.0	907.0	x
50-59 Culture, media and sports occupations	34	26	440.9	2.3	497.3	2.9	x	x	x	x	383.9	497.7	583.9	664.9	x	x
50-59 Business and public service associate professionals	35	391	639.3	0.2	738.7	0.8	342.1	432.0	470.8	500.4	571.9	717.6	811.3	873.8	955.1	1,253.5

4.15a Weekly pay - Gross (£) - For all employee jobs[a]: United Kingdom, 2016

Description	Code	Number of jobs[b] (000s)	Median	Annual % change	Mean	Annual % change	Percentiles 10	20	25	30	40	60	70	75	80	90
50-59 Administrative and secretarial occupations	4	743	358.4	2.0	384.0	2.9	153.9	206.4	234.7	264.9	315.1	398.0	450.4	480.8	517.5	638.0
50-59 Administrative occupations	41	562	377.7	2.3	404.1	3.5	158.0	224.6	258.7	288.2	336.1	419.9	469.5	500.4	539.4	661.2
50-59 Secretarial and related occupations	42	181	296.1	1.6	321.8	0.8	127.5	172.2	191.5	210.0	250.7	338.5	380.1	404.5	434.3	543.5
50-59 Skilled trades	5	430	513.1	1.5	542.5	3.1	252.1	345.0	378.4	404.4	460.2	569.7	634.5	672.7	721.0	846.6
50-59 Skilled agricultural and related trades	51	26	370.9	5.5	383.7	5.5	239.4	303.9	315.1	326.3	345.0	384.6	427.1	440.7	453.2	x
50-59 Skilled metal, electrical and electronic trades	52	237	611.9	6.0	639.4	4.3	387.6	454.7	483.8	508.6	556.0	660.7	716.9	749.1	789.0	911.9
50-59 Skilled construction and building trades	53	65	533.7	3.2	573.7	4.2	379.7	424.0	448.5	466.7	494.7	563.0	625.4	655.1	694.3	x
50-59 Textiles, printing and other skilled trades	54	102	326.1	3.0	336.4	-0.2	154.8	197.9	214.2	242.5	286.3	357.1	397.5	421.7	449.4	526.1
50-59 Caring, leisure and other service occupations	6	550	284.6	2.1	302.6	1.9	117.2	170.8	193.2	213.5	246.0	322.8	364.7	386.3	411.4	486.2
50-59 Caring personal service occupations	61	464	277.3	1.6	291.8	2.5	116.1	172.0	193.1	212.4	243.2	315.3	354.2	376.7	399.7	463.7
50-59 Leisure, travel and related personal service	62	86	324.2	0.2	361.2	0.0	118.9	163.6	193.7	219.1	274.7	368.6	425.7	456.8	500.2	626.7
50-59 Sales and customer service occupations	7	317	249.2	8.2	284.2	5.3	115.2	147.1	162.4	179.4	214.2	288.0	325.7	350.7	378.2	489.0
50-59 Sales occupations	71	236	219.8	6.6	246.8	5.7	108.0	136.1	149.4	162.9	189.8	254.2	288.9	306.0	329.2	403.0
50-59 Customer service occupations	72	81	352.0	0.1	393.7	2.7	156.1	221.7	247.5	274.8	318.7	385.6	447.2	485.2	528.6	665.0
50-59 Process, plant and machine operatives	8	386	461.5	2.0	493.3	2.5	269.9	325.2	347.3	372.6	416.2	514.8	577.5	602.3	646.5	766.1
50-59 Process, plant and machine operatives	81	164	432.3	3.0	472.6	3.4	270.0	306.4	329.4	349.3	389.2	487.4	549.9	582.7	615.3	747.8
50-59 Transport and mobile machine drivers and operatives	82	221	479.2	0.3	508.7	1.7	269.1	338.4	369.1	392.4	434.5	535.8	593.3	625.3	659.1	775.5
50-59 Elementary occupations	9	514	273.6	6.2	284.5	3.8	72.0	115.2	136.6	161.0	216.2	318.8	363.7	396.3	425.6	513.0
50-59 Elementary trades and related occupations	91	59	372.3	6.0	400.3	7.4	236.6	290.0	304.1	320.0	344.8	406.3	456.4	485.7	518.1	570.5
50-59 Elementary administration and service occupations	92	455	249.4	7.0	269.5	3.5	69.7	107.2	123.5	145.5	195.8	299.5	346.1	377.1	412.5	492.0
60+ ALL OCCUPATIONS		1,974	348.8	2.9	436.7	2.6	97.7	154.1	183.7	216.6	287.0	419.7	502.3	560.0	624.1	848.0
60+ Managers, directors and senior officials	1	228	580.4	-2.6	764.2	-2.8	161.0	276.0	318.8	374.6	472.6	718.8	887.3	1,009.5	1,149.9	1,524.3
60+ Corporate managers and directors	11	189	622.0	-4.0	805.8	-3.2	168.1	276.0	325.4	386.6	498.2	770.7	964.9	1,085.3	1,218.0	1,570.6
60+ Other managers and proprietors	12	39	476.8	3.8	561.9	0.5	147.2	267.7	297.7	335.5	400.4	546.6	632.6	688.8	754.1	x
60+ Professional occupations	2	340	543.0	-2.2	631.3	1.1	154.1	283.0	328.8	368.8	450.2	663.7	761.4	823.1	904.4	1,134.1
60+ Science, research, engineering and technology professionals	21	60	743.4	-1.8	776.8	0.3	354.0	489.7	539.5	575.0	675.1	830.5	932.4	973.5	1,042.9	x
60+ Health professionals	22	96	447.4	-1.8	581.7	-4.7	161.6	270.0	294.9	330.9	395.8	515.8	622.9	675.1	754.4	x
60+ Teaching and educational professionals	23	103	454.8	-1.4	570.4	3.8	98.4	167.4	230.0	284.4	362.9	623.2	725.8	802.1	891.3	1,134.4
60+ Business, media and public service professionals	24	81	576.2	-1.3	660.2	6.4	204.4	336.7	384.1	423.2	495.1	674.3	772.8	825.7	895.9	x
60+ Associate professional and technical occupations	3	177	489.2	1.2	540.2	3.1	172.4	279.9	326.9	357.9	429.2	561.9	629.4	671.3	729.9	910.4
60+ Science, engineering and technology associate	31	35	494.8	-4.8	544.4	-0.2	276.8	352.7	381.4	402.1	442.2	572.8	641.5	670.0	723.8	x
60+ Health and social care associate professionals	32	23	310.5	-11.0	352.9	-3.5	x	154.1	166.3	184.0	258.1	403.3	468.0	522.2	539.6	x
60+ Protective service occupations	33	8	530.4	0.7	546.9	-5.1	x	357.6	394.0	454.5	496.4	565.2	603.3	x	x	x
60+ Culture, media and sports occupations	34	10	x		386.2	22.3	x	x	x	x	x	x	x	x	x	x
60+ Business and public service associate professionals	35	101	524.4	3.9	595.5	5.1	199.7	321.6	354.9	392.6	462.7	603.7	670.8	733.9	803.3	1,026.8
60+ Administrative and secretarial occupations	4	304	270.0	4.2	301.0	3.1	76.7	138.0	154.9	179.0	221.7	328.6	378.7	411.1	442.1	542.8
60+ Administrative	41	220	286.6	2.8	309.7	3.0	73.6	138.7	156.8	183.1	228.4	344.8	392.9	425.2	454.4	550.3
60+ Secretarial and related occupations	42	84	234.8	3.3	278.0	3.2	84.6	137.1	154.1	170.0	201.2	276.1	335.1	367.5	402.7	507.9
60+ Skilled trades occupations	5	164	454.6	1.8	470.6	1.2	184.7	292.6	324.1	351.0	403.2	506.4	572.4	601.9	640.1	744.1
60+ Skilled agricultural and related trades	51	14	318.2	3.5	292.2	-1.2	114.8	141.3	153.3	185.8	259.3	337.2	362.3	373.4	x	x
60+ Skilled metal, electrical and electronic trades	52	85	554.8	2.6	560.5	1.3	319.8	395.1	425.0	448.0	499.3	594.7	644.0	681.5	712.5	811.7

4.15a Weekly pay - Gross (£) - For all employee jobs[a]: United Kingdom, 2016

Description	Code	Number of jobs[b] (000s)	Median	Annual % change	Mean	Annual % change	Percentiles 10	20	25	30	40	60	70	75	80	90
60+ Skilled construction and building trades	53	27	472.0	0.4	486.3	-2.0	287.6	387.3	406.7	423.4	446.3	503.4	545.2	567.7	608.3	x
60+ Textiles, printing and other skilled trades	54	39	313.3	0.1	325.5	4.2	115.1	149.7	193.9	232.5	268.2	334.3	371.5	402.9	430.3	x
60+ Caring, leisure and other service occupations	6	200	245.6	4.7	258.8	5.3	73.6	119.3	140.6	162.7	204.4	286.1	333.3	351.9	381.4	453.7
60+ Caring personal service occupations	61	159	248.1	6.1	259.9	6.5	75.7	122.3	147.2	167.6	210.1	286.4	333.7	351.6	381.2	450.5
60+ Leisure, travel and related personal service	62	41	226.6	-7.0	254.3	0.8	59.5	106.4	126.4	140.9	178.0	285.3	328.9	350.0	382.6	x
60+ Sales and customer service occupations	7	141	178.6	4.6	215.3	5.5	81.5	108.9	120.3	128.8	151.1	210.5	254.7	278.1	305.2	392.8
60+ Sales occupations	71	115	166.5	4.6	195.4	3.6	79.3	106.1	115.2	123.1	144.0	187.6	224.0	249.5	276.8	344.6
60+ Customer service occupations	72	26	274.4	1.6	304.6	5.9	101.6	134.0	161.0	194.8	233.5	328.8	377.7	398.0	422.6	x
60+ Process, plant and machine operatives	8	185	367.5	-0.8	386.9	-1.8	120.0	180.0	220.0	261.1	305.6	427.6	481.8	514.0	555.4	659.2
60+ Process, plant and machine operatives	81	62	366.1	0.1	399.7	2.0	162.8	249.8	273.1	288.0	313.1	409.3	469.7	503.0	534.5	630.8
60+ Transport and mobile machine drivers and operatives	82	123	368.4	-1.0	380.5	-3.8	104.0	165.0	192.4	224.2	300.8	433.3	490.9	522.1	565.4	666.5
60+ Elementary occupations	9	237	195.4	11.7	236.2	5.8	50.0	80.6	94.4	110.5	145.8	265.4	315.7	343.1	377.5	472.7
60+ Elementary trades and related occupations	91	25	341.9	5.7	354.5	6.9	143.5	204.6	263.7	288.0	316.6	376.5	420.3	447.0	479.1	x
60+ Elementary administration and service	92	211	175.5	13.1	222.0	5.8	47.6	74.1	88.8	102.5	131.6	232.8	295.2	323.8	358.1	455.9
Not Classified		:														

Source: Annual Survey of Hours and Earnings, Office for National Statistics.

a Employees on adult rates whose pay for the survey pay-period was not affected by absence.
b Figures for Number of Jobs are for indicative purposes only and should not be considered an accurate estimate of employee job counts.
KEY - The colour coding indicates the quality of each estimate; jobs, median, mean and percentiles but not the annual percentage change.
The quality of an estimate is measured by its coefficient of variation (CV), which is the ratio of the standard error of an estimate to the estimate.

Key	Statistical robustness
CV <= 5%	Estimates are considered precise
CV > 5% and <= 10%	Estimates are considered reasonably precise
CV > 10% and <= 20%	Estimates are considered acceptable
x = CV > 20%	Estimates are considered unreliable for practical purposes
.. = disclosive	
: = not applicable	
- = nil or negligible	

4.15b Hourly pay - Gross (£) - For all employee jobs[a]: United Kingdom, 2016

Description	Code	Number of jobs[b] (000s)	Median	Annual % change	Mean	Annual % change	Percentiles 10	20	25	30	40	60	70	75	80	90
All employees		25,758	12.16	3.3	15.73	3.1	7.30	8.18	8.69	9.22	10.50	14.20	16.77	18.37	20.33	26.43
18-21		1,273	7.48	5.3	8.26	4.5	5.57	6.50	6.70	6.83	7.20	7.85	8.38	8.76	9.21	10.74
22-29		4,471	10.55	4.6	12.37	4.8	7.20	7.84	8.20	8.56	9.45	11.92	13.47	14.37	15.43	18.87
30-39		5,916	13.62	1.9	16.34	2.2	7.68	8.88	9.50	10.16	11.80	15.69	18.16	19.61	21.46	27.17
40-49		6,300	13.95	2.9	17.76	2.8	7.70	8.88	9.51	10.22	11.87	16.43	19.36	21.12	23.15	30.42
50-59		5,581	13.22	3.7	17.28	4.0	7.67	8.78	9.35	10.00	11.45	15.54	18.49	20.31	22.30	29.48
60+		1,974	11.31	3.5	15.04	2.2	7.39	8.10	8.51	9.00	10.00	12.95	15.32	16.96	18.85	25.47
18-21 ALL OCCUPATIONS		1,273	7.48	5.3	8.26	4.5	5.57	6.50	6.70	6.83	7.20	7.85	8.38	8.76	9.21	10.74
18-21 Managers, directors and senior officials	1	19	8.77	2.2	9.10	2.8	x	7.31	7.50	7.73	7.96	9.26	9.44	9.62	9.72	x
18-21 Corporate managers and directors	11	16	8.81	11.2	9.27	8.8	x	7.27	7.35	7.54	8.12	9.36	9.62	9.69	x	x
18-21 Other managers and proprietors	12	x	7.92	-13.5	8.22	-14.4	x	x	x	x	x	x	x	x	x	x
18-21 Professional occupations	2	42	9.85	5.2	10.88	4.1	7.17	7.92	8.05	8.36	9.03	11.03	12.71	13.13	14.04	15.98
18-21 Science, research, engineering and technology professionals	21	16	9.18	6.9	9.89	-5.1	x	7.85	7.92	8.13	8.78	9.71	10.18	11.32	x	x
18-21 Health professionals	22	8	11.60	10.4	11.49	12.3	x	x	x	x	10.21	12.80	13.73	x	x	x
18-21 Teaching and educational professionals	23	x	15.93	43.0	16.33	65.0	x	x	13.11	13.11	14.08	17.05	x	x	x	x
18-21 Business, media and public service professionals	24	13	9.50	2.4	10.42	-4.2	x	7.70	7.93	8.12	8.72	9.90	10.61	x	x	x
18-21 Associate professional and technical occupations	3	110	9.18	0.7	10.10	1.0	7.08	7.59	7.73	8.01	8.48	9.63	10.49	10.99	11.58	13.32
18-21 Science, engineering and technology associate professionals	31	31	9.26	5.8	9.69	4.8	6.62	7.60	7.80	8.14	8.74	9.50	10.28	10.84	11.06	x
18-21 Health and social care associate professionals	32	11	8.44	-9.3	9.20	-5.2	x	7.65	x	7.96	8.25	9.02	9.24	x	x	x
18-21 Protective service occupations	33	x	10.83	-7.2	11.34	-7.8	x	x	x	x	x	x	x	x	x	x
18-21 Culture, media and sports occupations	34	15	9.66	2.7	12.47	5.8	x	7.50	7.84	8.01	8.58	10.75	12.38	x	x	x
18-21 Business and public service associate professionals	35	49	8.97	1.0	9.93	0.8	7.13	7.50	7.66	7.72	8.33	9.47	10.23	10.72	11.42	x
18-21 Administrative and secretarial occupations	4	123	8.10	3.3	8.71	4.8	6.25	6.99	7.18	7.30	7.68	8.52	9.20	9.67	10.01	11.85
18-21 Administrative occupations	41	100	8.22	3.5	8.90	6.2	6.50	7.11	7.21	7.46	7.80	8.74	9.50	9.90	10.29	12.14
18-21 Secretarial and related occupations	42	23	7.61	1.8	7.82	-1.1	5.96	6.70	6.78	6.99	7.21	7.97	8.25	8.47	8.69	x
18-21 Skilled trades occupations	5	83	7.61	-0.6	8.36	0.8	5.49	6.59	6.72	6.99	7.24	8.09	8.89	9.40	9.97	11.27
18-21 Skilled agricultural and related trades	51	x	7.75	0.1	7.70	-1.9	x	x	x	x	7.39	7.95	x	x	x	x
18-21 Skilled metal, electrical and electronic trades	52	45	8.02	-5.0	8.81	-1.1	5.49	6.70	7.00	7.18	7.59	8.86	9.81	10.28	10.74	12.21
18-21 Skilled construction and building trades	53	12	7.99	-0.2	8.60	0.4	5.30	6.25	6.69	6.99	7.58	8.65	9.65	10.21	10.95	x
18-21 Textiles, printing and other skilled trades	54	23	7.19	3.8	7.25	0.3	5.74	6.56	x	6.70	6.96	7.21	7.50	7.61	7.86	x
18-21 Caring, leisure and other service occupations	6	166	7.44	4.0	7.65	2.8	5.70	6.68	6.71	6.92	7.20	7.80	8.25	8.44	8.82	9.92
18-21 Caring personal service occupations	61	127	7.49	3.4	7.71	3.3	6.00	6.70	6.85	7.02	7.21	7.82	8.25	8.49	8.86	10.00
18-21 Leisure, travel and related personal service	62	39	7.13	2.3	7.41	0.9	5.30	6.00	6.32	6.59	6.85	7.57	8.13	8.37	8.64	x
18-21 Sales and customer service occupations	7	299	7.38	6.1	7.82	5.9	5.53	6.45	6.70	6.80	7.18	7.61	7.97	8.20	8.53	9.73
18-21 Sales occupations	71	254	7.31	6.1	7.74	6.9	5.50	6.25	6.70	6.75	7.13	7.51	7.87	8.14	8.41	9.61
18-21 Customer service occupations	72	45	7.67	4.6	8.15	0.8	6.14	6.70	6.98	7.14	7.45	7.98	8.40	8.66	9.05	10.27
18-21 Process, plant and machine operatives	8	33	7.84	4.6	8.62	7.1	6.12	6.78	7.04	7.20	7.43	8.37	8.96	9.28	9.51	11.43
18-21 Process, plant and machine operatives	81	26	7.91	4.7	8.65	7.5	6.25	7.00	7.19	7.20	7.45	8.43	9.05	9.36	9.64	11.62
18-21 Transport and mobile machine drivers and operatives	82	7	7.54	1.9	8.50	5.4	x	6.60	6.70	6.76	7.02	8.14	8.50	8.72	x	x
18-21 Elementary occupations	9	398	7.00	5.9	7.50	5.4	5.30	5.94	6.15	6.50	6.70	7.24	7.51	7.76	8.07	9.09
18-21 Elementary trades and related occupations	91	32	7.65	8.0	8.15	4.6	6.14	6.77	7.00	7.05	7.22	8.01	8.58	8.90	9.14	x
18-21 Elementary administration and service occupations	92	366	7.00	6.6	7.40	5.5	5.30	5.83	6.03	6.48	6.70	7.20	7.50	7.66	8.00	8.98

4.15b Hourly pay - Gross (£) - For all employee jobs[a]: United Kingdom, 2016

Description	Code	Number of jobs[b] (000s)	Median	Annual % change	Mean	Annual % change	Percentiles 10	20	25	30	40	60	70	75	80	90
22-29 ALL OCCUPATIONS		4,471	10.55	4.6	12.37	4.8	7.20	7.84	8.20	8.56	9.45	11.92	13.47	14.37	15.43	18.87
22-29 Managers, directors and senior officials	1	229	12.35	2.6	14.65	1.4	8.17	9.07	9.56	9.98	11.07	13.62	15.35	16.77	18.91	24.61
22-29 Corporate managers and directors	11	174	13.15	2.8	15.55	0.0	8.38	9.44	9.83	10.53	11.97	14.54	16.74	18.74	20.44	26.59
22-29 Other managers and proprietors	12	54	10.35	1.3	11.86	5.4	7.75	8.47	8.69	8.97	9.78	11.40	12.38	13.38	13.79	x
22-29 Professional occupations	2	935	15.55	1.5	16.51	1.7	10.77	12.43	13.10	13.48	14.54	16.75	18.20	19.18	20.32	23.66
22-29 Science, research, engineering and technology professionals	21	212	15.27	4.2	16.14	3.7	10.23	11.91	12.38	12.94	14.13	16.25	17.88	18.75	19.72	22.98
22-29 Health professionals	22	249	14.86	3.0	15.63	0.7	11.27	12.64	13.19	13.47	14.19	15.73	16.79	17.39	18.44	21.62
22-29 Teaching and educational professionals	23	218	16.77	1.2	17.09	1.8	11.89	13.15	14.13	14.37	15.55	17.84	19.32	20.15	20.91	23.78
22-29 Business, media and public service professionals	24	256	15.92	2.4	17.25	0.6	10.03	11.76	12.53	13.15	14.48	17.24	19.12	20.28	21.58	25.96
22-29 Associate professional and technical occupations	3	692	12.88	0.5	14.83	7.0	8.82	10.00	10.53	11.02	11.90	13.98	15.27	15.99	16.90	19.96
22-29 Science, engineering and technology associate professionals	31	134	12.19	1.8	12.70	1.7	8.24	9.28	9.70	10.27	11.22	13.14	14.15	14.70	15.45	17.70
22-29 Health and social care associate professionals	32	46	11.23	-1.6	11.97	-1.2	8.64	9.46	9.68	10.19	10.62	11.86	12.70	13.27	13.76	x
22-29 Protective service occupations	33	42	13.75	-2.6	13.96	-1.3	10.90	11.96	12.31	12.68	13.11	14.52	14.95	15.34	15.90	x
22-29 Culture, media and sports occupations	34	59	11.47	0.1	x		8.07	9.37	9.84	10.00	10.74	12.33	13.30	13.90	14.80	x
22-29 Business and public service associate professionals	35	412	13.52	1.3	14.80	2.0	9.10	10.33	10.94	11.43	12.43	14.72	16.21	17.03	18.21	21.83
22-29 Administrative and secretarial occupations	4	512	10.00	3.0	10.97	3.7	7.44	8.12	8.40	8.68	9.26	10.71	11.77	12.27	13.03	15.43
22-29 Administrative occupations	41	421	10.19	2.7	11.21	4.1	7.65	8.33	8.63	8.97	9.56	11.00	12.00	12.55	13.35	15.84
22-29 Secretarial and related occupations	42	91	8.75	2.8	9.75	2.6	7.20	7.43	7.59	7.82	8.22	9.21	10.10	10.68	11.60	13.77
22-29 Skilled trades occupations	5	380	10.36	3.2	11.36	2.5	7.41	8.08	8.48	8.80	9.51	11.33	12.55	13.24	14.03	16.24
22-29 Skilled agricultural and related trades	51	20	8.81	2.8	9.37	3.8	7.47	7.87	8.00	8.13	8.50	9.30	9.58	9.75	x	x
22-29 Skilled metal, electrical and electronic trades	52	190	12.02	0.4	12.71	1.5	8.21	9.19	9.68	10.00	11.03	13.09	14.22	14.93	15.74	17.66
22-29 Skilled construction and building trades	53	61	11.54	3.9	11.94	2.9	7.54	9.00	9.47	10.00	10.92	12.32	13.00	13.46	14.13	x
22-29 Textiles, printing and other skilled trades	54	109	8.41	5.1	8.92	5.2	7.20	7.37	7.50	7.72	8.00	8.86	9.38	9.79	10.23	11.11
22-29 Caring, leisure and other service occupations	6	474	8.40	4.7	8.98	3.8	7.18	7.30	7.47	7.63	8.00	8.91	9.48	9.88	10.39	11.95
22-29 Caring personal service occupations	61	389	8.41	4.4	8.92	3.9	7.18	7.33	7.49	7.67	8.02	8.93	9.47	9.86	10.34	11.95
22-29 Leisure, travel and related personal service	62	86	8.25	4.3	9.26	3.4	7.00	7.20	7.28	7.50	7.87	8.80	9.56	10.00	10.57	12.19
22-29 Sales and customer service occupations	7	509	8.28	6.2	9.25	5.3	7.10	7.21	7.36	7.50	7.86	8.82	9.48	9.93	10.43	12.06
22-29 Sales occupations	71	361	7.97	6.4	8.92	5.7	6.95	7.20	7.23	7.36	7.60	8.41	9.05	9.37	9.91	11.45
22-29 Customer service occupations	72	148	9.20	2.6	9.94	2.6	7.21	7.74	7.96	8.21	8.62	9.82	10.47	10.95	11.49	13.12
22-29 Process, plant and machine operatives	8	207	9.41	3.9	10.56	6.1	7.20	7.70	7.97	8.17	8.75	10.29	11.30	12.00	12.68	14.92
22-29 Process, plant and machine operatives	81	137	9.49	4.1	10.66	5.5	7.20	7.69	7.92	8.17	8.75	10.48	11.54	12.30	13.28	15.49
22-29 Transport and mobile machine drivers and operatives	82	70	9.35	5.2	10.38	7.2	7.20	7.72	8.00	8.17	8.75	10.04	11.00	11.47	12.00	x
22-29 Elementary occupations	9	533	7.75	6.1	8.61	5.6	6.94	x	7.20	7.21	7.45	8.14	8.71	9.09	9.50	10.87
22-29 Elementary trades and related occupations	91	68	8.32	6.5	9.04	6.9	7.20	7.20	7.36	7.50	7.96	8.96	9.48	9.92	10.17	11.69
22-29 Elementary administration and service occupations	92	465	7.68	6.0	8.53	5.5	6.89	x	x	7.20	7.40	8.03	8.60	8.97	9.40	10.72
30-39 ALL OCCUPATIONS		5,916	13.62	1.9	16.34	2.2	7.68	8.88	9.50	10.16	11.80	15.69	18.16	19.61	21.46	27.17
30-39 Managers, directors and senior officials	1	610	18.98	0.5	23.16	-0.2	9.58	11.82	12.90	14.04	16.34	22.22	26.58	29.36	32.83	42.85
30-39 Corporate managers and directors	11	509	20.80	-0.6	24.84	-0.2	10.08	12.71	13.98	15.28	17.72	24.34	29.08	32.04	35.66	45.82
30-39 Other managers and proprietors	12	102	13.52	2.2	14.88	0.9	8.78	9.98	10.51	10.83	12.06	14.66	16.67	17.73	18.94	22.18
30-39 Professional occupations	2	1,562	20.04	1.2	21.60	1.9	13.16	15.30	16.10	16.93	18.48	21.80	23.98	25.25	26.68	31.45

4.15b Hourly pay - Gross (£) - For all employee jobs[a]: United Kingdom, 2016

Description	Code	Number of jobs[b] (000s)	Median	Annual % change	Mean	Annual % change	Percentiles 10	20	25	30	40	60	70	75	80	90
30-39 Science, research, engineering and technology professionals	21	385	20.26	1.7	21.62	2.6	13.22	15.44	16.34	17.14	18.78	22.11	24.34	25.63	27.06	31.37
30-39 Health professionals	22	370	18.01	1.4	20.14	2.0	12.73	14.42	14.98	15.52	16.77	19.36	21.24	22.20	23.96	30.33
30-39 Teaching and educational professionals	23	391	22.28	1.5	22.35	1.7	14.28	17.32	18.34	19.39	20.77	23.81	25.54	26.58	27.98	31.14
30-39 Business, media and public service professionals	24	416	19.62	0.4	22.19	1.3	12.83	15.03	15.94	16.75	18.16	21.37	23.89	25.17	26.74	33.20
30-39 Associate professional and technical occupations	3	1,007	15.58	-0.2	17.77	0.1	10.12	11.77	12.42	13.05	14.31	17.02	18.65	19.73	21.13	25.98
30-39 Science, engineering and technology associate professionals	31	168	14.02	-0.6	15.09	0.0	9.33	10.96	11.62	12.09	13.05	15.23	16.38	17.50	18.48	21.36
30-39 Health and social care associate professionals	32	90	12.68	0.0	13.26	-2.0	9.06	10.01	10.45	11.07	11.80	13.30	14.31	14.88	15.31	17.95
30-39 Protective service occupations	33	125	17.13	2.3	17.10	1.6	12.81	14.21	14.84	15.32	16.20	18.03	18.74	19.24	19.83	21.24
30-39 Culture, media and sports occupations	34	60	14.06	0.5	19.05	4.0	9.53	11.23	11.71	12.27	13.02	15.18	16.37	17.06	18.08	x
30-39 Business and public service associate professionals	35	564	16.56	-1.0	19.28	-0.5	10.48	12.12	12.84	13.63	15.07	18.33	20.64	22.27	24.12	30.48
30-39 Administrative and secretarial occupations	4	605	10.99	1.7	12.50	2.7	7.85	8.70	9.08	9.45	10.10	12.00	13.22	14.01	15.01	18.12
30-39 Administrative occupations	41	501	11.24	2.2	12.71	3.1	8.04	8.96	9.27	9.62	10.30	12.23	13.46	14.32	15.30	18.34
30-39 Secretarial and related occupations	42	105	9.92	0.0	11.41	0.6	7.36	7.97	8.19	8.50	9.18	10.73	11.84	12.64	13.44	16.78
30-39 Skilled trades occupations	5	440	11.68	1.5	12.56	1.7	7.61	8.69	9.10	9.65	10.58	12.66	13.81	14.54	15.34	17.87
30-39 Skilled agricultural and related trades	51	19	9.57	2.5	9.88	-0.1	7.90	8.48	8.51	8.73	9.23	9.85	10.52	10.87	11.30	x
30-39 Skilled metal, electrical and electronic trades	52	220	13.51	1.2	14.33	2.7	9.09	10.50	11.12	11.68	12.56	14.54	15.71	16.43	17.15	20.28
30-39 Skilled construction and building trades	53	71	12.00	-0.1	12.32	-0.1	8.86	9.84	10.00	10.54	11.50	12.75	13.34	13.85	14.53	x
30-39 Textiles, printing and other skilled trades	54	131	8.88	3.6	9.84	1.8	7.20	7.41	7.59	7.90	8.41	9.55	10.27	10.68	11.39	13.04
30-39 Caring, leisure and other service occupations	6	469	8.99	4.7	9.83	4.5	7.22	7.60	7.81	8.03	8.50	9.52	10.26	10.78	11.40	13.19
30-39 Caring personal service occupations	61	392	8.96	4.6	9.66	4.2	7.24	7.62	7.82	8.05	8.50	9.46	10.12	10.60	11.22	12.80
30-39 Leisure, travel and related personal service	62	77	9.08	4.9	10.68	5.6	7.20	7.50	7.77	8.00	8.60	9.90	10.95	11.62	12.48	15.70
30-39 Sales and customer service occupations	7	389	8.76	4.4	10.24	4.3	7.20	7.35	7.50	7.68	8.20	9.45	10.36	10.97	11.88	14.35
30-39 Sales occupations	71	254	8.20	6.5	9.56	6.0	7.20	7.22	7.35	7.46	7.75	8.70	9.42	9.91	10.47	12.78
30-39 Customer service occupations	72	134	10.21	-0.1	11.40	0.6	7.33	8.07	8.49	8.83	9.39	11.01	12.24	13.00	13.77	15.78
30-39 Process, plant and machine operatives	8	310	10.28	3.6	11.33	4.6	7.40	8.20	8.51	8.84	9.57	11.04	12.19	12.95	13.74	16.03
30-39 Process, plant and machine operatives	81	164	10.05	4.8	11.13	4.1	7.37	8.00	8.33	8.64	9.25	10.91	12.23	13.10	13.82	16.08
30-39 Transport and mobile machine drivers and operatives	82	147	10.54	4.6	11.54	5.1	7.47	8.45	8.81	9.07	9.81	11.19	12.13	12.81	13.61	15.80
30-39 Elementary occupations	9	525	8.16	4.1	9.29	3.8	x	7.20	7.25	7.41	7.77	8.68	9.40	9.89	10.44	12.08
30-39 Elementary trades and related occupations	91	67	8.63	3.1	9.39	4.1	7.20	7.25	7.46	7.68	8.09	9.14	9.83	10.23	10.74	12.50
30-39 Elementary administration and service occupations	92	458	8.08	4.0	9.27	3.7	x	7.20	7.25	7.40	7.73	8.59	9.34	9.80	10.38	12.01
40-49 ALL OCCUPATIONS		6,300	13.95	2.9	17.76	2.8	7.70	8.88	9.51	10.22	11.87	16.43	19.36	21.12	23.15	30.42
40-49 Managers, directors and senior officials	1	802	22.62	3.2	28.29	4.3	10.45	13.67	15.02	16.50	19.49	26.57	31.80	35.06	38.74	51.68
40-49 Corporate managers and directors	11	704	24.04	3.4	29.58	3.9	10.85	14.42	15.96	17.46	20.67	28.31	33.48	36.58	40.69	53.23
40-49 Other managers and proprietors	12	98	15.67	2.3	18.84	3.0	8.81	10.69	11.50	12.23	14.05	17.93	20.68	21.84	23.60	x
40-49 Professional occupations	2	1,477	21.56	2.5	23.91	2.5	13.77	16.24	17.21	18.09	19.76	23.60	26.00	27.62	29.61	35.94
40-49 Science, research, engineering and technology professionals	21	340	22.72	2.7	23.95	1.1	14.31	17.12	18.21	19.17	20.84	24.44	26.79	28.24	29.71	34.42
40-49 Health professionals	22	419	18.87	2.5	22.77	3.5	13.42	14.99	15.76	16.49	17.92	20.70	22.36	23.94	25.90	38.62
40-49 Teaching and educational professionals	23	380	23.86	2.3	24.66	3.0	14.89	18.50	19.55	20.47	22.29	25.42	27.64	28.87	30.32	35.03
40-49 Business, media and public service professionals	24	338	21.23	1.9	24.45	2.4	12.94	15.94	16.91	17.91	19.47	23.51	26.25	27.96	30.31	37.19

4.15b Hourly pay - Gross (£) - For all employee jobs[a]: United Kingdom, 2016

Description	Code	Number of jobs[b] (000s)	Median	Annual % change	Mean	Annual % change	Percentiles 10	20	25	30	40	60	70	75	80	90
40-49 Associate professional and technical occupations	3	929	16.55	0.2	18.75	-1.5	10.44	12.09	12.85	13.58	14.94	18.18	19.93	21.03	22.37	27.73
40-49 Science, engineering and technology associate professionals	31	143	14.98	0.3	16.06	0.4	9.74	11.24	11.99	12.61	13.67	16.40	17.83	18.65	19.80	22.99
40-49 Health and social care associate professionals	32	90	13.03	2.2	14.08	0.5	9.27	10.45	10.92	11.38	12.09	13.88	14.75	15.59	16.69	18.85
40-49 Protective service occupations	33	137	18.52	0.3	18.26	-0.9	13.60	14.71	15.59	16.30	18.00	19.25	20.08	20.76	21.23	22.66
40-49 Culture, media and sports occupations	34	38	15.05	0.3	16.68	1.4	9.62	11.17	11.77	12.52	13.87	16.45	17.65	19.49	20.43	x
40-49 Business and public service associate professionals	35	521	17.27	-1.0	20.52	-2.6	10.75	12.37	13.08	13.93	15.48	19.20	21.75	23.48	25.55	33.79
40-49 Administrative and secretarial occupations	4	718	11.06	2.1	12.74	2.2	8.00	8.86	9.20	9.57	10.22	11.97	13.36	14.23	15.31	18.68
40-49 Administrative occupations	41	564	11.29	2.0	12.93	1.9	8.18	9.08	9.44	9.84	10.41	12.29	13.65	14.51	15.42	18.98
40-49 Secretarial and related occupations	42	154	10.07	1.1	11.96	3.5	7.67	8.25	8.58	8.89	9.45	11.09	12.04	13.03	14.11	17.90
40-49 Skilled trades occupations	5	470	12.10	0.9	13.41	1.4	7.78	8.88	9.45	10.00	11.06	13.33	14.58	15.40	16.30	19.19
40-49 Skilled agricultural and related trades	51	25	9.99	2.2	10.96	3.7	7.43	8.09	8.31	8.97	9.50	10.86	11.64	11.96	12.25	x
40-49 Skilled metal, electrical and electronic trades	52	242	14.05	3.3	15.07	2.6	9.67	10.97	11.43	12.00	12.99	15.11	16.49	17.25	18.12	21.21
40-49 Skilled construction and building trades	53	76	12.60	-1.1	13.39	-1.0	9.00	10.15	10.67	11.00	11.81	13.50	14.21	14.68	15.58	x
40-49 Textiles, printing and other skilled trades	54	127	8.75	0.9	10.16	3.1	7.20	7.50	7.65	7.87	8.33	9.39	10.42	10.95	11.55	13.90
40-49 Caring, leisure and other service occupations	6	597	9.05	2.9	9.99	3.6	7.31	7.75	7.93	8.12	8.61	9.63	10.40	10.90	11.50	13.38
40-49 Caring personal service occupations	61	516	9.03	3.2	9.77	4.6	7.35	7.77	7.95	8.13	8.62	9.56	10.30	10.80	11.34	13.02
40-49 Leisure, travel and related personal service	62	81	9.19	2.0	11.34	-2.8	7.20	7.50	7.75	8.01	8.59	10.01	11.31	12.28	13.21	x
40-49 Sales and customer service occupations	7	337	8.50	4.9	10.36	4.1	7.20	7.30	7.43	7.58	8.00	9.31	10.32	10.90	11.77	14.85
40-49 Sales occupations	71	238	8.06	6.1	9.47	5.1	7.20	7.21	7.32	7.41	7.65	8.48	9.24	9.69	10.35	12.65
40-49 Customer service occupations	72	99	10.49	-1.4	12.21	0.8	7.35	8.16	8.49	8.89	9.80	11.46	12.85	13.52	14.65	17.88
40-49 Process, plant and machine operatives	8	395	10.67	2.0	11.87	2.3	7.44	8.27	8.65	9.06	9.87	11.65	12.89	13.49	14.31	17.20
40-49 Process, plant and machine operatives	81	178	10.47	1.3	11.80	1.2	7.32	8.00	8.34	8.76	9.50	11.41	12.96	13.67	14.63	17.90
40-49 Transport and mobile machine drivers and operatives	82	217	10.83	3.2	11.92	3.2	7.60	8.50	8.93	9.35	10.05	11.73	12.83	13.36	14.06	16.78
40-49 Elementary occupations	9	574	8.18	4.3	9.47	3.4	x	7.20	7.26	7.41	7.78	8.75	9.50	10.06	10.57	12.60
40-49 Elementary trades and related occupations	91	66	8.62	2.4	9.58	2.1	7.20	7.32	7.50	7.70	8.09	9.29	9.99	10.48	11.00	13.21
40-49 Elementary administration and service occupations	92	509	8.12	4.2	9.45	3.7	x	7.20	7.24	7.38	7.74	8.68	9.44	10.00	10.52	12.53
50-59 ALL OCCUPATIONS		5,581	13.22	3.7	17.28	4.0	7.67	8.78	9.35	10.00	11.45	15.54	18.49	20.31	22.30	29.48
50-59 Managers, directors and senior officials	1	706	21.54	1.8	27.54	3.3	10.05	13.09	14.40	15.77	18.52	25.15	30.36	33.73	37.99	50.14
50-59 Corporate managers and directors	11	601	23.15	2.0	29.23	3.6	10.61	13.89	15.27	16.79	19.81	27.11	32.65	36.23	40.58	52.67
50-59 Other managers and proprietors	12	106	15.88	0.6	18.05	-0.6	8.85	10.42	11.50	12.46	14.06	17.69	20.02	21.49	23.35	29.35
50-59 Professional occupations	2	1,235	21.16	1.1	23.85	1.5	13.47	15.82	16.86	17.90	19.47	23.08	25.38	26.96	29.19	35.83
50-59 Science, research, engineering and technology professionals	21	244	22.05	1.7	23.91	2.3	14.22	16.53	17.72	18.43	20.29	24.32	26.83	28.50	30.15	36.01
50-59 Health professionals	22	388	18.98	3.4	23.11	0.7	13.42	14.99	15.75	16.53	17.99	20.70	21.83	22.95	24.56	35.53
50-59 Teaching and educational professionals	23	331	23.95	0.6	25.13	0.7	14.87	18.48	19.57	20.44	22.33	25.63	27.84	29.36	30.64	36.07
50-59 Business, media and public service professionals	24	271	20.49	3.0	23.46	2.8	12.16	14.73	15.83	16.88	18.69	22.63	25.10	27.07	29.07	35.85
50-59 Associate professional and technical occupations	3	702	16.02	0.6	18.65	0.7	10.11	11.76	12.51	13.08	14.52	17.86	19.74	21.10	22.60	28.88
50-59 Science, engineering and technology associate professionals	31	132	15.31	0.8	16.46	2.5	9.52	10.86	11.84	12.53	14.10	16.70	18.38	19.42	20.41	24.17
50-59 Health and social care associate professionals	32	93	12.99	-0.1	14.00	0.0	9.51	10.42	10.90	11.28	12.07	13.76	14.67	15.17	16.16	18.72
50-59 Protective service occupations	33	60	18.03	0.2	17.72	-1.5	11.26	13.63	14.36	14.76	15.90	19.14	20.26	20.89	21.51	x

4.15b Hourly pay - Gross (£) - For all employee jobs[a]: United Kingdom, 2016

Description	Code	Number of jobs[b] (000s)	Median	Annual % change	Mean	Annual % change	Percentiles 10	20	25	30	40	60	70	75	80	90
50-59 Culture, media and sports occupations	34	26	14.99	2.5	18.34	2.4	10.48	11.37	11.84	12.07	13.43	16.35	18.68	21.13	x	x
50-59 Business and public service associate professionals	35	391	17.29	0.0	20.58	0.4	10.63	12.52	13.08	13.88	15.55	19.21	21.86	23.39	25.81	33.67
50-59 Administrative and secretarial occupations	4	743	10.78	2.4	12.46	3.0	8.00	8.80	9.16	9.47	10.09	11.64	12.86	13.65	14.59	18.15
50-59 Administrative occupations	41	562	11.17	2.7	12.83	3.8	8.22	9.11	9.45	9.82	10.40	12.14	13.42	14.18	15.25	18.79
50-59 Secretarial and related occupations	42	181	9.83	-0.6	11.21	0.1	7.61	8.15	8.44	8.69	9.19	10.44	11.48	11.89	12.63	15.31
50-59 Skilled trades occupations	5	430	12.62	1.9	13.83	3.4	8.00	9.18	9.76	10.30	11.45	13.89	15.36	16.06	17.06	20.20
50-59 Skilled agricultural and related trades	51	26	9.86	4.6	10.48	5.8	7.50	8.19	8.44	8.62	9.33	10.23	10.89	11.28	11.97	x
50-59 Skilled metal, electrical and electronic trades	52	237	14.68	4.2	15.46	4.3	9.82	11.25	11.88	12.53	13.54	15.75	17.04	17.71	18.77	21.64
50-59 Skilled construction and building trades	53	65	12.84	2.8	14.02	4.5	9.90	10.83	11.25	11.61	12.23	13.79	14.91	15.53	16.30	19.41
50-59 Textiles, printing and other skilled trades	54	102	8.97	2.8	9.97	0.5	7.20	7.60	7.83	8.00	8.49	9.38	10.08	10.47	11.16	13.12
50-59 Caring, leisure and other service occupations	6	550	9.26	2.3	10.26	2.7	7.32	7.80	8.00	8.25	8.78	10.00	10.71	11.23	11.76	13.54
50-59 Caring personal service occupations	61	464	9.22	2.4	9.95	2.9	7.32	7.79	8.00	8.24	8.76	9.94	10.58	11.09	11.57	12.99
50-59 Leisure, travel and related personal service	62	86	9.54	-0.3	11.89	2.2	7.30	7.88	8.06	8.28	8.96	10.40	11.51	12.35	13.62	x
50-59 Sales and customer service occupations	7	317	8.20	4.7	9.87	4.2	7.20	7.26	7.39	7.48	7.78	8.80	9.56	10.12	10.90	13.66
50-59 Sales occupations	71	236	7.84	6.0	8.93	4.7	x	7.20	7.28	7.39	7.53	8.20	8.74	9.11	9.55	11.12
50-59 Customer service occupations	72	81	10.37	1.1	12.26	2.2	7.46	8.17	8.55	8.93	9.56	11.45	12.73	13.67	14.67	18.22
50-59 Process, plant and machine operatives	8	386	10.61	2.5	11.66	2.0	7.50	8.24	8.62	9.00	9.77	11.43	12.52	13.16	14.12	16.78
50-59 Process, plant and machine operatives	81	164	10.68	4.7	11.88	3.6	7.46	8.00	8.40	8.88	9.70	11.70	13.13	14.02	14.90	17.82
50-59 Transport and mobile machine drivers and operatives	82	221	10.58	1.7	11.52	1.0	7.57	8.37	8.79	9.09	9.79	11.27	12.20	12.72	13.38	15.94
50-59 Elementary occupations	9	514	8.24	4.7	9.46	2.5	x	7.20	7.31	7.48	7.85	8.80	9.64	10.19	10.68	12.51
50-59 Elementary trades and related occupations	91	59	9.08	5.4	10.03	5.5	7.20	7.50	7.70	7.96	8.50	9.66	10.70	11.38	11.95	13.76
50-59 Elementary administration and service occupations	92	455	8.15	3.9	9.36	2.0	x	7.20	7.28	7.43	7.80	8.65	9.47	10.05	10.54	12.35
60+ ALL OCCUPATIONS		1,974	11.31	3.5	15.04	2.2	7.39	8.10	8.51	9.00	10.00	12.95	15.32	16.96	18.85	25.47
60+ Managers, directors and senior officials	1	228	17.93	1.0	23.54	-0.6	9.00	10.57	11.68	12.68	15.35	20.84	25.76	27.96	32.03	42.60
60+ Corporate managers and directors	11	189	18.85	-0.6	24.62	-1.7	9.17	10.91	12.00	13.22	16.10	22.32	27.31	30.53	33.40	44.35
60+ Other managers and proprietors	12	39	15.30	15.3	18.03	7.0	8.63	9.80	10.42	11.45	12.69	17.27	19.23	20.65	22.76	x
60+ Professional occupations	2	340	20.46	0.7	22.76	0.4	12.44	14.77	15.84	16.85	18.39	22.42	24.97	26.58	28.94	34.96
60+ Science, research, engineering and technology professionals	21	60	21.15	1.0	22.44	0.8	12.86	15.31	16.30	17.73	19.51	23.42	25.64	27.34	29.45	x
60+ Health professionals	22	96	18.02	1.1	22.07	-2.2	12.68	14.53	15.00	15.58	17.12	19.30	21.16	22.38	24.55	x
60+ Teaching and educational professionals	23	103	23.70	-0.3	25.51	2.8	14.18	17.68	18.90	19.74	22.05	25.70	28.47	29.77	31.17	37.41
60+ Business, media and public service professionals	24	81	18.31	-2.9	21.20	0.7	10.91	12.56	13.58	14.85	16.97	20.95	23.41	24.38	26.96	x
60+ Associate professional and technical occupations	3	177	14.41	1.2	16.91	3.5	9.12	10.55	11.42	11.89	13.07	16.02	17.83	19.07	20.35	25.31
60+ Science, engineering and technology associate professionals	31	35	14.00	-0.1	15.23	2.6	9.18	10.36	11.06	11.42	12.25	15.67	16.73	17.54	19.20	x
60+ Health and social care associate professionals	32	23	12.63	-0.4	14.02	1.7	8.85	9.32	9.85	10.53	11.51	13.73	14.42	15.29	15.84	x
60+ Protective service occupations	33	8	14.35	0.6	15.02	-5.2	x	12.05	12.34	12.79	13.81	15.10	16.30	x	x	x
60+ Culture, media and sports occupations	34	10	14.46	2.3	15.70	3.2	x	9.83	10.11	11.19	12.35	16.21	x	x	x	x
60+ Business and public service associate professionals	35	101	15.31	3.5	18.30	4.3	9.30	11.31	11.84	12.47	13.61	16.89	19.44	20.45	22.38	28.47
60+ Administrative and secretarial occupations	4	304	10.30	2.5	11.74	1.7	7.76	8.50	8.84	9.16	9.81	11.20	12.26	12.93	13.77	16.73
60+ Administrative occupations	41	220	10.48	1.5	11.94	2.1	7.80	8.63	9.01	9.29	10.00	11.45	12.50	13.16	14.00	16.90
60+ Secretarial and related occupations	42	84	9.97	2.7	11.18	0.6	7.54	8.21	8.50	8.79	9.19	10.63	11.54	12.27	13.05	15.87

4.15b Hourly pay - Gross (£) - For all employee jobs[a]: United Kingdom, 2016

Description	Code	Number of jobs[b] (000s)	Median	Annual % change	Mean	Annual % change	Percentiles 10	20	25	30	40	60	70	75	80	90
60+ Skilled trades occupations	5	164	11.76	1.7	12.93	1.7	7.89	8.79	9.23	9.86	10.69	12.85	14.05	14.89	15.74	18.27
60+ Skilled agricultural and related trades	51	14	9.02	0.0	9.68	-0.5	7.20	7.68	7.86	8.13	8.68	9.72	10.00	10.01	x	x
60+ Skilled metal, electrical and electronic trades	52	85	13.55	0.3	14.29	1.3	9.14	10.58	11.10	11.64	12.79	14.75	15.76	16.50	17.19	19.56
60+ Skilled construction and building trades	53	27	11.98	2.0	12.81	0.4	9.52	10.12	10.50	10.75	11.27	12.68	13.43	13.74	14.85	x
60+ Textiles, printing and other skilled trades	54	39	8.75	-0.1	10.40	4.8	7.24	7.68	7.88	8.02	8.38	9.42	10.33	10.75	11.29	x
60+ Caring, leisure and other service occupations	6	200	9.21	3.6	10.00	4.0	7.31	7.81	8.05	8.25	8.75	9.78	10.55	11.16	11.71	13.43
60+ Caring personal service occupations	61	159	9.27	4.1	9.96	4.4	7.35	7.90	8.10	8.32	8.88	9.89	10.67	11.25	11.75	13.34
60+ Leisure, travel and related personal service occupations	62	41	8.91	2.9	10.16	3.1	7.20	7.64	7.85	8.08	8.34	9.30	10.23	10.79	11.51	x
60+ Sales and customer service occupations	7	141	7.94	6.6	9.23	5.7	x	7.20	7.27	7.39	7.59	8.27	8.98	9.58	10.16	12.51
60+ Sales occupations	71	115	7.71	5.6	8.69	4.4	x	7.20	7.22	7.30	7.48	8.10	8.42	8.77	9.31	10.85
60+ Customer service occupations	72	26	10.02	8.2	11.25	6.1	7.26	7.65	8.01	8.48	9.14	10.77	12.06	12.73	13.55	x
60+ Process, plant and machine operatives	8	185	9.75	2.6	10.83	-0.3	7.20	7.61	7.90	8.18	8.89	10.40	11.33	11.85	12.48	14.37
60+ Process, plant and machine operatives	81	62	9.98	1.6	11.22	3.1	7.25	7.70	7.91	8.18	9.00	11.03	12.21	13.12	13.54	15.49
60+ Transport and mobile machine drivers and operatives	82	123	9.61	2.9	10.63	-2.0	7.20	7.53	7.90	8.15	8.78	10.27	11.00	11.42	11.91	13.74
60+ Elementary occupations	9	237	8.00	4.2	9.24	3.7	x	7.20	7.22	7.39	7.68	8.47	9.13	9.58	10.18	11.97
60+ Elementary trades and related occupations	91	25	8.99	5.8	9.87	4.9	7.20	7.44	7.60	7.77	8.38	9.44	10.24	10.86	11.47	x
60+ Elementary administration and service occupations	92	211	7.95	4.6	9.13	3.5	x	x	7.20	7.35	7.61	8.31	9.00	9.40	10.00	11.76
Not Classified		:														

Source: Annual Survey of Hours and Earnings, Office for National Statistics.

a Employees on adult rates whose pay for the survey pay-period was not affected by absence.

b Figures for Number of Jobs are for indicative purposes only and should not be considered an accurate estimate of employee job counts.

KEY - The colour coding indicates the quality of each estimate; jobs, median, mean and percentiles but not the annual percentage change.

The quality of an estimate is measured by its coefficient of variation (CV), which is the ratio of the standard error of an estimate to the estimate.

Key	Statistical robustness
CV <= 5%	Estimates are considered precise
CV > 5% and <= 10%	Estimates are considered reasonably precise
CV > 10% and <= 20%	Estimates are considered acceptable
x = CV > 20%	Estimates are considered unreliable for practical purposes
.. = disclosive	
: = not applicable	
- = nil or negligible	

4.16 Median weekly and hourly earnings for all employees[a] by age group: United Kingdom April 2007 to 2016

	18-21	22-29	30-39	40-49	50-59	60+
Median gross weekly earnings						
All	**JRG9**	**JRH2**	**JRH3**	**JRH4**	**JEH5**	**JRH6**
2007	265.5	387.8	509.0	517.3	479.1	418.7
2008	271.6	400.0	532.7	539.9	504.1	437.5
2009	277.5	407.1	541.8	550.5	514.0	446.3
2010	277.4	411.2	547.8	559.6	528.2	457.3
2011	277.8	406.6	553.7	564.7	531.8	466.1
2012	279.7	412.0	557.7	573.1	535.9	476.1
2013	287.5	420.6	562.9	579.9	551.0	490.4
2014	290.0	424.8	566.0	588.2	556.1	491.3
2015	199.3	383.2	489.1	491.9	458.0	338.9
2016	206.8	400.0	498.3	503.7	473.4	348.8
Men	**JRH8**	**JRH9**	**JRI2**	**JRI3**	**JRI4**	**JRI5**
2007	275.9	402.5	539.0	574.9	534.4	440.9
2008	280.0	416.7	566.3	599.1	563.6	462.6
2009	285.7	421.6	571.1	605.2	569.7	469.0
2010	285.9	421.2	573.7	613.7	582.7	483.0
2011	288.2	413.7	574.9	618.9	586.7	496.3
2012	295.4	420.6	574.9	622.9	598.2	508.3
2013	299.0	430.6	579.6	637.8	613.3	527.5
2014	301.7	435.6	578.6	641.3	621.1	528.0
2015	233.0	411.6	556.5	618.8	593.9	443.1
2016	252.8	430.4	574.8	632.4	609.5	458.6
Women	**JRI7**	**JRI8**	**JRI9**	**JRJ2**	**JRJ3**	**JRJ4**
2007	254.3	374.1	460.6	420.3	395.6	356.1
2008	258.8	384.7	480.9	437.3	419.7	376.4
2009	268.3	392.9	497.9	457.7	432.8	382.1
2010	268.3	401.3	507.9	472.2	440.9	389.0
2011	264.7	398.5	519.4	477.1	449.1	399.6
2012	266.3	402.5	527.0	484.4	446.0	407.4
2013	276.2	405.7	533.8	494.1	463.5	416.1
2014	279.2	414.0	537.3	507.3	465.4	412.0
2015	166.6	347.5	401.0	365.2	342.8	235.7
2016	167.4	364.1	408.2	373.6	364.1	251.9

4.16 Median weekly and hourly earnings for all employee jobs[a] by age group: United Kingdom April 2007 to 2016

	18-21	22-29	30-39	40-49	50-59	60+
Median hourly earnings (excluding overtime)						
All	**JRJ6**	**JRJ7**	**JRJ8**	**JRJ9**	**JRK2**	**JRK3**
2007	6.60	9.80	12.77	12.77	11.87	10.09
2008	6.75	10.12	13.34	13.31	12.53	10.57
2009	7.00	10.43	13.82	13.83	12.95	10.97
2010	7.00	10.34	13.91	14.01	13.19	11.18
2011	6.97	10.23	14.07	14.16	13.34	11.46
2012	7.00	10.34	14.23	14.37	13.55	11.83
2013	7.20	10.60	14.37	14.63	13.89	12.13
2014	7.25	10.76	14.37	14.82	14.00	12.22
2015	7.08	10.03	13.31	13.49	12.68	10.88
2016	7.45	10.51	13.55	13.90	13.17	11.25
Men	**JRK5**	**JRK6**	**JRK7**	**JRK8**	**JRK9**	**JRL2**
2007	6.65	9.80	13.10	13.77	12.79	10.31
2008	6.85	10.13	13.70	14.37	13.52	10.89
2009	7.09	10.45	14.15	14.95	13.91	11.25
2010	7.05	10.26	14.07	14.95	14.25	11.50
2011	7.07	10.08	14.14	15.14	14.31	11.84
2012	7.24	10.22	14.28	15.27	14.68	12.15
2013	7.27	10.57	14.43	15.62	15.00	12.61
2014	7.42	10.73	14.35	15.69	15.13	12.78
2015	7.25	10.26	14.05	15.41	14.97	12.26
2016	7.50	10.87	14.34	15.86	15.39	12.56
Women	**JRL4**	**JRL5**	**JRL6**	**JRL7**	**JRL8**	**JRL9**
2007	6.55	9.79	12.28	11.14	10.54	9.48
2008	6.64	10.12	12.78	11.57	11.10	9.82
2009	6.93	10.40	13.29	12.21	11.52	10.23
2010	6.90	10.48	13.66	12.54	11.84	10.40
2011	6.76	10.45	13.99	12.77	12.02	10.64
2012	6.82	10.53	14.18	12.93	11.99	10.99
2013	7.15	10.64	14.28	13.18	12.38	11.10
2014	7.06	10.81	14.37	13.53	12.41	10.99
2015	7.00	9.83	12.41	11.55	10.84	9.60
2016	7.39	10.15	12.62	11.88	11.45	10.00

Source: Annual Survey of Hours and Earnings, Office for National Statistics

a. Employees on adult rates whose pay for the survey pay-period was not affected by absence.

4.17 Trade Unions 2016-17

Trade unions: distribution by size

			Number of Unions		*Membership of all Unions*	
Number of Members	*Number of Unions*	*Membership*	*Per cent*	*Cumulative Per cent*	*Per cent*	*Cumulative Per cent*
Under 100	25	571	16.5	16.5	0.0	0.0
100-499	24	5,989	15.9	32.4	0.1	0.1
500-999	14	9,275	9.3	41.7	0.1	0.2
1,000-2,499	26	39,674	17.2	58.9	0.6	0.8
2,500-4,999	9	34,803	6.0	64.9	0.5	1.3
5,000-9,999	11	84,599	7.3	72.2	1.2	2.6
10,000-14,999	3	37,125	2.0	74.2	0.5	3.1
15,000-24,999	10	201,087	6.6	80.8	2.9	6.0
25,000-49,999	13	444,032	8.6	89.4	6.5	12.5
50,000-99,999	3	193,329	2.0	91.4	2.8	15.3
100,000-249,999	6	975,556	4.0	95.4	14.2	29.5
250,000 and over	7	4,839,016	4.6	100.0	70.5	100.0
Total	151	6,865,056	100		100	

The trade union membership of 6,865,056 recorded in this annual report compares to 6,948,725 reported in the previous annual report. This indicates a decrease of 83,669 members or 1.2%. The total recorded membership of around 6.9 million compares with a peak of 13.2 million in 1979, a fall of about 48%.

The following table shows the trade unions whose membership has increased or decreased by 10,000 members or more since the previous reporting period.

4.17 Trade Unions 2016-17

Trade Union: Changes in Membership over 10,000 members

	Total Membership		
	2015-2016	*2014-2015*	*% changes*
Increases			
British Medical Association	169,908	154,603	+9.90
Association of Teachers and Lecturers	200,631	189,479	+5.89
Royal College of Nursing	444,685	429,414	+3.43
Decreases			
Union of Construction, Allied Trades and Technicians	47,433	61,229	-22.53
Public and Commercial Services Union	195,091	231,323	-15.66
Unite the Union	1,382,126	1,405,838	-1.69
UNISON: The Public Service Union	1,255,653	1,270,248	-1.15

The annual returns submitted by unions to the Certification Officer require each union to provide figures for both total membership and members who pay contributions. There can be significant differences between these figures. This is usually the result of total membership figures including retired and unemployed members, members on long term sick and maternity/child care leave and those on career breaks. The returns submitted by unions during this reporting period show that the total number of contributing members was around 94.2% of the total number of members. This compared to 91.7% in the preceding year.

Source: Annual Report of the Certification Officer 2016/17

this page is intentionally blank

Social protection

Chapter 5

Social Protection

(Tables 5.2 to 5.11, 5.13 and 5.15 to 5.19)

Tables 5.2 to 5.6, 5.9 to 5.11 and 5.13 to 5.19 give details of contributors and beneficiaries under the National Insurance and Industrial Injury Acts, supplementary benefits and war pensions.

There are five classes of National Insurance Contributions (NICs):

Class 1 Earnings-related contributions paid on earnings from employment. Employees pay primary Class 1 contributions and employers pay secondary Class 1 contributions. Payment of Class 1 contributions builds up entitlement to contributory benefits which include Basic State Pension; Additional State Pension (State Earnings Related Pension Scheme SERPS and from April 2002, State Second Pension, S2P); Contribution Based Jobseeker's Allowance; Bereavement Benefits and Employment and Support Allowance.

Class 1A or 1B Employers pay these directly on their employee's expenses or benefits

Primary class 1 contributions stop at State Pension age, but not Class 1 secondary contributions paid by employers. There are reduced contribution rates where the employee contracts out of S2P (previously SERPS). They still receive a Basic State Pension but an Occupational or Personal Pension instead of the Additional State Second Pension.

Class 2 Flat rate contributions paid by the self-employed whose profits are above the small earnings exception. Payment of Class 2 contributions builds up entitlement to the contributory benefits which include Basic State Pension; Bereavement Benefits; Maternity Allowance and the Employment and Support Allowance, but not Additional State Second Pension or Contribution Based Jobseeker's Allowance (JSA).

Class 2 contributions stop at State Pension age.

Class 3 Flat rate voluntary contributions, which can be paid by someone whose contribution record is insufficient. Payment of Class 3 contributions builds up entitlement to contributory benefits which include Basic State Pension and Bereavement Benefits. (Tables 5.2 to 5.11, 5.13 and 5.15 to 5.19) Tables 5.2 to 5.6, 5.9 to 5.11 and 5.13 to 5.19 give details of contributors and beneficiaries under the National Insurance and Industrial Injury Acts, supplementary benefits and war pensions.

Class 4 Profit-related contributions paid by the self employed in addition to Class 2 contributions. Class 4 contributions paid by self-employed people with a profit over £8,164 don't usually count towards state benefits.

Home Responsibilities Protection

Home Responsibilities Protection (HRP) was introduced to help to protect the basic State Pension of those precluded from regular employment because they are caring for children or a sick or disabled person at home. To be entitled to HRP, a person must have been precluded from regular employment for a full tax year. HRP reduces the amount of qualifying years a person would otherwise need for a Basic State Pension. **The scheme ceased on the 6th April 2010** and has been replaced by National Insurance credits which can be claimed if qualifying criteria are met.

National Insurance Credits

In addition to paying, or being treated as having paid contributions, a person can be credited with National Insurance contributions (NIC) credits. Contribution credits help to protect people's rights to State Retirement Pension and other Social Security Benefits.

A person is likely to be entitled to contributions credits if they are: a student in full time education or training, in receipt of Jobseeker's Allowance, unable to work due to sickness or disability, entitled to Statutory Maternity Pay or Statutory Adoption Pay, or they have received Carer's Allowance.

National Insurance Credits eligibility can be checked at: https://www.gov.uk/national-insurance-credits/eligibility

Jobseeker's Allowance (Table 5.6)

Jobseeker's Allowance (JSA) replaced Unemployment Benefit and Income Support for unemployed claimants on 7 October 1996. It is a unified benefit with two routes of entry: contribution-based, which depends mainly upon National Insurance contributions, and income-based, which depends mainly upon a means test. Some claimants can qualify by either route. In practice they receive income-based JSA but have an underlying entitlement to the contribution based element.

Employment and Support Allowance, and Incapacity Benefit (Table 5.7)

Incapacity Benefit replaced Sickness Benefit and Invalidity Benefit from 13 April 1995. The first condition for entitlement to these contributory benefits is that the claimants are incapable of work because of illness or disablement. The second is that they satisfy the contribution conditions, which depend on contributions paid as an employed (Class 1) or self-employed person (Class 2). Under Sickness and Invalidity Benefits the contribution conditions were automatically treated as satisfied if a person was incapable of work because of an industrial accident or prescribed disease. Under Incapacity Benefit those who do not satisfy the contribution conditions do not have them treated as satisfied. Class 1A contributions paid by employers are in respect of the benefit of cars provided for the private use of employees, and the free fuel provided for private use. These contributions do not provide any type of benefit cover.

Since 6 April 1983, most people working for an employer and paying National Insurance contributions as employed persons receive Statutory Sick Pay (SSP) from their employer when they are off work sick. Until 5 April 1986 SSP was payable for a maximum of eight weeks, since this date SSP has been payable for 28 weeks. People who do not work for an employer, and employees who are excluded from the SSP scheme, or those who have run out of SSP before reaching the maximum of 28 weeks and are still sick, can claim benefit. Any period of SSP is excluded from the tables.

Spells of incapacity of three days or less do not count as periods of interruption of employment and are excluded from the tables. Exceptions are where people are receiving regular weekly treatment by dialysis or treatment by radiotherapy, chemotherapy or plasmapheresis where two days in any six consecutive days make up a period of interruption of employment, and those whose incapacity for work ends within three days of the end of SSP entitlement.

At the beginning of a period of incapacity, benefit is subject to three waiting days, except where there was an earlier spell of incapacity of more than three days in the previous eight weeks. Employees entitled to SSP for less than 28 weeks and who are still sick can get Sickness Benefit or Incapacity Benefit Short Term (Low) until they reach a total of 28 weeks provided they satisfy the conditions.

After 28 weeks of SSP and/or Sickness Benefit (SB), Invalidity Benefit (IVB) was payable up to pension age for as long as the incapacity lasted. From pension age, IVB was paid at the person's State Pension rate, until entitlement ceased when SP was paid, or until deemed pension age (70 for a man, 65 for a woman). People who were on Sickness or Invalidity Benefit on 12 April 1995 were automatically transferred to Incapacity Benefit, payable on the same basis as before.

For people on Incapacity Benefit under State Pension age there are two short-term rates: the lower rate is paid for the first 28 weeks of sickness and the higher rate for weeks 29 to 52. From week 53 the Long Term rate Incapacity Benefit is payable. The Short Term rate Incapacity Benefit is based on State Pension entitlement for people over State Pension age and is paid for up to a year if incapacity began before pension age.

The long-term rate of Incapacity Benefit applies to people under State Pension age who have been sick for more than a year. People with a terminal illness, or who are receiving the higher rate care component of Disability Living Allowance, will get the Long Term rate. The Long Term rate is not paid for people over pension age.

Under Incapacity Benefit, for the first 28 weeks of incapacity, people previously in work will be assessed on the 'own occupation' test – the claimant's ability to do their own job. Otherwise, incapacity will be based on a personal capability assessment, which will assess ability to carry out a range of work-related activities. The test will apply after 28 weeks of incapacity or from the start of the claim for people who did not previously have a job. Certain people will be exempted from this test.

The tables exclude all men aged over 65 and women aged over 60 who are in receipt of State Pension, and all people over deemed pension age (70 for a man and 65 for a woman), members of the armed forces, mariners while at sea, and married women and certain widows who have chosen not to be insured for sickness benefit. The tables include a number of individuals who were unemployed prior to incapacity.

The Short Term (Higher) and Long Term rates of Incapacity Benefit are treated as taxable income. There were transitional provisions for people who were on Sickness or Invalidity Benefit on 12 April 1995. They were automatically transferred to Incapacity Benefit, payable on the same basis as before. Former IVB recipients continue to get Additional Pension entitlement, but frozen at 1994 levels. Also their IVB is not subject to tax. If they were over State Pension age on 12 April 1995 they may get Incapacity Benefit for up to five years beyond pension age.

Employment and Support Allowance (ESA) replaced Incapacity Benefit and Income Support paid on the grounds of incapacity for new claims from 27 October 2008. ESA consists of two phases. The first, the assessment phase rate, is paid for the first 13 weeks of the claim whilst a decision is made on the claimants capability through the 'Work Capability Asessment'. The second, or main phase begins after 14 weeks, but only if the 'Work Capability Assesment' has deemed the claimants illness or disability as a limitation on their ability to work.

Within the main phase there are two groups, 'The Work Related Activity Group' and 'The Support Group'. If a claimant is placed in the first, they are expected to take part in work focused interviews with a personal advisor. They will be given support to help them prepare for work and on gaining work will receive a work related activity component in addition to their basic rate. If the claimant is placed in the second group due to their illness or disability having a severe effect upon their ability to work, the claimant will not be expected to work at all, but can do so on a voluntary basis. These claimants will receive a support component in addition to their basic rate.

Child Benefits (Table 5.9a and 5.9b)

You get child benefit if you are responsible for a child under 16 (or under 20 if they stay in approved education or training.

Approved education

Education must be full-time (more than an average of 12 hours a week supervised study or course-related work experience) and can include:

A levels or similar - eg Pre-U, International Baccalaureate

Scottish Highers

NVQs and other vocational qualifications up to level 3

home education - if started before your child turned 16

traineeships in England

Courses are not approved if paid for by an employer or 'advanced', eg a university degree or BTEC Higher National Certificate.

Approved training

Approved training should be unpaid and can include:

Access to Apprenticeships in England

Foundation Apprenticeships or Traineeships in Wales

Employability Fund programmes or Get Ready for Work (if started before 1 April 2013) in Scotland

Training for Success, Pathways to Success or Collaboration and Innovation Programme in Northern Ireland

Courses that are part of a job contract are not approved.

Guardian's Allowance is an additional allowance for people bringing up a child because one or both of their parents has died. They must be getting Child Benefit (CB) for the child. The table shows the number of families in the UK in receipt of CB. The numbers shown in the table are estimates based on a random 5 per cent sample of awards current at 31 August, and are therefore subject to sampling error. The figures take no account of new claims, or revisions to claims that were received or processed after 31 August, even if they are backdated to start before 31 August.

Child and Working Tax Credits (New Tax Credits) (Table 5.10 and 5.11)

Child and Working Tax Credits (CTC and WTC) replaced Working Families' Tax Credit (WFTC) from 6th April 2003. CTC and WTC are claimed by individuals, or jointly by couples, whether or not they have children.

CTC provides support to families for the children (up to the 31 August after their 16th birthday) and the 'qualifying' young people (in full-time non-advanced education until their 20th birthday) for which they are responsible. It is paid in addition to CB.

WTC tops up the earnings of families on low or moderate incomes. People working for at least 16 hours a week can claim it if they: (a) are responsible for at least one child or qualifying young person, (b) have a disability which puts them at a disadvantage in getting a job or, (c) in the first year of work, having returned to work aged at least 50 after a period of at least six months receiving out-of-work benefits. Other adults also qualify if they are aged at least 25 and work for at least 30 hours a week.

Bereavement Benefits (Table 5.12 and 5.13)

If your husband, wife or civil partner died before 6 April 2017, you may be able to get one or more of the following:

Bereavement Payment (a one-off payment)
Bereavement Allowance (monthly payments)
Widowed Parent's Allowance (if you're bringing up children)

Bereavement Payment is a one-off, tax-free, lump-sum payment. The other two benefits are payable monthly. Widowed Parents' Allowance is payable if you are bringing up children. Eligibility requirements must be met. A full list of requirements can be viewed on gov.uk at: https://www.gov.uk/bereavement-allowance

You don't have to apply more than once - you'll be considered for all bereavement benefits when you apply for one.

5.1 National Insurance Fund (Great Britain)

For the year ended 31 March

£ 000

	2012	2013	2014	2015	2016
Receipts					
Opening balance	43,163,939	38,593,953	29,082,990	23,195,862	20,935,278
National Insurance Contributions	78,423,776	79,119,934	82,236,514	84,112,562	86,461,626
Treasury Grant	-	-	-	4,600,000	9,600,000
Compensation for statutory pay recoveries	3,008,707	2,559,760	2,319,000	2,465,000	2,634,000
Income from Investment Account	188,825	161,550	125,749	89,443	85,747
State Scheme Premiums[2]	36,733	30,861	56,408	32,622	29,318
Other receipts	46,401	36,164	29,586	23,292	786
Redundancy receipts	49,274	38,320	39,995	36,932	30,758
Total Receipts	**81,753,716**	**81,946,589**	**84,807,252**	**91,359,851**	**98,842,235**
Less					
Payments					
Benefit payments	82,357,733	87,464,810	88,933,118	91,759,523	94,656,169
of which					
State Pension	*74,110,982*	*80,008,745*	*82,522,101*	*85,893,497*	*88,688,966*
Incapacity Benefit	*4,981,255*	*3,355,345*	*1,213,380*	*233,704*	*61,610*
Employment and Support Alllowance	*1,410,890*	*2,312,374*	*3,554,301*	*4,130,282*	*4,460,807*
Jobseeker's Allowance (Contributory)	*757,582*	*669,184*	*533,630*	*375,940*	*307,176*
Bereavement Benefits	*605,011*	*598,431*	*587,821*	*579,061*	*569,630*
Maternity Allowance	*366,968*	*395,522*	*397,608*	*420,518*	*438,501*
Christmas Bonus	*123,203*	*123,308*	*122,356*	*124,521*	*127,458*
Guardian's Allowance and Child's Special Allowance	*1,842*	*1,901*	*1,921*	*2,000*	*2,021*
Personal Pensions[1]	2,139,042	2,124,560	15,913	1,448	-
Administrative costs	1,125,019	916,875	903,502	*806,386*	801,220
Redundancy payments	406,631	453,577	356,069	*276,708*	285,014
Transfers to Northern Ireland NIF	145,000	334,000	315,000	*609,000*	690,000
Other payments	150,277	163,730	170,778	*167,370*	171,217
Total Payments	**86,323,702**	**91,457,552**	**90,694,380**	**93,620,435**	**96,603,620**
Excess of payments over receipts	(4,569,986)	(9,510,963)	(5,887,128)	(2,260,584)	(2,238,615)
Opening balance	43,163,939	38,593,953	29,082,990	23,195,862	20,935,278
Less excess of payments over receipts	(4,569,986)	(9,510,963)	(5,887,128)	(2,260,584)	(2,238,615)
Closing balance	**38,593,953**	**29,082,990**	**23,195,862**	**20,935,278**	**23,173,893**

Source: HM Revenue and Customs, Department for Work and Pensions

1. On 5 April 2012 the abolition of contracting-out on a defined contribution basis took place resulting in these contributions no longer being received. As the payments were made a year in arrears, from April 2013, the number of transactions has greatly reduced as only late payments and recoveries are being dealt with.

2. State Scheme Premiums are payable to the Fund in respect of employed persons' who cease to be covered, in certain specified circumstances, by a contracted-out pension scheme.

3. Opening balance has been restated based on analysis of prior year data as better management information has become available.

5.2 National Insurance Contributions

For the year ended 31 March

	Notes	2012	2013	2014	2015	2016	2017
Contributions							
Class 1 (employed earner)	i	75,528,875	75,873,021	79,067,796	80,814,248	83,138,168	92,145,709
Class 1A and 1B	ii	987,226	1,047,965	1,118,263	1,078,274	1,119,605	1,227,184
Class 2 (Self-employed flat rate)	iii	229,516	341,361	327,180	353,608	191,127	400,864
Class 3 (Voluntary contributions)	iv	48,876	40,274	31,627	23,129	29,897	12,809
Class 3A (Voluntary contributions)	v	-	-	-	-	58,277	98,784
Class 4 (Self-employed earnings related	vi	1,629,283	1,817,313	1,689,648	1,842,303	1,924,552	1,967,644
		78,423,776	**79,119,934**	**82,236,514**	**84,112,562**	**86,461,626**	**95,852,994**

Source: HMRC National Insurance Fund Account Great Britain

Notes

i. **Class 1** contributions comprise two parts: primary contributions payable by employees and secondary contributions payable by employers.

ii. **Class 1A** contributions are paid by employers on most benefits provided to employees. Employers pay Class 1A contributions to HMRC via the Pay As You Earn scheme with their Class 1 contributions.
Class 1B contributions are payable by employers where they have entered into a PAYE settlement agreement for tax enabling them to settle their National Insurance and income tax liability in a lump sum after the end of the tax year. The figures for Class 1A and Class 1B have been combined.

iii. **Class 2** self-employed persons pay flat rate weekly contributions. From 6 April 2018, Class 2 contributions will be abolished.

iv. **Class 3** voluntary flat rate contributions are paid to maintain contributors' National Insurance record for certain benefit and/or pension purposes.

v. **Class 3A** allows pensioners who have reached state pension age before 6 April 2016 to boost their retirement incomes by making voluntary payments of NICs. The scheme was available for 18 months between October 2015 and April 2017.

vi. **Class 4** self employed persons pay earnings related contributions. From 6 April 2018, Class **4** contributions will be reformed to include a new threshold.

5.3 Main Features of National Insurance Contributions (NCIS) 1999-2000 to 2017-18

	Rate in 1999-2000	Rate in 2000-2001	Rate in 2001-2002	Rate in 2002-2003	Rate in 2003-2004	Rate in 2004-2005	Rate in 2005-2006	Rate in 2006-2007	Rate in 2007-2008	Rate in 2008-2009
Class 1										
Lower earnings limit (LEL) – a week	£66	£67	£72	£75	£77	£79	£82	£84	£87	£90
Primary threshold (PT) – a week	-	£76	£87	£89	£89	£91	£94	£97	£100	£105
Secondary threshold (ST) – a week	£83	£84	£87	£89	£89	£91	£94	£97	£100	£105
Upper Secondary Threshold (under 21) (UST) – a week (1)	-	-	-	-	-	-	-	-	-	-
Apprentice Upper Secondary Threshold (apprentice under 25) (AUST) – a week (2)	-	-	-	-	-	-	-	-	-	-
Upper accruals Point (UAP) – a week (3)	-	-	-	-	-	-	-	-	-	-
Upper earnings limit (UEL) – a week (4)	£500	£535	£575	£585	£595	£610	£630	£645	£670	£770
Primary contributions (employee)										
Main contribution rate (PT to UEL) (5)	10.0%	10.0%	10.0%	10.0%	11.0%	11.0%	11.0%	11.0%	11.0%	11.0%
Additional contribution rate (above UEL)	-	-	-	-	1.0%	1.0%	1.0%	1.0%	1.0%	1.0%
Contracted out rebate (LEL to UAP/UEL) (6) (7)	1.6%	1.6%	1.6%	1.6%	1.6%	1.6%	1.6%	1.6%	1.6%	1.6%
Reduced rate for married women and widow optants (8)	3.85%	3.85%	3.85%	3.85%	4.85%	4.85%	4.85%	4.85%	4.85%	4.85%
Secondary contributions (employer)										
Contribution rate (above ST)	12.2%	12.2%	11.9%	11.8%	12.8%	12.8%	12.8%	12.8%	12.8%	12.8%
Contracted out rebate (LEL to UAP/UEL) (7)										
- COSRS	3.0%	3.0%	3.0%	3.5%	3.5%	3.5%	3.5%	3.5%	3.7%	3.7%
- COMPS (9)	0.6%	0.6%	0.6%	1.0%	1.0%	1.0%	1.0%	1.0%	1.4%	1.4%
Class 1A and 1B										
Contribution rate (10)	12.2%	12.2%	11.9%	11.8%	12.8%	12.8%	12.8%	12.8%	12.8%	12.8%
Class 2										
Flat-rate contribution – a week	£6.55	£2.00	£2.00	£2.00	£2.00	£2.05	£2.10	£2.10	£2.20	£2.30
Small earnings exception / Small Profits Threshold – a year (13)	£3,770	£3,825	£3,955	£4,025	£4,095	£4,215	£4,345	£4,465	£4,635	£4,825
Class 3										
Flat-rate contribution – a week (11)	£6.45	£6.55	£6.75	£6.85	£6.95	£7.15	£7.35	£7.55	£7.80	£8.10
Class 4										
Lower profits limit (LPL) – a year	£7,530	£4,385	£4,535	£4,615	£4,615	£4,745	£4,895	£5,035	£5,225	£5,435
Upper profits limit (UPL) – a year (4)	£26,000	£27,820	£29,900	£30,420	£30,940	£31,720	£32,760	£33,540	£34,840	£40,040
Main contribution rate (LPL to UPL)	6%	7%	7%	7%	8%	8%	8%	8%	8%	8%
Additional contribution rate (above UPL)	-	-	-	-	1%	1%	1%	1%	1%	1%

Source: HM Revenue & Customs

5.3 Main Features of National Insurance Contributions (NCIS) 1999-2000 to 2017-18

	Rate in 2009-2010	Rate in 2010-11	Rate in 2011-12	Rate in 2012-13 (12)	Rate in 2013-14 (12)	Rate in 2014-15 (12)	Rate in 2015-16 (12)	Rate in 2016-17 (12)	Rate in 2017-18 (12)
Class 1									
Lower earnings limit (LEL) – a week	£95	£97	£102	£107	£109	£111	£112	£112	£113
Primary threshold (PT) – a week	£110	£110	£139	£146	£149	£153	£155	£155	£157
Secondary threshold (ST) – a week	£110	£110	£136	£144	£148	£153	£156	£156	£157
Upper Secondary Threshold (under 21) (UST) – a week (1)	-	-	-	-	-	-	£815	£827	£866
Apprentice Upper Secondary Threshold (apprentice under 25) (AUST) – a week (2)	-	-	-	-	-	-	-	£827	£866
Upper accruals Point (UAP) – a week (3)	£770	£770	£770	£770	£770	£770	£770	-	-
Upper earnings limit (UEL) – a week (4)	£844	£844	£817	£817	£797	£805	£815	£827	£866
Primary contributions (employee)									
Main contribution rate (PT to UEL) (5)	11.0%	11.0%	12.0%	12.0%	12.0%	12.0%	12.0%	12.0%	12.0%
Additional contribution rate (above UEL)	1.0%	1.0%	2.0%	2.0%	2.0%	2.0%	2.0%	2.0%	2.0%
Contracted out rebate (LEL to UAP/UEL) (6) (7)	1.6%	1.6%	1.6%	1.4%	1.4%	1.4%	1.4%	-	-
Reduced rate for married women and widow optants (8)	4.85%	4.85%	5.85%	5.85%	5.85%	5.85%	5.85%	5.85%	5.85%
Secondary contributions (employer)									
Contribution rate (above ST)	12.8%	12.8%	13.8%	13.8%	13.8%	13.8%	13.8%	13.8%	13.8%
Contracted out rebate (LEL to UAP/UEL) (7)									
- COSRS	3.7%	3.7%	3.7%	3.4%	3.4%	3.4%	3.4%	-	-
- COMPS (9)	1.4%	1.4%	1.4%	-	-	-	-	-	-
Class 1A and 1B									
Contribution rate (10)	12.8%	12.8%	13.8%	13.8%	13.8%	13.8%	13.8%	13.8%	13.8%
Class 2									
Flat-rate contribution – a week	£2.40	£2.40	£2.50	£2.65	£2.70	£2.75	£2.80	£2.80	£2.85
Small earnings exception / Small Profits Threshold – a year (13)	£5,075	£5,075	£5,315	£5,595	£5,725	£5,885	£5,965	£5,965	£6,025
Class 3									
Flat-rate contribution – a week (11)	£12.05	£12.05	£12.60	£13.25	£13.55	£13.90	£14.10	£14.10	£14.25
Class 4									
Lower profits limit (LPL) – a year	£5,715	£5,715	£7,225	£7,605	£7,755	£7,956	£8,060	£8,060	£8,164
Upper profits limit (UPL) – a year (4)	£43,875	£43,875	£42,475	£42,475	£41,450	£41,865	£42,385	£43,000	£45,000
Main contribution rate (LPL to UPL)	8%	8%	9%	9%	9%	9%	9%	9%	9%
Additional contribution rate (above UPL)	1%	1%	2%	2%	2%	2%	2%	2%	2%

Source: HM Revenue & Customs

5.3 Main Features of National Insurance Contributions (NCIS) 1999-2000 to 2017-18

(1) From 6 April 2015 employers with employees under 21 years old do not pay Class 1 secondary National Insurance contributions (NICs) on earnings up to the Upper Secondary Threshold (UST) for those employees. An employer must choose the appropriate National Insurance contribution category letter to have the exemption applied

(2) From 6 April 2016 employers of apprentices under 25 years old who are following an approved UK government statutory apprenticeship framework do not pay Class 1 secondary National Insurance contributions(NICs) on earnings up to the Apprentices Upper Secondary Threshold (AUST) for those apprentices. An employer must choose the appropriate National Insurance contribution category letter to have the exemption applied.

(3) The upper accruals point was introduced in April 2009 until April 2015-16. It is no longer needed after the contracting out rebates are abolished from 2016-17 onwards.

(4) From April 2009 the upper earnings limit and upper profits limit were aligned to the income tax higher rate threshold.

(5) Between LEL and UEL for 1999-2000.

(6) For Appropriate Personal Pension Schemes (APPS) both employer and employee pay NICs at the full contracted-out rate and in the following tax year on submission of the end-of-year returns HMRC pay an age related rebate direct to the schemes. The employee's share of this rebate is 1.6%.

(7) Up to and including 2008-09, the rebate applies between the LEL and the UEL. From 2009-10 onwards the rebate applies between the LEL and UAP. The rebates are abolished from 2016-17 onwards.

(8) Married women opting to pay contributions at the reduced rate earn no entitlement to contributory National Insurance benefits as a result of these contributions. No women have been allowed to exercise this option since 1977.

(9) For employers operating a COMPS, in addition to the reduction shown in secondary Class 1 contributions, in the following tax year on submission of end-of-year returns, HMRC pay an additional "top-up" rebate direct to the scheme. As with APPS, this rebate is age related. COMPs are abolished from 2012-13 onwards.

(10) From April 2000 the Class 1A liability for employers was extended from company cars and fuel to include other taxable benefits not already attracting a Class 1 liability. Class 1A and Class 1B contributions are paid in the year following accrual.

(11) Class 3 contribution rules changed in 2009-10 to allow those reaching state pension age before April 2015 with 20 qualifying years to purchase up to 6 additional years.

(12) From 2012-13 the default indexation assumption for NICs is CPI (excluding the secondary threshold up until 2016-17).

(13) The Small Profits Threshold replaced the Small Earnings Exception on 6 April 2015.

Notes:

Class 1 National Insurance Contributions (NICs)

Class 1 NICs are earnings related contributions paid by employed earners and their employers. Liability starts at age 16 and ends at Sate Pension age for earners; employers continue to pay beyond State Pension age. Up to April 2016 the contributions were paid at either the contracted-out rate or the not contracted-out rate. The contracted-out rate, abolished in April 2016, was payable payable only where the employee was a member of a contracted-out occupational scheme in place of State Second Pension (formerly SERPS).

Class 1 NICs are collected by HMRC along with income tax under the Pay As You Earn (PAYE) scheme.

Class 1A National Insurance Contributions (NICs)

Class 1A NICs are paid only by employers on the value of most taxable benefits-in-kind provided to employees, such as private use of company cars and fuel, private medical insurance, accommodation and loan benefits. They do not give any benefit rights.

Class 1B National Insurance Contributions (NICs)

Class 1B NICs were introduced on 6 April 1999. Like Class 1A they are also paid only by employers and cover PAYE Settlement Agreements (PSA) under which employers agree to meet the income tax liability arising on a restricted range of benefits. Class 1B is payable on the value of the items included in the PSA that would otherwise attract a Class 1 or Class 1A liability and the value of the income tax met by the employer. They do not give any benefit rights.

Class 2 National Insurance Contributions (NICs)

Class 2 contributions are a flat rate weekly liability payable by all self-employed people over 16 (up to State Pension age) with profits above the Small Profits Threshold. Self-employed people with profits below the Small Profits Threshold may pay Class 2 contributions voluntary. Voluntary payments of Class 2 NICs are typically collected through self-assessment but can usually be paid up to six years after the tax year. Class 4 NICs may also have to be paid by the self-employed if their profits for the year are over the lower profits limit (see below).

Class 3 National Insurance Contributions (NICs)

Class 3 NICs may be paid voluntarily by people aged 16 and over (but below State Pension age) to help them qualify for State Pension if their contribution record would not otherwise be sufficient. Contributions are flat rate and can be paid up to six years after the year in which they are due.

Class 4 National Insurance Contributions (NICs)

Class 4 NICS are paid by the self-employed whose profits are above the lower profits limit. They are profit related and do not count for any benefits themselves.

5.4 Proposed benefit and pension rates 2016 to 2017

(Weekly rates unless otherwise shown)	RATES 2015	RATES 2016
ATTENDANCE ALLOWANCE		
higher rate	82.30	82.30
lower rate	55.10	55.10
BEREAVEMENT BENEFIT		
Bereavement payment (lump sum)	2000.00	2000.00
Widowed parent's allowance	112.55	112.55
Bereavement Allowance		
standard rate	112.55	112.55
age-related		
age 54	104.67	104.67
53	96.79	96.79
52	88.91	88.91
51	81.04	81.04
50	73.16	73.16
49	65.28	65.28
48	57.40	57.40
47	49.52	49.52
46	41.64	41.64
45	33.77	33.77
BENEFIT CAP		
In Housing Benefit (weekly rate)		
Couples and lone parents	500.00	500.00
Single persons without children	350.00	350.00
In Universal Credit (monthly rate)		
Joint claimants and single claimants with children	2167.00	2167.00
Single claimants, no dependent children	1517.00	1517.00
CAPITAL LIMITS - rules common to Income Support, income based Jobseeker's Allowance, income-related Employment and Support Allowance, Pension Credit, and Housing Benefit, and Universal Credit unless stated otherwise		
upper limit	16000.00	16000.00
upper limit - Pension Credit and those getting Housing Benefit and Pension Credit Guarantee Credit	No limit	No limit
Amount disregarded - all benefits except Pension Credit and Housing Benefit for those above the qualifying age for Guarantee Credit	6000.00	6000.00
Amount disregarded - Pension Credit and Housing Benefit for those above the qualifying age for Pension Credit	10000.00	10000.00
child disregard (not Pension Credit, Employment and Support Allowance nor Housing Benefit)	3000.00	3000.00
Amount disregarded (living in RC/NH)	10000.00	10000.00

5.4 Proposed benefit and pension rates 2016 to 2017

(Weekly rates unless otherwise shown)	RATES 2015	RATES 2016
Tariff income		
£1 for every £250, or part thereof, between the amount of capital disregarded and the capital upper limit		
Tariff income - Pension Credit and Housing Benefit where claimant/partner is over Guarantee Credit qualifying age		
£1 for every £500, or part thereof, above or between the amount of capital disregarded and any capital upper limit applicable		
CARER'S ALLOWANCE	62.10	62.10
DEDUCTIONS - rules common to Income Support, Jobseeker's Allowance, Employment and Support Allowance, Pension Credit and Housing Benefit unless stated otherwise		
Non-dependant deductions from housing benefit and from IS, JSA(IB), ESA(IR) and Pension Credit		
aged 25 and over in receipt of IS and JSA(IB), or any age in receipt of main phase ESA(IR), aged 18 or over, not in remunerative work	14.55	14.65
aged 18 or over and in remunerative work		
- gross income: less than £133	14.55	14.65
- gross income: £133 to £194.99	33.40	33.65
- gross income: £195 to £252.99	45.85	46.20
- gross income: £253 to £337.99	75.05	75.60
- gross income: £338 to £419.99	85.45	86.10
- gross income: £420 and above	93.80	94.50
Deductions from housing benefit		
Service charges for fuel		
heating	28.80	28.80
hot water	3.35	3.35
lighting	2.30	2.30
cooking	3.35	3.35
Amount ineligible for meals		
three or more meals a day		
single claimant	26.85	26.85
each person in family aged 16 or over	26.85	26.85
each child under 16	13.60	13.60
less than three meals a day		
single claimant	17.85	17.85
each person in family aged 16 or over	17.85	17.85
each child under 16	9.00	9.00
breakfast only - claimant and each member of the family	3.30	3.30
Amount for personal expenses (not HB)	24.00	24.00
Third party deductions from IS, JSA(IB), ESA(IR) and Pension Credit for;		
arrears of housing, fuel and water costs council tax etc. and deductions for ELDS and ILS.	3.70	3.70
child support, contribution towards maintenance (CTM)		
standard deduction	7.40	7.40

5.4 Proposed benefit and pension rates 2016 to 2017

(Weekly rates unless otherwise shown)	RATES 2015	RATES 2016
lower deduction	3.70	3.70
arrears of Community Charge		
court order against claimant	3.70	3.70
court order against couple	5.75	5.75
fine or compensation order		
standard rate	5.00	5.00
lower rate	3.70	3.70
Maximum deduction rates for recovery of overpayments (not JSA(C)/ESA(C))		
ordinary overpayments	11.10	11.10
Fraud Overpayments	29.60	29.60
Deductions from JSA(C) and ESA (C)		
Arrears of Comm. Charge & overpayment recovery		
Age 16 - 24	19.30	19.30
Age 25 +	24.36	24.36
Arrears of Council Tax & Fines		
Age 16 - 24	23.16	23.16
Age 25 +	29.24	29.24
Max. deduction for arrears of Child Maintenance		
Age 16 - 24	19.30	19.30
Age 25 +	24.36	24.36
DEPENDENCY INCREASES		
Adult dependency increases for spouse or person looking after children - payable with;		
State Pension on own insurance (Cat A or B)	65.70	65.70
long term Incapacity Benefit	61.20	61.20
Severe Disablement Allowance	36.75	36.75
Carers Allowance	36.55	36.55
short-term Incapacity Benefit (over state pension age)	58.90	58.90
short-term Incapacity Benefit (under State Pension age)	47.65	47.65
Child Dependency Increases - payable with;		
State Pension; Widowed Mothers/Parents Allowance;	11.35	11.35
short-term Incapacity benefit - higher rate or over state pension age;		
long-term Incapacity Benefit; Carer's Allowance; Severe Disablement; Unemployability Supplement.		
NB - The rate of child dependency increase is adjusted where it is payable for the eldest child for whom child benefit is also paid. The weekly rate in such cases is reduced by the difference (less £3.65) between the ChB rates for the eldest and subsequent children.	8.00	8.00

5.4 Proposed benefit and pension rates 2016 to 2017

(Weekly rates unless otherwise shown)	RATES 2015	RATES 2016
DISABILITY LIVING ALLOWANCE		
Care Component		
Highest	82.30	82.30
Middle	55.10	55.10
Lowest	21.80	21.80
Mobility Component		
Higher	57.45	57.45
Lower	21.80	21.80
DISREGARDS		
Housing Benefit		
Earnings disregards		
standard (single claimant)	5.00	5.00
couple	10.00	10.00
higher (special occupations/circumstances)	20.00	20.00
lone parent	25.00	25.00
childcare charges	175.00	175.00
childcare charges (2 or more children)	300.00	300.00
permitted work higher	104.00	115.50
permitted work lower	20.00	20.00
Other Income disregards		
adult maintenance disregard	15.00	15.00
war disablement pension and war widows pension	10.00	10.00
widowed mothers/parents allowance	15.00	15.00
Armed Forces Compensation Scheme	10.00	10.00
student loan	10.00	10.00
student's covenanted income	5.00	5.00
income from boarders (plus 50% of the balance)	20.00	20.00
additional earnings disregard	17.10	17.10
income from subtenants (£20 fixed from April 08)	20.00	20.00
Income Support, income-based Jobseeker's Allowance, Income-related Employment and Support Allowance (ESA(IR)) and Pension Credit		
Earnings disregards		
standard (single claimant) (not ESA(IR))	5.00	5.00
couple (not ESA(IR))	10.00	10.00
higher (special occupations/circumstances)	20.00	20.00
partner of claimant (ESA(IR))	20.00 (maximum)	20.00 (maximum)
Other Income disregards		
war disablement pension and war widows pension	10.00	10.00
widowed mothers/parents allowance	10.00	10.00
Armed Forces Compensation Scheme	10.00	10.00
student loan (not Pension Credit)	10.00	10.00
student's covenanted income (not Pension Credit)	5.00	5.00
income from boarders (plus 50% of the balance)	20.00	20.00
income from subtenants (£20 fixed from April 08)	20.00	20.00

5.4 Proposed benefit and pension rates 2016 to 2017

(Weekly rates unless otherwise shown)	RATES 2015	RATES 2016
EARNINGS RULES		
Carers Allowance	110.00	110.00
Limit of earnings from councillor's allowance	104.00	115.50
Permitted work earnings limit - higher	104.00	115.50
- lower	20.00	20.00
Industrial injuries unemployability supplement permitted earnings level (annual amount)	5408.00	6006.00
Earnings level at which adult dependency (ADI) increases are affected with:		
short-term incap.benefit where claimant is		
(a) under state pension age	47.65	47.65
(b) over state pension age	58.90	58.90
state pension, long term incapacity benefit, severe disablement allowance, unemployability supplement - payable when dependant		
(a) is living with claimant	73.10	73.10
(b) still qualifies for the tapered earnings rule	45.09	45.09
Earnings level at which ADI is affected when dependant is not living with claimant;		
state pension,	65.70	65.70
long-term incapacity benefit,	61.20	61.20
unemployability supplement,	62.10	62.10
severe disablement allowance	36.75	36.75
Carers allowance	36.55	36.55
Earnings level at which child dependency increases are affected		
for first child	230.00	230.00
additional amount for each subsequent child	30.00	30.00
Pension income threshold for incapacity benefit	85.00	85.00
Pension income threshold for contributory Employment Support Allowance	85.00	85.00
EMPLOYMENT AND SUPPORT ALLOWANCE		
Personal Allowances		
Single		
under 25	57.90	57.90
25 or over	73.10	73.10
lone parent		
under 18	57.90	57.90
18 or over	73.10	73.10
couple		
both under 18	57.90	57.90

5.4 Proposed benefit and pension rates 2016 to 2017

(Weekly rates unless otherwise shown)	RATES 2015	RATES 2016
both under 18 with child	87.50	87.50
both under 18 (main phase)	73.10	73.10
both under 18 with child (main phase)	114.85	114.85
one 18 or over, one under 18 (certain conditions apply)	114.85	114.85
both over 18	114.85	114.85
claimant under 25, partner under 18	57.90	57.90
claimant 25 or over, partner under 18	73.10	73.10
claimant (main phase), partner under 18	73.10	73.10
Premiums		
enhanced disability		
single	15.75	15.75
couple	22.60	22.60
severe disability		
single	61.85	61.85
couple (lower rate)	61.85	61.85
couple (higher rate)	123.70	123.70
carer	34.60	34.60
pensioner		
single with WRAC	49.05	53.45
single with support component	41.90	46.30
single with no component	78.10	82.50
couple with WRAC	86.95	93.65
couple with support component	79.80	86.50
couple with no component	116.00	122.70
Components		
Work-related Activity	29.05	29.05
Support	36.20	36.20
HOUSING BENEFIT		
Personal allowances		
single		
under 25	57.90	57.90
25 or over	73.10	73.10
entitled to main phase ESA	73.10	73.10
lone parent		
under 18	57.90	57.90
18 or over	73.10	73.10
entitled to main phase ESA	73.10	73.10
couple		
both under 18	87.50	87.50
one or both 18 or over	114.85	114.85
claimant entitled to main phase ESA	114.85	114.85
dependent children	66.90	66.90

5.4 Proposed benefit and pension rates 2016 to 2017

(Weekly rates unless otherwise shown)	RATES 2015	RATES 2016
pensioner		
single/lone parent has attained the qualifying age for Pension Credit but under 65	151.20	155.60
couple – one or both has attained the qualifying age for Pension Credit but both under 65	230.85	237.55
single / lone parent - 65 and over	166.05	168.70
couple - one or both 65 and over	248.30	252.30
Premiums		
family	17.45	17.45
family (lone parent rate)	22.20	22.20
disability		
single	32.25	32.25
couple	45.95	45.95
enhanced disability		
single	15.75	15.75
disabled child	24.43	24.43
couple	22.60	22.60
severe disability		
single	61.85	61.85
couple (lower rate)	61.85	61.85
couple (higher rate)	123.70	123.70
disabled child	60.06	60.06
carer	34.60	34.60
ESA components		
work-related activity	29.05	29.05
support	36.20	36.20
INCAPACITY BENEFIT		
Long-term Incapacity Benefit	105.35	105.35
Short-term Incapacity Benefit (under state pension age)		
lower rate	79.45	79.45
higher rate	94.05	94.05
Short-term Incapacity Benefit (over state pension age)		
lower rate	101.10	101.10
higher rate	105.35	105.35
Increase of Long-term Incapacity Benefit for age		
higher rate	11.15	11.15
lower rate	6.20	6.20
Invalidity Allowance (Transitional)		
higher rate	11.15	11.15
middle rate	6.20	6.20
lower rate	6.20	6.20

5.4 Proposed benefit and pension rates 2016 to 2017

(Weekly rates unless otherwise shown)	RATES 2015	RATES 2016
INCOME SUPPORT		
Personal Allowances		
single		
under 25	57.90	57.90
25 or over	73.10	73.10
lone parent		
under 18	57.90	57.90
18 or over	73.10	73.10
couple		
both under 18	57.90	57.90
both under 18 - higher rate	87.50	87.50
one under 18, one under 25	57.90	57.90
one under 18, one 25 and over	73.10	73.10
both 18 or over	114.85	114.85
dependent children	66.90	66.90
Premiums		
family / lone parent	17.45	17.45
pensioner (applies to couples only)	116.00	122.70
disability		
single	32.25	32.25
couple	45.95	45.95
enhanced disability		
single	15.75	15.75
disabled child	24.43	24.43
couple	22.60	22.60
severe disability		
single	61.85	61.85
couple (lower rate)	61.85	61.85
couple (higher rate)	123.70	123.70
disabled child	60.06	60.06
carer	34.60	34.60
Relevant sum for strikers	40.50	40.50
INDUSTRIAL DEATH BENEFIT		
Widow's pension		
higher rate	115.95	119.30
lower rate	34.79	35.79
Widower's pension	115.95	119.30
INDUSTRIAL INJURIES DISABLEMENT BENEFIT		
Standard rate		
100%	168.00	168.00
90%	151.20	151.20
80%	134.40	134.40
70%	117.60	117.60
60%	100.80	100.80
50%	84.00	84.00

5.4 Proposed benefit and pension rates 2016 to 2017

(Weekly rates unless otherwise shown)	RATES 2015	RATES 2016
40%	67.20	67.20
30%	50.40	50.40
20%	33.60	33.60
Maximum life gratuity (lump sum)	11150.00	11150.00
Unemployability Supplement	103.85	103.85
increase for early incapacity		
higher rate	21.50	21.50
middle rate	13.90	13.90
lower rate	6.95	6.95
Maximum reduced earnings allowance	67.20	67.20
Maximum retirement allowance	16.80	16.80
Constant attendance allowance		
exceptional rate	134.40	134.40
intermediate rate	100.80	100.80
normal maximum rate	67.20	67.20
part-time rate	33.60	33.60
Exceptionally severe disablement allowance	67.20	67.20
JOBSEEKER'S ALLOWANCE		
Contribution based JSA - Personal rates		
under 25	57.90	57.90
25 or over	73.10	73.10
Income-based JSA - personal allowances		
under 25	57.90	57.90
25 or over	73.10	73.10
lone parent		
under 18	57.90	57.90
18 or over	73.10	73.10
couple		
both under 18	57.90	57.90
both under 18 - higher rate	87.50	87.50
one under 18, one under 25	57.90	57.90
one under 18, one 25 and over	73.10	73.10
both 18 or over	114.85	114.85
dependent children	66.90	66.90
Premiums		
family / lone parent	17.45	17.45
Pensioner		
Single	78.10	82.50
Couple	116.00	122.70
disability		
single	32.25	32.25
couple	45.95	45.95
enhanced disability		
single	15.75	15.75
disabled child	24.43	24.43

5.4 Proposed benefit and pension rates 2016 to 2017

(Weekly rates unless otherwise shown)	RATES 2015	RATES 2016
couple	22.60	22.60
severe disability		
single	61.85	61.85
couple (lower rate)	61.85	61.85
couple (higher rate)	123.70	123.70
disabled child	60.06	60.06
Carer	34.60	34.60
Prescribed sum for strikers	40.50	40.50
MATERNITY ALLOWANCE		
Standard rate	139.58	139.58
MA threshold	30.00	30.00
PENSION CREDIT		
Standard minimum guarantee		
Single	151.20	155.60
Couple	230.85	237.55
Additional amount for severe disability		
Single	61.85	61.85
couple (one qualifies)	61.85	61.85
couple (both qualify)	123.70	123.70
Additional amount for carers	34.60	34.60
Savings credit		
threshold - single	126.50	133.82
threshold - couple	201.80	212.97
maximum - single	14.82	13.07
maximum - couple	17.43	14.75
Amount for claimant and first spouse in polygamous marriage	230.85	237.55
Additional amount for additional spouse	79.65	81.95
Non-State Pensions (for Pension Credit purposes)		
Statutory minimum increase to non-state pensions	1.20%	0.00%
PERSONAL INDEPENDENCE PAYMENT		
Daily living component		
Enhanced	82.30	82.30
Standard	55.10	55.10
Mobility component		
Enhanced	57.45	57.45
Standard	21.80	21.80
SEVERE DISABLEMENT ALLOWANCE		
Basic rate	74.65	74.65
Age-related addition (from Dec 90)		
Higher rate	11.15	11.15
Middle rate	6.20	6.20
Lower rate	6.20	6.20

5.4 Proposed benefit and pension rates 2016 to 2017

(Weekly rates unless otherwise shown)	RATES 2015	RATES 2016
STATE PENSION		
Category A or B	115.95	119.30
Category B(lower) - spouse or civil partner's insurance	69.50	71.50
Category C or D - non-contributory	69.50	71.50
Additional pension	1.20%	0.00%
Increments to:-		
Basic pension	1.20%	0.00%
Additional pension	1.20%	0.00%
Graduated Retirement Benefit (GRB)	1.20%	0.00%
Inheritable lump sum	1.20%	0.00%
Contracted-out Deduction from AP in respect of pre-April 1988 contracted-out earnings	Nil	Nil
Contracted-out Deduction from AP in respect of contracted-out earnings from April 1988 to 1997	1.20%	0.00%
Graduated Retirement Benefit (unit)	0.1330	0.1330
Increase of long term incapacity for age	1.20%	0.00%
Addition at age 80	0.25	0.25
Increase of Long-term incapacity for age		
higher rate	21.50	21.50
lower rate	10.80	10.80
Invalidity Allowance (Transitional) for State Pension recipients		
higher rate	21.50	21.50
middle rate	13.90	13.90
lower rate	6.95	6.95
NEW STATE PENSION		155.65
STATUTORY ADOPTION PAY		
Earnings threshold	112.00	112.00
Standard Rate	139.58	139.58
STATUTORY MATERNITY PAY		
Earnings threshold	112.00	112.00
Standard rate	139.58	139.58
STATUTORY PATERNITY PAY		
Earnings threshold	112.00	112.00
Standard Rate	139.58	139.58
Additional statutory paternity pay	139.58	139.58
STATUTORY SHARED PARENTAL PAY		
Earnings threshold	112.00	112.00
Standard rate	139.58	139.58
STATUTORY SICK PAY		
Earnings threshold	112.00	112.00
Standard rate	88.45	88.45

5.4 Proposed benefit and pension rates 2016 to 2017

(Weekly rates unless otherwise shown)	RATES 2015	RATES 2016
UNIVERSAL CREDIT (monthly rates)		
Universal Credit Minimum Amount	0.01	0.01
Universal Credit Amounts		
Standard allowance		
Single		
Single under 25	251.77	251.77
Single 25 or over	317.82	317.82
Couple		
Joint claimants both under 25	395.20	395.20
Joint claimants, one or both 25 or over	498.89	498.89
Child element		
First child	277.08	277.08
Second/ subsequent child	231.67	231.67
Disabled child additions		
Lower rate addition	126.11	126.11
Higher rate addition	367.92	367.92
Limited Capability for Work element	126.11	126.11
Limited Capability for Work and Work-Related Activity element	315.60	315.60
Carer element	150.39	150.39
Childcare costs element		
Maximum for one child	532.29	646.35
Maximum for two or more children	912.50	1108.04
Non-dependants' housing cost contributions	69.37	69.37
Work allowances		
Higher work allowance (no housing element)		
Single		
Single claimant, no dependent children	111.00	Nil
Single claimant, one or more children	734.00	397.00
Single claimant, limited capability for work	647.00	397.00
Joint claimants		
Joint claimant, no dependent children	111.00	Nil
Joint claimant, one or more children	536.00	397.00
Joint claimant, limited capability for work	647.00	397.00
Lower work allowance		
Single		
Single claimant, no dependent children	111.00	Nil
Single claimant, one or more children	263.00	192.00
Single claimant, limited capability for work	192.00	192.00
Joint claimants		
Joint claimant, no dependent children	111.00	Nil
Joint claimant, one or more children	222.00	192.00
Joint claimant, limited capability for work	192.00	192.00
Assumed income from capital for every £250 or part thereof, between capital disregard and upper capital limit	4.35	4.35

Third Party Deductions at 5% of UC Standard Allowance (excludes deductions for rent and service charges included in rent)

5.4 Proposed benefit and pension rates 2016 to 2017

(Weekly rates unless otherwise shown)	RATES 2015	RATES 2016
Single		
Single under 25	12.59	12.59
Single 25 or over	15.89	15.89
Couple		
Joint claimants both under 25	19.76	19.76
Joint claimants, one or both 25 or over	24.94	24.94
Maximum deductions for Fines	108.35	108.35
Minimum deductions for rent and service charges included in rent at 10% of UC Standard Allowance (10% minimum introduced from Nov 2014)		
Single		
Single under 25	25.18	25.18
Single 25 or over	31.78	31.78
Couple		
Joint claimants both under 25	39.52	39.52
Joint claimants, one or both 25 or over	49.89	49.89
Maximum deductions for rent and service charges included in rent at 20% of UC Standard Allowance (20% maximum introduced from Nov 2014)		
Single		
Single under 25	50.35	50.35
Single 25 or over	63.56	63.56
Couple		
Joint claimants both under 25	79.04	79.04
Joint claimants, one or both 25 or over	99.78	99.78
Overall Maximum deduction Rate at 40% of UC Standard Allowance:		
Single		
Single under 25	100.71	100.71
Single 25 or over	127.13	127.13
Couple		
Joint claimants both under 25	158.08	158.08
Joint claimants, one or both 25 or over	199.56	199.56
Fraud Overpayments, Recoverable Hardship Payments and Administrative Penalties at 40% of UC Standard Allowance		
Single		
Single under 25	100.71	100.71
Single 25 or over	127.13	127.13
Couple		
Joint claimants both under 25	158.08	158.08
Joint claimants, one or both 25 or over	199.56	199.56
Ordinary Overpayments and Civil Penalties at 15% of UC Standard Allowance		
Single		
Single under 25	37.77	37.77
Single 25 or over	47.67	47.67
Couple		
Joint claimants both under 25	59.28	59.28
Joint claimants, one or both 25 or over	74.83	74.83
Ordinary Overpayments and Civil Penalties at 25% of UC Standard Allowance if claimant's and/or partner's earnings are over the Work Allowance		

5.4 Proposed benefit and pension rates 2016 to 2017

(Weekly rates unless otherwise shown)	RATES 2015	RATES 2016
Single		
Single under 25	62.94	62.94
Single 25 or over	79.46	79.46
Couple		
Joint claimants both under 25	98.80	98.80
Joint claimants, one or both 25 or over	124.72	124.72
WIDOW'S BENEFIT		
Widowed mother's allowance	112.55	112.55
Widow's pension		
standard rate	112.55	112.55
age-related		
age 54 (49)	104.67	104.67
53 (48)	96.79	96.79
52 (47)	88.91	88.91
51 (46)	81.04	81.04
50 (45)	73.16	73.16
49 (44)	65.28	65.28
48 (43)	57.40	57.40
47 (42)	49.52	49.52
46 (41)	41.64	41.64
45 (40)	33.77	33.77

Source: Department for Work and Pensions

Note: For deaths occurring before 11 April 1988 refer to age-points shown in brackets.

5.5 Number of Persons claiming benefits: Caseloads by age groups, thousands

	2005/06 Outturn	2006/07 Outturn	2007/08 Outturn	2008/09 Outturn	2009/10 Outturn	2010/11 Outturn	2011/12 Outturn	2012/13 Outturn	2013/14 Outturn	2014/15 Outturn	2015/16 Outturn
Benefits directed at Children											
Attendance Allowance (in payment)	-	-	-	-	-	-	-	-	-	-	-
Child Benefit & One Parent Benefit	-	-	-	-	-	-	-	-	-	-	-
number of children covered	-	-	-	-	-	-	-	-	-	-	-
Disability Living Allowance	286	292	300	310	322	331	339	350	362	381	406
of which in payment	286	292	300	310	322	331	339	350	362	381	406
of which entitlement without payment	-	-	-	-	-	-	-	-	-	-	-
Mobility Allowance	-	-	-	-	-	-	-	-	-	-	-
Benefits Directed at People of Working Age											
Armed Forces Independence Payment									1	1	1
Attendance Allowance (in payment)	-	-	-	-	-	-	-	-	-	-	-
Bereavement related benefits	163	147	129	117	108	103	100	97	95	92	92
Carer's Allowance	475	485	496	519	550	584	615	650	675	730	793
of which in payment	422	432	442	462	491	523	558	595	631	679	740
of which entitlement without payment	53	52	54	57	59	61	57	55	44	52	52
Christmas Bonus - non-contributory	1,912	1,920	2,003	3,164	3,246	3,227	3,212	3,240	3,215	3,329	3,565
Council Tax Benefit	2,603	2,570	2,533	2,566	2,940	3,172	3,254	3,368	-	-	-
Disability Living Allowance	1,627	1,657	1,692	1,733	1,780	1,819	1,847	1,877	1,866	1,761	1,566
of which in payment	1,612	1,641	1,676	1,715	1,761	1,800	1,828	1,858	1,846	1,742	1,547
of which entitlement without payment	15	16	16	17	19	19	20	20	20	19	18
Disability Working Allowance	-	-	-	-	-	-	-	-	-	-	-
Employment and Support Allowance	-	-	-	136	391	579	811	1,365	1,912	2,235	2,356
of which contributory	-	-	-	59	145	199	262	364	492	507	489
of which contributory and income-based	-	-	-	6	22	38	59	103	180	248	325
of which income-based	-	-	-	56	168	275	424	784	1,116	1,340	1,398
of which credits only	-	-	-	16	56	67	65	114	124	141	144
Family Credit	-	-	-	-	-	-	-	-	-	-	-
Housing benefits	2,495	2,518	2,527	2,625	2,981	3,224	3,356	3,502	3,520	3,457	3,360
Incapacity Benefit, Invalidity Benefit & Sickness Benefit	2,475	2,443	2,415	2,332	2,031	1,827	1,577	965	366	133	74
of which in payment	1,500	1,456	1,413	1,346	1,177	1,054	909	566	192	38	10
of which credits only	975	987	1,002	986	854	773	668	399	174	95	65
Income Support	2,142	2,135	2,117	2,087	1,935	1,803	1,619	1,254	939	799	706
Industrial Injuries benefits	182	176	170	164	157	152	146	137	137	131	126
Jobseeker's Allowance	870	927	818	1,025	1,538	1,415	1,515	1,507	1,273	885	643
of which contributory	165	157	142	244	321	234	212	178	145	111	77
of which contributory and income-based	15	15	13	21	30	22	19	18	15	11	9
of which income-based	632	691	609	695	1,072	1,069	1,208	1,242	1,045	710	522
of which credits only	58	64	54	66	114	91	77	69	68	53	35
Maternity Allowance	31	30	44	54	56	54	57	60	58	59	62
Mobility Allowance	-	-	-	-	-	-	-	-	-	-	-
Personal Independence Payment	-	-	-	-	-	-	-	-	12	184	569
of which in payment	-	-	-	-	-	-	-	-	12	182	563
of which entitlement without payment	-	-	-	-	-	-	-	-	-	2	6
Severe Disablement Allowance	246	234	221	210	200	191	184	177	167	134	75
Statutory Maternity Pay	154	154	193	245	250	269	266	275	271	264	267
Unemployment Benefit	-	-	-	-	-	-	-	-	-	-	-
Universal Credit (Total)									2	13	130
Benefits Directed at Pensioners											
Attendance Allowance	1,629	1,666	1,700	1,737	1,776	1,782	1,756	1,710	1,641	1,617	1,602
of which in payment	1,445	1,489	1,528	1,568	1,607	1,619	1,597	1,553	1,490	1,462	1,459
of which entitlement without payment	184	177	172	169	169	163	160	158	151	155	143
Bereavement related benefits	23	21	19	14	11	8	6	5	3	2	1
Carer's Allowance	279	319	356	388	411	420	417	405	396	378	378
of which in payment	24	26	28	30	31	30	26	22	22	20	19
of which entitlement without payment	255	292	327	357	381	390	391	383	374	358	359
Christmas Bonus - contributory	12,387	12,586	12,728	11,754	12,123	12,239	12,335	12,346	12,245	12,459	12,757
Council Tax Benefit	2,426	2,510	2,535	2,592	2,631	2,633	2,620	2,544	-	-	-
Disability Living Allowance	864	903	949	991	1,031	1,055	1,066	1,079	1,079	1,072	1,046
of which in payment	859	897	942	984	1,023	1,046	1,057	1,070	1,069	1,062	1,036
of which entitlement without payment	5	6	6	7	8	9	9	9	10	10	10
Housing benefits	1,491	1,503	1,509	1,541	1,566	1,574	1,576	1,551	1,505	1,464	1,417
Incapacity Benefit, Invalidity Benefit & Sickness Benefit	-	-	-	-	-	-	-	-	-	-	-
of which in payment	-	-	-	-	-	-	-	-	-	-	-
of which credits only	-	-	-	-	-	-	-	-	-	-	-
Industrial Injuries benefits	156	159	171	172	176	182	185	187	189	188	187

5.5 Number of Persons claiming benefits: Caseloads by age groups, thousands

	2005/06 Outturn	2006/07 Outturn	2007/08 Outturn	2008/09 Outturn	2009/10 Outturn	2010/11 Outturn	2011/12 Outturn	2012/13 Outturn	2013/14 Outturn	2014/15 Outturn	2015/16 Outturn
Income Support	-	-	-	-	-	-	-	-	-	-	-
Mobility Allowance	-	-	-	-	-	-	-	-	-	-	-
Over-75 TV Licence	3,965	3,982	3,993	4,079	4,206	4,236	4,277	4,316	4,414	4,493	4,360
Pension Credit	2,700	2,729	2,732	2,724	2,736	2,718	2,649	2,505	2,380	2,228	2,098
Personal Independence Payment	-	-	-	-	-	-	-	-	1	17	25
of which in payment	-	-	-	-	-	-	-	-	1	16	24
of which entitlement without payment	-	-	-	-	-	-	-	-	-	-	-
State Pension	11,585	11,715	11,938	12,160	12,410	12,566	12,667	12,810	12,888	12,958	12,957
of which contributory	11,563	11,692	11,914	12,134	12,382	12,537	12,634	12,774	12,846	12,912	12,908
of which basic element	11,492	11,617	11,837	12,053	12,285	12,460	12,556	12,737	12,814	12,887	12,890
of which earnings-related element ("Additional Pension", "SERPS" or	7,700	7,963	8,324	8,673	9,052	9,320	9,549	9,848	10,021	10,207	10,335
of which Graduated Retirement Benefit	9,439	9,594	9,842	10,087	10,358	10,563	10,702	10,874	10,984	11,096	11,145
of which lump sums (covering all contributory elements)	-	8	24	46	58	66	59	56	56	50	47
of which new State Pension (excluding protected payments)											
of which new State Pension Protected Payments											
of which non-contributory only ("Category D")	23	23	25	26	28	29	33	35	42	46	48
Severe Disablement Allowance	42	42	42	41	40	39	36	34	31	29	38
Winter Fuel Payments	11,555	11,750	12,123	12,421	12,681	12,783	12,686	12,683	12,585	12,467	12,215

Source: Department for Work and Pensions (DWP)

Caseloads:

Caseload figures represent an average over the full financial year; caseloads for benefits which commenced or ended during a financial year still reflect an average over the full year.

Revisions:

Some figures for past years may have changed since previous publications and from other sources owing to the incorporation of more up-to-date information, improvements in the methodology used to break down expenditure totals between sub-groups, or minor definitional differences.

Accounting basis:

Figures for 1999/00 onwards are on a Resource Accounting and Budgeting basis. There may be small differences between figures quoted in these tables and those quoted in Department for Work and Pensions Accounts.

Treatment of Universal Credit:

Universal Credit was introduced in October 2013. This will gradually replace Income Support, income-based Jobseeker's Allowance, income-based Employment and Support Allowance and Housing Benefit, along with Child Tax Credit and Working Tax Credit (delivered by Her Majesty's Revenue & Customs at present).

Benefit changes over time:

Where one benefit has been renamed or superseded by another, and the earlier benefit is not shown separately, the most recent name for the benefit is shown, but the figures cover all relevant benefits, as follows:

Bereavement benefits include Widows' Benefits and Bereavement Support Payment.
Carer's Allowance includes Invalid Care Allowance.
Child Benefit includes Family Allowance, and also One Parent Benefit where not shown separately.
Council Tax Benefit includes Community Charge Benefit and Rate Rebate.
Family Credit includes Family Income Supplement.
Income Support includes Supplementary Benefit and National Assistance.
Severe Disablement Allowance includes Non-Contributory Invalidity Pension.

Rounding: Caseloads stated in these tables are rounded to the nearest 1,000, as such totals may not sum due to this rounding.

5.6 Jobseeker's Allowance[1,2,3] claimants: by benefit entitlement
Great Britain

As at May of each year | Thousands

		2006	2007	2008	2009	2010	2011	2012	2013 *	2014 *	2015 *	2016
All Persons												
All with benefit - total	**KXDX**	812	730.8	718	1316.4	1237.3	1298.3	1377	1432.6	1035.3	719.1	562.4
Contribution-based JSA only	**KXDY**	134.6	113.6	127.8	341.8	205.3	182.7	159.5	142.4	97.3	72.7	63.7
Contribution based JSA & income-based JSA	**KXDZ**	13	11.9	12.8	34.6	21.1	19.9	16.8	14.9	10.9	7.1	8.3
Income-based JSA only payment	**KXEA**	664.5	605.3	577.4	940	1010.9	1095.7	1200.7	1156	842.4	583.2	446.0
No benefit in payment	**KXEB**	83.9	76.4	69.9	126.6	117.3	105.8	107.2	119.4	84.7	56.1	44.3
Males												
All with benefit - total	**KXED**	606.8	537.8	529.9	978.9	890.9	879.8	930	938.4	665.7	460.9	351.1
Contribution-based JSA only	**KXEE**	95.8	79.6	90.6	248.7	143.4	118.9	103.5	94.1	62	45.8	39.7
Contribution based JSA & income-based JSA	**KXEF**	12	10.7	11.7	31.2	18.1	16.9	13.7	12.6	8.9	5.9	6.7
Income-based JSA only payment	**KXEG**	498.9	447.5	427.6	698.9	729.5	744	812.8	753	539.1	374.1	277.2
No benefit in payment	**KXEH**	56.6	51.7	46.7	88.8	82.2	69.3	71.6	78.7	55.8	35.1	27.5
Females												
All with benefit - total	**KXEJ**	205.3	193	188.1	337.6	346.4	418.4	447	494.3	369.5	258.2	211.3
Contribution-based JSA only	**KXEK**	38.7	34	37.2	93.1	61.9	63.7	56	48.3	35.3	26.9	24.1
Contribution based JSA & income-based JSA	**KXEL**	1	1.2	1.2	3.4	3.0	3	3.1	2.3	2	1.3	1.7
Income-based JSA only payment	**KXEM**	165.5	157.8	149.8	241.1	281.4	351.7	387.9	403	303.3	209.1	168.8
No benefit in payment	**KXEN**	27.2	24.8	23.2	37.7	35.1	36.5	35.5	40.7	28.9	21	16.8

Sources: Department for Work and Pensions

1. Jobseeker's Allowance (JSA) is a benefit payable to unemployed people. In general, to be entitled to Jobseeker's Allowance, a person must be available for work for at least 40 hours a week, be actively seeking work, and have entered into a Jobseeker's Agreement with Jobcentre Plus.
JSA has two routes of entry: contrbution-based which depends mainly upon national insurance contributions and income-based which depends mainly on a means test. Some claimants can qualify by either route. In practice they receive income-based JSA but have an under lying entitlement to the contribution-based element.

2 Figures are given at May each year and have been derived by applying 5% proportions to 100% totals taken from the DWP 100% Work and Pensions Longitudinal Study (WPLS).

3 Figures are rounded to the nearest hundred and quoted in thousands. They may not sum due to rounding and are subject t sampling variation.

* 5% sample data - DWP recommends that, where the detail is only available on the 5% sample data, the proportions derived should be applied to the overall 100% total for the benefit.

5.7 Employment and Support Allowance and Incapacity Benefit claimants: by sex, age and duration of claim

Great Britain

As at May								Count
	2009	**2010**	**2011**	**2012**	**2013**	**2014**	**2015**	**2016**
Male								
All durations: All ages	**170312**	**301455**	**362360**	**608526**	**935744**	**1150176**	**1242802**	**1245241**
All durations:								
Under 18	1653	2479	2259	2271	2019	2050	2032	1991
18-24	24691	41131	49865	66498	81905	97424	106134	102265
25-34	33024	56314	65655	102628	145989	182064	200254	199231
35-44	38136	68818	81733	136130	192386	222224	238832	236166
45-49	19052	35649	43814	81729	128904	154682	163456	162624
50-54	18037	34339	42363	80507	134578	166363	181195	183348
55-59	20096	36254	43905	83117	142023	172524	184783	185164
Over 60	15619	26465	32762	55644	107932	152839	166109	174456
Unknown	..	6	..	..	6	7	..	..
Over six months:								
Under 18	219	1236	1189	1215	1051	1060	1110	1074
18-24	2330	19451	28819	42317	56118	70828	80459	81034
25-34	3545	26495	36581	57166	96660	138469	162711	166970
35-44	4108	34397	49754	76891	133915	176424	197010	203371
45-49	2106	17933	27191	45594	89026	126235	141176	143902
50-54	1919	17295	26986	44713	91595	136827	158176	164282
55-59	2191	18820	28371	46783	94839	143075	163248	166545
Female								
All durations: All ages	**117971**	**225268**	**299404**	**524288**	**807088**	**989471**	**1092604**	**1119183**
All durations:								
Under 18	1534	2184	2003	2056	1733	1748	1897	1804
18-24	18301	31746	38732	51544	62948	74429	81109	79194
25-34	19431	35806	48626	79634	118000	145272	160866	161629
35-44	29812	58042	77175	124690	171653	194602	209405	207171
45-49	17174	35235	47217	86097	128895	151227	159606	158636
50-54	16342	32168	42737	86361	139806	169241	185858	189239
55-59	15196	29399	38294	82127	144170	175266	190798	194372
Over 60	177	694	4623	11775	39888	77683	103060	127143
Unknown	..	..	..	..	..	6	6	..
Over six months:								
Under 18	**188**	**956**	**909**	**1023**	**832**	**828**	**852**	**898**
18-24	**1845**	**14725**	**22447**	**32575**	**42816**	**52970**	**60473**	**62119**
25-34	**2037**	**17007**	**26269**	**45025**	**79320**	**111593**	**131334**	**136079**
35-44	**2916**	**29034**	**45882**	**74290**	**123122**	**156426**	**173807**	**179403**
45-49	**1672**	**18040**	**29692**	**50423**	**92385**	**125223**	**138465**	**140852**
50-54	**1723**	**16961**	**27748**	**48938**	**98491**	**142033**	**163086**	**170864**
55-59	**1691**	**15893**	**25270**	**45892**	**98324**	**148542**	**170254**	**177561**
Over 60	**45**	**527**	**3181**	**8201**	**27149**	**66385**	**92827**	**117140**

Source: Stat-Xplore, Department for Work and Pensions

".." denotes a nil or negligible number of claimants or award amount based on a nil or negligible number of claimants.

Statistical disclosure control has been applied to this table to avoid the release of confidential data. Totals may not sum due to the disclosure control applied.

The move to publishing benefit data via the Stat-Xplore instead of the DWP Tabulation Tool has involved adopting a new disclosure control methodology, in line with other benefits published via this new tool. Although the data still comes from the same source there may be small differences in the outputs displayed using this new tool, when compared to the Tabulation Tool.

5.8 Attendance Allowance - cases in payment: Age and gender of claimant Great Britain
Great Britain

At May each year										Count
	2007	**2008**	**2009**	**2010**	**2011**	**2012**	**2013**	**2014**	**2015**	**2016**
Males: All ages	478,262	496,991	516,126	531,070	529,570	525,691	504,351	493,165	498,963	503,439
Unknown age	44	23	20	20	24	19	19	21	24	33
65-69	22,797	23,501	24,354	24,752	23,769	23,252	21,122	20,567	24,254	27,308
70-74	66,758	70,191	73,604	74,890	71,909	68,697	63,516	59,777	60,772	62,890
75-79	106,282	109,051	112,296	114,784	113,594	112,183	107,189	103,958	103,978	101,279
80-84	133,053	135,335	137,612	139,715	137,503	135,277	129,925	125,576	125,627	125,765
85-89	98,497	107,708	116,034	118,027	117,833	116,921	112,561	111,066	110,872	110,900
90 and over	50,827	51,192	52,205	58,883	64,942	69,344	70,022	72,204	73,444	75,261
Females: All ages	1,029,019	1,049,375	1,068,964	1,082,436	1,068,797	1,046,878	997,006	962,307	950,845	941,899
Unknown age	26	20	18	23	26	24	33	30	38	40
65-69	28,376	29,128	30,021	30,312	28,687	27,147	23,793	22,440	26,566	30,169
70-74	96,418	99,660	103,449	104,453	99,642	93,820	85,257	78,399	78,187	79,738
75-79	185,714	186,646	188,379	188,345	182,140	176,428	166,160	158,411	155,890	151,438
80-84	278,490	277,675	277,658	276,881	269,083	259,667	244,729	231,714	226,030	220,996
85-89	259,209	276,660	290,707	286,518	279,699	271,425	258,583	249,908	244,734	240,270
90 and over	180,784	179,590	178,729	195,903	209,519	218,367	218,457	221,400	219,397	219,245

Source: Stat-Xplore, Department for Work and Pensions

".." denotes a nil or negligible number of claimants or award amount based on a nil or negligible number of claimants.

Statistical disclosure control has been applied to this table to avoid the release of confidential data. Totals may not sum due to the disclosure control applied.
Description

The move to publishing benefit data via the Stat-Xplore instead of the DWP Tabulation Tool has involved adopting a new disclosure control methodology, in line with other benefits published via this new tool. Although the data still comes from the same source there may be small differences in the outputs displayed using this new tool, when compared to the Tabulation Tool.

5.9a Families and children receiving Child Benefit, in each country and English Region, 2003 to 2016

Time Series	Number of families and children																
					England												
	United Kingdom [1]	Great Britain	England and Wales	England	North East	North West	Yorkshire and the Humber	East Midlands	West Midlands	East	London	South East	South West	Wales	Scotland	Northern Ireland	Foreign and not known
Area Codes [2]	K02000001	K03000001	K04000001	E92000001	E12000001	E12000002	E12000003	E12000004	E12000005	E12000006	E12000007	E12000008	E12000009	W92000004	S92000003	N92000002	n/a
Number of families																	
August 2003	**7,246,335**	**7,000,770**	**6,394,870**	6,037,500	318,470	861,775	619,630	517,590	663,400	653,695	876,120	956,080	570,735	357,370	605,900	225,885	19,675
August 2004	**7,296,495**	**7,055,160**	**6,448,355**	6,087,500	317,515	863,070	622,065	520,870	667,175	660,390	894,090	965,480	576,845	360,855	606,805	226,850	14,485
August 2005	**7,315,165**	**7,074,665**	**6,470,575**	6,110,190	315,855	860,660	622,475	522,195	667,565	664,155	909,045	970,225	578,015	360,385	604,085	226,800	13,705
August 2006	**7,413,475**	**7,129,720**	**6,528,205**	6,168,010	316,665	864,650	626,740	527,105	672,220	671,850	926,055	981,015	581,705	360,195	601,515	230,140	53,615
August 2007	**7,475,035**	**7,212,565**	**6,605,270**	6,241,895	318,020	869,475	631,995	535,775	678,300	683,780	937,480	995,990	591,085	363,375	607,290	230,825	31,650
August 2008	**7,582,990**	**7,320,990**	**6,708,080**	6,341,345	319,815	876,795	640,670	543,350	686,910	696,485	964,180	1,013,595	599,550	366,735	612,910	233,830	28,165
August 2009	**7,769,880**	**7,485,730**	**6,864,935**	6,492,290	324,525	892,240	653,645	554,925	701,070	713,455	1,002,815	1,038,010	611,600	372,650	620,795	238,605	45,545
August 2010	**7,841,675**	**7,557,305**	**6,935,695**	6,562,705	324,265	894,940	657,700	559,645	705,640	723,030	1,028,265	1,051,885	617,340	372,985	621,615	240,985	43,385
August 2011	**7,884,760**	**7,600,115**	**6,979,465**	6,606,285	323,155	895,670	659,240	561,885	708,325	730,180	1,044,355	1,061,870	621,605	373,180	620,650	242,310	42,335
August 2012	**7,920,495**	**7,641,575**	**7,022,780**	6,650,070	321,310	895,845	661,370	564,385	711,110	737,485	1,061,620	1,071,795	625,145	372,705	618,795	243,185	35,735
August 2013	**7,550,265**	**7,279,100**	**6,691,985**	6,328,460	311,725	868,775	643,560	545,720	692,110	690,410	996,490	979,075	600,590	363,525	587,115	239,125	32,040
August 2014	**7,461,675**	**7,195,865**	**6,619,190**	6,259,275	307,860	862,015	640,080	542,575	688,340	681,035	982,060	959,600	595,710	359,910	576,675	237,865	27,945
August 2015	**7,416,800**	**7,153,935**	**6,584,675**	6,227,865	305,000	857,415	636,600	541,540	687,010	678,260	977,940	951,060	593,040	356,810	569,260	236,890	25,970
August 2016	**7,396,355**	**7,139,250**	**6,573,395**	6,219,065	302,920	856,100	635,760	542,215	688,655	677,570	978,825	945,350	591,665	354,335	565,850	236,280	20,825
Number of children																	
August 2003	**13,138,075**	**12,670,975**	**11,625,050**	10,983,290	552,970	1,549,900	1,116,630	934,450	1,219,985	1,200,175	1,613,235	1,754,585	1,041,360	641,755	1,045,925	439,870	27,230
August 2004	**13,096,760**	**12,635,505**	**11,600,380**	10,960,280	544,840	1,534,595	1,109,155	930,920	1,214,695	1,200,175	1,632,425	1,752,995	1,040,475	640,100	1,035,125	435,690	25,565
August 2005	**13,111,665**	**12,654,135**	**11,626,490**	10,988,765	540,940	1,528,255	1,109,150	932,310	1,215,315	1,204,750	1,658,755	1,758,520	1,040,780	637,725	1,027,640	431,995	25,535
August 2006	**13,233,320**	**12,706,365**	**11,685,995**	11,050,975	540,980	1,529,585	1,113,190	936,980	1,219,915	1,212,530	1,686,375	1,768,965	1,042,445	635,020	1,020,370	435,485	91,475
August 2007	**13,267,355**	**12,778,460**	**11,754,415**	11,117,770	540,610	1,529,060	1,117,760	946,090	1,225,025	1,225,485	1,699,215	1,782,530	1,052,000	636,645	1,024,045	433,370	55,525
August 2008	**13,340,565**	**12,857,555**	**11,831,255**	11,194,420	539,840	1,528,890	1,124,420	951,000	1,231,190	1,235,400	1,732,120	1,795,225	1,056,340	636,835	1,026,300	434,390	48,625
August 2009	**13,604,375**	**13,088,240**	**12,054,140**	11,409,950	546,125	1,549,625	1,143,245	967,010	1,251,900	1,258,520	1,794,220	1,827,530	1,071,775	644,190	1,034,095	440,570	75,565
August 2010	**13,685,250**	**13,170,155**	**12,138,365**	11,495,395	544,775	1,551,080	1,147,440	971,690	1,257,180	1,269,870	1,831,965	1,843,465	1,077,930	642,965	1,031,795	443,110	71,985
August 2011	**13,721,160**	**13,207,465**	**12,179,715**	11,537,505	542,680	1,549,475	1,148,450	973,310	1,259,770	1,276,525	1,853,670	1,852,950	1,080,680	642,210	1,027,750	444,285	69,410
August 2012	**13,771,635**	**13,267,355**	**12,243,960**	11,602,370	540,060	1,550,880	1,153,480	976,870	1,265,765	1,284,980	1,880,560	1,865,335	1,084,435	641,590	1,023,390	445,220	59,055
August 2013	**13,107,460**	**12,618,675**	**11,651,810**	11,026,465	525,215	1,505,780	1,124,295	943,980	1,233,780	1,198,215	1,763,895	1,693,670	1,037,630	625,345	966,865	437,440	51,345
August 2014	**12,962,175**	**12,482,260**	**11,532,980**	10,913,100	520,170	1,497,345	1,121,595	938,835	1,229,210	1,181,620	1,738,575	1,656,975	1,028,775	619,885	949,280	435,055	44,860
August 2015	**12,895,530**	**12,420,785**	**11,482,570**	10,867,625	517,125	1,494,870	1,118,980	938,125	1,229,805	1,176,055	1,729,510	1,639,590	1,023,565	614,945	938,215	433,940	40,805
August 2016	**12,877,170**	**12,410,910**	**11,476,565**	10,864,980	515,905	1,497,955	1,121,150	940,315	1,236,365	1,174,760	1,728,685	1,629,015	1,020,835	611,585	934,350	433,310	32,950

Source: HM Revenue and Customs

Footnotes

[1] Includes Foreign and not known

[2] Area codes implemented from 1 January 2011; in line with the new GSS Coding and Naming policy.

5.9b Families receiving Child Benefit nationally, in each country and English Region, August 2016

Area names	Area Codes [1]	Number of families, by size						Number of children in these families, by age				
		Total	One child	Two children	Three children	Four children	Five or more children	**Total**	Under 5	5-10	11-15	16 and over
United Kingdom [2]	K02000001	**7,396,355**	**3,532,955**	**2,698,780**	**840,995**	**235,310**	**88,315**	**12,877,170**	**3,475,365**	**4,354,460**	**3,263,900**	**1,783,445**
Great Britain	K03000001	**7,139,250**	**3,418,785**	**2,605,030**	**804,745**	**225,345**	**85,340**	**12,410,910**	**3,351,145**	**4,200,545**	**3,148,330**	**1,710,895**
England and Wales	K04000001	**6,573,395**	**3,128,510**	**2,400,975**	**749,475**	**212,770**	**81,665**	**11,476,565**	**3,100,965**	**3,878,840**	**2,900,945**	**1,595,810**
England	E92000001	6,219,065	2,958,025	2,271,105	709,600	202,360	77,975	10,864,980	2,939,685	3,674,720	2,744,460	1,506,115
North East	E12000001	302,920	150,575	108,315	32,100	8,705	3,220	515,905	138,280	173,435	130,750	73,440
North West	E12000002	856,100	411,735	304,880	98,685	29,125	11,680	1,497,955	405,675	504,395	378,385	209,500
Yorkshire and the Humber	E12000003	635,760	300,015	230,265	73,890	22,720	8,865	1,121,150	306,480	379,245	282,185	153,240
East Midlands	E12000004	542,215	258,730	200,825	59,710	16,665	6,285	940,315	254,915	317,005	237,280	131,110
West Midlands	E12000005	688,655	320,055	245,315	84,600	27,010	11,680	1,236,365	335,835	415,635	313,210	171,685
East	E12000006	677,570	317,995	257,140	76,300	19,700	6,435	1,174,760	318,125	396,285	297,565	162,785
London	E12000007	978,825	475,215	334,240	117,750	35,730	15,885	1,728,685	467,635	594,940	433,550	232,555
South East	E12000008	945,350	445,920	361,815	102,745	26,440	8,430	1,629,015	437,010	552,730	413,260	226,015
South West	E12000009	591,665	277,785	228,310	63,820	16,265	5,490	1,020,835	275,725	341,055	258,275	145,780
Wales	W92000004	354,335	170,490	129,870	39,875	10,415	3,690	611,585	161,280	204,125	156,485	89,695
Scotland	S92000003	565,850	290,275	204,055	55,270	12,575	3,675	934,350	250,180	321,700	247,385	115,085
Northern Ireland	N92000002	236,280	102,595	86,705	34,510	9,595	2,870	433,310	115,795	142,785	107,330	67,400
Foreign and not known	N/A	20,825	11,575	7,040	1,735	370	105	32,950	8,425	11,130	8,240	5,150

Source: HM Revenue and Customs

Footnotes

[1] Area codes implemented from 1 January 2011; in line with the new GSS Coding and Naming policy.

[2] Includes Foreign and not known.

5.10 Child Tax Credit and Working Tax Credit elements and thresholds

Annual rate (£), except where specified

	2007-08	2008-09	2009-10	2010-11	2011-12	2012-13	2013-14	2014-15	2015-16	2016-17
Child Tax Credit										
Family element	545	545	545	545	545	545	545	545	545	545
Family element, baby addition [1]	545	545	545	545	-	-	-	-	-	-
Child element [2]	1,845	2,085	2,235	2,300	2,555	2,690	2,720	2,750	2,780	2,780
Disabled child additional element [3]	2,440	2,540	2,670	2,715	2,800	2,950	3,015	3,100	3,140	3,140
Severely disabled child element [4]	980	1,020	1,075	1,095	1,130	1,190	1,220	1,255	1,275	1,275
Working Tax Credit										
Basic element	1,730	1,800	1,890	1,920	1,920	1,920	1,920	1,940	1,960	1,960
Couples and lone parent element	1,700	1,770	1,860	1,890	1,950	1,950	1,970	1,990	2,010	2,010
30 hour element [5]	705	735	775	790	790	790	790	800	810	810
Disabled worker element	2,310	2,405	2,530	2,570	2,650	2,790	2,855	2,935	2,970	2,970
Severely disabled adult element	980	1,020	1,075	1,095	1,130	1,190	1,220	1,255	1,275	1,275
50+ return to work payment [6]										
16 but less than 30 hours per week	1,185	1,235	1,300	1,320	1,365	-	-	-	-	-
at least 30 hours per week	1,770	1,840	1,935	1,965	2,030	-	-	-	-	-
Childcare element										
Maximum eligible costs allowed (£ per week)										
Eligible costs incurred for 1 child	175	175	175	175	175	175	175	175	175	175
Eligible costs incurred for 2+ children	300	300	300	300	300	300	300	300	300	300
Percentage of eligible costs covered	*80%*	*80%*	*80%*	*80%*	*70%*	*70%*	*70%*	*70%*	*70%*	*70%*
Common features										
First income threshold [7]	5,220	6,420	6,420	6,420	6,420	6,420	6,420	6,420	6,420	6,420
First withdrawal rate	*37%*	*39%*	*39%*	*39%*	*41%*	*41%*	*41%*	*41%*	*41%*	*41%*
Second income threshold [8]	50,000	50,000	50,000	50,000	40,000	-	-	-	-	-
Second withdrawal rate	*1 in 15*	*1 in 15*	*1 in 15*	*1 in 15*	41%	-	-	-	-	-
First income threshold for those entitled to Child Tax Credit only [9]	14,495	15,575	16,040	16,190	15,860	15,860	15,910	16,010	16,105	16,105
Income increase disregard [10]	25,000	25,000	25,000	25,000	10,000	10,000	5,000	5,000	5,000	2,500
Income fall disregard [10]	-	-	-	-	-	2,500	2,500	2,500	2,500	2,500
Minimum award payable	26	26	26	26	26	26	26	26	26	26

Source: HM Revenue and Customs

Footnotes

[1] Payable to families for any period during which they have one or more children aged under 1. Abolished 6 April 2011.

[2] Payable for each child up to 31 August after their 16th birthday, and for each young person for any period in which they are aged under 20 (under 19 to 2005-06) and in full-time non-advanced education, or under 19 and in their first 20 weeks of registration with the Careers service or Connexions.

[3] Payable in addition to the child element for each disabled child.

[4] Payable in addition to the disabled child element for each severely disabled child.

[5] Payable for any period during which normal hours worked (for a couple, summed over the two partners) is at least 30 per week.

[6] Payable for each qualifying adult for the first 12 months following a return to work.Abolished 6 April 2012.

[7] Income is net of pension contributions, and excludes Child Benefit, Housing benefit, Council tax benefit, maintenance and the first £300 of family income other than from work or benefits. The award is reduced by the excess of income over the first threshold, multiplied by the first withdrawal rate.

[8] For those entitled to the Child Tax Credit, the award is reduced only down to the family element, plus the baby addition where relevant, less the excess of income over the second threshold multiplied by the second withdrawal rate. Abolished 6 April 2012.

[9] Those also receiving Income Support, income-based Jobseeker's Allowance or Pension Credit are passported to maximum CTC with no tapering.

[10] Introduced from 6 April 2012, this drop in income is disregarded in the calculation of Tax Credit awards.

5.11 Number of families and children with Child Tax Credits or Working Tax Credits, by level of award, 2016-2017

Thousands

	Area Codes[1]	Total out-of-work families	In-work families				Total in receipt (out-of-work and in-work families)	Number of children in recipient families		
			With children		Of which, lone parents	With no children		Total out-of-work families	In-work families	
			receiving WTC and CTC	Receiving CTC only		Receiving WTC only			Receiving WTC and CTC	Receiving CTC only
United Kingdom [2]	**K02000001**	**1,190**	1,654	803	1,135	401	**4,047**	2,308	3,084	1,678
Great Britain	**K03000001**	**1,140**	1,596	773	1,094	382	**3,892**	2,212	2,982	1,612
England and Wales	**K04000001**	**1,047**	1,480	713	1,000	346	**3,586**	2,044	2,787	1,493
England	E92000001	**980**	1,401	671	943	322	**3,374**	1,917	2,645	1,406
North East	E12000001	**60**	72	32	52	23	**187**	115	127	64
North West	E12000002	**137**	210	92	141	57	**497**	268	398	190
Yorkshire and the Humber	E12000003	**110**	159	75	100	42	**385**	218	304	156
East Midlands	E12000004	**80**	122	68	82	32	**302**	159	224	141
West Midlands	E12000005	**123**	167	81	103	37	**408**	250	328	172
East	E12000006	**92**	132	74	94	26	**325**	180	241	159
London	E12000007	**178**	252	80	160	38	**549**	341	502	166
South East	E12000008	**122**	171	94	127	34	**421**	236	312	201
South West	E12000009	**77**	116	74	84	33	**300**	149	209	156
Wales	W92000004	**67**	80	42	57	23	**212**	127	143	87
Scotland	S92000003	**94**	116	59	94	36	**305**	168	194	119
Northern Ireland	N92000002	**49**	55	29	40	17	**150**	93	99	64
Foreign and not known		**1**	3	2	1	1	**6**	2	3	3

Source: HM Revenue and Customs
Child and Working Tax Credits Statistics: Finalised annual awards 2016 to 2017, Geographical Analysis

Footnotes

[1] Area codes implemented from 1 January 2011 in line with the new GSS Coding and Naming policy.

[2] Includes Foreign and not known

[3] All figures are rounded to the nearest integer therefore not all totals may exactly equal the sums of their respective components.

[4] "Foreign and not known" consists of a small proportion of recipient families and children who do not live within England, Scotland, Northern Island or Wales. They may for instance be a Crown servant posted overseas, or living in a British Crown Dependency. Due to the small size of this population we combine them into one group which also consists of those whom, at the time of publication, either have a UK postcode that does not match to a geographical office region code, or do not have a postcode in the available data.

5.12 Widows' Benefit (excluding bereavement payment[1,2,3]): by type of benefit

Great Britain

Number in reciept of widows benefit as at May each year

	2007	2008	2009	2010	2011	2012	2013	2014	2015	2016
All Widows' benefit (excluding breavement allowance)										
All ages	89,570	71,447	56,637	46,221	40,178	34,738	30,175	26,209	22,881	20,301
Unknown age	15	..	..	..	..	..	..	..	..	..
18-24	..	..	..	..	..	..	..	..	..	..
25-29	37	15	8	..	..	..	..	..	..	..
30-34	299	192	122	71	41	21	12	5	..	..
35-39	1,438	1,022	701	472	316	201	128	83	50	26
40-44	3,703	2,855	2,176	1,611	1,132	777	548	352	211	131
45-49	7,140	5,867	4,797	3,915	3,146	2,519	1,936	1,422	1,012	663
50-54	16,768	13,583	11,022	9,161	7,602	6,328	5,231	4,325	3,519	2,839
55-59	42,915	34,480	28,419	23,122	18,771	15,329	12,462	10,126	8,462	7,033
60-64	17,259	13,425	9,402	7,871	9,167	9,550	9,859	9,892	9,622	9,607
Widow's Pension - not age related										
All ages	9,389	6,536	4,451	3,389	2,984	2,636	2,370	2,077	1,795	1,643
Unknown age	5	..	..	..	..	..	..	..	..	..
18-24	..	..	..	..	..	..	..	..	..	..
25-29	..	..	..	..	..	..	..	..	..	..
30-34	..	..	..	..	..	..	..	..	..	..
35-39	..	..	..	..	..	..	..	..	..	..
40-44	..	..	..	..	..	..	..	..	..	..
45-49	..	..	..	..	..	..	..	..	..	..
50-54	186	104	43	13	9	5	..	..	..	..
55-59	3,230	2,553	2,116	1,741	1,372	1,122	919	708	559	459
60-64	5,978	3,878	2,289	1,633	1,602	1,509	1,451	1,372	1,237	1,187
Widow's Pension - age related										
All ages	64,927	52,638	42,466	35,125	31,235	27,609	24,556	21,851	19,563	17,728
Unknown age	12	..	..	..	..	..	..	..	..	..
18-24	..	..	..	..	..	..	..	..	..	..
25-29	..	..	..	..	..	..	..	..	..	..
30-34	..	..	..	..	..	..	..	..	..	..
35-39	..	..	..	..	..	..	..	..	..	..
40-44	53	31	12	5	..	..	..	..	..	..
45-49	2,533	2,099	1,745	1,382	1,155	1,012	851	678	528	400
50-54	13,061	10,454	8,496	7,117	5,956	5,041	4,262	3,621	3,032	2,515
55-59	38,150	30,634	25,195	20,479	16,653	13,597	11,104	9,087	7,663	6,419
60-64	11,119	9,425	7,015	6,145	7,472	7,961	8,334	8,460	8,338	8,391
Widowed Mother's Allowance - with dependants										
All ages	15,162	12,209	9,678	7,669	5,920	4,461	3,236	2,265	1,508	919
Unknown age	..	..	..	..	..	..	..	..	..	..
18-24	..	..	..	..	..	..	..	..	..	..
25-29	31	15	8	..	..	..	..	..	..	..
30-34	300	188	120	69	38	21	12	5	..	..
35-39	1,432	1,021	694	476	316	203	131	81	50	26
40-44	3,637	2,827	2,166	1,601	1,136	777	548	352	209	132
45-49	4,581	3,751	3,031	2,521	1,976	1,502	1,078	750	488	265
50-54	3,500	3,014	2,466	2,024	1,635	1,281	958	692	479	315
55-59	1,516	1,277	1,093	893	731	601	438	328	236	152
60-64	168	119	92	85	92	76	64	56	41	29
Widowed Mother's Allowance - without dependants										
All ages	85	57	46	40	33	26	22	18	13	10
Unknown age	..	..	..	..	..	..	..	..	..	..
18-24	..	..	..	..	..	..	..	..	..	..
25-29	..	..	..	..	..	..	..	..	..	..
30-34	..	..	..	..	..	..	..	..	..	..
35-39	6	..	..	..	..	..	..	..	..	..
40-44	9	6	5	..	..	..	..	..	..	..
45-49	20	17	15	14	13	7	6	..	..	..
50-54	24	13	10	7	5	7	9	8	5	6
55-59	21	20	14	13	11	10	6	6	..	6
60-64	6	..	..	..	..	7	8	8	..	..

Source: Stat-Xplore, Department for Work and Pensions

5.12 Widows' Benefit (excluding bereavement payment[1,2,3]): by type of benefit

Great Britain

Notes

".." denotes a nil or negligible number of claimants or award amount based on a nil or negligible number of claimants.

1. Statistical disclosure control has been applied to this table to avoid the release of confidential data. Totals may not sum due to the disclosure control applied.

2 Caseload (Thousands) All Claimants of Widows Benefit are female. No new claims for WA have been accepted since April 2001 when it was replaced by Bereavement Allowance
3 Figures include overseas cases.

Widow's Benefit (WB) is payable to women widowed on or after 11th April 1988 and up to and including 8th April 2001. Statistics are based on WB claims in payment in Great Britain on the reference date; this excludes cases in Northern Ireland.

Widowed Mother's Allowance: Weekly benefit payable to a widowed mother (providing she was widowed before 8th April 2001) if her husband paid enough NIC and receiving Child Benefit for one of her children, or her husband was in receipt of Child Benefit, or she was expecting her husbands baby, or if she was widowed before 11th April 1988 and has a young person under 19 living with her for whom she was receiving Child Benefit.

Widow's Pension: Weekly benefit payable to widows without dependant children providing she was widowed before 8th April 2001. A widow may be able to get widows pension if her husband paid enough NIC. She must be 45 or over when her husband died or when her Widowed Mother's Allowance ends, she cannot get Widow's Pension at the same time as Widowed Mother's Allowance.

5.13 Bereavement Benefit[1] (excluding bereavement payment): by sex, type of benefit and age of widow/er

Great Britain and Overseas

At May of each year | Count

	Male					Female				
	2012	2013	2014	2015	2016	2012	2013	2014	2015	2016
All Bereavement Benefit (exluding bereavement allowance)										
All ages	18822	18789	18570	18486	18427	47389	48804	49625	50832	51619
18-24	..	8	..	6	6	53	42	34	34	21
25-29	43	42	56	60	54	464	472	401	393	370
30-34	252	258	259	254	229	1694	1774	1759	1692	1640
35-39	845	791	754	745	747	3858	3819	3756	3732	3756
40-44	2155	2103	1939	1839	1724	7760	7663	7430	7291	6905
45-49	3917	3822	3751	3586	3469	11300	11182	11313	11016	11042
50-54	3974	4108	4177	4210	4379	10784	10944	11137	11366	11397
55-59	3539	3572	3598	3654	3784	9487	9790	9628	10083	10003
60-64	4091	4085	4038	4142	4043	1985	3117	4168	5222	6489
Widowed Parents' Allowance with dependants										
All ages	11700	11664	11475	11177	11059	33887	34306	34455	34416	34350
18-24	..	8	..	6	6	53	37	34	34	20
25-29	43	42	56	60	54	459	472	401	389	368
30-34	252	258	259	251	229	1684	1764	1761	1683	1635
35-39	845	791	754	745	747	3846	3809	3743	3728	3750
40-44	2151	2098	1939	1835	1724	7722	7640	7409	7271	6891
45-49	3415	3337	3253	3078	3001	9811	9817	9944	9671	9701
50-54	2862	2977	3036	2996	3096	7132	7307	7552	7762	7905
55-59	1465	1497	1558	1554	1562	2919	3091	3166	3364	3426
60-64	666	652	630	659	645	253	370	456	516	645
Widowed Parents' Allowance without dependants										
All ages	30	25	17	12	9	180	161	134	118	100
18-24	..	..	..	..	..	..	..	..	..	..
25-29	..	..	..	..	..	7	..	..	..	..
30-34	..	..	..	..	..	8	9	..	6	9
35-39	..	..	..	..	..	12	13	11	8	10
40-44	..	..	..	..	..	39	30	25	22	14
45-49	16	6	10	8	5	54	49	38	24	26
50-54	5	5	7	..	..	42	43	43	31	27
55-59	5	6	..	..	..	14	12	11	15	18
60-64	..	..	..	..	..	7	5	5	6	6
Bereavement allowance - age related										
All ages	1755	1755	1786	1894	1935	5547	5381	5371	5405	5282
18-24	..	..	..	..	..	..	..	..	..	..
25-29	..	..	..	..	..	..	..	..	..	..
30-34	..	..	..	..	..	..	..	..	..	..
35-39	..	..	..	..	..	..	..	..	..	..
40-44	..	..	..	..	..	..	..	..	..	..
45-49	490	476	493	500	464	1428	1313	1335	1316	1313
50-54	1109	1121	1131	1211	1281	3613	3593	3543	3572	3459
55-59	149	155	166	182	190	503	476	498	513	509
60-64	..	..	..	..	..	..	..	..	..	..
Bereavement allowance - not age related										
All ages	5342	5342	5286	5402	5429	7776	8955	9666	10896	11887
18-24	..	..	..	..	..	..	..	..	..	..
25-29	..	..	..	..	..	..	..	..	..	..
30-34	..	..	..	..	..	..	..	..	..	..
35-39	..	..	..	..	..	..	..	..	..	..
40-44	..	..	..	..	..	..	..	..	..	..
45-49	..	..	..	..	..	..	..	..	..	..
50-54	..	..	..	..	..	..	..	..	..	..
55-59	1918	1910	1875	1916	2028	6051	6206	5954	6192	6049
60-64	3423	3436	3408	3486	3400	1726	2747	3710	4704	5837

Source: Stat-Xplore, Department for Work and Pensions

5.13 Bereavement Benefit[1] (excluding bereavement payment): by sex, type of benefit and age of widow/er
Great Britain and Overseas

Footnotes
1 Figures are for Great Britain and Overseas and do not include figures for Northern Ireland
".." denotes a nil or negligible number of claimants or award amount based on a nil or negligible number of claimants.

Bereavement Benefit is payable to men/women widowed on or after 9th April 2001.

Widowed Parents Allowance: Weekly benefit payable to widowed parents. A widow/widower may be entitled to this if his/her late spouse/civil partner had paid enough NIC and the widow/widower is receiving Child Benefit or can be treated as entitled to Child Benefit, or the late spouse/civil partner was receiving child benefit, or expecting her husband's/civil partner's baby (pregnant from fertility treatment).

Bereavement Allowance: Weekly benefit payable to widows/widowers without dependant children and payable between age 45 and pensionable age. The amount payable to a widow/widower aged between 45 and 54 is related to their age at date of entitlement. The weekly rate is reduced by 7% for each year they are aged under 55, so they will get 93% rate at 54, falling to 30% at age 45. Those aged 55 or over at the date of entitlement will get their full rate of Bereavement Allowance.

Recording and clerical errors can occur within the data source - for this reason, no reliance should be placed on very small numbers obtained through Stat-Xplore.

Statistical disclosure control has been applied to this table to avoid the release of confidential data. Totals may not sum due to the disclosure control applied.

The move to publishing benefit data via the Stat-Xplore instead of the DWP Tabulation Tool has involved adopting a new disclosure control methodology, in line with other benefits published via this new tool. Although the data still comes from the same source there may be small differences in the outputs displayed using this new tool, when compared to the Tabulation Tool.

5.14 State Pension Caseload by Category of Pension, Age and Sex[1]

Great Britain

As at May each year — Count (000s)

	2007	2008	2009	2010	2011	2012	2013	2014	2014	2016
MALE										
Pre-2016 State Pension[2]										
Contributory State Pension[3]										
60-64	0.12	0.12	0.14	0.17	0.15	0.17	0.17	0.19	0.17	0.20
65-69	1206.02	1223.01	1261.61	1307.80	1362.91	1486.80	1592.27	1558.83	1608.48	1572.26
70-74	1062.01	1083.34	1104.68	1118.81	1114.94	1121.46	1192.21	1149.82	1235.52	1290.69
75-79	831.37	842.96	850.39	864.04	876.96	894.74	942.28	917.88	955.55	952.21
80-84	543.64	551.82	562.65	577.98	594.47	609.01	633.17	621.47	644.32	656.85
85-89	267.26	285.84	301.36	305.99	312.45	320.48	338.96	326.79	348.22	360.80
90 and over	96.87	95.72	95.61	109.25	122.23	132.09	146.32	138.09	150.65	157.20
Unknown	1.41	0.22	0.26	0.27	0.32	0.37	0.52	0.46	0.62	0.76
Total all ages	**4008.70**	**4083.03**	**4176.69**	**4284.30**	**4384.45**	**4565.14**	**4845.90**	**4713.53**	**4943.54**	**4990.95**
Non-contributory State Pension[4]										
60-64	..	..	..	..	..	..	..	..	..	..
65-69	..	..	..	..	..	..	..	..	..	..
70-74	..	..	..	..	..	..	0.01	0.01	0.01	0.01
75-79	0.08	0.07	0.09	0.04	0.10	0.17	0.11	0.24	0.23	0.17
80-84	2.81	3.17	3.55	4.08	4.93	6.05	6.86	7.68	8.22	8.56
85-89	1.67	1.85	1.88	1.90	1.95	2.08	2.48	2.77	3.08	3.57
90 and over	0.94	0.96	0.96	1.02	1.10	1.23	1.37	1.47	1.52	1.52
Unknown	..	..	0.01	0.01	0.01	0.01	0.02	0.02	0.03	0.04
Total all ages	**5.50**	**6.06**	**6.49**	**7.05**	**8.09**	**9.55**	**10.84**	**12.20**	**13.07**	**13.86**
New State Pension:										
60-64	..	..	..	..	..	..	..	..	..	0.01
65-69	..	..	..	..	..	..	..	..	..	46.48
70-74	..	..	..	..	..	..	..	..	..	..
75-79	..	..	..	..	..	..	..	..	..	..
80-84	..	..	..	..	..	..	..	..	..	..
85-89	..	..	..	..	..	..	..	..	..	..
90 and over	..	..	..	..	..	..	..	..	..	..
Unknown	..	..	..	..	..	..	..	..	..	0.02
Total all ages	**..**	**..**	**..**	**..**	**..**	**..**	**..**	**..**	**..**	**46.50**
Total	**4014.20**	**4089.08**	**4183.19**	**4291.35**	**4392.54**	**4574.69**	**4724.36**	**4858.10**	**4956.62**	**5004.82**
FEMALE										
Pre-2016 State Pension[2]										
Contributory State Pension[3]										
60-64	1523.77	1589.38	1628.72	1639.14	1521.08	1305.32	928.75	1105.41	758.49	567.98
65-69	1313.44	1338.95	1378.26	1423.22	1477.81	1608.72	1720.75	1684.33	1743.82	1762.22
70-74	1190.62	1207.57	1227.05	1238.54	1232.20	1238.38	1307.06	1266.45	1350.45	1403.35
75-79	1056.31	1056.13	1051.16	1051.83	1053.73	1063.81	1103.13	1081.85	1113.80	1108.39
80-84	830.66	822.96	822.26	829.14	837.33	842.70	843.91	843.99	841.77	844.79
85-89	537.36	564.66	582.60	572.79	565.40	561.34	564.72	558.15	568.77	576.29
90 and over	296.10	289.42	285.25	313.74	339.34	355.00	372.61	360.65	371.31	375.84
Unknown	1.71	0.51	0.48	0.53	0.59	0.85	1.41	1.12	1.71	2.10
Total all ages	**6749.96**	**6869.59**	**6975.76**	**7068.91**	**7027.49**	**6976.14**	**6842.33**	**6901.94**	**6750.11**	**6640.96**
Non-contributory State Pension[4]										
60-64	..	..	..	..	..	..	..	..	..	..
65-69	..	..	..	..	..	..	..	..	..	..
70-74	..	..	..	0.01	..	0.01	..	0.01	0.01	0.01
75-79	0.23	0.22	0.27	0.12	0.22	0.34	0.22	0.57	0.49	0.39
80-84	7.83	8.71	9.79	11.09	12.93	15.17	17.07	18.93	20.80	22.17
85-89	4.99	5.54	5.75	5.64	5.75	6.26	7.29	7.94	8.50	9.26
90 and over	4.00	4.03	3.91	4.01	4.13	4.35	4.97	5.18	5.08	5.12
Unknown	0.01	0.02	0.02	0.04	0.05	0.06	0.08	0.12	0.17	0.22
Total all ages	**17.07**	**18.53**	**19.76**	**20.92**	**23.09**	**26.19**	**29.64**	**32.74**	**35.03**	**37.15**
New State Pension:										
60-64	..	..	..	..	..	..	..	..	..	..
65-69	..	..	..	..	..	..	..	..	..	..
70-74	..	..	..	..	..	..	..	..	..	..
75-79	..	..	..	..	..	..	..	..	..	..
80-84	..	..	..	..	..	..	..	..	..	..
85-89	..	..	..	..	..	..	..	..	..	..
90 and over	..	..	..	..	..	..	..	..	..	..
Unknown	..	..	..	..	..	..	..	..	..	..
Total all ages	**..**	**..**	**..**	**..**	**..**	**..**	**..**	**..**	**..**	**..**
Total	6767.03	6888.11	6995.51	7089.83	7050.57	7002.33	6931.58	6875.07	6785.15	6678.11

Source: Stat-Xplore, Department for Work and Pensions

5.14 State Pension Caseload by Category of Pension, Age and Sex[1]

Great Britain

Footnotes:

1. Excludes Abroad cases

2. Pre-2016 State Pension: This is paid to people reaching their State Pension age (SPa) prior to 6th April 2016. There are two main types of SP: contributory and non-contributory. Contributory SP consists of any combination of a Basic Pension, Additional Pension or Graduated Retirement Benefit. Non-contributory SP consists of a Basic Pension plus any Graduated Retirement Benefit that is due.

3. Includes all categories of contributory state pension (Cat A, Cat B, Cat ABL, Cat BL, Cat AB and GRB only)

4. Includes all categories of non-contributory state pension (Cat C and Cat D)

5. New State Pension: This is paid to people reaching SPa on, or after, 6th April 2016. nSP is a contributory SP made up of an amount based upon the persons NI contributions. Where transitional arrangements apply, some individuals will receive a Protected Payment – which is an amount above the full rate of nSP.

".." denotes a nil or negligible number of claimants or award amount based on a nil or negligible number of claimants.

Statistical disclosure control has been applied to this table to avoid the release of confidential data. Totals may not sum due to the disclosure control applied.

The move to publishing benefit data via the Stat-Xplore instead of the DWP Tabulation Tool has involved adopting a new disclosure control methodology, in line with other benefits published via this new tool. Although the data still comes from the same source there may be small differences in the outputs displayed using this new tool, when compared to the Tabulation Tool.

From November 2017 State Pension data excludes persons with a 'suspended' account and should be treated as a break in series. A suspended account, when the department suspends payment, can occur for a number of reasons. Suspended cases may end and pensions put back into payment, at which point they will be shown in the next extract of data, or the suspension may end and the case terminated.

5.15a: War Pensions: estimated number of pensioners[1] Great Britain

At 31 March each year

Thousands

		2005	2006[2]	2007	2008	2009	2010	2011	2012	2013	2014	2015	2016
Disablement	**KADH**	191.75	182.8	173.85	165.17	157.13	148.95	141.72	134.43	127.6	121.9	116.05	111.23
Widows and dependants	**KADI**	43.55	41.05	38.69	36.1	33.62	31.45	29.2	27.11	25.1	23.11	21.17	19.55
Total	**KADG**	235.3	223.85	212.54	201.27	190.75	180.4	170.92	161.54	152.7	145.01	137.22	130.78

Source: War Pensions Computer System

1 See chapter text. From 1914 war, 1939 war and later service.
2 The discontinuity between 2005 and 2006 is due to improvements in data processing.
An additional validation check was introduced in 2014/15 on the 'not known' disablement pensioners to put them in the correct payment category.
The sum of the sub-totals may not sum to the totals due to rounding

5.15b: War Pensions in payment by type of pension, gender and financial year end, 31 March 2012 to 31 March 2016, numbers[1]

	Awards in payment at:				
	31-Mar-12	**31-Mar-13**	**31-Mar-14**	**31-Mar-15**	**31-Mar-16**
ALL IN PAYMENT	**161,537**	**152,695**	**145,004**	**137,216**	**130,774**
Men	**128,719**	**122,106**	**116,611**	**110,935**	**106,295**
Women	**32,818**	**30,589**	**28,393**	**26,281**	**24,479**
Disablement Pensioners	**134,431**	**127,590**	**121,900**	**116,049**	**111,228**
Men	128,128	121,531	116,057	110,409	105,788
Women	6,303	6,059	5,843	5,640	5,440
War Widow(er)s	**26,376**	**24,414**	**22,446**	**20,533**	**18,950**
Men	79	83	82	72	74
Women	26,297	24,331	22,364	20,461	18,876
Other Pensioners	**730**	**691**	**658**	**634**	**596**
Men	512	492	472	454	433
Women	218	199	186	180	163

Source: War Pensions Computer System

1 The sum of the sub-totals may not sum to the totals due to rounding.
2 Please note that pensioners can move from disablement pensions to other pensions and vice versa.

5.16 Income support by statistical group: number of claimants receiving weekly payment
Great Britain

As at May each year									Count (1000s)
	2008	**2009**	**2010**	**2011**	**2012**	**2013**	**2014**	**2015**	**2016**
All income support claimants	**2102.30**	**1990.00**	**1852.30**	**1703.20**	**1417.10**	**1021.70**	**840.77**	**734.76**	**665.68**
Incapacity Benefits	1191.40	1097.00	996.60	924.90	654.13	328.05	167.62	92.13	45.01
Lone Parent	738.60	720.50	679.20	595.40	577.08	499.63	474.73	441.60	416.48
Carer	87.30	93.80	103.90	115.70	129.75	145.89	156.53	165.37	173.22
Others on income related benefit	85.00	78.90	72.70	67.20	56.10	48.14	41.89	35.66	30.98

Source: Stat-Xplore, Department for Work and Pensions

Statistical disclosure control has been applied to this table to avoid the release of confidential data. Totals may not sum due to the disclosure control applied.

The move to publishing benefit data via the Stat-Xplore instead of NOMIS has involved adopting a new disclosure control methodology, in line with other benefits published via this new tool. Although the data still comes from the same source there may be small differences in the outputs displayed using this new tool, when compared to NOMIS.

Statistical Group refers to the client group which is based on the combination of benefits being claimed. It is based on receipt of certain other benefits:

- Incapacity Benefits: claimant receives Incapacity Benefit, Severe Disablement Allowance (IBSDA) or Employment and Support Allowance (ESA);
- Lone Parent: claimant receives Income Support with a child under 16 and no partner;
- Carer: claimant receives Carer's Allowance (CA);
- Others on Income Related Benefit: claimant receives Income Support (including IS Disability Premium) or Pension Credit (PC).

Benefits are arranged hierarchically and claimants are assigned to the topmost benefit they receive. Thus a person who is a lone parent and receives Incapacity Benefit would be classified in the Incapacity Benefits statistical group.

Others on Income Related Benefit: After August 2003, there was a sharp decline in this statistical group due to the migration of most existing Minimum Income Guarantee (MIG) claimants to Pension Credit. Some residual cases remain after this date.

Lone Parent Obligations: From November 2008, lone parent obligations (LPOs) were introduced and lone parents with a youngest child aged 12 or over were no longer able to make a new or repeat claim for Income Support solely on the basis of their parental status. Existing IS LPs with a youngest child aged 12 or over had their eligibility removed over a period of time commencing 2nd March 2009. From October 2009 this policy was extended to LPs with a youngest child aged 10 or 11 and from October 2010, to LPs with a youngest child aged 7 or over. The Welfare Reform Act 2012 introduced further changes and from 21 May 2012 lone parents will only be eligible to claim Income Support until their youngest child is five years old. Most effected LPs will leave IS and claim Jobseeker's Allowance (JSA). However, there are exceptions to these rules where the youngest child can legitimately be over the ages mentioned above. Similarly, some former LPs remain on IS for other reasons (e.g. they have a long term caring responsibility and claim Carer's Allowance).

5.17 Pension Credit: number of claimants
Great Britain

As at May each year										Count (1000s)
	2007	**2008**	**2009**	**2010**	**2011**	**2012**	**2013**	**2014**	**2015**	**2016**
All Pension Credit	2733.6	2719.1	2730.5	2734.1	2674.6	2541.4	2413.7	2270.2	2096.6	1948.5
Guarantee Credit only	805.9	882.1	925.7	954.3	936.9	1015.8	968.3	950.2	931.4	936.8
Both Guarantee and Savings Credit	1330.2	1246.2	1205.2	1202.4	1148.0	964.2	906.5	824.2	739.6	659.7
Savings Credit only	597.5	590.8	599.6	577.4	589.6	561.4	538.8	495.8	425.7	352.0

Source: Stat-Xplore, Department for Work and Pensions

Statistical disclosure control has been applied to this table to avoid the release of confidential data. Totals may not sum due to the disclosure control applied.

The move to publishing benefit data via the Stat-Xplore instead of the DWP Tabulation Tool has involved adopting a new disclosure control methodology, in line with other benefits published via this new tool. Although the data still comes from the same source there may be small differences in the outputs displayed using this new tool, when compared to the Tabulation Tool.

5.18 Income support: average amounts of benefit[1,2]

Great Britain

As at May										£ per week[3]
	2007	2008	2009	2010	2011	2012	2013	2014	2015	2016
Statistical Group[4]:										
Incapacity Benefits	80.04	81.85	89.22	91.81	93.66	93.69	82.12	67.47	63.68	65.93
Lone Parent	89.70	87.37	82.79	79.02	75.94	76.54	74.09	72.75	71.98	70.74
Carer	70.82	70.21	71.85	70.90	69.94	72.23	72.29	72.16	72.82	72.97
Others on income related benefit	62.47	63.02	66.35	67.87	68.82	73.19	74.11	74.86	75.21	75.44
Total	82.45	82.55	85.17	85.01	84.88	83.93	76.42	71.69	71.28	71.21

Source: Stat-Xplore, Department for Work and Pensions

".." denotes a nil or negligible number of claimants or award amount based on a nil or negligible number of claimants.

1 Figures prior to 2013 are taken from the DWP 100% Source: Department for Work and Pensions (DWP); Work and Pensions Longitudinal Study (WPLS) Work and Pensions Longitudinal Study (WPLS).
From 2013 onwards, data is sourced from Stat-Xplore, DWP. Although the data still comes from the same source there may be small differences in the outputs displayed using this new tool, when compared to NOMIS.

2 The amount of Income Support is affected by the introduction in April 2003 of Child Tax Credit. From that date there were no new child dependency increases awarded to IS claimants, although existing CDIs were transitionally protected.

3 Average amounts are shown as pounds per week and rounded to the nearest penny.

4 Statistical Group refers to the client group which is based on the combination of benefits being claimed. It is based on receipt of certain other benefits:

- Incapacity Benefits: claimant receives Incapacity Benefit, Severe Disablement Allowance (IBSDA) or Employment and Support Allowance (ESA)
- Lone Parent: claimant receives Income Support with a child under 16 and no partner
- Carer: claimant receives Carer's Allowance (CA);
- Others on Income Related Benefit: claimant receives Income Support (including IS Disability Premium) or Pension Credit (PC). After August 2003, there was a sharp decline in this statistical group due to the migration of most existing Minimum Income Guarantee (MIG) claimants to Pension Credit. Some residual cases remain after this date.

Income Support

Income Support (IS) is intended to help cover costs for people on low incomes who do not have to be available for employment. It is being replaced by Universal Credit (UC) and IS cannot be claimed at the same time as UC.
The main groups of people who receive it are lone parents, carer's and people on Incapacity Benefits.

The amount of IS that a claimant can receive depends mainly upon their age; whether they have a partner, whether they have special needs such as a disability or caring responsibilities; and whether they have liabilities for certain types of housing costs such as mortgage interest payments. The maximum amount that a claimant can receive is normally reduced by income from other types of benefits or other sources.

Recording and clerical errors can occur within the data source - for this reason, no reliance should be placed on very small numbers obtained through Stat-Xplore.

Statistical disclosure control has been applied with Stat-Xplore, which guards against the identification of an individual claimant.

5.19 Pension Credit: average weekly amounts of benefit[1]

Great Britain

As at May										£ per week[2]
	2007	2008	2009	2010	2011	2012	2013	2014	2015	2016
Type of Pension Credit										
Guarantee Credit only	83.75	85.08	88.87	90.75	92.52	90.13	90.07	89.19	87.59	86.25
Savings Credit only	13.36	13.62	13.71	14.01	13.57	11.37	10.87	9.85	8.51	7.29
Both Guarantee and Savings Credit	46.12	48.29	50.82	51.75	52.04	50.26	49.41	47.72	45.49	43.77
Residual MIG case	109.49	112.71	107.44	90.24	100.51	108.44	97.81	122.8	93.79	74.18
Total	50.05	52.69	55.57	57.39	57.74	57.61	57.12	56.75	56.64	57.61

Source: Stat-Xplore, Department for Work and Pensions

1 Figures are given in each May and are taken from the DWP 100% Work and Pensions Longitudinal Study (WPLS).
2 Average amounts are shown as pounds per week and rounded to the nearest penny.

Pension Credit:
Pension Credit is an income-related benefit made up of 2 parts - Guarantee Credit and Savings Credit.

Pension Credit (Guarantee Credit) tops up any other income to a standard minimum amount (Standard Minimum Guarantee). There are additional amounts for those who are severely disabled, have caring responsibilities or certain housing costs.

To be entitled to Guarantee Credit, the claimant must have reached the qualifying age (women's state pension age) and live in Great Britain. A couple, where only one has reached the qualifying age can currently chose to claim Pension Credit.

Partner in this term refers to; your husband, your wife, your civil partner or the person you live with as if they were your husband, wife or civil partner.

Pension Credit (Savings Credit) is an extra amount for those 65 and over, who reached state pension age before 5th April 2016 and have made some additional provision for their retirement, for example through a private pension or savings.

Pensioners receive 60 pence of Savings Credit for every pound of qualifying income between the savings credit threshold and the Standard Minimum Guarantee. For those who have income above the Standard Minimum Guarantee and any additional amounts they are entitled to (the Appropriate Amount) the Savings Credit Maximum is reduced by 40 pence for every pound of income above that level.

The savings credit is only applicable to people aged 65 or over. In the case of a couple if either of the couple is aged 65 or over the savings credit may be payable. Some people will be entitled to the guarantee credit, the savings credit or both.

Recording and clerical errors can occur within the data source - for this reason, no reliance should be placed on very small numbers obtained through Stat-Xplore.
Statistical disclosure control has been applied with Stat-Xplore, which guards against the identification of an individual claimant.

this page is intentionally blank

External trade and investment

Chapter 6

External trade and investment

External trade (Table 6.1 and 6.3 to 6.6)

The statistics in this section are on the basis of Balance of Payments (BoP). They are compiled from information provided to HM Revenue and Customs (HMRC) by importers and exporters on the basis of Overseas Trade Statistics (OTS) which values exports 'f.o.b.' (free on board) and imports 'c.i.f.' (including insurance and freight). In addition to deducting these freight costs and insurance premiums from the OTS figures, coverage adjustments are made to convert the OTS data to a BoP basis. Adjustments are also made to the level of all exports and European Union (EU) imports to take account of estimated under-recording. The adjustments are set out and described in the annual United Kingdom *Balance of Payments Pink Book* (Office for National Statistics (ONS)). These adjustments are made to conform to the definitions in the 6th edition of the IMF Balance of Payments Manual.

Aggregate estimates of trade in goods, seasonally adjusted and on a BoP basis, are published monthly in the ONS statistical bulletin UK Trade. More detailed figures are available from time series data on the ONS website (www.ons.gov.uk) and are also published in the *Monthly Review of External Trade Statistics*. Detailed figures for EU and non-EU trade on an OTS basis are published in *Overseas trade statistics: United Kingdom trade with the European Community and the world* (HMRC).

Overseas Trade Statistics

HMRC provide accurate and up to date information via the website:
www.uktradeinfo.com
They also produce publications entitled 'Overseas Trade Statistics'.

Import penetration and export sales ratios (Table 6.2)

The ratios were first introduced in the August 1977 edition of *Economic Trends* in an article entitled 'The Home and Export Performance of United Kingdom Industries'. The article described the conceptual and methodological problems involved in measuring such variables as import penetration.

The industries are grouped according to the 2007 Standard Industrial Classification at 2-digit level.

Table 6.3 to 6.6

The series are now available as datasets in the UK Trade release, which is updated monthly

International trade in services (Tables 6.7 and 6.8)

These data relate to overseas trade in services and cover both production and non-production industries (excluding the public sector). In terms of the types of services traded these include royalties, various forms of consultancy, computing and telecommunications services, advertising and market research and other business services. A separate inquiry covers the film and television industries. The surveys cover receipts from the provision of services to residents of other countries (exports) and payments to residents of other countries for services rendered (imports).

Sources of data

The International Trade in Services (ITIS) surveys (which consist of a quarterly component addressed to the largest businesses and an annual component for the remainder) are based on a sample of companies derived from the Inter-departmental Business Register in addition to a reference list and from 2007 onwards a sample of approximately 5000 contributors from the Annual Business Inquiry (ABI). The companies are asked to show the amounts for their imports and exports against the geographical area to which they were paid or from which they were received, irrespective of where they were first earned.

The purpose of the ITIS survey is to record international transactions which impact on the UK's BoP. Exports and imports of goods are generally excluded, as they will have been counted in the estimate for trade in goods. However earnings from third country trade – that is, from arranging the sale of goods between two countries other than the UK and where the goods never physically enter the UK (known as merchanting) – are included. Earnings from commodity trading are also included. Together, these two comprise trade related services.

Royalties are a large part of the total trade in services collected in the ITIS survey. These cover transactions for items such as printed matter, sound recordings, performing rights, patents, licences, trademarks, designs, copyrights, manufacturing rights, the use of technical know-how and technical assistance.

Balance of Payments (Tables 6.9 to 6.12)

Tables 6.9 to 6.12 are derived from *United Kingdom Balance of Payments: The Pink Book*. The following general notes to the tables provide brief definitions and explanations of the figures and terms used. Further notes are included in the Pink Book.

Summary of Balance of Payments

The BoP consists of the current account, the capital account, the financial account and the International Investment Position (IIP). The current account consists of trade in goods and services, income, and current transfers. Income consists of investment income and compensation of employees. The capital account mainly consists of capital transfers and the financial account covers financial transactions. The IIP covers balance sheet levels of UK external assets and liabilities. Every credit entry in the balance of payments accounts should, in theory, be matched by a corresponding debit entry so that total current, capital and financial account credits should be equal to, and therefore offset by, total debits. In practice there is a discrepancy termed net errors and omissions.

Current account

Trade in goods

The goods account covers exports and imports of goods. Imports of motor cars from Japan, for example, are recorded as debits in the trade in goods account, whereas exports of vehicles manufactured in the UK are recorded as credits. Trade in goods forms a component of the expenditure measure of gross domestic product (GDP).

Trade in services

The services account covers exports and imports of services, for example civil aviation. Passenger tickets for travel on UK aircraft sold abroad, for example, are recorded as credits in the services account, whereas the purchases of airline tickets from foreign airlines by UK passengers are recorded as debits. Trade in services, along with trade in goods, forms a component of the expenditure measure of GDP.

Income

The income account consists of compensation of employees and investment income and is dominated by the latter. Compensation of employees covers employment income from cross-border and seasonal workers which is less significant in the UK than in other countries. Investment income covers earnings (for example, profits, dividends and interest payments and receipts) arising from cross-border investment in financial assets and liabilities. For example, earnings on foreign bonds and shares held by financial institutions based in the UK are recorded as credits in the investment income account, whereas earnings on UK company securities held abroad are recorded as investment income debits. Investment income forms a component of gross national income (GNI) but not GDP.

Current transfers

Current transfers are composed of central government transfers (for example, taxes and payments to and receipts from, the EU) and other transfers (for example gifts in cash or kind received by private individuals from abroad or receipts from the EU where the UK government acts as an agent for the ultimate beneficiary of the transfer). Current transfers do not form a component either of GDP or of GNI. For example, payments to the UK farming industry under the EU Agricultural Guarantee Fund are recorded as credits in the current transfers account, while payments of EU agricultural levies by the UK farming industry are recorded as debits in the current transfers account.

Capital account

Capital account transactions involve transfers of ownership of fixed assets, transfers of funds associated with acquisition or disposal of fixed assets and cancellation of liabilities by creditors without any counterparts being received in return. The main components are migrants transfers, EU transfers relating to fixed capital formation (regional development fund and agricultural guidance fund) and debt forgiveness. Funds brought into the UK by new immigrants would, for example, be recorded as credits in the capital account, while funds sent abroad by UK residents emigrating to other countries would be recorded as debits in the capital account. The size of capital account transactions are quite minor compared with the current and financial accounts.

Financial account

While investment income covers earnings arising from cross-border investments in financial assets and liabilities, the financial account of the balance of payments covers the flows of such investments. Earnings on foreign bonds and shares held by financial institutions based in the UK are, for example, recorded as credits in the investment income account, but the acquisition of such foreign securities by UK-based financial institutions are recorded as net debits in the financial account or portfolio investment abroad. Similarly, the acquisitions of UK company securities held by foreign residents are recorded in the financial account as net credits or portfolio investment in the UK.

International Investment Position

While the financial account covers the flows of foreign investments and financial assets and liabilities, the IIP records the levels of external assets and liabilities. While the acquisition of foreign securities by UK-based financial institutions are recorded in the financial account as net debits, the total holdings of foreign securities by UK-based financial institutions are recorded as levels of UK external assets. Similarly, the holdings of UK company securities held by foreign residents are recorded as levels of UK liabilities.

Foreign direct investment (Tables 6.13 to 6.18)

Direct investment refers to investment that adds to, deducts from, or acquires a lasting interest in an enterprise operating in an economy other than that of the investor – the investor's purpose being to have an effective voice in the management of the enterprise. (For the purposes of the statistical inquiry, an effective voice is taken as equivalent to a holding of 10 per cent or more in the foreign enterprise.) Other investments in which the investor does not have an effective voice in the management of the enterprise are mainly portfolio investments and these are not covered here.

Direct investment is a financial concept and is not the same as capital expenditure on fixed assets. It covers only the money invested in a related concern by the parent company and the concern will then decide how to use the money. A related concern may also raise money locally without reference to the parent company.

The investment figures are published on a net basis; that is they consist of investments net of disinvestments by a company into its foreign subsidiaries, associate companies and branches.

ESA2010

The European System of National and Regional Accounts (ESA 2010) is the newest internationally compatible EU accounting framework for a systematic and detailed description of an economy. The ESA 2010 was published in the Official Journal on 26 June 2013. It was implemented in September 2014.

The ESA 2010 differs in scope as well as in concepts from its predecessor ESA 95 reflecting developments in measuring modern economies, advances in methodological research and the needs of users. The structure of the ESA 2010 is consistent with the worldwide guidelines on national accounting set out in the System of National Accounts 2008 (2008 SNA).

What are the main changes?

• Research and development expenditure is counted as investment. Expenditures on research and development (R&D) have the nature of an investment and contribute to future economic growth. This is the major improvement introduced by ESA 2010.

• Expenditure on weapon systems is counted as investment. The new system recognises the productive potential of expenditure on weapon systems for the external security of a country, over several years. This identifies them as investment.

• A more detailed analysis of pension schemes. A compulsory supplementary table transparently shows the liabilities of all pension schemes, including those of government whether unfunded or funded, in order to improve comparability between countries.

• Goods sent abroad for processing. The value of goods sent abroad for processing will no longer impact on gross exports and imports figures because ESA 2010 uses a change in ownership approach and is no more based on physical movements. ESA2010 just records an export processing service. This will reduce the level of exports and imports, but will not affect the overall current account balance. See https://ec.europa.eu/eurostat/documents/737960/738004/ESA2010-FAQ.pdf/fea21e81-a2cb-421a-8b9e-41aae7d02a14

Sources of data

The figures in Tables 6.13 to 6.18 are based on annual inquiries into foreign direct investment for 2016. These were sample surveys which involved sending approximately 1530 forms to UK businesses investing abroad, and 2370 forms to UK businesses in which foreign parents and associates had invested. The tables also contain some revisions as a result of new information coming to light in the course of the latest surveys. Further details from the latest annual surveys, including analyses by industry and by components of direct investment, are available in business monitor MA4.

Country allocation

The analysis of inward investment is based on the country of ownership of the immediate parent company. Thus, inward investment in a UK company may be attributed to the country of the intervening overseas subsidiary, rather than the country of the ultimate parent. Similarly, the country analysis of outward investment is based on the country of ownership of the immediate subsidiary; for example, to the extent that overseas investment in the UK is channeled through holding companies in the Netherlands, the underlying flow of investment from this country is overstated and the inflow from originating countries is understated.

Further information

More detailed statistics on foreign direct investment are available on request from Office for National Statistics, Telephone: +44 (0)1633 455923, email fdi@ons.gsi.gov.uk

6.1 Trade in goods[1]

United Kingdom
Balance of payments basis

£million and Indices 2013=100

		2004	2005	2006	2007	2008	2009	2010	2011	2012	2013	2014	2015	2016
Value (£ million)														
Exports of goods	**BOKG**	191 608	212 053	243 957	222 964	254 577	229 107	270 196	308 171	301 621	303 147	292 894	287 584	301 705
Imports of goods	**BOKH**	253 549	282 213	322 920	313 504	349 603	315 731	367 580	403 126	412 528	423 811	415 469	407 304	436 580
Balance on trade in goods	**BOKI**	-61 941	-70 160	-78 963	-90 540	-95 026	-86 624	-97 384	-94 955	-110 907	-120 664	-122 575	-119 720	-134 875
Price index numbers[2]														
Exports of goods	**BQKR**	70.3	72.8	74.0	73.6	83.7	84.5	90.3	97.4	97.3	100.0	95.6	88.7	93.7
Imports of goods	**BQKS**	72.5	75.7	78.1	78.2	89.2	90.2	94.5	102.5	102.7	100.0	96.0	90.6	93.5
Terms of trade[3]	**BQKT**	101.0	100.3	98.8	98.2	97.9	97.7	99.6	99.1	98.9	100.0	99.6	98.0	100.2
Volume index numbers[4]														
Exports of goods	**BQKU**	84.5	91.3	103.6	95.3	96.7	86.4	96.2	102.7	101.0	100.0	101.6	108.7	107.8
Imports of goods	**BQKV**	82.1	88.1	98.1	95.2	93.7	84.4	94.1	95.6	98.0	100.0	103.3	108.1	112.1

Source: Office for National Statistics: 01633 455635

1 These are provisional estimates subject to fluctuations when new or amended data become available. See chapter text. Statistics of trade in goods on a balance of payments basis are obtained by making certain adjustments in respect of valuation and coverage to the statistics recorded in the Overseas Trade Statistics. These adjustments are described in detail in The Pink Book.

2. Price index numbers - not seasonally adjusted.

3 Export price index as a percentage of the import price index.

4. Volume index numbers - seasonally adjusted.

Table 6.1 may show revisions to data going back over time. This is mainly to reflect revised data from HMRC and other data suppliers, later survey data and a re-assessment of seasonal factors.

6.2 Sales of products manufactured in the United Kingdom by Industry Division

Division	SIC(07) Division	2012	2013	2014	£ millions 2015
Other mining and quarrying	8	S	2,299	2,315	1,738
Manufacture of food products	10	62,898	66,030	67,053	66,176
Manufacture of beverages and tobacco products	11 & 12	14,169	14,109	S	14,599
Manufacture of textiles	13	4,134	S	S	4,193
Manufacture of wearing apparel	14	1,634	1,634	1,830	1,665
Manufacture of leather and related products	15	647	727	681	690
Manufacture of wood and of products of wood and cork, except furniture; manufacture of articles of straw and plaiting materials	16	5,740	6,097	S	6,534
Manufacture of paper and paper products	17	10,018	S	10,364	10,105
Printing and reproduction of recorded media	18	8,672	8,055	S	7,910
Manufacture of coke and refined petroleum products	19	S	S	S	0
Manufacture of chemicals and chemical products	20	S	S	21,431	20,453
Manufacture of basic pharmaceutical products and pharmaceutical preparations	21	12,289	12,047	10,914	10,799
Manufacture of rubber and plastic products	22	S	S	S	19,226
Manufacture of other non-metallic mineral products	23	10,168	10,359	11,468	12,436
Manufacture of basic metals	24	7,422	6,825	6,583	5,926
Manufacture of fabricated metal products, except machinery and equipment	25	S	24,266	25,551	26,439
Manufacture of computer, electronic and optical products	26	S	12,559	12,145	12,166
Manufacture of electrical equipment	27	S	S	S	10,288
Manufacture of machinery and equipment n.e.c.	28	26,921	S	27,581	24,756
Manufacture of motor vehicles, trailers and semi-trailers	29	39,297	S	47,382	48,424
Manufacture of other transport equipment	30	23,840	26,471	27,192	27,759
Manufacture of furniture	31	6,098	6,306	6,557	6,709
Other manufacturing	32	S	S	4,771	4,932
Repair and installation of machinery and equipment	33	S	13,987	14,086	14,221
Total		341,985	354,721	362,545	358,143

Source: Office for National Statistics
Email: prodcompublications@ons.gov.uk
Tel: (01633) 456720

Note: Information in this table relates to products corresponding to a division irrespective of which division the business making the product is classified to.

S A figure has been suppressed as disclosive

6.3 United Kingdom exports: by commodity[1,2]

Seasonally adjusted

		2006	2007	2008	2009	2010	2011	2012	2013	2014	2015	2016
0. Food and live animals	BOGG	**6974**	**7745**	**9104**	**9504**	**10881**	**12478**	**11651**	**12430**	**12531**	**12151**	**13441**
01. Meat and meat preparations	BOGS	784	859	1203	1278	1453	1749	1638	1697	1707	1477	1592
02. Dairy products and eggs	BQMS	724	804	895	848	1054	1299	1202	1423	1537	1329	1392
04 & 08. Cereals and animal feeding stuffs	BQMT	1601	1825	2322	2385	2653	2831	2838	2868	2926	3131	3495
05. Vegetables and fruit	BQMU	562	581	678	736	810	912	857	1022	950	1027	1120
1. Beverages and tobacco	BQMZ	**4385**	**4651**	**5136**	**5431**	**6166**	**7489**	**7268**	**7363**	**6934**	**6771**	**7274**
11. Beverages	BQNB	3916	4324	4661	5005	5790	7166	6964	7064	6638	6494	7030
12. Tobacco	BQOW	469	327	475	426	376	323	304	299	296	277	244
2. Crude materials	BQOX	**4393**	**5001**	**6042**	**4578**	**6716**	**8524**	**7875**	**6840**	**6287**	**5350**	**5710**
of which:												
24. Wood, lumber and cork	BQOY	140	146	131	87	115	113	100	109	114	100	104
25. Pulp and waste paper	BQOZ	313	401	471	342	530	625	536	486	474	498	558
26. Textile fibres	BQPA	473	439	470	511	626	739	798	695	636	500	524
28. Metal ores	BQPB	2497	3003	3758	2607	4213	5279	4660	4049	3722	3155	3433
3. Fuels	BOPN	**25664**	**24727**	**35898**	**27461**	**35907**	**43796**	**44653**	**41979**	**36005**	**23800**	**21100**
33. Petroleum and petroleum products	ELBL	23499	22789	32347	24958	31838	38996	40472	38396	32809	20720	18754
32, 34 & 35. Coal, gas and electricity	BOQI	2165	1938	3551	2503	4069	4800	4181	3583	3196	3080	2346
4. Animal and vegetable oils and fats	BQPI	**228**	**280**	**321**	**336**	**387**	**420**	**440**	**458**	**411**	**383**	**409**
5. Chemicals	ENDG	**37654**	**39533**	**44378**	**48021**	**51811**	**54385**	**53769**	**49885**	**48899**	**52726**	**53709**
of which:												
51. Organic chemicals	BQPJ	8202	7746	8527	9398	9204	9431	9217	7811	6971	8633	7744
52. Inorganic chemicals	BQPK	2167	2854	3000	2846	3513	3081	2937	2559	1877	1888	1733
53. Colouring materials	CSCE	1684	1746	1905	1740	2009	2229	2023	2045	2084	1911	2092
54. Medicinal products	BQPL	13757	14770	17479	20914	22566	23291	23690	21094	21374	24412	25473
55. Toilet preparations	CSCF	3479	3719	3916	4148	4330	4900	4885	5311	5240	4896	5478
57 & 58. Plastics	BQQA	4613	4772	5003	4553	5488	6142	5834	5719	5819	5556	5864
6. Manufactures classified chiefly by material	BQQB	**28050**	**29450**	**32469**	**24660**	**29523**	**35358**	**32477**	**31856**	**29312**	**27679**	**26990**
of which:												
63. Wood and cork manufactures	BQQC	273	263	247	221	230	265	274	257	264	241	275
64. Paper and paperboard manufactures	BQQD	2076	2182	2393	2335	2414	2473	2362	2340	2289	2035	2252
65. Textile manufactures	BQQE	2669	2563	2540	2346	2599	2822	2739	2811	2862	2730	2846
67. Iron and steel	BQQF	5197	6048	6896	4588	5070	6120	5812	6104	6091	4761	3688
68. Non-ferrous metals	BQQG	5071	5859	6887	3974	5879	8642	6806	6991	6885	7027	6629
69. Metal manufactures	BQQH	4617	4752	5161	4351	4636	5036	5046	5023	5479	5353	5605
7. Machinery and transport equipment[3]	BQQI	**111799**	**83892**	**89563**	**79942**	**93491**	**105095**	**105209**	**110794**	**109689**	**110017**	**122513**
71-716, 72, 73 & 74. Mechanical machinery	BQQK	28812	29647	32457	29537	33145	39295	39807	41864	40446	39111	41410
716, 75, 76 & 77. Electrical machinery	BQQL	55623	24168	25042	24022	25995	26547	24565	24711	24531	24205	25486
78. Road vehicles	BQQM	19838	21651	22909	17400	23660	27861	28957	31554	32603	32849	38080
79. Other transport equipment	BQQN	7526	8426	9155	8983	10691	11392	11880	12665	12109	13852	17537
8. Miscellaneous manufactures[3]	BQQO	**24574**	**25133**	**27108**	**26447**	**30547**	**33309**	**33582**	**35241**	**37957**	**41813**	**42953**
of which:												
84. Clothing	CSCN	2842	3017	3188	3322	3570	4149	4342	4881	5434	5786	6243
85. Footwear	CSCP	507	526	601	697	830	883	978	1154	1247	1444	1579
87 & 88. Scientific and photographic	BQQQ	7487	7243	8206	8474	9836	10931	10763	11445	11461	11747	12428
9. Other commodities and transactions	BOQL	**1038**	**2112**	**2240**	**984**	**1608**	**2950**	**2464**	**3544**	**5091**	**6062**	**4974**
Total United Kingdom exports	BOKG	**244759**	**222524**	**252259**	**227364**	**267037**	**303804**	**299388**	**300390**	**293116**	**286752**	**299073**

Source: Office for National Statistics
Email: trade@ons.gov.uk
Tel: 01633 651988

1 See chapter text. The numbers on the left hand side of the table refer to the code numbers of the Standard International Trade Classification, Revision 3, which was introduced in January 1988.

2 Balance of payments consistent basis.

3 Sections 7 and 8 are shown by broad economic category in table G2 of the Monthly Review of External Trade Statistics.

6.4 United Kingdom imports: by commodity [1,2]

Seasonally adjusted

		2006	2007	2008	2009	2010	2011	2012	2013	2014	2015	2016
0. Food and live animals	**BQQR**	**20308**	**21676**	**25556**	**26663**	**27492**	**29610**	**30693**	**32566**	**32432**	**32563**	**35827**
of which:												
01. Meat and meat preparations	BQQS	3918	4052	4641	4947	5041	5697	5663	5846	5976	5848	6195
02. Dairy products and eggs	BQQT	1843	1868	2286	2328	2432	2546	2665	2920	2852	2614	2724
04 & 08. Cereals and animal feeding stuffs	BQQU	2534	2951	3850	3979	4019	4210	4744	5522	5226	5034	5277
05. Vegetables and fruit	BQQV	5934	6321	7154	7191	7564	8101	8181	8449	8401	8745	10330
1. Beverages and tobacco	**BQQW**	**5542**	**5737**	**6210**	**6444**	**6937**	**7322**	**7379**	**7526**	**7626**	**7546**	**7947**
11. Beverages	EGAT	4152	4384	4767	5072	5231	5604	5734	5899	5932	5800	6154
12. Tobacco	EMAI	1390	1353	1443	1372	1706	1718	1645	1627	1694	1746	1793
2. Crude materials	**ENVB**	**7192**	**8777**	**9661**	**6655**	**9299**	**10606**	**9586**	**9875**	**9681**	**8648**	**8889**
of which:												
24. Wood, lumber and cork	ENVC	1504	1837	1399	1177	1497	1452	1514	1811	2186	2324	2569
25. Pulp and waste paper	EQAH	563	539	647	457	601	654	531	517	516	550	498
26. Textile fibres	EQAP	237	246	272	241	300	446	347	355	384	341	332
28. Metalores	EHAA	2862	4080	4917	2470	4151	4941	4250	4330	3793	2856	2739
3. Fuels	**BQAT**	**31649**	**32738**	**49245**	**36033**	**45430**	**63971**	**68684**	**64185**	**54202**	**38114**	**34254**
33. Petroleum and petroleum products	ENXO	26474	27360	38439	28346	36156	49901	54482	49493	43201	29196	26506
32, 34 & 35. Coal, gas and electricity	BPBI	5175	5378	10806	7687	9274	14070	14202	14692	11001	8918	7748
4. Animal and vegetable oils and fats	**EHAB**	**799**	**916**	**1408**	**1055**	**1126**	**1483**	**1409**	**1363**	**1184**	**1063**	**1158**
5. Chemicals	**ENGA**	**33583**	**36471**	**39893**	**41965**	**47063**	**50955**	**51311**	**49947**	**52150**	**51603**	**54105**
of which:												
51. Organic chemicals	EHAC	8073	8804	8562	8335	9452	10186	10232	8198	6993	6268	6390
52. Inorganic chemicals	EHAE	2111	2739	2760	2799	2947	3639	3325	2529	2272	2326	2002
53. Colouring materials	CSCR	1110	1171	1218	1152	1269	1322	1357	1391	1401	1388	1600
54. Medicinal products	EHAF	10603	11536	12983	16105	17484	18489	19403	19938	23278	23911	25563
55. Toilet preparations	CSCS	3369	3472	3916	4147	4403	4639	4734	5048	5203	5540	5867
57 & 58. Plastics	EHAG	5429	5709	6211	5552	6871	7657	7449	7942	8072	7617	8078
6. Manufactures classified chiefly by material	**EHAH**	**37538**	**39880**	**41703**	**35672**	**43732**	**49342**	**48730**	**47312**	**44507**	**42919**	**45776**
of which:												
63. Wood and cork manufactures	EHAI	1648	1782	1776	1549	1703	1728	1707	1857	2037	2186	2331
64. Paper and paperboard manufactures	EHAJ	5181	5351	5581	5630	6028	6133	5846	5949	6117	5768	5937
65. Textile manufactures	EHAK	4041	4093	4016	3794	4247	4568	4498	4697	4878	5007	5279
67. Iron and steel	EHAL	5132	6066	6646	3928	5243	6584	6284	5422	5915	5063	5192
68. Non-ferrous metals	EHAM	5948	6232	6343	6030	8787	10388	11473	10225	8327	7557	8073
69. Metal manufactures	EHAN	5881	6643	7018	6036	6908	7541	7647	8005	8359	8434	9292
7. Machinery and transport equipment[3]	**EHAO**	**141270**	**118193**	**120467**	**107500**	**128445**	**128621**	**131098**	**140423**	**146683**	**151767**	**169087**
71 - 716, 72, 73 & 74. Mechanical machinery	EHAQ	22920	26124	29083	24415	28783	33002	34522	35937	36969	36223	40765
716, 75, 76 & 77. Electrical machinery	EHAR	75466	46084	47001	44521	50793	51266	50796	52329	51679	53182	57431
78. Road vehicles	EHAS	33569	36811	34051	26737	33474	36399	36274	41182	45766	50006	53857
79. Other transport equipment	EHAT	9315	9174	10332	11827	15395	7954	9506	10975	12269	12356	17034
8. Miscellaneous manufactures[3]	**EHAU**	**42873**	**45324**	**47751**	**47365**	**51031**	**53866**	**55125**	**58077**	**61926**	**66186**	**69847**
of which:												
84. Clothing	CSDR	11662	11957	12716	13465	14125	15126	15141	16304	17052	17970	18946
85. Footwear	CSDS	2675	2583	2760	3021	3459	3491	3800	3929	4280	4753	4933
87 & 88. Scientific and photographic	EHAW	7724	7581	8307	8335	8984	9440	10033	10659	10855	11471	12474
9. Other commodities and transactions	**BQAW**	**1902**	**1396**	**2029**	**3317**	**2096**	**2391**	**2093**	**8106**	**4796**	**4153**	**4835**
Total United Kingdom imports	**BOKH**	**322656**	**311108**	**343923**	**312669**	**362651**	**398167**	**406108**	**419380**	**415187**	**404562**	**431725**

1 See chapter text. The numbers on the left hand side of the table refer to the code numbers of the Standard International Trade Classification, Revision 3, which was introduced in January 1988.

2 Balance of payments consistent basis.

3 Sections 7 and 8 are shown by broad economic category in table G2 of the Monthly Review of External Trade Statistics.

Source: Office for National Statistics

Email: trade@ons.gov.uk
Tel: 01633 651988

6.5 Trade in goods - exports

£ million

		2007	2008	2009	2010	2011	2012	2013	2014	2015	2016
Exports (Credits)											
Europe											
European Union (EU)											
Austria	QBRY	1376	1478	1295	1484	1732	1554	1659	1733	1625	1834
Belgium	QDOH	11829	13428	10869	13489	16257	14218	13613	12621	12015	11831
Bulgaria	QAMF	202	262	205	256	337	310	387	471	362	457
Croatia	QAMM	158	217	212	175	152	145	98	152	148	184
Cyprus	QDNZ	414	540	623	571	710	442	445	470	387	325
Czech Republic	QDLF	1403	1557	1447	1846	1968	1827	1904	2190	2048	2220
Denmark	QBSE	2182	2602	2485	2789	3079	2690	2838	2975	2418	2543
Estonia	QAMN	228	226	141	196	288	289	322	288	227	236
Finland	QBSH	1958	1915	1329	1517	1696	1547	1537	1701	1337	1314
France	QDJA	18142	18160	17258	19450	22484	20892	20709	19658	18606	20003
Germany	QDJD	25018	28260	24542	28720	34801	32504	29918	32315	31770	33068
Greece	QDJG	1355	1667	1630	1401	1237	910	1333	1050	968	937
Hungary	QDLI	862	1013	855	1099	1217	1094	1222	1290	1326	1370
Ireland	QDJJ	17810	19184	15966	17092	18229	17235	18373	19032	17416	17235
Italy	QDJM	9201	9436	8378	8950	10243	8043	8387	9265	8820	10078
Latvia	QAMO	144	171	109	172	246	256	375	356	223	238
Lithuania	QAMP	307	286	177	234	280	379	319	315	290	364
Luxembourg	QDOK	271	206	199	254	283	228	238	228	205	212
Malta	QDOC	363	445	400	402	462	393	442	434	391	399
Netherlands	QDJP	15203	20085	18299	22192	25010	25040	25516	23908	17601	18651
Poland	QDLL	2376	3026	2806	3847	4416	3418	3791	4090	3786	4281
Portugal	QDJT	1482	1650	1544	1860	1796	1376	1341	1417	1315	1467
Romania	QAMQ	666	759	691	792	981	942	917	998	1027	1053
Slovak Republic	QAMR	377	455	375	473	568	526	466	493	464	549
Slovenia	QAMS	203	231	181	227	252	221	209	258	212	249
Spain	QDJW	10066	10316	9252	10053	9954	8481	8554	9387	9260	9691
Sweden	QDJZ	4911	5236	4233	5632	6407	5725	5685	5820	4618	4682
European Central Bank	QARP	-	-	-	-	-	-	-	-	-	-
EU Institutions	EOAY	-	-	-	-	-	-	-	-	-	-
Total EU28	L87R	128507	142811	125501	145173	165085	150685	150598	152915	138865	145471
European Free Trade Association (EFTA)											
Iceland	QDKW	202	189	128	132	150	192	171	176	220	584
Liechtenstein	EPOW	3	9	5	25	13	9	4	20	10	3
Norway	QDKZ	2723	2827	2725	3102	3374	3561	3447	3537	3144	3180
Switzerland	QDLC	3864	4732	3976	5458	6210	7017	5954	5768	9832	8602
Total EFTA	EPOT	6792	7757	6834	8717	9747	10779	9576	9501	13206	12369
Other Europe											
Albania	QAMC	19	16	18	21	19	22	21	21	17	19
Belarus	QAME	69	90	81	120	134	129	97	87	66	53
Russia	QDLO	2850	4332	2455	3681	5212	5663	5337	4296	2758	2906
Turkey	QDLR	2346	2601	2371	3255	3937	3693	4066	3548	3483	4451
Ukraine	QAMT	443	612	589	473	566	600	594	371	283	393
Serbia and Montenegro	QAMW	107	130	101	98	123	127	150	139	140	149
of which: Serbia	KN2P	99	120	97	94	115	117	135	127	131	133
Montenegro	KN2M	8	10	4	4	8	10	15	12	9	16
Other	BOQE	294	564	508	809	977	1056	1112	1185	1116	1163
Total Europe	EPLM	141427	158913	138458	162347	185800	172754	171551	172063	159934	166974

6.5 Trade in goods - exports

£ million

		2007	2008	2009	2010	2011	2012	2013	2014	2015	2016
Exports (Credits) ***(contd.)***											
Americas											
Argentina	QAOM	225	318	255	358	417	384	374	314	297	321
Brazil	QDLU	1068	1691	1792	2222	2472	2667	2693	2301	2175	1975
Canada	QATH	3276	3247	3332	4132	4755	4156	3984	4043	3901	4876
Chile	QAMG	183	267	514	629	794	684	1157	494	460	477
Colombia	QAML	139	160	174	230	313	331	363	349	371	273
Mexico	QDLX	762	906	754	950	1007	1136	1164	1064	1307	1320
United States of America	J8V9	32094	35252	34028	38111	40089	41231	39579	38700	45898	47420
Uruguay	QAMU	36	66	60	79	121	115	169	120	223	136
Venezuela	QAMV	250	280	300	273	328	410	314	208	211	109
Other Central American Countries	BOQQ	862	1023	757	898	974	1214	881	844	948	1129
Other	BOQT	184	248	234	395	477	656	606	444	525	342
Total Americas	EPLO	39079	43458	42200	48277	51747	52984	51284	48881	56316	58378
Asia											
China	QDMA	4675	6015	5622	8293	10542	11533	13820	15473	12773	13478
Hong Kong	QDMD	2649	3661	3738	4463	5380	5394	5613	4962	5835	6336
India	QDMG	3771	4953	3086	4508	6633	5430	6384	5267	4018	3703
Indonesia	QDMJ	293	393	365	460	672	652	697	527	470	559
Iran	QAON	398	443	405	307	190	109	84	101	97	167
Israel	QDMM	1238	1339	1145	1391	1656	1545	1414	1117	1116	1186
Japan	QAMJ	3857	3910	3572	4343	4725	4933	4787	4501	4528	5041
Malaysia	QDMP	951	1135	1054	1276	1486	1541	1645	1536	1369	1365
Pakistan	QDMS	428	476	478	461	534	563	488	534	525	651
Philippines	QDMV	249	242	267	284	293	332	380	369	401	422
Saudi Arabia	QDMY	1853	2215	2367	2496	2704	3090	3378	5008	4638	4571
Singapore	QDNB	2438	2808	2931	3412	3742	4404	4208	3589	3818	4707
South Korea	QDNE	1858	2561	2172	2349	2686	4944	5172	4335	4880	4594
Taiwan	QDNH	937	889	796	1117	1387	1153	1231	1117	1185	1203
Thailand	QDNK	596	759	915	1138	1415	2008	1952	1467	1252	1141
Residual Gulf Arabian Countries	BOQW	4510	6035	5780	6604	7471	8535	9506	9461	9793	10453
Other Near & Middle Eastern Countries	QARJ	745	1031	1101	1319	1372	1347	1273	1205	1443	1169
Other	BORB	1598	843	983	1215	1363	1334	1465	1330	1422	1542
Total Asia	EPLP	33044	39708	36777	45436	54251	58847	63497	61899	59563	62288
Australasia & Oceania											
Australia	QDNN	2581	3103	2961	3364	4396	4752	4294	3834	3864	4108
New Zealand	QDNQ	359	387	350	414	541	616	646	671	580	743
Other	EGIZ	66	102	92	82	68	85	61	61	65	95
Total Australasia & Oceania	EPLQ	3006	3592	3403	3860	5005	5453	5001	4566	4509	4946
Africa											
Egypt	QDNT	690	945	1007	1200	1103	963	970	1091	1039	1323
Morocco	QAOO	313	516	312	566	567	650	475	594	507	880
South Africa	QDNW	2154	2650	2256	2894	3463	3213	2557	2434	2252	2414
Other North Africa	BORU	507	811	960	911	637	741	932	832	607	846
Other	BOQH	2744	3984	3734	4705	5598	6016	5902	4946	4043	4018
Total Africa	EPLN	6408	8906	8269	10276	11368	11583	10836	9897	8448	9481
International Organisations	EPLR	-	-	-	-	-	-	-	-	-	-
World total	LQAD	222964	254577	229107	270196	308171	301621	302169	297306	288770	302067

Source: Office for National Statistics

6.6 Trade in goods - imports

£ million

		2007	2008	2009	2010	2011	2012	2013	2014	2015	2016
Imports (Debits)											
Europe											
European Union (EU)											
Austria	**QBRZ**	2499	2365	2307	2665	2977	2621	2827	3206	3060	3287
Belgium	**QDOI**	15061	16542	15219	17301	19330	18408	20585	21832	21361	23491
Bulgaria	**QAMZ**	238	212	182	232	286	284	410	366	377	303
Croatia	**QANC**	73	88	78	97	106	77	126	71	97	103
Cyprus	**QDOA**	195	156	123	106	142	168	133	140	162	183
Czech Republic	**QDLG**	2994	3622	3377	4041	4288	4526	4606	4841	4953	5466
Denmark	**QBSF**	3454	3960	3891	4170	6145	5902	5753	4622	3501	4040
Estonia	**QAND**	237	151	128	167	225	234	188	184	189	249
Finland	**QBTG**	2627	2802	2140	2176	2462	2174	2461	2466	2079	2262
France	**QDJB**	22014	23421	20729	21852	23290	22764	24500	25711	24871	25503
Germany	**QDJE**	44780	45168	40736	47038	51040	53154	55710	61658	61465	65790
Greece	**QDJH**	649	672	565	715	674	692	745	742	727	809
Hungary	**QDLJ**	2382	2555	2575	3290	3116	2664	2610	2512	2556	2773
Ireland	**QDJK**	11369	12355	12597	13033	13187	12984	12294	12208	12741	13556
Italy	**QDJN**	13368	14280	12483	14123	14212	14416	14952	17093	15948	17467
Latvia	**QANE**	631	418	340	440	448	410	572	436	496	712
Lithuania	**QANF**	305	358	377	562	612	839	896	995	788	773
Luxembourg	**QDOL**	699	839	624	954	933	685	357	454	473	444
Malta	**QDOD**	181	137	106	172	169	128	105	133	187	205
Netherlands	**QDJQ**	23269	26124	22257	26796	28856	31578	34545	33550	31601	36194
Poland	**QDLM**	3707	4354	4737	6189	7149	7488	7799	7956	8222	9358
Portugal	**QDJU**	1518	1764	1448	1774	1824	1762	1943	2328	2389	2719
Romania	**QANG**	949	812	799	1261	1303	1286	1477	1529	1567	1805
Slovak Republic	**QANH**	1281	1649	1630	1646	1536	1597	1828	1982	2028	2727
Slovenia	**QANI**	317	324	257	362	363	346	319	323	331	422
Spain	**QDJX**	10529	10880	9710	10520	11925	11673	13924	15862	16799	14799
Sweden	**QDKA**	5324	6926	5804	6897	7792	9173	7467	7808	6920	6481
European Central Bank	**QARQ**	-	-	-	-	-	-	-	-	-	-
EU Institutions	**EOBS**	-	-	-	-	-	-	-	-	-	-
Total EU28	**L87T**	170650	182934	165219	188579	204390	208033	219132	231008	225888	241921
European Free Trade Association (EFTA)											
Iceland	**QDKX**	424	473	490	433	417	390	391	418	469	476
Liechtenstein	**EPOX**	38	34	21	10	7	2	3	7	7	8
Norway	**QDLA**	14680	22097	16262	21055	26846	24725	20240	15649	12325	13736
Switzerland	**QDLD**	4856	5402	5415	7471	7608	8999	8339	8624	8721	10126
Total EFTA	**EPOU**	19998	28006	22188	28969	34878	34116	28973	24698	21522	24346
Other Europe											
Albania	**QAMX**	-	-	-	-	1	-	8	7	-	-
Belarus	**QAMY**	599	105	20	37	48	89	76	54	24	34
Russia	**QDLP**	5476	7019	4660	5253	7424	8381	7073	6226	4220	4009
Turkey	**QDLS**	4719	4988	4678	5349	5536	5713	6308	6818	7038	7457
Ukraine	**QANJ**	119	151	145	282	353	295	398	413	247	305
Serbia and Montenegro	**QANM**	74	90	74	94	97	83	113	94	146	219
of which: Serbia	**KN2Q**	74	88	74	93	96	80	112	94	146	219
Montenegro	**KN2N**	-	2	-	1	1	3	1	-	-	-
Other	**BOQF**	194	217	259	243	285	339	342	623	252	389
Total Europe	**EPMM**	201829	223510	197243	228806	253012	257049	262423	269941	259337	278680

6.6 Trade in goods - imports

£ million

		2007	2008	2009	2010	2011	2012	2013	2014	2015	2016
Imports (Debits) *(contd.)*											
Americas											
Argentina	**QAOP**	424	572	669	664	616	638	653	584	600	673
Brazil	**QDLV**	2071	2667	2576	3110	2713	2434	2537	2260	2008	1990
Canada	**QATI**	5830	5757	4477	5772	6118	5498	5734	4912	6056	5375
Chile	**QANA**	502	592	600	585	618	588	643	627	584	673
Colombia	**QANB**	373	706	584	676	920	931	826	675	610	495
Mexico	**QDLY**	562	786	759	1034	1080	715	758	915	1016	1075
United States of America	**J8VA**	25775	25695	24300	26988	28630	29650	27587	28787	33124	36625
Uruguay	**QANK**	71	118	116	103	116	117	97	79	72	65
Venezuela	**QANL**	494	618	428	422	408	468	258	272	200	129
Other Central American Countries	**BOQR**	1168	1383	1252	1146	1068	829	1089	1010	952	1106
Other	**BOQU**	251	373	352	364	461	497	496	479	451	609
Total Americas	**EPMO**	37521	39267	36113	40864	42748	42365	40678	40600	45673	48815
Asia											
China	**QDMB**	19205	23913	25354	30944	31774	31490	35763	36458	36344	40547
Hong Kong	**QDME**	7037	8218	7784	8176	7598	7340	7326	6898	6579	6691
India	**QDMH**	4006	4959	5462	6203	6606	6483	9680	8169	6097	6369
Indonesia	**QDMK**	1010	1227	1243	1394	1345	1267	1245	1129	1096	1283
Iran	**QAOQ**	55	69	211	207	375	121	35	41	25	41
Israel	**QDMN**	1047	1177	1101	1565	2258	2396	1904	1208	1055	1046
Japan	**QAMK**	7956	8597	6691	8110	8832	8468	7611	7017	6822	8241
Malaysia	**QDMQ**	1718	1906	1673	1838	1772	1704	1673	1750	1866	1852
Pakistan	**QDMT**	506	642	706	809	883	838	956	1124	1076	1194
Philippines	**QDMW**	727	638	397	526	476	449	402	403	412	493
Saudi Arabia	**QDMZ**	920	724	677	794	1095	1707	2816	2573	1878	1555
Singapore	**QDNC**	4112	4069	3603	4141	3862	3705	2693	2488	1912	2575
South Korea	**QDNF**	3010	3534	2870	2562	2605	3220	3399	4086	4413	4762
Taiwan	**QDNI**	2431	2648	2272	3116	3474	3936	3607	3355	3188	3188
Thailand	**QDNL**	2033	2467	2333	2684	2581	2601	2718	2692	2597	2873
Residual Gulf Arabian Countries	**BOQX**	2148	2410	2831	5385	8818	7165	7345	6490	5724	5749
Other Near & Middle Eastern Countries	**QARK**	379	436	344	298	444	816	348	195	220	246
Other	**BORD**	2651	3181	3634	3909	4949	6439	7123	6911	8031	9083
Total Asia	**EPMP**	60951	70815	69186	82661	89747	90145	96644	92987	89335	97788
Australasia & Oceania											
Australia	**QDNO**	2205	2397	2231	2312	2427	2397	2225	1656	1911	2078
New Zealand	**QDNR**	664	753	821	843	868	887	890	926	911	883
Other	**HFKF**	117	170	168	107	198	161	184	213	151	155
Total Australasia & Oceania	**EPMQ**	2986	3320	3220	3262	3493	3445	3299	2795	2973	3116
Africa											
Egypt	**QDNU**	545	654	689	658	824	646	807	879	671	674
Morocco	**QAOR**	433	443	335	344	416	475	528	621	589	995
South Africa	**QDNX**	3158	4813	3868	4426	2942	3276	2128	2374	2867	3052
Other North Africa	**BORW**	1715	2386	1849	2851	2235	4213	5244	4154	1977	1103
Other	**BOQJ**	3688	3771	3018	3504	7533	8694	10201	6077	3974	3235
Total Africa	**EPMN**	9539	12067	9759	11783	13950	17304	18908	14105	10078	9059
International Organisations	**EPMR**	-	-	-	-	-	-	-	-	-	-
World total	**LQBL**	312826	348979	315521	367376	402950	410308	421952	420428	407396	437458

Source: Office for National Statistics

6.7 Total International Trade in Services all industries (excluding travel, transport and banking) analysed by product 2015-2016

£ million

	Exports		Imports		Balance	
	2015	2016	2015	2016	2015	2016
Agricultural and Mining Services						
Agricultural, forestry and fishing	15	15	10	12	4	3
Mining and oil and gas extraction services	1,679	1,157	168	236	1,510	921
Total Agricultural and Mining services	**1,693**	**1,172**	**179**	**248**	**1,515**	**924**
Manufacturing, Maintenance and On-site Processing Services						
Waste treatment and depolution services	121	117	130	165	-9	-49
Manufacturing services on goods owned by others	2,350	2,735	627	601	1,723	2,134
Maintenance and repair services	2,089	2,041	890	725	1,199	1,317
Total Manufacturing, Maintenance and On-site Processing services	**4,560**	**4,893**	**1,647**	**1,491**	**2,913**	**3,402**
Business and Professional Services						
Accountancy, auditing, bookkeeping and tax consulting services	2,058	2,395	893	1,070	1,165	1,326
Advertising, market research and public opinion polling services	5,258	7,085	3,166	3,495	2,092	3,590
Business management and management consulting services	7,249	8,921	3,060	5,254	4,189	3,666
Public relations services	338	386	123	168	215	218
Recruitment services	1,365	1,613	519	760	846	854
Legal services	4,966	4,982	741	1,132	4,225	3,850
Operating leasing services	342	358	624	503	-282	-144
Procurement services	188	217	289	266	-101	-49
Property management services	409	423	145	27	265	396
Other business and professional services	3,724	4,859	2,093	2,767	1,631	2,092
Services between related enterprises	11,970	14,668	9,676	11,520	2,294	3,147
Total Business and Professional Services	**37,867**	**45,907**	**21,329**	**26,961**	**16,538**	**18,945**
Research and Development Services						
Provision of R&D services	5,224	5,749	4,559	4,906	665	843
Provision of product development and testing activities	1,141	1,343	422	327	719	1,015
Total Research and Development Services	**6,364**	**7,092**	**4,980**	**5,233**	**1,384**	**1,858**
Intellectual Property						
Trade marks, franchises, brands or design rights						
Outright sales and purchases	371	724	720	1,141	-349	-417
Charges or payments for the use of	5,468	5,103	3,435	3,805	2,034	1,298
Copyrighted literary works, sound recordings, films, television prgrammes and databases						
Outright sales and purchases	248	549	109	322	139	227
Charges or payments for the use of	5,223	6,459	4,236	4,679	987	1,780
Patents and other intellectual property that are the end result of research and development						
Outright sales and purchases	90	86	133	74	-43	13
Charges or payments for the use of	1,737	1,455	686	919	1,051	536
Total intellectual property	**13,137**	**14,376**	**9,319**	**10,939**	**3,819**	**3,436**
Telecommunication, Computer and Information Services						
Postal and courier	1,574	1,757	1,015	1,082	559	675
Telecommunications	6,783	8,617	4,444	4,947	2,339	3,670
Computer Services	7,673	8,335	4,729	5,190	2,944	3,146
Publishing Services	693	1,032	118	151	575	880
News agency Services	605	674	56	50	549	624
Information Services	2,080	2,330	903	1,041	1,177	1,289
Total Telecommunication, Computer and Information Services	**19,409**	**22,744**	**11,266**	**12,461**	**8,143**	**10,283**
Construction Services						
Construction in the UK	177	381	701	798	-524	-417
Construction outside the UK	1,416	1,593	503	612	913	980
Total Construction Services	**1,594**	**1,974**	**1,205**	**1,410**	**389**	**563**

6.7 Total International Trade in Services all industries (excluding travel, transport and banking) analysed by product 2015-2016

£ million

	Exports		Imports		Balance	
	2015	2016	2015	2016	2015	2016
Financial Services						
Financial	14,896	18,415	3,283	3,430	11,612	14,985
Insurance and Pension Services						
Insurance and Pension Services Claims	2,322	3,008			2,322	3,008
Insurance and Pension Services Premiums			403	450	-403	-450
Merchanting and Other Trade related Services						
Merchanting	2,241	2,691	372	345	1,870	2,346
Other trade - related services	2,208	1,607	817	832	1,390	775
Total Merchanting and Other Trade related Services	**4,449**	**4,297**	**1,189**	**1,177**	**3,260**	**3,121**
Personal, Cultural and Recreational Services						
Audio- Visual and related services	1,546	1,438	682	755	864	684
Medical Services	26	41	8	12	18	28
Training and educational services	296	437	79	84	217	353
Heritage and recreational services	354	440	137	106	218	334
Social, domestic and other personal services	74	130	41	34	33	96
Total Personal, Cultural and Recreational Services	**2,296**	**2,486**	**946**	**990**	**1,350**	**1,495**
Technical and Scientific Services						
Architectural services	468	456	31	48	437	408
Engineering Services	7,348	7,314	1,249	1,963	6,099	5,350
Scientific and other techinical services inc surveying	1,379	1,431	598	445	781	986
Total Technical Services	**9,194**	**9,201**	**1,878**	**2,456**	**7,316**	**6,745**
Other Trade in Services						
Other trade in services	5,449	7,092	886	1,470	4,563	5,622
Total International Trade in Services	**123,231**	**142,657**	**58,509**	**68,718**	**64,722**	**73,939**

Source: Office for National Statistics

- Denotes nil or less than £500,000

.. Denotes disclosive data

The sum of constituent items may not always agree exactly with the totals shown due to rounding

Data from 2013 has been collected in accordance with BPM6 regulations

6.8 Total International Trade in Services (excluding travel, transport and banking) analysed by continents and countries 2014 - 2016

£ million

	Exports			Imports			Balance		
	2014	2015	2016	2014	2015	2016	2014	2015	2016
Europe									
European Union (EU)									
Austria	373	388	482	380	345	355	-6	43	127
Belgium	1,730	2,078	2,516	1,010	1,264	1,331	720	814	1,186
Bulgaria	96	159	137	57	89	138	39	70	-1
Croatia	55	53	72	16	21	23	40	33	49
Cyprus	230	287	413	141	181	135	89	106	278
Czech Republic	332	351	444	178	257	305	155	94	139
Denmark	1,514	1,427	1,976	713	553	638	801	874	1,337
Estonia	46	30	38	25	31	36	22	-1	3
Finland	791	604	623	216	181	226	574	423	397
France	4,650	5,346	6,516	3,586	3,568	4,392	1,064	1,778	2,124
Germany	7,171	7,276	9,719	5,287	4,910	6,395	1,883	2,366	3,324
Greece	398	342	425	111	119	106	287	223	319
Hungary	280	260	325	178	140	183	102	120	142
Irish Republic	6,598	7,188	9,092	3,335	3,791	4,736	3,263	3,398	4,357
Italy	2,292	3,035	2,680	1,542	1,401	1,664	750	1,634	1,016
Latvia	35	45	77	15	17	30	20	29	47
Lithuania	49	47	75	26	31	41	23	16	34
Luxembourg	2,255	2,189	2,589	1,693	1,905	2,078	562	284	511
Malta	207	240	410	55	73	153	152	168	256
Netherlands	7,580	6,854	7,672	2,393	2,720	3,751	5,187	4,134	3,921
Poland	818	805	1,004	506	619	759	312	186	245
Portugal	455	409	393	277	244	242	178	165	152
Romania	223	230	273	153	142	217	69	87	56
Slovakia	133	127	193	82	85	79	51	42	114
Slovenia	..	..	87	..	..	22	50	..	64
Spain	2,070	2,138	2,532	1,392	1,333	1,362	679	805	1,169
Sweden	2,009	2,123	2,496	1,167	1,824	1,482	841	299	1,014
EU Institutions	..	..	11	..	..	-	18	..	11
Total European Union (EU)	**42,475**	**44,098**	**53,267**	**24,554**	**25,866**	**30,879**	**17,921**	**18,232**	**22,389**
European Free Trade Association (EFTA)									
Iceland	96	118	155	24	16	47	72	102	109
Liechtenstein	36	65	84	2	23	39	34	42	45
Norway	2,212	1,624	1,708	466	400	559	1,746	1,224	1,149
Switzerland	7,204	6,863	7,737	1,791	2,603	2,480	5,413	4,261	5,257
Total EFTA	**9,548**	**8,670**	**9,684**	**2,283**	**3,041**	**3,124**	**7,265**	**5,629**	**6,560**
Other Europe									
Russia	1,133	1,080	900	288	294	304	845	786	596
Channel Islands	1,550	1,813	2,017	291	264	294	1,259	1,549	1,724
Isle of Man	435	197	239	14	9	40	421	188	199
Turkey	582	808	699	127	370	198	454	438	501
Rest of Europe	800	726	841	201	146	292	599	580	549
Europe Unallocated	2,188	2,126	2,437	1,326	1,494	1,580	862	632	858
Total Europe	**58,711**	**59,518**	**70,085**	**29,085**	**31,483**	**36,710**	**29,626**	**28,035**	**33,375**
America									
Brazil	797	781	507	149	184	220	648	597	287
Canada	1,414	1,476	2,089	791	563	707	623	913	1,383
Mexico	261	383	370	40	45	82	222	338	288
USA	27,821	27,991	32,733	12,945	13,880	16,734	14,875	14,110	15,999
Rest of America	2,806	3,094	3,533	861	683	808	1,945	2,412	2,725
America Unallocated	425	328	444	76	57	100	349	271	343
Total America	**33,523**	**34,053**	**39,675**	**14,863**	**15,413**	**18,650**	**18,661**	**18,641**	**21,025**

6.8 Total International Trade in Services (excluding travel, transport and banking) analysed by continents and countries 2014 - 2016

£ million

	Exports			Imports			Balance		
	2014	2015	2016	2014	2015	2016	2014	2015	2016
Asia									
China	1,058	1,647	1,600	521	861	832	537	785	767
Hong Kong	1,006	1,241	1,330	666	760	854	341	481	476
India	975	1,189	1,062	1,519	1,759	2,066	-544	-570	-1,004
Indonesia	171	180	153	55	72	63	115	108	89
Israel	351	452	581	241	375	279	109	77	302
Japan	2,456	2,370	2,743	1,410	1,702	2,443	1,046	668	300
Malaysia	438	406	477	191	147	335	247	259	143
Pakistan	181	150	243	93	35	35	88	115	208
Philippines	90	103	123	127	319	214	-37	-216	-91
Saudi Arabia	4,289	4,613	4,874	71	84	132	4,218	4,530	4,742
Singapore	2,077	2,311	1,767	1,507	1,196	1,389	570	1,115	378
South Korea	800	768	851	205	207	242	595	561	609
Taiwan	317	298	514	100	86	106	217	212	408
Thailand	286	317	212	172	64	73	114	253	140
Rest of Asia	4,494	4,634	7,388	946	1,188	1,373	3,548	3,446	6,015
Asia Unallocated	714	771	859	424	209	224	290	562	634
Total Asia	**19,703**	**21,452**	**24,778**	**8,248**	**9,065**	**10,662**	**11,454**	**12,386**	**14,116**
Australasia and Oceania									
Australia	1,863	1,787	1,968	873	1,096	824	990	691	1,143
New Zealand	220	175	223	39	70	62	181	106	161
Rest of Australia and Oceania	..	..	69	..	..	14	74	54	55
Oceania Unallocated	..	..	2	..	..	2	1	1	-1
Total Australasia and Oceania	**2,175**	**2,023**	**2,261**	**929**	**1,172**	**903**	**1,246**	**851**	**1,359**
Africa									
Nigeria	493	867	397	75	97	104	418	770	293
South Africa	1,167	1,037	1,111	325	408	424	842	629	687
Rest of Africa	3,160	3,216	3,242	574	520	865	2,585	2,696	2,377
Africa Unallocated	261	216	220	186	114	158	75	102	62
Total Africa	**5,081**	**5,335**	**4,970**	**1,160**	**1,138**	**1,551**	**3,921**	**4,196**	**3,419**
Total Unallocated	..	850	887	..	237	242	340	613	645
International Organisations	..	-	-	..	-	-	1	-	-
TOTAL INTERNATIONAL TRADE IN SERVICES	**119,703**	**123,231**	**142,657**	**54,455**	**58,508**	**68,718**	**65,248**	**64,722**	**73,939**

Source: Office for National Statistics

- Denotes nil or less than £500,000

.. Denotes disclosive data

The sum of constituent items may not always agree exactly with the totals shown due to rounding

Data from 2013 has been collected in accordance with BPM6 regulation

See quality and methodology section for geographical groupings

Excludes the activities of travel, transport and banking industries

Estimates for Croatia have been published for the first time in 2013. Previously this was included in the Rest of Europe.

6.9 Summary of balance of payments in 2015

£ million

	Credits	Debits
1. Current account		
A. Goods and services	510340	548908
1. Goods	284855	411186
2. Services	225485	137722
2.1. Manufacturing physical inputs owned by others	2191	536
2.2. Maintenance and repair	1164	413
2.3. Transport	24100	21739
2.4. Travel	29758	41415
2.5. Construction	1574	1154
2.6. Insurance and pension services	12907	151
2.7. Financial	50769	8695
2.8. Intellectual property	11480	8132
2.9. Telecommunications, computer and information services	15893	9248
2.10. Other business	70527	40411
2.11. Personal, cultural and recreational services	2505	3208
2.12. Government	2617	2620
B. Primary income	139656	176672
1. Compensation of employees	1295	1498
2. Investment income	136331	172087
2.1. Direct investment	66499	69427
2.2. Portfolio investment	48483	71228
2.3. Other investment	20494	31432
2.4. Reserve assets	855	
3. Other primary income	2030	3087
C. Secondary income	19012	43689
1. General government	5503	25981
2. Other sectors	13509	17708
Total current account	669008	769269
2. Capital account		
1. Capital transfers	915	1896
2. Acquisition/disposal of non-produced, non-financial assets	762	910
Total capital account	1677	2806

6.9 Summary of balance of payments in 2015

contd.

£ million

	Net acquisition of financial assets	Net incurrence of liabilities
3. Financial account		
1. Direct investment	-42018	33202
Abroad	-42018	
1.1. Equity capital other than reinvestment of earnings	-53	
1.2. Reinvestment of earnings	-3194	
1.3. Debt instruments[1]	-38771	
In United Kingdom		33202
1.1. Equity capital other than reinvestment of earnings		26065
1.2. Reinvestment of earnings		22209
1.3. Debt instruments[2]		-15072
2. Portfolio investment	-24398	240993
Assets	-24398	
2.1. Equity and investment fund shares	-25422	
2.2. Debt securities	1024	
Liabilities		240993
2.1. Equity and investment fund shares		74334
2.2. Debt securities		166659
3. Financial derivatives and employee stock options (net)	-31783	
4. Other investment	-107076	-358935
Assets	-107076	
4.1. Other equity	69	
4.2. Currency and deposits	-112533	
4.3. Loans	5794	
4.4. Trade credit and advances	-65	
4.5. Other accounts receivable	-341	
Liabilities		-358935
4.1. Currency and deposits		-121373
4.2. Loans		-238393
4.3. Insurance, pensions and standardised guarantee schemes		-254
4.4. Trade credit and advances		-
4.5. Other accounts payable		1085
4.6. Special drawing rights		-
5. Reserve assets	21079	
5.1. Monetary gold	-	
5.2. Special drawing rights	55	
5.3. Reserve position in the IMF	-172	
5.4. Other reserve assets	21196	
Total financial account	-184196	-84740

Source: Office for National Statistics

1 Debt instrument transactions on direct investment abroad represents claims on affiliated enterprises plus claims on direct investors.

2 Debt instrument transactions on direct investment in the United Kingdom represents liabilities to direct investors plus liabilities to affiliated enterprises

6.10 Summary of balance of payments: Balances (net credits less net debits)

£ million

	Current account												
	Trade in goods	Trade in services	**Total goods and services**	Compen- sation of employees	Invest- ment income	Other primary income	**Total primary income**	Second- ary income	**Current balance**	Current balance as % of GDP[1]	Capital account	Financial account	Net errors & omissions
	LQCT	KTMS	KTMY	KTMP	HMBM	MT5W	HMBP	KTNF	HBOG	AA6H	FKMJ	-HBNT	HHDH
1946	-101	-274	-375	-20	76	-	56	166	-153	..	-21	-181	-7
1947	-358	-197	-555	-19	140	-	121	123	-311	..	-21	-552	-220
1948	-152	-64	-216	-20	223	-	203	96	83	0.7	-17	58	-8
1949	-138	-43	-181	-20	206	-	186	29	34	0.3	-12	103	81
1950	-55	-4	-59	-21	378	-	357	39	337	2.6	-10	447	120
1951	-693	32	-661	-21	322	-	301	29	-331	-2.3	-15	-426	-80
1952	-274	123	-151	-22	231	-	209	169	227	1.5	-15	229	17
1953	-246	122	-124	-25	207	-	182	143	201	1.2	-13	177	-11
1954	-213	114	-99	-27	227	-	200	55	156	0.9	-13	174	31
1955	-318	41	-277	-27	149	-	122	43	-112	-0.6	-15	-34	93
1956	44	25	69	-30	203	-	173	2	244	1.2	-13	250	19
1957	-39	120	81	-32	223	-	191	-5	267	1.2	-13	313	59
1958	22	117	139	-34	261	-	227	4	370	1.6	-10	411	51
1959	-129	116	-13	-37	233	-	196	-	183	0.7	-5	68	-110
1960	-418	36	-382	-35	201	-	166	-6	-222	-0.8	-6	7	235
1961	-160	48	-112	-35	223	-	188	-9	67	0.2	-12	-23	-78
1962	-122	47	-75	-37	301	-	264	-14	175	0.6	-12	195	32
1963	-142	1	-141	-38	364	-	326	-37	148	0.5	-16	30	-102
1964	-573	-37	-610	-33	365	-	332	-74	-352	-1	-17	-392	-23
1965	-288	-70	-358	-34	405	-	371	-75	-62	-0.2	-18	-49	31
1966	-144	39	-105	-39	358	-	319	-91	123	0.3	-19	-22	-126
1967	-646	151	-495	-39	354	-	315	-118	-298	-0.7	-25	-179	144
1968	-770	333	-437	-48	303	-	255	-119	-301	-0.7	-26	-688	-361
1969	-283	382	99	-47	468	-	421	-109	411	0.8	-23	794	406
1970	-94	443	349	-56	527	-	471	-89	731	1.3	-22	818	109
1971	120	602	722	-63	454	-	391	-90	1023	1.6	-23	1330	330
1972	-829	703	-126	-52	350	-	298	-142	30	-	-35	-477	-472
1973	-2676	883	-1793	-68	970	-	902	-336	-1227	-1.5	-39	-1031	235
1974	-5357	1258	-4099	-92	1010	-	918	-302	-3483	-3.8	-34	-3185	332
1975	-3378	1663	-1715	-102	257	-	155	-313	-1873	-1.6	-36	-1569	340
1976	-4079	2815	-1264	-140	760	-	620	-534	-1178	-0.9	-12	-507	683
1977	-2439	3636	1197	-152	-678	-	-830	-889	-522	-0.3	11	3286	3797
1978	-1710	4132	2422	-140	-300	-	-440	-1420	562	0.3	-79	2655	2172
1979	-3514	4469	955	-130	-342	-	-472	-1777	-1294	-0.6	-103	-864	533
1980	1123	4284	5407	-82	-2268	-	-2350	-1653	1404	0.5	-4	2157	757
1981	2986	4616	7602	-66	-1883	-	-1949	-1219	4434	1.5	-79	5312	957
1982	1614	4075	5689	-95	-2336	-	-2431	-1476	1782	0.6	6	1233	-555
1983	-1892	5191	3299	-89	-1050	-	-1139	-1391	769	0.2	75	3287	2443
1984	-5736	5867	131	-94	-326	-	-420	-1566	-1855	-0.5	107	7130	8878
1985	-3755	8243	4488	-120	-2609	-	-2729	-2924	-1165	-0.3	185	1657	2637
1986	-9968	7878	-2090	-156	71	-	-85	-2094	-4269	-1	135	122	4256
1987	-12093	8610	-3483	-174	-785	-	-959	-3437	-7879	-1.6	159	-9690	-1970
1988	-22028	6934	-15094	-64	-1234	-	-1298	-3293	-19685	-3.6	-39	-15271	4453
1989	-25214	6891	-18323	-138	-2367	-	-2505	-4228	-25056	-4.1	-56	-9988	15124
1990	-19280	8163	-11117	-110	-4644	-	-4754	-4802	-20673	-3.1	222	-23090	-2639
1991	-10919	8369	-2550	-63	-5691	-	-5754	-999	-9303	-1.3	-55	-5711	3647
1992	-13788	8941	-4847	-49	-990	-	-1039	-5228	-11114	-1.5	35	-17720	-6641
1993	-13881	11223	-2658	35	-2488	-	-2453	-5056	-10167	-1.3	32	-23696	-13561
1994	-11972	11787	-185	-170	1625	-	1455	-5187	-3917	-0.5	-252	3259	7428
1995	-12985	15379	2394	-296	-435	-	-731	-7363	-5700	-0.7	97	-1297	4306

6.10 Summary of balance of payments: Balances (net credits less net debits)

£ million

	Current account												
	Trade in goods	Trade in services	**Total goods and services**	Compen- sation of employees	Invest- ment income	Other primary income	**Total primary income**	**Second- ary income**	**Current balance**	Current balance as % of GDP[1]	Capital account	Financial account	Net errors & omissions
	LQCT	**KTMS**	**KTMY**	**KTMP**	**HMBM**	**MT5W**	**HMBP**	**KTNF**	**HBOG**	**AA6H**	**FKMJ**	**-HBNT**	**HHDH**
1996	-14736	16340	1604	93	-2351	-	-2258	-4539	-5193	-0.6	806	-2030	2357
1997	-12892	16720	3828	83	-299	686	470	-6097	-1799	-0.2	509	6544	7834
1998	-22343	14433	-7910	-10	11792	819	12601	-8878	-4187	-0.4	-261	563	5011
1999	-29418	13249	-16169	201	-1530	711	-618	-7864	-24651	-2.4	-258	-21270	3639
2000	-33472	13033	-20439	150	6673	441	7264	-10053	-23228	-2.1	393	-13653	9182
2001	-41913	15805	-26108	66	10615	579	11260	-6893	-21741	-1.9	73	-30063	-8395
2002	-48953	16008	-32945	67	17861	968	18896	-9382	-23431	-2	-675	-22443	1663
2003	-50959	20573	-30386	59	19324	1272	20655	-10822	-20553	-1.7	-65	-14150	6468
2004	-61941	26544	-35397	-494	22696	1279	23481	-11090	-23006	-1.8	90	-13517	9399
2005	-70160	33658	-36502	-610	32094	1140	32624	-12865	-16743	-1.2	-843	-12304	5282
2006	-78963	42850	-36113	-958	16594	816	16452	-12702	-32363	-2.2	-1527	-28587	5303
2007	-90540	50598	-39942	-734	16626	537	16429	-13977	-37490	-2.4	-169	-26554	11105
2008	-95026	48837	-46189	-715	5634	362	5281	-14094	-55002	-3.5	220	-39261	15521
2009	-86624	52269	-34355	-259	4863	756	5360	-15836	-44831	-3	404	-29017	15410
2010	-97384	54791	-42593	-389	20468	114	20193	-20662	-43062	-2.7	3	-30276	12783
2011	-94955	67895	-27060	-173	19589	229	19645	-21673	-29088	-1.8	-380	-23455	6013
2012	-110907	73573	-37334	-148	-1765	-273	-2186	-21913	-61433	-3.7	-167	-52786	8814
2013	-120664	81426	-39238	-326	-9544	-471	-10341	-26863	-76442	-4.4	-472	-78558	-1644
2014	-122575	86352	-36223	-470	-22642	-654	-23766	-25009	-84998	-4.7	-415	-78589	6824
2015	-126331	87763	-38568	-203	-35756	-1057	-37016	-24677	-100261	-5.4	-1129	-99456	1934

Source: Office for National Statistics

1. Using series YBHA: GDP at current market prices.

6.11 Balance of payments: current account

£ million

		1994	1995	1996	1997	1998	1999	2000	2001	2002	2003	2004
Credits												
Exports of goods and services												
Exports of goods	**LQAD**	135,143	153,577	167,196	172,110	163,997	166,539	188,130	189,624	186,776	188,546	191,608
Exports of services	**KTMQ**	53,089	59,202	65,085	67,377	70,375	75,960	81,739	88,444	93,255	104,635	114,711
Total exports of goods and services	**KTMW**	188,232	212,779	232,281	239,487	234,372	242,499	269,869	278,068	280,031	293,181	306,319
Primary income												
Compensation of employees	**KTMN**	681	887	911	1,007	840	960	1,032	1,087	1,121	1,116	931
Investment income	**HMBN**	72,883	85,797	90,122	96,180	105,941	103,423	134,480	139,884	124,178	124,908	140,914
Other primary income	**MT5S**	-	-	-	3,068	2,937	2,781	2,571	2,679	2,912	3,227	3,449
Total primary income	**HMBQ**	73,564	86,684	91,033	100,255	109,718	107,164	138,083	143,650	128,211	129,251	145,294
Secondary income												
General government	**FJUM**	2,138	1,730	2,828	2,393	1,767	3,542	2,465	4,991	3,663	3,968	4,299
Other sectors	**FJUN**	8,918	10,213	11,372	8,503	8,439	6,215	6,280	6,020	7,695	8,148	8,563
Total secondary income	**KTND**	11,056	11,943	14,200	10,896	10,206	9,757	8,745	11,011	11,358	12,116	12,862
Total	**HBOE**	272,852	311,406	337,514	350,638	354,296	359,420	416,697	432,729	419,600	434,548	464,475
Debits												
Imports of goods and services												
Imports of goods	**LQBL**	147,115	166,562	181,932	185,002	186,340	195,957	221,602	231,537	235,729	239,505	253,549
Imports of services	**KTMR**	41,302	43,823	48,745	50,657	55,942	62,711	68,706	72,639	77,247	84,062	88,167
Total exports of goods and services	**KTMX**	188,417	210,385	230,677	235,659	242,282	258,668	290,308	304,176	312,976	323,567	341,716
Primary income												
Compensation of employees	**KTMO**	851	1,183	818	924	850	759	882	1,021	1,054	1,057	1,425
Investment income	**HMBO**	71,258	86,232	92,473	96,479	94,149	104,953	127,807	129,269	106,317	105,584	118,218
Other primary income	**MT5U**	-	-	-	2,382	2,118	2,070	2,130	2,100	1,944	1,955	2,170
Total primary income	**HMBR**	72,109	87,415	93,291	99,785	97,117	107,782	130,819	132,390	109,315	108,596	121,813
Secondary income												
General government	**FJUO**	4,795	4,811	5,081	8,370	10,701	10,913	11,819	11,056	11,968	13,648	13,803
Other sectors	**FJUP**	11,448	14,495	13,658	8,623	8,383	6,708	6,979	6,848	8,772	9,290	10,149
Total secondary income	**KTNE**	16,243	19,306	18,739	16,993	19,084	17,621	18,798	17,904	20,740	22,938	23,952
Total	**HBOF**	276,769	317,106	342,707	352,437	358,483	384,071	439,925	454,470	443,031	455,101	487,481
Balances												
Trade in goods and services												
Trade in goods	**LQCT**	-11,972	-12,985	-14,736	-12,892	-22,343	-29,418	-33,472	-41,913	-48,953	-50,959	-61,941
Trade in services	**KTMS**	11,787	15,379	16,340	16,720	14,433	13,249	13,033	15,805	16,008	20,573	26,544
Total exports of goods and services	**KTMY**	-185	2,394	1,604	3,828	-7,910	-16,169	-20,439	-26,108	-32,945	-30,386	-35,397
Primary income												
Compensation of employees	**KTMP**	-170	-296	93	83	-10	201	150	66	67	59	-494
Investment income	**HMBM**	1,625	-435	-2,351	-299	11,792	-1,530	6,673	10,615	17,861	19,324	22,696
Other primary income	**MT5W**	-	-	-	686	819	711	441	579	968	1,272	1,279
Total primary income	**HMBP**	1,455	-731	-2,258	470	12,601	-618	7,264	11,260	18,896	20,655	23,481
Secondary income												
General government	**FJUQ**	-2,657	-3,081	-2,253	-5,977	-8,934	-7,371	-9,354	-6,065	-8,305	-9,680	-9,504
Other sectors	**FJUR**	-2,530	-4,282	-2,286	-120	56	-493	-699	-828	-1,077	-1,142	-1,586
Total secondary income	**KTNF**	-5,187	-7,363	-4,539	-6,097	-8,878	-7,864	-10,053	-6,893	-9,382	-10,822	-11,090
Total (Current balance)	**HBOG**	-3,917	-5,700	-5,193	-1,799	-4,187	-24,651	-23,228	-21,741	-23,431	-20,553	-23,006

\- = nil or less than a million

Source: Office for National Statistics
Email: bop@ons.gsi.gov.uk
Tel: 01633 456333

6.11 Balance of payments: current account

(contd.)

£ million

		2005	2006	2007	2008	2009	2010	2011	2012	2013	2014	2015
Credits												
Exports of goods and services												
Exports of goods	**LQAD**	212,053	243,957	222,964	254,577	229,107	270,196	308,171	301,621	303,147	292,894	284,855
Exports of services	**KTMQ**	129,285	145,836	157,679	166,223	169,473	174,121	188,816	197,520	214,495	218,760	225,485
Total exports of goods and services	**KTMW**	341,338	389,793	380,643	420,800	398,580	444,317	496,987	499,141	517,642	511,654	510,340
Primary income												
Compensation of employees	**KTMN**	974	938	984	1,046	1,176	1,097	1,121	1,124	1,094	1,080	1,295
Investment income	**HMBN**	193,049	249,298	307,890	287,868	175,117	174,003	199,995	170,279	157,261	139,005	136,331
Other primary income	**MT5S**	3,408	3,221	2,952	3,051	3,411	3,059	3,166	2,625	2,455	2,306	2,030
Total primary income	**HMBQ**	197,431	253,457	311,826	291,965	179,704	178,159	204,282	174,028	160,810	142,391	139,656
Secondary income												
General government	**FJUM**	4,385	4,471	4,408	5,720	6,271	3,843	3,536	3,719	4,302	5,086	5,503
Other sectors	**FJUN**	10,665	15,806	9,416	14,568	10,602	11,699	10,699	12,737	15,324	14,161	13,509
Total secondary income	**KTND**	15,050	20,277	13,824	20,288	16,873	15,542	14,235	16,456	19,626	19,247	19,012
Total	**HBOE**	553,819	663,527	706,293	733,053	595,157	638,018	715,504	689,625	698,078	673,292	669,008
Debits												
Imports of goods and services												
Imports of goods	**LQBL**	282,213	322,920	313,504	349,603	315,731	367,580	403,126	412,528	423,811	415,469	411,186
Imports of services	**KTMR**	95,627	102,986	107,081	117,386	117,204	119,330	120,921	123,947	133,069	132,408	137,722
Total exports of goods and services	**KTMX**	377,840	425,906	420,585	466,989	432,935	486,910	524,047	536,475	556,880	547,877	548,908
Primary income												
Compensation of employees	**KTMO**	1,584	1,896	1,718	1,761	1,435	1,486	1,294	1,272	1,420	1,550	1,498
Investment income	**HMBO**	160,955	232,704	291,264	282,234	170,254	153,535	180,406	172,044	166,805	161,647	172,087
Other primary income	**MT5U**	2,268	2,405	2,415	2,689	2,655	2,945	2,937	2,898	2,926	2,960	3,087
Total primary income	**HMBR**	164,807	237,005	295,397	286,684	174,344	157,966	184,637	176,214	171,151	166,157	176,672
Secondary income												
General government	**FJUO**	15,596	16,063	16,382	16,966	19,268	20,900	21,716	21,989	27,015	25,930	25,981
Other sectors	**FJUP**	12,319	16,916	11,419	17,416	13,441	15,304	14,192	16,380	19,474	18,326	17,708
Total secondary income	**KTNE**	27,915	32,979	27,801	34,382	32,709	36,204	35,908	38,369	46,489	44,256	43,689
Total	**HBOF**	570,562	695,890	743,783	788,055	639,988	681,080	744,592	751,058	774,520	758,290	769,269
Balances												
Trade in goods and services												
Trade in goods	**LQCT**	-70,160	-78,963	-90,540	-95,026	-86,624	-97,384	-94,955	-110,907	-120,664	-122,575	-126,331
Trade in services	**KTMS**	33,658	42,850	50,598	48,837	52,269	54,791	67,895	73,573	81,426	86,352	87,763
Total exports of goods and services	**KTMY**	-36,502	-36,113	-39,942	-46,189	-34,355	-42,593	-27,060	-37,334	-39,238	-36,223	-38,568
Primary income												
Compensation of employees	**KTMP**	-610	-958	-734	-715	-259	-389	-173	-148	-326	-470	-203
Investment income	**HMBM**	32,094	16,594	16,626	5,634	4,863	20,468	19,589	-1,765	-9,544	-22,642	-35,756
Other primary income	**MT5W**	1,140	816	537	362	756	114	229	-273	-471	-654	-1,057
Total primary income	**HMBP**	32,624	16,452	16,429	5,281	5,360	20,193	19,645	-2,186	-10,341	-23,766	-37,016
Secondary income												
General government	**FJUQ**	-11,211	-11,592	-11,974	-11,246	-12,997	-17,057	-18,180	-18,270	-22,713	-20,844	-20,478
Other sectors	**FJUR**	-1,654	-1,110	-2,003	-2,848	-2,839	-3,605	-3,493	-3,643	-4,150	-4,165	-4,199
Total secondary income	**KTNF**	-12,865	-12,702	-13,977	-14,094	-15,836	-20,662	-21,673	-21,913	-26,863	-25,009	-24,677
Total (Current balance)	**HBOG**	-16,743	-32,363	-37,490	-55,002	-44,831	-43,062	-29,088	-61,433	-76,442	-84,998	-100,261

Source: Office for National Statistics

Email: bop@ons.gsi.gov.uk

Tel: 01633 456333

\- = nil or less than a million

6.12 Summary of international investment position, financial account and investment income

£ billion

		2005	2006	2007	2008	2009	2010	2011	2012	2013	2014	2015
Investment abroad												
International investment position												
Direct investment	**N2V3**	954.0	992.3	1148.6	1438.6	1261.9	1343.0	1363.5	1411.5	1437.4	1383.9	1396.7
Portfolio investment	**HHZZ**	1383.1	1556.2	1722.8	1696.8	1923.3	2144.2	2130.5	2347.5	2439.1	2546.9	2549.9
Financial derivatives	**JX96**	820.1	853.7	1378.2	4040.2	2176.4	2962.9	3617.8	3060.1	2424.4	2828.6	2430.8
Other investment	**HLXV**	2730.8	2929.7	3697.6	4160.5	3467.8	3753.1	4039.8	3711.2	3488.0	3547.3	3401.6
Reserve assets	**LTEB**	24.7	22.9	26.7	36.3	40.1	49.7	56.8	61.7	61.4	67.7	87.5
Total	**HBQA**	5912.8	6354.8	7973.9	11372.4	8869.6	10252.8	11208.3	10591.9	9850.4	10374.4	9866.6
Financial account transactions[1]												
Direct investment	**-N2SV**	87.8	77.0	184.1	200.1	-32.8	35.8	50.0	7.7	28.6	-73.1	-42.0
Portfolio investment	**-HHZC**	160.5	144.8	100.5	-113.0	179.8	100.8	12.5	131.9	-10.3	7.2	-24.4
Financial derivatives (net)	**-ZPNN**	-5.8	-20.6	27.0	121.7	-29.1	-25.5	3.0	-36.9	11.6	-0.6	-31.8
Other investment	**-XBMM**	498.3	394.8	660.5	-652.0	-350.1	238.5	103.2	-233.7	-209.2	110.8	-107.1
Reserve assets	**-LTCV**	0.7	-0.4	1.2	-1.3	5.8	6.1	4.9	7.6	5.0	7.1	21.1
Total	**-HBNR**	741.5	595.6	973.2	-444.6	-226.4	355.7	173.6	-123.5	-174.3	51.5	-184.2
Investment income												
Direct investment	**N2QP**	83.5	91.7	101.1	86.6	74.3	92.9	104.6	87.2	84.0	71.2	66.5
Portfolio investment	**HLYX**	46.9	57.0	68.8	69.7	56.1	50.0	53.9	50.8	47.0	44.3	48.5
Other investment	**AIOP**	61.9	99.9	137.5	130.8	43.9	30.3	40.7	31.6	25.6	22.9	20.5
Reserve assets	**HHCB**	0.7	0.6	0.6	0.8	0.8	0.7	0.8	0.7	0.6	0.6	0.9
Total	**HMBN**	193.0	249.3	307.9	287.9	175.1	174.0	200.0	170.3	157.3	139.0	136.3
Investment in the UK												
International investment position												
Direct investment	**N2UG**	692.0	774.4	788.1	944.3	881.2	948.2	994.1	1250.9	1265.3	1349.7	1389.8
Portfolio investment	**HLXW**	1499.1	1744.2	2023.7	2040.0	2437.6	2565.9	2549.3	2606.2	2585.7	2715.7	2871.7
Financial derivatives	**JX97**	831.1	890.5	1392.2	3915.3	2096.8	2895.0	3554.9	3032.2	2376.7	2806.5	2441.7
Other investment	**HLYD**	2975.5	3110.3	3906.3	4331.9	3614.5	3906.3	4206.6	4077.0	3904.5	3823.9	3432.5
Total	**HBQB**	5997.8	6519.4	8110.4	11231.6	9030.1	10315.4	11305.0	10966.4	10132.2	10695.8	10135.7
Financial account transactions												
Direct investment	**N2SA**	139.7	113.0	104.6	142.4	6.2	42.3	16.6	29.7	35.8	44.3	33.2
Portfolio investment	**HHZF**	206.6	199.3	206.9	132.4	210.8	87.0	5.4	-81.5	45.2	131.3	241.0
Other investment	**XBMN**	407.5	311.9	688.3	-680.2	-414.4	256.6	175.0	-18.9	-176.8	-45.5	-358.9
Total	**HBNS**	753.8	624.2	999.8	-405.3	-197.4	386.0	197.1	-70.7	-95.8	130.0	-84.7
Investment income												
Direct investment	**N2Q4**	32.1	51.9	61.7	60.5	50.6	45.1	51.1	52.3	56.2	57.9	69.4
Portfolio investment	**HLZC**	49.5	62.8	71.8	77.5	61.5	63.9	73.3	72.4	72.6	69.9	71.2
Other investment	**HLZN**	79.3	118.0	157.8	144.3	58.2	44.5	55.9	47.3	38.0	33.9	31.4
Total	**HMBO**	161.0	232.7	291.3	282.2	170.3	153.5	180.4	172.0	166.8	161.6	172.1
Net investment												
International investment position												
Direct investment	**MU7O**	262.0	217.9	360.5	494.2	380.7	394.8	369.4	160.6	172.2	34.2	6.9
Portfolio investment	**CGNH**	-116.0	-188.0	-300.9	-343.2	-514.3	-421.6	-418.9	-258.7	-146.6	-168.7	-321.8
Financial derivatives	**JX98**	-11.0	-36.8	-14.1	124.9	79.6	67.8	62.9	27.9	47.7	22.1	-10.9
Other investment	**CGNG**	-244.7	-180.6	-208.7	-171.3	-146.7	-153.2	-166.8	-365.9	-416.5	-276.6	-30.9
Reserve assets	**LTEB**	24.7	22.9	26.7	36.3	40.1	49.7	56.8	61.7	61.4	67.7	87.5
Net investment position	**HBQC**	-85.0	-164.6	-136.5	140.9	-160.5	-62.5	-96.7	-374.5	-281.8	-321.3	-269.1
Financial account transactions[1]												
Direct investment	**-MU7M**	-51.9	-36.0	79.5	57.7	-39.0	-6.5	33.3	-22.0	-7.2	-117.4	-75.2
Portfolio investment	**-HHZD**	-46.1	-54.4	-106.4	-245.4	-31.0	13.8	7.1	213.4	-55.5	-124.1	-265.4
Financial derivatives	**-ZPNN**	-5.8	-20.6	27.0	121.7	-29.1	-25.5	3.0	-36.9	11.6	-0.6	-31.8
Other investment	**-HHYR**	90.8	82.9	-27.9	28.1	64.3	-18.1	-71.8	-214.9	-32.4	156.3	251.9
Reserve assets	**-LTCV**	0.7	-0.4	1.2	-1.3	5.8	6.1	4.9	7.6	5.0	7.1	21.1
Net transactions	**-HBNT**	-12.3	-28.6	-26.6	-39.3	-29.0	-30.3	-23.5	-52.8	-78.6	-78.6	-99.5
Investment income												
Direct investment	**MU7E**	51.4	39.7	39.4	26.1	23.8	47.8	53.5	34.9	27.8	13.3	-2.9
Portfolio investment	**HLZX**	-2.6	-5.7	-3.0	-7.8	-5.4	-13.9	-19.4	-21.6	-25.6	-25.6	-22.7
Other investment	**CGNA**	-17.4	-18.1	-20.4	-13.4	-14.2	-14.2	-15.2	-15.8	-12.4	-10.9	-10.9
Reserve assets	**HHCB**	0.7	0.6	0.6	0.8	0.8	0.7	0.8	0.7	0.6	0.6	0.9
Net earnings	**HMBM**	32.1	16.6	16.6	5.6	4.9	20.5	19.6	-1.8	-9.5	-22.6	-35.8

1. When downloading data from the Pink Book dataset users should reverse the sign of series that have an identifier that is prefixed with a minus sign.

Source: Office for National Statistics
Email: bop@ons.gsi.gov.uk
Tel: 01633 456333

6.13 Net foreign direct investment flows abroad analysed by area and main country, 2007 to 2016 (Directional)

£ million

	2007	2008	2009	2010	2011	2012	2013	2014	2015	2016
EUROPE	**91,174**	**64,811**	**16,642**	**24,436**	**37,212**	**-3,964**	**-20,241**	**-107,766**	**-12,078**	**-25,789**
EU	65,695	54,853	-13,416	20,191	25,441	-5,459	-11,656	-83,140	-13,403	-22,462
AUSTRIA	109	-73	-42	472	-49	-287	14	-131	..	85
BELGIUM	2,246	1,784	-1,833	7,284	16,053	1,472	-4,054	373	1,610	..
BULGARIA	-1	48	16	-101	-10	-43	4	13	26	-1
CROATIA	-6	54	-2	-9	-3	-12	11	11	25	-13
CYPRUS	371	470	60	-308	-340	296	36	-83	25	..
CZECH REPUBLIC	63	387	-189	-175	-42	974	268	26	5	-49
DENMARK	2,463	3,178	-2,177	479	-1,018	536	-124	-5	-800	788
ESTONIA	-4	-21	24	6	-10	-29	15	8	..	-83
FINLAND	258	80	-88	-19	-615	-198	3	-107	-43	46
FRANCE	8,256	8,507	845	5,180	-4,215	-6,925	-9,700	-2,631	1,085	517
GERMANY	2,798	1,000	3,027	-2,793	3,513	2,593	732	4,222	-1,569	-129
GREECE	291	465	-349	106	-982	-46	35	-33	160	..
HUNGARY	60	186	89	116	-7	161	40	-115	-123	..
IRISH REPUBLIC	3,367	223	3,619	-560	6,372	-4,185	-2,223	-192	-81	-5,662
ITALY	7,266	508	-3,530	527	657	116	-341	1,883	..	319
LATVIA	..	144	-60	-23	-36	20	50	-10	-9	-15
LITHUANIA	-1	..	..	4	4	-22	23	-5	3	..
LUXEMBOURG	29,335	6,854	-2,760	6,945	11,717	3,267	-6,291	-76,928	-7,964	1,565
MALTA	-2,891	..	-422	-509	-266	350	278	505	216	46
NETHERLANDS	1,122	12,118	-15,664	949	-4,777	-4,549	8,966	-7,488	-6,807	-13,188
POLAND	-575	-19	923	155	213	832	879	237	1,123	-112
PORTUGAL	431	384	721	604	-252	82	173	-67	-338	-444
ROMANIA	126	241	..	96	-28	133	187	15	82	..
SLOVAKIA	..	112	-34	..	95	16	-26	-12	-12	-45
SLOVENIA	..	12	9	..	127	-34	6	-3	-6	10
SPAIN	6,518	16,191	2,961	2,182	-371	9	-1,100	-1,526	289	790
SWEDEN	3,738	735	1,116	-486	-290	11	997	-1,098	477	2,349
EFTA	3,966	2,321	4,613	2,052	1,156	-2,594	3,284	2,045	2,344	28
of which										
NORWAY	1,280	1,630	1,884	-311	2,536	-833	-704	134	1,023	1,020
SWITZERLAND	2,796	742	2,885	2,354	-1,379	-1,744	3,554	1,900	1,323	-989
OTHER EUROPEAN COUNTRIES	21,513	7,637	25,445	2,194	10,614	4,089	-11,869	-26,670	-1,020	-3,356
of which										
RUSSIA	860	3,747	-34	-2,497	373	3,382	..	4,144	764	-432
UK OFFSHORE ISLANDS	19,134	2,961	24,591	3,222	10,775	493	-2,509	-27,050	-1,615	-2,966
THE AMERICAS	**59,514**	**20,391**	**-3,872**	**-19,648**	**45,305**	**11,258**	**40,992**	**8,396**	**-21,418**	**1,969**
of which										
BERMUDA	2,122	4,254	-2,014	-65	-879	-334	1,785	1,269	-362	-406
BRAZIL	846	932	390	1,687	2,283	321	-115	1,646	950	346
CANADA	15,453	-153	-2,698	-11,664	9,042	-3,638	655	333	..	-1,031
CHILE	99	-290	-	211	805	160	111	200	-532	203
COLOMBIA	109	169	188	..	-694	-486	115	-15	-120	-124
MEXICO	302	498	29	501	965	654	279	601	698	422
PANAMA	-12	-2	59	29	58	10	59	-33	..	9
USA	35,410	11,486	7,805	-13,691	34,813	12,478	37,199	2,474	-11,227	728
ASIA	**11,315**	**12,738**	**7,835**	**11,466**	**-22,989**	**1,253**	**-6,498**	**8,666**	**-9,730**	**12,574**
NEAR & MIDDLE EAST COUNTRIES	1,859	3,309	1,637	-5,736	-1,123	9,675	-9,139	1,788	..	5,303
of which										
GULF ARABIAN COUNTRIES	706	928	1,559	-734	907	2,469	915	-1,450	..	4,817
OTHER ASIAN COUNTRIES	9,456	9,429	6,197	17,202	-21,866	-8,422	2,641	6,878	5,110	7,272
of which										
CHINA	1,114	1,116	179	569	1,135	1,702	352	-251	-807	1,131
HONG KONG	2,267	1,115	-1,201	1,786	3,545	6,832	277	1,454	3,346	2,860
INDIA	4,893	784	547	2,567	8,977	-165	611	314	651	..
INDONESIA	-91	40	662	3,184	3,933	277	426	92	-164	801
JAPAN	893	980	1,031	-559	1,760	-729	516	-102	..	-20
MALAYSIA	218	312	280	629	800	550	164	1,541	65	669
SINGAPORE	-2,155	2,417	1,572	4,882	-43,882	-18,893	-1,533	1,662	2,737	..

6.13 Net foreign direct investment flows abroad analysed by area and main country, 2007 to 2016 (Directional)

£ million

	2007	2008	2009	2010	2011	2012	2013	2014	2015	2016
SOUTH KOREA	436	672	498	937	370	1,725	196	350	..	1,226
THAILAND	-15	275	300	141	164	272	137	204	-32	586
AUSTRALASIA & OCEANIA	**1,894**	**9,548**	**-3,399**	**8,530**	**6,655**	**2,902**	**8,406**	**-2,570**	**92**	**983**
of which										
AUSTRALIA	1,790	8,450	-4,517	8,240	6,012	2,585	8,234	-2,840	122	901
NEW ZEALAND	105	127	1,140	237	555	257	142	126	-128	11
AFRICA	**3,969**	**318**	**1,388**	**6,339**	**-6,522**	**1,655**	**3,243**	**2,523**	**225**	**-6,270**
of which										
KENYA	77	56	43	93	-51	-69	39	94	84	38
NIGERIA	31	242	873	220	888	1,545	-940	-213	..	553
SOUTH AFRICA	1,406	1,394	-1,961	2,038	799	1,610	1,536	883	893	..
ZIMBABWE	2	-6	1	10	25	17	3	-10	..	10
WORLD TOTAL	**167,866**	**107,806**	**18,593**	**31,124**	**59,660**	**13,105**	**25,902**	**-90,751**	**-42,910**	**-16,532**
OECD	127,963	78,285	-4,300	8,088	81,558	4,832	35,927	-80,685	-36,365	..
CENTRAL & EASTERN EUROPE	4	8	36	13	22	-16	66	41	-65	182

Source: Office for National Statistics

The sum of constituent items may not always agree exactly with the totals shown due to rounding.
A negative sign before values indicates a net disinvestment abroad.
For countries listed within regions see Geography tab.

.. Indicates data are disclosive
- Indicates nil data

6.14 FDI International investment positions abroad analysed by area and main country, 2007 to 2016 (Directional)

£ million

	2007	2008	2009	2010	2011	2012	2013	2014	2015	2016
EUROPE	**547,294**	**670,112**	**586,151**	**645,252**	**643,536**	**586,061**	**551,832**	**525,230**	**534,045**	**619,414**
EU	429,073	538,044	504,202	564,615	557,436	504,848	454,904	445,048	456,163	526,135
AUSTRIA	2,711	3,069	3,932	1,119	1,036	347	862	993	986	1,006
BELGIUM	8,274	12,769	15,807	43,284	40,991	16,699	12,537	11,032	15,818	14,928
BULGARIA	48	141	116	..	95	74	137	160	89	54
CROATIA	..	282	282	246	244	185	248	224	230	239
CYPRUS	745	626	556	623	739	1,224	702	526	520	3,230
CZECH REPUBLIC	670	1,036	531	554	472	1,346	1,749	1,733	1,747	1,871
DENMARK	6,569	11,554	7,321	8,324	7,245	24,489	7,465	7,032	6,050	6,900
ESTONIA	10	28	41	70	97	63	109	113	164	207
FINLAND	2,437	610	417	1,265	1,659	193	721	1,054	735	880
FRANCE	44,624	56,017	49,796	63,767	58,951	70,853	25,477	57,030	60,488	71,741
GERMANY	20,576	25,711	28,029	23,625	22,222	15,526	20,217	20,698	17,738	20,899
GREECE	911	1,186	960	2,125	1,510	1,301	1,612	1,442	544	275
HUNGARY	2,135	2,328	728	673	825	1,038	673	969	702	1,075
IRISH REPUBLIC	24,854	24,777	35,008	41,200	45,737	44,223	27,660	31,896	42,839	48,199
ITALY	15,310	12,454	12,735	12,903	12,308	10,836	10,200	11,165	10,950	12,452
LATVIA	..	106	10	-17	66	71	143	101	73	118
LITHUANIA	11	..	28	..	45	45	49	60	52	43
LUXEMBOURG	103,818	134,048	133,212	149,180	151,827	121,881	104,572	108,192	93,837	112,774
MALTA	3,741	1,961	1,884	1,152	487	1,765	243	1,858	2,184	..
NETHERLANDS	126,843	136,218	131,505	132,179	132,464	128,725	111,882	121,884	128,707	141,738
POLAND	2,086	3,232	4,676	3,874	4,075	4,053	4,585	4,974	6,047	6,195
PORTUGAL	3,948	4,741	4,177	4,432	3,397	3,097	1,056	3,202	3,039	3,365
ROMANIA	422	721	578	565	567	591	820	847	884	989
SLOVAKIA	200	..	262	275	295	203	267	307	239	..
SLOVENIA	..	..	55	..	343	262	101	77	111	125
SPAIN	39,479	76,835	47,132	48,454	44,751	36,194	4,781	40,532	45,015	55,944
SWEDEN	18,372	27,345	24,428	24,163	24,988	19,562	20,257	16,947	16,374	18,561
EFTA	15,985	21,392	25,463	26,055	23,789	26,254	28,581	17,025	21,380	28,981
of which										
NORWAY	2,433	4,402	5,417	5,837	4,976	4,820	3,754	2,384	3,358	6,835
SWITZERLAND	13,270	16,723	19,564	20,189	18,787	21,415	19,676	14,608	18,020	22,125
OTHER EUROPEAN COUNTRIES	102,236	110,675	56,485	54,582	62,310	54,958	68,347	63,157	56,502	64,298
of which										
RUSSIA	7,219	11,328	9,973	9,698	8,108	5,705	13,668	13,798	8,266	11,725
UK OFFSHORE ISLANDS	86,586	88,937	36,220	34,530	42,255	38,440	42,019	39,889	38,363	42,840
THE AMERICAS	**285,615**	**337,475**	**296,105**	**263,684**	**288,127**	**293,686**	**326,729**	**367,527**	**342,900**	**353,863**
of which										
BERMUDA	14,784	25,552	16,943	17,333	17,017	15,391	15,923	26,435	14,877	21,249
BRAZIL	3,132	6,144	4,105	6,121	14,331	14,582	9,241	14,639	15,645	13,498
CANADA	30,902	31,764	29,607	36,461	31,760	30,925	28,074	28,517	17,206	21,071
CHILE	506	369	275	574	838	718	877	1,327	1,273	1,223
COLOMBIA	1,188	1,785	2,101	2,661	465	-117	673	602	580	586
MEXICO	1,619	1,439	607	980	2,544	5,093	898	6,581	7,348	7,515
PANAMA	..	..	196	196	318	..	..	..	..	..
USA	193,958	236,081	222,237	181,511	203,918	198,001	169,146	254,153	237,262	240,979
ASIA	**50,970**	**71,948**	**76,317**	**100,563**	**111,614**	**107,822**	**125,021**	**121,398**	**138,216**	**152,290**
NEAR & MIDDLE EAST COUNTRIES	8,771	13,745	17,524	22,733	25,977	13,428	28,705	13,415	16,437	24,275
of which										
GULF ARABIAN COUNTRIES	5,238	7,881	11,915	14,980	18,412	10,529	23,899	6,943	9,145	14,319
OTHER ASIAN COUNTRIES	42,199	58,203	58,794	77,829	85,637	94,394	96,316	107,983	121,779	128,015
of which										
CHINA	2,942	4,504	4,614	6,001	6,598	6,501	4,588	9,165	9,862	11,605
HONG KONG	14,689	19,029	16,750	19,434	20,572	42,640	15,197	52,142	55,047	61,317
INDIA	4,984	4,827	10,629	12,345	13,632	5,088	3,547	3,148	12,117	13,188
INDONESIA	853	1,093	1,897	2,712	5,976	4,089	3,331	4,303	4,575	5,877
JAPAN	666	1,552	2,936	2,697	6,003	6,308	3,776	4,106	4,497	4,399
MALAYSIA	1,035	1,380	879	1,433	1,874	1,910	3,984	3,266	3,213	3,427

6.14 FDI International investment positions abroad analysed by area and main country, 2007 to 2016 (Directional)

£ million

	2007	2008	2009	2010	2011	2012	2013	2014	2015	2016
SINGAPORE	7,684	14,639	8,850	9,791	10,658	9,060	10,939	16,409	18,698	10,670
SOUTH KOREA	3,302	3,376	3,175	3,857	4,192	4,468	2,528	4,652	3,450	6,137
THAILAND	1,351	1,653	1,174	1,308	1,395	1,496	1,151	2,545	1,758	2,417
AUSTRALASIA & OCEANIA	**17,334**	**19,891**	**19,218**	**34,036**	**39,716**	**43,490**	**50,632**	**21,814**	**29,951**	**42,138**
of which										
AUSTRALIA	16,401	17,654	16,191	33,267	38,532	42,388	48,495	20,369	28,248	41,042
NEW ZEALAND	777	780	1,624	601	758	664	677	834	1,073	876
AFRICA	**20,618**	**19,827**	**36,608**	**33,604**	**35,036**	**42,403**	**36,424**	**42,723**	**38,862**	**45,093**
of which										
KENYA	345	405	393	466	590	483	348	530	512	539
NIGERIA	853	1,233	2,096	1,854	2,148	1,743	1,169	1,483	4,122	5,136
SOUTH AFRICA	11,544	8,395	21,124	13,672	13,782	13,013	8,189	12,949	11,565	13,422
ZIMBABWE	36	39	20	5	12	32	14	83	..	109
WORLD TOTAL	**921,831**	**1,119,252**	**1,014,399**	**1,077,139**	**1,118,030**	**1,073,462**	**1,090,639**	**1,078,692**	**1,083,975**	**1,212,798**
OECD	692,313	855,854	809,588	854,859	876,229	822,719	815,767	785,585	780,870	880,184
CENTRAL & EASTERN EUROPE	16	7	46	7	25	-8	122	204	388	..

Source: Office for National Statistics

The sum of constituent items may not always agree exactly with the totals shown due to rounding.

A negative sign before values indicates a net disinvestment abroad.

For countries listed within regions see Geography tab.

.. Indicates data are disclosive

- Indicates nil data

6.15 Earnings from foreign direct investment abroad analysed by area and main country, 2007 to 2016 (Directional)

£ million

	2007	2008	2009	2010	2011	2012	2013	2014	2015	2016
EUROPE	**43,186**	**42,693**	**35,740**	**39,666**	**46,306**	**28,508**	**30,844**	**22,360**	**22,096**	**24,678**
EU	33,559	36,782	30,652	30,668	36,523	23,003	24,002	17,248	16,662	19,625
AUSTRIA	247	174	253	137	-14	-150	2	-8	12	168
BELGIUM	1,282	1,548	1,454	1,165	1,853	1,355	533	474	356	1,441
BULGARIA	-10	-4	5	-	8	-	21	24	15	7
CROATIA	-17	28	26	..	-13	-3	..	27	31	27
CYPRUS	367	331	56	-11	-86	133	30	-20	7	-22
CZECH REPUBLIC	72	-123	-122	-75	2	210	173	191	133	87
DENMARK	580	543	219	627	541	477	404	360	264	580
ESTONIA	5	6	27	17	22	14	6	16	11	1
FINLAND	281	131	120	184	218	62	67	152	103	101
FRANCE	3,012	1,956	1,406	3,222	3,566	2,859	795	554	2,563	2,353
GERMANY	2,748	2,783	2,743	1,474	1,392	207	1,126	-9	2,424	2,161
GREECE	218	114	204	-45	23	31	40	71	2	24
HUNGARY	91	72	34	21	89	114	71	1	88	92
IRISH REPUBLIC	2,940	1,892	-800	-2,857	730	1,318	2,429	1,211	1,184	4,481
ITALY	810	524	214	687	181	355	436	677	729	466
LATVIA	4	-18	-27	-20	-24	33	28	-6	-8	-9
LITHUANIA	2	-1	-	3	4	4	2	5	13	5
LUXEMBOURG	7,982	13,309	11,422	10,353	12,092	7,368	3,769	3,553	1,100	..
MALTA	-67	42	324	-5	-51	69	..	526	..	150
NETHERLANDS	9,441	10,363	7,915	11,820	11,796	4,739	8,462	5,985	3,934	2,321
POLAND	255	421	708	382	497	542	586	619	358	476
PORTUGAL	256	289	173	324	59	208	..	146	49	3
ROMANIA	79	108	93	12	61	76	126	103	128	..
SLOVAKIA	103	21	23	..	42	32	37	53	..	31
SLOVENIA	11	14	5	..	-32	-37	15	10	15	14
SPAIN	983	1,229	1,000	602	876	-366	518	988	878	1,075
SWEDEN	1,884	1,029	3,177	2,462	2,689	3,355	2,336	1,544	2,034	2,418
EFTA	4,591	4,392	2,739	5,251	5,090	3,410	4,219	1,755	2,459	2,656
of which										
NORWAY	297	602	580	538	472	-415	303	578	4	-180
SWITZERLAND	4,294	3,786	2,174	4,714	4,617	3,832	3,421	1,175	2,454	2,834
OTHER EUROPEAN COUNTRIES	5,037	1,520	2,348	3,746	4,693	2,094	2,623	3,358	2,975	2,396
of which										
RUSSIA	1,158	1,835	1,509	1,652	2,961	313	1,802	1,326	1,189	776
UK OFFSHORE ISLANDS	3,543	-86	165	1,620	1,120	1,257	477	1,670	1,422	1,524
THE AMERICAS	**28,104**	**13,573**	**15,510**	**21,212**	**26,439**	**23,625**	**24,233**	**22,785**	**16,783**	**8,733**
of which										
BERMUDA	1,563	1,549	1,183	2,339	1,455	2,159	2,612	2,447	..	794
BRAZIL	706	728	1,212	1,045	1,270	1,052	43	1,246	928	38
CANADA	1,644	-2,248	-485	471	-325	417	359	263	-462	1,929
CHILE	775	601	531	125	322	89	91	95	89	136
COLOMBIA	189	321	137	280	657	-441	36	13	-18	1
MEXICO	555	293	255	544	1,362	760	169	724	798	681
PANAMA	43	..	66	54	84	61	76	72	178	180
USA	18,763	9,470	10,927	14,424	20,344	17,314	12,976	15,940	11,615	2,561
ASIA	**11,389**	**10,271**	**10,967**	**14,636**	**18,208**	**16,888**	**14,851**	**16,525**	**14,446**	**11,953**
NEAR & MIDDLE EAST COUNTRIES	2,580	3,661	1,830	2,023	2,645	782	3,172	2,531	1,633	1,240
of which										
GULF ARABIAN COUNTRIES	1,000	1,719	961	762	928	653	1,929	1,216	1,300	967
OTHER ASIAN COUNTRIES	8,809	6,611	9,137	12,613	15,563	16,107	11,680	13,994	12,813	10,713
of which										
CHINA	502	293	539	778	773	1,291	360	1,223	1,191	1,938
HONG KONG	4,062	1,410	797	2,736	4,179	5,023	1,056	4,845	5,101	3,235
INDIA	914	790	1,015	1,512	1,696	1,259	895	1,365	1,568	1,129
INDONESIA	170	178	400	560	1,065	1,047	661	772	416	656
JAPAN	144	431	364	299	391	242	517	385	308	998
MALAYSIA	587	526	674	734	536	562	435	988	1,011	517
SINGAPORE	469	959	2,423	2,278	3,158	3,039	-635	1,675	1,279	230
SOUTH KOREA	488	608	381	676	564	764	320	572	230	460
THAILAND	11	-122	164	173	201	244	194	287	203	205

6.15 Earnings from foreign direct investment abroad analysed by area and main country, 2007 to 2016 (Directional)

£ million

	2007	2008	2009	2010	2011	2012	2013	2014	2015	2016
AUSTRALASIA & OCEANIA	**3,506**	**4,213**	**4,602**	**6,555**	**1,953**	**3,979**	**3,642**	**3,001**	**2,579**	**2,244**
of which										
AUSTRALIA	3,207	3,947	4,181	6,133	1,671	3,682	3,378	2,712	2,249	1,912
NEW ZEALAND	256	194	343	331	176	236	208	162	202	213
AFRICA	**4,449**	**3,792**	**2,885**	**5,581**	**6,060**	**7,506**	**5,113**	**3,801**	**1,289**	**2,784**
of which										
KENYA	82	93	68	87	114	5	25	83	117	52
NIGERIA	74	212	64	652	1,031	1,261	311	687	..	176
SOUTH AFRICA	2,190	1,173	1,025	2,358	2,494	3,180	1,803	1,590	1,725	1,676
ZIMBABWE	5	-5	-6	3	22	23	..	12	26	10
WORLD TOTAL	**90,634**	**74,542**	**69,704**	**87,649**	**98,966**	**80,507**	**78,682**	**68,473**	**57,193**	**50,392**
OECD	63,926	54,204	49,921	59,032	66,564	49,880	52,156	39,401	33,864	30,930
CENTRAL & EASTERN EUROPE	5	-	2	-1	6	-3	3	-6	..	..

Source: Office for National Statistics

The sum of constituent items may not always agree exactly with the totals shown due to rounding.
A negative sign before values indicates a net disinvestment abroad.
For countries listed within regions see Geography tab.

.. Indicates data are disclosive
- Indicates nil data

6.16 Net foreign direct investment flows into the United Kingdom analysed by area and main country, 2007 to 2016 (Directional)

£ million

	2007	2008	2009	2010	2011	2012	2013	2014	2015	2016
EUROPE	**38,565**	**22,115**	**22,584**	**8,957**	**-28,258**	**22,830**	**9,456**	**-8**	**-12,305**	**97,807**
EU	32,508	21,267	15,181	-922	-23,682	15,381	-466	2,911	-13,807	92,022
AUSTRIA	223	75	89	170	876	-74	21	-87	32	-75
BELGIUM	159	-533	86	416	5,416	2,048	724	-1,947	-540	..
BULGARIA	..	..	..	..	..	-2	-	-1	-2	-1
CROATIA	..	..	..	..	..	..	..	..	-	-
CYPRUS	84	73	27	..	-1,639	-192	265	61	388	77
CZECH REPUBLIC	1	1	-	1	-4	..	..	1	21	-
DENMARK	775	303	-432	-601	-822	506	-1,291	281	451	27
ESTONIA	..	..	-	..	..	..	..	..	-	-
FINLAND	75	41	170	62	42	44	139	46	68	-41
FRANCE	925	-4,291	12,121	-9,065	2,127	6,499	-5,115	4,290	..	458
GERMANY	12,545	6,421	4,056	11,221	561	1,358	2,790	976	4,978	2,468
GREECE	119	5	30	-193	-387	178	-10	3	21	9
HUNGARY	1	1	-	-34	5	..	-20	..	7	..
IRISH REPUBLIC	1,422	2,384	-629	3,408	216	634	98	35	681	-703
ITALY	885	-209	166	467	-1,372	1,082	775	226	228	-560
LATVIA	..	..	-	-	-	..	..	..	-1	1
LITHUANIA	-	-	-	-	-	..	..	..	-	1
LUXEMBOURG	2,455	1,785	-6,548	-4,246	3,693	4,870	-1,040	1,107	-850	21,579
MALTA	6	20	14	-16	346	-49	19	5	..	-33
NETHERLANDS	2,356	9,866	-729	-3,274	-35,732	-1,594	1,251	-2,714	-22,289	..
POLAND	-10	9	-1	1	23	-	11	12	19	-1
PORTUGAL	149	3	149	94	-81	63	-18	21	13	6
ROMANIA	..	1	-	-	-	..	-	-	-	2
SLOVAKIA	..	..	..	..	-1	-	..	..	21	2
SLOVENIA	..	1	1	-1	..	-	..	-1	-1	-
SPAIN	10,396	4,530	6,389	2,226	2,578	-84	978	630	2,288	1,876
SWEDEN	-66	785	222	115	469	329	-25	211	601	-10
EFTA	3,894	-4,930	3,209	5,194	-2,221	5,765	8,278	1,955	1,313	2,518
of which										
NORWAY	673	289	269	147	253	-384	483	477	..	..
SWITZERLAND	2,521	-5,258	2,985	4,176	-2,476	6,126	7,960	1,507	..	..
OTHER EUROPEAN COUNTRIES	2,163	5,778	4,194	4,686	-2,355	1,685	1,644	-4,875	188	3,266
of which										
RUSSIA	469	1,765	6	..	205	-40	-19	..	..	-48
UK OFFSHORE ISLANDS	1,690	4,115	4,003	4,322	-2,563	-691	1,662	-4,759	237	3,284
THE AMERICAS	**25,150**	**24,634**	**39,448**	**25,971**	**40,866**	**6,552**	**17,842**	**7,874**	**27,994**	**21,006**
of which										
BRAZIL	7	1	-	75	8	5	-4	-3	-2	..
CANADA	998	327	3	3,782	83	1,833	1,277	956	3,527	115
USA	20,309	24,073	37,575	17,131	40,118	4,237	16,528	9,159	21,113	18,562
ASIA	**23,046**	**3,530**	**-2,845**	**4,729**	**9,721**	**4,922**	**4,606**	**6,692**	**7,869**	**27,951**
NEAR & MIDDLE EAST COUNTRIES	-1,104	-880	333	1,049	5,070	498	542	..	739	..
OTHER ASIAN COUNTRIES	24,149	4,410	-3,178	3,680	4,651	4,423	4,065	..	7,130	..
of which										
CHINA	22	-23	100	12	..	845	..	604	460	409
HONG KONG	..	902	-323	1,030	878	623	1,009	276	927	..
INDIA	151	2,428	108	-8	1,470	94	-124	85	..	-587
JAPAN	3,048	1,001	-2,433	1,608	1,106	1,666	2,240	1,552	1,718	1,701
SINGAPORE	..	250	47	-164	1,137	103	-28	2,118	3,754	4,159
SOUTH KOREA	50	214	38	..	-92	146	-18	112	..	140
AUSTRALASIA & OCEANIA	**366**	**-1,137**	**-1,696**	**-2,083**	**3,175**	**810**	**934**	**36**	**..**	**-1,168**
of which										
AUSTRALIA	373	-1,102	-1,676	-2,047	3,333	804	..	247	..	-1,600
NEW ZEALAND	-8	-19	-16	-34	-20	-5	..	26	19	41
AFRICA	**1,252**	**990**	**95**	**92**	**835**	**-15**	**216**	**399**	**..**	**13**
of which										
SOUTH AFRICA	1,225	1,034	125	29	734	-60	216	370	353	-66
WORLD TOTAL	**88,379**	**50,131**	**57,586**	**37,666**	**26,339**	**35,099**	**33,054**	**14,993**	**25,309**	**145,609**
OECD	61,034	40,745	51,967	28,179	20,016	30,093	28,461	16,904	13,534	112,920
CENTRAL & EASTERN EUROPE	..	..	..	..	..	..	..	..	-	-

The sum of constituent items may not always agree exactly with the totals shown due to rounding.

Source: Office for National Statistics

A negative sign before values indicates a net disinvestment in the UK.

For countries listed within regions see Geography tab.

.. Indicates data are disclosive

\- Indicates nil data

6.17 FDI International investment positions in the United Kingdom analysed by area and main country, 2007 to 2016 (Directional)

£ million

	2007	2008	2009	2010	2011	2012	2013	2014	2015	2016
EUROPE	**327,421**	**363,898**	**387,753**	**398,821**	**431,298**	**540,839**	**557,987**	**600,935**	**544,394**	**675,651**
EU	290,801	317,375	344,344	347,469	366,400	452,276	462,342	490,245	440,832	541,561
AUSTRIA	1,025	1,105	931	1,076	2,419	5,235	2,565	2,165	1,810	1,317
BELGIUM	4,475	4,278	3,577	7,133	15,971	10,480	24,841	26,162	21,161	26,402
BULGARIA	..	..	..	..	..	..	7	7	5	39
CROATIA	..	..	..	..	..	..	..	..	-	-
CYPRUS	430	501	311	1,827	2,577	4,090	3,605	3,942	4,155	4,237
CZECH REPUBLIC	8	19	1	6	23	11	26	11	165	6
DENMARK	5,008	8,626	4,944	3,079	3,538	5,959	8,861	5,910	6,498	6,776
ESTONIA	..	..	-	..	..	..	..	..	-	1
FINLAND	692	727	752	741	838	2,178	1,474	1,401	1,132	592
FRANCE	50,142	45,752	69,101	61,212	54,725	73,521	66,776	75,797	69,600	59,929
GERMANY	58,341	68,928	61,992	46,752	45,312	62,123	49,290	51,033	50,496	59,829
GREECE	151	221	414	661	757	325	511	179	710	118
HUNGARY	12	20	5	..	115	55	..	-8	144	-17
IRISH REPUBLIC	7,192	8,613	9,248	7,565	10,619	9,008	11,911	13,825	12,309	11,485
ITALY	4,973	4,218	5,068	938	2,175	8,932	13,481	4,226	7,651	5,059
LATVIA	..	..	-	-	-	..	..	..	47	8
LITHUANIA	-	-	-	-	-	..	..	..	1	3
LUXEMBOURG	19,287	26,006	47,050	60,817	52,006	56,610	71,455	71,782	69,698	114,799
MALTA	62	143	48	606	271	913	969	514	633	675
NETHERLANDS	106,645	132,646	106,999	117,577	129,166	148,494	147,586	180,188	145,763	212,097
POLAND	75	78	18	24	88	76	209	105	290	120
PORTUGAL	217	301	558	761	308	479	515	486	544	417
ROMANIA	..	..	..	..	10	14	9	10	9	6
SLOVAKIA	..	..	..	..	-2	..	6	4	160	11
SLOVENIA	9	14	..	6	-1	..	7	9	6	3
SPAIN	27,681	10,731	26,825	32,997	39,895	56,116	49,470	43,062	38,347	30,276
SWEDEN	4,285	4,320	6,382	3,489	5,578	7,593	8,479	9,402	9,497	7,373
EFTA	23,913	22,773	20,078	25,167	31,056	35,368	45,986	46,916	46,420	53,969
of which										
NORWAY	1,503	1,425	1,764	1,600	2,229	4,852	3,861	4,954	4,523	5,335
SWITZERLAND	20,087	19,882	17,354	22,665	25,931	29,630	39,289	39,136	39,065	45,308
OTHER EUROPEAN COUNTRIES	12,707	23,750	23,331	26,186	33,841	53,195	49,659	63,774	57,142	80,120
of which										
RUSSIA	..	..	..	817	979	881	1,647	..	..	1,003
UK OFFSHORE ISLANDS	11,555	21,748	22,579	25,037	32,206	44,824	46,562	61,435	55,394	78,557
THE AMERICAS	**177,002**	**209,659**	**197,481**	**227,155**	**247,993**	**299,735**	**279,612**	**323,596**	**388,570**	**412,074**
of which										
BRAZIL	21	10	-	249	-5	-10	121	15	143	..
CANADA	19,843	18,625	18,833	18,201	17,012	14,606	19,656	20,872	16,924	18,576
USA	143,297	170,369	159,900	185,458	205,925	255,169	217,950	242,070	309,632	308,099
ASIA	**47,014**	**42,448**	**35,958**	**46,551**	**56,722**	**62,689**	**74,581**	**73,987**	**82,070**	**96,657**
NEAR & MIDDLE EAST COUNTRIES	5,278	3,397	2,991	3,646	4,445	3,710	4,900	5,983	6,295	6,526
OTHER ASIAN COUNTRIES	41,736	39,051	32,967	42,905	52,277	58,979	69,681	68,004	75,774	90,131
of which										
CHINA	196	199	607	367	767	1,118	..	1,100	2,261	1,524
HONG KONG	..	6,979	5,884	7,527	16,972	10,253	11,622	12,799	10,888	..
INDIA	1,323	3,284	1,875	2,749	2,774	2,072	1,676	1,942	2,643	1,488
JAPAN	20,321	24,801	19,263	22,501	26,071	36,036	36,194	39,756	41,260	46,489
SINGAPORE	12,202	1,518	3,454	5,739	3,635	4,064	3,655	8,482	15,363	18,224
SOUTH KOREA	768	884	696	2,752	889	2,516	2,389	2,076	1,836	1,852
AUSTRALASIA & OCEANIA	**8,601**	**7,026**	**11,468**	**8,399**	**10,879**	**8,230**	**3,953**	11858	**15,064**	**13,117**
of which										
AUSTRALIA	8,165	6,750	11,229	8,171	10,022	7,633	..	11,192	14,372	11,143
NEW ZEALAND	429	275	239	224	271	579	..	338	526	264
AFRICA	**1,332**	**1,994**	**1,009**	**1,403**	**1,769**	**1,368**	**2,345**	2887	**2,435**	**1,955**
of which										
SOUTH AFRICA	898	1,558	490	553	819	353	1,274	2,060	1,538	1,043
WORLD TOTAL	**561,370**	**625,025**	**633,669**	**682,330**	**748,661**	**912,861**	**918,478**	**1,013,263**	**1,032,534**	**1,199,453**
OECD	507,478	561,816	574,328	607,930	653,463	799,380	781,800	847,247	865,073	974,692
CENTRAL & EASTERN EUROPE	..	..	..	..	..	..	..	..	-	-2

The sum of constituent items may not always agree exactly with the totals shown due to rounding.

A negative sign before values indicates a net disinvestment in the UK.

For countries listed within regions see Geography tab.

.. Indicates data are disclosive

- Indicates nil data

Source: Office for National Statistics

6.18 Earnings from foreign direct investment in the United Kingdom analysed by area and main country, 2007 to 2016 (Directional)

£ million

	2007	2008	2009	2010	2011	2012	2013	2014	2015	2016
EUROPE	**30,028**	**14,778**	**25,216**	**23,706**	**20,112**	**22,752**	**27,190**	**26,346**	**21,969**	**21,905**
EU	25,525	17,640	20,488	18,038	16,747	21,071	24,951	23,931	18,263	16,494
AUSTRIA	275	130	98	104	168	207	141	119	32	80
BELGIUM	622	697	-169	427	911	961	1,964	1,469	1,547	2,080
BULGARIA	..	..	..	..	..	-	1	-	-1	3
CROATIA	..	..	..	..	..	..	..	..	-	-
CYPRUS	82	75	33	104	86	197	235	246	284	345
CZECH REPUBLIC	1	1	-	-	30	..	6	1	8	-
DENMARK	-69	-8	-256	89	-71	156	421	326	618	751
ESTONIA	..	..	-	..	..	..	..	..	-	-
FINLAND	189	92	94	93	77	198	146	149	76	-8
FRANCE	3,586	3,812	10,506	4,135	4,437	2,170	2,326	2,960	2,648	-116
GERMANY	6,386	5,905	2,045	4,373	3,582	5,601	6,441	5,615	4,281	5,236
GREECE	126	304	190	328	71	122	122	68	53	48
HUNGARY	2	-	..	1	2	1	15	2	12	1
IRISH REPUBLIC	1,473	2,004	264	-1,089	382	486	493	506	975	274
ITALY	620	596	513	264	151	1,145	1,223	575	273	289
LATVIA	..	..	-	-	-	..	-	..	3	1
LITHUANIA	-	-	-	-	-	..	..	..	-	1
LUXEMBOURG	301	496	882	1,528	754	2,077	1,853	1,146	1,177	1,214
MALTA	9	11	1	31	18	91	71	35	2	25
NETHERLANDS	8,528	-1,334	652	2,872	3,679	4,337	6,062	6,634	3,375	3,355
POLAND	7	4	1	2	4	3	6	8	10	4
PORTUGAL	70	101	71	58	-66	67	38	152	122	96
ROMANIA	..	..	..	..	1	-1	1	1	1	-
SLOVAKIA	..	..	..	..	..	-	..	..	7	-
SLOVENIA	3	..	..	-	1	-1	1	-	-	-
SPAIN	2,892	4,272	5,281	4,245	2,009	2,677	2,689	3,182	2,106	2,262
SWEDEN	413	478	284	471	519	573	698	736	654	551
EFTA	2,940	-4,587	2,823	1,780	1,380	-410	353	983	1,949	2,637
of which										
NORWAY	202	265	12	18	194	398	686	255	205	26
SWITZERLAND	2,376	-4,901	2,771	1,004	804	-795	-499	422	1,413	2,024
OTHER EUROPEAN COUNTRIES	1,563	1,726	1,905	3,889	1,984	2,091	1,886	1,432	1,757	2,774
of which										
RUSSIA	8	31	3	59	125	-2	129	-44	..	-47
UK OFFSHORE ISLANDS	1,531	1,769	1,852	3,809	1,855	1,875	1,661	1,438	1,787	2,776
THE AMERICAS	**19,481**	**32,264**	**21,404**	**16,914**	**20,972**	**19,829**	**20,844**	**16,947**	**21,508**	**24,761**
of which										
BRAZIL	9	-	-	28	16	12	17	5	7	9
CANADA	675	1,427	1,012	886	420	779	1,965	1,258	310	1,114
USA	16,566	29,498	19,135	14,648	18,894	17,889	17,608	12,659	18,236	18,744
ASIA	**289**	**471**	**-2,704**	**-742**	**4,051**	**3,198**	**2,486**	**4,781**	**4,855**	**5,521**
NEAR & MIDDLE EAST COUNTRIES	222	329	149	181	837	440	649	342	863	139
OTHER ASIAN COUNTRIES	67	142	-2,854	-923	3,213	2,758	1,836	4,439	3,992	5,382
of which										
CHINA	21	-20	38	21	34	106	202	207	42	4
HONG KONG	..	-358	-141	488	-4	589	1,179	949	1,590	1,578
INDIA	136	280	111	167	1,251	117	94	167	148	414
JAPAN	-257	-375	-3,126	-2,141	-147	1,441	640	1,733	1,604	3,147
SINGAPORE	597	161	-215	-101	1,508	230	-218	1,406	485	402
SOUTH KOREA	126	117	54	111	60	99	136	-96	30	99
AUSTRALASIA & OCEANIA	**1,254**	**683**	**1,913**	**-134**	**145**	**-99**	**272**	**-14**	**-259**	**-157**
of which										
AUSTRALIA	1,225	697	1,922	-151	159	-128	228	266	-284	-619
NEW ZEALAND	28	-11	-5	17	5	20	181	33	22	20
AFRICA	**159**	**226**	**121**	**73**	**199**	**-37**	**87**	**-49**	**85**	**43**
of which										
SOUTH AFRICA	103	171	119	20	110	-73	20	-108	52	-29
WORLD TOTAL	**51,211**	**48,423**	**45,949**	**39,817**	**45,478**	**45,644**	**50,878**	**48,011**	**48,158**	**52,073**
OECD	46,754	44,372	42,328	33,089	37,143	40,498	45,693	40,280	39,552	40,740
CENTRAL & EASTERN EUROPE	..	..	..	..	..	..	..	..	-	-

The sum of constituent items may not always agree exactly with the totals shown due to rounding.

Source: Office for National Statistics

A negative sign before values indicates a net disinvestment in the UK.

For countries listed within regions see Geography tab.

.. Indicates data are disclosive

- Indicates nil data

this page is intentionally blank

Chapter 7

Research and development

Research and development

(Tables 7.1 to 7.5)

Research and experimental development (R&D) is defined for statistical purposes as 'creative work undertaken on a systematic basis in order to increase the stock of knowledge, including knowledge of man, culture and society, and the use of this stock of knowledge to devise new applications'.

R&D is financed and carried out mainly by businesses, the Government, and institutions of higher education. A small amount is performed by non-profit-making bodies. Gross Expenditure on R&D (GERD) is an indicator of the total amount of R&D performed within the UK. Detailed figures are reported each year in a statistical bulletin published in July. Table 7.1 shows the main components of GERD.

ONS conducts an annual survey of expenditure and employment on R&D performed by government, and of government funding of R&D. The survey collects data for the reference period along with future estimates. Until 1993 the detailed results were reported in the *Annual Review of Government Funded R&D*. From 1997 to 2012, the results have appeared in the Science, Engineering and Technology (SET) Statistics published by the Department for Business, Innovation and Skills (BIS). From 2013, the results have appeared in the Government Expenditure on Science, Engineering and Technology Statistics published by ONS and the Department for Business, Energy and Industrial Strategy (BEIS). Table 7.2 gives some broad totals for gross expenditure by government (expenditure before deducting funds received by government for R&D). Table 7.3 gives a breakdown of net expenditure (receipts are deducted).

The ONS conducts an annual survey of R&D in business. Tables 7.4 and 7.5 give a summary of the main trends up to 2016.

Statistics on expenditure and employment on R&D in higher education institutions (HEIs) are based on information collected by Higher Education Funding Councils and the Higher Education Statistics Agency (HESA). In 1994 a new methodology was introduced to estimate expenditure on R&D in HEIs. This is based on the allocation of various Funding Council Grants. Full details of the new methodology are contained in science, engineering and technology (SET) Statistics available on the gov.uk website at: https://www.gov.uk/government/collections/science-engineering-and-technology-statistics

The most comprehensive international comparisons of resources devoted to R&D appear in Main Science and Technology Indicators published by the Organisation for Economic Co-operation and Development (OECD). The Statistical Office of the European Union and the United Nations also compile R&D statistics based on figures supplied by member states.

To make international comparisons more reliable the OECD have published a series of manuals giving guidance on how to measure various components of R&D inputs and outputs. The most important of these is the Frascati Manual, which defines R&D and recommends how resources for R&D should be measured. The UK follows the Frascati Manual as far as possible.

For information on available aggregated data on Research and Development please call Office for National Statistics on 01633 456767.

7.1a EXPENDITURE ON R&D IN THE UK BY PERFORMING AND FUNDING SECTORS, 2015

Current prices	Sector performing the R&D						£ million
	Government[1]	Research Councils	Higher Education	Business Enterprise	Private Non-Profit	**Total[1]**	Overseas
Sector funding the R&D							
Government	1,124	120	478	1,817	85	**3,624**	681
Research Councils	45	512	2,176	1	174	**2,908**	223
Higher Education Funding Councils	-	-	2,218	-	-	**2,218**	-
Higher Education	3	15	304	-	112	**433**	-
Business Enterprise[1]	19	28	349	15,069	19	**15,484**	7,423
Private Non-Profit	13	48	1,206	130	157	**1,553**	-
Overseas	121	50	1,279	3,868	87	**5,406**	-
TOTAL	**1,324**	**773**	**8,009**	**20,885**	**634**	**31,626**	-
of which:							
Civil	1,156	773	7,969	19,394	627	**29,919**	-
Defence	168	-	40	1,491	8	**1,707**	-

Source: Office for National Statistics

1. Estimates of launch investment loan repayments received by government from business have been removed following a review of how these payments should be reported. These loan repayments are in relation to loans given out in previous years and therefore should not be included in current totals of R&D expenditure. The total of loan repayments removed was £112 million, this value has also been removed from the total funding by business and the total performed by government.

- denotes nil, figures unavailable or too small to display.

Please note:

Differences may occur between totals and the sum of their independently rounded components.

7.1b EXPENDITURE ON R&D IN THE UK BY SECTOR OF PERFORMANCE:

2006 to 2015

£ million

		2006	2007	2008	2009	2010	2011	2012	2013	2014	2015
Sector performing the R&D											
Current prices											
TOTAL[3]	**GLBA**	**22,993**	**24,696**	**25,345**	**25,632**	**26,173**	**27,452**	**27,257**	**29,015 †**	**30,413**	**31,626**
Government[3]	GLBK	1,252	1,320	1,348	1,406	1,372	1,321	1,391	1,503 †	1,391	1,324
Research Councils	DMRS	1,061	1,034	1,041	1,097	1,141	1,035	804	814	819 †	773
Business Enterprise	GLBL	14,144	15,676	15,814	15,532	16,045	17,452	17,409	18,617 †	19,819	20,885
Higher Education	GLBM	6,022	6,119	6,545	6,931	6,963	7,117	7,133	7,593 †	7,835	8,009
Private Non-Profit[2]	GLBN	513	546	595	666	652	526	520	489 †	549	634
As % of GDP		1.56	1.60	1.64	1.67	1.64	1.68	1.61	1.65	1.66	1.68

		2006	2007	2008	2009	2010	2011	2012	2013	2014	2015
Sector performing the R&D											
Constant prices (2015)[1]											
TOTAL[3]	**GLBD**	**26,860**	**28,167**	**28,143**	**28,075**	**28,153**	**29,124**	**28,322**	**29,660**	**30,639**	**31,626**
Government[3]	GLBW	1,463	1,506	1,497	1,540	1,476	1,401	1,445	1,536	1,401	1,324
Research Councils	DMSU	1,239	1,179	1,156	1,202	1,227	1,098	835	832	825	773
Business Enterprise	GLBX	16,523	17,879	17,560	17,012	17,259	18,515	18,090	19,031	19,966	20,885
Higher Education	GLBY	7,035	6,979	7,267	7,592	7,490	7,550	7,412	7,762	7,893	8,009
Private Non-Profit[2]	GLBZ	599	623	661	729	701	558	540	500	553	634

Source: Office for National Statistics

	2006	2007	2008	2009	2010	2011	2012	2013	2014	2015
GDP deflator used to convert current prices to constant prices	85.604	87.677	90.059	91.298	92.968	94.259	96.238	97.825	99.262	100

1 Please note that the latest deflators have been applied to the business research and development estimates in this bulletin which has resulted in small differences being observed between the BERD and GERD publications.

2 Prior to 2011 PNP data was estimated. From 2011 data has been collected from a biennial survey with intermediate years being estimated. Estimates for 2015 have been published using survey data.

3 Estimates of launch investment loan repayments received by government from business have been removed following a review of how these payments should be reported. These loan repayments are in relation to loans given out in previous years and therefore should not be included in current totals of R&D expenditure. The total of loan repayments have been removed from the total performed by government and the UK total for 2013, and 2015, there were no repayments in 2014. In current prices the values removed were 2013 (£212 Million) and 2015 (£112 million).

† crosses denote earliest data revision.

Please Note:

Differences may occur between totals and the sum of their independently rounded components.

7.2 EXPENDITURE ON R&D IN THE UK BY PERFORMING AND FUNDING SECTORS, 2016

Current prices	Sector performing the R&D						£ million
	Government	Research Councils	Higher Education	Business Enterprise	Private[1] Non-Profit	**Total**	Overseas
Sector funding the R&D							
Government	1136	137	483	1,730	98	**3,584**	542
Research Councils	47	554	2,107	5	197	**2,909**	292
Higher Education Funding Councils	-	-	2,207	-	-	**2,207**	-
Higher Education	2	17	299	-	131	**449**	-
Business Enterprise	15	25	350	16,742	18	**17,151**	6,658
Private Non-Profit	13	42	1,242	188	170	**1,655**	-
Overseas	122	60	1,346	3,560	85	**5,174**	-
TOTAL	**1,335**	**837**	**8,035**	**22,224**	**699**	**33,130**	-
of which:							
Civil	1,178	837	7,994	20,658	688	**31,354**	-
Defence	156	-	42	1,567	11	**1,776**	-

Source: Office for National Statistics

1 Prior to 2011 PNP data was estimated. From 2011 data has been collected from a biennial survey with intermediate years being estimated using previous years data.

\- denotes nil, figures unavailable or too small to display.

Please note:

Differences may occur between totals and the sum of their independently rounded components.

7.3 UK GOVERNMENT EXPENDITURE ON R&D BY SOCIO-ECONOMIC OBJECTIVE, PERCENTAGE SHARE: 2007 TO 2016

Current prices										£ million
	2007	2008	2009	2010	2011	2012	2013	2014	2015	2016
TOTAL	**8,979**	**9,235**	**9,590**	**9,452**	**9,174**	**9,202**	**10,048**	**10,253**	**10,155** †	**10,330**

	2007	2008	2009	2010	2011	2012	2013	2014	2015	2016
Per cent										
TOTAL	**100**	**100**	**100**	**100**	**100**	**100**	**100**	**100**	**100**	**100**
General advancement of knowledge: R&D financed from General University Funds	25	24	25	24	25	24	23	22	22	21
Health	16	18	19	20	21	21	22	22	23	21
Defence	24	22	18	18	14	16	15	17	16	16
General advancement of knowledge: R&D financed from other sources	17	18	16	18	13	13	13	12	12	11
Industrial production and technology	2	2	4	3	4	3	4	4	4	5
Transport, telecommunication, other infrastructure	1	1	1	1	3	3	3	4	4	4
Exploration and exploitation of the earth	3	3	3	3	3	3	3	4	4	4
Exploration and exploitation of space	2	2	2	2	3	3	4	3	3	4
Agriculture	3	3	4	3	4	4	4	3	4 †	4
Energy	1	1	1	1	2	2	2	2	3 †	3
Political and social systems, structures and processes	1	2	2	2	1	3	3	3	3	3
Environment	2	3	3	3	3	3	3	2	2	2
Culture, recreation, religion and mass media	2	2	2	2	2	1	1	1	1	1
Education	1	1	1	1	-	-	-	-	-	-

Source: Office for National Statistics

- denotes nil, figures unavailable or too small to display.

† denotes earliest data revision.

Please Note:

Differences may occur between totals and the sum of their independently rounded components.

7.4 EXPENDITURE ON R&D PERFORMED IN UK BUSINESSES: BROAD PRODUCT GROUPS, 2005 TO 2016

£ million

		2005	2006	2007	2008	2009	2010	2011	2012	2013	2014	2015	2016
CURRENT PRICES													
TOTAL	**DLBX**	**13,734**	**14,144**	**15,676**	**15,814**	**15,532**	**16,045**	**17,452**	**17,409**	**18,617**	**19,982 †**	**21,038**	**22,224**
Manufacturing: Total	**DLDF**	**10,560**	**10,555**	**11,612**	**11,672**	**11,230**	**11,585**	**12,462**	**12,383**	**13,158**	**13,721 †**	**14,607**	**15,416**
Chemicals	DLDG	4,011	4,205	4,602	4,985	5,034	5,339	5,437	4,873	4,793	4,639	5,003 †	5,142
Mechanical engineering	DLDH	978	997	1,124	864	..	902	1,091	1,102	1,156	1,121	1,089 †	1,022
Electrical machinery	DLDI	1,274	1,273	1,297	1,400	1,275	1,144	1,200	1,339	1,535	1,649	1,799 †	1,592
Transport	DLDJ	892	913	1,097	1,344	..	1,468	1,800	2,040	2,398	2,785 †	3,201	3,775
Aerospace	DLDK	2,169	1,832	2,070	1,732	1,466	1,437	1,438	1,511	1,639	1,666	1,699 †	1,905
Other manufacturing	DLDL	1,236	1,336	1,422	1,348	1,251	1,295	1,495	1,518	1,638	1,860	1,816 †	1,981
Services	**DLDM**	**2,949**	**3,404**	**3,860**	**3,904**	**3,952**	**4,120**	**4,563**	**4,539**	**4,898**	**5,577 †**	**5,733**	**6,124**
Other: Total	**LABA**	**225**	**185**	**205**	**238**	**350**	**340**	**426**	**487**	**561**	**684 †**	**697**	**684**
Agriculture, hunting & forestry; Fishing	LADE	..	88	..	88	..	102	133	132	121	135	139	132
Extractive industries	LADM	59	59	82	90	140	152	195	172	209	230	206	186
Electricity, gas & water supply; Waste management	LAEB	15	21	35	40	75	72	68	118	140	168 †	196	156
Construction	LAEM	..	17	..	21	..	14	31	64	91	151	156 †	211

£ million

	2005	2006	2007	2008	2009	2010	2011	2012	2013	2014	2015	2016
CONSTANT PRICES (2016)												
TOTAL	**16,923 †**	**16,899**	**18,275**	**17,969**	**17,396**	**17,648**	**18,923**	**18,492**	**19,443**	**20,570**	**21,513**	**22,224**
Manufacturing: Total	**13,012 †**	**12,611**	**13,537**	**13,262**	**12,577**	**12,742**	**13,512**	**13,153**	**13,742**	**14,125**	**14,936**	**15,416**
Chemicals	4,942 †	5,024	5,365	5,664	5,638	5,872	5,895	5,176	5,006	4,776	5,116	5,142
Mechanical engineering	1,205 †	1,191	1,310	982	..	992	1,183	1,171	1,207	1,154	1,114	1,022
Electrical machinery	1,570 †	1,521	1,512	1,591	1,428	1,258	1,301	1,422	1,603	1,698	1,840	1,592
Transport	1,099 †	1,091	1,279	1,527	..	1,615	1,952	2,167	2,504	2,867	3,273	3,775
Aerospace	2,673 †	2,189	2,413	1,968	1,642	1,581	1,559	1,605	1,712	1,715	1,737	1,905
Other manufacturing	1,523 †	1,596	1,658	1,532	1,401	1,424	1,621	1,612	1,711	1,915	1,857	1,981
Services	**3,634 †**	**4,067**	**4,500**	**4,436**	**4,426**	**4,532**	**4,948**	**4,821**	**5,115**	**5,741**	**5,862**	**6,124**
Other: Total	**277 †**	**221**	**239**	**270**	**392**	**374**	**462**	**517**	**586**	**704**	**713**	**684**
Agriculture, hunting & forestry; Fishing	.. †	105	..	100	..	112	144	140	126	139	142	132
Extractive industries	73 †	70	96	102	157	167	211	183	218	237	211	186
Electricity, gas & water supply; Waste management	18	25 †	41	45	84	79	74	125	146	173	200	156
Construction	.. †	20	..	24	..	15	34	68	95	155	160	211

Source: Office for National Statistics

	2005	2006	2007	2008	2009	2010	2011	2012	2013	2014	2015	2016
GDP deflator used to convert current prices to constant prices	81.158 †	83.699	85.777	88.008	89.287	90.918	92.228	94.144	95.752	97.140	97.794	100

1 .. denotes disclosive figures.

2 † denotes earliest data revision.

3 Differences may occur between totals and the sum of their independently rounded components.

4 From 2016 onwards civil and defence figures are no longer separated due to limited data availability following changes in disclosure.

Please note: From 2016 onwards civil and defence figures are no longer separated due to disclosure and resulting issues in data availability and quality

7.5a SOURCES OF FUNDS FOR R&D PERFORMED IN UK BUSINESSES: 2013 TO 2016

CURRENT PRICES

		2013	2014	2015	2016
£ million					
TOTAL	**DLBX**	**18,617**	**19,982**	**21,018 †**	**22,587**
UK Government	DLDO	1,848	1,886	1,817 †	1,700
Overseas total of which:	DLHK	3,891	4,061	3,801 †	3,531
European Commission grants	DLDQ	65	64	67	93 †
Other Overseas	DLDS	3,826	3,996	3,734 †	3,438
Other UK Business	DLDU	364	391	384	507 †
Own funds	DLDW	12,407	13,515	14,805 †	16,605
Other [1]	DLDY	107	129	211 †	244

	2013	2014	2015	2016
Per cent				
TOTAL	**100**	**100**	**100**	**100**
UK Government	10	9	9	8
Overseas total of which:	21	20	18	16
European Commission grants	-	-	-	-
Other Overseas	21	20	18	15
Other UK Business	2	2	2	2
Own funds	67	68	70	74 †
Other [1]	1	1	1	1

Source: Office for National Statistics

- denotes nil, figures unavailable or too small to display.

† denotes earliest data revision.

Differences may occur between totals and the sum of their independently rounded components.

1 'Other' includes funds from UK Private Non-Profit organisations and Higher Education establishments, and from 2011, international organisations.

7.5b SOURCES OF FUNDS FOR R&D PERFORMED IN UK BUSINESSES: CIVIL AND DEFENCE, 2013 TO 2016

CURRENT PRICES £ million

		Civil					Defence			
		2013	2014	2015	2016		2013	2014	2015	2016
UK Government	DLFG	767	838	821 †	715	DLFN	1,081	1,047	997	985 †
Overseas total of which:	DLHS	3,732	3,914	3,651 †	3,396	DLIF	160	147	151	135
European Commission grants	DLFH	64	63	66	91	DLFO	1	1	1	1
Other Overseas	DLFI	3,668	3,850	3,585 †	3,304	DLFP	158	146	149	133
Other UK Business	DLFJ	..	339	328	428	DLFQ	..	53	56	80
Own	DLFK	12,096	13,225	14,524 †	16,245	DLFR	312	290	280	359 †
Other [1]	DLFL	..	118	203 †	237	DLFS	..	11	8	7
TOTAL	**DLBV**	**16,966**	**18,435**	**19,527 †**	**21,021**	**DLBW**	**1,651**	**1,548**	**1,491**	**1,566 †**

Source: Office for National Statistics

- denotes nil, figures unavailable or too small to display.

.. denotes disclosive figures.

† denotes earliest data revision.

Differences may occur between totals and the sum of their independently rounded components.

1 'Other' includes funds from UK Private Non-Profit organisations and Higher Education establishments, and from 2011, international organisations.

this page is intentionally blank

Chapter 8

Income and wealth

Personal income, expenditure and wealth

Distribution of total incomes (Table 8.1)

The information shown in Table 8.1 comes from the Survey of Personal Income. This is an annual survey covering approximately 600,000 individuals across the whole of the UK. It is based on administrative data held by HM Revenue & Customs (HMRC) on individuals who could be liable for tax.

The table relates only to those individuals who are taxpayers. The distributions only cover incomes as computed for tax purposes, and above a level which for each year corresponds approximately to the single person's allowance. Incomes below these levels are not shown because the information about them is incomplete.

Some components of investment income (for example interest and dividends), from which tax has been deducted at source, are not always held on HMRC business systems. Estimates of missing bank and building society interest and dividends from UK companies are included in these tables. The missing investment income is distributed to cases, so that the population as a whole has amounts consistent with evidence from other sources. For example, amounts of tax accounted for by deposit takers and the tendency to hold interest-bearing accounts as indicated by household surveys.

Superannuation contributions are estimated and included in total income. They have been distributed among earners in the Survey of Personal Incomes sample, by a method consistent with information about the number of employees who are contracted in or out of the State Earnings Related Pension Scheme (SERPS) and the proportion of their earnings contributed.

When comparing results of these surveys across years, it should be noted that the Survey of Personal Incomes is not a longitudinal survey. However, sample sizes have increased in recent years to increase precision.

Effects of taxes and benefits, by household type (Table 8.2)

Original income is the total income in cash of all the members of the household before receipt of state benefits or the deduction of taxes. It includes income from employment, self-employment, investment income and occupational pensions. Gross income is original income plus cash benefits received from government (retirement pensions, child benefit, and so on). Disposal income is the income available for consumption; it is equal to gross income less direct taxes (which include income tax, national insurance contributions, and council tax). By further allowing for taxes paid on goods and services purchased, such as VAT, an estimate of post-tax income is derived. These income figures are derived from estimates made by the Office for National Statistics (ONS) based largely on information from the Living Costs and Food Survey (LFC) and published each year on the ONS website.

In Table 8.2, a retired household is defined as one where the combined income of retired members amounts to at least half the total gross income of the household; where a retired person is defined as anyone who describes themselves as retired, or anyone over the minimum National Insurance (NI) pension age describing themselves as 'unoccupied' or 'sick or injured but not intending to seek work.

Children are defined as people aged under 16 or aged between 16 and 19, not married nor in a Civil Partnership, nor living with a partner; and living with parent(s)/guardian(s); and and receiving non-advanced further education or in unwaged-government training

Living Costs and Food Survey (Tables 8.3–8.5)

The Living Costs and Food Survey (LCF) is a sample survey of private households in the UK.The LCF sample is representative of all regions of the UK and of different types of households. The survey is continuous, with interviews spread evenly over the year to ensure that estimates are not biased by seasonal variation. The survey results show how households spend their money; how much goes on food, clothing and so on, how spending patterns vary depending upon income, household composition, and regional location of households. In previous releases, Family Spending has reported on a calendar year basis. However, data used in these tables and subsequent Family Spending releases will report on a financial year basis (April to March). This change has been made to reduce disparities in estimates. The methodology in sampling and collecting Living Costs and Food Survey data has remained consistent to ensure that data in this release remain comparable with that of previous Family Spending releases.

One of the main purposes of the LCF is to define the 'basket of goods' for the Retail Prices Index (RPI) and the Consumer Prices Index (CPI). The RPI has a vital role in the up rating of state pensions and welfare benefits, while the CPI is a key instrument of the Government's monetary policy. Information from the survey is also a major source for estimates of household expenditure in the UK National Accounts. In addition, many other government departments use LCF data as a basis for policy making, for example in the areas of housing and transport. The Department for Environment, Food and Rural Affairs (Defra) uses LCF data to report on trends in food consumption and nutrient intake within the UK. Users of the LCF outside government include independent research institutes, academic researchers and business and market researchers. Like all surveys based on a sample of the population, its results are subject to sampling variability and potentially to some bias due to non-response. The results of the survey are published in an annual report called Family spending in the UK. The report includes a list of definitions used in the survey, items on which information is collected, and a brief account of the fieldwork procedure.

8.1 Distribution of total income before and after tax by gender, 2014-15

Taxpayers only

Numbers: thousands; Amounts: £ million

Total

Range of total income (lower limit) £	Before tax, by range of total income before tax				After tax, by range of total income after tax			
	No. of taxpayers	Total income before tax	Total tax	Total income after tax	No. of taxpayers	Total income before tax	Total tax	Total income after tax
10,000 [(a)]	1,260	13,100	108	13,000	1,520	16,000	159	15,800
11,000	1,490	17,100	347	16,700	1,840	21,700	538	21,200
12,000	4,250	57,300	2,630	54,700	5,150	73,400	3,980	69,400
15,000	6,080	106,000	8,350	97,400	6,800	129,000	11,500	118,000
20,000	7,730	189,000	21,100	168,000	7,750	215,000	25,900	189,000
30,000	6,600	251,000	34,700	216,000	5,680	253,000	39,900	213,000
50,000	1,670	96,600	19,200	77,400	1,070	81,500	19,500	62,000
70,000	829	68,500	17,000	51,500	513	58,800	17,400	41,400
100,000	425	50,700	15,300	35,400	210	37,800	12,700	25,100
150,000	151	25,700	8,630	17,100	63	17,000	6,200	10,800
200,000	101	24,300	8,780	15,500	47	18,200	6,920	11,300
300,000	59	22,100	8,450	13,700	26	16,300	6,420	9,900
500,000	30	20,700	8,130	12,500	15	16,300	6,450	9,850
1,000,000	15	35,200	13,900	21,400	6	23,700	9,160	14,600
All ranges	30,700	977,000	167,000	811,000	30,700	977,000	167,000	811,000

Male

Range of total income (lower limit) £	Before tax, by range of total income before tax				After tax, by range of total income after tax			
	No. of taxpayers	Total income before tax	Total tax	Total income after tax	No. of taxpayers	Total income before tax	Total tax	Total income after tax
10,000 [(a)]	538	5,600	49	5,550	652	6,870	73	6,800
11,000	649	7,460	155	7,310	816	9,640	246	9,390
12,000	1,950	26,300	1,220	25,100	2,420	34,600	1,910	32,700
15,000	3,170	55,200	4,350	50,900	3,670	70,100	6,240	63,900
20,000	4,540	112,000	12,500	99,100	4,690	130,000	15,900	115,000
30,000	4,290	164,000	22,900	141,000	3,840	172,000	27,600	145,000
50,000	1,190	69,300	14,000	55,400	786	60,200	14,600	45,600
70,000	618	51,100	12,800	38,300	394	45,400	13,500	31,800
100,000	330	39,400	11,900	27,400	169	30,400	10,300	20,100
150,000	122	20,900	7,020	13,900	52	14,200	5,160	9,000
200,000	83	20,000	7,230	12,700	40	15,500	5,880	9,580
300,000	50	18,800	7,190	11,600	23	14,500	5,710	8,770
500,000	27	18,300	7,220	11,100	13	14,600	5,780	8,780
1,000,000	14	32,000	12,600	19,400	6	21,700	8,370	13,300
All ranges	17,600	640,000	121,000	519,000	17,600	640,000	121,000	519,000

8.1 Distribution of total income before and after tax by gender, 2014-15

Taxpayers only

Numbers: thousands; Amounts: £ million

Range of total income (lower limit) £	Female							
	Before tax, by range of total income before tax				After tax, by range of total income after tax			
	No. of taxpayers	Total income before tax	Total tax	Total income after tax	No. of taxpayers	Total income before tax	Total tax	Total income after tax
10,000 [(a)]	720	7,550	59	7,490	863	9,140	87	9,050
11,000	837	9,630	191	9,430	1,030	12,100	293	11,800
12,000	2,300	31,000	1,410	29,600	2,730	38,800	2,080	36,700
15,000	2,910	50,500	4,000	46,500	3,120	59,300	5,270	54,000
20,000	3,200	77,800	8,600	69,200	3,060	84,300	10,100	74,200
30,000	2,310	86,700	11,800	74,900	1,840	80,400	12,300	68,100
50,000	472	27,300	5,280	22,000	283	21,300	4,940	16,400
70,000	211	17,400	4,210	13,200	118	13,400	3,830	9,550
100,000	95	11,300	3,340	7,960	41	7,350	2,430	4,910
150,000	28	4,850	1,620	3,240	11	2,860	1,040	1,830
200,000	18	4,330	1,550	2,780	7	2,770	1,040	1,730
300,000	9	3,320	1,260	2,060	3	1,840	707	1,130
500,000	3	2,360	915	1,450	2	1,750	674	1,070
1,000,000	1	3,220	1,250	1,960	1	2,060	791	1,270
All ranges	13,100	337,000	45,500	292,000	13,100	337,000	45,500	292,000

Source: Survey of Personal Incomes 2014-15

Footnote

(a) Can include some taxpayers who are not entitled to a Personal Allowance whose total income can be less than the Personal Allowance of £10,000 for 2014-15 (see Annex B for details).

Notes on the Table
Distribution of total income before and after tax by gender, 2014-15

1. This table only covers individuals with some liability to tax.

2. It should be noted that individuals may not necessarily fall into the same total income range for before and after tax breakdowns. Total income before tax is used to assign people to an income range for columns 2 to 5, whereas total income after the deduction of tax is used to assign individuals to an income band for columns 6 to 9.

3. For more information about the SPI and symbols used in this table, please refer to Personal Income Statistics release: https://www.gov.uk/government/collections/personal-incomes-statistics

8.2 Summary of the effects of taxes and benefits, by household type,[1] 2015/16

	All households	Retired households			
		1 adult Men	1 adult Women	All 1 adult	2 or more adults
Average per household (£ per year)					
Original income	35 204	9 108	7 160	7 805	19 362
plus Cash benefits	6 341	9 015	10 025	9 691	13 297
Gross income	41 545	18 122	17 186	17 496	32 659
less Direct taxes and employees' NIC	7 767	2 063	1 751	1 854	4 266
Disposable income	33 778	16 059	15 435	15 642	28 393
Equivalised[3] disposable income	*31 441*	*24 010*	*23 152*	*23 436*	*27 702*
less Indirect taxes	6 126	3 341	2 381	2 699	6 035
Post-tax income	27 652	12 718	13 054	12 943	22 358
plus Benefits in kind	6 952	4 721	5 204	5 044	7 937
Final income	34 605	17 440	18 258	17 987	30 295

	Non-Retired households									
	1 adult Men[2]	1 adult Women[2]	All 1 adult[2]	2 adults[2]	3 or more adults[2]	1 adult with children[3]	2 adults with 1 child	2 adults with 2 children	2 adults with 3 or more children	3 or more adults with children
Average per household (£ per year)										
Original income	23 647	20 198	22 129	48 419	58 542	12 337	50 820	55 384	46 376	53 279
plus Cash benefits	2 631	3 512	3 019	2 731	4 338	11 595	4 155	4 987	9 180	7 479
Gross income	26 277	23 710	25 147	51 150	62 879	23 933	54 975	60 371	55 556	60 758
less Direct taxes and employees' NIC	5 248	4 516	4 926	10 736	11 163	2 213	11 713	13 253	11 030	10 914
Disposable income	21 030	19 194	20 222	40 414	51 716	21 720	43 262	47 118	44 525	49 844
Equivalised[4] disposable income	*31 544*	*28 792*	*30 333*	*40 414*	*34 616*	*20 992*	*34 975*	*32 582*	*25 814*	*27 538*
less Indirect taxes	3 616	3 794	3 694	7 298	10 063	3 935	6 898	7 733	7 732	9 399
Post-tax income	17 413	15 401	16 528	33 116	41 653	17 785	36 365	39 385	36 793	40 445
plus Benefits in kind	1 428	1 815	1 599	3 421	5 770	11 711	8 218	14 087	22 107	15 124
Final income	18 842	17 216	18 126	36 537	47 423	29 496	44 583	53 472	58 900	55 569

Source: Office for National Statistics

Notes:

1 See Methodology and Coherence section for definitions of retired households, adults and children.

2 Without children.

3 Children are defined as people aged under 16 or aged between 16 and 19, not married nor in a Civil Partnership, nor living with a partner; and living with parent(s)/guardian(s); and and receiving non-advanced further education or in unwaged-government training.

4 Using the modified-OECD scale.

8.3 Income and source of income for all UK households, 1977 to 2016/17

(2016/17 prices[1])

	Number of households in the population	Average annual household income		Sources of income[2]						
		Disposable	Gross	Wages and salaries	Imputed income from benefits in kind	Self-employment income	Private pensions, annuities	Investment income	Other income	Total cash benefits
Year[3,4,5]	000s	£	£	Percentage of gross household income						
1977	7,199	3,568	4,628	73	0	7	3	3	1	13
1978	7,001	4,156	5,295	0	0	0	3	3	1	13
1979	6,777	4,789	6,020	74	0	6	3	3	1	14
1980	6,944	5,773	7,293	73	0	7	3	3	1	13
1981	7,525	6,485	8,292	70	0	7	3	4	1	14
1982	7,428	6,813	8,733	69	0	7	3	4	1	16
1983	6,973	7,230	9,286	67	0	8	4	4	1	17
1984	7,081	7,649	9,788	67	0	7	4	4	1	17
1985	7,012	8,469	10,803	66	0	8	5	4	1	16
1986	7,178	9,156	11,639	65	0	9	5	4	1	16
1987	7,396	10,075	12,817	65	0	10	5	5	1	15
1988	7,265	11,289	14,252	64	0	12	5	5	1	13
1989	7,410	12,039	15,087	65	0	11	5	5	1	13
1990	7,046	13,607	17,069	64	1	11	5	6	1	13
1991	7,056	14,624	18,168	63	1	9	5	7	1	13
1992	7,418	14,913	18,493	62	1	9	6	6	1	15
1993	6,979	15,271	18,978	62	1	8	6	5	1	16
1994/95	6,853	15,752	19,805	62	1	10	6	4	1	16
1995/96	6,796	16,168	20,366	62	1	9	7	5	1	16
1996/97	24,253	17,397	21,691	63	1	10	6	5	1	15
1997/98	24,556	18,402	22,985	65	1	8	7	4	1	14
1998/99	24,664	19,230	24,250	66	1	8	7	4	1	14
1999/00	25,334	20,225	25,423	64	1	10	7	5	1	13
2000/01	25,030	21,242	26,728	65	1	10	7	4	1	13
2001/02	24,888	22,925	28,891	67	1	8	7	4	1	13
2002/03	24,346	23,483	29,229	66	1	8	7	3	1	14
2003/04	24,670	24,069	30,366	66	1	9	7	3	1	14
2004/05	24,431	25,360	32,035	66	1	8	7	3	1	14
2005/06	24,799	26,039	32,914	65	1	8	7	3	1	14
2006/07	24,836	27,370	34,806	66	1	9	7	3	1	14
2007/08	25,289	27,769	35,317	66	1	9	7	3	1	14
2008/09	25,874	28,428	35,758	65	1	9	7	3	1	15
2009/10	26,053	29,241	36,631	65	1	8	8	3	1	16
2010/11	26,265	30,416	38,021	63	1	9	8	2	1	16
2011/12	26,436	30,027	37,600	65	1	7	9	2	1	16
2012/13	26,823	30,786	38,232	62	1	9	9	3	1	16
2013/14	26,675	31,786	39,314	63	1	8	9	3	1	16
2014/15	26,856	33,326	41,027	63	1	8	9	3	1	15
2015/16	27,204	33,778	41,546	63	1	8	10	3	1	15
2016/17	27,210	35,247	43,645	62	1	9	10	3	1	15

Source: Office for National Statistics

Notes:

1 Income figures have been deflated to 2016/17 prices using the consumer prices index including owner-occupiers' housing costs (CPIH).

2 See Table 2 for information relating to the composition of different sources of income.

3 For 1978 it is not possible to provide a breakdown of income from employment into employee wages and salaries and self-employment income.

4 Prior to 1990 imputed income from benefits in kind was not included in gross household income.

5 Prior to 1996/97 income figures are unweighted. From 1996/97 onwards income figures are based on weighted data.

8.4 Household expenditure at current[1] prices

UK, financial year ending March 2002 to financial year ending 2016

	2001-02	2002-03	2003-04	2004-05	2005-06	2006[2]	2006[3]	2007	2008	2009	2010	2011	2012	2013[4]	2014	2014-15	2015-16
Weighted number of households (thousands)	24,450	24,350	24,670	24,430	24,800	24,790	25,440	25,350	25,690	25,980	26,320	26,110	26,410	26,840	26,600	26,760	27,220
Total number of households in sample	7,470	6,930	7,050	6,800	6,790	6,650	6,650	6,140	5,850	5,830	5,260	5,690	5,600	5,140	5,130	5,170	4,920
Total number of persons in sample	18,120	16,590	16,970	16,260	16,090	15,850	15,850	14,650	13,830	13,740	12,180	13,430	13,180	12,120	12,120	12,160	11,620
Total number of adults in sample	13,450	12,450	12,620	12,260	12,170	12,000	12,000	11,220	10,640	10,650	9,430	10,330	10,200	9,350	9,440	9,510	8,950
Weighted average number of persons per househ(	2.4	2.4	2.4	2.4	2.4	2.4	2.3	2.4	2.4	2.3	2.3	2.4	2.3	2.4	2.4	2.4	2.4
Commodity or service							Average weekly household expenditure (£)										
1 Food and non-alcoholic drinks	41.80	42.70	43.50	44.70	45.30	46.90	46.30	48.10	50.70	52.20	53.20	54.80	56.80	58.80	58.80	58.30	56.80
2 Alcoholic drinks, tobacco and narcotics	11.40	11.40	11.70	11.30	10.80	11.10	11.10	11.20	10.80	11.20	11.80	12.00	12.60	12.00	12.30	12.00	11.40
3 Clothing and footwear	22.90	22.30	22.70	23.90	22.70	23.20	23.00	22.00	21.60	20.90	23.40	21.70	23.40	22.60	23.70	23.70	23.50
4 Housing (net)[5], fuel and power	35.90	36.90	39.00	40.40	44.20	47.60	47.50	51.80	53.00	57.30	60.40	63.30	68.00	74.40	72.70	72.80	72.50
5 Household goods and services	30.50	30.20	31.30	31.60	30.00	30.30	29.90	30.70	30.10	27.90	31.40	27.30	28.50	33.10	35.40	36.70	35.50
6 Health	4.50	4.80	5.00	4.90	5.50	5.90	5.80	5.70	5.10	5.30	5.00	6.60	6.40	6.20	7.10	7.00	7.20
7 Transport	57.80	59.20	60.70	59.60	61.70	62.00	60.80	61.70	63.40	58.40	64.90	65.70	64.10	70.40	74.80	73.30	72.70
8 Communication	10.40	10.60	11.20	11.70	11.90	11.70	11.60	11.90	12.00	11.70	13.00	13.30	13.80	14.50	15.50	15.50	16.00
9 Recreation and culture	54.10	56.40	57.30	59.00	57.50	58.50	57.60	57.40	60.10	57.90	58.10	63.90	61.50	63.90	68.80	69.30	68.00
10 Education	5.60	5.20	5.20	6.50	6.60	7.20	7.00	6.80	6.20	7.00	10.00	7.00	6.80	8.80	9.80	9.00	7.00
11 Restaurants and hotels	33.40	35.40	34.90	36.10	36.70	37.90	37.60	37.20	37.70	38.40	39.20	39.70	40.50	40.40	42.50	42.50	45.10
12 Miscellaneous goods and services	30.70	33.10	33.60	34.90	34.60	36.00	35.70	35.30	35.60	35.00	35.90	38.60	38.40	39.10	40.00	40.40	39.70
1-12 All expenditure groups	338.80	348.30	356.20	364.70	367.60	378.30	373.80	379.80	386.30	383.10	406.30	413.90	420.70	444.30	461.20	460.50	455.30
13 Other expenditure items[6]	59.50	57.90	61.90	69.70	75.80	77.60	75.10	79.30	84.60	71.80	67.30	69.70	68.30	73.00	70.10	66.90	73.60
Total expenditure	**398.30**	**406.20**	**418.10**	**434.40**	**443.40**	**455.90**	**449.00**	**459.20**	**471.00**	**455.00**	**473.60**	**483.60**	**489.00**	**517.30**	**531.30**	**527.30**	**528.90**
Average weekly expenditure per person (£)																	
Total expenditure	**167.60**	**170.50**	**177.40**	**182.00**	**188.00**	**192.80**	**192.00**	**194.80**	**199.80**	**194.40**	**203.10**	**205.40**	**208.70**	**219.40**	**221.80**	**221.20**	**224.50**

Note: The commodity and service categories are not comparable to those in publications before 2001-02.

Source: Office for National Statistics

1 Data in Table 4.3 have not been deflated to 2015-16 prices and therefore show the actual expenditure for the year they were collected. Because inflation is not taken into account, comparisons between the years should be made with caution.
2 From 2001-02 to this version of 2006, figures shown are based on weighted data using non-response weights based on the 1991 Census and population figures from the 1991 and 2001 Censuses.
3 From this version of 2006 until 2012, figures shown are based on weighted data using non-response weights and population figures based on the 2001 Census.
4 From 2013, figures are based on weighted data using non-response weights based on the 2001 Census and population estimates based on the 2011 Census.
5 Excluding mortgage interest payments, council tax and Northern Ireland rates.
6 An improvement to the imputation of mortgage interest payments has been implemented for 2006 data onwards. This means there is a slight discontinuity between 2006 and earlier years.
Rounding: Individual figures have been rounded independently. The sum of component items does not therefore necessarily add to the totals shown.
Averages: These are averages (means) for all households included in the column or row, and unless specified, are not restricted to those households reporting expenditure on a particular item or income of a particular type.

8.5 Percentage of households with durable goods

UK, 1998-99 to financial year ending 2016

	Car/ van	Central heating[1]	Washing machine	Tumble dryer	Dish-washer	Micro-wave	Tele-phone	Mobile phone	DVD Player	Home computer	Internet connection
1998-99[2]	*72*	*89*	*92*	*51*	*23*	*79*	*95*	*27*	--	*33*	*10*
1999-2000	*71*	*90*	*91*	*52*	*23*	*80*	*95*	*44*	--	*38*	*19*
2000-01	*72*	*91*	*93*	*53*	*25*	*84*	*93*	*47*	--	*44*	*32*
2001-02[3]	*74*	*92*	*93*	*54*	*27*	*86*	*94*	*64*	--	*49*	*39*
2002-03	*74*	*93*	*94*	*56*	*29*	*87*	*94*	*70*	*31*	*55*	*45*
2003-04	*75*	*94*	*94*	*57*	*31*	*89*	*92*	*76*	*50*	*58*	*49*
2004-05	*75*	*95*	*95*	*58*	*33*	*90*	*93*	*78*	*67*	*62*	*53*
2005-06	*74*	*94*	*95*	*58*	*35*	*91*	*92*	*79*	*79*	*65*	*55*
2006[4]	*76*	*95*	*96*	*59*	*38*	*91*	*91*	*80*	*83*	*67*	*59*
2006[5]	*74*	*95*	*96*	*59*	*37*	*91*	*91*	*79*	*83*	*67*	*58*
2007	*75*	*95*	*96*	*57*	*37*	*91*	*89*	*78*	*86*	*70*	*61*
2008	*74*	*95*	*96*	*59*	*37*	*92*	*90*	*79*	*88*	*72*	*66*
2009	*76*	*95*	*96*	*58*	*39*	*93*	*88*	*81*	*90*	*75*	*71*
2010	*75*	*96*	*96*	*57*	*40*	*92*	*87*	*80*	*88*	*77*	*73*
2011	*75*	*96*	*97*	*56*	*41*	*92*	*88*	*87*	*88*	*79*	*77*
2012	*75*	*96*	*97*	*56*	*42*	*93*	*88*	*87*	*87*	*81*	*79*
2013	*76*	*96*	*97*	*56*	*42*	*92*	*89*	*92*	*85*	*83*	*82*
2014	*76*	*96*	*97*	*56*	*44*	*92*	*88*	*94*	*83*	*85*	*84*
2014-15	*76*	*96*	*97*	*56*	*44*	*92*	*88*	*94*	*83*	*85*	*84*
2015-16	*78*	*95*	*97*	*56*	*45*	*93*	*88*	*95*	*80*	*88*	*88*

Source: Office for National Statistics

Please see background notes for symbols and conventions used in this report.

-- Data not available.

1 Full or partial.

2 From this version of 1998-99, figures shown are based on weighted data and including children's expenditure.

3 From 2001-02 onwards, weighting is based on the population figures from the 2001 census.

4 From 1998-99 to this version of 2006, figures shown are based on weighted data using non-response weights based on the 1991 Census and population figures from the 1991 and 2001 Census.

5 From this version of 2006, figures shown are based on weighted data using updated weights, with non-response weights and population figures based on the 2001 Census.

this page is intentionally blank

Chapter 9

Lifestyles

Lifestyles

Expenditure by the Department for Culture, Media and Sport (Table 9.1)

The figures in this table are taken from the department's Annual Report and are outturn figures for each of the headings shown (later figures are the estimated outturn). The department's planned expenditure for future years is also shown.

International tourism and holidays abroad (Tables 9.8 and 9.9)

The figures in these tables are compiled using data from the International Passenger Survey (IPS). A holiday abroad is a visit made for holiday purposes. Business trips and visits to friends and relatives are excluded.

Domestic tourism (Table 9.10)

The figures in this table are compiled using data from the Visit England. Data includes total number of trips taken as well as number of bednights and expenditure, as well as average trip totals.

Gambling (Table 9.12a and b)

The figures in these tables are the latest released by The Gambling Commission at the time of going to press. The statistics come from the data provided by licence holders through their regulatory returns.

9.1 Expenditure by the Department for Culture, Media and Sport

(£'000s)

	2012-13 Outturn	2013-14 Outturn	2014-15 Outturn	2015-16 Outturn	2016-17 Outturn	2017-18 Plans	2018-19 Plans	2019-20 Plans
Resource DEL								
Support for the Museums and Galleries sector	12,664	16,267	16,003	20,314	16,198	25,777	29,267	26,887
Museums and Galleries sponsored ALBs (net)	355,854	351,059	326,032	339,528	362,966	392,331	403,479	409,240
Libraries sponsored ALBs (net)	110,753	101,374	98,369	113,571	115,172	122,684	124,209	126,201
Museums, libraries and archives council (net)	8,632	-	-	-	-	-	-	-
Support for the Arts sector[1]	(53,218)	(67,219)	(58,465)	(79,113)	(76,979)	(73,467)	783	583
Arts and culture ALBs (net)	452,545	448,788	433,475	439,548	442,231	431,528	368,784	369,211
Support for the Sports sector	6,847	21,147	18,075	11,159	7,585	7,124	7,124	7,124
Sport sponsored ALBs (net)	142,742	112,767	111,006	106,112	128,683	125,154	132,826	129,952
Ceremonial and support for the Heritage sector[2]	22,161	16,690	29,456	53,141	48,451	42,111	37,741	28,273
Heritage sponsored ALBs (net)[3]	90,277	105,685	115,478	84,350	99,814	80,964	77,315	75,691
The Royal Parks[4]	16,955	13,637	14,600	12,320	6,022	-	-	-
Support for the Tourism sector	70	10	(200)	-	-	-	-	-
Tourism sponsored ALBs (net)	47,824	48,200	46,502	66,374	57,095	45,992	56,232	33,732
Support for the Broadcasting and Media sector	15,607	15,862	42,315	19,498	28,346	24,591	13,745	10,892
Broadcasting and Media sponsored ALBs (net)[5]	188,279	101,810	88,099	95,600	82,204	72,166	41,185	40,811
Administration and Research	55,140	36,554	41,748	54,081	57,898	60,297	59,443	57,766
Support for Horseracing and the Gambling sector	(1,560)	(1,603)	(843)	(2,858)	(2,539)	(3,080)	-	-
Gambling Commission(net)	1,959	3,097	1,449	365	1,197	3,448	343	310
Olympics - legacy programmes[6]	501,628	(18,083)	(33,823)	(55,210)	(30,408)	4,492	-	-
London 2012(net)[6]	1,575,240	(29,477)	55,715	-	-	-	-	-
Office for Civil Society[7]	133,359	163,530	219,954	162,582	255,511	246,202	294,879	343,043
Spectrum Management Receipts[8]	(60,142)	(54,535)	(52,594)	(52,139)	(49,645)	(30,000)	-	-
Total Resource DEL	**3,623,616**	**1,385,560**	**1,512,351**	**1,389,223**	**1,549,802**	**1,578,314**	**1,647,355**	**1,659,716**
Of which:								
Staff costs	592,051	631,209	563,156	539,792	563,658	222,869	219,579	216,566
Purchase of goods and services	831,340	1,130,775	880,324	579,800	600,778	498,589	468,454	428,249
Income from sales of goods and services	(289,338)	(491,300)	(106,416)	(55,262)	(57,591)	-	-	-
Current grants to local government (net)	10,781	(6,900)	28,150	46,224	69,566	-	-	-
Current grants to persons and non-profit (net)	845,657	507,543	750,679	639,275	758,716	771,059	749,329	792,347
Current grants abroad (net)	-	(1,528)	13,269	(1,819)	(3,787)	-	-	-
Subsidies to private sector companies	-	157	-	-	-	-	-	-
Subsidies to public corporations	522,976	9,663	51,410	58,428	43,704	-	-	-
Rentals	3,537	37,420	27,624	22,996	19,699	-	-	-
Depreciation[9]	1,444,816	156,627	103,925	127,571	143,397	171,995	186,293	198,854
Change in pension scheme liabilities[10]	-	(44)	-	-	158	-	-	-
Unwinding of discount rate on pension scheme liabilities[10]	-	-	-	1,393	813	-	-	-
Other resource	(338,204)	(588,062)	(799,770)	(569,175)	(589,309)	(86,198)	23,700	23,700
Resource AME								
British Broadcasting Corporation(net)	3,204,478	3,046,611	3,363,162	3,138,249	3,117,377	3,342,268	3,661,584	3,604,113
Provisions, Impairments and other AME spend	21,385	18,523	11,157	31,004	14,024	49,401	-	-
Levy bodies[11]	(10,268)	(2,721)	4,021	8,139	7,490	330	-	-
London 2012(net)	(30,996)	102,138	-	-	-	-	-	-
Lottery Grants[12]	1,450,215	1,352,673	1,594,409	1,070,465	1,294,717	1,284,009	1,189,222	1,189,222
Total Resource AME	**4,634,814**	**4,517,224**	**4,972,749**	**4,247,857**	**4,433,608**	**4,676,008**	**4,850,806**	**4,793,335**
Of which:								
Staff costs	921,649	929,732	1,018,560	1,082,412	1,170,477	1,739,655	1,502,554	1,479,910
Purchase of goods and services	2,792,331	2,469,733	2,695,641	2,548,864	2,412,420	2,401,776	2,483,047	2,445,393
Income from sales of goods and services	(328,808)	-	-	-	-	(190,469)	(184,642)	(181,815)
Current grants to local government (net)	20,812	34,896	32,218	24,145	21,787	35,623	35,623	35,623
Current grants to persons and non-profit (net)	557,133	1,245,777	1,470,874	949,267	1,260,754	1,096,316	1,000,901	1,000,901
Current grants abroad (net)	-	-	-	37	-	-	-	-
Subsidies to public corporations	-	24	4,823	7,245	-	-	-	-
Rentals	80,775	104,496	106,848	51,535	34,284	-	-	-
Depreciation	237,372	274,590	245,068	212,835	221,081	175,686	-	-
Take up of provisions	592,197	29,932	21,167	46,670	44,783	-	-	-
Release of provision	(38,851)	(10,526)	(10,805)	(3,412)	-	-	-	-
Change in pension scheme liabilities[13]	162,422	178,831	192,115	165,013	195,426	15,334	-	-
Unwinding of discount rate on pension scheme liabilities[13]	730,035	82,412	70,393	43,555	47,882	-	-	-
Release of provisions covering pension benefits	(234)	(14,336)	(11,769)	(10,237)	-	-	-	-
Other resource	(1,092,019)	(808,337)	(862,384)	(870,072)	(975,286)	(597,913)	13,323	13,323
Total Resource Budget[14]	**3,623,616**	**1,385,560**	**1,512,351**	**1,389,223**	**1,549,802**	**1,578,314**	**1,647,355**	**1,659,716**
Of which								
Depreciation[15]	1,682,188	431,217	348,993	340,406	364,478	347,681	186,293	198,854

9.1 Expenditure by the Department for Culture, Media and Sport

(£'000s)

	2012-13 Outturn	2013-14 Outturn	2014-15 Outturn	2015-16 Outturn	2016-17 Outturn	2017-18 Plans	2018-19 Plans	2019-20 Plans
Capital DEL								
Support for the Museums and Galleries sector[16]	2,100	100	1,981	1,170	3,118	49,300	48,500	8,500
Museums and Galleries sponsored ALBs (net)[17]	80,184	19,887	42,177	30,031	65,867	27,865	27,115	26,273
Libraries sponsored ALBs (net)	17,167	7,173	12,561	3,408	8,050	3,221	3,221	3,221
Support for the Arts sector	-	3,932	-	723	314	305	-	-
Arts and culture ALBs (net)[18]	18,222	18,679	14,432	21,413	49,316	59,314	38,334	17,634
Support for the Sports sector	-	250	-	154	-	-	-	-
Sport sponsored ALBs (net)	33,898	30,120	29,019	38,916	37,131	37,265	42,765	43,265
Ceremonial and support for the Heritage sector	7,581	6,882	2,182	5,491	5,056	2,250	-	-
Heritage sponsored ALBs (net)[19]	36,369	24,095	106,864	17,421	25,401	23,795	21,959	20,359
The Royal Parks[20]	1,583	2,620	2,570	3,577	5,201	-	-	-
Tourism sponsored ALBs (net)	189	357	325	253	1,184	186	186	186
Support for the Broadcasting and Media sector[21]	9,136	55,198	229,066	213,138	51,779	166,594	183,338	306,480
Broadcasting and Media sponsored ALBs (net)[22]	41,638	23,525	4,290	4,720	30,522	79,342	163,857	154,857
Administration and Research	2,554	2,215	4,401	1,800	1,424	-	-	-
Support for Horseracing and the Gambling sector[23]	9,000	9,000	49,896	-	-	-	-	-
Gambling Commission(net)	737	302	335	633	724	-	-	-
Olympics - legacy programmes[24]	42,053	-	-	-	(6,435)	-	-	-
London 2012(net)[24]	54,056	(184,059)	(256,703)	-	-	-	-	-
Office for Civil Society[25]	926	12,553	20,357	6,136	(3,705)	-	-	-
Total Capital DEL	**357,393**	**32,829**	**263,753**	**348,984**	**274,947**	**449,437**	**529,275**	**580,775**
Of which:								
Staff costs	10,214	11,332	11,450	10,660	-	9,790	9,790	9,790
Purchase of goods and services	3,900	3,900	3,900	3,900	14,521	4,000	4,000	4,000
Release of provision	-	-	-	-	-	-	-	-
Capital support for local government (net)	1,237,270	50,452	217,082	202,987	82,509	-	-	-
Capital grants to persons & non-profit (net)	43,517	(103,067)	(100,388)	(81,098)	(76,394)	329,381	482,452	532,836
Capital grants to private sector companies (net)	34,383	(1,737)	41,159	43,204	(247)	-	-	-
Capital grants abroad (net)	(216)	(202)	-	-	-	-	-	-
Capital support for public corporations	46,818	-	80,050	-	-	-	-	-
Purchase of assets	457,473	314,247	178,115	191,713	276,438	106,266	33,033	34,149
Income from sales of assets	(1,352,679)	(115,685)	(322,599)	(42,176)	(3,322)	-	-	-
Net lending to the private sector and abroad	444	938	241	30,282	8,186	-	-	-
Other capital	(123,731)	(127,349)	154,743	(10,488)	(26,744)	-	-	-
Capital AME								
British Broadcasting Corporation(net)[26]	(60,056)	127,393	139,462	45,226	143,691	171,326	197,000	170,000
London 2012(net)	-	(3,815)	-	-	-	-	-	-
Levy bodies[27]	(8,411)	(1,763)	1,991	(2,079)	(2,737)	-	-	-
Lottery Grants[28]	536,954	523,705	601,444	453,717	503,897	496,540	447,593	447,593
Total Capital AME	**468,487**	**645,520**	**742,897**	**496,864**	**644,851**	**667,866**	**644,593**	**617,593**
Of which:								
Staff costs	20,324	20,324	23,078	23,078	-	17,885	-	-
Purchase of goods and services	-	-	-	-	14,000	-	-	-
Release of provision	(7,400)	(3,815)	-	-	-	-	-	-
Capital support for local government (net)	99,230	132,060	188,770	21,803	149,469	-	-	-
Capital grants to persons & non-profit (net)	355,026	311,789	329,681	30,932	280,753	496,400	407,454	407,454
Capital support for public corporations	-	18	417	-	-	-	-	-
Purchase of assets	135,451	129,856	124,090	120,203	126,206	153,581	237,139	210,139
Income from sales of assets	(208,487)	(14,264)	(6,342)	(96,311)	(8,067)	-	-	-
Net lending to the private sector and abroad	8,455	21,360	17,612	20,554	33,471	-	-	-
Other capital	65,888	48,192	65,591	376,605	49,019	-	-	-
Total Capital Budget[29]	**825,880**	**678,349**	**1,006,650**	**845,848**	**919,798**	**1,117,303**	**1,173,868**	**1,198,368**
Total Departmental Spending[30]	**2,767,308**	**1,632,692**	**2,170,008**	**1,894,665**	**2,105,122**	**2,347,936**	**2,634,930**	**2,659,230**
Of which:								
Total DEL[31]	2,536,193	1,261,762	1,672,179	1,610,636	1,681,352	1,855,756	1,990,337	2,041,637
Total AME[32]	4,865,929	4,888,154	5,470,578	4,531,886	4,857,378	5,168,188	5,495,399	5,410,928

Source: Department for Culture, Media and Sport

9.1 Expenditure by the Department for Culture, Media and Sport

These Tables present actual expenditure by the Department for the years 2012-13 to 2016-17 and planned expenditure for the years 2017-18 to 2019-20 (derived from the Spending Review 2015 and subsequent fiscal events). The data relates to the Department's expenditure on an Estimate and budgeting basis.

The format of the Tables is determined by HM Treasury, and the disclosure in Tables 1 and 2 follow that of the Supply Estimate Functions. All years have been restated for the effect of Machinery of Government Changes and the change in budgetary treatment of research and development (from resource to capital). Please note that the current year Statement of Parliamentary Supply has not been restated for any other prior period adjustments.

The current year numbers in these Tables reconcile to the outturn figures disclosed on the Statement of Parliamentary Supply and related notes.

Table 1 Public Spending – summarises expenditure on functions administered by the Department. Consumption of resources includes Departmental Expenditure Limits (DEL) for administration, programme and capital costs, and Annually Managed Expenditure (AME) both Voted and Non-Voted expenditure. The figures are derived from the OSCAR database and the mappings replicate the lines in SoPS Note 1.

Table 2 Administration Budgets – provides a more detailed analysis of the administration costs of the Department. It retains the high level functional analysis used in Table 1. The figures are derived from the OSCAR database and the mappings replicate the lines in SoPS Note 1.

Resource DEL

1. Support for the Art Sector. The income relates to contributions from the Department for Education towards the cost of Music Hubs and other programmes managed by the Arts Council England. The funding profile is agreed on a year by year basis.

2. Ceremonial and Support for the Heritage sector included funding for World War One commemorations in 2013-14 through to 2017-18 including the Battle of Jutland and the Somme.

3. The Heritage Sponsored Bodies line illustrates an initial reduction in 2012-13 as a result of the 2010 Spending Review cuts and also in 2015-16 following Spending Review 2013. In addition it includes funding for Church Roof repairs, announced in the 2014 Autumn Statement, via the National Heritage Memorial fund which commenced in 2015-16.

4. On 15 March 2017 The Royal Parks Charity took over the role of managing the parks from The Royal Parks Agency. The charity manages the parks on behalf of the government, however it now receives less exchequer funding than it raises in commercial income, consequently it has been reclassified as outside of central government and removed from the DCMS Supply Estimate. As a result The Royal Parks Agency has no planned expenditure after 2016-17.

5. Broadcasting and Media includes the clearance and auction of the 800MHz band, with additional funding in 2014-15 for Superfast Broadband. The reduction in expenditure between 2016-17 and 2017-18 is due to Ofcom becoming self funding from October 2017 and so will not need the funding it currently receives from the Exchequer.

6. Olympics legacy and London 2012 relate to the staging of the Olympic and Paralympic games 2012. This includes income from the sale of the Olympic Village, residual costs and final settlements with the Greater London Authority (GLA) and Olympic Lottery Distribution Fund (OLDF), most of which concluded by 2016-17.

7. On the 15 July 2016 the Office for Civil Society moved from the Cabinet Office to the Department for Culture, Media and Sport via a Machinery of Government transfer. The National Citizens Service participation levels are forecast to increase from 2018-19 onwards.

8. Spectrum Management receipts which partially offset Broadcasting Administration expenditure, will, from 2018-19, be treated as income by Ofcom.

9. Depreciation includes impairment. In 2012-13 this included impairments relating to London 2012.

10. Pension schemes report under IAS 19 Employee Benefits accounting requirements. These figures, therefore, include cash payments made and contributions received, as well as certain non-cash items.

Resource AME

11. Levy Bodies: Levy Expenditure is only recorded at year end via the annual accounts, hence no forward plans data.

12. Lottery Grants: The group accounts exclude the Devolved Administrations and records expenditure on an accruals basis since 2014-15.

13. Pension schemes report under IAS 19 Employee Benefits accounting requirements. These figures, therefore, include cash payments made and contributions received, as well as certain non-cash items.

14. Total Resource Budget is the sum of the Resource DEL budget and the Resource AME budget, including depreciation.

15. Depreciation includes impairment.

9.1 Expenditure by the Department for Culture, Media and Sport

Capital DEL

16. In the Spending Review 2015 it was announced that the government would invest £150 million to support the British Museum, Science Museum and Victoria and Albert Museum to replace out of date museum storage at Blythe House, this programme commenced in 2016-17.

17. Museums and Galleries Sponsored ALBs illustrate the efficiency savings made by the Museums & Galleries following spending reviews of 2010 & 2013. Additional Capital funding was allocated for 2016-17 in the Spending Review 2015, with reserves access granted to them as part of the new Museums Freedoms programme.

18. Arts and culture ALBs includes funding in 2016-17 for the Factory Manchester as part of the Northern Powerhouse.

19. Heritage Sponsored ALBs saw an additional £80m allocated in 2014-15 to Historic England (formerly English Heritage) on implementation of the New Model whereby the management of historic bodies was transferred to a charity, the English Heritage Trust.

20. On 15 March 2017 The Royal Parks Charity took over the role of managing the parks from The Royal Parks Agency. The charity manages the parks on behalf of the government, however it now receives less exchequer funding than it raises in commercial income, consequently it has been reclassified as outside of central government and removed from the DCMS Supply Estimate. As a result, The Royal Parks Agency has no planned expenditure after 2016-17.

21. Support for Broadcasting and Media sector related to the Broadband Delivery UK (BDUK) project. At the Autumn Statement 2016 it was announced that the Government would invest a further £740 million targeted at supporting the market to roll out full-fibre connections and future 5G communications.

22. Broadcasting and Media sponsored ALBs sees an increase for 2016-17 onwards as it includes funding for the clearance and auction of the 700MHz band.

23. Support for Horseracing and Gambling sector - following the sale of the Tote in 2011-12 it was agreed that the proceeds would be returned to the racing industry over a period of years. Initially, at £9m a year and then with the industry it was agreed that the balance of £49.9m be repaid in 2014-15.

24. Olympics legacy and London 2012 relate to the staging of the Olympic and Paralympic games 2012. This includes income from the sale of the Olympic Village, residual costs and final settlements with the GLA and OLDF.

25. On the 15 July 2016 the Office for Civil Society moved from the Cabinet Office to the Department for Culture, Media and Sport via a Machinery of Government transfer. Any future years expenditure will be reflected at the Supplementary Estimate.

Capital AME

26. BBC Capital expenditure is net of property disposals including the sale of Television Centre in White City in 2015-16.

27. Levy Bodies: Levy Expenditure is only recorded at year end via the annual accounts, hence no forward plans data.

28. Lottery Grants: The group accounts excludes the Devolved Administrations and records expenditure on an accruals basis since 2014-15.

Totals

29. Total Capital Budget is the sum of the Capital DEL budget and the Capital AME budget.

30. Total departmental spending is the sum of the resource budget and the capital budget less depreciation.

31. Total DEL is the sum of the resource budget DEL and capital budget DEL less depreciation in DEL.

32. Total AME is the sum of the resource budget AME and the capital budget AME less depreciation in AME.

Please note that the Department for Culture, Media and Sport changed it's name in July 2017 to the Department for Digital, Culture, Media and Sport.

9.2 Estimates of Average Issue Readership of National Daily Newspapers

NRS rolling 12 months' periods ending

000's

National Dailies (Mon-Sat. A.I.R.)		2013 Mar	2013 Jun	2013 Sep	2013 Dec	2014 Mar	2014 Jun	2014 Sep	2014 Dec	2015 Mar	2015 Jun	2015 Sep	2015 Dec	2016 Mar	2016 Jun	2016 Sep	2016 Dec	2017 Mar
The Sun	WSDV	6,707	6,435	6,123	5,841	5,685	5,508	5,421	5,347	5,178	4878	4664	4490	4,392	4,317	4,188	3,915	3,653
Daily Mail	WSEI	4,245	4,298	4,269	4,215	4,074	3,866	3,833	3,745	3,704	3657	3605	3546	3,444	3,456	3,354	3,294	3,215
Daily Mirror/Record[1]	WSEH	3,614	3,512	3,357	3,167	2,975	2,893	2,908	2,881	2,796	2554	2433	2337	2,287	2,325	2,283	2,151	2,064
Daily Mirror	WSEM	2,856	2,775	2,639	2,456	2,309	2,230	2,251	2,281	2,211	2029	1953	1848	1,813	1,851	1,818	1,773	1,691
Daily Record		783	764	747	736	688	679	679	624	608	550	496	504	487	486	484	406	406
The Daily Telegraph	WSEN	1,352	1,348	1,312	1,318	1,313	1,261	1,237	1,192	1,119	1154	1150	1165	1,190	1,191	1,183	1,139	1,171
The Times	WSES	1,300	1,261	1,240	1,147	1,155	1,110	1,047	1,062	995	985	1014	1036	1,054	1,092	1,047	1,014	1,049
Daily Express	WSEP	1,157	1,123	1,114	1,095	1,114	1,097	1,079	1,079	993	948	845	777	758	767	842	828	838
Daily Star	WSEQ	1,279	1,211	1,158	1,113	1,090	1,039	978	1,010	943	878	838	808	791	793	800	759	769
The Guardian	WSET	1,027	935	890	843	793	748	744	748	761	793	793	814	809	835	865	828	898
i (Newspaper)		579	545	568	559	563	584	573	579	549	561	533	536	569	518	541	499	475
The Independent[2]	WSEU	443	397	393	348	309	261	264	262	272	284	270	270	285	-	-	-	-
Financial Times[3]	WSEY	312	305	296	235	-	-	-	-	-	-	-	-	-	-	-	-	-
Any national morning[4]	WSEZ	17,403	20,852	20,181	19,347	19,092	18,384	18,106	17,929	17,331	16,716	16,161	15,794	15,591	15,306	15,124	14,455	14,165

The figures in this table are for printed media only.

Source: National Readership Surveys Ltd.

1. The combined figures for the DAILY MIRROR/RECORD are net readership figures for the Daily Mirror and the Daily Record.
2. The last published data for The Independent (print) was for the period ending March 2016, after that it became a digital only title.
3. NRS ceased to publish estimates for Financial Times as of 2014 data, so data cannot be provided for March 2014 onwards.
4. Gross national dailies.

Readership is an estimate of how many readers a publication has. As most publications have more than one reader per copy, the NRS readership estimate is very different from the circulation count (i.e. the count of how many copies of a particular publication are distributed).

The National Readership Survey was established in 1956 and today provides the most authoritative and valued audience research in use for print (and digital) advertising trading in Britain.

9.3 Creative Industries group jobs by gender and Creative Industries group: 2015[4]

	Male	Female	% Female
Advertising and marketing	109,000	73,000	40.3%
Architecture	59,000	31,000	34.3%
Design: product, graphic and fashion design	76,000	56,000	42.3%
Film, TV, video, radio and photography	139,000	92,000	39.9%
IT, software and computer services	503,000	137,000	21.4%
Museums, galleries and libraries	33,000	64,000	65.9%
Music, performing and visual arts	149,000	138,000	48.1%
Publishing	102,000	98,000	49.0%
Creative Economy Total	**1,145,000**	**694,000**	**37.2%**

Source: Department for Culture, Media and Sport

[4] Change for Crafts has not been shown due to small sample size.

9.4 Proportion of adults who participate in selected activities in their free time, 2015/16

	16 -24	25-44	45-64	65-74	75+	All aged 16+
	%	%	%	%	%	%
Watching TV	88.1	88.1	90.4	93.6	93.1	89.9
Spending time with friends/family	91.1	91.4	87.7	89.6	85.4	89.4
Listening to music	91.1	80.1	78.6	74.5	69.3	79.4
Shopping	75.5	77.1	75.4	81.4	74.8	76.6
Eating out at restaurants	76.2	77.5	75.3	78.3	68.3	75.8
Internet/emailing	85.3	82.8	71.0	59.4	30.4	71.5
Reading	55.1	66.3	70.5	78.3	73.2	68.1
Days out or visits to places	66.9	72.8	69.8	73.9	55.2	69.4
Sport/exercise	66.0	63.4	57.5	50.7	37.5	57.9
Going to the cinema	72.3	62.2	50.1	39.8	26.2	53.7
Going to pubs/bars/clubs	57.6	52.9	51.7	47.0	26.7	49.9
Gardening	11.1	43.1	61.9	69.7	59.1	49.2
Theatre/music concerts	38.5	41.9	50.5	52.2	34.7	44.6
DIY	20.5	44.3	49.6	45.4	26.2	40.9
Visiting historic sites	23.6	39.9	49.0	53.5	33.5	41.4
Visiting museums/galleries	27.5	40.9	44.5	47.2	28.5	39.6
Playing computer games	59.5	37.7	20.4	17.3	7.8	30.0
Arts and crafts	17.6	24.4	23.1	28.0	23.3	23.3
Playing a musical instrument	13.3	10.8	9.7	8.2	6.1	10.0

Source: Taking Part Survey, Department for Digital, Culture, Media and Sport

Please note - this table has not been updated since the last edition of AOS.
An updated table will appear in a following edition of this publication.

9.5 Films

United Kingdom

Numbers and £ million

	Production of UK films[1,4]		Expenditure on feature films			
	Films produced in the UK (numbers)	Production costs (current prices)	UK Box Office	Video[2] rental	Video retail[2,3]	Video on demand
	KWGD	KWGE	KWHU	KWHV	KWHW	
1998	83	389	547	437	453	33
1999	92	507	563	451	451	40
2000	80	578	583	601	601	50
2001	74	379	645	494	821	65
2002	119	551	755	494	1,175	63
2003	214	1,127	742	462	1,392	68
2004	198	879	770	476	1,557	73
2005	223	608	770	399	1,399	74
2006	208	827	762	340	1,302	67
2007	240	849	821	295	1,440	75
2008	297	723	850	284	1,454	89
2009	338	1,256	944	285	1,311	110
2010	374	1,154	988	278	1,267	127
2011	363	1,328	1,040	262	1,165	142
2012	373	1,009	1,099	221	968	208
2013	370	1,167	1,083	146	940	320
2014	364	1,575	1,058	87	861	397
2015	361	1,570	1,236	62	712	487
2016	327	1,840	1,228	48	589	578

Source: British Film Institute

1 Includes films with a production budget of £500,000 or more.

2 Video includes only rental and retail of physical discs, and does not include downloads.

3 In 2005 the British Video Association changed its methodology for producing market value which has necessitated a change to historical figures quoted.

4 Prior to 2010, the Research and Statistics Unit tracked all features shooting in the UK with a minimum budget of £500,000. However, evidence from avariety of sources (data on British film certification and the 2008 UK Film Council report Low and Micro-Budget Film Production in the UK) revealed a substantial number of films produced below this budget level. In order to broaden the evidence base, production tracking was extended to include feature films with budgets under £500,000 and data was collected from 2008 onwards.

Figures not adjusted for inflation

9.6 Box office top 20 films released in the UK and Republic of Ireland, 2015

Title	Country of origin	Box office gross (£ million)	Number of opening weekend cinemas	Opening weekend gross (£ million)	Distributor
1 Star Wars: The Force Awakens*	UK/USA	122.3	676	34.0+	Walt Disney
2 SPECTRE*	UK/USA	95.2	651	41.3+	Sony Pictures
3 Jurassic World	USA	64.5	619	19.4+	Universal
4 Avengers: Age of Ultron	UK/USA	48.3	585	18.0+	Walt Disney
5 Minions*	USA/Fra	47.7	601	11.7	Universal
6 Inside Out*	USA	39.3	608	7.4	Walt Disney
7 Fast & Furious 7	USA	38.6	537	12.7	Universal
8 Fifty Shades of Grey	USA	35.1	585	13.6	Universal
9 The Hunger Games: Mockingjay – Part 2	USA/Ger	29.2	579	11.3+	Lionsgate
10 Home	USA	25.4	531	6.0+	20th Century Fox
11 The Martian*	UK/USA	23.5	582	6.6+	20th Century Fox
12 The Theory of Everything	UK/USA	21.7	532	3.7+	Universal
13 Cinderella	UK/USA	21.3	556	3.8	Walt Disney
14 Mission: Impossible – Rogue Nation	UK/USA	21.2	572	5.4+	Paramount
15 Big Hero 6	USA	20.7	501		Walt Disney
16 Hotel Transylvania 2	USA	20.4	563	6.3+	Sony Pictures
17 Legend	UK/Fra/USA#	18.4	522	5.2+	StudioCanal
18 Taken 3	Fra	17.8	483	6.7+	20th Century Fox
19 Pitch Perfect 2	USA	17.4	497	5.0+	Universal
20 Mad Max: Fury Road	USA/Aus	17.4	546	4.5+	Warner Bros

Source: comScore, BFI RSU analysis

Notes:

Box office gross = cumulative total up to 21 February 2016.

* Film still on release on 21 February 2016.

Film made with independent (non-studio) US support or with the independent arm of a US studio.

+ Film had an extended opening weekend (the largest of which was a seven-day opening for *SPECTRE).*

9.7 Full year accommodation usage figures for 2004-2016 (excluding 2013)

Data	Accommodation	2004	2005	2006	2007	2008	2009	2010	2011	2012	2014	2015	2016
Total Visits (000s)	All staying visits	25,677	28,038	30,654	30,871	30,142	28,208	28,300	29,197	29,282	32,613	34,436	35,814
	Bed & Breakfast	1,177	1,221	1,242	1,174	1,118	1,065	1,083	996	1,003	1,043	1,349	1,570
	Free guest with relatives or friends	10,174	11,144	12,081	11,944	12,056	11,165	10,570	10,646	10,811	11,120	11,881	12,633
	Holiday village/Centre	37	60	44	67	59	77	41	49	59	170	60	63
	Hostel/university/school	949	1,096	1,167	1,203	1,138	1,218	1,102	1,180	1,174	1,144	1,267	1,217
	Hotel/guest house	11,451	12,465	13,939	14,156	13,472	13,001	13,841	14,446	14,406	16,383	16,796	16,886
	Other	1,815	1,855	2,143	2,073	1,930	1,470	1,518	1,360	1,439	1,971	2,317	2,886
	Own home	413	412	466	446	418	385	358	392	364	382	401	397
	Paying guest family or friends house	610	616	595	567	650	461	465	577	537	583	736	611
	Camping/caravan	295	381	425	394	298	333	312	302	284	335	300	292
	Rented house/flat	740	806	832	836	868	934	882	958	1,002	1,361	1,421	1,373
Total Nights (000s)	All staying visits	227,406	249,181	273,417	251,522	245,775	229,391	227,960	234,363	230,149	264,366	272,941	278,057
	Bed & Breakfast	8,576	7,840	7,411	7,078	6,500	5,804	6,341	5,639	5,307	5,809	8,041	9,566
	Free guest with relatives or friends	113,736	121,487	133,209	121,272	122,898	111,947	107,642	108,703	107,575	111,173	120,308	120,730
	Holiday village/Centre	222	346	336	576	329	448	321	321	393	1,522	362	329
	Hostel/university/school	16,757	17,863	21,103	15,680	15,443	16,775	16,305	18,670	18,236	18,543	18,796	21,888
	Hotel/guest house	45,291	51,069	57,540	57,174	55,133	54,246	58,741	60,365	60,081	72,640	73,414	73,926
	Other	5,546	7,078	6,930	6,452	6,597	4,397	4,982	4,990	4,635	10,428	10,007	11,410
	Own home	4,638	5,507	7,895	5,169	5,110	4,524	5,068	5,625	4,895	5,412	6,413	5,324
	Paying guest family or friends house	8,807	8,716	9,692	8,240	7,961	5,423	5,148	6,574	7,433	7,060	8,614	7,379
	Camping/caravan	3,015	4,705	4,350	4,182	2,988	3,296	2,904	3,229	2,757	3,047	2,763	2,272
	Rented house/flat	20,818	24,570	24,950	25,695	22,817	22,362	20,482	20,237	18,838	28,731	24,223	25,232
Total Spend (£m)	All staying visits	12,798	14,011	15,759	15,699	16,058	16,354	16,649	17,666	18,245	21,578	21,787	22,257
	Bed & Breakfast	481	511	512	488	470	459	522	470	457	562	732	829
	Free guest with relatives or friends	3,822	3,972	4,498	4,207	4,501	4,425	4,254	4,371	4,515	4,593	4,878	4,789
	Holiday village/Centre	9	12	17	27	22	27	23	23	27	84	21	16
	Hostel/university/school	739	848	937	829	813	1,055	1,004	1,122	1,083	1,350	1,253	1,445
	Hotel/guest house	5,826	6,547	7,580	7,916	7,914	7,773	8,577	9,138	9,626	11,254	11,594	11,812
	Other	263	308	245	328	337	328	272	307	265	529	466	516
	Own home	354	357	412	402	429	531	354	377	505	515	532	558
	Paying guest family or friends house	345	393	439	385	379	364	340	426	475	445	501	521
	Camping/caravan	97	112	142	146	111	144	129	128	111	134	143	98
	Rented house/flat	861	951	977	971	1,084	1,245	1,172	1,305	1,181	2,111	1,666	1,674
Sample	All staying visits	37,321	39,977	40,410	36,432	31,854	41,952	41,948	38,144	37,666	37,359	37,058	35,918
	Bed & Breakfast	1,570	1,617	1,471	1,266	1,137	1,469	1,518	1,252	1,224	1,129	1,417	1,511
	Free guest with relatives or friends	15,167	16,363	16,256	14,386	12,831	16,976	16,003	14,233	14,207	13,133	13,090	12,815
	Holiday village/Centre	45	64	53	59	46	99	49	55	82	177	60	55
	Hostel/university/school	1,232	1,372	1,348	1,261	1,153	1,616	1,510	1,382	1,381	1,158	1,230	1,171
	Hotel/guest house	18,716	19,971	20,585	18,560	15,641	20,885	21,998	19,765	19,458	19,842	19,110	18,330
	Other	965	893	910	864	873	1,008	1,033	1,136	1,174	1,314	1,649	1,818
	Own home	730	744	740	645	522	656	637	545	594	528	516	484
	Paying guest family or friends house	562	599	527	487	507	529	538	637	548	558	666	541
	Camping/caravan	250	322	339	320	298	363	378	379	325	360	383	324
	Rented house/flat	1,101	1,161	1,164	1,034	973	1,457	1,397	1,291	1,334	1,607	1,525	1,439

International Passenger Survey, Office for National Statistics

Please note for **2013** the accommodation categories were reduced therefore we have included the analysis separately on the next page. ONS reverted back to the full accommodation options for 2014 data onwards, therefore 2014 -2016 data is shown in this table.

9.7 Full year accommodation usage figures by visitors from overseas 2013

		Year
Data	Accommodation	**2013**
Total Visits (000s)	All staying visits	31,064
	Own Home	366
	Hotels or similar	16,852
	Camp/caravan sites	480
	Other Short Term Rented	2,100
	Friends or Relatives	10,569
	Other (Non Rented or Long Term Rented)	2,299
Total Nights (000s)	All staying visits	245,412
	Own Home	5,453
	Hotels or similar	77,553
	Camp/caravan sites	3,980
	Other Short Term Rented	34,680
	Friends or Relatives	105,763
	Other (Non Rented or Long Term Rented)	17,983
Total Spend (£m)	All staying visits	20,938
	Own Home	531
	Hotels or similar	11,956
	Camp/caravan sites	225
	Other Short Term Rented	2,514
	Friends or Relatives	4,656
	Other (Non Rented or Long Term Rented)	1,056
Sample	All staying visits	39,416
	Own Home	566
	Hotels or similar	22,514
	Camp/caravan sites	602
	Other Short Term Rented	2,561
	Friends or Relatives	13,609
	Other (Non Rented or Long Term Rented)	1,910

Source: International Passenger Survey, Office for National Statistics

Please note: For 2013 the accommodation categories were reduced therefore the analysis has been shown separately in this table. ONS reverted back to the full accommodation options for 2014. Therefore, 2014-2016 data is shown in the previous table.

9.8 International tourism[1]

Thousands and £ million

	Visits to the UK by overseas residents (thousands)	Spending in the UK by overseas residents		Visits overseas by UK residents (thousands)	Spending overseas by UK residents	
		Current prices	Constant 1995 prices[2]		Current prices	Constant 1995 prices[2]
2000	25,209	12,805	11,102	56,837	24,251	27,281
2001	22,835	11,306	9,528	58,281	25,332	27,710
2002	24,180	11,737	9,641	59,377	26,962	29,311
2003	24,715	11,855	9,451	61,424	28,550	28,677
2004	27,755	13,047	10,146	64,194	30,285	30,444
2005	29,970	14,248	10,714	66,441	32,154	30,954
2006	32,713	16,002	11,641	69,536	34,411	30,904
2007	32,778	15,960	11,389	69,450	35,013	32,477
2008	31,888	16,323	11,276	69,011	36,838	28,657
2009	29,889	16,592	11,032	58,614	31,694	22,673
2010	29,803	16,899	10,644	55,562	31,820	22,116
2011	30,798	17,998	10,870	56,836	31,701	20,569
2012	31,084	18,640	10,842	56,538	32,450	22,024
2013	32,692	21,258	11,740	57,792	34,510	23,613
2014	34,377	21,849	11,874	60,082	35,537	23,800
2015	36,115	22,072	11,730	65,720	39,028	24,381
2016	37,609	22,543	-	70,815	43,771	-

1 See chapter text

2. As of 2016 constant 1995 prices are no longer produced by ONS.

Sources: International Passenger Survey
Office for National Statistics;

9.9 Holidays abroad:[1] by destination

Percentages

		2003	2004	2005	2006	2007	2008	2009	2010	2011	2012	2013	2014	2015	2016
Spain	JTKC	29.8	28.4	27.2	27.8	26.5	26.6	26.5	25.9	25.8	27.0	27.5	28.2	27.1	28.7
France	JTKD	18.1	17.3	16.6	15.9	16.7	16.7	18.6	18.3	17.4	17.2	16.4	15.5	14.6	12.4
Greece	JTKF	6.6	5.7	5.1	5.0	5.0	4.2	4.4	4.8	4.8	4.5	4.4	4.5	4.9	4.9
USA	JTKE	5.5	6.1	6.0	5.1	5.2	5.4	5.4	4.9	5.2	5.2	5.0	5.4	5.4	5.1
Italy	JTKG	5	5	5.4	5.4	5.6	5.2	4.7	4.6	4.5	5.0	5.3	5.3	5.8	6.2
Irish Republic	JTKI	3.7	3.8	3.8	4.0	3.3	3.2	3.2	2.5	2.9	2.3	2.2	2.6	2.6	2.9
Portugal	JTKH	4	3.5	3.6	3.7	4.1	4.8	4.1	4.4	4.5	4.5	4.8	4.7	5.0	5.1
Cyprus	JTKL	2.7	2.6	2.8	2.4	2.4	2.4	2.1	2.1	2.2	2.0	1.5	1.3	1.3	1.5
Netherlands	JTKK	2.6	2.6	2.5	2.7	2.4	2.1	2.2	2.2	2.6	2.6	2.7	3.1	3.6	3.8
Turkey	JTKJ	2.3	2.3	2.7	2.7	2.8	3.7	3.5	4.7	3.7	3.3	2.8	2.9	2.8	1.6
Belgium	JTKM	2.2	1.8	1.9	2.0	2.2	2.0	1.9	1.7	2	2.5	2.3	2.5	2.2	1.7
Germany	JTKN	1.2	1.6	1.7	1.7	2.0	1.9	1.7	1.7	2.2	2.0	2.3	2.1	2.4	2.5
Austria	JTKP	1.1	1.4	1.3	1.2	1.2	1.4	1.4	1.5	1	1.1	1.2	1.0	1.0	1.4
Malta	JTKO	1	1	1.1	1.0	0.9	0.9	0.8	1.0	1	1.0	1.2	1.1	1.0	1.2
Other countries	JTKQ	14.2	16.8	18.4	20	19.6	19.5	19.5	19.6	20.2	13.3	13.4	13.3	12.5	11.9

1 See chapter text.

Sources: International Passenger Survey, Office for National Statistics;
01633 456032

9.10 All tourism trips in Great Britain, 2009 - 2016

	2009	2010	2011	2012	2013	2014	2015 (O)[1]	2015 (RP)[1]	2016
TRIPS (millions)	122.537	115.711	126.635	126.019	122.905	114.242	124.426	125.162	119.455
BEDNIGHTS (millions)	387.448	361.398	387.329	388.24	373.607	349.546	377.101	379.449	359.557
EXPENDITURE (£ millions)	£20,971	£19,797	£22,666	£23,976	£23,294	£22,692	£24,825	£24,100	£23,079
Av. Trip Length	3.16	3.12	3.06	3.08	3.04	3.06	3.03	3.03	3.01
Av. £/Night	54	55	59	62	62	65	66*	64	64
Av. £/trip	171	171	179	190	190	199	200*	194	193

Source: Visit England

1. When comparing between 2015 and 2016 it is recommended to use 2015 (RP) (Reprocessed 2015) figures. When comparing 2015 to earlier years use 2015 (O) (Original 2015) figures.

2. All figures for 2009 -2014 are original figures (O).

This table shows a breakdown of all domestic overnight tourism into trips, nights and spend.
The number of overnight tourism trips within GB decreased by -4.6% in 2016 compared with 2015, with the total number of trips taken being 119.5 million.
In the same period, the number of bednights spent during GB trips in 2016 decreased by -5.2% to 359.6 million.
Expenditure on GB overnight trips declined in 2016, decreasing by -4.2% to £23.1 billion.

9.11 All touism in Great Britain: 2015 - 2016

	Trips				Nights				Spend			
	GB	England	Scotland	Wales	GB	England	Scotland	Wales	GB	England	Scotland	Wales
	Millions				*Millions*				*£millions*			
All tourism - 2015	**124.426**	**102.730**	**11.988**	**10.449**	**377.101**	**299.569**	**41.336**	**36.197**	**£24,825**	**£19,571**	**£3,279**	**£1,975**
All tourism - 2016	**119.455**	**99.342**	**11.514**	**9.307**	**359.557**	**287.702**	**38.876**	**32.978**	**£23,079**	**£18,492**	**£2,897**	**£1,689**
Purpose												
Leisure	100.961	84.154	9.132	8.297	306.966	245.115	32.627	29.224	£18,008	£14,316	£2,199	£1,493
Total holiday	84.833	69.934	8.062	7.445	275.259	217.953	29.762	27.543	£16,585	£13,099	£2,064	£1,423
Holiday\pleasure\leisure	55.888	44.706	5.929	5.588	190.897	147.078	21.379	22.440	£13,313	£10,413	£1,676	£1,225
Visiting friends or relatives - mainly holiday	28.945	25.228	2.133	1.857	84.362	70.876	8.383	5.103	£3,272	£2,686	£388	£198
Visiting friends or relatives - mainly other reason	13.350	11.684	0.904	0.776	31.707	27.161	2.865	1.681	£1,423	£1,217	£135	£70
VFR	42.294	36.912	3.037	2.632	116.069	98.037	11.248	6.784	£4,695	£3,903	£523	£269
Total Business	16.765	14.125	1.912	0.790	38.717	31.606	4.659	2.453	£4,369	£3,632	£592	£145
To attend a conference	1.709	1.548	0.090	0.071	3.316	3.068	0.150	0.097	£392	£355	£25	£11
To attend an exhibition\trade show	1.324	1.204	0.087	0.033	2.791	2.466	0.208	0.117	£289	£253	£32	£3
Travel\transport is my work	0.518	0.439	0.060	0.030	1.398	1.128	0.196	0.075	£146	£118	£23	£5
To do paid work\on business	13.731	11.372	1.736	0.686	32.610	26.071	4.300	2.238	£3,689	£3,023	£535	£130
School trip	1.675	1.184	0.357	0.134	6.194	4.821	0.775	0.599	£176	£128	£15	£34
Other reason	1.675	1.460	0.141	0.086	4.513	3.791	0.319	0.403	£265	£214	£43	£8

Source: Visit England

GB trends by tourism type [2016]

- During 2016, GB residents took a total of 119.5m overnight tourism trips to destinations in England, Scotland or Wales; amounting to 359.6m nights and£23.1bn was spent during these trips.
- Examining tourism type, the category 'holidays' accounted for 55.9m of these trips and £13.3bn of spend.
- Those who took trips to 'visit friends and relatives' accounted for 42.3m trips and £4.7bn of spend.
- Tourism for the purpose of 'business' accounted for 16.8m trips and £4.4bn of spend.

GB trends by country [2015 vs 2016]

- At GB level, a percentage decrease in tourism trips taken, of -4.6% was observed between 2015 and 2016. In the same period, nights volume decreased by -5.2%, as did expenditure, by -4.2%.
- England saw an overall decline across the year compared to 2015, with 8 months out of 12 seeing a reduction in domestic trip volume. This equates to a fall in trip volume from 2015-2016 of -3.9%.
- The pattern in Scotland was one of six months increase and six months decline in domestic trips taken relative to 2015, overall down -4.7% between 2015 and 2016.
- Wales generally saw more months of declining trip volumes than increases compared to 2015, overall a decrease of -11.2% from 2015 to 2016.

9.12a Gambling industry data

Industry Statistics - November 2018

	Gambling Industry GGY by Sector (£m)									
	Apr 2008 Mar 2009	Apr 2009 Mar 2010	Apr 2010 Mar 2011	Apr 2011 Mar 2012	Apr 2012 Mar 2013	Apr 2013 Mar 2014	Apr 2014 Mar 2015	Apr 2015 Mar 2016	Apr 2016 Mar 2017	Apr 2017 Mar 2018
Arcades	480.35	455.96	392.00	381.06	358.71	379.11	387.22	418.06	421.64	417.98
Betting	2,903.24	2,811.36	2,957.32	3,029.59	3,198.60	3,176.77	3,266.91	3,318.19	3,391.79	3,254.17
Bingo	703.11	627.22	625.58	680.64	700.90	673.44	679.02	693.11	687.24	688.29
Casinos	796.17	751.13	797.43	872.80	961.41	1,111.06	1,159.79	999.38	1,163.54	1,191.22
Remote betting, bingo and casino - 2005 Act Regulated	816.86	632.22	653.06	710.19	932.61	1,134.66	753.53*			
Remote betting, bingo and casino - 2014 Act Regulated GB Customers only							1485.47**	4,230.76	4,742.80	5,351.04
National Lottery (remote and non-remote)	2,521.50	2,679.20	2,840.20	3,123.90	3,279.50	3,099.80	3,232.10	3,416.80	2,978.60	3,007.70
Lotteries (remote and non-remote)	143.69	158.55	170.12	228.61	273.00	293.79	349.74	379.77	442.34	502.87
Total	**8,364.92**	**8,115.64**	**8,435.70**	**9,026.80**	**9,704.74**	**9,868.62**	**11,313.78**	**13,456.05**	**13,827.95**	**14,413.26**

Source: Gambling Commission

Notes on this section:

* The figure represented reflects seven months data under the Gambling Act 2005 from 1 April 2014 to 31 October 2014, and represents the whole regulated market (regardless of where the customer was based).

** The figure represented reflects five months data under the Gambling (Licensing and Advertising) Act from 1 November 2014 to 31 March 2015, and relates to GB customers only.

For National Lottery and Lotteries, figures relate to the proceeds from ticket sales minus the amount given out in prizes, which is a GGY equivalent.

GGY = Gross Gambling Yield

9.12b Remote: Gambling (Licensing and Advertising) Act Data

Industry Statistics - November 2018

GB only remote data (£m)						
Turnover	Nov 2014 Mar 2015	Apr 2015 Mar 2016	Apr 2016 Mar 2017	Apr 2017 Mar 2018		
	Total	Total	Total	Proprietary	Revenue Share	Total
Betting	5,322.85	22,892.85	25,887.16	19,908.60	6,998.99	26,907.59
Bingo	330.51	1,468.81	1,413.52	680.23	645.62	1,325.85
Casino	6,761.34	62,227.59	71,344.68	24,383.12	58,531.44	82,914.55
Pool Betting	29.54	60.72	89.80	73.50	15.21	88.71
Total	12,444.23	86,649.96	98,735.16	45,045.45	66,191.26	111,236.71
GGY	Nov 2014 Mar 2015	Apr 2015 Mar 2016	Apr 2016 Mar 2017	Apr 2017 Mar 2018		
	Total	Total	Total	Proprietary	Revenue Share	Total
Betting	456.44	1,565.75	1,755.44	1,510.56	562.33	2,072.89
Betting Exchange	52.44	151.90	169.58	160.61	-	160.61
Bingo	66.98	122.41	160.57	73.76	91.04	164.80
Casino	899.79	2,364.44	2,624.33	913.48	2,010.58	2,924.05
Pool Betting	9.82	26.27	32.89	25.98	2.71	28.69
Total	1,485.47	4,230.76	4,742.80	2,684.38	2,666.65	5,351.04
Betting Turnover	Nov 2014 Mar 2015	Apr 2015 Mar 2016	Apr 2016 Mar 2017	Apr 2017 Mar 2018		
	Total	Total	Total	Proprietary	Revenue Share	Total
Cricket	238.11	492.39	507.70	558.53	190.85	749.38
Dogs	86.48	284.36	443.44	450.41	135.99	586.40
Financials	56.50	234.75	275.94	176.78	-	176.78
Football	2,119.33	5,890.46	8,189.06	8,093.59	2,348.83	10,442.43
Golf	34.93	182.44	193.94	209.18	49.36	258.53
Horses	1,631.01	5,354.42	6,388.31	6,731.01	2,154.52	8,885.54
Other	741.97	2,136.55	2,242.55	2,053.61	728.26	2,781.87
Tennis	444.05	1,467.74	1,619.09	1,600.22	743.41	2,343.63
Virtual	-	-	-	108.76	662.98	771.74
Unallocated rev share	-	6,910.45	6,116.92	-	-	-
Total	5,352.39	16,043.11	19,860.04	19,982.10	7,014.20	26,224.56
Betting GGY	Nov 2014 Mar 2015	Apr 2015 Mar 2016	Apr 2016 Mar 2017	Apr 2017 Mar 2018		
	Total	Total	Total	Proprietary	Revenue Share	Total
Cricket	4.22	21.23	20.67	26.39	5.32	31.71
Dogs	9.02	28.44	44.16	41.07	13.10	54.16
Financials	3.10	12.70	37.03	22.03	-	22.03
Football	160.71	577.80	663.02	812.81	224.93	1,037.73
Golf	2.62	14.39	14.10	10.89	3.21	14.10
Horses	115.47	346.06	435.09	469.26	140.70	609.96
Other	41.43	156.24	159.31	196.71	62.27	258.98
Tennis	22.80	72.21	92.20	103.84	40.74	144.58
Virtual	-	-	-	14.15	74.78	88.92
Unallocated rev share	159.35	514.84	492.32	-	-	-
Total	518.70	1,743.91	1,957.90	1,697.15	565.04	2,262.19
Casino Turnover	Nov 2014 Mar 2015	Apr 2015 Mar 2016	Apr 2016 Mar 2017	Oct 2016 Sep 2017		
	Total	Total	Total	Proprietary	Revenue Share	Total
Blackjack	-	-	-	488.91	1,749.34	2,238.25
Card Game	492.81	8,350.19	8,815.08	1,452.73	5,086.03	6,538.76
Other	223.16	3,464.10	5,594.32	1,604.97	5,155.27	6,760.24
Roulette	-	-	-	728.59	3,750.44	4,479.03
Slots	5,171.23	34,938.89	40,252.61	17,557.34	33,027.92	50,585.26
Table Game	874.14	15,474.41	16,682.68	2,550.58	9,762.43	12,313.01
Total	6,761.34	62,227.59	71,344.68	24,383.12	58,531.44	82,914.55
Casino GGY	Nov 2014 Mar 2015	Apr 2015 Mar 2016	Apr 2016 Mar 2017	Apr 2017 Mar 2018		
	Total	Total	Total	Proprietary	Revenue Share	Total
Blackjack	-	-	-	11.58	40.76	52.33
Card Game	66.45	184.23	203.62	28.09	126.40	154.49
Other	59.15	132.80	210.76	38.13	181.12	219.25
Peer to Peer	44.00	103.68	105.49	76.56	30.53	107.09
Roulette	-	-	-	17.60	89.02	106.62
Slots	594.31	1,559.10	1,688.64	679.74	1,334.20	2,013.93
Table Game	135.89	384.63	491.80	61.78	249.30	311.08
Total	899.79	2,364.44	2,700.31	901.90	2,010.58	2,912.48

9.12b Remote: Gambling (Licensing and Advertising) Act Data

Industry Statistics - November 2018

Total remote data (£m)						
Turnover	Nov 2014 Mar 2015	Apr 2015 Mar 2016	Apr 2016 Mar 2017	Apr 2017 Mar 2018		
	Total	Total	Total	Proprietary	Revenue Share	Total
Betting	5,460.64	23,345.92	26,310.78	20,398.70	7,031.48	27,430.17
Bingo	331.21	1,472.77	1,419.65	681.44	649.11	1,330.55
Casino	7,470.54	65,494.81	75,777.13	25,461.29	59,062.10	84,523.39
Pool Betting	92.78	214.63	267.01	251.71	16.35	268.06
Total	13,355.17	90,528.12	103,774.57	46,793.14	66,759.03	113,552.16
GGY	Nov 2014 Mar 2015	Apr 2015 Mar 2016	Apr 2016 Mar 2017	Apr 2017 Mar 2018		
	Total	Total	Total	Proprietary	Revenue Share	Total
Betting	478.71	1,625.29	1,813.96	1,561.72	565.88	2,127.60
Betting Exchange	56.88	171.82	184.05	164.90	-	164.90
Bingo	67.59	123.28	161.87	73.80	85.11	158.91
Casino	1,042.70	2,480.46	2,822.12	956.60	2,081.46	3,038.06
Pool Betting	37.29	73.95	96.09	126.27	3.67	129.94
Total	1,683.17	4,474.79	5,078.09	2,883.29	2,736.12	5,619.41
Betting Turnover	Nov 2014 Mar 2015	Apr 2015 Mar 2016	Apr 2016 Mar 2017	Apr 2017 Mar 2018		
	Total	Total	Total	Proprietary	Revenue Share	Total
Cricket	240.17	498.71	514.13	570.01	190.99	761.00
Dogs	95.75	294.32	447.87	456.67	136.01	592.68
Financials	61.72	255.19	290.03	186.11	-	186.11
Football	2,182.80	6,022.46	8,329.38	8,298.61	2,362.55	10,661.16
Golf	36.24	186.18	198.47	215.47	49.37	264.84
Horses	1,681.73	5,479.14	6,511.51	6,887.66	2,157.45	9,045.11
Other	804.55	2,359.37	2,488.25	2,299.41	730.79	3,030.20
Tennis	450.46	1,494.07	1,641.60	1,626.45	744.19	2,370.64
Virtual	-	-	-	110.02	676.47	786.49
Unallocated rev share	-	6,971.12	6,156.55	-	-	-
Total	5,553.42	16,589.43	20,421.24	20,650.41	7,047.82	26,911.74
Betting GGY	Nov 2014 Mar 2015	Apr 2015 Mar 2016	Apr 2016 Mar 2017	Apr 2017 Mar 2018		
	Total	Total	Total	Proprietary	Revenue Share	Total
Cricket	4.31	22.10	21.14	27.01	5.33	32.33
Dogs	10.97	30.51	44.91	41.84	13.10	54.94
Financials	3.42	13.93	37.88	22.61	-	22.61
Football	172.16	587.93	676.74	832.69	226.31	1,059.01
Golf	2.73	14.65	14.60	11.02	3.21	14.23
Horses	123.17	362.09	447.24	482.22	141.24	623.46
Other	70.61	240.05	249.86	315.60	62.58	378.18
Tennis	23.68	74.90	93.81	105.61	40.79	146.41
Virtual	-	-	-	14.28	76.99	91.27
Unallocated rev share	161.83	524.90	507.90	-	-	-
Total	572.88	1,871.05	2,094.10	1,852.88	569.55	2,422.43
Casino Turnover	Nov 2014 Mar 2015	Apr 2015 Mar 2016	Apr 2016 Mar 2017	Apr 2017 Mar 2018		
	Total	Total	Total	Proprietary	Revenue Share	Total
Blackjack	-	-	-	544.43	1,765.22	2,309.65
Card Game	544.62	8,465.38	8,968.17	1,497.25	5,191.53	6,688.78
Other	243.77	3,674.38	5,892.96	2,135.31	5,184.79	7,320.10
Roulette	-	-	-	746.47	3,786.37	4,532.83
Slots	5,721.67	37,260.22	43,500.60	17,929.52	33,298.44	51,227.97
Table Game	960.48	16,094.83	17,415.41	2,608.30	9,835.75	12,444.06
Total	7,470.54	65,494.81	75,777.13	25,461.29	59,062.10	84,523.39
Casino GGY	Nov 2014 Mar 2015	Apr 2015 Mar 2016	Apr 2016 Mar 2017	Apr 2017 Mar 2018		
	Total	Total	Total	Proprietary	Revenue Share	Total
Blackjack	-	-	-	13.43	41.26	54.69
Card Game	71.68	192.31	207.30	29.70	129.68	159.38
Other	139.19	212.54	287.68	58.69	190.73	249.41
Peer to Peer	49.44	113.37	111.52	77.78	33.30	111.08
Roulette	-	-	-	17.86	90.01	107.87
Slots	641.75	1,616.72	1,784.36	695.42	1,384.62	2,080.03
Table Game	140.64	345.52	508.97	63.73	253.13	316.86
Total	1,042.70	2,480.46	2,899.82	943.17	2,081.46	3,024.63

9.12b Remote: Gambling (Licensing and Advertising) Act Data

Industry Statistics - November 2018

Social responsibility data	Nov 2014 Mar 2015	Apr 2015 Mar 2016	Apr 2016 Mar 2017	Apr 2017 Mar 2018
Self Exclusions	179,142	612,427	1,117,322	1,382,857
Known breaches of self-exclusion	12,576	36,992	73,715	98,896
Number of individuals who cancelled their self-exclusion after minimum period	16,307	45,523	52,819	66,752
Challenged having gambled but unable to prove age	14,689	51,734	55,547	72,033
Accounts (Millions)	Nov 2014 Mar 2015	Apr 2015 Mar 2016	Apr 2016 Mar 2017	Apr 2017 Mar 2018
Funds held in customer accounts	498.49	607.38	875.48	784.78
New account registrations	8.97	23.94	30.94	35.39
Active number accounts GC Licensed Facilities	21.78	23.05	29.73	33.58
Headcount	Nov 2014 Mar 2015	Apr 2015 Mar 2016	Apr 2016 Mar 2017	Apr 2017 Mar 2018
GB workforce	7,645	6,373	7,813	10,273

Accounts (Millions)	Nov 2014 Mar 2015	Apr 2015 Mar 2016	Apr 2016 Mar 2017	Apr 2017 Mar 2018
Funds held in customer accounts	519.07	637.63	932.42	859.14
Active number accounts GC Licensed Facilities	24.08	24.55	31.83	35.59

Source: Gambling Commission

Notes on this section:

1. Since 1 November 2014 the Commission has been collecting GGY derived from revenue share agreements between licensed operators. To mitigate against the risk of double counting this revenue, the Commission requires operators to report only their relevant portion of the revenue share. Details of this arrangement can be seen in the remote regulatory returns consultation responses document, relevant sections are contained within Annex A.. The Commission is working with operators to ensure reported data complies with regulatory return requirements.
2. Revenue share is defined as GGY which is subject to a contractual arrangement to be shared between two or more Commission licensed operators.
3. Customers gambling on betting exchanges tend to maintain a significant balance in their account as they need to have sufficient funds to cover the liabilities of their bets, rather than just have sufficient funds to cover the stake of the bets they intend to make.
4. Active accounts are those that have been used by customers in the last 12 months. New registrants includes new individual customer registrations that occurred during the period, but may not have gambled.
5. The number of people who have self-excluded and the number of people who have cancelled their self-exclusion may be lower than these figures as individuals may have self-excluded from more than one site or operator and therefore been counted more than once. The number of breaches represents the number of separate incidents, rather than the number of individuals.
6. Customers may have accounts with more than one operator and therefore the data relates to accounts rather than the individuals.

9.13 Most Popular Boy and Girl Baby Names in England and Wales, 2015

BOYS				GIRLS			
Rank 1-50	Name	Rank 51-100	Name	Rank 1-50	Name	Rank 51-100	Name
1	OLIVER	51	REUBEN	1	AMELIA	51	ABIGAIL
2	JACK	52	HARLEY	2	OLIVIA	52	GEORGIA
3	HARRY	53	LUCA	3	EMILY	53	MAISIE
4	GEORGE	54	MICHAEL	4	ISLA	54	ELEANOR
5	JACOB	55	HUGO	5	AVA	55	HANNAH
6	CHARLIE	56	LEWIS	6	ELLA	56	HARRIET
7	NOAH	57	FRANKIE	7	JESSICA	57	AMBER
8	WILLIAM	58	LUKE	8	ISABELLA	58	BELLA
9	THOMAS	59	STANLEY	9	MIA	59	THEA
10	OSCAR	60	TOMMY	10	POPPY	59	ANNABELLE
11	JAMES	61	JUDE	11	SOPHIE	61	EMMA
12	MUHAMMAD	62	BLAKE	12	SOPHIA	62	AMELIE
13	HENRY	63	LOUIE	13	LILY	63	HARPER
14	ALFIE	64	NATHAN	14	GRACE	64	GRACIE
15	LEO	65	GABRIEL	15	EVIE	65	ROSE
16	JOSHUA	66	CHARLES	16	SCARLETT	66	SUMMER
17	FREDDIE	67	BOBBY	17	RUBY	67	MARTHA
18	ETHAN	68	MOHAMMAD	18	CHLOE	68	VIOLET
19	ARCHIE	69	RYAN	19	ISABELLE	69	PENELOPE
19	ISAAC	70	TYLER	20	DAISY	70	ANNA
21	JOSEPH	71	ELLIOTT	21	FREYA	71	NANCY
22	ALEXANDER	72	ALBERT	22	PHOEBE	72	ZARA
23	SAMUEL	73	ELLIOT	23	FLORENCE	73	MARIA
24	DANIEL	74	RORY	24	ALICE	74	DARCIE
25	LOGAN	74	ALEX	25	CHARLOTTE	75	MARYAM
26	EDWARD	76	FREDERICK	26	SIENNA	76	MEGAN
27	LUCAS	77	OLLIE	27	MATILDA	77	DARCEY
28	MAX	78	LOUIS	28	EVELYN	78	LOTTIE
29	MOHAMMED	79	DEXTER	29	EVA	79	MILA
30	BENJAMIN	80	JAXON	30	MILLIE	80	HEIDI
31	MASON	81	LIAM	31	SOFIA	81	LEXI
32	HARRISON	82	JACKSON	32	LUCY	82	LACEY
33	THEO	83	CALLUM	33	ELSIE	83	FRANCESCA
34	JAKE	84	RONNIE	34	IMOGEN	84	ROBYN
35	SEBASTIAN	85	LEON	35	LAYLA	85	BETHANY
36	FINLEY	86	KAI	36	ROSIE	86	JULIA
37	ARTHUR	87	AARON	37	MAYA	87	SARA
38	ADAM	88	ROMAN	38	ESME	88	AISHA
39	DYLAN	89	AUSTIN	39	ELIZABETH	89	DARCY
40	RILEY	90	ELLIS	40	LOLA	90	ZOE
41	ZACHARY	91	JAMIE	41	WILLOW	91	CLARA
42	TEDDY	92	REGGIE	42	IVY	92	VICTORIA
43	DAVID	93	SETH	43	ERIN	93	BEATRICE
44	TOBY	94	CARTER	44	HOLLY	93	HOLLIE
45	THEODORE	95	FELIX	45	EMILIA	95	ARABELLA
46	ELIJAH	96	IBRAHIM	46	MOLLY	96	SARAH
47	MATTHEW	97	SONNY	47	ELLIE	97	MADDISON
48	JENSON	98	KIAN	48	JASMINE	98	LEAH
49	JAYDEN	99	CALEB	49	ELIZA	99	KATIE
50	HARVEY	100	CONNOR	50	LILLY	100	ARIA

Source: Office for National Statistics (ONS)

Notes:

These rankings have been produced using the exact spelling of the name given at birth registration. Similar names with different spellings have been counted separately.

Births where the name was not stated have been excluded from these figures. Of the 339,716 baby girls in the 2015 dataset, 10 were excluded for this reason.

* denotes new entry to top 100

9.14a Libraries overview

Great Britain

Percentages

	2005/06	2006/07	2007/08	2008/09	2009/10	2010/11	2011/12	2012/13	2013/14	2014/15	2015/16
	%	%	%	%	%	% (1)	% (1)	% (1)	% (1)	% (1)	% (1)
Has visited a public library in the last year (2)	48.2	**46.1**	**45.0**	**41.1**	**39.4**	**39.7**	**38.8**	**37.0**	**35.4**	**34.5**	**33.4**
Frequency of attendance (2)											
1-2 times a year	10.4	10.3	10.5	**8.9**	**7.9**	**8.9**	**8.4**	**8.7**	**8.5**	**7.9**	**8.3**
3-4 times a year	13.4	12.9	13.0	**11.4**	**10.9**	**11.6**	**12.2**	**10.8**	**9.9**	**10.9**	**10.0**
At least once a month	16.4	15.7	**14.9**	**13.3**	**12.8**	**13.4**	**12.4**	**12.4**	**12.2**	**10.8**	**10.6**
At least once a week	7.9	**7.2**	**6.7**	**5.9**	**5.4**	**5.8**	**5.7**	**5.0**	**4.9**	**4.9**	**4.4**
Has not visited	51.8	**53.9**	**55.0**	**60.5**	**63.0**	**60.3**	**61.2**	**63.0**	**64.6**	**65.5**	**66.6**

Notes

(1) Figures in bold indicate a significant change from 2005/06.

(2) Figures exclude people who have visited a library for the purposes of paid work or academic study

Source: Department for Culture, Media and Sport - Taking Part Survey 2015/16 Q4
https://www.gov.uk/government/statistics/taking-part-201516-quarter-4-statistical-release

9.14b Proportion who have visited a public library in the last year - area-level breakdown

	2005/06	2006/07	2007/08	2008/09	2009/10	2010/11	2011/12	2012/13	2013/14	2014/15	2015/16
	%	%	%	%	%	% (1)	% (1)	% (1)	% (1)	% (1)	% (1)
Index of deprivation											
1- Most deprived	N/A	N/A	N/A	N/A	37.6	39.8	37.3	40.1	40.4	37.6	35.8
2	N/A	N/A	N/A	N/A	32.8	38.2	37.0	35.7	35.3	34.8	35.3
3	N/A	N/A	N/A	N/A	38.3	39.2	39.2	33.5	33.4	33.5	35.8
4	N/A	N/A	N/A	N/A	36.1	41.2	39.1	35.0	33.3	37.8	32.2
5	N/A	N/A	N/A	N/A	42.1	38.4	40.6	35.3	35.7	**33.9**	35.5
6	N/A	N/A	N/A	N/A	38.7	36.4	38.3	37.5	36.1	32.2	**30.4**
7	N/A	N/A	N/A	N/A	39.9	40.7	40.4	34.8	**33.3**	**31.8**	35.1
8	N/A	N/A	N/A	N/A	34.6	40.1	33.8	37.1	32.7	34.5	29.6
9	N/A	N/A	N/A	N/A	45.4	**38.7**	42.2	41.8	**37.1**	**35.7**	**32.9**
10- Least deprived	N/A	N/A	N/A	N/A	46.3	43.5	39.8	**38.4**	**36.8**	**33.8**	**31.4**
Region											
North East	44.9	43.9	**40.1**	**37.1**	42.9	**38.8**	**36.3**	**38.2**	**34.1**	**34.6**	**32.5**
North West	46.9	46.2	45.0	**42.1**	41.4	**43.0**	**37.5**	**37.8**	**35.4**	**34.0**	**34.9**
Yorkshire and Humberside	42.1	40.5	**36.6**	**33.7**	**30.0**	**33.6**	**33.4**	**34.9**	**33.1**	**31.0**	**31.2**
East Midlands	44.7	42.9	44.3	**38.8**	42.7	**35.8**	**37.7**	**34.9**	**32.3**	**30.9**	**27.9**
West Midlands	47.6	47.1	**43.5**	**39.3**	**38.0**	**36.6**	**40.1**	**35.5**	**34.8**	**35.0**	**33.1**
East of England	50.5	47.5	**45.5**	**42.9**	**39.5**	**42.4**	**41.2**	**37.5**	**37.0**	**32.2**	**33.0**
London	52.6	**49.2**	**49.5**	**43.6**	**38.1**	**43.1**	**43.1**	**41.9**	**40.9**	**40.2**	**37.4**
South East	51.0	48.3	48.5	**44.5**	**43.5**	**40.5**	**37.4**	**34.6**	**34.0**	**34.9**	**31.9**
South West	47.9	45.1	45.5	**41.8**	**38.8**	**38.8**	**40.0**	**36.3**	**33.6**	**34.4**	**35.2**
Urban	48.5	**46.5**	**45.6**	**41.6**	**40.1**	**40.0**	**39.2**	**37.8**	**36.4**	**35.4**	**34.2**
Rural	47.1	44.7	**42.8**	**38.9**	**36.5**	**38.2**	**36.9**	**33.7**	**31.4**	**30.9**	**29.9**
ACORN											
Wealthy Achievers	50.9	48.9	**47.4**	**42.1**	**39.9**	**40.7**	**40.6**	**38.4**	**33.8**	**32.9**	**33.5**
Urban Prosperity	57.3	**51.0**	**52.0**	**41.8**	**42.6**	**43.9**	**41.9**	**39.2**	**38.3**	**38.8**	**37.8**
Comfortably Off	48.5	**46.4**	**44.2**	**41.9**	**41.9**	**38.2**	**37.9**	**35.4**	**35.0**	**34.0**	**32.6**
Moderate Means	45.3	45.0	**42.4**	**41.5**	**37.7**	**41.3**	**38.9**	**36.9**	**35.7**	**35.1**	**30.7**
Hard-pressed	40.9	39.8	41.0	**37.5**	**33.9**	**36.9**	**35.8**	**36.4**	**35.9**	**34.5**	**33.9**
Unclassified	61.7	50.0	**62.7**	**46.9**	*	*	*	*	**40.3**	*	**29.9**
All	48.2	**46.1**	**45.0**	**41.1**	**39.4**	**39.7**	**38.8**	**37.0**	**35.4**	**34.5**	**33.4**

Notes

(1) Figures in bold indicate a significant change from 2005/06.

(2) Index of deprivation data not available pre-2009/10. For Index of Deprivation data, figures in bold indicate a significant change from 2009/10.

(3) *= N too small to report

Source: Department for Culture, Media and Sport - Taking Part Survey 2015/16 Q4
https://www.gov.uk/government/statistics/taking-part-201516-quarter-4-statistical-release

9.14c Proportion who have visited a public library in the last year - demographic breakdown

	2005/06	2006/07	2007/08	2008/09	2009/10	2010/11	2011/12	2012/13	2013/14	2014/15	2015/16
	%	%	%	%	%	% (1)	% (1)	% (1)	% (1)	% (1)	% (1)
Age											
16-24	51.0	**47.1**	**45.4**	**42.8**	**40.0**	**34.4**	**34.5**	**32.3**	**33.4**	**28.5**	**27.4**
25-44	51.2	50.2	49.5	**43.7**	**40.9**	**44.6**	**44.0**	**42.2**	**40.4**	**41.3**	**37.4**
45-64	45.7	44.3	**42.1**	**38.8**	**39.5**	**36.0**	**36.1**	**33.1**	**30.9**	**30.6**	**31.0**
65-74	46.7	44.4	44.7	**42.0**	**39.3**	44.3	**35.8**	**38.6**	**37.1**	**35.2**	**34.8**
75+	42.3	**37.1**	**37.6**	**35.0**	**32.9**	**37.1**	38.9	**36.5**	**33.3**	**31.6**	**34.3**
Sex											
Male	43.8	**42.1**	**40.2**	**35.3**	**35.5**	**34.3**	**33.6**	**31.4**	**29.7**	**29.8**	**29.2**
Female	52.3	**49.9**	**49.6**	**46.5**	**43.2**	**44.8**	**43.8**	**42.3**	**40.8**	**39.0**	**37.4**
NS-SEC											
Upper socio-economic group	52.1	**50.2**	**48.0**	**43.3**	**43.1**	**43.9**	**42.3**	**39.7**	**36.7**	**35.9**	**35.5**
Lower socio-economic group	40.1	**38.1**	38.7	**35.1**	**32.3**	**33.6**	**33.5**	**33.0**	**32.4**	**31.2**	**30.3**
Employment status											
Not working	49.7	**46.7**	**46.6**	**44.0**	**42.4**	**42.9**	**41.7**	**41.0**	**38.3**	**37.8**	**37.1**
Working	47.2	**45.7**	**44.0**	**39.0**	**37.4**	**37.5**	**36.8**	**34.3**	**33.4**	**32.3**	**31.0**
Tenure											
Owners	48.7	**46.4**	**44.8**	**41.1**	**39.8**	**40.1**	**39.2**	**37.0**	**34.9**	**33.8**	**33.2**
Social rented sector	41.9	40.5	42.2	39.0	**36.8**	**37.0**	**37.2**	38.6	**38.1**	39.1	**37.1**
Private rented sector	53.3	51.0	**49.2**	**43.0**	**39.8**	**40.2**	**38.7**	**35.8**	**35.0**	**33.4**	**31.3**
Ethnicity											
White	47.2	**44.9**	**43.6**	**40.1**	**37.9**	**38.3**	**37.8**	**35.9**	**33.8**	**32.9**	**31.6**
Black or ethnic minority	57.5	56.7	57.9	**50.2**	**50.6**	**50.0**	**46.5**	**45.1**	**47.8**	**47.5**	**45.6**
Religion											
No religion	46.8	45.5	45.3	**40.1**	**35.2**	**37.8**	**36.8**	**33.2**	**34.4**	**33.2**	**30.3**
Christian	47.3	**44.8**	**43.7**	**40.3**	**39.7**	**39.2**	**38.8**	**37.7**	**34.3**	**33.4**	**33.5**
Other religion	58.2	58.9	57.1	52.7	53.0	**48.2**	**44.4**	**46.9**	**48.3**	**49.7**	**46.7**
Long-standing illness or disability											
No	50.0	**48.0**	**46.0**	**42.1**	**40.4**	**40.1**	**39.2**	**36.9**	**36.0**	**35.7**	**33.2**
Yes	43.8	**41.5**	42.4	**38.4**	**36.8**	**38.5**	**37.9**	**37.3**	**34.2**	**31.6**	**33.8**
All	48.2	**46.1**	**45.0**	**41.1**	**39.4**	**39.7**	**38.8**	**37.0**	**35.4**	**34.5**	**33.4**

Notes

(1) Figures in bold indicate a significant change from 2005/06.

Source: Department for Culture, Media and Sport - Taking Part Survey 2015/16 Q4
https://www.gov.uk/government/statistics/taking-part-201516-quarter-4-statistical-release

9.15 Museums and Galleries overview

	2005/06	2006/07	2007/08	2008/09	2009/10	2010/11	2011/12	2012/13	2013/14	2014/15	2015/16
	%	%	%	%	%	% (1)	% (1)	% (1)	% (1)	% (1)	% (1)
Has visited a museum or gallery in the last year(2)	42.3	41.5	**43.5**	43.4	**46.0**	**46.3**	**48.9**	**52.8**	**53.1**	**52.0**	**52.5**
Frequency of attendance (2)											
1-2 times a year	25.6	25.3	26.3	26.1	**27.9**	**27.4**	**29.6**	**31.3**	**32.4**	**30.7**	**30.6**
3-4 times a year	13.2	12.9	13.8	13.9	14.1	**14.7**	**15.3**	**17.2**	**17.2**	**17.7**	**18.0**
At least once a month	3.2	2.8	3.2	2.9	3.6	**3.6**	3.4	3.5	3.1	3.1	3.6
At least once a week	0.3	**0.4**	0.3	0.4	0.4	**0.5**	**0.5**	**0.6**	0.4	**0.5**	0.4
Has not visited	57.7	58.5	**56.5**	56.7	**54.0**	**53.7**	**51.1**	**47.2**	**46.9**	**48.0**	**47.5**
Have been to an museum or gallery in last 12 months											
In your own - time	N/A	N/A	N/A	96.8	97.4	97.5	**98.1**	97.4	**97.9**	**98.1**	**98.3**
For paid work	N/A	N/A	N/A	2.5	2.0	2.6	2.5	2.8	2.1	2.4	2.4
For academic study	N/A	N/A	N/A	3.0	3.1	2.3	**2.2**	2.6	2.5	**2.1**	**2.0**
As a part of voluntary work ~	N/A	N/A	N/A	.6	0.4	0.5	0.5	0.6	0.4	0.6	0.5
For some other reason ~	N/A	N/A	N/A	.2	0.1	0.2	0.1	0.2	0.2	0.2	0.1

Notes

(1) Figures in bold indicate a significant change from 2005/06. For purpose of visit data, figures in bold indicate a significant change from 2008/09.

(2) Figures exclude people who have visited a library for the purposes of paid work or academic study

(3) * N to small to report

Source: Department for Culture, Media and Sport - Taking Part Survey 2015/16 Q4
https://www.gov.uk/government/statistics/taking-part-201516-quarter-4-statistical-release

9.16 Participation in voluntary activities, England 2005 to 2016-17

	England, 2001 to 2015-16											*England, 2013-14 to 2016-17*			
Percentages	**Face-to-Face Estimates**											**Online/Paper Estimates**			
	At least once a month											At least once a month			
	2001[1]	2003[1]	2005[1]	2007-08[1]	2008-09[1]	2009-10[1]	2010-11[1]	2012-13	2013-14	2014-15	2015-16	2013-14	2014-15	2015-16	2016-17
Informal volunteering[2]	34	37	37	35	35	29	29	36	35	34	34	31	28	29	27
Formal volunteering[3]	27	28	29	27	26	25	25	29	27	27	27	27	25	21	22
Any volunteering[4]	46	50	50	48	47	42	41	49	48	47	47	44	41	39	39

	England, 2001 to 2015-16											*England, 2013-14 to 2016-17*			
Percentages	At least once in last year											At least once in last year			
	2001[1]	2003[1]	2005[1]	2007-08[1]	2008-09[1]	2009-10[1]	2010-11[1]	2012-13	2013-14	2014-15	2015-16	2013-14	2014-15	2015-16	2016-17
Informal volunteering[2]	67	63	68	64	62	54	55	62	64	59	60	58	54	54	52
Formal volunteering[3]	39	42	44	43	41	40	39	44	41	42	41	45	40	37	37
Any volunteering[4]	74	73	76	73	71	66	65	72	74	69	70	70	65	65	63
Employer volunteering[5]	n/a	n/a	n/a	n/a	n/a	n/a	n/a	6	8	8	8	6	5	5	6
Respondents	*9,430*	*8,920*	*9,195*	*8,804*	*8,768*	*8,712*	*9,664*	*6,915*	*5,105*	*2,022*	*3,027*	*10,215*	*2,323*	*3,256*	*10,256*

Source: Community Life Survey 2016/17

[1]Data collected through the Citizenship Survey

[2] Informal volunteering: Giving unpaid help as an individual to people who are not relatives.

[3] Formal volunteering: Giving unpaid help through groups, clubs or organisations to benefit other people or the environment.

[4] Participated in either formal or informal volunteering

[5] Volunteering undertaken by employees that is encouraged by employers / companies

The Community Life Survey (CLS) is a national survey, capturing views on a range of issues critical for supporting stronger communities.
The data presented in these tables are based on findings from 10,256 online/paper self-completion questionnaires, completed between 2016 and 2017. The findings are representative of adults aged 16 and over in England.
Following thorough testing, the CLS has moved to an online and paper mixed method approach from 2016-17 onwards, with an end to the current face-to-face method.
As this change represents a break in the time series, differences observed between the two data collection modes mean that the data are not comparable; we have published online/paper data for the 3 years 2013-14 to 2015-16 to enable trend analysis.

This data was collected during the methodological testing of moving the survey to an online/paper mixed mode.
More information on this change can be found can be found in the Online/Postal Estimates Technical note:
https://www.gov.uk/government/publications/community-life-survey-2016-17

We would advise users to use the new online/postal estimates for any analysis.
We do not recommend appending the 2016-17 online/postal estimate onto the face-to-face backseries as any differences may be the result of a change in mode, not a true change.

9.17 UK residents' visits to friends and relatives[1] abroad: by destination

United Kingdom

Percentages[2]

	2006	2009	2011	2012	2013	2014	2015	2016
Irish Republic	15	14	13	10	10	11	10	9
France	11	11	10	10	10	11	9	9
Poland	6	9	9	9	9	9	10	10
Spain	9	8	7	8	8	8	7	7
Germany	6	5	5	5	5	5	5	4
USA	6	5	5	4	4	4	4	4
India	3	4	4	4	4	4	4	4
Italy	4	4	3	4	4	4	5	5
Netherlands	3	3	3	3	3	3	3	3
Pakistan	3	3	3	3	3	3	2	3
Other countries	35	36	39	39	39	37	35	42
All destinations (=100%) (millions)	12.0	11.6	11.6	11.8	12.3	13.3	14.7	16.6

Source: International Passenger Survey, Office for National Statistics

1 As a proportion of all visits to friends and relatives taken abroad by residents of the UK. Excludes business trips and other miscellaneous visits.

2 Percentages may not add up to 100 per cent due to rounding.

9.18 The Internet

Internet activities, by age group, sex, 2016
Within the last 3 months

%

	Age group						Sex		
	16-24	25-34	35-44	45-54	55-64	65+	Men	Women	All
Sending/receiving emails	88	88	90	85	78	53	80	78	**79**
Finding information about goods and services	74	85	86	85	77	53	76	75	**76**
Social networking (eg Facebook or Twitter)	91	89	75	66	51	23	62	64	**63**
Reading online news, newspapers or magazines	66	76	73	64	55	34	64	56	**60**
Internet banking	61	87	75	66	55	26	62	58	**60**
Looking for health-related information (eg injury, disease, nutrition, improving health etc)	49	68	66	53	51	28	47	56	**51**
Using services related to travel or travel related accommodation	46	61	61	60	55	31	53	49	**51**
Listening to music (eg internet radio, music streaming)	87	68	61	49	32	13	53	45	**49**
Using payment accounts (eg Paypal) to pay internet purchases	48	66	62	56	43	20	50	46	**48**
Uploading content created by you to a website to be shared	65	63	59	52	33	20	47	47	**47**
Watching video content from sharing services (eg YouTube)	77	64	60	47	35	13	54	40	**47**
Telephoning or making video calls over the internet via a webcam	59	58	55	44	35	18	43	43	**43**
Watching internet streamed TV (live or catch-up) from TV broadcasters	59	60	52	43	36	18	48	39	**43**
Playing or downloading games	54	43	39	31	21	14	35	30	**32**
Watching video on demand from commercial services (eg Netflix, HBO)	55	46	35	26	20	4	33	25	**29**
Selling goods or services over the internet	16	28	28	21	14	6	20	17	**18**
Making an appointment with a doctor or other healthcare practitioner via a website	7	19	19	18	20	10	15	16	**15**
Creating websites or blogs	11	11	8	7	5	2	10	4	**7**

Base: Adults (aged 16+) in Great Britain. Source: Office for National Statistics

1. Equality Act disabled refers to those who have a health condition or illness in line with the Equality Act definition of disability.

Online purchases, by age group, sex, 2016
Within the last 12 months

%

	Age group						Sex		
	16-24	25-34	35-44	45-54	55-64	65+	Men	Women	All
Clothes or sports goods	69	73	64	58	50	24	49	59	**54**
Household goods (eg furniture, toys etc)	34	65	65	56	49	24	47	49	**48**
Holiday accommodation	31	52	51	52	45	24	43	41	**42**
Travel arrangements (eg transport tickets, car hire)	33	50	47	45	41	19	39	38	**38**
Tickets for events	40	50	47	46	40	13	38	37	**38**
Films, music (including downloads)	43	46	43	35	22	6	34	29	**31**
Books, magazines, newspapers (including e-books and downloads)	27	33	37	37	35	19	29	32	**31**
Food or groceries	23	37	39	30	20	9	23	28	**26**
Electronic equipment (including cameras)	26	34	31	28	22	9	32	17	**24**
Video games software, other computer software and upgrades (including downloads)	36	27	27	22	12	4	25	15	**20**
Telecommunication services	13	25	24	24	16	8	22	15	**18**
Computer hardware	19	20	18	18	11	6	21	9	**15**
Medicine	8	10	14	16	15	9	11	13	**12**
E-learning material	11	9	11	9	6	1	8	7	**7**

Base: Adults (aged 16+) in Great Britain. Source: Office for National Statistics

1. Equality Act disabled refers to those who have a health condition or illness in line with the Equality Act definition of disability.

Households with internet access, 2005 to 2016

	Year	%	Year	%
GB	2005	55	2011	77
	2006	57	2012	80
	2007	61	2013	83
	2008	65	2014	84
	2009	70	2015	86
	2010	73	2016	89

GB estimates from 2005 to 2015. Source: Office for National Statistics

2015 and 2016 estimates relate to January, February and April. Previous estimates relate to January to March, except 1998 which relates to April to June and 2005 which relates to May. During 2005, estimates were published at irregular intervals as Topic Based Summaries. These are no longer available on the ONS website.

9.19 Radio Listening

United Kingdom (including Channel Islands and Isle of Man)

Adults aged 15 and over: population[1]: 54,466,000

	Weekly Reach[2] (000s)	Weekly Reach[3] %	Average Hours per head[4]	Average Hours per listener[5]	Total Hours[6] (000s)	Share of Listening in TSA %
Quarterly Summary of Radio Listening - Survey period ending June 2017						
All Radio	49206	90%	19.0	21.0	1033226	100.0%
All BBC Radio	34945	64%	9.9	15.5	539982	52.3%
BBC Local Radio	8632	16%	1.4	8.7	75340	7.3%
All Commercial Radio	35881	66%	8.5	13.0	464812	45.0%
All National Commercial[8]	19905	37%	3.2	8.7	172369	16.7%
All Local Commercial (National TSA)	27277	50%	5.4	10.7	292443	28.3%
All BBC Network Radio[8]	32136	59%	8.5	14.5	464642	45.0%
BBC Radio 1	9586	18%	1.2	6.7	64345	6.2%
BBC Radio 2	14884	27%	3.2	11.7	173955	16.8%
BBC Radio 3	2062	4%	0.2	6.1	12600	1.2%
BBC Radio 4	11551	21%	2.3	11.0	127114	12.3%
BBC Radio 4 (including 4 Extra)	11923	22%	2.6	11.7	139091	13.5%
BBC Radio 4 Extra	2093	4%	0.2	5.7	11977	1.2%
BBC Radio 5 live	5317	10%	0.6	6.6	35020	3.4%
BBC Radio 5 live (inc. sports extra)	5631	10%	0.7	6.8	38325	3.7%
BBC Radio 5 live sports extra	1246	2%	0.1	2.7	3305	0.3%
BBC 6 Music	2235	4%	0.4	8.7	19381	1.9%
1Xtra from the BBC	1031	2%	0.1	4.5	4659	0.5%
BBC Asian Network UK	646	1%	0.1	4.9	3162	0.3%
BBC World Service	1593	3%	0.2	6.0	9504	0.9%

Source: RAJAR/Ipsos MORI/RSMB

STATION SUMMARY ANALYSIS - RAJAR REPORTING PERIOD 2017 Q1

(Report 1690) All Radio, Adults Only

Quarterly Weighted Data

		Age Group of Respondent				
	Total	25-34	35-44	45-54	55-64	65+
Unw. Sample	21850	2989	3606	4568	4588	6099
Est. Pop'n	46030	8923	8343	9250	7606	11908
ALL RADIO						
Weekly Reach 000s	41578	7592	7509	8717	7103	10657
Weekly Reach %	452.2	85.1	90	94.2	93.4	89.5
Total Hours	931577	129620	148560	204513	179072	269812
Average Hours Per Head	100.6	14.5	17.8	22.1	23.5	22.7
Average Hours Per Listener	110.9	17.1	19.8	23.5	25.2	25.3
Market Share	500	100	100	100	100	100

1. The number of people aged 15+ who live within the TSA of a given station

Source: RAJAR

2. The number of people aged 15+ who listen to a radio station for at least 5 minutes in the course of an average week.
3. The Weekly Reach expressed as a percentage of the Population within the TSA.
4. The total hours of listening to a station during the course of a week, averaged across the total adult population of the UK.
5. The total hours of listening to a station during the course of a week, averaged across all those listening to the station for at least 5 minutes.
6. The overall number of hours of adult listening to a station in the UK in an average week.
7. The percentage of total listening time accounted for by a station in the UK in an average week.
8. Audiences in local analogue areas excluded from 'All BBC Network Radio' and 'All National Commercial' totals.

Total Survey Area (TSA): The area within which a station's audience is measured. This is defined by the station using postcode districts as building blocks.

Population: The number of people aged 15+ who live within the TSA of a given station.

RAJAR Ltd (Radio Joint Audience Research) was set up in 1992 to align, design and operate a single audience measurement system for the UK radio industry serving both the BBC and licensed commercial stations. The company is jointly owned by the BBC (British Broadcasting Corporation) and by the RadioCentre (the trade body representing the vast majority of Commercial Radio stations in the UK). For more information visit: www.rajar.co.uk

this page is intentionally blank

Chapter 10

Environment

Environment

Air emissions (Table 10.2 to 10.8)

Emissions of air pollutants arise from a wide variety of sources. The National Atmospheric Emissions Inventory (NAEI) is prepared annually for the Government and the devolved administrations by AEA Energy and Environment, with the work being co-ordinated by the Department for Business, Energy & Industrial Strategy (BEIS). Information is available for a range of point sources including the most significant polluters. However, a different approach has to be taken for diffuse sources such as transport and domestic emissions, where this type of information is not available. Estimates for these are derived from statistical information and from research on emission factors for stationary and mobile sources. Although for any given year considerable uncertainties surround the emission estimates for each pollutant, trends over time are likely to be more reliable.

UK national emission estimates are updated annually and any developments in methodology are applied retrospectively to earlier years. Adjustments in the methodology are made to accommodate new technical information and to improve international comparability.

Three different classification systems are used in the tables presented here; a National Accounts basis (Table 10.2), the format required by the Inter-governmental Panel on Climate Change (IPCC) (Table 10.3) and the National Communications (NC) categories (Tables 10.5-10.7).

The NC source categories are detailed below together with details of the main sources of these emissions:

Energy supply total: Power stations, refineries, manufacture of solid fuels and other energy industries, solid fuel transformation, exploration, production and transport of oils, offshore oil and gas – venting and flaring, power stations - FGD, coal mining and handling, and exploration, production and transport of gas.

Business total: Iron and steel – combustion, other industrial combustion, miscellaneous industrial and commercial combustion, energy recovery from waste fuels, refrigeration and air conditioning, foams, fire fighting, solvents, one components foams, and electronics, electrical insulation and sporting goods.

Transport total: Civil aviation (domestic, landing and take off, and cruise), passenger cars, light duty vehicles, buses, HGVs, mopeds & motorcycles, LPG emissions (all vehicles), other road vehicle engines, railways, railways – stationary combustion, national navigation, fishing vessels, military aircraft and shipping, and aircraft – support vehicles.

Residential total: Residential combustion, use of non aerosol consumer products, accidental vehicle fires, and aerosols and metered dose inhalers.

Agriculture total: Stationary and mobile combustion, breakdown of pesticides, enteric fermentation (cattle, sheep, goats, horses, pigs, and deer), wastes (cattle, sheep, goats, horses, pigs, poultry, and deer), manure liquid systems, manure solid storage and dry lot, other manure management, direct soil emission, and field burning of agricultural wastes.

Industrial process total: Sinter production, cement production, lime production, limestone and dolomite use, soda ash production and use, fletton bricks, ammonia production, iron and steel, nitric acid production, adipic acid production, other – chemical industry, halocarbon production, and magnesiun cover gas.

Land-use change: Forest land remaining forest land, forest land biomass burning, land converted to forest land, direct N2O emissions from N fertilisation of forest land, cropland liming, cropland remaining cropland, cropland biomass burning, land converted to cropland, N2O emissions from disturbance associated with land-use conversion to cropland, grassland biomass burning, grassland liming, grassland remaining grassland, land converted to grassland, wetlands remaining wetland, Non-CO2 emissions from drainage of soils and wetlands, settlements biomass burning, land converted to settlements, and harvested wood.

Waste management total: Landfill, waste-water handling, and waste incineration.

Atmospheric emissions on a National Accounts basis (Table 10.1)

The air and energy accounts are produced for ONS by AEA Technology plc based on data compiled for the National Atmospheric Emissions Inventory (NAEI)7 and UK Greenhouse Gas Inventory (GHGI)8. Every year a programme of development work is undertaken to optimise the methodologies employed in compiling the accounts. Assessments in previous years have indicated that a number of splits used to apportion road transport source data to more than one industry should be reviewed. The results of this review have been implemented in the 2011 UK Environmental Accounts for reference period 2009 and years back to 1990.

The industry breakdown used in the accounts has moved to using the Standard Industrial Classification 2007 (SIC 2007). Historically, the accounts were based on Environmental Accounts codes (EAcodes) based on SIC 2003. This change will allow the accounts which are broken down by industry to be more readily compared with other economic statistics. A methodology article that outlines this change in more detail was published on the ONS website in May 2011: http//www.statistics.gov.uk/cci/article.asp?id=2694. As a result while names given to the breakdown maybe similar they are not necessarily the same.

The National Accounts figures in Table 10.2 differ from those on an IPCC basis, in that they include estimated emissions from fuels purchased by UK resident households and companies either at home or abroad (including emissions from UK international shipping and aircraft operators), and exclude emissions in the UK resulting from the activities of non-residents. This allows for a more consistent comparison with key National Accounts indicators such as Gross Domestic Product (GDP).

Greenhouse gases include carbon dioxide, methane, nitrous oxide, hydro-fluorocarbons, perfluorocarbons and sulphur hexafluoride which are expressed in thousand tonnes of carbon dioxide equivalent.

Acid rain precursors include sulphur dioxide, nitrogen oxides and ammonia which are expressed as thousand tonnes of sulphur dioxide equivalent.

Road Transport Emissions (Table 10.2)

Various pollutants are emitted from road transport into the atmosphere. Table 10.2 shows emissions by pollutant generated from combustion by road vehicles.

Greenhouse gases are made up of carbon dioxide, methane and nitrous oxide

Acid rain precursors are made of sulphur dioxide, nitrogen oxides and ammonia

Estimated total emissions of greenhouse gases on an IPCC basis (Table 10.3)

The IPCC classification is used to report greenhouse gas emissions under the UN Framework Convention on Climate Change (UNFCCC) and includes Land Use Change and all emissions from Domestic aviation and shipping, but excludes International aviation and shipping bunkers. Estimates of the relative contribution to global warming of the main greenhouse gases, or classes of gases, are presented weighted by their global warming potential.

Greenhouse gas emissions bridging table (Table 10.4)

National Accounts measure to UNFCCC measure

The air and energy accounts are produced for ONS by AEA Technology plc based on data compiled for the National Atmospheric Emissions Inventory (NAEI)7 and UK Greenhouse Gas Inventory (GHGI)8. Every year a programme of development work is undertaken to optimise the methodologies employed in compiling the accounts. Assessments in previous years have indicated that a number of splits used to apportion road transport source data to more than one industry should be reviewed. The results of this review have been implemented in the 2011 UK Environmental Accounts for reference period 2009 and years back to 1990. There are a number of formats for the reporting and recording of atmospheric emissions data, including those used by the Department for Business, Energy & Industrial Strategy (BEIS) for reporting greenhouse gases under UNFCCC and the Kyoto Protocol, and for reporting air pollutant emissions to the UN Economic Commission for Europe (UNECE), which differ from the National Accounts consistent measure published by the Office for National Statistics (ONS).
Differences between the National Accounts measure and those for reporting under UNFCCC and the Kyoto Protocol, following the guidance of the IPCC, are shown in Table 10.4.

Emissions of carbon dioxide (Table 10.5)

Carbon dioxide is the main man-made contributor to global warming, with the highest source of emissions being energy supply.

Emissions of methane (Table 10.6)

The overall amount of methane emissions has fallen year on year since 2002, The highest source of emissions of methane for the 5th year running is Agriculture.

Emissions of nitrous oxide (Table 10.7)

Agriculture continues to be the highest source of nitrous oxide emissions for 2015.

Material Flow Account (Table 10.8)

Economy-wide material flow accounts estimate the physical flow of materials through our economy. As well as providing an aggregate overview of the annual extraction of raw materials, they also measure the physical amounts of imports and exports. This information is important in attempting to understand resource productivity. For example, they shed light on the depletion of natural resources and seek to promote a sustainable and more resource-efficient economy.

Annual rainfall (Table 10.9)

Regional rainfall is derived by the Met Office's National Climate Information Centre for the National Hydrological Monitoring Programme at the Centre for Ecology and Hydrology. These monthly area rainfalls are based initially on a subset of rain gauges (circa 350) but are updated after four to five months with figures using the majority of the UK's rain gauge network.

The regions of England shown in this table correspond to the original nine English regions of the National Rivers Authority (NRA). The NRA became part of the Environment Agency on its creation in April 1996. The figures in this table relate to the country of Wales, not the Environment Agency Welsh Region.

UK weather summary (Table 10.10)

Table 10.10 represents an initial assessment of the weather that was experienced across the UK and how it compares with the 1961 to 1990 average.

Final averages use quality controlled data from the UK climate network of observing stations. They show the Met Office's best assessment of the weather that was experienced across the UK during the years and how it compares with the 1961 to 1990 average. The columns headed 'Anom' (anomaly) show the difference from, or percentage of, the 1961 to 1990 long-term average.

Biological and chemical quality of rivers and canals (Table 10.11)

Table 10.11 shows a Summary of River Basin District Ecological and Chemical Status from 2009-2015. It looks at each river basin district in terms of Percent of surface water bodies that are at good chemical status or better and also Percent of surface water bodies are at good ecological status/potential or better. Improvements are measured in terms of the number of water bodies meeting good status

Status of Rivers and Canals in Scotland (Table 10.12)

Looks at the overall status of rivers & canals in Scotland, including water quality.

Reservoir stocks in England and Wales (Table 10.13)

Data are collected for a network of major reservoirs (or reservoir groups) in England and Wales for the National Hydrological Monitoring Programme at the Centre for Ecology and Hydrology. Figures of usable capacity are supplied by the Water PLCs and the Environment Agency at the start of each month and are aggregated to provide an index of the total reservoir stocks for England and Wales.

Water industry expenditure (Table 10.14)

So that water companies can benchmark themselves against each other, they collate and share historic information about their operations, investment and performance. Table 10.14 Water Industry Regulatory Capital Values.

Water pollution incidents (Table 10.15)

The Environment Agency responds to complaints and reported incidents of pollution in England and Wales. Each incident is then logged and categorised according to its severity. The category describes the impact of each incident on water, land and air. The impact of an incident on each medium is considered and reported separately. If no impact has occurred for a particular medium, the incident is reported as a category 4. Before 1999, the reporting system was used only for water pollution incidents; thus the total number of substantiated incidents was lower, as it did not include incidents not relating to the water environment.

Bathing waters (Table 10.16)

Table 10.16 shows statistics on UK bathing waters for 2016. These results summarise the compliance of coastal and inland bathing waters to the Bathing Water Directive (2006/7/EC) for the whole of the United Kingdom in 2016.

Surface and groundwater abstractions (Table 10.17)

Significant changes in the way data is collected and/or reported were made in 1991 (due to the Water Resources Act 1991) and 1999 (commission of National Abstraction Licensing Database). Figures are therefore not strictly comparable with those in previous/intervening years. From 1999, data have been stored and retrieved from one system nationally and are therefore more accurate and reliable. Some regions report licensed and actual abstracts for financial rather than calendar years. As figures represent an average for the whole year expressed as daily amounts, differences between amounts reported for financial and calendar years are small.

Under the Water Act 2003, abstraction of less than 20 m3/day became exempt from the requirement to hold a licence as of 1 April 2005. As a result over 22,000 licences were deregulated, mainly for agricultural or private water supply purposes. However, due to the small volumes involved, this has had a minimal affect on the estimated licensed and actual abstraction totals. The following changes have occurred in the classification of individual sources:

- Spray irrigation: this category includes small amounts of non-agricultural spray irrigation
- Mineral washing: from 1999 this was not reported as a separate category; licences for 'Mineral washing' are now contained in 'Other industry'
- Private water supply: this was shown as separate category from 1992 and includes private abstractions for domestic use and individual households
- Fish farming, cress growing, amenity ponds: includes amenity ponds, but excludes miscellaneous from 1991

Estimates of remaining recoverable oil and gas reserves (Table 10.18)

Only a small proportion of the estimated remaining recoverable reserves of oil and gas are known with any degree of certainty. The latest oil and gas data for 2015 shows that the upper range of total UK oil reserves was estimated to be around 1.6 billion tonnes, while UK gas reserves were around 1089 billion cubic metres. Of these, proven reserves of oil were 0.3 billion tonnes and proven reserves of gas were 207 billion cubic metres.

Local authority collected (Table 10.19)

Local authority collected includes household and non-household waste that is collected and disposed of by local authorities. It includes regular household collections, specific recycling collections, and special collections of bulky items, waste received at civic amenity sites, and waste collected from non-household sources that come under the control of local authorities.

Waste arisings from households (Table 10.20)

The 'waste from households' calculation was first published by Defra in May 2014. It was introduced for statistical purposes to provide a harmonised UK indicator with a comparable calculation in each of the four UK countries and to provide a consistent approach to report recycling rates at UK level on a calendar year basis under the Waste Framework Directive (2008/98/EC). The waste from household measure is a narrower measure than the 'household waste' measure which was previously used and excludes waste not considered to have come directly from households, such as recycling from street bins, parks and grounds.

Chartered Institute of Environmental Health Survey of Local Authority Noise Enforcement Activity (Table 10.21)

Every year the CIEH collects data on noise complaints made to local authorities and on the enforcement actions consequently taken by them. The data helps to inform policy and practice in environmental protection and public health and, in particular, the survey results provide the source of data for the Public Health England Outcome Indicator on noise. This, part of the Public Health Outcomes Framework, provides recognition of noise as one of the wider determinants of health.

Government revenue from environmental taxes (Table 10.22)

Environmental taxes data are based on the definition outlined in Regulation (EU) No 691/2011 on European environmental economic accounts. The European Statistical Office (Eurostat) define an environmental tax as a tax whose base is a physical unit (for example, a litre of petrol or a passenger flight) that has a proven negative impact on the environment. These taxes are designed to promote environmentally positive behaviour, reduce damaging effects on the environment and generate revenue that can potentially be used to promote further environmental protection.

In 2016, revenue from environmentally related taxes stood at £47 billion. This corresponded to 2.4% of the UK's gross domestic product (GDP). Looking over the time series as a whole, environmental taxes as a share of GDP has remained at a broadly consistent level of between 2% and 3%

10.1 Atmospheric emissions, 2015[1]

	Thousand tonnes CO_2 equivalent							Thousand tonnes of SO_2 equivalent			
	Total greenhouse gas emissions	Carbon Dioxide (CO_2)	Methane (CH_4)	Nitrous Oxide (N_2O)	Hydrofluoro-carbons (HFCs)	Perfluoro-carbons (PFCs)	Sulphur hexafluoride (SF_6)	Total acid rain precursors	Sulphur Dioxide (SO_2)	Nitrogen Oxides (NO_X)	Ammonia (NH_3)
Agriculture, forestry and fishing	51546	7519	27657	16321	48	0	0	497	0	20	477
Mining and quarrying	20495	17473	2659	354	9	0	0	55	6	49	0
Manufacturing	88529	85368	223	585	1887	327	139	215	103	104	8
Electricity, gas, steam and air conditioning supply; water supply, sewerage, waste management activities and remediation services	149500	126913	20142	2015	231	0	199	249	91	143	15
Construction	11905	11207	21	372	305	0	0	37	0	36	0
Wholesale and retail trade; repair of motor vehicles and motorcycles	17883	12555	36	167	5126	0	0	27	0	27	0
Transport and storage; information and communication	85727	83049	86	898	1693	0	0	466	108	357	1
Accommodation and food services	3742	3077	9	18	638	0	0	4	0	4	0
Financial and insurance activities	226	98	0	10	118	0	0	0	0	0	0
Real estate activities; professional scientific and technical activities; administration and support service activities	6158	5239	7	34	877	0	1	12	0	11	1
Public administration and defence; compulsory social security	5661	5298	7	49	189	0	118	24	1	17	6
Education	2916	2588	6	10	312	0	0	5	2	3	0
Human health and social work activities	5550	4465	9	598	476	0	1	5	0	5	0
Arts, entertainment and recreation; other service activities	2897	2659	5	14	220	0	0	12	0	4	7
Activities of households as employers; undifferentiated goods and services-producing activities of households for own use	240	238	1	1	0	0	0	0	0	0	0
Consumer expenditure	142223	136581	1311	627	3705	0	0	187	27	124	35
Total	595197	504327	52179	22072	15833	327	457	1794	341	903	550
Of which: emissions from road transport[2]	115394	114267	107	1020	..	..	..	229	0	218	10

Source: Ricardo Energy & Environment, ONS

Notes:

1. Components may not sum to totals due to rounding.
2. Includes emissions from fuel sources which are used by road vehicles (eg HGVs, LGVs, cars and motorcycles) across all industries.

10.1 Atmospheric emissions, 2015[1]

Continued

	Thousand tonnes						Tonnes		
	PM_{10}[3]	$PM_{2.5}$[3]	CO	NMVOC	Benzene	1,3-Butadiene	Lead	Cadmium	Mercury
Agriculture, forestry and fishing	18.98	7.56	52.69	180.43	0.11	0.04	0.42	0.04	0.02
Mining and quarrying	7.97	2.00	36.96	99.79	0.30	0.00	0.36	0.05	0.02
Manufacturing	32.49	24.36	415.25	264.61	2.13	0.19	52.14	1.76	2.02
Electricity, gas, steam and air conditioning supply; water supply, sewerage, waste management activities and remediation services	5.89	3.80	72.66	31.06	1.19	0.00	3.33	0.18	1.61
Construction	8.68	3.42	185.47	50.68	0.54	0.14	0.36	0.05	0.02
Wholesale and retail trade; repair of motor vehicles and motorcycles	2.35	1.61	15.45	36.49	0.08	0.02	1.33	0.03	0.02
Transport and storage; information and communication	34.50	31.66	92.40	27.89	2.26	0.19	3.12	1.29	0.13
Accommodation and food services	0.18	0.16	2.51	0.53	0.02	0.00	0.02	0.00	0.00
Financial and insurance activities	0.05	0.05	0.41	0.12	0.00	0.00	0.01	0.00	0.00
Real estate activities; professional scientific and technical activities; administration and support service activities	0.66	0.50	15.77	1.07	0.04	0.01	0.05	0.01	0.01
Public administration and defence: compulsory social security	0.81	0.72	18.73	1.87	0.11	0.02	0.12	0.02	0.01
Education	0.49	0.45	4.74	0.20	0.01	0.00	0.66	0.01	0.06
Human health and social work activities	0.15	0.13	2.94	0.98	0.02	0.00	0.01	0.00	0.00
Arts, entertainment and recreation; other service activities	0.30	0.24	4.84	1.92	0.01	0.00	0.09	0.01	0.60
Activities of households as employers; undifferentiated goods and services-producing activities of households for own use	0.00	0.00	50.70	0.98	0.07	0.01	0.00	0.00	0.00
Consumer expenditure	59.98	54.65	738.10	219.58	6.73	1.26	5.51	1.21	0.34
Total (excluding natural world)	173.48	131.31	1709.62	918.20	13.61	1.89	67.52	4.67	4.84
Of which: emissions from road transport[2]	20.53	13.88	334.26	26.26	0.92	0.24	1.67	0.36	0.23

Source: Ricardo Energy & Environment, ONS

Notes:
1. Components may not sum to totals due to rounding.
2. Includes emissions from fuel sources which are used by road vehicles (eg HGVs, LGVs, cars and motorcycles) across all industries.
3. PM_{10} and $PM_{2.5}$ is particulate matter arising from various sources including fuel combustion, quarrying and construction, and formation of 'secondary' particles in the atmosphere from reactions involving other pollutants - sulphur dioxide, nitrogen oxides, ammonia and NMVOCs.

10.2 Road transport[1] emissions by pollutant, 2002 to 2015

UK resident basis

Weights in thousand tonnes

Pollutant	2002	2003	2004	2005	2006	2007	2008	2009	2010	2011	2012	2013	2014	2015
Greenhouse gases	**120,469.4**	**120,042.5**	**120,772.9**	**121,495.4**	**121,804.9**	**123,474.3**	**119,473.1**	**115,730.2**	**114,911.7**	**113,215.1**	**112,471.9**	**112,024.7**	**113,939.5**	**115,429.1**
of which:														
Carbon dioxide	118,637.5	118,362.6	119,202.9	120,012.9	120,416.6	122,152.2	118,355.9	114,728.0	113,917.0	112,212.1	111,450.7	110,978.4	112,849.3	114,296.6
Methane	482.7	425.2	381.1	349.7	315.6	281.4	251.1	187.9	165.1	148.8	133.6	118.7	112.3	106.5
Nitrous oxide	1,349.2	1,254.7	1,188.8	1,132.8	1,072.7	1,040.7	866.0	814.3	829.6	854.3	887.6	927.7	978.0	1,026.1
Acid rain precursors	**503.8**	**474.0**	**451.7**	**428.6**	**411.6**	**392.3**	**365.3**	**302.9**	**284.9**	**267.5**	**254.0**	**243.7**	**235.9**	**227.0**
of which:														
Sulphur dioxide	3.0	3.0	2.7	2.4	2.1	1.7	1.0	0.5	0.5	0.5	0.5	0.4	0.4	0.5
Nitrogen Oxides as NO_2	462.3	435.9	416.2	396.0	381.5	364.9	341.5	280.7	265.3	250.6	239.4	231.1	224.8	217.2
Ammonia	38.5	35.1	32.8	30.1	28.1	25.7	22.8	21.8	19.1	16.5	14.2	12.2	10.7	9.4
PM_{10}	33.1	32.4	31.7	30.8	29.9	29.1	27.6	26.4	25.7	24.0	22.9	21.9	21.1	20.5
$PM_{2.5}$	26.9	26.1	25.4	24.5	23.5	22.6	21.3	20.2	19.5	17.8	16.9	15.8	14.9	14.2
Carbon monoxide	2,160.2	1,961.0	1,777.0	1,578.8	1,405.7	1,218.8	1,091.1	838.6	717.0	589.2	519.7	439.9	367.8	324.7
Non Methane VOC	298.2	253.3	215.7	183.4	158.6	133.8	117.7	81.6	68.9	57.3	49.5	42.5	37.7	34.9
Benzene	8.8	8.1	7.3	6.5	5.9	5.0	4.6	2.8	2.4	1.9	1.6	1.3	1.0	0.9
1,3-Butadiene	2.6	2.2	1.9	1.6	1.4	1.2	1.0	0.7	0.6	0.5	0.4	0.3	0.3	0.2
Cadmium	0.4	0.4	0.4	0.4	0.4	0.4	0.4	0.4	0.4	0.4	0.4	0.3	0.4	0.4
Lead	2.0	2.0	2.0	2.1	2.1	1.8	1.7	1.6	1.6	1.6	1.6	1.6	1.6	1.7
Mercury	0.3	0.3	0.3	0.3	0.3	0.3	0.2	0.2	0.2	0.2	0.2	0.2	0.2	0.2

Source: Ricardo Energy and Environment, Office for National Statistics

Notes

[1] Emissions from fuel sources which are used by road vehicles across industry groups.

Greenhouse gases are made up of carbon dioxide, methane and nitrous oxide. Weight in carbon dioxide equivalent

Acid rain precursors are made of sulphur dioxide, nitrogen oxides and ammonia. Weight in sulphur dioxide equivalent

All figures are reported to 1 decimal place. Total figures are based on raw data and therefore may not sum due to rounding.

Enquiries about these data can be sent by email to: **environment.accounts@ons.gsi.gov.uk**

10.3 UK greenhouse gas emissions headline results, UK 2001-2016

Million tonnes carbon dioxide equivalent ($MtCO_2e$)

Gas	2001	2002	2003	2004	2005	2006	2007	2008	2009	2010	2011	2012	2013	2014	2015	2016
Net CO_2 emissions (emissions minus removals)	561.8	545.4	556.1	556.7	553.3	550.4	540.8	527.0	476.2	492.7	449.7	469.9	459.0	419.1	402.5	378.9
Methane (CH_4)	104.3	101.8	96.6	92.3	87.6	83.2	79.2	73.5	69.1	64.5	61.8	60.1	55.5	53.1	51.6	51.6
Nitrous oxide (N_2O)	28.3	26.3	26.2	26.7	25.8	24.6	24.6	23.9	22.2	22.5	21.7	21.7	21.4	21.9	21.5	21.4
Hydrofluorocarbons (HFC)	10.8	11.3	12.8	11.8	13.1	14.0	14.4	14.9	15.5	16.4	14.9	15.4	15.7	16.0	15.9	15.2
Perfluorocarbons (PFC)	0.5	0.4	0.4	0.4	0.4	0.4	0.3	0.3	0.2	0.3	0.4	0.3	0.3	0.3	0.3	0.4
Sulphur hexafluoride (SF_6)	1.5	1.5	1.3	1.1	1.1	0.9	0.8	0.7	0.6	0.7	0.6	0.6	0.5	0.5	0.5	0.5
Nitrogen trifluoride (NF_3)	0.0	0.0	0.0	0.0	0.0	0.0	0.0	0.0	0.0	0.0	0.0	0.0	0.0	0.0	0.0	0.0
Total greenhouse gas emissions	**707.1**	**686.7**	**693.4**	**689.1**	**681.3**	**673.5**	**660.3**	**640.3**	**583.8**	**597.1**	**549.1**	**568.0**	**552.4**	**510.8**	**492.4**	**467.9**

Footnotes:

1. The entire time series is revised each year to take account of methodological improvements

2. In accordance with international reporting and carbon trading protocols, each of these gases are weighted by their global warming potential (GWP), so that total greenhouse gas emissions can be reported on a consistent basis (in carbon dioxide equivalent units). The GWP for each gas is defined as its warming influence relative to that of carbon dioxide. The GWPs used are from Working Group 1 of the IPCC Fourth Assessment Report: Climate Change 2007.

Uncertainty in estimates of UK Greenhouse Gas emissions, UK, Crown Dependencies and Overseas Territories 1990/2016[1]

Pollutant		GWP[2]	1990 emissions[3] (thousand tonnes CO2 equivalent)	2016 emissions[3] (thousand tonnes CO2 equivalent)	Uncertainty[4] in 2016 emissions	Range of uncertainty in 2016 emissions: 2.5 percentile	Range of uncertainty in 2016 emissions: 97.5 percentile	Percentage change between 1990 and 2016	Range of likely % change between 1990 and 2016[5]: 2.5 percentile	Range of likely % change between 1990 and 2016[5]: 97.5 percentile
Carbon dioxide[6]	CO_2	1	597,827	406,134	2%	397,771	414,041	-32%	-34%	-30%
Methane	CH_4	25	135,472	52,578	16%	45,054	61,615	-61%	-70%	-50%
Nitrous oxide	N_2O	298	51,550	23,604	28%	19,028	32,190	-53%	-68%	-34%
Hydrofluorocarbons	HFC	12 - 14,800	14,400	15,944	9%	14,426	17,452	11%	-7%	33%
Perfluorocarbons	PFC	7,390 - 17,340	1,651	327	23%	259	407	-80%	-84%	-75%
Sulphur hexafluoride	SF_6	22,800	1,280	457	13%	396	518	-64%	-70%	-58%
Nitrogen trifluoride	NF_3	17,200	0.4	0.4	47%	0.2	0.7	14%	-46%	108%
All greenhouse gases weighted by GWP			**802,180**	**499,044**	**3%**	**486,098**	**513,735**	**-38%**	**-41%**	**-35%**

Source: Deprtment of Energy and Climate Change (DECC)

Footnotes:

1. Figures include emissions for the UK, Crown Dependencies and the Overseas Territories. Uncertainties are not calculated for different geographical coverages but would be expected to be similar.

2. The GWP (Global Warming Potential) of a greenhouse gas measures its effectiveness in global warming over 100 years relative to carbon dioxide.

3. 1990 and 2016 estimates, and the percentage change, are presented as the central estimate from the model. These differ from the actual emissions estimates.

4. Expressed as a percentage relative to the mean value 2016 emissions. Calculated as 0.5*R/E where R is the difference between 2.5 and 97.5 percentiles and E is the mean.

5. Equivalent to a 95 per cent probability that the percentage change between 1990 and 2016 is between the two values shown. Values include uncertainties for overseas territories data.

6. CO_2 emissions are net emissions. Total emissions minus removals.

10.4 Summary Greenhouse Gas Emissions Bridging Table showing relationship of Environmental Accounts measure to UNFCCC[1] measure

United Kingdom [5 6 9]

Thousand tonnes CO_2 equivalent

	1995	2000	2005	2010	2014	2015	2016
Greenhouse gases[2] - CO_2, CH_4, N_2O, HFCs, PFCs SF_6 and NF_3							
Environmental Account	**795,059.77**	**772,522.56**	**771,786.46**	**687,185.30**	**609,975.94**	**599,451.09**	**576,277.02**
less							
Bunker emissions[3]	28,081.14	36,985.96	41,796.83	40,860.35	42,056.64	41,622.81	42,580.54
CO2 biomass[4]	5,710.50	6,642.65	11,874.98	20,753.98	30,844.00	36,009.10	37,542.72
Cross-boundary[5]	12,050.66	16,054.17	25,477.56	14,072.11	11,830.73	14,322.24	13,711.69
plus							
Land-Use, Land-Use Change and Forestry (LULUCF)[7]	-4,959.64	-7,852.72	-11,373.96	-14,447.54	-14,416.09	-15,104.04	-14,557.47
BEIS reported (Excluding Crown Dependencies & Overseas Territories)[8 9]	**744,257.83**	**704,987.06**	**681,263.13**	**597,051.32**	**510,828.49**	**492,392.90**	**467,884.59**
plus							
Crown Dependencies[6] (including net emissions from LULUCF)	1,928.86	2,033.72	1,858.41	1,834.43	1,787.93	1,668.33	1,721.27
Overseas Territories (including net emissions from LULUCF)	1,789.43	1,902.82	2,154.10	2,191.08	2,133.91	2,124.68	2,120.21
UNFCCC reported in the UK Greenhouse Gas Inventory[8]	**747,976.13**	**708,923.60**	**685,275.64**	**601,076.82**	**514,750.32**	**496,185.92**	**471,726.07**

Source: Ricardo Energy and Environment, Department for Business, Energy & Industrial Strategy, Office for National Statistics

Notes

1 United Nations Framework Convention on Climate Change https://unfccc.int/process/transparency-and-reporting/greenhouse-gas-data/ghg-data-unfccc

2 Carbon dioxide, methane, nitrous oxide, hydrofluorocarbons, perfluorocarbons, sulphur hexafluoride and nitrogen trifluoride expressed as thousand tonnes of carbon dioxide equivalent

3 Bunker emissions include IPCC memo items International Aviation and International Shipping

4 Emissions arising from wood, straw, biogases and poultry litter combustion for energy production

5 Emissions generated by UK households and business transport and travel abroad, net of emissions generated by non-residents travel and transport in the UK

6 Emissions of Crown dependencies; Guernsey, Jersey, Isle of Man.

7 Emissions from deforestation, soils and changes in forest and other woody biomass.

8 https://www.gov.uk/government/collections/final-uk-greenhouse-gas-emissions-national-statistics

9 This is the UK total for the sum of the 7 pollutants and differs slightly from the Kyoto greenhouse gas basket totals which uses a narrower definition of Land Use, Land Use Change and Forestry and includes emissions from UK Overseas Territories (Gibraltar, the Falkland Islands, the Cayman Islands, Montserrat, Bermuda)

All figures are reported to 2 decimal places. Total figures are based on raw data and therefore may not sum due to rounding.

10.5 Estimated emissions of carbon dioxide by source category, type of fuel and end user category, UK 2000-2015

Million tonnes carbon dioxide equivalent ($MtCO_2e$)

Sector	2000	2001	2002	2003	2004	2005	2006	2007	2008	2009	2010	2011	2012	2013	2014	2015
(a) By source																
Energy supply	203.4	214.4	212.4	219.9	218.0	218.9	224.3	219.3	213.0	190.0	197.1	182.6	193.0	181.0	156.3	136.7
Business	108.8	106.2	95.5	98.2	97.6	96.9	94.0	92.0	89.6	76.5	78.2	71.5	72.9	73.3	71.0	69.9
Transport	130.9	130.6	133.3	132.5	133.5	134.3	134.3	135.9	129.9	125.0	123.2	121.1	120.1	118.6	120.0	122.1
Public	12.1	12.2	10.3	10.2	11.2	11.1	10.1	9.4	9.7	8.8	9.4	8.0	8.9	9.1	7.7	8.0
Residential	85.6	87.9	84.4	85.2	87.0	82.5	79.9	76.3	78.2	75.0	84.5	67.3	73.7	74.5	62.0	64.5
Agriculture	5.5	5.4	5.5	6.2	6.2	6.1	5.9	5.7	5.5	5.4	5.4	5.6	5.4	5.2	5.6	5.5
Industrial processes	16.9	15.7	14.8	15.7	16.0	16.4	15.5	16.8	15.1	10.0	10.6	10.1	9.9	12.2	12.3	12.1
Land use, land use change and forestry	-10.0	-11.0	-11.4	-12.3	-13.2	-13.2	-13.7	-14.9	-14.2	-14.9	-16.1	-16.6	-14.2	-15.1	-15.9	-16.6
Waste management	0.5	0.5	0.5	0.5	0.5	0.4	0.3	0.3	0.3	0.3	0.3	0.3	0.3	0.3	0.3	0.3
Grand Total	**553.7**	**561.8**	**545.4**	**556.1**	**556.7**	**553.3**	**550.4**	**540.8**	**527.0**	**476.2**	**492.7**	**449.7**	**469.9**	**459.0**	**419.1**	**402.5**

Source: Department of Energy and Climate Change

Footnotes:

: means data are not available

1. The entire time series is revised each year to take account of methodological improvements.

10.6 Estimated emissions of methane (CH_4) by source category, type of fuel and end user category, UK 2000-2015

Million tonnes carbon dioxide equivalent ($MtCO_2e$)

Sector	2000	2001	2002	2003	2004	2005	2006	2007	2008	2009	2010	2011	2012	2013	2014	2015
(a) By source																
Energy supply	16.5	15.2	14.7	13.1	12.8	11.2	10.3	9.9	9.5	9.4	9.1	8.8	8.7	7.5	7.2	6.7
Business	0.1	0.1	0.1	0.1	0.1	0.1	0.1	0.1	0.1	0.1	0.1	0.1	0.1	0.1	0.1	0.1
Transport	0.6	0.5	0.5	0.4	0.4	0.4	0.3	0.3	0.3	0.2	0.2	0.2	0.1	0.1	0.1	0.1
Public	0.0	0.0	0.0	0.0	0.0	0.0	0.0	0.0	0.0	0.0	0.0	0.0	0.0	0.0	0.0	0.0
Residential	0.9	0.9	0.8	0.8	0.7	0.6	0.6	0.6	0.7	0.7	0.9	0.8	0.8	0.9	0.8	0.9
Agriculture	29.4	27.9	27.4	27.6	27.8	27.5	27.0	26.7	26.0	25.7	25.9	25.8	25.7	25.8	26.3	26.3
Industrial processes	0.2	0.1	0.1	0.2	0.1	0.1	0.1	0.1	0.1	0.1	0.1	0.1	0.1	0.1	0.1	0.1
Land use, land use change and forestry	0.0	0.0	0.0	0.1	0.0	0.0	0.0	0.0	0.0	0.0	0.0	0.0	0.1	0.0	0.0	0.0
Waste management	61.4	59.3	58.1	54.4	50.2	47.6	44.5	41.4	36.8	32.8	28.2	26.1	24.5	20.8	18.4	17.4
Grand Total	**109.1**	**104.3**	**101.8**	**96.6**	**92.3**	**87.6**	**83.2**	**79.2**	**73.5**	**69.1**	**64.5**	**61.8**	**60.1**	**55.5**	**53.1**	**51.6**

Source: Department of Energy and Climate Change

Footnotes:

1. The entire time series is revised each year to take account of methodological improvements.

10.7: Estimated emissions of nitrous oxide (N_2O) by source category, type of fuel and end user category, UK 2000-2015

Million tonnes carbon dioxide equivalent ($MtCO_2e$)

Sector	2000	2001	2002	2003	2004	2005	2006	2007	2008	2009	2010	2011	2012	2013	2014	2015
(a) By source																
Energy supply	1.2	1.2	1.3	1.3	1.2	1.2	1.3	1.2	1.1	1.0	1.0	1.0	1.2	1.1	1.0	1.0
Business	1.6	1.6	1.6	1.6	1.7	1.6	1.7	1.7	1.6	1.4	1.4	1.3	1.5	1.3	1.3	1.5
Transport	1.7	1.6	1.6	1.5	1.4	1.4	1.3	1.3	1.1	1.0	1.0	1.0	1.1	1.1	1.2	1.2
Public	0.0	0.0	0.0	0.0	0.0	0.0	0.0	0.0	0.0	0.0	0.0	0.0	0.0	0.0	0.0	0.0
Residential	0.2	0.2	0.2	0.2	0.2	0.1	0.1	0.1	0.2	0.2	0.2	0.2	0.2	0.2	0.2	0.2
Agriculture	16.8	16.0	16.0	16.0	15.7	15.5	14.9	14.6	14.4	14.5	14.6	14.7	14.6	14.6	15.1	14.6
Industrial processes	5.4	4.7	2.7	2.9	3.8	3.1	2.6	3.0	2.8	1.4	1.5	0.6	0.3	0.3	0.3	0.3
Land use, land use change and forestry	2.1	2.0	2.0	1.9	1.9	1.8	1.8	1.7	1.6	1.6	1.6	1.6	1.5	1.5	1.5	1.4
Waste management	0.9	1.0	1.0	0.9	1.0	1.0	1.1	1.1	1.1	1.2	1.2	1.3	1.3	1.3	1.3	1.3
Grand Total	**29.9**	**28.3**	**26.3**	**26.2**	**26.7**	**25.8**	**24.6**	**24.6**	**23.9**	**22.2**	**22.5**	**21.7**	**21.7**	**21.4**	**21.9**	**21.5**

Source: Department of Energy and Climate Change

Footnotes:

1. The entire time series is revised each year to take account of methodological improvements.

10.8 Material flows account for the United Kingdom: Domestic extraction, 2003 to 2015

UK

1,000 Metric tonnes

Domestic extraction	2003	2004	2005	2006	2007	2008	2009	2010	2011	2012	2013	2014	2015
Biomass	**138,291**	**139,307**	**138,420**	**134,642**	**129,458**	**138,406**	**134,338**	**131,555**	**136,493**	**128,897**	**132,684**	**143,435**	**138,504**
Crops	42,326	42,742	41,653	39,698	37,156	43,713	42,359	40,118	43,079	37,667	40,479	46,421	43,397
Crop residues (used), fodder crops and grazed biomass	90,546	90,995	91,058	89,357	86,371	89,139	86,296	85,095	86,906	84,635	85,202	89,676	88,171
Wood	4,775	4,915	5,039	4,963	5,311	4,958	5,092	5,730	5,907	5,963	6,371	6,583	6,231
Wild fish catch and aquatic plants/animals	644	655	670	625	620	596	591	613	601	632	632	756	705
Metal ores (gross ores)	**6**	**5**	**4**	**4**	**3**	**3**	**4**	**4**	**4**	**1**	**1**	**1**	**1**
Iron	1	1	0	0	0	0	0	0	0	0	0	0	0
Non-ferrous metal	6	4	3	3	3	3	4	4	4	1	1	1	1
Non-metallic minerals[1]	**287,885**	**300,018**	**290,601**	**291,300**	**295,217**	**261,116**	**210,290**	**204,761**	**207,706**	**192,183**	**196,181**	**211,206**	**221,210**
Limestone and gypsum	80,635	83,334	79,296	81,928	85,191	75,345	61,311	58,185	59,300	56,000	58,100	67,500	71,353
Clays and kaolin	14,224	14,504	14,221	13,437	13,135	11,014	7,226	8,084	8,536	7,491	8,419	8,758	9,084
Sand and gravel	164,899	174,227	170,603	169,275	173,861	155,996	126,935	122,202	123,756	112,228	113,938	121,275	126,300
Other	28,127	27,953	26,481	26,660	23,030	18,762	14,818	16,290	16,114	16,464	15,724	13,673	14,473
Fossil energy materials /carriers[2]	**237,434**	**216,500**	**193,352**	**175,195**	**165,368**	**158,965**	**144,388**	**136,587**	**114,538**	**98,864**	**89,189**	**87,434**	**92,797**
Coal and other solid energy materials/ carriers[2]	29,791	26,046	21,632	19,717	17,674	18,626	18,542	19,103	19,173	17,394	13,712	12,246	9,201
Crude oil, condensate and natural gas liquids	106,073	95,374	84,721	76,578	76,575	71,789	68,199	62,962	51,972	44,561	40,646	39,928	45,288
Natural gas	101,570	95,080	87,000	78,900	71,119	68,551	57,648	54,523	43,393	36,909	34,831	35,260	38,308
Total domestic extraction[3]	**663,616**	**655,830**	**622,377**	**601,140**	**590,047**	**558,490**	**489,020**	**472,907**	**458,741**	**419,944**	**418,055**	**442,076**	**452,511**

Source: Department for Environment, Food and Rural Affairs; Food and Agriculture Organization of the United Nations; Eurostat; Kentish Cobnuts Association; British Geological Survey

Notes

1. 2015 and 2016 data have been estimated due to unavailable data sources. Alternative data sources are being reviewed. In addition some non-metallic mineral data were not available in 2016. This may mean total figures are a slight underestimate. This is likely to be small, as the missing data was around 0.4% of total domestic extraction in 2015.

2. Data for peat, included in 'coal and other solid energy materials/carriers, was not available in 2016. This may mean total figures are a slight underestimate. This is likely to be small, as peat was around 0.1% of total domestic extraction in 2015.

3. Total domestic extraction for 2016 may be a slight underestimate due to small missing data sources as detailed above. This is estimated to be less than 0.5% of the total.

4. : denotes unavailable data.

5. All figures are reported to 1 decimal place. Total figures are based on raw data and may not sum due to rounding.

Enquiries about these data can be sent by email to: **environment.accounts@ons.gsi.gov.uk**

10.8 Material flows account for the United Kingdom: Imports, 2003 to 2015

UK

1,000 Metric tonnes

Imports	2003	2004	2005	2006	2007	2008	2009	2010	2011	2012	2013	2014	2015
Biomass and biomass products	52,631	53,671	53,935	53,710	53,867	52,312	49,423	51,425	50,468	52,387	58,477	59,603	58,982
Metal ores and concentrates, raw and processed	42,348	45,964	43,623	45,291	47,862	42,605	26,955	32,936	33,476	33,856	37,972	40,595	37,718
Non-metallic minerals, raw and processed	16,240	16,989	16,752	16,454	17,160	16,337	12,684	15,078	15,904	13,904	14,505	18,308	17,940
Fossil energy materials/ carriers, raw and processed	125,431	151,906	161,792	170,454	170,004	163,769	158,813	158,337	176,737	190,554	184,907	172,143	158,874
Other products	15,793	18,258	16,915	17,167	17,038	16,469	14,858	16,541	15,611	15,102	15,939	16,631	15,873
Waste imported for final treatment and disposal	2	1	1	15	10	13	19	22	5	5	30	17	19
Total imports	**252,445**	**286,790**	**293,018**	**303,090**	**305,941**	**291,504**	**262,752**	**274,339**	**292,200**	**305,808**	**311,830**	**307,297**	**289,406**

Exports	2003	2004	2005	2006	2007	2008	2009	2010	2011	2012	2013	2014	2015
Biomass and biomass products	20,289	19,118	20,005	20,704	21,374	21,543	20,159	22,413	21,950	22,103	21,239	21,978	22,950
Metal ores and concentrates, raw and processed	24,952	26,677	26,355	27,216	27,335	27,171	20,704	23,502	24,502	24,005	25,316	25,712	24,086
Non-metallic minerals, raw and processed	20,312	21,928	22,634	23,591	22,840	21,170	17,094	16,681	17,034	14,444	15,119	14,436	11,809
Fossil energy materials/ carriers, raw and processed	118,544	114,242	104,307	99,946	95,972	96,421	94,463	101,577	98,556	95,222	91,250	89,308	91,199
Other products	8,934	8,685	9,423	8,504	9,539	8,754	7,721	7,716	7,739	7,705	7,693	7,855	7,740
Waste exported for final treatment and disposal	2	4	2	3	0	1	3	3	4	5	124	509	467
Total exports	**193,033**	**190,653**	**182,726**	**179,964**	**177,061**	**175,060**	**160,145**	**171,892**	**169,784**	**163,484**	**160,740**	**159,797**	**158,249**

Indicators	2003	2004	2005	2006	2007	2008	2009	2010	2011	2012	2013	2014	2015
Domestic material consumption (domestic extraction plus imports minus exports)[1,2]	**723,027**	**751,967**	**732,669**	**724,267**	**718,926**	**674,935**	**591,626**	**575,355**	**581,157**	**562,268**	**569,144**	**589,576**	**583,668**
Biomass	172,267	176,101	174,131	169,680	163,660	171,134	165,603	163,075	167,277	161,303	172,392	183,641	176,864
Metal ores	17,569	19,541	17,450	18,298	20,747	15,616	6,331	9,585	9,101	9,984	12,840	15,096	13,815
Non-metallic minerals	286,530	298,884	287,661	287,607	292,593	259,251	208,399	206,329	209,414	194,197	198,409	218,143	230,376
Fossil fuels	246,661	257,441	253,428	248,682	241,927	228,934	211,293	196,365	195,366	196,785	185,504	172,696	162,613
Physical trade balance (imports minus exports)	**59,412**	**96,137**	**110,292**	**123,126**	**128,880**	**116,444**	**102,607**	**102,447**	**122,416**	**142,324**	**151,090**	**147,500**	**131,157**
Direct material input (domestic extraction plus imports)[2]	**916,060**	**942,620**	**915,395**	**904,231**	**895,987**	**849,995**	**751,771**	**747,247**	**750,941**	**725,752**	**729,885**	**749,373**	**741,917**

Sources: Office for National Statistics

Notes

: denotes unavailable data.

1. 'Other' and 'waste for final treatment and disposal' imports and exports have been allocated to categories within Domestic Material Consumption using the same method that is used by Eurostat:

http://ec.europa.eu/eurostat/statistics-explained/images/7/75/Raw_material_equivalents_2015.xlsx.

2. Total material input and consumption for 2016 may be slight underestimates due to small missing data sources on extraction for some minor materials. See domestic material consumption sheet for more information.

3. All figures are reported to 1 decimal place. Total figures are based on raw data and therefore may not sum due to rounding.

Enquiries about these data can be sent by email to: **environment.accounts@ons.gsi.gov.uk**

10.8 Material flows account for the United Kingdom: Per capita, 2003 to 2015

UK

Metric tonnes

Per capita (person)	2003	2004	2005	2006	2007	2008	2009
Mid-year population estimates (persons)	59,636,700	59,950,400	60,413,300	60,827,100	61,319,100	61,823,800	62,260,500
Domestic extraction	11.1	10.9	10.3	9.9	9.6	9.0	7.9
Total imports	4.2	4.8	4.9	5.0	5.0	4.7	4.2
Total exports	3.2	3.2	3.0	3.0	2.9	2.8	2.6
Domestic material consumption (DMC)	12.1	12.5	12.1	11.9	11.7	10.9	9.5
Direct material input (DMI)	15.4	15.7	15.2	14.9	14.6	13.7	12.1

Per capita (person)	2010	2011	2012	2013	2014	2015
Mid-year population estimates (persons)	62,759,500	63,285,100	63,705,000	64,105,700	64,596,800	65,110,000
Domestic extraction	7.5	7.2	6.6	6.5	6.8	6.9
Total imports	4.4	4.6	4.8	4.9	4.8	4.4
Total exports	2.7	2.7	2.6	2.5	2.5	2.4
Domestic material consumption (DMC)	9.2	9.2	8.8	8.9	9.1	9.0
Direct material input (DMI)	11.9	11.9	11.4	11.4	11.6	11.4

Source: Office for National Statistics

Notes

1. Mid-year population estimates available here:

www.ons.gov.uk/peoplepopulationandcommunity/populationandmigration/populationestimates/bulletins/annualmidyearp opulationestimates/mid2017

2. : denotes unavailable data.

3. All figures are reported to 1 decimal place. Total figures are based on raw data and therefore may not sum due to rounding.

Enquiries about these data can be sent by email to: **environment.accounts@ons.gsi.gov.uk**

10.9 Annual rainfall: by region

United Kingdom

Millimetres and percentages

Region		1971 - 2000[2] rainfall average (= 100%) millimetres	2002	2003	2004	2005	2006	2007	2008	2009	2010	2011	2012	2013	2014	2015	2016
United Kingdom	JSJB	1084	118	83	112	100	109	111	120	112	88	108	123	101	120	117	101
North West	JSJC	1177	121	85	116	96	114	110	126	113	84	116	136	97	111	128	106
Northumbria	JSJD	831	124	80	120	111	101	105	135	116	105	104	144	106	110	124	105
Severn Trent[1]	JSJE	759	119	81	110	92	103	123	121	103	84	74	139	100	121	99	103
Yorkshire	JSJF	814	126	82	114	96	110	115	130	105	91	89	143	91	114	115	106
Anglian	JSJG	603	118	86	115	89	102	118	116	99	97	73	138	93	122	95	101
Thames	JSLK	700	128	81	103	79	106	118	115	104	87	79	134	101	130	93	97
Southern	JSLL	782	129	85	97	79	101	106	108	109	94	81	130	107	137	100	92
Wessex	JSLM	866	132	83	98	89	100	113	116	107	80	84	140	101	128	95	93
South West	JSLN	1208	121	78	99	90	92	110	112	110	83	86	133	103	115	104	80
England	JSLO	819	123	83	109	91	103	114	120	107	89	87	137	99	120	106	100
Wales	JSLP	1373	119	83	108	95	107	108	121	109	82	94	124	98	113	114	100
Scotland	JSLQ	1440	112	84	117	110	114	109	120	117	87	131	112	102	122	129	104
Northern Ireland	JSLR	1111	127	84	98	96	104	99	114	114	94	115	107	103	117	119	95

Sources: Met Office; National Hydrological Monitoring Programme, Centre for Ecology and Hydrology

[1] The regions of England shown in this table correspond to the original nine English regions of the National Rivers Authority (NRA); the NRA became part of the Environment Agency upon its creation in April 1996. The exception to this is the Severn Trent region, part of which (the upper Severn) lies in Wales.

[2] 1971-2000 averages have been derived using arithmetic averages of Met Office areal rainfall.

10.10 UK Annual Weather Summary

	Max Temp		Min Temp		Mean Temp		Sunshine		Rainfall	
	Actual (degrees celsius)	Anomaly (degrees celsius)	Actual (degrees celsius)	Anomaly (degrees celsius)	Actual (degrees celsius)	Anomaly (degrees celsius)	Actual (hours/ day)	Anomaly (%)	Actual (mm)	Anomaly (%)
	WLRL	WLRM	WLRO	WLRP	WLRR	WLRS	WLRX	WLRY	WLSH	WLSI
1990	13.1	1.2	5.8	0.9	9.4	1.1	1490.7	111.4	1172.8	106.7
1991	12.1	0.3	5.1	0.2	8.6	0.3	1302.0	97.3	998.2	90.8
1992	12.3	0.4	5.2	0.4	8.7	0.4	1290.8	96.5	1186.8	107.9
1993	11.8	-0.1	5.0	0.1	8.4	0.0	1218.6	91.1	1121.1	102.0
1994	12.4	0.5	5.5	0.6	8.9	0.6	1366.9	102.2	1184.7	107.7
1995	13.0	1.1	5.4	0.6	9.2	0.9	1588.5	118.7	1023.7	93.1
1996	11.7	-0.1	4.7	-0.1	8.2	-0.2	1403.5	104.9	916.6	83.4
1997	13.1	1.3	5.8	1.0	9.4	1.1	1430.3	106.9	1024.0	93.1
1998	12.6	0.8	5.8	1.0	9.1	0.8	1268.4	94.8	1265.1	115.1
1999	13.0	1.1	5.9	1.0	9.4	1.1	1419.4	106.1	1239.1	112.5
2000	12.7	0.8	5.6	0.8	9.1	0.8	1367.5	102.2	1337.3	121.5
2001	12.4	0.6	5.3	0.5	8.8	0.5	1411.9	105.5	1052.8	95.5
2002	13.0	1.1	6.0	1.2	9.5	1.2	1304.0	97.5	1283.7	116.5
2003	13.5	1.6	5.6	0.7	9.5	1.2	1587.4	118.7	904.2	82.0
2004	13.0	1.2	6.0	1.2	9.5	1.2	1361.4	101.8	1210.1	110.1
2005	13.1	1.2	5.9	1.1	9.5	1.1	1399.2	104.6	1083.0	98.4
2006	13.4	1.5	6.1	1.3	9.7	1.4	1495.9	111.8	1175.9	106.8
2007	13.3	1.4	6.0	1.1	9.6	1.3	1450.7	108.4	1197.1	108.8
2008	12.7	0.8	5.5	0.6	9.1	0.7	1388.8	103.8	1295.0	117.7
2009	12.8	1.0	5.6	0.7	9.2	0.9	1467.4	109.7	1213.3	110.2
2010	11.7	-0.1	4.2	-0.6	8.0	-0.4	1456.0	108.8	950.5	86.4
2011	13.5	1.5	6.0	1.2	9.6	1.3	1406.2	105.0	1172.5	107
2012	12.4	0.5	5.2	0.4	8.8	0.4	1340.5	100	1334.8	121
2013	12.4	0.5	5.2	0.4	8.8	0.5	1421.1	106	1091	99
2014	13.5	1.7	6.3	1.5	9.9	1.6	1426.6	107	1300.5	118
2015	12.9	1.1	5.5	0.7	9.2	0.9	1456.7	109	1272.4	116
2016	13.0	1.1	5.7	0.9	9.3	1.0	1424.9	107	1099.8	100

Source: Met Office

10.11 Summary of River Basin District Ecological and Chemical Status 2009- 2016

Chemical Classification of surface waters at good or better status

Percentage

River Basin District	2009	2010	2011	2012	2013	2014	2015	2015*	2016*
Solway Tweed	50	89	89	88	91	91	95	99	99
Northumbria	50	68	72	68	70	75	66	92	91
Humber	77	79	83	77	76	77	76	97	96
Anglian	85	89	92	87	84	83	84	99	99
Thames	75	76	79	74	72	70	70	99	98
South East	88	91	93	88	88	87	80	98	99
South West	77	80	83	84	79	79	83	96	96
Severn	78	83	88	82	82	83	83	95	97
Dee	75	92	92	87	82	67	100	90	90
North West	70	75	72	71	74	76	79	98	97

Ecological classification of surface water bodies at good or better status

Percentage

River Basin District	2009	2010	2011	2012	2013	2014	2015	2015*	2016*
Solway Tweed	44	43	45	48	41	41	42	41	43
Northumbria	43	41	43	40	42	38	41	26	25
Humber	18	16	17	18	17	16	16	14	14
Anglian	18	19	18	18	17	13	13	10	9
Thames	23	22	22	18	19	14	14	7	6
South East	19	15	16	15	15	13	14	15	17
South West	33	31	34	32	31	27	25	23	23
Severn	29	30	30	30	29	26	27	19	9
Dee	28	26	30	30	25	15	15	0	10
North West	30	31	30	29	30	28	28	22	20

Source: Environment Agency

% of English water bodies only
Improvements measured in terms of the number of water bodies meeting good status
* Cycle 2 figures of each year. Data sourced from Catchment Data Explorer, Environment Agency (https://environment.data.gov.uk/catchment-planning/). These figures are not directly comparable to those of previous years. Therefore, 2015 data from this source is also provided to allow comparison with 2016 figures.

10.12 Overall status of rivers & canals in Scotland, 2014

	High	Max EP	Good	Good EP	Moderate	Moderate EP	Poor	Poor Ep	Bad	Bad EP
No. of river water bodies	166	0	999	133	465	116	321	79	76	52
Length of river water bodies (km)	1434	0	9832	1308	5647	1214	3472	862	891	454
% of length of river water bodies	5.7%	0.0%	39.2%	5.2%	22.5%	4.8%	13.8%	3.4%	3.5%	1.8%

Water Quality 2014

	High	Good	Moderate	Poor	bad
No. of river water bodies	827	1123	396	49	12
Length of river water bodies (km)	8331.6	11781.6	4370.7	505.7	122.8
% of length of river water bodies	33.2%	46.9%	17.4%	2.0%	0.5%

Source: Scottish Environment Protection Agency

Please note: This table has not been updated since the last edition of AOS.

10.13 Monthly reservoir stocks for England & Wales[1]

Percentages

		2004	2005	2006	2007	2008	2009	2010	2011	2012	2013	2014	2015	2016
January	JTAS	93.8	92.3	88.7	93.7	95.7	95.3	92.4	89.8	90.4	96.7	98.2	94.8	97
February	JTAT	92.1	92.1	91.2	96.7	95.6	93.4	91.8	93.7	92.0	93.8	98.1	95.5	95.6
March	JTAU	94.4	93.6	96.2	95.2	97.3	94.5	94.1	92.2	89.2	92.0	96.3	95.6	94.3
April	JTAV	94.7	95.0	93.4	91.9	95.1	92.0	91.9	88.8	94.0	94.5	95.4	93.1	94.5
May	JTAW	90.5	93.0	94.4	91.1	92.6	93.3	86.2	87.4	93.6	94.5	96.1	93.9	91.6
June	JTAX	84.8	85.6	88.4	94.4	90.6	88.6	79.0	86.7	97.8	90.8	91.3	88.7	89.6
July	JTAY	78.5	77.9	77.2	93.5	92.0	91.0	77.3	84.7	96.8	83.7	82.9	84.1	88
August	JTAZ	82.4	71.5	70.7	88.3	92.5	89.7	75.5	79.9	96.0	82.1	81.4	82.7	87
September	JTBA	84.2	67.4	67.8	86.1	90.9	84.0	81.1	81.0	95.3	77.7	73.5	79.7	83.6
October	JTBB	87.5	77.2	80.0	81.2	93.8	82.3	82.0	80.0	94.3	87.6	79.8	74.6	78.4
November	JTBC	86.2	83.8	89.8	82.4	93.1	93.0	86.9	79.7	95.8	88.3	83.5	89.4	81.6
December	JTBD	91.2	85.9	92.2	89.8	92.4	90.6	84.3	88.6	97.6	95.4	92.0	95.3	83.7

1 Reservoir stocks are the percentage of useable capacity based on a representative selection of reservoirs; the percentages relate to the end of each month.

Sources: Water PLCs;
Environment Agency;
National Hydrological Monitoring Programme, Centre for Ecology and Hydrology: 01491 838800

10.14 Water Industry Regulatory Capital Values

RCV roll forward for indexation (£ million)	
RCV at 31 March 2018 as published in April 2017[1]	70,208
Indexation	2,346
RCV at 31 March 2018 in March 2018 prices	72,554

Wholesale water RCV (£ million)	2015-16	2016-17	2017-18	2018-19	2019-20
Opening RCV	29,251	29,723	30,359	30,905	31,250
RCV additions (from totex)	1,710	1,888	1,790	1,614	1,385
Less RCV run-off and depreciation	-1,238	-1,251	-1,242	-1,267	-1,292
Other adjustments[2]	0	-2	-2	-2	-2
Closing RCV	29,723	30,359	30,905	31,250	31,341
Average RCV (year average)	29,127	29,675	30,258	30,698	30,914

Wholesale water RCV breakdown (£ million)	2015-16	2016-17	2017-18	2018-19	2019-20
2015 RCV	28,048	26,906	25,848	24,836	23,863
Totex RCV	1,675	3,453	5,057	6,413	7,478
Total	29,723	30,359	30,905	31,250	31,341

Wholesale wastewater RCV (£ million)	2015-16	2016-17	2017-18	2018-19	2019-20
Opening RCV	39,723	40,300	40,970	41,649	42,195
RCV additions (from totex)	2,330	2,430	2,442	2,320	1,923
Less RCV run-off and depreciation	-1,754	-1,760	-1,763	-1,774	-1,766
Other adjustments[2]	0	0	0	0	0
Closing RCV	40,300	40,970	41,649	42,195	42,352
Average RCV (year average)	39,524	40,140	40,806	41,411	41,758

Wholesale wastewater RCV breakdown (£ million)	2015-16	2016-17	2017-18	2018-19	2019-20
2015 RCV	38,010	36,377	34,831	33,362	31,981
Totex RCV	2,289	4,593	6,818	8,833	10,371
Total	40,300	40,970	41,649	42,195	42,352

Notes

Source: OFWAT

1 Presented in March 2017 prices

2 Impact of the reduction in allowed totex and the associated RCV run-off as included in the CMA's final determination for Bristol Water

Link to CMA final determination

10.15 Summary of pollution incidents by region and incident category, England 2016

Region	Water						Land						Air					
	Cat 1	Cat 2	Cat 3	Cat 4	Total	Cat 1 and 2 Total	Cat 1	Cat 2	Cat 3	Cat 4	Total	Cat 1 and 2 Total	Cat 1	Cat 2	Cat 3	Cat 4	Total	Cat 1 and 2 Total
Anglian	2	36	5	20	63	38	0	14	7	42	63	14	0	16	3	44	63	16
Midlands	14	46	11	45	116	60	2	35	8	71	116	37	4	22	19	71	116	26
North East	8	49	0	17	74	57	0	9	7	58	74	9	0	8	6	60	74	8
North West	5	25	4	19	53	30	4	18	9	22	53	22	2	7	6	38	53	9
South East	13	57	7	26	103	70	0	18	17	68	103	18	0	22	10	71	103	22
South West	11	55	8	32	106	66	0	19	13	74	106	19	1	27	11	67	106	28
Total	**53**	**268**	**35**	**159**	**515**	**321 0**	**6**	**113**	**61**	**335**	**515**	**119 0**	**7**	**102**	**55**	**351**	**515**	**109**

Source: Environment Agency

Details of all pollution incidents reported to the Environment Agency are held on the National Incident Reporting System. This dataset only includes substantiated and closed environmental protection incidents, where the environment impact level is either category 1 (major) ,category 2 (significant), category 3 (minor) or category 4 (no impact) to at least 1 media (i.e. water, land or air).

10.16 Bathing Water Complaince Results 2016

EA Area Name	Overall Water Body Class					Total Surface Water Bodies	Percentage of Total (%)				
	High	Good	Moderate	Poor	Bad		High	Good	Moderate	Poor	Bad
Cambridgeshire and Bedfordshire	0	23	144	16	4	187	0.0	12.3	77.0	8.6	2.1
Cumbria and Lancashire	1	159	251	45	11	467	0.2	34.0	53.7	9.6	2.4
Derbyshire Nottinghamshire and Leicestershire	0	26	152	49	5	232	0.0	11.2	65.5	21.1	2.2
Devon and Cornwall	2	116	276	55	4	453	0.4	25.6	60.9	12.1	0.9
Essex Norfolk and Suffolk	0	16	163	45	3	227	0.0	7.0	71.8	19.8	1.3
Greater Manchester Merseyside and Cheshire	1	7	203	49	10	270	0.4	2.6	75.2	18.1	3.7
Hertfordshire and North London	0	2	81	22	6	111	0.0	1.8	73.0	19.8	5.4
Kent and South London	0	23	119	33	7	182	0.0	12.6	65.4	18.1	3.8
Lincolnshire and Northamptonshire	0	20	147	58	10	235	0.0	8.5	62.6	24.7	4.3
Northumberland Durham and Tees	4	101	213	70	8	396	1.0	25.5	53.8	17.7	2.0
Shropshire Herefordshire Worcestershire and Gloucestershire	0	22	174	86	8	290	0.0	7.6	60.0	29.7	2.8
Solent and South Downs	0	35	126	37	10	208	0.0	16.8	60.6	17.8	4.8
Staffordshire Warwickshire and West Midlands	0	35	113	62	15	225	0.0	15.6	50.2	27.6	6.7
Wessex	0	55	230	60	11	356	0.0	15.4	64.6	16.9	3.1
West Thames	0	16	165	80	13	274	0.0	5.8	60.2	29.2	4.7
Yorkshire	0	82	414	55	15	566	0.0	14.5	73.1	9.7	2.7
England	**8**	**738**	**2971**	**822**	**140**	**4679**	**0.2**	**15.8**	**63.5**	**17.6**	**3.0**

Source: Environment Agency Catchment Planning System

	Bathing Water Classification				Total Designated Bathing Waters	Percentage of Total			
	Excellent	Good	Sufficient	Poor		Excellent	Good	Sufficient	Poor
Wales	**84**	**13**	**5**	**1**	**103**	**81.6**	**12.6**	**4.9**	**1.0**
Scotland	**17**	**38**	**12**	**17**	**84**	**20.2**	**45.2**	**14.3**	**20.2**
Northern Ireland	**11**	**9**	**2**	**1**	**23**	**47.8**	**39.1**	**8.7**	**4.3**

Source: Natural Resources Wales, Scottish Environment Protection Agency, Department of Agriculture, Environment and Rural Affairs (DAERA)

10.17 Estimated abstractions from all surface and groundwaters by purpose and source: 2004 to 2016 England

million cubic metres

Purpose Source	2004	2005	2006	2007	2008	2009	2010	2011	2012	2013	2014	2015	2016
Public water supply													
tidal waters	1	0	0	0	0	6	21	13	16	12	8	7	9
non-tidal surface waters	3,775	3,831	3,778	3,626	3,624	3,462	3,545	3,431	3,490	3,482	3,377	3,450	3,606
groundwaters	1,786	1,819	1,747	1,707	1,724	1,730	1,715	1,730	1,672	1,684	1,661	1,651	1,666
all sources except tidal	5,561	5,649	5,525	5,333	5,348	5,192	5,260	5,161	5,161	5,167	5,038	5,101	5,273
all surface and groundwaters	5,562	5,649	5,525	5,333	5,348	5,198	5,281	5,175	5,177	5,178	5,046	5,109	5,282
Spray irrigation (1)													
tidal waters	0	0	0	0	0	0	0	0	0	0	0	0	0
non-tidal surface waters	47	45	52	32	31	44	56	62	30	50	50	50	46
groundwaters	33	35	45	26	25	40	46	55	20	48	38	44	38
all sources except tidal	80	80	97	58	56	84	102	116	50	97	88	94	84
all surface and groundwaters	80	80	97	58	56	84	102	117	50	97	88	94	84
Agriculture (excl. spray irrigation)													
tidal waters	0	0	0	0	0	0	0	0	0	0	0	0	0
non-tidal surface waters	11	6	3	11	3	2	2	2	2	3	3	2	1
groundwaters	31	14	14	14	9	13	22	22	23	23	23	23	25
all sources except tidal	42	21	16	25	13	15	24	25	25	24	26	25	26
all surface and groundwaters	42	21	16	25	13	15	24	25	25	25	26	25	26
Electricity supply industry (2)													
tidal waters	6,940	7,292	7,942	8,083	6,677	6,803	6,518	6,806	6,906	5,968	4,514	4,398	4,977
non-tidal surface waters	2,190	1,715	1,073	1,072	1,662	1,508	1,781	1,424	2,040	1,799	2,140	2,474	2,642
groundwaters	5	10	13	13	10	7	7	9	8	5	4	4	8
all sources except tidal	2,195	1,725	1,086	1,085	1,672	1,515	1,788	1,433	2,048	1,805	2,144	2,478	2,650
all surface and groundwaters	9,136	9,017	9,028	9,168	8,349	8,318	8,305	8,239	8,954	7,772	6,659	6,876	7,628
Other industry													
tidal waters	742	783	1,018	887	717	822	926	1,065	888	955	955	943	980
non-tidal surface waters	1,202	1,100	933	586	753	874	573	434	813	563	679	630	686
groundwaters	260	271	241	233	205	188	189	184	169	163	168	171	176
all sources except tidal	1,462	1,371	1,174	819	958	1,061	762	618	983	726	847	801	862
all surface and groundwaters	2,204	2,154	2,192	1,706	1,675	1,884	1,688	1,683	1,871	1,681	1,802	1,744	1,842
Fish farming, cress growing, amenity ponds													
tidal waters	0	0	0	0	0	0	0	0	0	0	0	0	0
non-tidal surface waters	1,269	1,115	1,105	1,013	850	768	871	679	813	785	794	718	608
groundwaters	140	141	152	151	133	143	135	129	113	119	128	123	113
all sources except tidal	1,409	1,256	1,257	1,164	983	911	1,007	808	926	902	922	841	722
all surface and groundwaters	1,409	1,256	1,257	1,164	983	911	1,007	808	926	903	922	841	722
Private water supply													
tidal waters	0	0	0	0	0	0	0	0	0	0	0	0	0
non-tidal surface waters	1	1	3	1	1	1	0	1	0	1	2	1	1
groundwaters	9	9	9	10	8	9	8	9	8	8	8	9	9
all sources except tidal	11	9	12	11	8	10	9	9	9	9	10	10	9
all surface and groundwaters	11	9	12	11	8	10	9	9	9	9	10	10	9
Other													
tidal waters	0	0	0	0	0	0	0	0	0	0	0	0	0
non-tidal surface waters	13	8	13	25	13	12	10	9	10	12	10	13	18
groundwaters	15	14	17	14	14	14	10	13	16	22	18	16	21
all sources except tidal	28	22	30	39	27	25	20	22	27	33	28	29	40
all surface and groundwaters	28	22	30	39	27	25	20	22	27	33	28	29	40
Total												b	
tidal waters	7,683	8,075	8,961	8,971	7,394	7,631	7,465	7,885	7,810	6,935	5,477	5,349	5,967
non-tidal surface waters	8,509	7,821	6,959	6,366	6,936	6,670	6,838	6,042	7,199	6,693	7,056	7,338	7,609
groundwaters	2,279	2,313	2,238	2,167	2,129	2,143	2,133	2,152	2,029	2,070	2,047	2,042	2,057
all sources except tidal	10,789	10,133	9,197	8,533	9,065	8,814	8,971	8,193	9,228	8,764	9,103	9,379	9,666
all surface and groundwaters	18,472	18,208	18,158	17,504	16,458	16,445	16,437	16,078	17,038	15,699	14,580	14,728	15,633

Notes:

Source: Environment Agency

1. Includes small amounts of non-agricultural spray irrigation

Contact: enviro.statistics@defra.gsi.gov.uk

2. The 'Electricity supply industry' category includes hydropower licences

b. Indicates a break in the series where information concerning abstractions in the country of England and the Dee/Wye regional charge areas (formerly the Wales regional charge area) has been amalgamated into the 'North West' and 'Midlands' regional charge areas respectively.

10.18 Estimates of remaining recoverable oil and gas reserves and resources, 2004 to 2015

Oil (million tonnes)

	Reserves						Range of undiscovered resources		Range of total reserves and resources		Expected level of reserves[3]			
	Proven	Probable	Proven plus probable	Possible	Contingent Resources	Maximum	Lower	Upper	Lower[1]	Upper[2]	Opening stocks	Extraction[4]	Other volume changes	Closing stocks
	K7MI	K7MJ	K7MK	K7ML	-	K7MM	K7MN	K7MO	K7MP	K7MQ	K7MR	K7MS	K7MT	K7MU
2004	533	283	816	512	-	1328	396	1830	1724	3158	857	-95	54	816
2005	516	300	816	451	-	1267	396	1581	1663	2848	816	-85	85	816
2006	479	298	777	478	-	1255	438	1637	1693	2892	816	-77	38	777
2007	452	328	780	399	-	1179	379	1577	1558	2756	777	-77	80	780
2008	408	361	769	360	-	1129	454	1561	1583	2690	780	-72	61	769
2009	378	390	768	343	-	1111	397	1477	1508	2588	769	-68	67	768
2010	374	377	751	342	-	1093	475	1374	1568	2467	768	-63	46	751
2011	413	374	788	319	-	1106	422	1321	1528	2427	751	-52	89	788
2012	405	405	811	253	-	1064	455	1342	1519	2406	788	-45	68	811
2013	404	342	746	338	-	1084	172	755	1257	1840	811	-41	-24	746
2014	374	342	716	344	-	1060	156	755	1216	1816	746	-40	10	716
2015	349	217	566	161	216	943	156	755	1099	1698	716	-45	-105	566

Gas (billion cubic metres)

	Reserves						Range of undiscovered resources		Range of total reserves and resources		Expected level of reserves[3]			
	Proven	Probable	Proven plus probable	Possible	Contingent Resources	Maximum	Lower	Upper	Lower[1]	Upper[2]	Opening stocks	Extraction[4]	Other volume changes	Closing stocks
	K7MV	K7MW	K7MX	K7MY	-	K7MZ	K7N2	K7N3	K7N4	K7N5	K7N6	K7N7	K7N8	K7N9
2004	531	296	827	343	-	1170	293	1245	1463	2415	905	-95	17	827
2005	481	247	728	278	-	1006	226	1035	1232	2041	827	-86	-13	728
2006	412	272	684	283	-	967	301	1049	1268	2016	728	-78	34	684
2007	343	304	647	293	-	940	280	1039	1220	1979	684	-70	33	647
2008	292	309	601	306	-	907	319	1043	1226	1950	647	-68	22	601
2009	256	308	564	276	-	840	300	949	1140	1789	601	-57	20	564
2010	253	267	520	261	-	781	363	1021	1144	1802	564	-55	10	520
2011	246	246	493	216	-	709	353	977	1062	1686	520	-43	16	493
2012	244	217	461	238	-	699	369	1010	1068	1709	493	-37	5	461
2013	241	211	452	198	-	650	133	581	783	1231	461	-34	26	452
2014	205	201	407	187	-	594	120	581	713	1174	452	-39	-7	407
2015	207	126	333	113	62	508	120	581	628	1089	407	-38	-36	333

Notes:

Source: Department for Business, Energy and Industrial Strategy (BEIS)and Oil and Gas Authority

All data refer to end of year. Components may not sum to totals due to rounding

For further details see https://www.ogauthority.co.uk/data-centre/data-downloads-and-publications/reserves-and-resources/

1. The lower end of the range of total reserves and resources has been calculated as the sum of maximum and the lower end of the range of undiscovered resources. The lower range of total reserves and resources have decreased due to a new "Yet to Find" (YTF) reporting method for the years 2013 to 2016.
2. The upper end of the range of total reserves and resources has been calculated as the sum of maximum and the upper end of the range of undiscovered resources. The upper range of total res
3. Expected reserves are the sum of proven and probable reserves.
4. The negative of extraction is shown here for the purposes of the calculation only. Of itself, extraction should be considered as a positive value.

10.19a Local Authority Collected Waste Generation from 2003/04 to 2015/16

England *Thousand tonnes*

Household waste from:	**2003/04**	**2004/05**	**2005/06**	**2006/07r**	**2007/08**	**2008/09r**	**2009/10**	**2010/11**	**2011/12**	**2012/13**	**2013/14**	**2014/15**	**2015/16**
Regular household collection	16,066	15,470	14,616	14,050	13,046	12,076	11,432	11,048	10,586	10,317	10,308	10,392	10,532
Other household sources	1,244	1,205	1,314	1,173	1,073	1,026	1,070	1,047	997	1,027	1,099	1,058	1,142
Civic amenity sites	3,616	3,198	2,726	2,576	2,434	2,086	1,765	1,635	1,470	1,477	1,568	1,597	1,700
Household recycling	4,521	5,785	6,796	7,976	8,735	9,146	9,398	9,724	9,846	9,759	9,980	10,117	10,075
Total household	**25,448**	**25,658**	**25,454**	**25,775**	**25,287**	**24,334**	**23,666**	**23,454**	**22,899**	**22,580**	**22,967**	**23,169**	**23,449**
Non household sources (excl. recycling)	2,650	2,795	2,289	2,408	2,250	2,063	1,999	1,882	1,654	1,558	1,600	1,617	1,585
Non household recycling	1,016	1,167	1,003	961	969	936	877	864	866	817	950	950	998
Total LA collected waste	**29,114**	**29,619**	**28,745**	**29,144**	**28,506**	**27,334**	**26,541**	**26,200**	**25,419**	**24,955**	**25,518**	**25,737**	**26,032**

Source: Department for Environment, Food & Rural Affairs

There has been a revision to 2008/09 to include asbestos in "Other household sources" instead of "Non household sources".

10.19b Waste managed (tonnes) by management method and year, 2012-13 onwards

Area: Wales

	2013-14	2014-15	2015-16	2016-17
Total Municipal Waste Collected/Generated	1557229	1543357.32	1592177.684	1589794.99
Total Waste Reused/Recycled/Composted (Statutory Target) (1)	846091	868079.46	958258.84	1014454.76
Non-Household Waste Reused/Recycled (2)	128310	141705.77	176763.1	163312.12
Non-Household Waste Composted (3)	13653	14346.36	13391.66	12320.87
Household Waste Reused/Recycled (4)	429863	430264.88	482303.1	541444.93
Household Waste Composted (5)	274265	281762.43	285800.99	297376.84
Waste sent for other recovery (6)	4532	4923.87	3937.44	1010.14
Other recovery: Recycling (7)	.	1488.15	781.57	855.89
Other recovery: Composting (8)	.	3435.72	3155.87	154.25
Waste Incinerated with Energy Recovery	89907	182961.26	301905.74	389599.30
Waste Incinerated without Energy Recovery	341	245.08	655.93	495.59
Waste Landfilled	587390	453497.37	288820.05	150984.28
Percentage of Waste Reused/Recycled/Composted (Statutory Target) (9)	54.333108	56.246175	60.185421	63.810414
Percentage of Non-Household Waste Reused/Recycled (10)	8.239625	9.181657	11.101971	10.272527
Percentage of Non-Household Waste Composted (11)	0.876877	0.929555	0.841091	0.774997
Percentage of Household Waste Reused/Recycled (12)	27.604254	27.878501	30.29204	34.057532
Percentage of Household Waste Composted (13)	17.612416	18.256461	17.95032	18.705358

Source: WasteDataFlow, Natural Resources Wales

1 Total waste reused/recycled/composted as defined by the Statutory Local Authority Recovery Target (LART)

2 Non-Household waste sent to be reused/recycled as defined by the Statutory Local Authority Recovery Target (LART)

3 Non-Household waste sent to be composted as defined by the Statutory Local Authority Recovery Target (LART)

4 Household waste sent to be reused/recycled as defined by the Statutory Local Authority Recovery Target (LART)

5 Household waste sent to be composted as defined by the Statutory Local Authority Recovery Target (LART)

6 Other waste sent for recycling and/or composting that is not included in the statutory target definition

7 Other waste sent for recycling that is not included in the statutory target definition

8 Other waste sent for composting that is not included in the statutory target definition

9 Total waste reused/recycled/composted (as defined by the Statutory Local Authority Recovery Target, LART), as a percentage of total municipal waste collected/generated

10 Non-Household waste sent to be reused/recycled (as defined by the Statutory Local Authority Recovery Target, LART), as a percentage of total municipal waste collected/generated

11 Non-Household waste sent to be composted (as defined by the Statutory Local Authority Recovery Target, LART), as a percentage of total municipal waste collected/generated

12 Household waste sent to be reused/recycled (as defined by the Statutory Local Authority Recovery Target, LART), as a percentage of total municipal waste collected/generated

13 Household waste sent to be composted (as defined by the Statutory Local Authority Recovery Target, LART), as a percentage of total municipal waste collected/generated

. The data item is not applicable.

10.19c Household waste - Summary data 2016, Scotland

Local Authority	2016 Generated (tonnes)	2016 Recycled (tonnes)	2016 *Percentage Recycled (%)*	2016 Other diversion from landfill* (tonnes)	2016 *Percentage Other diversion from Landfill (%)*	2016 Landfilled (tonnes)	2016 *Percentage Landfilled (%)*	2015 *Percentage Recycled (%)*
Aberdeen City	96,123	37,498	*39.0*	604	*0.6*	58,021	*60.4*	38.5
Aberdeenshire	131,863	57,305	*43.5*	1,564	*1.2*	72,995	*55.4*	43.7
Angus	58,847	33,371	*56.7*	10,206	*17.3*	15,270	*25.9*	59.2
Argyll and Bute	53,684	18,188	*33.9*	8,182	*15.2*	27,315	*50.9*	33.8
City of Edinburgh	193,333	86,318	*44.6*	3,424	*1.8*	103,590	*53.6*	42.3
Clackmannanshire	27,091	15,306	*56.5*	3,898	*14.4*	7,887	*29.1*	48.1
Dumfries and Galloway	79,805	21,291	*26.7*	26,541	*33.3*	31,975	*40.1*	27.1
Dundee City	67,998	22,861	*33.6*	40,499	*59.6*	4,638	*6.8*	33.3
East Ayrshire	56,433	30,063	*53.3*	5,935	*10.5*	20,437	*36.2*	53.0
East Dunbartonshire	55,852	27,085	*48.5*	5,909	*10.6*	22,858	*40.9*	50.7
East Lothian	50,874	26,337	*51.8*	86	*0.2*	24,451	*48.1*	51.4
East Renfrewshire	47,724	29,010	*60.8*	791	*1.7*	17,923	*37.6*	56.4
Falkirk	71,783	36,832	*51.3*	11,229	*15.6*	23,723	*33.0*	53.9
Fife	187,746	102,610	*54.7*	8,183	*4.4*	76,955	*41.0*	52.3
Glasgow City	216,873	54,552	*25.2*	5,983	*2.8*	156,337	*72.1*	26.0
Highland	130,959	58,232	*44.5*	995	*0.8*	71,733	*54.8*	44.5
Inverclyde	29,363	15,692	*53.4*	900	*3.1*	12,769	*43.5*	54.7
Midlothian	42,636	22,804	*53.5*	5,752	*13.5*	14,079	*33.0*	47.9
Moray	51,968	30,698	*59.1*	0	*0.0*	21,253	*40.9*	57.4
Na h-Eileanan Siar	14,959	3,607	*24.1*	1,929	*12.9*	9,423	*63.0*	21.2
North Ayrshire	63,838	35,309	*55.3*	1,916	*3.0*	26,615	*41.7*	56.0
North Lanarkshire	160,916	66,207	*41.1*	25,297	*15.7*	69,410	*43.1*	40.0
Orkney Islands†	10,349	2,007	*19.4*	4,997	*48.3*	2,880	*27.8*	19.2
Perth and Kinross	78,730	43,095	*54.7*	8,627	*11.0*	27,008	*34.3*	54.2
Renfrewshire	83,661	40,547	*48.5*	22,869	*27.3*	20,245	*24.2*	43.9
Scottish Borders	51,921	20,264	*39.0*	955	*1.8*	30,702	*59.1*	37.3
Shetland Islands	9,996	787	*7.9*	6,953	*69.6*	2,256	*22.6*	9.2
South Ayrshire	56,485	28,190	*49.9*	5,974	*10.6*	22,320	*39.5*	51.5
South Lanarkshire	152,533	80,818	*53.0*	0	*0.0*	71,715	*47.0*	49.0
Stirling	44,267	24,233	*54.7*	7,835	*17.7*	12,201	*27.6*	53.9
West Dunbartonshire	44,936	21,785	*48.5*	4,282	*9.5*	18,869	*42.0*	46.4
West Lothian	75,436	36,591	*48.5*	4,893	*6.5*	33,952	*45.0*	47.4
Total Scotland	**2,498,981**	**1,129,493**	***45.2***	**237,205**	***9.5***	**1,131,806**	***45.3***	**44.2**

Source: Scottish Environment Protection Agency (SEPA)

10.19c Household waste - Summary data 2016, Scotland

* Other waste diverted from landfill is the fate of waste material not reused, recycled or landfilled. It includes household waste treated by incineration, mechanical biological and heat treatment. It also includes composted wastes that do not reach the quality standards set by PAS 100/110. It also includes any Incinerator Bottom Ash and Metals recycled as a result of treatment, and excludes the residue from incineration which is landfilled. It also includes any weight loss during the treatment process. It does not include temporary storage of treated waste pending a recycling or disposal market.

† Includes treated waste sent to interim storage pending a recycling or disposal market. More waste will be recorded as generated than managed.

Please note local authorities report the management of waste in the same period when that waste is collected to avoid discrepancies with the total waste generated and managed. The figures are accurate at the time of publication. Data may be updated in accordance with SEPA's revision policy.

10.19d-i: Local authority collected (LAC) municipal waste sent for preparing for reuse, dry recycling, composting, energy recovery and landfill by district council and waste management group

Northern Ireland, 2015/16

Units: Tonnes
KPI (j)

Authority	LAC municipal waste									
	preparing for reuse	dry recycling	composting	preparing for reuse, dry recycling and composting	energy recovery rate (mixed residual LACMW)	energy recovery rate (specific streams e.g. wood)	recovery rate	landfill rate	un-classified	arisings
Antrim & Newtownabbey	14	21,235	19,887	41,137	2,977	5,133	8,109	35,231	581	85,058
Ards & North Down	117	21,113	20,046	41,275	337	5,294	5,631	52,812	51	99,770
Armagh City, Banbridge & Craigavon	96	26,381	23,624	50,101	31,308	2,058	33,366	19,158	332	102,957
Belfast	139	39,553	20,987	60,679	34,691	965	35,656	72,937	693	169,964
Causeway Coast & Glens	121	18,979	11,542	30,642	14,031	2,533	16,563	30,966	191	78,363
Derry City & Strabane	76	19,348	5,310	24,734	23,450	2,955	26,405	19,648	113	70,901
Fermanagh & Omagh	22	16,993	8,278	25,292	177	495	672	28,059	-60	53,963
Lisburn & Castlereagh	35	14,280	15,918	30,234	2,786	1,990	4,776	35,129	342	70,480
Mid & East Antrim	46	16,933	16,615	33,593	3,659	2,477	6,136	35,741	71	75,541
Mid Ulster	0	18,174	18,908	37,082	8,198	1,469	9,667	30,814	138	77,701
Newry, Mourne & Down	15	18,633	11,995	30,643	21,785	2,147	23,932	29,762	121	84,459
arc21	366	131,746	105,449	237,561	66,235	18,005	84,240	261,611	1,859	585,271
NWRWMG	197	38,327	16,852	55,377	37,481	5,488	42,969	50,615	305	149,265
Northern Ireland	682	231,622	173,110	405,414	143,398	27,515	170,913	390,256	2,574	969,157

Source: NIEA

Notes: The tonnage of waste sent for recycling includes recycling from both clean/source segregated collection sources (as shown in Table 5) and recycling from residual waste processes.

Unclassified waste is calculated as a residual amount of municipal waste after municipal waste sent for preparing for reuse, for dry recycling, composting, energy recovery and to landfill have been accounted for.

It is not extracted directly from the WasteDataFlow system. The majority of the total unclassified tonnage can be attributed to moisture and/or gaseous losses.

Small negative tonnages can arise in the unclassified column if more waste is sent for treatment in the year than was actually collected as is more likely at councils operating transfer stations.

10.19d-ii: Percentage of local authority collected (LAC) municipal waste sent for preparing for reuse, dry recycling, composting, energy recovery and landfill by district council and waste management group

Northern Ireland, 2015/16

Units: Percentages

				KPI (e2)				KPI(f)	
Authority	LAC municipal waste								
	preparing for reuse rate	dry recycling rate	composting rate	preparing for reuse, dry recycling and composting rate	energy recovery rate (mixed residual LACMW)	energy recovery rate (specific streams e.g. wood)	recovery rate	landfill rate	un-classified
Antrim & Newtownabbey	0.0	25.0	23.4	48.4	3.5	6.0	9.5	41.4	0.7
Ards & North Down	0.1	21.2	20.1	41.4	0.3	5.3	5.6	52.9	0.1
Armagh City, Banbridge & Craigavon	0.1	25.6	22.9	48.7	30.4	2.0	32.4	18.6	0.3
Belfast	0.1	23.3	12.3	35.7	20.4	0.6	21.0	42.9	0.4
Causeway Coast & Glens	0.2	24.2	14.7	39.1	17.9	3.2	21.1	39.5	0.2
Derry City & Strabane	0.1	27.3	7.5	34.9	33.1	4.2	37.2	27.7	0.2
Fermanagh & Omagh	0.0	31.5	15.3	46.9	0.3	0.9	1.2	52.0	-0.1
Lisburn & Castlereagh	0.1	20.3	22.6	42.9	4.0	2.8	6.8	49.8	0.5
Mid & East Antrim	0.1	22.4	22.0	44.5	4.8	3.3	8.1	47.3	0.1
Mid Ulster	0.0	23.4	24.3	47.7	10.6	1.9	12.4	39.7	0.2
Newry, Mourne & Down	0.0	22.1	14.2	36.3	25.8	2.5	28.3	35.2	0.1
arc21	0.1	22.5	18.0	40.6	11.3	3.1	14.4	44.7	0.3
NWRWMG	0.1	25.7	11.3	37.1	25.1	3.7	28.8	33.9	0.2
Northern Ireland	0.1	23.9	17.9	41.8	14.8	2.8	17.6	40.3	0.3

Source: NIEA

Notes: Rates calculated by dividing total tonnage of LAC municipal waste sent in each category by total LAC municipal waste arisings.

Unclassified waste is calculated as a residual amount of municipal waste after municipal waste sent for preparing for reuse, for dry recycling, composting, energy recovery and to landfill have been accounted for.

It is not extracted directly from the WasteDataFlow system. The majority of the total unclassified tonnage can be attributed to moisture and/or gaseous losses.

Small negative tonnages can arise in the unclassified column if more waste is sent for treatment in the year than was actually collected as is more likely at councils operating transfer stations.

10.19d-iii: Household waste sent for preparing for reuse, dry recycling, composting and landfill by district council and waste management group

Northern Ireland, 2015/16

Units: Tonnes

Authority	Household waste preparing for reuse	Household waste dry recycling	Household waste composting	Household waste preparing for reuse, dry recycling and composting	Household waste landfilled	Household waste arisings
Antrim & Newtownabbey	14	15,437	19,862	35,314	31,918	75,536
Ards & North Down	117	14,872	19,919	34,907	46,359	86,816
Armagh City, Banbridge & Craigavon	96	21,978	23,027	45,101	17,678	93,925
Belfast	139	35,957	20,536	56,632	56,552	141,537
Causeway Coast & Glens	121	14,994	11,542	26,657	27,046	68,767
Derry City & Strabane	76	17,119	5,308	22,503	19,177	67,526
Fermanagh & Omagh	22	14,567	8,278	22,867	26,782	50,220
Lisburn & Castlereagh	35	10,877	15,918	26,830	32,399	64,102
Mid & East Antrim	46	11,862	16,615	28,522	32,339	66,442
Mid Ulster	0	16,021	18,908	34,929	26,745	70,357
Newry, Mourne & Down	15	17,426	11,944	29,385	25,138	75,556
arc21	366	106,430	104,794	211,590	224,704	509,990
NWRWMG	197	32,112	16,850	49,159	46,224	136,293
Northern Ireland	682	191,108	171,857	363,647	342,133	860,786

Source: NIEA

Note: The tonnages of waste sent for preparing for reuse, for dry recycling, composting and landfill may not always equal the waste arisings because the recycling measures were defined to capture outputs from recycling processes which exclude energy recovery.

10.19d-iv: Percentage of household waste sent for preparing for reuse, dry recycling, composting and landfill by district council and waste management group

Northern Ireland, 2015/16

Units: Percentages

Authority	Household waste preparing for reuse rate	Household waste dry recycling rate	Household waste composting rate	KPI (a2) Household waste preparing for reuse, dry recycling and composting rate	KPI (b) Household waste landfill rate
Antrim & Newtownabbey	0.0	20.4	26.3	46.8	42.3
Ards & North Down	0.1	17.1	22.9	40.2	53.4
Armagh City, Banbridge & Craigavon	0.1	23.4	24.5	48.0	18.8
Belfast	0.1	25.4	14.5	40.0	40.0
Causeway Coast & Glens	0.2	21.8	16.8	38.8	39.3
Derry City & Strabane	0.1	25.4	7.9	33.3	28.4
Fermanagh & Omagh	0.0	29.0	16.5	45.5	53.3
Lisburn & Castlereagh	0.1	17.0	24.8	41.9	50.5
Mid & East Antrim	0.1	17.9	25.0	42.9	48.7
Mid Ulster	0.0	22.8	26.9	49.6	38.0
Newry, Mourne & Down	0.0	23.1	15.8	38.9	33.3
arc21	0.1	20.9	20.5	41.5	44.1
NWRWMG	0.1	23.6	12.4	36.1	33.9
Northern Ireland	0.1	22.2	20.0	42.2	39.7

Source: NIEA

Notes: Rates calculated by dividing total tonnage of household waste sent in each category by total household waste arisings. The percentages of waste sent for preparing for reuse, for dry recycling, composting and landfill may not equal 100% because the recycling measures were defined to capture outputs from recycling processes which exclude energy recovery.

10.19d-v: Household waste per capita and per household by district council and waste management group

Northern Ireland, 2015/16

Units: Kilogrammes per capita and tonnes per household

Authority	Household waste arisings	Population (2015)	Household waste arisings (kg per capita) KPI (p)	Housing stock (at Apr 2016)	Household waste arisings (tonnes per household) KPI (h)
Antrim & Newtownabbey	75,536	140,467	538	55,742	1.355
Ards & North Down	86,816	158,797	547	66,223	1.311
Armagh City, Banbridge & Craigavon	93,925	207,797	452	77,776	1.208
Belfast	141,537	338,907	418	145,863	0.970
Causeway Coast & Glens	68,767	143,148	480	56,139	1.225
Derry City & Strabane	67,526	149,473	452	57,912	1.166
Fermanagh & Omagh	50,220	115,311	436	44,438	1.130
Lisburn & Castlereagh	64,102	140,205	457	55,636	1.152
Mid & East Antrim	66,442	137,145	484	55,925	1.188
Mid Ulster	70,357	144,002	489	50,058	1.406
Newry, Mourne & Down	75,556	176,369	428	64,314	1.175
arc21	509,990	1,091,890	467	443,703	1.149
NWRWMG	136,293	292,621	466	114,051	1.195
Northern Ireland	860,786	1,851,621	465	730,026	1.179

Source: NIEA, NISRA, LPS

Notes: The population figures are NISRA mid-year population estimates for 2015.
The number of occupied households is estimated from the total housing stock adjusted for vacant properties using the 2011 Census.

10.20a Waste arisings from households (Million tonnes) UK, 2010 – 2016

Waste from households arisings (million tonnes)	2010	2011	2012	2013	2014	2015	2016
UK	27.0	26.8	26.4	25.9	26.8	26.7	27.3
England	22.1	22.2	22.0	21.6	22.4	22.2	22.8
Scotland	2.6	2.5	2.4	2.3	2.3	2.4	2.4
Wales	1.3	1.3	1.3	1.3	1.3	1.3	1.3
NI	0.8	0.8	0.8	0.8	0.8	0.8	0.9

Source: Department for Environment, Food & Rural Affairs

1. The 'waste from households' calculation was first published by Defra in May 2014. It was introduced for statistical purposes to provide a harmonised UK indicator to be reported against the Waste Framework Directive (2008/98/EC). It is calculated on a calendar year basis by each of the four UK countries using almost identical methodologies.
2. The waste from household measure is a narrower measure than the 'household waste' measure which was previously used in England. Waste from households excludes waste not considered to have come directly from households, such as recycling from street bins, parks and grounds.

3. Waste arising from households in the UK increased by 2 per cent between 2015 and 2016 to 27.3 million tonnes.

Notes: Waste from households' includes waste from: Regular household collection, Civic amenity sites, 'Bulky waste' 'Other household waste'. It does not include street cleaning/sweeping, gully emptying, separately collected healthcare waste, asbestos waste. 'Waste from households' is a narrower measure than 'municipal waste' and 'council collected waste'.

10.20b Waste from households, England, 2011 to 2016 *(Waste Prevention Metric)*

	2011	2012	2013	2014	2015	2016
Total waste generated from households (Million tonnes)	22.2	22	21.6	22.4	22.2	22.8
Waste generated (kg per person)	421	412	402	413	406	412

1. Total waste from households amounted to 22.8 million tonnes in 2016, an increase of 2.5 per cent on 2015.
2. In 2016 the amount of 'other organics' sent for recycling has increased by 3.1 per cent to 3.8 million tonnes.
3. Separate food waste collected for recycling increased by 15.0 per cent in 2016 to 353 thousand tonnes from 307 thousand tonnes in 2015
4. This is equivalent to 412 kg per person, up from 406 kg per person in 2015, but similar to 2014 figure of 413 kg per person.
5. A breakdown of the previous measure of household waste covering national, regional and local authorities can be downloaded on the gov.uk website.

Source: Department for Environment, Food & Rural Affairs, Office for National Statistics

10.20c Waste from households, UK and country split, 2010 -2016

thousand tonnes and % rate

Year	Measure	UK	England	NI	Scotland	Wales
2010	Arisings ('000 tonnes)	26,954	22,131	829	2,649	1,344
	Of which recycled (excl. IBAm) ('000 tonnes)	10,878	9,112	314	861	591
	Recycling rate (excl. IBAm)	**40.4%**	**41.2%**	**37.8%**	**32.5%**	**44.0%**
2011	Arisings ('000 tonnes)	26,792	22,170	810	2,482	1,329
	Of which recycled (excl. IBAm) ('000 tonnes)	11,492	9,596	324	921	651
	Recycling rate (excl. IBAm)	**42.9%**	**43.3%**	**40.0%**	**37.1%**	**49.0%**
2012	Arisings ('000 tonnes)	26,428	21,956	783	2,383	1,306
	Of which recycled (excl. IBAm) ('000 tonnes)	11,594	9,684	319	911	681
	Recycling rate (excl. IBAm)	**43.9%**	**44.1%**	**40.7%**	**38.2%**	**52.1%**
2013	Arisings ('000 tonnes)	25,929	21,564	781	2,311	1,274
	Of which recycled (excl. IBAm) ('000 tonnes)	11,433	9,523	324	916	669
	Recycling rate (excl. IBAm)	**44.1%**	**44.2%**	**41.5%**	**39.6%**	**52.5%**
2014	Arisings ('000 tonnes)	26,797	22,355	808	2,349	1,285
	Of which recycled (excl. IBAm) ('000 tonnes)	12,035	10,025	344	962	704
	Recycling rate (excl. IBAm)	**44.9%**	**44.8%**	**42.5%**	**41.0%**	**54.8%**
2015	Arisings ('000 tonnes)	26,677	22,225	821	2,354	1,278
	Of which recycled (excl. IBAm) ('000 tonnes)	11,789	9,746	344	989	709
	Recycling rate (excl. IBAm)	**44.2%**	**43.9%**	**42.0%**	**42.0%**	**55.5%**
	Of which recycled (incl. IBAm)('000 tonnes)	11,891	9,843	z	990	713
	Recycling rate (incl. IBAm)	**44.6%**	**44.3%**	**z**	**42.1%**	**55.8%**
2016	Arisings ('000 tonnes)	27,306	22,770	850	2,378	1,307
	Of which recycled (excl. IBAm) ('000 tonnes)	12,192	10,067	366	1,017	741
	Recycling rate (excl. IBAm)	**44.6%**	**44.2%**	**43.0%**	**42.8%**	**56.7%**
	Of which recycled (incl. IBAm)('000 tonnes)	12,352	10,219	z	1,018	749
	Recycling rate (incl. IBAm)	**45.2%**	**44.9%**	**z**	**42.8%**	**57.3%**

z = Not applicable - see Notes for users

Source: Waste Data Flow

Recycling rate = 'Recycled' as a percentage of 'Arisings'

IBAm = Incineration bottom ash metal

Notes for users:

1) UK estimates for 'Waste from households' have been calculated in accordance with the Waste Framework Directive.

2) 'Waste from households' includes waste from:
   - Regular household collection
   - Civic amenity sites
   - 'Bulky waste'
   - 'Other household waste'

3) 'Waste from households' excludes waste from:
   - Street cleaning/sweeping
   - Gully emptying
   - Separately collected healthcare waste
   - Soil, Rubble, Plasterboard & Asbestos wastes

4) Whilst the general approach is consistent across UK countries, aggregation method and the wording of some questions completed by Local Authorities varies.

10.20c Waste from households, UK and country split, 2010 -2016

5) Users should be aware that individual UK countries other than England publish household recycling estimates using alternative measures and as such may differ from the estimates published here.

6) Local Authorities in England may also use an alternative measure to 'Waste from Households'.

7) a) The NI waste from households data previously reported in Dec 2015 used the England WfH calculation for the years 2013 and 2014.

b) A new WfH calculation specific to NI has been used for 2015 which now correctly excludes certain Construction & Demolition wastes from the Recycled tonnage.

c) In order to provide a uniform comparison ALL previous years for NI have been recalculated.

8) England figure for 2015 revised in February 2018 due to methodological changes.

9) Incineration bottom ash (IBA) metals are now included within the recycling rate calculations, though the date from which these have been included varies for each country:

England and Scotland have both included IBA metals for data from 2015 onwards, when Q100 was introduced. England data only includes IBA metals from April 2015, when Q100 came into full use by all local authorities.

For Wales, Q100 was introduced in 2012. Wales figures for 2012-2014 have been revised in this release to remove IBA metals. These are included for 2015 and 2016 in line with the other UK countries.

NI did not have any incinerators that burnt municipal waste collected by local authorities in this period, so no WfH IBA metal was counted as recycled.

10.20d Packaging waste and recycling / recovery, split by material, UK

	Packaging waste arising (thousand tonnes)		Total recovered / recycled (thousand tonnes)		Achieved recovery / recycling rate (%)		EU target recovery / recycling rate (%)	
	2014	2015	2014	2015	2014	2015	2014	2015
Metal	736	736	428	440	58.2%	59.8%	50.0%	50.0%
of which: Aluminium	177	177	73	76	41.0%	42.9%	n/a	z
of which: Steel	559	559	356	364	63.7%	65.1%	n/a	z
Paper and cardboard	4,749	4,749	3,470	3,667	73.1%	77.2%	60.0%	60.0%
Glass	2,399	2,399	1,613	1,577	67.2%	65.7%	60.0%	60.0%
Plastic	2,220	2,260	842	891	37.9%	39.4%	22.5%	22.5%
Wood	1,310	1,310	412	375	31.4%	28.6%	15.0%	15.0%
Other materials	23	23	0	0	0.0%	0.0%	n/a	z
Total (for recycling)	**11,436**	**11,476**	**6,765**	**6,950**	**59.2%**	**60.6%**	**55.0%**	**55.0%**
Energy from Waste		z	566	476	4.9%	4.1%	n/a	z
Total (for recycling and recovery)	**11,436**	**11,476**	**7,331**	**7,427**	**64.1%**	**64.7%**	**60.0%**	**60.0%**

Source: Defra Statistics

z = Not applicable

1) Theses statistics have been calculated to fulfil a reporting requirement to Eurostat at UK level in relation to the EC Packaging and Packaging Waste Directive (94/62/EC). The 2014 figures were submitted to Eurostat in June 2016. The 2013 figures were submitted to Eurostat in June

2) Figures are compiled from the National Packaging Waste Database (NPWD) and industry reports.

3) Only includes obligated packaging producers (handle 50 tonnes of packaging materials or packaging and have a turnover more than £2 million a year)

4) "Recovery' in these tables refer specifically to waste used for energy recovery.

5) The recovery figure includes waste sent to facilities that did not meet the R1 recovery energy efficiency thresholds, but were considered eligible based on the Packaging Directive, which states "'energy recovery' shall mean the use of combustible packaging waste as a means to generate energy through direct incineration with or without other waste but with recovery of the heat".

10.21 CIEH Survey of Local Authority Noise Enforcement Activity 2014-15

England and Wales - Data represents 130 (37%) of 348 local authorities

	INDUSTRY		COMMERCE / LEISURE			RESIDENTIAL			CONSTRUCTION ETC	VME's	TOTAL'S	
	Agricultural Premises	Industrial / Warehousing / Distribution Premises	"On"-licensed Premises e.g. Pubs, Clubs, Restaurants	Commercial Premises e.g. Offices, Shops, Public transport	Leisure Premises e.g. Sports Facilities, Funfairs	Single Family House / Bungalow	Flats / Maisonettes	Other Residential e.g. Hostels, HMOs, Boarding Schools	Construction / Demolition Sites	Vehicles, Machinery and Equipment in Streets	SUM OF COLUMNS [4]	TOTAL OF ALL COMPLAINTS [5]
COMPLAINTS												
Number of Noise Complaints Received in Year	635	2,081	7,292	6,353	2,242	60,723	17,895	1,965	4,956	3,114	107,256	115,315
Number of Noise Complaints Resolved in Year	600	1,668	6,045	5,335	1,852	51,994	14,693	1,490	4,085	2,764	90,526	94,974
Number of Noise Incidents Complained-of	565	1,602	5,483	5,057	1,728	49,656	12,247	1,369	3,926	2,547	84,180	87,954
Number of Noise Incidents Per Million Population	45	91	312	287	100	2,817	717	92	225	152	4,838	4,881
Incidents Confirmed as Potentially Actionable [1, 2]	139	459	1,640	1,625	461	15,494	3,056	358	1,322	652	25,230	
STATUTORY NUISANCES REMEDIED WITHOUT A NOTICE [3, 6]												
Nuisance Ceased and Not Likely to Recur	21	69	261	241	55	3,228	583	51	119	89	4,717	
Referred to Other Services		32	52	52	40	498	106	12	19	40	851	
Resolved Informally	60	167	573	705	144	5,232	932	154	644	181	8,792	
No Action Possible	20	56	213	178	92	2,241	471	56	114	97	3,538	
NOTICES SERVED [6]												
S.80 EPA 1990 Abatement Notice	4	14	152	92	28	776	263	27	14	37	1,407	1,515
S.60 & S.61 CoPA 1974 Control of Construction Noise									185	1	186	201
Noise Act 1996 Warning Notice			1			22	2	1			26	65
Noise Act 1996 Fixed Penalty							1				1	1
S.80(4A) EPA 1990 Fixed Penalty (Lond)			4	1		2	2				9	9
APPEALS AGAINST NOTICES [6]												
Number of Appeals Allowed in Whole or in Part			3	1	2		1				7	
PROSECUTIONS BEGUN [6]												
Breach of Abatement Notice	1		18	3	1	91	43	3	3	6	169	171
Breach of Restriction on, or Prior Consent for, Construction Noise									2		2	5
Noise Act 1996							1					2
Convictions Gained	1		3	1	1	44	11		3	2	66	
OTHER REMEDIES [6]												
Nuisance Remedied by the LA in Default			4	5		48	5	1	1	6	70	71
Number of Seizures			3	1		50	29				83	

[1] Incidents Confirmed as Potentially Actionable includes all those 'triggers' giving rise to formal enforcement power (described previously as "incidents confirmed as statutory nuisances etc")

[2] The sum of actions taken to resolve nuisances may exceed the Incidents Confirmed as Potentially Actionable figure because not all local authorities could provide data on incidents and more than one formal action may be taken to resolve a nuisance

[3] "Nuisances" here means statutory nuisances

[4] The sum of columns value is calculated, information provided by local authorities providing sub-total data only is not included here

[5] The Total of all Complaints column includes noise activity unaccounted for in previous columns

[6] Figures reported from 2005-06 may seem lower than previous years as they have not been subject to a 'grossing' calculation. Before 2005-06, where responding authorities were not able to provide data on the questions concerning outcome of noise incidents, estimates were made by pro-rating on number of noise incidents complained of

Source: Chartered Institute of Environmental Health.

Website: http://www.cieh.org

Note: The last year for which data was collected and analysed was 2014/15. However, CIEH have relaunched the noise survey this year (2019) after making several changes, with the aim of improving the response rate. The survey is open until July 31st and they plan to publish the results in the Autumn of 2019.

10.22: Government revenue from environmental taxes in the UK, 1997 to 2017

£ million

Environmental tax	2005	2006	2007	2008	2009	2010	2011	2012	2013	2014	2015	2016
Energy taxes	**24,666**	**24,859**	**26,035**	**26,503**	**27,731**	**29,114**	**29,336**	**29,795**	**31,132**	**32,518**	**34,012**	**35,255**
Tax on Hydrocarbon oils[1,2]	23,346	23,448	24,512	24,790	25,894	27,013	26,923	26,703	26,697	27,094	27,415	27,989
Climate Change Levy[3]	747	711	690	717	693	666	675	624	1,098	1,506	1,752	1,881
Fossil Fuel Levy	0	0	0	0	0	0	0	0	0	0	0	0
Gas Levy	0	0	0	0	0	0	0	0	0	0	0	0
Hydro-Benefit	10	0	0	0	0	0	0	0	0	0	0	0
Renewable Energy Obligations	563	700	833	996	1,099	1,243	1,423	1,842	2,391	2,931	3,691	4,479
Emmisions Trading Scheme (EU-ETS)	0	0	0	0	45	192	315	278	339	418	493	386
Carbon Reduction Commitment	0	0	0	0	0	0	0	348	607	569	661	520
Transport taxes	**5,899**	**6,233**	**7,667**	**7,853**	**8,099**	**8,910**	**9,597**	**10,108**	**10,534**	**10,854**	**10,869**	**11,043**
Air Passenger Duty	896	961	1,883	1,876	1,800	2,094	2,605	2,766	2,960	3,154	3,119	3,150
Rail Franchise Premia	98	125	244	285	496	792	993	1,275	1,275	1,501	1,611	1,656
Northern Ireland Driver Vehicle Agency	0	0	15	19	18	16	16	16	16	16	16	16
Motor vehicle duties paid by businesses	1,204	1,245	1,288	1,259	1,266	1,279	1,539	1,679	1,789	1,865	2,076	2,205
Motor vehicle duty paid by households	3,558	3,765	4,096	4,265	4,364	4,561	4,281	4,201	4,312	4,110	3,823	3,784
Boat Licenses	0	0	0	0	0	0	0	0	0	0	0	0
Vehicle Registration Tax	143	137	141	134	122	123	120	125	138	151	169	171
Air Travel Operators Tax	0	0	0	15	33	45	43	46	44	57	55	61
Pollution/Resources taxes	**1,080**	**1,145**	**1,236**	**1,308**	**1,137**	**1,375**	**1,403**	**1,379**	**1,494**	**1,506**	**1,403**	**1,450**
Landfill Tax	733	804	877	954	842	1,065	1,090	1,094	1,191	1,143	1,028	1,024
Fishing Licenses	20	20	20	20	20	20	23	21	21	21	21	21
Aggregates levy	327	321	339	334	275	290	290	264	282	342	354	405
Total environmental taxes	**31,645**	**32,237**	**34,938**	**35,664**	**36,967**	**39,399**	**40,336**	**41,282**	**43,160**	**44,878**	**46,284**	**47,748**
Total taxes and social contributions	462,167	491,036	517,355	521,308	491,236	527,465	556,950	559,333	578,930	598,690	622,076	658,475
As a percentage of total taxes and social contributions (%)	**6.9**	**6.6**	**6.8**	**6.8**	**7.5**	**7.5**	**7.2**	**7.4**	**7.5**	**7.5**	**7.4**	**7.3**
Gross Domestic Product (GDP)	1,386,386	1,463,435	1,536,565	1,572,467	1,529,536	1,579,877	1,635,062	1,685,225	1,752,554	1,837,062	1,888,737	1,963,311
As a percentage of GDP (%)	**2.3**	**2.2**	**2.3**	**2.3**	**2.4**	**2.5**	**2.5**	**2.5**	**2.5**	**2.4**	**2.5**	**2.4**

Source: Office for National Statistics

Notes

1. Includes unleaded petrol (including super unleaded), leaded petrol, lead replacement petrol, ultra low suplhur petrol, diesel and ultra low sulphur diesel.
2. Duty incentives have concentrated production on ultra low sulphur varieties.
3. Includes Carbon Price Floor from 2013.
4. All data are presented in current prices i.e. not adjusted for inflation.
5. Totals may not sum due to rounding.

this page is intentionally blank

Chapter 11

Housing

Housing

Permanent dwellings (Table 11.1, 11.3)

Local housing authorities include: the Commission for the New Towns and New Towns Development Corporations; Communities Scotland; and the Northern Ireland Housing Executive. The figures shown for housing associations include dwellings provided by housing associations other than the Communities Scotland and the Northern Ireland Housing Executive and include those provided or authorised by government departments for the families of police, prison staff, the Armed Forces and certain other services.

Mortgage possession actions by region (Table 11.6)

The table shows mortgage possession actions in the county courts of England and Wales and excludes a small number of mortgage actions in the High Court.

A claimant begins an action for an order for possession of a property by issuing a claim in the county court, either by using the Possession Claim Online system or locally through a county court. In mortgage possession cases, the usual procedure is for the claim being issued to be given a hearing date before a district judge. The court, following a judicial hearing, may grant an order for possession immediately. This entitles the claimants to apply for a warrant to have the defendant evicted. However, even where a warrant for possession is issued, the parties can still negotiate a compromise to prevent eviction.

Frequently the court grants the claimant possession but suspends the operation of the order. Provided the defendant complies with the terms of suspension, which usually require the defendant to pay the current mortgage instalments plus some of the accrued arrears, the possession order cannot be enforced.

The mortgage possession figures do not indicate how many houses have actually been repossessed through the courts. Repossessions can occur without a court order being made while not all court orders result in repossession.

A new mortgage pre-action protocol (MPAP), approved by the Master of the Rolls, was introduced for possession claims in the County Courts with effect from 19 November 2008. The MPAP gives clear guidance on what the courts expect lenders and borrowers to have done prior to a claim being issued.

Evidence from administrative records from Qtr4 2008 suggests that this date coincided with a fall of around 50% in the daily and weekly numbers of new mortgage repossession claims being issued in the courts.

It therefore seems highly likely that the launch of the MPAP has led to a fall in the number of new claims being issued since introduction of MPAP (19th November to 31st December 2008).

Mortgage possession orders are typically made (where necessary) around 8 weeks after the corresponding claims are issued.

Households in Temporary Accommodation under homelessness provisions (Tables 11.7, 11.8, 11.9)

Comprises households in accommodation arranged by local authorities pending enquiries or after being accepted as owed a main homeless duty under the 1996 Act (includes residual cases awaiting re-housing under the 1985 Act). Excludes "homeless at home" cases. The data shown for Wales includes "homeless at home" cases.

11.1a Dwelling stock: by tenure[1], England[2 3]

Thousands of dwellings

	Owner Occupied	Rented Privately or with a job or business	Rented from Private Registered Providers	Rented from Local Authorities	Other public sector dwellings	**All Dwellings**
31 March [3]						
2000	14,600	2,089	1,273	3,012	101	**21,075**
2001	14,735	2,133	1,424	2,812	103	**21,207**
2002	14,846	2,197	1,492	2,706	112	**21,354**
2003 [4]	14,752	2,549	1,651	2,457	104	**21,513**
2004 [4]	14,986	2,578	1,702	2,335	83	**21,684**
2005 [4]	15,100	2,720	1,802	2,166	82	**21,870**
2006 [4]	15,052	2,987	1,865	2,087	82	**22,073**
2007 [4]	15,093	3,182	1,951	1,987	75	**22,288**
2008 [4]	15,067	3,443	2,056	1,870	74	**22,511**
2009 [4]	14,968	3,705	2,128	1,820	74	**22,694**
2010 [4]	14,895	3,912	2,180	1,786	66	**22,839**
2011 [4]	14,827	4,105	2,255	1,726	63	**22,976**
2012 [4] P	14,754	4,286	2,304	1,693	75	**23,111**
2013 [4] P	14,685	4,465	2,331	1,682	73	**23,236**
2014 [4] P	14,674	4,623	2,343	1,669	64	**23,372**
2015 [4] PR	14,684	4,773	2,387	1,643	55	**23,543**
2016 [4] PR	14,801	4,832	2,430	1,612	57	**23,733**

Source: Department for Communities and Local Government

Contact: 0303 44 41864

E-Mail: housing.statistics@communities.gsi.gov.uk

1. For detailed definitions of all tenures, see Definitions of housing terms in Housing Statistics home page.
2. Figures for census years are based on census output.
3. Series from 1992 to 2001 for England has been adjusted so that the 2001 total dwelling estimate matches the 2001 Census. Series from 2002 to 2011 for England has been adjusted so that the 2011 total dwelling estimate matches the 2011 Census. Estimates from 2002 are based on local authority and Private Registered Provider (housing association) dwelling counts, the Labour Force Survey and, from 2003, the English Housing Survey. Estimates may not be strictly comparable between periods.
4. From 2003 the figures for owner-occupied and the private rental sector for England have been produced using a new improved methodology as detailed in the dwelling stock release. Previous to this vacancy was not accounted for.

R- Revised from previous publication

P - Provisional

Data for earlier years are less reliable and definitions may not be consistent throughout the series Stock estimates are expressed to the nearest thousand but should not be regarded as accurate to the last digit. Components may not sum to totals due to rounding.

11.1b Dwelling stock: by tenure[1,2], Wales

Thousands of dwellings

	Owner Occupied	Rented Privately or with a job or business	Rented from Housing Associations	Rented from Local Authorities	**All Dwellings**
31 March					
2000 [5]	914	106	54	193	**1,267**
2001 [5]	941	90	55	188	**1,275**
2002 [5]	957	89	57	183	**1,285**
2003 [5]	966	97	57	176	**1,296**
2004 [5]	979	104	64	160	**1,307**
2005 [5]	989	109	65	156	**1,319**
2006 [5]	997	113	66	154	**1,331**
2007 [5]	1,002	122	67	153	**1,343**
2008 [5]	1,001	135	89	130	**1,355**
2009 [5]	989	157	107	113	**1,366**
2010 [5]	984	170	110	111	**1,375**
2011 [5]	981	180	134	89	**1,384**
2012 [5]	977	189	135	88	**1,389**
2013 [5]	983	188	135	88	**1,394**
2014 [5]	981	196	135	88	**1,400**
2015 [5]	974	208	136	88	**1,406**
2016 [5 R]	986	202	137	87	**1,413**

Source: Welsh Assembly Government

Contact: 0303 44 41864

E-Mail: housing.statistics@communities.gsi.gov.uk

1. For detailed definitions of all tenures, see Definitions of housing terms in Housing Statistics home page.
2. Owner-occupied tenure includes owner-occupied, intermediate and other.
3. April data for census years are based on census output.
4. Data for years 1969 to 1990 sourced from Department of Environment publications:
   Housing and Construction Statistics, 1967-1979, 1977-1987,1980-1990 and 1990-1997.
5. The tenure split between owner-occupied and privately rented dwellings has been calculated from 1997 onwards using information from the Labour Force Survey. These figures were revised in January 2011 following a re-weighting of the Labour Force Survey data.

R - Revised

P - Provisional

These data are produced and published separately by the Welsh Assembly Government, and although the figures in this table are correct at the time of its latest update they may be superseded before the next update. Data for earlier years are less reliable and definitions may not be consistent throughout the series. Stock estimates are expressed to the nearest thousand but should not be regarded as accurate to the last digit. Components may not sum to totals due to rounding.

11.1c Dwelling stock: by tenure[1,2,3,4,5], Scotland

Thousands of dwellings

	Owner Occupied	Rented Privately or with a job or business	Rented from Housing Associations	Rented from Local Authorities	**All Dwellings**
31 December[4]					
2000	1,472	155	137	557	**2,322**
31 March[4]					
2001	1,439	181	139	553	**2,312**
2002	1,477	179	143	531	**2,329**
2003	1,505	188	238	416	**2,347**
2004	1,513	213	251	389	**2,367**
2005	1,536	225	251	374	**2,387**
2006	1,559	234	251	362	**2,406**
2007	1,562	259	261	346	**2,428**
2008	1,592	259	269	330	**2,451**
2009	1,590	285	268	326	**2,469**
2010	1,584	303	272	323	**2,482**
2011	1,580	320	275	320	**2,495**
2012	1,545	366	277	319	**2,508**
2013	1,537	389	277	318	**2,521**
2014	1,545	394	277	318	**2,534**
2015	1,552	402	278	317	**2,549**
2016	1,558	414	278	317	**2,567**

Source: Scottish Government

Contact: 0303 44 41864

E-Mail: housing.statistics@communities.gsi.gov.uk

1. For detailed definitions of all tenures, see Definitions of housing terms in Housing Statistics home page
2. April data for census years are based on census output
3. Data for years 1969 to 1989 sourced from Department of Environment publications: Housing and Construction Statistics, 1967-1979, 1977-1987,1980-1990 and 1990-1997.
4. Estimates from 1990 onwards are based on the Census (1991, 2001, 2011), council tax records and exemptions, social sector stock counts, and private tenure splits from the Scottish Household Survey and are not strictly comparable with earlier figures. These are not all collected for the same timescales and may not be exact counts, even rounded to the nearest thousand.
5. In order to include vacant private sector dwellings in table 107, estimates for vacant private sector stock in the Scottish statistics have been apportioned according to the % of occupied dwellings for the private sector tenures.

R- Revised from previous publication

P- Provisional

These data are produced and published separately by the Scottish Government, and although the figures in this table are correct at the time of its latest update they may be superseded before the next update. Data for earlier years are less reliable and definitions may not be consistent throughout the series. Stock estimates are expressed to the nearest thousand but should not be regarded as accurate to the last digit. Components may not sum to totals due to rounding.

11.1d Household Tenure 2008-09 to 2016-17[1,2,3,4,5] Northern Ireland

All households *Percentages*

Tenure	2008-09	2009-10	2010-11	2011-12	2012-13	2013-14	2014-15	2015-16	2016-17
Owned outright	36	36	35	35	36	38	37	37	39
Owned with mortgage[2]	33	34	33	31	30	29	31	28	27
Rented- NIHE[3]	14	13	12	14	12	12	11	13	13
Rented other[4]	16	16	19	19	20	19	20	21	20
rented from housing association	..	..	..	..	*4*	*3*	*4*	*4*	*4*
rented privately	..	..	..	..	*16*	*16*	*16*	*17*	*16*
Rent free[5]	1	2	1	1	1	1	1	1	1
Bases=100%	**2,474**	**2,761**	**2,718**	**2,778**	**2,710**	**2,736**	**2,521**	**2,494**	**2,532**

Source: Continuous Household Survey

1. See Appendix 1: Data Sources - Supply at https://www.communities-ni.gov.uk/sites/default/files/publications/communities/ni-housing-stats-16-17-appendix1.docx
2. Includes properties being purchased through the co-ownership scheme.
3. NIHE - Northern Ireland Housing Executive
4. Includes properties which are rented from a housing association, rented privately.
5. Includes squatting and rent free

11.2 Dwelling stock: by tenure[1], Great Britain

Thousands of dwellings

	Owner Occupied	Rented Privately or with a job or business	Rented from Housing Associations	Rented from Local Authorities	Other public sector dwellings	All Dwellings
1 April [2]						
1981	12,020	2,354	454	6,127	..	**20,954**
31 December [3]						
1981	11,936	2,288	468	6,388	..	**21,077**
1982	12,357	2,201	480	6,196	..	**21,233**
1983	12,740	2,121	497	6,060	..	**21,419**
1984	13,099	2,040	516	5,959	..	**21,615**
1985	13,440	1,963	537	5,863	..	**21,803**
1986	13,790	1,885	551	5,776	..	**22,002**
1987	13,968	2,139	586	5,599	..	**22,293**
1988	14,424	2,077	614	5,412	..	**22,527**
1989	14,832	2,069	652	5,190	..	**22,743**
1990	15,099	2,123	702	5,015	..	**22,940**
31 March [3,4]						
1991	15,155	1,990	701	4,966	167	**22,979**
1992	15,367	2,058	733	4,879	151	**23,190**
1993	15,523	2,120	811	4,759	153	**23,366**
1994	15,695	2,184	884	4,634	150	**23,546**
1995	15,869	2,255	976	4,496	145	**23,739**
1996	16,013	2,332	1,078	4,369	141	**23,931**
1997	16,215	2,361	1,132	4,273	132	**24,113**
1998	16,461	2,367	1,205	4,140	121	**24,296**
1999	16,734	2,324	1,319	3,983	110	**24,469**
2000	16,949	2,350	1,458	3,788	101	**24,645**
2001	17,115	2,404	1,618	3,553	103	**24,794**
2002	17,280	2,465	1,692	3,420	112	**24,968**
2003 [5]	17,223	2,834	1,946	3,049	104	**25,156**
2004 [5]	17,478	2,895	2,017	2,884	83	**25,358**
2005 [5]	17,625	3,054	2,118	2,696	82	**25,576**
2006 [5]	17,608	3,334	2,182	2,603	82	**25,810**
2007 [5]	17,657	3,563	2,279	2,486	75	**26,059**
2008 [5]	17,660	3,837	2,414	2,330	74	**26,317**
2009 [5]	17,547	4,147	2,503	2,259	74	**26,529**
2010 [5]	17,463	4,385	2,562	2,220	66	**26,696**
2011 [5]	17,388	4,605	2,664	2,135	63	**26,855**
2012 [5]	17,276	4,841	2,716	2,100	75	**27,008**
2013 [5]	17,205	5,042	2,743	2,088	73	**27,151**
2014	17,200	5,213	2,755	2,075	64	**27,306**
2015 R	17,210	5,383	2,801	2,048	55	**27,498**

Source: Ministry of Housing, Communities and Local Government
Welsh Assembly Government, Scottish Government
Department for Social Development (Northern Ireland)
Contact: 0303 44 41864
E-Mail: housing.statistics@Communities.gsi.gov.uk

1. For detailed definitions of all tenures, see Definitions of housing terms in Housing Statistics home page. 'Other public sector dwellings' figures are currently only available for England.
2. Figures for census years are based on census output
3. Data for years 1969 to 1990 sourced from Department of Environment publications:
Housing and Construction Statistics, 1967-1979, 1977-1987,1980-1990 and 1990-1997.
Great Britain totals from 2002 are derived by summing country totals at 31st March.
For 1991 to 2001 Scotland stock levels from the year before is added into the UK total.
4. Series from 1992 to 2011 for England has been adjusted so that the 2001 and 2011 total dwelling estimate matches the 2001 and 2011 Census. Estimates from 2002 are based on local authority and housing association dwelling counts, the Labour Force Survey and, from 2003, the English Housing Survey. Estimates may not be strictly comparable between periods.
5. From 2003 the figures for owner-occupied and the private rental sector for England have been produced using a new improved methodology as detailed in the dwelling stock release. Previous to this vacancy was not accounted for.

R- Revised from previous publication
P- Provisional

Data for earlier years are less reliable and definitions may not be consistent throughout the series. Stock estimates are expressed to the nearest thousand but should not be regarded as accurate to the last digit. Components may not sum to totals due to rounding.

11.3 House building: permanent dwellings completed, by tenure[1] and country[2, 3]

Number of dwellings

	Financial Year		United Kingdom	England	Wales	Scotland	Northern Ireland
All Dwellings							
	1994-95	R	195,580	157,970	9,070	21,810	6,730
	1995-96	R	197,710	154,600	9,170	24,690	9,250
	1996-97	R	185,940	146,250	10,090	20,700	8,910
	1997-98	R	190,760	149,560	8,430	22,590	10,180
	1998-99	R	178,290	140,260	7,740	20,660	9,640
	1999-00	R	184,010	141,800	8,710	23,110	10,400
	2000-01	R	175,370	133,260	8,330	22,110	11,670
	2001-02	R	174,200	129,870	8,270	22,570	13,490
	2002-03	R	183,210	137,740	8,310	22,750	14,420
	2003-04	R	190,590	143,960	8,300	23,820	14,510
	2004-05	R	205,400	155,890	8,490	26,470	14,540
	2005-06 [2]	R	210,320	163,400	8,250	24,960	13,710
	2006-07 [2]	R	215,220	167,680	9,330	24,280	13,930
	2007-08	R	215,860	170,610	8,660	25,790	10,800
	2008-09	R	178,560	140,990	7,120	21,020	9,430
	2009-10	R	151,230	119,910	6,170	17,120	8,020
	2010-11	R	136,020	107,870	5,510	16,430	6,210
	2011-12	R	145,800	118,510	5,580	16,000	5,720
	2012-13	R	133,030	107,980	5,450	14,080	5,530
	2013-14	R	138,540	112,330	5,840	15,060	5,320
	2014-15	R	153,020	124,640	6,170	16,700	5,500
	2015-16	R	169,160	139,670	6,900	16,810	5,790
	2016-17	R	178,470	147,930	6,830	17,230	6,470
	2017-18	P	187,560	160,470	6,660	13,320	7,110
Private Enterprise							
	1994-95	R	155,290	125,740	6,300	17,890	5,350
	1995-96	R	156,540	123,620	6,880	19,200	6,850
	1996-97	R	153,450	121,170	7,520	17,490	7,270
	1997-98	R	160,680	127,840	6,490	17,980	8,370
	1998-99	R	154,560	121,190	6,440	18,780	8,140
	1999-00	R	160,520	124,470	7,860	19,070	9,120
	2000-01	R	152,740	116,640	7,390	18,200	10,510
	2001-02	R	153,580	115,700	7,490	18,310	12,070
	2002-03	R	164,300	124,460	7,520	18,940	13,390
	2003-04	R	172,370	130,100	7,860	20,460	13,950
	2004-05	R	183,710	139,130	7,990	22,450	14,150
	2005-06 [2]	R	185,840	144,940	7,880	20,260	12,760
	2006-07 [2]	R	188,560	145,680	8,990	21,040	12,850
	2007-08	R	187,280	147,170	8,320	21,660	10,140
	2008-09	R	145,300	113,800	6,430	16,110	8,960
	2009-10	R	116,420	93,030	5,290	11,130	6,960
	2010-11	R	103,880	83,180	4,510	10,700	5,480
	2011-12	R	108,800	89,120	4,750	10,110	4,830
	2012-13	R	103,210	84,550	4,710	9,870	4,070
	2013-14	R	110,010	89,630	5,160	11,010	4,200
	2014-15	R	118,620	96,270	5,330	12,480	4,540
	2015-16	R	135,380	111,320	5,650	13,350	5,060
	2016-17	R	145,330	121,000	5,590	13,370	5,360
	2017-18	P	153,150	131,390	5,470	10,390	5,900
Housing Associations							
	1994-95	R	37,240	31,380	2,570	2,790	500
	1995-96	R	38,170	30,230	2,130	4,780	1,040
	1996-97	R	30,950	24,630	2,550	2,960	810
	1997-98	R	28,550	21,400	1,940	4,490	730
	1998-99	R	22,870	18,890	1,270	1,750	960
	1999-00	R	23,170	17,270	850	3,960	1,090
	2000-01	R	22,250	16,430	900	3,800	1,110

11.3 House building: permanent dwellings completed, by tenure[1] and country[2, 3]

Number of dwellings

	Financial Year		United Kingdom	England	Wales	Scotland	Northern Ireland
	2001-02	R	20,400	14,100	710	4,200	1,390
	2002-03	R	18,610	13,080	780	3,720	1,030
	2003-04	R	18,020	13,670	420	3,370	560
	2004-05	R	21,550	16,660	480	4,020	390
	2005-06 [2]	R	24,160	18,160	350	4,700	950
	2006-07 [2]	R	26,400	21,750	350	3,230	1,080
	2007-08	R	28,330	23,220	340	4,100	660
	2008-09	R	32,430	26,690	690	4,580	470
	2009-10	R	34,030	26,520	880	5,580	1,060
	2010-11	R	30,380	23,550	990	5,110	740
	2011-12	R	33,950	27,460	830	4,780	890
	2012-13	R	27,500	22,060	740	3,240	1,450
	2013-14	R	26,480	21,790	670	2,910	1,110
	2014-15	R	31,880	27,020	840	3,060	960
	2015-16	R	30,750	26,450	1,250	2,320	730
	2016-17	R	30,180	25,090	1,240	2,750	1,100
	2017-18	P	32,670	27,210	1,120	3,130	1,210
Local Authorities							
	1994-95	R	3,060	850	200	1,130	880
	1995-96	R	3,010	760	160	720	1,360
	1996-97	R	1,540	450	20	240	820
	1997-98	R	1,520	320	-	110	1,080
	1998-99	R	870	180	30	120	540
	1999-00	R	320	60	-	70	190
	2000-01	R	380	180	50	110	50
	2001-02	R	230	60	70	70	30
	2002-03	R	300	200	10	90	-
	2003-04	R	210	190	20	-	-
	2004-05	R	130	100	30	-	-
	2005-06 [2]	R	320	300	20	-	-
	2006-07 [2]	R	260	250	-	10	-
	2007-08	R	250	220	10	30	-
	2008-09	R	830	490	-	340	-
	2009-10	R	780	370	-	410	-
	2010-11	R	1,760	1,140	-	610	-
	2011-12	R	3,080	1,960	-	1,110	-
	2012-13	R	2,330	1,360	-	960	-
	2013-14	R	2,060	910	10	1,140	-
	2014-15	R	2,520	1,360	-	1,160	-
	2015-16	R	3,040	1,900	-	1,140	-

1. For detailed definitions of all tenures see definitions of housing terms on Housing Statistics home page
2. Northern Ireland data prior to 2005 is sourced from the Department of Communities, which use different definitions and adjust their data. Further information can be viewed at: https://www.communities-ni.gov.uk/publications/review-new-dwelling-starts-and-completions
3. These figures are for new build dwellings only. The Department also publishes an annual release entitled 'Housing Supply: net additional dwellings, England' which is the primary and most comprehensive measure of housing supply in England.
4. Figures from October 2005 to March 2007 in England are missing a small number of starts and completions that were inspected by independent approved inspectors. These data are included from June 2007.

Totals may not equal the sum of component parts due to rounding to the nearest 10

- \- Less than 5 dwellings
- P Figure provisional and subject to revision
- R Revised from previous release
- .. Not available

Source:
P2 returns from local authorities
National House-Building Council (NHBC)
Approved inspector data returns
Welsh Assembly Government
Scottish Government
Department of Finance and Personnel (DFPNI)
District Council Building Control (NI)

Contact: Rosie McGarrity
Telephone: 0303 444 6770
Email: housing.statistics@communities.gsi.gov.uk

11.4a Housebuilding: permanent dwellings completed, by house and flat, number of bedroom and tenure[1], England

Percentage of all dwellings

Financial Year	2003 /04 [2]	2004 /05 [2]	2005 /06 [2]	2006 /07[2]	2007 /08[2]	2008 /09[2]	2009 /10[2]	2010 /11[2]	2011 /12[2]	2012 /13[2]	2013 /14[2]	2014 /15[2]	2015 /16[2]
Private Enterprise													
Houses													
1 bedroom	1	1	-	0	-	1	0	1	0	1	1	1	0
2 bedrooms	11	8	8	7	7	9	9	11	10	10	11	12	10
3 bedrooms	32	30	25	24	23	25	25	28	32	36	33	38	38
4 or more bedrooms	36	29	23	24	23	23	28	32	29	33	32	33	31
All	79	67	56	56	53	58	63	72	71	79	76	83	80
Flats													
1 bedroom	4	7	10	10	8	10	10	4	6	4	6	4	6
2 bedrooms	15	25	32	33	38	31	26	23	22	17	18	12	14
3 bedrooms	1	1	1	1	1	1	1	1	1	0	0	0	0
4 or more bedrooms	-	-	-	-	-	0	0	0	0	0	0	0	0
All	21	33	44	44	47	42	37	28	29	21	24	17	20
Houses and flats													
1 bedroom	5	7	11	10	8	11	10	5	7	5	7	5	6
2 bedrooms	26	33	40	40	45	40	35	34	32	26	29	25	24
3 bedrooms	33	30	26	25	23	26	26	29	32	36	33	38	38
4 or more bedrooms	36	29	23	24	24	23	29	32	29	33	32	33	31
All	100	100	100	100	100	100	100	100	100	100	100	100	100
Housing Associations													
Houses													
1 bedroom	1	3	1	1	1	1	1	1	1	1	2	1	2
2 bedrooms	30	23	23	21	19	22	18	22	27	24	27	27	28
3 bedrooms	22	33	23	23	19	17	19	22	25	32	34	32	29
4 or more bedrooms	4	8	3	2	2	3	4	6	7	6	7	4	4
All	57	67	50	46	40	43	42	51	60	63	71	64	63
Flats													
1 bedroom	16	13	21	20	20	21	24	15	10	11	10	10	11
2 bedrooms	27	17	28	33	37	35	34	34	30	27	19	26	26
3 bedrooms	-	3	1	1	-	1	0	1	0	0	0	0	0
4 or more bedrooms	-	-	-	-	2	0	0	0	0	0	0	0	0
All	43	33	50	54	60	57	58	49	40	37	29	36	37
Houses and flats													
1 bedroom	17	16	21	21	21	22	25	16	10	11	12	11	13
2 bedrooms	57	40	52	54	55	57	52	56	57	51	46	53	53
3 bedrooms	23	36	24	24	19	18	20	22	26	32	34	32	29
4 or more bedrooms	4	8	3	2	4	3	4	6	7	6	7	4	4
All	100	100	100	100	100	100	100	100	100	100	100	100	100
All tenures													
Houses													
1 bedroom	**1**	**1**	**-**	**-**	**-**	**1**	**1**	**1**	**0**	**1**	**1**	**1**	**1**
2 bedrooms	**12**	**10**	**10**	**9**	**9**	**13**	**12**	**14**	**13**	**12**	**13**	**15**	**14**
3 bedrooms	**31**	**30**	**25**	**24**	**22**	**23**	**23**	**27**	**30**	**35**	**33**	**36**	**36**
4 or more bedroom	**34**	**26**	**20**	**21**	**20**	**18**	**21**	**25**	**24**	**28**	**28**	**27**	**26**
All	**78**	**67**	**55**	**54**	**51**	**54**	**57**	**67**	**68**	**76**	**75**	**79**	**77**
Flats													
1 bedroom	**5**	**7**	**12**	**11**	**10**	**13**	**14**	**7**	**7**	**5**	**7**	**5**	**7**
2 bedrooms	**16**	**24**	**32**	**33**	**38**	**32**	**29**	**26**	**24**	**18**	**18**	**15**	**17**
3 bedrooms	**1**	**1**	**1**	**1**	**1**	**1**	**0**	**1**	**1**	**0**	**0**	**0**	**0**
4 or more bedroom	**-**	**-**	**-**	**-**	**1**	**0**	**0**	**0**	**0**	**0**	**0**	**0**	**0**
All	**22**	**33**	**45**	**46**	**49**	**46**	**43**	**33**	**32**	**24**	**25**	**21**	**23**
Houses and flats													
1 bedroom	**6**	**8**	**12**	**12**	**10**	**14**	**15**	**8**	**8**	**6**	**8**	**6**	**7**
2 bedrooms	**28**	**34**	**41**	**42**	**47**	**45**	**40**	**40**	**38**	**31**	**32**	**30**	**30**
3 bedrooms	**32**	**31**	**26**	**25**	**23**	**23**	**24**	**27**	**31**	**36**	**33**	**37**	**36**
4 or more bedroom	**34**	**27**	**21**	**21**	**20**	**18**	**21**	**25**	**24**	**28**	**28**	**27**	**26**
All	**100**	**100**	**100**	**100**	**100**	**100**	**100**	**100**	**100**	**100**	**100**	**100**	**100**

Source: Department for Communities and Local Government
Telephone: 0303 444 1291
E-Mail: housing.statistics@communities.gsi.gov.uk

1. For detailed definitions of all tenures, see Definitions of housing terms in Housing Statistics home page
2. Figures for 2001/02 onwards are based on NHBC data only, so there is some degree of variability owing to partial coverage.
3. The England worksheet and charts have been corrected following initial publication.
4. Financial Year relates to April - April

Contact:
Contact: Rosie McGarrity
Telephone: 0303 444 6770

11.4b New dwellings completed by dwelling type and number of bedrooms, Wales

	Flats					Houses					Total Houses and flats
	Number of bedrooms					Number of bedrooms					
	1	2	3	4 or more	Total	1	2	3	4 or more	Total	
2002/2003	431	754	102	0	1,287	30	773	2,847	3,373	7,023	8,310
2003/2004	407	966	111	6	1,490	51	688	2,992	3,075	6,806	8,296
2004/2005	555	972	94	17	1,638	57	770	2,888	3,139	6,854	8,492
2005/2006	649	1,585	96	1	2,331	72	645	2,755	2,446	5,918	8,249
2006/2007	960	1,807	125	9	2,901	29	819	2,983	2,602	6,433	9,334
2007/2008	843	1,906	154	25	2,928	59	728	2,667	2,282	5,736	8,664
2008/2009	1,048	1,494	88	20	2,650	59	863	2,033	1,516	4,471	7,12
2009/2010	594	1,235	68	1	1,898	64	785	2,164	1,263	4,276	6,174
2010/2011	513	767	55	5	1,340	48	813	2,079	1,225	4,165	5,505
2011/2012	528	786	15	6	1,335	85	772	1,975	1,408	4,240	5,575
2012/2013	292	574	42	2	910	99	744	2,101	1,597	4,541	5,451
2013/2014	575	659	31	4	1,269	70	743	2,148	1,613	4,574	5,843
2014/2015	540	580	13	11	1,144	46	836	2,331	1,813	5,026	6,170
2015/2016	783	699	37	7	1,526	47	865	2,646	1,816	5,374	6,900

Source: New house building data collection, Welsh Government

.	The data item is not applicable.
Bedrooms	Breakdown by number of bedrooms within property.
Dwelling Type	Breakdown by Houses and Flats.
Period	Data on starts and completions of new permanent dwellings is only available at Wales level prior to 1996-97. From 1996-97, the information is available at a local authority level. Figures on housing starts are from records kept for building control purposes. It is often difficult for data providers to identify whether a dwelling is being built for RSLs or for a private developer and this may lead to an understatement of RSL

Contact email: stats.housing@gov.wales
Web link: http://gov.wales/statistics-and-research/new-house-building/?lang=en

In Wales, new house building is undertaken by the private sector, Registered Social Landlords (RSLs) and local authorities. The information presented here is based on the reports of local authority building inspectors and the National House Building Council (NHBC). It does not include information from private approved inspectors. The exclusion of this information means that there is currently an undercount in the number of dwellings completed though this is estimated to be quite small.

The information shows the number of new dwellings completed in Wales and is collected in order to assess the level of new house building across Wales during the period. The data is used to help monitor trends in both the overall level of Welsh housing stock and the changes in its tenure distribution over time. Data is also used by the Welsh Government and local authorities to assess levels of housing supply across Wales and as an indication as to whether housing need is being met.

Figures on housing completions are from records kept for building control purposes. It is sometimes difficult for data providers to identify whether a dwelling is being built for RSLs or for a private developer. This may lead to an understatement of RSL completions recorded in these tables, and a corresponding overstatement of private enterprise figures. This problem is more likely to occur with starts than completions.

New house building funded with capital grant funding includes funding via Social Housing Grant, Recycled Social Housing Grant and Strategic Capital Investment Fund.

11.5 Mortgage possession workload in the county courts of England and Wales, 2004 - 2016

Year (calendar)	Quarter	Claims Issued	Orders			Warrants[1]	Repossessions by county court bailiffs	Properties taken into possession[2] in
			Outright	Suspended	Total			
2004		76,993	20,048	26,639	46,687	33,042	7,074	8,200
2005		114,733	32,757	38,211	70,968	48,513	12,794	14,500
2006		131,248	46,288	44,895	91,183	66,060	20,960	21,000
2007		137,725	58,250	49,259	107,509	73,890	23,831	25,900
2008		142,741	70,804	61,994	132,798	89,748	35,792	40,000
2009		93,533	44,856	38,039	82,895	77,461	32,457	48,300
2010		75,431	32,940	29,235	62,175	63,532	23,612	38,100
2011		73,181	30,190	29,697	59,887	65,371	25,463	37,100
2012		59,877	24,129	23,935	48,064	59,040	19,728	34,000
2013		53,659	20,718	19,585	40,303	52,305	15,692	28,900
2014		41,151	16,120	13,519	29,639	41,900	11,976	20,900
2015		19,852	7,984	6,031	14,015	23,220	5,592	10,200
2016 (r)		18,456	7,274	4,481	11,755	17,627	4,754	7,700
2012	Q1	16,963	6,763	7,116	13,879	16,136	6,072	9,600
	Q2	14,615	6,032	6,152	12,184	14,373	4,825	8,500
	Q3	14,168	5,556	5,437	10,993	14,557	4,676	8,200
	Q4	14,131	5,778	5,230	11,008	13,974	4,155	7,700
2013	Q1	14,375	5,674	5,260	10,934	13,580	4,474	8,000
	Q2	12,881	5,187	5,059	10,246	13,529	4,087	7,600
	Q3	14,256	4,974	4,723	9,697	13,039	3,733	7,200
	Q4	12,147	4,883	4,543	9,426	12,157	3,398	6,100
2014	Q1	12,706	4,648	4,277	8,925	12,391	3,709	6,400
	Q2	10,773	4,400	3,539	7,939	11,121	3,028	5,400
	Q3	9,731	3,940	3,201	7,141	10,067	2,805	5,000
	Q4	7,941	3,132	2,502	5,634	8,321	2,434	4,100
2015	Q1	5,643	2,298	1,926	4,224	6,343	1,658	3,000
	Q2	4,849	1,951	1,475	3,426	5,646	1,363	2,500
	Q3	5,012	2,055	1,385	3,440	6,255	1,423	2,500
	Q4	4,348	1,680	1,245	2,925	4,976	1,148	2,200
2016	Q1	4,739	1,736	1,281	3,017	4,848	1,355	2,100
	Q2	4,430	1,901	1,200	3,101	4,848	1,183	1,900
	Q3	4,485	1,746	939	2,685	4,353	1,212	1,900
	Q4 (r)	4,802	1,891	1,061	2,952	3,578	1,004	1,800

Source:
HM Courts and Tribunals Service CaseMan,
Possession Claim On-Line (PCOL) and Council of Mortgage Lenders (CML)

Notes:

1 Multiple warrants may be issued per claim

2 Council of Mortgage Lenders (CML) statistics for the latest quarter are unavailable prior to this bulletin being published. This figure relates to all repossessions made in the United Kingdom whereas all other statistics in this bulletin relate to England and Wales. Please see the CML website http://www.cml.org.uk/ for more information about these statistics.

3 Data relating to 1999 onwards are sourced from county court administrative systems and exclude duplicate observations. Data prior to 1999 are sourced from manual counts made by court staff.

.. = data not available

(p) = provisional

(r) = revised

11.6 Mortgage arrears and repossessions

Year	2004	2005	2006	2007	2008	2009	2010	2011	2012	2013	2014	2015	2016
Number of mortgages													
at year end (000s)	11,515	11,608	11,746	11,852	11,667	11,504	11,478	11,384	11,284	11,186	11,147	11,126	11,107
of which homeowners	10,898	10,909	10,910	10,827	10,498	10,257	10,169	9,996	9,835	9,658	9,491	9,342	9,245
Repossessions during year	8,200	14,500	21,000	25,900	40,000	48,900	38,500	37,300	33,900	28,900	20,900	10,200	7,700
of which homeowners	–	–	19,900	23,900	37,000	44,100	33,900	31,200	27,000	23,300	15,900	7,200	5,400
Cases in mortgage arrears													
12+ months arrears	11,000	15,000	15,700	15,300	29,500	69,500	63,700	54,400	48,500	41,100	30,700	30,600	30,500
+ 6 - 12 months arrears	29,900	38,600	34,900	40,500	72,000	93,900	80,500	72,200	69,900	60,700	45,100	38,700	34,000
+ 3 - 6 months arrears	60,500	69,400	64,900	71,700	117,400	112,400	103,300	99,000	97,200	86,600	68,800	55,200	46,400
= All 3+ months arrears	101,400	122,900	115,600	127,500	219,000	275,800	247,500	225,600	215,700	188,300	144,500	124,400	110,900
of which homeowners	98,600	118,400	110,800	120,000	192,000	250,700	225,600	206,600	199,200	174,200	133,200	114,100	101,600

Sources: Compendium of Housing Finance Statistics,
Housing Finance and CML website, Council of Mortgage Lenders.

Notes: Properties taken into possession include those voluntarily surrendered. The CML arrears figures are for the end of the year. Changes in the mortgage rate have the effect of changing monthly mortgage repayments and hence the number of months in arrears which a given amount represents. Arrears figures are for both homeowners and buy to let mortgages except for bottom row (of all 3+ month arrears cases) which is exclusively for homeowners.

11.7 Households in temporary accommodation (1) by type of accommodation, and cases where duty owed but no accommodation has been secured at the end of each quarter[7] England, 2002 to 2016

number / *percent*

	Total in TA[1, 8, 9] (Temporary Accommodation)				Bed and breakfast hotels (including shared annexes)[2, 8]							Hostels (including women's refuges)		
	Total	% change on same quarter in previous year	*of which:* with children[4,7]	*Total number of children*[5,7]	**Total**	% of Total TA	*of which:* with children[4,7]	with children and resident more than 6 weeks	*of which:* pending review/ appeal[10]	*of which:* headed by a 16/17 year old[9]	*of which:* resident more than 6 weeks[9]	**Total**	% of Total TA	*of which:* with children[4]
Number and percentage of total households in TA (%)														
2002 Q1	**80,200**	*7%*	54,660	..	12,710	*16%*	6,960	..	..	..	..	9,570	*12%*	5,540
Q2	**81,660**	*8%*	58,870	..	12,720	*16%*	6,830	..	..	..	..	9,770	*12%*	6,030
Q3	**85,010**	*9%*	61,740	..	13,950	*16%*	6,970	..	..	..	..	9,720	*11%*	6,280
Q4	**85,140**	*10%*	60,310	..	13,240	*16%*	5,870	3,050	..	..	..	9,650	*11%*	5,770
2003 Q1	**89,040**	*11%*	61,510	..	12,440	*14%*	5,230	2,910	..	..	..	10,050	*11%*	6,040
Q2	**91,870**	*13%*	65,040	..	11,380	*12%*	3,940	2,120	..	..	..	10,420	*11%*	6,360
Q3	**94,440**	*11%*	67,260	..	10,310	*11%*	3,200	1,590	..	..	..	10,800	*11%*	6,450
Q4	**94,610**	*11%*	67,540	..	8,420	*9%*	1,730	940	..	..	..	10,370	*11%*	6,060
2004 Q1	**97,680**	*10%*	70,580	..	7,090	*7%*	820	30	..	..	..	10,790	*11%*	6,280
Q2	**99,530**	*8%*	71,640	121,590	7,240	*7%*	1,100	60	..	..	..	10,570	*11%*	6,090
Q3	**101,300**	*7%*	72,510	122,530	7,450	*7%*	1,420	180	..	..	..	10,380	*10%*	5,960
Q4	**101,030**	*7%*	72,800	124,630	6,450	*6%*	820	100	..	..	..	10,070	*10%*	5,650
2005 Q1	**101,070**	*3%*	72,670	125,860	6,780	*7%*	1,180	110	..	..	..	10,280	*10%*	5,830
Q2	**100,970**	*1%*	72,810	124,900	6,290	*6%*	1,300	130	50	..	..	9,870	*10%*	5,440
Q3	**101,020**	*0%*	74,180	127,990	6,100	*6%*	1,470	150	40	..	..	10,020	*10%*	5,410
Q4	**98,730**	*-2%*	72,920	127,620	4,950	*5%*	820	140	30	..	..	9,230	*9%*	4,990
2006 Q1	**96,370**	*-5%*	71,560	127,650	5,150	*5%*	1,020	110	30	..	..	9,010	*9%*	4,960
Q2	**93,910**	*-7%*	69,790	130,470	4,890	*5%*	1,050	100	50	..	..	8,940	*10%*	4,820
Q3	**93,090**	*-8%*	69,500	129,340	4,900	*5%*	1,100	120	40	..	..	8,460	*9%*	4,460
Q4	**89,510**	*-9%*	65,770	122,080	4,210	*5%*	650	110	40	..	..	7,850	*9%*	3,950
2007 Q1	**87,120**	*-10%*	65,210	125,430	4,310	*5%*	980	80	30	..	..	7,640	*9%*	4,030
Q2	**84,900**	*-10%*	64,020	117,340	4,070	*5%*	940	100	30	670	300	7,230	*9%*	3,890
Q3	**82,750**	*-11%*	62,830	117,090	4,090	*5%*	900	130	30	690	300	7,180	*9%*	3,850
Q4	**79,500**	*-11%*	59,990	112,260	3,530	*4%*	700	120	20	550	270	6,620	*8%*	3,490
2008 Q1	**77,510**	*-11%*	59,230	110,360	3,840	*5%*	1,030	160	30	560	250	6,450	*8%*	3,580
Q2	**74,690**	*-12%*	57,210	107,050	3,440	*5%*	1,030	180	30	420	160	6,020	*8%*	3,350
Q3	**72,130**	*-13%*	55,850	104,640	3,230	*4%*	940	160	30	400	150	5,800	*8%*	3,190
Q4	**67,480**	*-15%*	52,290	98,880	2,560	*4%*	520	100	20	330	150	5,250	*8%*	2,830
2009 Q1	**64,000**	*-17%*	49,030	92,590	2,450	*4%*	470	70	10	340	120	5,170	*8%*	2,740
Q2	**60,230**	*-19%*	45,940	87,030	2,150	*4%*	510	80	20	310	130	4,710	*8%*	2,430
Q3	**56,920**	*-21%*	43,400	82,780	2,050	*4%*	510	130	20	230	100	4,480	*8%*	2,330
Q4	**53,370**	*-21%*	40,560	77,990	1,880	*4%*	400	120	10	170	70	4,150	*8%*	2,150
2010 Q1	**51,310**	*-20%*	39,200	74,610	2,050	*4%*	630	100	10	180	60	4,240	*8%*	2,270
Q2	**50,400**	*-16%*	37,940	72,590	2,410	*5%*	740	160	10	190	70	4,320	*9%*	2,380
Q3	**49,680**	*-13%*	37,620	71,460	2,660	*5%*	930	140	10	210	80	4,360	*9%*	2,440
Q4	**48,010**	*-10%*	36,230	69,050	2,310	*5%*	660	150	10	140	50	4,160	*9%*	2,270
2011 Q1	**48,240**	*-6%*	36,640	69,660	2,750	*6%*	1,030	200	10	160	50	4,250	*9%*	2,330
Q2	**48,330**	*-4%*	35,950	68,770	3,120	*6%*	1,210	240	20	150	40	4,370	*9%*	2,340
Q3	**49,100**	*-1%*	36,680	69,850	3,370	*7%*	1,340	310	40	140	50	4,380	*9%*	2,370
Q4	**48,920**	*2%*	36,600	69,460	3,170	*6%*	1,310	450	60	100	30	4,310	*9%*	2,380
2012 Q1	**50,430**	*5%*	37,190	70,090	3,960	*8%*	1,660	480	60	150	50	4,360	*9%*	2,350
Q2	**51,630**	*7%*	39,470	73,890	4,230	*8%*	1,900	680	70	140	50	4,350	*8%*	2,610
Q3	**52,960**	*8%*	40,090	75,460	4,120	*8%*	1,920	870	100	120	50	4,390	*8%*	2,690
Q4	**53,140**	*9%*	40,830	76,740	3,820	*7%*	1,600	770	100	80	50	4,280	*8%*	2,610
2013 Q1	**55,320**	*10%*	40,450	76,040	4,510	*8%*	1,970	760	50	100	40	4,480	*8%*	2,710
Q2	**55,840**	*8%*	42,800	79,030	4,350	*8%*	2,090	740	70	80	20	4,590	*8%*	2,890
Q3	**57,410**	*8%*	42,210	78,770	4,610	*8%*	2,110	800	80	70	20	4,700	*8%*	2,960
Q4	**56,940**	*7%*	43,750	80,970	3,920	*7%*	1,560	500	60	70	20	4,710	*8%*	2,950
2014 Q1	**58,410**	*6%*	44,770	83,370	4,370	*7%*	1,900	440	40	60	20	4,880	*8%*	3,010
Q2	**59,570**	*7%*	45,940	87,890	4,590	*8%*	2,130	610	50	70	20	4,980	*8%*	3,100
Q3	**60,900**	*6%*	47,460	91,090	4,680	*8%*	2,140	470	60	70	20	5,010	*8%*	3,110
Q4	**61,930**	*9%*	48,460	93,980	4,540	*7%*	2,040	780	60	40	20	5,090	*8%*	3,360
2015 Q1	**64,710**	*11%*	51,210	98,620	5,270	*8%*	2,560	920	50	50	10	5,040	*8%*	3,360
Q2	**66,980**	*12%*	52,550	102,090	5,630	*8%*	2,660	880	40	40	10	5,180	*8%*	3,510
Q3	**68,560**	*13%*	53,480	103,440	5,910	*9%*	3,000	1,050	100	30	10	5,310	*8%*	3,510
Q4	**69,140**	*12%*	54,240	106,240	5,120	*7%*	2,270	910	100	40	20	5,360	*8%*	3,670
2016 Q1	**71,670**	*11%*	56,430	111,060	5,960	*8%*	2,890	950	60	60	10	5,570	*8%*	3,820
Q2	**73,050**	*9%*	58,140	114,810	6,490	*9%*	3,370	1,240	40	40	10	5,490	*8%*	3,860
Q3	**74,750**	*9%*	59,380	117,510	6,680	*9%*	3,450	1,450	100	30	10	5,690	*8%*	3,940
Q4	**75,740**	*10%*	60,240	118,930	5,990	*8%*	2,790	1,260	40	20	10	5,700	*8%*	4,080

Source: Department for Communities and Local Government; P1E Homelessness returns (quarterly)

email: homelessnessstats@communities.gsi.gov.uk

11.7 Households in temporary accommodation (1) by type of accommodation, and cases where duty owed but no accommodation has been secured at the end of each quarter[7] England, 2002 to 2016

number / *percent*

	Nightly paid, self contained accommodation			Local Authority or Housing Association (LA/HA) stock[6]			Leased from the Private Sector by an LA or HA[6]			Other accommodation[2] (including private landlord)		
	Total	% of Total TA	*of which:* with children[4]	**Total**	% of Total TA	*of which:* with children[4,7]	**Total**	% of Total TA	*of which:* with children[4,7]	**Total**	% of Total TA	*of which:* with children[4,7]
Number and percentage of total households in TA (%)												
2002 Q1	3,590	*4%*	2,550	27,760	*35%*	19,160	20,660	*26%*	17,070	5,920	*7%*	3,380
Q2	3,690	*5%*	2,840	28,470	*35%*	21,360	22,610	*28%*	18,570	4,400	*5%*	3,250
Q3	4,130	*5%*	3,170	28,870	*34%*	21,130	23,850	*28%*	20,600	4,490	*5%*	3,590
Q4	4,060	*5%*	3,020	27,580	*32%*	20,380	25,940	*30%*	21,630	4,680	*5%*	3,640
2003 Q1	4,110	*5%*	3,070	28,250	*32%*	19,690	28,370	*32%*	23,240	5,810	*7%*	4,240
Q2	5,020	*5%*	3,770	27,590	*30%*	19,900	31,460	*34%*	26,630	5,990	*7%*	4,450
Q3	4,690	*5%*	3,460	27,560	*29%*	19,650	35,140	*37%*	29,950	5,950	*6%*	4,560
Q4	3,250	*3%*	2,350	27,480	*29%*	19,450	38,730	*41%*	33,340	6,370	*7%*	4,600
2004 Q1	3,260	*3%*	2,350	27,890	*29%*	20,120	42,390	*43%*	36,390	6,270	*6%*	4,620
Q2	4,140	*4%*	2,970	27,960	*28%*	20,070	42,630	*43%*	35,900	6,990	*7%*	5,510
Q3	4,270	*4%*	2,920	28,220	*28%*	20,070	43,720	*43%*	36,650	7,260	*7%*	5,500
Q4	4,180	*4%*	2,760	27,730	*27%*	19,730	46,140	*46%*	38,750	6,460	*6%*	5,080
2005 Q1	4,190	*4%*	2,850	26,630	*26%*	18,610	46,530	*46%*	39,170	6,670	*7%*	5,030
Q2	4,520	*4%*	2,970	27,430	*27%*	19,070	46,990	*47%*	39,600	5,870	*6%*	4,420
Q3	4,520	*4%*	3,140	25,030	*25%*	17,620	48,860	*48%*	41,500	6,500	*6%*	5,060
Q4	4,450	*5%*	2,950	24,220	*25%*	17,110	49,910	*51%*	42,310	5,970	*6%*	4,750
2006 Q1	4,500	*5%*	2,990	22,350	*23%*	16,080	49,660	*52%*	41,960	5,700	*6%*	4,560
Q2	4,570	*5%*	3,020	20,790	*22%*	14,880	49,320	*53%*	41,740	5,400	*6%*	4,270
Q3	4,870	*5%*	3,190	20,180	*22%*	14,830	49,700	*53%*	41,980	4,980	*5%*	3,950
Q4	4,900	*5%*	3,310	18,840	*21%*	13,930	48,850	*55%*	40,130	4,870	*5%*	3,810
2007 Q1	5,140	*6%*	3,470	18,040	*21%*	13,510	45,600	*52%*	38,600	6,400	*7%*	4,620
Q2	5,410	*6%*	3,760	17,240	*20%*	12,970	44,610	*53%*	37,920	6,350	*7%*	4,540
Q3	5,650	*7%*	3,990	16,490	*20%*	12,410	43,430	*52%*	37,100	5,920	*7%*	4,590
Q4	5,780	*7%*	4,080	15,910	*20%*	11,780	41,730	*52%*	35,380	5,930	*7%*	4,560
2008 Q1	6,210	*8%*	4,450	14,740	*19%*	11,080	40,480	*52%*	34,610	5,790	*7%*	4,480
Q2	5,980	*8%*	4,220	14,030	*19%*	10,660	41,130	*55%*	34,900	4,090	*5%*	3,050
Q3	5,680	*8%*	4,120	13,420	*19%*	10,240	39,990	*55%*	34,390	4,020	*6%*	2,970
Q4	5,230	*8%*	3,720	11,930	*18%*	8,990	38,790	*57%*	33,560	3,720	*6%*	2,680
2009 Q1	4,980	*8%*	3,470	10,480	*16%*	7,800	37,450	*59%*	32,050	3,480	*5%*	2,500
Q2	4,570	*8%*	3,120	9,520	*16%*	6,970	35,920	*60%*	30,620	3,360	*6%*	2,290
Q3	4,180	*7%*	2,870	8,780	*15%*	6,390	34,130	*60%*	29,090	3,310	*6%*	2,210
Q4	3,620	*7%*	2,450	8,180	*15%*	5,950	32,430	*61%*	27,540	3,100	*6%*	2,070
2010 Q1	3,380	*7%*	2,320	7,790	*15%*	5,790	30,920	*60%*	26,310	2,940	*6%*	1,900
Q2	3,340	*7%*	2,220	7,650	*15%*	5,570	29,820	*59%*	25,210	2,860	*6%*	1,830
Q3	3,520	*7%*	2,380	7,610	*15%*	5,480	28,740	*58%*	24,570	2,800	*6%*	1,810
Q4	3,590	*7%*	2,430	7,430	*15%*	5,440	27,730	*58%*	23,620	2,790	*6%*	1,810
2011 Q1	3,920	*8%*	2,730	7,490	*16%*	5,500	26,960	*56%*	23,170	2,870	*6%*	1,890
Q2	4,200	*9%*	2,920	7,570	*16%*	5,460	26,240	*54%*	22,170	2,850	*6%*	1,860
Q3	4,350	*9%*	3,100	7,890	*16%*	5,810	26,380	*54%*	22,250	2,740	*6%*	1,810
Q4	4,460	*9%*	3,330	7,990	*16%*	5,840	26,080	*53%*	21,800	2,910	*6%*	1,950
2012 Q1	4,860	*10%*	3,670	8,270	*16%*	6,000	26,040	*52%*	21,490	2,940	*6%*	2,030
Q2	5,370	*10%*	4,100	8,600	*17%*	6,470	25,960	*50%*	22,240	3,130	*6%*	2,160
Q3	5,880	*11%*	4,580	8,930	*17%*	6,730	26,290	*50%*	21,880	3,360	*6%*	2,280
Q4	6,190	*12%*	4,900	9,090	*17%*	6,830	26,310	*50%*	22,490	3,440	*6%*	2,400
2013 Q1	7,000	*13%*	5,450	9,270	*17%*	7,020	26,260	*47%*	21,020	3,800	*7%*	2,290
Q2	7,630	*14%*	6,060	10,060	*18%*	7,860	24,780	*44%*	21,210	4,440	*8%*	2,690
Q3	8,400	*15%*	6,420	9,810	*17%*	7,290	25,660	*45%*	21,460	4,230	*7%*	1,970
Q4	8,660	*15%*	7,330	9,560	*17%*	7,280	25,460	*45%*	21,450	4,620	*8%*	3,190
2014 Q1	9,340	*16%*	7,960	9,880	*17%*	7,530	25,270	*43%*	21,150	4,680	*8%*	3,220
Q2	10,100	*17%*	8,630	10,120	*17%*	7,870	24,800	*42%*	20,730	4,990	*8%*	3,490
Q3	11,750	*19%*	10,100	10,070	*17%*	7,790	23,290	*38%*	19,550	6,110	*10%*	4,780
Q4	12,540	*20%*	10,770	10,530	*17%*	8,110	23,460	*38%*	19,790	5,780	*9%*	4,400
2015 Q1	13,620	*21%*	11,770	10,920	*17%*	8,540	23,990	*37%*	20,410	5,860	*9%*	4,570
Q2	14,870	*22%*	12,840	11,500	*17%*	8,750	23,820	*36%*	20,410	5,980	*9%*	4,390
Q3	15,760	*23%*	13,280	12,210	*18%*	9,600	23,520	*34%*	19,800	5,860	*9%*	4,290
Q4	16,210	*23%*	13,990	12,480	*18%*	9,790	25,580	*37%*	21,130	4,400	*6%*	3,400
2016 Q1	17,060	*24%*	14,640	13,130	*18%*	10,230	24,420	*34%*	20,500	5,530	*8%*	4,350
Q2	17,530	*24%*	15,120	13,540	*19%*	10,830	24,990	*34%*	21,170	5,020	*7%*	3,780
Q3	18,420	*25%*	15,740	13,610	*18%*	10,880	24,300	*33%*	20,600	6,060	*8%*	4,780
Q4	19,080	*25%*	16,340	14,040	*19%*	11,150	24,150	*32%*	20,440	6,790	*9%*	5,430

Source: Department for Communities and Local Government; P1E Homelessness returns (quarterly

email: homelessnessstats@communities.gsi.gov.uk

11.7 Households in temporary accommodation (1) by type of accommodation, and cases where duty owed but no accommodation has been secured at the end of each quarter[7] England, 2002 to 2016

number / *percent*

		Duty owed, no accommodation secured[3]					
	Of which: in TA in another local authority district	a main duty accepted	*% change from previous quarter*	*of which:* with children[4]	All including decision pending	*% change from previous quarter*	Total with children[4], including decision pending
Number and percentage of total households in TA (%)							
2002 Q1	9,670	8,620	*0%*	..	11,990	*0%*	3,320
Q2	8,190	8,890	*3%*	..	12,440	*4%*	4,450
Q3	11,550	10,390	*17%*	..	14,440	*16%*	6,760
Q4	12,310	9,760	*-6%*	..	14,800	*3%*	5,830
2003 Q1	11,470	10,580	*8%*	..	16,280	*10%*	7,550
Q2	10,880	13,310	*26%*	..	19,380	*19%*	9,410
Q3	9,880	15,370	*15%*	..	23,060	*19%*	10,140
Q4	10,440	17,500	*14%*	..	23,070	*0%*	10,990
2004 Q1	9,850	15,870	*-9%*	..	21,940	*-5%*	11,610
Q2	9,480	17,030	*7%*	..	23,000	*5%*	13,230
Q3	10,030	17,100	*0%*	..	23,200	*1%*	13,400
Q4	8,610	16,100	*-6%*	..	20,930	*-10%*	11,880
2005 Q1	11,660	15,290	*-5%*	..	20,910	*0%*	12,850
Q2	11,790	16,020	*5%*	10,470	..	..	..
Q3	13,430	15,140	*-6%*	10,270	..	..	..
Q4	10,700	11,570	*-24%*	7,840	..	..	..
2006 Q1	11,080	11,010	*-5%*	7,210	..	..	..
Q2	11,590	10,210	*-7%*	6,920	..	..	..
Q3	11,620	9,720	*-5%*	6,550	..	..	..
Q4	9,950	8,470	*-13%*	5,740	..	..	..
2007 Q1	10,130	8,780	*4%*	5,910	..	..	..
Q2	10,490	9,150	*4%*	6,280	..	..	..
Q3	11,130	9,540	*4%*	6,300	..	..	..
Q4	10,820	8,080	*-15%*	5,510	..	..	..
2008 Q1	10,200	7,470	*-8%*	5,180	..	..	..
Q2	8,720	7,890	*6%*	5,630	..	..	..
Q3	7,620	6,740	*-15%*	4,520	..	..	..
Q4	7,360	6,070	*-10%*	4,030	..	..	..
2009 Q1	7,960	5,560	*-9%*	3,740	..	..	..
Q2	7,880	4,560	*-18%*	2,940	..	..	..
Q3	6,550	4,350	*-5%*	2,770	..	..	..
Q4	5,780	4,150	*-5%*	2,540	..	..	..
2010 Q1	5,430	3,710	*-11%*	2,320	..	..	..
Q2	5,630	3,780	*2%*	2,510	..	..	..
Q3	5,880	4,100	*8%*	2,700	..	..	..
Q4	5,810	4,410	*8%*	2,970	..	..	..
2011 Q1	6,300	4,770	*8%*	3,270	..	..	..
Q2	6,290	4,770	*0%*	3,420	..	..	..
Q3	6,850	5,110	*7%*	3,590	..	..	..
Q4	7,350	5,490	*8%*	3,550	..	..	..
2012 Q1	7,870	5,400	*-2%*	3,860	..	..	..
Q2	8,170	5,500	*2%*	3,830	..	..	..
Q3	8,520	5,560	*1%*	4,080	..	..	..
Q4	9,270	5,690	*2%*	3,950	..	..	..
2013 Q1	9,130	5,930	*4%*	4,270	..	..	..
Q2	11,280	5,510	*-7%*	3,870	..	..	..
Q3	11,860	5,010	*-9%*	3,520	..	..	..
Q4	12,190	4,930	*-2%*	3,460	..	..	..
2014 Q1	12,910	5,620	*14%*	3,960	..	..	..
Q2	14,130	5,310	*-6%*	3,880	..	..	..
Q3	15,460	6,120	*15%*	4,420	..	..	..
Q4	15,990	5,820	*-5%*	4,290	..	..	..
2015 Q1	16,810	6,900	*19%*	5,060	..	..	..
Q2	17,640	6,370	*-8%*	4,640	..	..	..
Q3	18,600	6,610	*4%*	4,830	..	..	..
Q4	18,670	7,490	*13%*	4,800	..	..	..
2016 Q1	19,880	6,790	*-9%*	4,980	..	..	..
Q2	20,650	7,020	*3%*	5,280	..	..	..
Q3	21,400	7,590	*8%*	5,600	..	..	..
Q4	21,920	8,610	*13%*	6,540	..	..	..

Source: Department for Communities and Local Government; P1E Homelessness returns (quarterly
email: homelessnessstats@communities.gsi.gov.uk

11.7 Households in temporary accommodation (1) by type of accommodation, and cases where duty owed but no accommodation has been secured at the end of each quarter[7] England, 2002 to 2016

Notes

1 Households in accommodation arranged by local authorities pending enquiries or after being accepted as homeless under the 1996 Act (includes residual cases awaiting re-housing under the 1985 Act).

2 Other private sector accommodation includes accommodation that has been leased directly by the household from a private landlord where this arrangement is temporary, supported lodgings, and mobile homes such as caravans. The Homelessness (Suitability of Accommodation) (England) Order 2003 came into force on 1 April 2004. This prohibits the use of B&B accommodation for families except in an emergency and even then for no longer than six weeks.

3 "Duty owed, but no accommodation has been secured" are households accepted as owed a main duty but able to remain in their existing accommodation for the immediate future. Cases in the final two columns include those households awaiting a decision on their application. Since Q2 2005, this can only apply once an appeal has been accepted as owed a main duty.

4 Includes expectant mothers with no other dependent children.

5 Includes expected children.

6 Housing Association (HA) - this was previously known as "Registered Social Landlord".

7 Households in TA are as reported at the end of each quarter. Q1 represents March 31st, Q2 June 30th, Q3 September 30th, Q4 December

8 The temporary accomodation and B&B totals including those pending review / appeal Q2 2017 includes 335 hotel rooms made available to the residents Grenfell Tower and Grenfell Walk and the surrounding area. The number of hotel room bookings has been reported as households as this is the best available information for that date. In Q2 2017 breakdowns of household composition are not provided for the household moved from the Grenfell area. This means the total TA Q2 2017 breadowns are based on 77,840 households. The breakdowns of household composition for total in B&B are based on 6,260 households.

9 After data collection closedown for quarter ending March 2018, Milton Keynes reported an error resulting in 25 households headed by 16/17 year old being wrongly recorded as accommodated in B&B (including shared annexes) - in fact, these households were placed in the commissioned supported accommodation for young people. This correction is not reflected in this table and figures in cells N88 and O88 are overstated by 25 cases.

.. Data not collected.
R Revised data
P Provisional data
Q1 to Q4 refers to calendar year quarters.

Totals may not equal the sum of components because of rounding.
Totals include estimated data to account for non-response.

11.8 Homeless Households in temporary accomodation at the end of the period - as at 31 March each year, Wales

		2005-06 Annual	2006-07 Annual	2007-08 Annual	2008-09 Annual	2009-10 Annual	2010-11 Annual	2011-12 Annual	2012-13 Annual	2013-14 Annual	2014-15 Annual	2015-16 Annual
Total accommodated at the end of quarter		3440	3150	2880	2815	2490	2640	2770	2525	2295	2050	1875
Total accommodated at the end of quarter	Private sector accommodation (1)	505	710	900	1070	1050	1080	1065	1010	910	855	801
	Public sector accommodation (2)	615	575	445	415	390	435	380	380	440	440	411
	Hostels and women's refuges	450	405	475	510	400	415	485	505	510	475	498
	Bed and breakfast	595	380	280	255	235	240	310	300	185	195	108
	Other	300	230	190	105	*	*	5	10	*	*	*
	Homeless at home	980	855	585	465	415	470	525	320	245	85	60
	Accommodation type unknown	.	.	.	.	.	.	.	.	.	.	.

Source: Welsh Government, Homelessness data collection

Contact: stats.housing@wales.gsi.gov.uk

1. Private sector accommodation includes private sector accommodation leased by the local authority, RSLs and directly with a private sector landlord

2. Public sector accommodation includes within local authority stock and RSL stock on assured shorthold tenancies

. The data item is not applicable.

* The data item is disclosive or not sufficiently robust for publication

11.9 Households in temporary accommodation by accommodation type, Scotland

All households		Households in temporary accommodation by accommodation type									
		Social sector accommodation[1]		Hostel		Bed & Breakfast		Other[2]		Total	
		Number	%	Number	%	Number	%	Number	%	Number	%
2004	as at 31 March	3,537	*55*	1,586	*25*	1,190	*18*	132	*2*	**6,445**	***100***
	as at 30 June	3,754	*56*	1,514	*23*	1,273	*19*	105	*2*	**6,646**	***100***
	as at 30	3,894	*56*	1,590	*23*	1,331	*19*	110	*2*	**6,925**	***100***
	as at 31	4,071	*59*	1,521	*22*	1,243	*18*	117	*2*	**6,952**	***100***
2005	as at 31 March	4,136	*57*	1,490	*20*	1,516	*21*	159	*2*	**7,301**	***100***
	as at 30 June	4,324	*59*	1,340	*18*	1,413	*19*	264	*4*	**7,341**	***100***
	as at 30	4,606	*60*	1,320	*17*	1,424	*19*	333	*4*	**7,683**	***100***
	as at 31	4,525	*60*	1,295	*17*	1,323	*18*	356	*5*	**7,499**	***100***
2006	as at 31 March	4,747	*59*	1,328	*17*	1,494	*19*	416	*5*	**7,985**	***100***
	as at 30 June	4,732	*60*	1,342	*17*	1,362	*17*	452	*6*	**7,888**	***100***
	as at 30	4,880	*60*	1,301	*16*	1,491	*18*	439	*5*	**8,111**	***100***
	as at 31	4,981	*62*	1,235	*15*	1,391	*17*	482	*6*	**8,089**	***100***
2007	as at 31 March	5,164	*60*	1,242	*14*	1,528	*18*	643	*7*	**8,577**	***100***
	as at 30 June	5,075	*60*	1,170	*14*	1,588	*19*	690	*8*	**8,523**	***100***
	as at 30	5,104	*61*	1,134	*13*	1,492	*18*	671	*8*	**8,401**	***100***
	as at 31	5,460	*63*	1,104	*13*	1,348	*16*	721	*8*	**8,633**	***100***
2008	as at 31 March[3]	6,134	*64*	1,079	*11*	1,609	*17*	713	*7*	**9,535**	***100***
	as at 30 June	6,079	*62*	1,064	*11*	1,791	*18*	815	*8*	**9,749**	***100***
	as at 30	6,131	*62*	1,058	*11*	1,780	*18*	848	*9*	**9,817**	***100***
	as at 31	5,931	*62*	1,019	*11*	1,662	*17*	924	*10*	**9,536**	***100***
2009	as at 31 March	6,355	*63*	994	*10*	1,748	*17*	956	*10*	**10,053**	***100***
	as at 30 June	6,294	*62*	1,186	*12*	1,654	*16*	1,072	*11*	**10,206**	***100***
	as at 30	6,438	*62*	1,221	*12*	1,584	*15*	1,100	*11*	**10,343**	***100***
	as at 31	6,378	*62*	1,234	*12*	1,515	*15*	1,151	*11*	**10,278**	***100***
2010	as at 31 March	6,775	*63*	1,217	*11*	1,765	*16*	972	*9*	**10,729**	***100***
	as at 30 June	6,938	*62*	1,267	*11*	1,940	*17*	958	*9*	**11,103**	***100***
	as at 30	7,124	*63*	1,369	*12*	1,673	*15*	1,098	*10*	**11,264**	***100***
	as at 31	7,272	*66*	1,339	*12*	1,418	*13*	1,066	*10*	**11,095**	***100***
2011	as at 31 March	7,215	*64*	1,371	*12*	1,544	*14*	1,124	*10*	**11,254**	***100***
	as at 30 June	7,443	*67*	1,349	*12*	1,414	*13*	953	*9*	**11,159**	***100***
	as at 30	7,382	*67*	1,329	*12*	1,433	*13*	916	*8*	**11,060**	***100***
	as at 31	7,102	*66*	1,310	*12*	1,232	*12*	1,041	*10*	**10,685**	***100***
2012	as at 31 March	7,093	*66*	1,333	*12*	1,281	*12*	1,043	*10*	**10,750**	***100***
	as at 30 June	7,106	*68*	1,190	*11*	1,205	*12*	965	*9*	**10,466**	***100***
	as at 30	7,146	*68*	1,333	*13*	1,090	*10*	977	*9*	**10,546**	***100***
	as at 31	6,920	*67*	1,292	*13*	1,063	*10*	977	*10*	**10,252**	***100***
2013	as at 31 March	7,061	*67*	1,290	*12*	1,170	*11*	950	*9*	**10,471**	***100***
	as at 30 June	6,965	*66*	1,451	*14*	1,104	*11*	972	*9*	**10,492**	***100***
	as at 30	6,877	*67*	1,503	*15*	1,001	*10*	887	*9*	**10,268**	***100***
	as at 31	6,687	*67*	1,496	*15*	932	*9*	848	*9*	**9,963**	***100***
2014	as at 31 March	6,405	*62*	1,813	*18*	1,125	*11*	938	*9*	**10,281**	***100***
	as at 30 June	6,310	*62*	1,830	*18*	1,073	*11*	981	*10*	**10,194**	***100***
	as at 30	6,509	*63*	1,714	*17*	1,070	*10*	1,035	*10*	**10,328**	***100***
	as at 31	6,365	*62*	1,766	*17*	1,030	*10*	1,057	*10*	**10,218**	***100***
2015	as at 31 March	6,558	*62*	1,741	*16*	1,085	*10*	1,183	*11*	**10,567**	***100***
	as at 30 June	6,600	*63*	1,743	*17*	1,059	*10*	1,061	*10*	**10,463**	***100***
	as at 30	6,547	*62*	1,749	*17*	1,156	*11*	1,046	*10*	**10,498**	***100***
	as at 31	6,616	*63*	1,733	*17*	1,025	*10*	1,093	*10*	**10,467**	***100***
2016	as at 31 March	6,679	*63*	1,728	*16*	1,052	*10*	1,084	*10*	**10,543**	***100***

To note: All figures in the table are rounded to 5 for disclosure purposes

Source: Scottish Government

1. Includes Glasgow Housing Association stock from 2003, and all other housing associations from June 2005 onward.
2. The category 'other' includes mainly private landlords. Prior to June 1999 the figures may also include an unknown number of local authority-owned chalets or mobile homes.
3. From 31 March 2008 there is a break in comparability in numbers in temporary accommodation in Glasgow-see notes page.

Background to discontinuity in Glasgow data from 31 March 2008

From 31 March 2008 there is a break in comparability in the information on numbers of homeless applicants in temporary accommodation in Glasgow. The number of homeless households in temporary accommodation in Glasgow includes asylum applications given indefinite leave to remain in the United Kingdom and who are in temporary accommodation. From 31 March 2008 there was an significant increase in such households as a consequence of the 'legacy' case reviews undertaken by the Home Office. This introduces a discontinuity in the statistics for both Glasgow and for Scotland in the totals for all households and households with children. To bridge the discontinuity Glasgow have provided figures on the numbers of such households included at the end of each quarter from 31 March 2008. The additional numbers included are:-

Chapter 12

Banking, insurance

Banking, insurance

Industrial analysis of monetary financial institutions deposits and lending (Tables 12.4 and 12.5)

These data collate information from UK MFIs on deposits from and lending to UK residents other than MFIs and are separated into 18 broad industrial categories, based upon the SIC classification system. Until Q3 2007, the analysis of lending covered loans, advances (including under reverse repos), finance leasing, acceptances and facilities (all in sterling and other currencies) provided by reporting MFIs to their UK resident non-MFI customers, as well as MFI holdings of sterling and euro commercial paper issued by these resident customers. Following a review of statistical data collected, acceptances and holdings of sterling and euro commercial paper are no longer collected at the industry level detail with effect from Q4 2007 data. Total lending therefore reflects loans and advances (including under reverse repos) only, from Q4 2007 data.

Consumer credit (Excluding Student Loans) (Table 12.12)

Following an ONS review in August 1997, data for 'other specialist lenders' were improved and revised back to January 1995. Total outstanding consumer credit was revised upwards by £2.6bn. Flows were break adjusted. Monthly data are available for lending by retailers from January 1997 but are not available for lending by insurance companies. The missing monthly data have been interpolated from quarterly data.

Within total consumer credit (excluding student loans) outstanding, credit card lending had been underestimated and 'other' consumer credit overestimated prior to January 1999 as a result of a longstanding inconsistency. The credit card element had previously covered sterling credit card lending to the UK household sector by only UK banks and building societies. Credit card lending by other specialist lenders and retailers (where they finance lending themselves) could not be separately identified and so was included within the 'other' consumer credit component.

From January 1999 onwards this inconsistency has been corrected, as credit card lending by other specialist lenders can be separately identified. As a result, data from January 1999 onwards for credit card lending and for 'other' consumer credit are not directly comparable with those for earlier periods. The change affects all three measures of credit card lending (gross, net and amounts outstanding), with an equal offsetting change to 'other' consumer credit. In non-seasonally adjusted terms, gross credit card lending was on average around £800 million per month higher since January 1999, whilst the amount outstanding of credit card debt was boosted by £4.8 billion in January 1999. The changes to net credit card lending are much smaller in absolute terms, with no discernible change to trend.

From November 2006, the Bank of England ceased to update the separate data on consumer credit provided by other specialist lenders, retailers, and insurance companies, previously contained in Table A5.6 of Monetary and Financial Statistics. The final month for which separate data are available on the Bank's Statistical Interactive Database is November 2006. The three categories have been merged into "other consumer credit lenders".

Prior to January 2008, building societies' lending was unsecured lending to individuals including sterling bridging loans (prior to October 1998 this was class 3 lending to individuals). Building societies gross lending through overdrafts is no longer included from January 2008.

http://www.bankofengland.co.uk/boeapps/iadb/newintermed.asp

12.1a The Bank of England's Annual Balance Sheet 1958-2016

This sheet gives consistent annual series for the Bank's liabilities and assets from 1958 to 1966, which were first published in the June 1967 Quarterly Bulletin and extended to 2006 using subsequent Quarterly Bulletins. An extension to 2014 is made using the new reporting method introduced in 2006. The dates in each year to which the figures relate are: last Saturday in February; 1958-1966 - Published Bank Returns, last Wednesday in February: 1966-2006 - Published Bank Returns: third Wednesday in February (the dates on which the London Clearing Banks compiled their monthly figures); 2006-2016 - Published Bank Returns: third Wednesday in February. See links at the bottom of the table for more information on the data.

Assets, £

	Total	Government debt	Other Government securities	Other securities	Coin and bullion	Notes in the Bank
1958	2,327,196,165	11,015,100	2,222,675,614	49,533,147	5,727,986	38,244,318
1959	2,396,154,287	11,015,100	2,309,195,369	27,721,013	3,926,655	44,296,150
1960	2,509,611,487	11,015,100	2,412,801,707	44,040,161	3,309,613	38,444,906
1961	2,766,327,702	11,015,100	2,655,953,220	52,627,117	2,331,877	44,400,388
1962	2,920,525,859	11,015,100	2,819,589,302	65,236,067	1,468,171	23,217,219
1963	2,714,385,221	11,015,100	2,585,258,886	75,731,629	1,467,915	40,911,691
1964	2,831,080,950	11,015,100	2,738,352,963	58,944,838	1,451,304	21,316,745
1965	3,042,943,845	11,015,100	2,879,556,182	101,959,343	1,469,009	48,944,211
1966	3,302,225,248	11,015,100	3,165,623,387	102,383,926	1,460,584	21,742,251
3rd Wednesday in February						
1966	3,294,800,000	11,015,100	3,165,884,900	100,500,000	17,400,000	
1967	3,532,700,000	11,015,100	3,326,484,900	153,800,000	41,400,000	
1968	3,742,400,000	11,015,100	3,513,084,900	179,700,000	38,600,000	
1969	3,870,700,000	11,015,100	3,724,084,900	116,900,000	18,700,000	
1970	3,887,000,000	11,015,100	3,655,984,900	198,000,000	22,000,000	
1971	4,668,000,000	11,015,100	4,166,984,900	446,000,000	44,000,000	
1972	4,242,000,000	11,015,100	3,598,984,900	594,000,000	38,000,000	
1973	5,484,000,000	11,015,100	4,572,984,900	866,000,000	34,000,000	
1974	6,564,000,000	11,015,100	5,208,984,900	1,320,000,000	24,000,000	
1975	6,945,000,000	11,015,100	6,037,984,900	877,000,000	19,000,000	
1976	7,677,000,000	11,015,100	6,508,984,900	1,138,000,000	19,000,000	
1977	8,156,000,000	11,015,100	6,600,984,900	1,537,000,000	7,000,000	
1978	10,004,000,000	11,015,100	8,541,984,900	1,428,000,000	23,000,000	
1979	10,193,000,000	11,015,100	8,491,984,900	1,683,000,000	7,000,000	
1980	11,065,000,000	11,015,100	8,760,984,900	2,269,000,000	24,000,000	
1981	12,112,000,000	11,015,100	7,336,984,900	4,749,000,000	15,000,000	
1982	12,701,000,000	11,015,100	4,765,984,900	7,919,000,000	5,000,000	
1983	15,961,000,000	11,015,100	4,369,984,900	11,565,000,000	15,000,000	
1984	14,315,000,000	11,015,100	2,109,984,900	12,184,000,000	10,000,000	
1985	19,603,000,000	11,015,100	2,893,984,900	16,693,000,000	5,000,000	
1986	19,219,000,000	11,015,100	3,227,984,900	15,972,000,000	8,000,000	
1987	17,256,000,000	11,015,100	2,150,984,900	15,087,000,000	7,000,000	
1988	16,889,000,000	11,015,100	2,713,984,900	14,157,000,000	7,000,000	
1989	17,350,000,000	11,015,100	6,114,984,900	11,214,000,000	10,000,000	
1990	18,679,000,000	11,015,100	11,681,984,900	6,976,000,000	10,000,000	
1991	19,694,000,000	11,015,100	9,952,984,900	9,726,000,000	4,000,000	
1992	20,280,000,000	11,015,100	8,448,984,900	11,808,000,000	12,000,000	
1993	24,569,000,000	11,015,100	7,976,984,900	16,574,000,000	7,000,000	
1994	26,351,000,000	11,015,100	6,954,984,900	19,381,000,000	4,000,000	
1995	24,195,000,000	0	14,311,000,000	9,876,000,000	8,000,000	
1996	25,181,000,000	0	13,552,000,000	11,624,000,000	5,000,000	
1997	26,917,000,000	0	10,309,000,000	16,596,000,000	12,000,000	
1998	32,681,000,000	0	6,174,000,000	26,503,000,000	4,000,000	
1999	101,956,000,000	0	6,936,000,000	95,008,000,000	12,000,000	
2000	80,756,000,000	0	7,255,000,000	73,489,000,000	12,000,000	
2001	37,850,000,000	0	15,061,000,000	22,782,000,000	7,000,000	
2002	41,352,000,000	0	15,298,000,000	26,050,000,000	4,000,000	
2003	46,712,000,000	0	15,735,000,000	30,970,000,000	7,000,000	
2004	48,565,000,000	0	16,426,000,000	32,132,000,000	7,000,000	
2005	55,714,000,000	0	15,193,000,000	40,512,000,000	9,000,000	
2006	61,799,000,000	0	15,538,000,000	46,254,000,000	7,000,000	

12.1a The Bank of England's Annual Balance Sheet 1958-2016

This sheet gives consistent annual series for the Bank's liabilities and assets from 1958 to 1966, which were first published in the June 1967 Quarterly Bulletin and extended to 2006 using subsequent Quarterly Bulletins. An extension to 2014 is made using the new reporting method introduced in 2006. The dates in each year to which the figures relate are: last Saturday in February; 1958-1966 - Published Bank Returns, last Wednesday in February: 1966-2006 - Published Bank Returns: third Wednesday in February (the dates on which the London Clearing Banks compiled their monthly figures); 2006-2016 - Published Bank Returns: third Wednesday in February. See links at the bottom of the table for more information on the data.

Assets, £

		£ Short-term repo operations with BoE	£ long-term operations with BoE	Central Bank bonds and other securities acquired via market transactions	£ Ways and means advances to HM government	Other assets including loan to the Asset Purchase facility
3rd Wednesday in February, Q1 observation used from 2015[1]						
2007	76,991,000,000	30,110,000,000	15,000,000,000	6,727,000,000	13,370,000,000	18,511,000,000
2008	97,616,000,000	6,609,000,000	31,999,000,000	7,618,000,000	7,370,000,000	51,638,000,000
2009	168,404,000,000	0	126,261,000,000	11,873,000,000	9,392,000,000	32,751,000,000
2010	247,280,000,000	0	20,607,000,000	12,691,000,000	370,000,000	226,303,000,000
2011	241,642,000,000	0	14,102,000,000	13,273,000,000	370,000,000	227,169,000,000
2012	311,459,000,000	0	5,545,000,000	13,892,000,000	370,000,000	305,545,000,000
2013	404,228,000,000	0	2,085,000,000	13,248,000,000	370,000,000	401,773,000,000
2014	403,089,000,000	0	1,165,000,000	16,312,000,000	370,000,000	401,554,000,000
2015	410,775,000,000	0	5,180,000,000	-	370,000,000	405,225,000,000
2016	423,246,000,000	0	18,657,000,000	-	370,000,000	404,219,000,000

Source: Bank of England

1. Following Bank of England money market reform on 18 May 2006 the Bank of England 'Bank Return' was changed. This series forms part of the new Bank Return, with data starting on 24 May 2006. More information on changes made to the Bank's monetary policy operations and their impact on published data can be found in `The implications of money market reform for data published in Monetary and Financial Statistics' in the June 2006 issue of Bank of England: Monetary and Financial Statistics. From 2015 onwards the observations on the total balance sheet are only available quarterly and with a 5 quarter lag so the nearest proxies are used for February observations. Thomas Ryland (email: ryland.thomas@bankofengland.co.uk.)

For more information on the data please use the following links:

Original 1967 Quarterly Bulletin article: http://www.bankofengland.co.uk/archive/Documents/historicpubs/qb/1967/qb67q2159163.pdf

Bank of England Statistical Abstracts: http://www.bankofengland.co.uk/archive/Pages/digitalcontent/historicpubs/statisticalabst.aspx

The implications of money market reform for data published in Monetary and Financial Statistics' in the June 2006 issue of Bank of England: Monetary and Financial Statistics.: http://www.bankofengland.co.uk/statistics/Documents/ms/articles/artjun06.pdf

Changes to the Bank's weekly reporting regime - Quarterly Bulletin article, 2014Q3: http://www.bankofengland.co.uk/publications/Documents/quarterlybulletin/2014/qb300614.pdf

Other data

Weekly data on the Bank of England's balance sheet 1844-2006: http://www.bankofengland.co.uk/research/Documents/onebank/balanceweekly_final.xlsx

12.1b The Bank of England's Annual Balance Sheet 1958-2016

This sheet gives consistent annual series for the Bank's liabilities and assets from 1958 to 1966, which were first published in the June 1967 Quarterly Bulletin and extended to 2006 using subsequent Quarterly Bulletins. An extension to 2014 is made using the new reporting method introduced in 2006. The dates in each year to which the figures relate are: last Saturday in February; 1958-1966 - Published Bank Returns, last Wednesday in February: 1966-2006 - Published Bank Returns: third Wednesday in February (the dates on which the London Clearing Banks compiled their monthly figures); 2007-2016 - Published Bank Returns: third Wednesday in February. See links at the bottom of the table for more information on the data.

Liabilities, £

	Notes In circulation	Notes in the Bank	Capital	Rest	Deposits	o/w Public deposits	o/w Special deposits	o/w Bankers deposits	Other accounts	Total
1958	1,962,114,543	38,244,318	14,553,000	3,900,136	308,384,168					2,327,196,165
1959	2,006,062,831	44,296,150	14,553,000	3,900,441	327,341,865					2,396,154,287
1960	2,111,915,274	38,444,906	14,553,000	3,898,192	340,800,115					2,509,611,487
1961	2,205,960,632	44,400,388	14,553,000	3,880,391	497,533,291		155,100,000			2,766,327,702
1962	2,302,141,403	23,217,219	14,553,000	3,917,764	576,696,473		241,400,000			2,920,525,859
1963	2,309,448,249	40,911,691	14,553,000	3,894,802	345,577,479					2,714,385,221
1964	2,429,044,275	21,316,745	14,553,000	3,896,193	362,270,737					2,831,080,950
1965	2,601,417,528	48,944,211	14,553,000	3,881,812	374,147,294					3,042,943,845
1966	2,778,619,008	21,742,251	14,553,000	3,882,025	483,428,964					3,302,225,248
3rd Wednesday in February										
1966	2,783,800,000	16,600,000	14,553,000	3,747,000	476,100,000	12,600,000	97,500,000	274,800,000	91,200,000	3,294,800,000
1967	2,859,800,000	40,600,000	14,553,000	3,747,000	614,000,000	16,100,000	201,400,000	282,400,000	114,100,000	3,532,700,000
1968	3,012,500,000	38,000,000	14,553,000	3,747,000	673,600,000	14,400,000	218,200,000	308,400,000	132,600,000	3,742,400,000
1969	3,132,500,000	18,000,000	14,553,000	3,747,000	702,000,000	18,500,000	231,000,000	308,200,000	144,300,000	3,870,800,000
1970	3,231,000,000	20,000,000	14,553,000	0	621,447,000	15,000,000	220,000,000	248,000,000	138,000,000	3,887,000,000
1971	3,658,000,000	42,000,000	14,553,000	0	953,447,000	15,000,000	398,000,000	314,000,000	226,000,000	4,668,000,000
1972	3,663,000,000	37,000,000	14,553,000	0	527,447,000	15,000,000	0	178,000,000	334,000,000	4,242,000,000
1973	4,166,000,000	34,000,000	14,553,000	0	1,269,447,000	22,000,000	714,000,000	230,000,000	303,000,000	5,484,000,000
1974	4,552,000,000	23,000,000	14,553,000	0	1,974,447,000	28,000,000	1,368,000,000	266,000,000	312,000,000	6,564,000,000
1975	5,306,000,000	19,000,000	14,553,000	0	1,604,447,000	21,000,000	935,000,000	275,000,000	373,000,000	6,944,000,000
1976	5,981,000,000	19,000,000	14,553,000	0	1,662,447,000	20,000,000	980,000,000	269,000,000	394,000,000	7,677,000,000
1977	6,694,000,000	6,000,000	14,553,000	0	1,441,447,000	18,000,000	711,000,000	273,000,000	439,000,000	8,156,000,000
1978	7,652,000,000	23,000,000	14,553,000	0	2,315,447,000	25,000,000	1,229,000,000	386,000,000	675,000,000	10,005,000,000
1979	8,843,000,000	7,000,000	14,553,000	0	1,328,447,000	25,000,000	255,000,000	404,000,000	644,000,000	10,193,000,000
1980	9,651,000,000	24,000,000	14,553,000	0	1,376,447,000	26,000,000	104,000,000	579,000,000	667,000,000	11,066,000,000
1981	10,160,000,000	15,000,000	14,553,000	0	1,921,447,000	32,000,000	0	602,000,000	1,288,000,000	12,111,000,000
1982	10,570,000,000	5,000,000	14,553,000	0	2,111,447,000	39,000,000	0	518,000,000	1,554,000,000	12,701,000,000
1983	10,910,000,000	15,000,000	14,553,000	0	5,021,447,000	2,286,000,000	0	537,000,000	2,199,000,000	15,961,000,000
1984	11,400,000,000	10,000,000	14,553,000	0	2,890,447,000	742,000,000	0	778,000,000	1,371,000,000	14,315,000,000
1985	11,976,000,000	4,000,000	14,553,000	0	7,608,447,000	5,267,000,000	0	672,000,000	1,670,000,000	19,603,000,000
1986	11,962,000,000	8,000,000	14,553,000	0	7,234,447,000	4,885,000,000	0	823,000,000	1,527,000,000	19,219,000,000
1987	12,503,000,000	7,000,000	14,553,000	0	4,731,447,000	2,158,000,000	0	953,000,000	1,621,000,000	17,256,000,000

12.1b The Bank of England's Annual Balance Sheet 1958-2016

This sheet gives consistent annual series for the Bank's liabilities and assets from 1958 to 1966, which were first published in the June 1967 Quarterly Bulletin and extended to 2006 using subsequent Quarterly Bulletins. An extension to 2014 is made using the new reporting method introduced in 2006. The dates in each year to which the figures relate are: last Saturday in February; 1958-1966 - Published Bank Returns, last Wednesday in February: 1966-2006 - Published Bank Returns: third Wednesday in February (the dates on which the London Clearing Banks compiled their monthly figures); 2007-2016 - Published Bank Returns: third Wednesday in February. See links at the bottom of the table for more information on the data.

Liabilities, £

	Notes In circulation	Notes in the Bank	Capital	Rest	Deposits	o/w Public deposits	o/w Special deposits	o/w Bankers deposits	Other accounts	Total
1988	13,253,000,000	7,000,000	14,553,000	0	3,614,447,000	104,000,000	0	1,057,000,000	2,452,000,000	16,889,000,000
1989	14,140,000,000	10,000,000	14,553,000	0	3,185,447,000	112,000,000	0	1,319,000,000	1,755,000,000	17,350,000,000
1990	14,951,000,000	9,000,000	14,553,000	0	3,704,447,000	54,000,000	0	1,736,000,000	1,915,000,000	18,679,000,000
1991	15,266,000,000	4,000,000	14,553,000	0	4,410,447,000	44,000,000	0	1,729,000,000	2,637,000,000	19,695,000,000
1992	15,436,000,000	12,000,000	14,553,000	0	4,815,447,000	119,000,000	0	1,417,000,000	3,278,000,000	20,278,000,000
1993	16,163,000,000	7,000,000	14,553,000	0	8,384,447,000	2,948,000,000	0	1,535,000,000	3,902,000,000	24,569,000,000
1994	17,096,000,000	4,000,000	14,553,000	0	9,236,447,000	1,129,000,000	0	1,628,000,000	6,479,000,000	26,351,000,000
1995	18,062,000,000	8,000,000	14,553,000	0	6,110,447,000	1,202,000,000	0	1,812,000,000	3,096,000,000	24,195,000,000
1996	19,405,000,000	5,000,000	14,553,000	0	5,756,447,000	873,000,000	0	1,842,000,000	3,042,000,000	25,181,000,000
1997	20,578,000,000	12,000,000	14,553,000	0	6,312,447,000	969,000,000	0	1,934,000,000	3,409,000,000	26,917,000,000
1998	22,026,000,000	4,000,000	14,553,000	0	10,636,447,000	1,103,000,000	0	2,716,000,000	6,817,000,000	32,681,000,000
1999	23,098,000,000	11,000,000	14,553,000	0	78,831,447,000	153,000,000	0	1,339,000,000	77,339,000,000	101,955,000,000
2000	24,918,000,000	12,000,000	14,553,000	0	55,811,447,000	217,000,000	0	1,360,000,000	54,235,000,000	80,756,000,000
2001	26,983,000,000	7,000,000	14,553,000	0	10,846,447,000	409,000,000	0	1,402,000,000	9,036,000,000	37,851,000,000
2002	29,046,000,000	4,000,000	14,553,000	0	12,288,447,000	372,000,000	0	1,656,000,000	10,261,000,000	41,353,000,000
2003	31,033,000,000	7,000,000	14,553,000	0	15,656,447,000	469,000,000	0	1,756,000,000	13,431,000,000	46,711,000,000
2004	33,013,000,000	7,000,000	14,553,000	0	15,530,447,000	650,000,000	0	1,929,000,000	12,951,000,000	48,565,000,000
2005	35,021,000,000	9,000,000	14,553,000	0	20,670,447,000	561,000,000	0	2,008,000,000	18,102,000,000	55,715,000,000
2006	36,793,000,000	7,000,000	14,553,000	0	24,983,447,000	803,000,000	0	2,857,000,000	21,324,000,000	61,798,000,000

12.1b The Bank of England's Annual Balance Sheet 1958-2016

This sheet gives consistent annual series for the Bank's liabilities and assets from 1958 to 1966, which were first published in the June 1967 Quarterly Bulletin and extended to 2006 using subsequent Quarterly Bulletins. An extension to 2014 is made using the new reporting method introduced in 2006. The dates in each year to which the figures relate are: last Saturday in February; 1958-1966 - Published Bank Returns, last Wednesday in February: 1966-2006 - Published Bank Returns: third Wednesday in February (the dates on which the London Clearing Banks compiled their monthly figures); 2007-2016 - Published Bank Returns: third Wednesday in February. See links at the bottom of the table for more information on the data.

Liabilities, £	Notes In circulation	£ Short-term repo operations with BoE	FC public securities issued	Cash ratio deposits	£ reserve balances	Other liabilities	Total
3rd Wednesday in February, Q1 observation used from 2015[1]							
2007	38,214,000,000	0	3,314,000,000	2,568,000,000	17,716,000,000	15,180,000,000	76,992,000,000
2008	40,933,000,000	0	3,327,000,000	2,936,000,000	23,824,000,000	26,595,000,000	97,615,000,000
2009	44,494,000,000	43,940,000,000	2,893,000,000	2,427,000,000	33,700,000,000	40,951,000,000	168,405,000,000
2010	49,486,000,000	0	3,881,000,000	2,574,000,000	155,165,000,000	36,174,000,000	247,280,000,000
2011	51,542,000,000	0	3,783,000,000	2,444,000,000	138,015,000,000	45,857,000,000	241,641,000,000
2012	54,568,000,000	0	3,870,000,000	2,386,000,000	188,975,000,000	61,660,000,000	311,459,000,000
2013	57,242,000,000	0	3,943,000,000	2,479,000,000	279,727,000,000	60,836,000,000	404,227,000,000
2014	59,391,000,000	0	3,597,000,000	4,078,000,000	305,951,000,000	30,072,000,000	403,089,000,000
2015	64,639,000,000	0	4,060,000,000	4,098,000,000	304,207,000,000	33,771,000,000	410,775,000,000
2016	69,776,000,000	0	4,194,000,000	4,136,000,000	312,245,000,000	32,895,000,000	423,246,000,000

Source: Bank of England

1. Following Bank of England money market reform on 18 May 2006 the Bank of England 'Bank Return' was changed. This series forms part of the new Bank Return, with data starting on 24 May 2006. More information on changes made to the Bank's monetary policy operations and their impact on published data can be found in `The implications of money market reform for data published in Monetary and Financial Statistics' in the June 2006 issue of Bank of England: Monetary and Financial Statistics. From 2015 onwards the observations on the total balance sheet are only available quarterly and with a 5 quarter lag so the nearest proxies are used for February observations.
Thomas Ryland (email: ryland.thomas@bankofengland.co.uk.)

For more information on the data please use the following links:
Original 1967 Quarterly Bulletin article: http://www.bankofengland.co.uk/archive/Documents/historicpubs/qb/1967/qb67q2159163.pdf
Bank of England Statistical Abstracts: http://www.bankofengland.co.uk/archive/Pages/digitalcontent/historicpubs/statisticalabst.aspx

The implications of money market reform for data published in Monetary and Financial Statistics' in the June 2006 issue of Bank of England: Monetary and Financial Statistics.: http://www.bankofengland.co.uk/statistics/Documents/ms/articles/artjun06.pdf

Changes to the Bank's weekly reporting regime - Quarterly Bulletin article, 2014Q3:
http://www.bankofengland.co.uk/publications/Documents/quarterlybulletin/2014/qb300614.pdf

Other data
Weekly data on the Bank of England's balance sheet 1844-2006: http://www.bankofengland.co.uk/research/Documents/onebank/balanceweekly_final.xlsx

12.2a Annual clearing volumes and values

Clearing volumes thousands	Annual volumes			
	2016	2017	Change 2017 on 2016 %	
Bacs				
Direct Credits	2,146,835	2,120,519	-26,316	-1%
Direct Debits	4,071,911	4,226,661	154,750	4%
Total BACS	**6,218,746**	**6,347,180**	**128,433**	**2%**
CHAPS Clearing Company				
Retail and Commercial (MT 103)	30,322	32,396	2,074	7%
Wholesale Financial (MT202)	8,641	9,256	614	7%
Total CHAPS	**38,964**	**41,652**	**2,688**	**7%**
Faster Payments				
Standing Order Payments	357,411	372,866	15,455	4%
Single Immediate Payments	882,226	1,081,096	198,869	23%
Forward Dated Payments	183,675	199,315	15,640	9%
Return Payments	2,780	2,530	-250	-9%
Total Faster Payments	**1,462,093**	**1,655,807**	**229,714**	**16%**
Cheque and Credit Clearing Company (C&CCC)				
Cheques	344,621	292,961	-51,660	-15%
Credits	21,857	17,261	-4,596	-21%
Euro debits	80	55	-25	-32%
Total Cheque & Credit	**366,558**	**310,276**	-56,281	**-15%**
Belfast Bankers' Clearing Company Ltd (BBCCL)[1]				
Cheques	11,037	9,739	-1,298	-12%
Credits	221	180	-41	-19%
Total BBCCL	11,257	9,918	-1,339	-12%
Total all Clearing Companies	**8,061,617**	**8,364,833**	**303,216**	**4%**

Clearing values £ millions	Annual values			
	2016	2017	Change 2017 on 2016 %	
Bacs				
Direct Credits	3,514,313	3,619,384	105,070	3%
Direct Debits	1,262,235	1,304,647	42,412	3%
Total BACS	**4,776,549**	**4,924,030**	**147,482**	**3%**
CHAPS Clearing Company				
Retail and Commercial (MT 103)	18,879,635	22,083,495	3,203,860	17%
Wholesale Financial (MT202)	56,693,993	61,998,982	5,304,990	9%
Total CHAPS	**75,573,628**	**84,082,477**	**8,508,849**	**11%**
Faster Payments				
Standing Order Payments	113,558	122,314	8,757	8%
Single Immediate Payments	728,642	874,684	146,041	20%
Forward Dated Payments	345,630	401,476	55,846	16%
Return Payments	1,178	1,217	39	3%
Total Faster Payments	**1,189,008**	**1,399,691**	**210,683**	**18%**
Cheque and Credit Clearing Company (C&CCC)				
Cheques	400,158	356,438	-43,720	-11%
Credits	15,022	11,733	-3,290	-22%
Euro debits	1,274	1,139	-135	-11%
Total	**416,455**	**369,310**	**-47,145**	**-11%**
Belfast Bankers' Clearing Company Ltd (BBCCL)[1]				
Cheques	17,833	16,664	-1,169	-7%
Credits	1,306	1,255	-49	-4%
Total BBCCL	**19,139**	**17,920**	**-1,219**	**-6%**
Total all Clearing Companies	**81,974,778**	**90,793,429**	**8,818,651**	**11%**

Source: Cheque and Credit Clearing Company Ltd

1. The Belfast Bankers' Clearing Company was formed in May 2007 as a means of formalising existing rules and standards for sterling paper clearings and Euro debit clearing in Northern Ireland, and has 4 members. The role of the Company is to maintain the integrity of the clearing arrangements and ensure the system is efficient and effective.

(a) Totals, averages and percentages are calculated using unrounded data. The value of euro debit clearings are shown as £ sterling equivalent.

(b) 252 days were used to calculate the average daily statistics in 2017, with 253 in 2016. In terms of Faster Standing Orders and 365 days were used for the other payment types. Payments, 252 days were used for Inter-branch clearing volumes (i.e. items cleared between branches of the same bank) are shown separately. These data are less comprehensive due to changes in agency arrangements and individual member processing policies, for example, the increased use of electronic processing methods. It is likely, therefore, that a proportion of inter-branch transactions are not included in these totals.

12.2b Bacs volumes and values

Annual volumes thousands

	Bacs Direct Credits		Bacs Euro Credits		Direct Debits		Total volumes	
	Number	% Change	Number	% Change	Number	% Change	Number	% Change
2003	1,341,945	14.4	54	45.0	2,429,915	6.2	4,060,357	8.7
2004	1,710,673	27.5	84	55.5	2,589,934	6.6	4,602,570	13.4
2005	2,093,859	22.4	12	48.6	2,722,245	5.1	5,134,250	11.6
2006	2,171,586	3.7	157	25.9	2,857,761	5.0	5,361,749	4.4
2007	2,233,106	2.8	181	15.8	2,296,474	3.7	5,544,109	3.4
2008	2,254,875	1.0	176	-3.2	3,076,857	3.8	5,655,751	2.0
2009	2,289,813	1.5	193	10.0	3,149,153	2.3	5,638,919	-0.3
2010	2,292,942	0.1	143	26.0	3,229,338	2.5	5,672,730	0.6
2011	2,270,987	-1.0			3,322,360	2.9	5,716,999	0.8
2012	2,182,667	-3.9			3,416,651	2.8	5,616,392	-1.8
2013	2,151,718	-1.0			3,524,905	3.0	5,695,028	1.0
2014	2,150,557	-			3,671,997	4.0	5,841,232	3.0
2015	2,171,697	-			3,908,346	6.0	6,080,043	4.0
2016	2,146,835	-1.0			4,071,911	4.0	6,218,746	2.0
2017	2,120,519	-1.0			4,226,661	4.0	6,347,180	2.0

Average values £ millions

	Bacs Direct Credits [(a)]		Bacs Euro Credits		Direct Debits		Total volumes	
	Number	% Change	Number	% Change	Number	% Change	Number	% Change
2003	1,910,251	8.3	1,924	53.9	662,192	7.3	2,574,367	8.1
2004	2,131,031	11.6	2,040	6.0	750,381	13.3	2,883,452	12.0
2005	2,350,644	10.3	2,524	23.7	797,039	6.2	3,150,207	9.3
2006	2,581,682	9.8	2,819	11.7	844,832	6.0	3,429,333	8.9
2007	2,808,349	8.8	3,965	40.6	883,592	4.6	3,695,906	7.8
2008	3,006,159	7.0	4,806	21.2	935,356	5.9	3,946,321	6.8
2009	2,969,711	-1.2	5,255	9.3	885,708	-5.3	3,860,674	-2.2
2010	3,111,218	4.8	3,033	-42.3	948,137	7.0	4,062,388	5.2
2011	3,318,536	6.7			1,044,677	10.2	4,363,214	7.4
2012	3,036,714	-8.5			1,075,507	3.0	4,112,222	-5.8
2013	3,103,579	2.0			1,115,065	4.0	4,218,644	3.0
2014	3,253,279	5.0			1,167,266	5.0	4,420,546	5.0
2015	3,374,815	4.0			1,215,396	4.0	4,590,211	4.0
2016	3,541,313	4.0			1,262,235	4.0	4,803,548	5.0
2017	3,619,384	3.0			1,304,647	3.0	4,924,031	3.0

Sources: UK Payments Administration Ltd, Cheque and Credit Clearing Company Ltd

(a) Values represent standing orders and Bacs Direct Credits combined.

The Euro Debit Credit Service ceased operation on 29 October 2010.

Bacs has been maintaining the integrity of payment related services since 1968, with responsibility for the schemes behind the clearing and settlement of UK automated payment methods, Direct Debit and Bacs Direct Credit. A membership company limited by Guarantee, Bacs currently has 19 members from the UK, Europe, and the US. Bacs also provides managed services for third parties, such as the Cash ISA Transfer Service, and the company owns and manages the Current Account Switch Service which has 46 direct participants.

12.2c CHAPS volumes and values

Annual volumes thousands

	CHAPS Sterling [a]		CHAPS Euro						Total volumes [a]	
			Domestic (a)		Target					
					Transmitted to		Received from			
	Number	% Change	Number	% Change	Number	% Change	Number	% Change	Number	% Change
2003	27,215	6.5	1,399	13.1	2,904	19.2	1,685	4.7	33,202	7.6
2004	28,322	4.1	1,378	-1.5	3,314	14.1	1,849	9.7	34,862	5.0
2005	29,686	4.8	1,484	7.7	3,597	8.6	1,988	7.5	36,756	5.4
2006	33,030	11.3	1,461	-1.6	4,115	14.4	2,080	4.6	40,686	10.7
2007	35,588	7.7	1,455	-0.3	4,263	3.6	2,229	7.1	43,535	7.0
2008	34,606	-2.8	220	-84.9	379	-91.1	593	-73.4	35,797	-17.8
2009	31,926	-7.7							31,926	-10.8
2010	32,169	0.8							32,169	0.8
2011	34,024	5.8							34,024	5.8
2012	33,936	-0.3							33,936	-0.3
2013	34,976	3.0							34,976	3.0
2014	36,521	4.0							36,521	4.0
2015	37,548	3.0							37,548	3.0
2016	38,964	4.0							38,964	4.0
2017	41,652	7.0							41,652	7.0

Annual Values £ millions

	CHAPS Sterling [a]		CHAPS Euro (sterling equivalent)						Total values [a]	
			Domestic (a)		Target					
					Transmitted to		Received from			
	Number	% Change	Number	% Change	Number	% Change	Number	% Change	Number	% Change
2003	51,613,456	-0.5	5,114,198	22.7	15,924,879	21.5	15,923,974	21.5	88,576,506	7.7
2004	52,347,525	1.4	4,509,924	-11.8	17,238,602	8.2	17,238,737	8.3	91,334,788	3.1
2005	52,671,592	0.6	6,069,146	34.6	19,180,194	11.3	19,179,273	11.3	97,100,206	6.3
2006	59,437,370	12.8	7,365,558	21.4	21,415,027	11.7	21,419,195	11.7	109,637,149	12.9
2007	69,352,322	16.7	6,781,942	-7.9	25,266,729	18.0	25,268,856	18.0	126,669,848	15.5
2008	73,625,908	6.2	574,610	-91.5	4,413,570	-82.5	4,403,022	-82.6	83,017,110	-34.5
2009	64,616,956	-12.2							64,616,956	-22.2
2010	61,587,609	-4.7							61,587,609	-4.7
2011	63,876,772	3.7							63,876,772	3.7
2012	71,716,857	12.3							71,716,857	12.3
2013	70,138,927	-2.0							70,138,927	-2.0
2014	67,959,491	-3.0							67,959,491	-3.0
2015	68,411,178	1.0							68,411,178	1.0
2016	75,573,628	10.0							75,573,628	10.0
2017	84,082,477	11.0							84,082,477	11.0

Sources: UK Payments Administration Ltd, Cheque and Credit Clearing Company Ltd

(a) NewCHAPS was launched on 27 August 2001 and since this date CHAPS Sterling and CHAPS Euro Domestic figures include all CHAPS traffic.

CHAPS is the UK's same day high value payment system for both wholesale financial and retail payments. Payments of any value are settled individually and irrevocably in central bank funds, and transferred over SWIFT. CHAPS is focused on systemically important, high value and time-critical payments. Currently 26 domestic and international financial institutions are Direct Participants, with several future joiners planned. These serve over 5,000 Indirect Participants. Financial institutions such as banks, central counterparties and authorised non-bank payment service providers are eligible to join CHAPS. Most of CHAPS' value is accounted for by wholesale financial transactions and international sterling flows.

12.2d Faster Payments volumes and values

Annual volumes thousands

	Standing Order Payments		Single Immedicate Payments		Forward Dated Payments		Return Payments		Total Volumes (a)	
	Number	% change	Number	% change	Number	% change	Number	% change	Number	% change
2003										
2004										
2005										
2006										
2007										
2008	37,574	*	36,325	*	8,708	*	182	*	82,789	*
2009	156,865	*	109,337	*	27,912	*	673	*	294,787	*
2010	203,055	29.4	181,195	65.7	40,632	45.6	880	30.6	425,761	44.4
2011	235,654	16.1	237,718	31.2	50,861	25.2	1,092	24.2	525,325	23.4
2012	299,630	27.1	379,844	59.8	129,829	155.3	1,788	63.6	811,090	54.4
2013	312,995	4	502,025	32	150,381	16.0	2,228	25.0	967,629	19.0
2014	329,858	5	609,879	21	159,153	6.0	2,040	-8.0	1,100,930	14.0
2015	343,642	4	730,675	20	170,339	7.0	2,378	17.0	1,247,035	13.0
2016	357,411	4.0	882,226	21	183,675	8.0	2,780	17.0	1,426,093	14.0
2017	372,866	4.0	1,081,096	23	199,315	9.0	2,530	-9.0	1,655,807	16.0

Annual values £ millions

	Standing Order Payments		Single Immedicate Payments		Forward Dated Payments		Return Payments		Total Volumes (a)	
	Number	% change	Number	% change	Number	% change	Number	% change	Number	% change
2003										
2004										
2005										
2006										
2007										
2008	3,341	*	22,015	*	7,473	*	42	*	32,871	*
2009	26,527	*	59,015	*	20,544	*	136	*	106,223	*
2010	38,963	46.9	92,847	57.3	32,193	56.7	208	52.9	164,211	54.6
2011	50,206	28.9	135,101	45.5	49,492	53.5	308	47.9	235,044	43.1
2012	80,009	59.4	328,685	143.3	208,252	321.3	965	213	617,911	162.9
2013	88,885	11.0	423,571	29.0	257,794	24.0	1,111	15.0	771,361	25.0
2014	97,121	9.0	517,641	22.0	288,034	12.0	999	-10.0	903,794	17.0
2015	107,202	10.0	619,303	20.0	313,099	9.0	1,114	12.0	1,040,717	15.0
2016	113,558	6.0	728,642	18.0	345,630	10.0	1,178	6.0	1,189,008	14.0
2017	122,314	8.0	874,684	20.0	401,476	16.0	1,217	3.0	1,399,691	18.0

Sources: UK Payments Administration Ltd, Cheque and Credit Clearing Company Ltd

(a) The UK Faster Payments Service was launched on 27 May 2008

The Faster Payment Service, operated by Faster Payments Scheme Ltd, enables internet, mobile and telephone banking payments as well as standing order payments to move from account to account, normally within seconds, 24 hours a day, 365 days a year. As at the end of 2017 there were 18 direct settling participants, with a number more intending to join in 2018. Given its scale and reach, it is considered one of the most advanced real-time payment services in the world.

12.2e Inter-bank volumes and values

Annual volumes thousands

	Exchanged in Great Britain							
	Cheques		Credits		Euro Debits		Total Volumes	
	Number	% change	Number	% change	Number	% change	Number	% change
2003	1,519,117	-6.3	140,792	-6.4	759	3.6	1,519,876	-6.3
2004	1,423,742	-6.3	132,899	-5.6	724	-4.6	1,424,465	-6.3
2005	1,325,762	-6.9	123,280	-7.2	637	-12.0	1,326,399	-6.9
2006	1,237,401	-6.7	108,309	-12.1	586	-7.9	1,237,987	-6.7
2007	1,124,869	-9.1	96,90	-11.1	531	-9.5	1,125,400	-9.1
2008	1,007,379	-23.5	86,442	-10.2	445	-16.1	1,007,824	-10.4
2009	875,533	-11.4	73,686	-14.8	351	-21.2	875,884	-13.1
2010	775,643	-12.1	61,662	-16.3	279	-20.5	775,922	-11.4
2011	682,082	-12.1	53,934	-12.5	223	-20.1	6,822,305	-12.1
2012	597,076	-12.5	46,927	-12.9	165	-25.7	597,241	-12.5
2013	525,295	-12.0	40,569	-14.0	131	-21.0	525,426	-12.0
2014	464,191	-12.0	34,962	-14.0	108	-17.0	464,299	-12.0
2015	404,134	-13.0	28,049	-20.0	89	-18.0	432,273	-13.0
2016	344,621	-15.0	21,857	22.0	80	-10.0	366,558	-15.0
2017	292,961	-15.0	17,261	-21.0	55	-25.0	310,276	-15.0

Annual values £ millions

	Exchanged in Great Britain							
	Cheques		Credits		Euro Debits		Total Volumes	
	Number	% change	Number	% change	Number	% change	Number	% change
2003	1,240,685	-3.2	74,366	-7.6	3,898	13.8	1,244,583	-3.1
2004	1,210,057	-2.5	68,261	-8.2	3,456	-11.4	1,213,513	-2.5
2005	1,152,256	-4.8	61,844	-9.4	3,206	-7.2	1,155,642	-4.8
2006	1,171,062	1.6	59,309	-4.1	3,111	-3.0	1,174,174	1.6
2007	1,156,684	-1.2	57,347	-3.3	2,970	-4.6	1,159,653	-1.2
2008	1,075,694	-7.0	51,641	-9.9	2,980	0.4	1,078,674	-7.0
2009	870,591	-19.1	41,624	-19.4	2,993	0.4	873,584	-19.0
2010	761,081	-12.6	32,312	-22.4	1,767	-41	762,848	-12.7
2011	675,706	-11.2	27,990	-13.4	1,559	-11.8	667,226	-11.2
2012	601,256	-11	23,802	-15	1,188	-23.9	602,444	-11.0
2013	535,513	-11.0	21,109	-11.0	1,166	-2.0	536,679	-11.0
2014	498,729	-7.0	19,659	-7.0	1,289	11.0	500,018	-7.0
2015	454,838	-9.0	17,216	-12.0	1,208	-6.0	473,261	-8.8
2016	400,158	-12.0	15,022	-13.0	1,274	5.0	416,455	-12.0
2017	356,438	-11.0	11,733	-22.0	1,139	-11.0	369,310	-11.0

Source: Cheque and Credit Clearing Company Ltd

The Cheque and Credit Clearing Company has managed the cheque clearing system in England and Wales since 1985 and in Scotland since 1996. As well as clearing cheques, the system processes bankers' drafts, postal orders, warrants, government payable orders and travellers' cheques. The company also manages the systems for the clearing of paper bank giro credits and euro cheques (drawn on GB banks). There are 11 participants in the cheque clearing system and the credit clearing system and 10 in the euro debit clearing system. The Image Clearing System (ICS) was launched on 30th October with very low volumes going through the system. There are 17 Participants in ICS. More information on the ICS Participants can be found on our website: www.chequeandcredit.co.uk.

12.3a Monetary financial institutions' (excluding central bank) balance sheet

£ millions — Not seasonally adjusted

Amounts outstanding of sterling liabilities

	Notes outstanding and cash loaded cards	Sight deposits					Time deposits								Sale and repurchase agreements				
		UK MFIs	of which intragroup banks	UK public sector	Other UK residents	Non-residents	UK MFIs	of which intragroup banks	UK public sector	Other UK residents	of which SAYE	of which cash ISAs	Non-residents	UK MFIs	of which intragroup banks	UK public sector	Other UK residents	Non-residents
RPM	B3LM	B3GL	B8ZC	B3MM	B3NM	B3OM	B3HL	B8ZE	B3PM	B3QM	B3RM	B3SM	B3TM	B3IL	B8ZA	B3UM	B3VM	B3WM
2016 Jan	6,997	116,615	101,441	16,617	1,218,570	158,484	138,517	132,667	18,463	674,235	1,119	262,923	200,850	46,043	18,401	1,774	75,871	68,286
Feb	6,966	116,650	100,824	16,012	1,237,202	158,086	138,712	132,503	17,581	670,527	972	263,504	176,619	48,599	19,209	1,609	78,575	58,133
Mar	7,065	106,174	89,056	15,189	1,264,267	166,282	142,403	136,776	15,435	654,894	975	265,493	178,697	54,471	18,309	310	70,684	68,543
Apr	7,065	101,243	85,379	16,398	1,249,182	161,550	143,038	135,012	16,559	662,888	1,000	270,998	185,514	58,104	18,055	5,857	73,912	69,809
May	7,145	101,341	85,893	15,747	1,266,291	152,548	138,641	131,217	16,828	660,096	1,012	271,719	177,644	55,967	15,678	6,107	78,066	73,496
Jun	7,118	95,237	79,259	15,764	1,294,533	166,716	162,142	154,324	17,087	661,180	1,046	271,941	183,339	61,906	16,733	6,290	76,670	75,146
Jul	7,122	102,532	83,544	16,423	1,299,441	176,575	158,302	151,103	17,941	661,500	962	272,368	185,186	52,310	11,110	4,286	90,674	63,811
Aug	7,238	97,833	79,415	16,266	1,305,093	177,915	154,919	148,019	17,991	663,883	932	271,966	182,842	52,894	11,710	5,199	99,551	67,808
Sep	7,321	104,476	87,166	15,155	1,323,496	170,492	158,982	151,736	17,763	657,004	887	271,617	183,587	51,065	11,418	2,011	83,126	70,165
Oct	7,355	106,085	86,216	15,701	1,322,805	171,335	150,903	142,332	17,845	657,516	901	270,962	183,697	48,409	13,522	3,485	102,510	78,151
Nov	7,426	99,860	82,335	14,917	1,324,085	169,995	156,550	144,352	17,626	651,071	894	270,176	182,511	46,054	12,981	3,775	116,898	83,119
Dec	7,852	104,913	89,263	15,030	1,333,224	172,218	191,696	165,240	16,955	652,271	899	269,783	184,000	40,851	12,828	2,176	96,054	83,951
2017 Jan	7,696	111,503	94,478	15,241	1,316,897	174,390	199,656	159,778	16,586	642,895	911	268,988	179,714	43,286	17,314	1,765	122,405	84,315
Feb	7,704	120,382	104,905	14,312	1,319,172	172,824	220,016	171,176	15,772	639,394	904	268,217	179,606	41,658	16,843	3,815	123,232	85,681
Mar	7,718	138,906	123,951	13,916	1,353,802	177,016	247,893	186,401	14,051	634,702	926	268,855	173,634	41,275	14,102	2,613	123,066	95,220
Apr	7,804	140,045	123,758	15,609	1,345,004	173,275	249,930	185,931	14,052	645,780	931	272,693	176,180	40,387	14,752	2,108	138,104	87,075
May	7,721	145,488	128,334	15,310	1,353,523	179,365	263,949	195,214	14,261	639,384	946	272,963	176,003	43,006	13,953	4,551	129,669	90,796
Jun	7,695	149,562	133,677	15,413	1,374,429	182,993	292,279	212,168	14,852	641,232	943	273,545	176,983	38,401	12,167	4,945	121,744	99,990
Jul	7,853	161,110	144,328	19,190	1,363,667	179,581	293,178	209,608	15,883	638,708	915	272,697	169,628	39,522	16,176	8,121	130,035	91,255
Aug	8,051	162,469	146,447	19,068	1,375,962	181,096	305,692	218,069	16,100	640,168	924	272,005	173,867	35,032	13,285	8,943	136,861	92,958
Sep	8,106	163,962	149,673	19,847	1,395,331 (b)	171,892	314,775	224,425	16,093	635,763 (e)	1,090	271,864	172,002	33,501	12,532	1,847	140,839 (g)	107,841
Oct	8,153	139,367	125,612	19,899	1,392,222	169,642	317,746	221,798	15,465	641,736	1,100	271,156	161,953	34,544	10,285	5,101	154,876	98,028
Nov	8,107	121,486	107,770	19,549	1,404,113	172,043	279,268	182,207	15,180	643,224	1,063	270,465	155,791	37,197	10,787	5,937	150,148	103,667
Dec	8,279	106,670	93,247	19,805	1,409,530	181,934	293,013	185,383	14,371	641,684	1,049	269,991	157,201	43,590	12,904	3,500	132,701	108,887
2018 Jan	7,953	72,628	58,912	20,111	1,400,497 (c)	168,640	263,002	151,790	13,711	641,673	1,064	269,097	152,982	40,994	11,620	6,335	152,224	110,989
Feb	7,845	77,347	63,165	19,350	1,401,377	167,832	279,717	149,048	11,928	641,703	1,099	269,072	155,176	42,226	11,324	8,280	150,560	104,075
Mar	7,949	61,344	47,219	20,548	1,417,816	175,494	278,043	146,756	10,812	633,259	1,109	271,687	162,426	43,594	9,896	2,506	121,804	109,256
Apr	8,302	53,277	40,472	17,027	1,419,902	174,154	289,873	158,433	11,546	634,912	1,113	276,657	161,897	46,752	15,427	2,439	125,517	103,453

Source: Bank of England

12.3a Monetary financial institutions' (excluding central bank) balance sheet

£ millions — Not seasonally adjusted

Amounts outstanding of sterling liabilities

	Acceptances granted	CDs and other paper Issued				Total sterling deposits	Sterling items in suspense and transmission	Net derivatives	Accrued amounts payable	Sterling capital and other internal funds	Total sterling liabilities
		CDs and Commercial paper	Bonds with maturity of up to and incl. 5 years	Bonds with maturity of greater than 5 years	Total						
RPM	B3XM	B2TL	B6OI	B2TM	B3YM	B3ZM	B3GN	B3HN	B3IN	B3JN	B3KN
2016 Jan	185	96,077	26,313	35,670	**158,060**	**2,892,570**	54,025	-28,529	22,582	434,102	**3,381,747**
Feb	169	97,325	27,341	35,693	**160,359**	**2,878,833**	40,442	1,782	23,742	409,127	**3,360,891**
Mar	157	101,297	26,186	35,841	**163,325**	**2,900,830**	36,852	-56,499	21,771	411,758	**3,321,777**
Apr	163	102,166	27,012	36,191	**165,368**	**2,909,588**	41,766	-61,178	20,810	401,950	**3,320,001**
May	161	106,273	26,088	35,886	**168,247**	**2,911,180**	44,957	-68,283	22,189	411,919	**3,329,107**
Jun	198	106,257	25,970	36,581	**168,808**	**2,985,018**	45,506	11,460	22,337	392,682	**3,464,121**
Jul	204	115,539	25,914	36,276	**177,729**	**3,006,915**	52,385	4,332	22,022	379,922	**3,472,699**
Aug	207	117,437	26,009	36,379	**179,826**	**3,022,228**	37,638	-2,697	21,597	386,255	**3,472,259**
Sep	173	121,666	25,863	36,346	**183,875**	**3,021,369**	44,922	14,223	22,233	361,127	**3,471,195**
Oct	189	120,983	25,822	36,052	**182,857**	**3,041,488**	37,203	80,682	22,767	331,138	**3,520,634**
Nov	208	118,027	26,007	35,185	**179,219**	**3,045,889**	46,521	3,667	22,620	380,019	**3,506,142**
Dec	181	120,150	24,948	35,177	**180,275**	**3,073,797**	20,592	11,417	21,423	388,720	**3,523,800**
2017 Jan	186	119,299	24,223	34,520	**178,042**	**3,086,880**	42,929	-12,810	21,392	415,255	**3,561,342**
Feb	187	124,491	24,053	34,543	**183,087**	**3,119,136**	44,997	21,903	21,907	426,770	**3,642,417**
Mar	252	134,753	23,161	34,305	**192,219**	**3,208,566**	48,528	-3,748	19,133	407,664	**3,687,861**
Apr	258	137,516	20,958	34,136	**192,610**	**3,220,418**	48,361	-38,604	18,570	409,362	**3,665,911**
May	264	134,143	23,527	33,460	**191,130**	**3,246,700**	43,690	-17,707	19,237	431,746	**3,731,386**
Jun	263	128,125	24,027	33,460	**185,612**	**3,298,698**	47,097	-25,745	19,210	460,976 (p)(q)(r)	**3,807,931 (p)(q)(r)**
Jul	217	127,960	23,779	33,560	**185,298**	**3,295,393**	41,454	-9,258	19,022	434,939	**3,789,403**
Aug	207	128,659	23,505	33,629	**185,794**	**3,334,217**	34,662	-2,291	18,520	443,925	**3,837,085**
Sep	145	127,302	22,424	33,076	**182,802**	**3,356,641 (e)(i)**	37,043	-46,716	18,043	465,953	**3,839,070 (e)(i)**
Oct	148	120,678	22,844	33,442	**176,964**	**3,327,691**	35,432	-29,840	18,754	455,427	**3,815,617**
Nov	146	126,435	22,780	33,921	**183,136**	**3,290,885**	45,860	-56,444	19,626	460,447	**3,768,482**
Dec	152	127,913	23,411	33,943	**185,267**	**3,298,302**	15,149	-61,678	21,902	474,854	**3,756,809**
2018 Jan	144	130,653	26,786	33,437	**190,876**	**3,234,806 (c)**	36,069	-146,781 (j)	21,088	455,927	**3,609,060 (c)(j)**
Feb	170	129,102	25,025	34,312	**188,439**	**3,248,179**	33,490	2,475 (k)	21,797	436,898	**3,750,684 (k)**
Mar	178	133,067	28,199	32,877	**194,143**	**3,231,223**	36,093	-24,358 (l)	22,316	440,923	**3,714,146 (l)**
Apr	261	131,111	29,292	30,536	**190,939**	**3,231,949**	34,784	70,082	19,623	452,128	**3,816,868**

Source: Bank of England

12.3a Monetary financial institutions' (excluding central bank) balance sheet

£ millions | Not seasonally adjusted

Notes to table

Movements in amounts outstanding can reflect breaks in data series as well as underlying flows. For changes data, users are recommended to refer directly to the appropriate series or data tables. Further explanation can be found at: https://www.bankofengland.co.uk/statistics/details/further-details-about-changes-flows-growth-rates-data.

(b) Due to improvements in reporting by one reporting institution, the amounts outstanding increased by £6bn. This amount has been adjusted out of the flows for September 2017.
(c) Due to improvements in reporting at one institution, the amounts outstanding increased by £5bn. This effect has been adjusted out of the flows for January 2018.
(e) Due to a change in group structure by one reporting institution, the amounts outstanding increased by £6bn. This effect has been adjusted out of the flows for September 2017.
(g) Due to improvements in reporting by one reporting institution, the amounts outstanding increased by £5bn. This amount has been adjusted out of the flows for September 2017.
(i) Due to improvements in reporting by one institution, the amounts outstanding increased by £11bn. This amount has been adjusted out of the flows for September 2017.
(j) Due to improvements in reporting by one institution, amounts outstanding decreased by £66bn.
(k) Due to improvements in reporting by one institution, amounts outstanding increased by £8bn.
(l) Due to improvements in reporting by one institution, amounts outstanding increased by £9bn.
(m Due to improvements in reporting at one institution, the amounts outstanding increased by £5bn.
(n) Due to improvements in reporting at one institution, the amounts outstanding increased by £10bn.
(o) Due to improvements in reporting at one institution, the amounts outstanding increased by £10bn.
(p) Due to improvements in reporting at one institution, the amounts outstanding increased by £17bn. This effect has been adjusted out of the flows for June 2017.
(q) Due to improvements in reporting at one institution, the amounts outstanding decreased by £5bn. This effect has been adjusted out of the flows for June 2017.
(r) Due to improvements in reporting at one institution, the amounts outstanding increased by £10bn. This effect has been adjusted out of the flows for June 2017.
(s) Due to improvements in reporting at one institution, the amounts outstanding decreased by £5bn.
(t) Due to improvements in reporting at one institution, the amounts outstanding decreased by £10bn.
(u) Due to improvements in reporting at one institution, the amounts outstanding decreased by £10bn.

Explanatory notes can be found here:
https://www.bankofengland.co.uk/statistics/details/further-details-about-monetary-financial-institutions-excluding-central-bank-balance-sheet-data

12.3b Monetary financial institutions' (excluding central bank) balance sheet

£ millions — Not seasonally adjusted

Amounts outstanding of foreign currency liabilities (including euro)

	Sight and time deposits					Acceptances	Sale and repurchase agreements				
	UK MFIs	of which intragroup banks	UK public sector	Other UK residents	Non-residents	granted	UK MFIs	of which intragroup banks	UK public sector	Other UK residents	Non-residents
RPM	B3JL	B8ZM	B2UP	B2UV	B3NN	B3KQ	B3KL	B8ZK	B3PN	B3QN	B3RN
2016 Jan	208,903	145,866	2,353	274,162	1,692,801	2,405	79,019	49,908	1,414	112,701	510,595
Feb	220,714	153,042	2,575	280,680	1,734,659	2,085	78,876	48,844	1,268	116,940	500,825
Mar	209,638	147,854	2,341	282,593	1,696,245	2,380	72,791	43,819	112	116,514	485,146
Apr	218,926	157,901	2,484	279,813	1,649,995	2,508	75,762	44,160	1,293	118,184	494,252
May	198,818	138,756	2,474	283,405	1,639,167	2,554	74,490	40,150	695	114,914	508,905
Jun	214,995	143,433	3,048	316,335	1,836,238	3,331	79,468	42,394	341	121,389	557,941
Jul	215,741	149,522	3,027	322,784	1,849,173	3,010	80,325	43,607	1,414	126,677	559,416
Aug	224,844	158,074	3,229	332,357	1,854,568	2,962	81,244	43,715	1,134	125,868	563,987
Sep	214,530	146,290	2,437	331,529	1,855,029 (g)	3,618	76,859	37,621	250	138,404	580,709
Oct	219,974	152,278	2,531	345,850	1,885,003	3,558	78,399	36,074	626	140,847	621,158
Nov	215,864	152,245	2,667	341,390	1,820,717	3,691	72,668	34,845	1,588	145,662	606,381
Dec	217,773	149,050	2,518	324,792	1,836,539	4,015	75,148	33,036	530	139,651	609,476
2017 Jan	217,530	153,305	2,689	336,977	1,817,696	3,288	78,312	35,890	1,317	151,236	628,041
Feb	206,752	144,109	2,633	336,848	1,842,486	3,789	76,870	35,761	339	181,024	653,853
Mar	197,174	136,947	2,383	328,699	1,813,204	4,008	82,344	39,816	70	172,708	648,760
Apr	192,379	133,353	2,674	329,056	1,783,247	3,580	77,778	38,108	1,340	171,046	632,021
May	194,621	135,194	3,053	340,680	1,775,830	3,183	80,168	38,516	1,092	170,582	672,362
Jun	156,845	99,947	3,130	339,052	1,789,057	3,327	74,407	35,467	255	169,837	654,366
Jul	164,065	104,084	3,222	338,603	1,798,441	2,792	75,876	34,249	2,659	183,889	688,821 (x)
Aug	172,338	108,733	3,154	346,532	1,795,818 (v)	2,541	83,413	40,431	1,855	190,514	698,269
Sep	162,434	105,987	3,402	330,970	1,728,963 (w)	2,953	80,247	39,181	2,443	181,224	733,277 (y)
Oct	160,441	104,307	3,572	331,512	1,754,574	2,785	78,816	34,941	2,221	194,611	761,236
Nov	156,376	101,797	3,273	333,947	1,743,717	2,950	83,263	39,834	2,463	204,451	757,869
Dec	159,519	103,492	3,242	322,158	1,750,941	3,472	75,320	34,218	2,730	187,517	806,778
2018 Jan	179,405	121,511	3,408	321,105	1,726,383	2,857	73,935	31,506	1,926	208,415	756,581
Feb	178,394	123,977	3,457	320,597	1,748,101	3,286	82,567	36,109	1,417	216,374	808,525
Mar	189,435	135,474	3,137	314,447	1,721,439	3,221	79,540	33,311	1,850	199,036	812,382
Apr	196,618	142,505	3,636	323,308	1,755,649	3,725	78,802	34,779	3,487	202,024	765,265

Source: Bank of England

12.3b Monetary financial institutions' (excluding central bank) balance sheet

£ millions

Not seasonally adjusted

Amounts outstanding of foreign currency liabilities (including euro)

	CDs and other paper Issued				Total foreign currency deposits	Items in suspense and transmission	Net derivatives	Accrued amounts payable	Capital and other internal funds	Total foreign currency liabilities	Total liabilities
	CDs and Commercial paper	Bonds with maturity of up to and incl. 5 years	Bonds with maturity of greater than 5 years	Total							
RPM	B2TP	B6OK	B2TQ	B3SN	B3TN	B3UN	B3VN	B3WN	B3XN	B3YN	B3ZN
2016 Jan	104,410	174,158	223,095	**501,663**	**3,386,015**	187,523	-13,622	12,320	166,672	**3,738,908**	**7,120,654**
Feb	110,507	178,379	230,433	**519,319**	**3,457,942**	186,073	-38,983	12,265	190,236	**3,807,533**	**7,168,425**
Mar	108,703	172,030	229,819	**510,552**	**3,378,313**	175,831	16,255	12,075	179,606	**3,762,080**	**7,083,857 (i)**
Apr	108,985	174,550	231,396	**514,930**	**3,358,148**	205,202	20,055	12,088	192,957	**3,788,451**	**7,108,452 (j)**
May	110,243	170,178	226,793	**507,214**	**3,332,634**	195,730	23,939	12,924	174,757	**3,739,984**	**7,069,091**
Jun	117,122	184,737	249,064	**550,923**	**3,684,009**	209,928	-55,571	13,368	206,776	**4,058,510**	**7,522,631**
Jul	112,175	185,495	253,075	**550,746**	**3,712,312**	207,744	-49,869	13,397	218,433	**4,102,018**	**7,574,717**
Aug	109,377	187,228	253,232	**549,838**	**3,740,030**	199,952	-45,574	13,355	215,958	**4,123,721**	**7,595,980**
Sep	109,113	211,662	252,924	**573,699**	**3,777,065 (g)**	228,135	-54,715	14,051	229,804	**4,194,340 (g)**	**7,665,535 (g)**
Oct	118,695	217,314	263,901	**599,910**	**3,897,855**	230,663	-134,521	15,506	267,587	**4,277,090**	**7,797,724**
Nov	117,042	206,511	244,788	**568,340**	**3,778,969**	257,720	-53,599	15,710	219,775	**4,218,575**	**7,724,717**
Dec	112,712	208,052	247,044	**567,808**	**3,778,250**	107,579	-59,185	13,881	232,269	**4,072,795**	**7,596,595**
2017 Jan	113,498	207,223	247,708	**568,429**	**3,805,515**	231,738	-31,677	14,500	205,652	**4,225,728**	**7,787,070**
Feb	124,665	214,881	256,400	**595,945**	**3,900,539**	242,484	-67,864	16,901	224,225	**4,316,285**	**7,958,706**
Mar	125,439	208,200	252,862	**586,502**	**3,835,852**	205,851	-41,321	16,370	207,097	**4,223,848**	**7,911,709**
Apr	121,172	215,507	251,092	**587,771**	**3,780,891**	237,729	-3,803	17,474	190,064	**4,222,355**	**7,888,650**
May	127,906	209,566	257,713	**595,185**	**3,836,757**	230,037	-21,819	18,545	159,769	**4,223,290**	**7,954,676**
Jun	127,362	208,509	257,113	**592,983**	**3,783,260**	206,994	-26,309	17,117	174,215	**4,155,276**	**7,963,207**
Jul	131,238	204,754	260,514	**596,507**	**3,854,874 (x)**	187,327	-33,778	17,849	189,381	**4,215,653 (x)**	**8,005,056 (x)**
Aug	136,229	208,773	275,514	**620,517**	**3,914,952 (v)**	190,012	-47,255	17,447	171,594	**4,246,752 (v)**	**8,083,837 (v)**
Sep	131,124	202,427	259,948	**593,500**	**3,819,412 (w)(y)**	207,849	-9,192	16,299	151,743	**4,186,109 (w)(y)**	**8,025,180 (w)(y)(af)(ag)**
Oct	138,995	188,455	257,545	**584,995**	**3,874,764**	212,241	-21,741	16,535	159,591	**4,241,390**	**8,057,007**
Nov	140,662	206,840	253,559	**601,061**	**3,889,368**	253,712	9,997	16,751	159,740	**4,329,568**	**8,098,050**
Dec	138,958	202,216	254,763	**595,937**	**3,907,615**	98,055	21,463	16,374	158,920	**4,202,426**	**7,959,235**
2018 Jan	136,983	196,191	253,195	**586,369**	**3,860,382**	230,435	110,385 (z)	18,220	158,007	**4,377,429 (ac)**	**7,986,489 (ah)**
Feb	140,752	197,576	259,152	**597,481**	**3,960,200**	222,862	-55,396 (aa)	18,332	185,185	**4,331,183 (ad)**	**8,081,867**
Mar	140,118	225,402	255,360	**620,880**	**3,945,367**	184,818	-28,236 (ab)	25,323	164,533	**4,291,805 (ae)**	**8,005,952**
Apr	147,302	243,070	255,101	**645,473**	**3,977,986**	187,182	-131,581	19,006	174,469	**4,227,061**	**8,043,929**

Source: Bank of England

12.3b Monetary financial institutions' (excluding central bank) balance sheet

£ millions | Not seasonally adjusted

Notes to table

Movements in amounts outstanding can reflect breaks in data series as well as underlying flows. For changes data, users are recommended to refer directly to the appropriate series or data tables.
Further explanation can be found at: www.bankofengland.co.uk/statistics/Pages/iadb/notesiadb/Changes_flows_growth_rates.aspx.

(g) Due to a change in treatment at one institution, the amounts outstanding decreased by £14bn. This effect has been adjusted out of the flows for September 2016.
(h) Due to a transfer of business by one institution, amounts outstanding increased by £29 billion. This amount has been adjusted out of the flows for July 2017.
(i) Due to changes in reporting at one institution, the amounts outstanding decreased by £5bn. This effect has been adjusted out of the flows for March 2016.
(j) Due to a loan transfer by one reporting institution, the amounts outstanding increased by £7bn. This effect has been adjusted out of the flows for April 2016.
(v) Due to improvements in reporting by one institution, amounts outstanding decreased by £17 billion. This amount has been adjusted out of the flows for August 2017.
(w) Due to improvements in reporting by one institution, amounts outstanding decreased by £12bn. This amount has been adjusted out of the flows for September 2017.
(x) Due to a transfer of business by one institution, amounts outstanding increased by £29 billion. This amount has been adjusted out of the flows for July 2017.
(y) Due to improvements in reporting by one reporting institution, the amounts outstanding increased by £38bn. This amount has been adjusted out of the flows for September 2017.
(z) Due to improvements in reporting by one institution, amounts outstanding increased by £288bn.
(aa) Due to improvements in reporting by one institution, amounts outstanding increased by £29bn.
(ab) Due to improvements in reporting by one institution, amounts outstanding decreased by £14bn.
(ac) Due to improvements in reporting by one institution, amounts outstanding increased by £66bn.
(ad) Due to improvements in reporting by one institution, amounts outstanding decreased by £8bn.
(ae) Due to improvements in reporting by one institution, amounts outstanding decreased by £9bn.
(af) Due to improvements in reporting by one institution, the amounts outstanding increased by £11bn. This amount has been adjusted out of the flows for September 2017.
(ag) Due to a change in group structure by one reporting institution, the amounts outstanding increased by £6bn. This effect has been adjusted out of the flows for September 2017.
(ah) Due to improvements in reporting at one institution, the amounts outstanding increased by £5bn. This effect has been adjusted out of the flows for January 2018.

Explanatory notes can be found here:
https://www.bankofengland.co.uk/statistics/details/further-details-about-monetary-financial-institutions-excluding-central-bank-balance-sheet-data

12.3 c Monetary financial institutions' (excluding central bank) balance sheet

£ millions

Not seasonally adjusted

Amounts outstanding of sterling assets

	Notes coin	With UK central bank		Loans					Acceptances granted				Bills			
		Cash ratio deposits	Other	UK MFIs	of which intragroup banks	UK MFIs CDs	UK MFIs commercial paper	Non-residents	UK MFIs	UK public sector	Other UK residents	Non-residents	Treasury bills	UK MFIs bills	Other UK residents	Non-residents
RPM	B3UO	B3VO	B3WO	B3NL	B8ZI	B3OL	B3PL	B3XO	B3QL	B3YO	B3ZO	B3GP	B3HP	B3RL	B3IP	B3JP
2016 Jan	9,460	4,136	304,721	251,630	234,082	3,875	183	116,236	-	-	152	33	9,489	231	152	749
Feb	9,309	4,136	305,759	253,020	233,981	3,798	85	111,677	-	-	136	33	9,359	213	19	663
Mar	10,730	4,136	301,075	247,946	225,945	3,638	44	120,187	-	-	126	31	7,582	210	78	670
Apr	9,907	4,137	310,603	242,961	220,690	3,484	44	122,328	-	-	127	36	6,994	241	76	779
May	10,187	4,155	305,681	239,632	217,320	3,475	43	121,830	-	-	126	35	6,201	248	41	579
Jun	10,717	4,215	302,755	256,043	234,542	3,300	43	122,793	-	-	163	35	8,821	273	104	402
Jul	10,116	4,215	306,966	258,489	235,689	3,845	71	132,507	-	-	171	33	14,084	270	147	586
Aug	10,825	4,215	318,346	251,400	228,514	3,795	50	132,255	-	-	175	32	12,725	270	76	595
Sep	10,247	4,216	314,556	262,442	240,715	3,638	43	136,040	-	-	141	31	11,779	274	84	388
Oct	9,769	4,217	326,529	251,643	227,915	3,602	33	136,124	-	-	155	33	10,589	297	93	473
Nov	10,346	4,242	342,425	246,527	223,861	3,502	25	134,727	-	-	175	33	8,997	298	152	417
Dec	11,867	4,424	356,687	275,269	253,758	3,278	25	127,565	-	-	141	39	7,630	311	153	364
2017 Jan	10,365	4,424	375,664	273,300	250,356	3,478	27	136,718	1	-	146	40	5,357	269	126	619
Feb	10,186	4,424	393,306	295,742	273,393	3,219	21	127,280	-	-	145	41	4,131	265	188	426
Mar	10,263	4,424	409,678	329,741	310,074	3,139	21	127,998	1	-	142	110	3,751	265	138	595
Apr	10,246	4,426	415,419	329,307	308,686	2,837	21	134,581	1	-	147	110	2,167	294	183	666
May	10,743	4,428	413,198	344,516	322,877	2,840	22	132,701	-	-	154	110	2,637	284	233	511
Jun	10,437	4,581	424,012	365,168	345,633	3,039	26	128,208	2	-	159	102	2,570	315	155	477
Jul	10,326	4,584	427,044	373,115	351,969	2,992	22	122,580	-	-	117	100	3,292	-	484	366
Aug	10,909	4,583	419,209	379,093	358,816	2,932	18	134,334	-	-	115	92	3,283	-	377	416
Sep	10,439	4,584	423,784	392,276	373,536	2,892	91	123,248	-	-	117	28	4,045	-	381	530
Oct	10,818	4,584	436,432	360,424	342,590	2,676	59	126,726	-	-	121	27	5,287	-	414	615
Nov	11,039	4,586	445,652	304,479	286,570	2,740	16	122,255	-	-	118	27	4,820	-	434	271
Dec	11,920	4,708	450,708	295,719	277,942	2,771	15	122,170	-	-	115	37	4,862	-	440	250
2018 Jan	10,365	4,708	451,929	228,023	210,856	2,822	15	126,364	-	-	109	34	3,867	-	396	926
Feb	10,338	4,708	474,461	229,203	212,334	2,585	24	118,059	-	-	128	41	5,014	1	430	938
Mar	10,426	4,708	464,665	211,670	195,334	2,758	23	111,415	-	-	130	48	5,704	1	391	951
Apr	10,672	4,711	479,065	216,324	200,314	2,852	9	109,208	-	-	212	48	7,954	1	382	328

Source: Bank of England

12.3 c Monetary financial institutions' (excluding central bank) balance sheet

£ millions Not seasonally adjusted

Amounts outstanding of sterling assets

	Sales and repurchase agreements					Advances			Investments					Items in suspense and collection	Accrued amounts receivable	Other assets	Total sterling assets
	UK MFIs	of which intragroup banks	UK public sector	Other UK residents	Non-residents	UK public sector	Other UK residents	Non-residents	UK government bonds	Other UK public sector	UK MFIs	Other UK residents	Non-residents				
RPM	B3SL	B8ZG	B3KP	B3LP	B3MP	B2UK	B3OP	B3PP	B3QP	B3RP	B3TL	B3SP	B3TP	B3UP	B3VP	B3WP	B3XP
2016 Jan	30,696	18,831	75	123,963	52,458	8,577	1,849,610	90,255	138,282	235	52,931	197,906	47,819	52,625	14,729	28,597	**3,389,805**
Feb	33,874	19,491	102	129,285	46,728	8,607	1,861,142	88,432	141,394	260	50,889	193,750	50,205	39,343	15,445	28,808	**3,386,472**
Mar	35,338	18,457	35	131,574	48,390	8,565	1,866,642	88,688	141,039	236	50,165	195,393	50,315	36,483	14,641	29,469	**3,393,425**
Apr	38,433	18,203	29	130,010	52,215	8,618	1,860,447 (p)	90,280	143,385	233	50,336	195,431	47,414	43,176	14,444	29,463	**3,405,634** (p)
May	37,923	16,009	11	146,215	53,538	8,830	1,861,454	95,840	141,552	244	50,197	194,426	49,141	42,399	15,609	29,513	**3,419,126**
Jun	38,128	16,865	11	157,700	55,618	8,316	1,871,114	99,973	144,619	582	50,082	195,532	49,148	43,775	15,121	29,582	**3,468,966**
Jul	27,958	11,223	11	155,061	57,090	8,495	1,879,028	96,632	143,879	598	49,955	196,977	52,165	54,099	15,437	29,815	**3,498,700**
Aug	29,009	11,804	224	154,650	59,769	8,417	1,887,402	100,322	152,551	664	50,017	197,912	54,176	38,360	15,637	29,927	**3,513,797**
Sep	30,692	11,493	497	159,840	61,495	8,235	1,890,474	98,555	151,526	647	50,406	195,925	54,460	43,470	14,070	30,379	**3,534,547**
Oct	30,458	13,597	1,491	165,219	58,909	8,643	1,889,663	99,873	151,472	604	50,985	190,374	56,783	35,727	13,909	30,644	**3,528,309**
Nov	29,190	13,056	428	182,007	61,076	8,667	1,881,345	95,257	150,012	581	50,189	191,266	55,710	44,096	14,162	30,689	**3,546,544**
Dec	30,026	12,903	-	175,957	67,530	8,515	1,886,203	104,938	150,107	574	51,387	193,520	55,106	17,728	13,807	30,867	**3,574,017**
2017 Jan	34,699	17,364	2,388	182,328	61,003	8,460	1,891,296	102,614	144,060	548	29,133	223,121	57,269	39,719	13,789	30,795	**3,631,756**
Feb	32,510	17,098	530	180,222	65,973	8,344	1,893,382	106,713	143,570	590	27,934	220,789	56,822	46,371	13,965	30,451	**3,667,539**
Mar	29,889	14,177	1,372	194,529	73,256	8,312	1,899,967	106,385	145,809	484	28,183	219,078	54,960	52,979	13,013	30,552	**3,749,034**
Apr	27,148	14,827	422	194,147	71,776	8,359	1,907,448	109,180	147,043	435	27,899	223,042	55,334	48,866	13,163	30,484	**3,765,152**
May	28,819	14,028	508	199,668	72,318	7,903	1,908,994	106,687	148,848	453	28,446	222,940	55,372	48,801	13,735	30,606	**3,786,476**
Jun	26,587	12,242	498	201,751	77,865	8,201	1,916,592	108,916	149,239	497	39,077 (ay)(az)	243,291 (ba)	55,067	51,057	12,722	29,437	**3,860,046** (ay)(az)(ba)
Jul	30,040	16,251	511	199,359	66,692	42,597 (ar)	1,886,661 (at)	109,216	148,655	514	38,345	246,045	56,171	44,851	13,010	29,588	**3,857,279**
Aug	24,758	13,360	1,475	204,449	68,630	42,903	1,896,508	109,442	147,509	518	37,706	245,307	54,160	37,670 (bb)	14,443	29,669	**3,870,504** (bb)
Sep	26,072	12,607	517	220,854 (ao)	75,635	43,130	1,911,609 (au)(av)	109,537	142,711	460	36,924	239,695	54,345	40,691 (bc)	12,253	26,324	**3,903,173** (av)(bc)(bd)
Oct	28,186	10,360	388	215,970	68,389	43,032	1,908,355	112,245	145,949	495	37,749	238,845	46,560	37,246	12,501	26,483	**3,870,579**
Nov	32,642	10,862	593	219,426	72,679	42,663	1,917,128	113,364	136,681	525	37,557	234,563	46,582	49,726	13,404	26,653	**3,840,623**
Dec	37,750	12,979	793	222,053 (ap)	72,517	42,763	1,917,130 (aw)	112,323	133,823	543	38,391	235,168	45,254	20,241	13,740	26,964	**3,813,169**
2018 Jan	36,791	11,695	534	218,834	77,298	42,299	1,921,439	109,302	138,385	510	38,883	228,608	48,437	38,702	14,790	27,588	**3,771,957**
Feb	38,106	11,399	1,413	213,837	77,549	42,293	1,923,214	112,639	140,668	485	38,153	226,369	48,660	36,375	15,116	27,817	**3,788,624**
Mar	40,324	9,971	4,902	204,223	85,068	41,534	1,937,529	112,709	139,395	498	39,507	222,730	47,656	38,774	15,458	26,414	**3,769,612**
Apr	43,400	15,507	619	196,716	85,228	8,696 (as)	1,974,537 (ax)	111,178	138,606	498	39,689	222,442	47,700	39,393	13,790	26,546	**3,780,804**

Source: Bank of England

12.3 c Monetary financial institutions' (excluding central bank) balance sheet

£ millions Not seasonally adjusted

Notes to table

Movements in amounts outstanding can reflect breaks in data series as well as underlying flows. For changes data, users are recommended to refer directly to the appropriate series or data tables.
Further explanation can be found at: https://www.bankofengland.co.uk/statistics/details/further-details-about-changes-flows-growth-rates-data.

(p) Due to a loan transfer by one reporting institution, the amounts outstanding increased by £7bn. This effect has been adjusted out of the flows for April 2016.

(ao) Due to improvements in reporting by one reporting institution, the amounts outstanding increased by £5bn. This amount has been adjusted out of the flows for September 2017.

(ap) Due to improvements in reporting at one institution, the amounts outstanding increased by £4bn. This effect has been adjusted out of the flows for December 2017.

(ar) In order to bring reporting in line with the National Accounts, English housing associations were reclassified from PNFCs to public corporations with effect from July 2017 data. The amounts outstanding increased by £34bn. This effect has been adjusted out of the flows for July 2017.

(as) In order to bring reporting in line with the National Accounts, English housing associations were reclassified from public corporations to PNFCs with effect from April 2018 data. The amounts outstanding decreased by £34bn. This effect has been adjusted out of the flows for April 2018.

(at) In order to bring reporting in line with the National Accounts, English housing associations were reclassified from PNFCs to public corporations with effect from July 2017 data. The amounts outstanding decreased by £34bn. This effect has been adjusted out of the flows for July 2017.

(au) Due to improvements in reporting by one reporting institution, the amounts outstanding increased by £6bn. This amount has been adjusted out of the flows for September 2017.

(av) Due to a change in group structure by one reporting institution, the amounts outstanding increased by £6bn. This effect has been adjusted out of the flows for September 2017.

(aw) Due to improvements in reporting at one institution, the amounts outstanding decreased by £4bn. This effect has been adjusted out of the flows for December 2017.

(ax) In order to bring reporting in line with the National Accounts, English housing associations were reclassified from public corporations to PNFCs with effect from April 2018 data. The amounts outstanding increased by £34bn. This effect has been adjusted out of the flows for April 2018.

(ay) Due to improvements in reporting at one institution, the amounts outstanding increased by £15bn. This effect has been adjusted out of the flows for June 2017.

(az) Due to improvements in reporting at one institution, the amounts outstanding decreased by £5bn. This effect has been adjusted out of the flows for June 2017.

(ba) Due to improvements in reporting at one institution, the amounts outstanding increased by £10bn. This effect has been adjusted out of the flows for June 2017.

(bb) Due to improvements in reporting by one institution, amounts outstanding increased by £5 billion. This amount has been adjusted out of the flows for August 2017.

(bc) Due to improvements in reporting by one reporting institution, the amounts outstanding decreased by £5bn. This amount has been adjusted out of the flows for September 2017.

(bd) Due to improvements in reporting by one reporting institution, the amounts outstanding increased by £11bn. This amount has been adjusted out of the flows for September 2017.

Explanatory notes can be found here:
https://www.bankofengland.co.uk/statistics/details/further-details-about-monetary-financial-institutions-excluding-central-bank-balance-sheet-data

12.3d Monetary financial institutions' (excluding central bank) balance sheet

£ millions — Not seasonally adjusted

Amounts outstanding of foreign currency assets (including euro)

	Loans and advances						Sale and repurchase agreements					Acceptances granted	Total bills
	UK MFIs	of which intragroup banks	UK MFIs' CDs etc.	UK public sector	Other UK residents	Non-residents	UK MFIs	of which intragroup banks	UK public sector	Other UK residents	Non-residents		
RPM	B3UL	B8ZQ	B3VL	B2UN	B3ZP	B2UH	B3WL	B8ZO	B3HQ	B3IQ	B3JQ	B3KQ	B3LQ
2016 Jan	195,957	146,249	1,052	568	232,201	1,766,536	76,412	49,968	1,600	111,056	543,274	2,405	42,382
Feb	207,542	153,751	1,218	656	246,339	1,772,048	76,697	49,377	1,163	122,409	561,171	2,085	45,599
Mar	199,514	148,544	1,310	624	233,809	1,731,340	69,105	44,479	275	114,579	564,808	2,380	45,031
Apr	209,821	158,534	1,314	579	236,631	1,683,644	71,991	44,765	1,326	120,361	566,334	2,508	42,023
May	189,081	139,117	1,295	509	233,587	1,696,042	70,777	40,171	1,473	121,308	563,487	2,554	41,010
Jun	204,057	143,873	1,489	641	258,388	1,923,479	76,452	42,394	922	132,391	631,881	3,331	40,564
Jul	206,542	149,625	1,576	711	260,296	1,930,097	76,466	43,610	1,316	131,352	630,828	3,010	38,970
Aug	214,079	158,988	1,571	680	262,614	1,947,698	77,153	43,719	1,014	130,628	620,260	2,962	38,339
Sep	203,684	147,291	1,412	11	241,896	1,992,264 (u)	72,088	37,621	1,628	136,365	668,115	3,618	36,123
Oct	211,952	152,778	1,810	9	248,968	2,053,109	73,408	36,061	426	138,097	686,863	3,558	38,843
Nov	207,664	152,537	1,193	3	250,122	1,997,339	69,252	34,846	1,527	141,062	668,495	3,691	36,273
Dec	203,308	149,424	1,153	12	241,795	2,021,172	70,567	33,036	1,813	122,640	671,554	4,015	36,204
2017 Jan	206,911	154,446	1,201	7	248,512	1,978,013	74,364	35,740	1,989	137,091	687,479	3,288	39,168
Feb	199,983	144,529	1,112	35	254,679	2,028,597	75,379	35,565	1,072	159,167	698,801	3,789	37,152
Mar	194,249	137,113	1,037	11	245,880	1,970,277	81,217	39,816	197	154,816	705,335	4,008	36,559
Apr	187,594	133,417	896	24	247,590	1,935,696	75,737	38,118	3,253	158,797	678,921	3,580	32,843
May	188,201	135,662	817	58	243,432	1,947,331	79,461	38,388	2,861	164,829	692,111	3,183	35,796
Jun	151,243	100,452	797	58	238,187	1,954,968	72,436	35,467	1,017	164,375	687,493	3,327	38,006
Jul	156,411	104,436	909	122	238,871	1,987,300	73,391	34,263	3,154	165,094	723,094 (bf)	2,792	39,348
Aug	161,433	109,158	1,106	110	242,104	2,043,328 (be)	80,817	40,407	2,356	169,270	731,457	2,541	39,073
Sep	158,005	106,543	1,031	150	228,535	1,942,944	76,914	39,182	2,635	157,215	766,670 (bg)	2,953	38,875
Oct	155,334	104,453	840	108	230,376	1,954,418	72,491	34,946	2,839	166,615	810,156	2,785	35,281
Nov	150,058	101,895	919	168	224,766	1,953,149	78,774	39,832	2,680	176,826	827,889	2,950	35,405
Dec	151,671	103,814	948	113	217,015	1,992,422	71,822	34,219	3,208	160,861	844,890	3,472	36,008
2018 Jan	169,980	121,581	750	266	227,380	1,924,383	69,967	31,516	1,678	183,451	795,020	2,857	36,391
Feb	169,908	123,652	527	60	219,994	1,959,861	76,960	36,112	1,409	191,978	862,381	3,286	34,532
Mar	181,022	135,312	615	62	215,564	1,983,357	77,177	33,326	1,894	175,965	860,787	3,221	33,072
Apr	189,087	142,024	646	136	230,083	2,003,479	78,184	34,780	3,276	166,654	835,305	3,725	32,395

Source: Bank of England

12.3d Monetary financial institutions' (excluding central bank) balance sheet

£ millions

Not seasonally adjusted

Amounts outstanding of foreign currency assets (including euro)

	Investments					Items in suspense and collection	Accrued amounts receivable	Other assets	Total foreign currency assets	Total assets	Holdings of own sterling acceptances	Holdings of own foreign currency acceptances
	UK government bonds	Other UK public sector	UK MFIs	Other UK residents	Non-residents							
RPM	B3MQ	B3NQ	B3XL	B3OQ	B3PQ	B3QQ	B3RQ	B3SQ	B3TQ	B3UQ	B3IM	B3JM
2016 Jan	473	-	14,898	19,107	475,717	197,818	11,153	38,239	**3,730,849**	**7,120,654**	176	1,123
Feb	504	1	14,918	19,378	459,136	197,071	10,893	43,124	**3,781,952**	**7,168,425**	156	1,028
Mar	569	2	14,124	19,651	446,141	192,914	11,202	43,053	**3,690,431**	**7,083,857**	118	1,017
Apr	661	1	15,609	17,793	457,143	222,009	10,053	43,019	**3,702,819**	**7,108,452**	128	884
May	711	3	14,996	17,267	442,661	204,291	10,454	38,461	**3,649,966**	**7,069,091**	139	932
Jun	778	4	14,814	16,779	466,404	225,679	11,088	44,525	**4,053,665**	**7,522,631**	151	1,094
Jul	691	3	14,589	14,941	492,137	215,369	10,356	46,767	**4,076,017**	**7,574,717**	154	1,198
Aug	703	2	14,534	15,155	486,311	206,322	10,688	51,469	**4,082,182**	**7,595,979**	187	1,111
Sep	692	-	13,889	13,730	462,304	227,515	10,583	45,071	**4,130,988 (u)**	**7,665,535 (u)**	184	1,011
Oct	582	-	14,477	14,097	490,431	235,684	11,673	45,429	**4,269,415**	**7,797,724**	198	897
Nov	499	-	13,605	14,862	450,162	266,521	11,892	44,011	**4,178,173**	**7,724,717**	201	936
Dec	464	-	13,855	13,104	457,809	108,868	9,392	44,851	**4,022,578**	**7,596,595**	189	1,011
2017 Jan	426	-	13,113	12,548	459,369	239,807	9,653	42,375	**4,155,313**	**7,787,070**	193	920
Feb	401	-	15,007	13,465	484,150	264,093	12,637	41,647	**4,291,167**	**7,958,706**	184	1,113
Mar	473	-	13,240	12,917	461,730	228,757	11,733	40,240	**4,162,675**	**7,911,709**	158	1,436
Apr	438	-	12,953	11,541	452,033	268,152	12,883	40,569	**4,123,499**	**7,888,650**	160	1,096
May	484	-	13,289	11,478	473,080	259,937	12,909	38,942	**4,168,199**	**7,954,676**	161	1,403
Jun	464	-	13,969	10,629	472,273	243,682	12,750	37,486	**4,103,162**	**7,963,207**	146	1,238
Jul	461	-	13,681	11,143	457,269	219,783	12,833	42,121	**4,147,777 (bf)**	**8,005,056 (bf)**	143	1,045
Aug	353	-	13,263	11,751	445,670	209,232	16,673	42,794	**4,213,333 (be)**	**8,083,837 (bh)**	281	1,277
Sep	344	-	12,431	10,985	459,476	211,908	12,040	38,895	**4,122,007 (bg)**	**8,025,180 (bg)**	160	1,051
Oct	245	-	11,442	11,000	468,036	211,219	11,765	41,475	**4,186,427**	**8,057,007**	171	1,004
Nov	245	-	12,068	11,076	475,164	254,701	12,228	38,363	**4,257,427**	**8,098,050**	170	1,061
Dec	229	-	13,193	13,113	480,204	99,909	13,195	43,795	**4,146,067**	**7,959,235**	151	1,398
2018 Jan	232	-	11,935	12,197	491,593	233,801	12,718	39,933	**4,214,532**	**7,986,489**	150	1,260
Feb	331	-	12,445	11,197	461,088	233,902	12,356	41,029	**4,293,243**	**8,081,867**	151	1,637
Mar	313	-	12,305	10,527	434,754	190,043	13,116	42,545	**4,236,340**	**8,005,952**	156	2,108
Apr	321	-	12,370	10,603	447,331	193,120	14,411	41,999	**4,263,125**	**8,043,929**	154	2,294

Source: Bank of England

Notes to table

Movements in amounts outstanding can reflect breaks in data series as well as underlying flows. For changes data, users are recommended to refer directly to the appropriate series or data tables.
Further explanation can be found at: https://www.bankofengland.co.uk/statistics/details/further-details-about-changes-flows-growth-rates-data.

(u) Due to a change in treatment at one institution, the amounts outstanding decreased by £14bn. This effect has been adjusted out of the flows for September 2016.
(be) Due to improvements in reporting by one institution, amounts outstanding decreased by £17 billion. This amount has been adjusted out of the flows for August 2017.
(bf) Due to transfer of business by one institution, amounts outstanding increased by £34 billion. This amount has been adjusted out of the flows for July 2017.
(bg) Due to improvements in reporting by one reporting institution, the amounts outstanding increased by £38bn. This amount has been adjusted out of the flows for September 2017.
(bh) Due to improvements in reporting by one institution, amounts outstanding decreased by £11 billion. This amount has been adjusted out of the flows for August 2017.
(bi) Due to improvements in reporting by one reporting institution, the amounts outstanding decreased by £5bn. This amount has been adjusted out of the flows for September 2017.
(bj) Due to improvements in reporting by one reporting institution, the amounts outstanding increased by £11bn. This amount has been adjusted out of the flows for September 2017.
(bk) Due to a change in group structure by one reporting institution, the amounts outstanding increased by £6bn. This effect has been adjusted out of the flows for September 2017.

Explanatory notes can be found here:
https://www.bankofengland.co.uk/statistics/details/further-details-about-monetary-financial-institutions-excluding-central-bank-balance-sheet-data

12.3e Monetary financial institutions' (excluding central bank) balance sheet

£ millions | Not seasonally adjusted

Changes in sterling liabilities

	Notes	Sight deposits					Time deposits						
	outstanding & cash loaded cards	UK MFIs	of which intragroup banks	UK public sector	Other UK residents	Non-residents	UK MFIs	of which intragroup banks	UK public sector	Other UK residents	of which SAYE	of which cash ISAs	Non-residents
RPM	B4IJ	B4GA	B8ZD	B4CF	B4BH	B4DD	B4HA	B8ZF	B4DF	B4CH	B4FH	B4DH	B4ED
2016 Jan	-236	-3,677	-4,910	737	-1,586	264	-7,735	-7,698	-278	-8,443	-1	267	-7,442
Feb	-31	35	-617	-612	18,511	-432	195	-165	-892	-3,516	16	581	-24,251
Mar	99	-10,476	-11,768	-809	27,036	8,195	3,699	4,281	-2,146	-10,425	3	1,989	2,078
Apr	1	-4,752	-3,677	1,232	-16,073	-4,469	443	-1,764	1,103	7,179	24	5,505	6,487
May	80	98	514	-652	17,109	-9,002	-4,397	-3,796	269	-2,518	12	722	-7,870
Jun	-26	-6,104	-6,634	18	28,593	12,322	23,501	23,107	259	1,084	34	222	3,142
Jul	4	7,295	4,285	659	5,368	9,859	-3,840	-3,221	854	-140	-84	426	1,847
Aug	116	-4,699	-4,129	-157	5,752	1,240	-3,383	-3,083	50	2,383	-29	-402	-2,344
Sep	82	6,644	7,751	-1,110	18,058	-7,423	4,063	3,717	-229	-6,485	-45	-349	996
Oct	34	1,609	-950	736	-246	1,443	-8,079	-9,404	-108	-535	13	-656	109
Nov	71	-6,282	-3,881	-784	2,491	-1,040	5,647	2,020	-219	-6,261	-6	-620	-1,186
Dec	426	5,084	6,929	114	9,113	2,225	34,946	20,603	-648	2,618	5	-393	1,522
2017 Jan	-156	6,589	5,214	211	-16,328	2,172	7,960	-5,462	-370	-9,377	12	-795	-4,286
Feb	8	9,369	10,427	-907	1,763	-1,565	20,360	11,398	-814	-6,711	-7	-771	-108
Mar	14	18,524	19,046	-388	30,254	3,243	27,877	15,225	-1,721	-4,309	21	638	-5,971
Apr	86	1,139	-194	1,693	-9,026	-1,488	2,037	-470	1	11,247	5	3,838	4,143
May	-83	5,442	4,576	-299	8,882	6,091	14,019	9,283	209	-6,946	15	271	-177
Jun	-26	4,074	5,343	103	21,906	3,627	28,330	16,954	592	848	-3	-419	980
Jul	157	11,548	10,651	1,209	-8,195	-3,409	899	-2,559	746	-2,262	-28	-848	-7,333
Aug	199	1,759	2,519	-122	13,081	1,490	12,513	8,460	218	1,438	9	-692	4,262
Sep	55	1,493	3,227	113	13,252	-9,287	9,084	6,356	-7	-10,293	24	-141	-1,843
Oct	48	-24,594	-24,061	57	-3,428	-2,144	2,971	-2,627	-626	6,042	10	-709	-10,112
Nov	-46	-17,882	-17,842	-350	11,897	2,400	-37,626	-39,591	-285	509	-37	-691	-6,162
Dec	172	-14,816	-14,523	256	5,097	9,891	18,780	8,210	-810	-1,540	-14	-474	1,409
2018 Jan	-326	-33,582	-34,076	207	-14,402	-12,673	-30,172	-33,753	-500	3,829	15	-725	-4,679
Feb	-107	4,720	4,253	-761	880	-809	16,715	-2,742	-1,784	30	35	-25	2,194
Mar	104	-16,004	-15,946	1,198	16,439	7,662	-1,673	-2,292	-1,115	-8,444	10	2,615	7,248
Apr	353	-8,044	-6,746	-535	-936	-1,299	12,523	11,677	1,175	2,655	3	4,908	-527

Source: Bank of England

12.3e Monetary financial institutions' (excluding central bank) balance sheet

£ millions

Not seasonally adjusted

Changes in sterling liabilities

	Liabilities under sale and repurchase agreements					Acceptances	CDs and other paper issued									
	UK MFIs	of which intragroup banks	UK public sector	Other UK residents	Non-residents	granted	CDs and Commercial paper	Bonds with maturity of and up to incl. 5 years	Bonds with maturity of greater than 5 years	Total	Total sterling deposits	Sterling items in suspense and transmission	Net derivatives	Accrued amounts payable	Sterling capital and other internal funds	Total sterling liabilities
RPM	B4IA	B8ZB	B4EF	B4EH	B4FD	B4BK	B2SU	B6OH	B2TK	B4EJ	B4FJ	B4AK	B4GJ	B4CJ	B4DJ	B4JJ
2016 Jan	-2,627	-2,819	-78	2,491	6,501	-7	-1,249	570	-72	**-752**	**-22,631**	33,204	26,017	1,450	-14,222	23,583
Feb	2,556	809	-165	2,704	-10,152	-16	1,249	1,028	22	**2,299**	**-13,737**	-13,422	30,311	625	-24,086	-20,340
Mar	5,872	-900	-1,298	-7,892	10,409	-12	3,972	-1,155	148	**2,966**	**27,199**	-3,590	-58,281	-1,970	-3,467	-40,010
Apr	3,633	-255	5,547	3,297	1,267	6	869	748	12	**1,628**	**6,527**	5,155	-5,248	-1,020	-13,865	-8,450
May	-2,137	-2,377	250	4,155	3,687	-2	4,108	-924	-305	**2,878**	**1,867**	2,536	-7,105	1,379	10,130	8,886
Jun	5,939	1,055	183	-1,396	1,650	37	-16	-118	695	**562**	**69,791**	1,205	79,742	148	-32,889	117,970
Jul	-9,596	-5,623	-2,005	14,004	-11,335	6	9,281	-55	-305	**8,920**	**21,897**	6,879	-7,127	-315	-22,436	-1,099
Aug	584	600	913	8,877	3,997	3	1,899	95	103	**2,097**	**15,313**	-14,747	-7,030	-425	-1,793	-8,566
Sep	-1,829	-292	-3,188	-16,919	2,357	-34	4,228	-231	-33	**3,964**	**-1,136**	7,284	16,923	722	-18,203	5,672
Oct	-2,656	2,104	1,474	19,384	7,986	16	-682	-42	-293	**-1,017**	**20,116**	-7,718	66,459	533	-23,379	56,045
Nov	-2,355	-540	290	14,388	4,968	19	-2,956	185	-867	**-3,638**	**6,038**	9,318	-77,015	-147	56,387	-5,347
Dec	-5,288	-153	-1,599	-20,844	833	-27	2,122	-1,058	-8	**1,056**	**29,104**	-25,930	7,750	-835	1,431	11,946
2017 Jan	2,436	4,486	-411	26,351	364	5	-851	-725	-657	**-2,233**	**13,083**	22,337	-24,227	-31	30,126	41,132
Feb	-1,629	-471	2,049	-1,031	1,366	1	5,192	-170	23	**5,045**	**27,188**	2,118	35,703	1,193	1,644	67,855
Mar	-383	-2,740	-1,202	-166	9,538	66	10,262	-892	-238	**9,133**	**84,494**	3,531	-25,650	-2,775	-15,579	44,035
Apr	-1,532	649	-505	15,039	-7,500	5	2,763	-2,203	-170	**391**	**15,644**	-167	-34,850	-541	1,666	-18,161
May	2,619	-799	2,444	-8,436	3,721	6	-3,373	2,569	-676	**-1,480**	**26,094**	-4,671	20,891	644	20,290	63,164
Jun	-4,606	-1,785	394	-7,925	9,194	-1	-6,018	500	1	**-5,518**	**51,998**	3,407	-9,538	-28	7,233	53,047
Jul	946	4,008	3,176	8,231	-9,175	-46	-165	-249	99	**-315**	**-3,979**	-5,643	16,487	-188	-26,210	-19,376
Aug	-4,490	-2,891	823	6,826	1,703	-10	700	-273	69	**496**	**39,987**	-6,792	6,967	-502	7,008	46,867
Sep	-3,749	-753	-7,096	-1,166	10,891	-62	-1,357	-1,081	-553	**-2,992**	**-1,661**	3,663	-43,530	-799	27,538	-14,736
Oct	1,043	-2,247	3,254	14,037	-9,813	3	-6,624	420	366	**-5,838**	**-29,151**	-1,589	16,876	750	-8,569	-21,636
Nov	2,654	502	836	-4,728	5,640	-3	5,757	-63	479	**6,173**	**-36,926**	10,428	-26,204	873	8,814	-43,061
Dec	6,393	2,117	-2,437	-17,447	5,219	6	1,478	630	22	**2,131**	**12,132**	-30,711	-5,233	2,277	11,233	-10,131
2018 Jan	-2,596	-1,285	2,835	20,453	1,172	-8	2,740	3,375	-506	**5,609**	**-64,507**	20,920	-85,104	-814	-7,219	-137,050
Feb	1,232	-296	1,945	-1,664	-6,913	26	-1,550	-1,761	875	**-2,437**	**13,374**	-2,579	149,256	710	-16,096	144,558
Mar	1,367	-1,427	-5,775	-28,756	5,181	9	3,965	3,174	-1,435	**5,704**	**-16,959**	2,603	-26,833	519	2,801	-37,766
Apr	3,158	5,531	-66	2,640	-5,804	83	-1,868	1,104	-2,343	**-3,107**	**1,915**	-1,034	90,689	-2,496	16,648	106,075

Notes to table

Source: Bank of England

Explanatory notes can be found here:
https://www.bankofengland.co.uk/statistics/details/further-details-about-monetary-financial-institutions-excluding-central-bank-balance-sheet-data

12.3f Monetary financial institutions' (excluding central bank) balance sheet

£ millions | Not seasonally adjusted

Changes in foreign currency liabilities (including euro)

	Sight and time deposits					Acceptances	Sale and repurchase agreements				
	UK MFIs	of which intragroup banks	UK public sector	Other UK residents	Non-residents	granted	UK MFIs	of which intragroup banks	UK public sector	Other UK residents	Non-residents
RPM	B4GB	B8ZN	B2VP	B2VV	B2VJ	B4HM	B4HB	B8ZL	B4GG	B4GI	B4HE
2016 Jan	-5,606	-7,719	81	9,258	-1,288	-444	-8,501	-3,767	-173	3,989	34,433
Feb	7,619	3,999	176	829	5,211	-358	-1,777	-2,047	-174	1,249	-20,970
Mar	-9,991	-4,290	-286	6,191	-19,595	328	-6,044	-5,074	-1,155	-237	-7,846
Apr	11,021	12,400	179	3,189	-15,012	162	3,571	989	1,198	3,464	16,184
May	-18,299	-17,836	6	5,126	85	48	-395	-3,486	-584	-1,586	16,798
Jun	916	-6,127	369	9,548	64,505	583	-1,111	-901	-385	-3,577	5,520
Jul	-2,111	4,055	-63	2,226	-11,744	-355	-380	543	1,067	3,380	-6,002
Aug	7,613	7,169	171	5,634	-12,516	-73	126	-304	-294	-1,985	-1,440
Sep	-12,950	-13,684	-817	-4,560	-7,969	622	-5,481	-6,659	-890	8,788	10,010
Oct	-3,501	-615	-30	-2,564	-55,398	-230	-1,909	-3,042	367	-3,519	9,954
Nov	3,955	5,979	207	6,970	2,332	226	-2,434	446	993	11,889	7,047
Dec	-3,854	-4,940	-181	-17,014	-60	279	1,560	-2,177	-1,063	-7,458	-4,475
2017 Jan	4,959	5,615	213	8,957	987	-675	3,849	2,982	796	12,516	26,574
Feb	-12,411	-9,523	-74	-943	16,425	472	-1,554	-41	-975	25,197	22,265
Mar	-10,131	-6,995	-245	-7,369	-24,977	233	5,631	4,095	-272	-8,694	-3,197
Apr	-615	-404	358	9,071	13,871	-335	-2,760	-993	1,279	1,956	-1
May	-929	-473	353	7,556	-32,000	-415	762	-629	-289	-4,714	31,387
Jun	-38,229	-35,646	86	-983	14,846	150	-5,956	-3,250	-845	-1,165	-17,062
Jul	6,603	3,752	114	1,085	11,371	-516	-1,842	-1,594	1,576	4,864	1,402
Aug	4,377	1,983	-142	501	-38,273	-300	5,397	5,155	-877	1,236	-7,890
Sep	-3,644	1,590	371	-430	19,997	488	-605	445	670	-949	23,847
Oct	-2,206	-1,817	149	-2,745	21,482	-184	-1,603	-4,279	-221	13,652	25,492
Nov	-3,421	-2,065	-259	5,809	3,437	197	4,934	5,021	234	10,278	3,110
Dec	2,554	1,292	-39	-12,636	1,905	523	-8,323	-5,821	250	-17,855	46,716
2018 Jan	25,289	21,064	296	10,900	27,126	-503	690	-2,015	-778	25,872	-23,337
Feb	-4,066	151	-36	-8,014	-16,585	363	7,206	4,097	-525	4,309	34,071
Mar	13,095	13,054	-269	-1,515	-3,161	-23	-1,992	-2,398	448	-14,876	15,503
Apr	6,141	6,277	449	6,818	16,955	477	-1,219	1,341	1,607	1,140	-54,327

Source: Bank of England

12.3f Monetary financial institutions' (excluding central bank) balance sheet

£ millions — Not seasonally adjusted

Changes in foreign currency liabilities (including euro)

	CDs and other paper Issued										
	CDs and Commercial paper	Bonds with maturity of up to and incl. 5 years	Bonds with maturity of greater than 5 years	Total	Total foreign currency deposits	Items in suspense and transmission	Net derivatives	Accrued amounts payable	Capital and other internal funds	Total foreign currency liabilities	Total liabilities
RPM	B2TN	B6OJ	B2TO	B4CM	B4DM	B4GM	B4EM	B4AM	B4BM	B4FM	B4JM
2016 Jan	2,358	-4,401	-3,155	**-5,198**	**26,550**	101,753	-36,162	-2,113	10,281	**100,309**	123,891
Feb	3,798	-113	2,141	**5,826**	**-2,370**	-3,510	-26,192	190	9,836	**-22,046**	-42,385
Mar	-854	-4,838	-414	**-6,106**	**-44,741**	-11,346	55,926	-270	-11,548	**-11,979**	-51,989
Apr	2,026	835	8,137	**10,998**	**34,954**	30,918	4,079	-168	12,304	**82,087**	73,636
May	2,047	-2,813	-1,616	**-2,383**	**-1,183**	-7,532	4,730	943	-20,412	**-23,455**	-14,569
Jun	-1,941	593	3,968	**2,620**	**78,988**	7,081	-83,278	35	8,337	**11,163**	129,133
Jul	-6,757	-1,875	209	**-8,423**	**-22,405**	-3,796	4,912	-69	214	**-21,144**	-22,243
Aug	-3,950	-13	-2,173	**-6,136**	**-8,900**	-8,588	4,097	-93	-3,590	**-17,073**	-25,640
Sep	-1,669	20,468	-3,996	**14,803**	**1,556**	26,599	-11,644	626	17,073	**34,211**	39,883
Oct	4,412	-4,348	16	**80**	**-56,750**	-873	-79,577	1,252	36,517	**-99,431**	-43,386
Nov	2,931	-2,184	-7,803	**-7,056**	**24,129**	32,908	84,112	538	-29,123	**112,564**	107,217
Dec	-5,738	-855	-1,475	**-8,067**	**-40,333**	-150,332	-4,737	-1,606	6,497	**-190,511**	-178,565
2017 Jan	1,966	1,404	2,218	**5,589**	**63,764**	124,391	27,279	620	-23,761	**192,292**	233,424
Feb	10,850	6,608	8,403	**25,860**	**74,263**	11,241	-34,557	5,186	-1,059	**55,074**	122,929
Mar	990	-6,285	-3,403	**-8,698**	**-57,718**	-37,128	26,530	-551	-12,259	**-81,126**	-37,091
Apr	-1,318	12,947	3,732	**15,361**	**38,184**	33,661	37,829	1,218	-13,334	**97,558**	79,397
May	4,436	-8,703	1,181	**-3,086**	**-1,375**	-11,576	-16,993	786	-40,408	**-69,567**	-6,403
Jun	-766	-575	-1,064	**-2,404**	**-51,560**	-23,893	-4,047	-1,497	16,260	**-64,738**	-11,691
Jul	3,503	-3,186	1,754	**2,071**	**26,728**	-21,352	-5,790	574	9,499	**9,659**	-9,717
Aug	1,481	-1,030	-2,335	**-1,884**	**-37,855**	-210	-10,211	-1,201	2,170	**-47,308**	-441
Sep	491	2,186	-4,038	**-1,361**	**38,384**	22,112	30,642	-597	-3,679	**86,863**	72,127
Oct	7,673	-14,969	-2,565	**-9,860**	**43,956**	4,836	-12,583	258	4,015	**40,481**	18,845
Nov	2,507	20,580	-3,105	**19,982**	**44,301**	41,104	31,195	191	694	**117,484**	74,423
Dec	-2,338	-5,214	95	**-7,457**	**5,637**	-155,978	11,632	-423	-5,413	**-144,545**	-154,675
2018 Jan	2,053	3,315	2,456	**7,823**	**73,379**	133,552	86,448	1,934	4,740	**300,054**	163,003
Feb	1,089	-1,192	-1,234	**-1,337**	**15,386**	-8,785	-162,794	40	29,937	**-126,216**	18,342
Mar	1,232	30,891	-536	**31,588**	**38,799**	-37,049	26,717	7,065	-14,229	**21,303**	-16,463
Apr	6,349	13,081	240	**19,670**	**-2,288**	2,423	-100,243	-6,302	9,395	**-97,015**	9,060

Notes to table

Source: Bank of England

Explanatory notes can be found here:
https://www.bankofengland.co.uk/statistics/details/further-details-about-monetary-financial-institutions-excluding-central-bank-balance-sheet-data

12.3g Monetary financial institutions' (excluding central bank) balance sheet

£ millions — Not seasonally adjusted

Changes in sterling assets

	Notes and coin	With UK central bank		Loans					Acceptances granted				Bills			
		Cash ratio deposits	Other	UK MFIs	of which intragroup banks	UK MFIs' CDs etc	UK MFIs commercial paper	Non-residents	UK MFIs	UK public sector	Other UK residents	Non-residents	Treasury bills	UK MFIs bills	Other UK	Non-residents
RPM	B4II	B3YR	B3ZR	B4DC	B8ZJ	B4JB	B4BC	B4BD	B4EC	B4FF	B3TR	B4GD	B4BA	B4IB	B4HG	B4IC
2016 Jan	-1,483	-	2,250	-11,778	-12,612	397	19	-1,056	-	-	-5	-2	821	68	40	-76
Feb	-151	-	1,038	1,390	-101	-77	-98	-4,559	-	-	-17	-	-660	-17	-133	-86
Mar	1,420	-	-4,684	-5,013	-7,976	-160	-41	8,482	-	-	-10	-2	-1,777	-3	59	7
Apr	-822	1	9,514	-4,979	-5,254	-154	1	2,152	-	-	1	5	-588	31	-2	108
May	279	18	-4,938	-3,329	-3,370	-10	-1	-498	-	-	-1	-1	-793	7	-35	-200
Jun	230	60	-2,941	16,407	17,222	-175	-	-4,032	-	-	37	-	2,620	25	63	-176
Jul	-601	-	4,211	2,446	1,146	546	27	9,715	-	-	8	-2	5,262	-4	43	184
Aug	709	-	11,380	-7,089	-7,175	-50	-21	-252	-	-	4	-1	-1,359	1	-71	9
Sep	-578	-	-3,777	11,032	12,202	-158	-7	4,035	-	-	-34	-1	-951	4	7	-208
Oct	-478	1	11,973	-10,793	-12,800	-35	-10	83	-	-	14	2	-1,190	23	10	85
Nov	577	26	15,896	-5,599	-4,054	-100	-7	-1,397	-	-	19	-	-1,592	1	59	-56
Dec	1,553	182	14,262	28,569	29,612	-224	-	-7,161	-	-	-33	6	-1,346	12	-	-53
2017 Jan	-1,502	-	18,977	-1,969	-3,402	200	2	9,152	-	-	5	1	-2,273	-41	-27	255
Feb	-179	-	17,641	22,441	23,037	-259	-6	-9,438	-	-	-1	1	-1,227	-4	62	-193
Mar	77	-	16,359	35,248	36,682	-80	-	948	-	-	-3	69	-379	-	-50	169
Apr	-17	2	5,742	-433	-1,388	-302	-	10,331	-	-	5	-	-1,584	29	46	70
May	497	2	-2,221	15,209	14,192	3	1	-1,880	-	-	7	-	470	-10	50	-155
Jun	-306	154	10,814	20,632	22,749	199	4	-4,494	2	-	5	-8	-72	31	-78	-34
Jul	-111	3	3,033	7,951	6,336	-47	-4	-5,628	-2	-	-42	-2	722	-	14	-111
Aug	583	-1	-7,836	5,978	6,848	-61	-4	11,754	-	-	-2	-8	-9	-	-107	50
Sep	-469	-	4,576	12,655	14,717	-40	73	-11,086	-	-	2	-64	762	-	4	114
Oct	378	4	12,648	-31,853	-30,946	-216	-32	3,478	-	-	4	-1	1,243	-	33	85
Nov	222	1	9,220	-55,945	-56,020	64	-43	-4,471	-	-	-2	-	-467	-	20	-344
Dec	881	122	5,056	-3,700	-3,593	32	-	30	-	-	-4	10	42	-	6	-20
2018 Jan	-1,555	-	1,227	-69,796	-69,106	50	-	3,794	-	-	-5	-3	-994	-	-44	676
Feb	-27	-	22,533	1,180	1,478	-237	9	-8,305	-	-	19	7	1,147	-	34	12
Mar	88	-	-9,797	-17,536	-17,000	173	-1	-6,643	-	-	2	7	689	-	-39	13
Apr	246	3	14,401	4,721	4,980	94	-14	-2,207	-	-	82	-	2,250	-	-18	-575

Source: Bank of England

12.3g Monetary financial institutions' (excluding central bank) balance sheet

£ millions

Not seasonally adjusted

Changes in sterling assets

	Claims under sale and repurchase agreements					Advances			Investments					Items in suspense and collection	Accrued amounts receivable	Other assets	Total sterling assets
	UK MFIs	of which intragroup banks	UK public sector	Other UK residents	Non-residents	UK public sector	Other UK residents	Non-residents	UK government bonds	Other UK public sector	UK MFIs	Other UK residents	Non-residents				
RPM	**B4FA**	**B8ZH**	**B4BF**	**B4AH**	**B4CD**	**B2VK**	**B2VQ**	**B4HC**	**B4CA**	**B4IE**	**B4CC**	**B4IG**	**B4JC**	**B4BJ**	**B4HI**	**B4JI**	**B4AJ**
2016 Jan	-2,327	-2,519	66	-2,722	2,647	93	9,586	566	-2,527	57	-107	-1,468	-454	33,993	380	61	27,038
Feb	3,178	661	26	5,321	-5,730	30	12,404	-2,539	2,730	25	-1,759	-39	-742	-13,282	891	36	-2,817
Mar	1,464	-1,035	-67	2,289	1,662	-42	5,862	272	592	-24	-920	-485	474	-2,859	-804	366	6,057
Apr	3,287	-253	-6	-1,756	3,825	66	-12,975	707	3,298	-3	-26	-565	-2,284	6,692	-185	-8	5,338
May	-510	-2,195	-19	15,064	2,464	227	1,374	6,157	-3,520	10	-243	-244	1,573	-776	1,165	49	13,273
Jun	205	857	-	11,484	2,080	-214	10,048	4,993	-4,896	53	-86	849	-4,794	1,375	-488	67	32,795
Jul	-10,170	-5,642	-	-2,639	1,472	179	8,671	-3,466	-3,295	16	-554	-4,573	1,708	10,324	316	233	20,057
Aug	1,051	581	213	-411	2,679	-56	8,716	3,661	5,820	66	-143	-3,839	1,382	-15,739	200	112	6,971
Sep	1,683	-311	273	4,696	1,727	-183	3,841	-1,729	2,597	-17	501	477	21	5,111	-1,443	487	27,408
Oct	-234	2,104	994	5,379	-2,586	408	-639	1,336	5,855	-43	312	-2,741	283	-7,743	-161	265	368
Nov	-1,268	-540	-1,063	16,789	2,167	24	-6,045	-4,599	1,244	-23	-731	2,503	1,886	8,369	254	46	27,381
Dec	836	-153	-428	-6,051	6,453	-152	6,731	9,702	-2,608	-6	993	-1,480	-1,453	-26,368	-349	171	21,758
2017 Jan	4,673	4,461	2,388	6,372	-6,527	-54	5,020	-2,379	-3,029	-27	-22,212	29,208	3,215	21,991	-18	-71	61,330
Feb	-1,428	-266	-2,095	-3,805	4,288	-117	2,275	4,134	-3,887	43	-1,415	-4,787	-1,879	2,574	162	-344	22,558
Mar	-2,621	-2,921	842	14,306	7,283	-32	4,863	-1,241	1,754	-106	291	-1,943	-1,414	6,607	-952	97	80,090
Apr	-2,741	649	-950	-381	-1,480	48	7,292	1,193	885	-49	-230	5,472	597	-4,112	150	-61	19,522
May	1,671	-799	86	5,521	542	94	1,460	-2,467	1,095	18	300	-1,648	125	-65	572	122	19,398
Jun	-2,232	-1,785	-10	2,083	5,547	89	7,816	2,254	3,316	44	519	3,847	-122	2,256	-1,014	-1,170	50,071
Jul	3,385	4,008	13	-2,456	-11,761	-98	4,929	316	-609	-1	-428	1,726	1,431	-6,206	288	150	-3,543
Aug	-5,282	-2,891	964	5,090	1,938	236	11,598	15	-2,981	4	-645	-1,307	-3,739	-4,265	439	81	12,481
Sep	-903	-753	-958	11,261	3,013	-463	2,713	107	-1,003	-58	-602	-2,608	2,329	2,103	-2,307	-3,132	16,019
Oct	2,114	-2,247	-129	-4,884	-7,246	-98	-2,310	2,709	2,846	35	783	1,101	-8,453	-3,443	267	160	-30,776
Nov	4,456	502	205	3,455	4,290	-369	9,287	1,119	-8,958	30	-162	-1,725	684	12,480	902	170	-25,883
Dec	5,107	2,117	177	-1,842	-1,059	123	5,125	-142	-4,783	18	692	-1,118	-1,828	-29,485	336	313	-25,912
2018 Jan	-889	-1,285	-260	-3,130	4,631	-464	6,161	-3,312	7,620	-33	858	303	4,517	18,461	1,050	624	-30,512
Feb	1,315	-296	880	-4,997	251	-6	2,443	3,342	2,808	-24	-536	-559	-39	-2,326	325	350	19,600
Mar	2,219	-1,427	3,489	-9,614	7,519	-759	13,336	75	-4,152	13	1,446	-1,857	-247	2,398	343	-1,403	-20,240
Apr	3,764	5,536	-4,283	-7,507	160	503	4,374	-1,801	678	-5	264	338	-241	1,060	-1,785	132	14,637

Source: Bank of England

Notes to table

Explanatory notes can be found here:
https://www.bankofengland.co.uk/statistics/details/further-details-about-monetary-financial-institutions-excluding-central-bank-balance-sheet-data

12.3h Monetary financial institutions' (excluding central bank) balance sheet

£ millions | Not seasonally adjusted

Changes in foreign currency assets (including euro)

	Loans and advances						Claims under sale and repurchase agreements					Acceptances granted	Total Bills
	UK MFIs	of which intragroup banks	UK MFIs' CDs etc.	UK public sector	Other UK residents	Non-residents	UK MFIs	of which intragroup banks	UK public sector	Other UK residents	Non-residents		
RPM	B4EB	B8ZR	B4AF	B2VN	B2VT	B2VH	B4FB	B8ZP	B4EG	B4EI	B4FE	B4HM	B4GL
2016 Jan	-8,136	-7,722	-96	56	3,210	10,029	-3,780	-3,778	131	6,624	5,939	-444	-3,606
Feb	7,196	4,306	142	75	9,278	-32,502	-1,247	-1,582	-467	8,394	4,895	-358	843
Mar	-7,077	-4,472	82	-41	-8,909	-23,453	-7,491	-4,943	-880	-7,366	13,870	328	84
Apr	13,306	12,322	19	-38	6,314	-18,251	4,423	946	1,067	7,038	8,683	162	-2,623
May	-19,066	-18,097	-	-60	-1,523	25,526	-460	-4,067	162	2,508	-709	48	-660
Jun	424	-6,054	102	87	5,309	86,110	-54	-967	-599	446	18,324	583	-3,892
Jul	-214	3,706	66	59	-1,548	-19,997	-1,158	539	384	-3,034	-9,591	-355	-2,178
Aug	5,746	7,987	-16	-37	-915	-115	-79	-307	-314	-1,902	-17,294	-73	-1,012
Sep	-12,229	-13,622	-177	-672	-23,535	32,476	-6,075	-6,680	595	2,086	39,948	622	-2,745
Oct	-258	-1,181	349	-2	-4,613	-30,536	-1,883	-3,099	-1,281	-3,829	-15,827	-230	1,091
Nov	3,506	5,810	-562	-7	10,178	21,958	-1,093	493	1,129	9,943	6,471	226	-767
Dec	-6,556	-4,864	-48	10	-8,027	1,348	455	-2,187	265	-19,524	-4,937	279	-381
2017 Jan	5,246	6,372	54	-6	9,613	-23,703	4,417	2,846	199	15,213	24,494	-675	3,224
Feb	-7,356	-10,232	-90	28	4,837	41,081	924	-94	-922	17,464	6,937	472	-2,244
Mar	-5,454	-7,270	-74	-24	-7,618	-55,084	5,981	4,291	-882	-4,336	8,385	233	-531
Apr	-2,586	-550	-124	13	8,127	12,602	-3,703	-966	3,086	7,245	-8,239	-335	-2,807
May	-2,467	-83	-85	33	-7,271	-19,194	2,089	-768	-436	2,042	3,871	-415	2,480
Jun	-37,411	-35,608	-19	-	-4,820	8,531	-7,270	-3,117	-1,847	-911	-3,166	150	2,440
Jul	4,587	3,569	116	63	355	32,421	-2,421	-1,575	2,129	-2,778	-3,808	-516	1,417
Aug	1,412	2,071	188	-16	-1,252	12,570	6,171	5,108	-879	-581	-10,731	-300	-1,202
Sep	2,384	1,682	-57	45	-2,554	-653	-1,466	482	377	-4,760	25,803	488	1,491
Oct	-2,908	-2,237	-195	-43	948	6,756	-4,599	-4,282	216	9,656	41,037	-184	-3,777
Nov	-4,654	-2,124	83	61	-3,890	12,696	6,717	5,021	-165	10,504	25,092	197	438
Dec	1,069	1,519	29	-55	-8,418	32,479	-7,299	-5,815	511	-16,751	14,356	523	563
2018 Jan	23,735	20,933	-186	158	16,823	-9,794	146	-1,970	-1,497	26,729	-22,477	-503	1,516
Feb	-2,991	-218	-229	-210	-12,515	-5,744	6,061	4,059	-287	4,848	47,969	363	-2,520
Mar	13,765	13,214	90	3	-1,405	49,519	1,218	-2,366	500	-13,856	10,655	-23	-1,018
Apr	6,795	5,687	29	-23	14,777	4,994	799	1,282	1,361	-10,062	-33,249	477	-1,317

Source: Bank of England

12.3h Monetary financial institutions' (excluding central bank) balance sheet

£ millions

Not seasonally adjusted

Changes in foreign currency assets (including euro)

	Investments					Items in suspense and collection	Accrued amounts receivable	Other assets	**Total foreign currency assets**	**Total assets**	Holdings of own sterling acceptances	Holdings of own foreign currency acceptances
	UK government bonds	Other UK public sector	UK MFIs	Other UK residents	Non-residents							
RPM	B4EA	B4CG	B4AG	B4CI	B4DE	B4JL	B4FL	B4HL	**B4IL**	**B4IM**	B3VR	B3XR
2016 Jan	-15	-	220	-569	-14,737	104,504	6	-2,526	**96,810**	**123,849**	-13	-96
Feb	22	1	-278	113	-33,659	-4,884	-484	3,312	**-39,608**	**-42,425**	-20	-114
Mar	77	1	-826	250	-15,097	-2,972	430	940	**-58,050**	**-51,993**	-38	20
Apr	119	-1	584	-1,324	17,092	31,840	-675	573	**68,308**	**73,646**	10	-119
May	48	2	-412	-32	-13,181	-15,787	464	-4,719	**-27,851**	**-14,578**	11	44
Jun	15	1	366	-1,586	-18,226	5,624	-181	3,424	**96,278**	**129,072**	12	84
Jul	-95	-1	-416	-2,040	10,185	-13,346	-877	1,820	**-42,338**	**-22,281**	3	93
Aug	5	-1	-167	-253	-9,670	-10,977	234	4,224	**-32,617**	**-25,645**	32	-101
Sep	-16	-2	-812	-1,740	-26,839	18,448	-195	-6,665	**12,472**	**39,879**	-3	-108
Oct	-143	-	79	-574	16,366	-1,318	587	-1,793	**-43,815**	**-43,447**	14	-171
Nov	-71	-	-360	556	-11,880	40,480	658	-464	**79,901**	**107,282**	3	60
Dec	-40	-	152	-3,072	30	-158,118	-2,597	409	**-200,352**	**-178,594**	-12	62
2017 Jan	-30	-	-697	-752	8,164	129,083	356	-2,080	**172,122**	**233,452**	4	-73
Feb	-29	-	1,879	217	16,374	18,922	2,936	-1,070	**100,362**	**122,920**	-9	183
Mar	74	-	-1,750	125	-19,641	-34,487	-893	-1,203	**-117,178**	**-37,088**	-26	333
Apr	-21	-	-48	-830	-68	44,768	1,439	1,377	**59,895**	**79,417**	3	-303
May	45	-	146	8	8,389	-13,077	-188	-1,774	**-25,802**	**-6,404**	1	305
Jun	-17	-	692	-848	807	-16,641	-161	-1,268	**-61,759**	**-11,688**	-15	-160
Jul	2	-	-227	260	-18,032	-24,879	106	5,036	**-6,168**	**-9,711**	-3	-179
Aug	-117	-	-712	686	-25,478	10,705	-3,227	-169	**-12,932**	**-452**	138	209
Sep	4	-	-382	-213	31,002	10,806	-3,766	-2,418	**56,131**	**72,150**	-121	-181
Oct	-103	-	-1,015	-341	3,112	-1,003	-314	2,373	**49,618**	**18,842**	11	-57
Nov	4	-	694	183	9,565	44,924	556	-2,695	**100,309**	**74,426**	-1	75
Dec	-16	-	1,108	1,407	1,067	-155,719	940	5,445	**-128,764**	**-154,675**	-20	338
2018 Jan	14	-	-444	-842	24,210	138,269	-68	-2,275	**193,514**	**163,001**	-	-74
Feb	92	-	285	-387	-31,258	-4,134	-638	42	**-1,253**	**18,346**	1	24
Mar	-13	-	5	14	-17,458	-41,250	936	2,095	**3,777**	**-16,463**	5	500
Apr	3	-	52	-74	9,696	1,301	1,171	-2,309	**-5,577**	**9,060**	-2	146

Notes to table

Source: Bank of England

Explanatory notes can be found here:
https://www.bankofengland.co.uk/statistics/details/further-details-about-monetary-financial-institutions-excluding-central-bank-balance-sheet-data

12.4a Industrial analysis of monetary financial institutions' lending to UK residents

£ millions | Not seasonally adjusted

Amounts outstanding of lending in sterling

	Agriculture, hunting and forestry	Fishing	Mining and quarrying	Manufacturing									Electricity, gas and water supply			
				Food, beverages and tobacco	Textiles, wearing apparel and leather	Pulp, paper, and printing	Chemicals, pharma-ceuticals, rubber and plastics	Non-metallic mineral products and metals	Machinery, equipment and transport equipment	Electrical, medical and optical equipment	Other manu-facturing	**Total**	Electricity, gas steam and air conditioning	Water collection and sewerage	Waste management related services and remediation activities	Total
RPM	TBUC	TBUD	TBUE	TBUG	TBUH	TBUI	TBUJ	TBUK	TBUL	TBUM	TBUN	TBUF	TBUO	TBUP	B3F9	B3FN
2016 Jan	17,435	234	1,840	4,419	729	1,883	3,355	3,062	5,773	1,855	2,640	**23,715**	8,572	2,969	2,086	**13,627**
Feb	17,370	229	1,820	4,344	690	1,847	3,242	3,100	5,946	1,872	2,632	**23,672**	8,930	2,958	2,144	**14,032**
Mar	17,456	229	1,770	4,382	700	1,844	3,491	3,024	5,807	1,739	2,605	**23,592**	8,988	3,211	2,093	**14,292**
Apr	17,458	226	1,712	4,738	700	1,823	3,459	3,085	5,366	1,838	2,591	**23,600**	9,206	3,361	2,127	**14,694**
May	17,578	225	1,771	4,864	696	1,823	3,657	3,345	5,428	2,055	2,599	**24,467**	9,056	3,364	2,130	**14,550**
Jun	17,760	269	2,040	4,741	727	1,816	3,350	3,409	5,358	1,672	2,623	**23,696**	8,934	3,457	1,927	**14,317**
Jul	17,909	269	1,956	4,686	734	1,809	3,547	3,423	5,402	1,761	2,639	**23,999**	9,067	3,615	2,024	**14,705**
Aug	17,947	268	1,851	4,623	748	1,824	3,659	3,213	5,456	1,784	2,632	**23,937**	9,385	3,575	2,114	**15,074**
Sep	17,946	262	1,888	4,351	759	1,801	3,612	3,269	5,599	1,759	2,587	**23,737**	9,373	3,481	2,019	**14,874**
Oct	17,954	275	1,934	4,499	748	1,821	3,656	3,276	5,536	1,727	2,485	**23,746**	9,090	3,501	2,173	**14,763**
Nov	17,994	278	1,932	4,531	748	1,824	3,671	3,145	5,659	1,574	2,485	**23,637**	8,976	3,609	2,177	**14,762**
Dec	17,591	289	1,824	4,672	756	1,842	3,702	3,144	5,495	1,518	2,479	**23,609**	8,998	3,436	2,231	**14,666**
2017 Jan	17,698	286	1,812	4,542	721	1,862	4,055	3,218	5,443	1,420	2,487	**23,750**	9,005	3,442	2,299	**14,746**
Feb	17,814	285	1,895	4,453	723	1,839	3,570	3,201	5,681	1,541	2,505	**23,513**	9,207	3,175	2,350	**14,733**
Mar	17,934	285	1,833	4,297	744	1,865	3,352	3,336	5,814	1,737	2,486	**23,631**	10,936	2,972	2,230	**16,138**
Apr	18,048	282	1,849	4,630	733	1,787	3,292	3,340	5,874	1,627	2,615	**23,899**	11,054	2,982	2,245	**16,281**
May	18,206	281	1,818	5,697	734	1,948	3,431	3,262	5,601	1,568	2,680	**24,920**	10,936	2,980	2,261	**16,177**
Jun	18,351	275	1,765	5,620	742	1,945	3,209	3,235	5,425	1,606	2,711	**24,492**	11,175	3,011	2,266	**16,452**
Jul	18,443	272	1,802	8,703	742	1,664	3,252	3,077	5,260	1,450	2,684	**26,834**	11,385	2,947	2,234	**16,566**
Aug	18,379	276	1,840	8,690	751	1,707	3,173	3,242	5,070	1,544	2,648	**26,825**	11,665	2,906	2,199	**16,770**
Sep	18,402	283	2,082	8,292	793	1,804	3,290	3,698	5,851 (a)	2,065	2,731	**28,522 (a)**	10,891	3,177	2,237	**16,305**
Oct	18,341	282	1,897	8,044	799	1,854	3,434	3,495	5,837	2,331	2,693	**28,487**	10,950	3,204	2,201	**16,355**
Nov	18,454	289	1,850	7,962	751	1,741	3,401	3,548	6,029	2,136	2,799	**28,366**	11,085	3,256	2,210	**16,551**
Dec	18,095	293	1,792	8,604	686	1,785	3,453	3,473	6,010	1,908	2,741	**28,660**	11,705	3,145	2,261	**17,112**
2018 Jan	18,151	289	1,843	8,367	697	1,739	3,277	3,524	5,958	1,969	2,827	**28,359**	11,591	3,346	2,260	**17,196**
Feb	18,182	290	1,800	8,361	693	1,732	3,341	3,679	6,335	1,744	2,945	**28,831**	11,637	3,499	2,306	**17,442**
Mar	18,320	290	1,806	8,493	699	1,596	3,291	3,866	6,932	1,729	2,696	**29,302**	11,294	3,273	2,334	**16,902**
Apr	18,354	280	2,127	8,426	730	1,806	3,426	4,023	7,100	1,617	2,784	**29,911**	11,545	3,334	2,302	**17,181**

Source: Bank of England

12.4a Industrial analysis of monetary financial institutions' lending to UK residents

£ millions Not seasonally adjusted

Amounts outstanding of lending in sterling

	Construction						Wholesale and retail trade				Accommodation	Transport, storage and communication		
	Development of buildings	Construction of commercial buildings	Construction of domestic buildings	Civil Engineering	Other construction activities	Total	Wholesale and retail trade and repair of motor vehicles and motorcycles	Wholesale trade, excluding motor vehicles and motor cycles	Retail trade excluding motor vehicles and motor cycles	Total	and food service activities	Transportation and storage	Information and communication	Total
RPM	B7EB	B3I6	B3LX	B4PK	B4PX	TBUQ	TBUS	TBUT	TBUU	TBUR	TBUV	B5PK	B5PR	TBUW
2016 Jan	15,971	4,757	4,221	2,887	5,645	**33,481**	12,205	10,939	15,176	**38,319**	22,453	12,351	12,472	**24,823**
Feb	16,742	4,454	4,573	3,280	5,555	**34,603**	13,360	10,857	15,754	**39,971**	22,479	12,612	11,339	**23,952**
Mar	14,967	4,282	4,655	3,175	5,477	**32,556**	12,637	10,518	16,191	**39,345**	22,600	11,928	8,968	**20,896**
Apr	14,865	4,325	4,560	3,195	5,506	**32,451**	12,166	10,578	16,284	**39,028**	22,818	12,009	8,376	**20,386**
May	14,834	4,277	4,949	3,198	5,607	**32,865**	11,804	10,619	16,075	**38,498**	22,912	11,905	8,647	**20,553**
Jun	14,828	3,971	4,813	2,876	5,573	**32,061**	12,218	10,361	16,439	**39,019**	22,829	11,713	8,516	**20,229**
Jul	14,894	4,195	4,777	2,956	5,645	**32,467**	12,526	10,217	16,629	**39,372**	22,963	12,096	8,776	**20,872**
Aug	14,806	4,230	4,899	3,087	5,647	**32,670**	12,598	10,319	16,198	**39,114**	23,192	11,924	8,777	**20,700**
Sep	15,203	4,224	4,833	3,242	5,694	**33,196**	11,316	10,431	16,377	**38,124**	22,998	12,098	8,521	**20,620**
Oct	15,198	4,258	5,012	3,391	5,748	**33,607**	11,116	10,439	16,742	**38,297**	23,053	11,909	8,707	**20,616**
Nov	15,215	4,255	5,189	3,458	5,831	**33,948**	11,103	10,589	16,699	**38,390**	23,004	11,221	8,555	**19,776**
Dec	14,838	3,992	4,646	3,139	5,612	**32,227**	11,269	10,666	16,430	**38,365**	23,238	10,801	8,600	**19,402**
2017 Jan	15,159	4,260	4,974	3,209	5,703	**33,304**	11,620	10,641	17,019	**39,280**	23,786	11,044	8,108	**19,152**
Feb	15,237	4,302	5,285	3,303	5,755	**33,881**	12,873	10,679	16,738	**40,289**	24,236	11,241	7,760	**19,001**
Mar	15,323	4,248	5,475	3,681	5,674	**34,400**	12,086	10,957	17,049	**40,092**	24,163	11,526	7,435	**18,961**
Apr	15,375	4,224	5,552	3,326	5,701	**34,178**	11,827	10,533	17,010	**39,371**	24,287	11,477	7,651	**19,128**
May	15,353	4,201	5,680	3,432	5,586	**34,252**	11,794	10,348	17,328	**39,470**	24,022	11,471	7,966	**19,437**
Jun	15,273	4,094	5,122	3,357	5,638	**33,483**	12,280	9,826	17,371	**39,478**	24,153	11,354	8,198	**19,553**
Jul	15,443	4,115	4,946	3,406	5,743	**33,653**	12,065	10,062	17,248	**39,374**	24,197	11,083	8,736	**19,819**
Aug	15,260	4,237	4,988	3,042	5,821	**33,348**	12,475	10,099	17,535	**40,109**	24,377	10,991	8,773	**19,764**
Sep	15,343	4,291	5,129	3,163	5,878	**33,804**	12,174	10,771	18,520 (b)	**41,465 (b)**	24,287	10,959	9,548	**20,506**
Oct	15,245	4,294	5,110	3,086	5,752	**33,487**	11,856	10,879	18,489	**41,223**	24,629	11,432	9,630	**21,062**
Nov	15,213	4,419	5,425	3,136	5,639	**33,832**	11,773	11,134	17,920	**40,827**	24,784	11,073	9,340	**20,413**
Dec	14,865	4,240	4,982	2,875	5,593	**32,555**	11,851	11,068	17,957	**40,876**	25,210	11,606	9,081	**20,687**
2018 Jan	14,919	4,110	5,297	2,894	5,671	**32,892**	11,906	11,129	18,160	**41,195**	24,967	11,692	8,902	**20,594**
Feb	15,044	4,121	5,492	3,245	5,722	**33,624**	12,362	11,262	19,037	**42,662**	25,013	11,823	8,602	**20,426**
Mar	15,210	3,982	5,594	2,856	5,686	**33,328**	11,736	11,233	19,701	**42,670**	24,868	11,945	8,685	**20,631**
Apr	15,320	4,017	5,458	2,830	5,694	**33,319**	11,597	11,345	19,383	**42,325**	24,698	12,310	8,551	**20,861**

Source: Bank of England

12.4a Industrial analysis of monetary financial institutions' lending to UK residents

£ millions — Not seasonally adjusted

Amounts outstanding of lending in sterling

	Real estate, professional services and support activities							Recreational, personal and community service activities			Financial intermediation (excluding insurance and pension funds)				
	Buying, selling and renting of real estate	Professional, scientific and technical activities	Administrative and support services	**Total**	Public administration and defence	Education	Human health and social work	Recreational, cultural and sporting activities	Personal and community service activities	**Total**	Financial leasing corporations	Non-bank credit grantors excluding credit unions and SPVs	Credit unions	Factoring corporations	Mortgage and housing credit corporations excluding SPVs
RPM	**TBUY**	**B6PD**	**B6PO**	**TBUX**	**TBVD**	**TBVE**	**TBVF**	**TBVH**	**TBVG**	**B6PT**	**TBVJ**	**TBVK**	**TBVL**	**TBVM**	**TBVN**
2016 Jan	133,281	15,977	20,032	**169,289**	7,946	10,671	20,211	5,034	3,233	**8,267**	23,603	18,341	1	4,559	53,410
Feb	132,844	16,013	20,651	**169,508**	7,973	10,722	20,237	4,982	3,308	**8,290**	23,477	18,678	1	4,534	53,822
Mar	136,349	15,789	21,018	**173,156**	7,769	10,730	20,229	5,126	3,286	**8,412**	23,953	19,066	2	5,288	54,677
Apr	135,509	15,510	21,470	**172,488**	8,073	10,668	19,986	5,002	3,344	**8,345**	24,150	19,628	1	5,378	49,019
May	135,563	15,330	21,407	**172,299**	7,968	10,629	20,179	4,921	3,338	**8,259**	24,068	19,329	1	5,365	48,925
Jun	136,467	15,624	22,214	**174,305**	7,573	10,655	20,316	4,662	3,313	**7,975**	23,888	19,461	1	5,692	49,670
Jul	136,397	15,952	22,686	**175,035**	7,670	10,826	20,389	4,659	3,316	**7,976**	24,005	19,864	-	5,342	49,908
Aug	136,002	16,286	23,154	**175,442**	7,808	10,846	20,185	4,489	3,312	**7,801**	24,014	19,882	-	5,190	49,316
Sep	135,591	16,288	23,241	**175,119**	8,115	10,587	19,961	4,578	3,310	**7,888**	23,964	22,861	-	5,647	49,895
Oct	135,125	16,048	23,926	**175,099**	9,172	10,538	20,147	4,690	3,345	**8,035**	24,236	23,351	-	5,542	50,555
Nov	134,689	15,966	23,992	**174,648**	8,103	10,465	20,109	5,017	3,311	**8,328**	24,963	23,729	-	5,566	48,506
Dec	135,351	15,248	24,185	**174,784**	7,779	10,445	19,631	5,278	3,326	**8,604**	25,327	23,656	-	5,833	48,373
2017 Jan	134,203	16,154	24,081	**174,439**	10,078	10,351	19,976	5,311	3,297	**8,609**	24,880	23,495	1	5,257	48,768
Feb	134,408	16,014	24,270	**174,691**	8,122	10,321	20,005	5,265	3,206	**8,470**	24,752	19,841	1	5,579	43,605
Mar	134,749	15,821	24,320 (e)	**174,890 (e)**	8,988	10,330	20,183	5,517	3,358	**8,874**	24,700	20,329	1	5,825	47,639
Apr	135,473 (c)	15,706	25,383 (f)	**176,562 (c)(f)**	8,284	10,364	19,867	5,617	3,431	**9,049**	24,322	20,090	1	5,879	47,634
May	135,671	15,489	25,460	**176,620**	7,700	10,212	20,002	5,678	3,415	**9,093**	24,927	19,851	1	5,794	46,339
Jun	135,435	15,680	25,723	**176,837**	7,729	10,185	20,081	5,504	3,444	**8,948**	25,749	22,746	1	6,217	46,276
Jul	134,246	15,518	26,218	**175,981**	7,935	10,240	20,034	5,483	3,351	**8,834**	25,927	23,155	1	6,157	46,465
Aug	133,369	15,823	25,738	**174,930**	8,470	10,271	20,292	5,426	3,345	**8,772**	26,331	24,055	2	6,190	46,482
Sep	134,939 (d)	16,515	26,292	**177,746 (d)**	8,274 (h)	10,348	19,800	5,522	3,326	**8,848**	27,367	23,539	2	6,451	46,829
Oct	133,858	15,597	26,888	**176,343**	8,153	10,169	20,061	5,603	3,227	**8,830**	26,587	23,664	2	6,254	44,934
Nov	134,309	15,764	26,587	**176,660**	8,095	10,233	20,230	5,594	3,193	**8,787**	26,827	23,472	2	6,436	45,070
Dec	134,668	15,878	25,329	**175,875**	8,418	10,254	19,707	5,627	3,249	**8,876**	27,157	23,877	2	6,247	44,870
2018 Jan	134,841	15,652	26,085	**176,578**	8,023	10,077	19,870	5,494	3,139	**8,632**	27,547	24,733	2	5,765	45,284
Feb	134,773	15,843	25,869	**176,485**	8,935	9,966	20,095	5,486	3,198	**8,684**	31,081 (i)	24,745	2	9,929 (j)	45,214
Mar	135,319	15,372	25,787	**176,479**	12,216	10,068	19,944	5,244	3,195	**8,438**	31,964	25,144	2	9,837	45,528
Apr	135,555	14,853	25,945	**176,352**	8,361	9,980	20,059	4,964	3,181	**8,145**	32,549	25,638	2	9,565	46,396

Source: Bank of England

12.4a Industrial analysis of monetary financial institutions' lending to UK residents

£ millions | Not seasonally adjusted

Amounts outstanding of lending in sterling

	Financial intermediation (excluding insurance and pension funds)								Insurance companies & pension funds		
	Investment and unit trusts excluding money market mutual funds	Money market mutual funds	Bank holding companies	Securities dealers	SPVs related to securitisation	Other financial intermediaries	of which intragroup activity	**Total**	Insurance companies	Pension funds	**Total**
RPM	**TBVO**	**TBVP**	**TBVQ**	**TBVR**	**B6PY**	**TBVS**	**B3U8**	**TBVI**	**B3V6**	**B3W4**	**TBVT**
2016 Jan	8,510	49	19,531	25,197	19,787	46,637	39,732	**219,627**	6,054	11,108	**17,162**
Feb	8,678	53	20,071	26,491	19,708	47,131	40,218	**222,644**	6,971	13,158	**20,129**
Mar	9,683	97	19,984	27,885	19,702	43,234	36,330	**223,571**	7,553	13,120	**20,673**
Apr	9,802	78	20,192	30,386	16,072	40,662	34,179	**215,369**	6,540	11,323	**17,863**
May	11,152	86	18,954	26,160	15,593	42,487	33,916	**212,119**	7,356	11,572	**18,928**
Jun	11,173	72	11,767	29,303	16,259	41,614	33,164	**208,900**	8,592	14,763	**23,355**
Jul	10,812	77	13,382	29,332	16,036	41,573	32,388	**210,332**	7,980	15,719	**23,699**
Aug	10,364	112	13,241	26,726	13,893	42,696	33,397	**205,436**	9,933	15,947	**25,881**
Sep	10,814	100	13,258	25,592	13,409	41,882	32,424	**207,422**	10,013	16,318	**26,331**
Oct	11,040	158	13,546	23,923	11,340	40,457	31,902	**204,150**	8,632	14,270	**22,902**
Nov	11,563	146	13,543	25,773	10,266	35,981	28,557	**200,037**	8,622	15,906	**24,529**
Dec	10,719	119	16,068	22,659	9,876	37,598	29,906	**200,229**	8,592	18,920	**27,512**
2017 Jan	9,703	119	18,859	21,908	9,771	37,996	29,801	**200,758**	8,460	15,742	**24,202**
Feb	11,085	101	18,296	22,155	9,503	38,103	29,814	**193,022**	8,162	16,744	**24,906**
Mar	9,597 (k)	119	13,376	20,107	9,291	38,267 (n)	31,501	**189,250 (k)(n)**	8,713	25,179 (r)	**33,892 (r)**
Apr	9,735	92	13,509	21,308	10,417	38,386	31,906	**191,372**	9,898	27,311	**37,209**
May	9,440	92	14,502	22,246	9,895	37,688	31,533	**190,774**	9,092	27,494	**36,586**
Jun	10,219	102	14,146	21,681	7,876 (m)	39,251 (o)	33,345 (o)	**194,264 (m)(o)**	8,358	26,652	**35,010**
Jul	10,599	120	14,292	22,749	8,458	39,968	32,812	**197,892**	7,726	24,682	**32,409**
Aug	10,528	149	14,152	22,081	7,663	39,104	31,792	**196,736**	8,844	24,580	**33,424**
Sep	11,513	130	14,371	22,450	7,836	38,912	31,993	**199,400**	7,676	26,118	**33,795**
Oct	11,490	123	11,027	24,525	8,712	37,867	30,940	**195,184**	7,232	24,656	**31,888**
Nov	11,629	111	11,751	24,345	8,705	37,560	30,363	**195,908**	7,674	25,778	**33,452**
Dec	9,470	107	11,122	24,342	8,323	42,059	34,562	**197,575**	7,900	25,286	**33,186**
2018 Jan	9,828	112	11,115	25,588	7,055	43,065	34,389	**200,093**	7,384	24,961	**32,346**
Feb	10,111	109	11,050	23,526	7,012	40,598 (p)	31,845 (p)	**203,377**	7,106	25,507	**32,613**
Mar	10,180	101	11,216	26,414	7,330	45,589	36,619	**213,306**	7,921	25,151	**33,072**
Apr	9,874	126	11,257	24,717	7,101	47,471	38,772	**214,697**	7,991	24,772	**32,763**

Source: Bank of England

12.4a Industrial analysis of monetary financial institutions' lending to UK residents

£ millions | Not seasonally adjusted

Amounts outstanding of lending in sterling

	Activities auxiliary to financial intermediation						Individuals and individual trusts			
	Fund management activities	Other			Total	**Total financial and non-financial businesses**				**Total UK residents**
		Central clearing counterparties	Other auxiliary activities	Total			Lending secured on dwellings inc. bridging finance	Other loans and advances	Total	
RPM	TBVU	B7FX	B8FD	TBVV	B8FJ	Z949	TBVX	TBVY	TBVW	TBUA
2016 Jan	80,338	39,274	2,814	**42,088**	**122,426**	**751,525**	1,108,163	122,216	**1,230,379**	**1,981,904**
Feb	89,728	36,301	2,920	**39,221**	**128,948**	**766,580**	1,109,821	122,735	**1,232,556**	**1,999,136**
Mar	92,832	33,196	2,871	**36,067**	**128,899**	**766,178**	1,116,891	123,746	**1,240,637**	**2,006,815**
Apr	90,058	33,328	3,227	**36,555**	**126,613**	**751,778**	1,123,534	123,792	**1,247,326**	**1,999,104**
May	98,386	40,599	3,305	**43,904**	**142,290**	**766,089**	1,125,346	125,075	**1,250,421**	**2,016,510**
Jun	107,126	44,789	3,511	**48,301**	**155,426**	**780,726**	1,130,284	126,131	**1,256,415**	**2,037,141**
Jul	106,520	41,753	3,693	**45,446**	**151,965**	**782,406**	1,133,579	126,611	**1,260,189**	**2,042,595**
Aug	107,048	46,868	3,098	**49,966**	**157,015**	**785,166**	1,137,641	127,885	**1,265,526**	**2,050,693**
Sep	112,388	44,451	3,074	**47,525**	**159,913**	**788,980**	1,141,851	128,209	**1,270,060**	**2,059,039**
Oct	113,124	50,543	3,115	**53,659**	**166,783**	**791,071**	1,145,235	128,709	**1,273,944**	**2,065,016**
Nov	113,975	57,907	3,144	**61,052**	**175,027**	**794,968**	1,147,616	129,864	**1,277,480**	**2,072,447**
Dec	115,853	51,003	3,384	**54,387**	**170,239**	**790,436**	1,150,155	130,084	**1,280,238**	**2,070,674**
2017 Jan	113,025	63,583	3,017	**66,600**	**179,624**	**801,852**	1,152,375	130,246	**1,282,620**	**2,084,472**
Feb	113,115	65,067 (w)	4,066	**69,133 (w)**	**182,248 (w)**	**797,433 (w)**	1,154,709	130,336	**1,285,045**	**2,082,478 (w)**
Mar	116,626 (s)(t)(u)	70,283	3,434	**73,718**	**190,344 (s)(t)(u)**	**814,189 (e)**	1,159,064	130,926	**1,289,991**	**2,104,180 (e)**
Apr	111,909	73,265	3,301	**76,566**	**188,475**	**818,504 (c)(f)**	1,160,471	131,401	**1,291,872**	**2,110,376 (c)(f)**
May	116,118	71,979	3,038	**75,017**	**191,134**	**820,704**	1,164,418	131,950	**1,296,369**	**2,117,073**
Jun	116,430	73,111	3,054	**76,164**	**192,595**	**823,650 (m)(o)**	1,171,109	132,283	**1,303,392**	**2,127,042 (m)(o)**
Jul	112,026	72,991	2,941	**75,932**	**187,959**	**822,244**	1,174,102	132,783	**1,306,884**	**2,129,129**
Aug	117,100	78,205	3,088	**81,293**	**198,393**	**832,976**	1,179,193	133,166	**1,312,359**	**2,145,334**
Sep	121,009 (v)	85,733 (x)	3,080	**88,813 (x)**	**209,822 (v)(x)**	**853,687 (a)(b)(d)(h)(v)(x)**	1,189,317	133,106	**1,322,423**	**2,176,109 (a)(b)(d)(h)(v)(x)**
Oct	121,206	82,169	2,670	**84,838**	**206,044**	**842,435**	1,192,030	133,281	**1,325,311**	**2,167,746**
Nov	121,210	86,137	3,215	**89,352**	**210,562**	**849,293**	1,196,335	134,181	**1,330,516**	**2,179,809**
Dec	131,312	75,896	3,081	**78,977**	**210,288**	**849,461**	1,199,156	134,123	**1,333,279**	**2,182,739**
2018 Jan	123,534	81,605	2,576	**84,181**	**207,715**	**848,821**	1,200,966	133,319	**1,334,285**	**2,183,105**
Feb	115,693	78,139	2,532	**80,671**	**196,364**	**844,787**	1,201,985	133,985	**1,335,969**	**2,180,757**
Mar	119,057	64,636	2,638	**67,273**	**186,330**	**847,968**	1,206,924	133,294	**1,340,219**	**2,188,187**
Apr	111,475	65,009	2,641	**67,649**	**179,125**	**838,539**	1,208,091	133,938	**1,342,029**	**2,180,567**

Source: Bank of England

12.4a Industrial analysis of monetary financial institutions' lending to UK residents

£ millions Not seasonally adjusted

Notes to table

Movements in amounts outstanding can reflect breaks in data series as well as underlying flows. For changes data, users are recommended to refer directly to the appropriate series or data tables. https://www.bankofengland.co.uk/statistics/details/further-details-about-changes-flows-growth-rates-data.

(a) Due to improvements in reporting by one institution, amounts outstanding increased by £1bn. This amount has been adjusted out of the flows for September 2017.
(b) Due to improvements in reporting by one institution, amounts outstanding increased by £1bn. This amount has been adjusted out of the flows for September 2017.
(c) Due to reporting improvements at one institution, amounts outstanding increased by £1 billion. This has been adjusted out of the flows for April 2017.
(d) Due to a loan transfer by one reporting institution, the amounts outstanding increased by £1 bn. This amount has been adjusted out of the flows for September 2017.
(e) Due to loan transfers by one institution, amounts outstanding decreased by £1 billion. This amount has been adjusted out of the flows for March 2017.
(f) Due to loan transfers by one institution, amounts outstanding increased by £1 billion. This amount has been adjusted out of the flows for April 2017.
(h) Due to improvements in reporting by one institution, amounts outstanding increased by £1bn. This amount has been adjusted out of the flows for September 2017.
(i) Due to improvements in reporting at one institution, the amounts outstanding increased by £3bn. This effect has been adjusted out of the flows for February 2018.
(j) Due to improvements in reporting at one institution, the amounts outstanding increased by £4bn. This effect has been adjusted out of the flows for February 2018.
(k) Due to reporting improvements at one institution, amounts outstanding decreased by £2bn. This has been adjusted out of flows for March 2017.
(l) Previously, this series formed part of other financial intermediaries.
(m) Due to a change in accounting treatment at one reporting institution, the amounts outstanding decreased by £2bn. This effect has been adjusted out of the flows for June 2017.
(n) Due to reporting improvements at one institution, amounts outstanding decreased by £2bn. This has been adjusted out of flows for March 2017.
(o) Due to improvements in reporting at one institution, the amounts outstanding decreased by £2bn. This effect has been adjusted out of the flows for June 2017.
(p) Due to improvements in reporting at one institution, the amounts outstanding decreased by £6bn. This effect has been adjusted out of the flows for February 2018.
(q) From January 2019 onwards, this series no longer includes venture and development capital. As result, this series decreased by £1bn. This effect has been adjusted out the flows for January 2019
(r) Due to reporting improvements at one institution, amounts outstanding increased by £5bn. This has been adjusted out of flows for March 2017.
(s) Due to reporting improvements at one institution, amounts outstanding decreased by £5bn. This has been adjusted out of flows for March 2017.
(t) Due to reporting improvements at one institution, amounts outstanding increased by £2bn. This has been adjusted out of flows for March 2017.
(u) Due to reporting improvements at one institution, amounts outstanding increased by £2bn. This has been adjusted out of flows for March 2017.
(v) Due to improvements in reporting by one institution, amounts outstanding increased by £1bn. This amount has been adjusted out of the flows for September 2017.
(w) Due to improvements in reporting at one institution, the amounts outstanding increased by £2bn. This effect has been adjusted out of the flows for February 2017.
(x) Due to improvements in reporting by one institution, amounts outstanding increased by £4 bn. This amount has been adjusted out of the flows for September 2017.

Explanatory notes can be found here: http://www.bankofengland.co.uk/statistics/Pages/iadb/notesiadb/industrial.aspx

12.4b Industrial analysis of monetary financial institutions' lending to UK residents

£ millions — Not seasonally adjusted

Amounts outstanding of lending in all currencies

	Agriculture, hunting and forestry	Fishing	Mining and quarrying	Manufacturing										Electricity, gas and water supply			
				Food, beverages and tobacco	Textiles, wearing apparel and leather	Pulp, paper, and printing	Chemicals, pharma-ceuticals, rubber and plastics	Non-metallic mineral products and metals	Machinery, equipment and transport equipment	Electrical, medical and optical equipment	Other manu-facturing	**Total**	Electricity, gas steam and air conditioning	Water collection and sewerage	Waste management related services and remediation activities	Total
RPM	**TBSC**	**TBSD**	**TBSE**	**TBSG**	**TBSH**	**TBSI**	**TBSJ**	**TBSK**	**TBSL**	**TBSM**	**TBSN**	**TBSF**	**TBSO**	**TBSP**	**B3FA**	**B3FO**
2016 Jan	17,653	259	6,229	5,941	1,167	2,421	5,874	4,746	8,849	2,881	3,635	**35,513**	9,499	2,969	2,192	**14,660**
Feb	17,558	253	6,512	5,973	1,105	2,421	6,242	4,937	8,778	2,972	3,746	**36,174**	9,922	2,960	2,247	**15,129**
Mar	17,657	254	6,465	5,877	1,152	2,388	6,539	4,878	8,563	2,731	3,966	**36,095**	9,898	3,211	2,326	**15,436**
Apr	17,659	248	6,221	6,494	1,114	2,276	6,600	4,870	7,993	2,898	4,031	**36,277**	9,741	3,361	2,320	**15,422**
May	17,761	248	6,469	7,427	1,109	2,330	7,005	5,148	7,519	3,133	4,005	**37,676**	9,542	3,365	2,225	**15,132**
Jun	17,969	296	7,695	7,239	1,206	2,424	7,088	5,336	7,363	3,043	3,595	**37,294**	9,403	3,458	2,091	**14,952**
Jul	18,130	294	7,098	7,152	1,235	2,310	6,382	4,967	7,294	2,953	3,667	**35,960**	9,559	3,624	2,259	**15,442**
Aug	18,184	293	7,005	6,794	1,221	2,380	6,831	4,717	7,218	3,031	3,401	**35,593**	9,980	3,576	2,308	**15,864**
Sep	18,186	284	8,471	7,375	1,232	2,326	6,719	4,779	7,940	3,177	3,298	**36,847**	10,054	3,482	2,150	**15,687**
Oct	18,209	299	9,417	7,512	1,253	2,245	6,787	4,780	8,189	3,242	3,251	**37,258**	9,764	3,502	2,398	**15,664**
Nov	18,207	301	9,577	7,104	1,235	2,521	6,675	4,591	8,107	3,099	3,267	**36,599**	9,526	3,610	2,311	**15,446**
Dec	17,811	312	9,639	7,914	1,203	2,486	6,871	4,541	8,026	2,975	3,198	**37,214**	9,588	3,438	2,323	**15,349**
2017 Jan	17,924	309	10,251	6,655	1,179	2,463	7,193	4,685	8,018	2,850	3,233	**36,276**	9,580	3,443	2,462	**15,486**
Feb	18,030	309	9,886	6,990	1,114	2,502	6,791	4,730	8,257	2,805	3,256	**36,446**	9,748	3,177	2,365	**15,289**
Mar	18,159	308	9,613	6,448	1,134	2,483	7,198	5,206	8,042	2,868	3,416	**36,796**	11,516	2,973	2,323	**16,813**
Apr	18,295	304	7,212 (an)	6,852	1,130	2,393	7,133	4,787	8,380	2,835	3,382	**36,892**	11,644	2,983	2,349	**16,975**
May	18,472	303	7,184	8,074	1,183	2,577	7,201	4,843	8,099	2,794	3,467	**38,238**	11,480	2,981	2,391	**16,852**
Jun	18,566	297	7,057	7,723	1,261	2,599	11,930	4,834	7,843	2,779	3,486	**42,454**	11,749	3,012	2,373	**17,134**
Jul	18,653	294	6,961	15,443 (ao)	1,206	2,174	11,865	4,705	8,192	2,553	3,576	**49,714 (ao)**	11,997	2,948	2,322	**17,267**
Aug	18,600	298	7,244	11,078 (ap)	1,254	2,290	9,687	4,909	7,600	2,692	3,496	**43,006 (ap)**	12,259	2,907	2,286	**17,452**
Sep	18,628	304	8,021	10,569	1,338	2,318	9,229	4,949	7,967 (aq)	3,036	3,609	**43,015 (aq)**	11,428	3,178	2,323	**16,929**
Oct	18,551	303	8,592	10,389	1,355	2,316	9,174	4,652	8,493	3,342	3,456	**43,178**	11,518	3,205	2,257	**16,981**
Nov	18,655	310	7,882	10,187	1,509	2,165	9,307	4,640	8,749	3,046	3,526	**43,129**	11,631	3,258	2,239	**17,128**
Dec	18,290	314	7,791	10,850	1,277	2,212	9,575	4,739	8,181	2,790	3,419	**43,043**	12,307	3,146	2,273	**17,727**
2018 Jan	18,337	308	7,482	11,310	1,167	2,172	8,967	4,698	8,386	2,914	3,529	**43,143**	12,222	3,347	2,296	**17,864**
Feb	18,381	311	8,133	10,577	1,165	2,133	8,777	4,786	9,137	2,712	3,669	**42,957**	12,418	3,508	2,319	**18,245**
Mar	18,520	309	8,329	10,261	1,255	2,162	8,502	5,160	9,527	2,637	3,426	**42,930**	12,181	3,283	2,374	**17,838**
Apr	18,549	300	8,210	10,329	1,258	2,248	8,152	5,268	9,645	2,773	3,595	**43,268**	12,381	3,343	2,386	**18,110**

Source: Bank of England

12.4b Industrial analysis of monetary financial institutions' lending to UK residents

£ millions

Not seasonally adjusted

Amounts outstanding of lending in all currencies

	Construction						Wholesale and retail trade				Accommodation	Transport, storage and communication		
	Development of buildings	Construction of commercial buildings	Construction of domestic buildings	Civil Engineering	Other construction activities	**Total**	Wholesale and retail trade and repair of motor vehicles and motorcycles	Wholesale trade, excluding motor vehicles and motor cycles	Retail trade excluding motor vehicles and motor cycles	**Total**	and food service activities	Transportation and storage	Information and communication	**Total**
RPM	B7EC	B3I7	B3LY	B4PL	B4PY	TBSQ	TBSS	TBST	TBSU	TBSR	TBSV	B5PL	B5PS	TBSW
2016 Jan	16,164	4,838	4,225	3,230	5,764	**34,222**	12,828	15,019	16,666	**44,513**	22,798	15,412	17,197	**32,610**
Feb	16,909	4,549	4,578	3,627	5,681	**35,344**	13,996	15,146	17,537	**46,679**	22,832	16,400	15,813	**32,213**
Mar	15,097	4,382	4,660	3,537	5,600	**33,276**	13,288	14,741	18,145	**46,173**	22,986	15,414	13,418	**28,832**
Apr	14,995	4,429	4,564	3,570	5,629	**33,188**	12,919	14,634	18,482	**46,035**	23,163	15,470	12,114	**27,584**
May	14,962	4,382	4,953	3,587	5,760	**33,643**	12,495	15,191	18,336	**46,022**	23,509	15,364	12,269	**27,632**
Jun	14,971	4,084	4,818	3,301	5,718	**32,891**	12,947	15,436	18,686	**47,068**	23,451	15,405	12,570	**27,975**
Jul	15,042	4,316	4,782	3,392	5,798	**33,329**	13,174	15,274	18,804	**47,252**	23,511	16,309	12,989	**29,299**
Aug	14,954	4,354	4,904	3,529	5,789	**33,530**	13,255	15,732	18,515	**47,502**	23,561	15,627	12,911	**28,538**
Sep	15,352	4,350	4,833	3,619	5,769	**33,923**	11,970	15,541	18,881	**46,392**	23,765	16,192	12,722	**28,914**
Oct	15,354	4,387	5,016	3,738	5,871	**34,367**	11,816	16,161	19,161	**47,139**	23,832	16,292	13,869	**30,161**
Nov	15,359	4,376	5,193	3,803	5,908	**34,639**	11,771	16,233	18,933	**46,937**	23,817	15,140	14,591	**29,731**
Dec	14,986	4,139	4,657	3,489	5,683	**32,955**	12,058	16,056	18,810	**46,924**	24,138	14,585	14,066	**28,652**
2017 Jan	15,317	4,402	4,974	3,571	5,774	**34,039**	12,385	16,202	19,294	**47,882**	24,346	15,139	13,526	**28,665**
Feb	15,402	4,449	5,286	3,663	5,829	**34,628**	13,600	16,373	19,120	**49,094**	24,912	15,364	13,095	**28,458**
Mar	15,488	4,403	5,475	4,047	5,746	**35,160**	12,842	16,843 (ar)	19,477	**49,162 (ar)**	24,884	15,667	12,552	**28,220**
Apr	15,534	4,368	5,552	3,675	5,785	**34,915**	12,650	17,947 (as)	19,122	**49,720 (as)**	24,968	15,468	12,698	**28,166**
May	15,520	4,342	5,680	3,823	5,675	**35,040**	12,617	19,087	19,437	**51,141**	25,042	15,498	12,930	**28,428**
Jun	15,456	4,248	5,122	3,708	5,717	**34,250**	13,086	18,738	19,641	**51,465**	25,155	14,849	12,984	**27,833**
Jul	15,632	4,254	4,946	3,704	5,833	**34,369**	12,900	19,319	19,646	**51,865**	25,134	14,858	13,620	**28,478**
Aug	15,454	4,375	4,988	3,337	5,905	**34,059**	13,300	19,127	20,305	**52,732**	25,282	14,808	14,107	**28,914**
Sep	15,546	4,413	5,129	3,433	5,937	**34,459**	13,011	18,542	21,145 (at)	**52,698 (at)**	25,183	14,834	14,734	**29,568**
Oct	15,435	4,469	5,111	3,481	5,795	**34,291**	12,653	19,529	21,130	**53,311**	25,527	15,645	14,705	**30,349**
Nov	15,412	4,587	5,434	3,544	5,681	**34,657**	12,517	18,777	20,330	**51,625**	25,679	15,200	13,983	**29,182**
Dec	15,069	4,359	4,991	3,269	5,631	**33,320**	12,623	19,038	20,261	**51,922**	26,356	15,452	13,919	**29,371**
2018 Jan	15,112	4,215	5,306	3,267	5,706	**33,605**	12,699	18,507	19,987	**51,192**	26,294	15,536	13,470	**29,006**
Feb	15,383	4,234	5,501	3,640	5,796	**34,553**	13,142	18,834	21,122	**53,097**	26,661	15,661	13,030	**28,691**
Mar	15,555	4,129	5,602	3,232	5,744	**34,263**	12,499	19,448	21,595	**53,543**	26,316	15,580	12,747	**28,327**
Apr	15,667	4,163	5,467	3,191	5,761	**34,248**	12,565	20,553	21,274	**54,392**	26,299	15,519	12,573	**28,093**

Source: Bank of England

12.4b Industrial analysis of monetary financial institutions' lending to UK residents

£ millions

Not seasonally adjusted

Amounts outstanding of lending in all currencies

	Real estate, professional services and support activities							Recreational, personal and community service activities			Financial intermediation (excluding insurance and pension funds)			
	Buying, selling and renting of real estate	Professional, scientific and technical activities	Administrative and support services	**Total**	Public administration and defence	Education	Human health and social work	Recreational, cultural and sporting activities	Personal and community service activities	**Total**	Financial leasing corporations	Non-bank credit grantors excluding credit unions and SPVs	Credit unions	Factoring corporations
RPM	TBSY	B6PE	B6PP	TBSX	TBTD	TBTE	TBTF	TBTH	TBTG	B6H5	TBTJ	TBTK	TBTL	TBTM
2016 Jan	135,168	19,565	23,494	**178,226**	10,125	10,689	20,330	5,598	3,309	**8,907**	28,376	18,651	1	5,020
Feb	134,300	19,426	24,521	**178,247**	9,781	10,742	20,363	5,577	3,391	**8,969**	28,563	18,999	1	4,956
Mar	137,417	19,353	25,134	**181,905**	8,657	10,754	20,391	5,695	3,382	**9,077**	28,875	19,347	4	5,784
Apr	136,322	19,035	25,714	**181,071**	9,927	10,706	20,140	5,498	3,429	**8,926**	29,003	19,926	1	5,854
May	136,384	19,097	25,380	**180,862**	9,938	10,662	20,314	5,413	3,453	**8,866**	28,807	19,625	1	5,832
Jun	137,193	19,798	26,904	**183,895**	9,131	10,691	20,473	5,205	3,437	**8,642**	29,046	19,759	1	6,662
Jul	137,262	20,157	27,541	**184,961**	9,703	10,864	20,561	5,227	3,438	**8,664**	29,835	20,161	1	6,322
Aug	136,893	20,663	28,157	**185,713**	9,520	10,890	20,355	5,059	3,433	**8,493**	29,614	20,223	1	5,850
Sep	136,346	21,368	28,107	**185,821**	9,757	10,630	20,306	5,351	3,427	**8,778**	29,918	23,183	1	6,240
Oct	135,761	21,146	29,208	**186,115**	9,633	10,563	20,509	5,514	3,473	**8,987**	31,165	23,752	1	6,143
Nov	135,301	20,839	28,800	**184,941**	9,648	10,521	20,405	5,820	3,428	**9,248**	31,211	24,131	1	6,269
Dec	135,990	19,863	30,159	**186,011**	9,605	10,504	19,866	6,065	3,442	**9,506**	31,580	24,071	1	7,164
2017 Jan	134,831	20,771	29,994	**185,596**	12,073	10,403	20,179	6,095	3,411	**9,506**	31,054	23,942	1	6,265
Feb	135,104	20,639	29,909	**185,652**	9,222	10,375	20,209	6,077	3,324	**9,401**	30,586	20,243	1	6,462
Mar	135,514	20,248	29,252 (ax)	**185,015 (ax)**	9,196	10,379	20,405	6,284	3,476	**9,760**	30,473	20,764	1	6,763
Apr	136,035 (av)	20,085	29,712 (ay)(az)	**185,832 (av)(ay)(az)**	11,595	10,410	20,059	6,368	3,600	**9,968**	29,649	20,501	2	6,684
May	136,257	20,002	30,772	**187,031**	10,662	10,238	20,195	6,469	3,589	**10,058**	30,381	20,299	1	6,765
Jun	135,998	20,251	30,365	**186,614**	8,862	10,216	20,297	6,289	3,603	**9,891**	31,198	23,547	2	7,653
Jul	134,881	19,232	30,956	**185,069**	11,246	10,277	20,235	6,342	3,493	**9,835**	31,500	23,957	2	7,248
Aug	133,929	19,372	30,662	**183,962**	10,935	10,332	20,489	6,310	3,470	**9,780**	32,202	24,891	2	7,246
Sep	135,555 (aw)	19,830	31,237	**186,622 (aw)**	11,058 (bc)	10,412	19,940	6,358	3,469	**9,828**	32,971	24,392	2	7,351
Oct	134,417	19,071	31,764	**185,252**	11,100	10,233	20,186	6,478	3,302	**9,781**	32,684	24,485	2	7,259
Nov	134,816	19,533	31,591	**185,940**	10,926	10,298	20,409	6,442	3,266	**9,708**	32,688	24,279	2	7,283
Dec	135,140	19,499	30,078	**184,718**	11,724	10,310	19,902	6,689	3,347	**10,035**	32,699	24,754	2	7,318
2018 Jan	135,284	19,093	30,845	**185,222**	9,940	10,141	20,035	6,428	3,186	**9,614**	32,905	25,538	2	6,644
Feb	135,249	19,153	30,988	**185,389**	10,436	10,028	20,279	6,477	3,229	**9,707**	37,570 (bd)	25,607	3	10,925 (be)
Mar	135,805	19,261	31,175	**186,240**	14,171	10,132	20,238	6,206	3,233	**9,439**	38,293	25,996	3	11,103
Apr	136,105	19,365	31,402	**186,872**	11,705	10,067	20,254	5,946	3,212	**9,159**	38,760	26,491	2	11,209

Source: Bank of England

12.4b Industrial analysis of monetary financial institutions' lending to UK residents

£ millions | Not seasonally adjusted

Amounts outstanding of lending in all currencies

	Financial intermediation (excluding insurance and pension funds) (contd.)									Insurance companies & pension funds			Activities auxiliary to financial intermediation
	Mortgage and housing credit corporations excluding SPVs	Investment and unit trusts excluding money market mutual funds	Money market mutual funds	Bank holding companies	Securities dealers	SPVs related to securitisation	Other financial intermediaries	of which intragroup activity	**Total**	Insurance companies	Pension funds	**Total**	Fund management activities
RPM	TBTN	TBTO	TBTP	TBTQ	TBTR	B6PZ	TBTS	B3U9	TBTI	B3V7	B3W5	TBTT	TBTU
2016 Jan	54,374	13,530	76	30,252	117,325	20,453	83,373	67,685	**371,432**	11,857	12,158	**24,015**	152,697
Feb	54,865	13,320	77	31,706	124,430	20,443	85,484	69,861	**382,845**	14,299	14,388	**28,686**	167,131
Mar	55,731	14,226	163	31,074	117,994	20,470	78,936	63,819	**372,604**	14,930	14,144	**29,074**	167,690
Apr	50,002	14,327	130	30,865	129,828	16,854	82,784	67,798	**379,574**	13,594	12,149	**25,743**	165,282
May	49,790	16,121	155	29,310	121,890	16,168	85,141	68,463	**372,841**	14,850	12,795	**27,645**	174,228
Jun	50,659	16,648	154	20,354	135,599	16,871	88,370	70,305	**384,122**	16,912	16,136	**33,048**	188,209
Jul	50,926	15,957	146	21,858	135,968	16,607	88,034	69,321	**385,816**	16,676	17,192	**33,868**	189,902
Aug	50,343	15,295	208	22,278	128,888	14,472	89,414	71,023	**376,588**	18,767	17,536	**36,303**	193,809
Sep	50,940	15,433	172	21,834	135,687	13,985	88,691	69,363	**386,084**	16,515	17,929	**34,444**	177,567
Oct	51,653	15,858	226	21,789	137,565	12,263	90,258	71,583	**390,673**	14,431	15,590	**30,020**	174,835
Nov	48,991	16,295	203	21,487	147,781	11,002	84,948	67,968	**392,317**	13,912	17,110	**31,022**	172,659
Dec	48,863	15,323	197	23,615	132,197	12,074	82,800	66,739	**377,886**	13,823	20,263	**34,087**	176,823
2017 Jan	49,258	14,204	180	26,225	136,033	12,015	83,163	67,279	**382,340**	13,499	16,980	**30,478**	175,239
Feb	44,089	15,477	162	25,702	136,382	11,669	95,627	72,332	**386,399**	13,394	17,927	**31,321**	183,337
Mar	48,131	13,974 (bf)	191	20,854	137,486	11,425	89,378 (bi)	74,340	**379,440 (bf)(bi)**	13,785	26,393 (bm)	**40,178 (bm)**	187,607 (bn)(bo)(bp)
Apr	48,084	13,651	188	20,756	142,980	12,463	88,948	73,995	**383,906**	15,502	28,661	**44,163**	185,279
May	46,811	13,720	212	21,702	140,372	12,021	88,200	74,659	**380,484**	14,404	28,680	**43,083**	187,104
Jun	46,761	14,658	188	21,310	131,558	10,042 (bh)	86,645 (bj)	73,758 (bj)	**373,560 (bh)(bj)**	13,462	27,507	**40,968**	194,784
Jul	46,956	15,072	224	21,404	128,452	10,645	87,956	73,364	**373,416**	12,686	25,957	**38,642**	186,471
Aug	46,995	14,901	274	21,241	125,492	9,307	88,294	73,245	**370,847**	13,969	26,006	**39,975**	193,671
Sep	47,303	15,785	267	21,054	120,283	9,517	87,209	73,178	**366,135**	13,015	27,490	**40,504**	188,692 (bq)
Oct	45,403	15,715	250	18,104	124,077	9,533	86,576	72,930	**364,087**	12,179	26,099	**38,278**	189,450
Nov	45,547	15,918	254	19,289	130,532	9,537	87,077	73,213	**372,406**	12,850	27,163	**40,013**	191,202
Dec	45,348	13,327	151	17,881	121,278	9,401	90,102	76,781	**362,260**	12,868	26,510	**39,378**	203,306
2018 Jan	45,737	14,643	182	16,190	141,768	7,668	91,256	75,019	**382,533**	12,515	26,323	**38,837**	199,949
Feb	45,752	14,747	189	16,129	134,575	7,739	79,694 (bk)	63,318 (bk)	**372,930**	11,710	27,053	**38,762**	197,567
Mar	45,994	14,441	199	16,322	129,568	8,484	83,026	67,322	**373,427**	12,423	27,268	**39,690**	200,006
Apr	46,786	14,112	220	16,361	133,327	8,341	88,712	73,083	**384,321**	12,024	26,199	**38,223**	187,702

Source: Bank of England

12.4b Industrial analysis of monetary financial institutions' lending to UK residents

£ millions — Not seasonally adjusted

Amounts outstanding of lending in all currencies

	Activities auxiliary to financial intermediation (contd.)				Total financial and non-financial businesses	Individuals and individual trusts			Total UK residents
	Other			Total		Lending secured on dwellings inc. bridging finance	Other loans and advances	Total	
	Central clearing counterparties	Other auxiliary activities	Total						
RPM	B3X2	B8FE	TBTV	B5H8	Z92T	TBTX	TBTY	TBTW	TBSA
2016 Jan	94,171	16,875	**111,046**	**263,743**	**1,095,922**	1,108,314	122,974	**1,231,288**	**2,327,210**
Feb	99,323	17,398	**116,721**	**283,852**	**1,136,178**	1,109,972	123,552	**1,233,524**	**2,369,702**
Mar	90,045	17,072	**107,117**	**274,806**	**1,114,440**	1,117,040	124,621	**1,241,662**	**2,356,102**
Apr	90,802	11,692	**102,494**	**267,776**	**1,109,661**	1,123,678	124,662	**1,248,339**	**2,358,000**
May	96,380	12,154	**108,534**	**282,762**	**1,121,981**	1,125,483	125,922	**1,251,406**	**2,373,387**
Jun	111,499	12,679	**124,177**	**312,386**	**1,171,980**	1,130,427	127,075	**1,257,502**	**2,429,482**
Jul	107,530	12,756	**120,286**	**310,188**	**1,174,942**	1,133,722	127,606	**1,261,328**	**2,436,270**
Aug	114,201	13,004	**127,206**	**321,015**	**1,178,945**	1,137,784	128,900	**1,266,684**	**2,445,629**
Sep	109,304	12,521	**121,825**	**299,392**	**1,167,679**	1,141,990	129,256	**1,271,246**	**2,438,925**
Oct	118,451	11,217	**129,668**	**304,503**	**1,177,350**	1,145,380	129,785	**1,275,166**	**2,452,516**
Nov	129,379	11,071	**140,450**	**313,108**	**1,186,465**	1,147,753	130,943	**1,278,696**	**2,465,162**
Dec	107,185	11,042	**118,227**	**295,050**	**1,155,509**	1,150,306	131,121	**1,281,426**	**2,436,935**
2017 Jan	136,194	11,056	**147,250**	**322,489**	**1,188,241**	1,152,531	131,298	**1,283,829**	**2,472,070**
Feb	146,347 (br)(bs)	11,844	**158,191 (br)(bs)**	**341,529 (br)(bs)**	**1,211,160 (br)(bs)**	1,154,866	131,405	**1,286,271**	**2,497,432 (br)(bs)**
Mar	140,926	11,702	**152,628**	**340,235 (bn)(bo)(bp)**	**1,213,720 (ar)(ax)**	1,159,213	132,150	**1,291,363**	**2,505,083 (ar)(ax)**
Apr	146,561	11,642	**158,203**	**343,482**	**1,226,862 (av)(ay)(az)**	1,160,600	132,578	**1,293,177**	**2,520,040 (av)(ay)(az)**
May	150,395	10,612	**161,007**	**348,110**	**1,230,560**	1,164,549	133,143	**1,297,693**	**2,528,253**
Jun	145,802	10,696	**156,498**	**351,282**	**1,225,902 (bh)(bj)**	1,171,238	133,539	**1,304,777**	**2,530,679 (bh)(bj)**
Jul	149,796 (bt)	10,399	**160,194 (bt)**	**346,666 (bt)**	**1,228,124 (ao)(bt)**	1,174,234	134,012	**1,308,246**	**2,536,370 (ao)(bt)**
Aug	165,966	11,896	**177,862**	**371,532**	**1,245,440 (ap)**	1,179,327	134,408	**1,313,735**	**2,559,175 (ap)**
Sep	167,021 (bu)	11,869	**178,890 (bu)**	**367,582 (bq)(bu)**	**1,240,888 (aq)(at)(aw)(bc)(bq)(bu)**	1,189,444	134,313	**1,323,757**	**2,564,644 (aq)(at)(aw)(bc)(bq)(bu)**
Oct	170,984	10,672	**181,656**	**371,106**	**1,241,107**	1,192,167	134,410	**1,326,577**	**2,567,684**
Nov	176,157	7,149	**183,306**	**374,507**	**1,252,455**	1,196,473	135,321	**1,331,794**	**2,584,249**
Dec	152,769	6,799	**159,568**	**362,874**	**1,229,335**	1,199,296	135,306	**1,334,602**	**2,563,937**
2018 Jan	170,592	6,267	**176,859**	**376,808**	**1,260,362**	1,201,102	134,417	**1,335,519**	**2,595,881**
Feb	174,868	6,018	**180,886**	**378,453**	**1,257,014**	1,202,121	135,062	**1,337,183**	**2,594,197**
Mar	150,085	6,425	**156,510**	**356,517**	**1,240,229**	1,207,059	134,385	**1,341,443**	**2,581,672**
Apr	151,875 (bv)	5,936	**157,811 (bv)**	**345,513 (bv)**	**1,237,583 (bv)**	1,208,218	134,914	**1,343,132**	**2,580,715 (bv)**

Source: Bank of England

12.4b Industrial analysis of monetary financial institutions' lending to UK residents

£ millions Not seasonally adjusted

Notes to table

Movements in amounts outstanding can reflect breaks in data series as well as underlying flows. For changes data, users are recommended to refer directly to the appropriate series or data tables.
Further explanation can be found at: www.bankofengland.co.uk/statistics/Pages/iadb/notesiadb/Changes_flows_growth_rates.aspx.

(an) Due to reporting improvements at one institution, amounts outstanding decreased by £2 billion. This has been adjusted out of the flows for April 2017.
(ao) Due to loan transfers by one institution, amounts outstanding increased by £1 billion. This amount has been adjusted out of the flows for July 2017.
(ap) Due to loan transfers by one institution, amounts outstanding decreased by £1 billion. This amount has been adjusted out of the flows for August 2017.
(aq) Due to improvements in reporting by one institution, amounts outstanding increased by £1bn. This amount has been adjusted out of the flows for September 2017.
(ar) Due to changes in the reporting population, amounts outstanding increased by £1bn. This has been adjusted out of flows for March 2017.
(as) Due to reporting improvements at one institution, amounts outstanding increased by £2 billion. This has been adjusted out of the flows for April 2017.
(at) Due to improvements in reporting by one institution, amounts outstanding increased by £1bn. This amount has been adjusted out of the flows for September 2017.
(av) Due to reporting improvements at one institution, amounts outstanding increased by £1 billion. This has been adjusted out of the flows for April 2017.
(aw) Due to a loan transfer by one reporting institution, the amounts outstanding increased by £1 bn. This amount has been adjusted out of the flows for September 2017.
(ax) Due to loan transfers by one institution, amounts outstanding decreased by £1 billion. This amount has been adjusted out of the flows for March 2017.
(ay) Due to reporting improvements at one institution, amounts outstanding decreased by £1 billion. This has been adjusted out of the flows for April 2017.
(az) Due to loan transfers by one institution, amounts outstanding increased by £1 billion. This amount has been adjusted out of the flows for April 2017.
(bc) Due to improvements in reporting by one institution, amounts outstanding increased by £1bn. This amount has been adjusted out of the flows for September 2017.
(bd) Due to improvements in reporting at one institution, the amounts outstanding increased by £3bn. This effect has been adjusted out of the flows for February 2018
(be) Due to improvements in reporting at one institution, the amounts outstanding increased by £4bn. This effect has been adjusted out of the flows for February 2018.
(bf) Due to reporting improvements at one institution, amounts outstanding decreased by £2bn. This has been adjusted out of flows for March 2017.
(bg) Previously, this series formed part of other financial intermediaries.
(bh) Due to a change in accounting treatment at one reporting institution, the amounts outstanding decreased by £2bn. This effect has been adjusted out of the flows for June 2017.
(bi) Due to reporting improvements at one institution, amounts outstanding decreased by £2bn. This has been adjusted out of flows for March 2017.
(bj) Due to improvements in reporting at one institution, the amounts outstanding decreased by £2bn. This effect has been adjusted out of the flows for June 2017.
(bk) Due to improvements in reporting at one institution, the amounts outstanding decreased by £6bn. This effect has been adjusted out of the flows for February 2018.
(bm) Due to reporting improvements at one institution, amounts outstanding increased by £5bn. This has been adjusted out of flows for March 2017.
(bn) Due to reporting improvements at one institution, amounts outstanding decreased by £5bn. This has been adjusted out of flows for March 2017.
(bo) Due to reporting improvements at one institution, amounts outstanding increased by £2bn. This has been adjusted out of flows for March 2017.
(bp) Due to reporting improvements at one institution, amounts outstanding increased by £2bn. This has been adjusted out of flows for March 2017.
(bq) Due to improvements in reporting by one institution, amounts outstanding increased by £1bn. This amount has been adjusted out of the flows for September 2017.
(br) Due to improvements in reporting at one institution, the amounts outstanding increased by £2bn. This effect has been adjusted out of the flows for February 2017.
(bs) Due to improvements in reporting at one institution, the amounts outstanding increased by £4bn. This effect has been adjusted out of the flows for February 2017.
(bt) Due to a transfer of business by one reporting institution, the amounts outstanding increased by £2bn. This effect has been adjusted out of the flows for July 2017.
(bu) Due to improvements in reporting by one institution, amounts outstanding increased by £4 bn. This amount has been adjusted out of the flows for September 2017.
(bv) Due to improvements in reporting at one institution, the amounts outstanding increased by £1bn. This effect has been adjusted out of the flows for April 2018

Explanatory notes can be found here: http://www.bankofengland.co.uk/statistics/Pages/iadb/notesiadb/industrial.asp

12.4c Industrial analysis of monetary financial institutions' lending to UK residents

£ millions Not seasonally adjusted

Amounts outstanding of facilities granted in sterling

	Agriculture, hunting and forestry	Fishing	Mining and quarrying	Manufacturing									Electricity, gas and water supply			
				Food, beverages and tobacco	Textiles, wearing apparel and leather	Pulp, paper, and printing	Chemicals, pharma-ceuticals, rubber and plastics	Non-metallic mineral products and metals	Machinery, equipment and transport equipment	Electrical, medical and optical equipment	Other manu-facturing	**Total**	Electricity, gas steam and air conditioning	Water collection and sewerage	Waste management related services and remediation activities	**Total**
RPM	**TCCC**	**TCCD**	**TCCE**	**TCCG**	**TCCH**	**TCCI**	**TCCJ**	**TCCK**	**TCCL**	**TCCM**	**TCCN**	**TCCF**	**TCCO**	**TCCP**	**B3FE**	**B3FS**
2016 Jan	24,105	282	7,454	8,717	1,130	2,612	7,428	5,191	11,193	3,040	4,168	**43,477**	15,563	7,212	2,893	**25,669**
Feb	24,070	281	2,939	8,573	1,101	2,612	7,554	5,187	11,398	3,058	4,147	**43,629**	16,184	7,208	2,956	**26,347**
Mar	24,202	282	2,856	8,790	1,100	2,613	7,471	5,149	11,306	3,048	4,111	**43,589**	15,978	7,313	2,889	**26,180**
Apr	24,171	276	2,869	9,242	1,090	2,725	7,599	5,185	11,032	3,054	4,076	**44,003**	16,445	7,341	2,891	**26,677**
May	24,234	277	2,899	9,319	1,108	2,671	7,696	5,294	11,128	3,394	4,132	**44,742**	17,636	7,602	2,869	**28,107**
Jun	24,389	320	3,019	9,325	1,173	2,626	7,480	5,293	11,138	2,994	4,093	**44,122**	18,321	7,712	2,647	**28,680**
Jul	24,487	331	3,022	9,351	1,151	2,587	7,710	5,371	10,846	2,965	4,001	**43,981**	17,984	7,872	2,734	**28,590**
Aug	24,584	328	3,442	9,297	1,153	2,569	7,743	5,263	10,887	3,295	3,914	**44,121**	18,056	8,110	2,834	**29,001**
Sep	24,675	326	3,376	8,979	1,164	2,636	7,982	5,257	11,252	3,312	3,782	**44,364**	17,416	8,080	2,863	**28,359**
Oct	24,700	330	3,400	9,119	1,146	2,687	8,093	5,264	10,973	3,102	3,705	**44,089**	17,428	7,959	2,969	**28,355**
Nov	24,687	330	3,388	9,140	1,160	2,582	8,049	5,214	11,151	3,159	3,759	**44,216**	17,544	7,912	2,907	**28,362**
Dec	24,684	342	3,356	9,253	1,177	2,672	7,970	5,186	11,112	3,215	3,752	**44,336**	17,853	7,773	3,033	**28,659**
2017 Jan	24,722	339	3,197	9,640	1,151	2,666	7,999	5,458	11,195	3,139	3,729	**44,978**	18,468	7,766	2,998	**29,233**
Feb	24,772	339	3,240	9,623	1,135	2,687	7,972	5,426	11,399	3,156	3,740	**45,137**	18,334	7,428	3,054	**28,816**
Mar	24,883	343	3,192	9,512	1,186	2,747	8,032	5,497	11,518	3,467	3,836	**45,795**	20,307	7,320	2,945	**30,572**
Apr	24,917	333	3,120	10,434	1,180	2,731	7,971	5,471	11,705	3,164	3,843	**46,498**	20,273	7,320	2,885	**30,478**
May	25,089	332	3,128	10,744	1,198	2,856	8,131	5,379	11,215	3,093	3,906	**46,521**	19,853	7,282	2,921	**30,057**
Jun	25,238	339	3,196	10,653	1,201	3,003	7,938	5,375	10,829	3,162	3,985	**46,147**	20,297	7,452	2,932	**30,681**
Jul	25,349	341	3,359	13,910	1,182	2,661	8,008	5,260	10,607	3,149	3,977	**48,755**	20,370	6,999	2,857	**30,226**
Aug	25,378	337	3,285	13,863	1,204	2,696	8,170	5,277	10,787	3,127	3,878	**49,003**	20,456	7,347	2,798	**30,601**
Sep	25,491	329	3,480	13,750	1,231	2,844	8,263	5,789	11,385 (by)	3,627	4,080	**50,968 (by)**	19,728	7,455	2,848	**30,031**
Oct	25,515	364	3,228	13,877	1,233	2,927	7,940	5,613	11,258	3,871	3,999	**50,719**	19,615	7,562	2,822	**29,999**
Nov	25,504	385	3,217	14,092	1,215	2,863	7,490	5,640	11,418	3,793	4,070	**50,582**	19,494	7,696	2,863	**30,052**
Dec	25,413	391	3,183	13,983	1,103	2,837	7,692	5,737	11,659	3,535	3,993	**50,539**	20,028	7,620	2,896	**30,544**
2018 Jan	25,294	339	2,369	13,781	1,082	2,776	7,508	5,695	11,551	3,624	4,092	**50,108**	19,802	7,708	2,838	**30,348**
Feb	25,181	335	2,377	13,772	1,118	2,797	7,521	5,744	11,820	3,231	4,248	**50,249**	19,940	7,660	2,868	**30,468**
Mar	25,269	336	2,319	14,127	1,098	2,655	8,822	6,002	12,551	3,199	3,998	**52,452**	20,051	7,693	2,924	**30,668**
Apr	25,301	339	2,637	14,200	1,129	2,886	8,583	6,290	13,241	3,091	4,056	**53,476**	20,306	7,715	2,878	**30,899**

Source: Bank of England

12.4c Industrial analysis of monetary financial institutions' lending to UK residents

£ millions

Not seasonally adjusted

Amounts outstanding of facilities granted in sterling

	Construction						Wholesale and retail trade				Accom-	Transport, storage and communication		
	Development of buildings	Construction of commercial buildings	Construction of domestic buildings	Civil Engineering	Other construction activities	**Total**	Wholesale and retail trade and repair of motor vehicles and motorcycles	Wholesale trade, excluding motor vehicles and motor cycles	Retail trade excluding motor vehicles and motor cycles	**Total**	modation and food service activities	Transportation and storage	Information and communication	Total
RPM	**B7EG**	**B3ID**	**B4PC**	**B4PP**	**B5QH**	**TCCQ**	**TCCS**	**TCCT**	**TCCU**	**TCCR**	**TCCV**	**B5PP**	**B5PW**	**TCCW**
2016 Jan	19,971	6,347	8,066	5,032	7,836	**47,252**	14,888	19,597	27,007	**61,493**	27,305	20,760	20,405	**41,164**
Feb	21,587	5,405	9,065	5,316	7,694	**49,067**	16,285	20,068	27,332	**63,685**	27,204	20,835	19,216	**40,051**
Mar	19,015	5,188	9,252	5,175	7,625	**46,255**	15,719	19,948	27,445	**63,112**	27,478	20,218	17,654	**37,871**
Apr	19,165	5,287	9,224	5,179	7,718	**46,572**	16,473	19,414	27,705	**63,592**	27,636	20,377	16,301	**36,678**
May	19,092	5,191	9,508	5,212	7,870	**46,874**	16,227	19,619	27,460	**63,307**	27,756	20,332	14,329	**34,661**
Jun	19,298	4,908	9,683	5,152	7,872	**46,913**	16,702	19,243	27,525	**63,471**	27,766	20,519	14,396	**34,915**
Jul	19,568	5,166	9,625	5,056	7,888	**47,303**	16,725	18,937	27,706	**63,368**	27,852	20,757	14,453	**35,209**
Aug	19,508	5,234	9,774	5,104	7,897	**47,518**	16,489	19,334	27,133	**62,955**	28,314	20,560	14,644	**35,205**
Sep	20,305	5,165	9,851	5,123	8,028	**48,472**	15,697	18,987	27,216	**61,901**	28,419	20,630	13,981	**34,611**
Oct	20,290	5,190	10,047	5,353	8,064	**48,944**	15,268	19,419	27,555	**62,242**	28,476	20,534	14,677	**35,211**
Nov	20,143	5,230	10,028	5,388	8,166	**48,955**	15,593	19,348	27,930	**62,871**	28,303	19,754	14,595	**34,349**
Dec	19,801	4,952	9,990	5,232	8,053	**48,028**	15,642	19,194	28,081	**62,917**	28,631	19,198	14,241	**33,440**
2017 Jan	20,060	5,194	10,237	5,235	8,113	**48,840**	16,217	19,606	28,130	**63,953**	29,128	18,967	14,156	**33,123**
Feb	20,344	5,211	10,330	5,339	8,111	**49,335**	17,079	19,993	28,053	**65,124**	29,522	19,722	14,007	**33,729**
Mar	20,299	5,148	10,461	5,897	8,042	**49,847**	17,007	19,697	27,994	**64,698**	29,632	19,739	14,415	**34,153**
Apr	20,396	5,095	10,498	5,497	8,058	**49,544**	16,644	18,809	28,443	**63,896**	30,192	19,676	14,400	**34,076**
May	20,208	5,086	10,576	5,476	7,909	**49,255**	16,506	18,619	28,736	**63,860**	29,884	19,452	14,907	**34,359**
Jun	20,332	4,944	10,454	5,437	7,965	**49,132**	17,127	18,161	28,460	**63,748**	29,740	19,675	15,207	**34,882**
Jul	20,568	5,022	10,342	5,548	8,066	**49,546**	16,694	18,246	28,376	**63,315**	29,664	19,290	15,782	**35,072**
Aug	20,431	5,089	10,293	5,090	8,205	**49,108**	16,782	18,265	28,632	**63,679**	29,865	19,287	15,048	**34,335**
Sep	20,470	5,122	10,271	5,071	8,249	**49,183**	16,895	18,909	29,555 (bz)	**65,359 (bz)**	30,001	19,368	15,927	**35,295**
Oct	20,323	5,250	10,331	4,896	8,002	**48,801**	16,524	18,650	30,090	**65,264**	30,248	19,442	15,878	**35,320**
Nov	20,233	5,187	10,672	5,065	7,872	**49,031**	16,236	18,643	29,924	**64,803**	30,412	19,082	15,811	**34,894**
Dec	20,121	5,220	10,368	4,940	7,859	**48,508**	16,351	18,698	29,956	**65,005**	30,636	19,384	15,665	**35,049**
2018 Jan	19,973	4,999	10,379	4,698	7,749	**47,799**	16,463	18,447	30,007	**64,917**	30,289	19,337	15,482	**34,818**
Feb	20,075	4,987	10,627	5,151	7,827	**48,666**	16,370	18,373	30,625	**65,368**	30,291	19,928	15,573	**35,501**
Mar	20,516	4,869	10,775	4,737	7,797	**48,694**	16,376	18,248	31,385	**66,008**	30,526	20,164	15,781	**35,945**
Apr	20,616	4,951	10,574	4,497	7,744	**48,383**	16,300	18,360	31,097	**65,757**	30,377	20,322	15,767	**36,089**

Source: Bank of England

12.4c Industrial analysis of monetary financial institutions' lending to UK residents

£ millions — Not seasonally adjusted

Amounts outstanding of facilities granted in sterling

	Real estate, professional services and support activities							Recreational, personal and community service activities			Financial intermediation (excluding insurance and pension funds)			
	Buying, selling and renting of real estate	Professional, scientific and technical activities	Administrative and support services	**Total**	Public administration and defence	Education	Human health and social work	Recreational, cultural and sporting activities	Personal and community service activities	**Total**	Financial leasing corporations	Non-bank credit grantors excluding credit unions and SPVs	Credit unions	Factoring corporations
RPM	**TCCY**	**B6PH**	**B3S2**	**TCCX**	**TCDD**	**TCDE**	**TCDF**	**TCDH**	**TCDG**	**B3SR**	**TCDJ**	**TCDK**	**TCDL**	**TCDM**
2016 Jan	161,868	23,371	28,560	**213,799**	9,956	13,224	23,447	7,083	4,161	**11,244**	27,974	23,879	2	4,812
Feb	161,364	23,014	28,891	**213,269**	10,157	13,328	23,470	7,249	4,248	**11,497**	27,853	24,117	2	4,725
Mar	165,885	23,190	29,167	**218,242**	10,043	13,294	23,389	7,378	4,230	**11,608**	28,282	20,249	3	5,404
Apr	165,937	23,020	29,664	**218,621**	10,247	13,213	23,295	7,356	4,302	**11,659**	28,215	20,874	1	5,580
May	166,400	23,185	29,731	**219,316**	10,235	13,268	23,357	7,318	4,279	**11,596**	28,135	20,770	1	5,569
Jun	167,282	23,365	30,470	**221,118**	9,975	13,220	23,408	7,040	4,302	**11,343**	27,893	20,581	1	5,808
Jul	167,276	23,483	31,010	**221,769**	9,895	13,268	23,401	7,065	4,328	**11,393**	28,035	20,923	1	5,469
Aug	167,629	23,393	31,280	**222,301**	10,406	13,229	23,206	6,994	4,348	**11,342**	28,034	21,001	1	5,283
Sep	166,956	23,516	31,405	**221,876**	10,682	13,042	22,980	7,124	4,358	**11,482**	28,011	23,878	1	5,706
Oct	166,666	23,276	32,555	**222,497**	11,517	13,013	23,097	7,411	4,368	**11,779**	28,012	24,502	1	5,657
Nov	167,329	23,237	32,743	**223,309**	10,398	12,906	23,197	7,265	4,328	**11,593**	28,791	24,906	1	5,679
Dec	168,592	22,806	33,283	**224,681**	10,025	12,913	22,713	7,609	4,344	**11,953**	27,807	24,816	1	5,985
2017 Jan	167,262	23,591	33,285	**224,138**	12,404	12,865	23,336	7,678	4,295	**11,973**	27,443	25,028	3	5,369
Feb	166,919	23,180	32,756	**222,855**	10,639	12,866	23,021	7,709	4,129	**11,838**	27,290	21,293	3	5,730
Mar	166,799	23,360	33,133 (cd)	**223,292 (cd)**	11,918	12,904	23,237	7,714	4,328	**12,042**	26,406	21,844	3	5,949
Apr	167,428 (ca)	23,537	33,921 (ce)	**224,885 (ca)(ce)**	11,208	12,926	23,048	7,847	4,425	**12,272**	25,879	21,519	3	5,984
May	168,147	23,413	34,235	**225,795**	10,476	12,968	23,278	7,894	4,388	**12,283**	26,518	20,978	2	5,903
Jun	167,956	23,546	34,910	**226,411**	11,361	12,839	23,349	7,709	4,433	**12,142**	27,360	23,959	2	6,338
Jul	166,265	23,304	35,387	**224,957**	11,237	12,891	23,439	7,541	4,338	**11,879**	27,615	24,146	2	6,299
Aug	166,542	23,379	34,882	**224,803**	12,151	12,938	23,502	7,444	4,333	**11,776**	27,958	25,210	3	6,344
Sep	168,253 (cb)	24,314	35,748	**228,315 (cb)**	11,227 (cg)	13,093	23,244	7,519	4,299	**11,818**	29,896	24,600	3	6,531
Oct	166,761	23,834	36,105	**226,700**	10,892	13,107	23,385	7,584	4,213	**11,797**	29,075	24,748	3	6,346
Nov	166,410	23,916	35,805	**226,132**	10,870	13,061	23,588	7,564	4,139	**11,703**	30,075	24,510	3	6,595
Dec	166,840	24,226	34,924	**225,990**	11,069	13,105	22,914	7,760	4,222	**11,982**	30,290	24,947	3	6,406
2018 Jan	167,685	24,374	35,555	**227,614**	10,752	12,821	23,202	7,621	4,099	**11,720**	30,685	26,085	3	5,829
Feb	167,893	24,503	35,240	**227,635**	14,154	12,666	23,361	7,654	4,158	**11,812**	34,275 (ci)	26,224	4	9,962 (cj)
Mar	169,510	23,894	35,402	**228,806**	15,066	12,818	23,149	7,556	4,166	**11,722**	35,184	26,599	4	9,880
Apr	170,664	23,923	35,706	**230,293**	10,977	12,756	23,180	7,258	4,129	**11,386**	35,665	27,163	3	9,613

Source: Bank of England

12.4c Industrial analysis of monetary financial institutions' lending to UK residents

£ millions

Not seasonally adjusted

Amounts outstanding of facilities granted in sterling

	Financial intermediation (excluding insurance and pension funds) (contd.)									Insurance companies & pension funds		
	Mortgage and housing credit corporations excluding SPVs	Investment and unit trusts excluding money market mutual funds	Money market mutual funds	Bank holding companies	Securities dealers	SPVs related to securitisation	Other financial intermediaries	of which intragroup activity	**Total**	Insurance companies	Pension funds	Total
RPM	TCDN	TCDO	TCDP	TCDQ	TCDR	B8EX	TCDS	B7FF	TCDI	B7FK	B3W9	TCDT
2016 Jan	54,251	10,438	54	19,862	26,007	23,708 (di)	50,008	39,746	**240,997**	11,263	11,721	**22,984**
Feb	54,663	10,626	58	20,396	27,313	23,237	50,378	40,882	**243,368**	11,920	13,836	**25,756**
Mar	54,975	11,458	104	20,308	28,872	23,485	46,862	36,995	**240,001**	12,486	13,783	**26,269**
Apr	49,310	11,982	87	20,600	31,229	19,981	44,615	34,844	**232,474**	11,382	11,988	**23,370**
May	49,215	13,376	93	19,322	26,903	19,425	46,324	34,580	**229,133**	12,152	12,276	**24,428**
Jun	49,949	13,417	118	12,150	31,030	20,844	45,764	33,789	**227,556**	13,342	15,464	**28,805**
Jul	50,163	13,397	123	13,535	30,015	20,554	45,496	33,023	**227,711**	12,986	16,425	**29,411**
Aug	49,597	12,983	154	13,395	27,389	18,970	46,474	34,188	**223,282**	14,573	16,654	**31,227**
Sep	50,171	13,404	159	13,547	26,299	18,637	45,743	33,213	**225,556**	14,668	17,018	**31,686**
Oct	51,061	14,409	214	13,919	24,535	16,251	44,507	32,679	**223,071**	13,371	14,970	**28,342**
Nov	48,970	14,277	206	13,748	26,587	15,222	39,898	29,091	**218,285**	12,915	16,648	**29,563**
Dec	48,760	13,653	160	16,327	23,355	14,764	41,351	30,379	**216,977**	13,373	19,678	**33,051**
2017 Jan	49,147	12,830	164	19,114	22,851	14,397	41,794	30,276	**218,141**	13,440	16,552	**29,992**
Feb	44,004	13,854	169	18,536	23,022	14,108	41,731	30,311	**209,740**	12,949	17,505	**30,454**
Mar	47,998	12,177 (ck)	168	13,632	21,018	14,052	41,590 (cn)	31,987	**204,836 (ck)(cn)**	13,861	25,911 (cr)	**39,772 (cr)**
Apr	47,980	12,394	120	13,774	22,208	15,107	41,813	32,394	**206,781**	15,067	28,080	**43,147**
May	46,680	12,342	111	14,755	23,052	13,980	41,176	32,013	**205,497**	14,401	28,253	**42,654**
Jun	46,620	13,273	118	14,469	22,690	12,194 (cm)	42,699 (co)	33,869 (co)	**209,723 (cm)(co)**	13,134	27,411	**40,546**
Jul	46,794	13,878	140	14,587	23,645	12,827	43,217	33,416	**213,149**	12,357	25,431	**37,788**
Aug	46,831	13,695	164	14,474	22,875	12,122	42,578	32,356	**212,253**	13,151	25,331	**38,482**
Sep	47,183	15,263	143	14,670	23,263	12,457	42,134	32,557	**216,141**	14,512	26,869	**41,380**
Oct	45,275	15,063	142	11,318	25,273	13,564	41,551	31,505	**212,357**	12,046	25,404	**37,450**
Nov	45,534	15,067	131	12,041	25,119	11,284	40,956	30,874	**211,315**	12,470	26,417	**38,888**
Dec	45,335	12,855	124	11,385	25,199	11,277	45,209	35,069	**213,031**	14,757	25,979	**40,736**
2018 Jan	45,755	13,656	131	11,380	26,481	9,122	47,722	34,811	**216,850**	11,759	25,646	**37,405**
Feb	45,679	13,726	127	11,321	24,637	9,003	45,211 (cp)	32,346 (cp)	**220,169**	11,725	26,206	**37,931**
Mar	45,969	13,673	117	11,477	27,337	9,578	50,232	37,065	**230,050**	12,771	25,852	**38,623**
Apr	46,878	13,680	144	11,516	25,575	9,087	50,736	39,188	**230,061**	13,124	25,474	**38,598**

Source: Bank of England

12.4c Industrial analysis of monetary financial institutions' lending to UK residents

£ millions — Not seasonally adjusted

Amounts outstanding of facilities granted in sterling

	Fund management activities	Activities auxiliary to financial intermediation: Other: Central clearing counterparties	Other auxiliary activities	Total	Total	Total financial and non-financial businesses	Individuals and individual trusts: Lending secured on dwellings inc. bridging finance	Other loans and advances	Total	Total UK residents
RPM	TCDU	B3X6	B3Y4	TCDV	B8FO	Z94D	TCDX	TCDY	TCDW	TCCA
2016 Jan	81,983	39,532	4,078	**43,611**	**125,594**	**939,446**	1,160,485	199,024	**1,359,508**	**2,298,954**
Feb	91,390	36,539	3,930	**40,468**	**131,859**	**949,978**	1,163,166	200,123	**1,363,289**	**2,313,266**
Mar	94,585	33,517	3,890	**37,407**	**131,992**	**946,665**	1,169,891	201,195	**1,371,086**	**2,317,751**
Apr	91,875	33,503	4,234	**37,737**	**129,612**	**934,967**	1,178,808	201,962	**1,380,771**	**2,315,738**
May	99,856	40,764	4,352	**45,117**	**144,972**	**949,162**	1,182,762	202,771	**1,385,533**	**2,334,695**
Jun	108,813	45,084	5,084	**50,169**	**158,982**	**968,002**	1,189,355	203,780	**1,393,134**	**2,361,136**
Jul	107,998	42,082	5,117	**47,199**	**155,197**	**966,187**	1,192,336	204,633	**1,396,969**	**2,363,156**
Aug	108,377	47,141	4,482	**51,623**	**160,000**	**970,460**	1,194,588	205,871	**1,400,459**	**2,370,919**
Sep	113,893	44,664	4,530	**49,194**	**163,087**	**974,892**	1,198,478	204,981	**1,403,458**	**2,378,350**
Oct	114,693	50,751	4,591	**55,341**	**170,034**	**979,096**	1,201,672	205,496	**1,407,168**	**2,386,264**
Nov	115,626	58,167	4,575	**62,743**	**178,369**	**983,082**	1,206,523	206,461	**1,412,984**	**2,396,066**
Dec	117,544	51,256	4,888	**56,144**	**173,689**	**980,396**	1,207,758	206,822	**1,414,580**	**2,394,976**
2017 Jan	114,829	63,796	4,377	**68,174**	**183,003**	**993,365**	1,209,427	207,224	**1,416,650**	**2,410,015**
Feb	115,191	65,273 (cw)	5,688	**70,961 (cw)**	**186,152 (cw)**	**987,578 (cw)**	1,212,619	207,735	**1,420,354**	**2,407,932 (cw)**
Mar	118,714 (cs)(ct)(cu)	70,475	5,108	**75,583**	**194,297 (cs)(ct)(cu)**	**1,005,414 (cd)**	1,219,164	208,675	**1,427,839**	**2,433,253 (cd)**
Apr	114,149	73,433	4,880	**78,314**	**192,463**	**1,009,783 (ca)(ce)**	1,220,500	209,396	**1,429,896**	**2,439,679 (ca)(ce)**
May	118,016	72,151	4,637	**76,787**	**194,803**	**1,010,238**	1,226,046	209,351	**1,435,397**	**2,445,635**
Jun	118,308	73,332	4,695	**78,027**	**196,334**	**1,015,810 (cm)(co)**	1,234,203	209,866	**1,444,069**	**2,459,878 (cm)(co)**
Jul	113,652	73,220	4,650	**77,870**	**191,522**	**1,012,489**	1,232,797 (cz)	203,399 (db)	**1,436,196 (cz)(db)**	**2,448,685 (cz)(db)**
Aug	118,904	78,760	4,795	**83,555**	**202,459**	**1,023,954**	1,236,277	203,837	**1,440,114**	**2,464,069**
Sep	122,898 (cv)	86,405 (cx)	4,910	**91,315 (cx)**	**214,213 (cv)(cx)**	**1,049,567 (by)(bz)(cb)(cg)(cv)(cx)**	1,245,840	204,570	**1,450,410**	**2,499,977 (by)(bz)(cb)(cg)(cv)(cx)**
Oct	123,267	83,178	4,458	**87,635**	**210,903**	**1,036,050**	1,248,590	203,826	**1,452,417**	**2,488,467**
Nov	123,124	86,401	4,972	**91,374**	**214,498**	**1,038,933**	1,253,950	203,508	**1,457,457**	**2,496,391**
Dec	133,303	76,094	4,988	**81,081**	**214,385**	**1,042,479**	1,255,532	204,197	**1,459,729**	**2,502,208**
2018 Jan	125,626	81,888	4,496	**86,383**	**212,010**	**1,038,657**	1,253,941	200,648 (dc)	**1,454,588 (dc)**	**2,493,246 (dc)**
Feb	117,945	78,366	4,568	**82,934**	**200,879**	**1,037,044**	1,254,408	202,402	**1,456,810**	**2,493,853**
Mar	120,643	64,835	4,658	**69,493**	**190,136**	**1,042,588**	1,260,425	202,544	**1,462,969**	**2,505,557**
Apr	113,580	65,207	4,527	**69,734**	**183,313**	**1,033,822**	1,262,106	203,142	**1,465,247**	**2,499,069**

Source: Bank of England

12.4c Industrial analysis of monetary financial institutions' lending to UK residents

£ millions | Not seasonally adjusted

Notes to table

Movements in amounts outstanding can reflect breaks in data series as well as underlying flows. For changes data, users are recommended to refer directly to the appropriate series or data tables. Further explanation can be found at: www.bankofengland.co.uk/statistics/Pages/iadb/notesiadb/Changes_flows_growth_rates.aspx.

(by) Due to improvements in reporting by one institution, amounts outstanding increased by £1bn. This amount has been adjusted out of the flows for September 2017.
(bz) Due to improvements in reporting by one institution, amounts outstanding increased by £1bn. This amount has been adjusted out of the flows for September 2017.
(ca) Due to reporting improvements at one institution, amounts outstanding increased by £1 billion. This has been adjusted out of the flows for April 2017.
(cb) Due to a loan transfer by one reporting institution, the amounts outstanding increased by £1 bn. This amount has been adjusted out of the flows for September 2017.
(cc) Due to improvements in reporting at one institution, the amounts outstanding increased by £1bn. This effect has been adjusted out of the flows for November 2018.
(cd) Due to loan transfers by one institution, amounts outstanding decreased by £1 billion. This amount has been adjusted out of the flows for March 2017.
(ce) Due to loan transfers by one institution, amounts outstanding increased by £1 billion. This amount has been adjusted out of the flows for April 2017.
(cf) Due to improvements in reporting at one institution, the amounts outstanding increased by £1bn. This effect has been adjusted out of the flows for July 2018.
(cg) Due to improvements in reporting by one institution, amounts outstanding increased by £1bn. This amount has been adjusted out of the flows for September 2017.
(ch) Due to improvements in reporting at one institution, the amounts outstanding increased by £1bn. This effect has been adjusted out of the flows for November 2018.
(ci) Due to improvements in reporting at one institution, the amounts outstanding increased by £3bn. This effect has been adjusted out of the flows for February 2018.
(cj) Due to improvements in reporting at one institution, the amounts outstanding increased by £4bn. This effect has been adjusted out of the flows for February 2018.
(ck) Due to reporting improvements at one institution, amounts outstanding decreased by £2bn. This has been adjusted out of flows for March 2017.
(cl) Previously, this series formed part of other financial intermediaries.
(cm) Due to a change in accounting treatment at one reporting institution, the amounts outstanding decreased by £2bn. This effect has been adjusted out of the flows for June 2017.
(cn) Due to reporting improvements at one institution, amounts outstanding decreased by £2bn. This has been adjusted out of flows for March 2017.
(co) Due to improvements in reporting at one institution, the amounts outstanding decreased by £2bn. This effect has been adjusted out of the flows for June 2017.
(cp) Due to improvements in reporting at one institution, the amounts outstanding decreased by £6bn. This effect has been adjusted out of the flows for February 2018.
(cq) From January 2019 onwards, this series no longer includes venture and development capital. As result, this series decreased by £2bn. This effect has been adjusted out the flows for January 2019
(cr) Due to reporting improvements at one institution, amounts outstanding increased by £5bn. This has been adjusted out of flows for March 2017.
(cs) Due to reporting improvements at one institution, amounts outstanding decreased by £5bn. This has been adjusted out of flows for March 2017.
(ct) Due to reporting improvements at one institution, amounts outstanding increased by £2bn. This has been adjusted out of flows for March 2017.
(cu) Due to reporting improvements at one institution, amounts outstanding increased by £2bn. This has been adjusted out of flows for March 2017.
(cv) Due to improvements in reporting by one institution, amounts outstanding increased by £1bn. This amount has been adjusted out of the flows for September 2017.
(cw) Due to improvements in reporting at one institution, the amounts outstanding increased by £2bn. This effect has been adjusted out of the flows for February 2017.
(cx) Due to improvements in reporting by one institution, amounts outstanding increased by £4 bn. This amount has been adjusted out of the flows for September 2017.
(cy) Due to improvements in reporting at one institution, the amounts outstanding increased by £5bn. This effect has been adjusted out of the flows for September 2018.
(cz) Due to improvements in reporting at one institution, the amounts outstanding decreased by £4bn. This effect has been adjusted out of the flows for July 2017.
(da) Due to improvements in reporting at one institution, the amounts outstanding increased by £2bn. This effect has been adjusted out of the flows for October 2018.
(db) Due to improvements in reporting at one institution, the amounts outstanding decreased by £6bn. This effect has been adjusted out of the flows for July 2017.
(dc) Due to improvements in reporting at one institution, the amounts outstanding decreased by £3bn. This effect has been adjusted out of the flows for January 2018.

Explanatory notes can be found here: http://www.bankofengland.co.uk/statistics/Pages/iadb/notesiadb/industrial.aspx

12.4d Industrial analysis of monetary financial institutions' lending to UK residents

£ millions Not seasonally adjusted

Amounts outstanding of facilities granted in all currencies

	Agriculture, hunting and forestry	Fishing	Mining and quarrying	Manufacturing									Electricity, gas and water supply			
				Food, beverages and tobacco	Textiles, wearing apparel and leather	Pulp, paper, and printing	Chemicals, pharma-ceuticals, rubber and plastics	Non-metallic mineral products and metals	Machinery, equipment and transport equipment	Electrical, medical and optical equipment	Other manu-facturing	**Total**	Electricity, gas steam and air conditioning	Water collection and sewerage	Waste management related services and remediation activities	Total
RPM	**TCAC**	**TCAD**	**TCAE**	**TCAG**	**TCAH**	**TCAI**	**TCAJ**	**TCAK**	**TCAL**	**TCAM**	**TCAN**	**TCAF**	**TCAO**	**TCAP**	**B3FF**	**B3FT**
2016 Jan	24,431	312	32,661	17,856	1,814	3,745	16,689	8,723	18,416	5,090	5,867	**78,200**	23,900	7,891	3,244	**35,035**
Feb	24,380	311	28,697	18,202	1,746	3,726	17,901	8,880	18,507	5,178	5,973	**80,113**	24,155	7,899	3,207	**35,261**
Mar	24,508	315	28,223	18,150	1,778	3,708	17,690	8,833	18,330	5,161	6,241	**79,893**	23,830	7,938	3,290	**35,058**
Apr	24,479	307	25,933	19,147	1,716	3,826	17,206	8,792	18,069	5,157	6,324	**80,237**	22,571	7,944	3,239	**33,754**
May	24,525	308	25,898	20,863	1,716	3,793	17,546	8,849	17,318	5,449	6,453	**81,986**	24,062	8,229	3,096	**35,386**
Jun	24,706	356	28,309	21,523	1,841	3,782	18,252	8,758	17,826	5,485	6,064	**83,531**	25,101	8,377	2,951	**36,428**
Jul	24,797	365	27,614	21,300	1,849	3,687	17,613	8,716	17,607	5,467	6,125	**82,363**	24,813	8,435	3,095	**36,343**
Aug	24,911	361	27,953	21,236	1,826	3,789	18,158	8,596	17,403	5,631	5,818	**82,457**	25,129	8,716	3,133	**36,979**
Sep	25,002	356	29,533	22,713	1,871	3,915	18,491	8,570	18,176	6,131	5,631	**85,499**	25,140	8,666	3,120	**36,926**
Oct	25,048	368	31,828	23,342	1,892	4,100	18,911	8,706	18,346	5,964	5,724	**86,985**	26,117	8,554	3,339	**38,011**
Nov	24,983	359	30,871	24,662	1,921	4,268	18,727	8,550	18,207	6,292	5,693	**88,320**	25,635	8,481	3,189	**37,305**
Dec	24,987	371	32,056	23,385	1,884	4,263	19,333	8,512	18,442	6,285	5,741	**87,845**	26,097	8,349	3,279	**37,724**
2017 Jan	25,031	370	30,930	32,304	1,851	4,669	19,292	8,731	18,583	6,147	5,678	**97,255**	26,783	8,477	3,315	**38,575**
Feb	25,066	370	30,720	33,695	1,785	4,813	32,120	8,750	18,988	6,024	5,692	**111,867**	26,697	8,167	3,222	**38,087**
Mar	25,183	373	30,176	33,313	1,831	4,840	27,766	9,258	18,818	6,139	6,051	**108,016**	28,612	8,063	3,223	**39,898**
Apr	25,258	362	27,259 (dd)	36,031	1,826	4,801	28,194	8,728	19,050	6,037	5,701	**110,366**	28,049	8,173	3,113	**39,335**
May	25,451	361	28,415	36,206	1,894	4,935	30,079	8,697	19,406	5,950	5,814	**112,981**	27,685	8,136	3,180	**39,001**
Jun	25,552	368	27,826	36,270	1,974	4,584	26,269	8,745	19,097	6,013	6,342	**109,295**	27,730	8,290	3,167	**39,187**
Jul	25,663	370	27,719	29,936 (de)	1,908	4,244	25,803	8,751	19,078	5,569	5,893	**101,181 (de)**	27,943	8,077	3,067	**39,087**
Aug	25,693	366	28,271	26,991 (df)	1,993	4,337	23,379	8,814	18,678	5,651	5,749	**95,592 (df)**	28,406	8,246	2,999	**39,651**
Sep	25,799	357	28,178	25,835	2,057	4,349	22,753	8,895	18,736 (di)	6,039	6,002	**94,667 (di)**	27,318	8,355	3,056	**38,730**
Oct	25,811	395	28,288	25,970	2,002	4,407	21,835	8,766	18,795	6,097	5,843	**93,715**	27,186	8,402	2,995	**38,583**
Nov	25,811	411	27,721	25,530	2,175	4,232	22,098	8,802	19,159	6,047	5,749	**93,793**	27,100	8,530	3,018	**38,649**
Dec	25,720	417	27,659	25,735	1,975	4,173	22,397	8,915	18,875	5,822	5,666	**93,558**	27,695	8,473	3,036	**39,205**
2018 Jan	25,731	367	26,012	26,261	1,793	4,011	21,265	8,670	18,811	8,313	5,710	**94,834**	27,499	8,433	3,005	**38,937**
Feb	25,466	362	27,205	26,602	1,837	4,599	21,138	8,859	19,407	8,110	5,939	**96,491**	27,721	8,433	2,964	**39,117**
Mar	25,566	358	26,657	26,241	1,894	4,624	28,313	9,018	20,294	8,036	5,667	**104,086**	28,087	8,454	3,049	**39,589**
Apr	25,564	360	27,005	26,434	1,915	3,980	24,806	9,315	22,180 (dj)	5,588 (dk)	5,741	**99,959**	28,321	8,433	3,085	**39,839**

Source: Bank of England

12.4d Industrial analysis of monetary financial institutions' lending to UK residents

£ millions

Not seasonally adjusted

Amounts outstanding of facilities granted in all currencies

	Construction						Wholesale and retail trade				Accommodation	Transport, storage and communication		
	Development of buildings	Construction of commercial buildings	Construction of domestic buildings	Civil Engineering	Other construction activities	**Total**	Wholesale and retail trade and repair of motor vehicles and motorcycles	Wholesale trade, excluding motor vehicles and motor cycles	Retail trade excluding motor vehicles and motor cycles	**Total**	and food service activities	Transportation and storage	Information and communication	**Total**
RPM	B7EH	B3IE	B4PD	B3KK	B5PC	TCAQ	TCAS	TCAT	TCAU	TCAR	TCAV	B3NF	B5PX	TCAW
2016 Jan	20,494	6,926	8,260	5,800	8,048	**49,528**	16,077	27,660	33,424	**77,161**	29,171	27,803	36,467	**64,270**
Feb	22,155	5,876	9,317	6,013	7,909	**51,269**	17,479	28,771	33,951	**80,201**	29,078	28,267	35,475	**63,742**
Mar	19,550	5,703	9,494	6,031	7,830	**48,607**	16,954	28,603	34,151	**79,708**	29,417	27,530	33,719	**61,249**
Apr	19,694	5,766	9,489	5,974	7,918	**48,840**	17,941	28,008	34,568	**80,517**	29,504	27,698	31,620	**59,319**
May	19,613	5,682	9,756	5,959	8,135	**49,146**	17,608	28,400	34,613	**80,622**	29,624	27,699	29,481	**57,180**
Jun	19,835	5,627	9,946	6,046	8,143	**49,597**	18,244	29,266	34,713	**82,223**	29,708	28,321	30,778	**59,099**
Jul	20,120	5,655	9,864	5,944	8,147	**49,731**	18,188	28,570	34,733	**81,491**	29,797	28,967	30,669	**59,636**
Aug	20,057	5,694	9,994	6,012	8,179	**49,936**	18,082	29,287	33,997	**81,366**	30,258	28,228	31,395	**59,623**
Sep	20,837	5,576	10,079	5,916	8,265	**50,673**	17,345	28,800	34,594	**80,739**	31,165	29,011	31,136	**60,147**
Oct	20,832	5,626	10,278	6,167	8,375	**51,277**	16,779	30,481	34,463	**81,722**	31,435	29,307	33,746	**63,053**
Nov	20,517	5,650	10,244	6,201	8,369	**50,982**	16,978	30,030	34,795	**81,803**	31,244	28,111	31,955	**60,066**
Dec	20,178	5,558	10,222	6,156	8,300	**50,414**	16,973	29,146	35,555	**81,674**	31,999	27,522	31,474	**58,996**
2017 Jan	20,481	5,701	10,506	6,267	8,347	**51,302**	17,660	29,520	35,513	**82,693**	32,050	27,505	31,449	**58,954**
Feb	20,763	5,709	10,604	6,362	8,347	**51,785**	18,414	29,928	35,403	**83,746**	32,426	28,439	31,490	**59,928**
Mar	20,724	5,654	10,734	6,806	8,278	**52,196**	18,365	30,109 (dl)	35,260	**83,734 (dl)**	32,679	28,163	31,991	**60,154**
Apr	20,780	5,583	10,774	6,308	8,298	**51,744**	17,969	30,899 (dm)	35,274	**84,143 (dm)**	33,344	27,934	31,470	**59,404**
May	20,475	5,571	10,855	6,367	8,150	**51,418**	17,893	32,119	35,614	**85,626**	33,115	27,841	32,312	**60,153**
Jun	20,638	5,508	10,743	6,288	8,233	**51,411**	18,587	32,310	35,553	**86,450**	33,339	27,812	32,009	**59,821**
Jul	20,898	5,548	10,631	6,576	8,330	**51,982**	18,066	32,469	35,767	**86,303**	32,630	27,888	31,402	**59,291**
Aug	20,763	5,560	10,579	6,003	8,491	**51,395**	18,180	32,511	36,203	**86,894**	32,865	27,860	31,710	**59,570**
Sep	20,947	5,458	10,553	5,999	8,506	**51,463**	18,263	32,091	36,978 (do)	**87,332 (do)**	32,986	27,799	32,058	**59,858**
Oct	20,652	5,598	10,663	5,802	8,252	**50,967**	17,922	32,825	37,473	**88,220**	33,278	28,310	32,856	**61,166**
Nov	20,571	5,498	11,011	6,008	8,127	**51,214**	17,609	30,851	37,722	**86,182**	33,476	27,999	32,312	**60,311**
Dec	20,468	5,553	10,702	5,904	8,114	**50,741**	17,727	31,957	38,167	**87,851**	34,008	27,875	32,938	**60,812**
2018 Jan	20,319	5,290	10,701	5,622	7,985	**49,918**	17,821	30,896	37,392 (dp)	**86,108 (dp)**	33,689	27,455	31,894	**59,348**
Feb	20,649	5,278	10,976	6,066	8,104	**51,073**	17,715	31,326	39,743	**88,784**	33,784	28,237	31,818	**60,056**
Mar	21,134	5,298	11,017	5,632	8,041	**51,122**	17,663	33,974	38,713	**90,351**	34,078	28,198	31,843	**60,041**
Apr	21,278	5,349	10,820	5,392	7,989	**50,828**	17,801	34,418	38,567	**90,785**	34,002	28,025	31,321	**59,346**

Source: Bank of England

12.4d Industrial analysis of monetary financial institutions' lending to UK residents

£ millions — Not seasonally adjusted

Amounts outstanding of facilities granted in all currencies

	Real estate, professional services and support activities							Recreational, personal and community service activities			Financial intermediation (excluding insurance and pension funds)				
	Buying, selling and renting of real estate	Professional, scientific and technical activities	Admin-istrative and support services	Total	Public administration and defence	Education	Human health and social work	Recreational, cultural and sporting activities	Personal and community service activities	Total	Financial leasing corporations	Non-bank credit grantors excluding credit unions and SPVs	Credit unions	Factoring corporations	Mortgage and housing credit corporations excluding SPVs
RPM	TCAY	B3QF	B3S3	TCAX	TCBD	TCBE	TCBF	TCBH	TCBG	B3T2	TCBJ	TCBK	TCBL	TCBM	TCBN
2016 Jan	166,283	30,937	35,302	**232,521**	12,154	13,271	23,761	8,431	4,543	**12,974**	32,754	24,803	3	5,311	55,390
Feb	165,259	30,621	36,444	**232,324**	11,977	13,375	23,823	8,608	4,625	**13,233**	32,947	25,158	2	5,183	55,881
Mar	169,336	30,361	36,850	**236,547**	10,942	13,333	23,782	8,727	4,662	**13,389**	33,216	21,265	5	5,932	56,203
Apr	169,111	30,101	37,523	**236,735**	12,113	13,264	23,620	8,622	4,629	**13,251**	33,083	21,867	2	6,104	50,466
May	169,367	30,461	37,388	**237,217**	12,216	13,314	23,675	8,598	4,614	**13,212**	32,923	21,796	2	6,086	50,253
Jun	170,175	31,113	38,795	**240,083**	11,545	13,282	23,886	8,441	4,735	**13,177**	33,095	21,470	2	6,833	51,112
Jul	170,282	31,204	39,330	**240,816**	11,940	13,325	23,897	8,505	4,765	**13,270**	33,892	21,806	2	6,591	51,348
Aug	170,588	31,212	40,069	**241,869**	12,257	13,306	23,744	8,435	4,779	**13,214**	33,664	21,839	2	6,004	50,795
Sep	170,069	32,310	40,219	**242,597**	12,467	13,120	23,644	8,823	4,771	**13,593**	34,673	24,682	2	6,447	51,386
Oct	169,472	31,993	42,064	**243,529**	12,126	13,105	23,768	9,249	4,803	**14,052**	35,037	25,427	2	6,406	52,338
Nov	170,247	31,176	41,558	**242,981**	11,956	13,018	23,834	8,884	4,736	**13,620**	35,258	25,869	2	6,523	49,623
Dec	171,590	31,102	43,805	**246,497**	11,863	13,026	23,153	9,216	4,745	**13,961**	34,173	25,743	2	7,448	49,415
2017 Jan	170,347	31,621	43,648	**245,616**	14,412	12,969	23,746	9,309	4,713	**14,022**	33,744	26,251	3	6,542	49,802
Feb	170,011	31,128	42,984	**244,122**	11,751	12,966	23,420	9,429	4,487	**13,916**	33,252	22,421	3	6,747	44,654
Mar	169,639	31,391	42,640 (du)	**243,670 (du)**	12,142	13,001	23,643	9,247	4,710	**13,957**	32,330	23,046	3	7,068	48,654
Apr	170,163 (dr)	31,417	42,392 (dv)(dw)	**243,972 (dr)(dv)(dw)**	14,650	13,020	23,442	9,424	4,825	**14,249**	31,337	22,678	3	6,969	49,035
May	170,922	31,385	43,731	**246,039**	13,567	13,060	23,695	9,431	4,801	**14,232**	32,084	22,296	2	7,017	47,572
Jun	170,598	31,441	43,892	**245,931**	12,669	12,933	23,767	9,286	4,817	**14,103**	32,918	25,413	2	7,946	47,266
Jul	169,018	30,519	44,351	**243,888**	14,721	12,974	23,838	9,115	4,752	**13,867**	33,302	25,836	2	7,567	47,442
Aug	169,567	30,649	44,385	**244,600**	14,781	13,054	23,907	9,076	4,743	**13,819**	33,929	26,630	3	7,508	47,506
Sep	171,253 (ds)	31,376	45,289	**247,918 (ds)**	14,196 (dz)	13,225	23,629	9,134	4,700	**13,834**	35,595	25,984	3	7,610	47,819
Oct	169,651	30,691	45,267	**245,608**	14,028	13,228	23,710	9,239	4,453	**13,692**	35,273	26,057	3	7,538	45,903
Nov	169,125	31,001	45,167	**245,293**	13,899	13,171	23,979	9,198	4,406	**13,604**	36,152	25,748	3	7,610	46,170
Dec	169,877	31,422	44,325	**245,624**	14,574	13,211	23,377	9,629	4,460	**14,090**	35,962	26,265	3	7,537	45,973
2018 Jan	170,788	31,074	47,290	**249,152**	12,898	12,933	23,622	9,192	4,203	**13,395**	36,160	27,336	4	6,800	46,376
Feb	171,107	30,946	45,240	**247,293**	15,835	12,789	23,820	9,275	4,247	**13,521**	40,873 (eb)	27,454	4	11,146 (ec)	46,372
Mar	172,968	30,988	45,179	**249,136**	17,203	12,943	23,715	9,079	4,270	**13,350**	41,614	27,829	4	11,363	46,551
Apr	173,961	31,866	45,615	**251,443**	14,481	12,894	23,637	8,800	4,223	**13,023**	41,990	28,478	4	11,469	47,383

Source: Bank of England

12.4d Industrial analysis of monetary financial institutions' lending to UK residents

Not seasonally adjusted

Amounts outstanding of facilities granted in all currencies

	Financial intermediation (excluding insurance and pension funds) (contd.)								Insurance companies & pension funds			Activities auxiliary to financial intermediation			
	Investment and unit trusts excluding money market mutual funds	Money market mutual funds	Bank holding companies	Securities dealers	SPVs related to securit-isation	Other financial inter-mediaries	of which intragroup activity	**Total**	Insurance companies	Pension funds	**Total**	Fund management activities	Other: Central clearing counterparties	Other: Other auxiliary activities	Total
RPM	TCBO	TCBP	TCBQ	TCBR	B7FB	TCBS	B7FG	TCBI	B7FL	B7FQ	TCBT	TCBU	B3X7	B3Y5	TCBV
2016 Jan	18,638	135	30,632	119,914	24,811	98,803	70,293	**411,194**	20,723	12,773	**33,495**	155,912	94,430	19,004	**113,434**
Feb	18,795	122	32,150	127,023	24,531	100,749	72,519	**422,541**	22,963	15,067	**38,030**	170,699	99,561	19,284	**118,845**
Mar	19,481	193	31,501	120,520	24,747	95,167	68,437	**408,232**	23,498	14,808	**38,307**	171,096	90,367	18,932	**109,299**
Apr	20,009	164	31,385	137,673	21,376	99,024	71,971	**421,150**	21,922	12,816	**34,737**	168,896	90,977	13,533	**104,510**
May	21,662	176	29,780	129,941	20,540	100,867	72,837	**414,027**	23,178	13,502	**36,680**	178,038	96,545	14,009	**110,554**
Jun	22,063	202	20,815	145,185	22,006	104,521	74,880	**427,303**	25,432	16,839	**42,272**	192,754	111,794	15,231	**127,025**
Jul	21,380	205	22,074	146,215	21,670	103,884	73,818	**429,066**	25,385	17,901	**43,286**	194,220	107,859	15,478	**123,337**
Aug	21,244	298	22,470	139,229	20,151	100,139	75,395	**415,835**	27,301	18,246	**45,547**	197,932	114,475	15,617	**130,092**
Sep	21,290	322	22,138	146,705	19,775	99,899	74,161	**427,318**	25,171	18,632	**43,803**	181,779	109,639	15,461	**125,099**
Oct	22,785	407	22,189	148,947	18,053	101,433	76,396	**433,024**	23,282	16,293	**39,574**	179,067	118,813	14,025	**132,837**
Nov	22,017	350	21,719	157,109	16,706	94,705	71,219	**429,880**	22,309	17,855	**40,163**	177,142	129,755	13,793	**143,548**
Dec	21,617	350	23,901	141,134	17,437	92,045	69,484	**413,265**	22,620	21,580	**44,200**	181,132	107,555	13,751	**121,306**
2017 Jan	20,757	342	26,508	144,833	17,262	92,318	70,107	**418,361**	22,604	17,909	**40,512**	180,013	136,409	13,668	**150,076**
Feb	22,020	342	25,970	145,280	16,767	104,803	75,245	**422,260**	22,317	18,690	**41,006**	188,212	146,574 (ep)(eq)	14,578	**161,152 (ep)(eq)**
Mar	20,100 (ed)	346	21,137	145,852	16,823	97,733 (eg)	77,207	**413,093 (ed)(eg)**	22,953	27,127 (ek)	**50,080 (ek)**	192,443 (el)(em)(en)	141,123	14,514	**155,637**
Apr	20,073	320	21,048	151,075	17,760	97,519	76,765	**417,816**	24,560	29,431	**53,991**	189,333	146,738	14,507	**161,245**
May	20,715	380	22,003	148,397	16,287	97,409	77,626	**414,161**	23,657	29,440	**53,097**	190,781	150,821	13,626	**164,447**
Jun	21,786	368	21,701	139,798	14,595 (ef)	96,120 (eh)	76,916 (eh)	**407,914 (ef)(eh)**	22,298	28,268	**50,565**	198,576	146,164	13,654	**159,818**
Jul	22,222	412	21,766	135,792	15,246	97,478	76,725	**407,067**	21,270	26,707	**47,977**	189,933	150,103 (er)	13,577	**163,680 (er)**
Aug	21,843	409	21,632	132,778	14,013	99,333	76,595	**405,584**	22,028	26,759	**48,787**	197,397	166,525	15,153	**181,678**
Sep	23,256	373	21,404	127,546	14,385	98,506	76,483	**402,482**	24,952	28,241	**53,194**	192,491 (eo)	167,699 (es)	14,949	**182,648 (es)**
Oct	23,199	352	18,422	131,294	14,612	98,436	76,139	**401,088**	20,397	26,847	**47,243**	193,522	172,007	13,736	**185,743**
Nov	22,883	338	19,606	137,685	12,337	98,812	76,340	**407,344**	20,766	27,802	**48,568**	194,880	176,440	10,327	**186,767**
Dec	20,648	338	18,217	128,203	12,897	101,089	79,885	**397,133**	22,822	27,203	**50,026**	206,947	152,973	10,035	**163,008**
2018 Jan	22,320	351	16,528	148,798	9,873	105,256	77,993	**419,803**	19,774	27,008	**46,781**	205,200	170,881	9,397	**180,277**
Feb	22,191	340	16,427	141,787	9,927	92,510 (ei)	66,239 (ei)	**409,032**	19,379	27,752	**47,132**	203,319	175,100	9,269	**184,369**
Mar	22,041	433	16,609	136,639	10,957	96,352	70,298	**410,392**	20,344	27,969	**48,313**	205,278	150,290	9,624	**159,915**
Apr	21,820	395	16,834	136,970	10,544	100,394	76,247	**416,283**	20,227	26,901	**47,128**	193,952	152,077 (et)	8,915	**160,992 (et)**

Source: Bank of England

12.4d Industrial analysis of monetary financial institutions' lending to UK residents

Not seasonally adjusted

Amounts outstanding of facilities granted in all currencies

	Activities auxiliary to financial intermediation (contd.)		Individuals and individual trusts			
	Total	Total financial and non-financial businesses	Lending secured on dwellings inc. bridging finance	Other loans and advances	Total	Total UK residents
RPM	B3Z2	Z94H	TCBX	TCBY	TCBW	TCAA
2016 Jan	269,346	1,399,484	1,160,637	199,838	1,360,475	2,759,959
Feb	289,544	1,437,898	1,163,318	200,997	1,364,315	2,802,213
Mar	280,395	1,411,904	1,170,040	202,130	1,372,171	2,784,075
Apr	273,406	1,411,166	1,178,952	202,890	1,381,841	2,793,008
May	288,592	1,423,607	1,182,900	203,688	1,386,588	2,810,195
Jun	319,779	1,485,284	1,189,498	204,788	1,394,287	2,879,570
Jul	317,557	1,485,295	1,192,480	205,693	1,398,172	2,883,467
Aug	328,024	1,487,641	1,194,731	206,951	1,401,682	2,889,323
Sep	306,878	1,483,464	1,198,617	206,097	1,404,714	2,888,178
Oct	311,904	1,500,810	1,201,820	206,681	1,408,501	2,909,311
Nov	320,690	1,502,076	1,206,662	207,641	1,414,303	2,916,379
Dec	302,437	1,474,467	1,207,911	207,965	1,415,876	2,890,343
2017 Jan	330,089	1,516,889	1,209,585	208,372	1,417,957	2,934,845
Feb	349,364 (ep)(eq)	1,552,801 (ep)(eq)	1,212,778	208,883	1,421,661	2,974,462 (ep)(eq)
Mar	348,080 (el)(em)(en)	1,550,074 (dl)(du)	1,219,315	209,987	1,429,302	2,979,376 (dl)(du)
Apr	350,578	1,562,935 (dr)(dv)(dw)	1,220,632	210,664	1,431,296	2,994,231 (dr)(dv)(dw)
May	355,228	1,569,600	1,226,180	210,637	1,436,817	3,006,417
Jun	358,395	1,559,525 (ef)(eh)	1,234,334	211,237	1,445,571	3,005,096 (ef)(eh)
Jul	353,612 (er)	1,542,171 (de)(er)	1,232,931 (ev)	204,779 (ex)	1,437,710 (ev)(ex)	2,979,881 (de)(er)(ev)(ex)
Aug	379,075	1,563,906 (df)	1,236,415	205,236	1,441,651	3,005,556 (df)
Sep	375,139 (eo)(es)	1,562,987 (di)(do)(ds)(dz)(eo)(es)	1,245,970	205,917	1,451,886	3,014,874 (di)(do)(ds)(dz)(eo)(es)
Oct	379,265	1,558,284	1,248,731	205,104	1,453,835	3,012,119
Nov	381,647	1,565,075	1,254,091	204,795	1,458,886	3,023,960
Dec	369,955	1,547,962	1,255,677	205,531	1,461,208	3,009,170
2018 Jan	385,477	1,579,005 (dp)	1,254,080	201,887 (ey)	1,455,967 (ey)	3,034,972 (dp)(ey)
Feb	387,688	1,579,448	1,254,548	203,617	1,458,165	3,037,612
Mar	365,193	1,572,092	1,260,563	203,788	1,464,351	3,036,443
Apr	354,945 (et)	1,561,522 (et)	1,262,236	204,273	1,466,509	3,028,031 (et)

Source: Bank of England

12.4d Industrial analysis of monetary financial institutions' lending to UK residents

£ millions Not seasonally adjusted

Notes to table

Movements in amounts outstanding can reflect breaks in data series as well as underlying flows. For changes data, users are recommended to refer directly to the appropriate series or data tables.

(dd) Due to reporting improvements at one institution, amounts outstanding decreased by £2 billion. This has been adjusted out of the flows for April 2017.
(de) Due to loan transfers by one institution, amounts outstanding increased by £1 billion. This amount has been adjusted out of the flows for July 2017.
(df) Due to loan transfers by one institution, amounts outstanding decreased by £1 billion. This amount has been adjusted out of the flows for August 2017.
(di) Due to improvements in reporting by one institution, amounts outstanding increased by £1bn. This amount has been adjusted out of the flows for September 2017.
(dj) Due to improvements in reporting at one institution, the amounts outstanding decreased by £2bn. This effect has been adjusted out of the flows for April 2018
(dk) Due to improvements in reporting at one institution, the amounts outstanding increased by £2bn. This effect has been adjusted out of the flows for April 2018
(dl) Due to changes in the reporting population, amounts outstanding increased by £1bn. This has been adjusted out of flows for March 2017.
(dm) Due to reporting improvements at one institution, amounts outstanding increased by £2 billion. This has been adjusted out of the flows for April 2017.
(do) Due to improvements in reporting by one institution, amounts outstanding increased by £1bn. This amount has been adjusted out of the flows for September 2017.
(dp) Due to improvements in reporting at one institution, the amounts outstanding increased by £1bn. This effect has been adjusted out of the flows for January 2018.
(dr) Due to reporting improvements at one institution, amounts outstanding increased by £1 billion. This has been adjusted out of the flows for April 2017.
(ds) Due to a loan transfer by one reporting institution, the amounts outstanding increased by £1 bn. This amount has been adjusted out of the flows for September 2017.
(du) Due to loan transfers by one institution, amounts outstanding decreased by £1 billion. This amount has been adjusted out of the flows for March 2017.
(dv) Due to reporting improvements at one institution, amounts outstanding decreased by £1 billion. This has been adjusted out of the flows for April 2017.
(dw) Due to loan transfers by one institution, amounts outstanding increased by £1 billion. This amount has been adjusted out of the flows for April 2017.
(dz) Due to improvements in reporting by one institution, amounts outstanding increased by £1bn. This amount has been adjusted out of the flows for September 2017.
(eb) Due to improvements in reporting at one institution, the amounts outstanding increased by £3bn. This effect has been adjusted out of the flows for February 2018.
(ec) Due to improvements in reporting at one institution, the amounts outstanding increased by £4bn. This effect has been adjusted out of the flows for February 2018.
(ed) Due to reporting improvements at one institution, amounts outstanding decreased by £2bn. This has been adjusted out of flows for March 2017.
(ee) Previously, this series formed part of other financial intermediaries.
(ef) Due to a change in accounting treatment at one reporting institution, the amounts outstanding decreased by £2bn. This effect has been adjusted out of the flows for June 2017.
(eg) Due to reporting improvements at one institution, amounts outstanding decreased by £2bn. This has been adjusted out of flows for March 2017.
(eh) Due to improvements in reporting at one institution, the amounts outstanding decreased by £2bn. This effect has been adjusted out of the flows for June 2017.
(ei) Due to improvements in reporting at one institution, the amounts outstanding decreased by £6bn. This effect has been adjusted out of the flows for February 2018.
(ek) Due to reporting improvements at one institution, amounts outstanding increased by £5bn. This has been adjusted out of flows for March 2017.
(el) Due to reporting improvements at one institution, amounts outstanding decreased by £5bn. This has been adjusted out of flows for March 2017.
(em) Due to reporting improvements at one institution, amounts outstanding increased by £2bn. This has been adjusted out of flows for March 2017.
(en) Due to reporting improvements at one institution, amounts outstanding increased by £2bn. This has been adjusted out of flows for March 2017.
(eo) Due to improvements in reporting by one institution, amounts outstanding increased by £1bn. This amount has been adjusted out of the flows for September 2017.
(ep) Due to improvements in reporting at one institution, the amounts outstanding increased by £2bn. This effect has been adjusted out of the flows for February 2017.
(eq) Due to improvements in reporting at one institution, the amounts outstanding increased by £4bn. This effect has been adjusted out of the flows for February 2017.
(er) Due to a transfer of business by one reporting institution, the amounts outstanding increased by £2bn. This effect has been adjusted out of the flows for July 2017.
(es) Due to improvements in reporting by one institution, amounts outstanding increased by £4 bn. This amount has been adjusted out of the flows for September 2017.
(et) Due to improvements in reporting at one institution, the amounts outstanding increased by £1bn. This effect has been adjusted out of the flows for April 2018
(ev) Due to improvements in reporting at one institution, the amounts outstanding decreased by £4bn. This effect has been adjusted out of the flows for July 2017.
(ex) Due to improvements in reporting at one institution, the amounts outstanding decreased by £6bn. This effect has been adjusted out of the flows for July 2017.
(ey) Due to improvements in reporting at one institution, the amounts outstanding decreased by £3bn. This effect has been adjusted out of the flows for January 2018.

Explanatory notes can be found here: http://www.bankofengland.co.uk/statistics/Pages/iadb/notesiadb/industrial.aspx

12.5a Industrial analysis of monetary financial institutions' deposits from UK residents

£ millions | Not seasonally adjusted

Amounts outstanding of deposit liabilities (including under repo) in sterling

	Agriculture, hunting and forestry	Fishing	Mining and quarrying	Manufacturing									Electricity, gas and water supply			
				Food, beverages and tobacco	Textiles, wearing apparel and leather	Pulp, paper, and printing	Chemicals, pharma-ceuticals, rubber and plastics	Non-metallic mineral products and metals	Machinery, equipment and transport equipment	Electrical, medical and optical equipment	Other manu-facturing	**Total**	Electricity, gas steam and air conditioning	Water collection and sewerage	Waste management related services and remediation activities	Total
RPM	TDCB	TDCC	TDCD	TDCF	TDCG	TDCH	TDCI	TDCJ	TDCK	TDCL	TDCM	TDCE	TDCN	TDCO	BE2M	B3FI
2016 Jan	6,225	239	10,389	4,081	1,355	1,667	5,370	5,826	9,906	4,721	4,466	**37,392**	5,122	2,205	1,509	**8,836**
Feb	6,201	260	3,508	3,688	1,353	1,640	5,466	5,731	9,960	4,724	4,505	**37,068**	5,638	2,310	1,502	**9,450**
Mar	6,160	267	3,208	3,828	1,335	1,668	5,361	5,801	10,056	4,523	4,718	**37,290**	6,436	2,286	1,733	**10,455**
Apr	6,162	259	2,919	3,788	1,316	1,651	4,915	5,815	9,531	4,572	4,670	**36,257**	6,140	2,151	1,522	**9,812**
May	6,182	263	2,805	3,886	1,349	1,583	5,027	5,944	9,547	4,658	4,682	**36,676**	6,650	2,344	1,489	**10,483**
Jun	6,236	258	2,887	4,165	1,347	1,648	5,102	6,151	9,978	4,751	4,847	**37,989**	6,356	2,472	1,653	**10,481**
Jul	6,225	260	3,006	3,788	1,354	1,646	4,832	5,997	9,752	4,636	4,602	**36,608**	6,380	2,076	1,688	**10,145**
Aug	6,183	293	4,167	3,984	1,351	1,628	5,079	5,979	10,055	4,686	4,772	**37,535**	5,839	2,021	1,777	**9,637**
Sep	6,227	300	6,303	4,077	1,374	1,681	4,972	6,246	9,832	4,653	4,785	**37,621**	5,821	2,284	1,736	**9,842**
Oct	6,297	307	5,029	3,930	1,421	1,748	5,272	6,455	9,440	4,815	4,880	**37,960**	6,471	2,397	1,807	**10,675**
Nov	6,436	335	5,050	4,060	1,432	1,707	5,161	6,401	9,654	4,622	4,974	**38,011**	6,290	2,427	1,679	**10,396**
Dec	7,216	355	5,090	4,011	1,339	1,778	4,763	6,495	10,166	4,667	5,208	**38,426**	6,104	2,643	1,633	**10,381**
2017 Jan	7,066	354	4,325	3,904	1,254	1,685	4,642	6,392	9,791	4,666	4,860	**37,193**	6,548	2,738	1,752	**11,038**
Feb	6,924	368	4,930	3,571	1,183	1,675	4,527	6,127	9,318	4,561	4,732	**35,694**	6,169	2,434	1,768	**10,370**
Mar	6,873	370	5,291	3,502	1,173	1,736	5,053	6,316	9,972	4,573	5,116	**37,442**	7,771	2,105	1,779	**11,655**
Apr	6,801	348	4,772	3,567	1,138	1,678	4,867	6,009	9,367	4,807	4,949	**36,381**	7,788	2,130	1,699	**11,617**
May	6,834	348	4,087	3,991	1,167	1,658	5,505	6,061	9,506	4,674	5,002	**37,563**	7,791	2,503	1,754	**12,049**
Jun	6,897	345	4,256	5,472	1,137	1,672	5,502	6,035	10,032	4,903	5,319	**40,073**	6,677	2,665	1,843	**11,186**
Jul	6,856	349	3,818	3,938	1,131	1,734	5,463	5,964	9,493	4,785	5,247	**37,756**	7,041	2,408	1,844	**11,293**
Aug	6,868	355	4,000	4,391	1,164	1,706	5,431	6,169	10,103	4,874	5,669	**39,505**	7,524	2,187	1,820	**11,531**
Sep	6,927	374	4,623	4,122	1,188	1,694	5,650	6,609	11,315 (a)	5,245	5,418	**41,241 (a)**	6,664	2,175	1,846	**10,685**
Oct	7,180	372	4,751	4,314	1,242	1,977	5,432	6,539	11,453	5,618	5,428	**42,003**	6,275	2,398	1,760	**10,434**
Nov	7,175	399	4,925	4,242	1,310	1,911	5,681	6,661	11,921	5,768	5,549	**43,042**	6,389	2,706	1,889	**10,983**
Dec	8,013	372	4,900	4,610	1,206	1,897	5,431	6,548	11,838	5,677	5,590	**42,795**	5,921	2,886	1,905	**10,712**
2018 Jan	7,727	358	4,548	3,935	1,226	1,831	5,471	6,205	11,079	5,733	5,140	**40,620**	5,903	2,588	2,030	**10,522**
Feb	7,696	363	4,406	4,013	1,206	1,781	5,581	6,008	10,583	5,520	4,786	**39,479**	6,414	2,864	2,030	**11,308**
Mar	7,709	356	3,921	3,865	1,153	1,740	5,647	6,134	11,111	5,685	4,884	**40,219**	7,289	2,560	1,960	**11,809**
Apr	7,569	345	3,847	3,842	1,180	1,765	5,184	6,224	11,076	5,592	4,746	**39,608**	6,193	2,510	1,963	**10,667**

Source: Bank of England

12.5a Industrial analysis of monetary financial institutions' deposits from UK residents

£ millions | Not seasonally adjusted

Amounts outstanding of deposit liabilities (including under repo) in sterling

	Construction						Wholesale and retail trade				Accom-modation and food service activities	Transport, storage and communication		
	Development of buildings	Construction of commercial buildings	Construction of domestic buildings	Civil Engineering	Other construction activities	**Total**	Wholesale and retail trade and repair of motor vehicles and motorcycles	Wholesale trade, excluding motor vehicles and motor cycles	Retail trade excluding motor vehicles and motor cycles	**Total**		Transportation and storage	Information and communication	Total
RPM	B3FW	B7EK	B3LS	B3JO	B4PS	TDCP	TDCR	TDCS	TDCT	TDCQ	TDCU	B5PF	B3NI	TDCV
2016 Jan	7,781	3,795	3,607	5,192	11,214	**31,590**	5,086	15,314	15,493	**35,892**	7,881	13,720	22,843	**36,563**
Feb	7,774	3,860	3,650	5,260	11,037	**31,580**	5,529	15,277	16,483	**37,288**	7,945	13,848	25,630	**39,478**
Mar	8,118	4,046	3,647	5,714	11,181	**32,705**	5,427	15,344	16,015	**36,786**	8,325	14,049	25,820	**39,868**
Apr	7,954	4,045	3,610	5,438	11,386	**32,433**	5,545	14,665	16,166	**36,376**	7,916	13,435	24,415	**37,850**
May	7,885	4,136	3,641	5,403	11,462	**32,526**	5,648	15,031	17,553	**38,232**	8,402	13,882	24,123	**38,006**
Jun	8,216	4,503	4,647	5,655	11,935	**34,956**	6,207	15,199	16,754	**38,159**	8,523	13,801	23,088	**36,889**
Jul	8,144	4,364	4,213	5,539	12,003	**34,263**	5,851	15,076	16,688	**37,615**	8,551	13,239	23,404	**36,643**
Aug	8,138	4,438	4,083	5,783	12,257	**34,699**	6,215	15,203	17,700	**39,118**	9,092	13,180	23,390	**36,570**
Sep	8,273	4,662	4,351	5,580	12,539	**35,405**	5,904	16,360	16,113	**38,377**	8,917	13,513	23,057	**36,570**
Oct	8,291	4,815	4,296	5,754	12,835	**35,991**	6,131	16,186	15,404	**37,721**	9,189	13,178	23,119	**36,297**
Nov	8,150	4,545	4,517	5,905	13,073	**36,190**	6,101	16,134	17,887	**40,122**	9,432	14,287	23,123	**37,411**
Dec	8,616	4,954	5,091	6,303	13,238	**38,202**	5,921	17,113	20,273	**43,307**	8,903	13,378	23,100	**36,479**
2017 Jan	8,842	4,508	4,401	6,205	12,729	**36,685**	5,732	15,569	17,825	**39,126**	8,378	13,192	23,506	**36,698**
Feb	8,412	4,498	4,630	5,990	12,402	**35,932**	5,915	15,701	17,734	**39,350**	8,489	13,874	23,920	**37,794**
Mar	8,947	5,037	4,803	6,560	12,813	**38,161**	6,442	16,715	16,701	**39,858**	8,771	13,763	24,455	**38,218**
Apr	8,899	4,834	4,838	6,665	12,846	**38,082**	6,232	16,345	15,913	**38,490**	9,032	13,887	24,332	**38,219**
May	8,853	5,086	4,899	6,620	13,091	**38,549**	6,261	16,430	17,313	**40,004**	9,272	14,224	24,255	**38,479**
Jun	9,026	5,224	5,900	7,044	13,308	**40,502**	6,311	16,596	17,567	**40,474**	9,253	13,808	24,938	**38,746**
Jul	9,153	5,245	5,323	6,666	13,359	**39,747**	6,343	15,957	16,553	**38,852**	9,732	13,892	25,218	**39,111**
Aug	9,540	5,526	5,618	6,689	13,581	**40,954**	6,381	16,644	17,500	**40,525**	10,387	14,244	25,367	**39,611**
Sep	9,189	5,978	5,795	6,617	13,698	**41,277**	6,465	16,896	17,776 (b)	**41,138 (b)**	10,165	14,548	26,152	**40,699**
Oct	9,310	6,348	6,246	6,430	13,988	**42,322**	6,588	17,319	16,546	**40,453**	10,475	14,694	26,085 (d)	**40,779 (d)**
Nov	9,788	6,365	5,847	6,598	13,988	**42,586**	6,496	17,405	19,007	**42,907**	10,607	16,306	27,113	**43,419**
Dec	9,820	6,365	6,671	6,993	14,199	**44,049**	6,209	17,533	21,154	**44,896**	9,720	14,960	26,894	**41,854**
2018 Jan	9,716	5,555	6,009	6,569	13,823	**41,672**	6,396	16,904	16,812	**40,112**	9,431	14,163	26,263	**40,426**
Feb	9,663	5,651	5,885	6,457	13,419	**41,076**	6,532	17,035	18,409	**41,976**	9,374	13,911	26,888	**40,799**
Mar	9,775	6,166	6,157	6,639	13,640	**42,376**	6,631	16,890	17,666	**41,188**	8,952	14,346	26,895	**41,242**
Apr	9,927	5,832	5,898	6,378	13,832	**41,866**	6,919	16,809	17,055	**40,783**	9,258	14,271	26,986	**41,257**

Source: Bank of England

12.5a Industrial analysis of monetary financial institutions' deposits from UK residents

£ millions | Not seasonally adjusted

Amounts outstanding of deposit liabilities (including under repo) in sterling

	Real estate, professional services and support activities				Public administration and defence	Education	Human health and social work	Recreational, personal and community service activities			Financial intermediation (excluding insurance and pension funds)				
	Buying, selling and renting of real estate	Professional, scientific and technical activities	Administrative and support services	Total				Recreational, cultural and sporting activities	Personal and community service activities	Total	Financial leasing corporations	Non-bank credit grantors excluding credit unions and SPVs	Credit unions	Factoring corporations	Mortgage and housing credit corporations excluding SPVs
RPM	TDCX	B3ON	B6PK	TDCW	TDDB	TDDC	TDDD	TDDF	TDDE	B3S6	TDDH	TDDI	TDDJ	TDDK	TDDL
2016 Jan	41,705	72,505	22,315	**136,526**	30,361	19,768	19,216	11,138	18,041	**29,179**	8,967	3,323	1,059	960	9,336
Feb	40,940	73,319	23,015	**137,273**	28,983	20,180	19,466	11,181	18,246	**29,426**	9,026	3,562	1,089	861	9,285
Mar	44,000	79,880	24,136	**148,016**	25,512	18,926	19,470	11,104	18,142	**29,246**	8,987	3,581	1,103	981	8,823
Apr	42,164	71,673	23,895	**137,732**	33,459	20,083	19,630	10,996	18,251	**29,247**	9,067	3,761	1,104	1,052	8,954
May	41,576	72,993	24,529	**139,098**	32,918	22,012	19,884	11,046	18,163	**29,209**	9,110	3,540	1,100	1,033	8,831
Jun	44,837	75,350	25,954	**146,142**	33,403	21,209	20,177	11,300	18,046	**29,347**	8,560	3,925	1,079	951	8,944
Jul	42,963	74,594	26,102	**143,660**	32,988	20,240	20,377	11,956	18,035	**29,991**	8,414	3,642	1,068	912	8,796
Aug	42,503	74,012	26,526	**143,040**	33,617	19,874	20,392	12,148	17,999	**30,147**	8,371	3,799	1,078	925	8,037
Sep	45,181	74,601	26,700	**146,481**	29,529	20,859	20,363	11,961	17,916	**29,877**	8,119	3,837	1,098	1,129	8,618
Oct	43,097	75,034	26,704	**144,835**	31,752	22,102	20,410	11,774	18,206	**29,980**	8,357	3,987	1,113	942	8,652
Nov	42,741	75,742	26,378	**144,862**	30,474	20,797	20,928	11,885	18,304	**30,189**	8,153	4,019	1,073	895	8,611
Dec	46,050	73,461	26,158	**145,669**	29,121	19,477	21,246	12,406	18,024	**30,430**	8,247	3,931	1,049	1,026	7,360
2017 Jan	43,820	73,203	26,282	**143,305**	28,169	20,610	20,855	12,869	18,223	**31,092**	7,900	3,985	1,062	894	7,457
Feb	43,619	73,357	26,636	**143,612**	28,169	20,836	21,123	12,930	18,190	**31,120**	7,869	3,620	1,063	886	3,559
Mar	46,472	76,023	27,889	**150,384**	25,524	19,378	21,162	12,702	18,573	**31,275**	7,866	3,749	1,063	765	7,621
Apr	45,350	74,500	27,667	**147,517**	26,379	20,807	20,965	12,214	18,534	**30,748**	7,700	3,779	1,084	758	7,232
May	44,955	77,578	28,582	**151,116**	28,349	22,886	21,239	12,479	18,826	**31,305**	7,885	3,899	1,082	827	6,677
Jun	48,223	81,313	29,093	**158,630**	29,462	21,988	21,805	12,088	18,675	**30,763**	8,282	3,784	1,068	981	6,446
Jul	46,626	79,984	29,967	**156,577**	33,993	20,799	21,570	12,750	18,617	**31,367**	8,204	4,504	1,069	985	6,565
Aug	46,651	80,540	29,693	**156,884**	35,501	20,617	21,672	13,140	18,914	**32,054**	8,659	4,452	1,075	971	6,233
Sep	49,686	80,701	29,785	**160,172**	28,906 (f)	21,831	21,446	12,744	18,916	**31,659**	8,221	4,243	1,061	936	6,406
Oct	47,979	80,054	30,737	**158,770**	31,338	22,701	21,866	12,797	19,049	**31,847**	8,124	4,193	1,062	777	6,064
Nov	47,981	82,059	31,565	**161,605**	30,532	21,554	21,926	12,676	18,877	**31,553**	7,760	4,485	1,034	804	6,093
Dec	51,299	77,410	30,516	**159,226**	28,623	20,214	21,692	13,485	18,973	**32,458**	8,048	4,449	1,040	302	5,926
2018 Jan	48,676	78,805	32,544 (e)	**160,024 (e)**	30,825	21,283	21,325	13,893	18,988	**32,882**	7,846	5,240	1,049	809	5,864
Feb	48,373	78,338	32,434	**159,144**	30,385	21,554	21,220	14,001	18,682	**32,683**	8,186	4,925	1,070	1,210	5,714
Mar	51,540	79,301	33,017	**163,858**	24,914	20,386	21,502	14,042	18,737	**32,779**	7,222	4,955	1,083	1,100	5,776
Apr	50,492	80,788	32,665	**163,946**	25,229	21,315	21,353	13,912	18,893	**32,805**	7,310	5,083	1,086	840	5,715

Source: Bank of England

12.5a Industrial analysis of monetary financial institutions' deposits from UK residents

£ millions — Not seasonally adjusted

Amounts outstanding of deposit liabilities (including under repo) in sterling

	Financial intermediation (excluding insurance and pension funds) (contd.)								Insurance companies & pension funds		
	Investment and unit trusts excluding money market mutual funds	Money market mutual funds	Bank holding companies	Securities dealers	SPVs related to securitisation	Other financial intermediaries	of which intragroup activity	**Total**	Insurance companies	Pension funds	**Total**
RPM	TDDM	TDDN	TDDO	TDDP	B3T5	TDDQ	B3U3	TDDG	B7FI	B3VH	TDDR
2016 Jan	18,644	1,022	10,293	28,556	99,845	65,344	42,707	**247,348**	21,519	25,317	**46,835**
Feb	19,842	910	11,512	28,374	100,449	63,546	41,805	**248,455**	21,478	25,279	**46,757**
Mar	19,704	939	10,565	28,342	98,834	63,699 (f)	42,579	**245,557**	23,321	20,627	**43,948**
Apr	17,994	606	10,135	27,202	97,692	61,397	41,087	**238,965**	20,973	21,685	**42,657**
May	18,126	923	9,834	26,129	100,684	60,915	40,703	**240,226**	21,114	21,162	**42,277**
Jun	20,220	940	14,472	27,346	100,744	60,509	40,171	**247,691**	23,654	22,278	**45,932**
Jul	19,843	1,256	15,243	30,539	95,505	60,737	38,881	**245,956**	24,314	22,774	**47,088**
Aug	18,968	553	17,329	28,489	92,642	63,071	40,016	**243,263**	23,732	20,813	**44,544**
Sep	21,894	502	18,329	30,237	90,901	60,922	38,572	**245,587**	27,328	23,785	**51,113**
Oct	19,634	622	17,993	32,421	88,444	60,702	38,817	**242,869**	24,696	24,766	**49,462**
Nov	20,200	677	17,084	31,134	89,450	58,613	37,253	**239,910**	26,320	23,924	**50,244**
Dec	20,324	1,483	18,422	31,874	88,612	58,592	37,173	**240,921**	26,297	24,412	**50,709**
2017 Jan	19,541	868	17,141	31,628	82,137	57,942	36,785	**230,556**	25,204	26,248	**51,452**
Feb	18,941	1,047	17,122	32,537	77,728 (h)	59,012	37,176	**223,384 (h)**	24,529	26,638	**51,167**
Mar	20,435	398	14,602	35,114	78,135	60,350	37,442	**230,099**	26,749	28,541	**55,289**
Apr	22,208	648	15,235	32,588	76,705	59,350	37,769	**227,287**	23,591	27,929	**51,521**
May	21,354	900	14,128	31,257	75,327	60,246	38,180	**223,583**	23,583	29,755	**53,338**
Jun	21,953	522	13,940	38,089	76,904	58,365	35,683	**230,334**	23,647	28,202	**51,850**
Jul	21,332	851	13,862	34,546	77,683	57,554	35,749	**227,156**	22,112	27,648	**49,760**
Aug	21,716	1,972	14,109	34,529	75,365	57,636	36,000	**226,717**	23,281	27,142	**50,423**
Sep	22,520	936	13,592	33,967	83,171 (i)	57,150	36,239	**232,202 (i)**	23,897	27,905	**51,802**
Oct	22,516	696	10,934	36,814	81,520	54,812	34,656	**227,512**	24,326	27,543	**51,869**
Nov	23,010	697	10,446	39,392	82,012	52,110	31,167	**227,843**	24,152	27,127	**51,279**
Dec	25,577	1,085	10,251	39,267	82,754	51,673	31,685	**230,372**	25,216	28,988	**54,204**
2018 Jan	25,833	512	15,613	41,004	81,471	54,593 (j)	32,020	**239,835 (j)**	19,133 (l)	30,935	**50,068 (l)**
Feb	25,425	607	14,940	39,853	81,111	49,431	27,066	**232,472**	18,691	30,842	**49,533**
Mar	25,740	679	15,236	38,220	82,649	49,315	26,077	**231,974**	19,075	32,049	**51,124**
Apr	25,097	537	17,475	41,145	82,095	47,812	25,297	**234,194**	18,984	30,843	**49,827**

Source: Bank of England

12.5a Industrial analysis of monetary financial institutions' deposits from UK residents

£ millions Not seasonally adjusted

Amounts outstanding of deposit liabilities (including under repo) in sterling

	Activities auxiliary to financial intermediation							
	Fund management activities	Other			Total	Total financial and non-financial businesses	Individuals and individuals trusts	Total UK residents
		Central clearing counterparties	Other auxiliary activities	Total				
RPM	TDDS	B7FT	B7FY	TDDT	B3Y8	Z945	TDDU	TDCA
2016 Jan	72,871	60,589	16,514	**77,103**	**149,974**	**854,213**	1,151,007	**2,005,221**
Feb	77,978	65,712	17,512	**83,224**	**161,202**	**864,521**	1,156,985	**2,021,506**
Mar	76,955	51,431	18,302	**69,732**	**146,687**	**852,426**	1,168,353	**2,020,779**
Apr	76,988	54,906	17,666	**72,572**	**149,560**	**841,318**	1,183,479	**2,024,797**
May	83,049	59,551	18,264	**77,815**	**160,864**	**860,064**	1,183,071	**2,043,135**
Jun	85,468	58,251	18,364	**76,615**	**162,083**	**882,361**	1,189,164	**2,071,525**
Jul	94,051	66,946	18,040	**84,986**	**179,038**	**892,652**	1,197,613	**2,090,265**
Aug	94,202	84,253	18,929	**103,182**	**197,384**	**909,555**	1,198,428	**2,107,983**
Sep	88,844	58,209	19,483	**77,693**	**166,537**	**889,908**	1,208,647	**2,098,555**
Oct	92,763	75,363	20,469	**95,832**	**188,594**	**909,470**	1,210,392	**2,119,862**
Nov	86,709	89,479	20,346	**109,825**	**196,535**	**917,322**	1,211,050	**2,128,372**
Dec	81,879	67,747	20,785	**88,532**	**170,410**	**896,340**	1,219,371	**2,115,712**
2017 Jan	86,344	94,528	20,264	**114,792**	**201,135**	**908,036**	1,207,752	**2,115,788**
Feb	88,091	95,776 (n)	18,856	**114,633 (n)**	**202,724 (n)**	**901,986 (h)(n)**	1,213,710	**2,115,696 (h)(n)**
Mar	86,962	90,887 (o)	20,856	**111,743 (o)**	**198,706 (o)**	**918,456 (o)**	1,223,694	**2,142,150 (o)**
Apr	90,778	112,001	19,666	**131,668**	**222,446**	**931,411**	1,229,246	**2,160,657**
May	88,844	102,773	20,930	**123,703**	**212,547**	**931,548**	1,225,151	**2,156,698**
Jun	88,999	91,554	21,531	**113,085**	**202,084**	**938,649**	1,233,967	**2,172,615**
Jul	90,449	102,885	21,049	**123,933**	**214,383**	**943,118**	1,232,486	**2,175,603**
Aug	92,777	109,793	21,371	**131,164**	**223,940**	**961,545**	1,235,558	**2,197,103**
Sep	93,304 (m)	105,243 (p)	21,893	**127,135 (p)**	**220,440 (m)(**	**965,587 (a)(b)(f)(i)(m)(p)**	1,244,134	**2,209,721 (a)(b)(f)(i)(m)(p)**
Oct	97,115	121,392	21,728 (s)	**143,119 (s)**	**240,234 (s)**	**984,905**	1,244,394	**2,229,299**
Nov	96,085	119,199	22,446	**141,645**	**237,730**	**990,066**	1,248,085	**2,238,151**
Dec	93,558	96,053	21,801	**117,854**	**211,412**	**965,510**	1,256,079	**2,221,590**
2018 Jan	98,445	118,292	21,508	**139,799**	**238,245**	**989,901 (e)(j)(l)**	1,244,650	**2,234,551 (e)(j)(l)**
Feb	100,662	119,648	21,281	**140,929**	**241,591**	**985,060**	1,248,137	**2,233,197**
Mar	94,794	85,018	21,777	**106,795**	**201,588**	**945,897**	1,260,847	**2,206,744**
Apr	95,664	91,421 (q)	21,250	**112,671 (q)**	**208,335 (q)**	**952,205 (q)**	1,259,138	**2,211,343 (q)**

Source: Bank of England

12.5a Industrial analysis of monetary financial institutions' deposits from UK residents

£ millions Not seasonally adjusted

Notes to table

Movements in amounts outstanding can reflect breaks in data series as well as underlying flows. For changes data, users are recommended to refer directly to the appropriate series or data tables. www.bankofengland.co.uk/statistics/Pages/iadb/notesiadb/Changes_flows_growth_rates.aspx.

(a) Due to improvements in reporting by one institution, amounts outstanding increased by £1bn. This amount has been adjusted out of the flows for September 2017.
(b) Due to improvements in reporting by one institution, amounts outstanding increased by £1bn. This amount has been adjusted out of the flows for September 2017.
(d) Due to improvements in reporting by one institution, amounts outstanding decreased by £1 billion. This amount has been adjusted out of the flows for October 2017.
(e) Due to improvements in reporting at one institution, the amounts outstanding increased by £1bn. This effect has been adjusted out of the flows for January 2018.
(f) Due to improvements in reporting by one institution, amounts outstanding increased by £1bn. This amount has been adjusted out of the flows for September 2017.
(g) Previously, this series formed part of other financial intermediaries.
(h) Due to improvements in reporting at one institution, the amounts outstanding increased by £3bn. This effect has been adjusted out of the flows for February 2017.
(i) Due to a change in group structure by one reporting institution, the amounts outstanding increased by £6bn. This amount has been adjusted out of the flows for September 2017.
(j) Due to improvements in reporting at one institution, the amounts outstanding increased by £4bn. This effect has been adjusted out of the flows for January 2018.
(l) Due to improvements in reporting at one institution, the amounts outstanding decreased by £4bn. This effect has been adjusted out of the flows for January 2018.
(m) Due to improvements in reporting by one institution, amounts outstanding increased by £1 bn. This amount has been adjusted out of the flows for September 2017.
(n) Due to improvements in reporting at one institution, the amounts outstanding increased by £2bn. This effect has been adjusted out of the flows for February 2017.
(o) Due to reporting improvements at one institution, amounts outstanding increased by £1bn. This has been adjusted out of flows for March 2017.
(p) Due to improvements in reporting by one institution, amounts outstanding increased by £4 bn. This amount has been adjusted out of the flows for September 2017.
(q) Due to improvements in reporting at one institution, the amounts outstanding decreased by £2bn. This effect has been adjusted out of the flows for April 2018.
(s) Due to improvements in reporting by one institution, amounts outstanding increased by £1 billion. This amount has been adjusted out of the flows for October 2017.

Explanatory notes can be found here: http://www.bankofengland.co.uk/statistics/Pages/iadb/notesiadb/industrial.aspx

12.5b Industrial analysis of monetary financial institutions' deposits from UK residents

£ millions | Not seasonally adjusted

Amounts outstanding of deposit liabilities (including under repo) in all currencies

	Agriculture, hunting and forestry	Fishing	Mining and quarrying	Manufacturing									Electricity, gas and water supply			
				Food, beverages and tobacco	Textiles, wearing apparel and leather	Pulp, paper, and printing	Chemicals, pharma-ceuticals, rubber and plastics	Non-metallic mineral products and metals	Machinery, equipment and transport equipment	Electrical, medical and optical equipment	Other manu-facturing	**Total**	Electricity, gas steam and air conditioning	Water collection and sewerage	Waste management related services and remediation activities	Total
RPM	TDAB	TDAC	TDAD	TDAF	TDAG	TDAH	TDAI	TDAJ	TDAK	TDAL	TDAM	TDAE	TDAN	TDAO	BE2N	B3FJ
2016 Jan	6,384	256	21,783	5,110	1,686	2,153	10,716	7,107	13,086	7,421	5,473	**52,751**	6,057	2,231	1,627	**9,915**
Feb	6,368	284	11,922	4,645	1,602	2,163	11,163	7,113	13,769	7,193	5,769	**53,417**	6,695	2,334	1,656	**10,685**
Mar	6,320	289	12,480	4,812	1,602	2,064	10,990	6,990	14,004	6,979	5,916	**53,356**	7,363	2,304	1,909	**11,576**
Apr	6,345	285	11,713	4,770	1,578	2,112	10,426	6,970	13,209	6,695	6,062	**51,822**	7,103	2,170	1,691	**10,964**
May	6,352	289	14,406	5,051	1,645	2,168	11,236	7,145	12,610	6,885	5,988	**52,727**	7,636	2,362	1,673	**11,671**
Jun	6,392	282	14,716	5,378	1,774	2,368	12,007	9,719	14,140	7,068	6,067	**58,520**	7,591	2,496	1,828	**11,916**
Jul	6,373	286	14,540	4,954	1,756	2,114	10,635	7,398	13,033	6,980	6,284	**53,154**	7,671	2,094	1,861	**11,627**
Aug	6,323	318	15,370	5,447	1,756	2,084	11,068	7,428	13,344	7,084	5,797	**54,007**	7,079	2,047	2,021	**11,147**
Sep	6,352	315	21,457	5,484	1,643	1,983	11,024	7,475	13,455	7,235	5,833	**54,132**	7,066	2,303	1,977	**11,346**
Oct	6,437	323	19,552	4,704	1,725	2,048	11,573	7,728	13,752	7,677	6,031	**55,238**	7,986	2,419	2,022	**12,427**
Nov	6,609	365	21,657	5,105	1,874	2,115	11,254	7,676	13,818	7,595	5,949	**55,386**	7,929	2,446	1,919	**12,293**
Dec	7,427	384	22,565	5,106	2,005	2,137	11,609	7,775	15,545	7,863	6,398	**58,438**	7,725	2,662	1,955	**12,342**
2017 Jan	7,234	380	21,176	4,979	1,720	2,046	11,444	7,699	14,188	7,685	5,974	**55,735**	7,747	2,758	1,985	**12,490**
Feb	7,089	416	22,134	4,866	1,535	2,028	10,574	7,544	14,630	7,272	5,879	**54,329**	7,483	2,454	2,076	**12,013**
Mar	7,142	421	21,866	4,798	1,652	2,139	10,872	7,472	15,210	7,457	6,287	**55,887**	9,067	2,129	2,066	**13,262**
Apr	7,074	400	18,858 (ai)	4,740	1,622	2,073	10,931	7,228	14,529	7,503	5,958	**54,585**	8,958	2,147	1,942	**13,048**
May	7,086	391	19,481	5,304	1,670	1,952	12,014	7,253	15,019	7,841	6,089	**57,141**	9,124	2,518	1,974	**13,616**
Jun	7,113	389	23,140	6,928	1,703	1,984	11,547	7,159	16,123	7,739	6,224	**59,406**	7,748	2,723	2,044	**12,515**
Jul	7,076	393	21,901	5,542	1,631	2,196	11,535	7,171	15,130	7,749	6,405	**57,359**	8,102	2,425	2,033	**12,561**
Aug	7,112	402	24,136	6,222	1,660	1,995	10,783	7,521	14,161	8,300	6,805	**57,447**	8,636	2,211	2,008	**12,855**
Sep	7,189	419	23,120	5,496	1,654	1,968	11,074	7,532	15,554 (aj)	8,397	6,376	**58,050 (aj)**	7,713	2,193	2,025	**11,932**
Oct	7,497	415	23,134	5,679	1,721	2,309	10,887	7,533	15,776	8,685	6,415	**59,005**	7,195	2,413	1,972	**11,579**
Nov	7,462	454	23,879	5,747	1,844	2,186	11,381	7,693	16,800	8,882	6,879	**61,413**	7,396	2,720	2,143	**12,259**
Dec	8,312	420	23,469	5,884	1,643	2,296	11,322	7,583	17,011	9,225	6,718	**61,683**	6,831	2,902	2,107	**11,840**
2018 Jan	7,963	415	20,453	5,569	1,627	2,329	10,956	7,227	15,458	9,023	6,277	**58,466**	6,715	2,608	2,240	**11,563**
Feb	7,922	430	21,777	5,255	1,528	2,058	11,115	7,067	14,943	8,561	6,032	**56,559**	7,166	2,881	2,260	**12,307**
Mar	7,915	424	20,337	5,307	1,489	2,027	11,673	7,082	16,225	8,461	6,113	**58,376**	7,972	2,572	2,195	**12,739**
Apr	7,787	401	17,676	4,928	1,497	2,195	10,710	7,225	15,823	8,746	6,061	**57,186**	6,873	2,531	2,208	**11,612**

Source: Bank of England

12.5b Industrial analysis of monetary financial institutions' deposits from UK residents

£ millions | Not seasonally adjusted

Amounts outstanding of deposit liabilities (including under repo) in all currencies

	Construction						Wholesale and retail trade				Accom-modation and food service activities	Transport, storage and communication		
	Development of buildings	Construction of commercial buildings	Construction of domestic buildings	Civil Engineering	Other construction activities	**Total**	Wholesale and retail trade and repair of motor vehicles and motorcycles	Wholesale trade, excluding motor vehicles and motor cycles	Retail trade excluding motor vehicles and motor cycles	**Total**		Transportation and storage	Information and communication	Total
RPM	**B3FX**	**B7EL**	**B3LT**	**B4PG**	**B4PT**	**TDAP**	**TDAR**	**TDAS**	**TDAT**	**TDAQ**	**TDAU**	**B5PG**	**B3NJ**	**TDAV**
2016 Jan	7,834	3,846	3,617	5,688	11,403	**32,388**	5,444	20,135	17,257	**42,836**	8,364	17,166	27,846	**45,012**
Feb	7,833	3,916	3,661	5,822	11,238	**32,471**	5,961	20,605	18,297	**44,864**	8,454	17,254	31,332	**48,586**
Mar	8,179	4,121	3,659	6,215	11,388	**33,562**	5,845	20,514	17,861	**44,220**	8,797	17,120	32,020	**49,140**
Apr	8,013	4,085	3,620	5,834	11,549	**33,101**	5,895	19,905	17,987	**43,788**	8,395	16,280	29,775	**46,055**
May	7,939	4,177	3,650	5,807	11,635	**33,209**	6,158	19,883	19,281	**45,322**	8,822	16,629	29,706	**46,335**
Jun	8,277	4,566	4,668	6,082	12,127	**35,719**	6,748	20,330	18,473	**45,552**	8,970	17,037	30,017	**47,054**
Jul	8,198	4,419	4,219	5,963	12,175	**34,974**	6,337	20,625	18,487	**45,449**	9,266	16,397	30,838	**47,235**
Aug	8,190	4,475	4,092	6,266	12,448	**35,471**	6,636	21,166	19,693	**47,495**	9,882	16,361	29,936	**46,297**
Sep	8,330	4,702	4,359	5,980	12,744	**36,115**	6,346	23,044	17,998	**47,388**	9,755	16,926	29,652	**46,578**
Oct	8,356	4,857	4,305	6,269	13,054	**36,839**	6,789	23,770	17,500	**48,059**	10,150	16,938	31,448	**48,386**
Nov	8,219	4,592	4,527	6,474	13,375	**37,188**	6,736	22,711	20,265	**49,711**	10,398	18,490	30,419	**48,909**
Dec	8,690	5,003	5,107	6,752	13,652	**39,204**	6,479	24,935	22,475	**53,889**	9,630	16,485	30,647	**47,132**
2017 Jan	8,905	4,576	4,418	6,656	12,941	**37,495**	6,249	22,925	20,038	**49,212**	9,013	16,596	31,199	**47,794**
Feb	8,475	4,557	4,641	6,424	12,628	**36,724**	6,444	22,875	19,950	**49,270**	9,160	16,887	31,891	**48,779**
Mar	9,005	5,102	4,811	7,066	13,044	**39,029**	7,104	24,385	18,679	**50,168**	9,388	17,204	32,445	**49,649**
Apr	8,954	4,893	4,846	7,099	13,077	**38,869**	6,808	25,252 (ak)	17,926	**49,986 (ak)**	9,718	17,134	31,565	**48,699**
May	8,909	5,148	4,907	7,029	13,295	**39,289**	6,893	26,736	19,443	**53,072**	9,929	17,350	32,206	**49,556**
Jun	9,094	5,281	5,913	7,489	13,508	**41,285**	7,017	26,444	19,761	**53,222**	9,948	17,221	33,843	**51,064**
Jul	9,214	5,283	5,335	7,052	13,557	**40,441**	6,959	25,869	18,783	**51,612**	10,503	16,915	35,698	**52,613**
Aug	9,595	5,583	5,628	7,063	13,789	**41,657**	6,893	27,426	19,861	**54,180**	11,092	17,386	35,800	**53,186**
Sep	9,247	6,011	5,803	6,891	13,895	**41,846**	6,962	26,781	20,026 (al)	**53,770 (al)**	10,854	18,643	36,252	**54,895**
Oct	9,368	6,392	6,257	6,713	14,211	**42,940**	7,056	27,854	18,852	**53,762**	11,130	17,947	35,667 (ao)	**53,614 (ao)**
Nov	9,855	6,411	5,858	6,941	14,270	**43,335**	6,970	27,799	21,434	**56,203**	11,256	19,688	35,894	**55,582**
Dec	9,893	6,439	6,679	7,301	14,421	**44,732**	6,573	27,852	23,696	**58,121**	10,427	18,296	36,901	**55,197**
2018 Jan	9,780	5,614	6,017	6,971	14,059	**42,442**	6,825	25,971	19,400	**52,196**	10,142	17,253	36,537	**53,790**
Feb	9,777	5,705	5,901	6,924	13,685	**41,991**	6,910	25,901	21,191	**54,001**	10,051	17,026	37,477	**54,503**
Mar	9,885	6,219	6,172	7,072	13,865	**43,212**	6,994	25,836	20,256	**53,086**	9,558	17,141	37,149	**54,290**
Apr	10,013	5,889	5,931	6,771	14,051	**42,655**	7,306	27,055	19,622	**53,983**	9,938	19,225	36,832	**56,057**

Source: Bank of England

12.5b Industrial analysis of monetary financial institutions' deposits from UK residents

£ millions — Not seasonally adjusted — Not seasonally adjusted

Amounts outstanding of deposit liabilities (including under repo) in all currencies

	Real estate, professional services and support activities							Recreational, personal and community service activities			Financial intermediation (excluding insurance and pension funds)				
	Buying, selling and renting of real estate	Professional, scientific and technical activities	Administrative and support services	**Total**	Public administration and defence	Education	Human health and social work	Recreational, cultural and sporting activities	Personal and community service activities	**Total**	Financial leasing corporations	Non-bank credit grantors excluding credit unions and SPVs	Credit unions	Factoring corporations	Mortgage and housing credit corporations excluding SPVs
RPM	TDAX	B3TK	B6PL	TDAW	TDBB	TDBC	TDBD	TDBF	TDBE	B3S7	TDBH	TDBI	TDBJ	TDBK	TDBL
2016 Jan	42,621	79,936	26,592	**149,148**	34,061	20,554	20,053	12,618	18,917	**31,536**	9,585	3,616	1,060	1,031	9,458
Feb	41,771	80,519	27,701	**149,992**	32,719	20,964	20,250	12,724	19,240	**31,964**	9,753	3,872	1,090	942	9,437
Mar	44,780	87,206	29,485	**161,471**	27,841	19,742	20,279	12,888	19,049	**31,937**	9,678	3,886	1,104	1,055	8,969
Apr	43,007	78,612	29,110	**150,728**	37,132	20,844	20,445	12,744	19,194	**31,938**	9,756	4,260	1,105	1,144	9,097
May	42,553	79,946	30,173	**152,671**	35,995	22,788	20,720	12,855	19,091	**31,945**	9,705	3,861	1,101	1,122	8,950
Jun	45,611	82,683	32,442	**160,736**	36,638	21,976	21,102	13,430	19,001	**32,431**	9,169	4,301	1,080	1,021	9,109
Jul	43,958	82,118	32,185	**158,261**	37,301	21,059	21,267	13,932	19,005	**32,937**	9,160	4,167	1,069	986	8,950
Aug	43,360	81,653	33,103	**158,117**	37,839	20,743	21,326	13,593	19,004	**32,596**	9,060	4,215	1,079	1,025	8,251
Sep	46,089	82,201	33,195	**161,486**	32,081	21,842	21,343	13,824	18,918	**32,742**	8,823	4,206	1,099	1,178	8,907
Oct	44,073	83,038	33,119	**160,229**	34,460	23,149	21,337	13,684	19,231	**32,916**	9,447	4,376	1,114	993	8,969
Nov	43,633	83,839	32,075	**159,547**	33,634	21,746	21,855	13,744	19,248	**32,991**	8,980	4,411	1,074	951	8,874
Dec	46,947	82,667	32,112	**161,726**	32,087	20,592	22,195	14,258	19,052	**33,311**	8,926	4,359	1,054	1,137	7,556
2017 Jan	44,721	82,465	32,054	**159,240**	31,663	21,637	21,854	14,612	19,222	**33,834**	8,520	4,413	1,062	944	7,648
Feb	44,497	82,290	32,192	**158,979**	31,018	21,835	22,189	14,608	19,202	**33,810**	8,278	4,075	1,063	942	4,048
Mar	47,351	84,952	33,848	**166,151**	27,917	20,375	22,247	14,663	19,646	**34,309**	8,254	4,135	1,063	870	8,122
Apr	46,207	83,711	33,482	**163,400**	30,330	21,769	22,029	14,116	19,565	**33,681**	8,025	4,120	1,084	943	7,681
May	46,779	86,894	34,777	**168,450**	32,415	23,819	22,273	14,249	19,799	**34,048**	8,219	4,447	1,083	1,034	7,139
Jun	49,448	90,210	35,323	**174,981**	32,746	22,920	22,810	14,389	19,733	**34,122**	8,583	4,093	1,069	1,323	6,914
Jul	47,744	88,012	35,634	**171,390**	39,696 (as)	21,702	22,602	15,121	19,734	**34,855**	8,524	4,981	1,070	1,406	7,014
Aug	47,781	88,811	35,928	**172,520**	40,371	21,599	22,683	15,279	20,036	**35,315**	9,148	5,033	1,076	1,277	6,635
Sep	50,782	88,625	37,061	**176,467**	33,481 (at)	22,823	22,352	14,844	19,955	**34,800**	8,684	4,739	1,062	1,110	6,777
Oct	49,031	88,614	37,738	**175,383**	36,871	23,812	22,787	14,954	20,019	**34,972**	8,957	4,616	1,063	985	6,123
Nov	49,225	90,844	38,930	**178,999**	36,026	22,632	22,837	14,883	19,832	**34,714**	8,450	4,941	1,035	992	6,153
Dec	52,524	87,071	37,675	**177,270**	34,264	21,359	22,701	15,794	20,049	**35,842**	8,506	4,865	1,042	535	5,983
2018 Jan	49,616	87,808	39,595 (aq)	**177,019 (aq)**	35,871	22,505	22,294	16,326	20,012	**36,338**	8,302	5,713	1,051	1,015	5,922
Feb	49,243	87,440	39,952	**176,635**	34,932	22,771	22,282	15,881	19,664	**35,545**	8,649	5,467	1,072	1,449	5,774
Mar	52,412	87,794	39,169	**179,375**	29,596	21,574	22,558	16,084	19,881	**35,965**	7,698	5,516	1,084	1,248	5,835
Apr	51,406	89,273	39,047	**179,726**	30,777	22,475	22,444	15,839	19,898	**35,737**	7,947	5,660	1,087	1,023	5,772

Source: Bank of England

12.5b Industrial analysis of monetary financial institutions' deposits from UK residents

£ millions Not seasonally adjusted

Amounts outstanding of deposit liabilities (including under repo) in all currencies

	Financial intermediation (excluding insurance and pension funds) (contd.)								Insurance companies & pension funds		
	Investment and unit trusts excluding money market mutual funds	Money market mutual funds	Bank holding companies	Securities dealers	SPVs related to securitisation	Other financial intermediaries	of which intragroup activity	**Total**	Insurance companies	Pension funds	**Total**
RPM	**TDBM**	**TDBN**	**TDBO**	**TDBP**	**B3T6**	**TDBQ**	**B3U4**	**TDBG**	**B3V2**	**B7FO**	**TDBR**
2016 Jan	25,802	1,184	49,779	93,021	102,005	102,266	71,114	**398,806**	29,208	29,451	**58,659**
Feb	27,185	972	51,441	93,430	102,719	101,482	71,948	**402,325**	28,925	30,066	**58,991**
Mar	26,194	1,069	61,005	90,293	100,951	99,342	70,926	**403,546**	30,218	24,482	**54,700**
Apr	25,571	773	54,987	93,058	99,800	95,885	67,932	**395,437**	28,038	26,564	**54,602**
May	25,175	1,038	58,304	86,144	102,703	95,377	67,638	**393,479**	28,843	25,247	**54,089**
Jun	28,315	1,115	63,499	91,842	102,752	99,164	70,343	**411,367**	31,190	26,905	**58,095**
Jul	27,530	1,614	73,286	97,258	98,229	98,459	68,484	**420,710**	32,452	27,163	**59,614**
Aug	26,710	760	84,961	90,317	95,023	102,584	71,512	**423,984**	31,902	25,347	**57,249**
Sep	29,577	550	87,782	100,571	93,776	100,037	69,595	**436,506**	35,305	29,124	**64,429**
Oct	27,992	678	90,970	102,289	98,355	97,767	66,386	**442,949**	34,268	30,806	**65,074**
Nov	27,840	748	87,726	109,995	98,498	95,162	64,232	**444,259**	34,639	29,283	**63,923**
Dec	28,388	1,639	87,846	92,642	97,430	91,925	61,253	**422,900**	34,272	29,893	**64,164**
2017 Jan	27,286	898	97,072	99,934	90,715	90,697	60,955	**429,190**	33,530	31,106	**64,637**
Feb	26,805	1,066	98,909	92,825	86,365 (av)	94,261 (ax)	62,919 (ax)	**418,637 (av)(ax)**	32,788	31,453	**64,241**
Mar	29,035	418	89,221	96,233	87,356	94,401	63,427	**419,110**	34,838	33,673	**68,511**
Apr	30,613	684	87,521	96,984	85,593	96,443	66,999	**419,691**	32,206	33,362	**65,568**
May	29,903	927	92,346	92,149	84,330	99,253	69,100	**420,830**	32,496	35,026	**67,521**
Jun	30,767	739	94,320	101,383	86,096	95,647	64,518	**430,933**	32,036	33,172	**65,208**
Jul	30,140	900	93,128	89,461	86,492	97,137	67,578	**420,251**	30,429	33,625	**64,053**
Aug	30,124	2,327	95,054	91,971	84,299	96,872	67,405	**423,815**	31,751	31,936	**63,687**
Sep	30,983	1,188	85,927	95,435	91,917 (aw)	96,359	67,495	**424,180 (aw)**	31,706	32,653	**64,359**
Oct	31,215	1,155	80,282	98,586	90,876	96,343	68,819	**420,201**	32,235	32,391	**64,625**
Nov	32,248	1,191	76,020	110,216	92,005	94,648	65,842	**427,899**	32,459	31,858	**64,316**
Dec	34,138	1,628	76,856	102,562	92,114	92,404	64,317	**420,632**	32,590	34,018	**66,608**
2018 Jan	35,044	947	86,118	105,781	89,919	96,559 (ay)(az)	65,903	**436,369 (ay)(az)**	26,761 (bb)	36,103	**62,864**
Feb	35,090	897	88,075	106,305	89,754	88,291	58,236	**430,823**	26,081	35,455	**61,536**
Mar	34,335	1,003	90,833	104,363	92,179	83,563	52,015	**427,657**	26,501	37,076	**63,578**
Apr	34,318	763	87,226	119,552	91,738	84,417	53,721	**439,503**	26,246	36,080	**62,325**

Source: Bank of England

12.5b Industrial analysis of monetary financial institutions' deposits from UK residents

£ millions | Not seasonally adjusted

Amounts outstanding of deposit liabilities (including under repo) in all currencies

	Activities auxiliary to financial intermediation							
	Fund management activities	Other			Total	Total financial and non-financial businesses	Individuals and individuals trusts	Total UK residents
		Central clearing counterparties	Other auxiliary activities	Total				
RPM	TDBS	B7FU	B7FZ	TDBT	B5H5	Z8ZX	TDBU	TDAA
2016 Jan	153,437	127,205	26,213	**153,418**	**306,855**	**1,239,361**	1,157,062	**2,396,423**
Feb	162,933	135,008	27,851	**162,860**	**325,792**	**1,260,047**	1,162,923	**2,422,970**
Mar	159,546	120,337	28,874	**149,210**	**308,756**	**1,248,013**	1,174,327	**2,422,340**
Apr	162,821	122,689	27,853	**150,542**	**313,363**	**1,236,957**	1,189,615	**2,426,572**
May	168,929	126,645	28,854	**155,499**	**324,428**	**1,255,249**	1,189,373	**2,444,623**
Jun	178,535	136,880	29,963	**166,844**	**345,378**	**1,316,844**	1,195,795	**2,512,638**
Jul	188,679	147,501	29,597	**177,098**	**365,777**	**1,339,830**	1,204,337	**2,544,167**
Aug	191,104	165,566	30,536	**196,102**	**387,206**	**1,365,371**	1,205,199	**2,570,570**
Sep	186,301	133,809	31,573	**165,382**	**351,683**	**1,355,549**	1,215,627	**2,571,176**
Oct	190,781	152,317	31,449	**183,765**	**374,546**	**1,392,071**	1,217,645	**2,609,715**
Nov	181,348	167,885	31,685	**199,570**	**380,917**	**1,401,388**	1,218,291	**2,619,679**
Dec	178,128	138,410	31,682	**170,091**	**348,220**	**1,356,208**	1,226,995	**2,583,203**
2017 Jan	183,825	174,364	31,736	**206,100**	**389,926**	**1,392,510**	1,215,497	**2,608,007**
Feb	200,346	192,734 (bf)(bg)	31,129	**223,862 (bf)(bg)**	**424,208 (bf)(bg)**	**1,414,830 (av)(**	1,221,710	**2,636,540 (av)(ax)(bf)(bg)**
Mar	203,155	172,233 (bh)	33,262	**205,495 (bh)**	**408,650 (bh)**	**1,414,081 (bh)**	1,231,928	**2,646,009 (bh)**
Apr	204,287	192,878	32,382	**225,260**	**429,547**	**1,427,251**	1,237,522	**2,664,773**
May	198,177	188,175	33,056	**221,231**	**419,409**	**1,438,324**	1,233,782	**2,672,105**
Jun	202,926	163,691	33,979	**197,669**	**400,595**	**1,442,397**	1,242,492	**2,684,890**
Jul	208,199 (bc)	191,754 (bi)	33,872	**225,626 (bi)**	**433,825 (bc)(bi)**	**1,462,831 (as)(l**	1,241,146	**2,703,977 (as)(bc)(bi)**
Aug	210,775	207,905	34,084	**241,989**	**452,764**	**1,494,822**	1,244,336	**2,739,158**
Sep	205,683 (bd)	194,028 (bj)	34,866	**228,894 (bj)**	**434,577 (bd)(bj)**	**1,475,114 (aj)(a**	1,252,645	**2,727,759 (aj)(al)(at)(aw)(bd)(bj)**
Oct	217,344	214,376	34,681 (bn)	**249,058 (bn)**	**466,402 (bn)**	**1,508,130**	1,253,086	**2,761,216**
Nov	215,687	218,677	31,867	**250,544**	**466,231**	**1,525,498**	1,256,786	**2,782,284**
Dec	209,518	178,011	31,575	**209,586**	**419,104**	**1,471,982**	1,265,255	**2,737,237**
2018 Jan	221,622 (be)	212,190	31,496	**243,686**	**465,308 (be)**	**1,515,996 (aq)(**	1,253,408	**2,769,404 (aq)(ay)(az)(bb)(be)**
Feb	227,583	215,840	30,457	**246,296**	**473,879**	**1,517,945**	1,257,097	**2,775,042**
Mar	218,604	163,867	32,787	**196,654**	**415,259**	**1,455,498**	1,269,716	**2,725,214**
Apr	207,641	185,524 (bk)	32,155	**217,679 (bk)**	**425,320 (bk)**	**1,475,603 (bk)**	1,268,195	**2,743,798 (bk)**

Source: Bank of England

12.5b Industrial analysis of monetary financial institutions' deposits from UK residents

£ millions

Not seasonally adjusted

Notes to table

Movements in amounts outstanding can reflect breaks in data series as well as underlying flows. For changes data, users are recommended to refer directly to the appropriate series or data tables. www.bankofengland.co.uk/statistics/Pages/iadb/notesiadb/Changes_flows_growth_rates.aspx.

(ai) Due to reporting improvements at one institution, amounts outstanding decreased by £2 billion. This has been adjusted out of the flows for April 2017.
(aj) Due to improvements in reporting by one institution, amounts outstanding increased by £1bn. This amount has been adjusted out of the flows for September 2017.
(ak) Due to reporting improvements at one institution, amounts outstanding increased by £2 billion. This has been adjusted out of the flows for April 2017.
(al) Due to improvements in reporting by one institution, amounts outstanding increased by £1bn. This amount has been adjusted out of the flows for September 2017.
(ao) Due to improvements in reporting by one institution, amounts outstanding decreased by £1 billion. This amount has been adjusted out of the flows for October 2017.
(aq) Due to improvements in reporting at one institution, the amounts outstanding increased by £1bn. This effect has been adjusted out of the flows for January 2018.
(as) Due to a transfer of business by one reporting institution, the amounts outstanding increased by £1bn. This effect has been adjusted out of the flows for July 2017.
(at) Due to improvements in reporting by one institution, amounts outstanding increased by £1bn. This amount has been adjusted out of the flows for September 2017.
(au) Previously, this series formed part of other financial intermediaries.
(av) Due to improvements in reporting at one institution, the amounts outstanding increased by £3bn. This effect has been adjusted out of the flows for February 2017.
(aw) Due to a change in group structure by one reporting institution, the amounts outstanding increased by £6bn. This amount has been adjusted out of the flows for September 2017.
(ax) Due to improvements in reporting at one institution, the amounts outstanding decreased by £1bn. This effect has been adjusted out of the flows for February 2017.
(ay) Due to improvements in reporting at one institution, the amounts outstanding increased by £2bn. This effect has been adjusted out of the flows for January 2018.
(az) Due to improvements in reporting at one institution, the amounts outstanding increased by £4bn. This effect has been adjusted out of the flows for January 2018.
(bb) Due to improvements in reporting at one institution, the amounts outstanding decreased by £4bn. This effect has been adjusted out of the flows for January 2018.
(bc) Due to a transfer of business by one reporting institution, the amounts outstanding increased by £1bn. This effect has been adjusted out of the flows for July 2017.
(bd) Due to improvements in reporting by one institution, amounts outstanding increased by £1 bn. This amount has been adjusted out of the flows for September 2017.
(be) Due to improvements in reporting at one institution, the amounts outstanding decreased by £2bn. This effect has been adjusted out of the flows for January 2018.
(bf) Due to improvements in reporting at one institution, the amounts outstanding increased by £2bn. This effect has been adjusted out of the flows for February 2017.
(bg) Due to improvements in reporting at one institution, the amounts outstanding increased by £4bn. This effect has been adjusted out of the flows for February 2017.
(bh) Due to reporting improvements at one institution, amounts outstanding increased by £1bn. This has been adjusted out of flows for March 2017.
(bi) Due to a transfer of business by one reporting institution, the amounts outstanding increased by £6bn. This effect has been adjusted out of the flows for July 2017.
(bj) Due to improvements in reporting by one institution, amounts outstanding increased by £4 bn. This amount has been adjusted out of the flows for September 2017.
(bk) Due to improvements in reporting at one institution, the amounts outstanding decreased by £2bn. This effect has been adjusted out of the flows for April 2018.
(bn) Due to improvements in reporting by one institution, amounts outstanding increased by £1 billion. This amount has been adjusted out of the flows for October 2017.

Explanatory notes can be found here: http://www.bankofengland.co.uk/statistics/Pages/iadb/notesiadb/industrial.aspx

12.6a Components of M4

£ millions Seasonally adjusted

Amounts outstanding

	Retail deposits and cash in M4			Wholesale deposits in M4		**M4**	**M3**
	Deposits	Notes and coin	**Total**	Deposits	of which repos		**(estimate of EMU aggregate for the UK)**
LPM	B3SF	VQJO	VQWK **(a)**	VRGP	VZZQ	AUYN	VWYZ
2016 Aug	1,534,555	71,034	1,605,590	616,095	93,634	2,235,463	2,588,747
Sep	1,544,929	71,202	1,616,132	611,401	87,796	2,225,093	2,605,501
Oct	1,549,974	71,982	1,621,955	623,376	99,289	2,250,976	2,640,027
Nov	1,552,151	72,346	1,624,497	625,648	112,821	2,260,972	2,636,981
Dec	1,557,469	72,143	1,629,611	620,596	103,685	2,248,868	2,641,111
2017 Jan	1,558,669	73,523	1,632,192	636,058	122,457	2,270,907	2,661,279
Feb	1,558,876	73,434	**1,632,311**	628,200 (f)	116,732	**2,267,362 (f)**	**2,682,272 (f)(p)**
Mar	1,570,472	73,651	**1,644,123**	652,160	130,790	**2,281,422**	**2,708,094**
Apr	1,575,439	73,443	**1,648,881**	674,161	141,354	**2,311,119**	**2,731,231**
May	1,578,104	73,690	**1,651,795**	658,925	130,963	**2,305,327**	**2,723,720**
Jun	1,584,477	73,618	**1,658,095**	655,643	129,723	**2,303,194**	**2,735,547**
Jul	1,586,531 (b)	73,687	**1,660,217 (b)**	649,114	128,080	**2,313,357 (b)**	**2,741,782 (b)(q)**
Aug	1,592,998	74,163	**1,667,162**	658,856	129,715	**2,338,047**	**2,775,103**
Sep	1,596,471	73,824	**1,670,295**	683,740 (g)(h)	147,148 (m)	**2,351,112 (g)(h)**	**2,786,224 (g)(h)**
Oct	1,599,409	73,809	**1,673,218**	684,006	148,573	**2,364,892**	**2,802,702**
Nov	1,605,733	73,532	**1,679,265**	681,330	141,244	**2,370,637**	**2,800,239**
Dec	1,607,160	73,087	**1,680,247**	678,571	144,344	**2,354,148**	**2,805,514**
2018 Jan	1,620,193 (c)	73,555	**1,693,748 (c)**	692,307 (i)	145,727	**2,393,177 (n)(o)**	**2,829,663 (o)(r)**
Feb	1,623,875	73,241	**1,697,116**	679,222	141,741	**2,383,794**	**2,820,094**
Mar	1,623,331 (d)	72,882	**1,696,212 (d)**	664,997 (j)	128,626	**2,350,138**	**2,785,611**
Apr	1,628,050	72,516	**1,700,567**	665,908	128,261	**2,359,304**	**2,795,332**

Notes to table Source: Bank of England

Movements in amounts outstanding can reflect breaks in data series as well as underlying flows. For changes and growth rates data, users are recommended to refer directly to the appropriate series or data tables. Further details can be found at https://www.bankofengland.co.uk/statistics/details/further-details-about-changes-flows-growth-rates-data.

(b) In order to bring reporting in line with the National Accounts, English housing associations were reclassified from PNFCs to public corporations with effect from July 2017 data. The amounts outstanding decreased by £3bn. This effect has been adjusted out of the flows for July 2017.

(c) Due to improvements in reporting at one institution, the amounts outstanding increased by £8bn. This effect has been adjusted out of the flows for January 2018.

(d) Due to improvements in reporting at one institution, the amounts outstanding decreased by £4bn. This effect has been adjusted out of the flows for March 2018.

(f) Due to improvements in reporting at one institution, the amounts outstanding increased by £3bn. This effect has been adjusted out of the flows for February 2017.

(g) Due to improvements in reporting by one institution, the amounts outstanding increased by £11bn. This amount has been adjusted out of the flows for September 2017.

(h) Due to a change in group structure by one reporting institution, the amounts outstanding increased by £6bn. This effect has been adjusted out of the flows for September 2017.

(i) Due to improvements in reporting at one institution, the amounts outstanding decreased by £8bn. This effect has been adjusted out of the flows for January 2018.

(j) Due to improvements in reporting at one institution, the amounts outstanding increased by £4bn. This effect has been adjusted out of the flows for March 2018.

(m) Due to improvements in reporting by one institution, the amounts outstanding increased by £5bn. This amount has been adjusted out of the flows for September 2017.

(n) Due to improvements in reporting at one institution, the amounts outstanding increased by £5bn. This effect has been adjusted out of the flows for January 2018.

(o) Due to improvements in reporting at one institution, the amounts outstanding decreased by £4bn. This effect has been adjusted out of the flows for January 2018.

(p) Due to improvements in reporting at one institution, the amounts outstanding increased by £4bn. This effect has been adjusted out of the flows for February 2017.

(q) Due to a transfer of business by one reporting institution, the amounts outstanding increased by £6bn. This effect has been adjusted out of the flows for July 2017.

(r) Due to improvements in reporting at one institution, the amounts outstanding increased by £5bn. This effect has been adjusted out of the flows for January 2018.

Explanatory notes can be found here: http://www.bankofengland.co.uk/statistics/details/further-details-about-m4-data

12.6b Components of M4

£ millions | Not seasonally adjusted

Changes

	Retail deposits and cash in M4					Wholesale deposits in M4		M4	M3
	Deposits			Notes and coin	Total	Deposits	of which repos		(estimate of EMU aggregate for the UK)
	Total	of which: Private non-financial corporations	of which: Household sector						
LPM	VRLW	Z599	Z59A	VQLU	VQZA	VRLR	VWDN	AUZI	VWXK
2016 Jan	**-10,121**	-7,372	-1,399	-889	**-11,009**	236	2,491	**-10,773**	**4,406**
Feb	**11,877**	528	4,168	276	**12,153**	7,726	2,704	**19,880**	**20,985**
Mar	**22,444**	7,658	11,061	605	**23,049**	-12,840	-7,892	**10,209**	**14,010**
Apr	**4,036**	-8,035	15,465	1,188	**5,224**	-10,169	3,297	**-4,945**	**2,692**
May	**6,085**	3,429	27	-13	**6,071**	17,305	4,155	**23,377**	**26,568**
Jun	**15,544**	8,271	5,914	374	**15,918**	16,882	-1,396	**32,800**	**38,732**
Jul	**6,313**	-2,295	6,774	1,663	**7,976**	14,014	14,004	**21,990**	**27,233**
Aug	**5,022**	3,055	-56	-428	**4,594**	12,460	8,877	**17,054**	**18,014**
Sep	**15,678**	5,210	9,581	1,075	**16,752**	-17,240	-16,919	**-488**	**-445**
Oct	**2,693**	90	1,909	921	**3,614**	17,662	19,384	**21,276**	**15,257**
Nov	**4,901**	1,504	940	292	**5,193**	6,063	14,388	**11,256**	**28,990**
Dec	**11,475**	3,197	8,135	1,621	**13,096**	-20,902	-20,844	**-7,806**	**-28,151**
2017 Jan	**-18,116**	-5,853	-10,767	-2,054	**-20,170**	21,120	26,351	**950**	**18,526**
Feb	**3,228**	-622	5,316	170	**3,399**	-4,261	-1,031	**-862**	**26,341**
Mar	**22,311**	8,180	8,157	861	**23,172**	7,016	-166	**30,188**	**17,935**
Apr	**3,399**	-1,447	7,788	825	**4,224**	21,617	15,039	**25,841**	**33,602**
May	**2,426**	3,704	-5,282	-822	**1,604**	-7,841	-8,436	**-6,237**	**-1,972**
Jun	**12,542**	6,545	8,897	631	**13,173**	-5,935	-7,925	**7,238**	**3,391**
Jul	**-2,163**	-2,620	-1,310	291	**-1,873**	-1,795	8,231	**-3,668**	**5,788**
Aug	**5,376**	3,072	590	-196	**5,180**	17,896	6,826	**23,076**	**23,680**
Sep	**10,575**	2,750	10,002	326	**10,901**	-4,344	-1,166	**6,556**	**8,030**
Oct	**691**	-949	4,108	-648	**43**	8,666	14,037	**8,710**	**18,116**
Nov	**4,952**	2,612	2,983	417	**5,369**	-639	-4,728	**4,730**	**22,380**
Dec	**5,909**	1,564	7,357	1,327	**7,237**	-18,366	-17,447	**-11,130**	**-42,248**
2018 Jan	**-15,461**	-6,557	-10,598	-2,988	**-18,449**	33,472	20,453	**15,023**	**47,150**
Feb	**2,624**	-230	3,921	-230	**2,393**	-7,353	-1,664	**-4,960**	**-8,934**
Mar	**20,282**	4,162	12,309	1,418	**21,699**	-33,920	-28,756	**-12,220**	**-33,548**
Apr	**912**	2,299	-1,109	-1,127	**-216**	-4,056	2,640	**-4,271**	**6,573**

Notes to table

Source: Bank of England

Explanatory notes can be found here: http://www.bankofengland.co.uk/statistics/details/further-details-about-m4-data

12.7 Counterparts to changes in M4: alternative presentation

£ millions — Not seasonally adjusted

Changes

	Public sector net cash requirement (PSNCR)	M4 private sector net purchases (-) of Central Government debt: Gilts	Sterling treasury bills	Tax instruments	National Savings	Other	Total	M4 private sector net purchases of other public sector debt: Local government debt (-)	Public corporation debt (-)	Other public sector purchases of M4 private sector debt (+)	Total
LPM	ABEN (g)	AVBY	VQLK	VQLG	VQLJ	VQLI	RCMD	VQLL	VQLO	VQLQ	AVBV
2016 Jan	-21,121	7,316	2,722	-17	107	-2,415	7,714	59	-	455	514
Feb	1,821	-6,781	2,880	241	-690	3,134	-1,216	311	-	-634	-323
Mar	23,519	346	-3,901	19	-571	-5,583	-9,691	503	-	-1,662	-1,159
Apr	-1,435	-11,782	5,328	-47	-1,004	1,564	-5,941	-443	-	1,884	1,441
May	8,268	-13,912	84	-65	957	3,162	-9,774	-31	-	-1	-32
Jun	18,150	-3,062	-6,804	-67	319	-3,740	-13,354	-177	-	1,207	1,030
Jul	2,253	-11,033	473	-85	-322	6,721	-4,246	-165	-	752	587
Aug	4,807	13,033	-12,305	44	-719	8,017	8,069	119	-	-311	-192
Sep	22,165	36,134	-5,454	-81	-977	-21,092	8,530	-11	-	217	206
Oct	-4,689	16,896	1,626	-67	-1,745	8,041	24,752	182	-	321	503
Nov	10,245	14,582	1,261	-181	-2,257	1,026	14,431	-192	-	-441	-633
Dec	21,608	-7,787	-4,737	-62	-2,063	-5,816	-20,464	9	-	-371	-362
2017 Jan	-27,125	2,893	6,913	-18	-1,688	9,668	17,767	-105	-	353	248
Feb	-3,114	-9,636	5,500	179	-1,551	4,527	-980	369	-	-1,200	-831
Mar	22,441	-5,603	6,902	72	-599	-11,235	-10,463	576	-	-1,946	-1,370
Apr	-17,659	-6,961	12,343	-74	-884	10,208	14,632	-444	-	1,532	1,088
May	9,730	-2,098	4,862	-61	-396	-6,601	-4,293	-191	-	-387	-578
Jun	17,627	-4,800	-1,896	-79	-348	-4,818	-11,941	-64	-	623	559
Jul	-10,680	-12,027	6,629	-55	-575	5,043	-985	-163	-	185	22
Aug	2,902	-2,049	-7,580	58	-610	6,545	-3,637	-33	-	179	146
Sep	18,943	23,701	-3,558	-130	-591	-15,712	3,709	-329	-	-94	-423
Oct	-7,426	-4,277	-454	-15	-808	16,124	10,570	182	-	87	269
Nov	12,665	-544	-6,722	-65	-809	-4,494	-12,634	-119	-	-919	-1,038
Dec	20,215	-10,527	-7,134	15	-1,651	-361	-19,659	-52	-	448	396
2018 Jan	-27,439	-9,593	15,853	40	-335	9,472	15,437	221	-	133	354
Feb	573	5,950	2,127	326	-1,444	7,031	13,990	258	-	-674	-416
Mar	21,680	2,408	-3,985	208	-1,137	-24,195	-26,701	99	-	-577	-478
Apr	-8,306	-1,577	4,429	22	-1,073	3,386	5,186	-576	-	1,094	518

£ millions — Not seasonally adjusted

Changes

	Purchases of public sector net debt (-)	External and foreign currency finance of public sector: Non-residents' purchases of gilts (-)	Non-residents' purchases of £TBs (-)	Other	Total	Public sector contribution	M4 lending: Loans	of which reverse repos	Investments	Total
LPM	VQLN	VQCZ	VRME	VQOC	VQDC	VWZL (h)	Z5MB	VWDP	VYAP (i)	BF37 (j)(k)
2016 Jan	8,228	6,273	-750	1,348	6,871	-6,022	8,092	-2,722	-1,468	6,624
Feb	-1,539	3,029	1,320	3,426	7,776	8,058	17,447	5,321	-39	17,408
Mar	-10,850	-7,811	189	-2,032	-9,654	3,014	8,566	2,289	-485	8,081
Apr	-4,500	-249	-75	-989	-1,313	-7,248	-14,454	-1,756	-565	-15,018
May	-9,806	-3,748	-32	1,993	-1,787	-3,326	14,988	15,064	-244	14,745
Jun	-12,323	-8,140	-842	1,081	-7,901	-2,075	21,105	11,484	849	21,954
Jul	-3,659	4,403	-870	1,201	4,734	3,327	7,536	-2,639	-4,573	2,964
Aug	7,877	-1,793	-117	3,864	1,955	14,638	8,521	-411	-3,839	4,682
Sep	8,736	-13,272	-1,996	-5,011	-20,279	10,623	6,893	4,696	639	7,532
Oct	25,254	-10,515	3,272	3,437	-3,805	16,760	4,432	5,379	-1,722 (k)	2,710
Nov	13,797	-15,577	479	1,582	-13,516	10,526	10,251	16,789	3,488	13,739
Dec	-20,827	2,970	2,470	-7	5,432	6,214	1,001	-6,051	-942	59
2017 Jan	18,015	7,574	815	-2,887	5,502	-3,608	11,269	6,372	29,824	41,093
Feb	-1,811	-758	2,142	3,774	5,159	234	-1,022	-3,805	-3,716	-4,738
Mar	-11,834	-218	1,522	-15	1,288	11,896	19,902	14,306	-1,009	18,893
Apr	15,721	-1,949	547	630	-772	-2,711	5,714	-381	6,068	11,782
May	-4,872	-8,384	539	-17	-7,862	-3,003	8,616	5,521	-1,683	6,933
Jun	-11,382	-1,104	-1,213	568	-1,749	4,496	9,669	2,083	3,821	13,490
Jul	-963	3,133	1,695	43	4,872	-6,772	2,607	-2,456	1,731	4,338
Aug	-3,490	-6,526	-2,882	623	-8,784	-9,373	16,117	5,090	-1,293	14,824
Sep	3,286	-3,591	-2,982	-973	-7,546	14,683	13,820	11,261	-2,627	11,193
Oct	10,839	-1,773	-554	-1,483	-3,810	-398	-8,207	-4,884	1,025	-7,182
Nov	-13,672	-8,649	-318	921	-8,045	-9,052	14,105	3,455	-1,744	12,362
Dec	-19,262	-488	-3,051	1,672	-1,867	-914	3,005	-1,842	-1,142	1,862
2018 Jan	15,791	9,299	3,531	1,077	13,907	2,259	2,364	-3,130	290	2,655
Feb	13,574	-11,565	-152	1,197	-10,520	3,627	-2,124	-4,997	-539	-2,663
Mar	-27,179	3,972	-1,405	536	3,103	-2,396	2,824	-9,614	-1,884	940
Apr	5,704	2,442	2,552	310	5,305	2,703	-1,665	-7,507	334	-1,332

12.7 Counterparts to changes in M4: alternative presentation

£ millions | Not seasonally adjusted

Changes

	External and foreign currency flows			Total	Net	M4
	Net sterling deposits from non-residents (-)	Net foreign currency liabilities (-)	**Total**	external counterparts	non-deposit £ liabilities (-)	
LPM	**B69P**	**B72P**	**AVBW**	**VQLP**	**VWZV**	**AUZI**
2016 Jan	3,175	-3,236	**-61**	6,810	-11,314	**-10,773**
Feb	19,776	-17,344	**2,431**	10,207	-8,018	**19,880**
Mar	-13,563	-45,943	**-59,506**	-69,160	58,619	**10,209**
Apr	7,571	-13,716	**-6,145**	-7,458	23,466	**-4,945**
May	19,451	-4,610	**14,841**	13,054	-2,883	**23,377**
Jun	-21,420	84,966	**63,546**	55,645	-50,625	**32,800**
Jul	6,266	-21,976	**-15,710**	-10,976	31,409	**21,990**
Aug	4,393	-16,223	**-11,830**	-9,876	9,563	**17,054**
Sep	6,604	-22,610	**-16,005**	-36,284	-2,637	**-488**
Oct	-13,510	55,417	**41,907**	38,102	-40,101	**21,276**
Nov	-1,093	-33,134	**-34,227**	-47,743	21,217	**11,256**
Dec	9,024	-10,030	**-1,005**	4,427	-13,074	**-7,806**
2017 Jan	5,397	-20,642	**-15,245**	-9,743	-21,290	**950**
Feb	-2,106	45,416	**43,309**	48,468	-39,667	**-862**
Mar	-4,814	-35,790	**-40,604**	-39,316	40,005	**30,188**
Apr	15,797	-37,448	**-21,651**	-22,423	38,420	**25,841**
May	-13,445	43,850	**30,405**	22,543	-40,571	**-6,237**
Jun	-11,281	3,002	**-8,278**	-10,028	-2,469	**7,238**
Jul	4,354	-15,776	**-11,422**	-6,550	10,188	**-3,668**
Aug	-4,992	34,451	**29,459**	20,675	-11,834	**23,076**
Sep	3,482	-30,739	**-27,257**	-34,803	7,938	**6,556**
Oct	11,133	9,082	**20,215**	16,405	-3,926	**8,710**
Nov	1,415	-17,146	**-15,731**	-23,776	17,152	**4,730**
Dec	-18,047	15,516	**-2,531**	-4,397	-9,547	**-11,130**
2018 Jan	21,894	-106,246	**-84,352**	-70,445	94,461	**15,023**
Feb	2,397	125,223	**127,620**	117,100	-133,544	**-4,960**
Mar	-17,639	-17,307	**-34,946**	-31,843	24,182	**-12,220**
Apr	4,545	91,547	**96,092**	101,397	-101,735	**-4,271**

Source: Bank of England

Notes to table

(g) This estimate of the Public Sector Net Cash Requirement may differ from the headline measure published by the Office for National Statistics (ONS). The Bank of England's measure is maintained to ensure the 'Alternative Counterparts' analysis continues to balance. More details on this can be found in article www.bankofengland.co.uk/statistics/Documents/ms/articles/art2may09.pdf.

(h) Net sterling lending to the public sector includes holdings of coin. Coin is a liability of Central Government and therefore outside of the MFIs' consolidated balance sheet. Holdings of coin are a component of M4 and are therefore included here in order to reconcile the counterparts.

(i) This series includes purchases of bonds made as part of the Bank of England's Corporate Bond Purchase Scheme. Data on Central Bank holdings of securities can be found in Bankstats Table B2.2. For further information on the Bank's treatment of securities transactions in credit statistics, see: www.bankofengland.co.uk/statistics/Documents/articles/2015/2may.pdf.

(j) Please note that the compilation and descriptions of some credit series have changed from publication of April 2015 data, as described in Bankstats, April 2015, 'Changes to the treatment of loan transfers and lending to housing associations', available at www.bankofengland.co.uk/statistics/Documents/ms/articles/art1apr15.pdf.

(k) This series includes purchases of bonds made as part of the Bank of England's Corporate Bond Purchase Scheme. Data on Central Bank holdings of securities can be found in Bankstats Table B2.2. For further information on the Bank's treatment of securities transactions in credit statistics, see: www.bankofengland.co.uk/statistics/Documents/articles/2015/2may.pdf.

Explanatory notes can be found here: http://www.bankofengland.co.uk/statistics/Pages/iadb/notesiadb/M4_counterparts.aspx

12.8 Selected retail banks' base rate

Daily average of 4 UK Banks' base rates, IUDAMIH [a]

Date of change	New rate	Date of change	New rate	Date of change	New rate
09-Jan-86	12.5	17-Sep-92	10.5	05-Jul-07	5.75
19-Mar-86	11.5	18-Sep-92	10	06-Dec-07	5.5
08-Apr-86	11.13	22-Sep-92	9	07-Feb-08	5.25
09-Apr-86	11	16-Oct-92	8.25	10-Apr-08	5
21-Apr-86	10.5	19-Oct-92	8	08-Oct-08	4.5
23-May-86	10.25	13-Nov-92	7	06-Nov-08	3
27-May-86	10	26-Jan-93	6	04-Dec-08	2
14-Oct-86	10.5	23-Nov-93	5.5	08-Jan-09	1.5
15-Oct-86	11	08-Feb-94	5.25	05-Feb-09	1
10-Mar-87	10.5	12-Sep-94	5.75	05-Mar-09	0.5
18-Mar-87	10.25	07-Dec-94	6.25	04-Jan-10	0.5
19-Mar-87	10	02-Feb-95	6.63	31-Dec-10	0.5
28-Apr-87	9.88	03-Feb-95	6.75	04-Jan-11	0.5
29-Apr-87	9.5	13-Dec-95	6.5	30-Dec-11	0.5
11-May-87	9	18-Jan-96	6.25	03-Jan-12	0.5
06-Aug-87	9.25	08-Mar-96	6	31-Dec-12	0.5
07-Aug-87	10	06-Jun-96	5.75	02-Jan-13	0.5
23-Oct-87	9.88	30-Oct-96	5.94	31-Dec-13	0.5
26-Oct-87	9.5	31-Oct-96	6	02-Jan-14	0.5
04-Nov-87	9.38	06-May-97	6.25	31-Dec-14	0.5
05-Nov-87	9	06-Jun-97	6.44	02-Jan-15	0.5
04-Dec-87	8.5	09-Jun-97	6.5	31-Jul-15	0.5
02-Feb-88	9	10-Jul-97	6.75	04-Aug-16	0.25
17-Mar-88	8.63	07-Aug-97	7	02-Nov-17	0.5
18-Mar-88	8.5	06-Nov-97	7.25	02-Aug-18	0.75
11-Apr-88	8	04-Jun-98	7.5		
17-May-88	7.88	08-Oct-98	7.25		
18-May-88	7.5	06-Nov-98	6.75		
02-Jun-88	7.75	10-Dec-98	6.25		
03-Jun-88	8	07-Jan-99	6		
06-Jun-88	8.25	04-Feb-99	5.5		
07-Jun-88	8.5	08-Apr-99	5.25		
22-Jun-88	8.88	10-Jun-99	5		
23-Jun-88	9	08-Sep-99	5.19		
28-Jun-88	9.25	10-Sep-99	5.25		
29-Jun-88	9.5	04-Nov-99	5.5		
04-Jul-88	9.88	14-Jan-00	5.75		
05-Jul-88	10	10-Feb-00	6		
18-Jul-88	10.38	08-Feb-01	5.75		
19-Jul-88	10.5	05-Apr-01	5.5		
08-Aug-88	10.88	10-May-01	5.25		
09-Aug-88	11	02-Aug-01	5		
25-Aug-88	11.75	18-Sep-01	4.75		
26-Aug-88	12	04-Oct-01	4.5		
25-Nov-88	13	08-Nov-01	4		
24-May-89	14	07-Feb-03	3.75		
05-Oct-89	15	11-Jul-03	3.5		
08-Oct-90	14	06-Nov-03	3.75		
13-Feb-91	13.5	05-Feb-04	4		
27-Feb-91	13	07-May-04	4.25		
22-Mar-91	12.5	10-Jun-04	4.5		
12-Apr-91	12	05-Aug-04	4.75		
24-May-91	11.5	04-Aug-05	4.5		
12-Jul-91	11	03-Aug-06	4.75		
04-Sep-91	10.5	09-Nov-06	5		
05-May-92	10	11-Jan-07	5.25		
16-Sep-92	12	10-May-07	5.5		

Source: Bank of England

1 Data obtained from Barclays Bank, Lloyds/TSB Bank, HSBC Bank and National Westminster Bank whose rates are used to compile this series.

2 Where all the rates did not change on the same day a spread is shown.

[a] This series will end on 31-July-2015

12.9 Average three month sterling money market rates

Date	Monthly average rate of discount, 3 month Treasury bills, Sterling [a] IUMAAJNB	Monthly average of Eligible bills discount rate, 3 month IUMAAJND	Monthly average Sterling 3 month mean interbank lending rate [b] [c] [d] IUMAAMIJ	Monthly average of Sterling certificates of deposit interest rate, 3 months, mean offer/bid [b] [e] IUMAVCDA
31-Jan-00	5.7218	5.9	6.0578	6.0152
29-Feb-00	5.8346	6.01	6.1492	6.0991
31-Mar-00	5.8582	5.98	6.1458	6.0878
30-Apr-00	5.9178	6.05	6.2129	6.1728
31-May-00	5.9501	6.09	6.2289	6.187
30-Jun-00	5.8535	6.03	6.1423	6.0958
31-Jul-00	5.8333	5.97	6.1146	6.0826
31-Aug-00	5.8103	5.97	6.1365	6.0913
30-Sep-00	5.7798	5.95	6.1191	6.0811
31-Oct-00	5.7482	5.92	6.081	6.0485
30-Nov-00	5.6833	5.88	6.0007	5.9794
31-Dec-00	5.6229	5.78	5.8882	5.8512
31-Jan-01	5.4852	5.64	5.7642	5.7338
28-Feb-01	5.4582	5.56	5.6854	5.661
31-Mar-01	5.2286	5.37	5.473	5.4443
30-Apr-01	5.1158	5.21	5.3323	5.3037
31-May-01	4.9765	5.06	5.1727	5.1479
30-Jun-01	4.991	5.08	5.189	5.1621
31-Jul-01	5.0052	5.07	5.1917	5.1673
31-Aug-01	4.7198	4.82	4.9269	4.8991
30-Sep-01	4.4297	4.57	4.6485	4.6223
31-Oct-01	4.1567	4.26	4.3594	4.3304
30-Nov-01	3.7799	3.85	3.9326	3.9084
31-Dec-01	3.8296	3.88	3.9852	3.9568
31-Jan-02	3.8321	3.91	3.978	3.957
28-Feb-02	3.868	3.92	3.9805	3.9618
31-Mar-02	3.9672	3.99	4.0609	4.0413
30-Apr-02	3.9693	4.04	4.1086	4.0802
31-May-02	3.9525	4.01	4.0795	4.0627
30-Jun-02	3.9767	4.04	4.112	4.0889
31-Jul-02	3.8408	3.94	3.9925	3.9704
31-Aug-02	3.7663	3.86	3.9174	3.9005
30-Sep-02	3.7861	3.86	3.9315	3.9057
31-Oct-02	3.7509	3.82	3.9015	3.8802
30-Nov-02	3.8033	3.84	3.9091	3.8876
31-Dec-02	3.8418	3.71	3.9488	3.929
31-Jan-03	3.7993	3.87	3.9132	3.9036
28-Feb-03	3.4993	3.65	3.6888	3.675
31-Mar-03	3.4721	3.54	3.5838	3.5729
30-Apr-03	3.4537	3.52	3.576	3.567
31-May-03	3.4366	3.52	3.5665	3.556
30-Jun-03	3.4724	3.45	3.5702	3.5602
31-Jul-03	3.3119	3.39	3.42	3.4089
31-Aug-03	3.3998	3.42	3.4518	3.4413
30-Sep-03	3.5239	3.59	3.6311	3.6216
31-Oct-03	3.6514	3.69	3.727	3.7204
30-Nov-03	3.808	3.88	3.9085	3.9038
31-Dec-03	3.8298	3.9	3.949	3.9419
31-Jan-04	3.8983	3.94	3.986	3.9771
29-Feb-04	3.9788	4.06	4.101	4.0908
31-Mar-04	4.1025	4.19	4.2328	4.2235
30-Apr-04	4.1862	4.28	4.3288	4.321
31-May-04	4.34	4.42	4.4555	4.4505
30-Jun-04	4.5793	4.68	4.7305	4.7211

12.9 Average three month sterling money market rates

Date	Monthly average rate of discount, 3 month Treasury bills, Sterling [a] IUMAAJNB	Monthly average of Eligible bills discount rate, 3 month IUMAAJND	Monthly average Sterling 3 month mean interbank lending rate [b] [c] [d] IUMAAMIJ	Monthly average of Sterling certificates of deposit interest rate, 3 months, mean offer/bid [b] [e] IUMAVCDA
31-Jul-04	4.6424	4.75	4.7859	4.7859
31-Aug-04	4.7218	4.85	4.8938	4.8864
30-Sep-04	4.6937	4.83	4.8743	4.868
31-Oct-04	4.679	4.79	4.8336	4.8319
30-Nov-04	4.6578	4.78	4.8159	4.8098
31-Dec-04	4.677	4.77	4.8057	4.7967
31-Jan-05	4.6568	4.75	4.8045	4.801
28-Feb-05	4.6858	4.78	4.822	4.8183
31-Mar-05	4.7691	4.88	4.9186	4.9069
30-Apr-05	4.7047	4.84	4.8756	4.8645
31-May-05	4.6618	4.8	4.8253	4.821
30-Jun-05	4.6175	4.76	4.7777	4.782
31-Jul-05	4.4609	4.57	4.5948	4.5967
31-Aug-05	4.4057	4.51	4.533	4.5336
30-Sep-05	4.4037	-	4.5359	4.5377
31-Oct-05	4.402	-	4.525	4.5202
30-Nov-05	4.4169	-	4.5614	4.5627
31-Dec-05	4.4287	-	4.587	4.5845
31-Jan-06	4.3906	-	4.5369	4.5398
28-Feb-06	4.3839	-	4.5203	4.519
31-Mar-06	4.3956	-	4.5263	4.5257
30-Apr-06	4.4196	-	4.5725	4.5719
31-May-06	4.5012	-	4.6519	4.6467
30-Jun-06	4.5414	-	4.6927	4.692
31-Jul-06	4.534	-	4.6838	4.681
31-Aug-06	4.7544	-	4.8968	4.8945
30-Sep-06	4.8359	-	4.9819	4.9807
31-Oct-06	4.9357	-	5.0909	5.0886
30-Nov-06	5.0095	-	5.1791	5.1782
31-Dec-06	5.0759	-	5.2453	5.2429
31-Jan-07	5.304	-	5.4545	5.4491
28-Feb-07	5.3393	-	5.5248	5.5143
31-Mar-07	5.3274	-	5.5041	5.5177
30-Apr-07	5.4329	-	5.6058	5.6939
31-May-07	5.5516	-	5.7221	5.835
30-Jun-07	5.6702	-	5.8348	5.9379
31-Jul-07	5.7742	-	5.9789	6.1118
31-Aug-07	5.7943	-	6.3389	6.3464
30-Sep-07	5.6896	-	6.5813	6.537
31-Oct-07	5.6058	-	6.2122	6.2052
30-Nov-07	5.4986	-	6.3564	6.3445
31-Dec-07	5.3034	-	6.3542	6.3489
31-Jan-08	5.1215	-	5.6071	5.6059
29-Feb-08	5.0178	-	5.6083	5.6
31-Mar-08	4.8835	-	5.8555	5.8482
30-Apr-08	4.8258	-	5.8961	5.8882
31-May-08	4.9496	-	5.7933	5.787
30-Jun-08	5.1138	-	5.9002	5.8924
31-Jul-08	5.0843	-	5.803	5.7996
31-Aug-08	4.9539	-	5.7588	5.7535
30-Sep-08	4.7425	-	5.8698	5.8573
31-Oct-08	3.6788	-	6.1772	6.1598
30-Nov-08	1.9948	-	4.3955	4.4
31-Dec-08	1.2875	-	3.2143	3.2107

12.9 Average three month sterling money market rates

Date	Monthly average rate of discount, 3 month Treasury bills, Sterling [a] IUMAAJNB	Monthly average of Eligible bills discount rate, 3 month IUMAAJND	Monthly average Sterling 3 month mean interbank lending rate [b] [c] [d] IUMAAMIJ	Monthly average of Sterling certificates of deposit interest rate, 3 months, mean offer/bid [b] [e] IUMAVCDA
31-Jan-09	0.8945	-	2.28	2.2869
28-Feb-09	0.7177	-	2.0758	2.0625
31-Mar-09	0.6035	-	1.8273	1.7864
30-Apr-09	0.625	-	1.4838	1.425
31-May-09	0.5271	-	1.3026	1.2697
30-Jun-09	0.5037	-	1.2057	1.1386
31-Jul-09	0.4397	-	1.0293	0.9185
31-Aug-09	0.3946	-	0.7963	0.69
30-Sep-09	0.3761	-	0.617	0.5136
31-Oct-09	0.4315	-	0.5636	0.5023
30-Nov-09	0.4459	-	0.5976	0.575
31-Dec-09	0.3587	-	0.6071	0.575
31-Jan-10	0.4874	-	0.6013	0.575
28-Feb-10	0.4878	-	0.5995	0.575
31-Mar-10	0.5109	-	0.6002	0.6011
30-Apr-10	0.5083	-	0.6	0.625
31-May-10	0.4976	-	0.6645	0.6776
30-Jun-10	0.4839	-	0.7045	0.7682
31-Jul-10	0.498	-	0.75	0.775
31-Aug-10	0.4945	-	0.75	0.7655
30-Sep-10	0.4966	-	0.7545	0.725
31-Oct-10	0.5061	-	0.75	0.725
30-Nov-10	0.4935	-	0.75	0.725
31-Dec-10	0.4913	-	0.755	0.7655
31-Jan-11	0.5055	-	0.7785	0.825
28-Feb-11	0.5363	-	0.775	0.825
31-Mar-11	0.5603	-	0.7811	0.8315
30-Apr-11	0.5676	-	0.8	0.875
31-May-11	0.5265	-	0.8	0.875
30-Jun-11	0.5174	-	0.8464	0.875
31-Jul-11	0.4996	-	0.86	0.875
31-Aug-11	0.4531	-	0.8873	0.9114
30-Sep-11	0.4649	-	0.9664	1.0077
31-Oct-11	0.4608	-	1.0179	1.0593
30-Nov-11	0.4387	-	1.0511	1.0968
31-Dec-11	0.2996	-	1.0878	1.15
31-Jan-12	0.3239	-	1.1086	1.175
29-Feb-12	0.3912	-	1.0971	1.156
31-Mar-12	0.4248	-	1.0752	1.1164
30-Apr-12	0.4236	-	1.0558	1.0992
31-May-12	0.3561	-	1.0143	1.0891
30-Jun-12	0.3422	-	0.9658	1.0376
31-Jul-12	0.2943	-	0.8627	0.8691
31-Aug-12	0.2398	-	0.7048	0.7405
30-Sep-12	0.2478	-	0.6418	0.6825
31-Oct-12	0.2368	-	0.535	0.575
30-Nov-12	0.2243	-	0.5034	0.575
31-Dec-12	0.249	-	0.5	0.575
31-Jan-13	0.2677	-	0.4927	0.575
28-Feb-13	0.3147	-	0.49	0.575
31-Mar-13	0.3391	-	0.4865	0.5655
30-Apr-13	0.3447	-	0.485	0.5731
31-May-13	0.3065	-	0.485	0.5512
30-Jun-13	0.3066	-	0.485	0.525

12.9 Average three month sterling money market rates

Date	Monthly average rate of discount, 3 month Treasury bills, Sterling [a] IUMAAJNB	Monthly average of Eligible bills discount rate, 3 month IUMAAJND	Monthly average Sterling 3 month mean interbank lending rate [b] [c] [d] IUMAAMIJ	Monthly average of Sterling certificates of deposit interest rate, 3 months, mean offer/bid [b] [e] IUMAVCDA
31-Jul-13	0.3124	-	0.4839	0.525
31-Aug-13	0.2812	-	0.485	0.525
30-Sep-13	0.289	-	0.4931	0.525
31-Oct-13	0.3141	-	0.495	0.525
30-Nov-13	0.2865	-	0.5017	0.5512
31-Dec-13	0.2555	-	0.5335	0.575
31-Jan-14	0.3211	-	0.5318	0.575
28-Feb-14	0.3624	-	0.5288	0.575
31-Mar-14	0.3882	-	0.53	0.575
30-Apr-14	0.3688	-	0.532	0.575
31-May-14	0.284	-	0.55	0.575
30-Jun-14	0.3586	-	0.55	0.575
31-Jul-14	0.4271	-	0.5487	0.575
31-Aug-14	0.3978	-	0.545	0.575
30-Sep-14	0.4351	-	0.5505	0.567
31-Oct-14	0.3964	-	0.5426	0.5511
30-Nov-14	0.4114	-	0.53	0.5538
31-Dec-14	0.4101	-	0.53	0.5524
31-Jan-15	0.377	-	0.53	0.5512
28-Feb-15	0.338	-	0.53	0.55
31-Mar-15	0.4295	-	0.53	0.5511
30-Apr-15	0.4322	-	0.533	0.55
31-May-15	0.4511	-	0.54	0.5532
30-Jun-15	0.467	-	0.5505	0.55
31-Jul-15	0.4895	-	0.567	0.55
31-Aug-15	0.4643	-	0.57	0.55
30-Sep-15	0.4532	-	0.57	0.55
31-Oct-15	0.48	-	0.57	0.55
30-Nov-15	0.4806	-	0.57	0.55
31-Dec-15	0.4551	-	0.57	0.5786
31-Jan-16	0.4823	-	0.566	0.6475
28-Feb-16	0.4711	-	0.565	0.65
31-Mar-16	0.4505	-	0.565	0.6476
30-Apr-16	0.4489	-	0.565	0.65
31-May-16	0.4362	-	0.565	0.65
30-Jun-16	0.4046	-	0.563	0.6386
31-Jul-16	0.3689	-	0.5414	0.4869
31-Aug-16	0.2281	-	0.468	0.367
30-Sep-16	0.2104	-	0.3627	0.3509
31-Oct-16	0.1711	-	0.3748	0.3524
30-Nov-16	0.1385	-	0.38	0.3523
31-Dec-16	0.0518	-	0.3775	0.35
31-Jan-17	0.1441	-	0.3452	0.35
28-Feb-17	0.1131	-	0.34	0.35
31-Mar-17	0.0231	-	0.3304	0.3478
30-Apr-17	0.0709	-	0.33	0.35
31-May-17	0.0592	-	0.3267	0.35
30-Jun-17	0.0759	-	0.32	0.35
31-Jul-17	-	-	0.32	0.3324
31-Aug-17	-	-	0.3123	0.2977
30-Sep-17	-	-	0.3157	0.3
31-Oct-17	-	-	0.3491	0.3
30-Nov-17	-	-	0.4364	0.4818
31-Dec-17	-	-	-	0.5

Source: Bank of England

12.9 Average three month sterling money market rates

Date	Monthly average rate of discount, 3 month Treasury bills, Sterling [a]	Monthly average of Eligible bills discount rate, 3 month	Monthly average Sterling 3 month mean interbank lending rate [b] [c] [d]	Monthly average of Sterling certificates of deposit interest rate, 3 months, mean offer/bid [b] [e]
	IUMAAJNB	**IUMAAJND**	**IUMAAMIJ**	**IUMAVCDA**

Notes:

[a] These data have been discontinued with effect from 20th July 2017.

[b] Data provided is for general reference purposes. Every effort is made to ensure that it is up to date and accurate. The Bank of England does not warrant, or accept responsibility/liability for, the accuracy/completeness of content, or loss/damage, whether direct, indirect or consequential, which may arise from reliance on said data. We reserve the right to change information published, including timing and methods used. We give no assurance that data currently published will be in the future.

[c] No data is available because the Bank has been unable to source sufficient representative data to allow it to calculate an average rate.

[d] No data available from 5 December 2017 because the Bank has been unable to source sufficient representative data to allow it to calculate an average rate. This series has been discontinued.

[e] From 2 July 2018 the Bank ceased publishing these data. Further information can be found at https://www.bankofengland.co.uk/statistics/details/further-details-about-wholesale-sterling-certificates-of-deposit-data

12.10 Average Foreign Exchange rates

Date	Monthly average Old IMF-based Effective exchange rate index, Sterling (a) (1990 average = 100) [3] XUMAGBG	Monthly average Effective exchange rate index, Sterling (Jan 2005= 100)[1] XUMABK67	Monthly average Spot exchange rate, US$ into Sterling [2] XUMAUSS	Monthly average Spot exchange rate, Euro into Sterling [2] XUMAERS
31-Jan-00	108.55	102.5163	1.6402	1.6201
29-Feb-00	108.44	102.1478	1.5998	1.6266
31-Mar-00	108.41	101.9463	1.5802	1.6377
30-Apr-00	110.06	103.3007	1.5837	1.673
31-May-00	108.52	101.3378	1.5075	1.6655
30-Jun-00	104.64	98.3084	1.5089	1.5882
31-Jul-00	105.63	99.0767	1.5088	1.6052
31-Aug-00	107.38	100.188	1.491	1.6478
30-Sep-00	106.21	98.7465	1.4355	1.6471
31-Oct-00	109.19	101.3391	1.4511	1.6994
30-Nov-00	107.27	99.6623	1.4256	1.6664
31-Dec-00	106.39	99.4118	1.4625	1.6302
31-Jan-01	104.43	98.2362	1.4769	1.5753
28-Feb-01	104.14	97.7179	1.4529	1.5786
31-Mar-01	105.02	98.4528	1.4454	1.5901
30-Apr-01	105.85	99.0733	1.435	1.6084
31-May-01	106.56	99.3906	1.4259	1.6304
30-Jun-01	106.77	99.2172	1.4014	1.6434
31-Jul-01	107.18	99.7551	1.4139	1.6433
31-Aug-01	105.09	98.4283	1.4365	1.5955
30-Sep-01	106.08	99.5949	1.4635	1.606
31-Oct-01	105.78	99.3536	1.4517	1.6024
30-Nov-01	106.14	99.4505	1.4358	1.6166
31-Dec-01	106.49	100.0899	1.4409	1.6151
31-Jan-02	106.9	100.26	1.4323	1.6222
28-Feb-02	107.36	100.4838	1.4231	1.6348
31-Mar-02	106.48	99.7945	1.4225	1.6224
30-Apr-02	107.13	100.5217	1.4434	1.6282
31-May-02	105.32	99.1553	1.4593	1.5914
30-Jun-02	103.58	98.0057	1.4863	1.5515
31-Jul-02	105.29	100.1562	1.5546	1.5665
31-Aug-02	105.38	100.0907	1.5377	1.5723
30-Sep-02	106.46	101.2329	1.5561	1.5861
31-Oct-02	106.67	101.4447	1.5574	1.5868
30-Nov-02	105.87	100.8857	1.5723	1.5694
31-Dec-02	105.48	100.6652	1.5863	1.5566
31-Jan-03	104.04	99.8966	1.6169	1.5222
28-Feb-03	102.42	98.4726	1.6085	1.4924
31-Mar-03	100.6	96.8021	1.5836	1.4649
30-Apr-03	99.8	95.9557	1.5747	1.4505
31-May-03	97.9	94.8862	1.623	1.403
30-Jun-03	99.64	96.6136	1.6606	1.4234
31-Jul-03	99.4	95.9155	1.6242	1.4277
31-Aug-03	99.01	95.2462	1.595	1.4286
30-Sep-03	99.24	95.5651	1.6131	1.4338
31-Oct-03	99.82	96.7185	1.6787	1.4334
30-Nov-03	100.42	97.317	1.6901	1.4426
31-Dec-03	100.29	97.8697	1.7507	1.4246
31-Jan-04	102.38	100.1608	1.8234	1.4447
29-Feb-04	104.84	102.5025	1.8673	1.4774
31-Mar-04	104.99	102.1884	1.8267	1.489
30-Apr-04	105.18	102.137	1.8005	1.5022
31-May-04	104.63	101.7871	1.7876	1.4894
30-Jun-04	105.8	103.059	1.8275	1.505
31-Jul-04	105.89	103.1662	1.8429	1.5023
31-Aug-04	105.16	102.4289	1.8216	1.4933

12.10 Average Foreign Exchange rates

Date	Monthly average Old IMF-based Effective exchange rate index, Sterling (a) (1990 average = 100) [3] XUMAGBG	Monthly average Effective exchange rate index, Sterling (Jan 2005= 100)[1] XUMABK67	Monthly average Spot exchange rate, US$ into Sterling [2] XUMAUSS	Monthly average Spot exchange rate, Euro into Sterling [2] XUMAERS
30-Sep-04	103.32	100.7156	1.7922	1.4676
31-Oct-04	102.17	99.8303	1.8065	1.4455
30-Nov-04	101.73	99.7587	1.8603	1.4311
31-Dec-04	103.15	101.2974	1.9275	1.4401
31-Jan-05	102.1	100	1.8764	1.4331
28-Feb-05	103.29	100.9792	1.8871	1.4499
31-Mar-05	103.21	101.0494	1.9078	1.444
30-Apr-05	104.38	102.0108	1.896	1.4652
31-May-05	103.55	100.9896	1.8538	1.4611
30-Jun-05	104.92	101.7515	1.8179	1.4952
31-Jul-05	102.14	98.8169	1.7509	1.4547
31-Aug-05	102.85	99.7011	1.7943	1.4592
30-Sep-05	103.91	100.6456	1.8081	1.4761
31-Oct-05	103.09	99.6486	1.764	1.4674
30-Nov-05	103.16	99.4195	1.7341	1.4719
31-Dec-05	103.32	99.5011	1.7462	1.4725
31-Jan-06	102.67	99.0364	1.7678	1.4582
28-Feb-06	102.83	98.9167	1.747	1.4637
31-Mar-06	102.09	98.3582	1.7435	1.45
30-Apr-06	101.87	98.3685	1.7685	1.4402
31-May-06	104.14	101.2652	1.8702	1.4637
30-Jun-06	-	100.9564	1.8428	1.456
31-Jul-06	-	100.9424	1.8447	1.454
31-Aug-06	-	102.9584	1.8944	1.4785
30-Sep-06	-	103.0141	1.8847	1.4811
31-Oct-06	-	103.1453	1.8755	1.4869
30-Nov-06	-	103.4686	1.9119	1.4834
31-Dec-06	-	104.5334	1.9633	1.486
31-Jan-07	-	105.5735	1.9587	1.5079
28-Feb-07	-	105.0313	1.9581	1.4969
31-Mar-07	-	103.5671	1.9471	1.4703
30-Apr-07	-	104.2682	1.9909	1.4713
31-May-07	-	103.9117	1.9836	1.4677
30-Jun-07	-	104.5063	1.9864	1.4805
31-Jul-07	-	105.2357	2.0338	1.4821
31-Aug-07	-	104.5357	2.0111	1.4762
30-Sep-07	-	103.3042	2.0185	1.4515
31-Oct-07	-	102.8113	2.0446	1.437
30-Nov-07	-	101.8978	2.0701	1.4106
31-Dec-07	-	99.9273	2.0185	1.3863
31-Jan-08	-	96.6594	1.9698	1.3383
29-Feb-08	-	96.1702	1.9638	1.3316
31-Mar-08	-	94.7859	2.0032	1.2897
30-Apr-08	-	93.0097	1.9817	1.258
31-May-08	-	93.0105	1.9641	1.2633
30-Jun-08	-	93.1297	1.9658	1.2636
31-Jul-08	-	93.2514	1.988	1.2615
31-Aug-08	-	91.6752	1.8889	1.2614
30-Sep-08	-	90.0272	1.7986	1.2531
31-Oct-08	-	89.6321	1.69	1.2718
30-Nov-08	-	83.8159	1.5338	1.2041
31-Dec-08	-	78.4569	1.4859	1.1043
31-Jan-09	-	77.2822	1.4452	1.0919
28-Feb-09	-	79.1632	1.4411	1.1264
31-Mar-09	-	77.2402	1.4174	1.0867
30-Apr-09	-	79.1169	1.4715	1.1157

12.10 Average Foreign Exchange rates

Date	Monthly average Old IMF-based Effective exchange rate index, Sterling (a) (1990 average = 100) [3] XUMAGBG	Monthly average Effective exchange rate index, Sterling (Jan 2005= 100)[1] XUMABK67	Monthly average Spot exchange rate, US$ into Sterling [2] XUMAUSS	Monthly average Spot exchange rate, Euro into Sterling [2] XUMAERS
31-May-09	-	80.65	1.5429	1.1295
30-Jun-09	-	84.1934	1.6366	1.1682
31-Jul-09	-	83.777	1.6366	1.1622
31-Aug-09	-	83.66	1.6539	1.1597
30-Sep-09	-	81.3425	1.6328	1.1212
31-Oct-09	-	79.5602	1.6199	1.0928
30-Nov-09	-	81.1213	1.6597	1.1126
31-Dec-09	-	80.4832	1.6239	1.1127
31-Jan-10	-	81.0259	1.6162	1.1327
28-Feb-10	-	80.305	1.5615	1.1415
31-Mar-10	-	77.526	1.5053	1.1092
30-Apr-10	-	79.3964	1.534	1.1436
31-May-10	-	79.2556	1.4627	1.1685
30-Jun-10	-	81.0387	1.4761	1.2082
31-Jul-10	-	81.4282	1.5299	1.1959
31-Aug-10	-	82.643	1.566	1.2132
30-Sep-10	-	81.219	1.5578	1.1901
31-Oct-10	-	79.5102	1.5862	1.1412
30-Nov-10	-	80.9631	1.5961	1.1701
31-Dec-10	-	80.4151	1.5603	1.1802
31-Jan-11	-	80.7146	1.5795	1.1817
28-Feb-11	-	81.4914	1.613	1.1815
31-Mar-11	-	80.2504	1.6159	1.1527
30-Apr-11	-	79.6662	1.6345	1.1331
31-May-11	-	79.7728	1.6312	1.1403
30-Jun-11	-	78.875	1.6214	1.1261
31-Jul-11	-	78.7586	1.6145	1.1308
31-Aug-11	-	79.633	1.6348	1.1422
30-Sep-11	-	79.259	1.5783	1.147
31-Oct-11	-	79.5315	1.576	1.1487
30-Nov-11	-	80.472	1.5804	1.1659
31-Dec-11	-	80.9061	1.5585	1.1843
31-Jan-12	-	81.1135	1.551	1.2034
29-Feb-12	-	80.9907	1.5802	1.1941
31-Mar-12	-	81.4144	1.5823	1.1981
30-Apr-12	-	82.5592	1.6014	1.2161
31-May-12	-	83.8064	1.5905	1.244
30-Jun-12	-	83.09	1.5571	1.2416
31-Jul-12	-	84.0002	1.5589	1.2688
31-Aug-12	-	84.0151	1.5719	1.2676
30-Sep-12	-	84.2259	1.6116	1.2524
31-Oct-12	-	83.6192	1.6079	1.2393
30-Nov-12	-	83.6804	1.5961	1.244
31-Dec-12	-	83.5787	1.6144	1.231
31-Jan-13	-	82.1836	1.5957	1.2
28-Feb-13	-	79.7009	1.5478	1.1594
31-Mar-13	-	79.1385	1.5076	1.1634
30-Apr-13	-	80.1286	1.5316	1.175
31-May-13	-	80.4282	1.5285	1.1777
30-Jun-13	-	80.9963	1.5478	1.174
31-Jul-13	-	79.9695	1.5172	1.16
31-Aug-13	-	80.989	1.5507	1.1649
30-Sep-13	-	82.7389	1.5865	1.1883
31-Oct-13	-	82.6672	1.6094	1.1797
30-Nov-13	-	83.5614	1.6104	1.1938
31-Dec-13	-	84.4199	1.6375	1.1947

12.10 Average Foreign Exchange rates

Date	Monthly average Old IMF-based Effective exchange rate index, Sterling (a) (1990 average = 100) [3] XUMAGBG	Monthly average Effective exchange rate index, Sterling (Jan 2005= 100)[1] XUMABK67	Monthly average Spot exchange rate, US$ into Sterling [2] XUMAUSS	Monthly average Spot exchange rate, Euro into Sterling [2] XUMAERS
31-Jan-14	-	85.4256	1.647	1.2097
28-Feb-14	-	85.7374	1.6567	1.2122
31-Mar-14	-	85.5266	1.6622	1.2021
30-Apr-14	-	86.1739	1.6743	1.2125
31-May-14	-	86.8392	1.6844	1.2267
30-Jun-14	-	87.6791	1.6906	1.2436
31-Jul-14	-	88.7384	1.7069	1.2611
31-Aug-14	-	87.7641	1.6709	1.2542
30-Sep-14	-	87.5035	1.6305	1.2639
31-Oct-14	-	87.353	1.6068	1.2678
30-Nov-14	-	86.9779	1.578	1.2646
31-Dec-14	-	87.5043	1.564	1.2686
31-Jan-15	-	87.7721	1.5143	1.3045
28-Feb-15	-	90.0828	1.5334	1.3503
31-Mar-15	-	90.4409	1.4957	1.3825
30-Apr-15	-	90.1919	1.4967	1.3856
31-May-15	-	91.3478	1.547	1.3852
30-Jun-15	-	92.1334	1.5568	1.3879
31-Jul-15	-	93.3352	1.556	1.4139
31-Aug-15	-	93.482	1.5583	1.4004
30-Sep-15	-	91.8347	1.5326	1.3665
31-Oct-15	-	91.5953	1.5339	1.3657
30-Nov-15	-	93.4031	1.519	1.4168
31-Dec-15	-	91.551	1.4983	1.3769
31-Jan-16	-	88.4994	1.4379	1.3257
28-Feb-16	-	86.6959	1.4296	1.289
31-Mar-16	-	85.7815	1.425	1.2809
30-Apr-16	-	84.9485	1.4312	1.2622
31-May-16	-	86.6711	1.4518	1.2846
30-Jun-16	-	84.9386	1.4209	1.2646
31-Jul-16	-	79.3988	1.3141	1.1884
31-Aug-16	-	78.3767	1.31	1.1687
30-Sep-16	-	78.6967	1.3142	1.1722
31-Oct-16	-	74.7185	1.2329	1.119
30-Nov-16	-	76.7407	1.2431	1.1533
31-Dec-16	-	78.3438	1.2488	1.1838
31-Jan-17	-	77.0524	1.2351	1.1613
28-Feb-17	-	77.6679	1.249	1.1732
31-Mar-17	-	76.6272	1.2348	1.1548
30-Apr-17	-	78.2617	1.2652	1.1798
31-May-17	-	78.6576	1.2933	1.1696
30-Jun-17	-	77.0608	1.2813	1.1403
31-Jul-17	-	76.9841	1.2994	1.1281
31-Aug-17	-	75.4841	1.2955	1.0974
30-Sep-17	-	77.1281	1.3324	1.1186
31-Oct-17	-	77.2558	1.3197	1.1227
30-Nov-17	-	77.5956	1.3219	1.1259
31-Dec-17	-	78.2736	1.3402	1.133

(a) This series was discontinued in May 2006

Source: Bank of England

(1): Please see notes and definitions for Effective exchange rate index, Sterling (Jan 2005 = 100)
https://www.bankofengland.co.uk/statistics/details/further-details-about-effective-exchange-rate-indices-data

(2): Please see notes and definitions for Spot exchange rates
https://www.bankofengland.co.uk/statistics/details/further-details-about-spot-exchange-rates-data

(3): Please see notes and definitions for Effective exchange rates
https://www.bankofengland.co.uk/statistics/details/further-details-about-effective-exchange-rate-indices-data

12.11 Average zero coupon yields

	End month level of yield from British Government Securities			Monthly average yield from British Government Securities	
	5 year Nominal Zero Coupon [c]	10 year Nominal Zero Coupon [c]	20 year Nominal Zero Coupon [c]	10 year Real Zero Coupon [a] [b]	20 year Real Zero Coupon [a] [b]
Date	IUMSNZC	IUMMNZC	IUMLNZC	IUMAMRZC	IUMALRZC
31 Jan 01	4.978	4.6718	4.3694	2.2154	1.8684
28 Feb 01	4.9824	4.7079	4.378	2.2144	1.8523
31 Mar 01	4.8425	4.7218	4.5984	2.2702	1.9601
30 Apr 01	5.126	5.065	4.8872	2.5368	2.2434
31 May 01	5.2777	5.1627	5.0197	2.5735	2.3112
30 Jun 01	5.4376	5.2329	5.0078	2.5725	2.2817
31 Jul 01	5.1702	5.0002	4.7653	2.5826	2.2629
31 Aug 01	4.9746	4.8652	4.682	2.3919	2.1494
30 Sep 01	4.8735	4.9172	4.8559	2.4992	2.3047
31 Oct 01	4.5126	4.5368	4.4576	2.5713	2.3376
30 Nov 01	4.6523	4.6479	4.5089	2.3844	2.1178
31 Dec 01	5.0788	5.0326	4.782	2.5171	2.2145
31 Jan 02	4.9044	4.8138	4.6689	2.4923	2.2395
28 Feb 02	4.9428	4.923	4.7928	2.4722	2.2767
31 Mar 02	5.3046	5.2456	5.0823	2.5074	2.3014
30 Apr 02	5.1522	5.1553	5.0257	2.4157	2.2401
31 May 02	5.2156	5.2282	5.1364	2.4142	2.2421
30 Jun 02	5.0148	4.9715	4.8164	2.3162	2.1556
31 Jul 02	4.7231	4.9201	4.8015	2.409	2.2475
31 Aug 02	4.4976	4.6394	4.4857	2.3109	2.1482
30 Sep 02	4.1825	4.412	4.3797	2.1834	2.0609
31 Oct 02	4.3315	4.5992	4.5466	2.3919	2.236
30 Nov 02	4.5062	4.6898	4.6549	2.3853	2.2838
31 Dec 02	4.1583	4.3967	4.4607	2.3083	2.2482
31 Jan 03	4.0136	4.2807	4.374	2.0797	2.0936
28 Feb 03	3.7987	4.227	4.4687	1.7905	1.9801
31 Mar 03	3.9584	4.3549	4.5931	1.8418	2.0679
30 Apr 03	4.0086	4.4202	4.6491	1.9411	2.1236
31 May 03	3.7737	4.1579	4.4323	1.7954	2.0315
30 Jun 03	3.8401	4.2698	4.6015	1.6503	1.9703
31 Jul 03	4.2291	4.6075	4.8344	1.8311	2.1601
31 Aug 03	4.4574	4.6562	4.6988	1.9459	2.141
30 Sep 03	4.3404	4.5844	4.6736	2.0418	2.1832
31 Oct 03	4.9274	5.0093	4.859	2.1484	2.2234
30 Nov 03	4.911	5.0473	4.8909	2.2143	2.2058
31 Dec 03	4.612	4.7733	4.7034	2.034	2.0784
31 Jan 04	4.7324	4.8572	4.7485	1.9359	1.9606
29 Feb 04	4.5996	4.735	4.7232	1.959	1.901
31 Mar 04	4.6154	4.7184	4.6453	1.8077	1.7684
30 Apr 04	4.8491	4.9564	4.839	1.9295	1.848
31 May 04	5.1163	5.1062	4.8917	2.0517	1.8784
30 Jun 04	5.039	5.0587	4.84	2.1008	1.8799
31 Jul 04	5.0958	5.0518	4.7933	2.0733	1.8713
31 Aug 04	4.8585	4.881	4.6547	2.0347	1.8228
30 Sep 04	4.7433	4.7878	4.6312	1.9736	1.798
31 Oct 04	4.6267	4.7002	4.5693	1.8884	1.7651
30 Nov 04	4.473	4.5606	4.4453	1.8755	1.7059
31 Dec 04	4.4287	4.4872	4.4097	1.7552	1.5992
31 Jan 05	4.4769	4.5419	4.4811	1.7474	1.5862
28 Feb 05	4.6761	4.6514	4.5249	1.7701	1.5918
31 Mar 05	4.6106	4.6382	4.5618	1.874	1.7246
30 Apr 05	4.444	4.4749	4.4264	1.7638	1.6408
31 May 05	4.2051	4.2811	4.3326	1.6959	1.5704

12.11 Average zero coupon yields

	End month level of yield from British Government Securities			Monthly average yield from British Government Securities	
	5 year Nominal Zero Coupon [c]	10 year Nominal Zero Coupon [c]	20 year Nominal Zero Coupon [c]	10 year Real Zero Coupon [a] [b]	20 year Real Zero Coupon [a] [b]
Date	IUMSNZC	IUMMNZC	IUMLNZC	IUMAMRZC	IUMALRZC
30 Jun 05	4.0387	4.1508	4.2073	1.6498	1.5324
31 Jul 05	4.2154	4.2884	4.3179	1.6469	1.5442
31 Aug 05	4.0641	4.1238	4.1705	1.6094	1.4946
30 Sep 05	4.1884	4.2464	4.2336	1.5097	1.4043
31 Oct 05	4.2874	4.2823	4.238	1.5665	1.3974
30 Nov 05	4.2061	4.1665	4.0854	1.541	1.2925
31 Dec 05	4.1019	4.0476	3.9626	1.4668	1.2015
31 Jan 06	4.172	4.0783	3.8631	1.2921	0.9687
28 Feb 06	4.2134	4.1192	3.9088	1.3237	0.9897
31 Mar 06	4.3946	4.3444	4.1388	1.4135	1.1011
30 Apr 06	4.6102	4.5845	4.3286	1.542	1.2818
31 May 06	4.6302	4.5389	4.2978	1.6291	1.3321
30 Jun 06	4.7356	4.6532	4.4151	1.6832	1.3862
31 Jul 06	4.6631	4.5484	4.2984	1.6457	1.3078
31 Aug 06	4.6343	4.4357	4.163	1.5515	1.2077
30 Sep 06	4.6412	4.4466	4.1548	1.4912	1.1173
31 Oct 06	4.6979	4.4204	4.0629	1.5735	1.1274
30 Nov 06	4.6926	4.4059	4.0858	1.4768	1.0326
31 Dec 06	4.9131	4.6261	4.2526	1.5656	1.116
31 Jan 07	5.1482	4.8488	4.4219	1.7909	1.2376
28 Feb 07	4.9735	4.6832	4.3078	1.8103	1.2555
31 Mar 07	5.1338	4.8558	4.4697	1.7137	1.2048
30 Apr 07	5.194	4.9249	4.5536	1.9163	1.3708
31 May 07	5.448	5.1262	4.6951	2.0546	1.4654
30 Jun 07	5.6348	5.3592	4.8891	2.2134	1.5466
31 Jul 07	5.3529	5.1163	4.6572	2.1929	1.5126
31 Aug 07	5.1209	4.9352	4.5484	1.9573	1.3084
30 Sep 07	4.9798	4.9505	4.6447	1.7847	1.2423
31 Oct 07	4.9395	4.8693	4.5916	1.7411	1.2508
30 Nov 07	4.5718	4.6382	4.5157	1.476	1.0932
31 Dec 07	4.4137	4.5176	4.3859	1.493	1.0805
31 Jan 08	4.2964	4.489	4.4193	1.3008	0.9196
29 Feb 08	4.1991	4.5271	4.503	1.329	1.0273
31 Mar 08	3.9541	4.4245	4.6048	1.0269	0.8891
30 Apr 08	4.4429	4.7338	4.7139	1.2039	1.0222
31 May 08	4.94	4.9995	4.8293	1.3551	0.9951
30 Jun 08	5.1659	5.168	4.8995	1.3521	0.8387
31 Jul 08	4.7675	4.8489	4.7434	1.2828	0.8239
31 Aug 08	4.4108	4.5304	4.5953	1.1547	0.6732
30 Sep 08	4.208	4.523	4.6924	1.2467	0.8046
31 Oct 08	3.9697	4.6995	4.9258	2.051	1.3361
30 Nov 08	3.3664	4.0107	4.5731	2.5578	1.3677
31 Dec 08	2.708	3.3892	4.066	2.1573	1.2343
31 Jan 09	2.8834	4.0768	4.7012	1.5136	1.0594
28 Feb 09	2.6227	3.8151	4.7151	1.2268	1.2058
31 Mar 09	2.4459	3.3015	4.2558	1.172	1.202
30 Apr 09	2.594	3.6361	4.5822	1.0457	1.1446
31 May 09	2.7154	3.8141	4.7127	1.0491	1.0401
30 Jun 09	2.9717	3.703	4.5708	1.0368	0.9954
31 Jul 09	3.083	3.9125	4.7431	1.1672	0.9737
31 Aug 09	2.6877	3.6313	4.1118	1.0943	0.8452
30 Sep 09	2.6807	3.7123	4.1499	1.003	0.8653
31 Oct 09	2.7662	3.7684	4.2789	0.6518	0.7198

12.11 Average zero coupon yields

Date	End month level of yield from British Government Securities 5 year Nominal Zero Coupon [c] IUMSNZC	10 year Nominal Zero Coupon [c] IUMMNZC	20 year Nominal Zero Coupon [c] IUMLNZC	Monthly average yield from British Government Securities 10 year Real Zero Coupon [a] [b] IUMAMRZC	20 year Real Zero Coupon [a] [b] IUMALRZC
30 Nov 09	2.6607	3.6987	4.2359	0.7194	0.6875
31 Dec 09	2.9821	4.203	4.5939	0.7586	0.7456
31 Jan 10	2.9411	4.1135	4.5279	0.8386	0.8509
28 Feb 10	2.7834	4.2373	4.7692	1.0099	1.0893
31 Mar 10	2.7852	4.1764	4.6577	0.8325	0.9807
30 Apr 10	2.7534	4.1034	4.6279	0.7105	0.9059
31 May 10	2.4101	3.7919	4.4818	0.7262	0.9368
30 Jun 10	2.2133	3.5853	4.3767	0.761	0.975
31 Jul 10	2.2281	3.5691	4.4956	0.8592	1.0467
31 Aug 10	1.7575	3.0217	3.9415	0.6655	0.9099
30 Sep 10	1.813	3.1512	4.0071	0.4585	0.7377
31 Oct 10	1.878	3.3042	4.3031	0.3731	0.7128
30 Nov 10	2.0313	3.4591	4.4002	0.4724	0.8109
31 Dec 10	2.314	3.6174	4.3314	0.6677	0.8226
31 Jan 11	2.5858	3.8827	4.5822	0.6391	0.8706
28 Feb 11	2.6508	3.8872	4.5184	0.7246	0.8861
31 Mar 11	2.6575	3.8975	4.5078	0.5509	0.8083
30 Apr 11	2.4534	3.7116	4.3435	0.5741	0.8267
31 May 11	2.2507	3.5655	4.3125	0.4157	0.8022
30 Jun 11	2.2036	3.6665	4.4964	0.2648	0.6877
31 Jul 11	1.7512	3.1755	4.2227	0.1862	0.5977
31 Aug 11	1.6065	2.9038	4.0173	-0.1472	0.4051
30 Sep 11	1.4048	2.5096	3.5397	-0.2034	0.3054
31 Oct 11	1.3719	2.5642	3.4276	-0.1199	0.3441
30 Nov 11	1.2752	2.4275	3.1294	-0.3125	0.1156
31 Dec 11	1.001	2.105	3.0454	-0.4715	-0.0284
31 Jan 12	0.9544	2.0983	3.0189	-0.5915	-0.1548
29 Feb 12	1.001	2.2582	3.2967	-0.5792	-0.0198
31 Mar 12	1.0698	2.3026	3.447	-0.5298	0.0418
30 Apr 12	1.1164	2.2225	3.3938	-0.5906	-0.0172
31 May 12	0.6748	1.6781	2.8994	-0.6885	-0.0622
30 Jun 12	0.8284	1.8651	2.9815	-0.5981	-0.0537
31 Jul 12	0.566	1.6111	2.7932	-0.6425	-0.0247
31 Aug 12	0.5849	1.6236	2.8217	-0.6936	-0.0165
30 Sep 12	0.6798	1.7105	2.9454	-0.6624	0.0823
31 Oct 12	0.8255	1.8749	3.0256	-0.5891	0.1512
30 Nov 12	0.8264	1.7969	2.9544	-0.629	0.098
31 Dec 12	0.8853	1.8876	3.023	-0.7249	-0.0074
31 Jan 13	1.098	2.1883	3.3222	-0.8252	-0.093
28 Feb 13	0.9145	2.1117	3.2498	-1.0107	-0.1884
31 Mar 13	0.7439	1.9006	3.0961	-1.2516	-0.2985
30 Apr 13	0.73	1.7922	2.9541	-1.3174	-0.4836
31 May 13	1.02	2.1634	3.2631	-1.0712	-0.348
30 Jun 13	1.3933	2.6171	3.5337	-0.6342	-0.1241
31 Jul 13	1.2511	2.5581	3.5392	-0.5751	-0.0065
31 Aug 13	1.5644	2.8293	3.6373	-0.3741	0.0945
30 Sep 13	1.5498	2.7591	3.5437	-0.2171	0.1536
31 Oct 13	1.5122	2.7045	3.4942	-0.3777	0.0186
30 Nov 13	1.6323	2.8776	3.6515	-0.2864	0.0642
31 Dec 13	1.9931	3.1571	3.7316	-0.1927	0.1004
31 Jan 14	1.7819	2.8347	3.5521	-0.1593	0.1263
28 Feb 14	1.798	2.8561	3.5484	-0.1815	0.1037

12.11 Average zero coupon yields

	End month level of yield from British Government Securities			Monthly average yield from British Government Securities	
	5 year Nominal Zero Coupon [c]	10 year Nominal Zero Coupon [c]	20 year Nominal Zero Coupon [c]	10 year Real Zero Coupon [a] [b]	20 year Real Zero Coupon [a] [b]
Date	IUMSNZC	IUMMNZC	IUMLNZC	IUMAMRZC	IUMALRZC
31 Mar 14	1.8714	2.8687	3.5515	-0.2982	0.0133
30 Apr 14	1.857	2.8078	3.4992	-0.3476	-0.0308
31 May 14	1.7997	2.7029	3.412	-0.3825	-0.0841
30 Jun 14	1.9945	2.812	3.4523	-0.2886	-0.0462
31 Jul 14	1.9847	2.7598	3.3233	-0.3072	-0.0794
31 Aug 14	1.6987	2.3916	2.9663	-0.4659	-0.2378
30 Sep 14	1.781	2.4682	3.0612	-0.5305	-0.2812
31 Oct 14	1.5647	2.3054	2.9766	-0.6111	-0.4436
30 Nov 14	1.3003	1.9853	2.6605	-0.7293	-0.5389
31 Dec 14	1.1987	1.8196	2.4808	-0.9257	-0.7589
31 Jan 15	0.9086	1.3867	2.0083	-1.0857	-0.9306
28 Feb 15	1.2811	1.8567	2.4648	-0.8858	-0.7547
31 Mar 15	1.0851	1.6605	2.2909	-0.92	-0.7803
30 Apr 15	1.3017	1.9447	2.5347	-1.1025	-0.9588
31 May 15	1.263	1.9178	2.5294	-0.9409	-0.8146
30 Jun 15	1.4567	2.1552	2.7485	-0.8422	-0.7103
31 Jul 15	1.3892	2.0074	2.5863	-0.829	-0.7394
31 Aug 15	1.3454	1.9669	2.5998	-0.8785	-0.8826
30 Sep 15	1.184	1.7919	2.5118	-0.9077	-0.8598
31 Oct 15	1.2853	1.9457	2.6502	-0.89	-0.8081
30 Nov 15	1.2399	1.8741	2.5946	-0.7969	-0.74
31 Dec 15	1.3752	2.0097	2.7092	-0.7875	-0.7594
31 Jan 16	0.9573	1.6355	2.3858	-0.8497	-0.7912
29 Feb 16	0.6909	1.4096	2.3061	-0.9706	-0.8878
31 Mar 16	0.8064	1.5041	2.3188	-1.0452	-0.9193
30 Apr 16	0.9684	1.6947	2.4476	-1.0659	-0.8943
31 May 16	0.9044	1.5474	2.2818	-1.0012	-0.8729
30 Jun 16	0.3959	1.0263	1.7905	-1.2024	-1.055
31 Jul 16	0.2752	0.7998	1.567	-1.638	-1.4033
31 Aug 16	0.2182	0.6615	1.2793	-1.9604	-1.6859
30 Sep 16	0.2591	0.7968	1.5211	-2.052	-1.8127
31 Oct 16	0.6341	1.2877	1.9205	-2.1096	-1.832
30 Nov 16	0.6747	1.4765	2.1026	-1.8772	-1.6208
31 Dec 16	0.5495	1.2955	1.9308	-1.8447	-1.551
31 Jan 17	0.7134	1.4858	2.1078	-1.9408	-1.6249
28 Feb 17	0.4196	1.1303	1.8546	-1.9647	-1.6763
31 Mar 17	0.4384	1.1343	1.8285	-1.9685	-1.6775
30 Apr 17	0.4062	1.1067	1.8271	-2.1515	-1.8587
31 May 17	0.3898	1.0669	1.7856	-2.0011	-1.7461
30 Jun 17	0.6352	1.2971	1.9618	-1.9715	-1.7026
31 Jul 17	0.5555	1.2613	1.9555	-1.7799	-1.5366
31 Aug 17	0.4195	1.0758	1.7913	-1.9318	-1.6783
30 Sep 17	0.7839	1.4009	2.0041	-1.8845	-1.6416
31 Oct 17	0.7923	1.3894	1.9978	-1.7722	-1.5743
30 Nov 17	0.8269	1.3844	1.9538	-1.8259	-1.6367
31 Dec 17	0.7444	1.258	1.8281	-1.8414	-1.6789

Source: Bank of England

[a] Calculated using the Variable Roughness Penalty (VRP) model.

[b] Users should note that on 15/02/2018 these yields were revised to the beginning of 2015.

[c] Calculated by the Bank of England using the Variable Roughness Penalty (VRP) model.

Please see notes and definitions for Yields:
https://www.bankofengland.co.uk/statistics/details/further-details-about-yields-data

12.12 Consumer credit excluding student loans

£ millions Not seasonally adjusted

Net lending - monthly changes

	Monthly changes of					
					of which:	
Date	MFIs sterling net consumer credit lending to individuals [a] [d] [c] LPMVVXP	of which: mutuals [a] [b] [c] LPMB3VC	Other consumer credit lenders (excluding the Student Loans Company) sterling net consumer credit lending to individuals [a] LPMB4TH	**Total (excluding the Student Loans Company) sterling net consumer credit lending to individuals LPMB3PT**	credit card lending to individuals LPMVZQS	other consumer credit lending to individuals LPMB4TV
31 Jan 13	-534	-6	-277	-811	-1052	241
28 Feb 13	244	75	-447	-202	-22	-180
31 Mar 13	-46	38	901	855	-40	895
30 Apr 13	729	45	93	822	374	448
31 May 13	250	7	171	421	268	153
30 Jun 13	314	13	289	603	522	81
31 Jul 13	718	14	123	841	-43	884
31 Aug 13	584	-1	53	637	544	93
30 Sep 13	941	-9	961	1902	276	1627
31 Oct 13	-327	-27	316	-11	-151	140
30 Nov 13	269	-35	511	780	999	-219
31 Dec 13	1259	-	582	1840	917	924
31 Jan 14	-762	-	-17	-780	-825	46
28 Feb 14	4	-	-160	-155	-90	-66
31 Mar 14	787	-	1012	1799	-276	2075
30 Apr 14	528	-	-18	510	602	-92
31 May 14	501	-	230	731	210	521
30 Jun 14	840	-	143	983	352	630
31 Jul 14	751	-	346	1097	166	931
31 Aug 14	480	-	216	696	542	154
30 Sep 14	1021	-	1125	2146	143	2003
31 Oct 14	59	-	316	375	92	283
30 Nov 14	862	-	522	1384	851	533
31 Dec 14	1115	-	496	1611	1150	461
31 Jan 15	-732	-	41	-691	-920	229
28 Feb 15	47	-	-138	-91	-118	27
31 Mar 15	1397	-	1140	2537	-203	2740
30 Apr 15	590	-	400	990	823	167
31 May 15	303	-	418	721	94	627
30 Jun 15	1327	-	418	1745	552	1193
31 Jul 15	833	-	510	1343	345	997
31 Aug 15	916	-	172	1088	580	508
30 Sep 15	999	-	1455	2454	234	2220
31 Oct 15	75	-	456	532	14	518
30 Nov 15	1579	-	755	2334	1267	1067
31 Dec 15	860	-	771	1630	1130	501
31 Jan 16	-202	-	256	54	-662	715
29 Feb 16	596	-	80	676	-143	819
31 Mar 16	1260	-	1651	2911	324	2588
30 Apr 16	201	-	561	762	470	292
31 May 16	1371	-	510	1881	601	1280
30 Jun 16	1207	-	658	1864	649	1215
31 Jul 16	743	-	462	1206	420	786
31 Aug 16	1563	-	185	1748	763	985
30 Sep 16	753	-	1712	2464	368	2096
31 Oct 16	736	-	639	1375	388	987
30 Nov 16	1523	-	1134	2657	1327	1330
31 Dec 16	144	-	860	1005	1040	-35

[a] These series may be affected by securitisations and loan transfers up to December 2009.

Source: Bank of England

[b] This series will be discontinued with effect from December 2013 data. Further information can be found in Bankstats, December 2013, `Changes to publication of data for mutually owned monetary financial institutions', available at www.bankofengland.co.uk/statistics/Documents/ms/articles/art1dec13.pdf.

[c] Separate data for banks and building societies have been discontinued from January 2010 onwards. For details, see the Monetary and Financial Statistics articleÂ http://www.bankofengland.co.uk/statistics/documents/ms/articles/artjan10.pdf. (31 Jan 2010)

[d] Please note that the compilation and descriptions of some credit series have changed from publication of April 2015 data, as described in Bankstats, April 2015, 'Changes to the treatment of loan transfers and lending to housing associations', available at www.bankofengland.co.uk/statistics/Documents/ms/articles/art1apr15.pdf.

12.13a INVESTMENT TRUSTS' ASSETS AND LIABILITIES AT MARKET VALUES

£ million

		2005	2006	2007	2008	2009	2010	2011	2012	2013	2014	2015	2016
ASSETS													
UK government securities denominated in sterling	RLLT	768	533	715	628	585	466	681	857	487	302	244	415
Index-linked	AFIS	0	0	0	0	0	8	95	c	45	47	c	c
Other[1]	K5HJ	768	533	715	628	585	458	586	c	442	255	c	c
UK government securities denominated in foreign currency	CBPP	0	0	0	0	0	0	0	0	0	0	0	0
UK local authority investments[2]	AHBR	0	0	0	0	0	0	0	0	0	0	0	c
Other UK public sector investments[3]	AHBS	0	0	0	0	0	0	0	0	0	0	0	0
UK ordinary shares													
Quoted[4]	AHBM	24,021	21,843	21,848	13,428	16,297	17,547	17,329	18,655	18,907	19,384	20,551	22,918
Unquoted	AHBQ	1,016	1,027	1,186	938	1,349	1,336	1,437	1,363	1,323	1,616	2,224	3,940
Overseas ordinary shares	AHCC	23,065	21,659	25,795	18,385	23,865	29,341	29,083	30,758	31,859	31,491	36,880	47,519
Other corporate securities[5]													
UK	CBGZ	673	1,071	1,259	813	665	560	529	470	498	350	427	529
Overseas	CBHA	937	741	1,038	623	939	1,304	1,344	1,129	1,217	775	698	531
UK authorised unit trust units	AHBT	140	24	0	28	33	42	76	53	86	119	331	394
Overseas government, provincial and municipal securities	AHBY	168	4	151	410	256	410	254	251	118	107	c	c
UK existing buildings, property, land and new construction work	CBHB	117	252	154	142	141	197	1,522	1,538	158	202	216	379
Other longer-term assets not elsewhere classified[6]	AMSE	2,359	2,898	3,462	3,684	3,824	4,618	5,439	5,744	6,240	8,168	c	8,665
LONGER-TERM ASSETS	**AHBD**	**53,264**	**50,052**	**55,608**	**39,079**	**47,954**	**55,821**	**57,694**	**60,818**	**60,893**	**62,514**	**68,830**	**85,474**
Short-term assets	CBGX	3,032	2,138	3,303	3,397	2,522	2,174	2,893	3,015	2,848	3,377	3,194	4,743
TOTAL ASSETS	**CBGW**	**56,296**	**52,190**	**58,911**	**42,476**	**50,476**	**57,995**	**60,587**	**63,833**	**63,741**	**65,891**	**72,024**	**90,217**
LIABILITIES													
Borrowing from UK and overseas banks[7]	CBHD	2,771	2,900	2,708	2,553	2,216	2,359	2,897	2,845	3,652	3,373	3,189	3,598
Other UK borrowing[8]	CBHG	670	952	988	1,012	1,062	1,123	914	865	989	1,099	1,432	1,631
Other overseas borrowing[9]	CBHI	0	2	0	225	185	186	126	117	11	c	162	213
Issued share and loan capital[10]	CBHK	7,155	5,492	5,659	3,834	3,627	3,361	4,395	4,345	3,741	3,237	3,133	4,468
TOTAL LIABILITIES	**CBHO**	**10,596**	**9,346**	**9,355**	**7,624**	**7,090**	**7,029**	**8,332**	**8,172**	**8,393**	**7,810**	**7,916**	**9,910**
NET ASSETS	**CBHM**	**45,700**	**42,844**	**49,556**	**34,852**	**43,386**	**50,966**	**52,255**	**55,661**	**55,348**	**58,081**	**64,108**	**80,307**

c Suppressed to avoid the disclosure of confidential data.

Source: Office for National Statistics

1 Includes securities of: 0 up to 15 years maturity; over 15 years maturity and undated maturity. Excludes treasury bills and index-linked securities.

2 Includes local authority securities; negotiable bonds; loans and mortgages.

3 Includes public corporation loans and mortgages and other public sector investments not elsewhere classified.

4 Includes investment trust securities.

5 Includes corporate bonds and preference shares.

6 Includes UK unauthorised unit trust units; UK open-ended investment companies; overseas mutual fund investments; other UK fixed assets; overseas fixed assets; overseas direct investment and other UK and overseas assets not elsewhere classified.

7 Sterling and foreign currency. Includes foreign currency liabilities on back-to-back loans and overdrafts.

8 Includes sterling and foreign currency borrowing from building societies; issue of securities (other than ordinary shares); issue of sterling commercial paper and other borrowing not elsewhere classified (such as borrowing from parent, subsidiary and associate companies and other related concerns).

9 Includes borrowing from related companies and other borrowing not elsewhere classified.

10 Quoted and unquoted. Includes ordinary shares; preference shares; deferred stocks; bonds; debentures and loan stocks.

12.13b UNIT TRUSTS AND PROPERTY UNIT TRUSTS' BALANCE SHEET ASSETS AND LIABILITIES AT MARKET VALUES

£ million

		2005	2006	2007	2008	2009	2010	2011	2012	2013	2014	2015	2016
ASSETS													
UK government securities denominated in sterling[1]	CBHT	25,181	31,603	32,120	33,466	29,331	33,306	37,116	36,033	37,275	44,970	41,824	49,352
Ordinary shares[2]													
UK	RLIB	157,149	185,637	195,009	143,550	167,401	204,616	179,940	201,822	234,866	241,783	249,355	268,812
Overseas	RLIC	105,443	127,409	142,211	113,667	150,863	200,028	187,714	215,705	265,209	288,079	298,515	361,606
Other corporate securities[3]													
UK	CBHU	29,293	29,876	30,626	30,174	36,646	52,786	52,735	63,546	60,803	66,686	64,615	65,598
Overseas	CBHV	16,057	25,617	30,029	30,442	43,301	49,098	48,388	62,870	67,946	78,566	88,047	94,286
Overseas government, provincial and municipal securities	CBHW	3,412	3,532	3,880	5,754	5,810	9,251	14,797	19,604	19,698	23,184	26,171	38,918
UK existing buildings, property, land and new construction work	RLIE	9,623	12,781	12,480	8,518	7,248	9,484	13,220	13,498	13,576	15,706	17,432	24,207
Other longer-term assets not elsewhere classified[4]	CBHX	22,327	29,765	38,707	42,670	49,417	60,029	66,640	81,849	105,015	110,193	118,554	146,158
Short-term assets	CBHS	16,417	20,653	27,969	35,224	37,263	48,382	45,001	53,734	62,021	56,686	65,130	78,978
of which:													
Derivative contracts with UK and overseas counterparties which have a positive (asset) value5	KUU5	4,745	4,552	7,271	13,151	17,132	25,944	18,168	25,644	27,923	13,320	12,550	18,266
TOTAL ASSETS	**CBHR**	**384,902**	**466,873**	**513,031**	**443,465**	**527,280**	**666,980**	**645,551**	**748,661**	**866,409**	**925,853**	**969,643**	**1,127,915**

12.13b UNIT TRUSTS AND PROPERTY UNIT TRUSTS' BALANCE SHEET ASSETS AND LIABILITIES AT MARKET VALUES

£ million

		2005	2006	2007	2008	2009	2010	2011	2012	2013	2014	2015	2016
LIABILITIES													
Borrowing from UK and overseas banks[6]	RLLF	1,456	2,544	2,603	3,486	1,541	991	1,992	3,430	3,154	2,834	2,072	c
Other UK borrowing[7]	RLLH	130	16	36	80	26	74	350	83	34	109	c	c
Other overseas borrowing[8]	RLLI	1	0	0	0	54	0	0	0	0	0	c	0
Derivative contracts with UK and overseas counterparties which have a negative (liability) value5	KUU6	2,814	3,701	6,382	11,890	15,294	23,676	17,464	22,832	26,255	12,122	14,265	20,559
Other creditors, provisions and liabilities not elsewhere classified	KUU7	2,425	3,370	2,562	3,442	5,524	7,228	14,087	5,460	1,740	4,424	5,880	2,540
Liability attributable to unit and share holders	RLLG	378,076	457,242	501,448	424,567	504,841	635,011	611,658	716,856	835,226	906,364	947,406	1,101,587
TOTAL LIABILITIES	**RLLE**	**384,902**	**466,873**	**513,031**	**443,465**	**527,280**	**666,980**	**645,551**	**748,661**	**866,409**	**925,853**	**969,643**	**1,127,915**

Source: Office for National Statistics

c Suppressed to avoid the disclosure of confidential data. Components may not sum to totals due to rounding.

1 Includes securities of: 0 up to 15 years maturity; over 15 years maturity; undated maturity and index-linked. Excludes treasury bills.

2 Quoted and unquoted. Includes investment trust securities.

3 Includes corporate bonds and preference shares.

4 UK and overseas. Includes UK government securities denominated in foreign currency; local authority and public corporation securities; mutual fund investments; other UK fixed assets; overseas fixed assets; direct investment and other assets not elsewhere classified.

5 Includes credit default products; employee stock options; other options; other swaps; futures; forwards and other derivative contracts not elsewhere classified.

6 Sterling and foreign currency. Includes foreign currency liabilities on back-to-back loans and overdrafts.

7 Includes sterling and foreign currency borrowing from building societies; issue of securities (other than ordinary shares); issue of sterling commercial paper and other borrowing not elsewhere classified (such as borrowing from parent, subsidiary and associate companies and other related concerns).

8 Includes borrowing from related companies and other borrowing not elsewhere classified.

12.14 SELF-ADMINISTERED PENSION FUNDS'[1] BALANCE SHEET ASSETS AND LIABILITIES AT MARKET VALUES

£ million

		2005	2006	2007	2008	2009	2010	2011	2012	2013	2014	2015	2016
ASSETS													
UK government securities denominated in sterling	AHVK	94,325	104,910	113,617	98,577	108,871	122,007	167,372	199,400	227,528	260,553	289,169	374,651
Index-linked	AHWC	48,821	53,858	64,797	58,564	70,317	83,016	110,808	142,565	159,843	178,465	195,291	262,818
Other[2]	J8Y5	45,504	51,052	48,820	40,013	38,554	38,991	56,564	56,835	67,685	82,088	93,878	111,833
UK government securities denominated in foreign currency	RYEX	45	27	42	4	126	89	1,287	5,695	275	351	32	52
UK local authority investments[3]	AHVO	4	2	5	0	2	274	113	263	291	284	276	286
Other UK public sector investments[4]	JE5J	846	1,118	1,351	1,259	2,347	2,911	1,703	1,611	3,862	582	224	4,176
UK PUBLIC SECTOR SECURITIES	**RYHC**	**95,220**	**106,057**	**115,015**	**99,840**	**111,346**	**125,281**	**170,475**	**206,969**	**231,956**	**261,770**	**289,701**	**379,165**
UK corporate bonds[5]	JX62	47,912	54,626	57,306	55,741	64,351	59,469	61,586	64,508	64,581	76,987	74,441	83,548
Sterling	GQFT	47,061	53,190	55,550	53,765	62,073	57,086	59,322	61,896	61,938	73,601	71,297	79,855
Foreign currency	GQFU	851	1,436	1,756	1,976	2,278	2,383	2,264	2,612	2,643	3,386	3,144	3,693
UK ordinary shares[6]	AHVP	199,199	208,473	152,048	110,571	116,710	121,882	108,631	111,913	109,777	95,981	84,403	87,581
UK preference shares[6]	J8YF	153	276	235	775	833	16	11	29	51	77	53	537
Overseas corporate securities	JRS8	203,562	224,514	215,068	175,747	214,230	222,751	211,562	226,274	232,277	259,644	245,442	259,266
Bonds	RLPF	19,891	30,867	44,387	47,612	57,920	60,826	61,129	60,424	61,655	70,977	75,726	72,539
Ordinary shares	AHVR	183,060	192,978	169,598	127,525	155,577	161,043	149,638	165,141	170,007	187,923	169,255	186,159
Preference shares	RLPC	611	669	1,083	610	733	882	795	709	615	744	461	568
Mutual fund investments	JRS9	192,033	215,218	254,936	211,724	286,493	369,955	385,337	448,583	476,623	449,664	499,047	588,774
UK	J8Y7	150,316	168,635	194,833	148,798	203,523	266,058	264,652	293,071	302,024	283,997	317,215	382,681
Unit trust units[7]	JX63	105,429	115,872	147,536	110,558	148,642	178,027	172,120	208,155	212,566	191,218	207,703	234,424
Other[8]	JX64	44,887	52,763	47,297	38,240	54,881	88,031	92,532	84,916	89,458	92,779	109,512	148,257
Overseas	JE4P	41,717	46,583	60,103	62,926	82,970	103,897	120,685	155,512	174,599	165,667	181,832	206,093

12.14 SELF-ADMINISTERED PENSION FUNDS'[1] BALANCE SHEET ASSETS AND LIABILITIES AT MARKET VALUES

£ million

		2005	2006	2007	2008	2009	2010	2011	2012	2013	2014	2015	2016
CORPORATE SECURITIES	**RYHN**	**642,859**	**703,107**	**679,593**	**554,558**	**682,617**	**774,073**	**767,127**	**851,307**	**883,309**	**882,353**	**903,386**	**1,019,706**
Overseas government, provincial and municipal securities	AHVT	19,037	21,776	22,434	21,527	16,900	17,335	21,424	23,768	23,462	22,643	22,306	26,762
Loans	JRT4	9	42	417	518	1,768	2,343	1,656	1,313	324	94	601	944
UK[9]	JE5E	6	6	12	0	116	81	77	170	c	c	c	c
Overseas[10]	AHVZ	3	36	405	518	1,652	2,262	1,579	1,143	c	c	c	c
Fixed assets[11]	JRT5	31,742	34,608	30,466	22,892	24,957	30,159	32,991	30,705	33,695	37,734	40,630	42,138
UK	JE5F	31,616	34,435	30,306	22,818	24,718	28,991	32,178	30,372	33,064	36,937	39,655	40,990
Overseas	GOLB	126	173	160	74	239	1,168	813	333	631	797	975	1,148
Investment in insurance managed funds, insurance policies and annuities	RYHS	86,336	92,387	103,610	86,541	70,318	80,613	93,823	99,896	110,723	122,194	134,665	143,489
Other longer-term assets not elsewhere classified[12]	J8YA	21,423	31,234	41,455	45,301	51,100	69,419	81,562	90,893	109,368	84,875	82,323	107,971
OTHER LONGER-TERM ASSETS	**RYHW**	**158,547**	**180,047**	**198,382**	**176,779**	**165,043**	**199,869**	**231,456**	**246,575**	**277,572**	**267,540**	**280,525**	**321,304**
LONGER-TERM ASSETS	**RYHX**	**896,626**	**989,211**	**992,990**	**831,177**	**959,006**	**1,099,223**	**1,169,058**	**1,304,851**	**1,392,837**	**1,411,663**	**1,473,612**	**1,720,175**

Source: Office for National Statistics

c Suppressed to avoid the disclosure of confidential data. Components may not sum to totals due to rounding.

1 Combined public and private sector. Data from the pension funds surveys are of lower quality than equivalent data from other institutional groups because of the difficulties in constructing a suitable sampling frame of pension funds.

2 Includes securities of: 0 up to 15 years maturity; over 15 years maturity and undated maturity. Excludes treasury bills and index-linked securities.

3 Includes local authority securities; negotiable bonds; loans and mortgages.

4 Includes public corporation loans and mortgages and other public sector investments not elsewhere classified.

5 Issued by: banks; building societies and other corporates.

6 Quoted and unquoted.

7 Authorised and unauthorised.

8 Includes property unit trusts; investment trust securities; open-ended investment companies; hedge funds and other mutual fund investments not elsewhere classified.

9 Includes sterling asset backed loans; loans to individuals secured on dwellings; other loans to individuals (including policy loans); loans to businesses and other loans not elsewhere classified. Excludes loans to UK associate companies; bank term deposits and building society investments.

10 Includes loans to parent companies; subsidiaries; associates and other loans not elsewhere classified. Excludes loans categorised as direct investment; loans covered by Export Credit Guarantee Department (ECGD), specific bank guarantees or ECGD buyer credit guarantees.

11 UK and overseas. Includes existing buildings; property; land; new construction work; vehicles; machinery and equipment; valuables and intangibles. Includes the capital value of assets bought on hire purchase or acquired (as lessee) under a finance leasing arrangement and assets acquired for hiring, renting and operating leasing purposes. Excludes the capital value of assets acquired but leased out to others under finance leasing arrangements.

12 UK and overseas. Includes certificates of tax deposit; insurance policies; annuities and loans covered by Export Credit Guarantee Department (ECGD), specific bank guarantees or ECGD buyer credit guarantees. Excludes pre-payments and debtors.

12.14 SELF-ADMINISTERED PENSION FUNDS[1] BALANCE SHEET ASSETS AND LIABILITIES AT MARKET VALUES

continued

£ million

		2005	2006	2007	2008	2009	2010	2011	2012	2013	2014	2015	2016
ASSETS													
Cash	GNOR	0	0	0	0	0	0	0	0	0	0	0	0
Balances with banks and building societies in the UK	JX5Q	17,789	22,823	25,974	20,133	23,054	23,736	23,854	22,929	22,701	25,881	22,433	21,274
Sterling	JX5S	15,510	20,211	22,615	16,802	19,099	20,043	20,159	18,901	18,193	21,841	17,525	15,757
Foreign currency	JX5U	2,279	2,612	3,359	3,331	3,955	3,693	3,695	4,028	4,508	4,040	4,908	5,517
Balances with overseas banks	GNOW	361	525	807	351	134	197	72	157	349	c	137	86
Other liquid deposits[13]	GNOX	3,010	3,891	5,392	4,300	12,431	9,631	11,956	15,265	20,505	15,084	13,133	16,182
Certificates of deposit issued by banks and building societies in the UK[14]	IX8H	2,649	4,932	8,156	6,480	2,269	2,472	6,498	2,069	1,288	455	522	804
Money market instruments issued by HM Treasury[15]	IX9J	89	22	304	548	1,709	1,109	1,734	4,116	1,167	1,698	1,828	3,767
UK local authority debt	AHVF	270	221	205	323	210	116	157	232	130	c	408	396
Commercial paper issued by UK companies[16]	GQFR	476	401	857	367	664	1,135	993	1,254	334	286	551	1,278
Other UK money market instruments[17]	GOZR	883	1,174	1,893	1,959	2,822	3,416	3,936	2,716	4,655	3,928	4,406	2,397
Money market instruments issued by non-resident businesses	GOZS	384	449	1,279	911	963	2,067	3,709	2,752	2,752	6,099	4,149	7,293
Other short-term assets not elsewhere classified[18]	JX5W	1,854	1,898	1,304	3,474	3,113	3,644	2,311	1,904	1,788	2,592	1,462	1,452
Balances outstanding from stockbrokers and securities dealers[19]	RYIL	18,879	24,812	28,297	30,536	11,281	7,145	8,241	6,213	5,989	5,379	7,740	9,767
Income accrued on investments and rents	RYIM	1,970	2,303	2,744	2,576	2,714	2,761	2,930	2,872	3,169	2,651	2,921	3,274
Amounts outstanding from HM Revenue and Customs[19]	RYIN	29	16	15	23	32	37	53	67	54	65	88	82
Other debtors and assets not elsewhere classified	RYIO	25,006	35,224	22,454	24,565	21,464	13,159	8,902	11,387	7,543	5,933	4,398	4,757
Derivative contracts with UK counterparties which have a positive (asset) value[20]	JRO3	22,157	24,357	29,789	35,194	61,862	99,420	170,170	186,184	191,511	222,296	225,060	252,227
Derivative contracts with overseas counterparties which have a positive (asset) value[20]	GOJU	2,668	5,995	8,652	5,835	20,534	19,803	29,445	38,324	49,910	79,679	87,428	74,623
TOTAL ASSETS	**RYIR**	**995,100**	**1,118,254**	**1,131,112**	**968,752**	**1,124,262**	**1,289,071**	**1,444,019**	**1,603,292**	**1,706,682**	**1,784,104**	**1,850,276**	**2,119,834**

12.14 SELF-ADMINISTERED PENSION FUNDS'[1] BALANCE SHEET ASSETS AND LIABILITIES AT MARKET VALUES

continued

£ million

Source: Office for National Statistics

c Suppressed to avoid the disclosure of confidential data. Components may not sum to totals due to rounding.

1 Combined public and private sector. Data from the pension funds surveys are of lower quality than equivalent data from other institutional groups because of the difficulties in constructing a suitable sampling frame of pension funds.
13 Includes money market funds; liquidity funds and cash liquidity funds.
14 Sterling and foreign currency.
15 Includes treasury bills. Excludes UK government securities.
16 Sterling and foreign currency commercial paper issued by: banks; building societies; other financial institutions and other issuing companies.
17 Includes floating rate notes maturing within one year of issue.
18 UK and overseas. Excludes derivative contracts.
19 Gross value.
20 Includes credit default products; employee stock options; other options; other swaps; futures; forwards and other derivative contracts not elsewhere classified.

12.14 SELF-ADMINISTERED PENSION FUNDS'[1] BALANCE SHEET ASSETS AND LIABILITIES AT MARKET VALUES

continued — £ million

		2005	2006	2007	2008	2009	2010	2011	2012	2013	2014	2015	2016
LIABILITIES													
Borrowing[21]	GQED	11,678	14,661	16,180	4,461	3,859	2,830	3,361	10,603	16,050	27,135	39,141	45,947
Balances owed to stockbrokers and securities dealers[19]	RYIS	18,722	25,954	33,965	37,912	13,707	7,312	9,688	7,816	8,267	9,869	12,346	18,251
Pensions due but not paid[22]	RYIT	86	285	220	167	280	271	300	5,152	2,672	3,693	3,783	5,283
Derivative contracts with UK counterparties which have a negative (liability) value[20]	JRP9	16,818	17,231	26,187	27,533	37,689	78,322	147,217	149,493	161,962	181,946	196,477	199,739
Derivative contracts with overseas counterparties which have a negative (liability) value[20]	GKGR	2,785	7,036	11,275	6,335	41,110	37,345	42,712	60,725	73,848	109,217	114,944	118,657
Other creditors, provisions and liabilities not elsewhere classified	RYIU	24,834	36,208	18,327	20,577	21,603	18,889	9,905	9,011	13,236	3,006	6,866	17,627
Market value of pension funds[23]	AHVA	920,177	1,016,879	1,024,958	871,767	1,006,014	1,144,102	1,230,836	1,360,492	1,430,647	1,449,238	1,476,719	1,714,330
TOTAL LIABILITIES	**RYIR**	**995,100**	**1,118,254**	**1,131,112**	**968,752**	**1,124,262**	**1,289,071**	**1,444,019**	**1,603,292**	**1,706,682**	**1,784,104**	**1,850,276**	**2,119,834**

Source: Office for National Statistics

c Suppressed to avoid the disclosure of confidential data. Components may not sum to totals due to rounding.

1 Combined public and private sector. Data from the pension funds surveys are of lower quality than equivalent data from other institutional groups because of the difficulties in constructing a suitable sampling frame of pension funds.

19 Gross value.

20 Includes credit default products; employee stock options; other options; other swaps; futures; forwards and other derivative contracts not elsewhere classified.

21 UK and overseas. Includes from a UK perspective: sterling and foreign currency borrowing from UK banks and building societies; borrowing arising from the issue of floating rate notes and preference shares; foreign currency liabilities on back-to-back loans; overdrafts and other borrowing not elsewhere classified. Includes from an overseas perspective: borrowing from banks and other borrowing not elsewhere classified.

22 Excludes any estimated future liabilities.

23 Net value as found in statement of net assets.

12.15a INSURANCE COMPANIES' BALANCE SHEET: LONG-TERM BUSINESS ASSETS AND LIABILITIES AT MARKET VALUES

£ million

		2005	2006	2007	2008	2009	2010	2011	2012	2013	2014	2015	2016
ASSETS													
UK government securities denominated in sterling	AHNJ	161,906	161,641	158,694	166,879	167,247	182,506	205,223	187,145	170,950	179,602	163,502	175,735
Index-linked	AHQI	33,722	41,104	45,902	54,387	57,157	66,115	78,354	72,499	71,234	81,181	72,840	80,206
Other[1]	J5HZ	128,184	120,537	112,792	112,492	110,090	116,391	126,869	114,646	99,716	98,421	90,662	95,529
UK government securities denominated in foreign currency	RGBV	206	12	0	0	0	0	0	0	0	0	c	0
UK local authority investments[2]	AHNN	1,840	1,614	998	776	655	768	813	770	3,168	8,390	c	10,477
Other UK public sector investments[3]	RGCS	801	651	634	872	1,461	2,189	2,207	2,197	3,684	2,496	2,129	1,130
UK PUBLIC SECTOR SECURITIES	**RYEK**	**164,753**	**163,918**	**160,326**	**168,527**	**169,363**	**185,463**	**208,243**	**190,112**	**177,802**	**190,488**	**173,188**	**187,342**
UK corporate bonds[4]	IFLF	165,918	159,073	159,273	159,789	160,532	158,987	163,348	178,627	167,021	177,937	176,016	176,182
Sterling	IFLG	158,995	150,907	153,694	154,525	155,184	156,477	160,842	174,682	165,453	176,486	175,269	174,804
Foreign currency	IFLH	6,923	8,166	5,579	5,264	5,348	2,510	2,506	3,945	1,568	1,451	747	1,378
UK ordinary shares[5]	IFLI	273,679	299,717	293,655	188,430	209,992	207,971	177,480	162,949	170,841	160,294	145,908	143,479
UK preference shares[5]	RLOL	1,228	1,231	983	724	624	648	536	375	340	271	230	196
Overseas corporate securities	IFLJ	165,452	194,997	234,388	219,957	266,280	278,930	262,823	303,565	315,453	331,122	339,248	391,047
Bonds	RLOP	45,970	57,774	69,696	85,077	111,866	112,338	115,744	127,629	119,631	122,217	119,028	129,841
Ordinary shares	AHNQ	119,207	136,652	163,249	134,211	153,500	165,216	145,932	173,982	194,250	207,643	219,253	259,793
Preference shares	RLOM	275	571	1,443	669	914	1,376	1,147	1,954	1,572	1,262	967	1,413
Mutual fund investments[6]	IFLK	168,896	192,516	222,081	186,950	230,247	259,457	265,750	328,657	360,502	390,694	449,493	506,913
CORPORATE SECURITIES	**RYEO**	**775,173**	**847,534**	**910,380**	**755,850**	**867,675**	**905,993**	**869,937**	**974,173**	**1,014,157**	**1,060,318**	**1,110,895**	**1,217,817**
Overseas government, provincial and municipal securities	AHNS	16,065	21,078	25,787	29,053	24,601	25,363	23,727	26,928	30,013	34,234	36,854	33,332
Other longer-term assets not elsewhere classified[7]	JX8D	83,665	92,326	99,316	76,139	67,531	74,900	81,916	81,039	74,737	80,064	78,488	95,239
OTHER LONGER-TERM ASSETS	**RYER**	**99,730**	**113,404**	**125,103**	**105,192**	**92,132**	**100,263**	**105,643**	**107,967**	**104,750**	**114,298**	**115,342**	**128,571**
LONGER-TERM ASSETS	**RYES**	**1,039,656**	**1,124,856**	**1,195,809**	**1,029,569**	**1,129,170**	**1,191,719**	**1,183,823**	**1,272,252**	**1,296,709**	**1,365,104**	**1,399,425**	**1,533,730**

c Suppressed to avoid the disclosure of confidential data. Components may not sum to totals due to rounding.

Source: Office for National Statistics

1 Includes securities of: 0 up to 15 years maturity; over 15 years maturity and undated maturity. Excludes treasury bills and index-linked securities.

2 Includes local authority securities; negotiable bonds; loans and mortgages.

3 Includes public corporation loans and mortgages and other public sector investments not elsewhere classified.

4 Issued by: banks; building societies and other corporates.

5 Quoted and unquoted.

6 UK and overseas. Includes authorised and unauthorised unit trust units; investment trust securities; open-ended investment companies; hedge funds and other mutual fund investments not elsewhere classified.

7 UK and overseas. Includes loans; fixed assets and other longer-term assets not elsewhere classified.

12.15a INSURANCE COMPANIES' BALANCE SHEET: LONG-TERM BUSINESS ASSETS AND LIABILITIES AT MARKET VALUES

continued

£ million

		2005	2006	2007	2008	2009	2010	2011	2012	2013	2014	2015	2016
ASSETS													
Cash	HLGW	29	0	0	0	0	0	0	0	0	0	0	0
Balances with banks and building societies in the UK	JX2C	31,606	34,454	48,619	51,139	44,483	34,026	34,998	35,424	26,785	26,456	25,901	26,985
Sterling	JX3R	30,221	32,653	45,948	47,456	42,097	32,387	32,698	33,805	24,616	23,842	22,896	24,941
Foreign currency	JX3T	1,385	1,801	2,671	3,683	2,386	1,639	2,300	1,619	2,169	2,614	3,005	2,044
Balances with overseas banks	HLHB	1,454	1,022	1,484	2,816	3,758	2,766	1,726	1,381	3,143	3,884	1,703	1,562
Other liquid deposits[8]	HLHC	1,215	333	678	1,638	12,385	14,076	15,891	17,257	38,843	39,791	46,570	48,885
Certificates of deposit issued by banks and building societies in the UK[9]	AHND	14,200	17,256	15,177	11,401	8,177	8,622	6,158	5,769	5,318	6,080	6,483	4,680
Money market instruments issued by HM Treasury[10]	RGBM	537	685	785	179	1,344	509	1,392	1,081	2,688	1,261	1,312	1,310
UK local authority debt	AHNF	0	0	0	0	0	0	0	0	1	c	c	0
Commercial paper issued by UK companies[11]	JF77	5,130	2,714	2,723	2,268	1,806	646	891	496	648	458	696	271
Other UK money market instruments[12]	HLHL	2,670	3,538	3,071	3,159	2,959	3,208	5,501	3,540	2,055	2,212	2,358	c
Money market instruments issued by non-resident businesses	HLHM	1,681	405	859	689	1,755	2,956	1,530	2,068	907	1,047	c	c
Other short-term assets not elsewhere classified[13]	JX2E	10,432	10,749	20,965	19,555	10,076	5,232	6,159	6,008	5,582	c	3,407	3,762
Balances due from stockbrokers and securities dealers[14]	RGBU	-1,052	-345	140	-399	-1,159	-834	-1,245	-1,145	-1,228	-1,604	-737	-3,675

12.15a INSURANCE COMPANIES' BALANCE SHEET: LONG-TERM BUSINESS ASSETS AND LIABILITIES AT MARKET VALUES

continued £ million

		2005	2006	2007	2008	2009	2010	2011	2012	2013	2014	2015	2016
SHORT-TERM ASSETS (excluding derivatives)	**RYEW**	**67,902**	**70,811**	**94,501**	**92,445**	**85,584**	**71,207**	**73,001**	**71,879**	**84,742**	**82,966**	**89,292**	**91,087**
Derivative contracts with UK and overseas counterparties which have a positive (asset) value[15]	IFKX	5,739	5,937	5,205	17,892	10,317	12,399	24,060	20,805	18,144	39,790	30,148	53,829
Agents' balances and outstanding premiums in respect of direct insurance and facultative reinsurance contracts[16]													
UK	RYPA	500	669	738	535	467	515	554	620	769	652	c	432
Overseas	RYPB	-103	-136	-177	0	1	3	3	0	0	0	c	0
Reinsurance, coinsurance and treaty balances[17]													
UK	RYPC	2,607	3,462	-413	-1,000	3,817	-838	-1,147	-1,778	2,109	7,699	-1,078	c
Overseas	RYPD	929	1,105	836	-7,355	-8,232	-6,020	-6,035	-6,425	-5,590	-5,562	-5,077	c
Outstanding interest, dividends and rents[18]	RYPH	7,897	7,330	8,690	9,256	9,158	8,591	8,511	8,716	7,762	7,216	6,186	6,276
Other debtors and assets not elsewhere classified[19]	RYPF	19,694	44,923	51,373	37,342	33,162	30,366	28,806	27,717	28,595	21,833	29,100	18,685
Direct investment for non-insurance subsidiary and associate companies in the UK[20]	RYET	8,390	13,016	9,186	11,484	10,129	5,097	7,249	8,880	8,125	5,434	6,368	9,375
Direct investment for UK insurance subsidiary, associate and holding companies[20]	RYEU	2,528	6,114	7,578	7,890	7,234	6,720	7,152	4,275	3,865	6,873	2,057	1,455
Direct investment for overseas subsidiaries, associates, branches and agencies[20]	RYEV	4,455	3,341	3,832	5,011	4,141	4,131	3,340	3,470	4,296	3,542	2,762	2,988
TOTAL ASSETS	**RKBI**	**1,160,194**	**1,281,428**	**1,377,158**	**1,203,069**	**1,284,948**	**1,323,890**	**1,329,317**	**1,410,411**	**1,449,526**	**1,535,547**	**1,559,670**	**1,717,351**

c Suppressed to avoid the disclosure of confidential data. Components may not sum to totals due to rounding.

Source: Office for National Statistics

8 Includes money market funds; liquidity funds and cash liquidity funds.
9 Sterling and foreign currency.
10 Includes treasury bills. Excludes UK government securities.
11 Sterling and foreign currency commercial paper issued by: banks; building societies; other financial institutions and other issuing companies.
12 Includes floating rate notes maturing within one year of issue.
13 UK and overseas. Excludes derivative contracts.
14 Net of balances owed. Includes amounts due on securities bought and sold for future settlement.
15 Includes credit default products; employee stock options; other options; other swaps; futures; forwards and other derivative contracts not elsewhere classified.
16 Net of insurance liabilities.
17 Net of reinsurance bought and sold.
18 Net value.
19 Includes deferred acquisition costs.
20 Net asset value of attributable companies.

12.15a INSURANCE COMPANIES' BALANCE SHEET: LONG-TERM BUSINESS ASSETS AND LIABILITIES AT MARKET VALUES

continued

£ million

		2005	2006	2007	2008	2009	2010	2011	2012	2013	2014	2015	2016
LIABILITIES													
Borrowing	AHNI	15,224	14,369	12,426	12,467	10,866	12,542	12,084	10,660	10,112	9,578	8,983	10,892
Banks and building societies in the UK[9]	JX2G	5,043	2,867	3,801	5,089	3,305	2,099	1,980	961	1,011	461	776	1,288
Other UK[21]	ICXU	9,030	9,537	6,699	4,832	5,460	8,112	8,730	9,075	8,368	8,340	7,692	9,295
Overseas[22]	RGDD	1,151	1,965	1,926	2,546	2,101	2,331	1,374	624	733	777	515	309
Long-term business insurance and investment contract liabilities[23]	RKDC	1,037,658	1,125,221	1,205,183	1,069,993	1,153,944	1,178,823	1,171,844	1,241,671	1,277,415	1,346,456	1,380,449	1,523,568
Claims admitted but not paid[23]	RKBM	3,481	3,513	3,848	3,426	4,637	2,946	3,072	3,387	3,608	3,649	3,594	2,896
Provisions for taxation and dividends payable[24]	KVE9	8,245	8,120	7,489	60	1,781	2,973	1,993	2,400	2,919	4,041	2,520	4,716
Other creditors, provisions and liabilities not elsewhere classified[25]	RYPL	16,907	33,192	39,527	52,849	47,803	53,826	66,466	69,971	68,289	89,296	79,994	97,778
Excess of total assets over liabilities in respect of: long-term business; minority interests in UK subsidiary companies; shareholders' capital and reserves and any other reserves[26]	A4YP	78,679	97,013	108,685	64,274	65,917	72,780	73,858	82,322	87,183	82,527	84,130	77,501
TOTAL LIABILITIES	**RKBI**	**1,160,194**	**1,281,428**	**1,377,158**	**1,203,069**	**1,284,948**	**1,323,890**	**1,329,317**	**1,410,411**	**1,449,526**	**1,535,547**	**1,559,670**	**1,717,351**

c Suppressed to avoid the disclosure of confidential data. Components may not sum to totals due to rounding.

Source: Office for National Statistics

9 Sterling and foreign currency.

21 Includes issue of securities (other than ordinary shares); issue of sterling commercial paper and other borrowing not elsewhere classified.

22 Includes borrowing from banks; related companies and other borrowing not elsewhere classified.

23 Net of reinsurers share.

24 UK and overseas. Includes deferred tax net of amounts receivable.

25 UK and overseas. Includes derivative contracts which have a negative (liability) value.

26 Includes unallocated divisible surplus and the 'net worth' of UK branches of overseas companies, including profit and loss account balances.

12.15b INSURANCE COMPANIES' BALANCE SHEET: GENERAL BUSINESS ASSETS AND LIABILITIES AT MARKET VALUES

£ million

		2005	2006	2007	2008	2009	2010	2011	2012	2013	2014	2015	2016
ASSETS													
UK government securities denominated in sterling	AHMJ	19,818	19,296	16,026	18,441	16,969	13,631	13,384	11,774	12,855	14,712	13,308	14,561
Index-linked	AHMZ	538	603	297	1,622	1,991	1,731	1,724	2,150	2,355	3,009	2,724	3,022
Other[1]	J8EX	19,280	18,693	15,729	16,819	14,978	11,900	11,660	9,624	10,500	11,703	10,584	11,539
UK government securities denominated in foreign currency	RYMQ	12	72	69	3	0	0	c	13	18	0	c	0
UK local authority investments[2]	AHMN	44	0	3	0	0	0	c	0	0	0	c	c
Other UK public sector investments[3]	RYMU	6	0	10	0	65	249	c	252	209	446	184	c
UK PUBLIC SECTOR SECURITIES	**RYMV**	**19,880**	**19,368**	**16,108**	**18,444**	**17,034**	**13,880**	**13,907**	**12,039**	**13,082**	**15,158**	**13,521**	**14,608**
UK corporate bonds[4]	IFVV	10,815	11,797	13,397	12,060	13,550	10,487	10,817	12,127	12,355	12,462	11,530	12,617
Sterling	IFVW	9,932	11,057	12,647	11,009	12,288	9,544	10,217	11,264	11,610	11,716	10,671	11,817
Foreign currency	IFVX	883	740	750	1,051	1,262	943	600	863	745	746	859	800
UK ordinary shares[5]	IFVY	9,864	10,138	9,006	10,501	9,963	9,525	8,435	8,732	7,846	3,500	3,402	3,092
UK preference shares[5]	RLOT	40	9	44	29	26	26	25	21	21	25	20	20
Overseas corporate securities	IFVZ	12,645	18,636	14,773	20,258	23,002	17,594	18,636	24,380	24,638	27,748	28,637	30,822
Bonds	RLOX	10,866	16,128	12,872	18,081	21,017	15,847	16,939	21,872	21,834	24,276	25,307	27,200
Ordinary shares	AHMQ	1,779	2,507	1,901	2,175	1,976	1,741	1,692	2,501	c	3,462	c	c
Preference shares	RLOU	0	1	0	2	9	6	5	7	c	10	c	c
Mutual fund investments[6]	IFWA	1,270	1,256	1,780	1,911	3,498	4,878	5,802	4,236	4,686	4,951	4,610	3,384
CORPORATE SECURITIES	**RYNF**	**34,634**	**41,836**	**39,000**	**44,759**	**50,039**	**42,510**	**43,715**	**49,496**	**49,546**	**48,686**	**48,199**	**49,935**
Overseas government, provincial and municipal securities	AHMS	7,341	8,035	4,869	8,505	7,204	5,126	5,524	9,355	9,584	8,373	9,079	8,519
Other longer-term assets not elsewhere classified[7]	JX8E	6,362	6,746	7,059	8,269	7,338	9,158	9,938	10,148	9,606	10,518	10,686	9,067
OTHER LONGER-TERM ASSETS	**RYNO**	**13,703**	**14,781**	**11,928**	**16,774**	**14,542**	**14,284**	**15,462**	**19,503**	**19,190**	**18,891**	**19,765**	**17,586**
LONGER-TERM ASSETS	**RYNP**	**68,217**	**75,985**	**67,036**	**79,977**	**81,615**	**70,674**	**73,084**	**81,038**	**81,818**	**82,735**	**81,485**	**82,129**

c Suppressed to avoid the disclosure of confidential data. Components may not sum to totals due to rounding.

Source: Office for National Statistics

1 Includes securities of: 0 up to 15 years maturity; over 15 years maturity and undated maturity. Excludes treasury bills and index-linked securities.
2 Includes local authority securities; negotiable bonds; loans and mortgages.
3 Includes public corporation loans and mortgages and other public sector investments not elsewhere classified.
4 Issued by: banks; building societies and other corporates.
5 Quoted and unquoted.
6 UK and overseas. Includes authorised and unauthorised unit trust units; investment trust securities; open-ended investment companies; hedge funds and other mutual fund investments not elsewhere classified.
7 UK and overseas. Includes loans; fixed assets and other longer-term assets not elsewhere classified.

12.15b INSURANCE COMPANIES' BALANCE SHEET: GENERAL BUSINESS ASSETS AND LIABILITIES AT MARKET VALUES

continued

£ million

		2005	2006	2007	2008	2009	2010	2011	2012	2013	2014	2015	2016
ASSETS													
Cash	HLMN	63	0	0	0	0	0	0	0	0	0	0	0
Balances with banks and building societies in the UK	JX3H	9,116	9,327	8,949	9,871	10,227	7,961	7,619	7,032	6,970	5,161	4,744	4,899
Sterling	JX43	7,952	6,501	6,907	8,170	8,763	6,730	6,532	5,988	5,583	3,974	3,480	3,363
Foreign currency	JX45	1,164	2,826	2,042	1,701	1,464	1,231	1,087	1,044	1,387	1,187	1,264	1,536
Balances with overseas banks	HLMS	1,116	1,031	1,015	1,250	1,138	981	1,150	1,841	1,369	617	976	565
Other liquid deposits[8]	HLMT	70	396	375	869	2,476	3,326	2,916	3,753	3,021	3,390	4,271	4,526
Certificates of deposit issued by banks and building societies in the UK[9]	IX8K	8,402	7,708	8,264	7,775	2,002	558	843	1,223	1,403	2,557	2,372	1,330
Money market instruments issued by HM Treasury[10]	ICWI	1,670	379	342	708	979	327	237	1,675	1,214	1,659	1,899	1,586
UK local authority debt	AHMF	0	0	0	0	0	0	0	0	0	0	0	0
Commercial paper issued by UK companies[11]	JF75	610	732	2,682	1,640	1,630	275	281	509	461	498	178	92
Other UK money market instruments[12]	HLNC	139	68	90	278	346	359	360	253	340	324	266	c
Money market instruments issued by non-resident businesses	HLND	2,429	3,516	3,261	2,277	2,321	545	745	449	1,120	570	562	c
Other short-term assets not elsewhere classified[13]	JX2I	2,992	1,733	612	1,576	718	725	933	1,064	781	1,413	797	963
Balances due from stockbrokers and securities dealers[14]	RYMA	3	-66	25	891	52	90	26	-1	37	-48	-34	-45

12.15b INSURANCE COMPANIES' BALANCE SHEET: GENERAL BUSINESS ASSETS AND LIABILITIES AT MARKET VALUES

continued

£ million

		2005	2006	2007	2008	2009	2010	2011	2012	2013	2014	2015	2016
SHORT-TERM ASSETS (excluding derivatives)	**RYME**	**26,610**	**24,824**	**25,615**	**27,135**	**21,889**	**15,147**	**15,110**	**17,798**	**16,716**	**16,141**	**16,031**	**14,792**
Derivative contracts with UK and overseas counterparties which have a positive (asset) value[15]	IFVJ	44	45	208	685	455	906	629	3,032	4,099	3,608	238	604
Agents' balances and outstanding premiums in respect of direct insurance and facultative reinsurance contracts[16]													
UK	RYMF	7,991	9,060	8,216	9,022	8,171	8,470	8,222	9,584	9,089	8,829	10,212	10,453
Overseas	RYMG	572	480	575	55	73	-15	-200	711	868	702	750	858
Reinsurance, coinsurance and treaty balances[17]													
UK	RYMH	934	1,290	1,164	1,092	1,730	-165	-258	-182	-233	-921	-2,926	1,698
Overseas	RYMI	-1,501	-48	-23	537	491	375	921	-4	217	244	-262	-1,344
Outstanding interest, dividends and rents[18]	RYPN	905	1,067	1,255	1,108	958	765	726	724	881	581	657	436
Other debtors and assets not elsewhere classified[19]	RKAC	12,405	15,814	19,096	17,189	10,785	11,064	10,683	14,281	12,905	11,407	10,179	11,642
Direct investment for non-insurance subsidiary and associate companies in the UK[20]	RYNR	20,530	20,111	21,954	21,259	21,181	18,206	18,627	19,876	20,510	7,674	8,297	5,683
Direct investment for UK insurance subsidiary, associate and holding companies[20]	RYNS	6,071	4,745	6,936	7,669	7,159	6,252	6,795	6,365	6,886	c	5,152	5,753
Direct investment for overseas subsidiaries, associates, branches and agencies[20]	RYNT	6,446	9,657	9,445	10,815	12,124	9,868	9,073	8,004	7,147	c	7,737	8,586
TOTAL ASSETS	**RKBY**	**149,224**	**163,030**	**161,477**	**176,543**	**166,631**	**141,547**	**143,412**	**161,227**	**160,903**	**142,025**	**137,550**	**141,290**

Source: Office for National Statistics

c Suppressed to avoid the disclosure of confidential data. Components may not sum to totals due to rounding.
8 Includes money market funds; liquidity funds and cash liquidity funds.
9 Sterling and foreign currency.
10 Includes treasury bills. Excludes UK government securities.
11 Sterling and foreign currency commercial paper issued by: banks; building societies; other financial institutions and other issuing companies.
12 Includes floating rate notes maturing within one year of issue.
13 UK and overseas. Excludes derivative contracts.
14 Net of balances owed. Includes amounts due on securities bought and sold for future settlement.
15 Includes credit default products; employee stock options; other options; other swaps; futures; forwards and other derivative contracts not elsewhere classified.
16 Net of insurance liabilities.
17 Net of reinsurance bought and sold.
18 Net value.
19 Includes deferred acquisition costs.
20 Net asset value of attributable companies.

12.15b INSURANCE COMPANIES' BALANCE SHEET: GENERAL BUSINESS ASSETS AND LIABILITIES AT MARKET VALUES

continued

£ million

		2005	2006	2007	2008	2009	2010	2011	2012	2013	2014	2015	2016
LIABILITIES													
Borrowing	AHMI	14,790	19,052	18,597	20,214	15,602	14,431	14,281	12,460	12,133	7,081	5,816	4,402
Banks and building societies in the UK[9]	JX3J	893	3,148	675	343	744	621	606	819	794	734	393	461
Other UK[21]	IFHX	11,080	10,445	10,885	13,179	9,965	9,835	8,991	8,401	8,792	5,200	4,062	2,505
Overseas[22]	RYMD	2,817	5,459	7,037	6,692	4,893	3,975	4,684	3,240	2,547	1,147	1,361	1,436
General business technical reserves[23]	RKCT	71,710	77,221	71,146	76,980	70,947	58,484	57,539	61,771	59,738	59,744	56,639	57,950
Provisions for taxation and dividends payable[24]	KVF2	1,806	2,656	2,486	858	345	40	7	240	424	595	487	450
Other creditors, provisions and liabilities not elsewhere classified[25]	RYPR	10,718	16,226	22,069	21,149	19,976	18,367	19,362	25,757	24,989	16,985	16,601	18,720
Excess of total assets over liabilities in respect of minority interests in UK subsidiary companies, reserves[26]	A8SI	50,200	47,875	47,179	57,342	59,761	50,225	52,223	60,999	63,619	57,620	58,007	59,768
TOTAL LIABILITIES	**RKBY**	**149,224**	**163,030**	**161,477**	**176,543**	**166,631**	**141,547**	**143,412**	**161,227**	**160,903**	**142,025**	**137,550**	**141,290**

Source: Office for National Statistics

c Suppressed to avoid the disclosure of confidential data. Components may not sum to totals due to rounding.
9 Sterling and foreign currency.
21 Includes issue of securities (other than ordinary shares); issue of sterling commercial paper and other borrowing not elsewhere classified.
22 Includes borrowing from banks; related companies and other borrowing not elsewhere classified.
23 Net of reinsurers share.
24 UK and overseas. Includes deferred tax net of amounts receivable.
25 UK and overseas. Includes derivative contracts which have a negative (liability) value.
26 Includes the 'net worth' of UK branches of overseas companies, including profit and loss account balances.

12.16a Individual insolvencies

England and Wales, not seasonally adjusted

	Total individual insolvencies	Bankruptcies[1]	Debt relief orders[2]	Individual voluntary arrangements[3]
2008	106,544	67,428	z	39,116
2009	134,142	74,670	11,831	47,641
2010	135,045	59,173	25,179	50,693
2011	119,943	41,876	29,009	49,058
2012	109,640	31,787	31,179	46,674
2013	100,998	24,571	27,546	48,881
2014	99,223	20,345	26,688	52,190
2015	80,404	15,845	24,175	40,384
2016	90,657	15,044	26,196	49,417

z Not applicable

Source: The Insolvency Service.

[1] Figures from 2011 Q2 onwards based on the date the bankruptcy order was granted by the court or the Adjudicator. From 6 April 2016, the process for people making themselves bankrupt moved online and out of the courts.

[2] Debt Relief Orders (DROs) came into effect on 6 April 2009 as an alternative route into individual insolvency. In April 2011 a change was introduced to the legislation to allow those who have built up value in a pension scheme to apply for debt relief under these provisions.

[3] Includes Deeds of Arrangement.

12.16b Individual insolvencies

Scotland, not seasonally adjusted

	Total individual insolvencies	Sequestrations (of which LILA/MAP)[1, 2]		Protected trust deeds
2008	19,991	12,449	(7,133)	7,542
2009	23,541	14,415	(8,774)	9,126
2010	20,344	11,906	(6,801)	8,438
2011	19,650	11,128	(4,812)	8,522
2012	18,402	9,630	(3,886)	8,772
2013	14,250	7,189	(2,728)	7,061
2014	11,622	6,747	(2,533)	4,875
2015	8,785	4,477	(1,509)	4,308
2016	9,779	4,474	(1,795)	5,305

Source: Accountant in Bankruptcy.

[1] On 1 April 2008, Part 1 of the Bankruptcy and Diligence etc. (Scotland) Act 2007 came into force making significant changes to some aspects of sequestration (bankruptcy), debt relief and debt enforcement in Scotland. This included the introduction of the new route into bankruptcy for people with low income and low assets (LILA). Of the number or sequestrations, individuals who meet LILA criteria are shown in brackets.

[2] On 1 April 2015, part of the Bankruptcy and Debt Advice (Scotland) Act came into force making significant changes to some aspects of sequestration (bankruptcy). This included the introduction of the Minimal Asset Process (MAP), which replaced the LILA route into sequestration; mandatory debt advice for people seeking statutory debt relief; a new online process for applying for sequestration; and an additional year for people to make contributions to repaying their debts (increasing from three years to four, in line with protected trust deeds).

12.16c Individual insolvencies

Northern Ireland, not seasonally adjusted

	Total individual insolvencies	Bankruptcies	Debt relief orders[1]	Individual voluntary arrangements
2008	1,638	1,079	z	559
2009	1,958	1,236	z	722
2010	2,323	1,321	z	1,002
2011	2,839	1,615	112	1,112
2012	3,189	1,452	506	1,231
2013	3,373	1,347	593	1,433
2014	3,395	1,367	536	1,492
2015	2,690	1,071	472	1,147
2016	2,582	997	366	1,219

Source: Department for Enterprise, Trade and Investment, Northern Ireland.

z Not applicable

1 Debt relief orders came into effect on 30 June 2011.

12.17a Company insolvencies[1,2]

England and Wales, not seasonally adjusted

	Total new company insolvencies[2,3]	Compulsory liquidations[3,4]	New creditors' voluntary liquidations[3]	Administrations[5,6,7]	Company voluntary arrangements[8]	Receivership appointments[9]
2008	21,072	5,494	9,995	4,808	586	189
2009	24,011	5,643	13,509	4,019	723	117
2010	19,795	4,792	11,506	2,682	766	49
2011	20,285	5,003	11,947	2,539	748	48
2012	19,349	4,261	11,906	2,334	816	32
2013	17,682	3,632	11,453	2,009	571	17
2014	16,317	3,755	10,399	1,587	554	22
2015	14,661	2,889	9,995	1,402	364	11
2016	16,551 r	2,930	11,893 r	1,377 r	346	5

Sources: Insolvency Service (compulsory liquidations only); Companies House (all other insolvency types).

r Revised

1 Data from 2000Q1 are not consistent with earlier data because of a change to the methodology. This does not affect compulsory liquidations.

2 Excludes creditors' voluntary liquidations following administration (See Table 2).

3 Includes partnership winding-up orders.

4 Figures from 2011 Q2 onwards based on the date the winding-up order was granted by the court.

5 Releases prior to 2012 Q4 showed administrations separately as "Administrator Appointments" and "In Administration - Enterprise Act".

6 The figure for Q4 2006 includes 844 separate, limited companies created and managed by "Safe Solutions Accountancy Limited" for which Grant Thornton was appointed administrator.

7 The figure for Q3 2008 includes 728 separate managed service companies.

8 The figure for Q2 2012 includes 104 new CVAs recorded under "Health and Social Work" in June reflecting the fact that on 20 June 2012 156 companies in the Southern Cross Healthcare Group had CVAs approved.

9 Data before 2000 Q1 include Law of Property Act and fixed charge receiverships, which are not insolvencies but which cannot be identified separately to insolvent receiverships under the previous methodology.

12.17b Company insolvencies[2]

Scotland, not seasonally adjusted

	Total new company insolvencies[2]	Compulsory liquidations[3]	New creditors' voluntary liquidations[2]	Administrations	Company voluntary arrangements	Receivership appointments
2008	893	561	104	190	4	34
2009	1,027	556	171	259	8	33
2010	1,301 r	779 r	252	212	7	51
2011	1,451	921	269	211	13	37
2012	1,377	920	233	169	24	31
2013	896	483	258	122	16	17
2014	963	650	207	87	14	5
2015	947 r	575 r	253	109	4	6
2016	1,036	591	284	145	13	3

Source: Companies House.

r Revised

1 Data from 2000 Q1 are not consistent with earlier data because of a change to the methodology.

2 Data before 2000 Q1 includes creditors' voluntary liquidations following administration as under the previous methodology it is not possible to separate these CVLs out.

3 Includes provisional liquidations.

12.17c Company insolvencies[1,2]

Northern Ireland, not seasonally adjusted

	Total new company insolvencies[4]	Compulsory liquidations[3]	New creditors' voluntary liquidations[4,5]	Administrations[4]	Company voluntary arrangements[4]	Administrative receiverships[4]
2008	:	158	51	:	:	:
2009	:	164	86	:	:	:
2010	495	250	117	78	42	8
2011	437	208	116	68	26	19
2012	526	252	136	83	41	14
2013	357	178	98	47	33	1
2014	380	221	90	29	37	3
2015	378	225	76	35	39	3
2016	395 r	243	89	32	27 r	4

Source: Department for Enterprise, Trade and Investment, Northern Ireland; Companies House

r Revised

1 Includes partnerships.

2 Data from 2009 Q4 are not consistent with earlier data because of a change to the methodology. This does not affect compulsory liquidations. Data for Northern Ireland prior to 2010 are not available under the new methodology.

3 Source: Department for Enterprise, Trade and Investment, Northern Ireland.

4 Source: Companies House.

5 Data before 2009 Q4 includes creditors' voluntary liquidations following administration as under the previous methodology it is not possible to separate these CVLs out.

12.18a Monetary financial institutions' consolidated balance sheet

£ millions — Not seasonally adjusted

Amounts outstanding of liabilities

	Currency, deposits and money market instruments						Financial derivatives (net)		Other securities issued		Other liabilities		Total liabilities/ assets
	Private sector		Public sector		Non-residents								
	Sterling	Foreign currency	Sterling	Foreign currency	Sterling	Foreign currency	Sterling	Foreign currency	Sterling	Foreign currency	Sterling	Foreign currency	
LPM	VYAX	VYAY	VYAZ	VYBA	VYBB	VYBC	VWKM	VWKN	VWKO	VWKP	VWKQ	VWKR	VYBF
2016 Jan	2,103,709	448,793	43,256	4,165	481,514	2,426,142	5,172	-13,794	35,670	223,095	460,059	179,012	**6,396,792**
Feb	2,123,558	460,909	41,638	4,372	448,076	2,466,958	41,133	-39,043	35,693	230,433	436,441	203,328	**6,453,495**
Mar	2,128,434 (v)	458,653	37,235	2,787	472,627	2,404,210	-18,147	16,777	35,841	229,819	437,545	191,690	**6,397,472 (v)**
Apr	2,125,195	458,240	47,402	4,105	469,387	2,370,539	-31,444	20,394	36,191	231,396	426,774 (ac)	205,058	**6,363,237 (ac)**
May	2,148,693	459,325	46,498	3,585	459,282	2,376,140	-32,261	23,825	35,886	226,793	438,191	187,700	**6,373,656**
Jun	2,186,240 (w)	502,635	45,800	3,797	481,787	2,636,668	67,183	-55,297	36,581	249,064	419,353	220,168	**6,793,978 (w)**
Jul	2,207,952	515,132	44,587	4,865	485,403	2,650,594	68,127	-49,553	36,276	253,075	406,487	231,860	**6,854,804**
Aug	2,224,788	525,091	46,421	4,783	488,900	2,662,013	70,967	-45,365	36,379	253,232	412,451	229,348	**6,909,008**
Sep	2,224,869	545,796	40,018	2,820	485,923	2,701,375 (ab)	78,794	-54,554	36,346	252,924	387,780	243,870	**6,945,961 (ab)**
Oct	2,246,503	563,526	43,686	3,273	498,638	2,780,936	125,231	-134,589	36,052	263,901	358,295	283,112	**7,068,564**
Nov	2,256,203	559,766	44,200	4,630	498,083	2,691,192	42,454	-53,667	35,185	244,788	406,917	235,508	**6,965,259**
Dec	2,246,902	540,650	40,362	3,322	497,082	2,712,601	57,778	-59,585	35,177	247,044	414,410	246,180	**6,981,922**
2017 Jan	2,247,924	561,878 (x)	39,543	4,246	495,978	2,707,400	23,929	-31,287	34,520	247,708	441,077	220,183	**6,993,100**
Feb	2,249,401 (al)	589,970 (aq)	42,028	3,278	496,227	2,769,649	72,207	-68,084	34,543	256,400	453,121	241,162	**7,139,900**
Mar	2,283,910	569,228	36,220	2,673	508,240	2,728,068	47,413	-41,079	34,305	252,862	431,358	223,483	**7,076,683**
Apr	2,310,127	569,250	37,310	4,276	498,933	2,679,311	9,730	-3,770	34,136	251,092	432,910	207,560	**7,030,864**
May	2,303,924	579,559	42,127	4,599	508,772	2,715,474	32,377	-21,323	33,460	257,713	455,412	178,343	**7,090,438**
Jun	2,311,207	575,621	41,095	3,697	523,016	2,706,952	15,614	-26,022	33,460	257,113	484,509 (bb)(bc)(bd)	191,364	**7,117,627**
Jul	2,305,404	590,314	50,849	6,180	503,241	2,753,945 (ar)	32,960	-32,891	33,560	260,514	458,513	207,268	**7,169,858 (ar)**
Aug	2,329,544	610,594	51,500	5,421	517,404	2,774,660 (as)	48,142	-46,930	33,629	275,514	467,126	189,089	**7,255,695 (be)**
Sep	2,351,608 (am)	584,931	42,430	6,125	512,452	2,738,423 (at)(au)	-8,080	-9,111	33,076	259,948	488,408	168,062	**7,168,271 (am)(au)(bf)**
Oct	2,360,636	597,048	46,780	6,052	491,520	2,793,114	5,635	-21,809	33,442	257,545	478,701	176,152	**7,224,816**
Nov	2,366,129	614,867	46,282	6,124	491,471	2,791,404	-20,012	10,139	33,921	253,559	484,618	176,519	**7,255,023**
Dec	2,355,197	583,265	42,850	6,362	506,578	2,842,107	-19,614	21,677	33,943	254,763	501,156	175,336	**7,303,622**
2018 Jan	2,370,271 (ao)	601,667	46,269	5,620	495,318	2,759,450	-114,129 (av)	110,738 (ay)	33,437	253,195	481,803	176,268	**7,219,907 (ao)**
Feb	2,365,433	609,031	47,361	5,213	488,133	2,837,146	35,651 (aw)	-55,394 (az)	34,312	259,152	463,101	203,569	**7,292,709**
Mar	2,353,262	593,946	39,863	5,208	506,299	2,834,275	16,571 (ax)	-28,235 (ba)	32,877	255,360	467,243	189,886	**7,266,555**
Apr	2,353,592	609,912	41,565	7,361	496,897	2,838,995	103,695	-131,823	30,536	255,101	476,095	193,514	**7,275,440**

Source: Bank of England

12.18a Monetary financial institutions' consolidated balance sheet

£ millions | Not seasonally adjusted

Notes to table

Movements in amounts outstanding can reflect breaks in data series as well as underlying flows. For changes data, users are recommended to refer directly to the appropriate series or data tables.
Further explanation can be found at: www.bankofengland.co.uk/statistics/Pages/iadb/notesiadb/Changes_flows_growth_rates.aspx.

(v) Due to changes in reporting at one institution, the amounts outstanding decreased by £5bn. This effect has been adjusted out of the flows for March 2016.
(w) Due to improvements in reporting at one institution, the amounts outstanding increased by £8bn. This effect has been adjusted out of the flows for June 2016.
(x) Due to improvements in reporting at one institution, the amounts outstanding increased by £8bn. This effect has been adjusted out of the flows for January 2017.
(aa) Due to changes in reporting at one institution, the amounts outstanding decreased by £18bn. This effect has been adjusted out of the flows for November 2015.
(ab) Due to a change in treatment at one institution, the amounts outstanding decreased by £14bn. This effect has been adjusted out of the flows for September 2016.
(ac) Due to a loan transfer by one reporting institution, the amounts outstanding increased by £7bn. This effect has been adjusted out of the flows for April 2016.
(al) Due to improvements in reporting at one institution, the amounts outstanding increased by £3bn. This effect has been adjusted out of the flows for February 2017.
(am) Due to a change in group structure by one reporting institution, the amounts outstanding increased by £6bn. This effect has been adjusted out of the flows for September 2017.
(an) Due to improvements in reporting by one institution, the amounts outstanding increased by £11bn. This amount has been adjusted out of the flows for September 2017.
(ao) Due to improvements in reporting at one institution, the amounts outstanding increased by £5bn. This effect has been adjusted out of the flows for January 2018.
(aq) Due to improvements in reporting at one institution, the amounts outstanding increased by £4bn. This effect has been adjusted out of the flows for February 2017.
(ar) Due to a transfer of business by one institution, amounts outstanding increased by £29 billion. This amount has been adjusted out of the flows for July 2017.
(as) Due to improvements in reporting by one institution, amounts outstanding decreased by £17 billion. This amount has been adjusted out of the flows for August 2017.
(at) Due to improvements in reporting by one reporting institution, the amounts outstanding increased by £38bn. This amount has been adjusted out of the flows for September 2017.
(au) Due to improvements in reporting by one institution, amounts outstanding decreased by £12bn. This amount has been adjusted out of the flows for September 2017.
(av) Due to improvements in reporting by one institution, amounts outstanding decreased by £66bn.
(aw) Due to improvements in reporting by one institution, amounts outstanding increased by £8bn.
(ax) Due to improvements in reporting by one institution, amounts outstanding increased by £9bn.
(ay) Due to improvements in reporting by one institution, amounts outstanding increased by £66bn.
(az) Due to improvements in reporting by one institution, amounts outstanding decreased by £8bn.
(ba) Due to improvements in reporting by one institution, amounts outstanding decreased by £9bn.
(bb) Due to improvements in reporting at one institution, the amounts outstanding increased by £17bn. This effect has been adjusted out of the flows for June 2017.
(bc) Due to improvements in reporting at one institution, the amounts outstanding decreased by £5bn. This effect has been adjusted out of the flows for June 2017.
(bd) Due to improvements in reporting at one institution, the amounts outstanding increased by £10bn. This effect has been adjusted out of the flows for June 2017.
(be) Due to improvements in reporting by one institution, amounts outstanding decreased by £34 billion. This amount has been adjusted out of the flows for August 2017.
(bf) Due to improvements in reporting by one institution, the amounts outstanding increased by £98bn. This amount has been adjusted out of the flows for September 2017.

Explanatory notes can be found here: www.bankofengland.co.uk/statistics/details/further-details-about-monetary-financial-institutions-consolidated-balance-sheet-contributions-data

12.18b Monetary financial institutions' consolidated balance sheet

£ millions Not seasonally adjusted

Amounts outstanding of assets

	Loans						Securities (other than financial derivatives)						Other assets	
	Private sector		Public sector		Non-residents		Private sector		Public sector		Non-residents			
	Sterling	Foreign currency	Sterling	Foreign currency	Sterling	Foreign currency	Sterling	Foreign currency	Sterling	Foreign currency	Sterling	Foreign currency	Sterling	Foreign currency
LPM	VYBG	VYBH	VYBI	VYBJ	VYBK	VYBL	VYBM (bg)	VYBN	VYBO	VYBP	VYBQ	VYBR	VYBS	VYBT
2016 Jan	1,971,390	343,714	18,534	2,169	258,686	2,383,122	197,906	19,107	551,779	473	47,946	481,025	85,260	35,681
Feb	1,988,011	369,669	18,429	1,819	246,392	2,414,046	193,750	19,378	564,855	505	50,332	465,036	84,264	37,008
Mar	1,996,196	350,676	16,532	899	256,817	2,378,322	195,392	19,651	560,108	572	50,567	452,454	83,232	36,054
Apr	1,988,741 (ai)	359,437	16,008	1,905	264,290	2,330,742	195,431	17,793	557,763	662	47,539	464,077	82,944	35,905
May	2,004,319	356,063	15,382	1,981	270,344	2,331,529	194,426	17,267	562,445	713	49,266	449,618	83,931	36,370
Jun	2,028,408 (aj)	393,287	17,516	1,563	278,705	2,632,461	195,532	16,779	583,134	782	49,272	474,023	83,289	39,227
Jul	2,035,188	392,944	22,946	2,027	287,077	2,635,179	196,976	14,941	591,342	694	52,289	499,600	83,912	39,689
Aug	2,043,367	393,778	21,758	1,694	293,539	2,646,503	197,911	15,155	621,774	705	54,299	493,898	84,392	40,233
Sep	2,049,984	378,685	20,877	1,639	296,913	2,725,452 (ak)	196,086	13,730	611,511	692	54,742	469,613	83,446	42,592
Oct	2,054,241	388,360	21,072	435	295,660	2,813,453	191,548	14,097	608,802	583	57,892	497,465	83,659	41,297
Nov	2,062,369	392,925	18,478	1,530	291,779	2,737,328	193,402	14,862	613,938	499	57,505	456,801	83,145	40,699
Dec	2,061,468	363,774	16,542	1,826	300,851	2,759,544	196,238	13,104	625,768	464	57,350	464,714	81,114	39,165
2017 Jan	2,072,809	385,805	16,586	1,995	301,412	2,737,797	226,409	12,548	610,527	426	60,028	465,869	63,446	37,442
Feb	2,074,570	418,126 (bo)	13,390	1,107	301,333	2,802,631	225,227	13,465	633,323	401	60,196	491,557	62,327	42,249
Mar	2,095,761	407,141	13,791	223	308,916	2,748,652	224,450	12,917	636,643	473	58,695	468,360	61,818	38,843
Apr	2,101,362	412,545	11,313	3,277	316,688	2,685,603	228,983	11,541	639,479	438	59,472	458,598	61,901	39,662
May	2,110,113	413,646	11,446	2,919	312,815	2,712,171	228,928	11,478	643,009	484	59,555	479,762	62,411	41,700
Jun	2,119,587	409,425	11,640	1,076	315,894	2,717,630	249,148 (bu)	10,629	631,862	464	59,173	478,937	70,800 (bu)	41,363
Jul	2,087,663 (bh)	409,178	46,699 (bp)	3,321	299,097	2,790,918 (br)	251,920	11,143	632,471	461	60,286	464,194	71,290	41,216
Aug	2,101,200	413,100	48,099	2,466	312,541	2,852,236 (bs)	251,272	11,751	634,274	353	58,220	452,901	72,130	45,153
Sep	2,133,311 (bi)(bj)	388,078	48,169	2,785	308,698	2,781,709 (bt)	245,499	10,985	620,717	344	58,314	465,867	66,220	37,576
Oct	2,124,113	397,236	49,177	2,947	307,574	2,830,557	244,574	11,000	625,337	245	50,507	474,657	67,387	39,505
Nov	2,137,998	402,302	48,553	2,848	308,466	2,845,752	240,248	11,076	617,247	245	50,518	481,661	68,479	39,630
Dec	2,140,390	379,784	49,002	3,321	307,161	2,904,640	240,906	13,113	617,145	229	49,218	486,992	69,871	41,848
2018 Jan	2,141,503 (bk)(bl)	411,349	47,007	1,944	314,115	2,784,071	234,265	12,197	612,169	232	52,351	498,204	71,390	39,112
Feb	2,138,710	413,915	48,970	1,469	309,397	2,889,874	231,966	11,197	615,169	331	52,535	467,978	71,847	39,352
Mar	2,142,514	392,632	52,381	1,956	310,062	2,911,742	228,327	10,527	611,675	313	51,565	440,830	71,500	40,530
Apr	2,173,961 (bm)	399,340	17,525 (bq)	3,412	306,319	2,906,898	228,008	10,603	615,716	321	51,567	453,436	69,549	38,784

Source: Bank of England

12.18b Monetary financial institutions' consolidated balance sheet

£ millions | Not seasonally adjusted

Notes to table

Movements in amounts outstanding can reflect breaks in data series as well as underlying flows. For changes data, users are recommended to refer directly to the appropriate series or data tables. Further explanation can be found at: www.bankofengland.co.uk/statistics/Pages/iadb/notesiadb/Changes_flows_growth_rates.aspx.

(ai) Due to a loan transfer by one reporting institution, the amounts outstanding increased by £7bn. This effect has been adjusted out of the flows for April 2016.

(aj) Due to improvements in reporting at one institution, the amounts outstanding increased by £3bn. This effect has been adjusted out of the flows for June 2016.

(ak) Due to a change in treatment at one institution, the amounts outstanding decreased by £14bn. This effect has been adjusted out of the flows for September 2016.

(bg) This series includes purchases of bonds made as part of the Bank of England's Corporate Bond Purchase Scheme. Data on Central Bank holdings of securities can be found in Bankstats Table B2.2. For further information on the Bank's treatment of securities transactions in credit statistics, see: www.bankofengland.co.uk/statistics/Documents/articles/2015/2may.pdf.

(bh) In order to bring reporting in line with the National Accounts, English housing associations were reclassified from PNFCs to public corporations with effect from July 2017 data. The amounts outstanding decreased by £34bn. This effect has been adjusted out of the flows for July 2017.

(bi) Due to a change in group structure by one reporting institution, the amounts outstanding increased by £6bn. This effect has been adjusted out of the flows for September 2017.

(bj) Due to improvements in reporting by one institution, the amounts outstanding increased by £11bn. This amount has been adjusted out of the flows for September 2017.

(bk) Due to improvements in reporting at one institution, the amounts outstanding decreased by £2bn. This effect has been adjusted out of the flows for January 2018.

(bl) Due to improvements in reporting at one institution, the amounts outstanding decreased by £2bn. This effect has been adjusted out of the flows for January 2018.

(bm) In order to bring reporting in line with the National Accounts, English housing associations were reclassified from public corporations to PNFCs with effect from April 2018 data. The amounts outstanding increased by £34bn. This effect has been adjusted out of the flows for April 2018.

(bn) Due to improvements in reporting at one institution, the amounts outstanding increased by £5bn. This effect has been adjusted out of the flows for September 2018.

(bo) Due to improvements in reporting at one institution, the amounts outstanding increased by £4bn. This effect has been adjusted out of the flows for February 2017.

(bp) In order to bring reporting in line with the National Accounts, English housing associations were reclassified from PNFCs to public corporations with effect from July 2017 data. The amounts outstanding increased by £34bn. This effect has been adjusted out of the flows for July 2017.

(bq) In order to bring reporting in line with the National Accounts, English housing associations were reclassified from public corporations to PNFCs with effect from April 2018 data. The amounts outstanding decreased by £34bn. This effect has been adjusted out of the flows for April 2018.

(br) Due to transfer of business by one institution, amounts outstanding increased by £34 billion. This amount has been adjusted out of the flows for July 2017.

(bs) Due to improvements in reporting by one institution, amounts outstanding decreased by £17 billion. This amount has been adjusted out of the flows for August 2017.

(bt) Due to improvements in reporting by one reporting institution, the amounts outstanding increased by £38bn. This amount has been adjusted out of the flows for September 2017.

(bu) Due to improvements in reporting at one institution, the amounts outstanding increased by £10bn. This effect has been adjusted out of the flows for June 2017.

Explanatory notes can be found here: www.bankofengland.co.uk/statistics/details/further-details-about-monetary-financial-institutions-consolidated-balance-sheet-contributions-data

12.18c Monetary financial institutions' consolidated balance sheet

£ millions | Not seasonally adjusted

Changes in liabilities

	Currency, deposits and money market instruments						Financial derivatives (net)		Other securities issued		Other liabilities		Total liabilities/ assets
	Private sector		Public sector		Non-residents								
	Sterling	Foreign currency	Sterling	Foreign currency	Sterling	Foreign currency	Sterling	Foreign currency	Sterling	Foreign currency	Sterling	Foreign currency	
LPM	VYAA	VYAB	VYAC	VYAD	VYAE	VYAF	VWKG	VWKH	VWKI	VWKJ	VWKK	VWKL	VYAI
2016 Jan	-10,772	10,846	193	-8	-1,114	29,558	37,614	-36,119	-72	-3,155	-26,217	8,065	**8,818**
Feb	19,880	2,386	-1,619	124	-33,531	-11,472	35,961	-26,157	22	2,141	-28,871	10,669	**-30,466**
Mar	10,197	2,406	-4,388	-1,570	24,583	-34,776	-59,280	56,534	148	-414	-813	-13,124	**-20,496**
Apr	-4,951	6,133	10,167	1,376	-3,350	4,382	-13,866	3,930	12	8,137	-10,075	12,197	**14,090**
May	23,368	4,868	-904	-481	-10,089	20,446	-817	4,313	-305	-1,616	4,958	-19,207	**24,533**
Jun	32,785	6,339	-698	-57	19,474	69,211	99,444	-83,104	695	3,968	-50,113	7,946	**105,890**
Jul	21,985	5,651	-1,213	1,013	3,684	-21,272	943	4,902	-305	209	-31,511	-161	**-16,074**
Aug	17,027	4,532	1,834	-131	3,420	-14,357	2,841	3,959	103	-2,173	-12,119	-3,682	**1,253**
Sep	-502	11,894	-6,403	-1,997	-2,761	20,339	7,829	-11,737	-33	-3,996	-5,920	17,602	**24,314**
Oct	21,271	-7,582	3,669	314	13,374	-46,425	46,437	-79,940	-293	16	-5,796	38,015	**-16,939**
Nov	11,192	17,103	514	1,470	-204	7,806	-82,777	84,258	-867	-7,803	61,913	-28,161	**64,444**
Dec	-7,859	-22,844	-3,816	-1,347	-950	-5,819	15,324	-5,105	-8	-1,475	-4,340	4,893	**-33,347**
2017 Jan	966	21,178	-818	974	-1,118	27,151	-33,848	28,087	-657	2,218	38,100	-23,247	**58,985**
Feb	-827	23,541	2,202	-983	87	50,832	49,268	-35,163	23	8,403	-10,789	4,158	**90,751**
Mar	30,056	-20,702	-5,800	-603	10,873	-35,602	-24,794	26,998	-238	-3,403	-15,479	-12,853	**-51,547**
Apr	25,835	13,653	1,089	1,682	-4,733	17,413	-37,683	37,675	-170	3,732	-451	-12,293	**45,750**
May	-6,225	1,189	4,818	244	9,752	-1,082	22,647	-16,608	-676	1,181	19,009	-39,948	**-5,699**
Jun	7,239	-3,638	-1,032	-904	14,191	-5,933	-18,263	-4,273	1	-1,064	18,923	14,647	**19,894**
Jul	-3,628	7,080	6,902	1,671	-20,235	15,807	17,346	-5,230	99	1,754	-27,124	9,751	**4,193**
Aug	23,107	-587	651	-916	14,243	-48,125	15,182	-10,866	69	-2,335	-3,549	843	**-12,282**
Sep	6,565	283	-9,690	926	-8,987	49,588	-55,327	30,527	-553	-4,038	42,169	-4,245	**47,216**
Oct	8,764	8,919	4,357	-93	-20,758	47,430	13,715	-12,725	366	-2,565	-8,980	4,357	**42,788**
Nov	4,790	22,060	-498	104	81	20,857	-25,246	31,398	479	-3,105	8,705	637	**60,261**
Dec	-11,149	-33,505	-3,432	210	14,995	42,414	398	11,689	22	95	10,456	-5,913	**26,281**
2018 Jan	15,060	37,555	3,418	-581	-11,408	5,156	-94,515	86,612	-506	2,456	2,315	6,299	**51,860**
Feb	-4,935	-4,479	1,092	-512	-7,209	17,952	149,780	-163,162	875	-1,234	-16,460	30,340	**2,048**
Mar	-12,199	-7,476	-7,498	63	18,156	35,528	-19,080	26,736	-1,435	-536	-3,958	-7,229	**21,072**
Apr	-4,272	11,299	5,106	2,080	-9,077	-22,868	83,373	-100,488	-2,343	240	18,653	3,264	**-15,032**

Notes to table

Source: Bank of England

Explanatory notes can be found here: www.bankofengland.co.uk/statistics/details/further-details-about-monetary-financial-institutions-consolidated-balance-sheet-contributions-data

12.18d Monetary financial institutions' consolidated balance sheet

£ millions

Not seasonally adjusted

Changes in assets

	Loans						Securities (other than financial derivatives)						Other assets	
	Private sector		Public sector		Non-residents		Private sector		Public sector		Non-residents			
	Sterling	Foreign currency	Sterling	Foreign currency	Sterling	Foreign currency	Sterling	Foreign currency	Sterling	Foreign currency	Sterling	Foreign currency	Sterling	Foreign currency
LPM	**VYAJ**	**VYAK**	**VYAL**	**VYAM**	**VYAN**	**VYAO**	**VYAP (bv)**	**VYAQ**	**VYAR**	**VYAS**	**VYAT**	**VYAU**	**VYAV**	**VYAW**
2016 Jan	8,092	10,120	1,001	187	2,520	12,714	-1,468	-475	-6,828	-15	-460	-14,322	11	-2,259
Feb	17,447	17,783	-640	-392	-13,009	-23,931	-39	113	7,081	23	-746	-33,275	-905	26
Mar	8,566	-14,667	-1,898	-921	10,420	-6,415	-485	250	512	78	600	-14,715	-1,325	-496
Apr	-14,454	14,370	-511	1,030	6,629	-9,296	-565	-1,324	3,423	118	-2,408	17,800	-463	-259
May	14,988	-320	-611	102	7,790	16,384	-244	-32	-3,628	50	1,572	-13,118	952	646
Jun	21,105	6,044	2,434	-511	2,861	101,777	849	-1,586	-5,222	16	-4,808	-18,228	-597	1,756
Jul	7,536	-5,971	5,430	443	8,246	-33,747	-4,573	-2,040	-3,321	-97	1,704	9,772	537	7
Aug	8,521	-3,833	-1,166	-352	6,433	-14,212	-3,839	-253	17,611	4	1,380	-9,601	388	170
Sep	6,893	-21,507	-887	-76	3,663	58,027	639	-1,740	5,092	-18	181	-27,171	-762	1,981
Oct	4,432	-8,319	195	-1,283	-1,235	-42,559	-1,722 (ar)	-574	20,228	-143	1,099	15,912	247	-3,217
Nov	10,251	21,055	-2,594	1,122	-3,928	30,066	3,488	556	13,570	-72	2,631	-11,873	-514	684
Dec	1,001	-28,951	-1,916	275	9,107	-8,191	-942	-3,072	4,260	-40	-1,032	184	-2,098	-1,931
2017 Jan	11,269	24,384	44	193	505	5,416	29,824	-752	-4,454	-30	3,774	7,857	-17,696	-1,351
Feb	-1,022	25,761	-3,433	-893	-685	49,420	-3,716	217	5,904	-29	-1,334	17,138	-1,165	4,589
Mar	19,902	-9,348	400	-891	7,084	-48,214	-1,009	125	5,562	74	-1,026	-20,379	-506	-3,321
Apr	5,714	15,575	-2,477	3,084	10,048	4,851	6,068	-830	850	-21	1,016	6	117	1,748
May	8,616	-6,169	684	-403	-3,869	-14,568	-1,683	8	1,142	45	176	8,325	409	1,589
Jun	9,669	-4,213	-21	-1,847	3,094	7,402	3,821	-848	3,485	-17	-184	808	-1,808	552
Jul	2,607	-4,009	565	2,236	-17,346	34,374	1,731	260	-395	2	1,466	-17,821	508	15
Aug	16,117	-1,107	1,331	-940	13,175	3,054	-1,293	686	-10,021	-117	-3,924	-25,377	-132	-3,734
Sep	13,820	-6,292	-651	423	-7,907	23,682	-2,627	-213	5,653	4	2,402	30,417	-5,774	-5,720
Oct	-8,207	8,412	1,008	173	-1,100	41,187	1,025	-341	3,006	-103	-8,524	3,271	1,176	1,805
Nov	14,105	7,292	-625	-105	766	37,508	-1,744	183	-8,866	4	730	9,469	1,089	454
Dec	3,005	-24,035	450	456	-1,207	49,239	-1,142	1,407	-4,815	-16	-1,844	1,303	1,329	2,154
2018 Jan	2,364	42,972	-1,995	-1,340	5,818	-32,813	290	-842	7,709	14	4,668	24,192	1,755	-932
Feb	-2,124	-6,148	1,963	-497	-4,713	42,690	-539	-387	2,780	92	-99	-30,999	650	-622
Mar	2,824	-15,595	3,411	503	670	61,328	-1,884	14	-13,284	-13	-153	-18,155	-291	1,696
Apr	-1,665	5,643	-1,497	1,338	-4,223	-28,120	334	-74	9,305	3	-308	9,693	-2,053	-3,407

Notes to table

Source: Bank of England

(ar) The data for PNFCs M4 lending in October 2016 take account of a redemption of MFIs UK equity holdings of £4bn, following a merger of a UK corporate with a non-UK entity.

(bv) This series includes purchases of bonds made as part of the Bank of England's Corporate Bond Purchase Scheme. Data on Central Bank holdings of securities can be found in Bankstats Table B2.2. For further information on the Bank's treatment of securities transactions in credit statistics, see: www.bankofengland.co.uk/statistics/Documents/articles/2015/2may.pdf.

Explanatory notes can be found here: www.bankofengland.co.uk/statistics/details/further-details-about-monetary-financial-institutions-consolidated-balance-sheet-contributions-data

12.19 Selected interest rates, exchange rates and security prices

	Monthly average of 4 UK Banks' base rates	Monthly average rate of discount, 3 month Treasury bills, Sterling	Monthly average yield from British Government Securities, 20 year Nominal Par Yield	Monthly average Spot exchange rate, US$ into Sterling
	IUMAAMIH [a] [b]	**IUMAAJNB**	**IUMALNPY [c] [d]**	**XUMAUSS**
31-Jan-09	1.5952	0.8945	4.2758	1.4452
28-Feb-09	1.075	0.7177	4.3394	1.4411
31-Mar-09	0.5682	0.6035	4.007	1.4174
30-Apr-09	0.5	0.625	4.2419	1.4715
31-May-09	0.5	0.5271	4.3752	1.5429
30-Jun-09	0.5	0.5037	4.471	1.6366
31-Jul-09	0.5	0.4397	4.4588	1.6366
31-Aug-09	0.5	0.3946	4.2164	1.6539
30-Sep-09	0.5	0.3761	4.0688	1.6328
31-Oct-09	0.5	0.4315	4.05	1.6199
30-Nov-09	0.5	0.4459	4.2177	1.6597
31-Dec-09	0.5	0.3587	4.3306	1.6239
31-Jan-10	0.5	0.4874	4.4161	1.6162
28-Feb-10	0.5	0.4878	4.5158	1.5615
31-Mar-10	0.5	0.5109	4.5698	1.5053
30-Apr-10	0.5	0.5083	4.558	1.534
31-May-10	0.5	0.4976	4.3143	1.4627
30-Jun-10	0.5	0.4839	4.2079	1.4761
31-Jul-10	0.5	0.498	4.1754	1.5299
31-Aug-10	0.5	0.4945	3.9824	1.566
30-Sep-10	0.5	0.4966	3.8954	1.5578
31-Oct-10	0.5	0.5061	3.8876	1.5862
30-Nov-10	0.5	0.4935	4.1149	1.5961
31-Dec-10	0.5	0.4913	4.2568	1.5603
31-Jan-11	0.5	0.5055	4.3204	1.5795
28-Feb-11	0.5	0.5363	4.405	1.613
31-Mar-11	0.5	0.5603	4.298	1.6159
30-Apr-11	0.5	0.5676	4.2933	1.6345
31-May-11	0.5	0.5265	4.1371	1.6312
30-Jun-11	0.5	0.5174	4.1277	1.6214
31-Jul-11	0.5	0.4996	4.0974	1.6145
31-Aug-11	0.5	0.4531	3.7132	1.6348
30-Sep-11	0.5	0.4649	3.4205	1.5783
31-Oct-11	0.5	0.4608	3.2581	1.576
30-Nov-11	0.5	0.4387	3.0313	1.5804
31-Dec-11	0.5	0.2996	2.9803	1.5585
31-Jan-12	0.5	0.3239	2.906	1.551
29-Feb-12	0.5	0.3912	3.089	1.5802
31-Mar-12	0.5	0.4248	3.1744	1.5823
30-Apr-12	0.5	0.4236	3.1259	1.6014
31-May-12	0.5	0.3561	2.9073	1.5905
30-Jun-12	0.5	0.3422	2.725	1.5571
31-Jul-12	0.5	0.2943	2.6453	1.5589
31-Aug-12	0.5	0.2398	2.65	1.5719
30-Sep-12	0.5	0.2478	2.7497	1.6116
31-Oct-12	0.5	0.2368	2.7969	1.6079
30-Nov-12	0.5	0.2243	2.7846	1.5961
31-Dec-12	0.5	0.249	2.8391	1.6144

12.19 Selected interest rates, exchange rates and security prices

	Monthly average of 4 UK Banks' base rates	Monthly average rate of discount, 3 month Treasury bills, Sterling	Monthly average yield from British Government Securities, 20 year Nominal Par Yield	Monthly average Spot exchange rate, US$ into Sterling
	IUMAAMIH [a] [b]	**IUMAAJNB**	**IUMALNPY [c] [d]**	**XUMAUSS**
31-Jan-13	0.5	0.2677	3.0069	1.5957
28-Feb-13	0.5	0.3147	3.1035	1.5478
31-Mar-13	0.5	0.3391	2.9654	1.5076
30-Apr-13	0.5	0.3447	2.776	1.5316
31-May-13	0.5	0.3065	2.9096	1.5285
30-Jun-13	0.5	0.3066	3.1584	1.5478
31-Jul-13	0.5	0.3124	3.2719	1.5172
31-Aug-13	0.5	0.2812	3.4083	1.5507
30-Sep-13	0.5	0.289	3.4662	1.5865
31-Oct-13	0.5	0.3141	3.3198	1.6094
30-Nov-13	0.5	0.2865	3.3978	1.6104
31-Dec-13	0.5	0.2555	3.497	1.6375
31-Jan-14	0.5	0.3211	3.4287	1.647
28-Feb-14	0.5	0.3624	3.3668	1.6567
31-Mar-14	0.5	0.3882	3.3469	1.6622
30-Apr-14	0.5	0.3688	3.3127	1.6743
31-May-14	0.5	0.284	3.2387	1.6844
30-Jun-14	0.5	0.3586	3.3055	1.6906
31-Jul-14	0.5	0.4271	3.228	1.7069
31-Aug-14	0.5	0.3978	2.9986	1.6709
30-Sep-14	0.5	0.4351	2.978	1.6305
31-Oct-14	0.5	0.3964	2.7955	1.6068
30-Nov-14	0.5	0.4114	2.7235	1.578
31-Dec-14	0.5	0.4101	2.4744	1.564
31-Jan-15	0.5	0.377	2.1112	1.5143
28-Feb-15	0.5	0.338	2.2503	1.5334
31-Mar-15	0.5	0.4295	2.2853	1.4957
30-Apr-15	0.5	0.4322	2.2061	1.4967
31-May-15	0.5	0.4511	2.4791	1.547
30-Jun-15	0.5	0.467	2.6379	1.5568
31-Jul-15	0.5	0.4895	2.5968	1.556
31-Aug-15	-	0.4643	2.4307	1.5583
30-Sep-15	-	0.4532	2.4175	1.5326
31-Oct-15	-	0.48	2.4421	1.5339
30-Nov-15	-	0.4806	2.5375	1.519
31-Dec-15	-	0.4551	2.4749	1.4983
31-Jan-16	-	0.4823	2.386	1.4379
29-Feb-16	-	0.4711	2.1972	1.4296
31-Mar-16	-	0.4505	2.222	1.425
30-Apr-16	-	0.4489	2.2451	1.4312
31-May-16	-	0.4362	2.1985	1.4518
30-Jun-16	-	0.4046	1.9487	1.4209
31-Jul-16	-	0.3689	1.5432	1.3141
31-Aug-16	-	0.2281	1.2661	1.31
30-Sep-16	-	0.2104	1.3562	1.3142
31-Oct-16	-	0.1711	1.655	1.2329
30-Nov-16	-	0.1385	1.9506	1.2431
31-Dec-16	-	0.0518	1.9985	1.2488

Source: Bank of England

[a] Data obtained from Barclays Bank, Lloyds Bank, HSBC, and National Westminster Bank whose rates are used to compile this series. Where all the rates did not change on the same day a spread is shown.
[b] This series will end on 31-July-2015
[c] Calculated using the Variable Roughness Penalty (VRP) model.
[d] The monthly average figure is calculated using the available daily observations within each month.

12.20 Mergers and Acquisitions in the UK by other UK Companies: Category of Expenditure

£ million

	Expenditure[2]					Percentage of Expenditure[2]		
		Cash						
	Total	Independent Companies	Subsidiaries	Issues of Ordinary Shares[2]	Issues of Fixed Interest Securities[2]	Cash	Issues of Ordinary Shares	Issues of Fixed Interest Securities
	DUCM	DWVW	DWVX	AIHD	AIHE	DWVY	DWVZ	DWWA
Annual								
2005	25,134	13,425	8,510	2,768	431	87	11	2
2006	28,511	14,573	8,131	5,472	335	..	..	2
2007	26,778	13,671	6,507	4,909	1,691	76	18	6
2008	36,469	31,333	2,851	1,910	375	94	5	1
2009	12,195	2,937	709	8,435	114	30	69	1
2010[1]	12,605	6,175	4,520	1,560	350	85	12	3
2011	8,089	4,432	2,667	719	271	87	10	4
2012	3,413	1,937	789	419	268	82	10	8
2013	7,665	3,690	3,475	353	147	92	6	2
2014	8,032	3,249	1,947	2,782	51	65	35	–
2015	6,920	3,365	1,871	1,418	265	74	22	4
2016	24,688	5,493	5,308	13,471	418	43	55	2
Quarterly								
2010 Q1[1]	1,361	765	525	58	13	95	4	1
2010 Q2	2,032	986	714	275	57	83	14	3
2010 Q3	2,949	1,165	814	839	131	68	28	4
2010 Q4	6,263	3,259	2,467	388	149	92	6	2
2011 Q1	1,500	552	651	240	57	80	16	4
2011 Q2	3,346	2,355	704	204	83	92	6	2
2011 Q3	1,452	828	462	75	87	89	5	6
2011 Q4	1,791	697	850	200	44	87	11	2
2012 Q1	1,070	518	199	323	30	67	30	3
2012 Q2	1,041	575	269	54	143	81	5	14
2012 Q3	610	409	100	8	93	84	1	15
2012 Q4	692	435	221	34	2	95	5	–
2013 Q1	2,825	567	2,216	26	16	98	1	1
2013 Q2	2,438	1,992	316	80	50	95	3	2
2013 Q3	1,166	587	332	230	17	79	20	1
2013 Q4	1,236	544	611	17	64	94	1	5
2014 Q1	1,613	896	103	612	2	62	38	–
2014 Q2	1,625	478	1,051	50	45	94	3	3
2014 Q3	3,152	476	656	2,019	–	36	64	–
2014 Q4	1,642	1,399	137	101	4	94	6	–
2015 Q1	1,755	1,075	314	281	84	79	16	5
2015 Q2	2,739	854	789	1,019	77	60	37	3
2015 Q3	1,195	666	464	64	2	95	5	–
2015 Q4	1,231	770	304	54	102	88	4	8
2016 Q1	11,871	630	3,603	7,617	22	36	64	–
2016 Q2	6,780	1,983	388	4,237	172	35	62	3
2016 Q3	3,575	1,610	943	875	148	71	24	5
2016 Q4	2,462	1,270	374	742	76	67	30	3
2017 Q1	3,295	2,615	419	138	122	92	4	4

Source: Mergers and Acquisitions Surveys, Office for National Statistics

† indicates earliest revision, if any
– indicates data is zero or less than £0.5m
Disclosive data indicated by ..

1 The deal identification threshold has been increased from Q1 2010 from £0.1m to £1.0m and as a consequence there may be a discontinuity in the number and value of transactions reported.
2 A new method for compiling M&A statistics was introduced from Q1 2018, and as a consequence there is a discontinuity in the number of transactions reported.

Chapter 13

Service industry

Service industry

Annual Business Inquiry (Tables 13.1, 13.3 and 13.4)

The Annual Business Inquiry (ABI) estimates cover all UK businesses registered for Value Added Tax (VAT) and/or Pay As You Earn (PAYE). The businesses are classified to the 2007 Standard Industrial Classification (SIC(2007)) headings listed in the tables. The ABI obtains details on these businesses from the Office for National Statistics (ONS) Inter-Departmental Business Register (IDBR).

As with all its statistical inquiries, ONS is concerned to minimise the form-filling burden of individual contributors and as such the ABI is a sample inquiry. The sample was designed as a stratified random sample of about 66,600 businesses; the inquiry population is stratified by SIC(2007) and employment using the information from the register.

The inquiry results are grossed up to the total population so that they relate to all active UK businesses on the IDBR for the sectors covered.

The results meet a wide range of needs for government, economic analysts and the business community at large. In official statistics the inquiry is an important source for the national accounts and input-output tables, and also provides weights for the indices of production and producer prices. Additionally, inquiry results enable the UK to meet statistical requirements of the European Union.

Data from 1995 and 1996 were calculated on a different basis from those for 1997 and later years. In order to provide a link between the two data series, the 1995 and 1996 data were subsequently reworked to provide estimates on a consistent basis.

Revised ABI results down to SIC(2007) 4 digit class level for 1995–2007, giving both analysis and tabular detail, are available from the ONS website at: www.statistics.gov.uk, with further extracts and bespoke analyses available on request. This service replaces existing publications.

From 2008 to 2014 the Total net capital expenditure, Total capital expenditure - acquisitions, and Total capital expenditure - disposals published values included a small element of Not yet in production (NYIP). From 2015 onwards NYIP is not estimated for and is no longer included in the published values.

Retail trade: index numbers of value and volume (Table 13.2)

The main purpose of the Retail Sales Inquiry (RSI) is to provide up-to-date information on short period movements in the level of retail sales. In principle, the RSI covers the retail activity of every business classified in the retail sector (Division 52 of the 2007 Standard Industrial Classification (SIC(2007)) in Great Britain. A business will be classified to the retail sector if its main activity is one of the individual 4 digit SIC categories within Division 52. The retail activity of a business is then defined by its retail turnover, that is the sale of all retail goods (note that petrol, for example, is not a retail good).

The RSI is compiled from the information returned to the statutory inquiries into the distribution and services sector. The inquiry is addressed to a stratified sample of 5,000 businesses classified to the retail sector, the stratification being by 'type of store' (the individual 4 digit SIC categories within Division 52) and by size. The sample structure is designed to ensure that the inquiry estimates are as accurate as possible. In terms of the selection, this means that:

- each of the individual 4 digit SIC categories are represented – their coverage depending upon the relative size of the category and the variability of the data
- within each 4 digit SIC category the larger retailers tend to be fully enumerated with decreasing proportions of medium and smaller retailers

The structure of the inquiry is updated periodically by reference to the more comprehensive results of the Annual Business Inquiry (ABI). The monthly inquiry also incorporates a rotation element for the smallest retailers. This helps to spread the burden more fairly, as well as improving the representativeness between successive benchmarks.

13.1a Retail Trade, except of motor vehicles and motorcycles

Standard Industrial Classification (Revised 2007) - Divison	Description	Year	Number of enterprises	Total turnover	Approximate gross value added at basic prices (aGVA)	Total purchases of goods, materials and services	Total employment			Total capital expenditure			Total stocks and work in progress		
							point in time[1]	average during the year[1]	costs	net [2]	acquisitions [2]	disposals [2]	value at end of year	value at beginning of year	increase during year
			Number	£ million	£ million	£ million	Thousand	Thousand	£ million	£ million	£ million	£ million	£ million	£ million	£ million
47	Retail trade, except of motor vehicles and motorcycles	2008	194,677	311,745	65,123	246,237	3,054	3,106	38,466	9,069	10,495	1,426	26,110	25,519	591
		2009	187,890	319,318	69,924	249,058	3,073	3,139	38,914	7,784	9,113	1,330	26,539	25,759	781
		2010	187,230	332,131	71,500	261,676	3,016	3,040	39,816	6,149	9,258	3,108	28,743	26,425	2,317
		2011	189,119	342,147	70,871	271,203	3,032	3,060	41,592	9,051	10,879	1,828	30,356	28,964	1,392
		2012	187,616	349,327	73,876	275,052	3,029	3,062	42,184	9,477	10,789	1,312	30,021	28,720	1,301
		2013	189,828	359,088	81,368	278,326	3,052	3,084	43,441	9,510	10,627	1,117	31,791	29,863	1,929
		2014	186,737	371,522	83,728	288,613	3,130	3,154	44,996	11,228	12,543	1,314	33,571	32,461	1,110
		2015	186,922	375,289	85,967	290,764	3,143	3,191	47,233	11,145	12,265	1,120	34,774	32,952	1,822
		2016	195,491	385,351	86,737	299,090	3,108	3,157	47,755	13,155	14,005	851	36,487	35,423	1,064

Source: Annual Business Survey (ABS)

The sum of constituent items in tables may not always agree exactly with the totals shown due to rounding.

1. Total employment - point in time and Total employment - average during the year are from the Business Register and Employment Survey (BRES). Caution should be taken when combining financial data from the ABS with employment data from BRES due to differences in methodology. More information can be found in the ABS Technical Report.

2. From 2008 to 2014 the Total net capital expenditure, Total capital expenditure - acquisitions, and Total capital expenditure - disposals published values included a small element of Not yet in production (NYIP). From 2015 onwards NYIP is not estimated for and is no longer included in the published values.

13.1b Retail trade, except of motor vehicles and motor-cycles

£ million (Inclusive of VAT)

	2008	2009	2010	2011	2012	2013	2014	2015
TOTAL TURNOVER	**346,002**	**350,269**	**367,446**	**385,692**	**393,423**	**404,534**	**418,185**	**421,708**
RETAIL TURNOVER	**325,847**	**331,256**	**347,144**	**363,280**	**368,176**	**378,917**	**387,983**	**393,439**
Fruit (including fresh, chilled, dried, frozen, canned and processed)	5,949	6,469	6,821	7,662	6,846	7,132	7,351	8,515
Vegetables (including fresh, chilled, dried, frozen canned and processed)	10,070	9,949	10,533	10,677	12,380	13,219	13,273	12,660
Meat (including fresh, chilled, smoked, frozen, canned and processed)	17,243	17,855	17,909	19,541	20,254	21,230	21,794	21,700
Fish, crustaceans and molluscs (including fresh, chilled, smoked, frozen, canned and processed)	2,936	2,989	2,978	3,295	3,453	3,458	3,486	3,676
Bakery products and cereals (including rice and pasta products)	15,816	16,719	17,875	18,818	20,078	20,352	20,372	22,104
Sugar, jam, honey, chocolate and confectionery (including ice-cream)	8,192	8,618	8,844	8,688	9,162	9,829	10,233	9,701
Alcoholic drink	14,965	15,609	16,618	17,445	18,184	19,219	19,605	18,981
Non-alcoholic beverages (including tea, coffee, fruit drinks and vegetable drinks)	7,793	7,756	8,018	9,176	9,161	9,652	9,860	9,894
Tobacco (excluding smokers requisites e.g. pipes, lighters etc)	10,343	11,411	11,369	11,838	11,885	11,405	11,607	11,420
Milk, cheese and eggs (including yoghurts and cream)	10,813	11,562	10,918	11,219	11,441	11,579	11,767	11,779
Oils and fats (including butter and margarine)	1,488	1,440	1,444	1,613	1,611	1,695	1,826	1,693
Food products not elsewhere classified (including sauces, herbs spices, soups)	4,969	5,149	4,427	4,528	3,890	3,858	3,971	4,352
Pharmaceutical products	3,519	3,636	3,946	4,390	4,725	4,916	5,359	4,994
National Health Receipts	11,479	11,792	12,067	11,405	11,680	11,100	12,262	11,828
Other medical products and therapeutic appliances and equipment	3,822	3,213	4,210	3,638	4,067	3,913	3,712	4,782
Other appliances, articles and products for personal care	12,596	13,148	14,109	15,107	15,702	16,776	17,172	17,828
Other articles of clothing, accessories for making clothing	3,011	2,505	3,395	3,781	4,051	4,317	4,321	5,369
Garments	34,121	35,556	36,706	37,976	38,730	41,466	43,253	42,713
Footwear (excluding sports shoes)	6,858	7,685	7,458	7,720	8,720	8,765	9,213	10,229
Travel goods and other personal effects not elsewhere classified	1,512	1,722	2,352	2,518	2,506	3,183	3,081	3,103
Household textiles (including furnishing fabrics, curtains etc)	4,368	4,535	4,862	4,188	4,158	4,731	4,786	5,266
Household and personal appliances whether electric or not	6,362	6,736	6,917	7,278	7,367	6,768	8,351	8,189
Glassware, tableware and household utensils (including non-electric)	2,768	2,824	2,754	3,369	3,668	3,899	3,622	3,578
Furniture and furnishings	13,839	13,226	12,313	13,475	12,395	13,606	14,492	16,674
Audio and visual equipment (including radios, televisions and video recorders	6,215	6,016	6,245	5,353	5,821	4,916	4,124	3,864
Recording material for pictures and sound (including audio and video tapes, blank and pre recorded records etc)	3,622	3,052	2,787	2,547	2,668	2,560	2,034	2,027
Information processing equipment (including printers, software, calculators and typewriters)	4,423	4,384	4,530	5,425	4,862	5,475	5,058	4,678
Decorating and DIY supplies	6,176	6,820	7,319	7,528	5,580	6,500	6,952	6,870
Tools and equipment for house and garden	3,131	2,964	3,088	3,566	3,887	4,235	3,916	4,458
Books	2,497	2,623	2,648	2,579	3,084	2,623	2,636	2,928
Newspapers and periodicals	3,971	3,405	3,947	3,675	3,410	2,906	3,022	2,872
Stationery and drawing materials and miscellaneous printed matter	4,446	4,423	4,025	4,432	4,397	4,620	4,304	4,426
Carpets and other floor coverings (excluding bathroom mats, rush and door mats)	3,493	2,840	2,824	3,159	3,144	2,806	3,114	3,389
Photographic and cinematographic equipment and optical instruments	2,274	1,854	1,625	1,643	1,298	736	809	986
Telephone and telefax equipment (including mobile phones)	3,264	3,249	3,143	3,665	4,437	4,481	3,277	3,488
Jewellery, silverware and plate; watches and clocks	5,091	5,693	6,045	6,235	6,626	6,340	7,449	7,323
Works of art and antiques (including furniture, floor coverings and jewellery)	1,391	1,347	1,756	1,493	1,254	1,807	2,374	3,503
Equipment and accessories for sport, camping, recreation and musical instruments	4,019	4,416	4,864	5,118	4,944	4,355	5,350	4,378
Spare parts and accessories for all types of vehicle and sales of bicycles	1,159	924	1,148	983	950	1,244	1,520	1,613
Games, toys, hobbies (including video game software, video game computers that plug into the tv, video-games cassettes and CD-ROM'S)	7,961	7,484	7,514	7,492	7,154	7,018	7,855	8,117
Other goods not elsewhere classified (including sale of new postage stamps and sales of liquid and solid fuels)	4,307	5,007	5,896	5,929	5,788	6,689	7,570	8,438
Non-durable household goods (including household cleaning, maintenance products) & paper products and other non-durable household goods	4,942	5,280	4,727	4,923	4,936	5,596	6,199	5,750
Natural or artificial plants and flowers	4,192	2,973	3,609	4,023	3,501	3,772	3,523	5,631
Pets and related products (including pet food)	3,601	3,884	3,896	4,166	4,154	4,664	4,697	4,696
Petrol, diesel, lubricating oil and other petroleum products	30,840	30,515	36,664	40,001	40,171	39,507	37,432	32,977

Source: Annual Business Survey (ABS)

The sum of constituent items in tables may not always agree exactly with the totals shown due to rounding.

13.2 Retail trade: index numbers of value and volume of sales[1]

Great Britain

Non-seasonally adjusted

Weekly average (2013=100)

		Sales in 2016 £ thousand	2007	2008	2009	2010	2011	2012	2013	2014	2015	2016
Value												
All retailing	**J5AH**	387,696,081	84.3	87.5	88.2	90.6	95.3	97.5	100	103	104.1	107.6
Large	**J5AI**	306,068,697	80.5	84.4	85.8	89.9	94.6	97.2	100	102.5	104.3	107.1
Small	**J5AJ**	81,627,384	98.9	99.6	97.4	93.4	97.9	98.7	100	104.9	103.4	109.6
All retailing excluding automotive fuel	**J43S**	350,846,937	84.5	87.1	88.9	91.1	94.3	96.8	100	103.8	105.7	109.3
Predominantly food stores	**EAFS**	154,445,506	79.9	84.5	89.1	90.5	94.4	97.1	100	101.1	101.2	102.9
Predominantly non-food stores	**EAFT**	163,199,444	94.1	94.5	93	95.3	96.7	98.3	100	105.4	107.9	110.5
Non specialised predominantly non-food stores	**EAGE**	34,180,001	81.9	79.7	81.1	86.8	90.2	95.7	100	105.4	109.7	115.5
Textile, clothing, footwear and leather	**EAFU**	45,728,484	87.2	86.9	87.9	92.7	96.2	97.7	100	103.6	106.8	104.4
Household goods stores	**EAFV**	32,673,518	119.4	116.8	111	106.6	104.2	103.2	100	105.6	111.2	112.3
Other specialised non-food stores	**EAFW**	50,617,441	92.5	97.1	94	96.1	96.8	97.3	100	107	105.6	112
Non-store retailing	**J596**	33,201,987	54	57.7	61.5	68	78.1	85.6	100	111.4	121.6	142
Automotive fuel	**J43H**	36,849,144	82.6	90.7	82.9	86.8	103.4	103.2	100	96.3	90.6	94.3
Volume												
All retailing	**J5DD**	387,696,081	98.6	98.6	99.0	98.0	98.2	98.7	100	103.7	108.2	113.7
All retailing excluding automotive fuel	**J448**	350,846,937	96.5	97.0	97.6	97.7	97.4	98.3	100	104.0	108.2	113.5
Predominantly food stores	**EAGW**	154,445,506	103.4	102.4	103.5	101.7	100.5	100.3	100	100.8	103.1	106.9
Predominantly non-food stores	**EAGX**	163,199,444	96.5	97.7	97.2	98.2	97.4	98.2	100	106.1	110.7	114.7
Non specialised predominantly non-food stores	**EAHI**	34,180,001	88.4	85.3	86.0	90.0	91.1	95.8	100	106.1	112.8	120.3
Textile, clothing, footwear and leather	**EAGY**	45,728,484	84.2	86.8	92.6	97.5	98.4	98.9	100	103.5	107.1	105.0
Household goods stores	**EAGZ**	32,673,518	124.7	122.4	115.7	108.5	103.8	102.2	100	106.7	115.7	118.6
Other specialised non-food stores	**EAHA**	50,617,441	95.9	100.5	97.1	97.6	96.3	96.6	100	108.4	109.4	117.8
Non-store retailing	**J5CL**	33,201,987	56.9	60.0	64.5	70.0	78.7	85.9	100	111.8	125.3	148.0
Automotive fuel	**J43V**	36,849,144	117.8	113.2	111.5	100.5	104.8	102.4	100	101.1	108.8	115.7

1 See chapter text.

Source: Office for National Statistics

Please note that the indices have been re-referenced so the value of 100 is in 2013

13.3 Wholesale and retail trade and repair of motor vehicles and motorcycles

Standard Industrial Classification (Revised 2007) - Divison	Description	Year	Number of enterprises	Total turnover	Approximate gross value added at basic prices (aGVA)	Total purchases of goods, materials and services	Total employment			Total capital expenditure			Total stocks and work in progress		
							point in time[1]	average during the year[1]	costs	net [2]	acquis-itions [2]	disposals [2]	value at end of year	value at beginning of year	increase during year
			Number	£ million	£ million	£ million	Thousand	Thousand	£ million	£ million	£ million	£ million	£ million	£ million	£ million
45	Wholesale and retail trade and repair of motor vehicles and motorcycles	2008	67,683	135,669	20,957	115,372	532	535	10,925	1,044	2,110	1,066	16,136	15,402	735
		2009	66,372	125,764	18,348	105,457	500	539	10,445	885	1,669	784	13,624	15,545	-1,921
		2010	66,239	132,077	22,150	111,243	511	510	10,439	1,035	1,747	711	15,008	13,640	1,368
		2011	67,298	137,364	23,419	115,292	523	535	10,658	1,292	2,067	775	16,451	15,107	1,344
		2012	67,274	142,461	22,347	120,649	510	522	10,615	1,174	1,927	753	17,067	16,490	577
		2013	67,754	152,510	24,236	129,877	525	537	11,570	1,530	2,296	766	18,139	16,525	1,613
		2014	68,108	168,247	26,857	143,563	547	521	11,895	2,155	2,873	718	20,692	18,606	2,086
		2015	70,517	180,214	30,983	152,154	559	573	12,361	2,444	3,379	935	23,139	20,322	2,817
		2016	74,675	193,388	32,418	162,591	577	591	13,118	2,285	3,151	867	23,992	22,511	1,481

Source: Annual Business Survey (ABS)

The sum of constituent items in tables may not always agree exactly with the totals shown due to rounding.

1. Total employment - point in time and Total employment - average during the year are from the Business Register and Employment Survey (BRES). Caution should be taken when combining financial data from the ABS with employment data from BRES due to differences in methodology. More information can be found in the ABS Technical Report.

2. From 2008 to 2014 the Total net capital expenditure, Total capital expenditure - acquisitions, and Total capital expenditure - disposals published values included a small element of Not yet in production (NYIP). From 2015 onwards NYIP is not estimated for and is no longer included in the published values.

13.4 Accommodation and food service activities

Standard Industrial Classification (Revised 2007) Section, Division, Group, Class	Description	Year	Number of enterprises	Total turnover	Approximate gross value added at basic prices (aGVA)	Total purchases of goods, materials and services	Total employment		
							point in time[1]	average during the year[1]	costs
			Number	£ million	£ million	£ million	Thousand	Thousand	£ million
I	Accommodation and food service activities	2010	127,844	68,346	31,435	36,883	1,869	1,855	19,074
		2011	130,336	72,322	34,826	37,563	1,937	1,869	19,987
		2012	128,831	74,355	37,764	37,272	1,970	1,910	21,132
		2013	131,322	77,033	38,357	38,625	2,029	1,970	21,611
		2014	131,979	81,937	42,842	39,433	2,108	2,044	22,743
		2015	135,740	85,526	45,214	40,376	2,182	2,134	24,832
		2016	149,066	90,408	47,688	42,648	2,312	2,263	26,459
55	Accommodation	2010	15,075	17,650	9,087	8,603	388	377	5,075
		2011	15,159	18,566	9,838	8,775	429	407	5,331
		2012	15,205	19,822	11,149	8,677	426	409	5,752
		2013	15,365	20,222	11,353	8,860	433	416	5,646
		2014	15,513	22,646	13,964	8,866	440	419	5,857
		2015	15,842	23,132	13,943	9,292	455	444	6,286
		2016	16,809	24,738	15,027	9,766	485	473	6,893
55.1	Hotels and similar accommodation	2010	9,559	13,493	7,102	6,399	321	316	4,173
		2011	9,575	14,150	7,619	6,532	358	342	4,424
		2012	9,449	15,186	8,572	6,609	351	339	4,823
		2013	9,364	15,764	8,925	6,852	356	344	4,703
		2014	9,300	17,391	10,715	6,784	357	347	4,758
		2015	9,312	17,535	10,657	6,912	369	366	5,133
		2016	9,583	18,401	11,421	6,987	391	388	5,574
55.2	Holiday and other short stay accommodation	2010	3,318	1,603	846	776	29	26	339
		2011	3,296	1,476	726	774	33	30	351
		2012	3,247	1,497	913	590	33	31	344
		2013	3,411	1,562	969	601	32	30	343
		2014	3,582	1,864	1,276	598	36	31	417
		2015	3,821	2,103	1,356	780	36	33	430
		2016	4,291	2,011	1,265	756	40	36	457
55.3	Camping grounds, recreational vehicle parks and trailer parks	2010	1,735	2,325	1,031	1,307	*	*	495
		2011	1,775	2,739	1,385	1,378	34	31	507
		2012	1,796	2,771	1,415	1,360	37	34	516
		2013	1,818	2,630	1,292	1,310	39	37	524
		2014	1,854	2,950	1,659	1,319	*	*	582
		2015	1,915	2,867	1,607	1,294	42	39	568
		2016	2,039	3,530	1,901	1,662	46	42	709
55.9	Other accommodation	2010	463	229	108	121	*	*	69
		2011	513	200	108	92	4	4	49
		2012	713	368	250	118	5	4	70
		2013	772	265	168	98	6	5	76
		2014	777	440	314	166	*	*	101
		2015	794	627	324	305	8	7	155
		2016	896	796	439	361	8	7	153
56	Food and beverage service activities	2010	112,769	50,696	22,348	28,281	1,481	1,478	13,998
		2011	115,177	53,756	24,988	28,787	1,507	1,462	14,656
		2012	113,626	54,533	26,615	28,594	1,544	1,501	15,380
		2013	115,957	56,811	27,003	29,765	1,596	1,553	15,964
		2014	116,466	59,291	28,878	30,567	1,668	1,625	16,886
		2015	119,898	62,395	31,270	31,084	1,727	1,690	18,546
		2016	132,257	65,670	32,661	32,882	1,828	1,789	19,566
56.1	Restaurants and mobile food service activities	2010	61,387	23,017	10,407	12,623	705	684	6,306
		2011	63,712	25,690	12,301	13,447	767	765	6,886
		2012	64,460	25,934	13,367	13,332	782	783	7,187
		2013	67,144	28,740	14,328	14,454	859	860	8,067
		2014	68,876	29,571	14,975	14,789	885	834	8,531
		2015	72,793	32,326	16,562	15,924	937	901	9,601
		2016	83,635	34,929	17,901	17,149	1,005	966	10,479

13.4 Accommodation and food service activities

Standard Industrial Classification (Revised 2007) Section, Division, Group, Class	Description	Year	Number of enterprises	Total turnover	Approximate gross value added at basic prices (aGVA)	Total purchases of goods, materials and services	Total employment		
							point in time[1]	average during the year[1]	costs
			Number	£ million	£ million	£ million	Thousand	Thousand	£ million
56.2	Event catering and other food service activities	2010	7,031	7,971	4,003	3,970	227	253	3,149
		2011	7,967	8,553	4,418	4,138	231	212	3,204
		2012	7,651	8,925	4,430	4,521	262	249	3,688
		2013	8,003	8,269	3,928	4,343	233	222	3,381
		2014	8,221	9,122	4,644	4,474	255	260	3,682
		2015	8,753	9,439	5,082	4,357	253	256	4,004
		2016	10,501	9,821	5,132	4,703	269	274	4,026
56.21	Event catering activities	2010	5,767	7,289	3,710	3,581	211	236	2,957
		2011	6,267	7,837	4,119	3,715	213	196	2,993
		2012	5,514	7,844	3,879	3,968	241	228	3,411
		2013	5,885	3,196	1,394	1,809	86	82	967
		2014	6,149	3,465	1,534	1,934	96	99	1,004
		2015	6,906	3,458	1,684	1,784	88	89	1,061
		2016	8,542	4,950	2,541	2,427	140	142	1,917
56.29	Other food service activities	2010	1,264	682	293	389	16	17	192
		2011	1,700	716	299	422	18	17	211
		2012	2,137	1,081	551	552	21	20	278
		2013	2,118	5,073	2,534	2,534	147	140	2,414
		2014	2,072	5,657	3,110	2,540	159	162	2,678
		2015	1,847	5,981	3,398	2,573	165	167	2,943
		2016	1,959	4,870	2,590	2,276	128	132	2,109
56.3	Beverage serving activities	2010	44,351	19,709	7,938	11,688	549	540	4,543
		2011	43,498	19,513	8,269	11,203	509	484	4,566
		2012	41,515	19,675	8,817	10,742	501	469	4,504
		2013	40,810	19,802	8,748	10,968	503	471	4,516
		2014	39,369	20,599	9,259	11,303	527	531	4,674
		2015	38,352	20,630	9,626	10,803	538	533	4,941
		2016	38,121	20,921	9,628	11,030	554	549	5,061

Source: Annual Business Survey (ABS)

The following symbols and abbreviations are used throughout the ABS releases;

- * Information suppressed to avoid disclosure
- .. not available
- \- nil or less than half the level of rounding

The sum of constituent items in tables may not always agree exactly with the totals shown due to rounding.

1. Total employment - point in time and Total employment - average during the year are from the Business Register and Employment Survey (BRES). Caution should be taken when combining financial data from the ABS with employment data from BRES due to differences in methodology. More information can be found in the ABS Technical Report.

2. From 2008 to 2014 the Total net capital expenditure, Total capital expenditure - acquisitions, and Total capital expenditure - disposals published values included a small element of Not yet in production (NYIP). From 2015 onwards NYIP is not estimated for and is no longer included in the published values.

13.4 Accommodation and food service activities

Standard Industrial Classification (Revised 2007) Section, Division, Group, Class	Description	Year	Total capital expenditure			Total stocks and work in progress		
			net [2]	acquisitions [2]	disposals [2]	value at end of year	value at beginning of year	increase during year
			£ million	£ million	£ million	£ million	£ million	£ million
I	Accommodation and food service activities	2010	2,807	3,804	997	1,481	1,403	79
		2011	3,311	4,339	1,028	1,484	1,368	117
		2012	3,930	4,704	774	1,716	1,713	3
		2013	3,946	4,837	891	1,544	1,523	21
		2014	5,629	6,888	1,259	1,585	1,494	92
		2015	7,212	8,046	835	1,587	1,460	126
		2016	7,639	8,498	859	1,953	1,842	112
55	Accommodation	2010	1,301	1,489	188	488	445	43
		2011	1,416	1,641	225	506	443	63
		2012	1,898	2,050	152	469	452	17
		2013	1,836	2,045	209	397	413	-16
		2014	1,656	2,275	619	472	438	34
		2015	2,869	3,167	298	431	385	46
		2016	3,309	3,547	238	660	632	28
55.1	Hotels and similar accommodation	2010	936	1,072	136	250	231	20
		2011	946	1,137	191	201	176	25
		2012	1,282	1,397	115	185	172	13
		2013	1,173	1,335	162	207	189	18
		2014	1,159	1,728	569	195	190	5
		2015	2,034	2,283	250	184	187	-3
		2016	2,508	2,690	182	220	221	-2
55.2	Holiday and other short stay accommodation	2010	186	214	28	75	66	9
		2011	169	184	15	59	45	15
		2012	254	269	16	64	58	6
		2013	195	216	21	37	34	3
		2014	223	234	11	54	48	6
		2015	372	388	16	83	59	24
		2016	203	223	20	54	51	3
55.3	Camping grounds, recreational vehicle parks and trailer parks	2010	160	181	21	159	145	14
		2011	238	257	18	245	222	23
		2012	258	279	21	217	219	-3
		2013	254	278	24	152	190	-38
		2014	237	269	32	220	198	22
		2015	359	390	31	163	138	25
		2016	553	586	33	383	356	27
55.9	Other accommodation	2010	19	22	4	3	3	-
		2011	62	63	1	1	1	-
		2012	104	105	1	3	3	-
		2013	214	216	2	1	-	-
		2014	36	44	8	3	2	1
		2015	104	105	1	1	1	-
		2016	44	48	4	3	3	-
56	Food and beverage service activities	2010	1,507	2,316	809	993	958	35
		2011	1,895	2,698	803	978	925	54
		2012	2,032	2,654	622	1,247	1,261	-13
		2013	2,110	2,792	682	1,147	1,110	37
		2014	3,973	4,613	640	1,113	1,056	58
		2015	4,343	4,880	537	1,155	1,075	80
		2016	4,331	4,951	621	1,294	1,210	84
56.1	Restaurants and mobile food service activities	2010	998	1,185	187	429	402	27
		2011	1,203	1,327	123	412	379	33
		2012	1,380	1,512	132	562	532	30
		2013	1,449	1,645	196	480	454	26
		2014	2,427	2,600	173	451	418	34
		2015	2,555	2,687	133	593	524	69
		2016	2,503	2,712	209	688	650	39

13.4 Accommodation and food service activities

Standard Industrial Classification (Revised 2007) Section, Division, Group, Class	Description	Year	Total capital expenditure			Total stocks and work in progress		
			net [2]	acquisitions [2]	disposals [2]	value at end of year	value at beginning of year	increase during year
			£ million	£ million	£ million	£ million	£ million	£ million
56.2	Event catering and other food service activities	2010	135	176	41	126	122	4
		2011	175	188	14	145	140	5
		2012	127	135	8	158	154	4
		2013	110	117	7	176	167	9
		2014	125	158	32	179	180	-1
		2015	148	168	20	160	150	10
		2016	248	275	28	165	153	12
56.21	Event catering activities	2010	117	155	38	111	107	4
		2011	116	129	13	123	124	-1
		2012	113	120	7	133	131	2
		2013	48	52	5	77	68	9
		2014	73	95	22	75	72	3
		2015	106	114	7	73	65	9
		2016	147	164	17	85	74	11
56.29	Other food service activities	2010	18	21	2	15	15	-
		2011	59	60	1	22	16	6
		2012	14	15	1	24	23	1
		2013	62	65	3	100	99	1
		2014	52	63	11	103	107	-4
		2015	42	54	13	86	85	1
		2016	100	111	11	80	79	1
56.3	Beverage serving activities	2010	374	955	581	438	434	5
		2011	517	1,183	666	421	405	16
		2012	524	1,007	483	527	575	-47
		2013	551	1,030	479	491	488	2
		2014	1,420	1,855	434	483	458	25
		2015	1,640	2,024	384	403	402	1
		2016	1,580	1,964	384	441	407	33

Source: Annual Business Survey (ABS)

The following symbols and abbreviations are used throughout the ABS releases;

* Information suppressed to avoid disclosure

.. not available

\- nil or less than half the level of rounding

The sum of constituent items in tables may not always agree exactly with the totals shown due to rounding.

1. Total employment - point in time and Total employment - average during the year are from the Business Register and Employment Survey (BRES). Caution should be taken when combining financial data from the ABS with employment data from BRES due to differences in methodology. More information can be found in the ABS Technical Report.

2. From 2008 to 2014 the Total net capital expenditure, Total capital expenditure - acquisitions, and Total capital expenditure - disposals published values included a small element of Not yet in production (NYIP). From 2015 onwards NYIP is not estimated for and is no longer included in the published values.

Sources:

This index of sources gives the titles of official publications or other sources containing statistics allied to those in the tables of this Annual Abstract. These publications provide more detailed analyses than are shown in the Annual Abstract. This index includes publications to which reference should be made for short–term (monthly or quarterly) series.

Table number	Government department or other organisation

Chapter 1: Area

1.1	ONS Geography Codes; Office for National Statistics - Standard Area Measurement for UK Local Authority Districts (SAM 2016)

Chapter 2: Parliamentary elections

2.1	British Electoral Facts 1832-2012; Plymouth University for the Electoral Commission
2.2a	Chronology of British Parliamentary By-elections 1833-1987; British Electoral Facts 1832-2006;
	House of Commons Library, RP10/50 By-election results 2005-10; SN05833 By-elections since 2010 General Election
	CBP 7417 By-elections since the 2015 General Election; CBP-8280 By-elections since the 2017 General Election
2.2b	British Parliamentary Election Results; House of Commons Library By-election results
2.3a	House of Commons Library Briefing Paper CBP7594, National Assembly for Wales Elections: 2016
2.3b	British Electoral Facts 1832-2006; House of Commons Library Research and Briefing Papers
2.4	British Electoral Facts 1832-2006; Electoral Office for Northern Ireland

Chapter 3 International Development

3.1	Department for International Development
3.2	Department for International Development
3.3	Department for International Development

Chapter 4 Labour Market

4.1	Labour Force Survey, Office for National Statistics
4.2	Labour Force Survey, Office for National Statistics
4.3	Labour Force Survey, Office for National Statistics
4.4	Labour Force Survey, Office for National Statistics
4.5a	Eurostat, OECD, National Statistical Offices. Labour market statistics
4.5b	Labour Disputes Survey, Office for National Statistics
4.6	Annual Civil Service Employment Survey, Office for National Statistics
4.7	Labour Force Survey, Office for National Statistics
4.8	Labour Force Survey, Office for National Statistics
4.9	Office for National Statistics
4.10	Labour Market Statistics,Office for National Statistics; Nomisweb
4.11a	Annual Survey of Hours and Earnings, Office for National Statistics
4.11b	Annual Survey of Hours and Earnings, Office for National Statistics
4.12a	Annual Survey of Hours and Earnings, Office for National Statistics
4.12b	Annual Survey of Hours and Earnings, Office for National Statistics
4.13	Office for National Statistics
4.14a	Monthly wages and salaries survey
4.14b	Monthly wages and salaries survey
4.14c	Monthly wages and salaries survey
4.14d	Monthly wages and salaries survey
4.15a	Annual Survey of Hours and Earnings, Office for National Statistics
4.15b	Annual Survey of Hours and Earnings, Office for National Statistics
4.16	Annual Survey of Hours and Earnings, Office for National Statistics
4.17	Certification Officer Annual Report 2016/17

Chapter 5 Social Protection

5.1	HM Revenue and Customs; Department for Work and Pensions
5.2	HM Revenue and Customs; National Insurance Fund Account Great Britain
5.3	HM Revenue and Customs
5.4	Department for Work and Pensions
5.5	Department for Work and Pensions
5.6	Department for Work and Pensions
5.7	Stat-Xplore, Department for Work and Pensions
5.8	Stat-Xplore, Department for Work and Pensions
5.9a	HM Revenue and Customs
5.9b	HM Revenue and Customs
5.10	HM Revenue and Customs
5.11	HM Revenue and Customs
5.12	Stat-Xplore, Department for Work and Pensions
5.13	Stat-Xplore, Department for Work and Pensions

Table number	Government department or other organisation
5.14	Stat-Xplore, Department for Work and Pensions
5.15a	War Pensions Computer System
5.15b	War Pensions Computer System
5.16	Stat-Xplore, Department for Work and Pensions
5.17	Stat-Xplore, Department for Work and Pensions
5.18	Stat-Xplore, Department for Work and Pensions
5.19	Stat-Xplore, Department for Work and Pensions

Chapter 6 External Trade

6.1	Office for National Statistics
6.2	Office for National Statistics
6.3	Office for National Statistics
6.4	Office for National Statistics
6.5	Office for National Statistics
6.6	Office for National Statistics
6.7	Office for National Statistics
6.8	Office for National Statistics
6.9	Office for National Statistics
6.10	Office for National Statistics
6.11	Office for National Statistics
6.12	Office for National Statistics
6.13	Office for National Statistics
6.14	Office for National Statistics
6.15	Office for National Statistics
6.16	Office for National Statistics
6.17	Office for National Statistics
6.18	Office for National Statistics

Chapter 7 Research and development

7.1a	Office for National Statistics
7.1b	Office for National Statistics
7.2	Office for National Statistics
7.3	Office for National Statistics
7.4	Office for National Statistics
7.5a	Office for National Statistics
7.5b	Office for National Statistics

Chapter 8 Personal income, expendiure & wealth

8.1	Survey of Personal Incomes, HM Revenue and Customs
8.2	Office for National Statistics
8.3	Office for National Statistics
8.4	Office for National Statistics
8.5	Office for National Statistics

Chapter 9 Lifestyles

9.1	Department for Culture, Media and Sport
9.2	National Readership Surveys Ltd.
9.3	Department for Culture, Media and Sport
9.4	Taking Part Survey, Department for Digital, Culture, Media and Sport
9.5	British Film Institute Statistical Yearbook
9.6	comScore, BFI RSU analysis
9.7	International Passenger Survey, Office for National Statistics
9.8	International Passenger Survey, Office for National Statistics
9.9	International Passenger Survey, Office for National Statistics
9.10	Visit England
9.11	Visit England
9.12	Gambling Commission
9.13	Office for National Statistics
9.14a	Taking Part Survey, Department for Culture, Media and Sport
9.14b	Taking Part Survey, Department for Culture, Media and Sport
9.14c	Taking Part Survey, Department for Culture, Media and Sport
9.15	Taking Part Survey, Department for Culture, Media and Sport
9.16	Community Life Survey, Cabinet Office
9.17	International Passenger Survey, Office for National Statistics
9.18	Office for National Statistics
9.19	RAJAR/Ipsos MORI/RSMB

Table number	Government department or other organisation

Chapter 10 Environment

10.1	Ricardo Energy & Environment, Office for National Statistics
10.2	Ricardo Energy & Environment, Office for National Statistics
10.3	Department for Business, Energy & Industrial Strategy
10.4	Ricardo Energy and Environment, Department for Business, Energy & Industrial Strategy, Office for National Statistics
10.5	Department for Business, Energy & Industrial Strategy
10.6	Department for Business, Energy & Industrial Strategy
10.7	Department for Business, Energy & Industrial Strategy
10.8	Department for Environment, Food and Rural Affairs; Food and Agriculture Organization of the United Nations; Eurostat; Kentish Cobnuts Association; British Geological Survey; Office for National Statistics;
10.9	Met Office; National Hydrological Monitoring Programme, Centre for Ecology and Hydrology
10.10	Met Office
10.11	Environment Agency
10.12	Scottish Environment Protection Agency
10.13	Water PLCs; Environment Agency; National Hydrological Monitoring Programme, Centre for Ecology and Hydrology
10.14	Office of Water Services (OFWAT)
10.15	Environment Agency
10.16	Environment Agency; Natural Resources Wales, Scottish Environment Protection Agency, Department of Agriculture, Environment and Rural Affairs (DAERA)
10.17	Environment Agency
10.18	Department for Business, Energy and Industrial Strategy (BEIS); Oil and Gas Authority
10.19a	Department for Environment, Food and Rural Affairs
10.19b	WasteDataFlow, Natural Resources Wales
10.19c	Scottish Environment Protection Agency
10.19d	Northern Ireland Environment Agency, NISRA, LPS
10.20a	Department for Environment Food and Rural affairs
10.20b	Department for Environment Food and Rural affairs; Office for National Statistics
10.20c	WasteDataFlow, Department for Environment, Food and Rural Affairs
10.20d	Department for Environment Food and Rural affairs
10.21	The Chartered Institute of Environmental Health
10.22	Office for National Statistics

Chapter 11 Housing

11.1a	Department for Communities and Local Government
11.1b	Welsh Assembly Government
11.1c	Scottish Government
11.1d	Continuous Household Survey
11.2	Ministry of Housing, Communities and Local Government; Welsh Assembly Government, Scottish Government; Department for Social Development (NI)
11.3	P2 returns from local authorities; National House Building Council (NHBC); Approved inspector data returns; Welsh Assembly Government; Scottish Government; Department of Finance and Personnel (DFPNI); District Council Building Control (NI)
11.4a	Department for Communities and Local Government
11.4b	New house building data collection, Welsh Government
11.5	HM Courts and Tribunals Service CaseMan; Possession Claim OnLine (PCOL); Council of Mortgage Lenders (CML)
11.6	Compendium of Housing Finance Statistics; Housing Finance and CML website; Council of Mortgage Lenders
11.7	Department for Communities and Local Government; P1E Homelessness returns (quarterly)
11.8	Welsh Government, Homelessness data collection
11.9	Scottish Government

Chapter 12 Banking and Finance

12.1a	Bank of England
12.1b	Bank of England
12.2a	Cheque and Credit Clearing Company Ltd
12.2b	UK Payments Administration Ltd, Cheque and Credit Clearing Company Ltd
12.2c	UK Payments Administration Ltd, Cheque and Credit Clearing Company Ltd
12.2d	UK Payments Administration Ltd, Cheque and Credit Clearing Company Ltd
12.2e	Cheque and Credit Clearing Company Ltd
12.3a	Bank of England
12.3b	Bank of England
12.3c	Bank of England
12.3d	Bank of England
12.3e	Bank of England
12.3f	Bank of England
12.3g	Bank of England
12.3h	Bank of England
12.4a	Bank of England
12.4b	Bank of England
12.4c	Bank of England
12.4d	Bank of England
12.5a	Bank of England

Table number	Government department or other organisation
12.5b	Bank of England
12.6a	Bank of England
12.6b	Bank of England
12.7	Bank of England
12.8	Bank of England
12.9	Bank of England
12.10	Bank of England
12.11	Bank of England
12.12	Bank of England
12.13a	Office for National Statistics
12.13b	Office for National Statistics
12.14	Office for National Statistics
12.15a	Office for National Statistics
12.15b	Office for National Statistics
12.16a	Insolvency Service
12.16b	Accountant in Bankruptcy (AiB), Companies House
12.16c	Department for Enterprise, Trade and Investment, Northern Ireland (DETINI)
12.17a	Insolvency Service; Companies House
12.17b	Companies House
12.17c	Department for Enterprise, Trade and Investment Northern Ireland (DETINI); Companies House
12.18a	Bank of England
12.18b	Bank of England
12.18c	Bank of England
12.18d	Bank of England
12.19	Bank of England
12.20	Mergers and Acquisitions Surveys, Office for National Statistics

Chapter 13 Services

13.1a	Annual Business Survey (ABS), Office for National Statistics
13.1b	Annual Business Survey (ABS), Office for National Statistics
13.2	Office for National Statistics
13.3	Annual Business Survey (ABS), Office for National Statistics
13.4	Annual Business Survey (ABS), Office for National Statistics